A-Z TYNE and

Key to Map Pages	2-3
Large Scale City Centres	4-7
Map Pages	8-183
Postcode Map	184-185
Index to Streets, and selected Pla	
Index to Hospita	
Tyne and Wear Metro and Rail Connections	see Inside Back Cover

REFERENCE

Motorway	A1(M)
Primary Route	A194
A Road	A1
B Road	B1288
Dual Carriageway	
Tunnel	
One-way Street Traffic flow on A Roads is also indicated by a heavy line on the driver's left.	
Road Under Construction Opening dates are correct at the time of publication.	
Proposed Road	
Restricted Access	
Pedestrianized Road	
Track / Footpath	
Residential Walkway	
Railway	Level Crossing, Tunnel, Station, Heritage Sta.
Metro Line	Tunnel, M
Local Authority Boundary	
Posttown Boundary	
Postcode Boundary (within Posttown)	
Built-up Area	MILL ST.
Map Continuation	54
Large Scale City Centre	4

Airport	
Car Park (selected)	P
Church or Chapel	†
City Wall (Large Scale Only)	
Cycleway (selected)	
Fire Station	
Hospital	H
House Numbers (selected Roads)	13 8 4
Information Centre	i
National Grid Reference	420
Park & Ride	Kingston Park P+R
Police Station	▲
Post Office	★
Safety Camera with Speed Limit Fixed cameras & long term road works cameras. Symbols do not indicate camera direction.	30
Toilet: without facilities for the Disabled with facilities for the Disabled Disabled use only	
Viewpoint	
Educational Establishment	
Hospital or Healthcare Building	
Industrial Building	
Leisure or Recreational Facility	
Place of Interest	
Public Building	
Shopping Centre or Market	
Other Selected Buildings	

SCALES

Map Pages 8-183	Map Pages 4-5	Map Pages 6-7
1:14,908 4¼ inches (10.8 cm) to 1 mile	1:10,560 6 inches (15.24 cm) to 1 mile	1:7,454 8½ inches (21.6 cm) to 1 mile
6.7 cm to 1 km	9.47 cm to 1 km	13.42 cm to 1 km
0 – ¼ Mile	0 – ⅛ – ¼ Mile	0 – ⅛ – ¼ Mile
0 – 250 – 500 Metres	0 – 250 Metres	0 – 250 Metres

A-Z AZ AtoZ
registered trade marks of Geographers' A-Z Map Company Ltd

www.az.co.uk

EDITION 5 2014

Telephone: 01732 781000 (Enquiries & Trade Sales)
01732 783422 (Retail Sales)

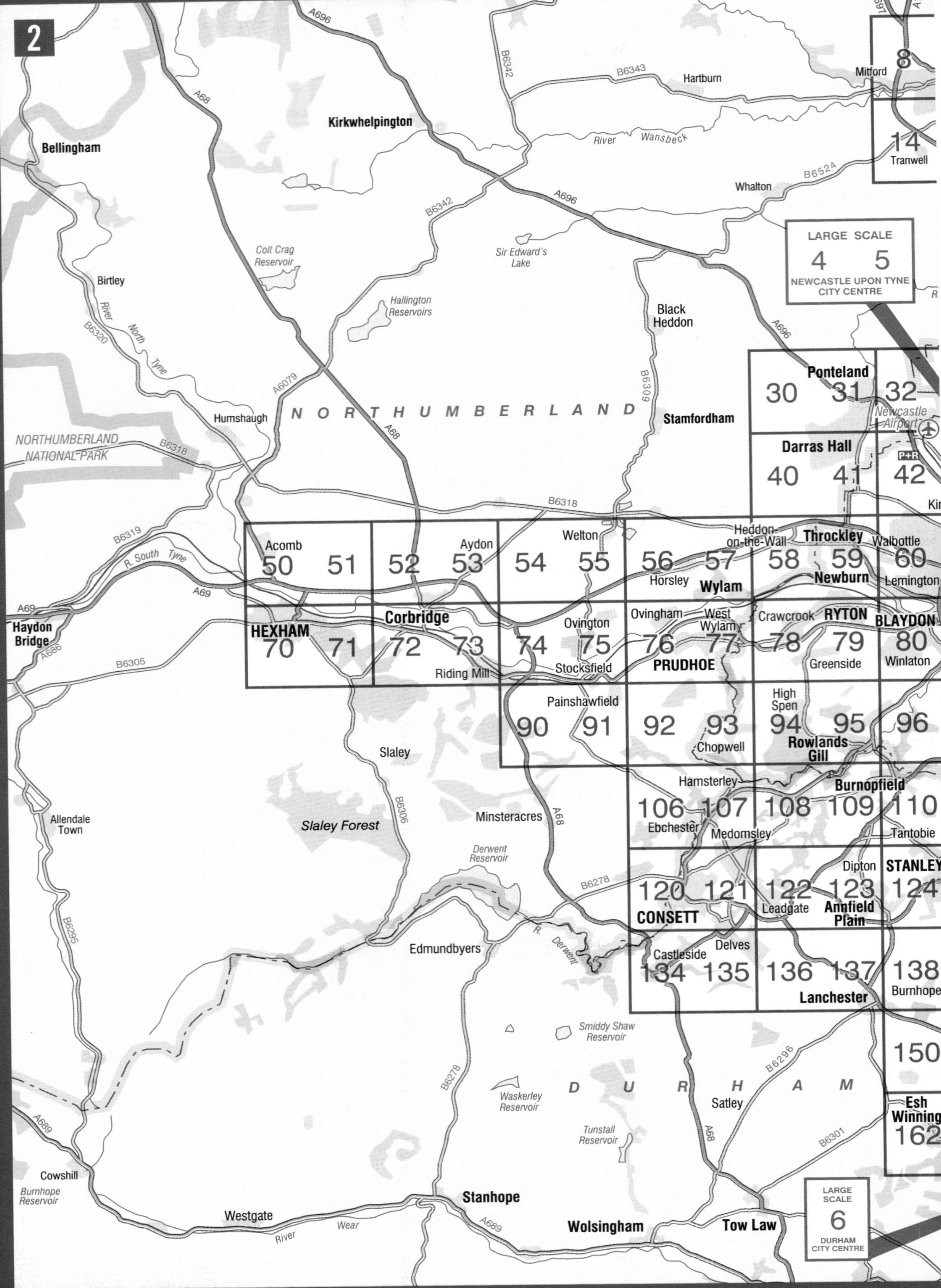

Bellingham
Kirkwhelpington
Hartburn
Mitford
Tranwell
River Wansbeck
Whalton
LARGE SCALE
4 5
NEWCASTLE UPON TYNE CITY CENTRE
Colt Crag Reservoir
Sir Edward's Lake
Birtley
Hallington Reservoirs
Black Heddon
River North Tyne
NORTHUMBERLAND
Humshaugh
Stamfordham
Ponteland
Newcastle Airport
Darras Hall
NORTHUMBERLAND NATIONAL PARK
Acomb
Aydon
Welton
Heddon-on-the-Wall
Throckley
Walbottle
R. South Tyne
Horsley
Wylam
Newburn
Lemington
Haydon Bridge
HEXHAM
Corbridge
Ovington
Ovingham
West Wylam
Crawcrook
RYTON
BLAYDON
Riding Mill
Stocksfield
PRUDHOE
Greenside
Winlaton
Painshawfield
High Spen
Slaley
Chopwell
Rowlands Gill
Hamsterley
Burnopfield
Allendale Town
Slaley Forest
Minsteracres
Ebchester
Medomsley
Tantobie
Derwent Reservoir
Dipton
STANLEY
CONSETT
Leadgate
Annfield Plain
Edmundbyers
R. Derwent
Castleside
Delves
Lanchester
Burnhope
Smiddy Shaw Reservoir
DURHAM
Waskerley Reservoir
Satley
Esh Winning
Tunstall Reservoir
Cowshill
Burnhope Reservoir
Stanhope
Westgate
River Wear
Wolsingham
Tow Law
LARGE SCALE
6
DURHAM CITY CENTRE
8 14 30 31 32 40 41 42 50 51 52 53 54 55 56 57 58 59 60 70 71 72 73 74 75 76 77 78 79 80 90 91 92 93 94 95 96 106 107 108 109 110 120 121 122 123 124 134 135 136 137 138 150 162
A696 A68 A1 A697 B6342 B6343 B6524 A6079 B6309 B6318 B6320 B6319 A69 A686 B6305 B6306 B6295 B6278 B6296 B6301 A689

KEY TO MAP PAGES

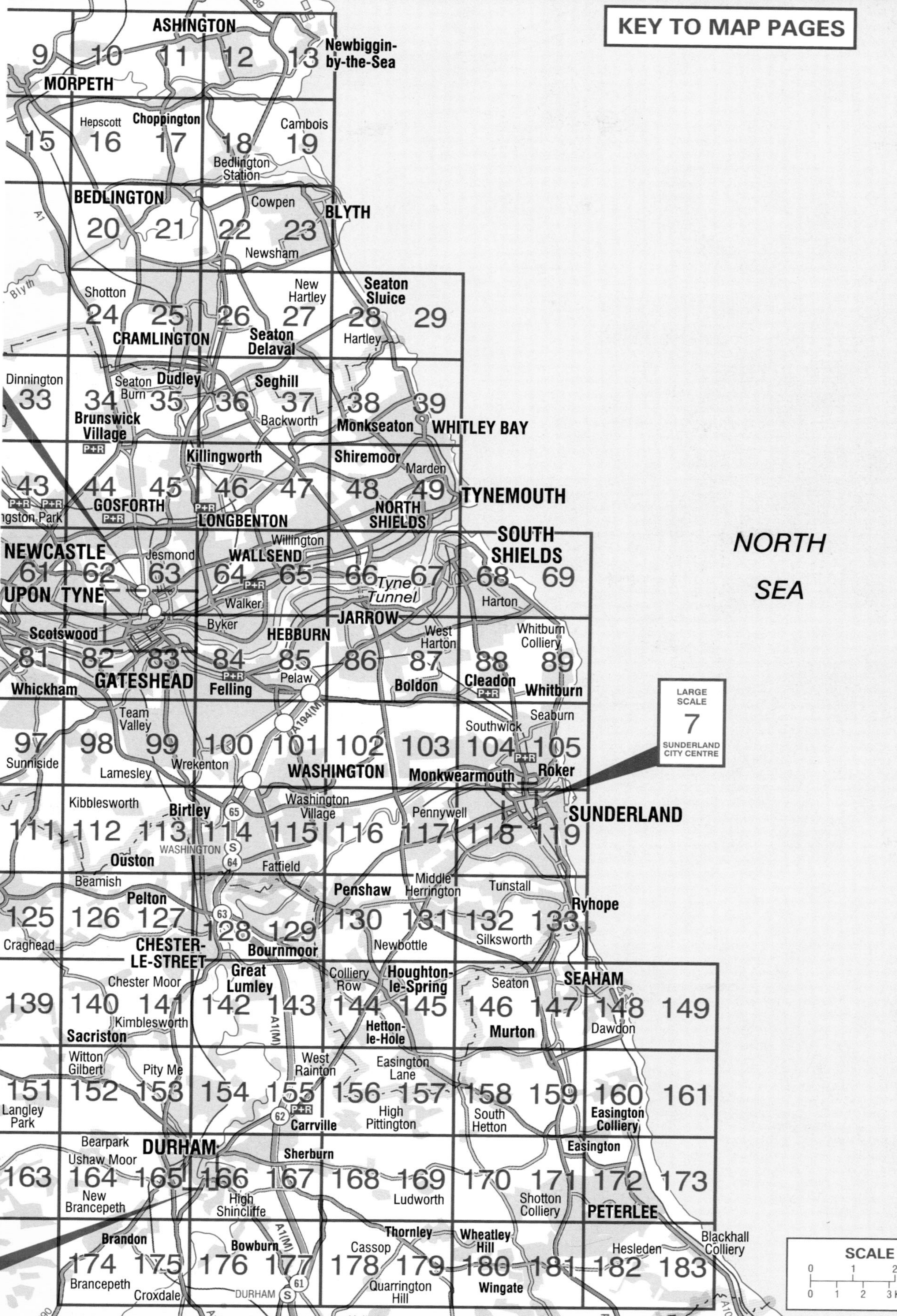

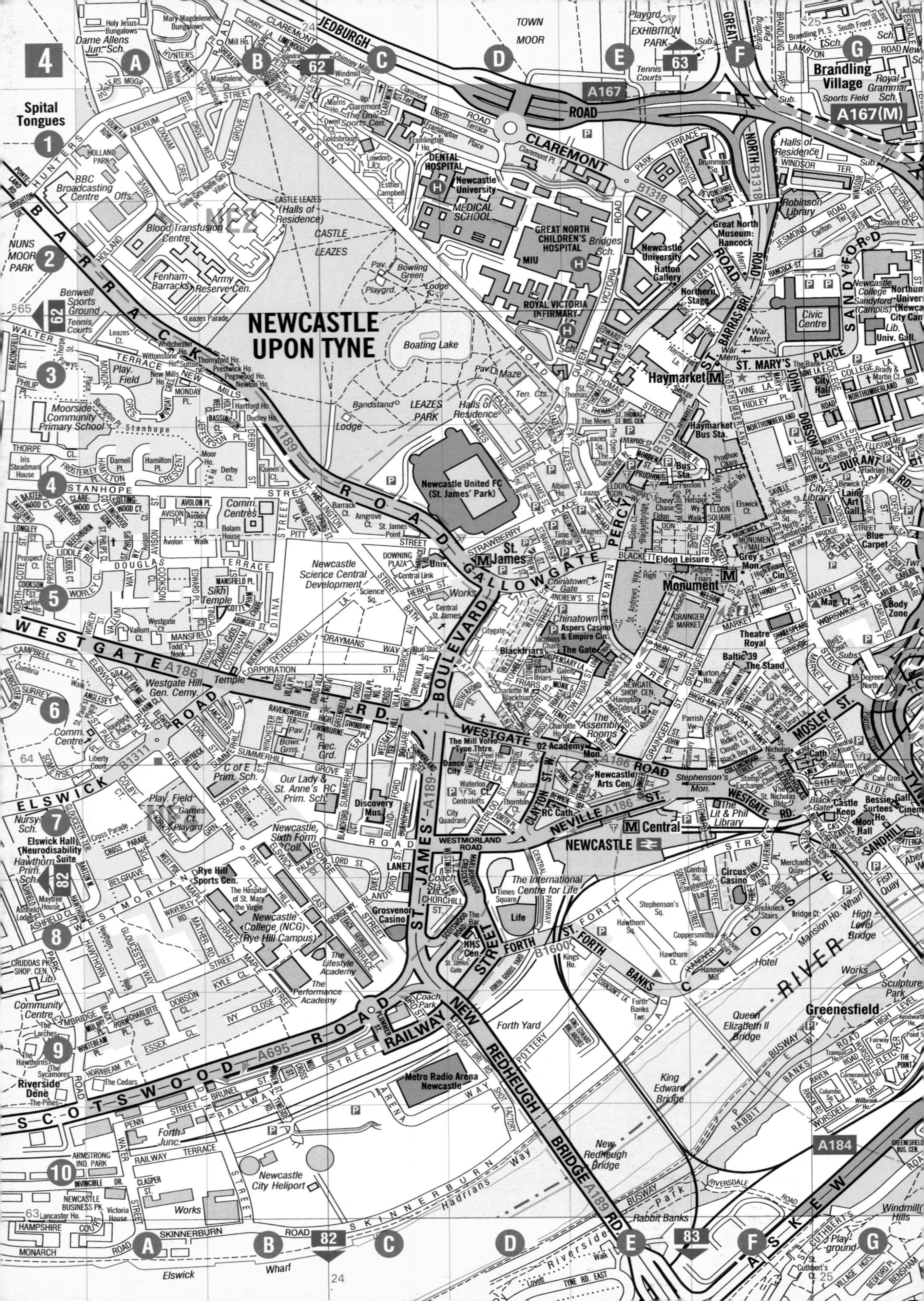

4
NEWCASTLE UPON TYNE
Spital Tongues
Brandling Village
Newcastle United FC (St. James' Park)
Leazes Park
Castle Leazes
Town Moor
Exhibition Park
Haymarket
Monument
Central
Newcastle Science Central Development
Metro Radio Arena Newcastle
River Tyne
Queen Elizabeth II Bridge
King Edward Bridge
New Redheugh Bridge
High Level Bridge
Greenesfield
Newcastle City Heliport
Forth Yard
24
25

H
J
K
L
M
N
P
5
26
27
63
Jesmond
Central Newcastle High Sch. (Junior)
St. Catherines Prim. Sch.
Newcastle General Cemetery
A1058
JESMOND ROAD
SANDYFORD ROAD
Bus Depot
Bowling Green Pavilion
King John's Palace (remains of)
St. Teresa's Catholic Prim. Sch.
HEATON PARK
Jesmond Vale
Ouseburn Park
Newington Road Depot
Depots
Newcastle upon Tyne
NE2
City Stadium
Hotspur Prim. Sch.
Comm. Cen.
Heaton Bingo
Tynemouth Ct.
64
65
1
2
3
4
6
7
8
9
10
Shieldfield
Univ.
Northumbria University
A167(M)
MOTORWAY
CENTRAL
Sports Central
Manors
NEW BRIDGE STREET
BYKER BRIDGE
NE1
Battle Field
St. Ann's
Ouseburn Viaduct
Seven Stories
Cluny Gall.
Superstore
Gala Bingo
SHIELDS RD.
A193 BY-PASS
Byker
Climb Newcastle
Library
East End Pool
NE6
BYKER
Ballast Hills Park
St. Lawrence Park
HOULTS ESTATES
Brinkburn Cen.
Youth Cen.
A186
WALKER ROAD
CITY ROAD
QUAYSIDE
Holy Jesus Hosp.
The Castlegate
The Law Courts
TYNE
NEWCASTLE UPON TYNE
GATESHEAD
Byker Ouseburn Regeneration Centre
St. Lawrence
BALTIC Centre for Contemporary Art
Gateshead Millennium Bridge
Quayside
Baltic Square
Tyne Bridge
Swing Bridge
The Sage Gateshead
Heritage Cen.
Saltmeadows
BALTIC BUSINESS QUARTER
Baltimore House
Gateshead College (Baltic Campus)
Gateshead
NE8
Mecca Bingo
A167
GATESHEAD
Anytime Fitness
Superstore
Old Town Hall
Vue Cin.
Bus Station
Gateshead
East Gateshead
SALTMEADOWS INDUSTRIAL PARK
HAWICK CRES. INDUSTRIAL EST.
RIVERSIDE EAST INDUSTRIAL ESTATE
St. Peter's
84
PARK LANE
A184
PARK ROAD
BALTIC BUSINESS CENTRE
SALTMEADOWS TRADE PARK
STADIUM INDUSTRIAL PARK
Gateshead International Stadium (Gateshead FC)
Games Court
83
Playing Field
Civic Centre
Supermarket
College

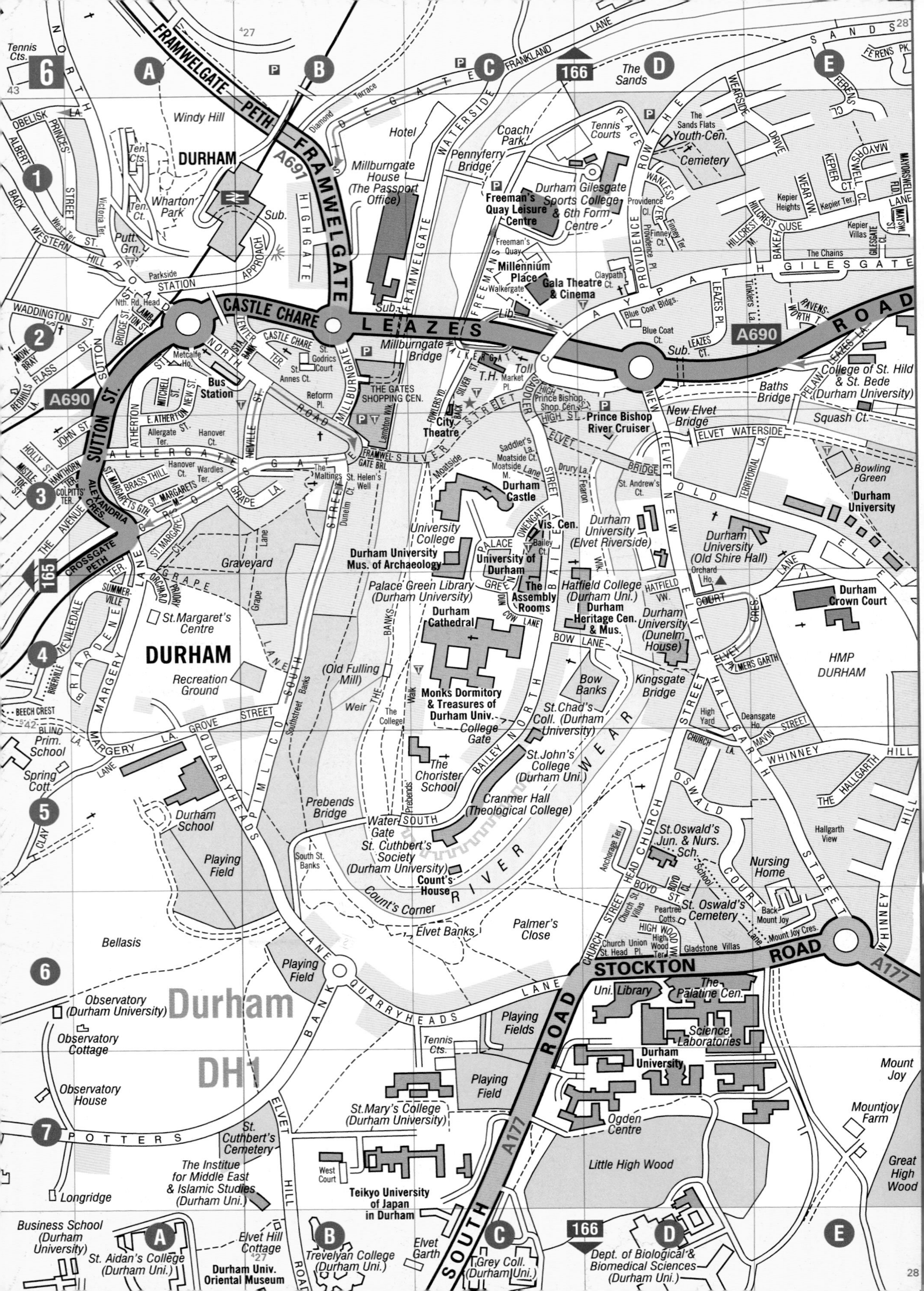

6
DURHAM
Windy Hill
Wharton Park
Putt. Grn.
Sub.
FRAMWELGATE PETH
A691
FRAMWELGATE
Millburngate House (The Passport Office)
Hotel
Diamond Terrace
FRANKLAND LANE
166
The Sands
SANDS
Coach Park
Tennis Courts
Pennyferry Bridge
Freeman's Quay Leisure Centre
Durham Gilesgate Sports College & 6th Form Centre
The Sands Flats
Youth Cen.
Cemetery
WEARSIDE DRIVE
FERENS CL.
FERENS PK.
KEPIER CT.
MAYORSWELL CL.
Kepier Heights
Kepier Ter.
Kepier Villas
HILLCREST
BAKEHOUSE
The Chains
GILESGATE
Freeman's Quay
Millennium Place
Gala Theatre & Cinema
Walkergate
Claypath Ct.
PROVIDENCE ROW
CLAYPATH
Blue Coat Bldgs.
Blue Coat Ct.
LEAZES PL.
Tinklers La.
RAVENSWORTH TER.
ROAD
A690
CASTLE CHARE
LEAZES
Millburngate Bridge
THE GATES SHOPPING CEN.
Lambton Wlk.
T.H.
Market Pl.
Bus Station
Metcalfe Ho.
NORTH ROAD
STATION APPROACH
Parkside
WESTERN HILL
WADDINGTON ST.
SUTTON ST.
A690
Reform Pl.
St. Godrics Court
St. Annes Ct.
City Theatre
SILVER ST.
Prince Bishop Shop. Cen.
Prince Bishop River Cruiser
HIGH ST.
ELVET BRIDGE
New Elvet Bridge
ELVET WATERSIDE
Baths Bridge
College of St. Hild & St. Bede (Durham University)
Squash Ct.
Bowling Green
Durham University
ALLERGATE
CROSSGATE
Hanover Ct.
Wardles Ter.
BRASS THILL
ST. MARGARETS
GRAPE LA.
The Maltings
St. Helen's Well
FRAMWELGATE BRIDGE
Saddler's La.
Moatside Ct.
Moatside Lane
Drury La.
Durham Castle
OWENGATE
Vis. Cen.
University College
Durham University Mus. of Archaeology
University of Durham
The Assembly Rooms
PALACE GREEN
Palace Green Library (Durham University)
Durham University (Elvet Riverside)
Hatfield College (Durham Uni.)
Durham Heritage Cen. & Mus.
Durham University (Dunelm House)
Durham University (Old Shire Hall)
Orchard Ho.
Durham Crown Court
HMP DURHAM
Durham Cathedral
DUN COW LANE
BOW LANE
Bow Banks
Kingsgate Bridge
(Old Fulling Mill)
Monks Dormitory & Treasures of Durham Univ.
College Gate
St. Chad's Coll. (Durham University)
St. John's College (Durham Uni.)
Cranmer Hall (Theological College)
The Chorister School
Prebends Bridge
Water Gate
St. Cuthbert's Society (Durham University)
Count's House
Count's Corner
RIVER WEAR
Graveyard
St. Margaret's Centre
DURHAM
Recreation Ground
CROSSGATE PETH
165
Weir
The College
Elvet Banks
Palmer's Close
High Yard
Deansgate Ho.
MAVIN STREET
WHINNEY HILL
THE HALLGARTH
Hallgarth View
OSWALD COURT
Nursing Home
St. Oswald's Jun. & Nurs. Sch.
St. Oswald's Cemetery
Mount Joy Cres.
Gladstone Villas
CHURCH STREET
STOCKTON ROAD
A177
Uni. Library
The Palatine Cen.
Science Laboratories
Durham University
Ogden Centre
Little High Wood
Mount Joy
Mountjoy Farm
Great High Wood
Bellasis
Playing Field
QUARRYHEADS LANE
Durham School
Playing Field
Observatory (Durham University)
Observatory Cottage
Observatory House
Durham
DH1
POTTERS BANK
St. Cuthbert's Cemetery
The Institute for Middle East & Islamic Studies (Durham Uni.)
Longridge
ELVET HILL ROAD
St.Mary's College (Durham University)
Tennis Cts.
Playing Fields
Playing Field
West Court
Teikyo University of Japan in Durham
SOUTH ROAD
Business School (Durham University)
St. Aidan's College (Durham Uni.)
Elvet Hill Cottage
Durham Univ. Oriental Museum
Trevelyan College (Durham Uni.)
Elvet Garth
Grey Coll. (Durham Uni.)
166
Dept. of Biological & Biomedical Sciences (Durham Uni.)
Spring Cott.
Prim. School
MARGERY LANE
GROVE STREET
CLAY LANE
BEECH CREST
A B C D E
1 2 3 4 5 6 7

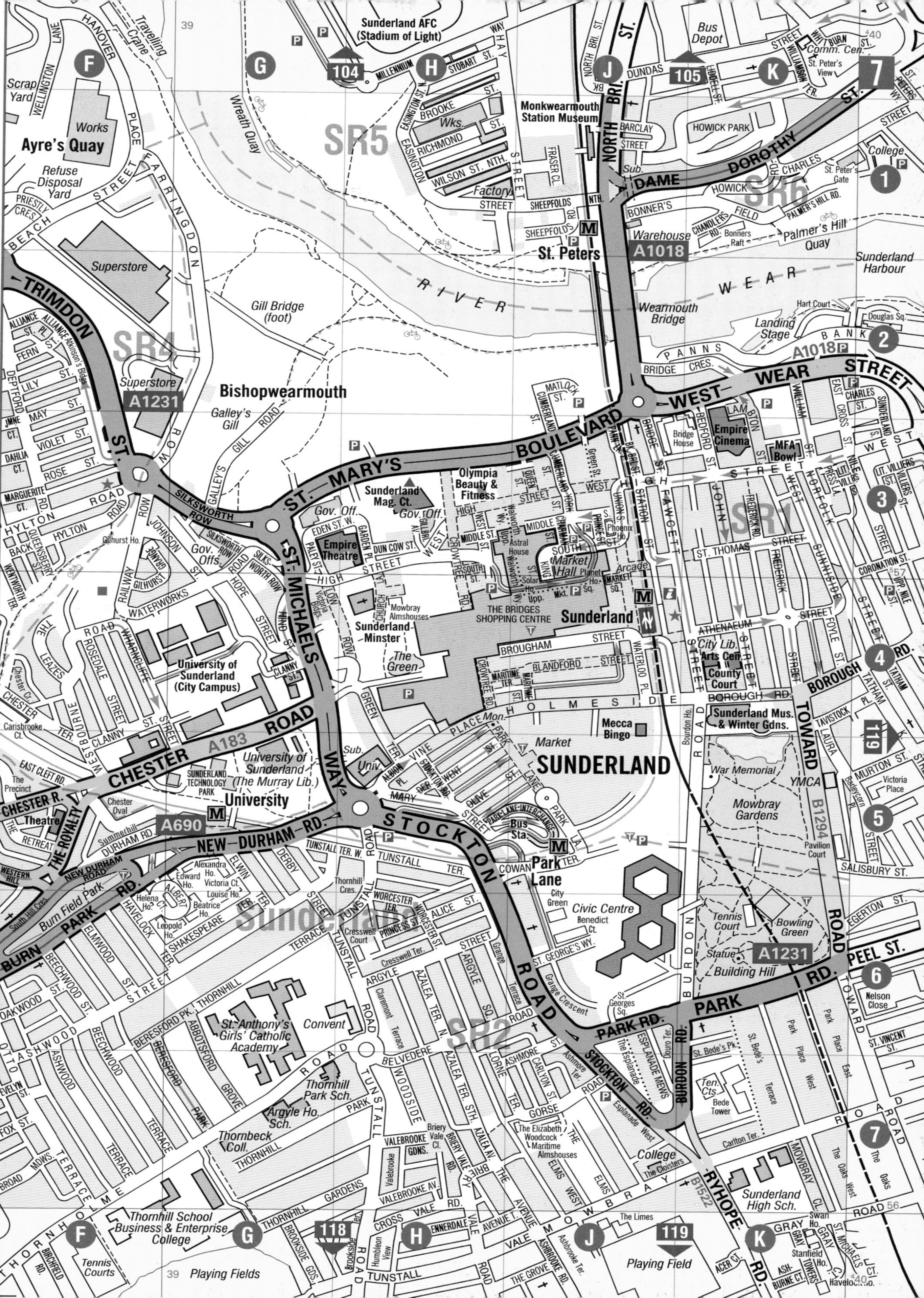

39
Sunderland AFC
(Stadium of Light)
104
105
F
G
H
J
K
7
Scrap Yard
Works
Ayre's Quay
Travelling Crane
Wreath Quay
SR5
Monkwearmouth
Station Museum
Bus Depot
Comm. Cen.
St. Peter's View
Howick Park
College
St. Peter's Gate
1
SR6
Refuse Disposal Yard
Superstore
St. Peters
A1018
Warehouse
Palmer's Hill Quay
Sunderland Harbour
River Wear
Gill Bridge (foot)
Wearmouth Bridge
Landing Stage
Hart Court
Douglas Sq.
2
SR4
Superstore
A1231
Bishopwearmouth
Galley's Gill
St. Mary's Boulevard
West Wear Street
Bridge House
Empire Cinema
MFA Bowl
Olympia Beauty & Fitness
Sunderland Mag. Ct.
Gov. Off.
Empire Theatre
SR1
3
The Bridges Shopping Centre
Sunderland
Market Hall
Mowbray Almshouses
Sunderland Minster
The Green
City Lib. Arts Cen.
County Court
4
University of Sunderland (City Campus)
Sunderland Mus. & Winter Gdns.
Mecca Bingo
Market
SUNDERLAND
War Memorial
YMCA
Mowbray Gardens
119
Victoria Place
5
University of Sunderland (The Murray Lib.)
Sunderland Technology Park
University
A183
A690
The Royalty Theatre
Chester Oval
Bus Sta.
Park Lane
Pavilion Court
B1294
Civic Centre
City Green
Benedict Ct.
Tennis Court
Bowling Green
Statue
Building Hill
A1231
6
Nelson Close
St. Anthony's Girls' Catholic Academy
Convent
SR2
Thornhill Park Sch.
Argyle Ho. Sch.
Thornbeck Coll.
The Elizabeth Woodcock Maritime Almshouses
Bede Tower
Ten. Cts.
College
The Cloisters
7
Sunderland High Sch.
B1522
Thornhill School Business & Enterprise College
Tennis Courts
Playing Fields
118
119
Playing Field
The Limes
Stanfield Ho.
Havelock Ho.
40
56
57
Ryhope Rd.
Stockton Road
Burdon Rd.
Toward Road
Park Rd.
Chester Road
New Durham Rd.
Burn Park Rd.
St. Michaels Way
Hylton Road
Trimdon St.
Holmeside
Borough Rd.
Mowbray Road
Thornhill Gardens
Tunstall Road

Quarry Hill
Banktop Plantation
A697
A1
Low Heighley
Warreners House
Low Heighley Rigg
West Shield Hill
HAG WOOD
HEIGHLEY WOOD
Heighley Wood
Kenneth Day Centre
Fairmoor Cemetery
NORTHGATE HOSPITAL
Silver Hill
Tennis Cts.
Sports Ground
Fair Moor
Nursery
Sewage Wks.
Kater Dean
Southernwood
(Proposed)
Fulbeck Grange
East Benridge
Benridge Bridge
Middle Benridge
East Lane End
West Lane End
Fulbeck
A192
Peacock Gap
POTTERY BANK
First Sch.
East Grange
Potterybank Wood
Davie's Wood
Playing Field
Morpeth Newminster Middle School
Rugby Football Grounds
Lowford Bridge
Mother's Wood
Dean House
Spital Hill Farm
Spital Hall
Mitford Bri.
Spital Hill
Scotch Gill
MITFORD ROAD
Community Centre
Pole Banks
MITFORD
Mill Farm
RIVER WANSBECK
B6343
Highford Bridge
Newminster Abbey House
Spring Hill
Inkles Heugh
Adders Haugh
Water Works
Newminster Abbey (remains of)
Abbey Banks
Stank Hill
Stable Green
Abbey Well
Abbeyfields First Sch.
Borough Wood
High House
Borough & Scotch Gills Nature Reserve
Mitford Castle (remains of)
Carlisle Park & Castle Wood
Highouse Dean
14
Mitford Park

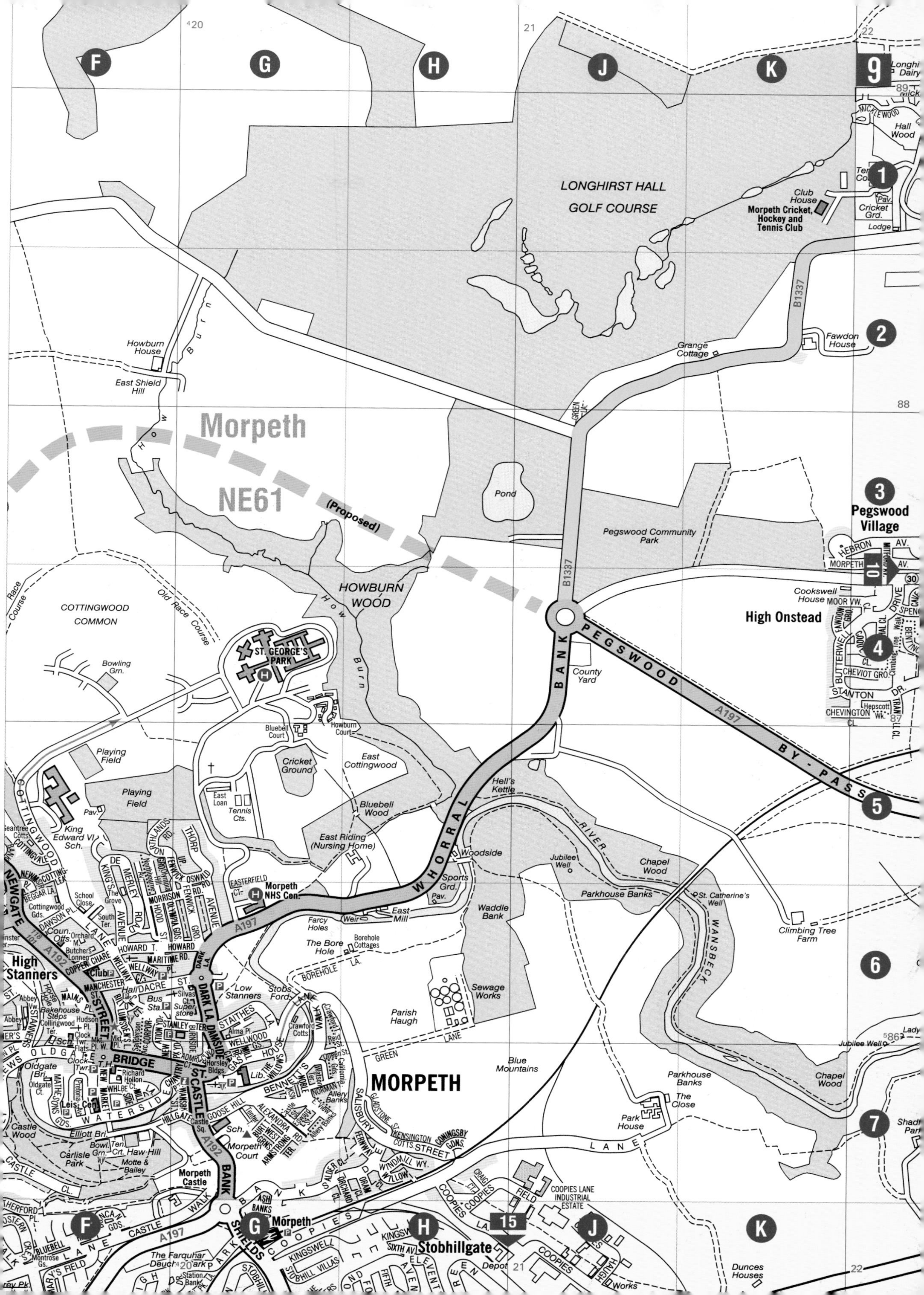

9
Morpeth
NE61
(Proposed)
LONGHIRST HALL
GOLF COURSE
Morpeth Cricket, Hockey and Tennis Club
Club House
Cricket Grd.
Pav.
Lodge
Hall Wood
Fawdon House
Grange Cottage
Howburn House
East Shield Hill
Pond
Pegswood Community Park
Pegswood Village
High Onstead
Cookswell House
HOWBURN WOOD
COTTINGWOOD COMMON
Old Race Course
Race Course
ST. GEORGE'S PARK
Bowling Grn.
Playing Field
Cricket Ground
East Cottingwood
Bluebell Court
Howburn Court
Bluebell Wood
East Riding (Nursing Home)
East Loan
Tennis Cts.
King Edward VI Sch.
Morpeth NHS Cen.
County Yard
Hell's Kettle
Woodside
Sports Grd.
East Mill
Weir
Farcy Holes
The Bore Hole
Borehole Cottages
Jubilee Well
Chapel Wood
Parkhouse Banks
St. Catherine's Well
Waddle Bank
Sewage Works
Parish Haugh
Climbing Tree Farm
Blue Mountains
Park House
The Close
Jubilee Well
Chapel Wood
MORPETH
High Stanners
Low Stanners
Stobs Ford
Morpeth Castle
Castle Wood
Carlisle Park
Motte & Bailey
Haw Hill
Morpeth Court
COOPIES LANE INDUSTRIAL ESTATE
Stobhillgate
Dunces Houses
Depot
Works
Morpeth
WHORRAL BANK
PEGSWOOD BY-PASS
B1337
A197
A192
RIVER WANSBECK
BRIDGE ST.
CASTLE BANK
NEWGATE
COTTINGWOOD
LANE
COOPIES
KINGSWELL
STOBHILL VILLAS
SHIELDS
15
10
20
21
22
88
87
86
89

10
Longhirst
Longhirst Village
Longhirst Farm
Longhirst Dairy
The Hainan
War Mem.
Old Vicarage
Council Off.
Stable Cl.
Micklewood Ho.
Hotel
Ford
Hall Wood
Pav.
Weir
Tennis Courts
Club House
Cricket Grd.
Lodge
Morpeth Cricket, Hockey and Tennis Club
B1337
Butcher's Lane
Sewage Works
Pipers Field
Longhirst Burn
Brocks Burn
Bothal Burn
The Brocks
Hall
Straker Ter.
Brocks Hill
Fawdon House
Morpeth
NE61
Monument
Playing Field
Pegswood First School
Pegswood Village
Pegswood Ind. Est.
Longhirst Road
Hebron
Morpeth Av.
Mitford Av.
Harewood Gdns.
Blenheim Gs.
Kirkharle
Petworth
Stowe Gs.
Trentham Gds.
Burghley Drive
Croome Gs.
Langwell Ter.
Beaumont Ct.
Lindisfarne
Dilston Ct.
Ford Cl.
Warkworth Dr.
Chipchase Cl.
Callaly Cl.
Castle Dr.
Belsay Cl.
Bamburgh Dr.
Walden
North Fm.
East Farm
Front St.
Cooperative Ter.
Subway
Bothal Park
Park Banks
Sewage Works
Cookswell House
Moor Vw.
High Onstead
Spencer Dr.
Whitefield
Charles
John St.
Edward
Ellis Sq.
William St.
South View
Patton Wy.
Wansbeck Cr.
Howburn Cres.
West Drive
Cheviot Gro.
Stanton
Chevington Cl.
Hepscott Wk.
Tranwell Cl.
De Walden Sq.
Bentinck Cres.
Bothal Cl.
Butterwell
Fawdon Gro.
Coquetdale Cl.
Climbing Tree Walk
30
Pegswood
Pav.
Pegswood Miners' Welfare Park.
Bothal Rd.
Cemy.
PEGSWOOD
Pegswood By-Pass
A197
Bothal
Park Wood
Bothal Bank
Bothal Barns
Bothal Bridge
War. Mem.
Bothal Castle
Bothal Banks
The Oaks
Whitefield
Twin Trees
Whitefield Dene
Bothal Mill
Weir
Wansbeck River
Bothal Mill Bridge
Climbing Tree Farm
Climbingtree Dean
Northstead Banks
Shadfen Cottage
Shadfen Bank
West Wood
Kennels
Bothalhaugh
The Woodlands
The Bungalow
Lady Well
Jubilee Well
Parkhouse Banks
Chapel Wood
Shadfen Park
Shadfen
South Lodge
West Fen
A196
Morpeth Rd.
16
9
Norbreck
Paddock Hall
North Farm
22
23
24
89
88
87
586
A B C D E
1 2 3 4 5 6 7

425
26
27
F
G
H
J
K
89
88
87
86
1
2
3
4
5
6
7
12
17
Portland
Burn
Abyssinia Wood
ELLINGTON ROAD
A1068
Hawthorn Cottage
Abyssinia House
Portland Terrace
Rec. Ground
WANSBECK BUSINESS PARK
NETWORK BUS. CEN.
WANSBECK BUSINESS CEN.
Depot
Eleventh Row
ROTARY — PARKWAY
A197
MORPETH ROAD
NEW MOOR CL.
HIGH MARKET
NINTH ROW
EIGHTH ROW
SEVENTH ROW
STATION ROAD
Bothal Middle Sch.
Bothal Cottages
Aged Miners' Cotts.
WELLHEAD TER.
Wellhead Court
Playing Field
ASHINGTON
Ashington Wansbeck First Sch.
Leis. Cen.
PARK VIEW
Park Villas
Cemy.
Bowl Grn.
Cricket Ground
ASHINGTON PARK
DARNLEY RD.
Ashington High Sch.- Annexe
Ashington
NE63
Ashington High Sch.
Lawn Court
COUPLAND RD.
GREEN LANE
HOLMDALE
Coney Garth
Coneygarth Cottage
SHEEPWASH ROAD
Bothal Barns Drift
Glebe Cottage
Ten Cts.
Sports Ground
The Steadings
WEST PASTURES
FALLOWFIELD
EAST PASTURES WAY
BLACKTHORN WAY
WANSBECK ROAD
Ashington Gardens
WELLHEAD DEAN ROAD
Wellhead Dean
WANSBECK RIVERSIDE PARK
WANSBECK RIVERSIDE CARAVAN PK
Playgrd.
Play. Field
Sheepwash Wood
Thieves Bank
RIVER WANSBECK
RIDING LANE
WELBECK WOOD
Riding Plantation
Bothal Riding
Sheepwash
Sheepwash Bri.
Sheepwash Gdns.
Weir
SHEEPWASH BANK
Choppington
NE62
Stakeford Bridge
Wansbeck Cottages
WESTFORD ROAD
A196
HALF MOON ST.
STAKEFORD
Rec. Grd.
Hall
Mowbray First Sch.
Youth Cen.
Choppington Wood
STAKEFORD
Windsor Villas
CAMBRIDGE RD.
NELSON RD.
OXFORD RD.
COLLINGWOOD
CRESCENT
Riverside Apts.
Leander

12
27
28
29
89
88
87
86
A
B
C
D
E
1
2
3
4
5
6
7
11
18
A189
A197
A196
A1147
B1334
Third House Farm
QUEEN ELIZABETH II COUNTRY PARK
Narrow Gauge Railway
Woodhorn Museum & Northumberland Archives
Woodhorn Colliery Houses
Aged Miners' Homes
NORTHUMBRIA CENTRE FOR ENTERPRISE
PARKWAY
LINTONVILLE ENT. CEN.
LINTONVILLE TER.
Depot
ASHINGTON
Army Reserve Centre
Superstores
Government Offices
Gov. Offs.
Superstore
Bus Depot
Health Club
Woodbridge
Maple Cl.
Elm Court
WANSBECK GENERAL HOSPITAL
ECC
Football Ground
Hirst Welfare Sports Ground
Ashington
NE63
WOODHORN ROAD
ST. PAULS CL.
HOWARD
CONEYGARTH PL.
CHRISTOPHERS
NICHOLAS CL.
WOODHORN LA.
BLYTH TER.
TYNE ST.
Woodhorn Villas
Hirst Castle M.
CHEVIOT VW.
ASHFIELD MEWS
STATION RD.
STATION
HALDANE ST.
LANGWELL CR.
YMCA
North View
Wansbeck Sq.
Lib.
Library Garden
SOUTH VW.
Offs.
Cricket Ground
Pav.
KENILWORTH
PARK VW.
EAST VIEW
ASHBOURNE
Arundel Sq.
Ridsdale Sq.
DARNLEY
Ashington High Sch. - Annexe
Ashington High Sch.
ELSDON DR.
KIELDER DR.
CHILLINGHAM
BAMBURGH T.
WARKWORTH CR.
ROSENEATH
VIEW
COUPLAND RD.
GREEN LA.
GREEN LANE
A J Cook Court
Greenacres Residential Home
HOLMDALE
Ten Cts.
Sports Ground
STONECROSS
GREENCROFT
LYNCROFT
CHELTENHAM CT.
GOODWOOD CT.
ASCOT GRO.
WETHERBY CL.
ALDERWOOD
ORCHID CL.
SORREL CL.
ORPINE CT.
EPSOM DR.
PASTURES
RYEDALE CL.
FALLOWFIELD WY.
CHAFFINCH
BLACKTHORN WY.
DENE
PLOVER FIELD CL.
KESTREL
FALCON
CELANDINE
BURNET CT.
PRIMROSE CT.
HAWKSMOOR CL.
JASMINE CT.
LILAC CT.
LARCHWOOD DR.
MAGNOLIA DR.
LAUREL DR.
LAVENDER CT.
REMSCHEID WAY
JUBILEE INDUSTRIAL ESTATE
Blackclose Dean
SENET ENTERPRISE CEN.
NORTH SEATON ROAD
WINDY GYLE
KIDLAND CL.
Eslington M.
BERRYMOOR
MOORHOUSE
Moor House Farm
Northumberland C of E Academy (Thomas Bewick Campus)
St. Benedict's RC Middle Sch.
Playing Fields
Ashington Hirst Park Middle Sch.
St. Andrews Ter.
Playing Field
HIRST PARK
Hirst
Pav.
Bowl. Grns.
Mem.
Ten. Cts.
Colliers Cl.
Northumberland C of E Academy (Josephine Butler Campus)
FALDO DR.
TORRANCE CL.
HARRINGTON
LYLE
GARCIA DRIVE
OAKMONT RISE
SUNNINGDALE RD.
SLALEY DR.
WENTWORTH WY.
NOUSTIE
SCOULAR
HARVEY CL.
BRENNAN CL.
BURNSIDE DRIVE
BEECHWAY
THORNTREE GDNS.
RIDGEWAY
MANLEY
OAKVILLE
ACADEMY RD.
LICHFIELD CL.
NORWICH
EXETER CL.
HIGHFIELD
WINCHESTER
ROCHESTER
ST. ALBANS
Windsor Wk.
St. Clements Ct.
MEADOWFIELD
SALISBURY CL.
CHICHESTER CL.
GLENDALE
BELGRAVE
WOODLANDS
FAIRFIELD DRIVE
AVONDALE
PEMBROKE
CARLTON
LYNDHURST RD.
Fox Cover
ANCROFT PL.
COLWELL RD.
FALSTONE CR.
WALLINGTON
Simonburn Lane
Kirkley Dr.
PARKSIDE COURT
SWEETHOPE
RUSKIN AV.
BROOMLEE
REDWOOD CT.
COLLEGE ROAD
Northumberland College
Playing Field
FIFTH AVENUE
SIXTH
SEVENTH
EIGHTH AV.
Monkseaton Terrace
CASTLE TER.
HAWTHORN
FIRST AVENUE
SECOND
THIRD AVENUE
FOURTH AVENUE
CAVENDISH TER.
GARDEN CITY
Welbeck
TITCHFIELD TER.
FARNE AV.
MITFORD DR.
NORHAM
ROWLINGTON
BYWELL
HAYDON
DILSTON DR.
ROTHLEY AV.
ELDER SQ.
BEECH T.
Cedar T.
Richardson
St. Aidan's RC & Hawthorn C of E Schs.
Depot
NEWBIGGIN ROAD
ROAD
PARK
Terrace
Coronation
HERON CL.
CORMORANT CL.
SWALLOW CL.
WATERFORD GRN.
MALLARD CL.
CYGNET
CURLEW
NURSERY
KINGFISHER CL.
SANDMARTIN
Cemetery
Rowlington Dean
Viaduct
BLACKCLOSE EST.
BLACKCLOSE BANK
ROAD
WESTFORD ROAD
Factories
Hall
Stakeford Bridge
Wansbeck Cottages
Playing Field
Stakeford First School
RIVER BANK
BANK
DR.
NAVAN CL.
WICKLOW CT.
ENNIS CL.
CARLOW
Choppington
NE62
HALF MOON ST.
CRESCENT
EAST FORD RD.
Dereham Ter.
Aged Miners' Homes
Pavs.
Bowl. Grn.
Ten. Cts.
Rec. Grd.
Hall
STAKEFORD
West Sleekburn
Wansbeck T.
Marshes Houses
Chanton Wynd
CHURCH AV.
Marcheys House Junction
Cemy.
Church
RIVER WANSBECK
Castle Island
CASTLE ISLAND WAY
Institute
Depot
WATERSIDE COURT
North Seaton Colliery
Community Centre
LINKS VIEW
Sea View
Wansbeck St.
ARMSTRONG WAY
ARMSTRONG CT.
FREEMAN CT.
FREEMAN WAY
NORTH SEATON INDUSTRIAL ESTATE
MERCHANT COURT
HEDLEY WY.
LOWTHER CL.
HAMBLETON CL.
VERN CL.
PENNINE DR.
COTSWOLD
BRECON CL.
MENDIP CL.
PENTLAND CL.
CHILTERN CL.
ASHWOOD BUSINESS PARK
BIRCHWOOD
Factory
168

13
F
G
H
J
K
1
2
3
4
5
6
7
430
31
32
89
88
87
586
Quarry Whiteoaks Cotts.
Woodhorn Mews
Woodhall Quarry Bungalow
Woodhorn Mill
Church Farm
Woodhorn
Woodhorn Church Museum
A197
NEWBIGGIN MOOR
NEWBIGGIN GOLF COURSE
Vesta Quarry
Hunkleton Side
Outer Carrs
White Holes
Way Foot
Newbiggin-by-the-Sea
NE64
Woodhorn Demesne
WOODHORN ROAD
Smallholdings
ALEXANDRA WY.
Alexandra Park
OAKWOOD AV.
MEMORIAL SQ.
War Mem.
COLLINGWOOD
KING GEORGES RD.
ALLAN RD.
OSWALD RD.
EMERSON ROAD
STOREY CR.
LATIMER WY.
STORE FARM R.
Newbiggin Sports & Comm. Cen.
Police Ho's
WOODLEA
Keir Hardie Court
MANOR DR.
SEA CREST ROAD
RICHARD ASHLEY CL.
QUEEN ST.
PROSPECT PL.
Club House
CHURCH POINT CARAVAN PARK
HIGH ST.
FRONT ST.
Vis. Cen.
Victoria Ter.
Promenade
Lifeboat Sta.
Newbiggin Maritime Cen.
Church Point
Newbiggin Point
Beacon End
Jefferson's Hully
Mary's Dub
Hully Rocks
Down Over Rocks
Little Bay
SUMMERHOUSE LA.
SUMMERHOUSE LANE
CENTRAL PARKWAY
Playground
The Northumberland C of E Academy (Grace Darling Campus)
Newbiggin Central Welfare FC
WELFARE CR.
CLEVELAND AV.
WILLIAM WAY
HOPKINSON WAY
SUTHERLAND AV.
BUTELAND T.
LONG PARK
ARGYLE TER.
B1334
HAVEN VW.
Sea Bank
Jubilee
WINDSOR RD.
GIBSON ST.
Lib.
Offs.
NEWBIGGIN-BY-THE-SEA
NEWBIGGIN BAY
A189
HAWESWATER CR.
RYDAL MOUNT
DERWENTWATER RD.
CONISTON RD.
WESTMORLAND AV.
NORTHUMBERLAND AV.
SEATON AV.
WESTFIELD CRES.
NORTH VIEW
NTH. SEATON R.
SPITAL CR.
HEPPLE RD.
Spital Burn
Spital House Farm
ROTHSAY TER.
MELROSE TER.
MELDON TER.
BEACH TERRACE
Aged Miners Homes
Bowl. Green
Milburn Pk.
Tennis Courts
Spital Carrs
Needle's Eye
Spital Point
Black Score
Sewage Works
Tanks
Links Quarry
TAYLOR AV.
KEEBLE CT.
BARNSTON VIEW
WEALLEANS CL.
Community Centre
NORTH SEATON
THE HOLLOW
THE DEMESNE
SOUTH RIDGE
SANDY LA.
South Side
B1334
ASHWOOD DR.
OAKWOOD WAY
North Seaton Links
Hawks Cliff
NORTH SEA
A189
SANDY BAY CARAVAN PARK
19
East View
Cambois House

14
8
A1
MORPETH
North Common
Tranwell
Tranwell Woods
MORPETH COMMON
MORPETH GOLF COURSE
N1 GOLF COURSE
GUBEON PLANTATIONS
COCKHILL MOOR
TRAMWELL AIRFIELD (disused)
WHALTON ROAD
B6524
Adders Haugh
Stank Hill
Stable Green
Water Works
Borough Wood
Borough & Scotch Gills Nature Reserve
Highouse Dean
Athy's Dean
West High House
High House
Abbey Well
Abbeyfields First Sch.
Mitford Castle (remains of)
Carlisle Park & Castle Wood
Mitford Park
Parkburn Plantation
Collingwood Plantation
Mitford Steads
Park Burn
The Grandstand
Star Plantation
Football Ground
Playing Field
Silver Hill
High Common House
Grindle Hill
Loansdean Hill Farm
Factory
COCK HILL
Rock Cottages
Reservoir (covered)
Tranwell Cottages
Deepdene
Newholm
Tranwell Farm
Tranwell Ct.
Tranwell House
Ash Grove House
Pump House
Gubeon
Commongate Plantation
Catch Burn
Runnymede
Schonbrunn
Camsen
Bromily
Ashwick House
Lindisfarne
Tall Trees
Woodside Cott.
Club House
Driving Range
Cockhill Plantation
Havis House
Threeways
Westwood Cott.
Skogen
Bramblings
Belt Plantation
Silver Birches
Welhill
Birchwood
Newlands
Whintings
Welhill Plantation
Cedar Cottage
Heatherlea
Redstacks
Kylemore
Seaton Ryde
Tranwell Woods
Stonewell
Fox Covert
Saltwick Plantation
Well Hill
Glororum Flats
Glororum Manor
Whitehouse Farm Cen.
North Whitehouse Farm
THE DRIVE
BETTS LANE
GUBEON WOOD
ABBEY MEADOWS
PASTURES
HIGH MOOR
SPELVIT
STOBHILL
QUEENSWAY
PILGRIMS WY.
TOWNSEND CRESCENT
GATE
SYLVAN CL.
MAYFIELD
SPRINGHILL
CASTLE MEADOWS
WESTFIELD
PRIORS WK.
CRAWHALL
GREEN ACRES
SWANSFIELD
WEST HILL
LELAND PL.
MONKS RIDGE
FRIARS GA.
FALCON
VANBURGH GDS.
TURNERS
DOWNING DR.
WOODHILL
CLARKS FIELD
RIDLEY CL.
ABBOTS WAY
HIGH HOUSE RD.
Renwick Ho.
St. Christopher's House
Abbey Banks
A B C D E
1 2 3 4 5 6 7
17 18 19
585 84 83 82

15
Morpeth
NE61
Morpeth Castle
Castle Wood
Carlisle Park
Elliott Bri.
Haw Hill
Motte & Bailey
Morpeth Court
Castle Sq.
Sch.
CASTLE BANK
CASTLE LANE
CASTLE CL.
BANK
ASH BANKS
Station Cotts.
COOPIES
KINGSWELL
SIXTH AV.
Stobhillgate
Depot
COOPIES LANE INDUSTRIAL ESTATE
COOPIES FIELD
COOPIES HAUGH
COOPIES WAY
Works
Dunces Houses
South Park
Park House
KENSINGTON COTTS.
STREET
CONINGSBY GDNS.
FENWAY
ALDER CL.
ORCHARD CL.
WINDMILL
WILLOW
LANE
A196
A192
A197
A1
SHIELDS ROAD
The Farquhar Deuchar Park
PARK
Station Bank
ST. MARY'S FIELD
BLUEBELL
RISE
Montrose Gs.
Comm. Cen.
High Church
THE WHALTON UNIT
Club House
RECTORY PK.
RECTORY DENE
HIGH PARK
HILLSIDE
ACOTT CL.
LOW STOBHILL
STOBHILL VILLAS
WHITEACRES
LINDISFARNE
ST. AIDAN'S
GRANGE
HEATHFIELD
BOUNDARY DR.
SECOND
FOURTH
FIFTH AV.
ELEVENTH
THIRD
FIRST AV.
SEVENTH AV.
EIGHTH AV.
NINTH AV.
TENTH AV.
GREEN
CHARLTON GS.
BEECH AV.
BROOM LANE
Morpeth Stobhillgate First Sch.
Collingwood School & Media Arts Coll.
Play. Fld.
Elliott Ct.
Noosi Ho.
CHOPPINGTON RD.
TURNER SQ.
CRES.
EASTGATE
JOBLING
Grange Ct.
Cheviot Ct.
EDEN
KENDOR GRO.
Southfield
SWEETHOPE
DENE
KYLINS
LOANSDEAN
WOOD
THE STEADS
MERLEY GATE
Merley Croft
Telford Ct.
Church Burn Drive
MIDDLE GATE
THE CRES.
THE AVENUE
THE CROSS WY.
LONG DR.
THE TURN
FAIRWAY
THE CHIP
Loansdean
Somersby Grange
SOUTHGATE
SOUTHGATE WOOD
Southgate
Northumberland County Hall
Pond
Burn
Catchburn
Catchburn Farm
Catch Burn
ROOKSWOOD
GROVE
SPINNEY
HIGH STOBHILL
EDGEHILL
WAY
THORNTON
SWINTON CL.
EGLINGHAM
CHATHILL CL.
WHITTINGHAM
FELTON CL.
High Stobhill Farm
Stobhill
REMINGTON CL.
Grange Mews
Grange Ho.
CROOKHAM
WHALTON CL.
NORHAM
ACOMB
CHATTON
The Knoll
Barmoor Farm
Barmoor Bank
Hepscott Bridge
Barmoor
New Houses
Coalburn Ter.
Coalburn Farm
Coal Burn
Hazeldene
DIAMOND HILL
Farndale
Wychwood
Baroda
HORNLEA
STONELEIGH
Hepscott Red House
THE ORCHARD
CROFT
South Lodge Wood
South Lodge
Fir Tree Copse
16
Hepscott Manor Farm
Hepscott Manor Cottages
Hepscott Manor
Greenland Plantation
Railway Cottage
Clifton Crossing
CLIFTON LANE
Clifton Lodge
Clifton
The Shires
Clifton Fm.
Clifton Ho.
Clifton Bridge
GT. NORTH RD.
Crag Plantation
High Clifton
High Clifton Farm
COLDWELL HILL
PARK DR.
9
F G H J K
1 2 3 4 5 6 7
420 21 22
585 84 83 82

16
Shadfen Park
22
23
24
10
South Lodge
Shadfen
West Fen
A196
MORPETH RD.
Norbreck
Paddock Hall
North Farm
Johnson Villas
New Cottages
South Farm
Willow
Burn
Healeywood
Hepscott Red House
Morpeth
NE61
Lea Crest
Works
High Holding Wood
Willow Burn
THE ORCHARD
CROFTS PK.
SIDE LA.
FIELD HOUSE LA.
FIELDHOUSE CL.
Park Side
South Ter.
15
South Lodge Wood
South Lodge
Fir Tree Copse
HEPSCOTT
The White House
Sewage Works
Hepscott Burn
BLUEHOUSE WOOD
HORNLEA
BRIARLEA
Baroda
STONELEIGH
Burnthouse Wood
Farm Cotts.
Field House Farm
Burnside Livery Stables & Kennels
Gas Valve Compound
Burnt House
A192
83
Netherton Letch
Coquet Day Centre
DRIVE
Northumberland PRU
BLYTH DR.
TWEED DR.
PARK
Hepscott Park
Blue House Farm Cottages
Howard House
NETHERTON
Blue House Farm
LANE
NETHERTON LANE
West Farm
THE GRANGE
North Farm Estate
Netherton Hall
NORTH FARM
Nedderton
B1331
OAKDALE
20
THE CROFT
HALLWOOD CL.
SOUTH FARM
The New Bungalow
STATION ROAD
The Cottage
The Bungalow
82
A
B
C
D
E
1
2
3
4
5
6
7

Choppington
NE62
Bedlington
NE22
STAKEFORD
GUIDE POST
CHOPPINGTON
Scotland Gate
Willow Bridge
Whinney Hill
BEDLINGTON
BEDLINGTON STATION
BARRINGTON INDUSTRIAL ESTATE
GALLAGER PARK
Bothal Riding
Riding Plantation
Choppington Wood
RIVER WANSBECK
Whinneyhill Plantation
Whinney Hill Farm
Whinneyhill Cottage Farm
Moor House
Bomarsund Farm
Sleekburn Cottage Farm
Windmill Farm
Glebe Farm
Windmill Farm Cottages
Sleek Burn
Willow Water
BARRINGTON ROAD
A1068
A196
A1147
B1331
CHOPPINGTON RD.
FRONT ST.
HIGH ST.
STAKEFORD
Cricket Field
Playing Field
Playing Fields
Meadowdale Middle School
St. Benet Biscop RC High School
Cemetery
Bedlington Terriers FC Welfare Pk.
Bebside Wood
17
11
18
21

STAKEFORD
Choppington
NE62
West Sleekburn
Castle Island
RIVER
A189
A1147
Bomarsund
Bedlington
NE22
Grange Park
East Sleekburn
BEDLINGTON STATION
Cowpen New Town
COWPEN
RIVER BLYTH
Bebside Viaduct
Kitty Brewster Bridge
Bedlingtonshire High School
Sleekburn Grange Farm
Mount Pleasant Farm
Cowpen Pool
Staithes Quay
Blyth Helipark
BLYTH RIVERSIDE BUSINESS PARK
SLEEKBURN BUSINESS CENTRE
WEST SLEEKBURN INDUSTRIAL ESTATE
High Brockland Farm
FERGUSONS BUS. PK. WEST
Sewage Works
Sports Ground
Football Ground
Stakeford First School
Stead Lane Prim. Sch.
Bebside Wood
12
17
22

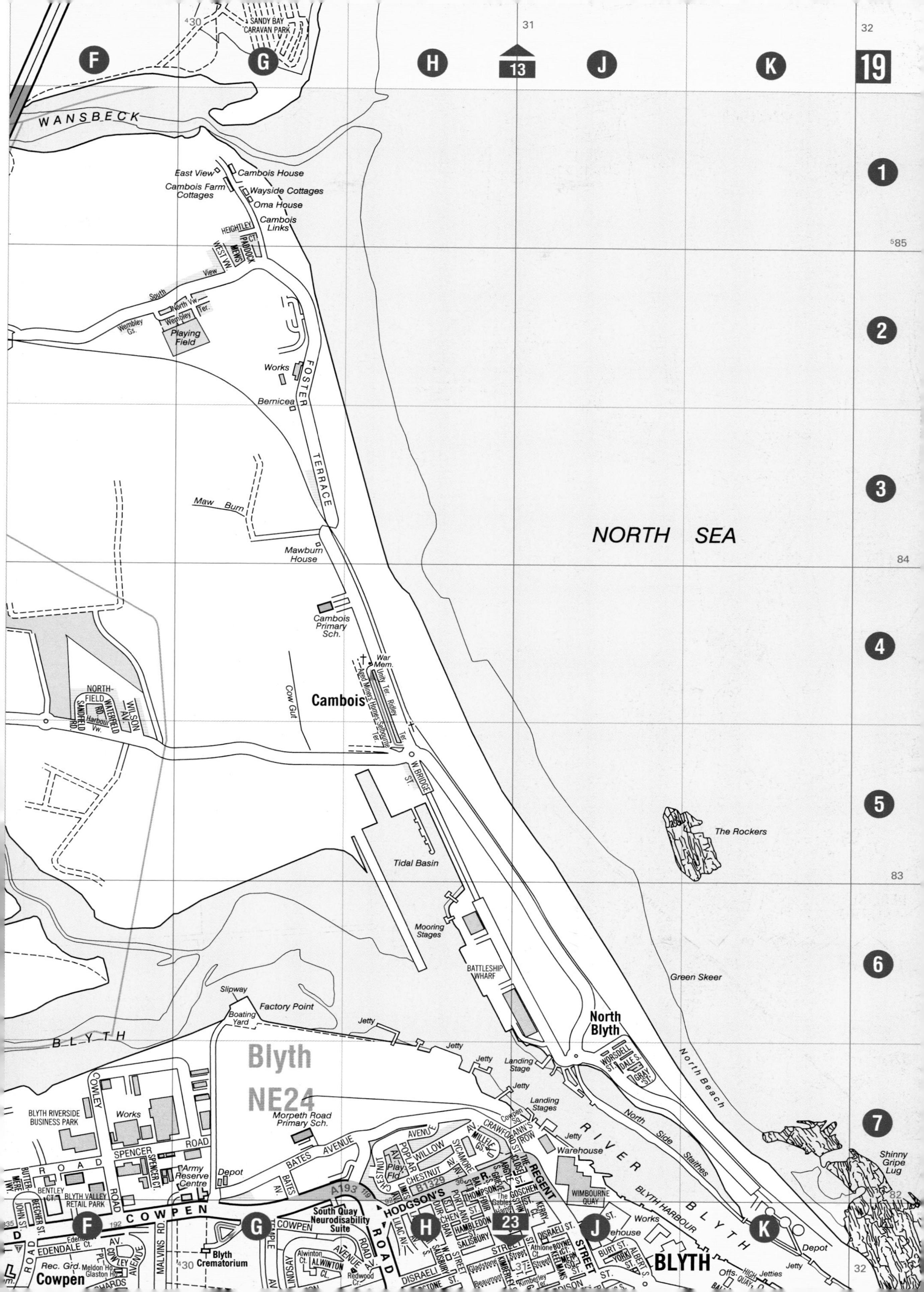
19
13
23
SANDY BAY CARAVAN PARK
WANSBECK
East View
Cambois House
Cambois Farm Cottages
Wayside Cottages
Oma House
Cambois Links
HEIGHTLEY
PADDOCK CT.
MEWS
WEST VW.
View
South
North Vw.
Wembley
Ter.
Wembley Gs.
Playing Field
Works
FOSTER
Bernicea
TERRACE
Maw Burn
Mawburn House
Cambois Primary Sch.
War Mem.
Aged Miners Homes
Unity Ter.
Ridley
Selbourne Ter.
Cambois
Cow Gut
NORTH-FIELD
WATERFIELD RD.
WILSON AV.
SANDFIELD RD.
Harbour Vw.
W. BRIDGE ST.
Tidal Basin
Mooring Stages
BATTLESHIP WHARF
NORTH SEA
The Rockers
Green Skeer
North Blyth
WORSDELL ST.
DALE S.
GRAY ST.
North Beach
North Side Staithes
Shinny Gripe Lug
Depot
Jetties
Jetty
Slipway
Factory Point
Boating Yard
BLYTH
Blyth NE24
Landing Stage
Landing Stages
Cowpen Sq.
RIVER BLYTH
BLYTH HARBOUR
Warehouse
WIMBOURNE QUAY
Works
Morpeth Road Primary Sch.
BLYTH RIVERSIDE BUSINESS PARK
COWLEY
Works
SPENCER
SPENCER CT.
ROAD
Army Reserve Centre
Depot
BATES AVENUE
BATES AV.
AVENUE
WILLOW
CHESTNUT
SYCAMORE AV.
POPLAR AV.
Play. Fld.
LIMES
CRAWFORD
MILLFIELD GS.
ANN'S ROW
THE REGENT
ARGYLE ST.
GOSCHEN
KERRY
THOMPSON
PORTLAND
HAMBLEDON
SALISBURY
B1329
A193
HODGSON'S ROAD
South Quay Neurodisability Suite
COWPEN
BUTTER-MERE WAY
JOHN ST.
BEECHER ST.
BENTLEY CT.
BLYTH VALLEY RETAIL PARK
ROAD
MALVINS RD.
EDENDALE CT.
AV.
COWLEY AVENUE
Rec. Grd.
Meldon Ho.
Glaston Ho.
Cowpen
Blyth Crematorium
TEMPLE
LINDSAY
Alwinton Ct.
ALWINTON CL.
AVENUE
Redwood Cr.
LILAC AV.
DISRAELI ST.
Gladstone
Beaumont
Kimberley Ter.
Athlone Ct.
BOYNE
KEELMANS
DISRAELI ST.
STREET
BURT ST.
YORK
ALBERT S.
BLYTH
HIGH QUAY
Offs.
F
G
H
J
K
1
2
3
4
5
6
7
31
32
430
585
84
83
82

Hepscott Park
Nedderton
North Farm Estate
Netherton Hall
West Farm
16
NETHERTON LANE
THE GRANGE
NORTH FARM
OAKDALE
THE CROFT
HALLWOOD CL.
SOUTH FARM
West Plantation
B1331
A192
The New Bungalow
STATION ROAD
STANNINGTON
Moor Farm Estate
The Cottage
The Bungalow
NETHERTON WOOD
Works
Fox Covert
South Plantation
Netherton Moor
Pegwhistle Burn
Netherton Park
Spts. Grd.
Netherton Park Childrens Home
Netherton Moor Farm
HARTFORD CARAVAN SITE
SHIELDS ROAD
Hartford Bridge
A1068
Visitors Centre
HARTFORD DR.
HARTFORD BRIDGE FM.
Hartford Wood
Hartford Hall
Four Acres
Low Middle Moor
Morpeth
PLESSEY WOODS COUNTRY PARK
East Moor
HARTFORD
Ford
NE61
Plessey Mill Farm
Chapel Close
Stannington Banks
Briery Hill
BLYTH
Plessey Banks
Plessey Flats
VALE
RIVER
Plessey Hall Farm
Plessey Wood
BANK
LANE
Fox Hill
Viaduct
Plessey Hall Dene
Stottford Dene
SHOTTON
WINDMILL INDUSTRIAL ESTATE
Chemical Works
24
FISHER

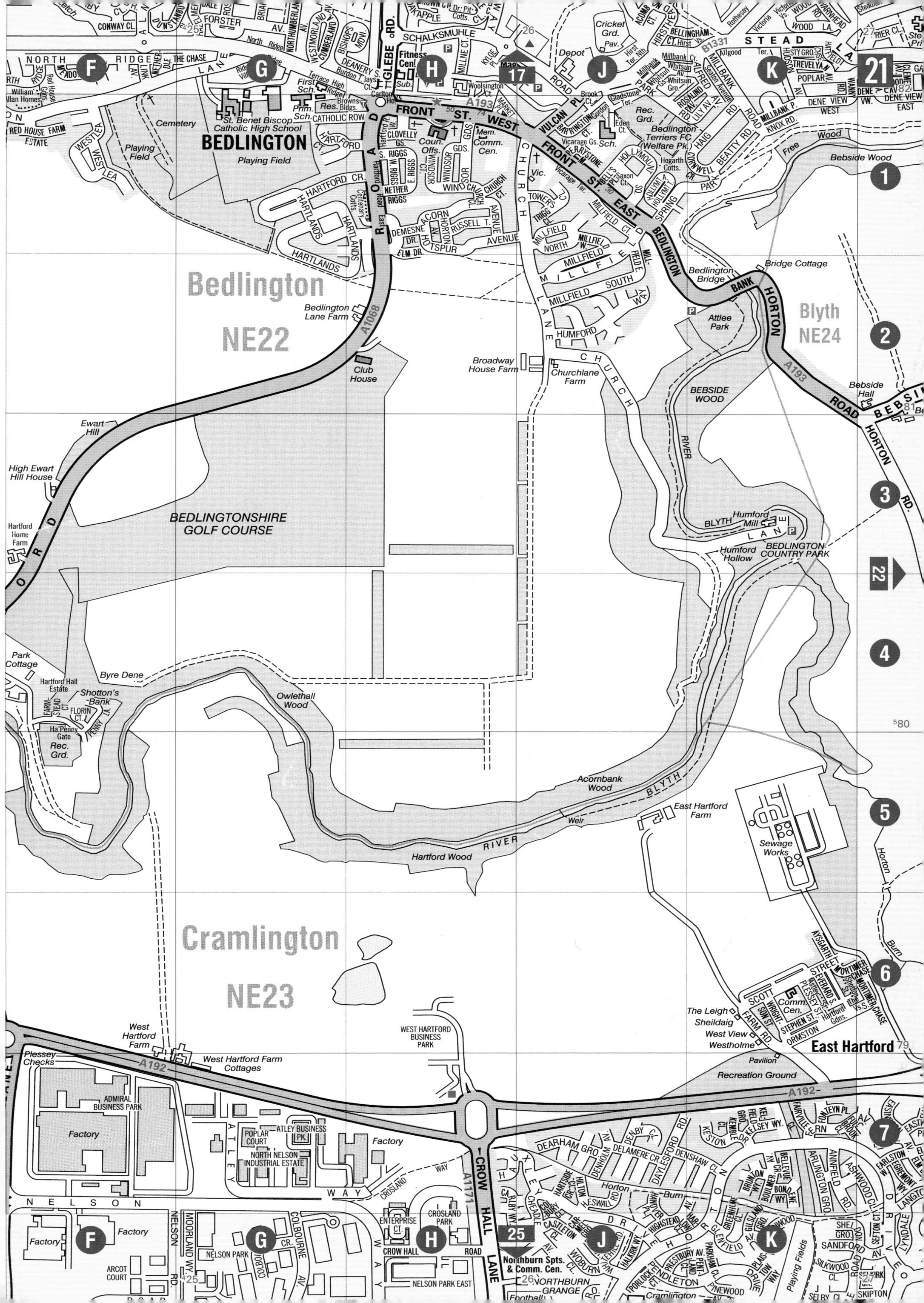
BEDLINGTON
Bedlington
NE22
Blyth
NE24
Cramlington
NE23
BEDLINGTONSHIRE
GOLF COURSE
BEDLINGTON
COUNTRY PARK
East Hartford
Bebside Wood
BEBSIDE
WOOD
Hartford Wood
Acornbank
Wood
Owlethall
Wood
Sewage
Works
Recreation Ground
ADMIRAL
BUSINESS PARK
NORTH NELSON
INDUSTRIAL ESTATE
WEST HARTFORD
BUSINESS
PARK
Cemetery
Playing Field
St. Benet Biscop
Catholic High School
Club
House
Broadway
House Farm
Churchlane
Farm
Bedlington
Lane Farm
Ewart
Hill
High Ewart
Hill House
Hartford
Home
Farm
Park
Cottage
Byre Dene
Hartford Hall
Estate
Shotton's
Bank
East Hartford
Farm
West
Hartford
Farm
West Hartford Farm
Cottages
Bedlington
Bridge
Bridge Cottage
Attlee
Park
Bebside
Hall
Humford
Mill
Humford
Hollow
Weir
RIVER BLYTH
FRONT ST. WEST
FRONT ST. EAST
BEDLINGTON BANK
HORTON ROAD
CHURCH LANE
A193
A1068
A192
A1171
B1331
CROW HALL LANE
NELSON
Northburn Spts.
& Comm. Cen.
17
22
25

Cowpen New Town
Blyth
NE24
Bebside
Chase Farm
East Hartford
Shankhouse
BLYTH GOLF COURSE
A189
A193
A192
A1061
B1505
B1331
HORTON ROAD
LAVEROCK HALL ROAD
BEBSIDE FRONT STREET
COWPEN ROAD
HATHERY LANE
FURNACE ROAD
RIVER BLYTH
Bebside Wood
Bebside Viaduct
Kitty Brewster Bridge
Kitty Brewster Farm
Blyth Helipark
Stead Lane Prim. Sch.
Furnace Bri.
High House Farm
Railway Cotts.
Recycling Centre
Bebside Hall
Bebside North Farm
Horton Grange Prim. Sch.
The Dales School
Superstore
Sporting Club, Blyth
Playing Field
The Blyth Academy
Blyth Riverside Business Park
Factory
Low Horton Farm
High Horton Farm
Vicarage
Horton Bridge
Bog Houses
Sewage Works
Shankhouse Bridge
Laverock Hall
Laverock Hall Cottages
Old Plessey Wagonway
Playing Fields
NE23

18
21
26

23
BLYTH
Cowpen
Isabella Pit
NEWSHAM
New Delaval
South Newsham
BLYTH RIVERSIDE BUSINESS PARK
BLYTH VALLEY RETAIL PARK
Morpeth Road Primary Sch.
Army Reserve Centre
South Quay Neurodisability Suite
Blyth Crematorium
BLYTH COMM. HOSPITAL
MIU
ALBION RETAIL CEN.
Malvin's Close Prim. Sch.
Blyth Sports Centre
St. Wilfrid's Cen. RC Prim Sch.
Civic Cen.
Mecca Bingo
KEEL ROW
Blyth Spartans AFC (Croft Pk.)
Patterson House
Bede Academy
Bede Academy South
Newsham Prim. Sch.
Miners' Welfare Park
New Delaval Prim. Sch.
PLESSEY RD. WORKSHOPS
Royal Northumberland Yacht Club
RIDLEY PARK
South Harbour
Blyth Cemetery
Newsham South Farm
Newsham North Farm
South Newsham Nature Reserve
Park Farm Cotts.
Newsham Junction
Reservoir (disused)
Camping Site
Fort House
Promenade
WIMBOURNE QUAY
RIVER BLYTH
North Side Staithes
BLYTH HARBOUR
COWPEN ROAD
WATERLOO ROAD
BRIDGE STREET
REGENT STREET
RENWICK ROAD
BROADWAY
BROADWAY CIRCLE
PLESSEY ROAD
ROTARY WAY
LINKS ROAD
SOUTH NEWSHAM ROAD
NEWCASTLE ROAD
NEWSHAM ROAD
RIDLEY AVENUE
WENSLEYDALE TER.
QUAYSIDE
HIGH QUAY
PRINCESS LOUISE RD.
BARRAS AVENUE WEST
AMERSHAM ROAD
WALKLEY ROAD
A193
A1061
B1329
B1328
B1327
B1523
Playing Field
Playing Fields
Cricket Ground
Play. Field
Rec. Grd.
Warehouse
Warehouses
Depot
Works
Jetty
Jetties
27
F
G
H
J
K
1
2
3
4
5
6
7
430
31
32
82
81
80
79

20
34
A
B
C
D
E
1
2
3
4
5
6
7
22
23
24
78
77
76
75
Morpeth
NE61
Shotton
Shotton North Farm
Shotton South Farm
SHOTTON LANE
SHOTTON LANE
Chemical Works
WINDMILL INDUSTRIAL ESTATE
A1068
FISHER LANE
Cale Cross
North Lodge
A1
Coal Wood
Down Hill
Northumberlandia
(The Lady of the North)
Factor
Trebor
Stonewall Plantation
North Wood
Weir
Newcastle upon Tyne
Smithy Plantation
Snitter Burn
Fusilier Plantation
Bog Plantation
Moor Plantation
BLAGDON LANE
50
Shotton Edge
North Wood
OLD GREAT NORTH ROAD
SOUTH DRIVE
BLAGDON PARK
NE13
Thornhill Cottage
South Lodge
Park House
Shotton Grange
NORTHUMBERLAND
NEWCASTLE UPON TYNE
Harehill Plantation
Jubilee Wood
Princess Royal Plantation
WHITE WOOD
Waterloo Plantation
Moor Farm Cottages
Plessey South Moor Farm
Shotton Edge South
HOYS WOOD
New Jubilee Plantation
Sir Jasper's Plantation
New Sally Nanny Plantation
Sandy's Letch
Brenkley
North Farm
BRENKLEY LANE
East Brenkley Farm Cottages
East Brenkley Farm
Crow Wood
Seven Mile House
Hotel
ARCOT
FISHER LANE

25
21
26
35
CRAMLINGTON
Cramlington
NE23
Nelson Village
Cramlington Village
Factory
POPLAR COURT
ATLEY BUSINESS PK.
NORTH NELSON INDUSTRIAL ESTATE
NELSON WAY
CROSLAND WAY
ENTERPRISE CT.
CROSLAND PARK
CROW HALL ROAD
CROW HALL LANE
A1171
Northburn Spts. & Comm. Cen.
NORTHBURN GRANGE
Football Pitch
NELSON PARK
ARCOT COURT
NELSON PARK WEST
NELSON PARK EAST
NELSON INDUSTRIAL ESTATE
Nelson Park Networkcentre
BAKER ROAD
EASTER PARK
NELSON DRIVE
SOUTH NELSON INDUSTRIAL ESTATE
RHODES CT.
SOUTH NELSON ROAD
Football Field
Get U Started Training
BASSINGTON LANE INDUSTRIAL ESTATE
Bassington
BOLAM BUSINESS CEN.
Works
Stother
Plantation
BASSINGTON INDUSTRIAL ESTATE
HUBBWAY BUSINESS CEN.
BASSINGTON AVENUE
A1172
Cramlington
Aged Miners Homes
Westwood Park
WESTWOOD GRANGE
Fanhouse
Superstore
BROCKWELL CENTRE
NORTHUMBRIAN ROAD
Cramlington Northburn Prim. Sch.
Burnside Prim. Sch.
Playing Fields
Playing Field
Cramlington Eastlea Prim. Sch.
PARKSIDE GRANGE
PARKSIDE DALE
Central Park
PARKSIDE CHASE
Cramlington Shanklea Prim. Sch.
PARKSIDE GLADE
CUMBRIAN ROAD
B1326
STATION ROAD
Osborne Ter.
WESTMORLAND WAY
WESTMORLAND RETAIL PK.
TOWN CENTRE
MANOR WALKS SHOPPING CENTRE
Concordia Leisure Cen.
FORUM
SOUTH MALL
Vue Cin.
Lib.
Cramlington Hall
HALL CLOSE DALE
Court Offs.
PARADISE ROW
Cramlington Hillcrest Sch.
Comm. Cen.
Play. Fld.
BEACONHILL GRANGE
BEACONHILL GREEN
Beacon Farm
Beacon Mews
Beaconhill Prim. Sch.
Comm. Centre
BEACONHILL GLADE
Westfield Park
BEACON LANE
BEACONHILL LEA
Garden Centre
Whitehall Farm
WHITELEA GRANGE
WHITELEA DALE
WHITELEA CHASE
WHITELEA GLADE
Hareside Prim. Sch.
DUDLEY LANE
B1319
LANCASTRIAN ROAD
St. Pauls RC First Sch.
HALL CLOSE GRANGE
HALL CLOSE GLADE
STONELAW DALE
STONELAW GRANGE
All Weather Pitch
St. Peter's RC Middle Sch.
Alexandra Park
Cramlington Learning Village
The Sporting Club of Cramlington
SOUTHFIELD GREEN
COLLINGWOOD GRANGE
Cragside C of E Prim. Sch.
Cragside Prim. Sch.
ARCOT HALL GOLF COURSE
Arcot Hall (Club House)
BARNS PARK
Damdykes
Plantation Farm
Manor Farm
SOUTHFIELD LEA
A19
B1505

26
22
25
36
A
B
C
D
E
1
2
3
4
5
6
7
27
28
29
Cramlington
NE23
East Cramlington
A189
A192
A1061
B1505
B1326
LAVEROCK HALL ROAD
Laverock Hall
Laverock Hall Cottages
Stickley Farm
North Moor Farm
East Cramlington Farm
Nature Reserve
EAST CRAMLINGTON INDUSTRIAL ESTATE
Depot
Works
East Cramlington Pond (Nature Reserve)
CRAMLINGTON HOSPITAL
COLLINGWOOD CHASE
The Grange
Middle Farm
Mare Close
Mare Close Farm
DURKEN BUSINESS PK.
Atkinson Ho. Sch.
Reservoir (Disused)
EASTFIELD LEA
Playing Field
EASTFIELD DALE
EASTFIELD CHASE
EASTFIELD GREEN
MAYFIELD DALE
MAYFIELD GLADE
KLONDYKE
HIGH PIT RD.
VILLAGE DRIVE
MAYFIELD ROAD
FRONT ST.
LAMB STREET
OLDSTONE
Lamb St.
Helen St.
MARJORIE ST.
ELIZABETH ST.
ALSTON
LANERCOST PK.
REEDSWOOD CRESCENT
WELDON RD.
ROWAN GRO.
BEECH AVENUE
THE PADDOCK
Cramlington Eastlea Prim. Sch.
Cramlington Village Prim. Sch.
Cramlington Hillcrest Sch.
Cramlington Ann Welfare Rec. Grd.
South Cramlington Farm
Cragside C of E Prim. Sch.
Cragside Prim. Sch.
Comm. Cen.
Cemy.
Blue Top Cotts.
NORTHUMBRIAN RD.
DURHAM ROAD
PORCHESTER DRIVE
OXFORD AVENUE
CLIFTON ROAD
CATERAN WAY
CRAMOND

27
23
28
37
Blyth
NE24
Whitley Bay
NE25
NE26
New Hartley
Seaton
SEATON DELAVAL
Seaton Terrace
Holywell
Meggie's Burn
Lysdon Burn
Reservoir (disused)
Camping Site
Playing Fields
Lysdon Farm
Lysdon Farm Cottages
Round Plantation
Seaton Red House Farm
New Hartley First Sch.
Hall
Aged Miners' Cottages
DELAVAL TRADING ESTATE
Factory
Depot
Harehope Court
Wheatridge Park Football Ground
Avenue North Farm
Seaton Delaval Hall
Seaton Village Farm
Harbord Ter.
Avenue Head Farm
Whytrig Middle Sch.
Seaton Delaval First Sch.
Astley High Sch.
Astley Park
Holywell Pond Nature Reserve
Holywell Village First Sch.
Bates Welfare Sports Ground
Vicarage
A190
A192
A193
THE AVENUE
ASTLEY ROAD
DOUBLE ROW
THE BRAMBLES

Gloucester Lodge Cottages
Gloucester Lodge Farm
Blyth NE24
LINKS ROAD
A193
Mile Hill
Hartley Links
Seaton Sluice Middle Sch.
The Sumps
Rocky Island
Sandy Island
Charley's Garden
COLLYWELL BAY
Collywell Sands
Crag Point
THE AVENUE
FOUNTAIN HEAD BANK
A190
Lookout Farm
Avenue North Farm
Seaton Delaval Hall
Mausoleum
Seaton
Harbord Ter.
Seaton Village Farm
Whitley Bay
NE26
Seaton Sluice Bridge
Seaton Lodge
Seaton Lodge Farm
Seaton Burn
SEATON SLUICE
BERESFORD ROAD
Hartley
Crag Park Play. Field
Fort House
OLD HARTLEY CARAVAN SITE
Old Hartley
Hartley East Farm
WEST END
EAST END
Obelisk Plantation
Obelisk
Holywell Dene
B1325
NORTHUMBERLAND
NORTH TYNESIDE
HARTLEY LANE
BLYTH ROAD
Transmitting Station
Hartley West Farm Cotts.
Hartley West Farm
Dark Plantation
NE25
Holywell Pond Nature Reserve
Playing Field
Holywell
Seaton Burn
WHITLEY BAY HOLIDAY PARK
27
38

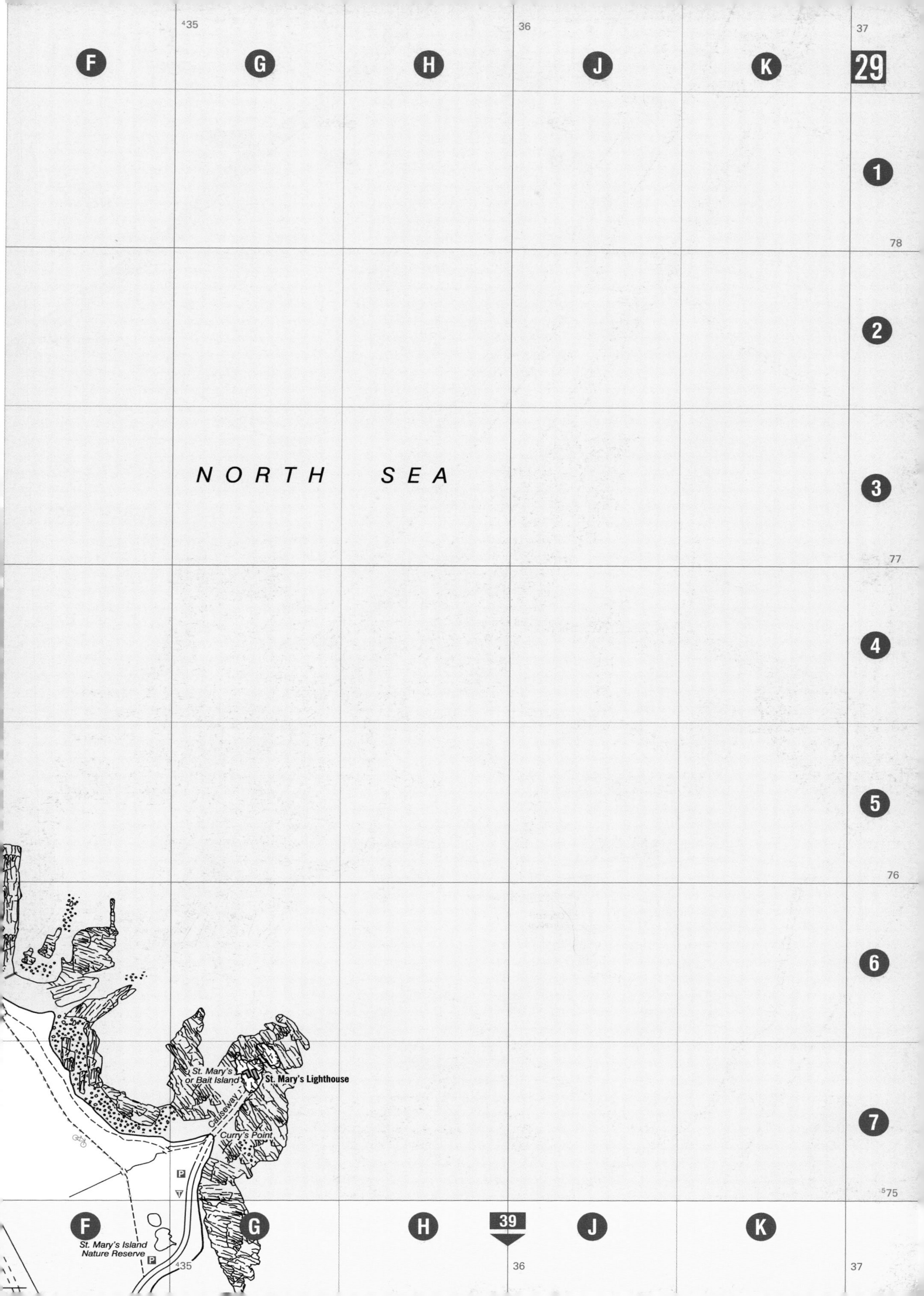

F
G
H
J
K
435
36
37
1
2
3
4
5
6
7
78
77
76
575
NORTH SEA
St. Mary's
or Bait Island
St. Mary's Lighthouse
Causeway
Curry's Point
St. Mary's Island
Nature Reserve
P
39

Milbourne
Higham Dykes
BLACK LANE
Mill Burn
Coldcoats Burn
A696
Middle Coldcoats
Coldcoats Covert
West Cotes
West Coldcoats Bridge
Charlton's Wood
Black Hill
Brick Kiln Wood
Shortridge
Woodside
Milbourne Lodge
BOTANY BAY WOOD
Striker's Bank
Bates' Plantation
South East Farm
Coldcoats Moor
Larch Wood
Newcastle
THORNY COVERT
Small Burn
Eastfield House
Redhouse Farm
FORSTER'S PLANTATION
Field Houses
LIMESTONE
Long Plantation
Dissington East Houses
NE18
PADDOCK LA.
Dissington
North Lodge
Benacres Plantation
RICHMOND WAY
Richmond Fields
REGENCY WY.
PEMBROKE
WESTERN
GRENVILLE CT.
RUN
KING JOHN'S CT.
East Lodge
Dissington Cottages
DISSINGTON PARK
Pont
River
Hall
Weir
40
THE CRESCENT
Donkins Houses

Swallow Sike
East Coldcotes
Hiddlestone
Coldcoats Burn
River Pont
Ecklindale
Smallburn Lodge
Smallburn
East Smallburn Bridge
Berwickhill Bridge
NORTHUMBRIA POLICE HEADQUARTERS
Ashcroft
Tudor Croft
North Court
North View
South Coldcoates
West Smallburn Bridge
upon Tyne
Grange Lea
Eland Green
Keepers Cottage
West Farm
NE20
Eland Hall Farm
Eland Hall
Eland Close
Richard Coates C of E Middle School
Ponteland First Sch.
Collingwood Cotts.
Woodside Farm
A696
THE BEECHES
WEST ROAD
MAIN ST.
BELL VS.
PONTELAND
Clickemin Br
West Houses
PONTELAND
Ponteland Leisure Centre
Playing Fields
Coat Hill
Ponteland Middle Sch.
Ponteland High Sch.
Nursery
ROTARY WAY
B6545
B6323
DARRAS HALL
RECREATION AREA
Darras Station
Darras Mews
41
32

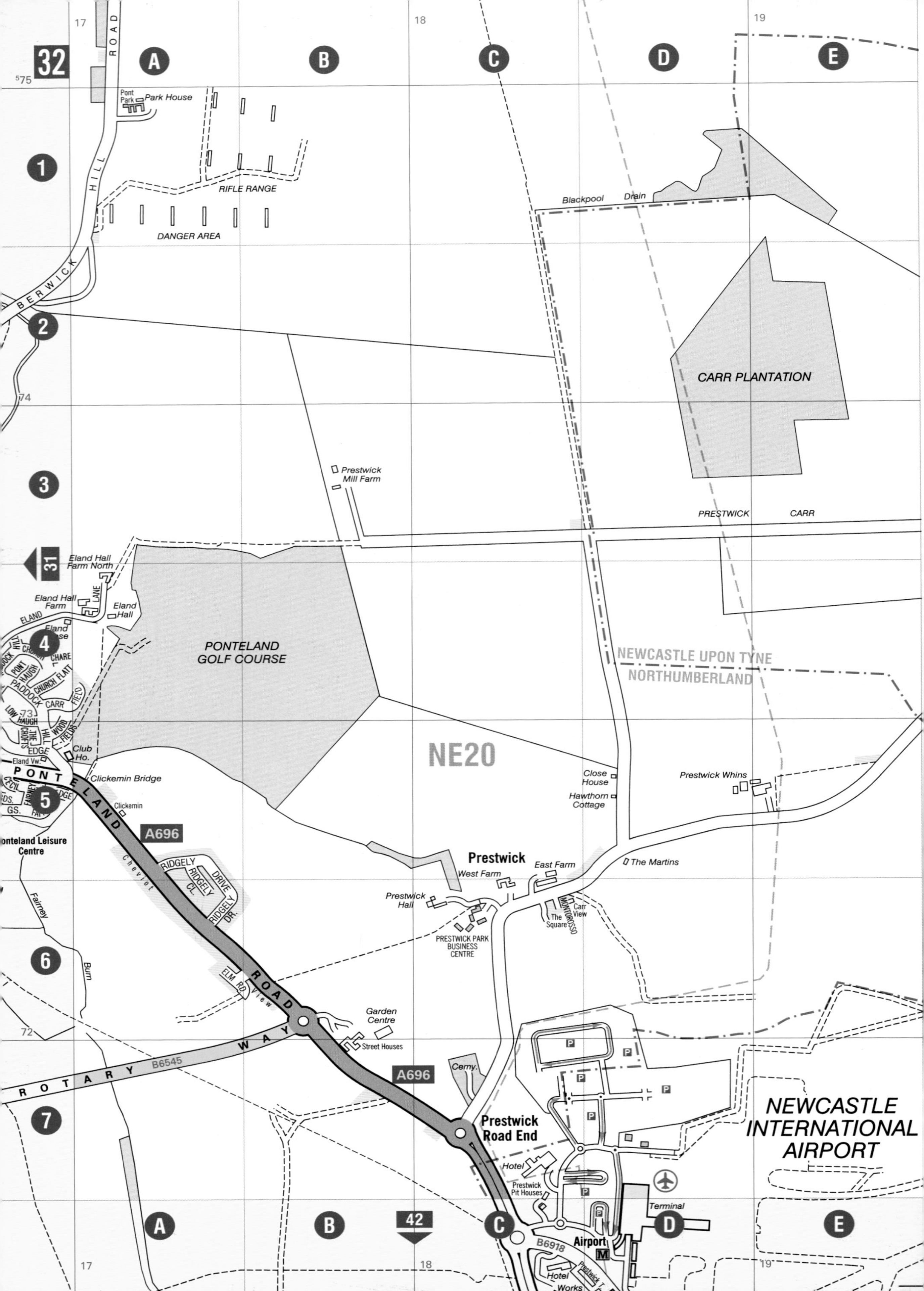

A
B
C
D
E
1
2
3
4
5
6
7
17
18
19
75
74
73
72
Park House
Pont Park
HILL ROAD
RIFLE RANGE
DANGER AREA
BERWICK
Blackpool Drain
CARR PLANTATION
Prestwick Mill Farm
PRESTWICK CARR
31
Eland Hall Farm North
Eland Hall Farm
Eland Hall
ELAND LANE
PONTELAND GOLF COURSE
NEWCASTLE UPON TYNE
NORTHUMBERLAND
NE20
Club Ho.
Clickemin Bridge
Clickemin
PONTELAND ROAD
A696
Ponteland Leisure Centre
Fairney Burn
Cheviot View
RIDGELY DRIVE
RIDGELY CL.
RIDGELY DR.
ELM RD
Close House
Hawthorn Cottage
Prestwick Whins
Prestwick
West Farm
East Farm
The Martins
Prestwick Hall
PRESTWICK PARK BUSINESS CENTRE
The Square
MONTROSSO
Carr View
Garden Centre
Street Houses
ROTARY WAY
B6545
Cemy.
Prestwick Road End
NEWCASTLE INTERNATIONAL AIRPORT
Hotel
Prestwick Pit Houses
Terminal
Airport
B6918
Works
42

33
Brenkley
Brenkley Lane
North Farm
South Brenkley Cottages
East Brenkley Farm
Fox Covert
Trinidad Plantation
Steve Smiths Shooting Ground
Horton Grange Road
Gardener's Houses Farm
Blackpool Drain
Curlew Cottage
Carr Grange Farm
Carr Road
Newcastle upon Tyne
The Venture
Marsfen
Mason
Prestwick
Prestwick Road
March Ter.
South View
DINNINGTON
NE13
Main Road
East Acres
West Acres
Beech Avenue
Sycamore Av.
Dinnington First Sch.
Rec. Grd.
Cycle Track
Youth Cen.
Hartley Burn
34
Moory Spot
Mill Hill
Sandy Lane
Greencroft
Hack Hall
Toft Hill
Dinnington Road
Coach Lane
Hawthorn Cottage
Woodlands
Havannah
Works
Beeftub Plantation
Lane Plantation
Foxcover Wood
High Sunnyside Plantation
43

34
Brenkley
North Farm
East Brenkley Farm Cottages
Crow Wood
Seven Mile House
24
A
B
C
D
E
1
2
3
4
5
6
7
33
44
A1
A19
A1068
A1056
B1318
B1321
Hotel
FISHER LANE
ARCOT LANE
FRONT STREET
Seaton Burn Recreation Ground
Bowling Green
Playground
Tennis Court
Football Ground
Factory
BLEZARD BUSINESS PARK
SEATON BURN
Newcastle upon Tyne
North - East Mason Farm
Hartley Burn
Seaton Burn
Big Waters Nature Reserve
NE13
NEWCASTLE UPON TYNE
NORTH TYNESIDE
Recreation Ground
BRIDGE ST.
PATIENCE AV.
MEADOW DRIVE
RAYLEIGH DR.
CHANTRY DRIVE
McCRACKEN DRIVE
MORPETH AV.
TAYLOR AV.
STALKS ROAD
SANDY LANE
BRUNSWICK INDUSTRIAL ESTATE
BRUNSWICK PARK IND. ESTATE
Depots
BRUNSWICK VILLAGE
WIDE OPEN
Sports Ground
Lockey Park
NORTH ROAD
WORCESTER WAY
Hazlewood Prim. Sch.
Lib. Comm. Cen.
Subway
BEACON DRIVE
Morley Hill Farm
Morley Hill Cottage
Recreation Ground
MELNESS ROAD
COACH LANE
Hawthorn Cottage
Woodlands
Havannah Nature Reserve
Three Mills Picnic Site
Strawberry Ter.
Comm. Cen.
NEWHAM AVENUE
CASTLE ST.
HIGH RIDGE
HAZLERIGG
Cemetery
Gosforth Park Villas
Nursery
Garden Centre
Dark Plantation
The Hawthorns
Letch Plantation
NORTH PARK
Offices
OAKWOOD DRIVE
HAZELWOOD RD.
BIRCHWOOD CHASE
ROTARY WAY
Hotel
22
23
24
72
73
74
75

35
36
25
45
Cramlington
NE23
NE12
NE3
DUDLEY
Annitsford
Fordley
Burradon
A19
A1171
A189
A1056
B1319
B1321
B1505
NORTHUMBERLAND
NORTH TYNESIDE
NORTHUMBERLAND BUSINESS PARK
PARKLANDS GOLF COURSE
SANDY LANE
KILLINGWORTH WAY

36
26
35
46
A
B
C
D
E
1
2
3
4
5
6
7
A189
A19
A190
A1056
B1505
B1321
B1322
B1317
Annitsford
Cramlington
NE23
NE12
SEGHILL
Burradon
Camperdown
KILLINGWORTH
ANNITSFORD ROAD
STATION ROAD
BACKWORTH LANE
BACKWORTH WAY
KILLINGWORTH WAY
BURRADON ROAD
FRONT STREET
Seghill Hall
Rose Park
Reservoir (Disused)
Weir
The Grange
Middle Farm
Mare Close Farm
DURKEN BUSINESS PK.
Recreation Ground
Youth Club
Scout Hut
Seghill First Sch.
Burradon Farm Cottages
Burradon House
Abattoir
Playing Field
Hard Games Pitches
Burradon Prim. Sch.
West Farm
High Farm
Poultry Farm
Seatonburn Wagonway
Seaton Burn
Amberley Prim. Sch.
Grasmere Academy
Superstore
White Swan Cen.
East House Farm

37
SEATON DELAVAL
Seaton Terrace
Holywell
Holywell Pond Nature Reserve
Whitley Bay
NE25
NORTHUMBERLAND
NORTH TYNESIDE
Newcastle upon Tyne
NE27
East Holywell
West Holywell
BACKWORTH
EARSDON
SHIREMOOR
BACKWORTH GOLF COURSE
EARSDON ROAD
ROTARY WAY
A190
A192
A186
B1322
27
38
47
F
G
H
J
K
1
2
3
4
5
6
7

38
32
33
34
A
B
C
D
E
1
2
3
4
5
6
7
28
37
48
Dark Plantation
Hartley West Farm
Holywell Nature Reserve
Playing Field
HOLYWELL DENE RD.
EAST GRANGE
Strother Farm
Holy Well
Seaton Burn
Holywell Dene
Seaton Burn
Weir
Crow Hall Farm
HARTLEY LANE
B1325
NORTH TYNESIDE
NORTHUMBERLAND
Whitley Bay
BLYTH ROAD
A193
WHITLEY BAY HOLIDAY PARK
Whitley Crematorium
Brierdene Farm
WHITLEY BAY GOLF COURSE
Brierdene Burn
Club House
Whitley Lodge First Sch.
EARSDON ROAD
A192
Brierdene Burn
Nursery
NE25
East Farm
Earsdon Cemetery
Comm. Cen.
CHURCH WAY
Hall
West Farm
FRONT STREET
War Mem.
Eastfield House
Wellfield
EARSDON
A186
Playground
South Wellfield
Recreation Ground
Wellfield Middle Sch.
South Wellfield First Sch.
Bertram Grange Community Centre
Recreation Ground
NE27
Stanton Lodge
SHIREMOOR
BEAUMONT DRIVE
HADDINGTON
GAINSBOROUGH CL.
HILLSDEN RD.
DIPTON ROAD
WOODBURN
ST. LUCIA CL.
CARAGSIDE DRIVE
MONKRIDGE
LONGRIDGE
Southridge First Sch.
A1148
Whitley Bay High Sch.
Running Track
Tennis Courts
Valley Gardens Middle Sch.
MONKSEATON DRIVE
HEPSCOTT
Superstore
NEWSTEADS DRIVE
FAIRWAYS
SUNNINGDALE
HOLLYWELL AVENUE
HILLCREST
THE DENE
West Monkseaton
Monkseaton
EARSDON ROAD
A192
SEATONVILLE RD.
Dickey's Holm
Crawford Ten. Park
Appletree Gdns. First Sch.
Mid. Sch.
West Monkseaton
Woodlawn Sch.
THORNTREE DRIVE
MARINA DRIVE
SANDRINGHAM DR.
Orchid M. Wilton Manse
HAREWOOD
OTTERBURN

NORTH SEA
WHITLEY BAY
Whitley Sands
St. Mary's Island Nature Reserve
Curry's Point
Miniature Golf Course
NE26
Monkseaton
Waves at Whitley Bay
Coquet Pk. First Sch.
Panama Gdns.
War Mem.
Whitley Pk.
Paddling Pool
Outfall
Table Rocks
Swimming Pool
Brown's Bay
Brown's Point
Superstore
Sports Cen.
Marden Bri. Mid. Sch.
Play. Fld.
Marden Quarry Nature Reserve
Cricket Ground
Ice Rink
Nursery
Whitley Bay (Hillheads)
Cullercoats
Lifeboat Sta.
North Pier
Dove Marine Lab
CULLERCOATS BAY
Whitley Bay
Running Track
Marlborough House
THE LINKS
PARK AVENUE
MARDEN ROAD SOUTH
HILLHEADS ROAD
MONKSEATON DRIVE
NORTHERN PROMENADE

29
49

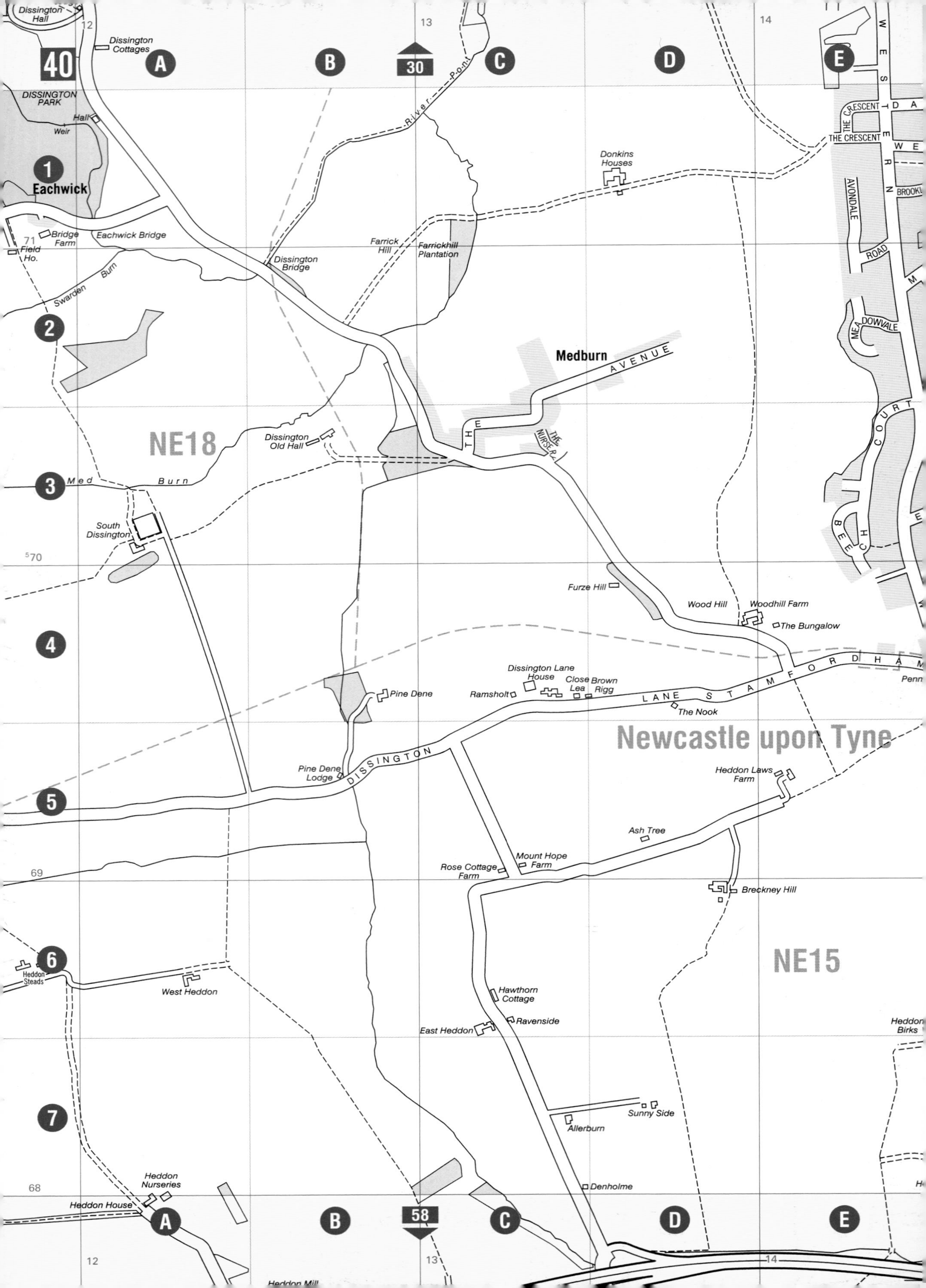

Dissington Hall
Dissington Cottages
DISSINGTON PARK
Hall
Weir
Eachwick
Bridge Farm
Eachwick Bridge
Field Ho.
Swarden Burn
River Pont
Farrick Hill
Farrickhill Plantation
Dissington Bridge
Donkins Houses
Medburn
THE AVENUE
THE NURSERY
NE18
Dissington Old Hall
Med Burn
South Dissington
Furze Hill
Wood Hill
Woodhill Farm
The Bungalow
Dissington Lane House
Close Lea
Brown Rigg
Ramsholt
Pine Dene
The Nook
STAMFORDHAM
LANE
DISSINGTON
Pine Dene Lodge
Newcastle upon Tyne
Heddon Laws Farm
Ash Tree
Mount Hope Farm
Rose Cottage Farm
Breckney Hill
NE15
Heddon Steads
West Heddon
Hawthorn Cottage
Ravenside
East Heddon
Heddon Birks
Sunny Side
Allerburn
Denholme
Heddon Nurseries
Heddon House
Heddon Mill
WESTERN
THE CRESCENT
AVONDALE ROAD
BROOKL
MEADOWVALE
COURT
BEECH
Penn

30

58

41
31
42
59
DARRAS HALL
NE20
NE5
High Callerton
Dissington March
Callerton Lane End
NORTHUMBERLAND
NEWCASTLE UPON TYNE
CALLERTON LANE
PONTELAND ROAD
STAMFORDHAM ROAD
B6323
B6324
RECREATION AREA
Darras Hall First Sch.
High Callerton Farm
Callerton Hall
Brough Hill
Braid Hill
Hold House Farm
Birney Hill
Birney Hill Farm
Forge Cottage
Fell House
Resr. (Cov.)
CALLERTON COMMON
Callerton Grange
Throckley Marsh
Broom Hall
Callerton Lane End Cotts.
Stoneville
Crescent Farm
THROCKLEY COMMON
FOX COVERT
West Woodside
Birks Cottage
Lough House
Field House
Holmside
Birds Hill
Pineglades
Long Plantation
Dewley Hill
Dewley Burn
Dewley Farm
Dewley Farm Cotts.

Prestwick Road End
Hotel
Prestwick Pit Houses
A696
32
B6918
Airport
Terminal
NEWCASTLE INTERNATIONAL AIRPORT
Hotel
Works
PRESTWICK INDUSTRIAL ESTATE
WOOLSINGTON
PONTELAND
NORTHUMBERLAND
NEWCASTLE UPON TYNE
Dark Plantation
Maintenance Area
Hold House Farm
Black Callerton Hill
NE20
AIRPORT
FREIGHTWAY
FREIGHT VILLAGE
Sports Ground
Pav.
Hotel
Hawthorn Cottage
Callerton Station Cotts.
LANE
Callerton Parkway
P+R
Callerton Parkway
Luddick Cottages
CALLERTON
Low Luddick House
Depot
ROAD
41
East Farm
West Farm
Black Callerton
WOOLSINGTON
A696
DUKES MDW
BY-PASS
NE5
Andrew Plantation
Armstrong St.
Short Row
WHORLTON
Butterlaw Farm
Callerton Burn Close
Club
STAMFORDHAM
Callerton
Severs Ter.
Morton Cr.
Lough Bridge
Loughbridge House
Whorlton House
Whorlton Hall
Whorlton Hall Cottages
Whorlton
B6324
Playing Field
Lowbiggin
WESTERHOPE GOLF COURSE
LANE
MANDARIN
MARQUIS
MAGENTA
CRESCENT
CL.
60
CLOSE
MALAGA
MAGENTA
AVENUE
CRES.
ROAD
Graveyard
JEDBURGH
CLOSE
INGRAM
DR.
MEADOWS
Whorlton Grange Cotts.
Whorlton Grange
Club House
Fell House Farm
FELL HO. FARM RD.
WALBOTTLE
17
18
19
71
70
69
68
A
B
C
D
E
1
2
3
4
5
6
7

NE13
WOOLSINGTON PARK
Newcastle upon Tyne
Woolsington Hall
Beeftub Plantation
Havannah
Foxcover Wood
High Sunnyside Plantation
Lane Plantation
West Brunton Farm Cottages
West Brunton Farm
BRUNTON LANE
DINNINGTON ROAD
Sunnyside
High Beeches
Whiteoaks
Oak Lea
Trees
Old Trees
Braeside
Riftswood
South Lodge Plantation
Hill Crest
Ouse Burn
Woolsington Bridge
Weir
Lakeside
Lakeside Cottage
Battery Plantation
Brinkburn
Park Broom
Ravendale
Cherrytrees
Brunton Bridge
Brunton Mill
Brunton Bridge Farm
KINGSTON PARK ROAD
PONTELAND ROAD
B6918
Nursery
Red Runner Plantation
UNIVERSITY OF NORTHUMBRIA SPORTS GROUND
Tennis Courts
Pavilion
Bullock Steads
Bullock Steads Cottages
Rugby Football Grounds
Newcastle Falcons RUFC (Kingston Park)
WOOLSINGTON BY-PASS
Kenton Bankfoot
Bank Foot
Kingston Park
Kingston Park Prim. Sch.
SpringsLite Gym
Comm. Cen.
Superstore
NE3
Factory
Belvedere Retail Park
Airport Industrial Estate
Kingston Retail Park
Army Reserve Centre
Training Centre
Bank Top
Hotels
NEWCASTLE WESTERN BY-PASS
A1
A696
Low Newbiggin Farm
HAREYDENE LANE
Hareydene
Pecks House Farm
Teasdale Ho.
THE NEIGHBOURHOOD CENTRE
Playing Field
Cheviot Prim. School
Newbiggin Hall Estate
Kenton Bar Prim. Sch.
St. Cuthbert's Catholic Primary School
Playing Fields
Kenton School
Subway
Hartburn
Medwood
Comm. Cen.
33
44
61
F G H J K
1 2 3 4 5 6 7
420 21 22
570 71 69 68

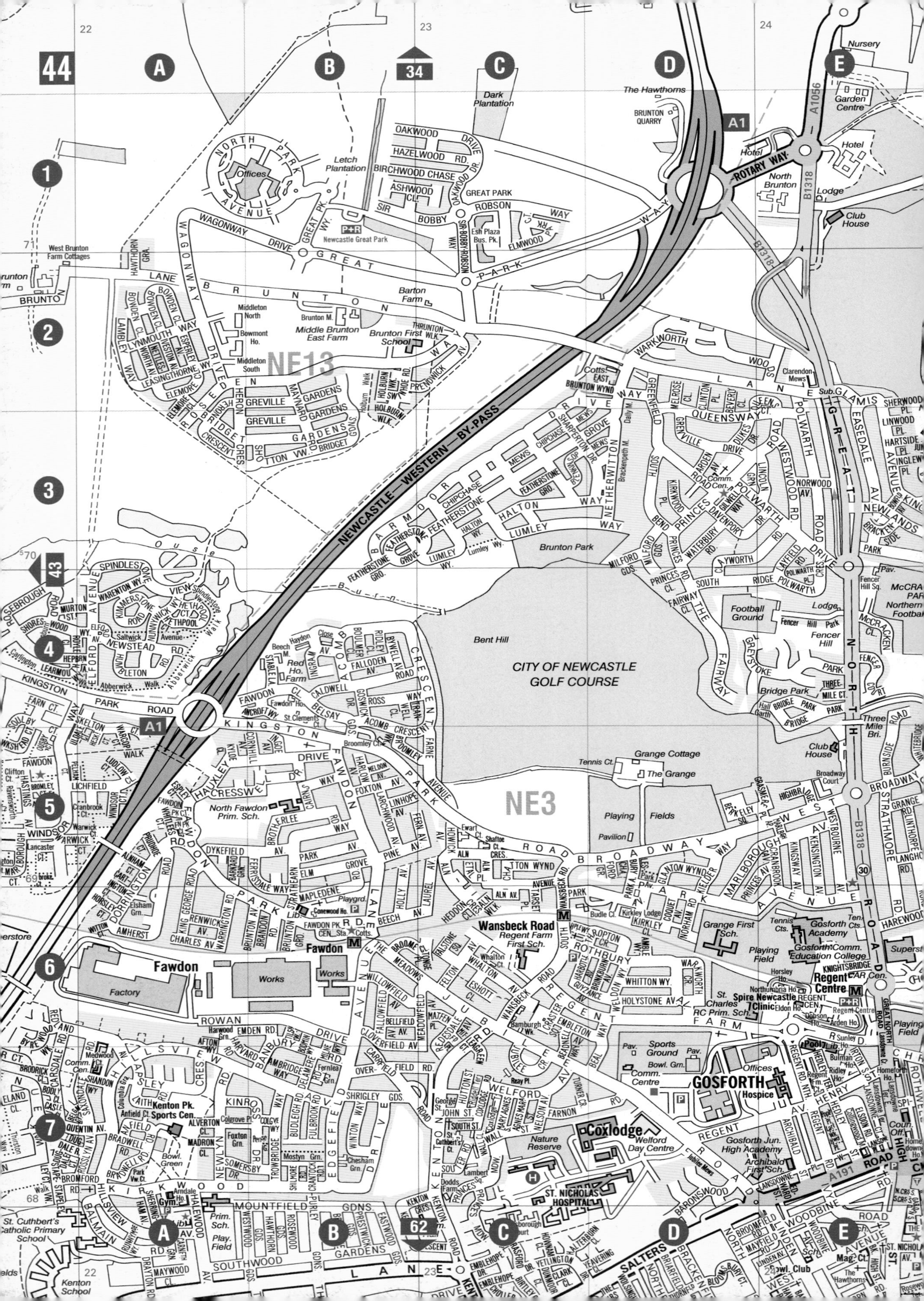

44
A
B
C
D
E
34
43
62
1
2
3
4
5
6
7
22
23
24
71
70
69
68
Dark Plantation
The Hawthorns
BRUNTON QUARRY
A1
Nursery
Garden Centre
A1056
Hotel
ROTARY WAY
North Brunton
B1318
Lodge
Club House
NORTH PARK AVENUE
Offices
Letch Plantation
OAKWOOD DRIVE
HAZELWOOD RD.
BIRCHWOOD CHASE
ASHWOOD CL.
OAKWOOD DR.
GREAT PARK
ROBSON WAY
SIR BOBBY ROBSON WAY
Esh Plaza Bus. Pk.
ELMWOOD
P+R
Newcastle Great Park
WAGONWAY DRIVE
GREAT PARK WAY
West Brunton Farm Cottages
BRUNTON LANE
Barton Farm
Middleton North
Bowmont Ho.
Middleton South
Brunton M.
Middle Brunton East Farm
Brunton First School
THRUNTON WALK
PRENDWICK AV.
NE13
HAWTHORN GRA.
BOWDEN CL.
LYNMOUTH WAY
LAMBLEY WAY
ESPERLEY
LEASINGTHORNE WY.
ELEMORE
ROSEDEN DRIVE
HERON
GREVILLE GARDENS
MAYNARD GARDENS
BRIDGET GDNS.
SHOTTON VW.
RIDGET CRES.
CRESCENT
HOLBURN WLK.
NEWCASTLE WESTERN BY-PASS
WARKWORTH WOODS LANE
Clarendon Mews
Cotts. EAST
BRUNTON WYND
BARMOOR DRIVE
CHIPCHASE MEWS
SHARPERTON DR.
GROVE
MEWS
FEATHERSTONE GRO.
HALTON WAY
NETHERWITTON WAY
Brackenpeth M.
Dally M.
GREENFIELD
MELROSE CL.
CLINTON PL.
BEVERLY CT.
QUEENSWAY
GRENVILLE DRIVE
DUKES DR.
ARDEN
Comm. Cen.
POLWARTH ROAD
WESTWOOD RD.
NORWOOD AV.
LINCOLN
KIRKWOOD PL.
PRINCES
GILWELL WAY
DAVENPORT DR.
WATERBURY RD.
CLAYWORTH
LAYFIELD RD.
POLWARTH CRES
SOUTH RIDGE
POLWARTH
LUMLEY WAY
Lumley Wy.
Brunton Park
MILFORD GDS.
PRINCES CL.
FAIRWAY
THE FAIRWAY
Football Ground
Fencer Hill Park
Fencer Hill
GREYSTOKE
PARK
Bridge Park
THREE MILE CT.
BRIDGE PARK
Hall Garth
Three Mile Bri.
Club House
GREAT NORTH ROAD
GLAMIS
EASEDALE AV.
SHERWOOD PL.
LINWOOD PL.
HARTSIDE
INGLEWOOD PL.
AVENUE
NEWLANDS
BRACKENSIDE
Pav.
Fencer Hill Sq.
McCRACKEN CL.
Lodge
Northern Football
Ouse Burn
SPINDLESTONE
WARENTON WY.
KIMMERSTONE ROAD
VIEW
NUNNYKIRK WY.
YETHPOOL CT.
Spindlestone Walk
Saltwick
Avenue
NEWSTEAD RD.
HUMBLETON
Abberwick
Abberwick Walk
ROSEBROUGH ROAD
MURTON ST.
AVENUE
SHORESWOOD
ROYLE ST.
LEARMOUTH
HEPBURN
Cartington
KINGSTON PARK ROAD
Bent Hill
CITY OF NEWCASTLE GOLF COURSE
Beech M.
Haydon Close
Red Ho. Farm
BOULMER CL.
RIDLEY AV.
BYWELL AV.
FALLODEN AV.
ACOMB CRESCENT
CALDWELL
ROSS WAY
FAWDON CL.
Fawdon Ho.
ACROFT WY.
BELSAY GDS.
St. Clements
GOSWICK DR.
ACOMB CRESCENT
BROOMLEY WALK
KINGSTON PARK
Broomley Ct.
FARNE AVENUE
FARN CT.
SKELTON
WARCOP CT.
WALK
LUDLOW
FAWDON
Clifton
HASTINGS
BROMLEY
LICHFIELD
Cranbrook
Warwick Ct.
WINDSOR
WINDSOR CT.
WARWICK CT.
Lancaster
MARLBOROUGH
KYLOE
CORNHILL
INGOE
HAUXLEY DRIVE
CRESSWELL DR.
FAWDON PARK
HARLOW
FOXTON WAY
LINHOPE
LARCHWOOD AV.
FERN AV.
CAIRNS WAY
North Fawdon Prim. Sch.
Grange Cottage
Tennis Ct.
The Grange
Playing Fields
Pavilion
NE3
GRASMERE
HIGHBRIDGE
BERKLEY SQ.
WEST WAY
WESTBOURNE AV.
BROADWAY
Broadway Court
STRATHMORE
GRANGE
LINTHORPE
B1318
30
ALNHAM CT.
FAWDON RD
BROTHERLEE
DYKEFIELD AV.
PARK AV.
GROVE
PINE AV.
ELM
MAPLEDENE
BARNARD GRN.
FERNSIDE WAY
STRATHEARN
Ewart Ct.
Shaftoe Ct.
ALN CRES.
ALN PL.
CHATTON WYND
BROADWAY
LESBURY
GLANTON WYND
KIELDER
MARLBOROUGH
CRANBROOK
KINGSWAY
KENSINGTON
PRINCES AV.
AVENUE
Grange First Sch.
Tennis Cts.
Gosforth Academy
Gosforth Comm. Education College
Playing Field
HAREWOOD
Superstore
DORRINGTON
Elsham Grn.
KING GEORGE ROAD
RENWICK AV.
WARRINGTON RD.
BRUNTON AV.
BRANDON
BRUNTON RD.
Conewood Ho.
Playgrd.
Lib.
FAWDON PK. RD.
CEN. Sta. Cotts.
AMHERST
CHARLES AV.
HOLLY AV.
LAUREL AV.
BEECH AV.
HEDDON CL.
TARSET
WANSBECK RD. SOUTH
PARK AV.
Budle Cl.
Kirkley Lodge
KIRKLEY CL.
COQUET AV.
NORHAM RD.
Wansbeck Road
Regent Farm First Sch.
ROTHBURY
ROPTON
Fawdon
Factory
Works
THE BROOME
THE MEADOWS
FALSTONE
FELTON
WHALTON
ESHOTT
WANSBECK
WHITTON WY.
HOLYSTONE AV.
WARKWORTH
WELDON WY.
KNIGHTSBRIDGE
Regent Centre
Horsley Ho.
Northumbria Ho.
St. Charles RC Prim. Sch.
Spire Newcastle Clinic
Eldon Ho.
Dobson Ho.
Regent Centre
Arden Ho.
Playing Field
ROWAN DRIVE
Harwood Grn.
EMDEN RD
AFTON
HARVARD
BANBURY
WILLOWFIELD AV.
FALLOWFIELD AV.
BELLFIELD AV.
MEADOWFIELD AV.
CLOVERFIELD AV.
MATFEN PL.
REDESDALE
JUBILEE RD.
REGENT FARM ROAD
EMBLETON AV.
BEAL
Bamburgh Wk.
Sports Ground
Pav.
Bowl. Grn.
Comm. Centre
Offices
GOSFORTH
Hospice
REGENT RD. NTH.
Sunley Ho.
Pool Lib.
Bulman Ho.
Ridley Ho.
Regent Ho.
HILLSVIEW
CARSDALE
BRODRICK
Medwood
Comm. Cen.
SHANDON WY.
APSLEY
Columbia Grs.
KINROSS
Kenton Pk. Sports Cen.
ALVERTON CL.
Colgrove Pl.
MADRON CL.
Foxton Grn.
NEWLYN
BUDLEIGH RD.
FULBROOK RD.
EDGEFIELD AV.
WINTON WAY
SHRIGLEY GDS.
CARRFIELD RD.
OVERFIELD RD.
DELAMERE
Fernlea
AMBRIDGE WAY
QUENTIN AV.
BRADWELL
BROADWELL RD.
SOMERSBY DR.
TROWBRIDGE
Mostyn Grn.
Chesham Grn.
Green
Bowl.
Park Vw. Ct.
BROMFORD
KIRKWOOD
Arndale Ho.
Gym.
HALEWOOD
MOUNTFIELD GDNS.
PURLEY
PRESTWICK
EASTWOOD GDNS.
Prim. Sch.
Play. Field
WESTWOOD
HAWTHORN
ROSEWOOD
SHILMORE
CRANTOCK
George St.
JOHN ST.
SOUTH ST.
St. Cuthbert's Ct.
HUTTON ST.
COXLODGE
MARY AGNES
NELSON AV.
WELFORD
FARNON
TURNER CR.
Reay Pl.
Nature Reserve
Coxlodge
Welford Day Centre
ST. NICHOLAS HOSPITAL
Jubilee Mews
REGENT AV.
HENRY
HEDLEY
ELSDON RD.
Gosforth Jun. High Academy
Archibald First Sch.
ARCHIBALD
A191
ROAD
HIGH
Coun. Off.
Homeforth Ho.
LANSDOWNE TER.
WARD
BARONSWOOD
WOODBINE ROAD
AVENUE
Mag. Ct.
ST. NICHOLAS
Dodds Farm
Lambert Sq.
PRINCES
KENTON ROAD
KENTON CRES.
St. Cuthbert's Catholic Primary School
BALMAIN
Kenton School
MAYWOOD CL.
SOUTHWOOD GARDENS
DRAYTON RD
LANE
SALTERS
BRACKENFIELD
BROOMFIELD
MAYFIELD
LINDEN
Bowl. Club
The Hawthorns
WEST
EMBLEHOPE DR.
GRASFORD
YETLINGTON
DUNMOOR
CLARK
HALTERBURN
YEAVERING
Borough Court

45
35
46
63
F
G
H
J
K
1
2
3
4
5
6
7
KILLINGWORTH
LANE
Blackroad Plantation
Driving Range
Club House
PARKLANDS GOLF COURSE
Gosforth Wood
Park Cottages
Newcastle Racecourse Exhibition Centre
Complete Football
Football Pitches
NEWCASTLE RACECOURSE
NORTHUMBERLAND GOLF COURSE
HIGH GOSFORTH PARK
Race Course
GOSFORTH WOOD
GOSFORTH LAKE
Woodland Cottage
Bathing Pool
Garden Centre
GREAT LIME ROAD
A189
STATION ROAD
B1505
Council Offices
KILLINGWORTH INDUSTRIAL AREA
Government Training Centre
Whitehouse Farm
Nellie Gormley House
Grasmere Academy
KILLINGWORTH DRIVE
GREAT LIME RD.
West Moor
Comm. Cen.
BENTON LANE
GREENHAUGH
SALTERS LANE INDUSTRIAL ESTATE
QUORUM BUSINESS PARK
BALLIOL BUSINESS PARK
DUKES WALK
The Letch
Longbenton College
NE12
Newcastle upon Tyne
NEWCASTLE UPON TYNE
NORTH TYNESIDE
SALTERS' LANE
GOSFORTH BUSINESS PARK
Nuffield, Fitness & Wellbeing Cen. (Gosforth)
Benton North Farm
St. Stephen's RC Prim. Sch.
A188
MELTON PARK
Fencerhill Wood
Black Plantation
Low Gosforth Home Farm
White Bri. Club House
Gosforth Park & Broadway East First Schs.
St. Oswald's RC Primary School
GOSFORTH GOLF COURSE
Gosforth East Middle Sch.
Heathery Lane Cottages
HEATHERY LANE
Ouse Burn
BRIDLE PATH
Dentsmires Bri.
GOSFORTH GOLF COURSE
Cemetery
Shield Grove
HOLLYWOOD AVENUE
Gosforth Metro Depot
Salters Bridge
Gosforth Central Mid Sch.
Archbishop Runcie C of E First Sch.
Council Depot
GOSFORTH IND. EST.
Gasholder
Superstore
Aged Miners Homes
Longbenton
Liby. Oxford Cen.
Balliol Primary School
Four Lane Ends
WEST FARM AVENUE
CHESTERS AVENUE
PARK ROAD
A191
BENTON ROAD
NE7
BENTON PARK VIEW
St. Mary's Catholic Sch.
Playing Field
Benton Park Prim. Sch.
STATION RD.
CHURCH RD.
S. Gosforth
South Gosforth
KILLINGWORTH RD.
HADDRICKS MILL RD.
Trinity School
West Jesmond
Offices

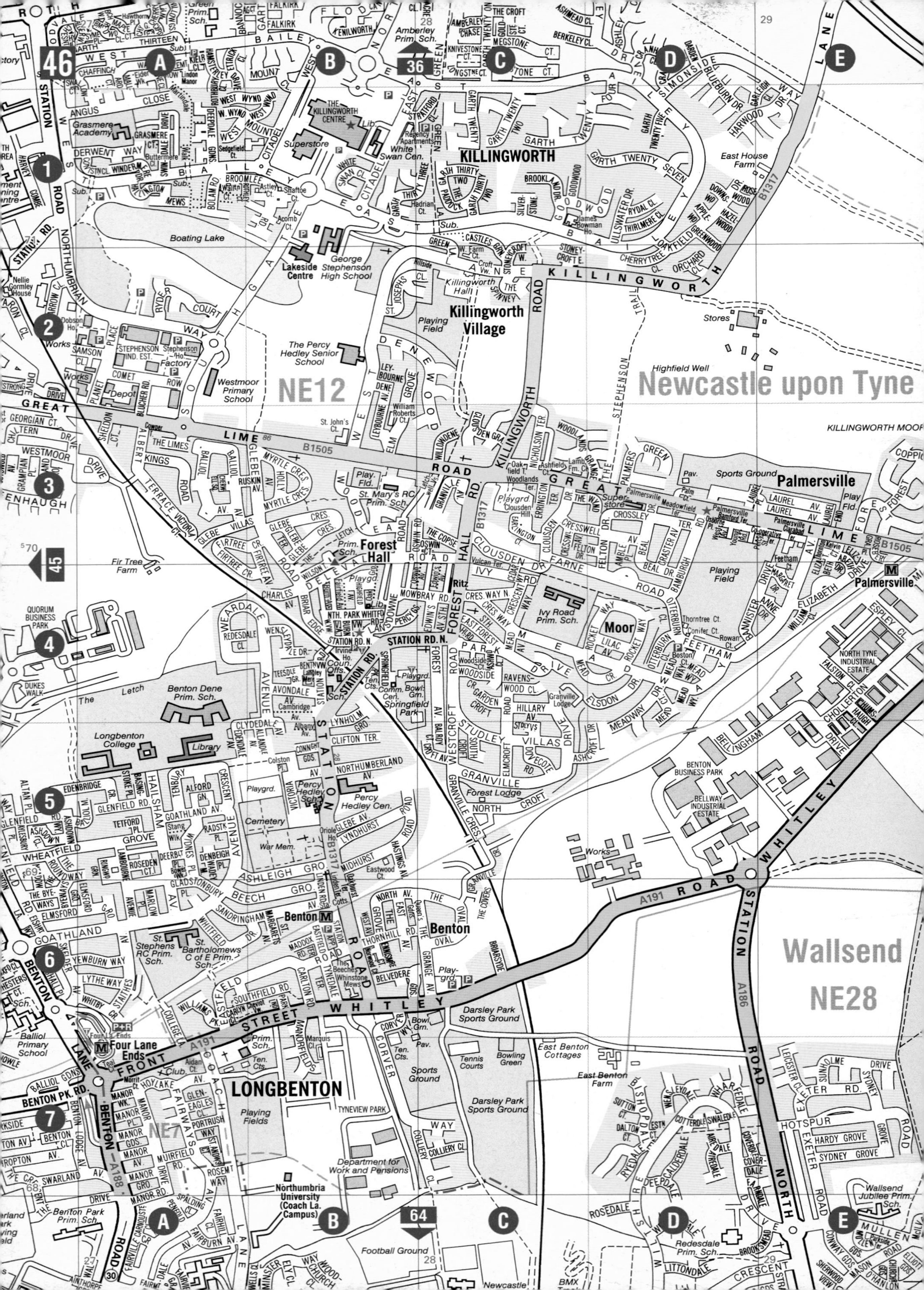

46
KILLINGWORTH
Killingworth Village
Forest Hall
Newcastle upon Tyne
NE12
Palmersville
Moor
Benton
LONGBENTON
Wallsend
NE28
NE7
36
45
64
Boating Lake
Lakeside Centre
George Stephenson High School
The Percy Hedley Senior School
Westmoor Primary School
Benton Dene Prim. Sch.
Longbenton College
Library
Cemetery
Percy Hedley Cen.
Darsley Park Sports Ground
Northumbria University (Coach La. Campus)
Department for Work and Pensions
North Tyne Industrial Estate
Benton Business Park
Bellway Industrial Estate
Ivy Road Prim. Sch.
Four Lane Ends
Football Ground
Redesdale Prim. Sch.
Wallsend Jubilee Prim. Sch.
Balliol Primary School
Benton Park Prim. Sch.
KILLINGWORTH MOOR
Highfield Well
East House Farm
Fir Tree Farm
Quorum Business Park
East Benton Farm
East Benton Cottages

BACKWORTH GOLF COURSE
Holystone Farm
Northumberland Park
NE27
Shiremoor
SHIREMOOR
Stanton Lodge
BOUNDARY MILL STORES
Benton Square
BENTON SQUARE INDUSTRIAL ESTATE
Holystone
Holystone Prim. Sch.
West Allotment
The Allotment
COBALT HOSPITAL
ALGERNON INDUSTRIAL ESTATE
Silverlink Park
Council Offices
COBALT BUSINESS CENTRE
SILVERLINK BUSINESS PARK
Superstore
Scaffold Hill Mill Farm
Scaffold Hill Farm
Rising Sun Countryside Centre
Swallow Pond Nature Reserve
RISING SUN COUNTRY PARK
Rising Sun Farm
Hadrian Park Prim Sch.
HADRIAN PARK ESTATE
BATTLE HILL ESTATE
Battle Hill
Battle Hill Primary Sch.
Recreation Ground
Metropolitan College
Willington Square
MIDDLE ENGINE LANE RETAIL PARK
Gala Bingo
COASTWAY SHOPPING FORUM
Hill Fields
Churchill Community College
Willington
Holy Cross RC Prim. School
St. Bernadette's RC Prim. Sch.
Beacon Hill School
Playing Fields
A19
A191
A186
A1058
B1322
37
48
65

38
47
66
A
B
C
D
E
1
2
3
4
5
6
7
SHIREMOOR
West Monkseaton
Newcastle upon Tyne
NE27
Murton
Murton Steads Farm
Riding Sch.
North Farm
Moorlands
Murton Nurseries
Playing Field
NEW YORK
NEW YORK INDUSTRIAL PARK
Electricity Sub. Sta.
SILVERLINK BUSINESS PARK
Shiremoor Farm
New York Prim. Sch.
Preston Grange
Rake House Farm
NORTH TYNESIDE GENERAL HOSPITAL
ECC
North Shields
Reservoir (covered)
Pumping Sta.
Billymill Res. (covered)
Whitehouse Prim. Sch.
The Cedars
St. Thomas More RC Academy
Tennis Court
Billy Mill
NE29
Tynemouth Squash Club
Moor Park House
WEST CHIRTON NORTH INDUSTRIAL ESTATE
NORTH BALKWELL FARM IND. EST.
Stephenson Railway Museum
Factories
Works
WEST CHIRTON (MIDDLE) TRADING ESTATE
Wallsend
NE28
Odeon Cinema
SILVERLINK RETAIL PK.
Bluehouse Bridges
WEST CHIRTON INDUSTRIAL ESTATE (SOUTH)
Willington Square
MIDDLE ENGINE LANE RETAIL PARK
Gala Bingo
VROOM CAR RETAIL PARK
ORION BUSINESS PARK
EVANS BUSINESS CENTRE
Silverdale School
Warehouses
TYNE TUNNEL TRADING ESTATE
North Tyneside Steam Railway
BUGATTI INDUSTRIAL PARK
Collingwood Prim. Sch.
Playing Field
Norham High Sch.
West Chirton
Factory
Electricity Sub. Sta.
TYNE TUNNEL TRADE PARK
Holy Cross RC Prim. School
Langley First Sch.
Woodlawn Sch.
Langley Play. Field
Star of the Sea RC Prim. Sch.
Monkseaton High School
Preston Gate
Crawford Ten. Park
Appletree Gdns. First Sch.
Bertram Grange Community Centre
BOUNDARY MILL STORES
Stanton Lodge
NEW YORK ROAD
NEW YORK BY-PASS
RAKE LANE
BILLY MILL LANE
LYNN ROAD
COAST ROAD
A191
A19
A1058
A192
A193
A1108
B1316
SEATONVILLE ROAD
BEACH ROAD
REGENT TER.
FRONT ROAD
WALLSEND ROAD
MURTON LANE
NORHAM ROAD
SILVER LINK
MIDDLE ENGINE LANE

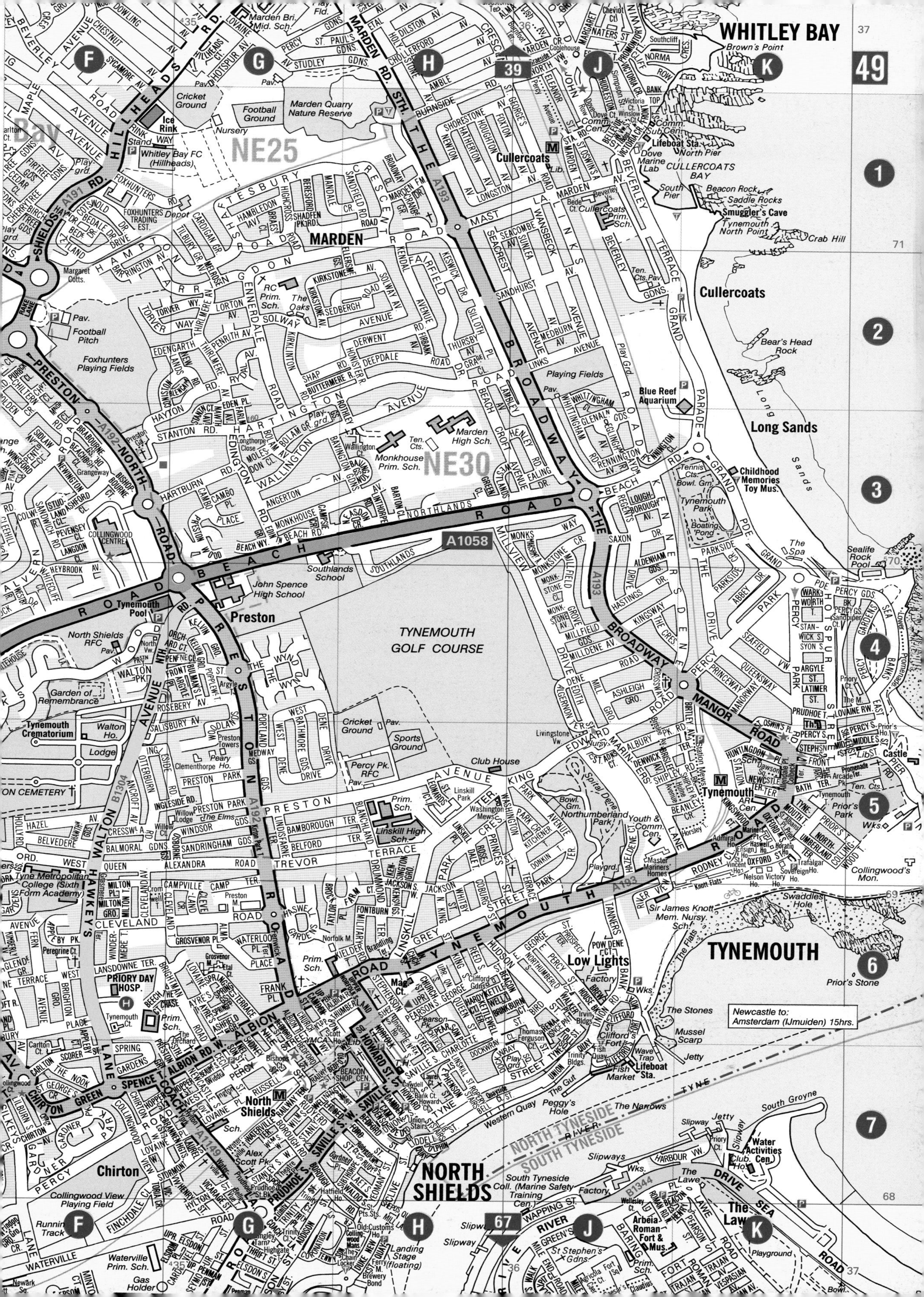
WHITLEY BAY
Brown's Point
Cullercoats
CULLERCOATS BAY
Lifeboat Sta.
North Pier
South Pier
Beacon Rock
Saddle Rocks
Smuggler's Cave
Tynemouth North Point
Crab Hill
Bear's Head Rock
Long Sands
Blue Reef Aquarium
Childhood Memories Toy Mus.
Tynemouth Park
The Spa
Sealife Rock Pool
Castle
Prior's Park
Collingwood's Mon.
Swaddles Hole
TYNEMOUTH
Prior's Stone
The Flats
The Stones
Mussel Scarp
Jetty
Newcastle to: Amsterdam (IJmuiden) 15hrs.
South Groyne
The Narrows
Peggy's Hole
Western Quay
The Gut
Fish Quay
Fish Market
Lifeboat Sta.
Clifford's Fort
Low Lights
NORTH TYNESIDE
SOUTH TYNESIDE
RIVER TYNE
Water Activities Cen.
The Lawe
Arbeia Roman Fort & Mus.
South Tyneside Coll. (Marine Safety Training Cen.)
NORTH SHIELDS
North Shields
Chirton
Collingwood View Playing Field
Running Track
Waterville Prim. Sch.
Gas Holder
Landing Stage (floating)
Old Customs Ho.
Priory Day Hosp.
Tynemouth Crematorium
Preston Cemetery
Garden of Remembrance
North Shields RFC
Tynemouth Pool
Preston
John Spence High School
Southlands School
TYNEMOUTH GOLF COURSE
Club House
Cricket Ground
Sports Ground
Percy Pk. RFC
Linskill High Sch.
Northumberland Park
Tynemouth
Monkhouse Prim. Sch.
Marden High Sch.
NE30
MARDEN
Foxhunters Playing Fields
Football Pitch
Collingwood Centre
Foxhunters Trading Est.
Whitley Bay FC (Hillheads)
Ice Rink
Cricket Ground
Football Ground
Marden Quarry Nature Reserve
NE25
Cullercoats
Playing Fields
BROADWAY
BEACH ROAD
A1058
A193
A192
A191
A1304
B1304
A1149
B1344
PRESTON ROAD
HAWKEY'S LANE
TYNEMOUTH ROAD
MANOR ROAD
GRAND PARADE
THE BROADWAY
MARDEN RD. STH.
HILLHEADS RD.
ALBION RD. W.
SAVILLE ST. W.
HOWARD ST.
SEA ROAD
RIVER DRIVE
39
67
F
G
H
J
K
1
2
3
4
5
6
7
35
36
37
68
69
70
71

50
Shaft Wood
The Scroggs
A
B
C
D
E
Codlawdean Cottage
High Barns
Barns Wood
EAST WOOD
Fallowfield Dene Cottages
Dene
FALLOWFIELD DENE CARAVAN PARK
Fallowfield
Acomb Buildings
A6079
Low Barns
Halfway House
East Wood House
Mariner's Cottage
Sunniside
Westfield House
Red Burn
New Rift Farm
Belmont
High Salmons Well
East Salmons Well
Salmons Well Farm
Acomb Steading
Acomb Dene
Hexham
NE46
CROSS BANK
BISHOPS HILL
Bishops Hill
Reservoir (covered)
Acomb First Sch.
ACOMB
MILLERSFIELD
NORTHUMBERLAND CT.
THE GAPS
THE GREEN
STREET
MAIN
Chapel Ct.
Rutter T.
West Vw.
Acomb House
Orchard Ter.
Townfoot Farm
Depot
Old Farm
Broom Park
LANE
Howford Quarry
ACOMB INDUSTRIAL ESTATE
COLLIERY R.
HOWFORD
Depot
Redburn Vs.
REDBURN CRES
Birkey
Burn
Branse's Well
Acomb Mill
The Lantern
RIDING BANK
GARDEN HOUSE DR.
HOUSE BANK
Alnmouth Ter.
Garden House Farm
Riding Farm
Riding Cottages
The Riding
Hall
Rectory
Target Cottage
Target House
A69
St. John Lee Bridge
West Oakwood Cottages
Peasley Gates
Kingshaw Green
70
Old Bridge End
Hermitage Lodge
The Hermitage
OAKWOOD
The Priory
PRIORY
Priest's Seat
HEXHAM GOLF COURSE
RIVER
Club House
CHERRY
LANE
Cemetery
Nursery
Caravan Site
RIVERSIDE LEISURE PARK
TYNEDALE GOLF COURSE
FRENCH GARDEN IND. EST.
WEST
B6531
SPITAL
HEXHAM GOLF COURSE
Railway Cotts.
Club House
Cockshaw Burn
TYNE
Tyne Green Country Park
Bridge End
BRIDGE END INDUSTRIAL ESTATE
A695
ROTARY WAY
FERRY ROAD
BURN HAUGH ESTATE
Auction Mart
Boat House
Hexham Bridge
FOUNDRY IND EST.
The Shaws Farm
Cobbler's Hall
Priors Flat
HEXHAM
TYNE MILLS IND. EST.
Tyne Mills
Hexham
DUKES ROAD
QUEENSWAY
THE LINK
West Quarter
SHAWS PK.
70
Superstore
Wentworth
Broomhaugh Island
LEAZES LANE
SHAWS LANE
Leazes Cottages
High Burswell
OSBORNE AV.
ALEMOUTH RD.
STATION ROAD
Wentworth Leisure Centre
Station Cottages
The Sele
COCKSHAW
GILESGATE
92
93
94
68
67
66
65
1
2
3
4
5
6
7

395
96
97
68
67
66
65
F
G
H
J
K
1
2
3
4
5
6
7
Hangman's Hill
ACOMB FELL
Fawcet Hill
Fawcethill
Fern Hill Farm
Fern Hill Cottages
Silver Hill
Carr Hill
Acomb Fell Farm
Birkey Burn
Black Hill
Beaufront Hill Head
Chesterholme
The Kennels
Highwood Hotts
Sandhoe
The Coach House
High Ho.
Sandhoe House
Tennis Court
Beaufront First Sch.
Beaufront Wood Head Cottages
Beaufront Wood Head Farm
CLARTY LANE
Haybarn Wood
Mill
Hollyhill Wood
North Lodge
Tennis Courts
Beaufront Castle
TARGET WOOD
Viewlands
Tosstree Wood
Rhododendron Wood
Cedarholm
THE PARK
Oakwood
EAST OAKWOOD
FAIRFIELD CRES.
Anick House
Anick Old House
Anick Farm
OAKWOOD
Anick Hall
The Cottage
Knoll Hill
Anick
Reservoir (covered)
Anick Farm
Anick Grange
Anick Grange Cottages
CORCHESTER LANE
Red
ROAD
Bank Foot
Subway
Beaufront Red House
A69
The Oaklands
BEAUFRONT BUS. PK.
Oaklands
The Timbers
Harwood Meadows
RIVER TYNE
Prior Thorns
Factory
Sewage Works
71
Wide Haugh
Anickgrange Haugh

52
71

52
A
B
C
D
E
1
2
3
4
5
6
7
97
98
99
68
67
66
65
Fawcet Hill
Fawcethill
Stagshawbank Bridge
Fair Hill Cottage
Stagshawbank Burn
Stagshaw Kennels
STAGSHAW BANK CATTLE FAIR
A68
Stagshaw High House
Plantation Cottage
Fox & Hounds Cottage
Low Houses
Hexham
NE46
Street Houses
Black Hill
Lodge
Stagshaw House
Chantry Farm
Holly Hall
The Courtyard
The Pot Holes
51
The Coach House
Sandhoe
High Ho.
Sandhoe House
Tennis Court
The Chalet
Leazes Cottage
Shawwell Farm
Shawwell Ho.
LEAZES LANE
Hampstead House
White Barns
Burn
Ford
Cor
COW LANE
MILKWELL
Dere Street Roman Road
Corburn Bridge
South Lodge
CORCHESTER
Redhouse
Bishop Rigg
Red House Plantation
Beaufront Red House
Burn
A69
STAGSHAW ROAD
B6529
Corbridge Middle Sch.
Playing Field
Corchester Towers
The Coach House
Corchester Ter.
Prior Thorns
Redhouse Burn
Shordon Brae
Redhouse Haughs
Corbridge Mill
Corbridge Roman Town Hadrian's Wall
Corbridge Old Pottery Kilns
Milkwell Farm
First Sch.
CHANTRY ESTATE
THE RIGGS
ST. HELEN'S LANE
Town Farm Field
Orchard Vale
West Green
RIVER TYNE
Green Pool
WELL BANK
WATLING ST.
HILL ST.
PRINCES ST.
MIDDLE ST.
MAIN ST.
FRONT ST.
AYDON RD.
B6530
72
Wide Haugh
Randle

53
54
Halton Castle (remains of)
Tennis Court
Halton
Carr Houses
Shildon Cottage
Hollywell Dene
Stagshawbank Burn
Lady's Well
The Cottage
West Bank
White House
Park Well
Fox Covert
Green
Peaslings Plantation
Cor Burn
Rye Hill
Aydon Castle
Shildon Bog
B6321
Aydon
Aydon North Farm
Aydon South Farm
Corbridge
NE45
Aydon Dene
Meg's Well
Aydon House
ROAD
Gallow Hill
Gallowhill
Thornbrough High Barns
Kiln House Cottage
Thornbrough Kiln House
LANE
CRAGSIDE
JAMESON
DRIVE
WOODSIDE AV.
BEECH DR.
Piperclose House
Aydon Grange
Didridge
Quarry Wood
Linn Burn Wood
A69
CORBRIDGE
Howden Dene Farm
Linn Burn House
CROOKS HILL
Stocksfield
NE43
THE CROFTS
Howden Close
Eastfield
The Hayes
Cricket Plantation
B6530
ROAD
73
Thornbrough
AYDON CR.
AVENUE
Aydon Ct.

Corbridge
NE45
Stocksfield
NE43
Shildon Cottage
Shildon
Kip Hill
CARRS FELL
Carrsfell Plantation
SHILDONHILL PLANTATION
Sunnyside
B6321
Shildon Grange Cottage
Shildon Grange
Greenleighton
Black Plantation
Shildon Hill
Low Shildon
Fort
Shildonhill
Well House Farm
Shildon Bog
Brockhole Burn
Newton Fell House
Homestead
Heathery Edge
The Rookery
Whittington Hill Reservoir
Whittington Hill
Pav.
Cricket Ground
Observatory
Brockhole Burn
Newtonkiln House
Round Hill
Newton Hall
Beech Close Farm
North Lodge
Newton High House
Rectory
Mowden Hall School
Mount Spen
Forge Cottage
West Lodge
Newton Hall Cottages
Boat House
Tofts Hill
Toftshill Plantation
Newton
Newton Town Farm
Brockhole Wood
Brockhole Burn
THE OLD FORGE
02
03
04
68
67
66
65

53
74

East Wallhouse
405
06
07
F
G
H
J
K
68
Whittle Dene Cottage
Whittle Dene Watercourse
NE18
Whittle
Burn
B6309
Welton
Welton Hall
Slate House
Cobblers Cottage
Welton Farm
COBBLER'S LANE
Newcastle upon Tyne
Whittle Burn
Laker Hall
Largs Cottage
Orchard House
Hollywell
Burn
Boggle Burn
NE15
67
Bogle
B6309
66
North Wood
East Lodge
North Lodge
Stelling Hall (Children's Home)
West Lodge
Stelling Farm
Stelling Cottages
Nafferton Farm
A69
Playing Field
East Lodge
Old Nafferton
East Crookhill
Crookhill Farm
Playing Field
Swarden Dene
565
South Lodge
DRIVE
The Oaks
Prudhoe
OVERDENE
Overdene
NE42
Hunter's Hill
A69
B6309
South Croft
Benlow Hill
Bearl Farm
1
2
3
4
5
6
7

56

75

Tresco
B6318
Whittle Dene Watercourse
Whittle Dene Water Treatment Works
North Side Farm
Lousy
Spital Villas
OATENS BANK
Newcastle upon Tyne
NE15
Bogle Burn
Spital
Marlow Sike
Whittle Burn
Whirl Dub
Duns Law
Horsley Hills
Horsley Hill
Stoney Hill
Horsley Fell
Hill Croft
Dukes Cotts.
Fellside House
A69
B6528
High Barns Farm
South Farm
HORSLEY
Water Treatment Works
Lonkin's Hall (remains of)
Whittle Dene
Whittle Farm
Pike Hill
Nelson's Hill
Swarden Dene
Gallow Hill
Prudhoe
Gills Crag
Hunter's Bank
Weir
Hunter's Hill
Eddybroth Well
GALLOW HILL LANE
NE42
Mount Huly
Duke's Dene
Playing Field

55

76

57
F
G
H
J
K
410
11
12
68
67
66
65
1
2
3
4
5
6
7
Heddon House
Hollins Hill
EPPIES HILL
Iron Sign
High Seat
Tollgate Cottage
MILITARY ROAD
B6318
HERDS HILL
Hill
Rudchester Farm
Rudchester
Quarry House
Low Seat
March Burn
A69
Rudchester Burn
Howdene Burn
Horsley Marsh
Blakeley Plantation
Blakeley Hill
Well House
Houghton Moor Cottages
B6528
58
Oakwood Lodge
March House
Holeyn Hall Cottage
Holeyn Hall
HOLEYN HALL ROAD
Hopside Farm
STONECROFT
East Holme
Horsley Banks
HORSLEY BUSINESS CENTRE
WEST WOOD
Burn Cottage
Ox Close
Oakwood House
High Close House
Ralby Hill
Well
Wylam
Oakwood
Burn
ACOMB DR.
NE41
Dayhole Dene
How Dene
The Rift
Rift Dene
Kitty's
Horsley Wood Cottages
Holly Hill
Howlway Burn
Howdene Burn
MILL WAY
Burn
BLUEBELL CL.
DENECROFT
Engine Dene
TYNEDALE CL.
DENE RD.
ROAD
BELL RD.
PARSON RD.
Wylam First School
Howdene Bridge
Wylam Hills Farm
CHURCH ROAD
ALGERNON TER.
WOODVALE GDNS.
MARK GS.
JACKSON RD.
HACKWORTH GDNS.
HEDLEY
WYLAM
Wylam Railway Mus.
Lib.
Comm. Cen.
STEPHENSON TER.
The Orchard
THE ORCHARD
BLACKETT COTTS.
South Vw.
Cherry Tree La.
Burgoyne Ter.
Blackett Ct.
Wylam Hall
CHAPEL LA.
MAIN ROAD
FALCON TER.
Ingham Ter.
War Mem.
STEPHENSON CT.
THE DENE
West View
TYNE VIEW
Horsley Wood
Wildwood Mount
Works
Tynewood
RIVER TYNE
Hagg Farm
The Park
FRONT STREET
OVINGHAM ROAD
WOODCROFT
Wylam Lodge
Ten. Pav. Ct.
Jubilee Field Rec. Grd.
Wylam Bridge
STATION ROAD
P
Wylam
Weir
High Hermitage
The Hermitage
HIGH HERMITAGE CARAVAN PARK
Hagg Bank
77
Hagg Bank
Railway Cotts.
The Haughs
Wylam Tennis Club
Pav.
ELM BANK ROAD
THE CRESCENT
Mill Wood
Bythorne
Burn

A
B
C
D
E
1
2
3
4
5
6
7
40
57
78
12
13
14
68
67
66
65
Sunny Side
Allerburn
Denholme
Heddon House
Heddon Nurseries
Heddon Mill
Hassockbog Plantation
HERDS HILL
MILITARY ROAD
B6318
A69
MILITARY
B6528
Bays Leap Farm
MILL LANE
BLACKROW
HEXHAM ROAD
HEXHAM
Great Hill
War Meml. Grd.
Knott Meml. Hall
Lib.
Prim. Sch.
Playgrd.
Houghton
North Farm
South Farm
Hill Head
Heddon Common
Burn
TRAJAN WLK.
TRAJAN AV.
REMUS
AQUILA
CAMPUS
KILLIEBRIGS
DRIVE
WALK
MARTIUS
MITHRAS GS.
TABERNA CL.
THE TOWNE
BANKS
CENTURION
Overhill
WAY
HEATH HILL
GATE
MARIUS
CALVIS DR.
VALERIAN AV.
CAMILLA RD.
ANTONINE WALK
ANTONINE WK.
STATION ROAD
HEDDON BANKS
Heddon Banks Farm
HEDDON-ON-THE-WALL
Newcastle upon Tyne
NE15
Heddon Hall
Lodge
Broomy Hill
Slacks Plantation
HEDDON
Close Lea
West Acres
Garden House
Ravens Dean
Ashbank Wood
CLOSE HOUSE ESTATE
Close House
Heddon Low Farm
Works
Clayton's Wood
High Close House
Club House
Hemmel Wood
CLOSE HOUSE GOLF COURSE
WEST WOOD
Club House
Heddon Haugh
Wylam
Cathouse Plantation
Reeth
RYTON GOLF COURSE
Club House
Doctor's Stanners
The Rift
Rift Dene
Close House Riverside Nature Reserve
TYNE
Wylam
NE41
Street Houses
George Stephenson's Birthplace
Bythorne Farm Cottage
Wylam First School
Fish Ponds
Bythorne Farm
WYLAM
Wylam Railway M
STEPHENSON CT.
STEPHENSON T.
STATION
War Mem.
Wylam Bridge
Wylam
Rose Cottage
RIVER
Eels Wood
Recreation Ground
Tennis Courts
Stanners Vw.
North View
South View
Tyne Vw.
Maryside Pl.
CLARA VALE COMPLEX
West Vw.
East Vw.
Edington Gs.
STANNERFORD
Clara Vale
Bog Wood
Edington Well
Maryside Hill
TYNESIDE GOLF COURSE
ROAD
Ryton
NE40
Building Farm
STANNERFORD ROAD
BANK
ROAD
THE CRESCENT
Mill Wood
Castle Hill House
Charles Thorpe Comprehensive School
Ryton Jun.

59
F
G
H
J
K
41
415
16
17
68
67
66
65
1
2
3
4
5
6
7
60
79
NE5
NE21
A69
A6085
B6323
B6528
PONTELAND ROAD
BIRKS
Holmside
Birds Hill
Heddon View
Burnside Farm
Pineglades
Dewley Hill
Dewley
Burn
Long Plantation
Dewley Farm
Dewley Farm Cotts.
Dewley Park House
LANE
DROVE RD.
Black Row Farm
Throckley North Farm
Works
THROCKLEY
THROCKLEY IND. EST.
DEWLEY CT.
WESTWAY IND. PARK
High Dewley Burn
Ford
Sub.
Small Burn
Playing Field
Walbottle Campus Technology College
Talbot House School
Dene Head Farm
Walbottle Dene Bridge
WESTWAY
GRADYS YD.
LIME S.
LILY ESTATE
LAUREL ST.
Bowl. Grn.
Pine St.
Rec. Grd.
SYCAMORE ST.
Comm. Cen
Poplar St.
WESLEY WY.
Oak St.
Hadrian Ho.
Stephenson T.
FINCHALE GDNS.
NORTHWAY
ALSTON
LANERCOST GDS.
BRAMPTON GDS.
AMBLESIDE
Throckley Primary School
FRENCHMANS ROW
INGLETON DR.
Aged Miners Homes
AINDERBY RD.
HEXHAM ROAD
Tenter Garth
OLLERTON DR.
SHERINGHAM GS.
HORNCLIFFE PL.
WESTVALE
HILL HOUSE RD.
THE MOUNT
GROVE
COACH
CLIPSTONE CL.
STUART GDNS.
Ravensburn Wk.
BROOMY
Rec. Grd.
Woodlands Ct.
Trinity School
Rec. Grd.
Superstore
HADRIAN PL.
VALLUM RD.
AVENUE
Field Ter.
Victoria Ter.
Bank Top
VALESIDE
WOODLANDS
WILSWAY
COQUET
THE BRIARY
REETH WAY
WELLFIELD CL.
HALLOW
ALLMOUTH PK.
THE BY-WAY
MT. PLEASANT CT.
APPIAN PL.
MAYFIELD
EVERSLEIGH PL.
ELMFIELD RD.
WOODSIDE
Walbottle Dene
Little Whinstone Dike
Small Burn
HOLEYN RD.
COLLIER CL.
Bolam Ct.
THE WILLOWS
THE WYND
Rec. Grd.
ROAD
HEWLEY
THE CAUSEWAY
CRESCENT
DRIVE
WINSHIELDS WY.
LYDNEY CT.
PARKWAY
Tyne Wk.
South Farm
LEAZES
THE LEAZES
Rec. Grd.
RICHARD ST.
GROWELL RD.
LAW
FOSSE
BRIAR LA.
MAYFIELD AV.
PARKSIDE GDNS.
New Burn
WALBOTTLE
Hawthorn St.
GEORGE ST.
BRAEBURN
APPLE TREE CT.
Burt Ter.
Beverley
RC Prim. Sch.
WHITEHALL RD.
Richmond Ter.
Prim. Sch.
GREEN
VILLAGE FARM
THE PADDOCK
PADDOCK
BANK HEAD
Comm. Cen.
QUEENS RD.
New Winning
Dene Terrace
WALBOTTLE
Picnic Area
Engine Plantation
Five Acre Field
Hallow Hill
Rye Hill
Burn
Ten Acre Field
Throckley Pond Nature Reserve
Seven Acre Field
Newburn Grange
NEWBURN
Winning Farm
Newburn Hall Motor Mus.
Newburn Manor Prim. Sch.
Nursy. Sch.
CORPORATION YD.
Rupert Ter.
RUPERT CT.
Rupert Ho.
TOWNFIELD GS.
ALNWICK ST.
Manor Av.
Reigh Burn
TYNE RIVERSIDE COUNTRY PARK
GRANGE
AZALEA WY.
WESTMA.
COTT ST.
PARK RD.
Community Centre
BOYD
Rec. Grd.
CHAPEL CT.
DAVISON S.
Foot Path
MILLFIELD
BERKLEY
HARESIDE CT.
MANOR GRO.
MILL
Blayney Row
Newburn Activity Centre
Newburn Sands
Sports Field
Coniston
Grasmere Cl.
Hareside
Library
CLARKS HILL WK.
CHURCH BANK
CHURCH
Almshouses
STEWARTS
VALE
Wagonway
NEWCASTLE UPON TYNE
NORTHUMBERLAND
Moore Ct.
Boat Ho.
WATER ROW
STATION RD.
The Retreat
HIGH STREET
Factory
ROAD
RIVER TYNE
Ryton Island
GATESHEAD
RYTON WILLOWS
Newburn Bridge
Works
SHELLEY ROAD
Warehouse
Works
NEWBURN INDUSTRIAL
Weir
Boat House
Ryton Willows
LANE
Church Dene
Parson's Haugh
Club House
Hall Banks
War Mem.
BANK
Reed Side
Engineering Works
Peth La.
NEWBURN BRIDGE ROAD
Warehouse
Stella West Sub Station
HAUGH
Whinhaven
LANE
Blaydon-on-Tyne
RIVER
Rectory Cotts.
Ryton Village West
Comm. Cen.
Village Green
STATION
Ryton Village
ELVASTON
Ryton Village East
VILLAGE EAST
PETH LANE
WESTFIELD
LANE
East Grange
Three Gables
CYPRESS GRO.
ASH
GROVE
CROSS TER.
NORTHUMBERLAND
THE LAWN
South Ferndene Park
Ferndene Gro.
WILLOW CT.
Holburn Dene
Peth Lane Farm
NEWBURN
Caravan Park
BRIDGE
Factory
CEDAR
LIME
Holly Av.
Ivy Cl.
HOLBURN
BURN
CRESCENT
REEDSIDE
Burn Head DR.
ROAD
KING
Ryton Grange
GRANGE LONNEN
BARMOOR
OAKFIELD
PARK
FIELD
ORCHARD CT.
WHITEWELL
Ryton Twr.
TOWER GARDENS
Pav.
Bowl. Grn.
DENE
MEADOW
MEADOWS
HOLBURN WAY
HOLBURN TER.
HOLBURN WK.
HOLBURN GS.
PRIMROSE GDS.
High Hedgefield Ter.
THE WILLOWS BUS. CEN.
RYTON IND. EST.
Works
HAUGH
ADDISON INDUSTRIAL ESTATE
Addison
Works
BLACKHOUSE LA.
Woodbine Cotts.
The Brambles
Dean Ter.

42
80
59
A
B
C
D
E
1
2
3
4
5
6
7
17
18
19
68
67
66
65
STAMFORD HAM ROAD
B6324
WHORLTON LANE
WALBOTTLE ROAD
Fell House Farm
Whorlton Grange Cotts.
Whorlton Grange
Club House
WESTERHOPE GOLF COURSE
Westerhope Community Rec. Grd.
Comm. Rec. Centre
Westerhope Prim. Sch.
Chapel Park
North Walbottle
Small Burn
Talbot House School
Knop Law Prim. Sch.
Milecastle Prim. Sch.
Comm. Cen.
Shop. Cen.
Knoplaw Prim. Sch.
HILLHEAD PARKWAY
HILLHEAD ROAD
GROSVENOR
Reservoir (covered)
West Denton
All Saints C of E College
Tennis Courts
Playing Field
Outer West Pool
DENTON PARK SHOP. CEN.
Lib.
St. John Vianney RC Prim. Sch.
Comm. Centre
West Denton Primary School
Playing Fields
A69
HEXHAM ROAD
B6528
Depot
Walbottle Hall
Walbottle Hall Gds.
Pumping Station
Blucher Village
Works
WALBOTTLE
WESTLANDS
WESTERN AVENUE
THE ROMAN WAY
WEST DENTON ROAD
Alan Shearer Cen.
Play. Field
Knop Law
NEWBURN
HOSPITAL LANE
Cemetery
Memorial
Playing Field
NE15
Sandy Banks
Bowling Green
Letch Way
HIGH ST.
LEMINGTON ROAD
A6085
SHELLEY ROAD
Warehouse
NEWBURN INDUSTRIAL ESTATE
Factory
RIVER TYNE
NEWCASTLE UPON TYNE
GATESHEAD
NE21
NEWBURN HAUGH INDUSTRIAL ESTATE
The Leamington Cen.
HIGH ROW
SCOTSWOOD ROAD
Sugley Dene
Waverley Primary School
LEMINGTON
Bell's Close
A1
WESTERN BYPASS
BELLS CLOSE INDUSTRIAL ESTATE
Caravan Park
Lemington Gut
THE WILLOWS BUS. CEN.
RYTON IND. EST.
OSWALD ROAD
HAUGH ROAD

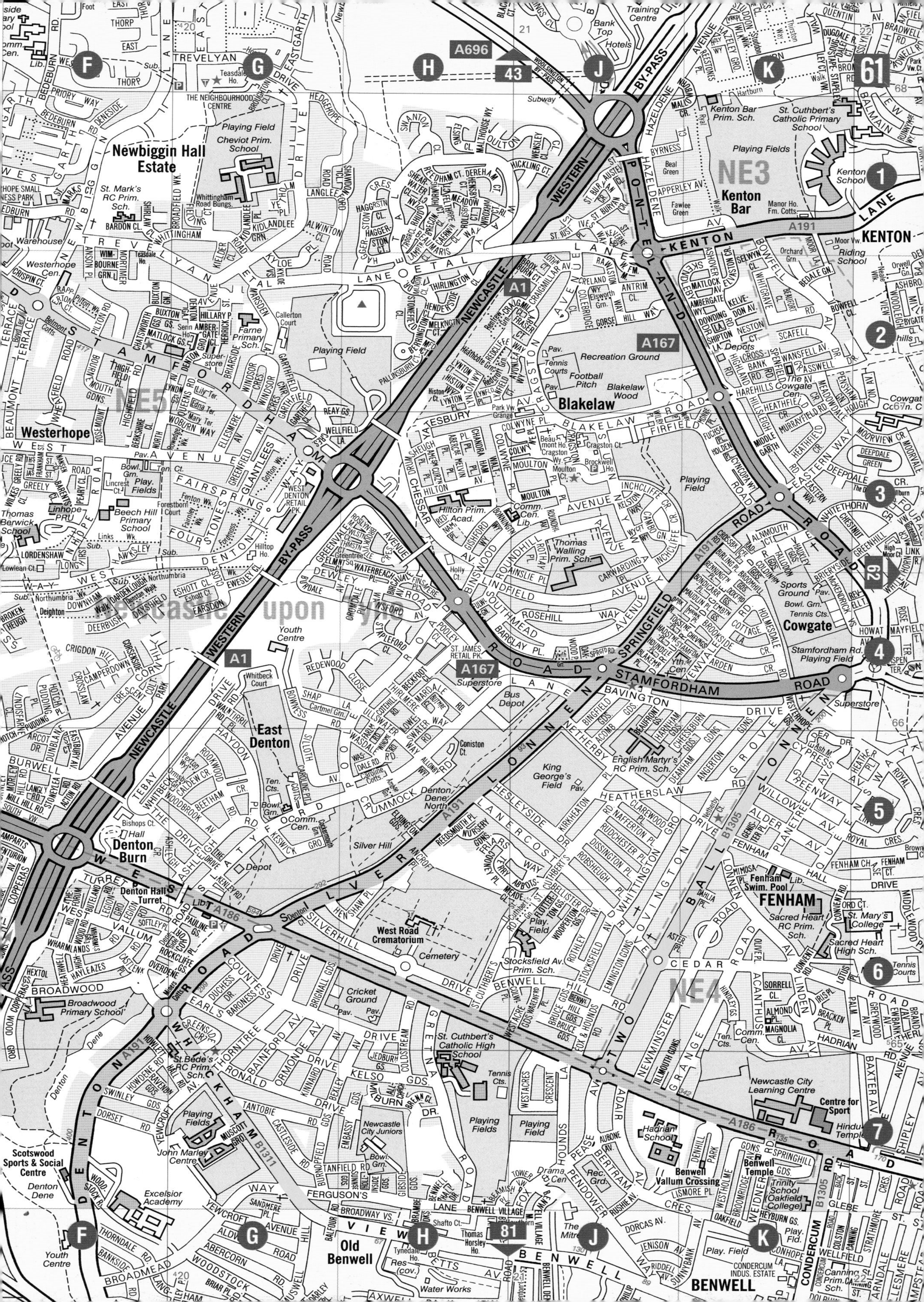

61
A696
43
F
G
H
J
K
1
2
3
4
5
6
7
Newbiggin Hall Estate
Cheviot Prim. School
THE NEIGHBOURHOOD CENTRE
Playing Field
St. Mark's RC Prim. Sch.
Whittingham Road Bungs.
TREVELYAN
Teasdale Ho.
WOOLSINGTON BY-PASS
Training Centre
Bank Top
Hotels
Subway
BY-PASS
Kenton Bar Prim. Sch.
St. Cuthbert's Catholic Primary School
Playing Fields
Kenton School
NE3
Kenton Bar
Beal Green
Fawlee Green
Manor Ho. Fm. Cotts.
KENTON
A191
LANE
Riding School
PONTELAND
HAZELDENE
WESTERN
NEWCASTLE
A1
A167
Recreation Ground
Football Pitch
Tennis Courts
Blakelaw
Blakelaw Wood
BLAKELAW ROAD
Cowgate Cen.
Cowgate
Westerhope
Westerhope Cen.
NE5
STAMFORD
Farne Primary Sch.
Superstore
Calleron Court
Playing Field
WEST AVENUE
Bowl. Grn.
Play. Fields
Beech Hill Primary School
Thomas Berwick School
Linhope PRU
LORDENSHAW
Northumbria Walk
Newcastle upon Tyne
WEST DENTON RETAIL PK.
BY-PASS
Hilton Prim. Acad.
Comm. Cen. Lib.
Thomas Walling Prim. Sch.
Playing Field
Sports Ground
Bowl. Grn.
Tennis Cts.
Stamfordham Rd. Playing Field
STAMFORDHAM ROAD
SPRINGFIELD
Superstore
Youth Centre
ST. JAMES RETAIL PK.
Bus Depot
East Denton
Whitbeck Court
King George's Field
English Martyr's RC Prim. Sch.
WESTERHOPE
Denton Dene North
Silver Hill
Depot
Comm. Cen.
Denton Burn
Denton Hall Turret
A186
WEST ROAD
West Road Crematorium
Cemetery
Stocksfield Av. Prim. Sch.
Play. Field
FENHAM
Fenham Swim. Pool
Lib.
Sacred Heart RC Prim. Sch.
St. Mary's College
Sacred Heart High Sch.
Tennis Courts
NE4
Broadwood Primary School
BROADWOOD
Cricket Ground
St. Cuthbert's Catholic High School
St. Bede's RC Prim. Sch.
Playing Fields
Playing Field
John Marley Centre
B1311
Newcastle City Juniors
Hadrian School
Newcastle City Learning Centre
Centre for Sport
Hindu Temple
Benwell Temple
Benwell Vallum Crossing
Trinity School (Oakfield College)
B1305
Scotswood Sports & Social Centre
Denton Dene
Excelsior Academy
Youth Centre
Old Benwell
Water Works
Thomas Horsley Ho.
Tynedale Ho.
81
BENWELL
Play. Field
CONDERCUM INDUS. ESTATE
Canning St. Prim. Sch.
CONDERCUM
DENTON
A191

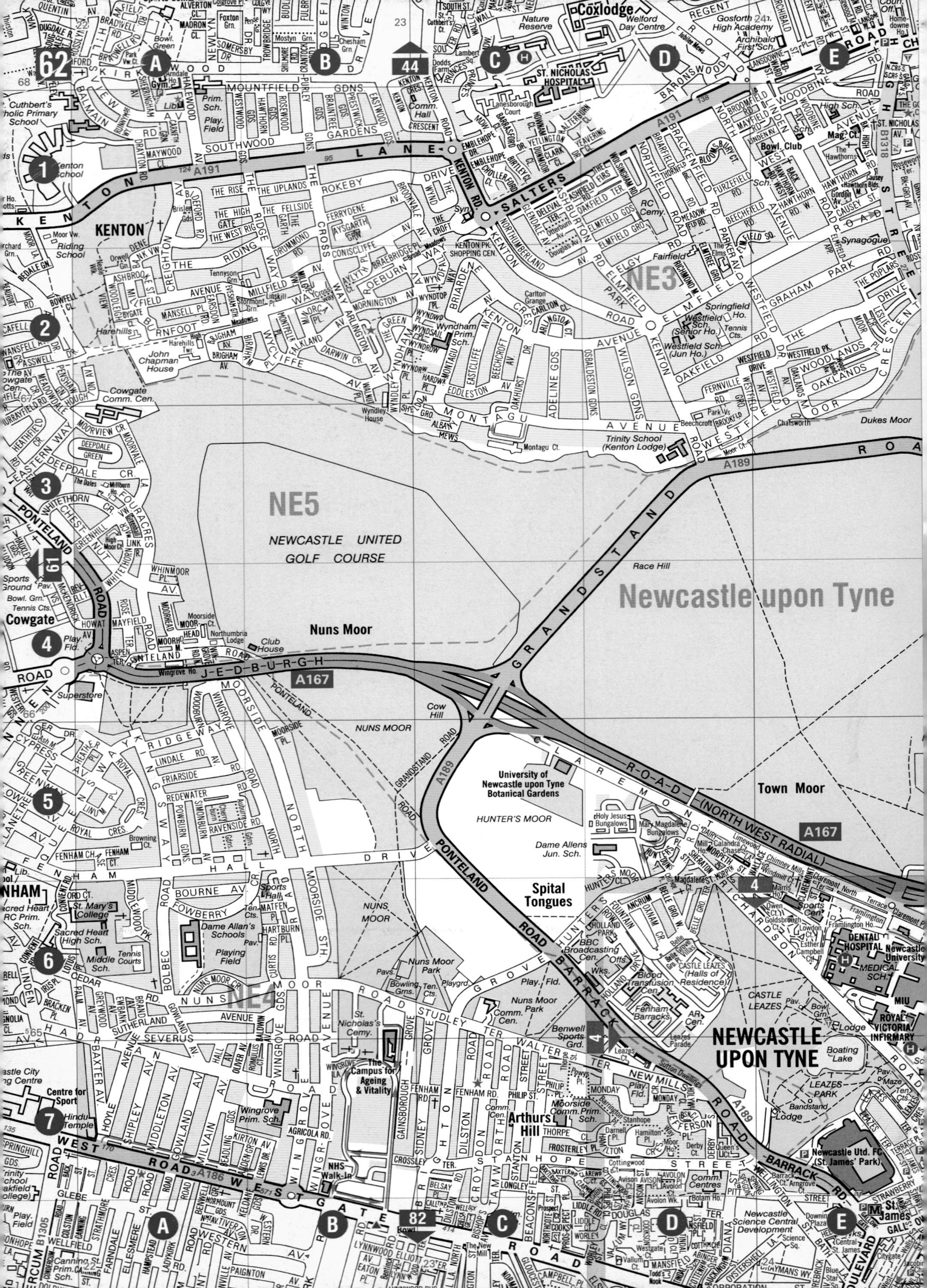
Coxlodge
Welford Day Centre
Nature Reserve
Gosforth High Academy
Archibald First Sch.
ST. NICHOLAS HOSPITAL
KENTON LANE
A191
Kenton School
KENTON
SALTERS ROAD
NE3
Riding School
Moor Vw.
KENTON PK. SHOPPING CEN.
Wyndham Prim. Sch.
John Chapman House
Cowgate Comm. Cen.
Westfield Sch. (Senior Ho.)
Westfield Sch. (Jun Ho.)
Trinity School (Kenton Lodge)
Montagu Ct.
Dukes Moor
A189
GRANDSTAND ROAD
NE5
NEWCASTLE UNITED GOLF COURSE
Race Hill
Newcastle upon Tyne
Cowgate
Nuns Moor
Club House
JEDBURGH ROAD
A167
Superstore
Cow Hill
NUNS MOOR
University of Newcastle upon Tyne Botanical Gardens
HUNTER'S MOOR
Town Moor
CLAREMONT ROAD (NORTH WEST RADIAL)
Dame Allens Jun. Sch.
Spital Tongues
PONTELAND ROAD
BARRACK ROAD
DENTAL HOSPITAL
Newcastle University
MEDICAL SCH.
ROYAL VICTORIA INFIRMARY
NE4
St. Mary's College
Sacred Heart RC Prim. Sch.
Sacred Heart High Sch.
Dame Allan's Schools
Playing Field
Nuns Moor Park
St. Nicholas' Cemy.
The Campus for Ageing & Vitality
BBC Broadcasting Cen.
Blood Transfusion Cen.
Fenham Barracks
CASTLE LEAZES (Halls of Residence)
NEWCASTLE UPON TYNE
Boating Lake
LEAZES PARK
Newcastle Utd. FC (St. James' Park)
Arthurs Hill
Moorside Comm. Prim. Sch.
Wingrove Prim. Sch.
Centre for Sport
Hindu Temple
NHS Walk-In
WEST ROAD A186
WESTGATE ROAD
STANHOPE STREET
Newcastle Science Central Development
St. James
Canning St. Prim. Sch.
44
61
82
4

South Gosforth
West Jesmond
Jesmond
High Heaton
Heaton
Jesmond Vale
Sandyford
Brandling Village
Shieldfield
Haymarket
Byker
Manors
Battle Field
Jesmond Dene
Freeman Hospital
Northern Cen. for Cancer Care
David Lloyd Leisure Centre
Sports Ground
Newcastle Clinic
The Northumberland Club
Heaton Manor School
Newcastle Nuffield Health Hospital
Northumberland Co. Cricket Club (County Ground)
All Saints' Cemetery
Newcastle General Cemetery
The Fleming Nuffield Unit
Royal Grammar Sch.
Northern Counties Coll.
Armstrong Park
King John's Palace (rems. of)
Ouseburn Park
City Stadium
Northumbria University (Newcastle City Campus)
Newcastle University
Hatton Gall.
Northern Stage
Civic Cen.
Exhibition Park
Boating Lake
Exhibition Building
Mootacres Playing Field
Little Moor
Sutherland Park Playing Field
The Gym Newcastle East
Great North Children's Hosp.
Ouseburn Viaduct
Jesmond Dene Road
Osborne Road
Benton Road
Matthew Bank
Haddricks Mill Road
Stephenson Road
Shields Road By-Pass
New Bridge St.
Central Motorway
Jesmond Road
Jesmond Dene Road
Great North Road
Chillingham Road
Heaton Road
Heaton Park Road
A167(M)
A1058
A189
A188
A193
B1600
B1307
B1312
B1318
NE2
NE6
45
64
5
83
F G H J K
1 2 3 4 5 6 7

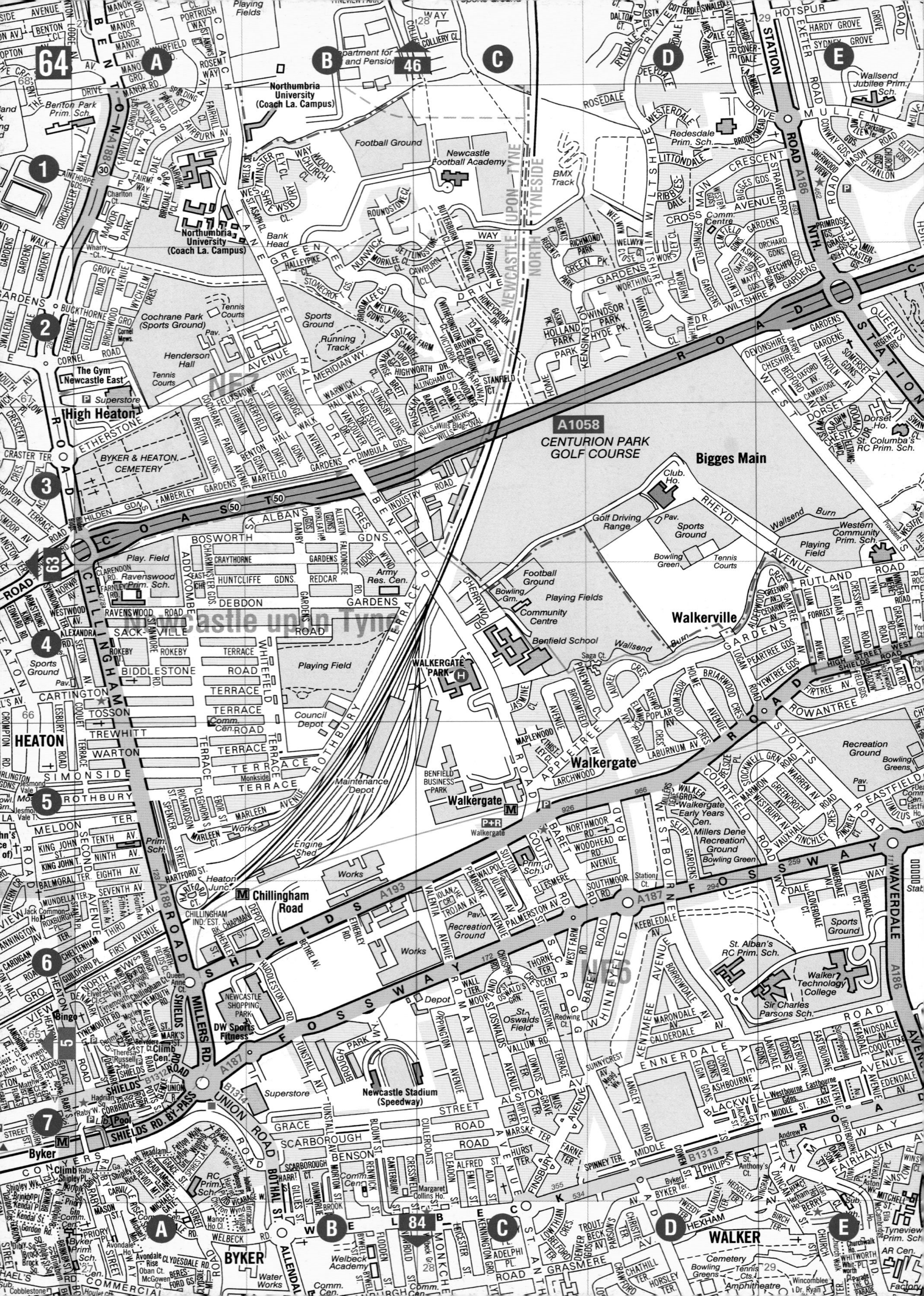
46
84
63
5
A
B
C
D
E
1
2
3
4
5
6
7
Northumbria University (Coach La. Campus)
Football Ground
Newcastle Football Academy
Benton Park Prim. Sch.
Redesdale Prim. Sch.
Wallsend Jubilee Prim. Sch.
BMX Track
NEWCASTLE UPON TYNE
NORTH TYNESIDE
Cochrane Park (Sports Ground)
Henderson Hall
Sports Ground
Running Track
The Gym Newcastle East
Superstore
High Heaton
NE7
A1058
CENTURION PARK GOLF COURSE
Bigges Main
BYKER & HEATON CEMETERY
COAST ROAD
Club Ho.
Golf Driving Range
Sports Ground
Bowling Green
Tennis Courts
Playing Field
Western Community Prim. Sch.
Play. Field
Ravenswood Prim. Sch.
Army Res. Cen.
Football Ground
Playing Fields
Community Centre
Benfield School
Walkerville
Newcastle upon Tyne
Sports Ground
Playing Field
WALKERGATE PARK
Council Depot
HEATON
Maintenance Depot
Benfield Business Park
Walkergate
Recreation Ground
Engine Shed
Works
Heaton Junc.
Chillingham Road
Walker Early Years Cen.
Millers Dene Recreation Ground
Bowling Green
Recreation Ground
CHILLINGHAM ROAD
SHIELDS ROAD
FOSSWAY
A187
A193
NE6
St. Alban's RC Prim. Sch.
Sports Ground
Walker Technology College
Sir Charles Parsons Sch.
Newcastle Shopping Park
DW Sports Fitness
Depot
St. Oswalds Field
Superstore
Newcastle Stadium (Speedway)
Byker
BYKER
WALKER
Welbeck Academy
Water Works
Cemetery
Bowling Greens
Amphitheatre
Tyneview Prim. Sch.
SHIELDS RD. BY-PASS
UNION ROAD
WAVERDALE
STATION ROAD
A186
A188

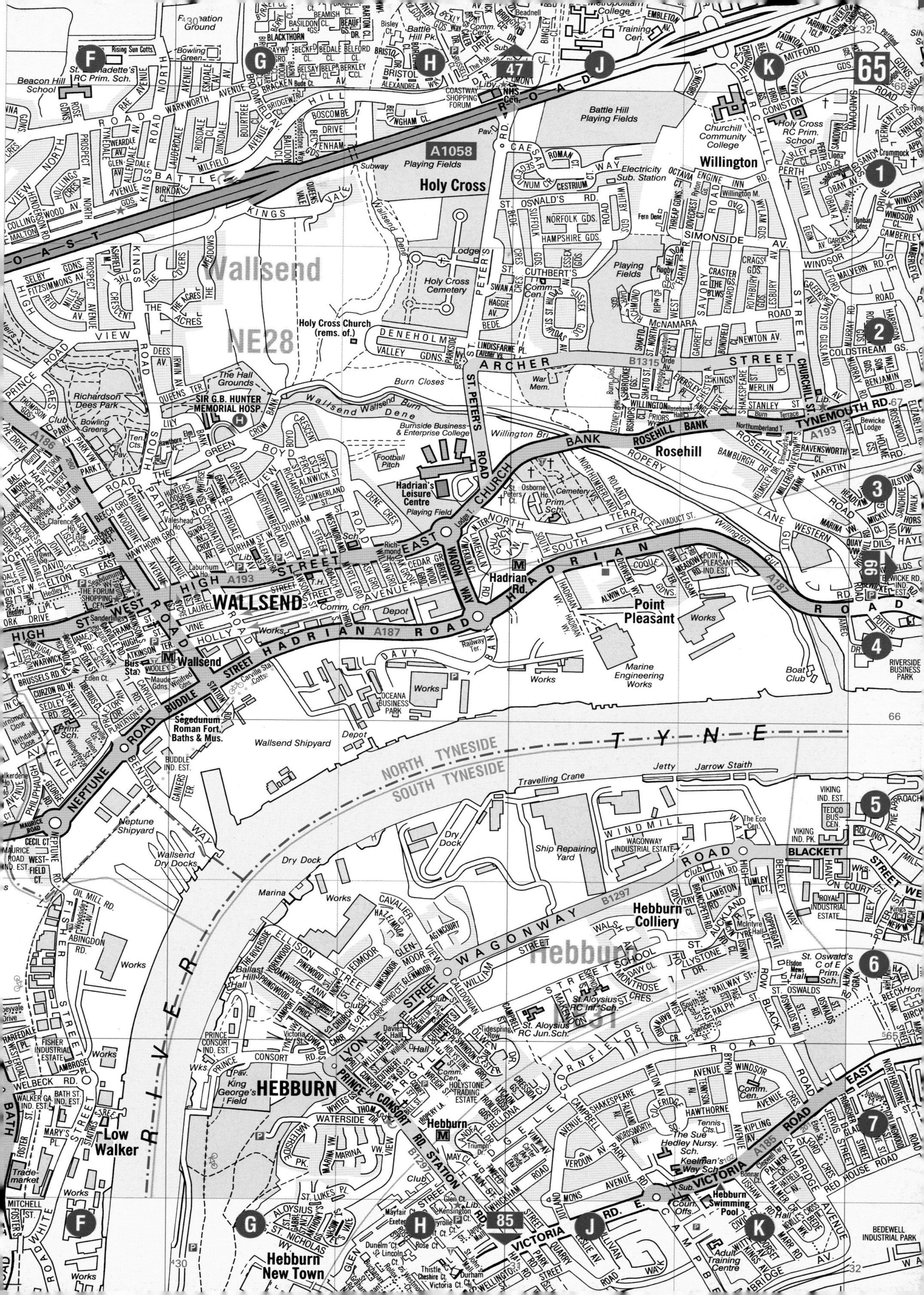
47
85
66
A1058
A186
A193
A187
A185
B1315
B1297
NE28
Wallsend
WALLSEND
Holy Cross
Willington
Rosehill
Point Pleasant
Hebburn Colliery
HEBBURN
Hebburn New Town
Low Walker
COAST ROAD
BATTLE HILL
Battle Hill Playing Fields
Playing Fields
Churchill Community College
Holy Cross RC Prim. School
Holy Cross Cemetery
Holy Cross Church (rems. of.)
Lodge
Wallsend Dene
Burn Closes
The Hall Grounds
SIR G.B. HUNTER MEMORIAL HOSP.
Richardson Dees Park
Bowling Greens
Burnside Business & Enterprise College
Football Pitch
Hadrian's Leisure Centre
Playing Field
Electricity Sub. Station
ARCHER STREET
TYNEMOUTH RD.
ROSEHILL BANK
CHURCH BANK
HIGH STREET EAST
HIGH STREET WEST
HADRIAN ROAD
WAGON WAY
ST. PETER'S ROAD
NEPTUNE ROAD
BUDDLE ROAD
STATION ROAD
THE FORUM SHOPPING CEN.
Wallsend
Hadrian Rd.
Segedunum Roman Fort, Baths & Mus.
Wallsend Shipyard
Neptune Shipyard
Wallsend Dry Docks
Marine Engineering Works
Works
Boat Club
RIVERSIDE BUSINESS PARK
OCEANA BUSINESS PARK
BUDDLE IND. EST.
POINT PLEASANT IND. EST.
Depot
RIVER TYNE
NORTH TYNESIDE
SOUTH TYNESIDE
Jetty
Jarrow Staith
Travelling Crane
Ship Repairing Yard
WAGONWAY INDUSTRIAL ESTATE
WINDMILL WAY
Dry Dock
Marina
BLACKETT STREET
VIKING IND. EST.
VIKING IND. PK.
TEDCO BUS. CEN.
ROYAL INDUSTRIAL ESTATE
WAGONWAY
Hebburn
St. Aloysius RC Inf. Sch.
St. Aloysius RC Jun. Sch.
St. Oswald's C of E Prim. Sch.
PRINCE CONSORT IND. EST.
PRINCE CONSORT RD.
King George's Field
HOLYSTONE TRADING ESTATE
Hebburn Swimming Pool
The Sue Hedley Nursy. Sch.
Keelman's Way Sch.
VICTORIA RD. EAST
VICTORIA RD. WEST
STATION RD.
CAMPBELL PARK ROAD
Adult Training Centre
BEDEWELL INDUSTRIAL PARK
FISHER INDUSTRIAL ESTATE
WALKER GA. IND. EST.
BATH ST. IND. EST.
Trade-market
MAURICE ROAD IND. EST.
Beacon Hill School
COASTWAY SHOPPING FORUM
F
G
H
J
K
1
2
3
4
5
6
7

66
48
65
86
A
B
C
D
E
1
2
3
4
5
6
7
32
33
34
66
65
Silverdale School
Holy Cross RC Prim. School
MELROSE
RIDLEY
WINDSOR DRIVE
WINDSOR COTTS.
WINDSOR CL.
Denbigh Prim. Sch.
Comm. Cen.
HOWDON
ROAD
TYNEMOUTH
A193
Wallsend
NE28
WALLSEND
ROAD
Stephenson Mem. Prim. Sch.
Howdon
Children's Nursery
Howdon Gas Works
MARTIN
Refuse Tip
BREWERS
WILLINGTON QUAY
A19
Toll
East End Park
HADRIAN
ROAD
A187
BEWICKE ST.
TYNE VIEW TER.
STEPHENSON STREET
POTTER STREET
RIVERSIDE BUSINESS PARK
Works
Boat Club
Howdon Pans
CAR RETAIL PARK
SATURN CT.
Warehouses
TYNE TUNNEL TRADING
Warehouse
TYNE TUNNEL TRADE PARK
BUGATTI INDUSTRIAL PARK
Factory
Electricity Sub Sta.
Playing Field
West Chirton
Norham High
Play. Field
WALLSEND ROAD
A193
Percy Main
EAST HOWDON BY-PASS
A187-HOWDON
HOWDON
St. Mark's Ct.
Percy Main Prim. Sch.
ST. JOHN'S
Cricket Ground
Meadow Well
County Court
BALTIC IND. PARK
HAYHOLE
ROYAL QUAYS OUTLET SHOPPING
DW Sports Fitness
East Howdon
Sewage Works
Settling Tanks
NORTHUMBERLAND DOCK ROAD
Works
Northumberland Dock
Jetty
Howdon Staithe
NORTH TYNESIDE
SOUTH TYNESIDE
RIVER
The Tyne Pedestrian & Cycle Tunnels
VIKING IND. EST.
VIKING IND. PK.
BLACKETT
WESTERN ROAD
B1297
ROYAL INDUSTRIAL ESTATE
BAILEY INDUSTRIAL ESTATE
TYNESIDE WORKS
Jarrow Riverside Park
CHAYTOR ST.
PRIORY
ELLISON ST.
THE VIKING SHOP. CEN.
Jarrow
Tanks
Bedes World
Oil Depot
Bede's World
Drewett Playing Fields
CHURCH BANK
St. Paul's Monastery (rems. of)
Tyne Car Terminal
Jarrow Slake
SLAKE ROAD
River Don
ALBERT ROAD
A185
HOWARD ST.
STRAKER
SWINBURNE ST.
East Jarrow
Jarrow Park
Bowling Greens
Bandstand
Tennis Courts
BEDEWELL INDUSTRIAL PARK
JARROW
Jarrow Cross C of E Prim. Sch.
Epinay Business & Enterprise School
Jarrow Cemetery
War Mem.
Jarrow Comm. Pool
Jarrow School
BEDE INDUSTRIAL ESTATE
South Shields FC
Bede
SIMONSIDE INDUSTRIAL ESTATE
Overrid Skate Pk.
TYNE POINT IND. ESTATE
MONKSWAY
SHAFTESBURY

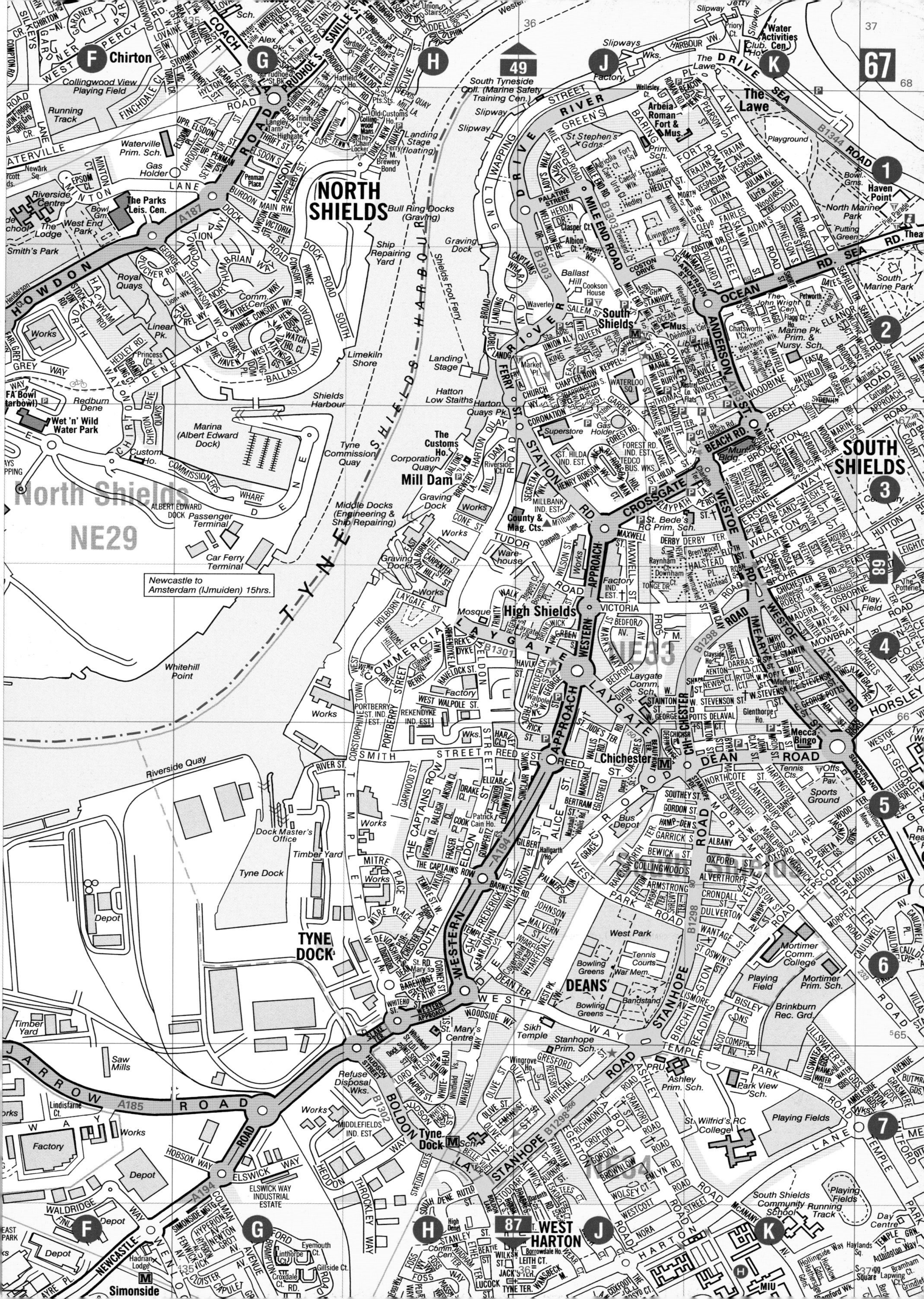
36
37
49
F
G
H
J
K
Chirton
North Shields
NORTH SHIELDS
NE29
South Shields Coll. (Marine Safety Training Cen.)
Water Activities Club Cen.
The Lawe
Arbeia Roman Fort & Mus.
SEA DRIVE
B1344
1
Haven Point
North Marine Park
South Marine Park
OCEAN RD.
2
3
SOUTH SHIELDS
68
4
5
6
7
Collingwood View Playing Field
Running Track
Waterville Prim. Sch.
Gas Holder
The Parks Leis. Cen.
Riverside Centre
West End Park
Smith's Park
HOWDON RD.
A187
Royal Quays
Linear Pk.
Redburn Dene
Wet 'n' Wild Water Park
Marina (Albert Edward Dock)
ALBERT EDWARD DOCK
Passenger Terminal
Car Ferry Terminal
Newcastle to Amsterdam (IJmuiden) 15hrs.
Bull Ring Docks (Graving)
Ship Repairing Yard
Shields Foot Ferry
Limekiln Shore
Shields Harbour
Landing Stage
Hatton Low Staiths
Tyne Commission Quay
TYNE
SHIELDS HARBOUR
The Customs Ho.
Corporation Quay
Mill Dam
Middle Docks (Engineering & Ship Repairing)
Graving Docks
Whitehill Point
Riverside Quay
Dock Master's Office
Timber Yard
Tyne Dock
TYNE DOCK
Depot
Saw Mills
JARROW ROAD
A185
A194
Factory
Works
ELSWICK WAY INDUSTRIAL ESTATE
Simonside
NEWCASTLE RD.
South Shields
Market Pl.
Superstore
Mus.
Lib.
County & Mag. Cts.
High Shields
Mosque
LAYGATE
B1301
NE33
Chichester
Laygate Comm. Sch.
Bus Depot
WESTERN APPROACH
STANHOPE ROAD
B1298
Mecca Bingo
DEAN ROAD
Sports Ground
West Park
Bowling Greens
Tennis Courts
War Mem.
DEANS
Bandstand
Sikh Temple
Stanhope Prim. Sch.
Mortimer Comm. College
Mortimer Prim. Sch.
Playing Field
Brinkburn Rec. Grd.
Park View Sch.
Ashley Prim. Sch.
St. Wilfrid's RC College
Playing Fields
South Shields Community School
Running Track
NE34
87
WEST HARTON
B1302
BOLDON LA.
MIDDLEFIELDS IND. EST
Day Centre
TEMPLE PARK RD.
A1018
A183
B1303
St. Bede's RC Prim. Sch.
St. Mary's Centre
Refuse Disposal Wks.

37
38
39
A
B
C
D
E
1
2
3
4
5
6
7
South Pier
Slipway
Watch Ho.
Amusement Pk. Caravan Site
Bus and Coach Pk.
Dunes
Adventure Island
Dunes Bowl.
Quasar
Haven Point
North Marine Park
Putting Green
Thtre.
Ocean Beach Pleasure Park
Herd Sand
Yachting Lake
South Marine Park
Bents Park
Caravan Park
Amphitheatre
Bents Recreation Ground
Lifeguard Station
Gypsies Green Sports Ground
The Waters Edge
Trow Point
Graham's Sand
Trow Lea
Coastguard Station
Frenchman's Bay
Frenchman's Lea
Man Haven
SOUTH SHIELDS
NE33
Cemetery
WINNINGS
Westoe Crown Prim. Sch.
Playing Field
Fulmar Lodge
Bents Cottages
Rec. Grd.
South Shields Bowls Centre
Play. Field
The Potteries
WESTOE
South Tyneside College (Westoe Campus)
Playing Flds.
Dr. Winterbottom Hall
Mecca Bingo
Robert Readhead Park
Cauldwell
War Mem.
HARTON CEMETERY
Nursery
AR Centre
Horsley Hill
Bamburgh School
Sea View Prim. Sch.
Harton Down Hill
Bramble Court
Woodhouse Court
St. Gregory's RC Prim. Sch.
Tabernacle
Aged Miners Homes
Bulmer Ho.
South Shields
NE34
The Cloisters
HARTON
Playing Fields
Harton School
Hall
Harton Prim. Sch.
Mortimer Comm. College
Mortimer Prim. Sch.
Playing Fields
Running Track
Day Centre
Harton Nook
88
67
MARSDEN
Marsden Old Local Nature
SEA ROAD
B1344
A183
COAST ROAD
ROAD
KINGSWAY
BAMBURGH AV.
HORSLEY HILL RD.
B1301
HIGHFIELD RD.
GROSVENOR
SUNDERLAND RD.
KING GEORGE ROAD
A1018
CHEVIOT ROAD
MARSDEN LANE
PRINCE EDWARD ROAD
A1300
TWO RIVERS
PROMENADE
Broadway
READHEAD AV.
HARTON HOUSE RD.
MOOR LA.
HIGH ST.
LINCOLN
FULWELL AV.
AVENUE
LUMLEY

440
41
42
F
G
H
J
K
68
1
2
67
3
4
66
5
6
565
7
42
NORTH SEA
Natural Arch
Natural Arch
Velvet Beds
sden Lea
Marsden Sands
Marsden
MARSDEN BAY
COAST
REDWELL LANE
Cliff
GROTTO GS.
GROTTO GS.
LIZARD
GROTTO
FALLOW
ROAD
RD.
GROTTO RD.
AVENUE
LAKESIDE
The Leas
Natural Arch
Marsden Rock
Smugglers' Cave
LIZARD LANE CARAVAN & CAMPING SITE
A183
Marsden Craggs
Quarry Reserve
Whitburn Golf Course
North Lizard Cottages
North Lizard Riding School
LANE
ROAD
89
440
41
Souter
Lizard Point

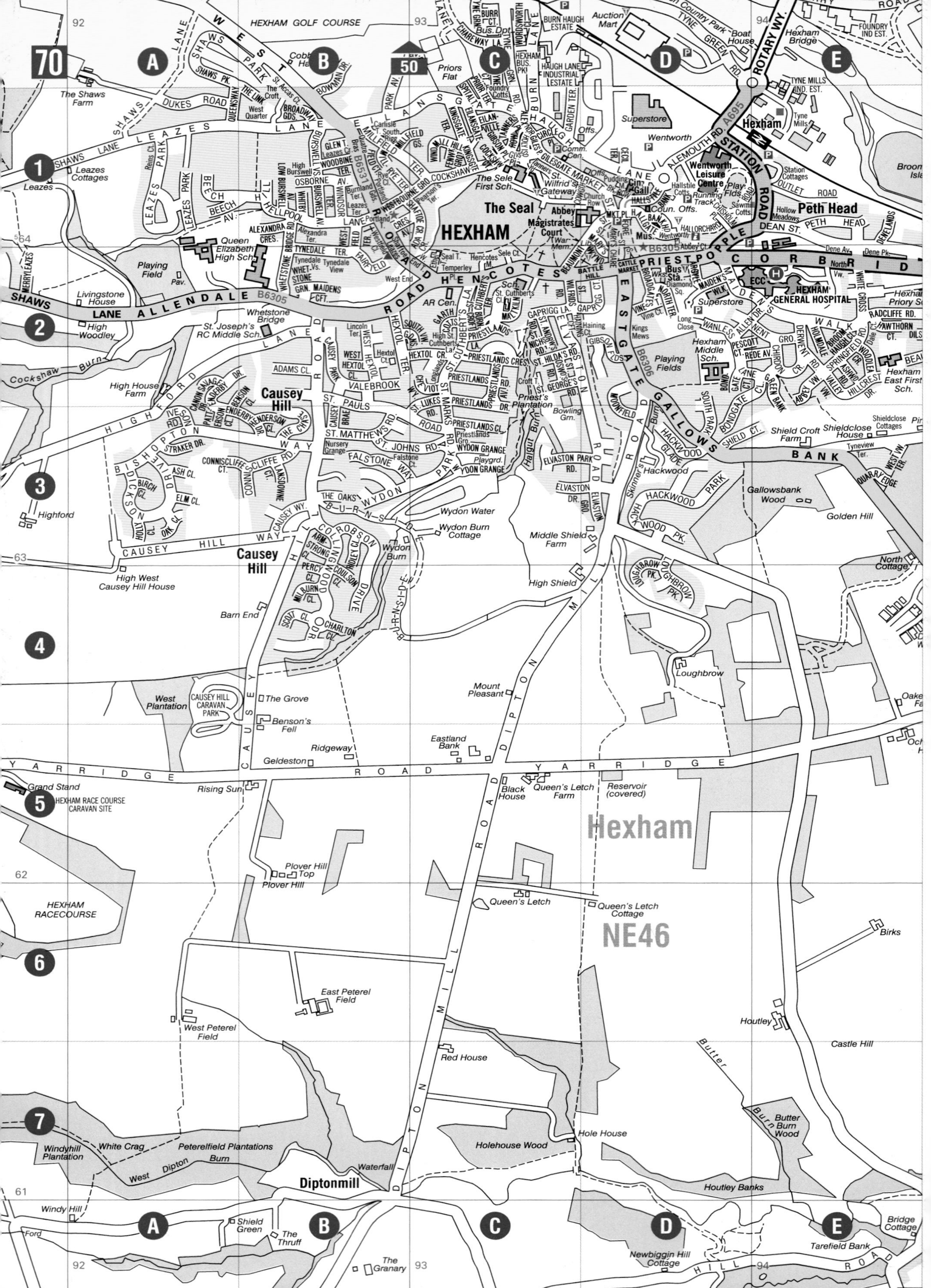

92
93
94
A
B
C
D
E
1
2
3
4
5
6
7
61
62
63
64
HEXHAM GOLF COURSE
50
Priors Flat
Auction Mart
Country Park
TYNE GREEN
Boat House
ROTARY WY.
Hexham Bridge
FOUNDRY IND EST.
BURN HAUGH ESTATE
HAUGH LANE INDUSTRIAL ESTATE
HEXHAM BUS. PK.
CHAREWAY LA.
Bus. Dpt.
Superstore
TYNE MILLS IND. EST.
Tyne Mills
Hexham
A695
STATION ROAD
Wentworth
Wentworth Leisure Centre
ALEMOUTH RD.
Station Cottages
OUTLET ROAD
Broom Isl
The Shaws Farm
SHAWS LANE
LEAZES LANE
DUKES ROAD
SHAWS PARK
SHAWS PK.
QUEENSWAY
THE LINK
West Quarter
The Croft
BROADWAY GDS.
BOWMAN DR.
WEST ROAD
Cobb Ha
Leazes Cottages
Leazes
LEAZES PARK
BEECH AV.
HELLPOOL
LOW BURSWELL
HIGH BURSWELL
OSBORNE AV.
WOODBINE TER.
WINDSOR TER.
MILLFIELD
COCKSHAW
KINGSGATE
ELANSGATE
The Sele First Sch.
The Seal
HEXHAM
Abbey
Magistrates Court
War Mem.
St. Wilfrid's Gateway
GILESGATE
MARKET ST.
Cin. Gall.
HALLSTILE BANK
Coun. Offs.
Mus.
Running Track
Play Flds.
Hallstile Cotts.
Sawmill Cotts.
Hollow Meadows
HALLORCHARD
Peth Head
DEAN ST.
PETH HEAD
DENELANDS
B6305
Abbey Ct.
PRIESTPOPPLE
CORBRIDGE ROAD
Dene Av.
Dene Pk.
North Vw.
ECC
HEXHAM GENERAL HOSPITAL
WHITE CROSS
Hexham Priory Sch.
RADCLIFFE RD.
HAWTHORN CT.
MERRYLEAZES
Queen Elizabeth High Sch.
ALEXANDRA CRES.
Alexandra Ter.
TYNEDALE TER.
Tynedale View
WHETSTONE BRIDGE RD.
GRN. MAIDENS CFT.
West End
Playing Field
Pav.
Livingstone House
SHAWS LANE
ALLENDALE ROAD
B6305
Whetstone Bridge
High Woodley
St. Joseph's RC Middle Sch.
HENCOTES
Seal T.
Temperley Pl.
Hencotes M.
Sele Ct.
AR Cen.
Sch.
St. Cuthberts Cl.
Battle Hill
CATTLE MARKET
Bus Sta.
Diamond Sq.
Superstore
Vine Ct.
NORTH TER.
MAIDEN'S WLK.
Long Close
Kings Mews
Playing Fields
Hexham Middle Sch.
B6306
EASTGATE
GALLOWS BANK
Cockshaw Burn
High House Farm
HIGHFORD LANE
Causey Hill
ADAMS CL.
VALEBROOK
Lincoln Ter.
WEST HEXTOL
HEXTOL TER.
HEXTOL CR.
PRIESTLANDS
PRIESTLANDS CRES.
PRIESTLANDS DR.
PRIESTLANDS CL.
ST. PAULS
ST. MATTHEWS RD.
ST. JOHNS RD.
ST. LUKES RD.
ST. MARKS RD.
Nursery Grange
FALSTONE WAY
Falstone Ct.
WYDON GRANGE
Playgrd.
WYDON PARK
GAPRIGG LA.
ST. NICHOLAS RD.
ST. ANDREWS RD.
ST. HILDA'S RD.
ST. GEORGE'S RD.
ELVASTON
Haining Cl.
GIBSON FLDS.
Croft T.
Priest's Plantation
Bowling Grn.
Halgut Burn
MOUNFIELD
HACKWOOD GLADE
Hackwood
SOUTH PARK
BONDGATE
Shield Croft Farm
Shieldclose House
Shieldclose Cottages
Tyneview Ter.
QUARRY EDGE
WEST VW. TER.
Hexham East First Sch.
HILLCREST DR.
SPRINGFIELD RD.
WOODLEA
ASHWOOD
BISHOPTON WAY
STRAKER DR.
CONNISCLIFFE RD.
CONNISCLIFFE CT.
LANSDOWNE
DICKSON DR.
BIRCH CL.
ASH CL.
ELM CL.
OAK CL.
HOLLY CL.
Highford
CAUSEY WY.
CAUSEY HILL WAY
THE OAKS
WYDON
BURNSIDE
Wydon Water
Wydon Burn Cottage
Wydon Burn
ELVASTON PARK RD.
ELVASTON DR.
Middle Shield Farm
HACKWOOD PARK
Skinner's Burn
Gallowsbank Wood
Golden Hill
North Cottage
Causey Hill
ROBSON DR.
COLLINGWOOD
ARMSTRONG
PERCY CL.
MILBURN CL.
SCOTT CL.
CHARLTON CL.
COULSON CL.
HIDLEY CL.
High West Causey Hill House
High Shield
LOUGHBROW PK.
Barn End
Loughbrow
DIPTON MILL ROAD
Mount Pleasant
West Plantation
CAUSEY HILL CARAVAN PARK
The Grove
Benson's Fell
Ridgeway
Geldeston
Eastland Bank
Oake Fa
Och
YARRIDGE ROAD
Grand Stand
HEXHAM RACE COURSE CARAVAN SITE
Rising Sun
Black House
Queen's Letch Farm
Reservoir (covered)
Hexham
Plover Hill Top
Plover Hill
HEXHAM RACECOURSE
Queen's Letch
Queen's Letch Cottage
NE46
Birks
East Peterel Field
West Peterel Field
Houtley
Castle Hill
Butter Burn
Red House
Butter Burn Wood
Windyhill Plantation
White Crag
Peterelfield Plantations
West Dipton Burn
Holehouse Wood
Hole House
Waterfall
Diptonmill
Houtley Banks
Windy Hill
Ford
Shield Green
The Thruff
The Granary
Newbiggin Hill Cottage
Tarefield Bank
Bridge Cottage
HILL ROAD

71
51
72
F
G
H
J
K
1
2
3
4
5
6
7
395
96
97
564
63
62
61
Factory
Sewage Works
Anickgrange Haugh
RIVER TYNE
RIVER
Sam's Island
Widehaugh Banks
Wide Haugh
A695
ROAD
Dilston Plains
Widehaugh
DILSTON PLAINS
Brick House
Craneshaugh
Roma Bungalow
Corbridge
Dilston Park
Woodlands
EAST WOODS
MONK'S TER.
Woodside
CHLDS
HILLSIDE
EASTFIELDS
CRANESHAUGH CL.
DOTLAND
CL.
ROAD
DIPTON CL.
GRANGE
EASTWOOD
EASTWOOD GRANGE CT.
MONKS MDWS
FAIRWOOD RD.
EDGEWOOD
GLANTON RD.
ELDONE RD.
HUDSHAW GDNS.
WOODSIDE VS.
Hudshaw
HUDSHAW
AV.
Bogle Hole
Delegate Cottage
Delegate Hall
COCK WOOD
Lodg
Dilston South Park
NE45
HALFMILE WOOD
Bowlingally Green
North Lodge
Garden Cottage
Duke's House
Park Wood
Heathery Hill
DILSTON PARK
East Haugh
Pinewood Haven
Coalpits Flat
DUKESHOUSE WOOD
Sunnyside Plantation
Milking Hill
Birchside Wood
Roma
West Haugh
Devil's Water
B6306
Swallowship House
Sunnyside
Tennis Court
Broomy Haugh
Hallstock Dean
Swallowship Wood
Swallowship Hill
Peggysbank Dene
Bridge Haugh
Linnels Cottages
Peggy's Bank
B6307
Old Fell
Barley Hill
Teasdale Fell
Linnels
Linnels Bridge
Weir
Broomy Bank
Borleywell Strand
LINNELS BANK
Linnels Head
Mill Haugh
Linnel Dene
Linnels Farm
Lamb Shield
Oaky Bank
Lambshield Banks
Water
Devil's
DIPTON WOOD
Hexham Levels
Site of Battle
1464
Hollybush Cottage
Hollybush Cottages
Brocks Bank
Ford
Newbiggin Bridge
Black Bank
Round Wood
Saw Mill
Waterfall
The Breeches
Newbiggin

72
52
71
Redhouse Haughs
Wide Haugh
DILSTON HAUGHS
RIVER TYNE
Green Pool
Town Farm Field
Orchard Vale
West Green
Vicars Pele
Market Pl.
HILL ST.
MIDDLE ST.
MAIN ST.
B6530
WATLING ST.
PRINCES ST.
ST. HELEN'S ST.
WELL BANK
APPLETREE
AYDON RD.
GLEBELANDS
WINDSOR TER.
Princes Ct.
Corbridge Bridge
Bythorne House
Randle Ho.
SPOUTWELL LA.
CORBRIDGE
A695
B6321
ROAD
Cemetery
STATION RD.
TINKLER'S BANK
THE STANNERS
Little Croft
Pav.
Daniel Stephens Memorial Sports Ground
ORCHARD HOLIDAY HOME PK.
Eales
Corbridge
Tynedale Park
STA. YD.
Works
Cliffe
TINKLERS YARD
B6529
The Scrogs
Priest's Bank
Dilston Crossing House
Dilston Haugh Cottages
Dilston Bridge
Dilston Haugh Farm
Dilston Newtown
Lodge
Dilston Mill House
Waterfall
Dilston
Dilston Mill
Earl's Bridge
Dilston Castle
Dilston Cott.
Dilston College of Further Education
Dilston Hall
Dilston House
Scurl Hill
Corbridge
Dilston Vale
Farnley
Farnley Grange
Bowlingally Green
LADYCUTTERS LANE
Ravenstone
Roecliff Lodge
Lauder Grange
The Cottage
High Town
West Fell
Dilston West Bungalow
East Haugh
NE45
Fellside
Whinney
The Mount
Mount Cottage
Birchside Wood
Dilston West Cottages
B6307
Snokoehill Plantation
Snokoe Hill
Highlevel Cottage
Kilbryde
Nixon's Belt
Highlevel Cottage
Prospect Hill
Quarry Cottage
Quarry Cottage Belt
Birchy
BIRCHY WOOD
Blossom Plantation
East Cottage
Fell Top
Temperley Grange
Temperley Grange Farm
Sike
Pit Allotment Wood
Old Fell
West Farm
Park Plantation
Middle Plantation
Corbridge Common
High Dipton
Seventy Acre Wood
Dipton Cottage
DIPTON WOOD
Dipton House
Lodge
A B C D E
1 2 3 4 5 6 7
397 98 99
564 63 62 61

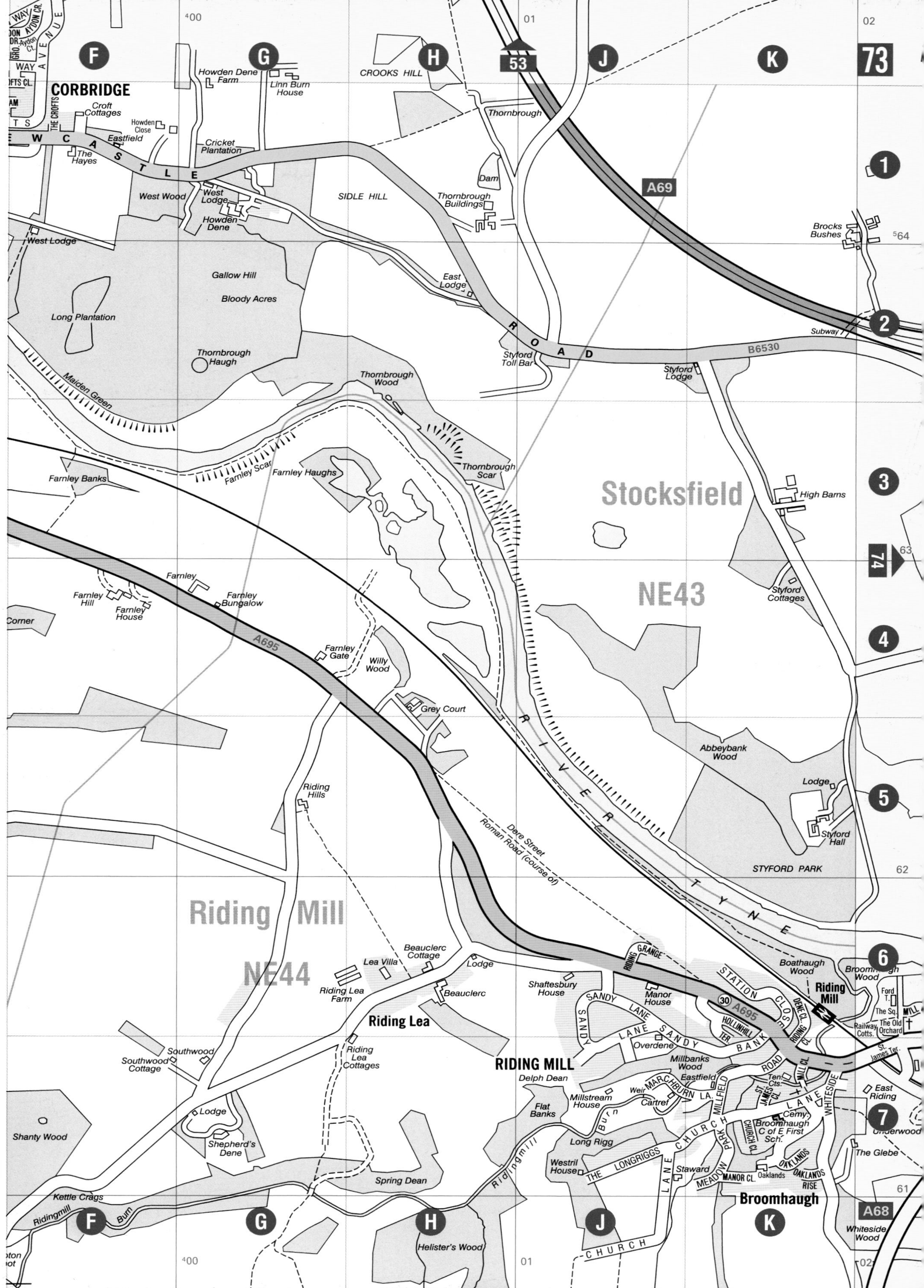
CORBRIDGE
Howden Dene Farm
Linn Burn House
CROOKS HILL
Thornbrough
Croft Cottages
Howden Close
Eastfield
Cricket Plantation
The Hayes
NEWCASTLE ROAD
West Wood
West Lodge
Howden Dene
SIDLE HILL
Thornbrough Buildings
Dam
A69
Brocks Bushes
Gallow Hill
Bloody Acres
Long Plantation
East Lodge
Thornbrough Haugh
Styford Toll Bar
Styford Lodge
B6530
Subway
Maiden Green
Thornbrough Wood
Thornbrough Scar
Farnley Scar
Farnley Haughs
Farnley Banks
Stocksfield
High Barns
NE43
Styford Cottages
Farnley
Farnley Hill
Farnley Bungalow
Farnley House
Corner
A695
Farnley Gate
Willy Wood
Grey Court
RIVER TYNE
Abbeybank Wood
Lodge
Riding Hills
Dere Street Roman Road (course of)
Styford Hall
STYFORD PARK
Riding Mill
NE44
Beauclerc Cottage
Lea Villa
Lodge
Riding Lea Farm
Beauclerc
Riding Lea
Shaftesbury House
Manor House
STATION CLOSE
RIDING GRANGE
Boathaugh Wood
Broomhaugh Wood
Riding Mill
SANDY LANE
HOLLINHILL TER.
BANK
DENE CL.
RIDING CL.
Overdene
Southwood
Southwood Cottage
Riding Lea Cottages
RIDING MILL
Millbanks Wood
ROAD
MILL CL.
Ten Cts.
Railway Cotts.
The Sq.
The Old Orchard
St. James Ter.
Delph Dean
Eastfield
Millstream House
Weir
Cartref
MARCHBURN LA.
MILLFIELD
ST. JAMES CL.
CHURCH LANE
WHITESIDE
East Riding
Cemy.
Broomhaugh C of E First Sch.
Underwood
Flat Banks
Lodge
Shanty Wood
Shepherd's Dene
Long Rigg
CHURCH CL.
OAKLANDS
The Glebe
Westril House
THE LONGRIGGS
Staward
PARK
Oaklands
OAKLANDS RISE
Spring Dean
Ridingmill
MEADOW
MANOR CL.
Broomhaugh
A68
Kettle Crags
Ridingmill Burn
Helister's Wood
Whiteside Wood
CHURCH
53
74
Ford

Plantation
Newton
Newton Town Farm
The Old Forge
Brockhole Wood
Brockhole
Burn
Brockhole Dean
Brocks Bushes
Shaw House
Newton Burn
Beam
Burn
A69
B6530
Wager Wood
Planetree Banks
Stonyverge Wood
Planetreebanks Plantation
High Barns
A68
Stocksfield
Styford Wood
Beam
Peepy Cottages
Peepy
Stonyverge
NE43
Burn
Burn
SUNNY BANK
Lodge
Peepy Dene
Sod Hall
Styford Hall
Hellhaugh Wood
Clockey
STYFORD PARK
Weir
Megsmill Plantation
Styford Bridge
Sewage Works
RIVER TYNE
Broomhaugh Wood
Riding Mill
Ford
The Sq.
Mill Grange
Water Flat
Railway Cotts.
The Old Orchard
A695
Low Shilford
Shilford Cottage
Catdean Bridge
St. James Ter.
East View
NE44
Broomhaugh
East Riding
A68
A695
Underwood
Shilford Middle Wood
The Glebe
Shilford East Wood
Oaklands
Shilford West Wood
Whiteside Wood
Juniperhill Wood
Smithy

54
73
90

75
55
91
76
Prudhoe
NE42
OVINGTON
Bearl
STOCKSFIELD
Stocksfield
Bywell
Birches Nook
Branch End
PAINSHAWFIELD
A69
B6309
A695
RIVER TYNE
MAIN ROAD
The Oaks
Overdene
South Croft
Benlow Hill
Bearl Farm Cottages
North Acomb
The Nurseries
Ovington Lodge
Ovington House
Acomb Cottage
West Dean
Bywell Home Farm
Bearl Wood
SHORT WOOD
Cottagebank Wood
Bywell Haughs
Alder Wood
Cockermere Burn
Bullion Hills
Crook Wood
Common Bank
Bellasis
Strawberry Wood
Lowclose Wood
Low Bank Cottages
Ezerley Well
Bywell Park
Bywell Bridge
Northumberland County Showground
Bywell Castle (rems. of)
Bywell Cottage
Stocksfield Hall
Green Hill
Merryshield Common
Merry Shield
Playing Field
Broomley First Sch.
Tennis Cts.
Winter Hill
Whinny Bank
Mickley Bank Farm
Mickley Common
Painshawfield Wood
Bywell House
Vicarage
Bywell Hall
Stocksfield House
Beaumont House
Hunter's Hill
OVERDENE
COAL LANE
ST. ANDREW'S LANE
Jubilee Rd.
GREEN RISING
BURNSIDE
Little Bldgs.
OLD BREWERY SQ.
THE GREEN
SPRINGFIELD
SPRINGFIELD CL.
Leazes Vw.
THE PASTURES
HALL FARM CL.
War Mem.
SOUTH VW.
Merryshields Ter.
BRETTONBY AV.
STONYBANK WAY
Meadowfield T.
Bywell View
Branch End T.
NEW RIDLEY ROAD
BIRCHES NOOK RD.
CRABTREE ROAD
CADEHILL ROAD
APPERLEY ROAD
PAINSHAWFIELD ROAD
BALLIOL RD.
NEVILLE RD.
Dale Vw. T.
BIRKDENE
LAYTON CL.
HALTON CL.
Kimberley Gdns.
Birches Nook Cotts.
GUESSBURN
BRUMWELL CT.
SOUTH PDE.
Mount Vw. Ter.
Burnside Cotts.
Stocksfield Burn
F
G
H
J
K
1
2
3
4
5
6
7
405
06
07
64
63
62
61

OVINGHAM
Eltringham
Stocksfield
NE43
Mickley Square
West Mickley
Mount Pleasant
High Mickley
PRUDHOE
Prudhoe
NE42
Prudhoe Castle
Prudhoe Mill
River Tyne
A695
B6395
Cherryburn (Mus.)
Ovingham Middle Sch.
Ovingham C of E First Sch.
Tyne Riverside Country Park
Prudhoe Castle First Sch.
Highfield Middle Sch.
St. Matthew's Catholic Prim Sch.
Mickley First Sch.
Water Pumping Station
Ovingham Bridge
Sewage Works
Football Ground
Cricket Ground
Cemetery
Playing Field
Field House
Alder Cottage
Alder Wood
Ferry Landing
Riverdale Nurseries
Eltringham Scar
Eltringham House
Oakwood
Horseclose Wood
Bullshaugh Wood
Knows Wood
The Knows
Broom Wood
Lowclose Wood
Highclose Wood
Clauchlands
Greenlaw Farm
Aged Mineworkers' Homes
Collieryclose Wood
Hall Yards
Tinkler's Row
Mickley Farm
High Mickley House Farm
East Farm
Mickley West Side Farm
South Side Farm
South Side Cotts.
Mickley Moor
Mickley Moor Farm Cottage
Edgewell House Farm
Highfield House Farm
Riding High Wood
Riding Low Wood
Toft Hill
Hunter's Hill
Bullion Hills
Whittle Dene
Duke's Dene
Mount H
Ovington Ho.
Orchard Hill
Wellburn House
Burnfoot
Cherryburn Cottages
Edgewell Road
Bowler's Hill
Stonybank Way
Main Road
West Road
Princess Way
Station Road
Castle Road
Highfield Road
Horsley Road
Gallowhill Lane
St. Andrew's Lane
Coal Lane
Eastgate Bank
Lumley's Lane
Ward Lane
56
75
92

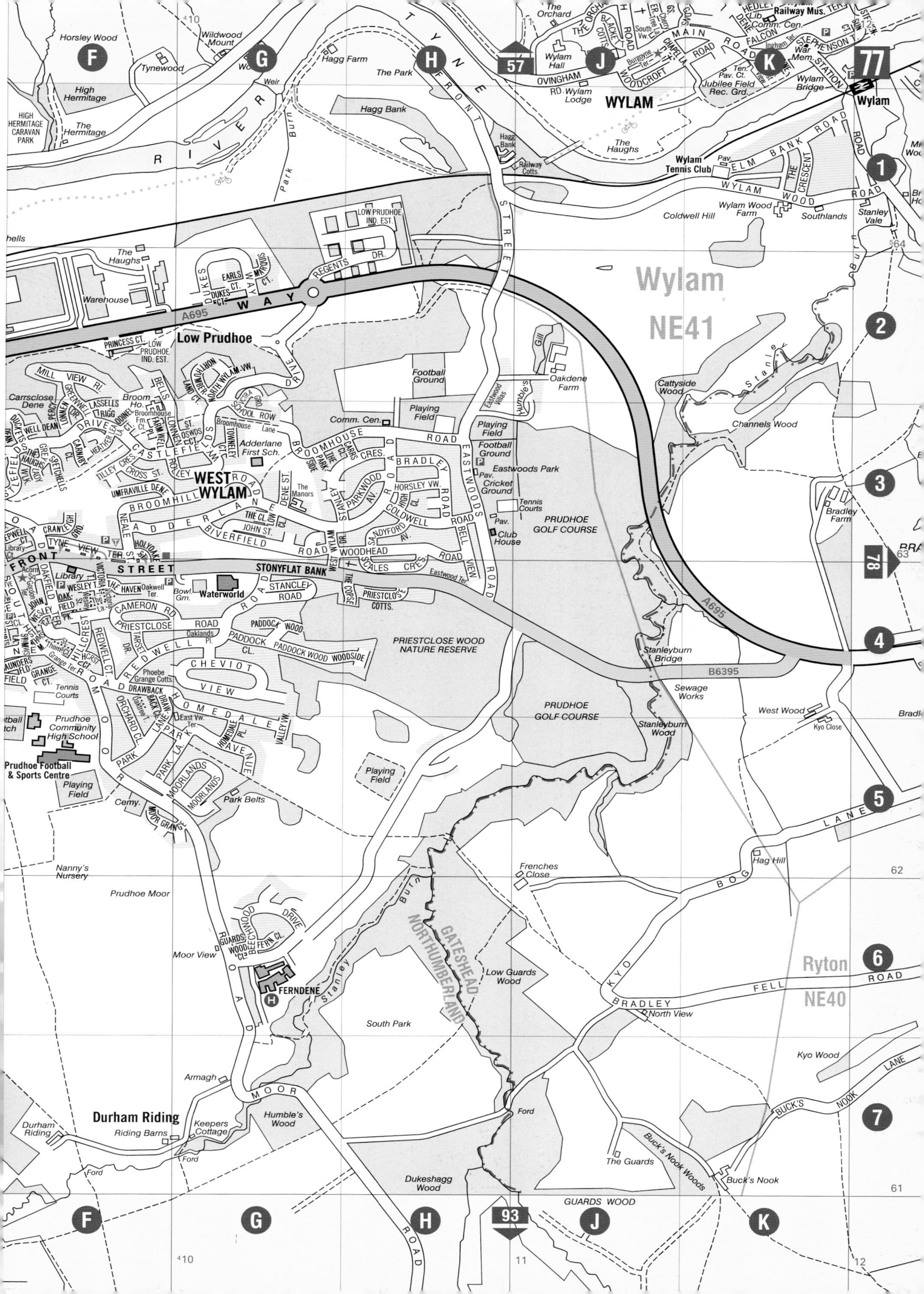

77
WYLAM
Wylam
NE41
Low Prudhoe
WEST WYLAM
PRUDHOE GOLF COURSE
PRIESTCLOSE WOOD NATURE RESERVE
Durham Riding
Ryton
NE40
57
78
93

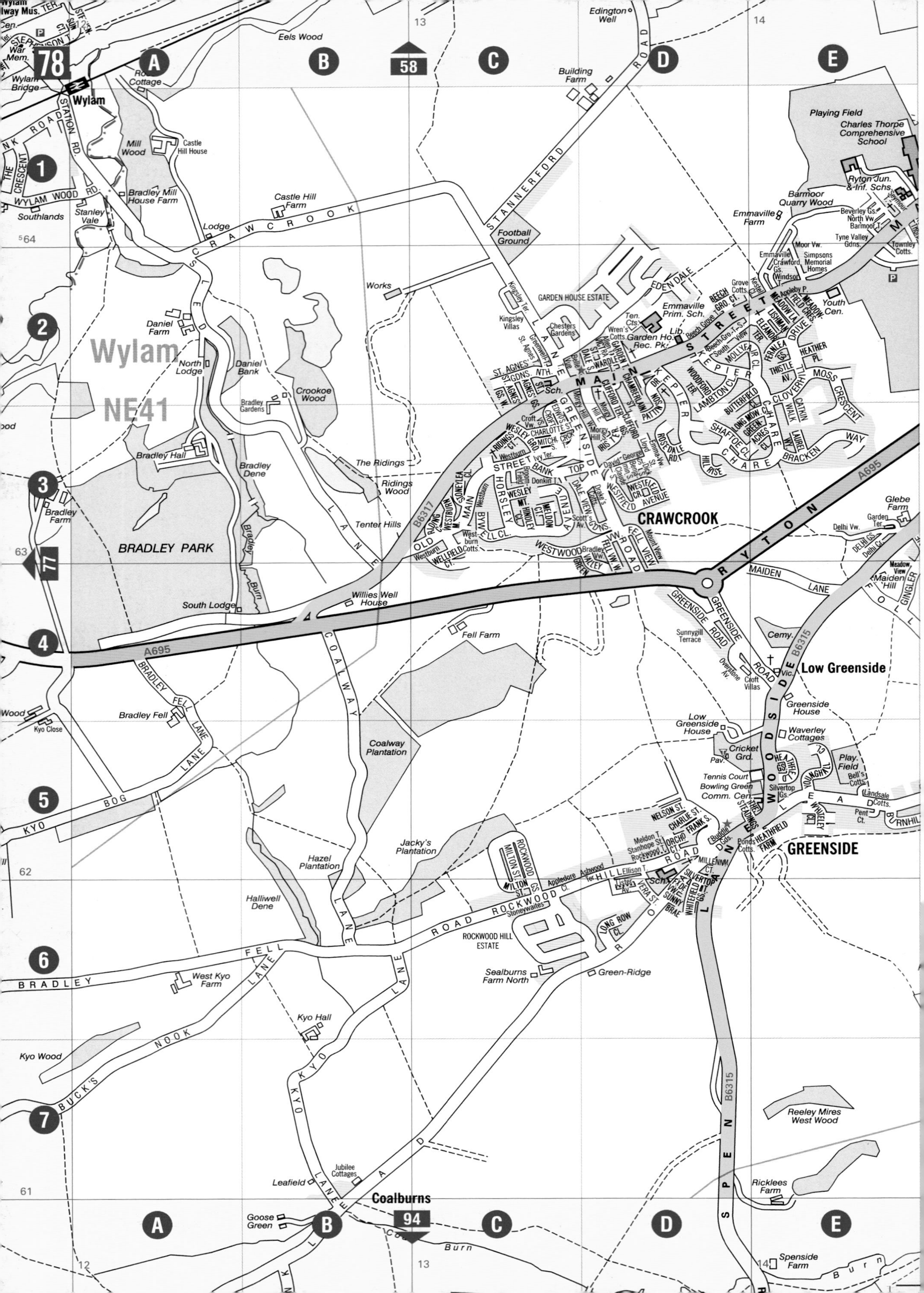

78
58
94
77
A
B
C
D
E
1
2
3
4
5
6
7
Wylam
NE41
CRAWCROOK
GREENSIDE
Low Greenside
Coalburns
BRADLEY PARK
Wylam Bridge
Eels Wood
Edington Well
Building Farm
Castle Hill House
Mill Wood
Bradley Mill House Farm
Castle Hill Farm
Southlands
Stanley Vale
Lodge
CRAWCROOK
STANNERFORD ROAD
Football Ground
Playing Field
Charles Thorpe Comprehensive School
Ryton Jun. & Inf. Schs.
Barmoor Quarry Wood
Emmaville Farm
Works
Daniel Farm
North Lodge
Daniel Bank
Crookoe Wood
Bradley Gardens
Bradley Hall
Bradley Dene
The Ridings
Ridings Wood
Tenter Hills
Bradley Farm
South Lodge
Willies Well House
Fell Farm
GARDEN HOUSE ESTATE
Kingsley Villas
Chesters Gardens
Emmaville Prim. Sch.
Youth Cen.
MAIN STREET
RYTON
A695
B6317
B6315
Glebe Farm
MAIDEN LANE
Cemy.
Sunnygill Terrace
Croft Villas
Greenside House
Low Greenside House
Waverley Cottages
Cricket Grd.
Play. Field
Tennis Court
Bowling Green
Comm. Cen.
Bradley Fell
Kyo Close
KYO BOG LANE
Coalway Plantation
COALWAY LANE
Jacky's Plantation
Hazel Plantation
Halliwell Dene
ROCKWOOD HILL ROAD
ROCKWOOD HILL ESTATE
Sealburns Farm North
Green-Ridge
BRADLEY FELL LANE
West Kyo Farm
Kyo Hall
Kyo Wood
BUCK'S NOOK LANE
KYO LANE
Reeley Mires West Wood
Ricklees Farm
Leafield
Jubilee Cottages
Goose Green
Spenside Farm
SPEN LANE
12
13
14
61
62
63
64

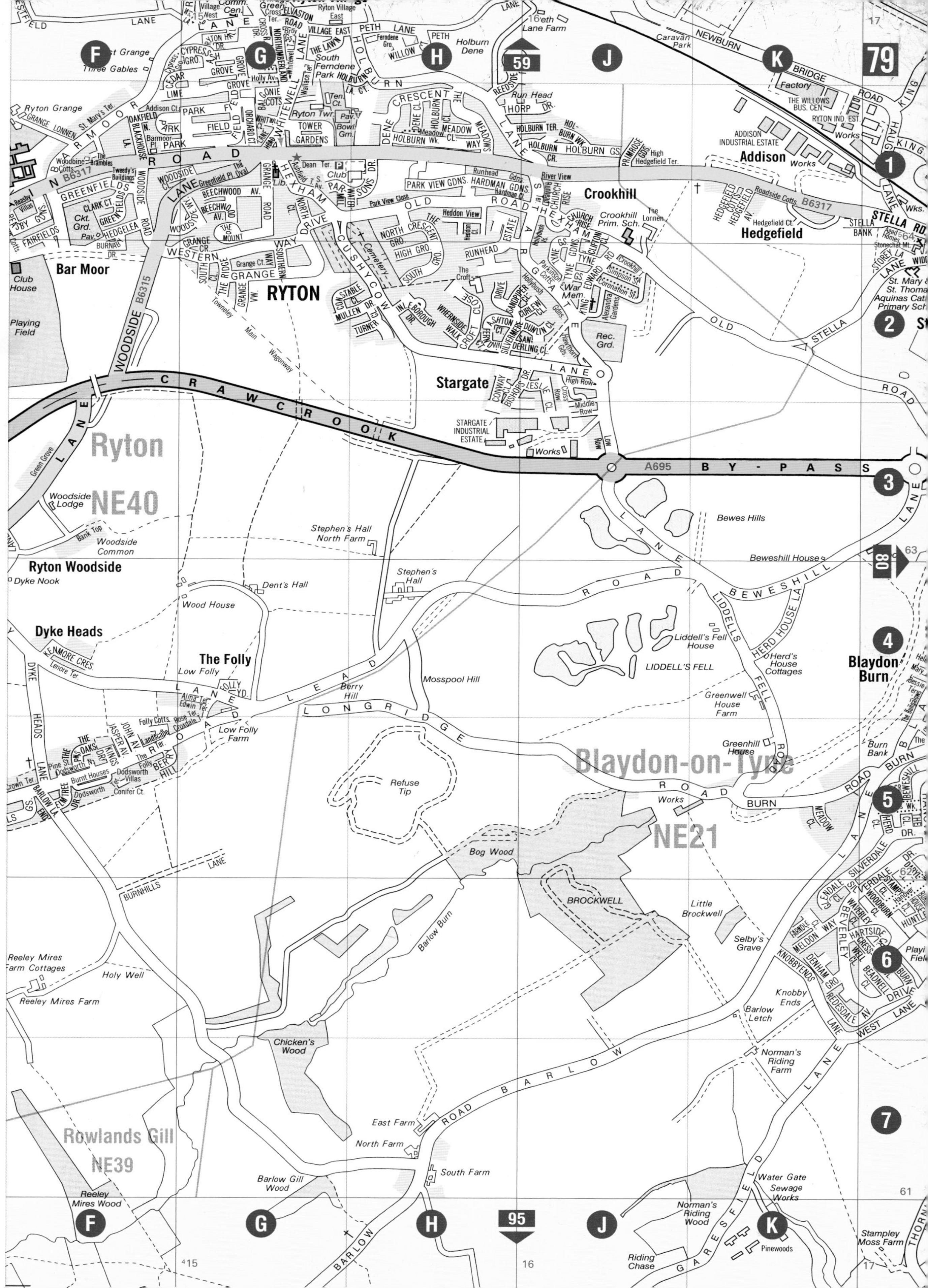

Ryton
NE40
RYTON
Crookhill
Addison
Hedgefield
Stargate
Bar Moor
Ryton Woodside
Dyke Heads
The Folly
Blaydon Burn
Blaydon-on-Tyne
NE21
Rowlands Gill
NE39
CRAWCROOK LANE
A695 BY-PASS
B6317
B6315
WOODSIDE LANE
HEXHAM ROAD
STELLA RD.
OLD STELLA ROAD
BEWESHILL LANE
LIDDELLS FELL ROAD
LEAD ROAD
LONGRIDGE ROAD
BURN ROAD
BARLOW ROAD
BARLOW LANE
GARESFIELD LANE
DYKE HEADS LANE
BURNHILLS LANE
Bewes Hills
Beweshill House
LIDDELL'S FELL
Liddell's Fell House
Herd's House Cottages
Greenwell House Farm
Greenhill House
Stephen's Hall North Farm
Stephen's Hall
Dent's Hall
Wood House
Low Folly
Low Folly Farm
Berry Hill
Mosspool Hill
Refuse Tip
Bog Wood
BROCKWELL
Little Brockwell
Selby's Grave
Knobby Ends
Barlow Letch
Norman's Riding Farm
Chicken's Wood
East Farm
North Farm
South Farm
Barlow Gill Wood
Reeley Mires Wood
Reeley Mires Farm
Reeley Mires Farm Cottages
Holy Well
Water Gate Sewage Works
Norman's Riding Wood
Riding Chase
Pinewoods
Stampley Moss Farm
Woodside Lodge
Woodside Common
Dyke Nook
Playing Field
Club House
STARGATE INDUSTRIAL ESTATE
ADDISON INDUSTRIAL ESTATE
Crookhill Prim. Sch.
Rec. Grd.
Caravan Park
St. Mary & St. Thomas Aquinas Cath. Primary Sch.
59
80
95
1 2 3 4 5 6 7
F G H J K

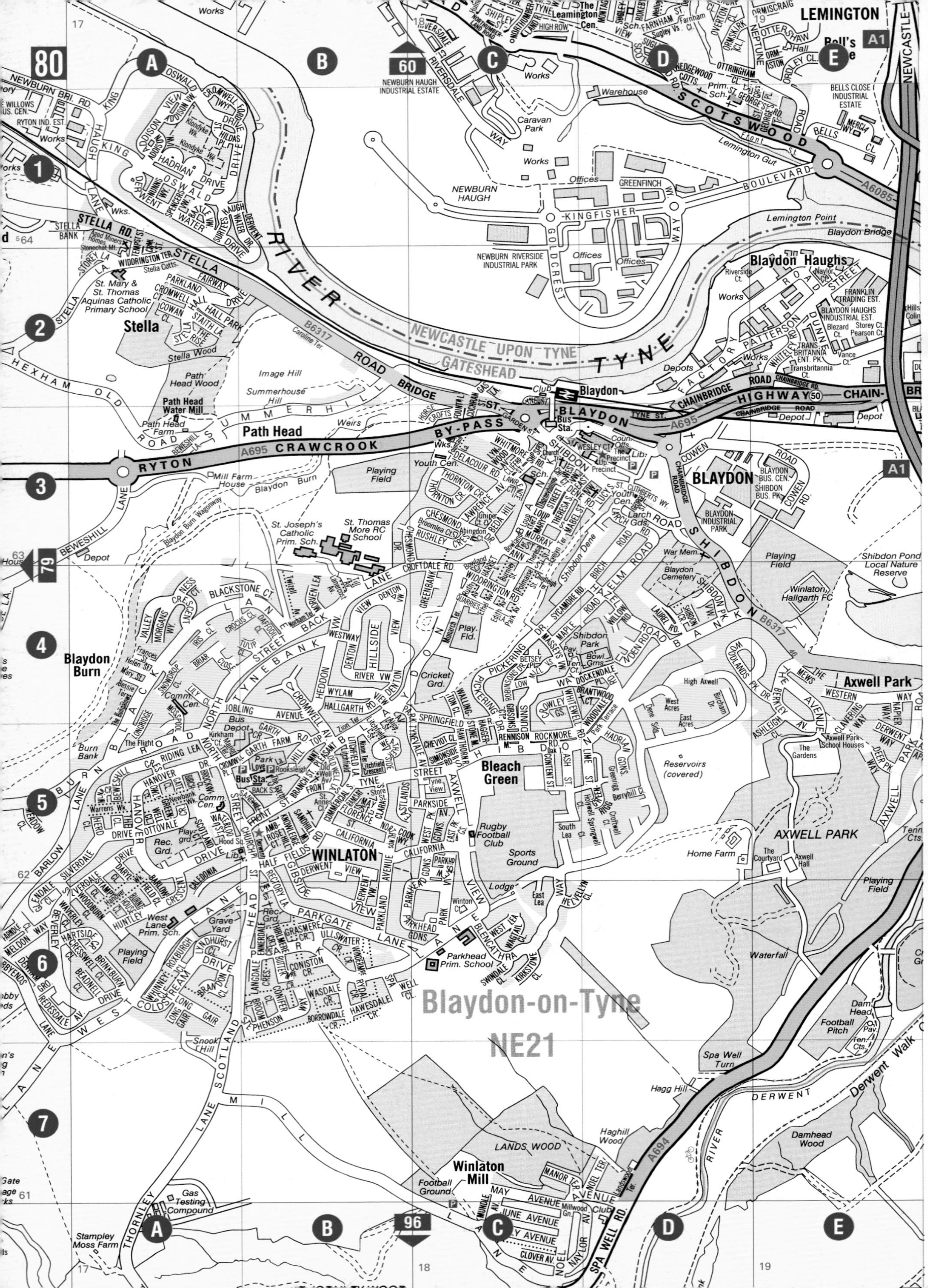
80
LEMINGTON
NEWCASTLE
A1
60
NEWBURN HAUGH INDUSTRIAL ESTATE
The Leamington Cen.
Works
Warehouse
SCOTSWOOD ROAD
BELLS CLOSE INDUSTRIAL ESTATE
Bell's Close
Caravan Park
Lemington Gut
BOULEVARD
A6085
NEWBURN HAUGH
KINGFISHER
GREENFINCH
Offices
NEWBURN RIVERSIDE INDUSTRIAL PARK
GOLDCREST
Lemington Point
Blaydon Bridge
Blaydon Haughs
BLAYDON HAUGHS INDUSTRIAL EST.
FRANKLIN TRADING EST.
TRANSBRITANNIA ENT. PK.
RIVER TYNE
NEWCASTLE UPON TYNE
GATESHEAD
NEWBURN BRI. RD.
RYTON IND. EST.
HAUGH LANE
STELLA RD.
Stella Bank
STELLA ROAD BRIDGE
B6317
St. Mary & St. Thomas Aquinas Catholic Primary School
Stella
Stella Wood
HEXHAM OLD ROAD
Path Head Wood
Path Head Water Mill
Path Head Farm
Image Hill
Summerhouse Hill
SUMMERHILL
Path Head
Weirs
A695 CRAWCROOK BY-PASS
RYTON
Mill Farm House
Blaydon Burn
Blaydon
BLAYDON
CHAINBRIDGE ROAD
HIGHWAY
50
Depot
Bus Sta.
Youth Cen.
Playing Field
BLAYDON
BLAYDON BUS. CEN.
SHIBDON BUS. PK.
BLAYDON INDUSTRIAL PARK
SHIBDON ROAD
St. Joseph's Catholic Prim. Sch.
St. Thomas More RC School
79
Depot
BEWESHILL LANE
CROFTDALE RD.
Shibdon Dene
War Mem.
Blaydon Cemetery
Playing Field
Shibdon Pond Local Nature Reserve
Winlaton Hallgarth FC
BLACKSTONE CT.
Play. Fld.
Blaydon Burn
Cricket Grd.
Shibdon Park
High Axwell
Axwell Park
West Acres
East Acres
Burn Bank
Bus Depot
Bus Sta.
Bleach Green
Reservoirs (covered)
WINLATON
Rugby Football Club
Sports Ground
AXWELL PARK
Home Farm
Axwell Hall
Playing Field
West Lane Prim. Sch.
Grave Yard
Playing Field
Parkhead Prim. School
Waterfall
Blaydon-on-Tyne
NE21
Football Pitch
Spa Well Turn
Hagg Hill
Snook Hill
SCOTLAND LANE
MILL LANE
LANDS WOOD
Haghill Wood
A694
DERWENT RIVER
Derwent Walk
Damhead Wood
Winlaton Mill
Football Ground
Gas Testing Compound
Stampley Moss Farm
THORNLEY
96
SPA WELL RD.
17
18
19
61
62
63
64
A
B
C
D
E
1
2
3
4
5
6
7

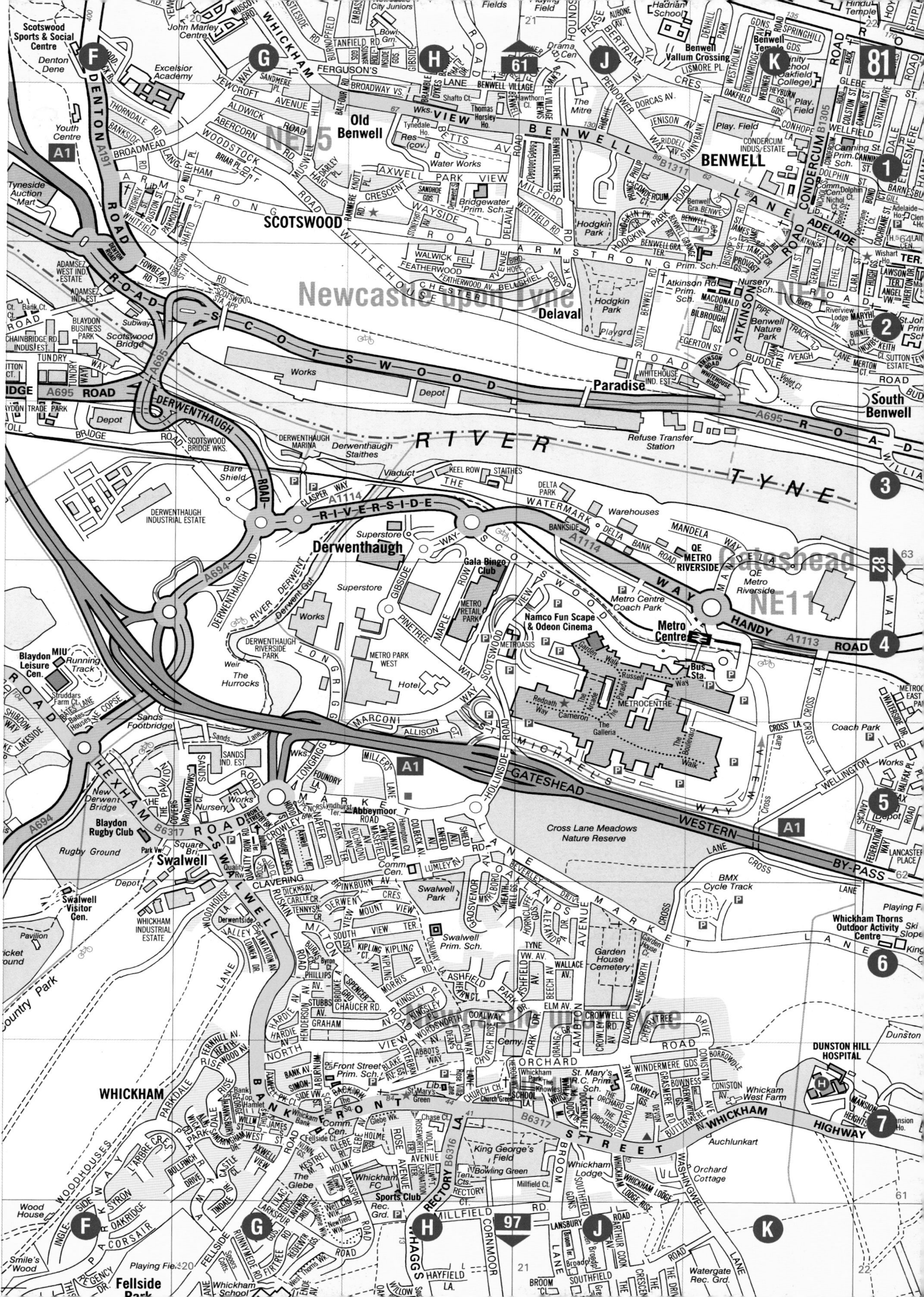
Scotswood Sports & Social Centre
Denton Dene
Excelsior Academy
John Marley Centre
Youth Centre
A1
DENTON ROAD
Tyneside Auction Mart
NE15
Old Benwell
SCOTSWOOD
BENWELL
Benwell Vallum Crossing
Benwell Temple
Hadrian School
Bridgewater Prim. Sch.
Water Works
Hodgkin Park
Atkinson Rd. Prim. Sch.
Benwell Nature Park
NE4
Newcastle upon Tyne
Delaval
Paradise
South Benwell
ADAMSEZ WEST IND. ESTATE
BLAYDON BUSINESS PARK
Scotswood Bridge
SCOTSWOOD ROAD
A695
DERWENTHAUGH ROAD
RIVER TYNE
DERWENTHAUGH MARINA
Derwenthaugh Staithes
Refuse Transfer Station
DERWENTHAUGH INDUSTRIAL ESTATE
RIVERSIDE WAY
A1114
Derwenthaugh
Superstore
Gala Bingo Club
METRO RETAIL PARK
QE METRO RIVERSIDE
Gateshead
NE11
Metro Centre Coach Park
Metro Centre
Namco Fun Scape & Odeon Cinema
METROCENTRE
HANDY ROAD
A1113
A694
DERWENTHAUGH RIVERSIDE PARK
The Hurrocks
METRO PARK WEST
Hotel
Blaydon Leisure Cen.
Running Track
Sands Footbridge
SANDS IND. EST.
New Derwent Bridge
Blaydon Rugby Club
Rugby Ground
Swalwell
Swalwell Visitor Cen.
WHICKHAM INDUSTRIAL ESTATE
Abbeymoor
GATESHEAD WESTERN BY-PASS
Cross Lane Meadows Nature Reserve
BMX Cycle Track
Coach Park
Whickham Thorns Outdoor Activity Centre
Swalwell Park
Swalwell Prim. Sch.
Garden House Cemetery
Country Park
WHICKHAM
DUNSTON HILL HOSPITAL
Whickam West Farm
Front Street Prim. Sch.
St. Mary's R.C. Prim. Sch.
King George's Field
Bowling Green
Whickham FC
Sports Club
Whickham Lodge
Orchard Cottage
Auchlunkart
WHICKHAM HIGHWAY
B6317
FRONT STREET
Wood House
Smile's Wood
Fellside Park
Playing Field
Watergate Rec. Grd.
61
97
82

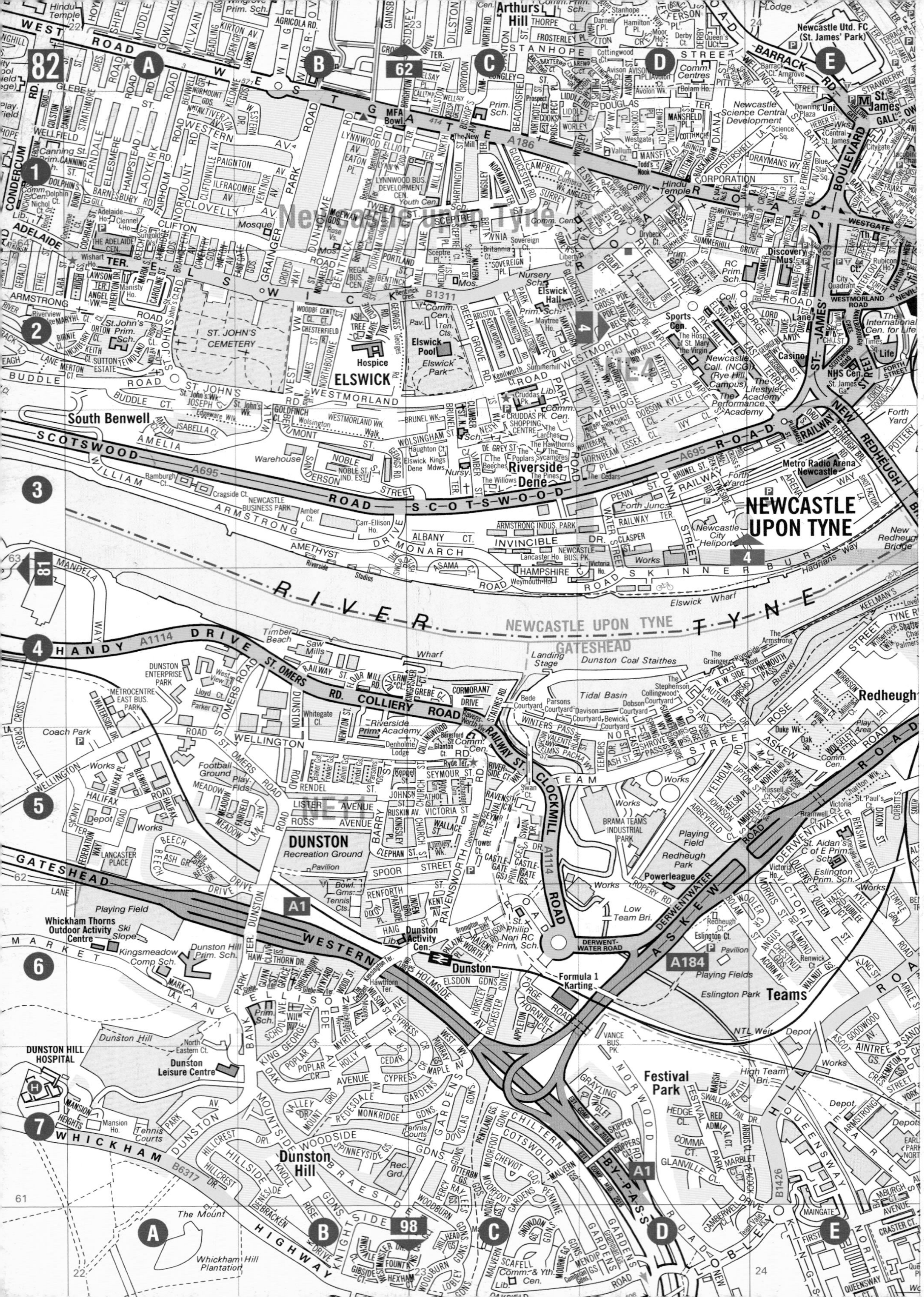

Arthurs Hill
Newcastle Utd. FC (St. James' Park)
WEST ROAD
WESTGATE ROAD
A186
62
MFA Bowl
Newcastle Science Central Development
St. James
BARRACK RD.
STRAWBERRY PL.
Hindu Temple
Mosque
ST. JOHN'S CEMETERY
ELSWICK
Hospice
Elswick Pool
Elswick Park
ELSWICK RD.
B1311
Discovery Mus.
Sports Cen.
Newcastle Coll. (NCG) (Rye Hill Campus)
The Lifestyle Academy
The Performance Academy
Casino
NHS Cen.
The International Cen. for Life
WESTMORLAND ROAD
NE4
South Benwell
SCOTSWOOD ROAD
A695
Riverside Dene
Metro Radio Arena Newcastle
NEWCASTLE UPON TYNE
NEWCASTLE BUSINESS PARK
ARMSTRONG INDUS. PARK
Newcastle City Heliport
New Redheugh Bridge
Hadrians Way
Forth Yard
Forth Junc.
Elswick Wharf
RIVER TYNE
NEWCASTLE UPON TYNE
GATESHEAD
81
HANDY DRIVE
A1114
Timber Beach
Saw Mills
Wharf
Landing Stage
Dunston Coal Staithes
Tidal Basin
DUNSTON ENTERPRISE PARK
METROCENTRE EAST BUS. PARK
Coach Park
COLLIERY ROAD
Riverside Prim. Academy
Redheugh
Football Ground
NE11
DUNSTON
Recreation Ground
BRAMA TEAMS INDUSTRIAL PARK
Playing Field
Redheugh Park
Powerleague
GATESHEAD
CLOCKMILL ROAD
A1
WESTERN
Playing Field
Whickham Thorns Outdoor Activity Centre
Ski Slope
Dunston Hill Prim. Sch.
Kingsmeadow Comp Sch.
Dunston Activity Cen.
Dunston
Formula 1 Karting
DERWENTWATER ROAD
A184
Playing Fields
Eslington Park
Teams
St. Aidan's C of E Prim. Sch.
Eslington Prim. Sch.
Low Team Bri.
NTL Weir
Dunston Hill
DUNSTON HILL HOSPITAL
Dunston Leisure Centre
Festival Park
High Team Bri.
WHICKHAM HIGHWAY
B6317
Dunston Hill
The Mount
Whickham Hill Plantation
98
BY-PASS
B1426
QUEENSWAY
LOBLEY HILL ROAD
A B C D E
1 2 3 4 5 6 7
22 23 24
61 62 63

83
F
G
H
J
K
1
2
3
4
5
6
7
63
4
5
84
99
Shieldfield
Monument
Theatre Royal
Blue Carpet
Manors
Seven Stories
Battle Field
St. Ann's
Baltic 39
NEWCASTLE
Central
Castle Keep
Moot Hall
Quayside
Baltic Centre
Gateshead Millennium Bridge
RIVER
St. Lawrence
The Sage Gateshead
Saltmeadows
BALTIC BUSINESS QUARTER
Greenesfield
Queen Elizabeth II Bridge
High Level Bridge
King Edward Bridge
Mecca Bingo
Anytime Fitness
GATESHEAD
East Gateshead
Gateshead International Stadium (Gateshead FC)
Gateshead Stadium
Old Fo
Civic Cen.
BENSHAM
NE8
Mount Pleasant
Shipcote
DECKHAM
Shipley Art Gallery
Elgin Centre
Sheriff Mt.
Carr Hill
SALTWELL PARK
Saltwell Park Mansion (Museum)
Saltwell
SALTWELL CEMETERY
BENSHAM HOSPITAL
TEAM VALLEY BUS. CEN.
GATESHEAD COMM. TEAT. CEN.
NE9
Dryden School
Gateshead Fell Cricket Club
A167(M)
A167
A184
A186
A189
A193
B1426
B1296
B1600
NEW BRIDGE
CITY ROAD
TYNE BRIDGE
QUAYSIDE
PARK LANE
SUNDERLAND ROAD
DURHAM ROAD
OLD DURHAM ROAD
ASKEW ROAD
PRINCE CONSORT ROAD
COATSWORTH ROAD
SHIELDS RD.
Byker
BYKER BRIDGE
WALKER ROAD
SALTMEADOWS ROAD
SOUTH SHORE ROAD
ALBANY ROAD
SALTWELL ROAD
SHERIFFS HIGHWAY

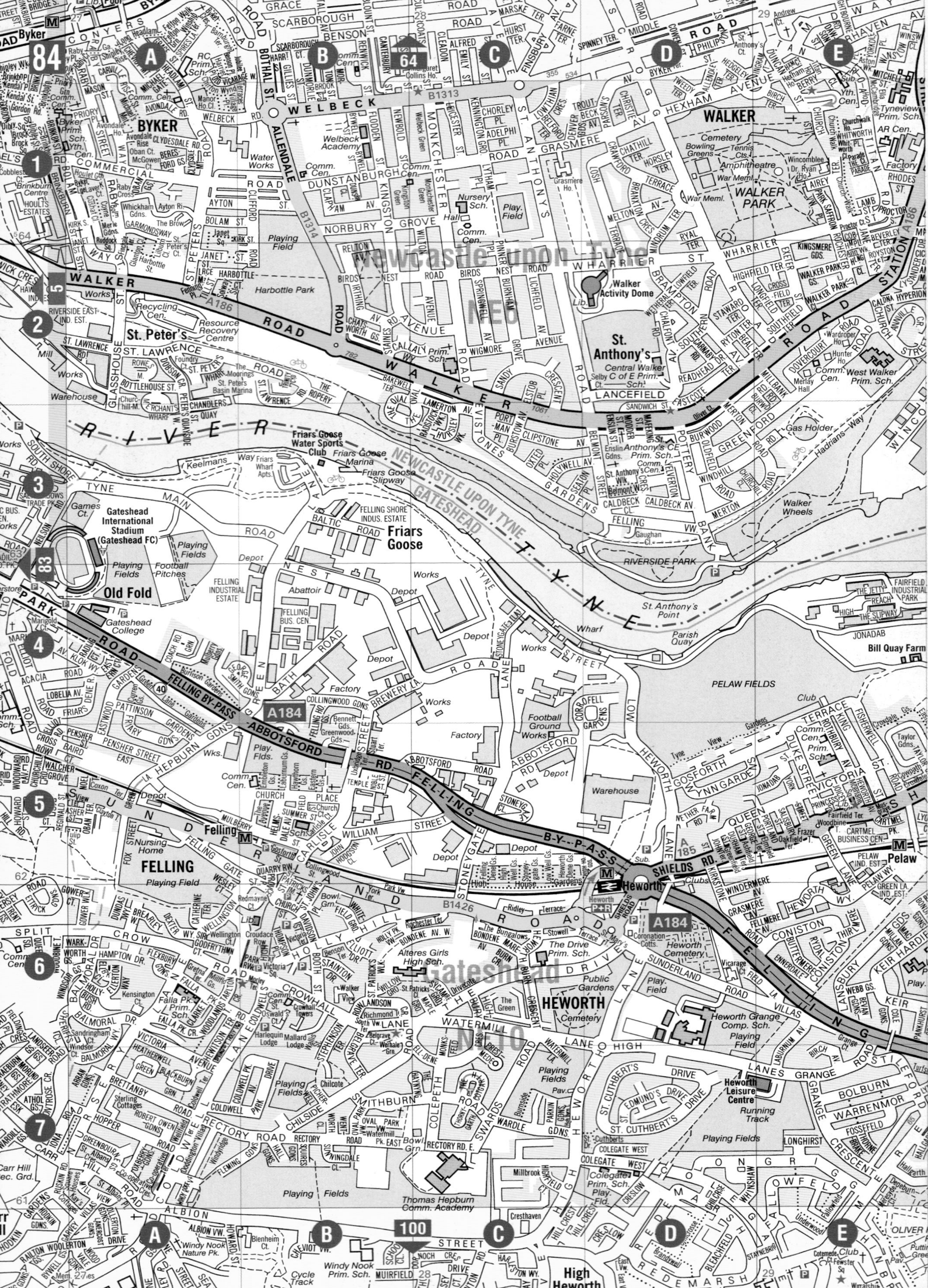

84
A
B
C
D
E
1
2
3
4
5
6
7
64
83
100
27
28
29
62
61
Byker
BYKER
WALKER
WALKER PARK
Newcastle upon Tyne
NE6
NE10
St. Peter's
St. Anthony's
RIVER
TYNE
NEWCASTLE UPON TYNE
GATESHEAD
Friars Goose
Old Fold
Gateshead International Stadium (Gateshead FC)
Gateshead College
FELLING
Felling
Gateshead
HEWORTH
High Heworth
Heworth
Pelaw
PELAW FIELDS
Bill Quay Farm
RIVERSIDE PARK
St. Anthony's Point
Parish Quay
Walker Wheels
Walker Activity Dome
Welbeck Academy
Harbottle Park
Playing Field
Playing Fields
Thomas Hepburn Comm. Academy
Heworth Grange Comp. Sch.
Heworth Leisure Centre
Heworth Cemetery
Alteres Girls High Sch.
Friars Goose Water Sports Club
Friars Goose Marina
FELLING SHORE INDUS. ESTATE
FELLING INDUSTRIAL ESTATE
FAIRFIELD INDUSTRIAL PARK
RIVERSIDE EAST IND. EST.
WELBECK RD.
WALKER ROAD
SHIELDS RD.
FELLING BY-PASS
ABBOTSFORD RD.
SUNDERLAND ROAD
HIGH LANE
ALBION STREET
A186
A184
A185
B1313
B1314
B1426

Low Walker
Hebburn
HEBBURN RIVERSIDE PARK
Hebburn New Town
HEBBURN
Hebburn NE31
Campbell Park
Hartleyburn Estate
Walker Riverside
Bill Quay
PELAW
Wardley
East Boldon NE36
Heworth
RIVER TYNE
A185
A184
A194
A194(M)
A195
B1306
B1288
SOUTH TYNESIDE
GATESHEAD
65
86
101

JARROW
Jarrow Cross C of E Prim. Sch.
Epinay Business & Enterprise School
66
A
B
C
D
E
1
2
3
4
5
6
7
32
33
34
Campbell Park
CAMPBELL PARK
BEDEWELL INDUSTRIAL PARK
Jarrow Park
Bowling Greens
Bandstand
Tennis Courts
Jarrow Comm. Pool
Jarrow School
Playing Field
Springwell Park
Jarrow Cemetery
War Mem.
Hill Park Estate
A19
South Shields FC
Bilton Hall
SIMONSIDE INDUSTRIAL ESTATE
Override Skate Pk.
TYNE POINT IND. ESTATE
BEDE TRADING ESTATE
BEDE INDUSTRIAL ESTATE
Factory
Warehouse
Bakery
PRIMROSE HILL HOSPITAL
King George's Field
Jarrow
NE32
St. Bede's Old People's Hostel
Primrose
Monkton Dene Park
Bede Burn Prim. Sch.
Running Track
Monkton Stadium
Sports Ground
Monkton
Valley Vw Prim. Sch.
B1516
B1516
ROMAN ROAD
LEAM LANE
A194
Simonside Prim. Sch.
St. Mary's RC Prim. Sch.
Community Centre
Jarrow FC
Hedworth
Primrose Bridge
Calf Close House
RC Prim. Sch.
Playing Fields
Luke's Lane Community Centre
Hebburn
NE31
85
Monkton Fell
Fellgate
St. Joseph's RC Prim. Sch.
Fellgate Prim. Sch.
Playing Field
Hagan Hall
Hedworthfield Primary School
West Fellgate Farm
Fellgate
Calfclose Burn
Burn
Hedworth Lane Prim. Sch.
BOLDON BUSINESS PK
Cineworld Cinema
BOLDON BUSINESS PARK
HI-TEC VILLAGE
The Quadrus Centre
Boldon Business Park Lake Nature Reserve
Hotel
B1298
A184
NEWCASTLE ROAD
NEWCASTLE
West House Farm Cottage
West House Farm
Colin House
Pikes Hole Farm
Boldon Fellgate Farm
High House Farm
Lodge
102
Mount Pleasant
Electricity Sub Station
61
62
63
64

87
67
88
103
F
G
H
J
K
1
2
3
4
5
6
7
Tyne Dock
WEST HARTON
Simonside
South Shields
NE34
NE35
NE36
Brockley Whins
Biddick Hall
Whiteleas
BOLDON COLLIERY
Boldon Colliery
East Boldon
BOLDON
New Town
West Boldon
South Boldon
EAST BOLDON
NEWCASTLE ROAD
A194
JOHN REID ROAD
A1300
B1298
A184
HARTON LANE
WHITELEAS WAY
BOLDON LANE
NEW ROAD
BENTON ROAD
NEVINSON AVENUE
GALSWORTHY ROAD
TILESHED LANE
SUNDERLAND ROAD
STATION TERRACE
FRONT STREET
WESTERN TERRACE
ADDISON ROAD
HYLTON LANE
SOUTH TYNESIDE DISTRICT HOSP.
South Shields Community School
Temple Park Leisure Centre
TEMPLE MEMORIAL PARK
Harton & Westoe Collieries' Welfare Ground
South Tyneside Crematorium
Monkton Jun. Sch.
Monkton Infants Sch.
Youth Cen.
Biddick Hall Jun. Sch.
Holy Trinity CofE Prim. Sch.
Chuter Ede Education Cen.
The Galsworthy Cen.
St. Oswald's RC Prim. Sch.
Forest View Prim. Sch.
Brockley Whins Junction
Newton Garths
River Don
Boldon Level Crossing
Tileshed Farm
Railway Cottages
The Shed Crossing
Piggery
Playing Field
All Weather Pitch
Cricket Ground
Football Ground
Jarrow Roofing FC
Boldon School
West Boldon Primary School
CLEADON LANE INDUSTRIAL ESTATE
Grange Park
Beggar's Bridge
Low House Farm
Cemetery
Club House
Bridleholme
North Road Bridge
Boldon Bridge
Crow Garth
The Meadows
Turners Hill
Factory
Depot
Works
LEEWICK WAY INDUSTRIAL ESTATE
MIDDLEFIELDS IND. EST

88
68
87
104
A
B
C
D
E
1
2
3
4
5
6
7
37
38
39
61
62
63
64
A1018
A1300
B1299
A184
KING GEORGE ROAD
JOHN REID ROAD
PRINCE EDWARD ROAD
SHIELDS ROAD
SUNDERLAND ROAD
WHITBURN ROAD
MOOR LANE
Harton Nook
South Shields
MARSDEN
Marsden Old Quarry Local Nature Reserve
SOUTH SHIELDS GOLF COURSE
Club House
Cleadon Hill
Cleadon Park
Playing Field
Tennis Courts
Bowling Greens
Elderly Persons' Cen.
Temple Park Leisure Centre
All Weather Pitch
TEMPLE MEMORIAL PARK
Ridgeway Primary Sch.
NE34
Works
Cleadon Lizards
Sunniside Farm
Sunniside Farm Cottage
Cleadon Hills Farm
South Shields Community School
Westholme
Cleadon North Farm
Cleadon Grange
Hexham House
CLEADON
Sunderland
SR6
East Farm Cottages
East Farm
Undercliff
Peacock Lodge
West Hall Farm
Hill Water Farm
Cleadon Village C of E Prim. Sch.
Piggery
TILESHED LANE
CLEADON LANE INDUSTRIAL ESTATE
Boldon Flats
Beggar's Bridge
East Boldon
NE36
EAST BOLDON
Cricket Ground
Bowling Green
Low House Farm
Sunderland Greyhound Stadium
Blue House Crossing
Blue House Farm
Ivy Cottage
West Moor Farm
Wil-Mena
Whitburn Moor
Football Pitches
The Academy of Light (Football Centre)
The Cottage
Dene Bridge
Harton Prim. Sch.
Rec. Grd.

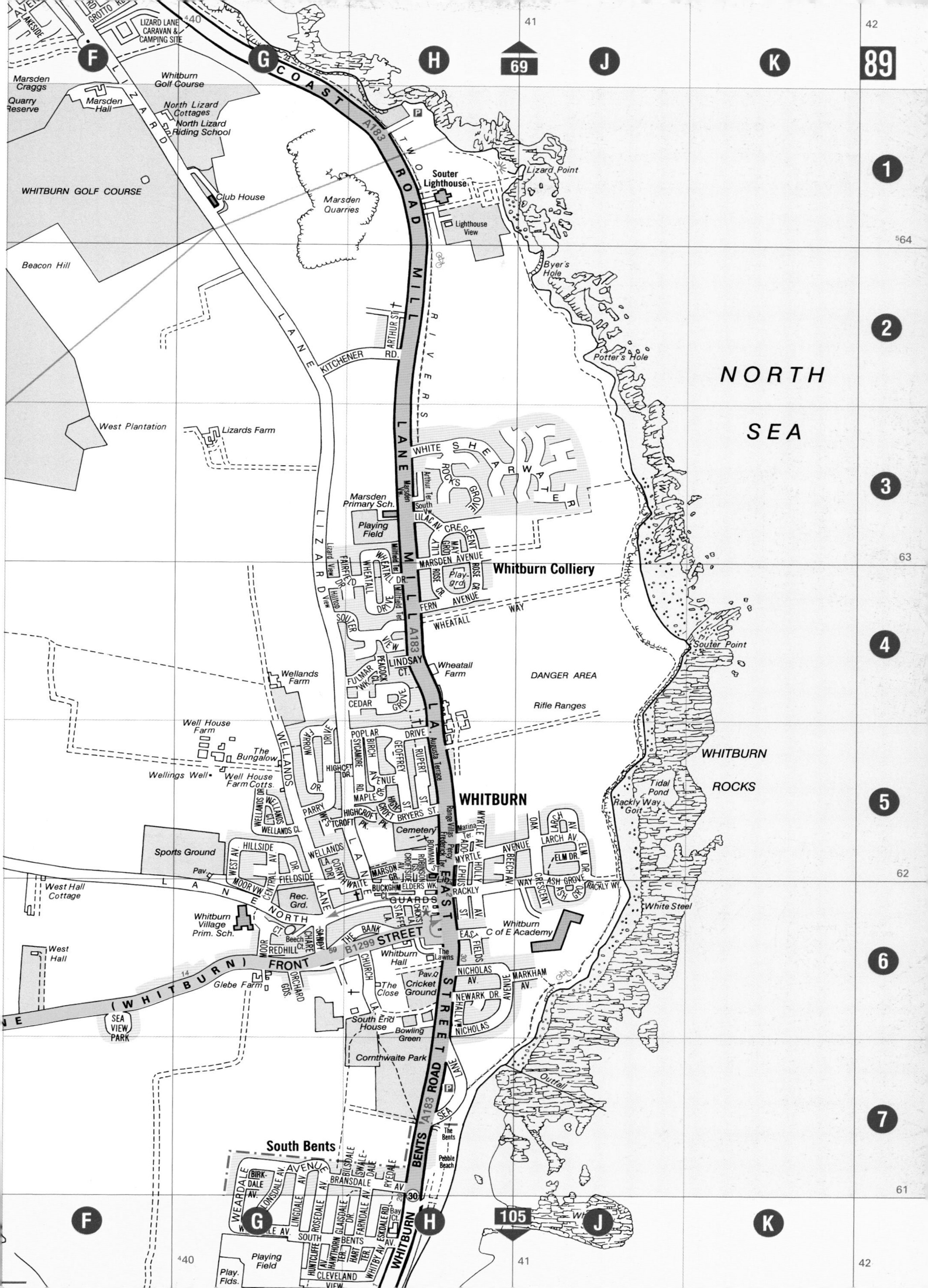

F
G
H
J
K
69
105
1
2
3
4
5
6
7
440
41
42
564
63
62
61
NORTH
SEA
WHITBURN
ROCKS
COAST ROAD
MILL LANE
EAST STREET
BENTS ROAD
A183
B1299
FRONT STREET
LIZARD LANE
NORTH LANE
LIZARD LANE CARAVAN & CAMPING SITE
Marsden Craggs
Quarry Reserve
Marsden Hall
Whitburn Golf Course
North Lizard Cottages
North Lizard Riding School
WHITBURN GOLF COURSE
Club House
Marsden Quarries
Souter Lighthouse
Lighthouse View
Lizard Point
Beacon Hill
Byer's Hole
Potter's Hole
West Plantation
Lizards Farm
KITCHENER RD.
ARTHUR ST.
TWO RIVERS
WHITE SHEARWATER
ROCKS GROVE
Marsden Primary Sch.
Playing Field
LILAC AV.
CRESCENT
MARSDEN AVENUE
Whitburn Colliery
ROSE CR.
FERN AVENUE
WHEATALL WAY
WHEATALL DR.
SOUTER VIEW
LINDSAY CT.
Wheatall Farm
DANGER AREA
Rifle Ranges
Souter Point
Wellands Farm
FULMAR WK.
PEACOCK CL.
CEDAR GROVE
POPLAR DRIVE
Augusta Terrace
Well House Farm
The Bungalow
Wellings Well
Well House Farm Cotts.
WELLANDS DR.
ARROW DR.
HIGHCROFT DR.
SYCAMORE RD.
BIRCH AVENUE
GEOFFREY ST.
RUPERT ST.
MAPLE
BRYERS ST.
HIGHCROFT PK.
WHITBURN
Range Villas
Tidal Pond
Rackly Way Goit
Cemetery
MYRTLE AV.
LARCH AV.
OAK AVENUE
BEECH AV.
ELM DR.
ASH GROVE
RACKLY WY.
WELLANDS CL.
HILLSIDE
Sports Ground
WEST AV.
FIELDSIDE
MOOR VW
CENTRAL AV.
Pav.
West Hall Cottage
Rec. Grd.
CORNTHWAITE
MARSDN AV.
BUCKGHM CL.
ELDERS WK.
GUARDS
RACKLY
CRESCENT
White Steel
Whitburn Village Prim. Sch.
Beech Ct.
THE BANK
REDHILL
SANDY CHARE
Whitburn C of E Academy
West Hall
Whitburn Hall
The Lawns
EAST FIELDS
NICHOLAS AV.
MARKHAM AV.
(WHITBURN)
Glebe Farm
ORCHARD GDS.
CHURCH LA.
The Close
Cricket Ground
NEWARK DR.
NICHOLAS
SEA VIEW PARK
South End House
Bowling Green
Cornthwaite Park
Outfall
SEA LANE
The Bents
Pebble Beach
South Bents
WEARDALE AV.
BIRKDALE AV.
LONSDALE AV.
AVENUE
BILSDALE
SWALEDALE
BRANSDALE
RYEDALE AV.
LINGDALE AV.
ROSEDALE AV.
GLAISDALE DR.
FARNDALE AV.
ESKDALE RD.
Bay CL.
SOUTH BENTS AV.
Playing Field
Play. Flds.
HUNTCLIFFE AV.
HAWTHORN TER.
HART TER.
WHITBY AV.
CLEVELAND VIEW
WHITBURN

90
74
A
B
C
D
E
1
2
3
4
5
6
7
02
03
04
560
59
58
61
Underwood
The Glebe
Shilford West Wood
Shilford Middle Wood
Shilford East Wood
Whiteside Wood
Juniperhill Wood
A68
High Shilford
High Shilford Fell
Dere Street
Roman Road
West Broomley
Roe House
Roe House Cottages
Smithy Burn
Broomley Wood
Broomley
West Farm
Riding Mill
NE44
Broomley Fell Farm
Gallaw Hill Farm
Dere Street
Roman Road (course of)
Bank Foot
Brookside Farm
Brookside
Jubilee Buildings
Jubilee Cottage
BROOMLEYFELL PLANTATION
Broomley Fell Wood
Sandyford Cottage
North Sandyford Plantation
South Sandyford Plantation
Hindley Burn
Fell House
Lingey Field
Lingeyfield Plantation
Fotherley Gill
Penn's Hill
Low Fotherley
A68
WHEELBIRKS
Bridges Farm
COLONEL'S PLANTATION
High Fotherley

91
75
92
F
G
H
J
K
1
2
3
4
5
6
7
A695
B6309
Stocksfield
NE43
PAINSHAWFIELD
New Ridley
Hindley
Apperley Dene
Mickley Bank Farm
Ruffside
Mickley Common
Wallockbirk Dene
Mickley Grange
Click-em-in Dene
Troughstone Hill
Painshawfield Wood
Glen View
Ridley Mill Cottages
Old Ridley
Hall Woods
Hopper's Gill
Cademuir
Carson House
Cranford
The Grange
East Ridley
Kinellan
Carnwath
The Mews
Lodge
Broomley Grange
Hindley Bridge
Hall Woods
Braeside
Hillcot
Rec. Grd.
Crag Wood
Hindley Hall
New Ridley Farm
White Cottage
Metal Bridge
Club House
STOCKSFIELD GOLF COURSE
Apperley Wood
West Riding
The Bungalows
Hindley Farm
Hindley
Craghead Cottages
Redshaw Foot
Bale Hill
Apperley Bank
New Frizzle Close
Henry Spring
Young Wood
Wheelbirks Bridge
Apperley
Apperley Farm Cottages
Cockshot Hill
Wheelbirks Cottages
Wheelbirks
Lynn Bogs
Apperley Dene
Pump Ho.
The Bungalow
Apperley House
Apperley Bank
Fox Hill
Wood Cottage
Roman Fortlet
Castle Hill
Shirley Croft
Apperleybankfoot Wood
Bleaberryh Wood
Woodlands Farm
Woodlands Bungalow
Kipper Lynn
WOODS
The Bridges
Lodge
Shortycroft Gill
Lynn Crags
Watchhill Plantation
Watch Hill
WHITTONSTALL COMMON
Greenfield Gill
Lawson's Farm
Lynn Burn
Stocksfield Burn
RIDLEY MILL ROAD
BATT HOUSE ROAD
APPERLEY ROAD
MEADOWFIELD ROAD
NEW RIDLEY ROAD
LEAD ROAD
CADEHILL
CRABTREE RD.
BIRCHES NOOK RD.
GUESSBURN
TYNEDALE GARDENS
LADYWELL
WELTON CL.
HALTON CL.
AYTON CL.
BIRKDENE
BALIOL RD.
NEWHILL
Dale Vw
Mount Vw. Ter.
SOUTH PDE.
PAINSHAWFIELD RD.
WELL RD.
MEADOWFIELD PARK STH.
THE PADDOCK
THE GROVE
WINSTON WAY
Ford
405
06
07
61
560
59
58

High Mickley
Mickley Farm
House Farm
East Farm
BOWLER'S
HILL
EDGEW
WARD
LANE
Mickley West Side Farm
South Side Cotts
South Side Farm
76
LUMLEY'S LA.
LUMLEY'S
Toft Hill
Mickley Common
Riding High Wood
Riding Low Wood
Burn
LANE
Wallockbirk Dene
Broom Hill
Hyons East
Stanley
Hyons West Wood
Click-em-in Dene
Mickley Grange
Fox Hill
LANE
MODIGARS
Stocksfield
91
North Farm
Hedley Park
Works
NE43
Field House
HIGH VW
MDWS CRST
Hall
CLARE LEA
East Farm
Crossbanks Plantation
Airyhill Plantation
West Riding
School Row
Hedley Hill Farm
West Farm
Hedley on the Hill
Hedley Reservoir
Airey Hill
Hedley Grange
Cockshot Hill
Fox Hill
Fishpond Wood
WESTRIDING WOOD
Woodhead
Spring House
Paddock Wood
Bleaberryhill Wood
RYEHILL WOOD
Hollings
Consett DH8
Duckpool Plantation
Haystackhill Wood
Millhill Wood
106
Lawson Farm
B6309
Redwaybanks Wood
Mill
Whittonstall
Redwaybanks
A
B
C
D
E
1
2
3
4
5
6
7
07
08
09
61
60
59
58

Durham Riding
Durham Riding
Riding Barns
Keepers Cottage
Ford
Humble's Wood
Dukeshagg Wood
GUARDS WOOD
The Guards
Buck's Nook Woods
Buck's Nook
77
Prudhoe
NE42
MOOR ROAD
Duke's Hagg
Dukeshagg Farm
CLINTY WOOD
Penny Hill
Pennyhill Plantation
ENGINE ROAD
Hedley Fell
Northumbria Gliding Club
Washwell Hill
Leadgate Plantation
The Bungalow
Leadgate Farm
Boundary House
Leadgate Gill
Leadgate Cotts.
Leadgate
LEAD ROAD
Shop Plantation
Currock Hill
Moss Plantation
Moorgate Plantation
94
GREENHEAD ROAD
Labourn's Fell
Broom
Newcastle upon Tyne
Bowser's Hole
Ashtree
NE17
Green Head
North Terrace
Greenhead Terrace
Club
RAMSAY ROAD
West Chopwell
HALL ROAD
Monument Ct.
Football Ground
SOUTH ROAD
Newhouse Farm
WHITTONSTALL ROAD
DERWENT STREET
RICHARDSON TER.
BURNWOOD CL.
Havelock Ter.
WILLIAM ST.
ELIZABETH ST.
JOSEPH TER.
Library
Comm. Cen.
The Pioneer Centre
Chopwell Prim. Sch.
Beaconsfield T.
DISRAELI TER.
SCOTT T.
Hillford Ter.
Nelson Ter.
Tennis Courts
Chopwell Park
CHOPWELL
BROOMFIELD CR.
FREDERICK ST.
Lesbury Ter.
Dalton Ter.
Symon Ter.
Woodside Terrace
Marx Ter.
South Terrace
Lenin Ter.
WHINNEY LEAS
South View
The Green
MOORLAND VW.
BOLTON'S BUNGALOWS
Playing Field
VALLEY ROAD
RUNNYMEDE GS.
WEST CR.
EAST TER.
NORTHUMBERLAND
GATESHEAD
Ravenside
MILKWELLBURN WOOD
Milkwell Burn
Hollings Hill
Rye Hill
107
Tongue Plan
F G H J K
1 2 3 4 5 6 7
410
11
12
61
60
59
58

Coalburns
Leafield
Goose Green
Ryton
NE40
Penny Hill
Brass Castle Farm Cottage
Brass Castle Farm
Coalburn Plantation
Pennyhill Plantation
Horsegate Plantation
Clayton Plantation
Horsegate Edge
Strothers Farm
Recreation Ground
Shop Plantation
Horsegate
Bail Hill
GARESFIELD GOLF COURSE
Miller's Wood
Club House
HIGH SPEN
Field House
Broomfield
Heavy Gate
Broomfield House
Vicarage
Newcastle upon Tyne
NE17
West Chopwell
CHOPWELL WOOD
Chopwell Park
Cricket Ground
Football Ground
Chopwell Wood House
Carr House
Playing Field
Tongue Burns Plantation
Craghead Wood
Chopwell Villa
Hooker Gate
Chopwellgate Cottage
Comb Wood
Ricklees Farm
Spenside Farm
West Wood
Pawston Cottage
Aged Miners' Homes
Collingdon Green
North View
HIGH SPEN IND. EST.
SPEN LANE
ROGUES LANE
COLLINGDON ROAD
HOOKERGATE
B6315

78
93
108

95
79
109
96
F
G
H
J
K
1
2
3
4
5
6
7
16
17
415
61
560
59
58
Blaydon-on-Tyne
Rowlands Gill
Newcastle upon Tyne
GATESHEAD
DURHAM
NE21
NE39
NE16
ROWLANDS GILL
Highfield
Barlow
Lockh
Low Friarside
East Farm
North Farm
South Farm
Low Gill Wood
Reeley Mires Wood
Norman's Riding Wood
Riding Chase
Pinewoods
Stampley Moss Farm
Gate Sewage Works
Pawston Birks
The Bungalow
BARLOW ROAD
BARLOW CR.
BARLOW FELL ROAD
BARLOW FELL
LANE
GARESFIELD LANE
Garesfield
Lillycrook Hill
High Thornley
HOLLINHILL LANE
Reservoir (covered)
Thornley House
WEST WOOD
HIGH HORSE CL.
HIGH HORSE
SPEN BANKS
Sherburn Tower Farm
Hollin Hill Farm
LOCKHAUGH ROAD
A694
Derwent
Works
Playing Field
Betty Plantation
Spen
Sherburn Green Wood
GLEN CL.
ASHTREE CL.
SHERBURN PARK DRIVE
PONTHAUGH
AVON CL.
SHERBURN GN.
THORNFIELD PL.
CHAPEL VIEW
HILLSIDE CL.
CARNFIELD GS.
ROOKSWOOD GS.
SNIPES DENE
DOMINIES CLOSE
Rowlands Gill Prim. Sch.
GARESFIELD GS.
LILLEYCROFT CR.
SOUTHWOOD CR.
Lilley Ter.
Cowen Ter.
GILL BURN
BROCKWELL DR.
ROWLAND BURN WAY
Burn
Croft
Oaktree Farm
Spen Burn
Low Spen Burn
NORWOOD CR.
THORNLEY VIEW
Cappy Scar
DERWENT
WILLIAM MORRIS AV.
Cooks Cotts
Engel St.
WOODLEA RD.
Hardie St.
North Vw. W.
North View East
South Vw. W.
South Vw.
COWELL GRO.
DENE VW.
THE GRN.
EAST VW.
BARKWOOD
HOLLINSIDE
BRIAR R.
PONTOP VW.
LEAZES
WHINFIELD
VALLEY
PARK RD.
Pipe Bridge Rec. Gd.
TOWNLEY RD.
VIEW TER.
BURNSIDE RD.
WOODLANDS ROAD
Rowland's Gill
Cemy.
LANE SMAILES
HILLCROFT
HIGHFIELD
WELLFIELD RD.
Margaret Ter.
RED KITE WAY
Football Ground
Pav.
B6315
Highfield Prim. & St. Josephs RC Prim. Schs.
Rec. Grd.
VIEW
Stewartsfield
Comm. Cen.
SOUTH
KELL'S WY.
SHERBURN
TOWNELEY FIELDS
HOLLYDENE
THE CRESCENT
Windsor Cl.
DERWENT PK.
ALLOY T.
GLENCOE RISE
GLENCOE TER.
OLGA
Victoria T.
ROAD
WAY
Pipe Bridge
Library
NORMAN AV.
MIDDLE
THE AV.
TAYLOR AV.
Bowling Green
Tennis Court
BURNOPFIELD RD.
RIVER
Palladium Chapel
STRATHMORE ROAD
STATION ROAD
SMAILES LA.
STIRLING AV.
THE GROVE
DERWENT AV.
LANE
Beda Hills
WOODSIDE WALK
WHINFIELD
WHINFIELD INDUSTRIAL ESTATE
LOW WEST AV.
WEST AV.
DENE CROSS
ORCHARD ROAD
Elgen Vs.
Orchard Ter.
ORCHARD AV.
ORCHARD RD.
DIPWOOD WY.
LINTZFORD GS.
BOWES LYON
FRIARSIDE CR.
DIPWOOD RD.
LINTZFORD CL.
RIVERSIDE WAY
Derwent Bridge
Viaduct
BUSTY BANK
B6314
Friarside Plantation
Strother Hills
Victoria Garesfield
School Houses
Low Friarside Farm
Lintzford Wood
SCAIFE'S WOOD
Friarside Wood
LINTZFORD ROAD
Lockside Burn
FORD
LANE
30
Sewage
Warren's

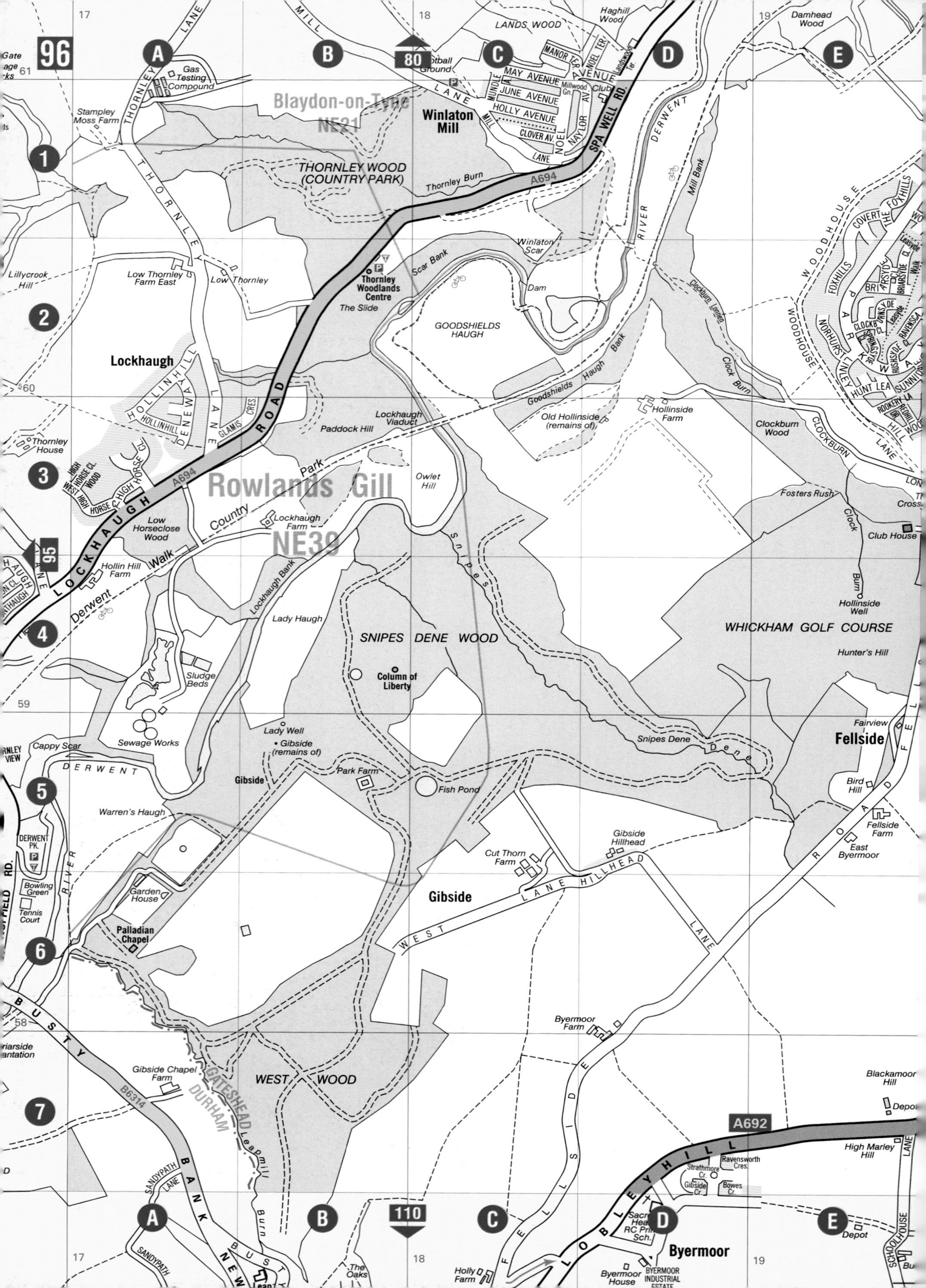

Blaydon-on-Tyne
NE21
Winlaton Mill
THORNLEY WOOD (COUNTRY PARK)
Thornley Woodlands Centre
Lockhaugh
Rowlands Gill
NE39
GOODSHIELDS HAUGH
SNIPES DENE WOOD
Column of Liberty
WHICKHAM GOLF COURSE
Fellside
Gibside
Palladian Chapel
WEST WOOD
Byermoor
LOCKHAUGH ROAD
SPA WELL RD.
A694
A692
B6314
BUSTY BANK
LOBLEY HILL
FELLSIDE
WEST LANE
HILLHEAD LANE
GATESHEAD
DURHAM
RIVER DERWENT
Derwent Walk Country Park
Sewage Works
Sludge Beds
Fish Pond
Park Farm
Gibside Chapel Farm
Byermoor Farm
Hollinside Farm
Clockburn Wood
Lockhaugh Farm
Hollin Hill Farm
Low Thornley
Lillycrook Hill
Thornley House
Damhead Wood
Haghill Wood
LANDS WOOD
80
95
110

WHICKHAM
Fellside Park
Whickham School
Playing Field
Watergate Estate
Washingwell Prim. Sch.
Buck's Hill Plantation
Buck's Hill
Marshall Lands Farm
Washingwell Wood
Black Burn
NE11
A692
Little Dene Cottage
Fugarfield Wood
Fugar Bar Cottages
Ponticherry
Streetgate Farm
Streetgate
Whickham Parochial C of E Prim. Sch.
Clover Hill Prim. Sch.
Reservoir (covered)
Gladeley Hill
Lambing Hill
WHICKHAM FELL
Paddy's Bridge
Long Hill
Limekiln Hill
Clover Hill Farm
Gellesfield Plantation
Gellesfield Hole
Dene Farm
Cuthbert's Hill
Tea Well
Riding Barns
High Park Farm
Newcastle upon Tyne
NE16
Penny Fine
BLACKBURN FELL
SUNNISIDE
Sunniside
Lingeyfine Stables
West Acre Stables
Hillcrest Stables
Burdon Moor
Vicarage
Bowling Green
Comm. Cen.
Football Ground
Aged Miners Homes
The Grange
Greenfield House
Marley Hill
Redlands
Tanfield Railway
Longfield House Farm
Engine Shed
GATESHEAD ROAD
CHURCH STREET
BURDON PLAIN
BIRKLAND LANE
ST. CUTHBERT'S ROAD
SUNNISIDE ROAD
RECTORY LANE
WHAGGS LANE
FRONT STREET
WASHINGWELL LANE
BROOM LANE
FELLSIDE ROAD
BROADWAY
KINGSWAY
HOLE LANE
PENNYFINE ROAD
MILLFIELD RD.
CORNMOOR ROAD
Auchlunkart
Orchard Cottage
King George's Field
Whickham FC
Sports Club
Washingwells
Watergate Rec. Grd.
B6316
A6076
81
111
98
F G H J K
1 2 3 4 5 6 7
20 21 22
61 60 59 58

98
WHICKHAM HIGHWAY
Dunston Hill
82
The Mount
Whickham Hill Plantation
B6317
HIGHWAY
Nursery
Playing Field
Washingwells
Emmanuel College
Play Fld.
Green's Farm
Playing Field
A692
CONSETT RD.
LOBLEY HILL ROAD
Lobley Hill Prim. Sch.
Lobley Hill
OAKFIELD
Comm. & Yth. Cen.
Lib.
GATESHEAD
LOBLEY
B1426
Team Valley
MAINGATE
QUEENSWAY
KINGSWAY
Factory
Bakery
Works
PRINCESWAY
PRINCES PARK
WESTERN BY-PASS
A1
DUKESWAY
COACH ROAD
Beggars Wood Recreation Area
Beggar Wood
Watergate Wood
North Lodge
WATERGATE BANK
Washingwell Wood
Coxclose Wood
Cox Close
The Trench
RAVENSWORTH PARK ESTATE
Beggar Bank
Black Burn
Golf Driving Range
Playing Fields
Millgreen Cottage
Lodge
Ravensworth
Trenchside Cottage
Trench Hall
Gateshead
Little Dene Cottage
Fugarfield Wood
97
Arboretum
CROSS LANE
Sawmill Cottage
Fish Pond
HILL HEAD WOOD
Mary's Well
Ravensworth Castle
Shanks Wood
South Lodge
THE PARK
Greenhouse Walks
Millers Park
Penny Fine
FELL
Hill Head
Robin's Wood
Park Farm Plantation
Lady Park
HIGH PARK WOOD
NE11
Ravensworth Park Country Club
Springfield
Hillcrest Stables
Oak Plantation
Newcastle upon Tyne
Silverhills
Silverhill Well
Blackman's Wood
Silverhill Wood
Holly Cottage
BANESLEY LANE
Banesley Lane Farm
NE16
The Peak
Banesley Lane Plantation
Bolams Gill
Cheviot Wood
HAGGS LANE
Old Ravensworth Farm
Beldy
Hagg Wood
Nursery
OUSLAW
Chapel Banks
BIRKLAND LANE
112
Mitcheson's Gill Wood
Strandy
Mitcheson's Gill
Briar Dene

99
83
100
113
Saltwell
Low Fell
Sheriff Hill
High Fell
Carr Hill
Team Valley
Lyndhurst
Chowdene
Harlow Green
Beacon Lough
Allerdene
Lamesley
NE8
NE9
QUEEN ELIZABETH HOSPITAL
RAVENSWORTH GOLF COURSE
Angel of the North
TYNE MARSHALLING YARD
Longacre Wood
GATESHEAD WESTERN BY-PASS
DURHAM ROAD
A167
A1
B1296
B1295

84
99
114
A
B
C
D
E
1
2
3
4
5
6
7
NE10
NE9
Gateshead
Windy Nook
High Heworth
Whitehills
Leam Lane Estate
Springwell Estate
Beacon Lough
WREKENTON
Eighton Banks
SPRINGWELL
The Mount
ARMSTRONG
Wallace Village
GATESHEAD
SUNDERLAND
QUEEN ELIZABETH HOSPITAL
St. Bede's Unit (Hospice)
Thomas Hepburn Comm. Academy
Windy Nook Prim. Sch.
Windy Nook Nature Pk.
Furrowfield School
Larkspur Prim. Sch.
Cardinal Hume Cath. Sch.
St. Oswald's RC Prim. Sch.
Fell Dyke Prim. Sch.
Hill Top School
Roman Rd. Prim. Sch.
Colegate Prim. Sch.
Springwell Village Prim. Sch.
Bowes Railway Centre
Refuse Disposal Works
Springwell Quarries
Brysons Animal Refuge
Beacon Lough Plantation
Mossheap Recreation Ground
RAVENSWORTH GOLF COURSE
High Eighton Farm
Eighton Lodge
Low Mount Farm
Usworth House
Peareth Hall Farm
Blackham's Hill
Mount Farm
Sheddonshill Well
Dunkirk
Havannah
Bowes Manor
South Leam Farm
Sorting Office
ARMSTRONG INDUSTRIAL ESTATE
A194(M)
A194(M) MOTORWAY
A1
A182
B1288
B1296
B1295
ALBION STREET
WHITEHILL DRIVE
SPRINGWELL ROAD
SPRINGWELL LANE
LEAM LANE
DURHAM ROAD
HIGH STREET
LONG BANK
RECTORY ROAD
WHITEHOUSE LANE
AYCLIFFE AVENUE
AYCLIFFE CRESCENT
GALLOPING GREEN ROAD
ROCK CLIFFE
MOUNT LANE
WASHINGTON HIGHWAY
PEARETH HALL ROAD
Wrekendike (Roman Road)
Bowes Railway
Camp Ground
Graveyard
Playing Fields

HEWORTH GOLF COURSE
Club House
Jingling Gate
A194(M)
A194(M) MOTORWAY
NEW ROAD
LINGEY LANE
LEAM LANE
(ROMAN ROAD)
HENDERSON PARK
White Mere Prim. Sch.
Lingey House Prim. Sch.
SHERBURN
B1288
85
Police Training Centre
Follingsby
Warehouse
FOLLINGSBY PARK
FOLLINGSBY LANE
WHITE ROSE WAY
SHOTTON WY.
South Follingsby Farm
SOUTH TYNESIDE
GATESHEAD
NEWCASTLE ROAD
LAVERICK LANE
High House Farm
River Don
Whittle Burn
GEORGE WASHINGTON GOLF COURSE
NORTHERN PLAYING FIELDS
Washington Disabled Riding Centre
East House Farm
East House Farm Cottages
102
NORTHUMBERLAND WAY
A195
Driving Range
Club Ho.& Country Club
STEPHENSON ROAD
Athletic Ground
Usworth Sixth Form College
Playing Field
STEPHENSON INDUSTRIAL ESTATE
Usworth Hall
WATERLOO ROAD
CELLAR ROAD
PEARETH HALL RD.
Cemetery
USWORTH
Washington
COACH ROAD ESTATE
St. Bede's RC Prim. Sch.
Army Res. Cen.
RUTHERFORD ROAD
SULGRAVE ROAD
SULGRAVE
Village Centre
Donwell Village
George Washington Prim. Sch.
Rec. Grd.
NE37
DONWELL
CONCORD
Usworth Colliery Prim. Sch. & Nursery
SULGRAVE IND. EST.
Usworth Grange Prim. Sch.
The Oval Washington Millennium Cen.
Usworth Rec. Park
Tennis Cts.
BLUE HOUSE LANE
A1290
WASHINGTON
Concord Bus Sta.
Lifespan
VERMONT
GLOVER
PARSONS INDUSTRIAL ESTATE
Washington 'F' Pit
Washington FC (Albany Park)
ALBANY PARK
ALBANY
115
Warehouse
BENTALL BUSINESS PARK
GLOVER NETWORK CENTRE
Hillthorn Farm
F G H J K
1 2 3 4 5 6 7

Gateshead
NE10
East Boldon
NE36
Washington
NE37
NEWCASTLE ROAD
A184
SUNDERLAND BY-PASS
A19
WASHINGTON ROAD
A1290
FOLLINGSBY LANE
WEST PASTURES
DOWNHILL LANE
Pikes Hole Farm
Boldon Fellgate Farm
Lodge
Scot's House
West House Farm Cottage
Colin House
HI-TEC VILLAGE
The Quadrus Centre
Boldon Business Park Lake Nature Reserve
WITNEY WAY
DIDCOT
ABINGDON WAY
B1298
Mount Pleasant
Electricity Sub Station
Strother House
Make-me-rich
Elliscope Farm
Hylton Grove Farm
Hylton Bridge
Hylton Bridge Farm
North Moor Farm
North East Land, Air & Sea Museums
Usworth Cotts.
West Moor Farm
MOTOR WORKS
Works
Depot
BLOSSOM WAY
CHERRY
CHERRY BLOSSOM WAY
BARMSTON LANE
NISSAN WAY
Peepy Plantation
Hylton Plantation
Severn Houses
Hillthorn Farm
GLOVER
GLOVER NETWORK CENTRE
Warehouse
TURBINE BUSINESS

86
101
116

103
West Boldon
Boldon
South Boldon
Boldon Golf Course
Turners Hill
Cemetery
Electricity Sub Station
Downhill Farm
Boldon Hills
Down Hill
Nanny Cow Hill
Reservoirs (covered)
Downhill Quarry
Quarry Hill
The Meadows
Belle Vue Villa
South Lodge
Mundles
Camp
Field Ho
Low House Farm
Bridleholme
Club House
Tennis Courts
Boldon Bridge
Crow Garth
Ascot Court
Glebe Farm Court
Addison Road
Hylton Lane
Mundles Lane
Sunderland Rd.
A184
87
South Tyneside
Sunderland
BMX Track
Football Pitch
Football Pitches
Community North Sports Complex
All Weather Pitches
Playing Field
Town End Farm
Town End Academy
Bexhill Academy
St. John Bosco RC Prim. Sch.
Downhill
Bunny Hill Prim. Care Cen.
Bunny Hill Wellness Cen.
Council Offices
SR5
Kingsway
Washington Road
Rotherfield Spa Well
Redcar Road
Ramsgate Road
Red House Academy
104
Pickersgill House
Hylton Red Ho. Nursy. Sch.
Northern Saints CofE Prim. Sch.
Aged Miners' Homes
Castlegreen Sch.
Hylton Castle (remains of)
St. Catherine's Chapel (remains of)
Sunderland
Hylton Dene Local Nature Reserve
Hylton Red House
Hylton Castle
Hylton Dene
Hylton Dene Burn
North Hylton Road Ind. Est.
Riverside Road
Works
Castle View Enterprise Academy
Playing Field
Tilesheds
Castletown
Cemetery
Castletown Prim. Sch.
Wessington Way
Wessington Ind. Est.
Hylton Riverside Retail Park
Hylton Park
Riverside Bowling
River Wear Bri. (Proposed)
River Wear
Sunderland Enterprise Park
Sunrise Enterprise Park
Ckt. Grd.
Football Grd.
A1231
A19
Baron's Quay Wood
Claxheugh Rock
117
Ford Quarry Recreation Area
Pallion West Industrial Estate
Pallion Industrial Estate
Riverside Pallion Retail Park
Tennis Court
Bowling Green
Sports Ground
SR4
European Way
B1405
Pallion
St. Luke's

104
EAST BOLDON
East Boldon
NE36
A
B
C
D
E
1
2
3
4
5
6
7
88
103
118
SUNDERLAND ROAD
NEWCASTLE ROAD
A184
A1018
A1231
A1290
B1405
B1291
SUNDERLAND ROAD
SHIELDS ROAD
NEWCASTLE ROAD
SOUTH TYNESIDE
SUNDERLAND
Low House Farm
Cricket Ground
Bowling Green
Sunderland Greyhound Stadium
Blue House Crossing
Blue House Farm
Whitburn Moor
The Academy of Light (Football Centre)
Football Pitches
The Cottage
Dene Bridge
Reservoir
Pumping Station
Stella Maris
Field House
Nine Wells Gds.
Rifle Range
White House Farm
Sunderland Golf Centre
Fulwell Quarry Local Nature Reserve
Maple Lodge Nursing Home
Willow Fields Primary Sch.
Red House Academy
Witherwack
Playing Field
Red Ho. Comm. Cen.
Carley Hill
SR5
Namey Hill
Seaburn
Sports Grd.
Res. (cov.)
Fulwell Windmill
Carley Hill Education Centre
Southwick Cemetery
Playing Field
High Southwick
Marley Pots
College
English Martyrs RC Prim. Sch.
Play. Flds.
Aged Miners' Homes
Grace Ho. Hospice
Carley Hill Cricket Ground
Nurs. Home
Margaret Thompson Park
MONKWEARMOUTH HOSPITAL
Southwick Prim. Sch.
Hahnemann Ct.
SOUTHWICK
Recreation Ground
Playing Fld.
Works
SOUTHWICK INDUSTRIAL ESTATE
Climb. Cen.
WESSINGTON WAY
QUEEN'S ROAD
KEIR HARDIE WAY
THOMPSON ROAD
RIVERSIDE ROAD
SUNDERLAND ENTERPRISE PK.
ALEXANDRA Wks.
BUS. & INNOVATION CEN.
HYLTON PARK
SILVERBRIAR
Low Southwick
Southwick Goods Yd.
RIVER WEAR
River Wear Bri. (Proposed)
ALEXANDRA BUS. PARK
Sunderland Wall Climbing Cen.
Pallion Quay
Quay
Jetties
Queen Alexandra Bridge
Warehouses
Shipbuilding Yard
Shipbuilding Yard
Travelling Cranes
MONKWEARMOUTH
Sunderland Aquatic Cen. & Wellness Centre
Sunderland AFC (Stadium of Light)
RIVERSIDE PALLION RETAIL PARK
Superstore
Pallion
SR4
Bowling Green
Sports Ground
EUROPEAN WAY
PALLION NEW ROAD
Webster Bank
Bus Depot
Gas Works
Scrap Yard
Deptford
Ayre's Quay
Superstore
Gala Bingo
University of Sunderland
PALLION INDUSTRIAL ESTATE
RIVERGREEN IND. EST.
PALLION
Gill Bridge
Bishopwearmouth
Millfield
TRIMDON ST.
BRIDGE APP.
QUEEN ALEXANDRA BRIDGE

South Bents
Whitburn Steel
Pebble Beach
89
SR6
Monkwearmouth School
Playing Field
Play. Flds.
Sports Ground
Superstore
Cemetery
Seaburn Dene Prim. Sch.
Tennis Courts
Nursery
Seaburn
Seaburn Centre
WHITBURN SANDS
WHITBURN BAY
Outfalls
Mere Knolls Cemetery
DYKELANDS ROAD
B1291
SEAFIELDS
QUEENS RD.
WHITBURN BENTS
WHITBURN ROAD
A183
Fulwell
Fulwell Jun. Sch.
Seaburn Park
War Mem.
Lighthouse
Roker Cliff Park
Parson's Rocks
NORTH SEA
Fire Station Cotts.
Coast Guard Station
Platform
Outfall
Miniature Railway
Bandstand
Bowl. Grns.
Roker Park
ROKER
Tennis Courts
Paddling Pool
Roker Rocks
Roker Pier
Roker Pier Lighthouse
ROKER TERRACE
MARINE WALK
Redby Prim. Sch.
St. Benet's RC Prim. Sch.
Comm. Cen.
HARBOUR VIEW
Mus.
Marine Activities Cen.
North Dock
Yacht Club
North Dock Basin
North Pier
North Pier Lighthouse
A1018
Stadium of Light
Superstore
Sunderland Retail Pk.
Wave Basin
Works
Swinging Basin
New South Pier
North Tidal Basin
North Half Tide Basin
SR1
Maud's Hole
St. Peter's Riverside Sculpture Trail
National Glass Cen.
North Sands Bus. Cen.
Burial Ground
University of Sunderland (Sir Tom Cowie Campus at St. Peter's)
Oil Depot
Gladstone Swing Bridge
Corporation Quay
Strand Quay
RIVER WEAR
South Rocks
Bus Depot
Station Mus.
St. Peters
B1293
119
Hudson Dock North
SOUTH DOCKS
HIGH STREET EAST
WEST WEAR ST.
PANNS BANK
LOW STREET

92
120
Whittonstall
Lawson's Farm
B6309
Whittonstall First Sch.
Old Hall Farm
Grove Plantation
Vicarage
ANVIL CT
Hall Farm
Dere Street (Roman Road)
Whittonstall Hall Farm
Whittonstall Sproats
Duckpool Plantation
Haystackhill Wood
Hollings
Millhill Wood
NE43
Redwaybanks Wood
Redwaybanks Wood
Mill Burn
Howlets Gill
Hoodsclose
Ashybank Wood
Wood House
Coatlandguards Wood
Meirs Wood
Pethhead Wood
LEAD LANE
Consett
DH8
PARK
Broom Hill
Old Wood
Works
FINE LANE
New Wood
Morrowfield Farm
Brockwell Heads
Brockwell House
Beechcroft
Seldom Seen
Small Burn
Haugh Farm
Newlands
Fellclose
Newlands Bridge
Burnside Cottage
Weir
Waterfall
Waterfall
BOUNDARY LANE
FINE LANE
Newlands South Farm
Mill Dene
Jerrysleap Wood
Waterfall
Stoopquarry Plantation
Yecklish Burn
Clarkspasture Plantation
Longriggs Wood
Foxridge Plantation
Mereburn Bridge
Black Plantation
Mere Burn
Low Northfield Plantation
Whinnynook Plantation
Northfield Plantation
Mereburn Plantation
Battershawfield Plantation
PIKE HILL
WASKERLEYEDGE PLANTATION
Mereburn Cottage
Hill Top
Ford
Panshields Cottage
Panshield
Pikehill Plantation
Spring Wood
RIVER
Derwent Le Cottage
Camperdown
Panshield Wood
Spa Pleasure Grounds

107
CHOPWELL
MILKWELLBURN WOOD
Hollings Hill
F
G
H
93
J
K
Rye Hill
GATESHEAD
NORTHUMBERLAND
Newcastle upon Tyne
Blackhall Farm
Tongue Burns
Peartree Farm
Blackhall Mill
East Howdenway Wood
Whitehill Wood
Broad Oak
NE17
Broadoak Quarry (Sand & Gravel)
Chester Hills
Playing Field
Derwentside Park
Coltpark Wood
COLTPARK WOODS
Derwent Valley Villas
Cemy.
War Mem.
Victoria T.
Denesider
A694
Thorney Brow
Hepper Hill
Underhills Wood
DERWENT
HAMSTERLEY
Heugh Wood
Low Westwood
Langdale Ter.
Ennerdale T.
WESTWOOD
Derwent Cote
Derwent Haven
CRONNIEWELL
CRESCENT
Colt Park
OAKWELL CT.
WOOD
The Haughs
Broadoak Mews
Summerfield
Cemetery
Whinny Bank
Westwood Plantation
Sherburn Terrace
LANE
RIVER
Ralph's Wood
Byersi Caravan
108
Heugh Bank
Haugh Wood
NORTHUMBERLAND
DURHAM
ROAD
THROAT
LANE
CUT
The Bungalows
High Westwood
LONSDALE CT.
Ebchester Bridge
Cricket Ground
Football Ground
B6309
Bridge End
VINDOMORA VILLAS
GARDEN CR.
Bridge End Wood
Briar Dene
Vindomora Roman Fort (Rems.)
Lane Head
The Bungalows
Allendale Farm
Allendale Cottages
SHAW
DIXON AV.
TEMPERANCE YD.
CHURCH CL.
FARBRIDGE CR.
Longbank Wood
Rectory La.
Long Bank
Ebchester C of E Prim. Sch.
EBCHESTER
VINDOMORA (FRONT ST.)
Fox Flatlets
The Haughs
Ebchester
Hill Bank Wood
CHESTERS DENE
WAY COHORT CL.
St. Mary's Convent
SYCAMORE ST.
Derwentside Wood
Summerson's Hole
FOSS WY.
HADRIANS WAY
The Hill
ST. EBBA'S
THE CHESTERS
Ebchester Hill Cottages
Allendale Cottages
West Wood
Sewage Works
SPRING
LANE
Station Bank
Ebchester Station Picnic Site
Slade's Ho.
Station Houses
CLOSE
Broomhill Dene
Burn
Westwood House
Westwood Farm
Derwent Dene Farm
The Dene
Fairholme
DENECREST
THE DENE
Adams T.
DENESYDE
Derwent Hill
SPRINGHOUSE
Broom Hill
HILL
Manorhouse Wood
West Farm
Grange
Manor Ho.
EAST LAW
Holly Lodge
Broomhill Farm
Bishop Ian Ramsey C of E Prim. Sch.
Grange Farm
War Mem.
B6310
ROAD
MANOR
HUNTERS CL.
East Law
WHINNY
Westlaw Wood
Gate House Cottage
A694
ROAD
Crossroads
Co-operative Ter.
MEDOMSLEY
North View
Rothley Ter.
Grange Ter.
RD.
NORTH MAGDALENE
West Law
LANE
B6309
B6310
HIGHSTEADS
FINES
B6308
SOUTH MAGDALENE
Derwent Lodge
Glebe Farm
Springfield Lodge
LAW
Ebchester Glebe
Medomsley Cross Roads
BROOMHILL TERRACE
Medomsley Edge
F
Greenwood
G
H
121
Belle Vue
J
K
WEST
Piper Wood
Park
Fern House
Fines House
PITHOUSE
410
11
12
57
56
55
54
1
2
3
4
5
6
7

Blackhall Mill
Hamsterley
Rowlands Gill
NE39
Hamsterley Mill
Newcastle upon Tyne
NE17
Consett
DH8
Medomsley
Tongue Burns Plantation
Tongue Burns
Peartree Farm
Armondside
Carr House
Craghead Wood
Galleyburn Wood
Ponthaugh Wood
Haggdene Wood
Hagg Banks Wood
Hagg Dene
Hagg Farm
Hagg
Mill Wood
Coltpark Wood
Pickle Bank Wood
Derwentcote Farm
Derwentcote Lodge
Derwentcote Steel Furnace
Forge Banks Wood
Derwent Cote
Derwentcote Cottage
Owlet Gill
Bairn's Gill
Ridgewood
Rough Pasture Wood
High Wood
Picnic Site
White Byerside
Byerside Caravan Site
Longclose Cottage
Byerside Wood
Longclose Wood
Crabtree Hill
High Hamsterley
HAMSTERLEY PARK
Longclose Trough
Make-me-Rich Plantation
Cut Throat Wood
Paddock Wood
Hamsterley Hall Wood
Hamsterley Hall
Fan Wood
White Well Wood
White Well
Scot's Bog Wood
Black Bog Wood
Black Byerside Wood
Peel Flats
Peelflats Plantation
Rabbit Shaws
Hamsterleyhall Spring Wood
Derwent Wood
Bath House Plantation
Bullion's Close Wood
Southfield Farm
Southfield Wood
North Wood
Struthers' Wood
Manorhouse Wood
West Farm Grange
Manor Ho.
Bishop Ian Ramsey C of E Prim. Sch.
War Mem.
Oakey Bank
Cowclose Wood
Pontop Low Wood
Shipmaster's Hill
Hollin Hill
South Moor Plantation
Little Kipling Plantation
Cockshot Wood
South Moor
Intake Plantation
Black Bog
Bradley Wood
A694
B6310
B6308
LINTZFORD ROAD
BANK
LONGCLOSE ROAD
CUT THROAT LANE
TOLLGATE ROAD
PARKLANDS
SOUTHFIELD LANE
HOUSING LANE
MANOR ROAD
RIVER DERWENT
GATESHEAD
DURHAM
94
107
122
A B C D E
1 2 3 4 5 6 7
12 13 14
54 55 56 57

Lintzford Wood
Lintzford
Low Friarside
High Friarside
Friarside Wood
Jockside Wood
SCAIFE'S WOOD
Bryan's Leap
Leazes
BURNOPFIELD
Lintz
Lintz Green
Priestfield Wood
Cockshot Wood
Sliding Braes
Steelclose Mill Farm
Steelclose Wood
Fogoesburn Wood
Pontburn Wood Nature Reserve
Oldmill Wood
Lofthouse Wood
The Beeches
Lintz Hall Farm
Loft House
Lintzhall Dene
Newcastle upon Tyne
NE16
Toft Gate
Pickering Nook
Black Hill
Upper Lintz
Old Papermill Cottage
Low Ewehurst
Bonner's Wood
Collierley Wood
Straightneck Wood
Mountsett
Mountsett Crematorium
Ewehurst Wood
Four Acre Wood
Six Acre Wood
Stanley
DH9
Hill Top
Flint Hill
Dipton Wood
Ewehurst Head
Sewage Works
Collierley
Coachroad Gill
Recreation Ground
Ivy Cottage
DIPTON
Sports Field
A694
A692
B6310
B6311
B6168
B6173
95
110
123

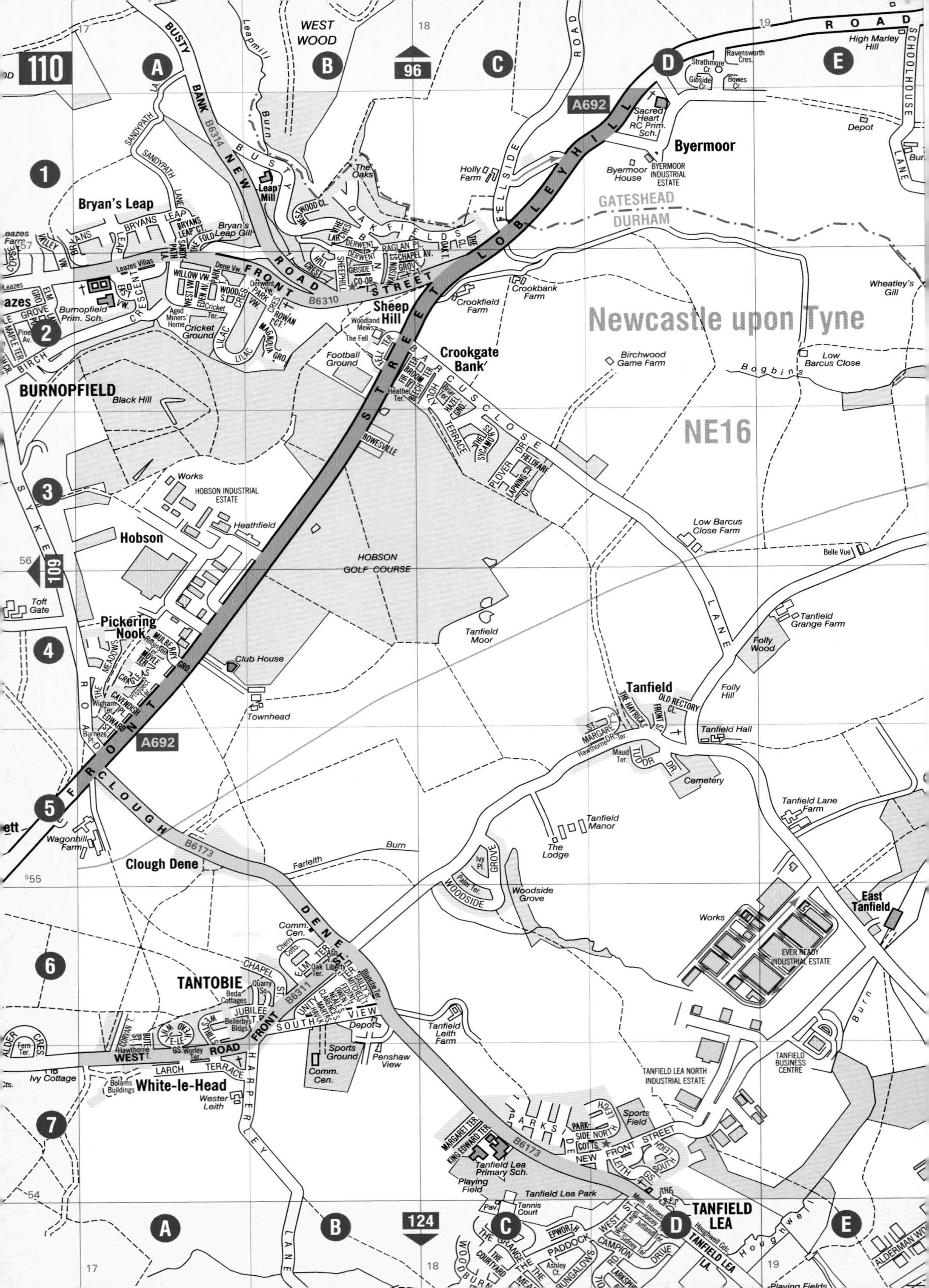

96
124
109
A
B
C
D
E
1
2
3
4
5
6
7
17
18
19
57
56
55
54
WEST WOOD
Leapmill Burn
BUSTY BANK
B6314
NEW ROAD
SANDYPATH
SANDYPATH LANE
Leap Mill
The Oaks
OAKFIELDS
Bryan's Leap
BRYANS LEAP
BRYANS LEAP CT.
Bryan's Leap Gill
THE FOLD
Leazes Farm
Leazes Villas
Leazes
GROVE
ELM
MAPLE TER.
BIRCH
CRESCENT
EAST VW.
Burnopfield Prim. Sch.
Aged Miners' Home
Cricket Ground
Cricket Ter.
WILLOW VW.
WEST VW.
EDEN AV.
PARK
WOODS
Dene Vw.
Derwent Vw.
DERWENT PARK
ROWAN CT.
LILAC
MAGNOLIA GRO.
FRONT STREET
B6310
DERWENT
RAGLAN PL.
CHAPEL AV.
GROVE
WATSON ST.
SHEEPHILL
GIBSIDE T.
CO-OP
OAK T.
Sheep Hill
Woodland Mews
The Fell
Football Ground
Crookgate Bank
BARCUS CLOSE
HAZEL GRO.
Heather Ter.
BOWESVILLE
TERRACE
THE SYCAMORES
PLOVER DR.
FIELDFARE CT.
LAPWING CT.
BURNOPFIELD
Black Hill
Works
HOBSON INDUSTRIAL ESTATE
Heathfield
Hobson
HOBSON GOLF COURSE
Toft Gate
SYKE
Pickering Nook
MULBERRY GRO.
Club House
Townhead
THE MEADOWS
CAVENDISH PL.
EDWARD ST.
Burneze Pl.
ROAD
A692
FRONT STREET
LOBLEY HILL
ROAD
FELLSIDE ROAD
Holly Farm
Crookfield Farm
Crookbank Farm
D
Strathmore Cr.
Ravensworth Cres.
Gibside Cr.
Bowes Cr.
Sacred Heart RC Prim. Sch.
Byermoor
Byermoor House
BYERMOOR INDUSTRIAL ESTATE
GATESHEAD
DURHAM
High Marley Hill
SCHOOLHOUSE LANE
Depot
Wheatley's Gill
Newcastle upon Tyne
Birchwood Game Farm
Low Barcus Close
Bogbins
NE16
Low Barcus Close Farm
Belle Vue
Tanfield Moor
LANE
Tanfield Grange Farm
Folly Wood
Folly Hill
Tanfield
THE HAYRICKS
OLD RECTORY CL.
FRONT ST.
ST. MARGARET'S
Hawthorne Dr.
Ter.
Maud Ter.
TUDOR DR.
Tanfield Hall
Cemetery
Tanfield Lane Farm
Tanfield Manor
The Lodge
Wagonhill Farm
CLOUGH
B6173
Clough Dene
Farleith Burn
Ivy Pl.
GROVE
Palm Ter.
WOODSIDE
Woodside Grove
Works
EVER READY INDUSTRIAL ESTATE
East Tanfield
DENE
Comm. Cen.
Cherry Cotts.
ELM TER.
Ash
Oak Ter.
Liberty
CHAPEL ST.
TANTOBIE
Beda Cottages
Quarry Sq.
B6311
JUBILEE
Bellerbys Bldgs.
FRONT
SOUTH VIEW
UNITY
Depot
Sports Ground
Comm. Cen.
Penshaw View
Tanfield Leith Farm
ALDER CRES.
Fern Ter.
Hawthorne
WEST
ROAD
LARCH TERRACE
Worley Ter.
Ivy Cottage
Bolams Buildings
White-le-Head
Wester Leith
HARPERLEY LANE
TANFIELD LEA NORTH INDUSTRIAL ESTATE
TANFIELD BUSINESS CENTRE
Burn
PARKSIDE
PARK SIDE
NORTH COTTS.
NEW
FRONT STREET
LEITH
SOUTH LEIGH
Sports Field
MARGARET TER.
KING EDWARD TER.
Tanfield Lea Primary Sch.
Playing Field
Tanfield Lea Park
Pav.
Tennis Court
THE GRANGE
EPWORTH
PADDOCK
WEST ST.
Sidney Ter.
CAMPION DRIVE
Ashley Ct.
BUNGALOWS
THE COURTYARD
TANFIELD LEA
TANFIELD LEA LA.
Houghwell Gds.
Houghwell
ALDERMAN
Playing Fields

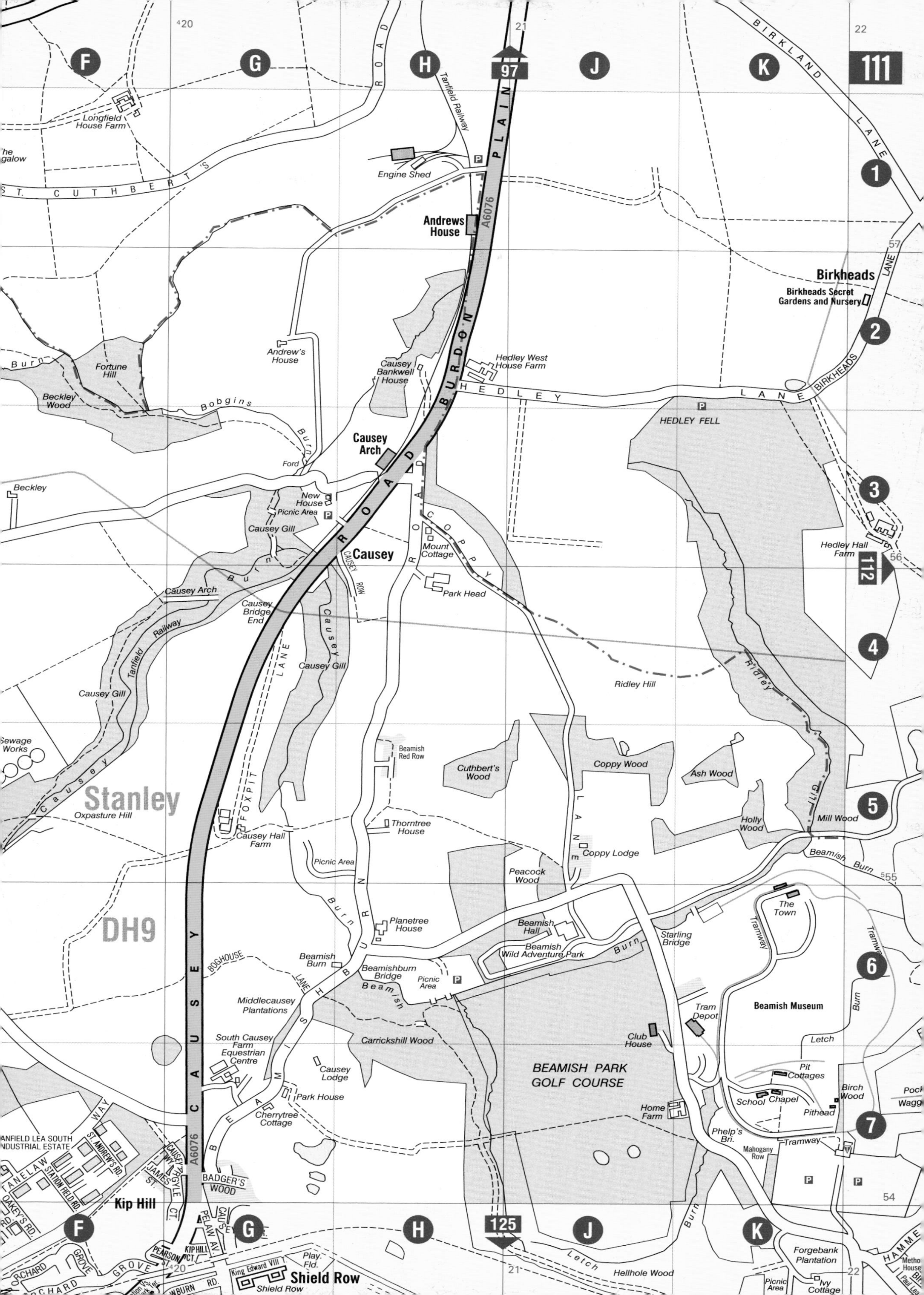

F
G
H
J
K
97
125
112
Longfield House Farm
St. Cuthbert's Road
Tanfield Railway
Engine Shed
Plain
Andrews House
A6076
Birkland Lane
Birkheads
Birkheads Secret Gardens and Nursery
Birkheads Lane
Fortune Hill
Beckley Wood
Burn
Bobgins Burn
Andrew's House
Causey Bankwell House
Hedley West House Farm
Burdon Road
Hedley Lane
Hedley Fell
Causey Arch
Ford
Beckley
New House
Picnic Area
Causey Gill
Causey
Coppy Road
Mount Cottage
Causey Row
Hedley Hall Farm
Park Head
Causey Arch
Causey Bridge End
Tanfield Railway
Causey Gill
Causey Gill
Lane
Ridley Hill
Ridley Gill
Sewage Works
Causey Burn
Stanley
Oxpasture Hill
Foxpit Lane
Beamish Red Row
Cuthbert's Wood
Coppy Wood
Ash Wood
Causey Hall Farm
Thorntree House
Holly Wood
Mill Wood
Coppy Lane
Coppy Lodge
Picnic Area
Beamish Burn
Peacock Wood
DH9
Planetree House
Beamish Hall
Beamish Wild Adventure Park
Starling Bridge
The Town
Tramway
Boghouse Lane
Beamish Burn
Beamishburn Bridge
Picnic Area
Beamish Museum
Middlecausey Plantations
Tram Depot
Club House
Letch Burn
South Causey Farm Equestrian Centre
Carrickshill Wood
Beamish Park Golf Course
Causey Lodge
Pit Cottages
Birch Wood
School
Chapel
Pithead
Park House
Home Farm
Cherrytree Cottage
Causey Road
Beamish Lane
Tanfield Lea South Industrial Estate
Way
St. Andrew's Rd.
Station Field Rd.
Tanelaw
Oakey's Rd.
St. James Ct.
Causey Way
Argyle St.
Badger's Wood
Phelp's Bri.
Mahogany Row
Tramway
Kip Hill
Pelaw Av.
Caus.
Kip Hill Ct.
Pearson Pl.
Orchard
Grove
Play. Fld.
King Edward VIII Ter.
Shield Row
Letch
Hellhole Wood
Forgebank Plantation
Picnic Area
Ivy Cottage
Hammer
Pock
Wagg
420
21
22
57
56
555
54
1
2
3
4
5
6
7

Cheviot Wood
HAGGS BANK
Old Ravensworth Farm
Beldy
Hagg Wood
Nursery
98
A
B
C
D
E
Chapel Banks
Burn
BIRKLAND LANE
OUSLAW LANE
Mitcheson's Gill Wood
Strandy
Mitcheson's Gill
Briar Dene
1
Ravensworth Grange Farm
57
Birkheads
Birkheads Secret Gardens and Nursery
2
NE BIRKHEADS LANE
Coltspool
High Hills
Kibblesworth West Farm
Lochfield Gdns.
Liddell Ter.
Valley Vw.
The Crescent
Coronation
Prospect T.
ROSE GS.
Comm. Cen.
Aged Miners' Homes
GRANGE ESTATE
The Grange
Grange Ter.
Gardiner Square
LABURNUM CR.
Pav.
Bowl. Grn.
KIBBLESWORTH
Whinnel Hill
KIBBLESWORTH
NE11
3
Opencast
Hedley Hall Farm
Kibblesworth Grange
111
56
NE16
RIDING LANE
Red Burn
Cooper House
4
Redburn Banks
Redburn Banks Wood
Burn
Riding Farm
Mossfield Plantation
Kibblesworth Common
5
Mill Wood
Beamish East Moor
Beamish
West Banks
Wallace's Gill Wood
55
The Town
Pockerley Hills
Pockerleyhill Wood
Stanley DH9
Broomy Banks Wood
Tramway
Burn
6
Pockerley Buildings
Burn
Beamish Museum
Flint Mill
Pockerley Old Hall
Bog Hill
Greenburn Howl
Team Valley
Letch
Pit Cottages
Birch Wood
Pockerley Waggonway
Cranberry Bog Plantation
BOBBY SHAFTO CARAVAN PK.
Money Hill
Money Plantation
Chapel
7
Tramway
High Forge
HAMMER SQUARE BANK
Urpeth Forge
Hammer Square
Hammer Square House
Upper Forge Bri.
Urpeth North Farm
MIRE DUBS
P
P
54
Martin Scar
Horse Shoe
Ousbrough Wood
Minstrel Farm
Doll's Hole
Urpeth House
Coach Ho.
Lodge
Ousbrough Hill
Urpeth Hall
High Urpeth
126
Urpeth South Farm
A
B
C
D
E
Forgebank Plantation
Urpeth
Burn
Weather Hill
Forgebank Plantation
Methold Houses
Beamish Woods
HEUGHS PLANTATION
22
23
24
Picnic Area
Ivy Cottage
URPETH COMMON

Lamesley
Gateshead
NE9
BIRTLEY
DH3
Chester-le-Street
OUSTON
Urpeth
DH2
Perkinsville
Tyne Marshalling Yard
Sewage Works
Bewick Main Caravan Park
Urpeth Wood
Birtley Crematorium
Birtley Cemetery
Westline Industrial Estate
Birtley Leisure Centre
Newtown Ind. Estate
Durham Road Trading Estate
Gateshead Western By-Pass
Newcastle Bank
Durham Road
Station Lane
Ouston Prim. School
St. Benet's RC Prim. Sch.
Kibblesworth Academy
St. Joseph's Catholic Inf. Sch.
IMEX Bus. Cen.
Spencer Industrial Estate
Ouston Spring Farm
Ouston Bank Farm
Low Urpeth
Sledge Hill
Team Valley
Cooper Wood
Target Wood
Beggardene Wood
Longacre Dene
Long Acre Farm
Moor Mill Farm
South Farm
Sandy Fords

99
114
127

100
113
128
Gateshead
NE9
SUNDERLAND
GATESHEAD
A1
BIRTLEY BY-PASS
A194(M)
A194(M) MOTORWAY
Junc. 65
A1(M)
A1231
Chester-le-Street
DH3
BIRTLEY
ARMSTRONG
ARMSTRONG INDUSTRIAL ESTATE
BLACKFELL
Blackfell Prim. Sch.
Bowes Manor Equestrian Centre
Northside Farm
Dunkirk
Sheddonshill Well
Sheddon's Hill
Havannah
Sorting Office
CROWTHER INDUSTRIAL EST.
Oxclose Village
OXCLOSE VILLAGE CEN.
Oxclose Community Academy
St. John Boste RC Prim. Sch.
Oxclose Village Prim. Sch.
HOLLEY PARK
Holley Park Academy
AYTON
EMERSON
Washington Service Area
Junc. 64
WESTERN
A195
A1(M) MOTORWAY
Portmeads
Portobello
PORTOBELLO INDUSTRIAL ESTATE
Lord Lawson of Beamish School
Ravensworth Ter. Prim. Sch.
St. Joseph's Catholic Inf. Sch.
Birtley East Prim. Sch.
Birtley Swimming Centre
BIRTLEY GOLF COURSE
Portobello Primary School
Birtley Leisure Cen.
NEWTOWN INDUSTRIAL ESTATE
Vigo
Barley Mow
Barley Mow Prim. Sch.
Vigo Wood
RICKLETON
RICKLETON VILLAGE CEN.
Rickleton Prim. Sch.
WASHINGTON SPIRE HOSP.
New Vigo Wood
DURHAM ROAD TRADING ESTATE
Nova Scotia
A167
DURHAM ROAD
VIGO LANE
BIRTLEY LANE
PICKTREE LANE
MOUNT PLEASANT ROAD
B1288
B1288
SUNDERLAND ROAD
BLACKFELL ROAD
CROWTHER ROAD
EMERSON ROAD
PORTOBELLO ROAD
RADIAL PARK RD.
Factory
Works
Depots
Sports Ground
Rec. Grd.
Playing Field
Football Ground
A B C D E
1 2 3 4 5 6 7
27 28 29
54 55 56

WASHINGTON
WASHINGTON VILLAGE
TOWN CENTRE
ALBANY
BARMSTON
COLUMBIA
GLEBE
BIDDICK
OXCLOSE
LAMBTON
WEAR
HARRATON
FATFIELD
MOUNT PLEASANT
NE37
NE38
DH4
Washington
101
116
129
A1290
A195
A182
A1231
BLUE HOUSE LANE
VICTORIA RD.
FRONT ST
USWORTH
GLOVER
VERMONT
HAVANNAH ROAD
SUNDERLAND HIGHWAY
WASHINGTON HIGHWAY
NORTHUMBERLAND WAY
NORTHUMBERLAND HIGHWAY
PARKWAY
BONEMILL LANE
PATTINSON ROAD
HORSLEY ROAD
Washington 'F' Pit
Washington FC (Albany Park)
ALBANY PARK
Washington Sch.
Playing Fields
HERTBURN INDUSTRIAL ESTATE
BENTALL BUSINESS PARK
PEEL RETAIL PARK
THE PEEL CEN.
GLOVER NETWORK CENTRE
GLOVER IND. EST.
PARSONS INDUSTRIAL ESTATE
ALBANY VILLAGE CENTRE
Albany Village Prim. Sch.
THE GALLERIES RETAIL PK.
THE GALLERIES
DURHAM HOUSE (Government Offices)
Bus Station
Bowl. Alley
Gala Bingo
Washington Leisure Centre
St. Joseph's RC Sch.
Glebe Park
Washington Old Hall
Cemetery
JOHN F. KENNEDY ESTATE
Wessington Prim. Sch.
Biddick Prim. Sch.
Barmston Village Prim. Sch.
BARMSTON CENTRE
John F. Kennedy Prim. Sch.
Glebe Colliery Welfare Park
Columbia Grange School
SWAN INDUSTRIAL ESTATE (NORTH)
SWAN INDUSTRIAL ESTATE (SOUTH)
PATTINSON INDUSTRIAL ESTATE
PATTINSON SOUTH INDUSTRIAL ESTATE
The Princess Anne Park
BIDDICK VILLAGE CENTRE
Biddick Sch. Spts. Coll.
Sports Pitches
St. Robert of Newminster RC School
Arts Cen.
Fatfield Primary School
Warehouse
Pattinson South Pond
The James Steel Park
Victoria Bridge House
Victoria Viaduct
River Wear
Mount Pleasant Lake
Low Lambton Farm
Railway Cottages
WEAR INDUSTRIAL ESTATE
Harraton Skills Centre
Fatfield House
ST. GEORGE'S ESTATE
Shiphouse Wood
Worm Hill
War Mem.
Lambton Sch.
Lambton Cen.

WASHINGTON
Severn Houses
Works
Hylton Plantation
A
B
C
D
E
102
Hillthorn Farm
Warehouse
GLOVER NETWORK CENTRE
MOTOR WORKS
TURBINE BUSINESS PARK
NE37
Barmston Pond
Barmston Pond Local Nature Reserve
BARMSTON MERE TRAINING CENTRE
SR5
PEEL RETAIL PARK
THE PEEL CEN.
A1231
SUNDERLAND HIGHWAY
WASHINGTON
Warehouse
Works
PATTINSON INDUSTRIAL ESTATE
Warehouse
Low Barmston Fm.
High Wood
Toby Gill
Offerton Haugh
ALSTON ROAD
MANDARIN WAY
Middle Barmston Farm
WATERVIEW PARK
Govt. Offs.
Spring Gill
The James Steel Park
PATTINSON NORTH INDUSTRIAL ESTATE
Washington
Washington Wetland Centre
Sub.
Playground
WASKERLEY ROAD
Works
Spa Well Gill
Ponds
WEARSIDE GOLF COURSE
RIVER WEAR
Stoney
SWAN INDUSTRIAL ESTATE (NORTH)
Sheringham Ho.
Sewage Works
Leat House
PATTINSON INDUSTRIAL ESTATE
NE38
Copperas Gill
PATTINSON SOUTH INDUSTRIAL ESTATE
Washington Staithes
Subway
Club House
Sunderland
Offerton
Wood House Farm
Waterside
Depot
Glebe Ho. Fm.
Cox Green
Alice Well Villas
Coxgreen Gill
Ayton's Wood
Offerton Hall
OFFERTON LANE
The James Steel Park
Jubilee Ter.
Railway Cotts.
Grimestone Banks
Low Lambton
OFFERTON ROAD
Dawson's Plantation
Victoria Bridge House
Penshaw North House Farm
Victoria Viaduct
Penshaw Wood
Flinton Hill Farm
Bore Hole
PENSHAW HILL
Houghton-le-Spring
Penshaw Hill House
Penshaw Monument
A183
CARR HILL
Low Lambton Farm
DH4
COXGREEN
East Barnwell Farm
CHESTER ROAD
Railway Cottages
Care Home
130
Village Farm
The Cedars
Penshaw Hill Farm
Burn Hill
Foxcover Plantation
115
32
33
34
57
56
55
54
1
2
3
4
5
6
7

117
103
118
131
SR4
SR3
North Hylton
South Hylton
PENNYWELL
Grindon
Hastings Hill
Springwell
Thorney Close
Ford Quarry Recreation Area
Sunderland Crematorium
Pennywell Industrial Estate
Pallion West Industrial Estate
Pallion Industrial Estate
Claxheugh Rock
Baron's Quay Wood
Sports Ground
Hasting Hill
Offerton Grange Farm
Wood House
The Bottoms
Transformer Station
A19
A1231
A183
A690
B1405

Pallion
Shipbuilding Yard
Works
Gas Works
Scrap Yard
Deptford
Ayre's Quay
EUROPEAN WAY
PALLION NEW RD.
104
PALLION INDUSTRIAL ESTATE
RIVERGREEN IND. EST.
University of Sunderland
The Forge
Gala Bingo
Superstore
A1231
TRIMDON ST.
Gill Bridge
Bishopwearmouth
RIVER
Wreath Quay
A183
ST. MARY'S BOU
Olympia
Millfield
Park
ST. LUKE'S RD.
OXFORD RD.
MIDMOOR RD.
Inf. & Jun. Schs.
University of Sunderland (City Campus)
Chester Ct.
The Precinct
University
The Green
CHESTER ROAD
STOCKTON RD.
Ford Estate
Playing Field
Tennis Court
Pav.
SUNDERLAND ROYAL HOSPITAL
Burial Ground
BISHOPWEARMOUTH CEMETERY
War Mem.
Sunderland Crematorium
High Barnes
CHESTER ROAD
THE BROADWAY
117
A183
Convent
School
Schs.
Thornhill Sch. Bus. & Ent. College
7
Ashbrooke
Ashbrooke Grounds
Barnes Jun. & Inf. Schs.
Richard Avenue Prim. Sch.
Barbara Priestman School
Playing Fields
St. Mary's RC Prim. Sch.
St. Aidan's Cath. Sch.
BARNES PARK
Barnes Burn
Nursery
Bowling Greens
Children's Cen. (Speech Therapy)
City of Sunderland College (Bede Centre)
Springwell
Springwell Dene Sch.
A690
DURHAM ROAD
QUEEN ALEXANDRA ROAD
Humbledon Hill Reservoirs
Humbledon Hill Farm
Tudor Gro. Cen. & PRU
Superstore
Sunningdale Sch.
ESSEN WAY
LEECHMERE WAY
PREMIER ROAD
B1405
Plains Farm Academy
Plains Farm
SR3
Superstore
Elstob Farm Caravans
Elstob House
Tunstall Hills
Maiden Paps
Rock Cottage Farm
Playing Field
THE PRECINCT
Thorney Close Prim. Sch.
Silksworth Comm. Pool, Tennis & Wellness Centre
Running Track
Sports Ground
Playing Fields
Tennis Cts.
Silksworth Sports Complex & Ski Slope
Ski Slope
Newport Hill
HIGH NEWPORT
132
Community Centre
Cricket Ground
TUNSTALL HOPE ROAD

F
G
H
J
K
1
2
3
4
5
6
7
42
57
56
55
54
105
133
A1018
A1231
B1293
B1294
B1522
B1405
SR1
SR2
NORTH
SEA
SUNDERLAND
HENDON
Grangetown
RYHOPE
COLLIERY
St. Peters
University of Sunderland
(Sir Tom Cowie Campus
at St. Peter's)
Tide Basin
Oil Depot
Gladstone
South Rocks
WEAR
Wearmouth Bridge
Hudson Dock North
SOUTH DOCKS
HUDSON DOCK
Works
South Outlet
North East Pier
Hudson Dock South
South West Breakwater
Warehouses
Hendon Dock
Spur Barrier
Factory
Sewage Works
Breakwater
Tanks
Oil Depot
Sub.
Gas Works
Outfall
Sports Grd.
Depot
Salterfen Rocks
Ryhope Nook
Salterfen Dene
Sunderland
Market
Bingo
Bus Sta.
Park La.
Civic Cen.
Sunderland Mus. & Winter Gardens
Mowbray Gdns.
Comm. Cen.
Town Moor
Stanfield Bus. Cen.
Bus Depot
Sports Cen.
Valley Rd. Prim. Sch. & PRU
Warehouse
Jack Crawford Ho.
Playing Field
Sunderland High Sch.
Barley Mow Park
Backhouse Park
Sports Ground
Southmoor Academy
SUNDERLAND EYE INFIRMARY
Playing Fields
Grangetown Prim. Sch.
Hill View Jun. Sch.
Play. Fld.
Community Centre
Stannington Centre
Hill View Inf. Sch.
Cemetery
North Lodge
South Lodge
Hypermarket
LEECHMERE INDUSTRIAL ESTATE
Rehab Unit
Nurs. Home
Res.
Tunstall Hills East
Tunstall Hills Local Nature Reserve
Field
Ryhope Grange Junc.
Superstore
Subway
WEST WEAR ST.
HIGH ST.
BOROUGH RD.
HOLMESIDE
TOWARD ROAD
BURDON ROAD
PARK RD.
PEEL ST.
SALEM RD.
WHITE HOUSE RD.
HENDON RD.
COMMERCIAL ROAD
MOWBRAY RD.
VILLETTE RD.
HUNTER TER.
STRATFORD AV.
ALEXANDRA ROAD
OCEAN ROAD
RYHOPE ROAD
SAINT-NAZIRE WAY
LEECHMERE ROAD
TUNSTALL ROAD
ROAD
B A R R O A D
WELLMERE RD.
SALTERFEN ROAD
HENDON VALLEY ROAD
CORPORATION RD.
ROBINSON TERRACE
PARADE
ADDISON ST.
W. LAWRENCE ST.
SANS ST.
LOW STREET
PANNS BANK
HENDON BURN AV.
GRANGE CRESCENT
THE RANGE
CEDARS
HOLLYCARRSIDE
ORKNEY

106
134
A
B
C
D
E
1
2
3
4
5
6
7
Consett
DH8
Waskerleyedge Plantation
Pikehill Plantation
Pike Lane
Camperdown
Hammermill
East Hammermill Plantation
Burnmillbank Plantation
Burnmill
Shotleyfield Burn
Burnmill Gill
Burnmill Bank
B6278
Burnmill Bridge
Ford
Burnhousegill Plantation
Burnhouse Gill
Weir
Burn House
Bluehouses Plantation
Blue House
Bluehouses Well
Hollin Hill
High Waskerley
Hill
Spring Wood
Spring Cottages
Low Waskerley
Waskerley Lodge
Hill Top
Panshields Cottage
Panshield
Panshield Wood
Northumberland
Durham
Derwent River
Derwent Lodge Cottage
Spa Pleasure Grounds
Cricket Ground
Snow's Greenburn Bridge
Shotley Park
Paddock Wood
Shotley Bridge Jun. Sch.
Shotley Hall
Shotley Bridge
Hall Park
Hall Wood
Benfieldside
Slonk's Plantation
Cutlers Hall Road
A691
Snodsedge Plantation
Fieldhead Plantation
Fieldhead Farm
Laings Loaning
Oakybank Wood
Shotley Grove Road
Derwentside Cottage
Bridgehill
Playing Field
Sandypath Cottage
The Mill House
The Forge
Weir
North Snods
Letch Burn
Orchardfield Wood
Southfield Plantation
Snods Dene
Whinney Bank
Orchard Field
Brownsbog Wood
Horseshoe Plantation
Brown's Hill
Sodfine Wood
The Old Barn
Bridgehill Farm Court
St. Mary's RC Prim. Sch.
Reservoir (covered)
Bulbeck Plantation
Bulbeck Cottage
Howden Burn
Howden Wood
Holerow Fell
Broom Hill
Holerow Banks
Holerow Haughs
River Derwent
Hole Row
Allensford Cottage
Consett Plantation
Pemberton Road
Consett Road
A68
Mosswood
Mosswood Cottages
Field Cott.
Wallishwalls Burn
Mosswood Farm
Allensford Bank
Allensford Mill Farm
Allensford Bridge
Allensford Mill
Allensford Country Park
Allensford
Daneburn Wood
West Wood
Aqueduct
Willerby Grange
Selby Lodge
Hall Cotts.
The Grove
Palmer Ct.
Oakfield
The Grove Prim. Sch.

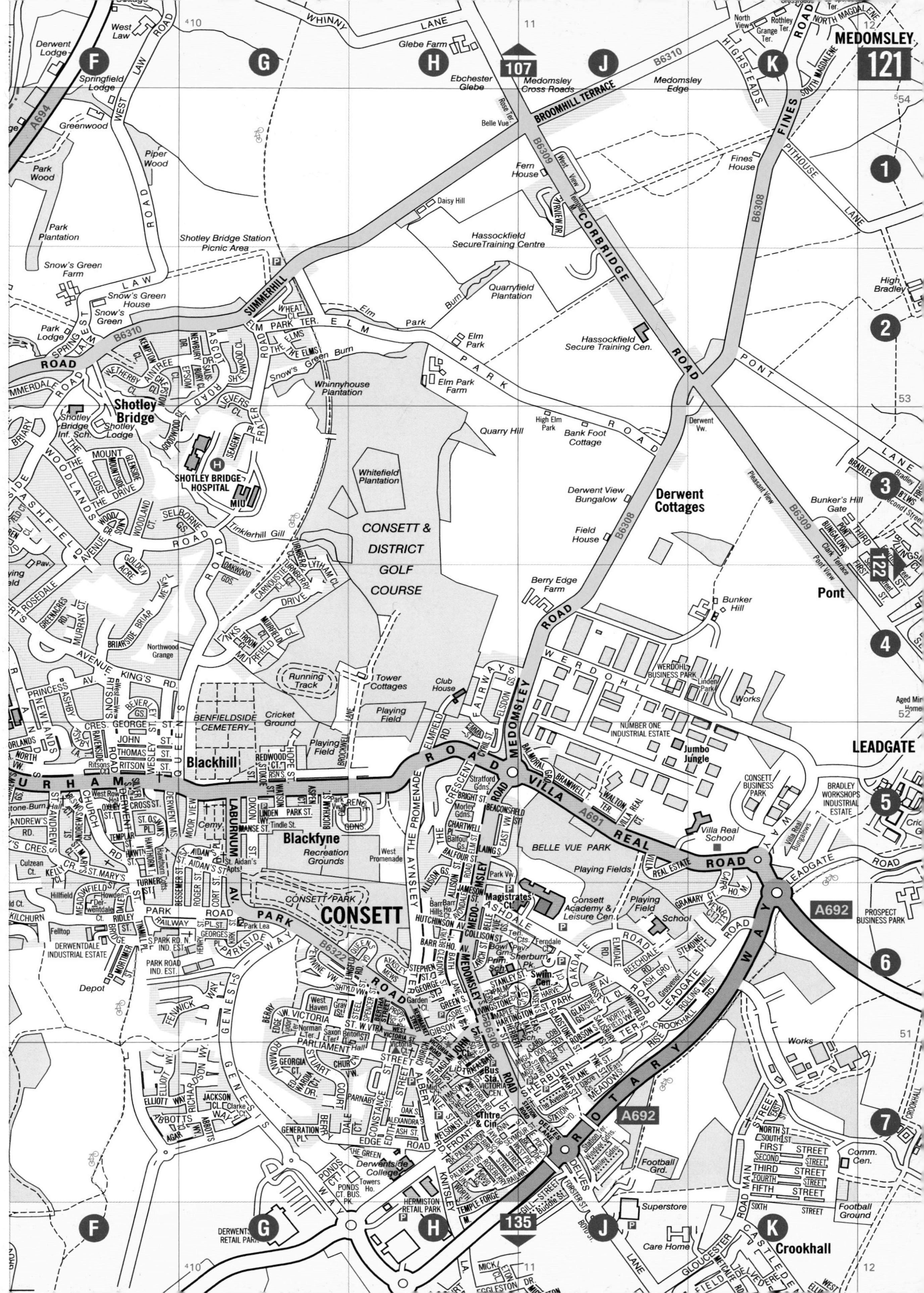

MEDOMSLEY
121
107
135
122
F
G
H
J
K
1
2
3
4
5
6
7
410
11
12
54
53
52
51
A694
B6310
B6309
B6308
B6322
A691
A692
West Law
Derwent Lodge
Springfield Lodge
Greenwood
Piper Wood
Park Wood
Park Plantation
Snow's Green Farm
Snow's Green House
Snow's Green
Park Lodge
Shotley Bridge Station Picnic Area
Glebe Farm
Ebchester Glebe
Medomsley Cross Roads
Medomsley Edge
BROOMHILL TERRACE
WHINNY LANE
HIGHSTEADS
NORTH MAGDALENE
SOUTH MAGDALENE
North View
Rothley Ter.
Grange Ter.
Belle Vue
Fern House
Fines House
PITHOUSE LANE
FINES ROAD
Daisy Hill
Hassockfield Secure Training Centre
Quarryfield Plantation
Hassockfield Secure Training Cen.
CORBRIDGE ROAD
SUMMERHILL
ELM PARK TER.
ELM PARK ROAD
Elm Park
Elm Park Farm
Whinnyhouse Plantation
Snow's Green Burn
High Bradley
PONT LANE
Quarry Hill
High Elm Park
Bank Foot Cottage
Derwent Vw.
Pleasant View
Derwent View Bungalow
Derwent Cottages
Bunker's Hill Gate
Field House
Berry Edge Farm
Bunker Hill
Pont
Shotley Bridge
Shotley Bridge Inf. Sch.
Shotley Lodge
SHOTLEY BRIDGE HOSPITAL
MIU
Whitefield Plantation
CONSETT & DISTRICT GOLF COURSE
Tinklerhill Gill
WOODLANDS
ASHFIELD
ROSEDALE
GOLDEN ACRE
Northwood Grange
Running Track
Tower Cottages
Club House
Playing Field
Cricket Ground
BENFIELDSIDE CEMETERY
Blackhill
WERDOHL BUSINESS PARK
NUMBER ONE INDUSTRIAL ESTATE
Jumbo Jungle
Works
Aged Mine Homes
LEADGATE
DURHAM ROAD
MEDOMSLEY ROAD
VILLA REAL ROAD
CONSETT BUSINESS PARK
BRADLEY WORKSHOPS INDUSTRIAL ESTATE
Villa Real School
BELLE VUE PARK
Playing Fields
LEADGATE ROAD
PROSPECT BUSINESS PARK
Blackfyne
Recreation Grounds
West Promenade
THE PROMENADE
CONSETT PARK
CONSETT
Magistrates Ct.
Consett Academy & Leisure Cen.
Playing Field
School
PARK ROAD
LABURNUM AV.
DERWENTDALE INDUSTRIAL ESTATE
PARK ROAD IND. EST.
Depot
PARKSIDE WAY
GENESIS WAY
Bus Sta.
Cthtre. & Cin.
Derwentside College
HERMISTON RETAIL PARK
DERWENTSIDE RETAIL PARK
ROTARY WAY
Football Grd.
Superstore
Care Home
Works
Comm. Cen.
Football Ground
FIRST STREET
SECOND STREET
THIRD STREET
FOURTH STREET
FIFTH STREET
SIXTH STREET
Crookhall

122
MEDOMSLEY
Consett
DH8
LEADGATE
Pont
Iveston
Crookhall
108
136
121
A692
A693
A691
B6309
South Moor Plantation
Little Kipling Plantation
Cockshot Wood
Hollin Hill
Shipmaster's Hill
Pontop Low Wood
South Moor
Intake Plantation
Black Bog
Bradley Wood
Bradley Hall
Low Bradley
Pithouse Plantation
Pontop Springpit Wood
High Bradley
Tewit Hill
Billingside Wood
Works
West Billingside
Pontop High Stables
BILLINGSIDE PLANTATION
Bunker's Hill Gate
Pont House Farm
Playground
Brooms Farm
Aged Miners' Homes
Redwell Hills Farm
Our Lady & St. Joseph's RC Prim. Sch.
Brooms Dene
High Brooms
Low Brooms Farm
BRADLEY WORKSHOPS INDUSTRIAL ESTATE
Cricket Grd.
Football Ground
Leadgate Jun. Sch.
Playing Fields
PROSPECT BUSINESS PARK
Copwell House Farm
Stonyheap Wood
Crook Hall Farm
Comm. Cen.
Sewage Works
Opencast Workings
LEADGATE INDUSTRIAL ESTATE
Handwell Hill
Bank Foot Farm
Rose Cottage
Bank Top Farm
Woody Close Farm
Lope Hill
Johnson's Buildings
Parker's Buildings
Townhead Farm
Whitehall Farm

123
DIPTON
A692
Pontop
Pontop Hall
Pontop Pike
TV & Wireless Transmission Station
Pontop Pike Farm
West Pike Well
Pontop Pike Park
Rec. Grd.
Collierley Prim. Sch.
Sports Field
Play. Fld.
Vicarage
Simpson's Hill
Grave Yard
Fondley Set
Stob House
St. Patrick's RC Prim. Sch.
Works
HARELAW INDUSTRIAL ESTATE
Bush Blades
Bushblades Mews
Hare Law
Hare Law Farm
Harelaw Watering Place
Harelaw
Cemetery
Carrmyers Farm
Burn
Playing Field
Hare Law Sch.
Catchgate
West Kyo
Ridings Hills
Stanley
DH9
Football Field
ANNFIELD PLAIN
East Castle
Catchgate Prim. Sch.
Playing Field
Loud Farm
Annfield House
Loud Hill
Loud Reservoir (cov.)
Oakwood Court
Cricket Ground
Greencroft
War Memorial
Annfield Plain Inf. Sch.
Football Ground
Annfield Plain Park
Playground
Stony Heap
Coronation House
Hanging Stone
Barley Banks
Sunnyside
Boxers' Hill
Gorecock Plantation
Pit House
Barley Hill
Humber Vw.
Works
GREENCROFT INDUSTRIAL PARK
GREENCROFT INDUSTRIAL ESTATE
THE GREENHOUSE
Park Head
Durham Hill
Durhamhill Wood
A693
PLAIN BY-PASS
FRONT STREET
NORTH ROAD
B6168
BUSHBLADES LANE
FONDLYSET LA. or THE AVENUE
DELIGHT BANK
PONTOP PIKE LANE
STONYHEAP LANE
HANGINGSTONE LANE
ANNFIELD PLAIN BY-PASS
WEST ROAD
NEW FRONT ST.
FRONT ST.
STATION RD.
GORECOCK LANE
TOWER ROAD
GREENCROFT ROAD
PARKWAY
PARKHEAD
KYO HEUGH RD.
HARPERLEY
109
124
137
F
G
H
J
K
1
2
3
4
5
6
7
415
16
17
554
53
52
51

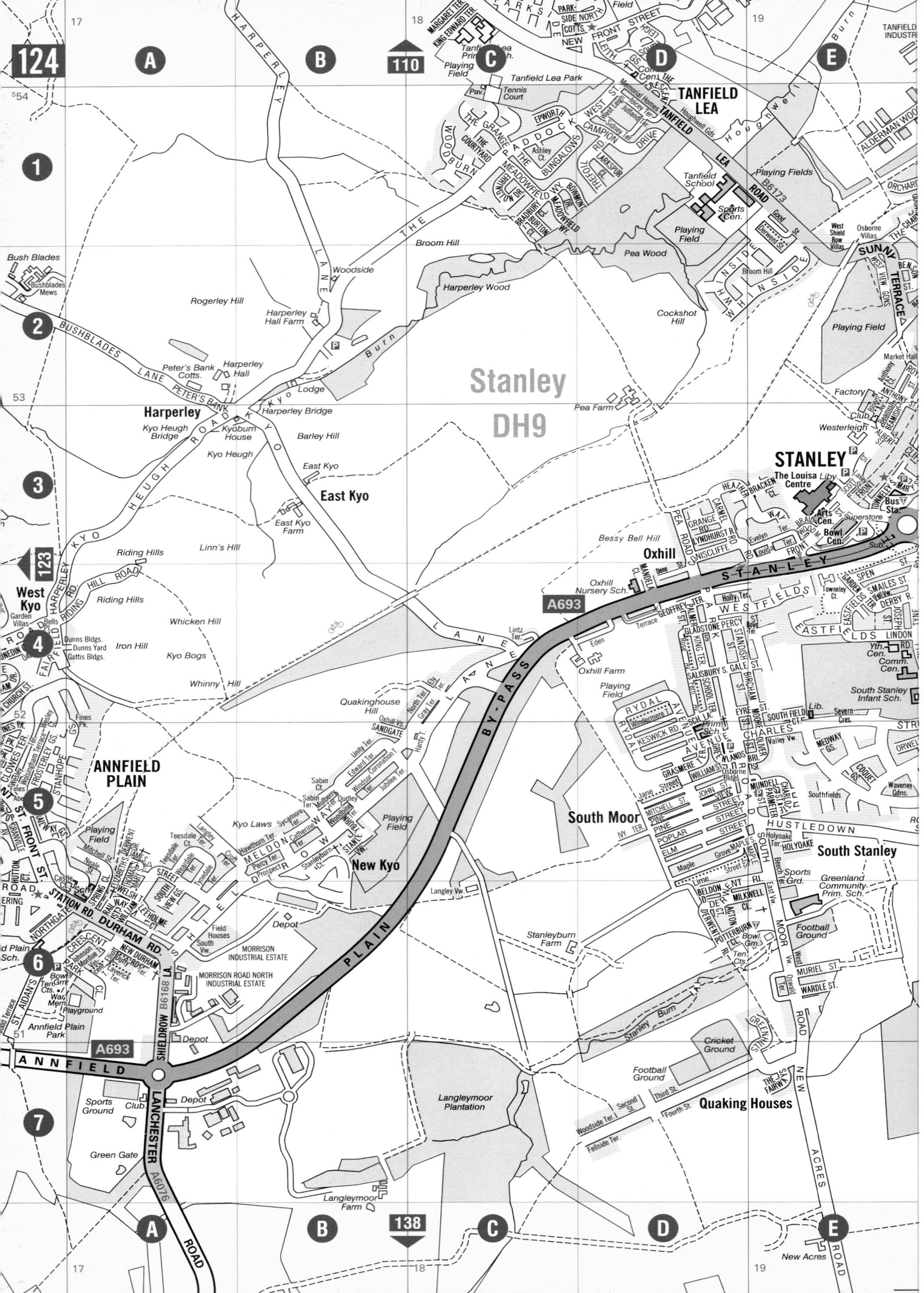
Stanley
DH9
STANLEY
TANFIELD LEA
Annfield Plain
Harperley
East Kyo
West Kyo
New Kyo
Oxhill
South Moor
South Stanley
Quaking Houses
Tanfield Lea Park
Tanfield School
Playing Fields
Harperley Wood
Pea Wood
Broom Hill
Cockshot Hill
Rogerley Hill
Harperley Hall Farm
Bush Blades
Peter's Bank Cotts.
Harperley Hall
Harperley Bridge
Kyo Heugh Bridge
Kyoburn House
Kyo Heugh
Barley Hill
East Kyo Farm
Linn's Hill
Riding Hills
Whicken Hill
Iron Hill
Kyo Bogs
Whinny Hill
Bessy Bell Hill
Pea Farm
Oxhill Farm
Oxhill Nursery Sch.
The Louisa Centre
South Stanley Infant Sch.
Kyo Laws
Quakinghouse Hill
Stanleyburn Farm
Morrison Industrial Estate
Morrison Road North Industrial Estate
Annfield Plain Park
Sports Ground
Green Gate
Langleymoor Plantation
Langleymoor Farm
Cricket Ground
Football Ground
Greenland Community Prim. Sch.
New Acres
A693
B6173
B6168
A6076
Annfield Plain By-Pass
Stanley Burn
110
123
138

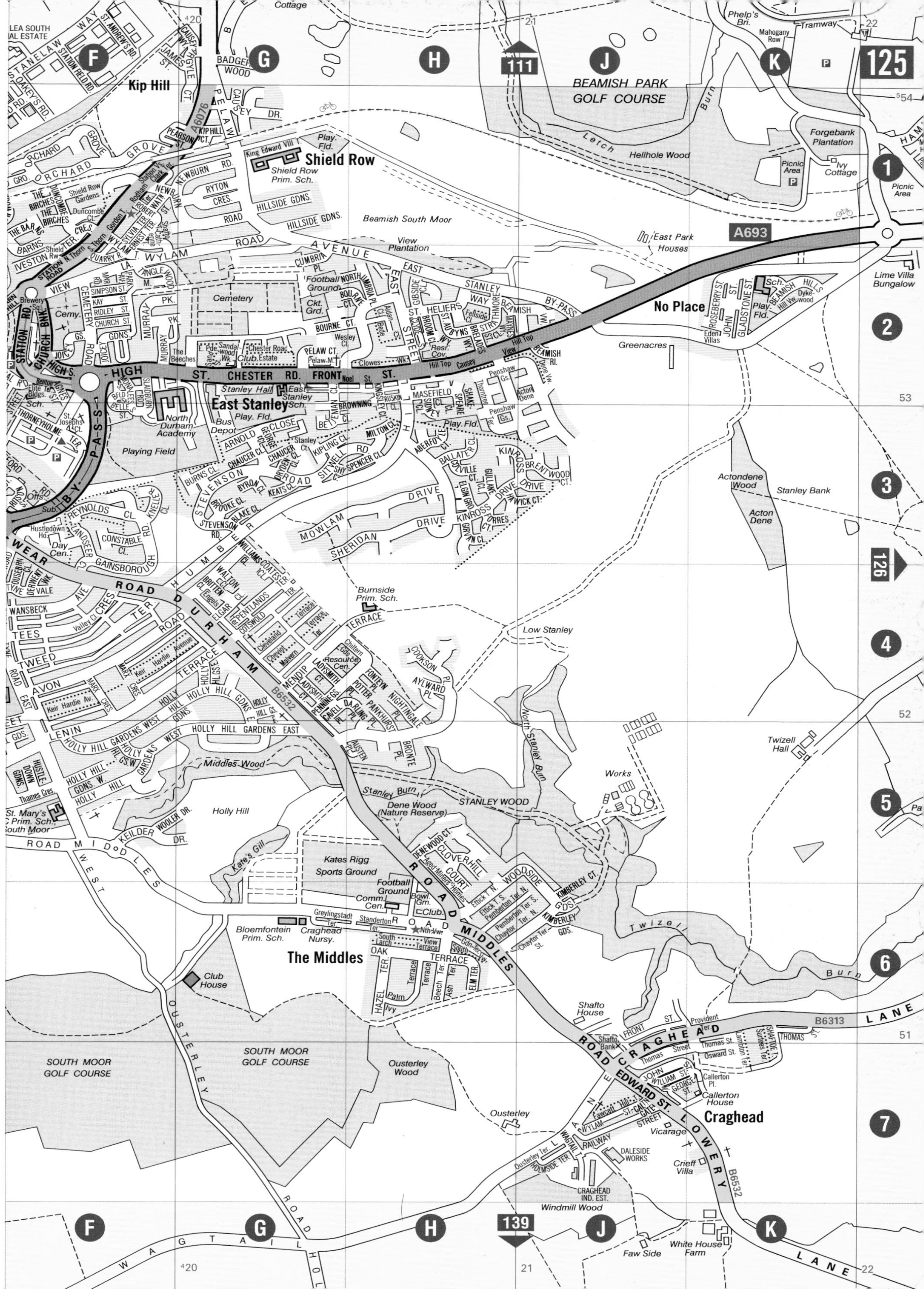
Kip Hill
Shield Row
Shield Row Prim. Sch.
BEAMISH PARK GOLF COURSE
Hellhole Wood
Forgebank Plantation
Ivy Cottage
Beamish South Moor
View Plantation
East Park Houses
A693
No Place
Lime Villa Bungalow
Greenacres
Cemetery
East Stanley
North Durham Academy
Playing Field
Stanley Hall
Actondene Wood
Stanley Bank
Acton Dene
Burnside Prim. Sch.
Low Stanley
Twizell Hall
Works
North Stanley Burn
Stanley Burn
Dene Wood (Nature Reserve)
STANLEY WOOD
Middles Wood
Holly Hill
Kate's Gill
Kates Rigg Sports Ground
Football Ground
The Middles
Bloemfontein Prim. Sch.
Craghead Nursy.
Club House
SOUTH MOOR GOLF COURSE
Ousterley Wood
Ousterley
Shafto House
Craghead
Callerton House
Vicarage
Crieff Villa
DALESIDE WORKS
CRAGHEAD IND. EST.
Windmill Wood
Faw Side
White House Farm
Twizell Burn
B6532
B6313
A6076
DURHAM ROAD
MIDDLES ROAD
WAGTAIL LANE
LOWERY LANE
F G H J K
1 2 3 4 5 6 7
111
126
139

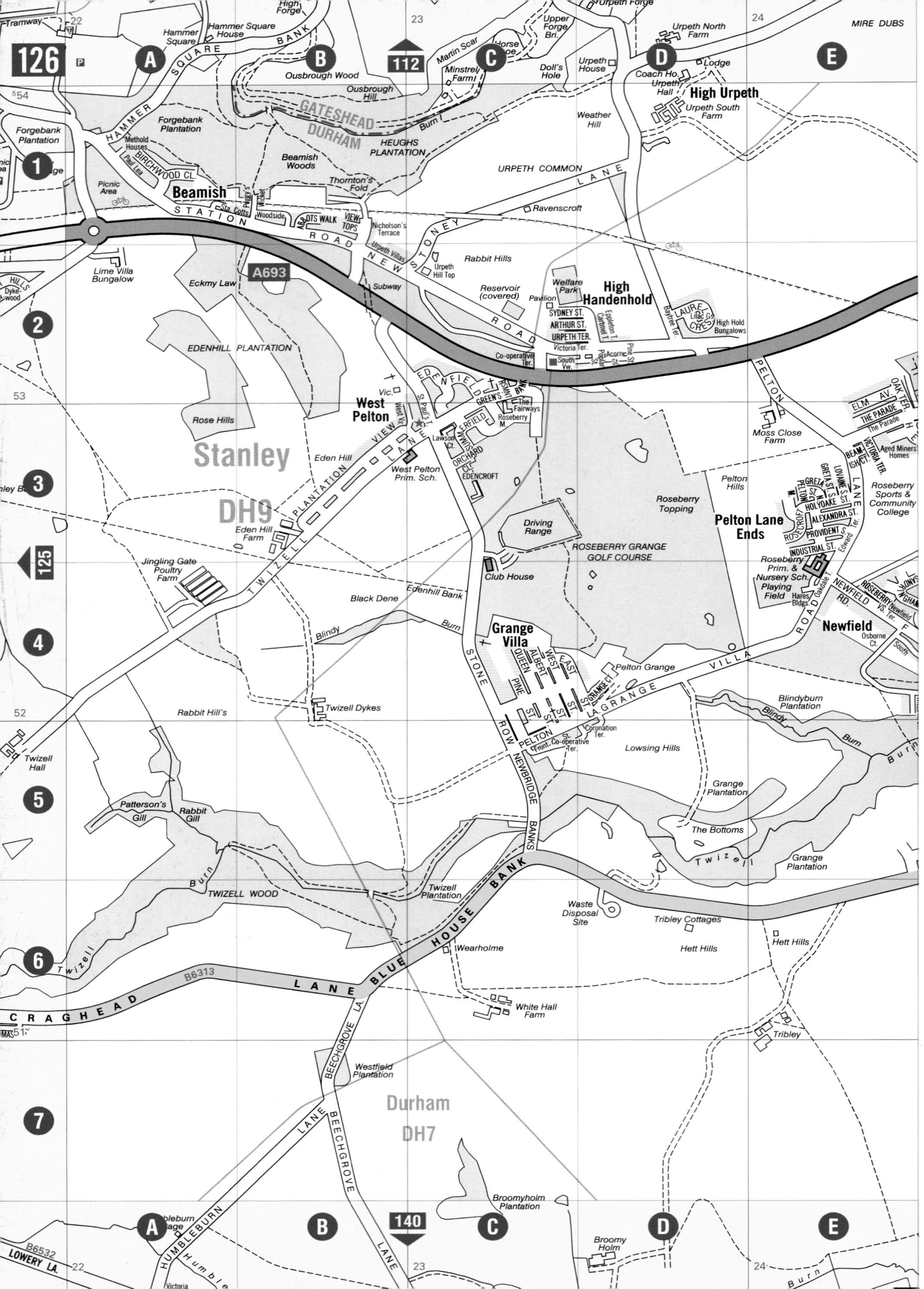
112
140
125
High Forge
Hammer Square House
Hammer Square
HAMMER SQUARE BANK
Ousbrough Wood
Ousbrough Hill
GATESHEAD
DURHAM
Martin Scar
Horse Shoe
Minstrel Farm
Upper Forge Bri.
Doll's Hole
Urpeth House
Urpeth Forge
Urpeth North Farm
MIRE DUBS
Lodge
Coach Ho.
Urpeth Hall
High Urpeth
Urpeth South Farm
Weather Hill
Forgebank Plantation
Forgebank Plantation
HEUGHS PLANTATION
Beamish Woods
Burn
Methold Houses
BIRCHWOOD CL.
Paul Lea
URPETH COMMON
LANE
Picnic Area
Beamish
Thornton's Fold
Sta. Cotts
Woodside
ABBOTS WALK
VIEW TOPS
STATION ROAD
Nicholson's Terrace
Ravenscroft
STONEY
NEW ROAD
Urpeth Villas
Rabbit Hills
Urpeth Hill Top
Lime Villa Bungalow
Eckmy Law
A693
Subway
Reservoir (covered)
Welfare Park
High Handenhold
Pavilion
SYDNEY ST.
ARTHUR ST.
URPETH TER.
Victoria Ter.
Eppleton T.
Carmel T.
Bayfree Ter.
LAUREL CRES.
Lilac Gs.
High Hold Bungalows
EDENHILL PLANTATION
Co-operative Ter.
South Vw.
Poplar St.
Acorn St.
Pine St.
PELTON
53
Vic.
West Pelton
West Vs.
St. Paul's T.
EDENFIELD
GREEN'S
ROSEMOUNT
BANK
The Fairways
Roseberry M.
Rose Hills
Lawson Ct.
WINSHIELDS
ORCHARD
CL.
EDENCROFT
OAK TER.
ELM AV.
THE PARADE
The Parade
Moss Close Farm
Aged Miners' Homes
Stanley
Eden Hill
PLANTATION VIEW
LANE
West Pelton Prim. Sch.
BEAMISH CT.
VICTORIA TER.
Pelton Hills
LOVAINE ST.
GRETA ST.
PELTON ST.
HOLYOAKE ST.
ALEXANDRA ST.
PROVIDENT ST.
ROSECROFT
INDUSTRIAL ST.
Edward Ter.
Roseberry Topping
Pelton Lane Ends
Roseberry Sports & Community College
DH9
Eden Hill Farm
Driving Range
ROSEBERRY GRANGE GOLF COURSE
Jingling Gate Poultry Farm
TWIZELL
Club House
Roseberry Prim. & Nursery Sch.
Playing Field
Hares Bldgs
Oakdale T.
NEWFIELD RD.
ROSEBERRY
Newfield Ter.
Edenhill Bank
Black Dene
Blindy
Burn
Grange Villa
Newfield
Osborne Ct.
South
STONE
QUEEN
ALBERT
WEST
EAST
PINE
ST.
GRANGE CT.
Pelton Grange
LA. GRANGE VILLA ROAD
Blindyburn Plantation
52
Rabbit Hill's
Twizell Dykes
ROW
PELTON
NEWBRIDGE
Front St.
Co-operative Ter.
Coronation Ter.
Lowsing Hills
Twizell Hall
Grange Plantation
Patterson's Gill
Rabbit Gill
BANKS
The Bottoms
Twizell
Grange Plantation
TWIZELL WOOD
Twizell Plantation
BLUE HOUSE BANK
Waste Disposal Site
Tribley Cottages
Wearholme
Hett Hills
Hett Hills
B6313
CRAGHEAD LANE
White Hall Farm
Tribley
51
BEECHGROVE LA.
Westfield Plantation
Durham
DH7
BEECHGROVE LANE
Broomyholm Plantation
Humbleburn Cottage
HUMBLEBURN LANE
B6532
LOWERY LA.
Broomy Holm
Victoria
22
23
24

F
G
H
J
K
Perkinsville
Recreation Ground
Playing Fld.
Football Ground
SANDY FORDS
Ouston Villa Farm
Works
DRUM INDUSTRIAL ESTATE
DRUM PARK
Pelaw Grange Stadium
PELTON
Pelton Comm. Prim. Sch.
East Farm
HARE LAW
A693
HIGH FLATTS
High Flatts Farm
Warehouse
Playing Field
PELTON HOUSE FARM ESTATE
Chester-le-Street
DH2
Newfield Farm
South Pelaw
128
Memorial Park
STELLA GILL INDUSTRIAL ESTATE
Pelton Fell Banks
Stella Gill
Stellagill Wood
PELTON FELL
PELTON FELL ROAD
B6313
Chester Furnace Bridge
Furnace Farm
Whitehill Hall
The Old Hall
Playing Field
Rutter's Plantation
Whitehill
Lindisfarne Nurs. Home
The Hermitage Academy
CHESTER-LE-STREET
Whitehill Villa
Newker Primary School
Waldridge House
Congburn Plantation
Dene Cottages
113
141
1
2
3
4
5
6
7

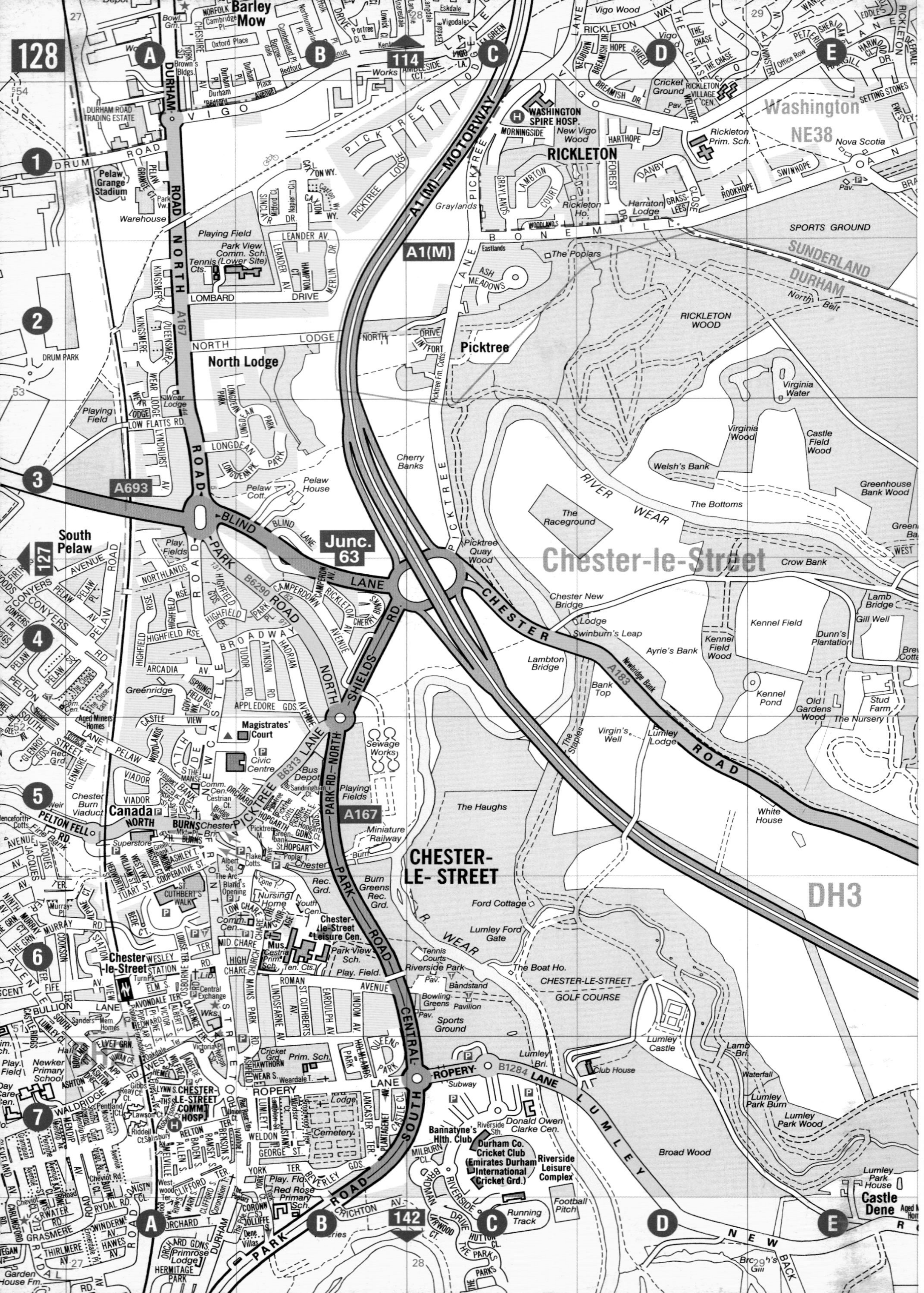
Barley Mow
114
Vigo Wood
RICKLETON WAY
Washington
NE38
WASHINGTON SPIRE HOSP.
RICKLETON
Rickleton Prim. Sch.
Nova Scotia
DURHAM ROAD TRADING ESTATE
VIGO
DRUM ROAD
Pelaw Grange Stadium
A1(M) MOTORWAY
A1(M)
Playing Field
Park View Comm. Sch. (Lower Site)
SPORTS GROUND
SUNDERLAND
DURHAM
RICKLETON WOOD
NORTH LODGE
North Lodge
Picktree
DRUM PARK
A167
Virginia Water
Virginia Wood
Castle Field Wood
Cherry Banks
Welsh's Bank
A693
Pelaw House
RIVER WEAR
The Raceground
The Bottoms
Greenhouse Bank Wood
South Pelaw
127
Junc. 63
BLIND LANE
Picktree Quay Wood
Chester-le-Street
Crow Bank
B6290
Chester New Bridge
Kennel Field
Lamb Bridge
Gill Well
Swinburn's Leap
Ayrie's Bank
Kennel Field Wood
Dunn's Plantation
Lambton Bridge
A183
Newbridge Bank
CHESTER ROAD
Kennel Pond
Old Gardens Wood
Stud Farm
The Nursery
Bank Top
Virgin's Well
Lumley Lodge
The Staples
Magistrates' Court
Civic Centre
Sewage Works
B6313
Canada
Bus Depot
Playing Fields
A167
The Haughs
White House
PELTON FELL RD.
Chester Burn Viaduct
Miniature Railway
CHESTER-LE-STREET
DH3
Nursing Home
Ford Cottage
Chester-le-Street Leisure Cen.
Lumley Ford Gate
R. WEAR
Chester-le-Street
The Boat Ho.
CHESTER-LE-STREET GOLF COURSE
Riverside Park
Bandstand
Sports Ground
Lumley Castle
Lamb Bri.
Lumley Bri.
B1284
ROPERY LANE
Club House
Waterfall
Lumley Park Burn
Lumley Park Wood
CHESTER-LE-STREET COMM. HOSP.
Cemetery
Bannatyne's Hlth. Club
Durham Co. Cricket Club (Emirates Durham International Cricket Grd.)
Riverside Leisure Complex
Broad Wood
Lumley Park House
Castle Dene
Running Track
Football Pitch
LUMLEY
Red Rose Primary Sch.
142
NEW BACK
PARK ROAD
SOUTH CENTRAL ROAD
Primrose Lodge
Garden House Fm.

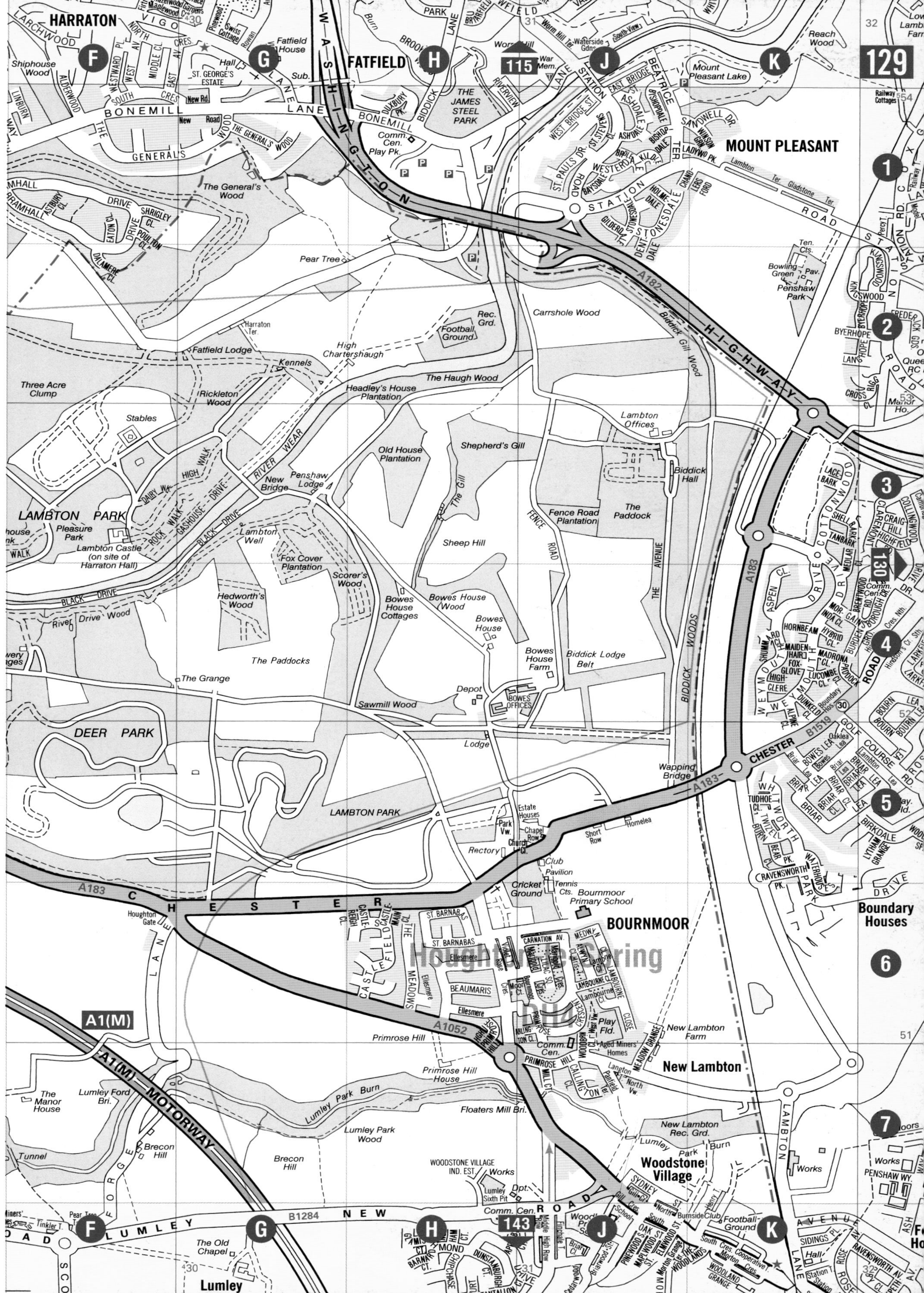
HARRATON
FATFIELD
MOUNT PLEASANT
LAMBTON PARK
DEER PARK
BOURNMOOR
Houghton-le-Spring
DH4
New Lambton
Woodstone Village
Boundary Houses
Lumley
WASHINGTON HIGHWAY
A182
A183
A1(M)
A1(M) MOTORWAY
A1052
B1519
B1284
CHESTER
NEW ROAD
LUMLEY
RIVER WEAR
BONEMILL LANE
STATION ROAD
115
130
143

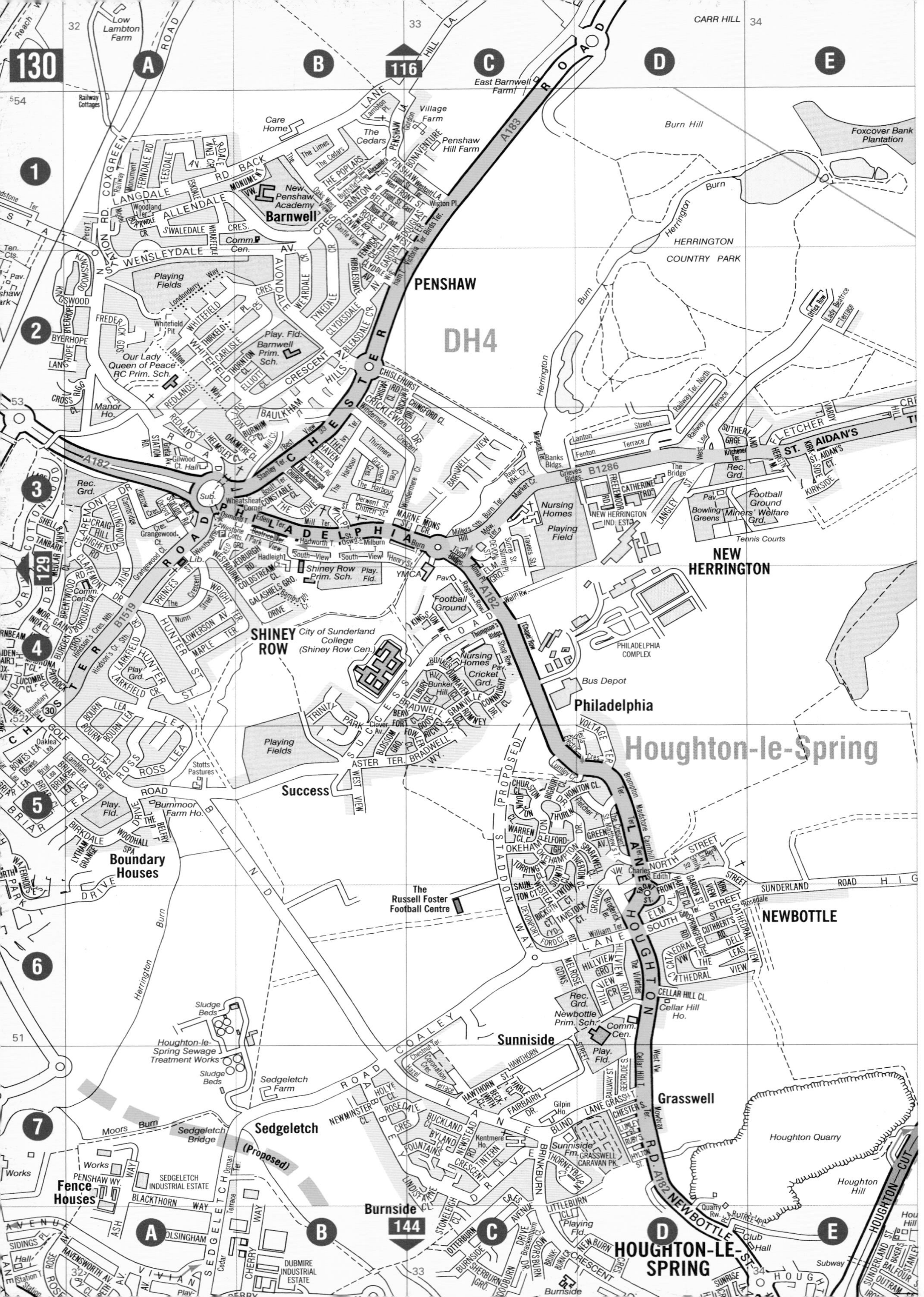

116
129
144
A
B
C
D
E
1
2
3
4
5
6
7
32
33
34
54
53
52
51
CARR HILL
Low Lambton Farm
Railway Cottages
Care Home
Village Farm
The Cedars
Penshaw Hill Farm
East Barnwell Farm
Burn Hill
Foxcover Bank Plantation
New Penshaw Academy
Barnwell
HERRINGTON COUNTRY PARK
PENSHAW
Playing Fields
Play. Fld. Barnwell Prim. Sch.
Our Lady Queen of Peace RC Prim. Sch.
DH4
Manor Ho.
A182
A183
B1286
B1519
Rec. Grd.
Nursing Homes
Playing Field
NEW HERRINGTON IND. EST.
Football Ground
Miners' Welfare Grd.
Bowling Greens
Tennis Courts
NEW HERRINGTON
Shiney Row Prim. Sch.
Play. Fld.
YMCA
Football Ground
SHINEY ROW
City of Sunderland College (Shiney Row Cen.)
PHILADELPHIA COMPLEX
Bus Depot
Philadelphia
Houghton-le-Spring
Cricket Grd.
Nursing Homes
Playing Fields
Stotts Pastures
Success
Burnmoor Farm Ho.
Boundary Houses
The Russell Foster Football Centre
NEWBOTTLE
Cellar Hill Ho.
Rec. Grd.
Newbottle Prim. Sch.
Comm. Cen.
Sunniside
Play. Fld.
Grasswell
Houghton Quarry
Houghton Hill
Sludge Beds
Houghton-le-Spring Sewage Treatment Works
Sedgeletch Farm
Sedgeletch
Sedgeletch Bridge
(Proposed)
Moors Burn
Works
Fence Houses
SEDGELETCH INDUSTRIAL ESTATE
DUBMIRE INDUSTRIAL ESTATE
Burnside
Sunniside Fm.
GRASSWELL CARAVAN PK.
Playing Fld.
Club Hall
Subway
HOUGHTON-LE-SPRING
HOUGHTON CUT

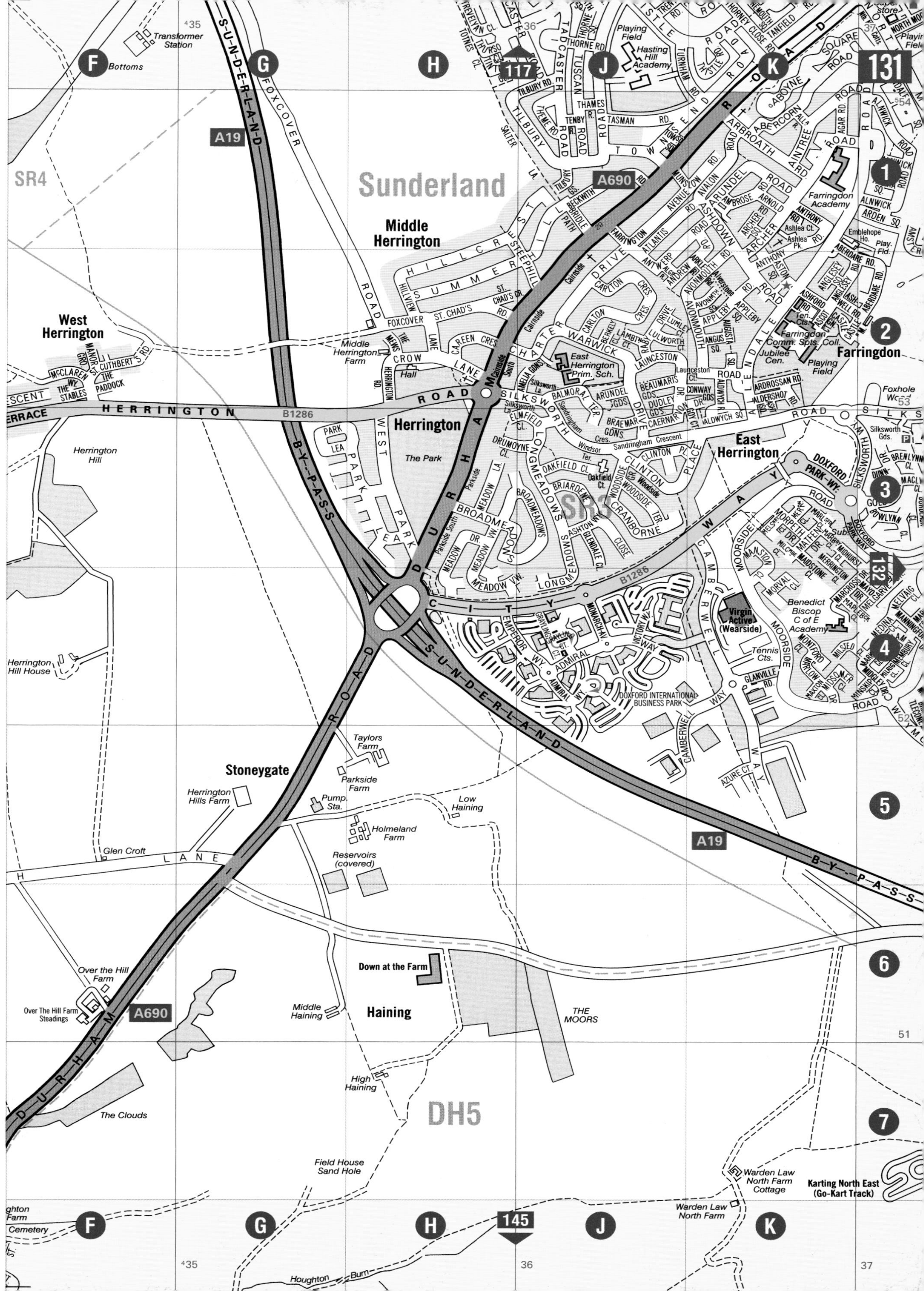

Sunderland
Middle Herrington
West Herrington
Herrington
East Herrington
Farringdon
Stoneygate
Haining
SR4
SR3
DH5
A19
A690
B1286
SUNDERLAND BY-PASS
DURHAM ROAD
HERRINGTON ROAD
CITY WAY
DOXFORD PARK WAY
SILKSWORTH ROAD
TOWNEND ROAD
FOXCOVER ROAD
Bottoms
Transformer Station
Playing Field
Hasting Hill Academy
Farringdon Academy
Ashlea Ct.
Ashlea Pk.
Emblehope Ho.
Play. Fld.
Middle Herrington Farm
Crow Hall
East Herrington Prim. Sch.
Farringdon Comm. Spts. Coll.
Jubilee Cen.
Ten. Cts.
Herrington Hill
The Park
Foxhole Wood
Benedict Biscop C of E Academy
Virgin Active (Wearside)
Tennis Cts.
DOXFORD INTERNATIONAL BUSINESS PARK
Herrington Hill House
Taylors Farm
Parkside Farm
Herrington Hills Farm
Pump. Sta.
Low Haining
Holmeland Farm
Glen Croft
Reservoirs (covered)
LANE
Down at the Farm
Over the Hill Farm
Over The Hill Farm Steadings
Middle Haining
THE MOORS
High Haining
The Clouds
Field House Sand Hole
Warden Law North Farm Cottage
Warden Law North Farm
Karting North East (Go-Kart Track)
Cemetery
Houghton Burn
117
132
145
F
G
H
J
K
1
2
3
4
5
6
7
435
36
37
51
52
53
54

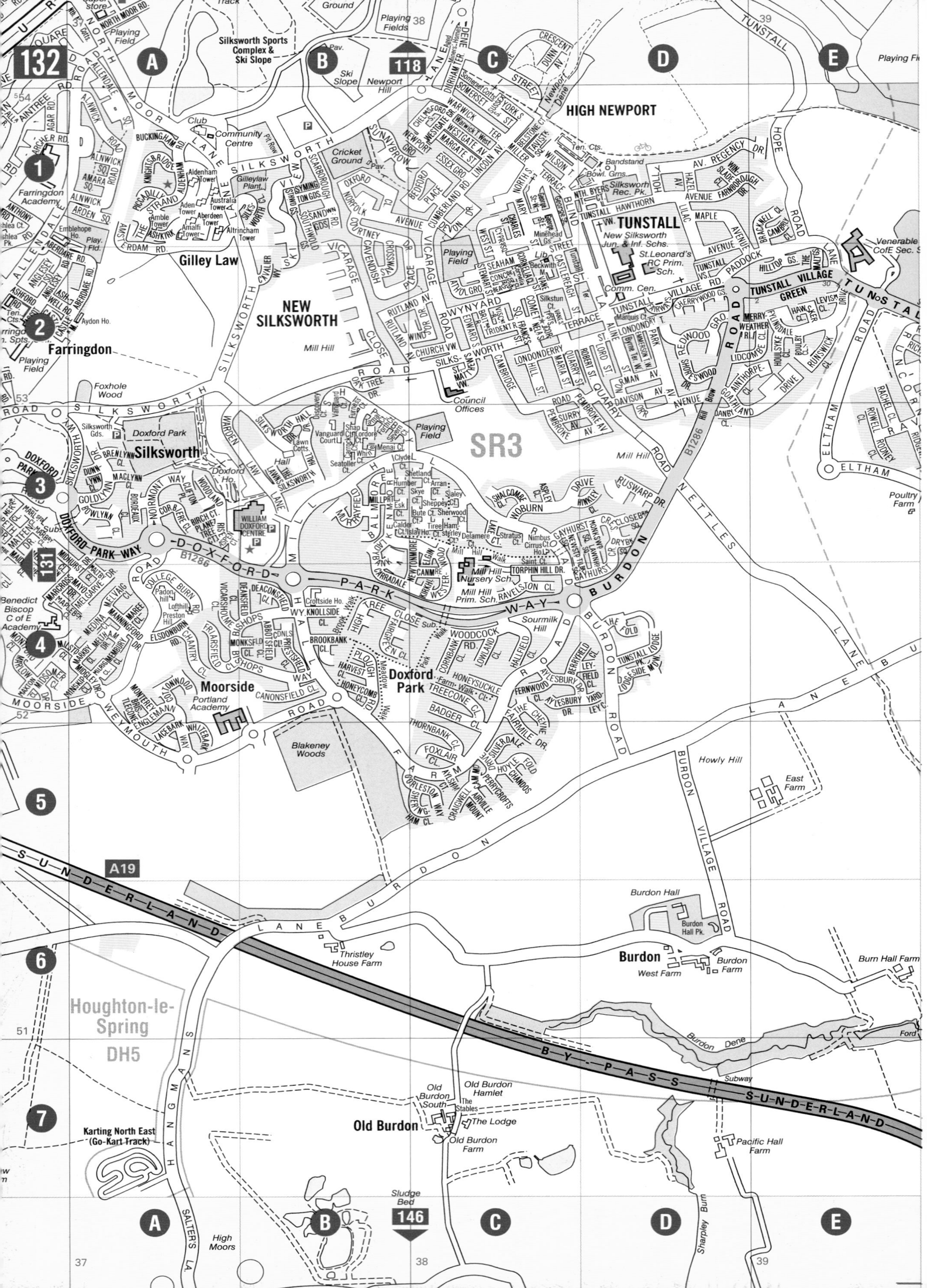

132
118
146
131
A
B
C
D
E
1
2
3
4
5
6
7
Silksworth Sports Complex & Ski Slope
Ski Slope
Newport Hill
HIGH NEWPORT
TUNSTALL
Tunstall Village
NEW SILKSWORTH
Gilley Law
Farringdon
Farringdon Academy
Silksworth
Doxford Park
SR3
Moorside
Portland Academy
Blakeney Woods
William Doxford Centre
Mill Hill
Mill Hill Nursery Sch.
Mill Hill Prim. Sch.
Council Offices
Cricket Ground
Playing Field
Silksworth Rec. Pk.
New Silksworth Jun. & Inf. Schs.
St.Leonard's RC Prim. Sch.
Venerable CofE Sec. Sch.
Benedict Biscop C of E Academy
Foxhole Wood
Sourmilk Hill
Howly Hill
East Farm
Poultry Farm
Burdon Hall
Burdon Hall Pk.
Burdon
West Farm
Burdon Farm
Burn Hall Farm
Thristley House Farm
Burdon Dene
Ford
Subway
Houghton-le-Spring
DH5
Old Burdon
Old Burdon Hamlet
Old Burdon South
The Stables
The Lodge
Old Burdon Farm
Pacific Hall Farm
Karting North East (Go-Kart Track)
High Moors
Sludge Bed
Sharpley Burn
A19
SUNDERLAND BY-PASS
DOXFORD PARK WAY
B1286
BURDON LANE
BURDON ROAD
BURDON VILLAGE ROAD
NETTLES LANE
HANGMANS LA.
SALTERS LA.
SILKSWORTH ROAD
SILKSWORTH LANE
MOOR LANE
MOORSIDE ROAD
WEYMOUTH ROAD
FARM ROAD
TUNSTALL ROAD
ELTHAM ROAD
37
38
39
51
52
53
54

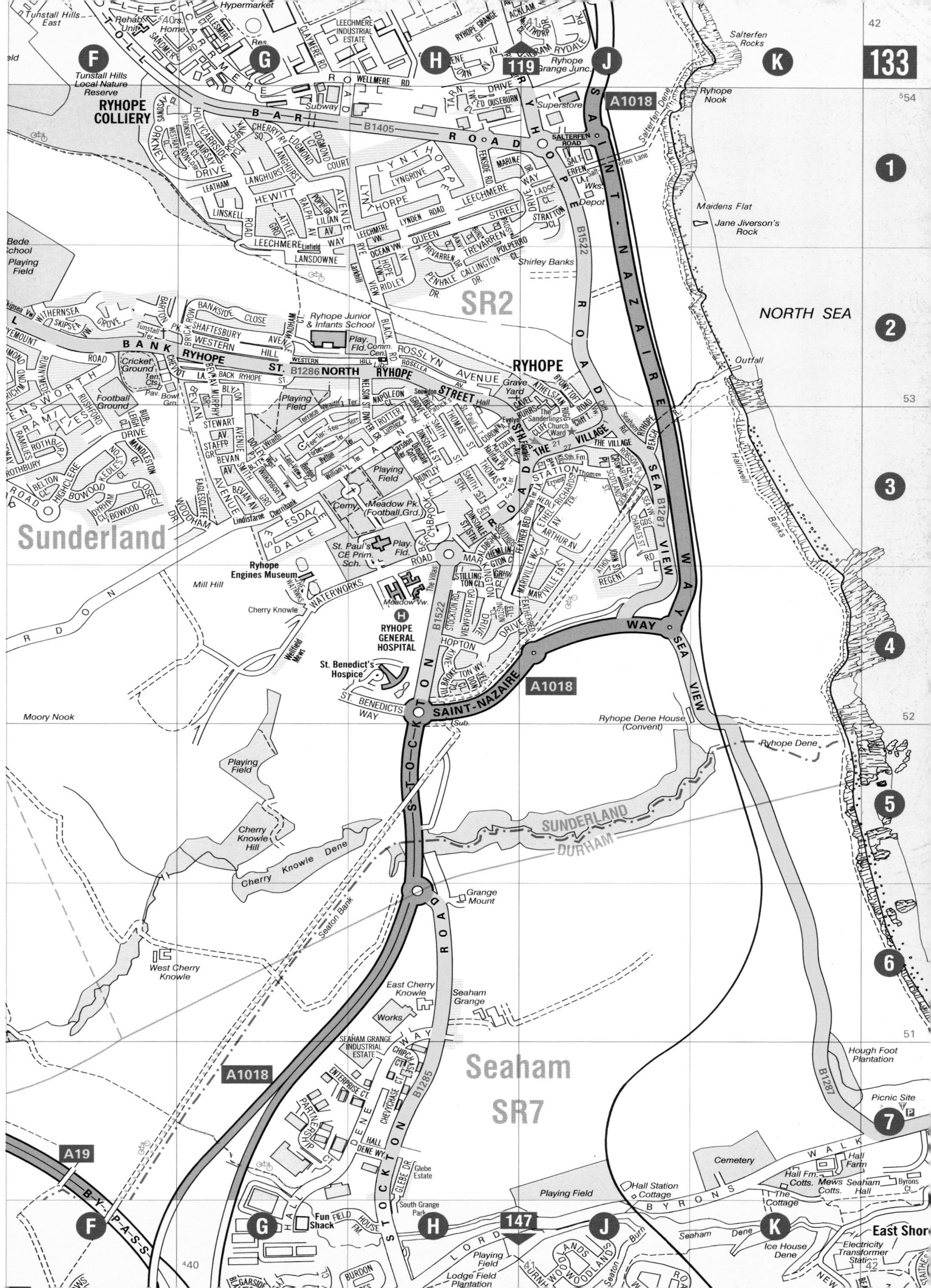
133
42
F
G
H
J
K
119
Hypermarket
Tunstall Hills East
Rehab. Unit
Home
Tunstall Hills Local Nature Reserve
RYHOPE COLLIERY
LEECHMERE INDUSTRIAL ESTATE
Ryhope Grange Junc.
Salterfen Rocks
Ryhope Nook
A1018
Superstore
BARNES ROAD
B1405
Subway
SALTERFEN ROAD
Depot
Maidens Flat
Jane Jiverson's Rock
Shirley Banks
Bede School
Playing Field
SR2
NORTH SEA
Ryhope Junior & Infants School
RYHOPE
B1286
RYHOPE STREET NORTH
Cricket Ground
Football Ground
Grave Yard
Outfall
THE VILLAGE
Church
Playing Field
Cemy.
Meadow Pk. (Football Grd.)
St. Paul's CE Prim. Sch.
Sunderland
Ryhope Engines Museum
Mill Hill
Cherry Knowle
RYHOPE GENERAL HOSPITAL
St. Benedict's Hospice
SAINT-NAZAIRE WAY
B1522
B1287
SEA VIEW
Hallwell Banks
Moory Nook
Ryhope Dene House (Convent)
Ryhope Dene
Playing Field
Cherry Knowle Hill
Cherry Knowle Dene
SUNDERLAND
DURHAM
Grange Mount
Seaton Bank
STOCKTON ROAD
West Cherry Knowle
East Cherry Knowle
Seaham Grange
Works
SEAHAM GRANGE INDUSTRIAL ESTATE
Seaham
SR7
B1285
Hough Foot Plantation
Picnic Site
A19
BY-PASS
Cemetery
Hall Farm
Playing Field
Hall Station Cottage
Seaham Hall
BYRONS WALK
Fun Shack
South Grange Park
Glebe Estate
147
Seaham Dene
Ice House Dene
East Shore
Electricity Transformer Station
Lodge Field Plantation
1
2
3
4
5
6
7
554
53
52
51
440
41
42

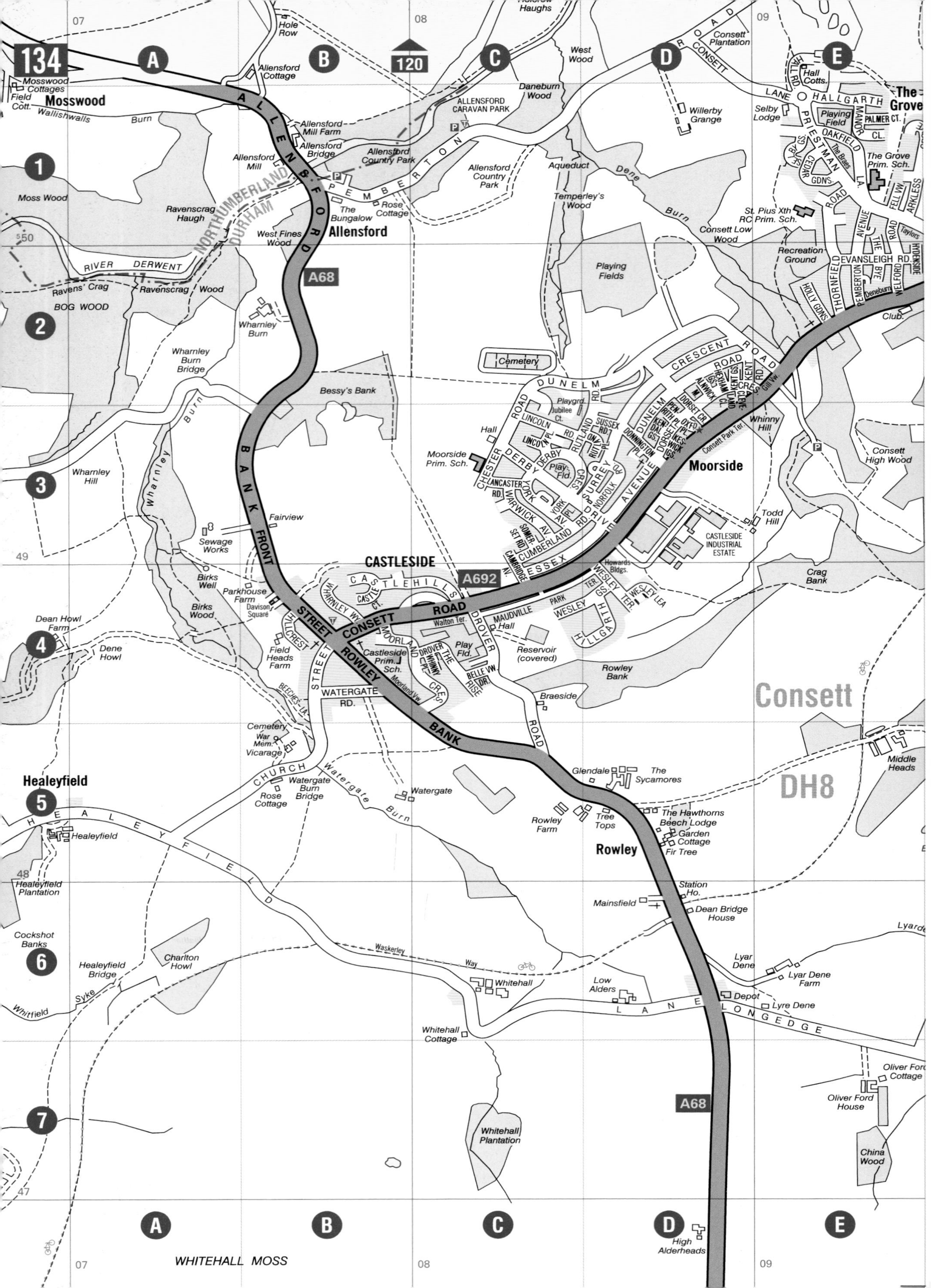
120
Mosswood
Allensford
Castleside
Moorside
Consett
DH8
Rowley
Healeyfield
The Grove
A68
A692
Allensford Bank
Front Street
Consett Road
Rowley Bank
Drover Road
Church Street
Healeyfield Lane
Longedge Lane
Pemberton Road
River Derwent
Northumberland
Durham
Allensford Country Park
Allensford Caravan Park
Moorside Prim. Sch.
Castleside Prim. Sch.
Castleside Industrial Estate
Waskerley Way
Whitehall Moss
Whitehall Plantation
China Wood
Crag Bank
Middle Heads
Bessy's Bank
Playing Fields
Cemetery
Sewage Works
Reservoir (covered)
Whitehall
Rowley Farm
Mainsfield
High Alderheads

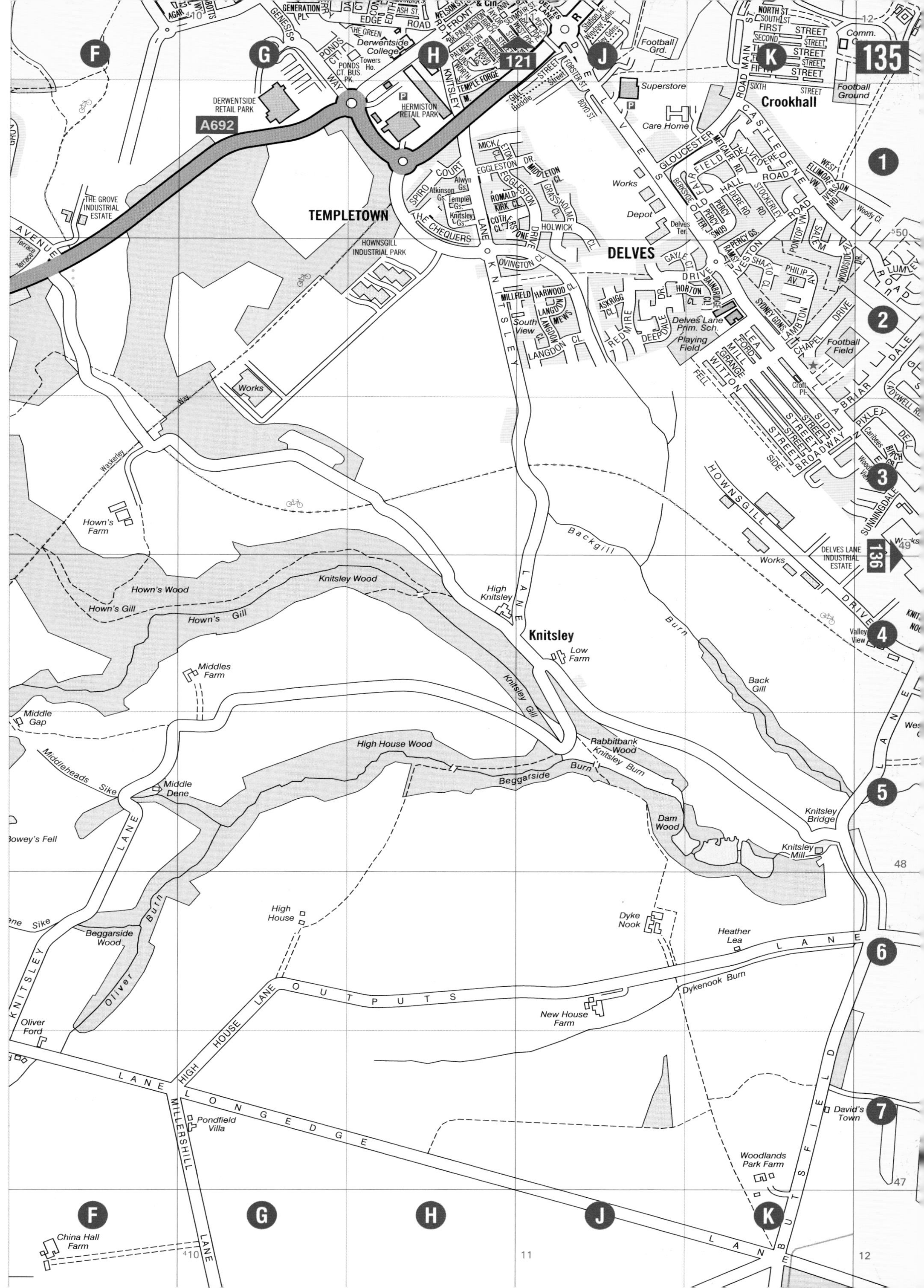

135
121
136
A692
TEMPLETOWN
DELVES
Crookhall
Knitsley
Derwentside College
DERWENTSIDE RETAIL PARK
HERMISTON RETAIL PARK
THE GROVE INDUSTRIAL ESTATE
HOWNSGILL INDUSTRIAL PARK
DELVES LANE INDUSTRIAL ESTATE
Superstore
Care Home
Football Grd.
Football Ground
Football Field
Delves Lane Prim. Sch.
Playing Field
Works
Depot
Hown's Farm
Hown's Wood
Hown's Gill
Knitsley Wood
High Knitsley
Low Farm
Knitsley Gill
Middles Farm
Middle Gap
Middle Dene
Middleheads Sike
Bowey's Fell
High House Wood
Rabbitbank Wood
Knitsley Burn
Beggarside Burn
Beggarside Wood
Oliver Burn
Oliver Ford
Dam Wood
Knitsley Mill
Knitsley Bridge
Back Gill
Backgill Burn
High House
Dyke Nook
Heather Lea
New House Farm
Dykenook Burn
OUTPUTS LANE
HIGH HOUSE LANE
LONGEDGE LANE
MILLERSHILL LANE
KNITSLEY LANE
BUTSFIELD LANE
Pondfield Villa
China Hall Farm
Woodlands Park Farm
David's Town
Valley View
Waskerley Way
F
G
H
J
K
1
2
3
4
5
6
7

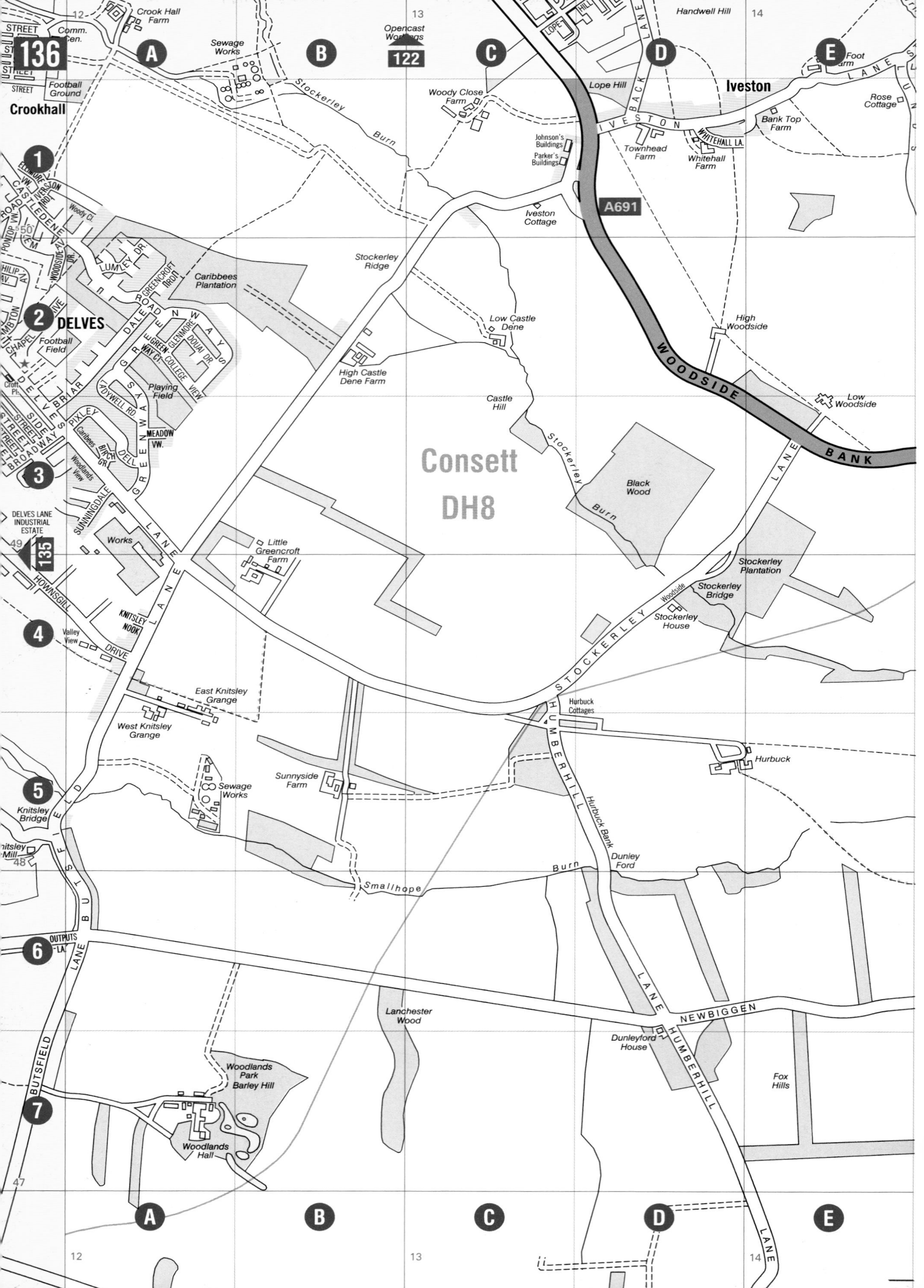
Crook Hall Farm
Comm. Cen.
Sewage Works
Opencast Workings
122
Football Ground
Crookhall
Stockerley Burn
Woody Close Farm
Lope Hill
Iveston
Handwell Hill
Rose Cottage
Bank Top Farm
Townhead Farm
Whitehall Farm
WHITEHALL LA.
Johnson's Buildings
Parker's Buildings
Iveston Cottage
A691
DELVES
Football Field
Caribbees Plantation
Stockerley Ridge
Low Castle Dene
High Castle Dene Farm
High Woodside
WOODSIDE BANK
Low Woodside
Playing Field
Castle Hill
Consett
DH8
Black Wood
DELVES LANE INDUSTRIAL ESTATE
135
Works
Little Greencroft Farm
Stockerley Plantation
Stockerley Bridge
Stockerley House
KNITSLEY NOOK
Valley View
East Knitsley Grange
West Knitsley Grange
Hurbuck Cottages
Hurbuck
Sewage Works
Sunnyside Farm
Knitsley Bridge
Knitsley Mill
Hurbuck Bank
Dunley Ford
Smallhope Burn
OUTPUTS LA.
BUTSFIELD LANE
NEWBIGGEN LANE
HUMBERHILL LANE
Lanchester Wood
Dunleyford House
Fox Hills
Woodlands Park Barley Hill
Woodlands Hall
A B C D E
1 2 3 4 5 6 7
12 13 14
47 48 49 50

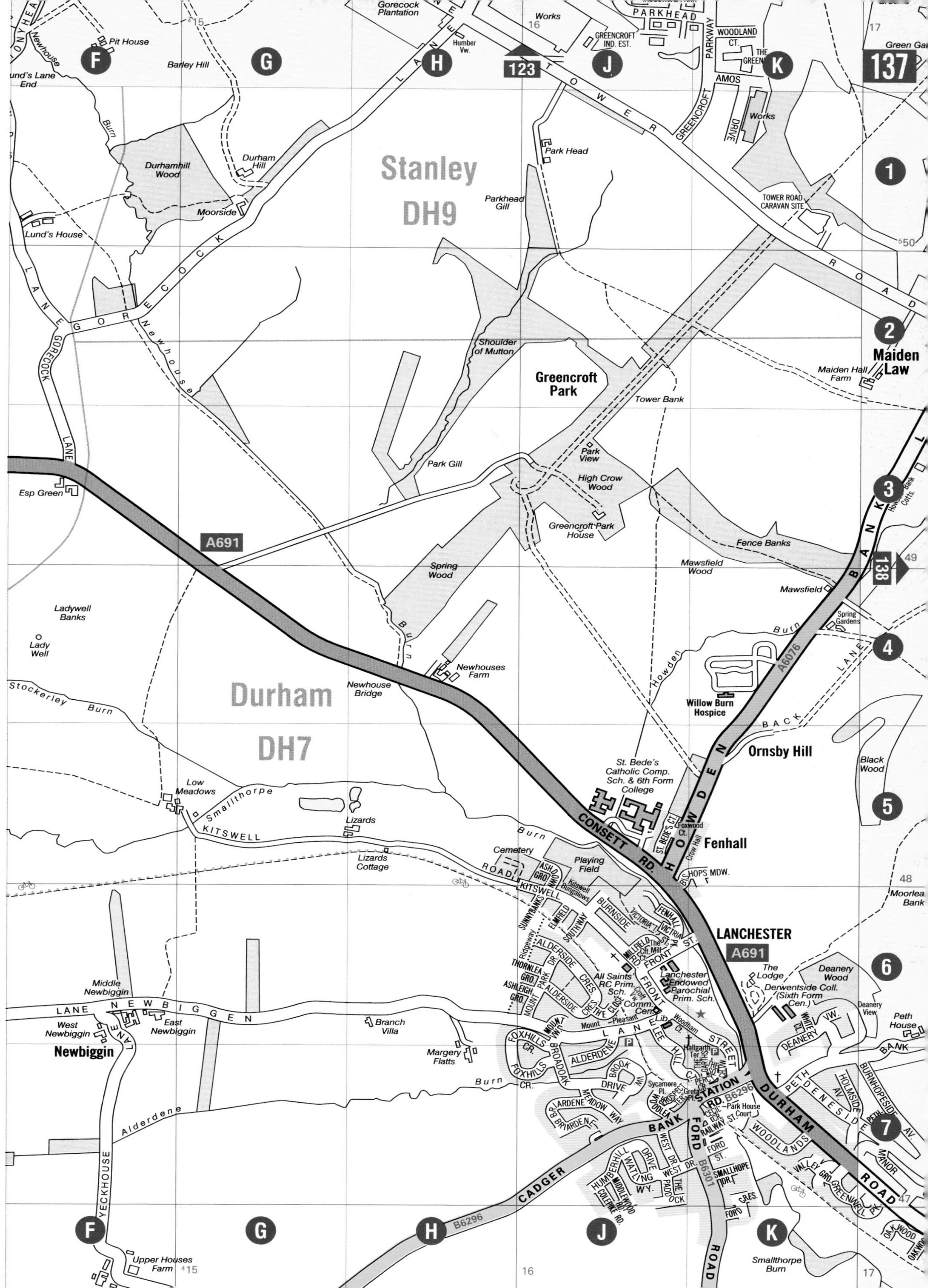
Stanley
DH9
Durham
DH7
Greencroft Park
Maiden Law
Ornsby Hill
Fenhall
LANCHESTER
Newbiggin
Gorecock Plantation
Works
PARKHEAD
GREENCROFT IND. EST.
WOODLAND CT.
THE GREEN
AMOS
PARKWAY
GREENCROFT
DRIVE
Pit House
Barley Hill
Lund's Lane End
Humber Vw.
TOWER ROAD
Durhamhill Wood
Durham Hill
Park Head
Parkhead Gill
Moorside
Lund's House
TOWER ROAD CARAVAN SITE
GORECOCK LANE
Newhouse
Shoulder of Mutton
Maiden Hall Farm
Tower Bank
Park View
High Crow Wood
Park Gill
Esp Green
A691
Greencroft Park House
Fence Banks
Spring Wood
Mawsfield Wood
Mawsfield
Spring Gardens
Ladywell Banks
Lady Well
Newhouses Farm
Howden Burn
Newhouse Bridge
Willow Burn Hospice
A6076
Stockerley Burn
BACK LANE
HOWDEN BANK
Black Wood
St. Bede's Catholic Comp. Sch. & 6th Form College
Low Meadows
Smallthorpe
Lizards
KITSWELL ROAD
Lizards Cottage
Cemetery
Playing Field
CONSETT RD.
Moorlea Bank
Middle Newbiggin
NEWBIGGEN LANE
West Newbiggin
East Newbiggin
Branch Villa
Margery Flatts
All Saints' RC Prim. Sch.
Lanchester Endowed Parochial Prim. Sch.
The Lodge
Deanery Wood
Derwentside Coll. (Sixth Form Cen.)
Deanery View
Peth House
Burn
Alderdene
YECKHOUSE
CADGER BANK
B6296
STATION RD.
FORD ROAD
B6301
DURHAM ROAD
WOODLANDS
Upper Houses Farm
Smallthorpe Burn
123
138

138
124
137
150
A
B
C
D
E
1
2
3
4
5
6
7
17
18
19
49
48
47
Green Gate
Depot
Langleymoor Plantation
Langleymoor Farm
Woodside Ter.
Fellside Ter.
Stanley
DH9
New Acres
NEW ACRES ROAD
GREEN
WAY
TOWER ROAD CARAVAN SITE
TOWER ROAD
A6076
LANCHESTER ROAD
BANK
HOWDEN
Langley Moor
Rose Cottage
Maiden Law Farm
Maiden Hall Farm
Maiden Law
THE CRESCENT
EDGE
Burnhope Road
Newacres Plantation
Morrowedge Plantation
Morrow Edge
Reservoirs (covered)
Langley Close
Howdenbank Farm
Howden Bank Cotts.
Chapman's Well Farm
Burnhope Flatts Farm
Cobble Farm
Tait's House
LANE EDGE
Spring Gardens
BACK LANE
ST. JOHNS
HOLM
War Mem.
EDWARDS
LANE
VALE VW.
Fellside Vw.
PARKSIDE
PAVILION TERRACE
CO-OPERATIVE TER.
Cricket Ground
THE AVENUE
Black Wood
Moor Leazes
Barrons Way
WEST TER.
Whitehouse Ter.
Langley Ter.
South View
BURNHOPE CT.
Front Street
Play. Fields
Burnhope Prim. Sch.
BURNHOPE
THE VILLAS
LANGLEY
WHITEHOUSE
THE GROVE
AVENUE
ROAD
HOLMSIDE
THE GABLES
MOUNT PLEASANT
THE HAVEN
PLEASANT VIEW
Hillcrest
BRAESIDE
HOLMLEA
MEADOWFIELD
Moorleazes Bank
Deanery Wood
Deanery View
LANE
Peth House
BANK PETH
Burnhope Television Station & Transmitter
BEECH GROVE
GREENWOOD AV.
Recreation Ground
Fair View
LANCHESTER
Black Wood
Manorhouse Gill
Burn
HOLMSIDE AV.
BURNHOPESIDE
PETH SIDE
DENE SIDE
AVENUE
MANOR
Playing Field
Manor House
Foxcover Wood
DURHAM
A691
GRANGE
GREENWELL PK.
OAKWOOD
OAK WOOD
Warriors Bridge
ROAD
Square Wood
Oak Wood
High Burnhopeside Plantation
High

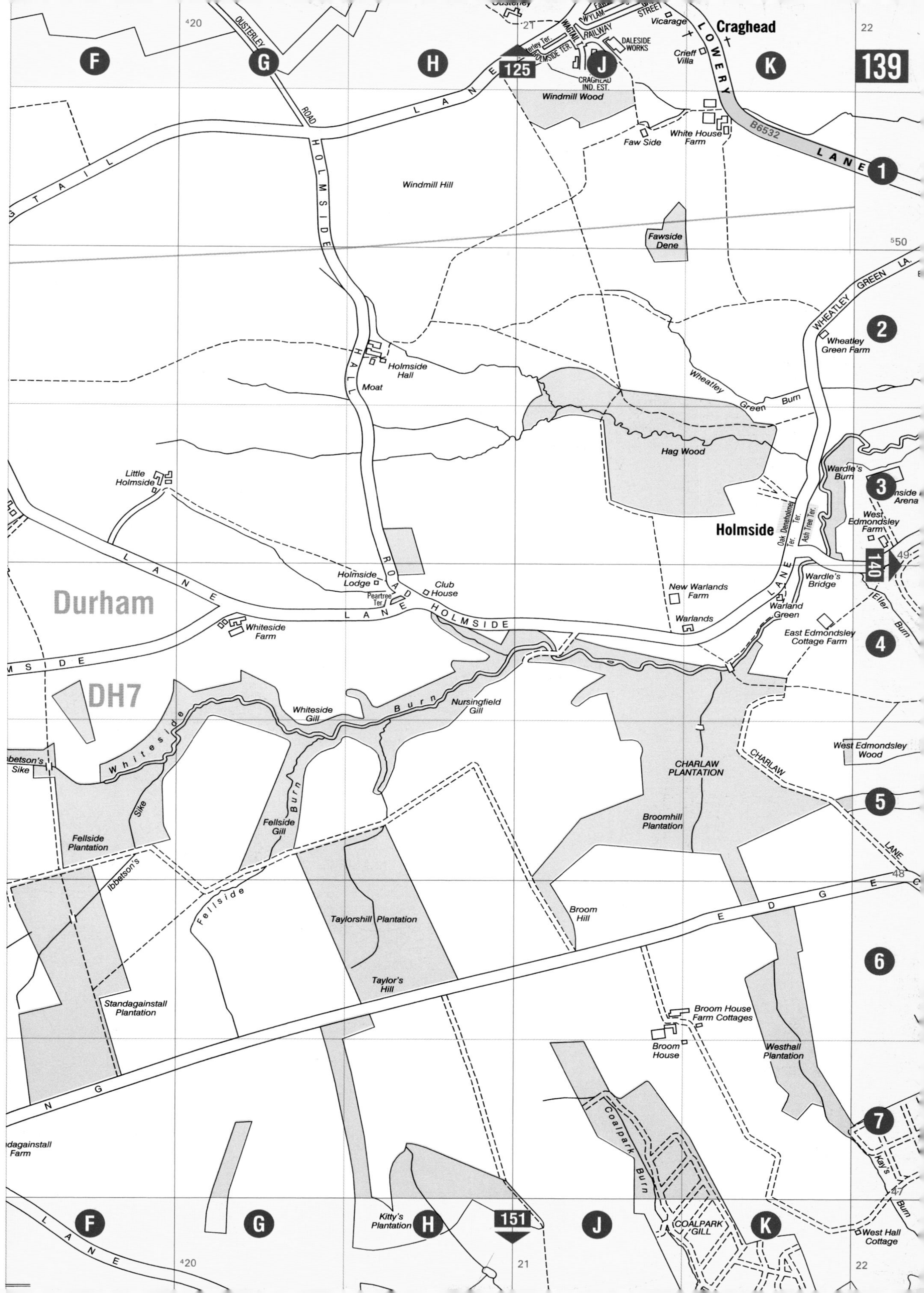
Craghead
Vicarage
Crieff Villa
LOWERY
DALESIDE WORKS
CRAGHEAD IND. EST.
RAILWAY
WYLAM
STREET
Windmill Wood
125
OUSTERLEY
ROAD
LANE
TAIL
HOLMSIDE
Windmill Hill
Faw Side
White House Farm
B6532
LANE
Fawside Dene
WHEATLEY GREEN LA.
Wheatley Green Farm
Holmside Hall
Moat
HALL
Wheatley Green Burn
Hag Wood
Little Holmside
Wardle's Burn
West Edmondsley Farm
Holmside
Oak Tree Ter.
Deneholme Ter.
Ash Tree Ter.
140
Wardle's Bridge
Eller Burn
Holmside Lodge
Peartree Ter.
ROAD
Club House
New Warlands Farm
Warland Green
Warlands
East Edmondsley Cottage Farm
Durham
LANE
HOLMSIDE
Whiteside Farm
DH7
Whiteside Gill
Burn
Nursingfield Gill
West Edmondsley Wood
Ibbetson's Sike
Whiteside
CHARLAW PLANTATION
CHARLAW
LANE
Sike
Fellside Gill
Burn
Broomhill Plantation
Fellside Plantation
Ibbetson's
Fellside
Broom Hill
EDGE
Taylorshill Plantation
Taylor's Hill
Standagainstall Plantation
Broom House Farm Cottages
Broom House
Westhall Plantation
Coalpark Burn
Kay's Burn
dagainstall Farm
Kitty's Plantation
151
COALPARK GILL
West Hall Cottage
LANE
F
G
H
J
K
1
2
3
4
5
6
7
420
21
22
550
49
48
47

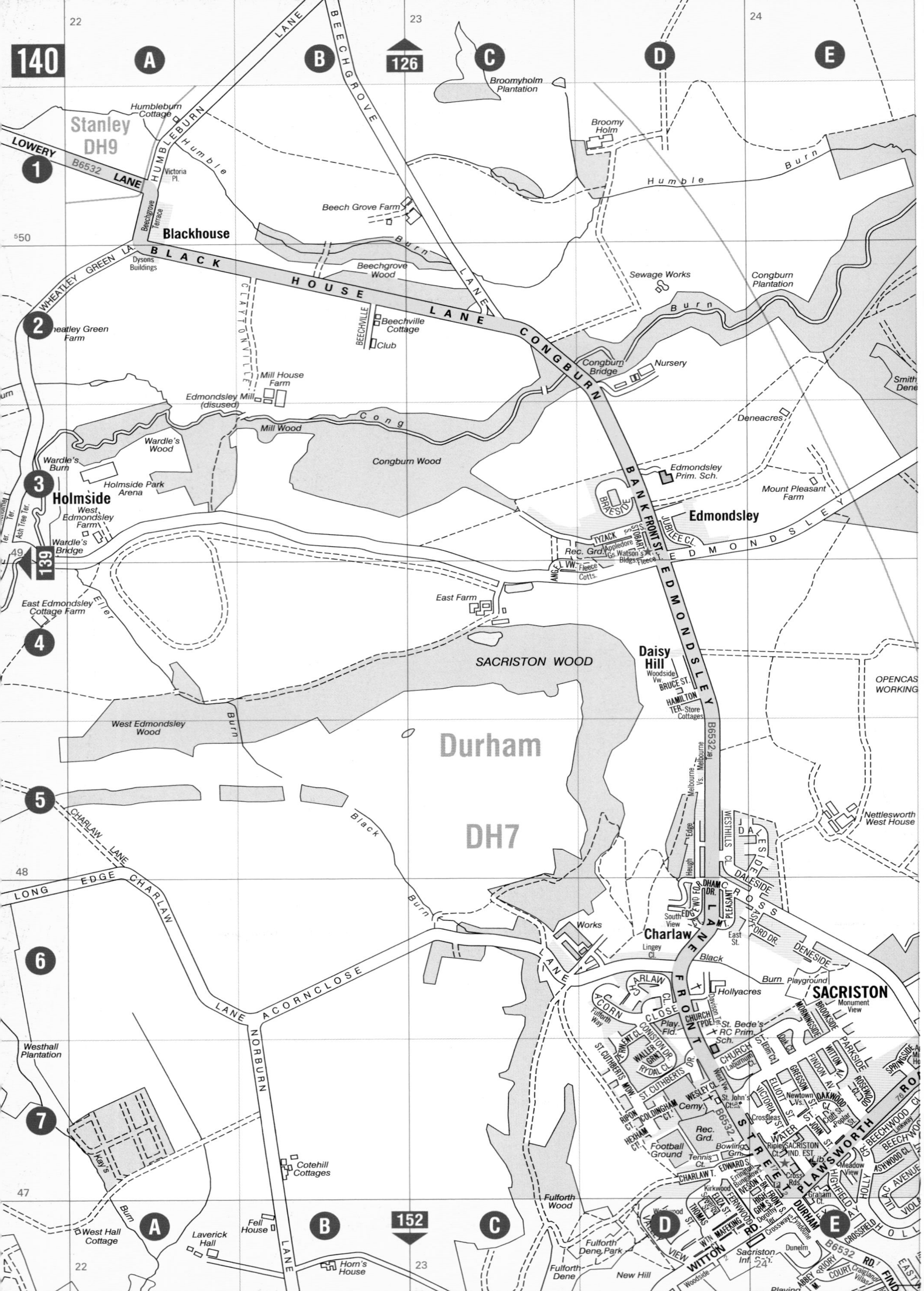

140
A
B
C
D
E
22
23
24
126
139
152
1
2
3
4
5
6
7
550
49
48
47
Stanley
DH9
Durham
DH7
LOWERY LANE
B6532
HUMBLEBURN LANE
Humbleburn Cottage
Victoria Pl.
Beechgrove Terrace
Blackhouse
BLACK HOUSE LANE
WHEATLEY GREEN LA
Dysons Buildings
Wheatley Green Farm
BEECHGROVE LANE
Beech Grove Farm
Beechgrove Wood
Humble Burn
Broomyholm Plantation
Broomy Holm
Sewage Works
Congburn Plantation
CONGBURN BANK
Congburn Bridge
Nursery
Beechville Cottage
BEECHVILLE
Club
CLAYTONVILLE
Mill House Farm
Edmondsley Mill (disused)
Mill Wood
Cong Burn
Congburn Wood
Wardle's Wood
Wardle's Burn
Holmside
Holmside Park Arena
West Edmondsley Farm
Wardle's Bridge
Ash Tree Ter.
East Edmondsley Cottage Farm
Eller
Deneacres
Smith Dene
Edmondsley Prim. Sch.
Mount Pleasant Farm
Edmondsley
BRAESIDE
FRONT ST.
JUBILEE CL.
TYZACK
STOBART ST.
Appledore Gs.
Watson's Bldgs.
Fleece T.
Rec. Grd.
ANGEL VW.
Fleece Cotts.
EDMONDSLEY
East Farm
SACRISTON WOOD
Daisy Hill
Woodside Vw.
BRUCE ST.
HAMILTON TER.
Store Cottages
OPENCAST WORKING
West Edmondsley Wood
Burn
Melbourne Ter.
Melbourne Vs.
Edge
Heugh
WESTHILLS CL.
DALESIDE
Nettlesworth West House
CHARLAW LANE
Black Burn
LONG EDGE
Works
Charlaw
South View
DHAM DR.
PLEASANT
East St.
ROSS
ASHFORD DR.
DENESIDE
Lingey Cl.
Black Burn
Playground
SACRISTON
Monument View
ACORNCLOSE LANE
NORBURN LANE
CHARLAW CL.
ACORN CLOSE
Fulforth Way
FRONT
Hollyacres
Play. Fld.
CHURCH PDE.
Davison Ter.
St. Bede's RC Prim. Sch.
CONISTON DR.
WALLER GRN.
RYDAL CL.
ST. CUTHBERTS DR.
ST. CUTHBERTS MDW.
MORNINGSIDE
BROOKSIDE
PARKSIDE
WITTON AV.
FINDON AV.
GREGSON
ELLIOTT ST.
Laburnum Ct.
West Vw.
WESLEY CL.
St. John's Ct.
Cemy.
COLDINGHAM CT.
RIPON CT.
HEXHAM CT.
Rec. Grd.
Football Ground
Tennis Ct.
Bowling Grn.
VICTORIA ST.
Crossleas
Newtown Vs.
OAKWOOD
Craft St.
Poplar St.
ROSEWOOD
SPRINGSIDE
PLAWSWORTH
BEECHWOOD
Linkway
SACRISTON IND. EST.
Ripley Ct.
Lib.
Cross Rds.
Meadow View
ASHWOOD
HOLLY
LILAC AVENUE
HIGHFIELD
Graham Ct.
DURHAM
CHARLAW T.
EDWARD S.
Errington Bungalows
IVESON T.
Kirkwood
THOMAS
ELIZA ST.
FERNWOOD
MAFEKING
HIGH GRN.
FRONT ST.
Dorothy Ter.
Crossways
WITTON RD
Sacriston Inf. Sch.
Dunelm
CROSSFIELD
B6532 RD.
PRIORY
ABBEY
COURT
Craigland Villas
FINDON
Playing
Westhall Plantation
Kay's
Burn
West Hall Cottage
Laverick Hall
Fell House
Horn's House
Cotehill Cottages
Fulforth Wood
Fulforth Dene Park
Fulforth Dene
New Hill
Woodside
VIEW

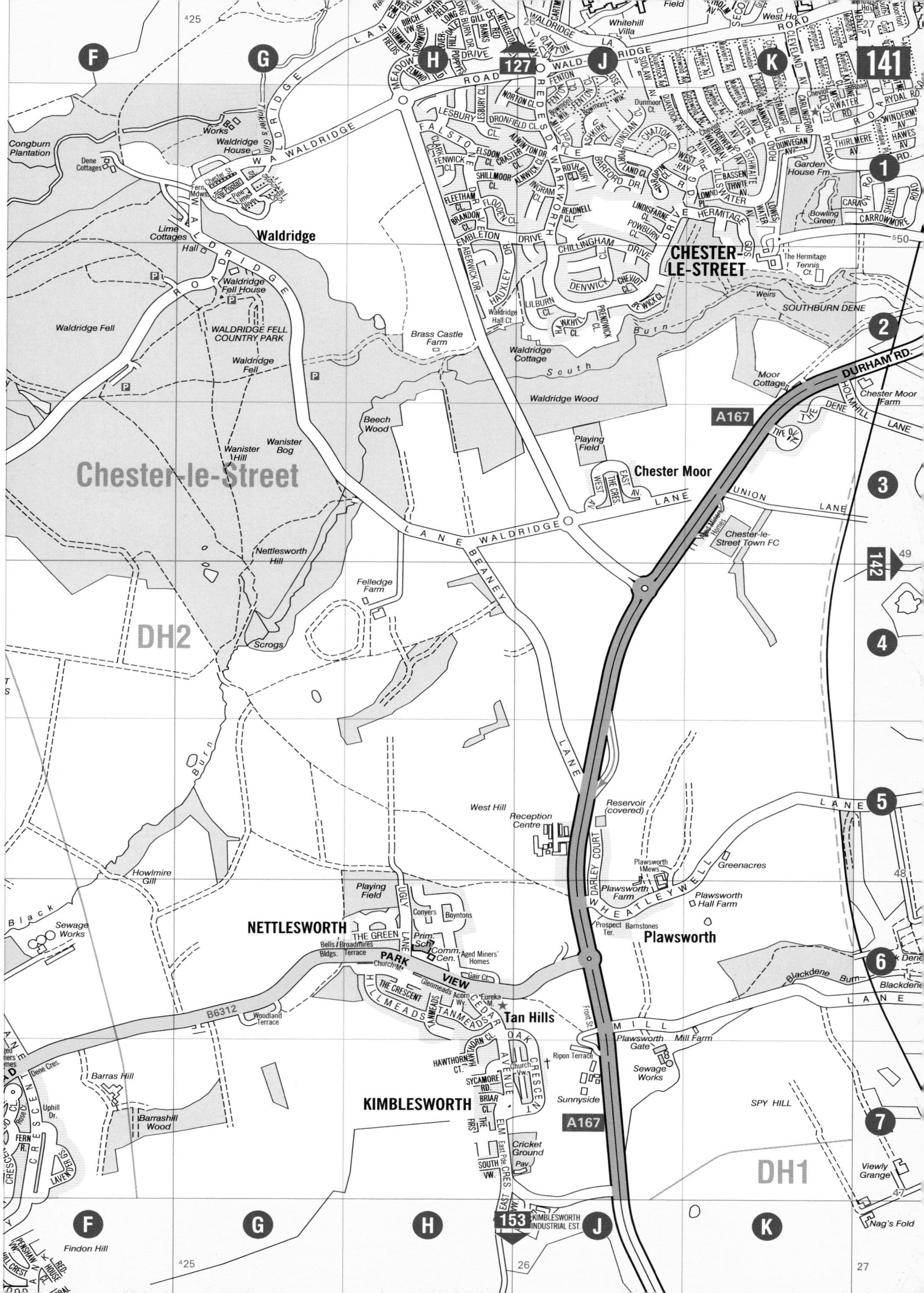

F
G
H
J
K
127
153
142
1
2
3
4
5
6
7
Waldridge
CHESTER-LE-STREET
Chester-le-Street
Waldridge Fell
WALDRIDGE FELL COUNTRY PARK
Waldridge Fell
Wanister Hill
Wanister Bog
Nettlesworth Hill
Scrogs
DH2
DH1
Chester Moor
Chester-le-Street Town FC
Waldridge Wood
Brass Castle Farm
Beech Wood
Felledge Farm
Moor Cottage
Chester Moor Farm
SOUTHBURN DENE
The Hermitage
Garden House Fm.
Bowling Green
A167
DURHAM RD.
B6312
WALDRIDGE LANE
BEANEY LANE
UNION LANE
WHEATLEYWELL
MILL LANE
PARK VIEW
Congburn Plantation
Dene Cottages
Works
Waldridge House
Lime Cottages
Waldridge Fell House
West Hill
Reception Centre
Reservoir (covered)
Plawsworth
Plawsworth Farm
Plawsworth Hall Farm
Greenacres
Plawsworth Gate
Mill Farm
Sewage Works
NETTLESWORTH
Tan Hills
KIMBLESWORTH
KIMBLESWORTH INDUSTRIAL EST.
Cricket Ground
Sunnyside
Ripon Terrace
SPY HILL
Viewly Grange
Nag's Fold
Howlmire Gill
Barras Hill
Barrashill Wood
Findon Hill
Woodland Terrace
Blackdene Burn
Playing Field
Aged Miners' Homes

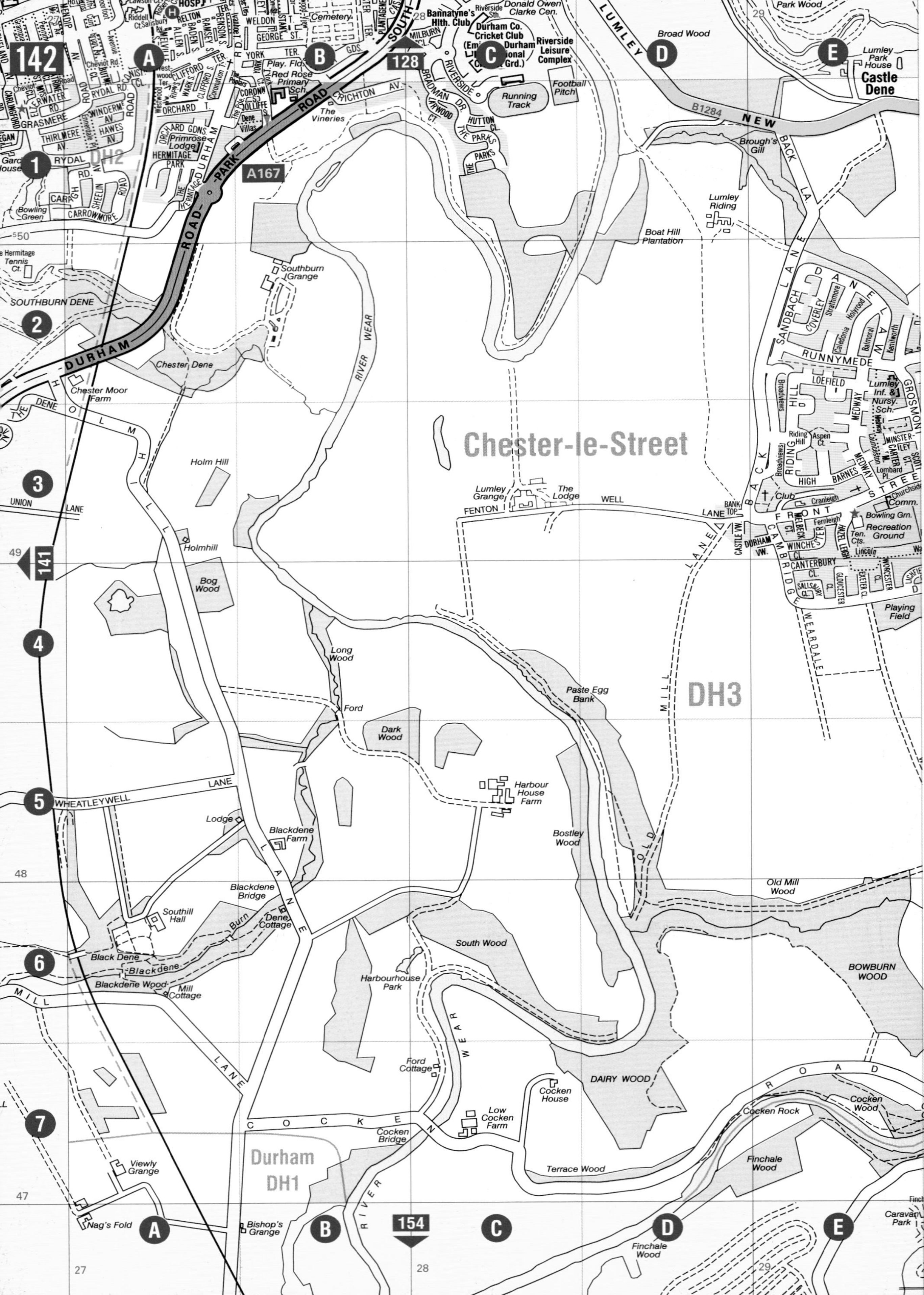
142
128
141
154
A
B
C
D
E
1
2
3
4
5
6
7
27
28
29
50
49
48
47
Chester-le-Street
DH2
DH3
Durham
DH1
A167
B1284
DURHAM ROAD
PARK ROAD
SOUTH
NEW
Bannatyne's Hlth. Club
Donald Owen Clarke Cen.
Durham Co. Cricket Club
Riverside Leisure Complex
Cemetery
Red Rose Primary Sch.
The Vineries
Running Track
Football Pitch
Broad Wood
Park Wood
Lumley Park House
Castle Dene
Brough's Gill
Lumley Riding
Boat Hill Plantation
Southburn Grange
SOUTHBURN DENE
The Hermitage Tennis Ct.
Bowling Green
Primrose Lodge
HERMITAGE PARK
Chester Dene
Chester Moor Farm
DENE
HOLM HILL
Holm Hill
Holmhill
Bog Wood
UNION LANE
RIVER WEAR
Lumley Grange
The Lodge
FENTON WELL LANE
BANK TOP
Long Wood
Ford
Dark Wood
Paste Egg Bank
Harbour House Farm
Bostley Wood
OLD MILL LANE
WHEATLEYWELL LANE
Lodge
Blackdene Farm
Blackdene Bridge
Southill Hall
Dene Cottage
Burn
Black Dene
Blackdene
Blackdene Wood
Mill Cottage
MILL LANE
South Wood
Harbourhouse Park
Old Mill Wood
BOWBURN WOOD
Ford Cottage
WEAR
DAIRY WOOD
Cocken House
Low Cocken Farm
COCKEN
Cocken Bridge
Terrace Wood
ROAD
Cocken Rock
Cocken Wood
Finchale Wood
Finchale Wood
Caravan Park
Viewly Grange
Nag's Fold
Bishop's Grange
RIVER
SANDBACH
DANE
RUNNYMEDE
LOEFIELD
Lumley Inf. & Nursy. Sch.
RIDING HILL
HIGH BARNES
BACK LANE
FRONT STREET
Club
Bowling Grn.
Recreation Ground
Ten. Cts.
WINCHESTER
CAMBRIDGE
CANTERBURY
WEARDALE
Playing Field
MEDWAY
GROSMONT
CASTLE VW.
DURHAM VW.
Grasmere
THIRLMERE AV.
RYDAL
CARROWMORE
ORCHARD
WELDON
GEORGE ST.
YORK TER.
CRICHTON AV.
BRADMAN DR.
RIVERSIDE
HUTTON CL.
THE PARKS

Lumley Park Wood
New Lambton Rec. Grd.
Lumley Park Burn
Brecon Hill
Tunnel
WOODSTONE VILLAGE IND. EST.
129
Works
Lumley Sixth Pit
Comm. Cen.
Aged Miners' Homes
Pear Tree Ter.
Tinkler T.
FORGE LANE
ROAD LUMLEY NEW ROAD
B1284
The Old Chapel
Lumley Thicks
SCORER'S LANE
A1(M) MOTORWAY
A1(M)
Woodstone House
Woodstone Village
Woodlea Prim. Sch.
School
Burnside Club
Football Ground
Depot
MORTON
The Rookery
THE WALLED GDN.
Morton Ho.
Morton Wood
DURHAM
SUNDERLAND
Dubmire Primary Sch.
Houghton-le-Spring
GREAT LUMLEY
Trent Cres.
Water Treatment Works
Pea Flatts Farm
PEA FLATTS LANE
Morton Grange Farm
DH4
Morton Cottage
High Dubmire
NEWBOTTLE LANE
Chilton Moor House
Black Boy Bridge
BLACK BOY ROAD
Morton Acres
Lumley Jun. Sch.
Crossways
GEORGE PIT LANE
144
OPENCAST WORKINGS
Lumley Moor Farm
Charles Pit Houses
Cocken Ride
Cocken White House Farm
Tibby's Gill
RYE HILL
MARK'S LANE
PIT HOUSE LANE
Lane House Farm
Blue House Farm
West Rainton Stables Farm
Carr Row
COCKEN LANE
COCKEN ROAD
Cocken Cottage
Toll
Finchale Priory (Remains of)
Golf Driving Range
Cocken Lodge Golf Course
Caravan Park
Whitehouse Farm
Finchale Banks
Jellico Ter.
Broom House
155
ADVENTURE LANE
WEST RAINTON
Bowl. Grn.
Playing Field
Village Farm
CRESCENT
Leamside
F G H J K
1 2 3 4 5 6 7
430 31 32
50 49 48 47

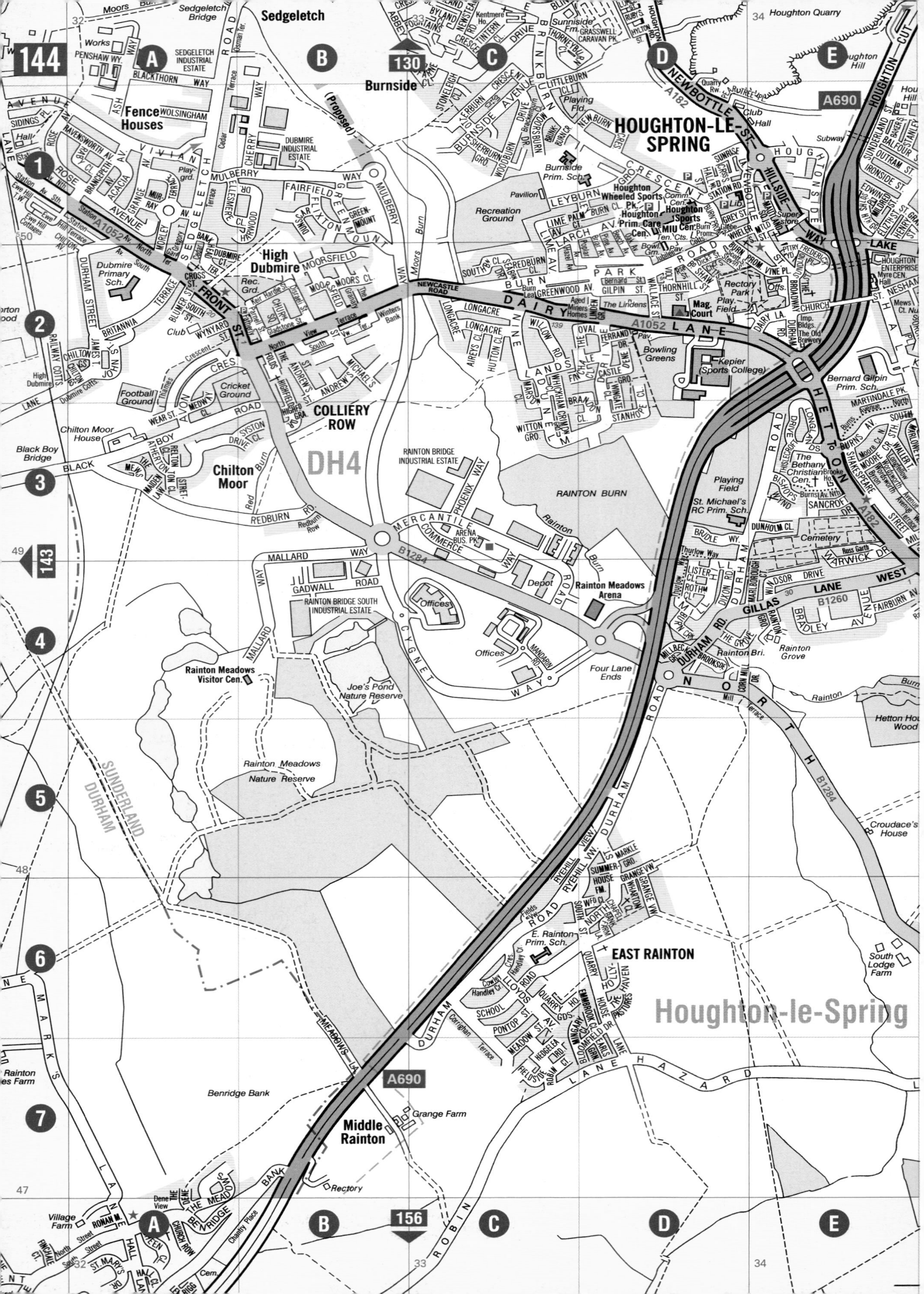
Sedgeletch
Fence Houses
Burnside
HOUGHTON-LE-SPRING
High Dubmire
COLLIERY ROW
DH4
Chilton Moor
RAINTON BRIDGE INDUSTRIAL ESTATE
RAINTON BRIDGE SOUTH INDUSTRIAL ESTATE
Rainton Meadows Visitor Cen.
Joe's Pond Nature Reserve
Rainton Meadows Nature Reserve
Rainton Meadows Arena
Four Lane Ends
Kepier (Sports College)
EAST RAINTON
Middle Rainton
Benridge Bank
Grange Farm
Houghton-le-Spring
A690
A1052
B1284
B1260
A182
130
143
156

Field House Sand Hole
131
Warden Law North Farm Cottage
Warden Law North Farm
Karting North East (Go-Kart Track)
Cemetery
Houghton Burn
Earsdon Grange
Field House Farm
Warden Law
New Town
White House Farm
SEAHAM ROAD
B1404
The Cottage
LOW MOORS
Club House
GILLAS LANE
EAST GILLAS LANE
HOUGHTON-LE-SPRING GOLF COURSE
Copt Hill
Rough Dene Burn
THE MOORS
Dene House Farm
146
Rough Dene
Rescue Station Cotts.
Low Downs
Playing Field
Eppleton Academy Prim. Sch.
High Downs
Broom Hill
Hetton Downs
Cricket Ground
Eppleton
DH5
WINDMILL HILL
Hetton Bogs Local Nature Reserve
Hetton Park
PIT LANE
Great Eppleton
Cemetery
HOUGHTON ROAD
A182
HETTON LYONS COUNTRY PARK
Lyons Lake
Hetton Sports Complex
Eppleton Colliery Football Grd.
Hetton Lyons Park Playing Field
Blossom Pond
RYE HILL
BRACKEN HILL
HETTON-LE-HOLE
Stephenson Lake
Playing Field
Hetton School
Hetton Prim. Sch.
HETTON LYONS IND. EST.
STATION ROAD
Grotto Plantation
ORCHARD HILL
157
COLLIERY LANE
B1285
B1284
Eppleton Hall
Little Eppleton Farm
WHITE HILL
Lyons
CONSTITUTION HILL

Old Burdon
The Lodge
Old Burdon Farm
Pacific Hall Farm
132
Karting North East (Go-Kart Track)
High Moors
Sharpley Burn
SUNDERLAND
DURHAM
Warden Law
B1404
Sharpley Hall Farm
Nursery
Warden Law
LOW MOORS
Seaton Plantation
Seaton Bank Top
High Sharpley
The Maples
Seaton Moor House
Northside
Stotfold Farm
145
Sharpley Plantations
GREEN LANE
Haverley House
South Sharpley
Houghton-le-Spring
DH5
Slingley Hill West
Slingley Hill East
Slingley Hill South
Great Eppleton
CARRHOUSE LANE
Water Gate
SALTERS LANE
Sandy Hill
Carr House Farm
Carr House Plantations
Murton Bridge
MURTON
BRACKEN HILL
RYE HILL
ORCHARD HILL
Murton Moor Farm
158
STATION ROAD
CHURCH LANE
The Village
Murton Mews
Cemetery
St. Joseph's Catholic Prim. Sch.
Little Eppleton Farm
CONSTITUTION HILL
Ribbon Academy Trust
Lib
Aged Miners' Homes
War. Mem.
Vicarage
B1285

133
159
148
A19
A1018
A182
B1285
B1404
B1287
B1432
SEATON LANE
STATION ROAD
STOCKTON ROAD
LORD BYRONS WALK
THE GRAHAM WAY
DENE ROAD
Seaton
Seaham
SR7
Westlea
Deneside
SEAHAM
Northlea
East Shore Village
Dalton-le-Dale
Cold Hesledon
Glebe Estate
South Grange Park
Fun Shack
Playing Field
Lodge Field Plantation
Cricket Ground
New Seaham Prim. Sch.
Seaham School of Technology
Football Ground
Aged Miners Homes
Bowling Green
War Mem.
St. Cuthbert's RC Prim. Sch.
Westlea Primary School
Comm. Cen.
Seaview Primary School
Seaham Leisure Cen.
Dawdon Dene Park
Recreation Ground
KINGFISHER INDUSTRIAL ESTATE
Hall Station Cottage
Cemetery
Seaham Dene
Ice House Dene
Electricity Transformer Station
Cricket Ground
Ten. Cts.
Youth Cen.
The Dene
Dalden Tower (remains of)
Dawdon Dene
Ewe Hill
Ewe Hill Gutter
West Farm
Cragdale Vs.
Dalton Bridge
Burnside Cottages
East Farm
Pumping Station
Glebe Farm
South Hill
Dalton Hill
Hesledon Plantation
SEAHAM GOLF COURSE
Stoney Cut Bank
Depot
COLD HESLEDON INDUSTRIAL ESTATE
The Waterworks
Dalton Moor
Burnside
Dalton Dene
CORNWALL ESTATE
DALTONPARK
The Glebe Cen.
MURTON ST.
Seaton Burn
Scawpie Dene
Seaham
F
G
H
J
K
1
2
3
4
5
6
7

East Shore Village
Seaham Hall
Byrons Ct.
Community Home
Greystones
Lodge
Lord Byron's Walk
Electricity Transformer Station
Featherbed Ct.
Harbour Lodge
The Castlereagh Homes
Promenade
Outfall
Featherbed Rocks
Bessy's Hole
North Road
SEAHAM
War Mem.
Marquess Point
The Waterside
Seaham Harbour Marina
North Dock
North Pier
Seaham Lighthouse
Outer Harbour
Lifeboat House
South Dock
South Pier
Byron Place Shop. Cen.
Superstores
Tempest Road
Harbour Walk
Seaham
Station
Cricket Ground
Seaham Cen.
Prim. Sch.
Youth Cen.
George St. Ind. Est.
Jubilee Cen.
St. John's Sq.
Lib.
Coun. Offs.
Seaham Leisure Cen.
Dawdon Dene Park
Seaham Trinity Prim. Sch.
Cemetery
The Dene
Dene Farm
Dalden Tower (remains of)
Playing Field
Lindisfarne Ho.
Club House
Dawdon
Cargodurham Distribution Centre
Liddle Stack
Seaham Fleet Rock
Parkside
Comm. Cen.
Bowling Greens
Football Ground
Cricket Ground
Dawdon Business Park
Nose's Point
Spectrum Business Park
Sewage Works
Lighthouse Vw.
Works
Seaham Golf Course
Fox Cover
Stoney Cut Bank
Fox Cover Industrial Park
Seaham
SR7
Admiralty Way
Hesledon East House
A182
Kinley Hill Tower
147
160

161

LANCHESTER
Playing Field
Manor House
Foxcover Wood
138
Square Wood
DURHAM
A691
Warriors Bridge
Smalthorpe Burn
Oak Wood
High Burnhopeside
High Burnhopeside Plantation
Nursery
Langley West House
Sewage Works
Manor House Bridge
Waters' Meeting
Greenwell Ford
Burnhopeside Cottages
River Browney
Hollybush Wood
Browney Bridge
Official Terrace
Works
LANCHESTER VALLEY
Burnhopeside Hall
Burnhopeside Farm
Hollybush Gill
Hollybush
Love's Wood
River Browney
Durham
DH7
Biggen Farm
Biggen House Farm
West Hamsteels
Hamsteels Hall
HAMSTEELS LANE
HAMSTEELS BANK
Malton House
HAMSTEELS LANE
Biggin Terrace
Blackburn
Hamsteels Beck
Weather Hill
Dere Street
LOW ESH
ROAD
BANK
Esh Glebe House
B6301
Wilk's Hill
Quarry House Farm
Greenland
FRONT STREET
Recreation Ground
Factory
Church View
The Fold
Marleys Houses
Quebec
Playing Field
Play-Grd
Esh Laude
Greenland Bank
GREENLAND
LAUDE BANK
STEADMAN'S LANE
Red Stacks
COMMERCIAL LANE
Clifford's House Farm
CLIFFORD'S BANK
Moorhouse
DERE STREET
162
Cornsay Colliery
Hawkshill Ter.
KNOX ST.

F
G
H
139
J
K
Kitty's Plantation
COALPARK GILL
West Hall Cottage
Coalpark Squares
Old Hall Wood
Langley Hall (remains of)
Ox Wood
Beech Wood
Kaysburn Plantation
Drift Plantation
Waterfall Wood
Langley
Stainsbybank Plantation
Park House Plantation
Long Plantation
Bleach Green
Bleachgreen Plantation
Langley House Belts
Buckham Ct.
Langley House
Castleways Bridge
Parkhouse Cottages
Kaysburn
Parkhouse Villas
Copper Beeches
Stobbilee House
Lane Ends Bridge
A691
Newlands
Langley Cott.
LANGLEY PARK NORTH INDUSTRIAL ESTATE
Stobbilee Farm
152
Hedley's Wood
River Browney
RIVERSIDE INDUSTRIAL ESTATE
Diggerland
LANGLEY PARK SOUTH IND. EST.
Wallnook Mill Farm
Wall Nook
The Firs
LANGLEY PARK
WALLNOOK
WITTON STATION CT.
Blackburn
Lime Garth
DAVIS CRES.
THE HAVEN
Sports Ground
Cricket Grd.
GARDEN AV.
THE CRESCENT
Finings Avenue
Cemetery
Stringer Terrace
MOOR ROAD
Tennis Court
Rec. Grd.
Playing Field
Langley Park Prim. Sch.
EASTERN AVENUE
HILLTOP VW.
West House
EAST CLERE
Springwell
Esh Hill Top Farm
North Farm
Hill Top
Groove Bank
FRONT ST.
Hilltop
Broom Cottages
Esh C of E Prim. Sch.
Glebe Farm
Esh Court Vw.
Consett Rutter Ter.
Sq.
STREET
St. Michael's RC Prim. Sch.
Esh Laude
Esh
Low Esh
Esh Hall
COLLEGE ROAD
The Rookery
Millgate Cottages
Mill House
St. John's
Ushaw Farm
Ushaw College
BROADGATE ROAD
Farm Plantation
Fortypence Plantation
163
East Lodge
Sports Grou
1
2
3
4
5
6
7

152
140
151
164
DH7
SACRISTON
WITTON GILBERT
BEARPARK
Kaysburn
Wall Nook
A691
B6312
FRONT STREET
DENE BANK
WITTON LANE
DURHAM ROAD
FINDON HILL
NORBURN LANE
WALLNOOK LANE
RIVER BROWNEY
COLLIERY ROAD
BEAUREPAIRE ROAD
Cotehill Cottages
West Hall Cottage
Laverick Hall
Fell House
Horn's House
Fulforth Farm
Fulforth Wood
Fulforth Dene Park
Fulforth Dene
New Hill
Beech Wood
Kaysburn Plantation
Kaysburn House
Newlands
Langley Cott.
Blackcliff Hill
Wallnook Bridge
The Firs
Witton Gilbert Prim.Sch.
Sacriston Inf. Sch.
Fyndoune Community College
Sports Cen.
Reservoir (covered)
Playing Fields
Playing Field
New Close
Football Ground
Rec. Grd.
Rectory
Picnic Site
Witton Dene Local Nature Reserve
High Church Hill
Witton Hall
Low Church Hill
Bog Wood
Sewage Works
St. John's Green
Ford
Lodge Hill
BEAR PARK
Lodge Farm
Esh Hill Top Farm
The Rookery
Ushaw College
USHAW PARK
Park Wood
East Lodge
Red House Farm
White House Farm
Sports Ground
Recreation Ground
Bowling Greens
Depot
Bearpark Prim. Sch.
Sleight's House
Dene Bridge
Bests Yard
Low Mdws.
Coach La.
Witton Station Ct.

153
KIMBLESWORTH
Chester-le-Street
DH2
Durham
DH1
A167
A691
B6532
141
154
165
Findon Hill
Barrasholl Wood
Cricket Ground
KIMBLESWORTH INDUSTRIAL EST.
Nag's Fold
Kimblesworth Grange
Wellsprings Farm
Red House Farm
Hartside
Little Gill
STANK LANE
Sewage Works
Poultry Farm
Folly Bridge
Inglewild
Kennels
Potter House
POTTERHOUSE LANE
Folly Plantation
Civic Amenity Site
BY-PASS
(GREAT NORTH ROAD)
ARNISON RETAIL CENTRE
Superstore
Hotel
ABBEY RD. BUS. PK.
ABBEYWOODS BUS. PK.
ABBEY ROAD INDUSTRIAL ESTATE
Harvest View
ROTARY WAY
ABBEY ROAD
Hartside Farm
Durham Trinity School
Black Lodge Cottages
Earl's House Cottages
LANCHESTER ROAD HOSPITAL
Half-Way Houses
Lodge
LANCHESTER ROAD
Pity Me Local Nature Reserve
PITY ME
Playing Field
Newton Hall
Framwellgate School
Sports Cen.
Running Track
King George's Field
Framwellgate Moor Prim. Sch.
Low Carrs Park
New College Durham
FRAMWELLGATE MOOR
The Oaks
The Cottage
Sniperley Farm
Sniperley Park
Sniperley P+R
Aykley Heads
Durham County Constabulary Headquarters
Durham Trinity Sch.
UNIVERSITY HOSPITAL OF NORTH DURHAM
AYKLEY HEADS BUSINESS CENTRE
Bowling Greens
Tennis Courts
Sports Ground
Rivergreen Centre
County Hall
Durham Light Infantry Museum & Durham Art Gallery
Aden Cottage
Stotgate Farm
Bearpark Hall Farm
Western Lodge
Southfield Ho. Govt. Offs.
Whitesmocks
NEWCASTLE ROAD
SOUTHFIELD WAY
DRYBURN RD.
Fernhill
North End
St. Leonard's
F G H J K
1 2 3 4 5 6 7

Cocken Bridge
Cocken Farm
Cocken Road
142
Viewly Grange
Nag's Fold
Bishop's Grange
Terrace Wood
Finchale Wood
River Wear
Redhouse Wood
Stockley Heugh
Finchale Training College
Sewage Works
Low Moor Cottages
Red House Farm
Harvest View
Hag House
Rotary Way
Arnison Retail Centre
Superstore
Mercia Retail Park
Abbey Road
Abbey Leisure Cen.
Bowls Cen.
Pity Me
Brasside
Green Acres
Finchale Avenue
Finchale Road
HMP & YOI Low Newton
HMP Frankland
Low Newton Farm
Finchale Primary Sch.
Abbey Road Ind. Est.
153
Low Carrs Park
Newton Hall
Sports Cen.
Running Track
Blue Coat C of E Jun. Sch.
Durham Newton Hall Inf. Sch.
Low Newton Local Nature Reserve
DH1
Frankland Wood
Frankland Lane
Kepier Wood
The Scroggs
Frankland Farm
Frankland Park
Frankland Park Farm
Aykley Heads
Durham County Constabulary Headquarters
Hopper's Wood
Rivergreen Centre
Sports Ground
Playing Field
Signal Bridge
Durham Light Infantry Museum & Durham Art Gallery
Crook Hall & Gardens
166
Sewage Works
Kepier
NEDL Training Centre
A690
Carrville
Belmont
Gilesgate
Durham Gilesgate Sports College & 6th Form Centre
Durham Gilesgate Primary School
High Grange
The Paddock
Playing Fields

Finchale Priory (Remains of)
Cocken Lodge Golf Course
Caravan Park
Carr Row
Whitehouse Farm
143
COCKEN ROAD
Jellico Ter.
Finchale Banks
Broom House
PIT HOUSE LANE
ADVENTURE LANE
Village Farm
RONAN M.
A1(M)-MOTORWAY
A1(M)
DH4
WEST RAINTON
Bowl. Grn.
Playing Field
Leamside
STATION ROAD
CRESCENT
Playgrd.
LOW STATION RD.
Currys Bldgs.
Leamside House
PROSPECT VW.
Play. Field
Sch.
Salters Cottage
Works
Houghton-le-Spring
Raintonpark Wood
Woodside Farm
WOODSIDE
Wood Side
Rainton Gate
Lambton View
TOLLGATE
The Bungalow
East Moor Leazes
Mallygill Wood
Mally Gill
Mallygill Craig
A690
PITTINGTON ROAD
Pitfield House
Adventure Valley
Union Hall Farm
Moor House Farm
Homer Hill Farm
Durham
RIVER WEAR
Black Wood
Mallygill Turn
Mally Gill
Winch Gill
DH5
156
Grange Wood
Woodwell House
The Rift
Sewage Works
Low Grange
Belmont Viaduct
RAMSIDE GOLF COURSE
Lodge
LANE
Maureen Ter.
Durham Grange Caravan & Camping Site
P+R Belmont
Ramside Hall Hotel
Driving Range
Junc. 62
MEADOW LA.
Depot
ROAD
Club House
EVANS BUSINESS CENTRE
Factory
Fatfield House Farm
PITTINGTON
DH6
BELMONT INDUSTRIAL ESTATE
Pittington Beck
MANDALE PARK
A1(M)
CARRVILLE
Hilltop Farm
Belmont Cheveley Park Prim. Sch.
City FC (s Stadium)
CATHEDRAL PARK
Broomside
County Durham & Darlington Fire & Rescue Service H.Q.
BELMONT BUSINESS PARK
Moor End
BROOMSIDE
CHEVELEY PARK SHOPPING CENTRE
Belmont C of E Jun. & Inf. Sch.
Belmont Community Sch.
Bannatyne Health Club
Community Centre
Playing Field
Belmont
167
Pittington Bridge
Broomside House

WEST RAINTON
Middle Raunton
Grange Farm
Rectory
144
Houghton-le-Spring
A690
Robin House
Greengables
Field House Farm
Pitfield House
Homer Hill Farm
Pittington Bank
High Moorsley
Moorsley Banks
Playing Field
High Moorsley Farm
Reservoir (covered)
155
Pittington
SUNDERLAND
DURHAM
COBBLER'S HILL
Low Pittington
Glenmoor Farm
Pittington Crossing
Coronation Crescent
Pump House
Hillside Farm
PITTINGTON HILL
Carriage Drive Plantation
Durham
DH6
DH4
Fatfield House Farm
Pittington Beck
HIGH PITTINGTON
Playing Field
Hall
Willow Garth
The Moor
Horseshoe Wood
Coalford Bridge
Sewage Works
Hallgarth Manor Farm
Hallgarth
Hallgarth House
Coalford Lane Farm
Cricket Ground
Moor Cottages
White's Wood
Littletown Bank
168
Littletown Farm Cotts.
Littletown Farm
Littletown House
Littletown
Hastings House
Pittington Bridge
Broomside House
Village Farm
Dene View
Fair Vw.
Woodland View
Lambton View
Cem.

HETTON-LE-HOLE
Lyons
Low Moorsley
EASINGTON LANE
Elemore Vale
High Haswell
DH5
ELEMORE GOLF COURSE
HETTON-LE-HILL WOOD
ELEMORE WOOD
COLLIERY LANE
HIGH STREET SOUTH
HETTON RD.
Hetton School
Hetton Prim. Sch.
Hetton Lyons Prim. & Nursy. Schs.
Easington Lane Primary School
Elemore Hall School
Cemetery
Eppleton Hall
Little Eppleton Farm
Hetton Moor Farm
Hetton Moor House
Coal Bank Farm
Elmside Villa
Hetton le Hill
Quarryhouse Wood
Club House
Elemore Grange Farm
Elemore Grange
Red House
Dog Kennel Bank
Brown's Plantation
Lily Hill Plantation
LILY HILL
Low Haswell
Low Haswell Banks
Chapel Garth
Colliery Farm
Store Farm
Dabble Bank
Cat Hole
Cherry Garth
East Wood
Elemore
Pig Hill
White Hill
Sheriff's Moor
WHITE HILL
ORCHARD HILL
CONSTITUTION HILL
Grotto Plantation
Stephenson Lake
Haswell Lodge
145
158
169
F G H J K
1 2 3 4 5 6 7
435 36 37
47 46 45 44

146
157
170
The Village
SOUTH HETTON
HASWELL
High Haswell
Durham
DH5
DH6
SUNDERLAND
DURHAM
EAST DURHAM LINK ROAD (Proposed)
STATION ROAD
CHURCH LANE
FRONT STREET
SOUTH HETTON ROAD
SALTER'S LANE
EASINGTON ROAD
A182
B1285
B1280
Murton Moor Farm
Murton Moor East Farm
Murton Moor West Farm
MURTON MOOR
Croup Hill
Dobson's Bridge
Constitution Hill
Sandy Gate
Hetton Moor Farm
Whitesgates Equestrian Centre
Cockhill Plantation
Cock Hill
High Fallowfield
Low Fallowfield
Pig Hill
Coldwell Burn Farm
Coldwell Burn
NORTH HILL
Duncombe Moor
Heathery Hill
Holy Cross Farm
Cove Holes
Pesspool Hall
PESSPOOL
Rymer's Moor Farm
RYMER'S MOOR
West Moor House
Milestone House
Linton House
Carr's Farm
Coop House Wood
Woodlands
Football Ground
Miners' Welfare Grounds
Aged Peoples Homes
Aged Miners' Homes
Murton Mews
Cemetery
St. Joseph's Catholic Prim. Sch.
Football Grounds
Murton Rec. Grd.
Comm. Cen.
SOUTH HETTON INDUSTRIAL ESTATE
Prim. Sch.
Play. Fld.
Play-ground
CHARTERS CRESCENT
HIGH HESWELL
STATION ST.
Vicarage

159
MURTON
Seaham
SR7
Peterlee
SR8
Cold Hesledon
Hawthorn
The Village
EASINGTON
Easington Service Area
A19
A182
B1432
B1285
B1283
147
160
171
DURHAM LINK ROAD
WEST LANE
SUNDERLAND ROAD
STOCKTON ROAD
SOUTH HETTON ROAD
HALL WALKS
DURHAM LA.
DALTONPARK
BATTER LAW HILL
COOP HILL
ROUND HILL
MILESTONE HILL
BRIDGE HILLS
Little Coop House Farm
East Batter Law Farm
West Batter Law Farm
Great Coop House Farm
Hallfield
Hallfield Burn
Loaning Burn
Easington Greyhound Stadium
Junction House Farm
Jackson's Mill
Garden Centre
Four Winds
Hesledon Moor East
West Farm
East Farm
South Farm
Batter Law
Hillcrest Mews
Rectory
Eagle Hall
Hawthorn Bridge
Dearham
North Hill
Nyree
Moorfield
Larches
Long Run
High West Lane
Seaton Holme
Fitness Cen.
The Waterworks
Pumping Station
COLD HESLEDON INDUSTRIAL ESTATE
Dalton Hill
Depot
Plantation

A182
Hesledon East House
148
Kinley Hill Tower
Kinley Hill
Seaham
SR7
Quarry (disused)
Chourdon Point
Natural Arch
Hawthorn Hive
Hive Point
New Plantation
Haythorne's Plantation
Old Plantation
Keeper's Cottage
Denehurst
North
Dene
HAWTHORN DENE NATURE RESERVE
Blue House Plantation
Hawthorn
Coop's Farm
159
Thompson's Plantation
Thorpe Lea East
Burn
Hawthorn
WEST LANE
The Village
South Farm
Hawthorn Dene
Tongue Gill
Beacon Hill
Beacon Point
Shippersea Bay
Shippersea Point
Thorpe Lea West
Easington Lea
Easington Lea
Easington Lea Farm
Peterlee
SR8
White Lea
Shot Rock
Brickyard Farm
LANE
BLIND LANE
PETWELL
Loom
EASINGTON COLLIERY
North Hill
Nyree
HOLMHILL
Reservoir (covered)
Holm Hill
Glendene School
Club
Rutherford House
Lib.
Hall
Vicarage
Townfield Hill
STATION ROAD
B1283
Busiers Holes
Fox Holes Dene
Playing Field
Prim. Sch.
Fitness Cen.
Coun. Offs.
Cricket Grd.
Football Grounds
Playgrounds
Easington Colliery Welfare Grounds
Glenhurst Cottages
Glenhurst Farm
172
Dene Villa
Rec. Grd.
Dene Hall
Horden Dene
EASINGTON
Paradise Gardens
Paradise

445
46
47
F
G
H
149
J
K
47
1
2
46
3
NORTH SEA
4
545
5
6
44
7
Fox Holes
F
G
H
173
J
K
445
46
47

Cornsay Colliery
Quebec
Waterhouses
Hamilton Row
ESH WINNING
Crook
DL15
150
STEADMAN'S LA.
COMMERCIAL STREET
B6301
B6302
Hedleyhope Burn
HEDLEYHILL LANE
CLIFFORD'S BANK
LAUDE BANK
DERE STREET
Red Stacks
Clifford's House Farm
Moorhouse
Heugh
Heugh Wood
Castle Steads
Moat
Rowley
Chapel Garth
Rowley Gillots
Rottenrow Plantation
Ivesley Wood
Old Ivesley Farm
IVESLEY LANE
Park Wood
Parkwood Cemetery
New Ivesley
Sports Ground
NEWHOUSE ROAD
DURHAM ROAD
WOODLAND ROAD
FAIR VIEW
ESH WINNING INDUSTRIAL ESTATE
STATION VIEW
Esh Winning Prim. Sch.
Woodlands Ter.
Water House Bank
Rabbit Hill
RUSSELL STREET
DEERNESS VALLEY
Deerness River
HEDLEY HILL ROAD
Playing Fld.
Hedley Hill Terrace
Ivesley Cottages
WOLSINGHAM RD.
BUTTON'S BANK
WATERHOUSES WOOD
LITTLE BRIER WOOD
STANDALONE WOOD
Crow Gill
STANLEY WOOD
Stanley Beck
WEST WOOD
Wooley Hill
WATER HOUSE RD.

Hall
F
G
H
151
J
K
St. John's
Ushaw Farm
Ushaw College
Fortypence Plantation
Farm Plantation
Hag Wood
Hag House
BROADGATE ROAD
Sports Ground
Farhill Plantation
East Flass
ESH ROAD
COCKHOUSE LANE
B6302
Deerness Vw.
Joyce Ter.
Flass Gardens
Deerness View
Durham DH7
FLASSHALL LANE
Flass Lodge
Broadgate Farm
Ushaw Moor Picnic Site
RIVER DEERNESS
Flass Ter.
Flass Hall
River Deerness
Sewage Works
RAG PATH WOOD
Hareholme Ct.
Hare Holme Farm
TERRACE
CASTLEFIELDS
Recreation Ground
Coronation Homes
COPPICE
PINE VIEW
Biggin Farm
Park Lodge
The Mound
Playgrd.
The Lodge
Eshwood Hall
Redburn Wood
Red Burn
Red Burn Bridge
Woodbine Ter.
Holburn Bri.
Holburn Wood
ESH WOOD
Holburn Beck
Hill House
LONG HILL WOOD
Long Hill
Standalone
NORTH WOOD
PIT LANE
MORLEY LANE
Keepers Cottages
BRANDON LANE
Tallyho Gate
PITHOUSE PLANTATION
Pithouse East Plantation
West Brandon
Brancepeth Manor Farm
East Brandon Wood
164

USHAW PARK
Park Wood
152
BEARPARK
Depot
Bowling Greens
Bearpark Prim. Sch.
Playing Field
COLLIERY
East Lodge
White House Farm
Red House Farm
Sports Ground
Farhill Plantation
COLLEGE VW.
BEAUREPAIRE
PARKWOOD AV.
WOODSIDE AV.
EAST SIDE AV.
QUARRY CRES.
Comm. Cen.
Whitehouse Vw.
Woodland Croft
RITSON
KINGSTON
AVENUE
TAYLOR
TAYLOR AV.
AVENUE
BURTON CT.
RYLAND CT.
MULLIN CL.
WAYSIDE CT.
Aged Miners' Homes
North Vw.
Woodland Ter.
Victor T.
South Vw.
SOUTH VW. TER.
Linden Rd.
AUTON
AUTON CL.
Field Vw.
Comm. Cen.
STILE
Institute T.
George Ter.
ALDIN GRANGE TER.
ALDIN RISE
Oak Lea Ter.
Club
WOODLAND ROAD
LANE
Durham Community Business College for Technology & Enterprise
Works
WHITEHOUSE CT.
BRACKEN CT.
BRACKEN
The Sir Bobby Robson Sports Centre
Football Pitch
Victoria Court
COURT
Middlewood
ALDRIDGE CT.
COCKHOUSE LANE
B6302
Ladysmith Ter.
WELBY DR.
PRINCE BISHOP
WELBY DR. M.
ST. LUKE'S MEWS
TEMPERANCE TER.
Scholars Ct.
Cook's Cotts.
South Vw.
USHAW TER.
DALE
ARTHUR ST.
WHITEHOUSE
HALL AV.
Whitehouse Av.
HUNTER
Flass Ter.
FLASS
NEW ACRES
USHAW MOOR
Silver Tree Prim. Sch.
Prim. Sch.
OAKRIDGE
ASH AV.
Broom Hall
HOLLY PK.
FIR PK.
LABURNUM
MAPLE PARK
BAY CT.
MDW.
SKIPPERS MDW.
HOLLYWELL CT.
DURHAM ROAD
BROOM ROAD
CHESTNUT GRO.
CRESCENT
Leisure Cen.
Breckon Hill
Cemy.
BOUNDARY CL.
VIEW
ESH WOOD
Rosewood
High View Wlk.
Cochrane T.
Cochrane M.
USHAW VS.
Ushaw Villas
HIGHFIELD
Terrace
Middlefield
Sports Ground
STATION
Holywell Sike
Deerness Valley
DEERNESS
RIVER
Ushaw Moor Site
THORNLEY CL.
GROVE
ELM GROVE
BROOM HALL DR.
ELDER CL.
WOOLEY DR.
BRANCEPETH CL.
CASTLE VW.
OCKLEY CT.
ALDERDENE CL.
Rec. Grd.
BROOM LANE
Burn
Plantation View
Scout House Bank
Ford
BARLEY RISE
Hall
Playgrd.
Red
Redburn Bridge
Woodbine Ter.
Prospect Place
Bewley Ter.
Benvile Ter.
Fairfalls Ter.
ROCK TERRACE
Edward Ter.
Prospect Ter.
The Bungalows
Walton's Ter.
CO-OPERATIVE TER.
JUBILEE CL.
BRAUNESPATH ESTATE
BRAUNESPATH ESTATE
ROAD
New Brancepeth Prim. Sch.
DORIC
ROWLEY CL.
PRINGLE PLACE
PRINGLE GRO.
PRINGLE CL.
Folds Close
Playing Field
NEW BRANCEPETH
Scouthouse Farm
MILL LANE
Alum Waters
Unthank Farm
Bolton Farm
Bleach Green Farm
DH7
Primrose Side Farm
Primrose Side Cottage
West Broom Farm
Broom Farm
WEST FARM CT.
HILL VW.
Broom Fm. W.
Brandon Vw.
Broompark
COOKE'S
Cooke's West Wood
DEERNESS
Pringle House
Stob House Farm
Stob House
Playing Field
High Shaws
ST. AGATHAS CL.
Stack Garth
Hemmel Courts
Tiree Close
The Rig
Stobb House View
NORTH END
Brandon Village
Old Gardens
East Farm
West Farm
Cemetery
PIT LANE
HIGH MEADOWS
DEERNESS
HEIGHTS
Football Ground
Playgrd.
Bowl. Grn.
Pav.
SYCAMORE PARK
Commercial St.
CHURCH
LANE
BRANDON
Depot
Market Pl.
AVENUE
Aged Miners' Homes
Lodge
HIGH CROFT
CARR
GABLES Courts
RIDGES
Pithouse East Plantation
MORLEY LA.
174
Brandon Hall
Brandon Hall Cottage
SAWMILLS LA.
PEAR LEA
PALM LEA
PINE LEA
OAK GREEN FLATS
LINDEN PK.
HOLLY PARK
HAWTHORN PK.
POPLAR LEA
REDWOOD FLATS
ROWAN LEA
RED FIRS
BROCKWELL CT.
Playground
GREY
COMMERCIAL SQ.
STATION AVENUE
DEERNESS CT.
FRENSHAM WAY
163
A
B
C
D
E
1
2
3
4
5
6
7
22
23
24
43
42
41
40

F
G
H
J
K
153
175
166
6
1
2
3
4
5
6
7
425
26
27
540
Stotgate Farm
River Browney
Sewage Works
Moorsley Banks
Aldin Grange Bridge
Aldin Grange Farm
Aldin Grange Hall
Old Arbour House
Arbour House
Moorsley Banks Farm
Weir
Toll House Road
Quarry House
Baxter Wood
Quarry House La.
Browney House
Railway Cotts.
Viaduct
Laundry
Durham
M1
B6302
Relly Farm
Relley Gill
Broompark Picnic Site
Relley Mill
Cooke's East Wood
Relley Wood
Langley Wood
Sleetburn
Field Hall
Langley Old Hall
Langley Hall Farm
Old Hall Cotts.
Front Street
North Brancepeth Ter.
Woodbridge
Prim. Sch. & Nursy.
Play. Fld.
Blair Cl.
St. Bedes Way
St. Cuthberts Wk.
Langley Moor
Langley Moor Ind. Est.
Mill Road
Co-operative Villas
Prim. Sch.
Littleburn
Cricket Ground
Sports Ground
Goat's Bridge
Football Pitch
Meadowfield Leisure Centre
Lobley Hill
High Street
A690
Church Mdw.
Cemy.
Towngate Bus. Cen.
Littleburn Road
Rosebay Road
Warehouses
Goat's Beck
Saw Mill
Thistle Rd.
West Durham Office Pk.
Farewellhall
The Garth
Borehole Wood
Moorhouse Wood
Langley Bri.
Holiday Park
Neville's Cross
Grove Ter.
Durham Dairy
Stone Bridge Gdns.
River Browney
North Wood
Sewage Works
Stone Bri.
Lowe's Barn
Whitesmocks
Western Lodge
Southfield Way
Southfield Ho. Govt. Offs.
Long Garth
St. Nicholas Dr.
Aykley Heads Sports Cen.
County Hall
County Hall Buildings
Durham Light Infantry Museum & Durham Art Gallery
Bowling Greens
Tennis Courts
Hosp.
Dryburn
Brackenbury
B6532
Framwellgate Peth
A691
North End
St. Leonard's RC Comp. Sch.
Western Hill
Windy Hill
Fernhill
Friarside
A167
Springwell Rd.
Club Lane
Durham Johnston Comp. School
Pitches
Maiden's Bower
Flass Bog
Bus Depot
Miners' Hall
Flass Vale
Crossgate Moor
Redhills
Cemetery
St. Monica Grove
St. Bede's Cl.
Durham
Wharton Park
Station App.
Castle Chare
Bus Sta.
Allergate
Crossgate
Crossgate Peth
A690
St. Margaret's Centre
Grave Yard
Neville's Cross Prim. Sch.
St. Margaret's C of E Prim. Sch.
DURHAM
Tennis Cts.
Playing Field
Durham Sch.
Prebends Bridge
Playing Fields
Bellasis
Neville's Cross
Observatory (Durham University)
Observatory House
Darlington Road
Potters Bank
Merryoaks
DH1
St Aidan's College (Durham Uni.)
Durham Business School
Durham University Oriental Museum
Nickleby Chare
St. Cuthbert's Hospice
Rec. Grd.
Mill Hill Lane
Van Mildert College (Univ. of Durham)
Science Park
Mount Oswald Golf Course
Club House
Elvet Moor Farm
Lodge
Blaidwood
Money Slack
A177
South Road
South Road Cemetery
Durham Crematorium
Durham High Sch. for Girls
Tennis Courts
Farewell Hall
St. Oswald's Dr.
Roundhaven
Farewell Hall West Farm
Farewell Hall East Farm
Blaid's Wood
Saltwell Gill
Ustinov Coll.
The Howlands Building
St. Mary's (Durham)
The Institute
Elvet Hill
Teikyo

166
A
B
C
D
E
1
2
3
4
5
6
7
27
28
29
154
176
165
Sports Ground
Signal Bridge
Durham Light Infantry Museum & Durham Art Gallery
Playing Field
Sewage Works
Nursery
Crook Hall & Gardens
The Riverside Centre
FRANKLAND LA.
FRAMWELGATE PETH
FRAMWELGATE
Kepier Hosp.
NEDL Training Centre
KEPIER LANE
CARRVILLE LINK ROAD
A690
Gilesgate
Durham Gilesgate Sports College & 6th Form Centre
High Grange
Durham Gilesgate Primary School
The Sands
Durham
Millburngate Ho.
Pennyferry Bri.
Leisure Cen.
Millennium Place
LEAZES RD.
CLAYPATH
GILESGATE
SHERBURN ROAD
SUNDERLAND ROAD
A181
Bus Sta.
The Gates Shop. Cen.
Cemetery
College of St. Hild & St. Bede (Univ. of Durham)
Malvern Villas
Pelaw Wood Beck
DURHAM
RIVER WEAR
Laurel Avenue Primary Sch.
Durham Castle
Durham University
Durham Cathedral
Durham Uni.
Hatfield College
Durham Crown Court
HMP DURHAM
Durham County Courts
Sports Ground
Hilton Cottage
Cricket Ground
Rugby Football Ground
Durham Amateur Rowing Club
Pelaw Wood
Sherburn Road Estate
Hockey Ground
Hollow Drift
Rugby Ground
Old Durham
Old Durham Farm
The Old Barn
Farm Cottage
St. Margaret's Centre
Prebends Bridge
St. Chad's Coll.
St. John's Coll.
Cranmer Hall Theological Coll.
St. Cuthbert's Society (Durham Uni.)
Count's Ho.
The Chorister School
Durham Johnston Comp. Sch. (Lower)
Maiden Castle Wood
Maiden Castle Promontory Fort
Whinney Hill
Playing Fields
OLD DURHAM BECK
Durham University Rowing Club
Running Track
The Graham Sports Centre (University of Durham)
Playing Field
Broom Hill
STOCKTON ROAD
A177
Palatine Cen.
Science Laboratories
Durham University
Mount Joy
Mountjoy Farm
St. Mary's College (Durham Uni.)
POTTERS BANK
The Institute for Middle East & Islamic Studies
Durham University Oriental Museum
Teikyo Univ. of Japan in Durham
Trevelyan College
Dept. of Biological & Biomedical Sciences (Durham Uni.)
Grey College (Durham Uni.)
John Snow Ho. (Durham Uni.)
Mountjoy Research Centre
Mount Joy Cottage
Mount Joy Reservoir
East Durham & Houghall Community College (Houghall Cen.)
World of Trees & Houghall Gdns.
DH1
Shincliffe Bridge
B1198
MILL LANE
Shincliffe Park
Sandy Cut
SHINCLIFFE
WILLOW TREE AV.
BANK FOOT
Science Park
University of Durham Botanic Garden
GREAT HIGH WOOD
Collingwood College (Durham Uni.)
Hollingside Cottage
Hollingside House
HOLLINGSIDE LANE
SOUTH ROAD
Howlands
The Howlands Building
Josephine Butler Coll.
Ustinov Coll.
Hollinside Wood
Student Accomodation
Blaidwood
Lodge
South Road Cemetery
Sewage Works
Nursery
Blaid's Wood
Saltwell Gill
FARM ROAD
Houghall Houses
Houghall Farm
Houghall
RIVER WEAR
Old England
Playground
Nursery
HIGH STREET
Rose Acre
The Croft
Houghton Hole
Shincliffe Hall
SHINCLIFFE WOOD
West Grange
East Grange

167
Moor End
Belmont
Broomside
Gilesgate Moor
Belmont Business Park
Durham City Retail Park
Dragonville Industrial Estate
Dragonville Retail Park
Superstore
A1(M) MOTORWAY
A1(M)
FRONT STREET
B1283
A181
SHERBURN
Seconds Out Sherburn ASET Centre
DH6
Durham
Sherburn Hospital (Residential Care Home)
Sherburn House
Sherburnhouse Plantation
Sherburn Grange
Naysmith Cottage
Sherburn Beck
Pittington Beck
Sewage Works
SHINCLIFFE LANE
B1198
Whitwell Grange Farm
Whitwell Grange
Whitwell House Farm
Whitwell Farm
Whitwell East House Farm
Chapman Beck
Chapman Bridge
Byers Garth
A688
HIGH SHINCLIFFE
Manor Farm
Manor Farm Cottage
Mill Cottages
Mill House
Oak Wood Cottage
Bent House Farm
Broomside Cottages
Broomside House
Pittington Bridge
Rosemeade
155
168
177
F G H J K
1 2 3 4 5 6 7
430 31 32
43 42 41 40

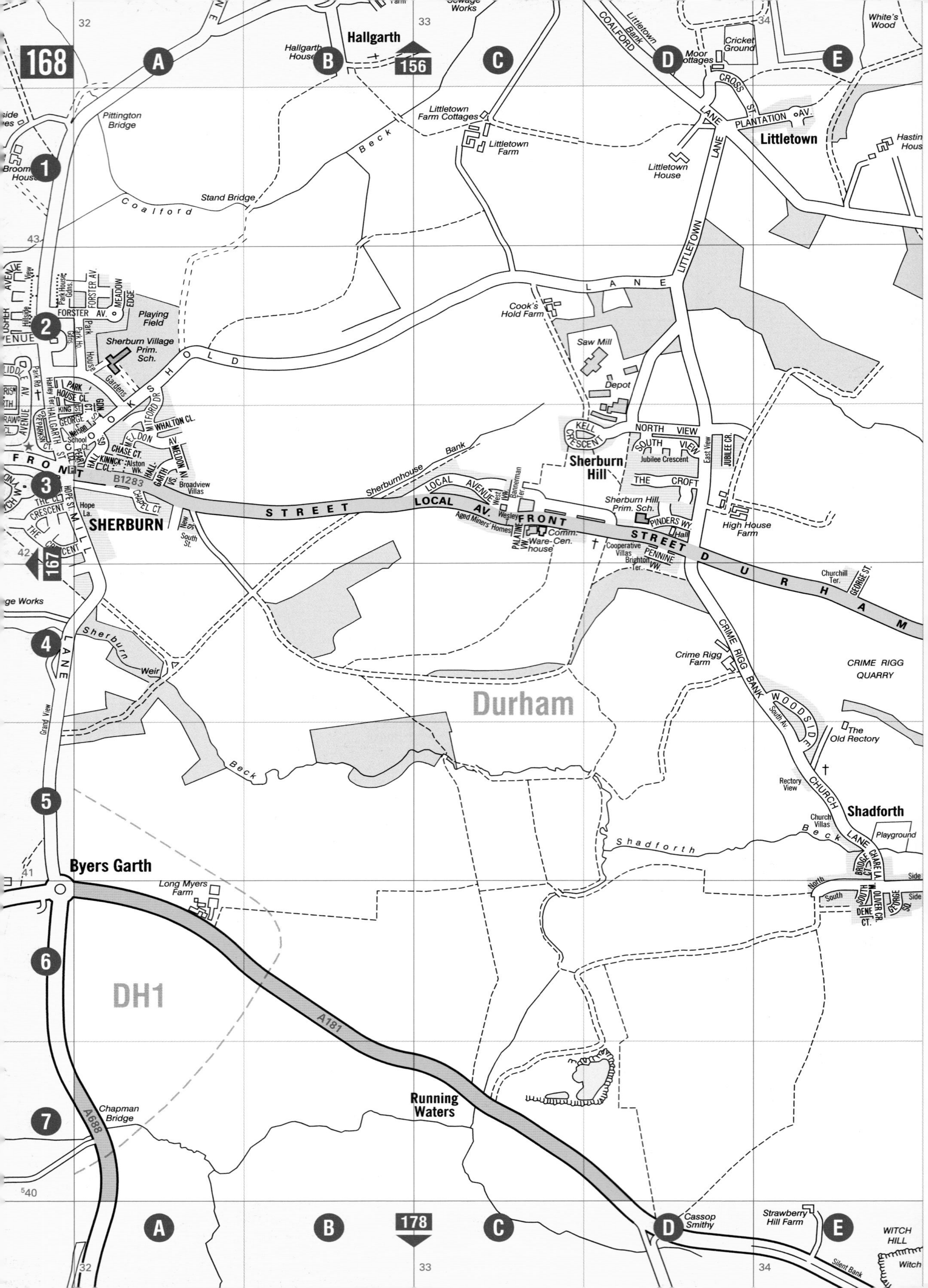
Hallgarth
156
Hallgarth House
Littletown Farm Cottages
Littletown Farm
Littletown
Littletown House
Cricket Ground
Moor Cottages
White's Wood
Pittington Bridge
Broom House
Stand Bridge
Coalford Beck
Playing Field
Sherburn Village Prim. Sch.
Cook's Hold Farm
Saw Mill
Depot
Sherburn Hill
Sherburn Hill Prim. Sch.
High House Farm
SHERBURN
FRONT STREET
LOCAL AV.
DURHAM
167
Sherburn Weir
Crime Rigg Farm
CRIME RIGG QUARRY
Durham
The Old Rectory
Shadforth
Playground
Byers Garth
Long Myers Farm
DH1
A181
A688
Chapman Bridge
Running Waters
Cassop Smithy
Strawberry Hill Farm
WITCH HILL
178

169
F
G
H
J
K
157
179
170
1
2
3
4
5
6
7
35
36
37
43
42
41
40
Dog Kennel Bank
Brown's Plantation
Lily Hill Plantation
LILY HILL
GREEN LANE
Colliery Farm
Store Farm
Cat Hole
Dabble Bank
Haswell Lodge
Red Brick Garth
High Row
WATSON'S HILL
Black Banks
Haswell Moor Farm
The Bottoms
Haswell Plough
B1283
LANE
GLOUCESTER
Crescent
TERRACE
West Vw.
Rutland Ter.
LIMEKILN HILL
PROSPECT HILL
Sevenacres Farm
Harehill Plantation
B1283
TOWER HILL
Playing Field
Ludworth
Hall
Hill House Farm
USHER
NTH. MARGARET ST.
S. VW.
War Mem.
St. Andrews Ct.
BARNARD AV.
Ludworth Tower
Ludworth Tower (remains of)
Hare Hill
DH6
Sch.
MOOR CRESCENT
MOOR CRES.
Greystones
BARNARD
BARNARD AV.
AVENUE
EAST VIEW
Playing Field
SPRINGFIELD MDW.
THORNTON CL.
NEW ROAD
Ford
DENE
Fatclose Plantation
LIMEKILN HILL
Ox Close Cottage
Ox Close Farm
Fatclose House
LANE
Shadforth Dene
Harrow Bank
SHEPHERD'S HILL
Cemetery
Whinny Banks
HORSE HILL
THORNLEY
EAST
Emmerson Sq.
LEA
COOPER'S TER.
SCHOOL GRN.
Gore Hill
Gore Hill Estate
Thornley Primary School
Gore Hall
GORE LA.
PASSFIELD SQ.
Hill Quarry
HILLSYDE
Bow St.
Garden Ter.
ASHFORD
Moor Vw.
Percy St.

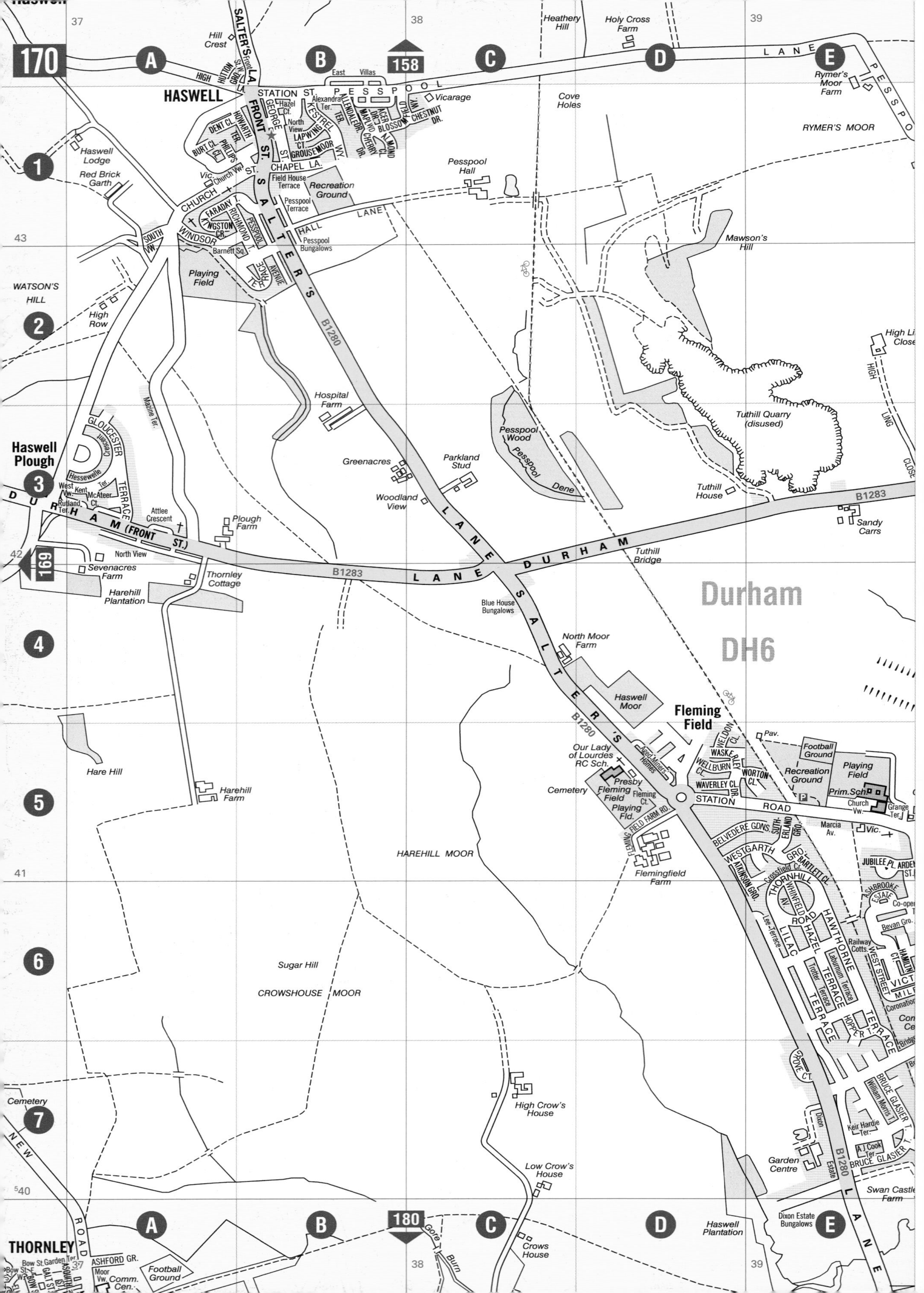
HASWELL
Haswell Plough
Fleming Field
THORNLEY
Durham
DH6
158
169
180
Hill Crest
Heathery Hill
Holy Cross Farm
Rymer's Moor Farm
RYMER'S MOOR
Cove Holes
Vicarage
Haswell Lodge
Red Brick Garth
Pesspool Hall
Recreation Ground
Mawson's Hill
WATSON'S HILL
High Row
Playing Field
Hospital Farm
Tuthill Quarry (disused)
Pesspool Wood
Greenacres
Parkland Stud
Woodland View
Tuthill House
Sandy Carrs
Attlee Crescent
Plough Farm
North View
Sevenacres Farm
Thornley Cottage
Harehill Plantation
Tuthill Bridge
Blue House Bungalows
North Moor Farm
Haswell Moor
Hare Hill
Harehill Farm
Our Lady of Lourdes RC Sch.
Cemetery
Football Ground
Playing Field
Recreation Ground
Prim.Sch
HAREHILL MOOR
Flemingfield Farm
Sugar Hill
CROWSHOUSE MOOR
High Crow's House
Low Crow's House
Crows House
Garden Centre
Haswell Plantation
Dixon Estate Bungalows
Swan Castle Farm
SALTER'S LANE
DURHAM LANE
B1280
B1283
STATION ROAD
PESSPOOL LANE

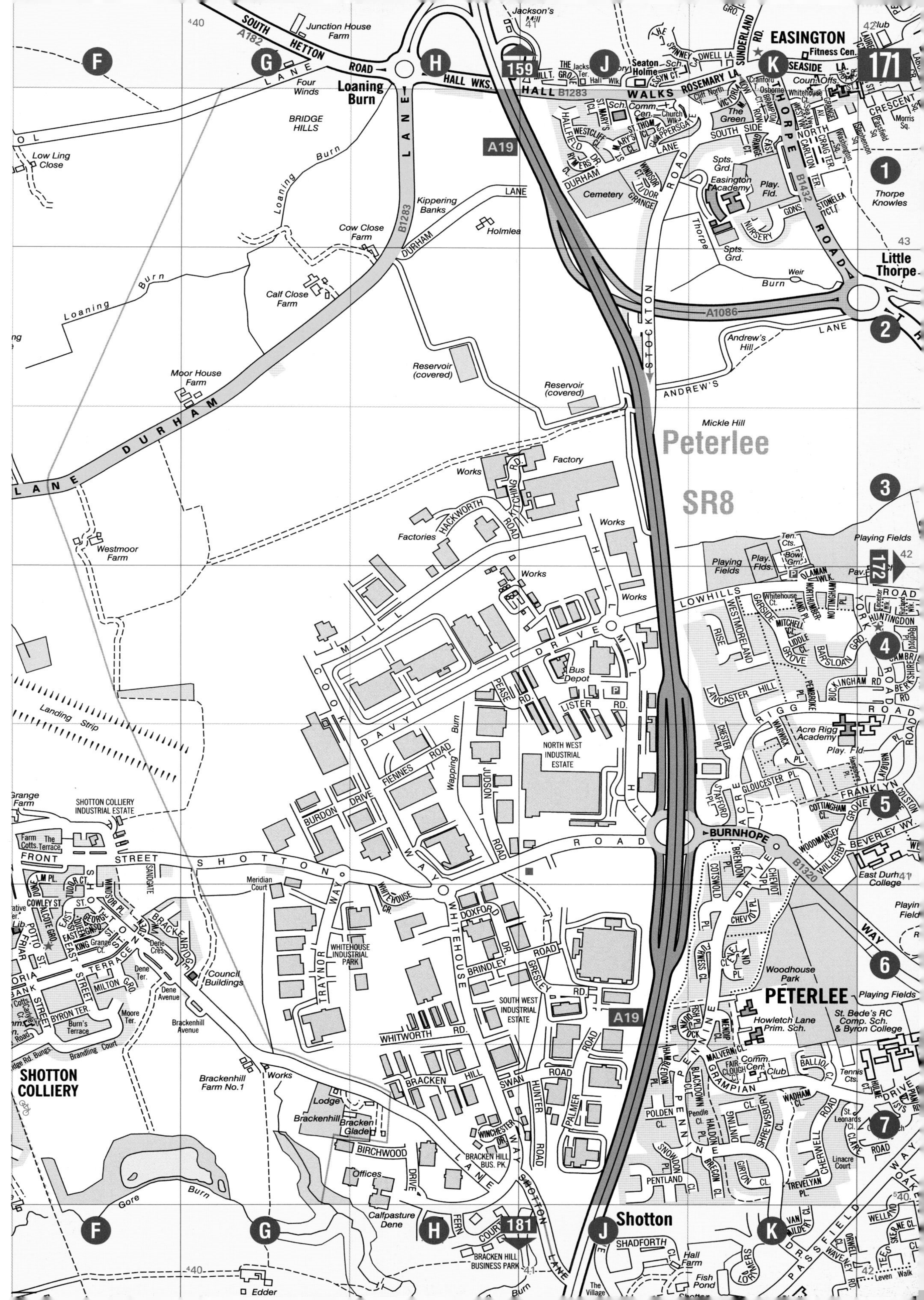
171
159
172
181
EASINGTON
Peterlee
SR8
PETERLEE
SHOTTON COLLIERY
Shotton
Little Thorpe
Loaning Burn
A19
A182
A1086
B1283
B1432
B1320
SOUTH HETTON ROAD
HALL WALKS
DURHAM LANE
STOCKTON ROAD
SHOTTON ROAD
BURNHOPE
Junction House Farm
Four Winds
BRIDGE HILLS
Low Ling Close
Kippering Banks
Holmlea
Cow Close Farm
Calf Close Farm
Moor House Farm
Westmoor Farm
Reservoir (covered)
Mickle Hill
Andrew's Hill
Thorpe Knowles
Easington Academy
Cemetery
NORTH WEST INDUSTRIAL ESTATE
SOUTH WEST INDUSTRIAL ESTATE
WHITEHOUSE INDUSTRIAL PARK
SHOTTON COLLIERY INDUSTRIAL ESTATE
BRACKEN HILL BUS. PK.
BRACKEN HILL BUSINESS PARK
Bus Depot
Landing Strip
Acre Rigg Academy
Woodhouse Park
Howletch Lane Prim. Sch.
St. Bede's RC Comp. Sch. & Byron College
East Durham College
Council Buildings
Brackenhill Farm No.1
Calfpasture Dene
Gore Burn
Edder
Hall Farm
Fish Pond
Jackson's Mill
Grange Farm
Playing Fields

EASINGTON
Little Thorpe
Thorpe Knowles
Dairy Farm
Littlethorpe Farm
Thorpe Gill
Thorpe Burn
Horden Burn
Horden Dene
Spring Bank
Thorpe Wood
Horden Hall
Horden Hall Farm
The Cottages
Cemetery
Paradise
Paradise Gardens
Easington Colliery Welfare Grounds
Glenhurst Farm
Playgrounds
Football Grounds
Townfield Hill
Fox Holes Dene
Dene Villa
Dene Hall
Rec. Grd.
Sewage Works
Warren House
Ash Gill
Black Plantation
SEAVIEW INDUSTRIAL ESTATE
NORTH EAST IND. EST.
Factory
Works
Day Centre
Playing Fields
Training Cen.
Peterlee
Eden Lane Playing Fields
HORDEN
PHOENIX WORKSHOPS
Welfare Park Ckt. Grd.
Football Ground
Acre Rigg Academy
Huntercombe Ho.
Seascape Primary School
East Durham College
Playing Field
Running Track
East Durham College (Burnhope Way Cen.)
Hypermarket
Bus Sta.
Superstore
Dene Park
St. Bede's RC Comp. Sch. & Byron College
Our Lady of the Rosary RC Prim. Sch.
Peterlee Leis.Cen.
PETERLEE
Peterlee Magistrates' Court
North Blunts
PETERLEE COMM. HOSP.
Hawthorns Nursing Home
Round Plantation
Dene House Prim. Sch.
Dene School
Long Plantation
Blunts Plantation
The Garden of Eden Cottage
Garden of Eden Bridge
Castle Eden Dene National Nature Reserve
Craggy Bank
Blunts Point
Blunts Dene
Cricket Ground
Club House
Playing Field
Edenvale Estate
Saw Mill
Cemy.
A1086
B1283
B1320
B1432
THORPE ROAD
SUNDERLAND ROAD
YODEN WAY
BURNHOPE WAY
PASSFIELD WAY
COAST ROAD
SR8
160
171
182

Fox Holes
F
G
H
J
K
161
445
46
47
1
2
3
4
5
6
7
43
42
41
540
NORTH SEA
House Gill
Blackhills Farm
South East View
Cotsford Junior School
ALMOND TER.
PARADISE ST.
BEACH GRO.
Azalea TER.
ASPEN AV.
CEDAR
ADAM ST.
EVE S.
WINDSOR TER.
Windsor Cnr.
Marlborough Cr.
ACACIA AV.
Bay AV.
Blackthorne
CHERRY AV.
ALDER RD.
Sandringham Cr.
Langthorne Av.
LANE
SEYMOUR ST.
Hall
Yohden Prim. Sch.
Cotsford Grange
Playing Field
Cotsford Inf. Sch.
Horden Nursy. Sch.
REYNOLDS CT.
RISE
Macbeth
DIXON Wk.
COTSFORD ESTATE
PARK
STAPYLTON DR.
Station Cottages
Limekiln Gill
Hartlepool Point
Dene Mouth
WILLOW GROVE
A1086
Burn
Eden
Scotchman's Gill
Ash Gill
Hartlepool
TS27
Wordsworth Av.
Tennyson Av.
Shakespeare Av.
SHAFTESBURY
Milton Av.
Kipling Av.
Coleridge Av.
Chaucer Av.
Burns Av.
ROAD
SHAFTESBURY AV.
BYRON AV.
ARNOLD AV.
ELEVENTH STREET
HACKWORTH RD.
BLACKHALL COLLIERY INDUSTRIAL ESTATE
183
Hardwick Dene
Welfare Park
Cricket
War Mem.

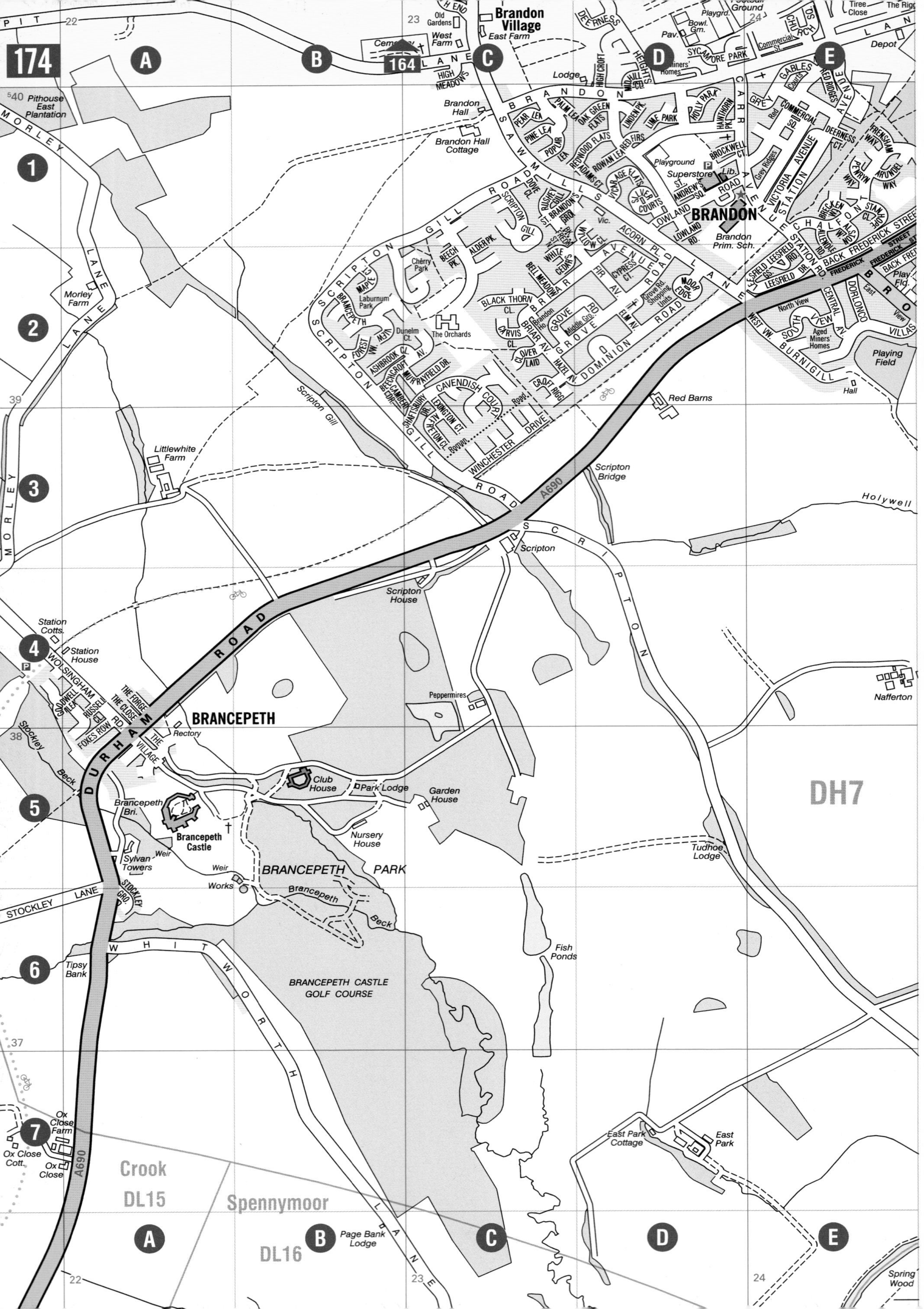
Brandon Village
BRANDON
BRANCEPETH
Brancepeth Castle
BRANCEPETH PARK
BRANCEPETH CASTLE GOLF COURSE
DURHAM ROAD
A690
DH7
Crook DL15
Spennymoor DL16
164

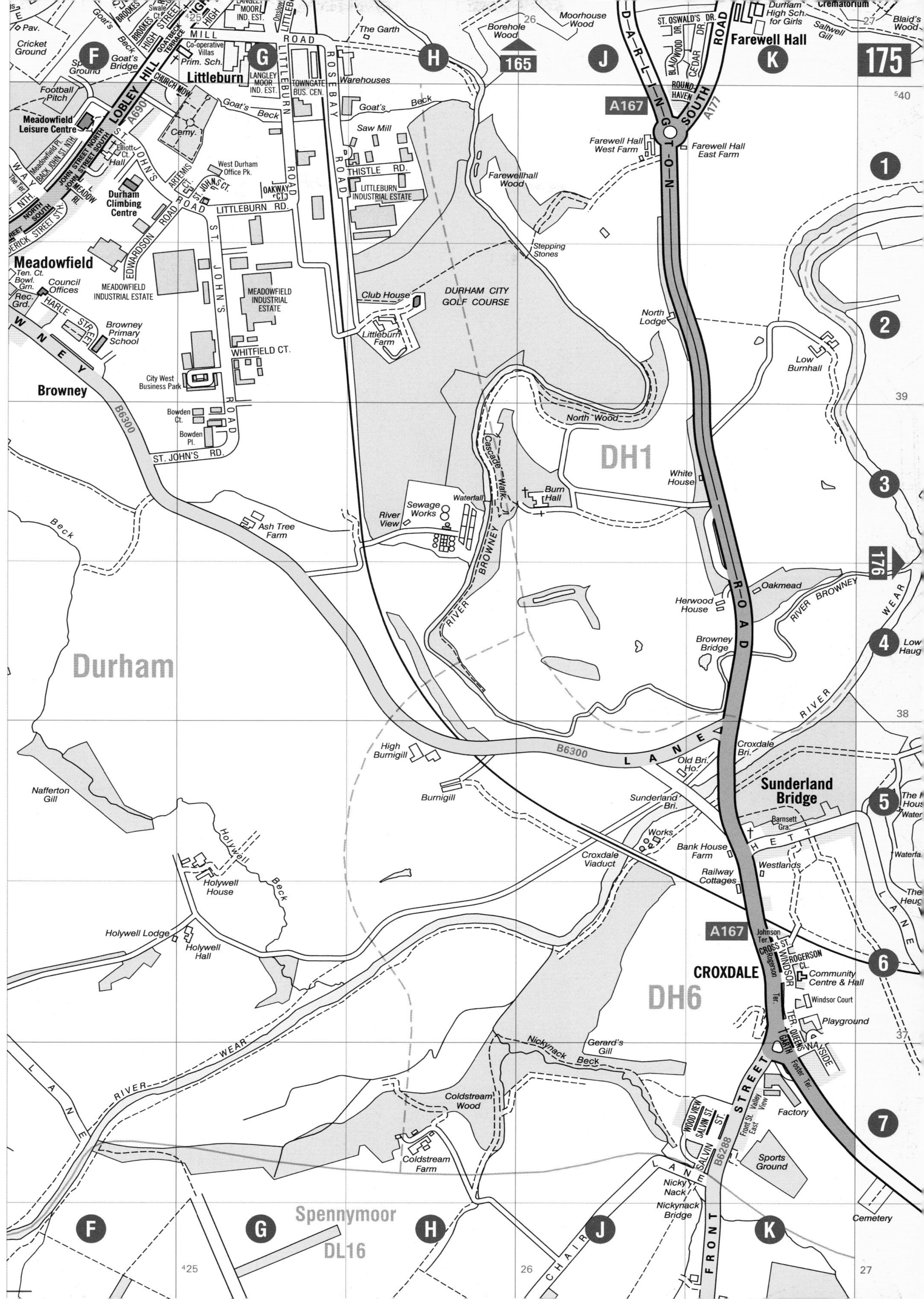
Meadowfield
Littleburn
Browney
Durham
Farewell Hall
Sunderland Bridge
CROXDALE
DH1
DH6
Spennymoor
DL16
DURHAM CITY GOLF COURSE
Meadowfield Leisure Centre
Durham Climbing Centre
MEADOWFIELD INDUSTRIAL ESTATE
LITTLEBURN INDUSTRIAL ESTATE
City West Business Park
Browney Primary School
Council Offices
Ash Tree Farm
Sewage Works
Burn Hall
North Wood
Farewellhall Wood
Croxdale Viaduct
Coldstream Wood
Coldstream Farm
Holywell House
Holywell Hall
Holywell Lodge
Nafferton Gill
High Burnigill
Burnigill
Low Burnhall
Herwood House
Oakmead
White House
North Lodge
Farewell Hall West Farm
Farewell Hall East Farm
Durham High Sch. for Girls
Moorhouse Wood
Borehole Wood
Crematorium
Saltwell Gill
Blaid's Wood
Community Centre & Hall
Windsor Court
Playground
Sports Ground
Factory
Cemetery
Nicky Nack
Nickynack Bridge
Gerard's Gill
Nickynack Beck
Westlands
Railway Cottages
Bank House Farm
Barnsett Gra.
Works
Sunderland Bri.
Old Bri. Ho.
Croxdale Bri.
Browney Bridge
RIVER WEAR
RIVER BROWNEY
LANE
B6300
A167
A177
A690
B6288
DARLINGTON ROAD
SOUTH ROAD
FRONT STREET
ST. JOHN'S ROAD
LITTLEBURN ROAD
ROSEBAY ROAD
MILL ROAD
EDWARDSON ROAD
WHITFIELD CT.
THISTLE RD.
HETT
F G H J K
1 2 3 4 5 6 7
165
176

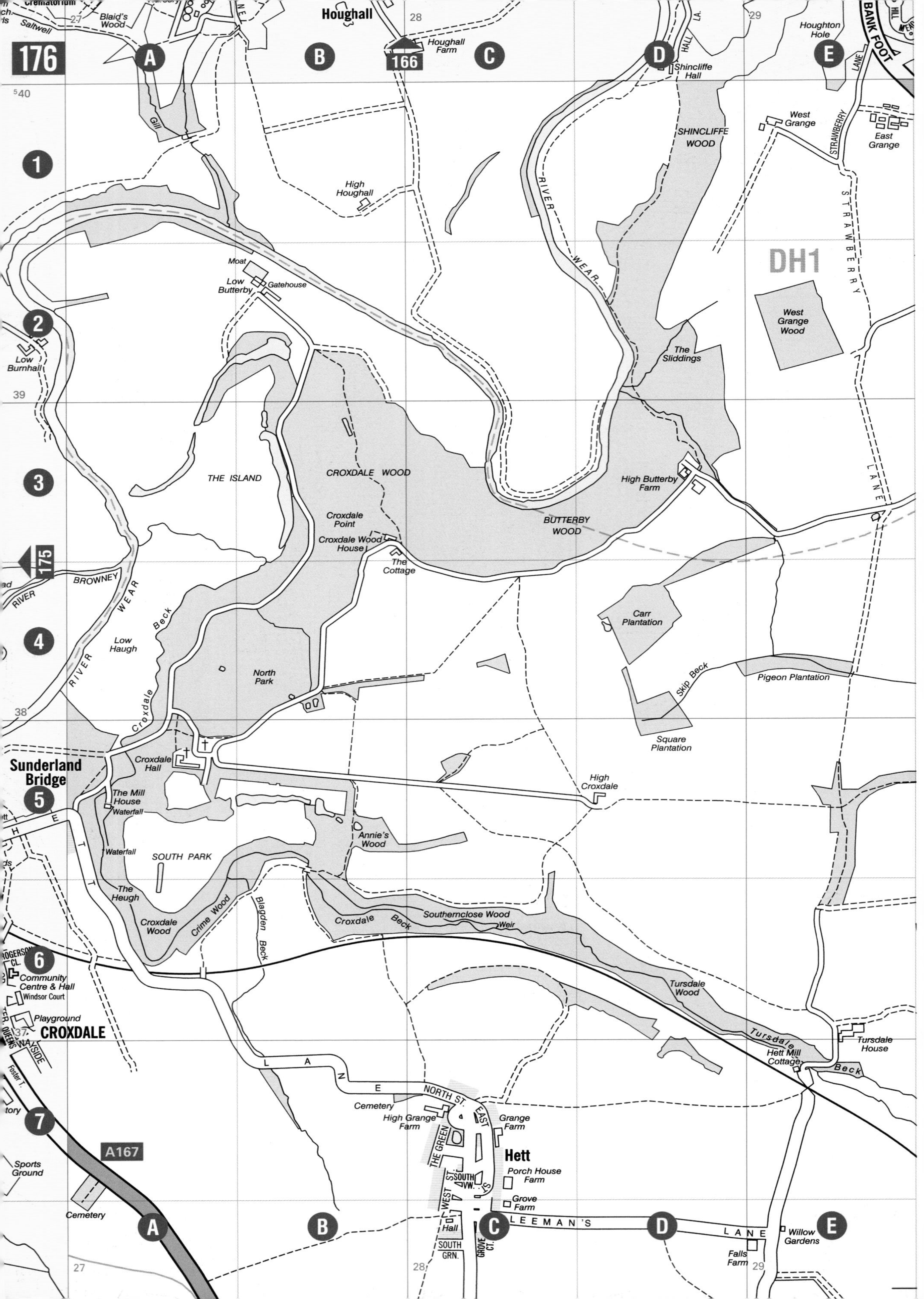

Houghall
Blaid's Wood
Saltwell
Houghall Farm
166
Shincliffe Hall
Houghton Hole
BANK FOOT
West Grange
East Grange
SHINCLIFFE WOOD
STRAWBERRY
High Houghall
RIVER WEAR
DH1
Moat
Low Butterby
Gatehouse
West Grange Wood
Low Burnhall
The Sliddings
THE ISLAND
CROXDALE WOOD
High Butterby Farm
STRAWBERRY LANE
Croxdale Point
Croxdale Wood House
The Cottage
BUTTERBY WOOD
175
BROWNEY
RIVER WEAR
Carr Plantation
Low Haugh
Croxdale Beck
North Park
Skip Beck
Pigeon Plantation
Square Plantation
Sunderland Bridge
Croxdale Hall
High Croxdale
The Mill House
Waterfall
Annie's Wood
SOUTH PARK
The Heugh
Croxdale Wood
Crime Wood
Blagden Beck
Southernclose Wood
Weir
Croxdale Beck
Community Centre & Hall
Windsor Court
Playground
CROXDALE
Tursdale Wood
Tursdale House
Hett Mill Cottage
Tursdale Beck
HETT LANE
NORTH ST.
EAST ST.
Cemetery
High Grange Farm
Grange Farm
THE GREEN
Hett
Porch House Farm
SOUTH VW.
WEST ST.
Grove Farm
A167
Sports Ground
Cemetery
LEEMAN'S LANE
Hall
Willow Gardens
SOUTH GRN.
GROVE CT.
Falls Farm

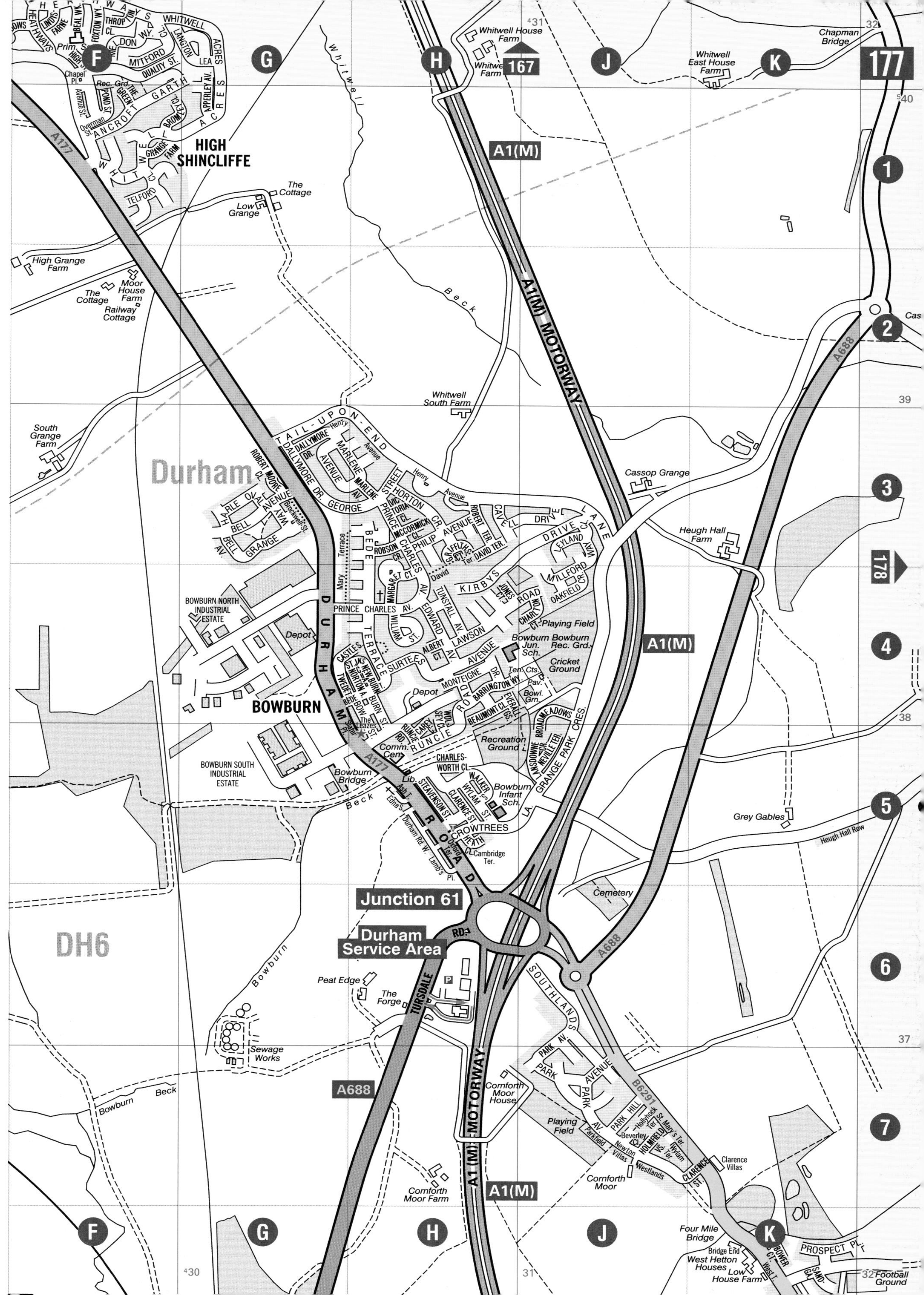
HIGH SHINCLIFFE
Durham
BOWBURN
DH6
Junction 61
Durham Service Area
A1(M) MOTORWAY
A1(M)
A177
A688
B6291
DURHAM ROAD
TURSDALE RD.
BOWBURN NORTH INDUSTRIAL ESTATE
BOWBURN SOUTH INDUSTRIAL ESTATE
Whitwell House Farm
Whitwell East House Farm
Chapman Bridge
The Cottage
Low Grange
High Grange Farm
Moor House Farm
Railway Cottage
South Grange Farm
Whitwell South Farm
Cassop Grange
Heugh Hall Farm
Grey Gables
Heugh Hall Row
Cemetery
Recreation Ground
Cricket Ground
Playing Field
Bowburn Jun. Sch.
Bowburn Rec. Grd.
Bowburn Infant Sch.
Bowburn Bridge
Depot
Peat Edge
The Forge
Sewage Works
Cornforth Moor House
Cornforth Moor Farm
Cornforth Moor
Clarence Villas
Four Mile Bridge
Bridge End
West Hetton Houses
Low House Farm
Football Ground
PROSPECT PL.
Bowburn Beck
Whitwell Beck
TAIL-UPON-END
DALLYMORE DR.
MARLENE AVENUE
GEORGE STREET
PRINCE CHARLES AV.
BEDE TERRACE
SURTEES AVENUE
RUNCIE RD.
GRANGE PARK CRES.
STEAVENSON ST.
CROWTREES LA.
SOUTHLANDS
PARK AVENUE
PARK HILL
CLARENCE ST.
Westlands
ANCROFT GARTH
WHITWELL ACRES
167
178
F G H J K
1 2 3 4 5 6 7
430 431 32
37 38 39 540

Chapman Bridge
Running Waters
168
A
B
C
D
E
1
2
3
4
5
6
7
177
A688
A181
Cassop Smithy
Strawberry Hill Farm
WITCH HILL
Silent Bank
Old Cassop
Pilmore Farm
Hill Croft
Cassop Farm
Grange Farm
Cassop Moor
Chapman
Beck
Durham
DH6
CASSOP VALE
Sewage Works
Comm. Hall
Quality Row
LUKE AV.
Quarrington Quarry
Beacon Hill
CHURCH
Res.
Cassop Hill
Cassop Primary School
Quarrington Farm
Old Quarrington
Heugh Hall Row
Quarrington Heights
BELLE VUE
Playing Field
QUARRINGTON HILL INDUSTRIAL ESTATE
Quarrington Hill
STREET
St. Helen's Cl.
Aged Miners' Homes
Comm. Cen.
QUARRY PLANTATION
Steetley Terrace
FRONT
Carole Dunes
NEIL CR.
TER.
DAVID
MALCOLM AV.
HAZEL AV.
HAWTHORN CR.
Welfare Ground
Bowling Green
Football Ground
Refuse Tip
B6291
MORLEY CRES.
ANN
SCHOOL AV.
MARY
CRESCENT
Kelloe Prim. Sch.
Playing Fields
Cemy.
Church Farm
PROSPECT PL.
SANDGATE
Football Ground
Coxhoe Bank Plantation
RAMONA AV.
WOODLAND CRES.
KELLOE
East Hetton Aged Workmen's Homes
BURNETT CR.
Front St.
Kelloe
32
33
34
37
38
39
40

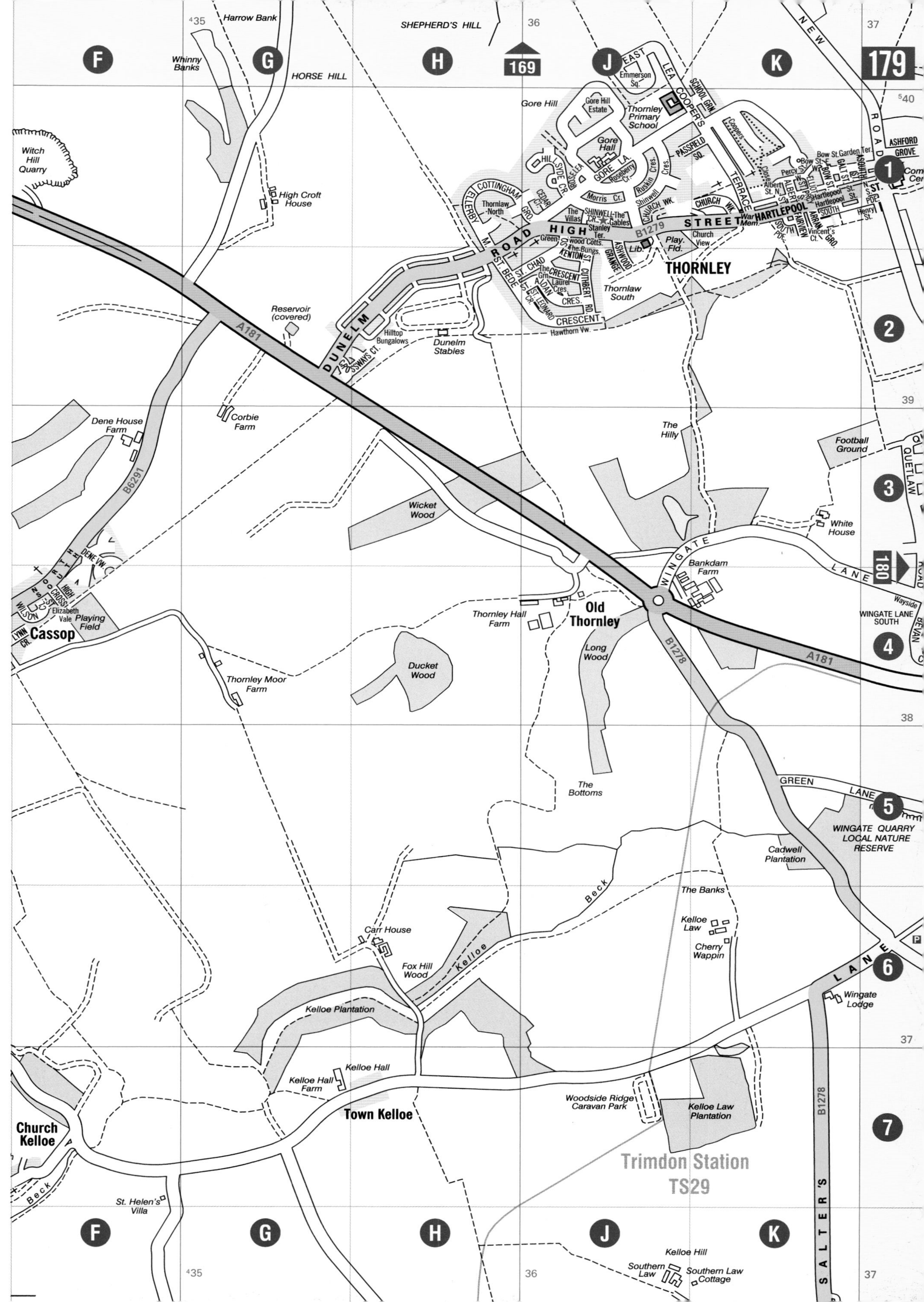
THORNLEY
Old Thornley
Cassop
Town Kelloe
Church Kelloe
Trimdon Station
TS29
169
180
A181
B1279
B1278
B6291
Harrow Bank
Whinny Banks
Shepherd's Hill
Horse Hill
Gore Hill
Witch Hill Quarry
High Croft House
Reservoir (covered)
Corbie Farm
Dene House Farm
Hilltop Bungalows
Dunelm Stables
Wicket Wood
Thornley Hall Farm
Ducket Wood
Long Wood
Thornley Moor Farm
Playing Field
The Hilly
Football Ground
White House
Bankdam Farm
Wingate Lane South
The Bottoms
Green Lane
Wingate Quarry Local Nature Reserve
Cadwell Plantation
The Banks
Kelloe Law
Cherry Wappin
Carr House
Fox Hill Wood
Kelloe Beck
Kelloe Plantation
Kelloe Hall
Kelloe Hall Farm
Woodside Ridge Caravan Park
Kelloe Law Plantation
Wingate Lodge
Salter's Lane
St. Helen's Villa
Kelloe Hill
Southern Law
Southern Law Cottage
Thornley Primary School
Gore Hill Estate
Gore Hall
Thornlaw North
Thornlaw South
Church View
Play. Fld.
Lib.
High Street
Hartlepool St.
Dunelm Road
Wingate Lane
New Road
Ashford Grove
Quetlaw
Crescent
Hawthorn Vw.
F
G
H
J
K
1
2
3
4
5
6
7
435
36
37
540
39
38
37

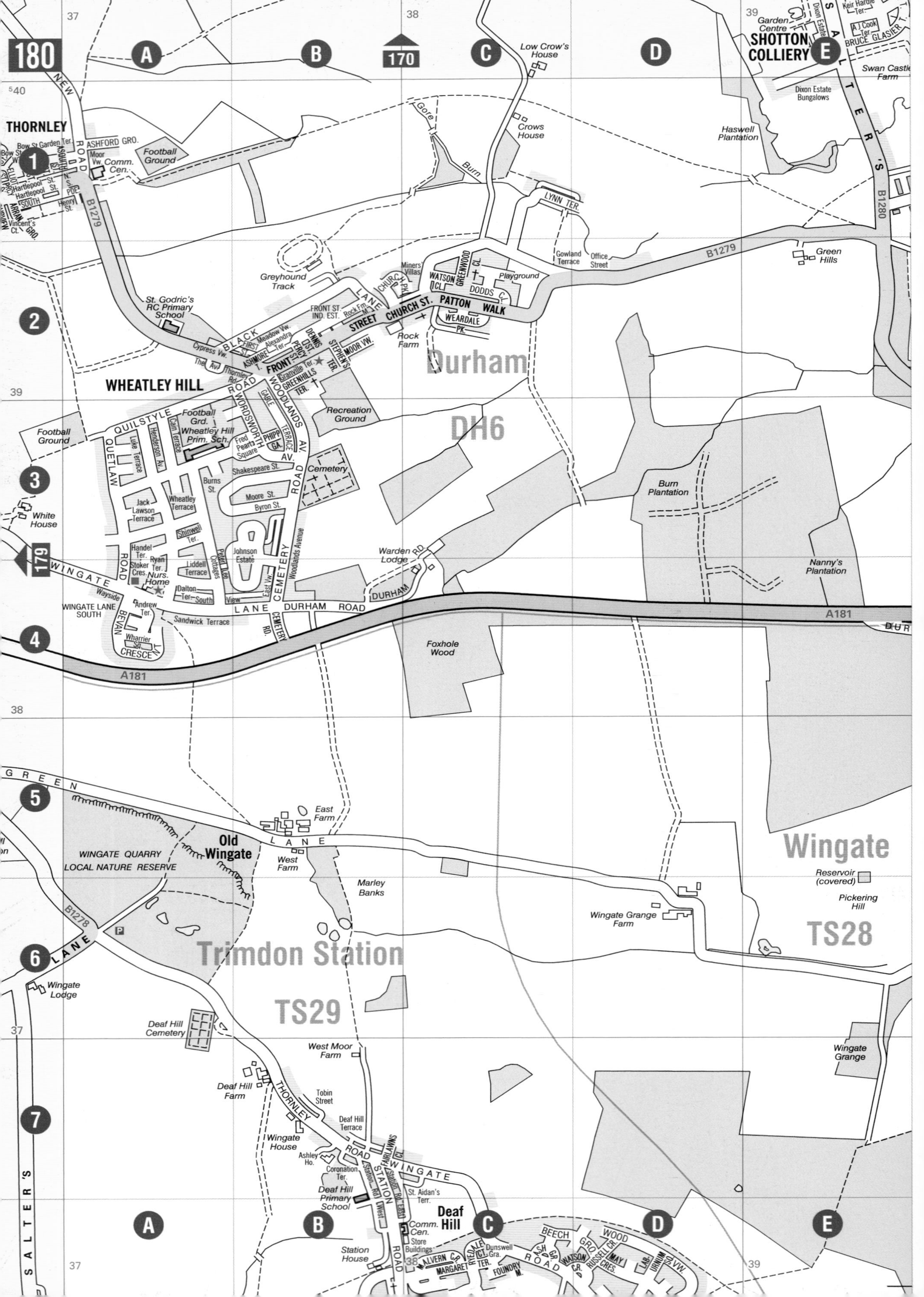
170
179
A
B
C
D
E
1
2
3
4
5
6
7
37
38
39
40
THORNLEY
SHOTTON COLLIERY
WHEATLEY HILL
Durham
DH6
Wingate
TS28
Trimdon Station
TS29
Old Wingate
Deaf Hill
Low Crow's House
Crows House
Garden Centre
Dixon Estate
Keir Hardie Ter.
A J Cook Ter.
BRUCE GLASIER
Swan Castle Farm
Dixon Estate Bungalows
Haswell Plantation
SALTER'S
B1280
B1279
Green Hills
Football Ground
ASHFORD GRO.
Moor Vw.
Comm. Cen.
NEW ROAD
Gore Burn
LYNN TER.
Gowland Terrace
Office Street
Miners Villas
Greyhound Track
Playground
WATSON CL.
GREENWOOD CL.
DODDS CL.
CHURCH ST.
PATTON WALK
WEARDALE PK.
Rock Farm
FRONT ST. IND. EST.
FRONT STREET
BLACK LANE
St. Godric's RC Primary School
Cypress Vw.
ASHMORE T.
Meadow Vw.
Alexandra Ter.
STEPHENS TER.
MOOR VW.
Granville Ter.
GREENHILLS TER.
Recreation Ground
QUILSTYLE
QUETLAW
Football Grd.
Wheatley Hill Prim. Sch.
Luke Terrace
Henderson Av.
Cain Terrace
WORDSWORTH AV.
WOODLANDS ROAD
TERRACE
Fred Peart Square
Cemetery
Shakespeare St.
Burns St.
Moore St.
Byron St.
Jack Lawson Terrace
Wheatley Terrace
Shinwell Ter.
Johnson Estate
Handel Ter.
Ryan Ter.
Stoker Cres.
Nurs. Home
Liddell Terrace
Dalton Ter.
CEMETERY ROAD
Woodlands Avenue
Warden Lodge
RD.
White House
WINGATE ROAD
Wayside
WINGATE LANE SOUTH
Andrew Ter.
BEVAN
Sandwick Terrace
LANE
DURHAM ROAD
DURHAM
Wharrier Sq.
CRESCENT
A181
Burn Plantation
Nanny's Plantation
Foxhole Wood
GREEN LANE
East Farm
West Farm
WINGATE QUARRY LOCAL NATURE RESERVE
Marley Banks
Wingate Grange Farm
Reservoir (covered)
Pickering Hill
B1278
LANE
Wingate Lodge
Deaf Hill Cemetery
West Moor Farm
Wingate Grange
Deaf Hill Farm
THORNLEY ROAD
Tobin Street
Deaf Hill Terrace
Wingate House
Ashley Ho.
Coronation Ter.
FAIRLAWNS
WINGATE
STATION ROAD
Deaf Hill Primary School
St. Aidan's Terr.
Comm. Cen.
Store Buildings
Station House
MALVERN CR.
MARGARET TER.
Dunswell Gra.
FOUNDRY M.
BEECH GRO.
ASH GR.
WATSON CR.
RUSSEL CR.
WOOD ROAD
MAY CRES.
LAB.
URNUM
SU VW.

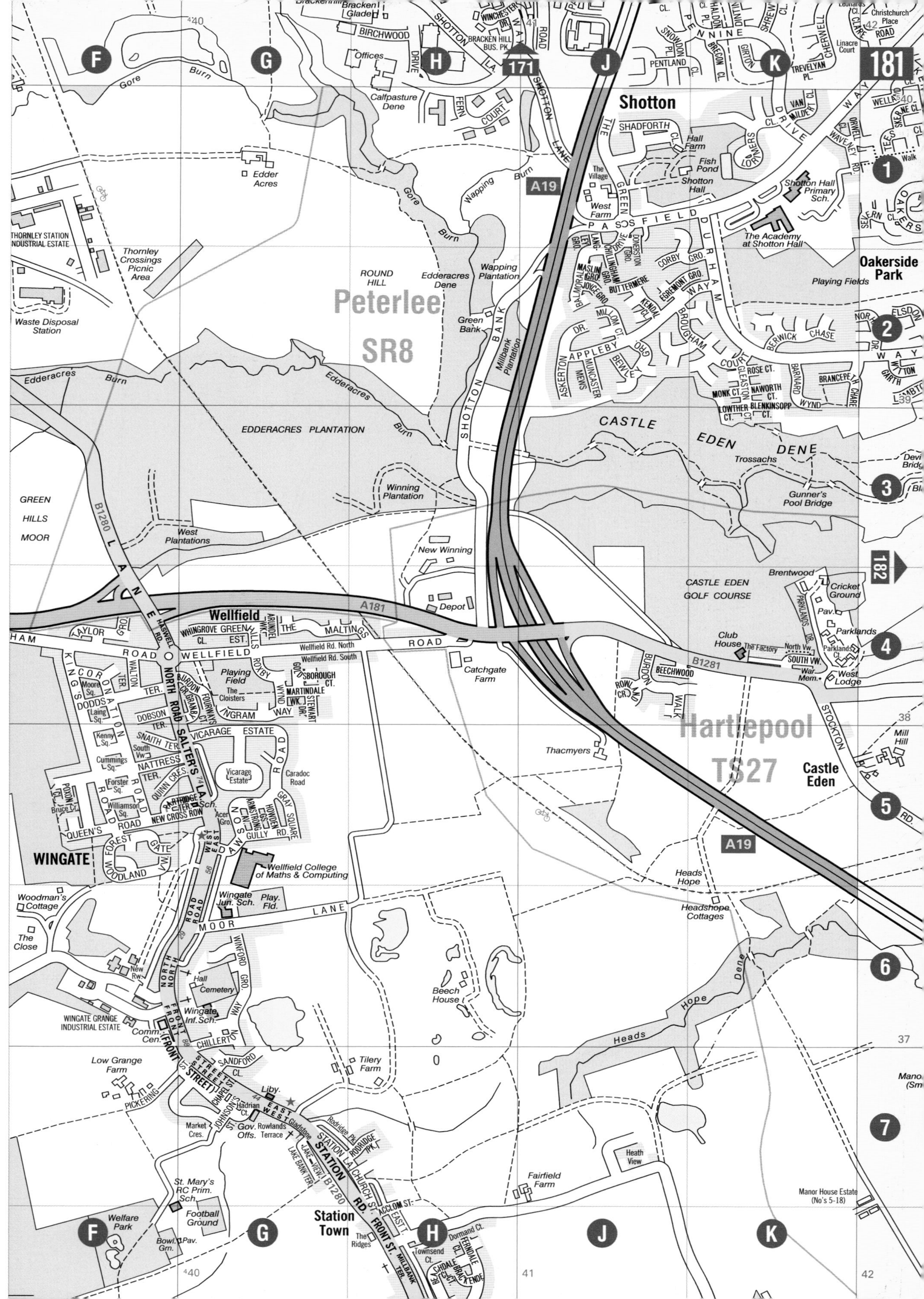
Shotton
Peterlee
SR8
Hartlepool
TS27
Oakerside Park
Castle Eden
WINGATE
Wellfield
Station Town
CASTLE EDEN DENE
EDDERACRES PLANTATION
CASTLE EDEN GOLF COURSE
GREEN HILLS MOOR
Thornley Crossings Picnic Area
Waste Disposal Station
THORNLEY STATION INDUSTRIAL ESTATE
WINGATE GRANGE INDUSTRIAL ESTATE
Wellfield College of Maths & Computing
The Academy at Shotton Hall
Shotton Hall Primary Sch.
A19
A181
B1280
B1281
171
182
Manor House Estate (No's 5-18)

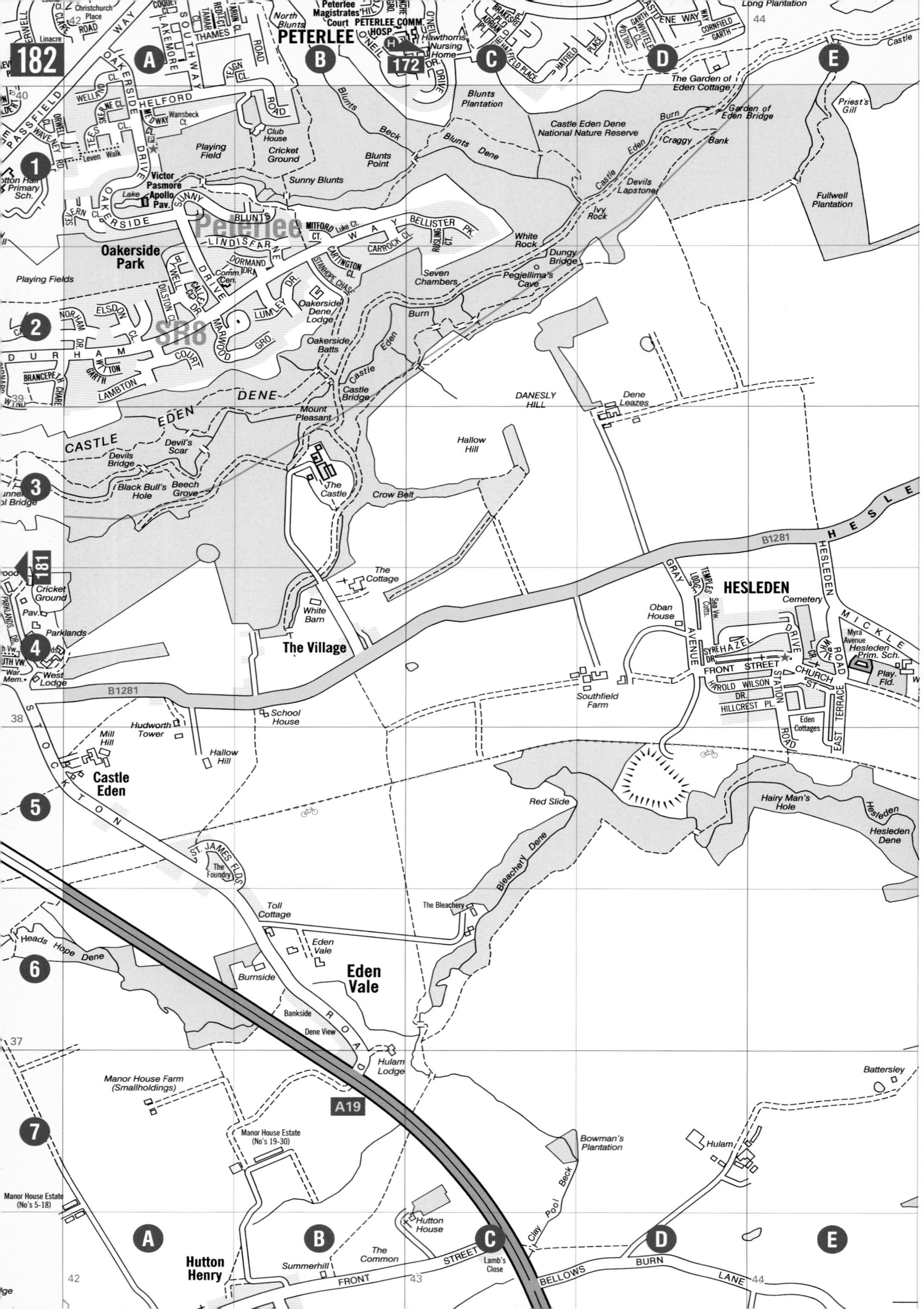

A
B
C
D
E
1
2
3
4
5
6
7
42
43
44
40
39
38
37
Christchurch Place
Linacre
PASSFIELD WAY
WAVENEY RD.
ORWELL CL.
TEES CL.
WELLAND CL.
OAKERSIDE DRIVE
HELFORD ROAD
MEDWAY
Wansbeck Ct.
Leven Walk
LAKEMORE
SOUTHWAY
THAMES CL.
TAMAR CL.
REDE CL.
ARUN CL.
TEIGN CL.
ROAD
North Blunts
Peterlee Magistrates' Court
PETERLEE
PETERLEE COMM. HOSP.
172
Hawthorns Nursing Home
O'NEILL DR.
O'NEILL DRIVE
BRAKESPEARE PL.
ADRIAN PL.
HATFIELD PLACE
EASTDENE WAY
GARTH
CORNFIELD GARTH
Long Plantation
Castle
The Garden of Eden Cottage
Garden of Eden Bridge
Priest's Gill
Blunts Plantation
Castle Eden Dene National Nature Reserve
Burn
Craggy
Bank
Eden
Blunts Beck
Blunts Dene
Playing Field
Club House
Cricket Ground
Blunts Point
Sunny Blunts
Victor Pasmore Apollo Pav.
Lake
Castle
Devils Lapstone
Ivy Rock
Fullwell Plantation
Otton Hall Primary Sch.
SEVERN CL.
OAKERSIDE
SUNNY BLUNTS
Peterlee
MITFORD CT.
Luke Ct.
BELLISTER PK.
WAY
LINDISFARNE
CARROCK CL.
RISLING CT.
White Rock
Dungy Bridge
Oakerside Park
DORMAND DR.
CARTINGTON CL.
STANHOPE CHASE
Comm. Cen.
Pegjellima's Cave
Seven Chambers
Playing Fields
DILSTON CL.
DRIVE
LUMLEY DR.
Oakerside Dene Lodge
Burn
ELSDON CL.
NORHAM DR.
SR8
MARWOOD GRO.
Oakerside Batts
Eden
Castle
DURHAM COURT
WITTON GARTH
BRANCEPETH CHARE
LAMBTON
Castle Bridge
DANESLY HILL
Dene Leazes
DENE
EDEN
CASTLE
Mount Pleasant
Hallow Hill
Devil's Scar
Devils Bridge
Black Bull's Hole
Beech Grove
The Castle
Crow Belt
HESLE
B1281
181
Cricket Ground
Pav.
PARKLANDS DR.
Parklands
The Cottage
White Barn
The Village
GRAY AVENUE
TEMPLES LODGE
HESLEDEN
Sea Vw. Cotts.
Cemetery
HESLEDEN ROAD
MICKLE
Oban House
Myra Avenue
Hesleden Prim. Sch.
HAZEL DRIVE
SYRE DR.
FRONT STREET
CHURCH ST.
Play. Fld.
West Lodge
War Mem.
B1281
HAROLD WILSON DR.
STATION ROAD
HILLCREST PL.
Eden Cottages
EAST TERRACE
Southfield Farm
School House
Hudworth Tower
Mill Hill
Hallow Hill
Castle Eden
STOCKTON ROAD
Red Slide
Hairy Man's Hole
Hesleden
Hesleden Dene
ST. JAMES FLDS
The Foundry
Bleachery Dene
Toll Cottage
The Bleachery
Heads Hope Dene
Eden Vale
Eden Vale
Burnside
Bankside
Dene View
Hulam Lodge
Manor House Farm (Smallholdings)
A19
Battersley
Manor House Estate (No's 19-30)
Bowman's Plantation
Hulam
Pool Beck
Clay
Manor House Estate (No's 5-18)
Hutton House
Hutton Henry
The Common
Summerhill
FRONT STREET
Lamb's Close
BELLOWS
BURN
LANE

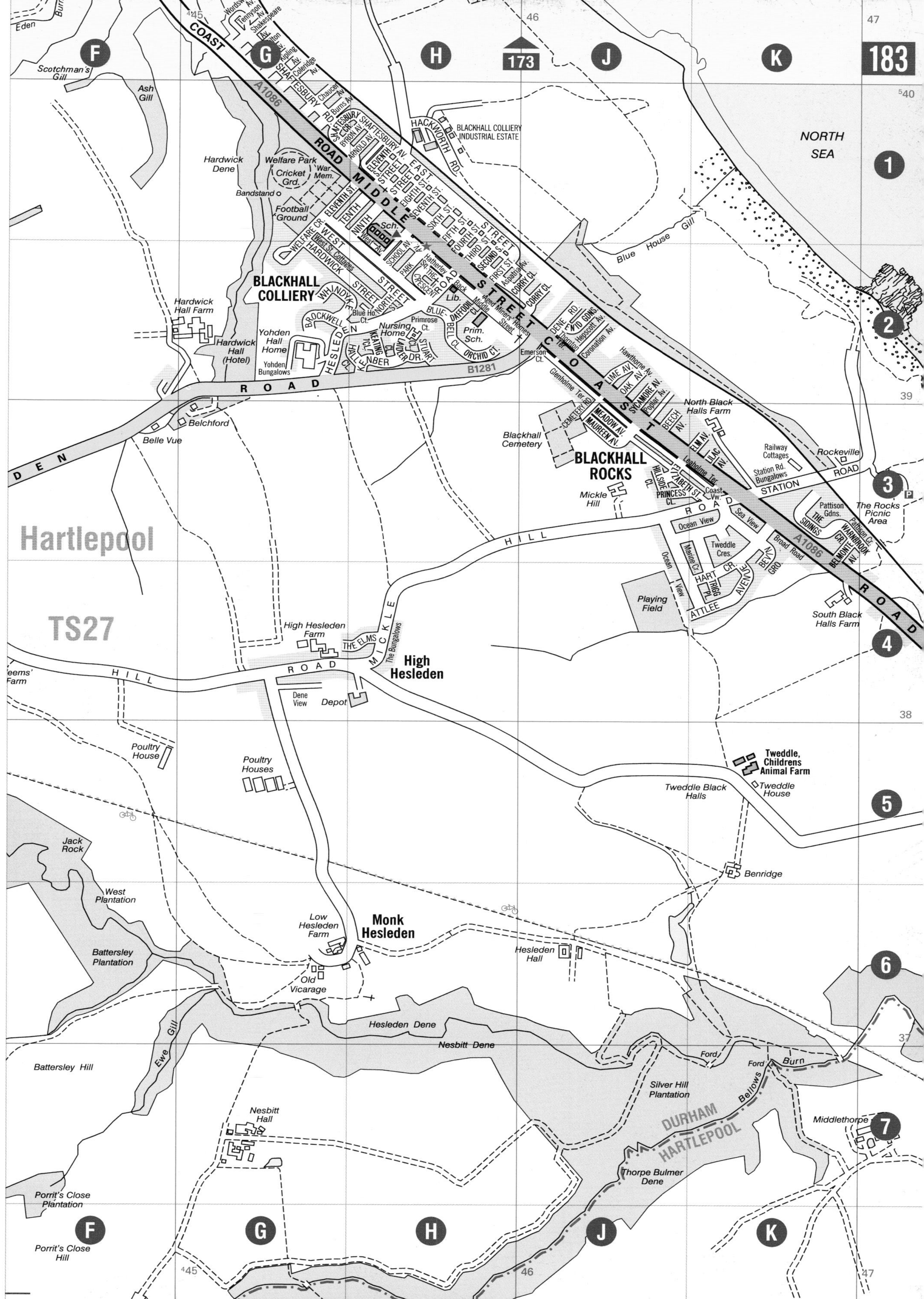
183
173
F
G
H
J
K
1
2
3
4
5
6
7
NORTH SEA
BLACKHALL COLLIERY
BLACKHALL ROCKS
High Hesleden
Monk Hesleden
Hartlepool
TS27
COAST ROAD
MIDDLE STREET
A1086
B1281
HESLEDEN ROAD
HILL ROAD
MICKLE HILL ROAD
STATION ROAD
Blackhall Colliery Industrial Estate
Hardwick Dene
Welfare Park
Cricket Grd.
War Mem.
Bandstand
Football Ground
Hardwick Hall Farm
Hardwick Hall (Hotel)
Yohden Hall Home
Yohden Bungalows
Belchford
Belle Vue
Blackhall Cemetery
North Black Halls Farm
Railway Cottages
Station Rd. Bungalows
Rockeville
The Rocks Picnic Area
Mickle Hill
Playing Field
South Black Halls Farm
High Hesleden Farm
Dene View
Depot
Poultry House
Poultry Houses
Tweddle, Childrens Animal Farm
Tweddle House
Tweddle Black Halls
Benridge
Low Hesleden Farm
Old Vicarage
Hesleden Hall
Hesleden Dene
Nesbitt Dene
Silver Hill Plantation
Bellows Burn
Ford
DURHAM
HARTLEPOOL
Thorpe Bulmer Dene
Middlethorpe
Nesbitt Hall
Ewe Gill
Battersley Hill
Battersley Plantation
West Plantation
Jack Rock
Porrit's Close Plantation
Porrit's Close Hill
Scotchman's Gill
Ash Gill
Blue House Gill
Eden
Weems' Farm

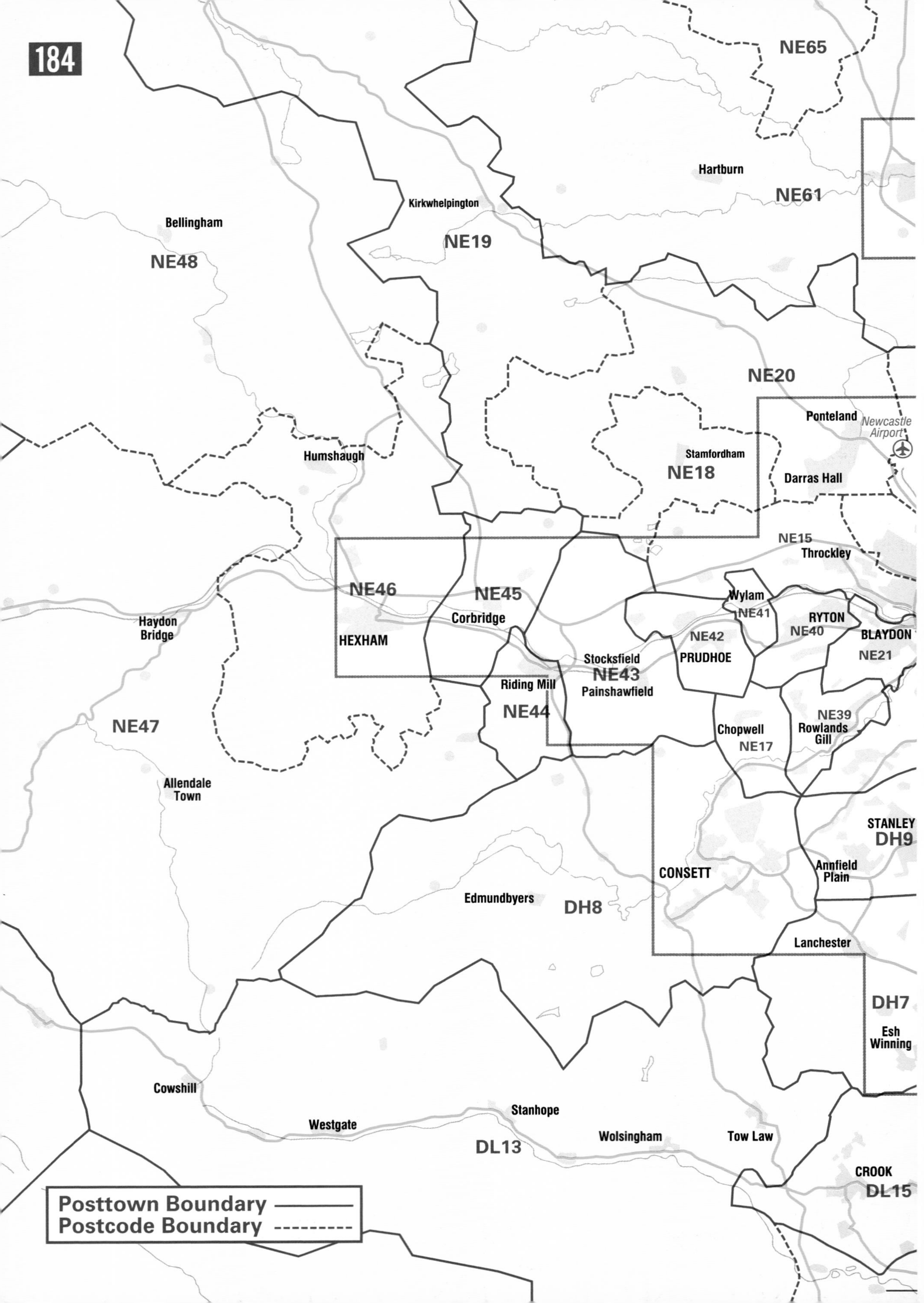
NE65
Hartburn
NE61
Kirkwhelpington
NE19
Bellingham
NE48
NE20
Ponteland
Newcastle Airport
Humshaugh
Stamfordham
NE18
Darras Hall
NE15
Throckley
NE46
NE45
Wylam
NE41
RYTON
NE40
BLAYDON
Haydon Bridge
Corbridge
HEXHAM
NE42
NE21
Stocksfield
PRUDHOE
NE43
Riding Mill
Painshawfield
NE44
NE39
NE47
Chopwell
Rowlands Gill
NE17
Allendale Town
STANLEY
DH9
CONSETT
Annfield Plain
Edmundbyers
DH8
Lanchester
DH7
Esh Winning
Cowshill
Stanhope
Westgate
Wolsingham
Tow Law
DL13
CROOK
DL15
Posttown Boundary
Postcode Boundary

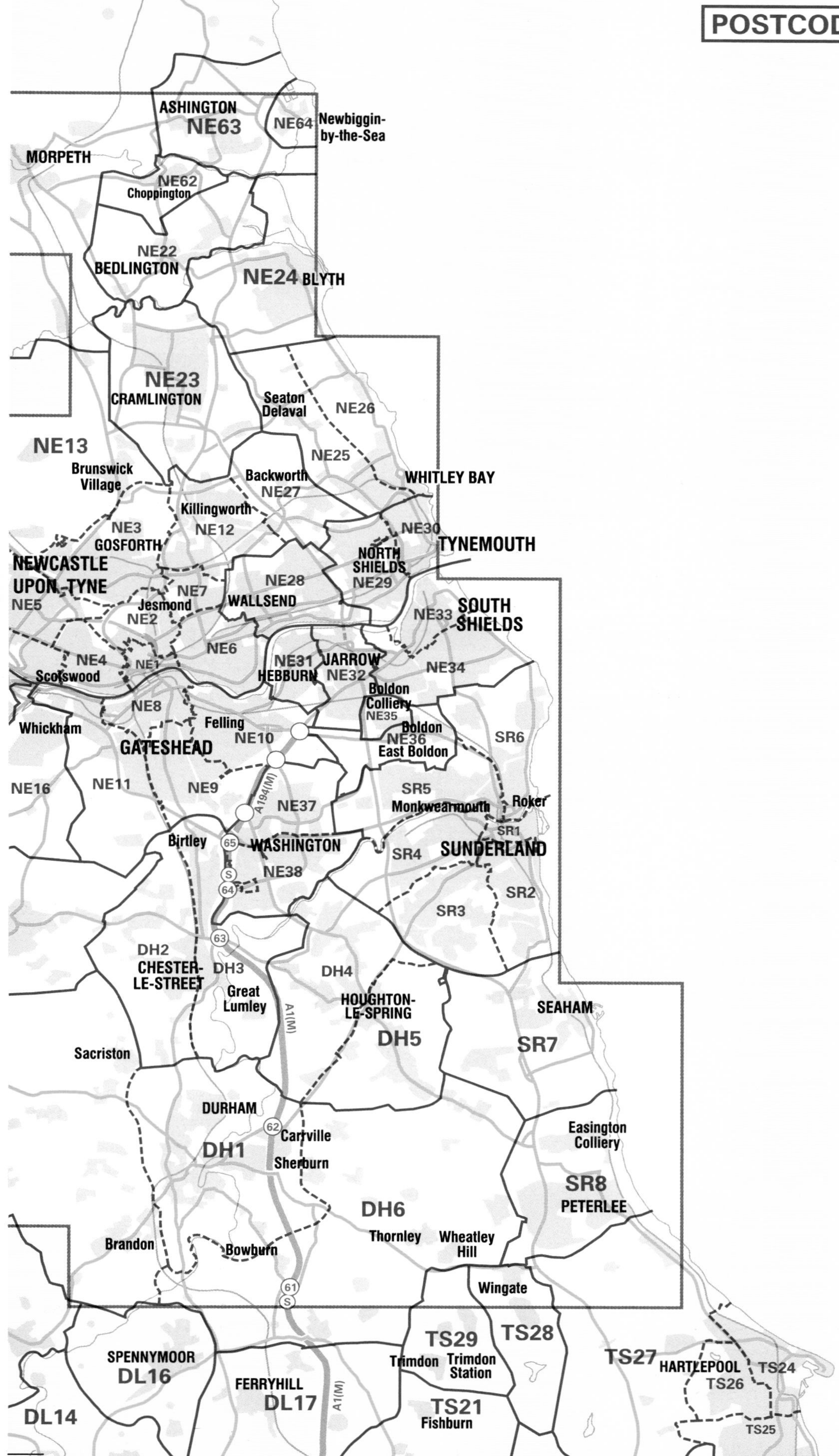
ASHINGTON
NE63
NE64
Newbiggin-by-the-Sea
MORPETH
NE62
Choppington
NE22
BEDLINGTON
NE24
BLYTH
NE23
CRAMLINGTON
Seaton Delaval
NE26
NE13
NE25
Brunswick Village
Backworth
NE27
WHITLEY BAY
Killingworth
NE3
GOSFORTH
NE12
NE30
TYNEMOUTH
NEWCASTLE UPON TYNE
NORTH SHIELDS
NE28
NE29
NE7
NE5
Jesmond
WALLSEND
NE33
SOUTH SHIELDS
NE2
NE6
NE4
NE1
NE31
JARROW
NE34
Scotswood
HEBBURN
NE32
Boldon Colliery
NE8
NE35
Whickham
Felling
Boldon
NE36
SR6
NE10
GATESHEAD
East Boldon
A194(M)
SR5
NE16
NE11
NE9
NE37
Monkwearmouth
Roker
SR1
Birtley
65
WASHINGTON
SUNDERLAND
SR4
NE38
64
SR2
SR3
63
DH2
CHESTER-LE-STREET
DH3
DH4
Great Lumley
HOUGHTON-LE-SPRING
SEAHAM
A1(M)
DH5
SR7
Sacriston
DURHAM
62
Carrville
Easington Colliery
DH1
Sherburn
SR8
PETERLEE
DH6
Brandon
Thornley
Wheatley Hill
Bowburn
Wingate
61
TS29
TS28
SPENNYMOOR
TS27
HARTLEPOOL
TS24
DL16
Trimdon
Trimdon Station
TS26
FERRYHILL
DL17
A1(M)
TS21
DL14
Fishburn
TS25

INDEX

Including Streets, Places & Areas, Industrial Estates,
Selected Flats & Walkways, Service Areas, Stations and Selected Places of Interest.

HOW TO USE THIS INDEX

1. Each street name is followed by its Postcode District and then by its Locality abbreviation(s) and then by its map reference; e.g. **Abbey Dr.** DH4: Hou S . . . 7B **130** is in the DH4 Postcode District and the Houghton-le-Spring Locality and is to be found in square 7B on page **130**. The page number is shown in bold type.

2. A strict alphabetical order is followed in which Av., Rd., St., etc. (though abbreviated) are read in full and as part of the street name; e.g. **Acornclose La.** appears after **Acorn Cl.** but before **Acorn Cft.**

3. Streets and a selection of flats and walkways that cannot be shown on the mapping, appear in the index with the thoroughfare to which they are connected shown in brackets; e.g. **Abbey Vw. Yd.** *NE61: Mor . . . 6E **8** (off Buller's Grn.)*

4. Addresses that are in more than one part are referred to as not continuous.

5. Places and areas are shown in the index in **BLUE TYPE** and the map reference is to the actual map square in which the town centre or area is located and not to the place name shown on the map; e.g. **ACOMB . . . 4B 50**

6. An example of a selected place of interest is Anker's House Mus. . . . 6B 128

7. Examples of stations are:
   Blaydon Station (Rail) . . . .2C 80; Whitley Bay Station (Metro) . . . . 7H 39; Bus Station, Eldon Sq. . . . .4E 4; Belmont (Park & Ride) 5H 155

8. Service Areas are shown in the index in **BOLD CAPITAL TYPE**; e.g. **DURHAM SERVICE AREA 6H 177**

9. Map references for entries that appear on large scale pages **4-7** are shown first, with small scale map references shown in brackets; e.g. **55 Degrees Nth.** NE1: Newc T 6G **4** (1G **83**)

GENERAL ABBREVIATIONS

All. : Alley
App. : Approach
Arc. : Arcade
Av. : Avenue
Bk. : Back
Blvd. : Boulevard
Bri. : Bridge
Bldg. : Building
Bldgs. : Buildings
Bungs. : Bungalows
Bus. : Business
Cvn. : Caravan
Cen. : Centre
Chu. : Church
Chyd. : Churchyard
Circ. : Circle
Cl. : Close
Comn. : Common
Cnr. : Corner
Cott. : Cottage
Cotts. : Cottages
Ct. : Court
Cres. : Crescent
Cft. : Croft
Dr. : Drive
E. : East
Ent. : Enterprise
Est. : Estate
Fld. : Field
Flds. : Fields
Gdn. : Garden
Gdns. : Gardens
Gth. : Garth
Ga. : Gate
Gt. : Great
Grn. : Green
Gro. : Grove
Hgts. : Heights
Ho. : House
Ho's. : Houses
Ind. : Industrial
Info. : Information
Intl. : International
La. : Lane
Lit. : Little
Lwr. : Lower
Mnr. : Manor
Mans. : Mansions
Mkt. : Market
Mdw. : Meadow
Mdws. : Meadows
M. : Mews
Mt. : Mount
Mus. : Museum
Nth. : North
No. : Number
Pde. : Parade
Pk. : Park
Pas. : Passage
Pl. : Place
Pct. : Precinct
Prom. : Promenade
Ri. : Rise
Rd. : Road
Shop. : Shopping
Sth. : South
Sq. : Square
Sta. : Station
St. : Street
Ter. : Terrace
Twr. : Tower
Trad. : Trading
Up. : Upper
Va. : Vale
Vw. : View
Vs. : Villas
Vis. : Visitors
Wlk. : Walk
W. : West
Yd. : Yard

LOCALITY ABBREVIATIONS

Acomb : **Acomb**
Allen : **Allensford**
Anic : **Anick**
Ann P : **Annfield Plain**
Ash : **Ashington**
Ayd : **Aydon**
Back : **Backworth**
Barl : **Barlow**
Beam : **Beamish**
Bearp : **Bearpark**
Bed : **Bedlington**
Benw : **Benwell**
Bill Q : **Bill Quay**
Bir : **Birtley**
B Col : **Blackhall Colliery**
B'hill : **Blackhill**
Blak : **Blakelaw**
Blay : **Blaydon**
Bly : **Blyth**
Bol C : **Boldon Colliery**
Both : **Bothal**
Bour : **Bournmoor**
Bowb : **Bowburn**
Bran : **Brancepeth**
B'don : **Brandon**
Bras : **Brasside**
B End : **Bridge End**
B'ley : **Broomley**
Bro : **Broompark**
Bru V : **Brunswick Village**
Bur : **Burdon**
B'hpe : **Burnhope**
Burn : **Burnopfield**
Byke : **Byker**
Call : **Callerton**
Camb : **Cambois**
Carr : **Carrville**
Cass : **Cassop**
Cas E : **Castle Eden**
C'sde : **Castleside**
Cha P : **Chapel Park**
Ches S : **Chester-le-Street**
Ches M : **Chester Moor**
Chop : **Choppington**
C'wl : **Chopwell**
C Vale : **Clara Vale**
Clead : **Cleadon**
Coal : **Coalburns**
Cold H : **Cold Hesledon**
Cons : **Consett**
Corb : **Corbridge**
Corn : **Cornsay**
Corn C : **Cornsay Colliery**
Cow : **Cowpen**
Cox G : **Cox Green**
Coxh : **Coxhoe**
Crag : **Craghead**
Cra : **Cramlington**
Craw : **Crawcrook**
Crook : **Crook**
Crox : **Croxdale**
Cull : **Cullercoats**
Dalt D : **Dalton-le-Dale**
Darr H : **Darras Hall**
Den M : **Denton Burn**
Din : **Dinnington**
Dip : **Dipton**
Diss : **Dissington**
Dox P : **Doxford Park**
Dud : **Dudley**
Dun : **Dunston**
Dur : **Durham**
Ears : **Earsdon**
E Bol : **East Boldon**
E Cram : **East Cramlington**
E Har : **East Hartford**
E Her : **East Herrington**
E Rain : **East Rainton**
E Sle : **East Sleekburn**
Eas : **Easington**
Eas C : **Easington Colliery**
Eas L : **Easington Lane**
Ebc : **Ebchester**
Edm : **Edmondsley**
Eigh B : **Eighton Banks**
Elsw : **Elswick**
Esh : **Esh**
Esh W : **Esh Winning**
Fair M : **Fair Moor**
Fawd : **Fawdon**
Fell : **Felling**
Fen : **Fenham**
Fest P : **Festival Park**
Ful : **Fulwell**
Gate : **Gateshead**
Gos : **Gosforth**
Gra V : **Grange Villa**
Gt Lum : **Great Lumley**
G'sde : **Greenside**
Ham : **Hamsterley**
Ham M : **Hamsterley Mill**
Harp : **Harperley**
H Bri : **Hartford Bridge**
H'pool : **Hartlepool**
Has : **Haswell**
Hawt : **Hawthorn**
Haz : **Hazelrigg**
Heat : **Heaton**
Heb : **Hebburn**
Hed W : **Heddon-on-the-Wall**
Hed : **Hedley**
Hep : **Hepscott**
Hes : **Hesleden**
Hett : **Hett**
Hett H : **Hetton-le-Hole**
Hew : **Heworth**
Hex : **Hexham**
H Cal : **High Callerton**
H Hea : **High Heaton**
H Pitt : **High Pittington**
H Shin : **High Shincliffe**
H Spen : **High Spen**
Hob : **Hobson**
H'wll : **Holywell**
Hord : **Horden**
Hor : **Horsley**
Hou S : **Houghton-le-Spring**
Hutt : **Hutton Henry**
Jar : **Jarrow**
Jes : **Jesmond**
Kel : **Kelloe**
Ken : **Kenton**
K Bank : **Kenton Bankfoot**
Kib : **Kibblesworth**
Kil : **Killingworth**
Kim : **Kimblesworth**
Ki Pk : **Kingston Park**
Lam P : **Lambton Park**
Lame : **Lamesley**
Lan : **Lanchester**
Lang M : **Langley Moor**
Lang P : **Langley Park**
Lead : **Leadgate**
Leam : **Leamside**
Lem : **Lemington**
Litt : **Littletown**
Loan : **Loansdean**
Lob H : **Lobley Hill**
Longb : **Longbenton**
Lngh : **Longhirst**
Low F : **Low Fell**
Low P : **Low Pittington**
Ludw : **Ludworth**
Maid L : **Maiden Law**
Marl H : **Marley Hill**
Mead : **Meadowfield**
Medb : **Medburn**
M'sly : **Medomsley**
Mic : **Mickley**
Mil : **Milbourne**
Mit : **Mitford**
Monks : **Monkseaton**
Monkw : **Monkwearmouth**
Mor : **Morpeth**
Mur : **Murton**
Nedd : **Nedderton**
Nel V : **Nelson Village**
Nett : **Nettlesworth**
Newb S : **Newbiggin-by-the-Sea**
Nbot : **Newbottle**
New B : **New Brancepeth**
Newb : **Newburn**
Newc T : **Newcastle upon Tyne**
Newf : **Newfield**
New Hart : **New Hartley**
New H : **New Herrington**
New L : **New Lambton**
News : **Newsham**
New S : **New Silksworth**
Newt : **Newton**
N Sea : **North Seaton**
N Shi : **North Shields**
Oakw : **Oakwood**
Old C : **Old Cassop**
Old Q : **Old Quarrington**
Ous : **Ouston**
O'ham : **Ovingham**
Oving : **Ovington**
Page B : **Page Bank**
Pains : **Painshawfield**
Peg : **Pegswood**
Pel : **Pelaw**
Pelt : **Pelton**
P Fel : **Pelton Fell**
Pen : **Penshaw**
Pet : **Peterlee**
P Me : **Pity Me**
Plaw : **Plawsworth**
Pon : **Ponteland**
Pres : **Prestwick**
Pru : **Prudhoe**
Quar H : **Quarrington Hill**
Queb : **Quebec**
Rave : **Ravensworth**
Rid M : **Riding Mill**
Roker : **Roker**
Row G : **Rowlands Gill**
Ryh : **Ryhope**
Ryton : **Ryton**
Sac : **Sacriston**
Sand : **Sandhoe**
Sco G : **Scotland Gate**
Scot : **Scotswood**
Seab : **Seaburn**
S'hm : **Seaham**
Seat : **Seaton**
Sea B : **Seaton Burn**
Sea D : **Seaton Delaval**
Sea S : **Seaton Sluice**
Seg : **Seghill**
Shad : **Shadforth**
S'burn : **Sherburn**
S Hil : **Sherburn Hill**
S Hou : **Sherburn House**
Shin : **Shincliffe**
S Row : **Shiney Row**
Shir : **Shiremoor**
Shot B : **Shotley Bridge**
Shot C : **Shotton Colliery**
Silk : **Silksworth**
S Het : **South Hetton**
S Shi : **South Shields**
S'wck : **Southwick**
Spri : **Springwell**
Stake : **Stakeford**
Stly : **Stanley**
S Cro : **Stanley Crook**
Stan : **Stannington**
Sta T : **Station Town**
Stoc : **Stocksfield**
Ston : **Stoneygate**
Sund : **Sunderland**
Sun B : **Sunderland Bridge**
Sun : **Sunniside**

Swa : **Swalwell**
Tanf : **Tanfield**
Tan L : **Tanfield Lea**
Tant : **Tantobie**
T Vall : **Team Valley**
Thor : **Thornley**
Thro : **Throckley**
Tra W : **Tranwell Woods**
Trim G : **Trimdon Grange**
Trim S : **Trimdon Station**
Tudh : **Tudhoe**
Tuns : **Tunstall**
Tyne : **Tynemouth**
Ush M : **Ushaw Moor**
Walb : **Walbottle**
Wald : **Waldridge**
Walk : **Walker**
W'snd : **Wallsend**
Ward : **Wardley**
Wash : **Washington**
Wat : **Waterhouses**
Well : **Wellfield**
Welt : **Welton**
W Bol : **West Boldon**
W Dent : **West Denton**
W Herr : **West Herrington**
W Holy : **West Holywell**
W Pelt : **West Pelton**
W Rai : **West Rainton**
W Sle : **West Sleekburn**
West : **Westerhope**
Whe H : **Wheatley Hill**
Whi : **Whickham**
Whit : **Whitburn**
Whit B : **Whitley Bay**
W'stll : **Whittonstall**
W Op : **Wide Open**
Wind N : **Windy Nook**
Win : **Wingate**
Winl : **Winlaton**
W Mill : **Winlaton Mill**
Wit G : **Witton Gilbert**
Wood : **Woodhorn**
Wool : **Woolsington**
Wrek : **Wrekenton**
Wylam : **Wylam**

55 Degrees Nth. NE1: Newc T 6G **4** (1G **83**)

A

Abbay St. SR5: S'wck 6C **104**
Abberwick Wlk. NE13: Ki Pk 4A **44**
Abbey Cl. NE25: Monks 7D **38**
NE38: Wash 3H **115**
Abbey Ct. NE8: Gate 5H **83**
NE27: Shir 1J **47**
NE46: Hex 2D **70**
Abbeydale Gdns. DH6: S Het 4C **158**
Abbey Dr. DH4: Hou S 7B **130**
NE5: Cha P 2B **60**
NE30: Tyne 4K **49**
NE32: Jar .6C **66**
Abbeyfield Cl. NE8: Gate 5D **82**
Abbey Ga. NE61: Mor 1D **14**
Abbey Leisure Cen.
Pity Me .3A **154**
Abbey Mdws. NE61: Mor 1D **14**
Abbey M. DH7: Sac 1E **152**
Abbey Rd. DH1: P Me 3K **153**
NE28: W'snd 5A **48**
NE38: Wash 3H **115**
Abbey Rd. Bus. Pk. DH1: P Me 3K **153**
Abbey Rd. Ind. Est. DH1: P Me 3K **153**
Abbey Ter. NE27: Shir 1J **47**
NE61: Mor .6F **9**
Abbeyvale Dr. NE6: Walk 6F **65**
Abbey Vw. NE46: Hex 2E **70**
NE61: Mor .6F **9**
Abbey Vw. Yd. *NE61: Mor* *6E 8*
(off Buller's Grn.)
Abbeywoods DH1: P Me 3A **154**
Abbeywoods Bus. Pk. DH1: P Me 3K **153**
Abbie Ct. *NE24: Bly* *2H 23*
(off Lynn St.)
Abbot Ct. NE8: Gate 10K **5** (3H **83**)
Abbots Cl. NE62: Stake 7K **11**
Abbotsfield Cl. SR3: Dox P 4B **132**
Abbotsford Gro. SR2: Sund 6G **7** (3E **118**)
Abbotsford Ho. NE24: Bly 3G **23**
Abbotsford Pk. NE25: Monks 7F **39**
Abbotsford Rd. NE10: Fell 5B **84**
Abbotsford Ter. NE2: Jes 5F **63**
Abbots Hill NE8: Gate 8K **5** (2H **83**)
Abbotside Cl. DH2: Ous 6F **113**
Abbotside Pl. NE5: Cha P 4D **60**
Abbotsmeade Cl. NE5: Fen 5J **61**
Abbots Row DH1: Dur 1D **166**
Abbot St. SR8: Eas C 6D **160**
Abbots Wlk. DH9: Beam 1B **126**
Abbots Way NE16: Whi 7H **81**
NE29: N Shi 3D **48**
NE61: Mor .7E **8**
Abbotsway NE32: Jar 7E **66**
Abbotts Way DH8: Cons 7F **121**
Abbs St. SR5: Monkw 6F **105**
Abercorn Pl. NE28: W'snd 6J **47**
Abercorn Rd. NE15: Scot 1G **81**
SR3: E Her 1K **131**
Abercrombie Pl. NE5: Blak 3H **61**
Aberdare Rd. SR3: E Her 2A **132**
Aberdeen DH2: Ous 7H **113**
Aberdeen Ct. NE3: Ki Pk 4K **43**
Aberdeen Dr. NE32: Jar 2E **86**
Aberdeen Twr. SR3: New S 1A **132**
Aberford Cl. NE5: Cha P 1B **60**
Aberfoyle DH2: Ous 7H **113**
Aberfoyle Ct. DH9: Stly 3H **125**
Abergele Pl. DH9: Ann P 5K **123**
Abernethy DH2: Ous 6H **113**
Aberwick Dr. DH2: Ches S 2H **141**
Abigail Ct. NE3: Gos 7G **45**
Abingdon Ct. NE3: Ki Pk 5K **43**
NE21: Blay 3C **80**
Abingdon Rd. NE6: Walk 6F **65**
Abingdon Sq. NE23: Cra 1A **26**
Abingdon St. SR4: Sund 3B **118**
Abingdon Way NE35: Bol C 5D **86**
Abinger St. NE4: Newc T 5B **4** (1D **82**)
Abington DH2: Ous 7H **113**
Aboyne Sq. SR3: E Her 7K **117**
Acacia Av. DH4: Hou S 1A **144**
SR8: Hord .6F **173**
Acacia Gro. NE31: Heb 2J **85**
NE34: S Shi 1B **88**
Acacia Rd. NE10: Gate 4K **83**
Acacia Ter. NE63: Ash 4B **12**
Academy of Light, The (Football Centre)
. . . . .7E **88**
Academy Rd. NE63: N Sea 5D **12**
Acanthus Av. NE4: Fen 6K **61**
Acclom St. TS28: Sta T 7H **181**
Acer Ct. SR2: Sund 7K **7** (4F **119**)
Acer Dr. DH6: Has 1B **170**
Acer Gro. TS28: Win 5G **181**
Acklam Av. SR2: Sund 7J **119**
ACOMB 4B **50**
Acomb Av. NE25: Sea D 1H **37**
NE28: W'snd 5H **47**
Acomb Cl. NE61: Hep 3J **15**
Acomb Ct. NE9: Low F 5K **99**
NE12: Kil .1B **46**
NE22: Bed .7J **17**
SR2: Sund 7H **119**
Acomb Cres. NE3: Fawd 4B **44**
Acomb Dr. NE41: Wylam 6J **57**
Acomb Gdns. NE5: Fen 5J **61**
Acomb Ind. Est. NE46: Acomb 4B **50**
Acorn Av. NE8: Gate 6E **82**
NE22: Bed .1H **21**
Acorn Cl. DH7: Sac 6D **140**
NE9: Wrek .4B **100**
Acornclose La. DH7: Sac 6B **140**
Acorn Cft. DH7: Wit G 3C **152**
Acorn La. NE27: Shir 7K **37**
Acorn Pl. DH1: P Me 4J **153**
DH7: B'don 1D **174**
Acorn Rd. NE2: Jes 3G **63**
Acorn Sq. NE42: Pru 4F **77**
Acorn St. DH2: Pelt 2D **126**
Acorn Wlk. DH7: Wit G 3D **152**
Acorn Way DH2: Nett 6H **141**
Acreford Ct. NE62: Chop 2G **17**
Acre Rigg Rd. SR8: Pet 5K **171**
Acres, The NE28: W'snd 2F **65**
Acton Ct. DH9: Stly 6D **124**
Acton Dene DH9: Stly 2J **125**
Acton Dr. NE29: N Shi 4D **48**
Acton Pl. NE7: H Hea 3K **63**
Acton Rd. DH7: Esh W 4E **162**
NE5: W Dent 5F **61**
Ada Cres. NE46: Hex 1C **70**
Adair Av. NE15: Benw 7J **61**
Adair Way NE31: Heb 1K **85**
Adams Bldgs. DH9: Dip 1G **123**
Adamsez Ind. Est. NE15: Scot 2F **81**
Adamsez West Ind. Est. NE15: Scot 2F **81**
Adams Ter. DH8: M'sly 6J **107**
Adam St. SR8: Hord 6F **173**
Ada St. NE6: Walk 7C **64**
NE33: S Shi 4K **67**
Ada St. E. SR7: Mur 1F **159**
Ada St. W. SR7: Mur 1F **159**
Adderlane Rd. NE42: Pru 3F **77**
Adderstone Av. NE23: Cra 5K **25**
Adderstone Ct. NE2: Jes 2H **63**
Adderstone Cres. NE2: Jes 3H **63**
Adderstone Gdns. NE29: N Shi 3B **48**
Addington Cres. NE29: N Shi 6E **48**
Addington Dr. NE24: News 4J **23**
NE28: W'snd 5H **47**
ADDISON 1K **79**
Addison Cl. NE6: Byke 3P **5** (7K **63**)
Addison Ct. NE28: W'snd 4B **66**
NE40: Ryton 1F **79**
Addison Gdns. NE10: Ward 6F **85**
Addison Ind. Est. NE21: Blay 1K **79**
Addison Rd. NE6: Byke 3P **5** (7K **63**)
NE15: Lem .6D **60**
NE36: W Bol 7G **87**
Addison St. NE29: N Shi 1G **67**
SR2: Sund 2H **119**
Addison Vw. NE21: Blay 1A **80**
Addison Wlk. NE34: S Shi 4G **87**
Addycombe Ter. NE6: Heat 3A **64**
Adelaide Cen., The NE4: Benw 1A **82**
Adelaide Cl. SR1: Sund 1H **119**
Adelaide Ct. NE8: Gate 10H **5** (3G **83**)
Adelaide Ho. NE4: Benw 1A **82**
Adelaide Pl. SR1: Sund 1H **119**
Adelaide Row SR7: S'hm 3B **148**
Adelaide St. DH3: Ches S 7A **128**
Adelaide Ter. NE4: Benw 1K **81**
Adeline Gdns. NE3: Ken 2C **62**
Adelphi Cl. NE29: N Shi 4C **48**
Adelphi Pl. NE6: Walk 1C **84**
Aden Ct. DH7: Bearp 7C **152**
Aden Twr. SR3: New S 1A **132**
Adfrid Pl. SR8: Pet 5B **172**
Admington Ct. NE62: Chop 1H **17**
Admiral Bus. Pk. NE23: Nel V 7F **21**
Admiral Collingwood Ct. NE61: Mor 7G **9**
Admiral Ho. NE30: Tyne 5K **49**
Admiralty Way SR7: Cold H, S'hm 6B **148**
Admiral Way SR3: Dox P 4J **131**
Adolphus Pl. DH1: Dur 2F **167**
SR7: S'hm .3C **148**
Adolphus St. SR6: Whit 5H **89**
Adolphus St. W. SR7: S'hm 3B **148**
Adrian Pl. SR8: Pet 7C **172**
Advent Courtyard *NE8: Gate* *5D 82*
(off Pacha Way)
Adventure La. DH4: W Rai 7K **143**
Adventure Valley 3F **155**
Affleck St. NE8: Gate 4G **83**
Afton Ct. NE34: S Shi 1J **87**
Afton Way NE3: Ken 6A **44**
Agar Cl. DH8: Cons 7F **121**
Agar Rd. SR3: E Her 1K **131**
Aged Miners Cotts. NE25: New Hart 4J **27**
NE27: Shir .3H **47**
NE42: Pru *5D 76*
(off Edgewell Rd.)
NE63: Ash 3J **11**
Aged Miner's Home DH5: Hett H 4F **145**
Aged Miners' Home NE16: Burn 2A **110**
Aged Miners Homes DH2: Ches M 3K **141**
DH2: Ches S 5A **128**
DH2: Nett .6H **141**
DH2: Pelt .3E **126**
DH3: Gt Lum 1E **142**
DH4: Bour .7J **129**
DH4: Hou S 2C **144**
DH4: S Row *3B 130*
(off Chester Rd.)
DH5: Hett H 1G **157**
DH5: Hou S 2F **145**
DH6: Quar H 6D **178**
DH6: S Hil .3C **168**
DH6: Shot C 5D **170**
DH7: B'don 7D **164**
DH7: Bearp 1C **164**
DH7: Lang P 5J **151**
DH7: Mead .2E **174**
DH7: Sac 7E **140**
DH8: Lead .4A **122**
DH9: Stly .5H **125**
NE5: West .2D **60**
NE7: Longb .7J **45**
NE11: Kib .2E **112**
NE13: Bru V 5D **34**
NE15: Thro 3F **59**
NE16: Marl H 6G **97**
NE21: Blay .1A **80**
NE23: Cra *5B 26*
(off Front St.)
NE23: Nel V 3H **25**
NE24: Bly .4F **23**
NE24: Camb 4H **19**
NE25: Sea D *7H 27*
(off Ryal Cl.)
NE27: Back 6G **37**
NE27: Shir .1K **47**
NE34: S Shi 6C **68**
NE35: Bol C 5D **86**
NE37: Wash 7G **101**
NE39: H Spen 3E **94**
NE40: Ryton *2J 79*
(off Stargate La.)
NE62: Stake 1A **18**
NE63: Wood 2D **12**
NE64: Newb S 4H **13**
SR2: Ryh *2G 133*
(off Cheviot La.)
SR3: New S 7C **118**
SR5: Sund 5A **104**
SR7: Mur .7D **146**
SR7: S'hm 1H **147**
(East Vw.)
SR7: S'hm 5B **148**
(Shrewsbury St.)
SR8: Hord .5D **172**
TS27: B Col 2H **183**
Aged Miners Homes (Annitsford)
NE23: Dud .2K **35**
Aged Miners' Homes (Dudley)
NE12: Dud .5J **35**
Aged Miners' Homes (Wallsend)
NE28: W'snd *7J 47*
(off Embleton Av.)
Aged Mineworkers' Homes
NE43: Mic .6B **76**
Aged Peoples Homes DH6: S Het 4D **158**
Agincourt NE12: Kil 7B **36**
NE31: Heb .6H **65**
Agnes Maria St. NE3: Gos 7C **44**
Agnes St. DH9: Stly 2F **125**
Agricola Ct. NE33: S Shi 1J **67**
Agricola Gdns. NE28: W'snd 6H **47**
Agricola Rd. NE4: Fen 7B **62**
Aidan Av. NE26: Sea S 4B **28**
Aidan Cl. DH9: Stly 2H **125**
NE13: W Op 5D **34**
NE27: Longb 3G **47**
Aidan Ct. NE7: Longb 7A **46**
NE32: Jar .7D **66**
Aidan Ho. NE8: Gate 4H **83**
Aidan Wlk. NE3: Gos 7F **45**
Aiden Way DH5: Hett H 5G **145**
Ailesbury St. SR4: Sund 1C **118**
Ainderby Rd. NE15: Thro 3F **59**
Ainsdale Gdns. NE5: Cha P 3C **60**
Ainsley St. DH1: Dur 2K **165**
Ainslie Pl. NE5: Blak 4J **61**
Ainsworth Av. NE34: S Shi 3G **87**
Ainthorpe Cl. SR3: Tuns 2D **132**
Ainthorpe Gdns. NE7: Longb 1K **63**
NE9: Low F .2H **99**
Aintree Cl. NE37: Wash 1H **115**
NE63: Ash .5A **12**
Aintree Dr. DH8: Shot B 2F **121**
Aintree Gdns. NE8: Gate 7E **82**
Aintree Rd. SR3: E Her 1K **131**
Airedale NE28: W'snd 7D **46**
Airedale Gdns. DH5: Hett H 1F **157**
Aireys Cl. DH4: Hou S 2C **144**
Airey Ter. NE6: Walk 1E **84**
NE8: Gate .5F **83**
Airport Freightway NE13: Wool 2E **42**
Airport Ind. Est. NE3: Ki Pk 6K **43**
Airport Station (Metro) 1D **42**
Airville Mt. SR3: Dox P 5C **132**
Aisgill Cl. NE23: Cra 4K **25**
Aisgill Dr. NE5: Cha P 4C **60**
Aiskell St. SR4: Sund 2C **118**
Aitken's Bldgs. DH9: Dip 1G **123**
A J Cook Ct. NE63: Ash 4A **12**
A J Cooks Cotts. NE39: Row G 5F **95**
A J Cook Ter. DH6: Shot C 7E **170**
Akeld Cl. NE23: Cra 5K **25**
Akeld Ct. NE3: Gos 1G **63**
Akeld M. SR6: Roker 6G **105**
Akenside Hill NE1: Newc T 7H **5** (2G **83**)
Akenside Ter. NE2: Jes 1J **5** (5H **63**)
Alanbrooke Row NE31: Heb 3G **85**
Alansway Gdns. NE33: S Shi 5K **67**
ALBANY 1G **115**
Albany Av. NE12: Longb 5B **46**
Albany Ct. NE4: Newc T 3C **82**
Albany Gdns. NE26: Whit B 7H **39**
Albany Ho. NE37: Wash 1G **115**
SR5: Monkw 6E **104**
Albany M. NE3: Ken 3C **62**
Albany Rd. NE8: Gate 9L **5** (3J **83**)
Albany St. E. NE33: S Shi 5K **67**
Albany St. W. NE33: S Shi 5K **67**
Albany Ter. NE32: Jar 2K **85**
Albany Village Cen. NE37: Wash 2F **115**
Albany Way NE37: Wash 1G **115**
Albatross Way NE24: News 6J **23**
Albemarle Av. NE2: Jes 2F **63**
Albemarle St. NE33: S Shi 2J **67**
Albert Av. NE28: W'snd 3F **65**
Albert Ct. DH6: Bowb 4H **177**
SR2: Sund 6G **7** (3E **118**)
Albert Dr. NE9: Low F 3H **99**
Albert Edward Dock
NE29: N Shi 3F **67**
Albert Edward Ter. NE35: Bol C 4E **86**
Albert Pl. NE9: Low F 3H **99**
NE38: Wash 4K **115**
Albert Rd. DH8: Cons 7H **121**
NE22: Bed .6C **18**
NE26: Sea S 4D **28**
NE32: Jar .6B **66**
(Chapel Rd.)
NE32: Jar .7A **66**
(Pine St.)
SR4: Sund 1C **118**
Albert Sq. DH3: Ches S 5A **128**
Albert St. DH1: Dur 1A **6** (1K **165**)
DH2: Gra V 4C **126**
DH3: Ches S 6A **128**
DH6: Thor .1K **179**
DH7: Esh W 4E **162**
DH9: Stly .3E **124**
NE2: Newc T 4J **5** (7H **63**)
NE24: Bly .1J **23**
NE31: Heb .6H **65**
NE39: Row G 6E **94**
SR7: S'hm .4C **148**
Albert St. Nth. DH6: Thor 1K **179**
Albert Ter. DH7: Esh W 4E **162**
NE12: Longb 3A **46**
NE26: Whit B 7H **39**
NE33: S Shi 3J **67**
Albion Ct. NE6: Byke 5N **5** (1K **83**)
NE16: Burn 3K **109**
NE24: Cow .2H **23**
NE33: S Shi 1J **67**
Albion Gdns. NE16: Burn 3K **109**
Albion Ho. NE1: Newc T 4D **4** (7E **62**)
Albion Pl. SR1: Sund 5H **7** (2E **118**)
Albion Retail Cen. NE24: Cow 1H **23**
Albion Rd. NE29: N Shi 6G **49**
NE30: N Shi 6G **49**
Albion Rd. W. NE29: N Shi 7G **49**
Albion Row NE6: Byke 5M **5** (1J **83**)
(not continuous)
Albion St. NE10: Hew, Wind N 1A **100**
SR4: Sund 2G **117**
Albion Ter. NE9: Spri 6D **100**
NE23: Cra .7B **22**
NE29: N Shi 6G **49**
NE46: Hex *1C 70*
(off Glovers Pl.)
Albion Vw. NE10: Wind N 1A **100**

Albion Way NE23: Cra . . . 1B 26
NE24: Bly, Cow . . . 2G 23
Albion Yd. NE1: Newc T . . . 6E 4 (1F 83)
Albury Pk. Rd. NE30: Tyne . . . 5J 49
Albury Pl. NE16: Whi . . . 2G 97
Albury Rd. NE2: Jes . . . 2F 63
Albyn Gdns. SR3: Sund . . . 5C 118
Alcester Cl. NE62: Chop . . . 1H 17
Alconbury Cl. NE24: News . . . 4J 23
Alcote Gro. DH6: Shot C . . . 6F 171
Alcroft Cl. NE5: Cha P . . . 2B 60
Aldborough St. NE24: Bly . . . 2J 23
Aldbrough Cl. SR2: Ryh . . . 3H 133
Aldeburgh Av. NE15: Lem . . . 5C 60
Aldeburgh Way SR7: S'hm . . . 2B 148
Aldenham Gdns. NE30: Tyne . . . 3J 49
Aldenham Rd. SR3: New S . . . 1A 132
Aldenham Twr. SR3: New S . . . 1A 132
Alder Av. NE4: Fen . . . 5K 61
Alder Cl. DH5: Hett H . . . 7F 145
NE61: Mor . . . 7G 9
Alder Ct. NE25: Monks . . . 7E 38
Alder Cres. DH9: Tant . . . 7K 109
Alderdene DH7: Lan . . . 7J 137
Alderdene Cl. DH7: Ush M . . . 3E 164
Alder Gro. DH8: Lead . . . 6B 122
NE25: Monks . . . 5E 38
SR7: S'hm . . . 5A 148
Alderlea Cl. DH1: Dur . . . 1E 166
Alderley Cl. NE35: Bol C . . . 5E 86
SR2: Sund . . . 6H 119
Alderley Dr. NE12: Kil . . . 7C 36
Alderley Rd. NE9: Low F . . . 2G 99
Alderley Way NE23: Cra . . . 1A 26
Alderman Fenwicks House . . . 6G 4
(off Pilgrim St.)
Alderman Wood Rd. DH9: Tan L . . . 1E 124
Alderney Gdns. NE5: Cha P . . . 3C 60
Alder Pk. DH7: B'don . . . 2C 174
Alder Rd. NE28: W'snd . . . 6J 47
NE29: N Shi . . . 5A 48
SR8: Hord . . . 6F 173
Aldershot Rd. SR3: E Her . . . 2K 131
Aldershot Sq. SR3: E Her . . . 2K 131
Alderside Cres. DH7: Lan . . . 6J 137
Alder St. SR5: Sund . . . 6H 103
Alderton Ct. NE62: Chop . . . 1H 17
Alder Wlk. NE34: S Shi . . . 2B 88
Alder Way NE12: Kil . . . 7A 36
Alderwood NE8: Gate . . . 5F 83
NE38: Wash . . . 1F 129
NE63: Ash . . . 5A 12
Alderwood Cres. NE6: Walk . . . 4D 64
Alderwood Pk. NE23: Dud . . . 3H 35
Alderwyk NE10: Hew . . . 1F 101
Aldhome Ct. DH1: Dur . . . 5J 153
Aldin Grange Hall DH7: Bearp . . . 2F 165
Aldin Grange Ter. DH7: Bearp . . . 1E 164
Aldin Ri. DH7: Bearp . . . 2E 164
Aldridge Ct. DH7: Ush M . . . 2C 164
Aldsworth Cl. NE9: Spri . . . 6D 100
Aldwick Rd. NE15: Scot . . . 1G 81
Aldwych Dr. NE29: N Shi . . . 5B 48
Aldwych Rd. SR3: E Her . . . 2K 131
Aldwych Sq. SR3: E Her . . . 3K 131
Aldwych St. NE33: S Shi . . . 3A 68
Alemouth Rd. NE46: Hex . . . 1D 70
Alexander Dr. DH5: Hett H . . . 7F 145
Alexander Pl. NE46: Hex . . . 1C 70
Alexander Ter. NE13: Haz . . . 6C 34
SR6: Ful . . . 4F 105
Alexandra Av. SR5: Sund . . . 6B 104
Alexandra Bus. Pk. SR4: Sund . . . 6A 104
Alexandra Chase NE23: Cra . . . 5J 25
Alexandra Cl. DH1: Dur . . . 5J 153
Alexandra Cres. NE46: Hex . . . 1B 70
Alexandra Dr. NE16: Swa . . . 6J 81
Alexandra Gdns. NE29: N Shi . . . 6E 48
NE40: Ryton . . . 2J 79
Alexandra Ho. SR2: Sund . . . 5G 7
Alexandra Pk. NE64: Newb S . . . 2H 13
SR3: Sund . . . 4D 118
Alexandra Pl. NE61: Mor . . . 7G 9
(off Alexandra Rd.)
Alexandra Rd. NE6: Heat . . . 4K 63
NE8: Gate . . . 4G 83
NE61: Mor . . . 7G 9
NE63: Ash . . . 3C 12
Alexandra St. DH2: Pelt . . . 3E 126
DH8: Cons . . . 7H 121
NE28: W'snd . . . 3G 65
NE39: Row G . . . 6E 94
Alexandra Ter. DH4: Pen . . . 1B 130
DH6: Has . . . 1B 170
DH6: Whe H . . . 2B 180
NE9: Spri . . . 6D 100
NE16: Sun . . . 5J 97
NE22: Bed . . . 7K 17
NE26: Whit B . . . 7H 39
NE43: Pains . . . 7K 75
NE46: Hex . . . 1B 70
Alexandra Way NE23: Cra . . . 5J 25
NE64: Newb S . . . 2H 13
Alexandrea Way NE28: W'snd . . . 7H 47
Alexandria Cres. DH1: Dur . . . 3A 6 (3K 165)
Alexandrina St. SR7: S'hm . . . 3B 148
Alford DH2: Ous . . . 6H 113
Alford Grn. NE12: Longb . . . 5A 46
Alfred Av. NE22: Bed . . . 7K 17
Alfred St. NE6: Walk . . . 7C 64
NE24: Bly . . . 3J 23
NE31: Heb . . . 1H 85
SR7: S'hm . . . 4C 148
SR8: Eas C . . . 6C 160
Alfred St. E. SR7: S'hm . . . 4C 148
Alfreton Cl. DH7: B'don . . . 3C 174
Algernon NE12: Kil . . . 6B 36
Algernon Cl. NE6: Byke . . . 6A 64
Algernon Ct. NE6: Byke . . . 6A 64
(off North Cl.)
Algernon Dr. NE27: Back . . . 1H 47
Algernon Ind. Est. NE27: Shir . . . 3K 47
Algernon Pl. NE26: Whit B . . . 7H 39
Algernon Rd. NE6: Byke . . . 6A 64
NE15: Lem . . . 7C 60
Algernon Ter. NE30: Tyne . . . 4J 49
NE41: Wylam . . . 7J 57
Algiers Rd. SR3: E Her . . . 2J 131
Alice St. NE21: Winl . . . 5B 80
NE33: S Shi . . . 5J 67
SR2: Sund . . . 6H 7 (3E 118)
Alice Well Vs. SR4: Cox G . . . 5B 116
Aline St. SR3: New S . . . 2D 132
SR7: S'hm . . . 3C 148
Alington Pl. DH1: Dur . . . 2E 166
Alisha Va. SR8: Eas C . . . 7D 160
Alison Ct. NE6: Heat . . . 2P 5
Alison Dr. NE36: E Bol . . . 7K 87
Allandale Av. NE12: Longb . . . 5B 46
Allandale Cotts. NE17: Ebc . . . 5J 107
Allan Rd. NE64: Newb S . . . 2H 13
Allan St. SR8: Eas C . . . 6D 160
Allanville NE12: Kil . . . 6K 35
Allchurch NE15: Benw . . . 7H 61
Allchurch Dr. NE63: N Sea . . . 4E 12
Allen Av. NE11: T Vall . . . 7F 83
Allendale Av. NE28: W'snd . . . 1F 65
ALLENDALE COTTAGES . . . 5J 107
Allendale Cres. DH4: Pen . . . 1A 130
NE27: Shir . . . 1A 48
NE62: Stake . . . 6J 11
Allendale Dr. NE34: S Shi . . . 5C 68
Allendale Pl. NE30: Tyne . . . 5K 49
Allendale Rd. DH7: Mead . . . 1E 174
NE6: Byke . . . 1B 84
NE24: Bly . . . 3K 23
NE46: Hex . . . 2A 70
SR3: E Her . . . 2K 131
Allendale Sq. SR3: E Her . . . 7A 118
Allendale St. DH5: Hett H . . . 1G 157
Allendale Ter. DH6: Has . . . 1B 170
DH9: Ann P . . . 5K 123
NE6: Walk . . . 1D 84
Allen Dr. NE46: Hex . . . 2D 70
Allenheads NE5: W Dent . . . 4E 60
NE25: Sea D . . . 6G 27
NE38: Wash . . . 7J 115
ALLENSFORD . . . 1B 134
Allensford Bank DH8: Allen . . . 1B 134
Allensford Cvn. Pk. DH8: Allen . . . 1C 134
Allensford Country Pk. . . . 1C 134
Allensgreen NE23: Cra . . . 4K 25
Allen St. DH3: Ches S . . . 7A 128
Allen Ter. NE40: Craw . . . 2D 78
Allerdean Cl. NE15: Lem . . . 6B 60
NE25: Sea D . . . 1H 37
ALLERDENE . . . 6J 99
Allerdene Wlk. NE16: Whi . . . 1G 97
Allergate DH1: Dur . . . 3A 6 (3K 165)
Allergate Ter. DH1: Dur . . . 3A 6
Allerhope NE23: Cra . . . 5K 25
Allerton Gdns. NE6: Heat . . . 3B 64
Allerton Pl. NE16: Whi . . . 2F 97
Allerwash NE5: W Dent . . . 4E 60
Allery Banks NE61: Mor . . . 7G 9
Allgood Ter. NE22: Bed . . . 7K 17
All Hallows La. NE1: Newc T . . . 6H 5 (1G 83)
Alliance Pl. SR4: Sund . . . 2F 7 (1D 118)
Alliance St. SR4: Sund . . . 2F 7 (1D 118)
Allingham Ct. NE7: H Hea . . . 2C 64
Allison Ct. NE11: Dun . . . 5H 81
Allison Gdns. DH8: Cons . . . 6H 121
Allison St. DH8: Cons . . . 6H 121
Alloa Rd. SR3: E Her . . . 1K 131
Allonby M. NE23: Cra . . . 7B 22
Allonby Way NE5: Den M . . . 5H 61
ALLOTMENT, THE . . . 3K 47
Alloy Ter. NE39: Row G . . . 6G 95
All Saints Bus. Cen. NE1: Newc T . . . 6H 5
All Saints Ct. NE29: N Shi . . . 6D 48
SR6: Roker . . . 6F 105
All Saints Dr. DH5: Hett H . . . 5G 145
All Saints Ho. SR6: Roker . . . 6F 105
Allwork Ter. NE16: Whi . . . 7H 81
Alma Pl. DH1: Dur . . . 1F 167
DH4: S Row . . . 4C 130
NE26: Whit B . . . 7H 39
NE29: N Shi . . . 6G 49
NE61: Mor . . . 6G 9
Alma St. SR4: Sund . . . 1G 117
Alma Ter. DH1: Dur . . . 4J 165
(off Neville's Cross Bank)
DH1: Dur . . . 2C 166
(Gilesgate)
NE40: G'sde . . . 4G 79
Almond Cl. DH6: Has . . . 1B 170
Almond Cres. NE8: Gate . . . 6E 82
Almond Dr. SR5: Sund . . . 7G 103
Almond Gro. NE24: News . . . 5G 23
Almond Pl. NE4: Fen . . . 6K 61
Almond Ter. SR8: Hord . . . 5F 173
Almond Way SR7: S'hm . . . 5A 148
Almoners Barn DH1: Dur . . . 5J 165
Almshouses NE15: Newb . . . 6K 59
Aln Av. NE3: Gos . . . 5C 44
Aln Ct. NE15: Lem . . . 7C 60
Aln Cres. NE3: Gos . . . 5C 44
Aln Gro. NE15: Lem . . . 6C 60
Alnham Ct. NE3: Fawd . . . 5A 44
Alnham Grn. NE5: Cha P . . . 3C 60
Alnmouth Av. NE29: N Shi . . . 1D 66
NE63: Ash . . . 2J 11
Alnmouth Ct. NE5: Fen . . . 3K 61
Alnmouth Dr. NE3: Gos . . . 1G 63
Alnmouth Ter. NE46: Acomb . . . 4B 50
Alnmouth Way SR7: S'hm . . . 1A 148
Aln St. NE31: Heb . . . 7H 65
(not continuous)
NE63: Ash . . . 3C 12
Aln Wlk. NE3: Gos . . . 6C 44
Alnwick Av. NE26: Whit B . . . 6G 39
NE29: N Shi . . . 1D 66
Alnwick Cl. DH2: Ches S . . . 1J 141
NE16: Whi . . . 7G 81
Alnwick Ct. NE38: Wash . . . 3E 114
Alnwick Dr. NE22: Bed . . . 6F 17
Alnwick Gro. NE32: Jar . . . 4B 86
Alnwick Ho. NE29: N Shi . . . 1D 66
Alnwick M. DH8: C'sde . . . 2D 134
Alnwick Rd. DH1: Dur . . . 4A 154
NE34: S Shi . . . 7J 67
SR3: E Her . . . 1A 132
Alnwick Sq. SR3: E Her . . . 1A 132
Alnwick St. NE15: Newb . . . 5K 59
NE28: W'snd . . . 3G 65
SR8: Eas C . . . 6C 160
SR8: Hord . . . 3D 172
Alnwick Ter. NE13: W Op . . . 4E 34
Alpine Cl. DH4: S Row . . . 4K 129
Alpine Ct. DH2: Ches S . . . 6A 128
Alpine Gro. NE36: W Bol . . . 7H 87
Alpine Way SR3: Sund . . . 5C 118
Alresford NE12: Kil . . . 7B 36
Alston Av. NE6: Walk . . . 7C 64
NE23: E Cram . . . 5B 26
Alston Cl. NE28: W'snd . . . 1A 66
NE29: N Shi . . . 5C 48
Alston Cres. SR6: Seab . . . 2E 104
Alstone Ct. NE62: Chop . . . 1H 17
Alston Gdns. NE15: Thro . . . 2H 59
Alston Gro. NE26: Sea S . . . 3D 28
Alston Rd. DH8: Shot B . . . 5D 120
NE25: New Hart . . . 4H 27
NE38: Wash . . . 2B 116
Alston St. NE8: Gate . . . 5E 82
Alston Ter. DH8: Shot B . . . 5E 120
Alston Wlk. DH6: S'burn . . . 3A 168
SR8: Pet . . . 5C 172
Alston Way DH7: Mead . . . 1E 174
Altan Pl. NE12: Longb . . . 5K 45
Altree Grange SR5: Ful . . . 4E 104
Altrincham Twr. SR3: New S . . . 1A 132
ALUM WATERS . . . 4C 164
Alum Well NE9: Low F . . . 2H 99
Alum Well Rd. NE9: Low F . . . 2H 99
(Alum Well)
NE9: Low F . . . 2G 99
(Belle Vue Cotts.)
Alverston Cl. NE15: Lem . . . 5C 60
Alverstone Av. NE9: Low F . . . 3G 99
Alverstone Rd. SR3: E Her . . . 2K 131
Alverthorpe St. NE33: S Shi . . . 5K 67
Alverton Cl. NE3: Ken . . . 7A 44
Alveston Cl. NE62: Chop . . . 1H 17
Alwin NE38: Wash . . . 7E 114
Alwin Cl. NE28: W'snd . . . 4J 65
Alwin Grange NE31: Heb . . . 6K 65
Alwinton Av. NE29: N Shi . . . 4D 48
Alwinton Cl. NE5: West . . . 1G 61
NE24: Cow . . . 1G 23
Alwinton Ct. NE24: Cow . . . 1G 23
Alwinton Dr. DH2: Ches S . . . 1J 141
Alwinton Gdns. NE11: Lob H . . . 2C 98
Alwinton Rd. NE27: Shir . . . 1A 48
Alwinton Sq. NE63: Ash . . . 5D 12
Alwinton Ter. NE3: Gos . . . 7F 45
Alwyn Cl. DH4: Bour . . . 6J 129
Alwyn Gdns. DH8: Cons . . . 1H 135
Amalfi Twr. SR3: New S . . . 1A 132
Amara Sq. SR3: E Her . . . 1A 132
Ambassadors Way NE29: N Shi . . . 4B 48
Amber Ct. NE4: Elsw . . . 3B 82
NE24: Bly . . . 3G 23
Amberdale Av. NE6: Walk . . . 5E 64
Ambergate Cl. NE5: West . . . 2G 61
Ambergate Way NE3: Ken . . . 2K 61
Amberley Chase NE12: Kil . . . 7C 36
Amberley Cl. NE28: W'snd . . . 1A 66
Amberley Gdns. NE7: H Hea . . . 3A 64
Amberley Gro. NE16: Whi . . . 2G 97
Amberley St. NE8: Gate . . . 5D 82
SR2: Sund . . . 3G 119
Amberley St. Sth. SR2: Sund . . . 3G 119
Amberley Wlk. NE16: Whi . . . 2H 97
Amberley Way NE24: News . . . 4J 23
Amble Av. NE25: Whit B . . . 7H 39
NE34: S Shi . . . 5D 68
Amble Cl. NE24: Bly . . . 4G 23
NE29: N Shi . . . 1D 66
Amble Gro. NE2: Newc T . . . 1L 5 (6J 63)
Amble Pl. NE12: Longb . . . 3D 46
Ambleside NE15: Thro . . . 3H 59
Ambleside Av. NE34: S Shi . . . 7A 68
SR7: S'hm . . . 2G 147
Ambleside Cl. NE25: Sea D . . . 7H 27
SR8: Pet . . . 5C 172
Ambleside Ct. DH3: Ches S . . . 7C 114
Ambleside Gdns. NE9: Low F . . . 3J 99
Ambleside Grn. NE5: Den M . . . 5H 61
Ambleside M. DH8: Lead . . . 5B 122
Ambleside Ter. SR6: Seab . . . 3E 104
Amble Twr. SR3: New S . . . 1A 132
Amble Way NE3: Gos . . . 6D 44
Ambridge Way NE3: Ken . . . 7B 44
NE25: Sea D . . . 6E 26
Ambrose Ct. DH9: Ann P . . . 6J 123
NE21: Winl . . . 5B 80
Ambrose Pl. NE6: Walk . . . 7F 65
Ambrose Rd. SR3: E Her . . . 1K 131
Amec Dr. NE28: W'snd . . . 4K 65
Amelia Cl. NE4: Benw . . . 3A 82
Amelia Gdns. SR3: E Her . . . 2J 131
Amelia Wlk. NE4: Benw . . . 3A 82
(not continuous)
Amen Corner NE1: Newc T . . . 7G 4 (2G 83)
Amersham Cres. SR8: Pet . . . 5B 172
Amersham Pl. NE5: Blak . . . 3H 61
Amersham Rd. NE24: News . . . 5H 23
Amesbury Cl. NE5: Cha P . . . 2B 60
Amethyst Rd. NE4: Newc T . . . 3B 82
Amethyst St. SR4: Sund . . . 1B 118
AMF Bowling
Washington . . . 3G 115
Amherst Rd. NE3: Fawd . . . 6A 44
Amos Ayre Pl. NE34: S Shi . . . 1F 87
Amos Dr. DH9: Ann P . . . 7K 123
Amphitheatre . . . 2B 68
Amsterdam Rd. SR3: New S . . . 1A 132
Amusement Pk. Caravan Site
NE33: S Shi . . . 1A 68
Amy St. SR5: S'wck . . . 5D 104
Ancaster Av. NE12: Longb . . . 6K 45
Ancaster Rd. NE16: Whi . . . 1F 97
Anchorage, The DH3: Ches S . . . 6B 128
DH4: S Row . . . 3B 130
NE38: Wash . . . 4J 115
Anchorage Ter. DH1: Dur . . . 5D 6 (4B 166)
Anchor Chare NE1: Newc T . . . 6J 5
Ancona St. SR4: Sund . . . 7B 104
Ancroft Av. NE29: N Shi . . . 5F 49
Ancroft Gth. DH1: H Shin . . . 1F 177
Ancroft Pl. NE5: Fen . . . 5H 61
NE63: Ash . . . 6D 12
Ancroft Rd. NE25: Sea D . . . 7F 27
Ancroft Way NE3: Fawd . . . 4B 44
Ancrum St. NE2: Newc T . . . 1A 4 (6D 62)
Ancrum Way NE16: Whi . . . 2F 97
Anderson Ct. NE16: Burn . . . 2B 110
(off Sheephill)
Anderson Grn. NE9: Low F . . . 1H 99
Anderson St. NE33: S Shi . . . 2K 67
Anderson St. Nth. NE33: S Shi . . . 2J 67
Andover Pl. NE28: W'snd . . . 6J 47
Andrew Ct. NE6: Walk . . . 7E 64
Andrew Rd. SR3: E Her . . . 2J 131
Andrews House Station
Tanfield Railway . . . 1H 111
Andrew's La. SR8: Eas . . . 2J 171
Andrew St. SR8: Eas C . . . 7C 160
Andrew Ter. DH6: Whe H . . . 4A 180
Andromeda Ct. NE6: Walk . . . 2F 85
Anemone Cl. NE24: Bly . . . 4K 23
Anfield Ct. NE3: Ken . . . 7A 44
Anfield Rd. NE3: Ken . . . 7A 44
Angelica Cl. DH8: Cons . . . 7J 121
Angel of the North . . . 7J 99
Angel Pk. DH2: Ous . . . 2J 127
Angel Vw. DH7: Edm . . . 4C 140
NE4: Benw . . . 2A 82
Angel Way DH3: Bir . . . 2B 114
Angerstein Ct. DH1: Carr . . . 7G 155
Angerton Av. NE27: Shir . . . 2K 47
NE30: Cull . . . 3G 49
Angerton Gdns. NE5: Fen . . . 5K 61
Angerton Ter. NE23: Dud . . . 3H 35
Anglesey Gdns. NE5: Cha P . . . 3C 60
Anglesey Pl. NE4: Newc T . . . 6A 4 (1D 82)
Anglesey Rd. SR3: E Her . . . 2K 131
Anglesey Sq. SR3: E Her . . . 2K 131
Angle Ter. NE28: W'snd . . . 3K 65
Angram Dr. SR2: Sund . . . 7J 119
Angram Wlk. NE5: Cha P . . . 3C 60
Angrove Gdns. SR4: Sund . . . 3B 118
Angus DH2: Ous . . . 6H 113
Angus Cl. NE12: Kil . . . 1A 46
Angus Cres. NE29: N Shi . . . 1D 66
Angus Rd. NE8: Gate . . . 6E 82
Angus Sq. DH7: Lang M . . . 7F 165
SR3: E Her . . . 2K 131
Angus St. DH7: Lang M . . . 6G 165
SR8: Eas C . . . 6C 160
Angus Ter. SR8: Eas C . . . 1D 172
ANICK . . . 5G 51
Anick Rd. NE46: B End . . . 7F 51
Anker's House Mus. . . . 6B 128
Annand Ct. NE34: S Shi . . . 2G 87
Annand Rd. DH1: Dur . . . 1D 166
Annaside M. DH8: Lead . . . 5B 122
Ann Av. DH6: Kel . . . 7D 178
Anne Dr. NE12: Longb . . . 4E 46
Annfield Pl. DH9: Ann P . . . 5J 123
ANNFIELD PLAIN . . . 5K 123
Annfield Plain By-Pass DH9: Ann P . . . 5G 123
Annfield Rd. NE23: Cra . . . 7K 21
Annfield Ter. DH9: Ann P . . . 4J 123
Annie St. SR6: Ful . . . 3F 105
ANNITSFORD . . . 2K 35
Annitsford Dr. NE23: Dud . . . 3K 35
Annitsford Pond Nature Reserve . . . 2J 35
Annitsford Rd. NE23: Seg . . . 3A 36
Ann's Pl. DH7: Lang M . . . 6G 165
Ann's Row NE24: Bly . . . 7J 19
Ann St. DH8: Cons . . . 7H 121
NE8: Gate . . . 10J 5 (4H 83)
NE21: Blay . . . 3C 80
NE27: Shir . . . 7J 37
NE31: Heb . . . 6G 65
Annville Cres. NE6: Walk . . . 2E 84
Ann Wlk. NE6: Walk . . . 2E 84
Anolha Ho. NE1: Newc T . . . 5J 5 (1H 83)

Anscomb Gdns. NE7: H Hea 3J **63**
Anson Cl. NE33: S Shi 5H **67**
Anson Pl. NE5: West 2F **61**
Anson St. NE8: Gate 5K **83**
Anson Wlk. NE6: Walk 2F **85**
Anstead Cl. NE23: Cra 4K **25**
Anthony Ct. DH9: Stly 2E **124**
Anthony Rd. SR3: E Her 1K **131**
Anthony St. DH9: Stly 2E **124**
SR8: Eas C 6D **160**
Antliff Ter. DH9: Ann P 5K **123**
Antonine Wlk. NE15: Hed W 3D **58**
Anton Pl. NE23: Cra 5K **25**
Antrim Cl. NE5: Blak 2J **61**
Antrim Gdns. SR7: S'hm 2A **148**
Antwerp Rd. SR3: E Her 2J **131**
Anvil Ct. DH1: P Me 4J **153**
DH8: W'stll 1A **106**
Anytime Fitness 3H **83**
Apex Bus. Village NE23: Dud 2K **35**
Apollo Ct. NE31: Heb 5K **85**
Apperley NE5: W Dent 4E **60**
Apperley Av. DH1: H Shin 1G **177**
NE3: Ken 1J **61**
APPERLEY DENE 6G **91**
Apperley Rd. NE43: Pains 1J **91**
Appian Pl. NE9: Low F 7K **83**
NE15: Thro 3H **59**
(not continuous)
Appleby Ct. DH4: Hou S 1H **143**
NE12: Longb 6J **45**
NE29: N Shi 7F **49**
Appleby Gdns. NE9: Low F 4J **99**
NE28: W'snd 1A **66**
Appleby Pk. NE29: N Shi 6F **49**
Appleby Pl. NE40: Craw 2E **78**
Appleby Rd. SR3: E Her 2K **131**
Appleby Sq. SR3: E Her 2K **131**
Appleby St. NE29: N Shi 1G **67**
Appleby Way SR8: Pet 2J **181**
Apple Cl. NE15: Lem 5C **60**
Apple Ct. NE25: New Hart 4H **27**
Appledore Cl. NE40: G'sde 6C **78**
Appledore Gdns. DH3: Ches S 4B **128**
DH7: Edm 3D **140**
NE9: Low F 4H **99**
Appledore Rd. NE24: News 4J **23**
Appleforth Av. SR2: Sund 7J **119**
Appleton Cl. NE11: Gate 6C **82**
Appletree Ct. *NE8: Gate* *4G 83*
(off Bensham Rd.)
NE15: Walb 3A **60**
Appletree Dr. NE42: Pru 3E **76**
Appletree Gdns. NE6: Walk 5C **64**
NE25: Monks 1E **48**
Appletree La. NE45: Corb 1E **72**
Appletree Ri. NE45: Corb 1E **72**
Applewood NE12: Kil 1D **46**
Appley Ter. SR6: Roker 5G **105**
April Courtyard *NE8: Gate* *5D 82*
(off North Side)
Apsley Cres. NE3: Ken 7A **44**
Aqua Ter. NE64: Newb S 3H **13**
Aquila Dr. NE15: Hed W 3B **58**
Arbeia Roman Fort & Mus. 1J **67**
Arbourcourt Av. DH7: Esh W 4D **162**
Arbroath DH2: Ous 7H **113**
Arbroath Rd. SR3: E Her 1K **131**
Arcade, The DH3: Ches S 5A **128**
NE11: Dun 4J **81**
NE24: Bly *2J 23*
(off Waterloo Rd.)
NE30: Tyne 5K **49**
Arcade Pk. NE30: Tyne 5K **49**
Arcadia DH2: Ous 7H **113**
Arcadia Av. DH3: Ches S 4A **128**
Arcadia Ter. NE24: Bly 3J **23**
Archbold Ter. NE2: Jes, Newc T 1H **5** (6G **63**)
Archer Rd. SR3: E Her 1K **131**
Archers Ct. DH1: Dur 2J **165**
Archer Sq. SR3: E Her 1K **131**
Archer St. NE28: W'snd 2H **65**
Archer Vs. NE28: W'snd 2H **65**
Archery Ri. DH1: Dur 4J **165**
Archibald St. NE3: Gos 7E **44**
Arcot Av. NE23: Nel V 2G **25**
NE25: Monks 1E **48**
Arcot Ct. NE23: Nel V 1F **25**
Arcot Dr. NE5: W Dent 5F **61**
NE25: Monks 1E **48**
Arcot La. NE23: Dud, Sea B 1D **34**
Arcot Ter. NE24: Bly 1H **23**
Arden Av. NE3: Gos 3D **44**
Arden Cl. NE28: W'snd 5H **47**
Arden Cres. NE5: Fen 4K **61**
Arden Ho. NE3: Gos 6E **44**
Arden Sq. SR3: E Her 1A **132**
Arden St. DH6: Shot C 5E **170**
Ardrossan DH2: Ous 7H **113**
Ardrossan Rd. SR3: E Her 2K **131**
Arena Bus. Pk. DH4: Hou S 3C **144**
Arena Way NE4: Newc T 9C **4** (3E **82**)
Argent St. SR8: Eas C 6D **160**
Argus Cl. NE11: Fest P 7D **82**
Argyle Ct. DH9: Stly 7G **111**
Argyle M. *NE24: Bly* *7J 19*
(off Argyle St.)
Argyle Pl. DH6: S Het 4B **158**
NE29: N Shi 4G **49**
Argyle Sq. SR2: Sund 6H **7** (3E **118**)
Argyle St. NE1: Newc T 5H **5** (1G **83**)
NE24: Bly 7H **19**
NE30: Tyne 4K **49**
NE31: Heb 7H **65**
SR2: Sund 6H **7** (3E **118**)
Argyle Ter. NE29: N Shi 4G **49**
NE46: Hex 2D **70**
NE64: Newb S 3H **13**
Argyll DH2: Ous 7H **113**
Ariel St. NE63: Ash 3C **12**
(Juliet St.)
NE63: Ash 4C **12**
(St Andrews Ter.)
Arisaig DH2: Ous 7H **113**
Arklecrag NE37: Wash 2G **115**
Arkle Rd. SR3: E Her 2K **131**
Arkleside Pl. NE5: Cha P 4D **60**
Arkless Gro. DH8: C'sde 1E **134**
Arkle St. NE8: Gate 6E **82**
NE13: Haz 7C **34**
Arkwright St. NE8: Gate 7F **83**
Arlington Av. NE3: Ken 2B **62**
Arlington Cl. DH4: Bour 6J **129**
Arlington Ct. NE3: Ken 2C **62**
Arlington Gro. NE16: Whi 1G **97**
NE23: Cra 7K **21**
Arlington Rd. NE31: Heb 2K **85**
Arlington St. SR4: Sund 2B **118**
Arlott Ho. NE29: N Shi 2D **66**
Armitage Gdns. NE9: Eigh B 6A **100**
Armonside Rd. NE17: C'wl 2A **108**
ARMSTRONG 1E **114**
Armstrong, The NE8: Gate 4E **82**
Armstrong Av. NE6: Heat 4K **63**
NE34: S Shi 7A **68**
TS28: Win 5G **181**
Armstrong Cl. NE46: Hex 3B **70**
Armstrong Ct. NE63: N Sea 6D **12**
Armstrong Dr. NE12: Kil 2K **45**
Armstrong Ho. NE37: Wash 1E **114**
Armstrong Ind. Est. NE37: Wash 1E **114**
Armstrong Ind. Pk.
NE4: Newc T 10A **4** (3C **82**)
Armstrong Rd. NE4: Benw 2J **81**
NE15: Benw, Scot 1F **81**
NE28: W'snd 4A **66**
NE37: Wash 1D **114**
SR8: Pet 3B **172**
Armstrong St. NE5: Call 5B **42**
NE8: Gate 7E **82**
(not continuous)
Armstrong Ter. NE33: S Shi 6J **67**
NE61: Mor 7G **9**
Armstrong Way NE63: N Sea 7D **12**
Arncliffe Av. SR4: Sund 4A **118**
Arncliffe Gdns. NE5: Cha P 3C **60**
Arndale Arc. NE32: Jar 6B **66**
Arndale Ho. NE3: Ken 7A **44**
Arndale Ho's. DH3: Bir 4A **114**
Arngrove Ct. NE4: Newc T 4C **4** (7E **62**)
Arnham Gro. SR4: Sund 6F **117**
Arnison Retail Cen.
DH1: P Me 3K **153**
Arnold Av. TS27: B Col 1H **183**
Arnold Cl. DH9: Stly 3G **125**
Arnold Rd. SR3: E Her 1K **131**
Arnold St. NE35: Bol C 6F **87**
Arnside Wlk. NE5: Cha P 3C **60**
(not continuous)
Arran Ct. SR3: Silk 3C **132**
Arran Dr. NE32: Jar 3E **86**
Arran Gdns. NE10: Wind N 7A **84**
Arran Gro. DH6: Thor 1K **179**
Arran Pl. NE29: N Shi 4C **48**
Arras La. SR1: Sund 1G **119**
Arrol Pk. SR4: Sund 2D **118**
Arrow Cl. NE12: Kil 2K **45**
Artemis Ct. DH7: Mead 1F **175**
Arthington Way NE34: S Shi 1A **88**
Arthur Av. SR2: Ryh 3J **133**
Arthur Cook Av. NE16: Whi 1J **97**
ARTHURS HILL 7C **62**
Arthur St. DH2: Pelt 2C **126**
DH7: Ush M 2B **164**
NE8: Gate 4H **83**
NE24: Bly 1J **23**
(not continuous)
NE32: Jar 7B **66**
SR2: Ryh 3J **133**
SR6: Whit 2H **89**
Arthur Ter. SR6: Whit 3H **89**
Arun Cl. SR8: Pet 7A **172**
Arundel Cl. NE13: W Op 6C **34**
NE22: Bed 5A **18**
Arundel Ct. NE3: K Bank 5J **43**
NE12: Longb 6J **45**
Arundel Dr. NE15: Lem 6E **60**
NE25: Monks 7B **38**
Arundel Gdns. NE9: Low F 2J **99**
SR3: E Her 2J **131**
Arundel Rd. SR3: E Her 1K **131**
Arundel Sq. NE63: Ash 4A **12**
Arundel Wlk. DH2: Ous 2H **127**
NE16: Whi 2G **97**
TS28: Win 4G **181**
Arundel Way DH7: Mead 1E **174**
Asama Ct. NE4: Newc T 3C **82**
Ascot Cl. NE28: W'snd 6H **47**
Ascot Ct. NE3: K Bank 5J **43**
NE36: W Bol 1F **103**
SR3: E Her 2K **131**
(not continuous)
Ascot Cres. NE8: Gate 6E **82**
Ascot Gdns. NE34: S Shi 6K **67**
Ascot Gro. NE63: Ash 5B **12**
Ascot Pl. DH2: Ous 1H **127**
Ascot Rd. DH8: Shot B 2G **121**
Ascot St. SR8: Eas C 7D **160**
Ascott Ct. NE12: Longb 6K **45**
Ascot Wlk. NE3: K Bank 5J **43**
Ash Av. DH1: Dur 3E **166**
DH7: Ush M 2C **164**
NE13: Din 4H **33**
Ash Banks NE61: Mor 1G **15**
Ashberry Gro. SR6: Ful 6F **105**
Ashbourne Av. NE6: Walk 7D **64**
Ashbourne Cl. NE27: Back 6G **37**
Ashbourne Cres. NE63: Ash 4K **11**
Ashbourne Rd. NE32: Jar 1C **86**
Ashbrook Cl. DH7: B'don 2B **174**
ASHBROOKE 4E **118**
Ashbrooke NE25: Monks 6E **38**
Ashbrooke Cl. NE25: Monks 6E **38**
Ashbrooke Cres. SR2: Sund 4F **119**
Ashbrooke Cross SR2: Sund 5E **118**
Ashbrooke Dr. NE20: Pon 4J **31**
Ashbrooke Est. DH6: Shot C 6E **170**
Ashbrooke Gdns. NE28: W'snd 2J **65**
Ashbrooke Mt. SR2: Sund 4E **118**
Ashbrooke Range SR2: Sund 5E **118**
Ashbrooke Rd. SR2: Sund 7J **7** (4E **118**)
Ashbrooke St. NE3: Ken 2A **62**
Ashbrooke Ter. NE36: E Bol 7K **87**
SR2: Sund 7J **7** (4F **119**)
Ashburne Ct. SR2: Sund 7K **7** (4F **119**)
Ashburn Rd. NE28: W'snd 6J **47**
Ashburton Rd. NE3: Gos 1C **62**
Ashbury NE25: Monks 5C **38**
Ashby Cres. DH8: B'hill 4F **121**
Ashby La. DH8: B'hill 5F **121**
Ashby St. SR2: Sund 5H **119**
Ashby Vs. NE36: W Bol 1F **103**
Ash Cl. NE46: Hex 3A **70**
Ash Ct. NE29: N Shi 3E **48**
Ash Cres. SR7: S'hm 5A **148**
SR8: Hord 6E **172**
Ashcroft NE20: Pon 2H **31**
Ashcroft Dr. NE12: Longb 5C **46**
Ashdale DH4: Pen 1J **129**
NE20: Darr H 1G **41**
Ashdale Ct. SR6: Roker 5G **105**
Ashdale Cres. NE5: Cha P 3D **60**
Ashdale Rd. DH8: Cons 6H **121**
Ashdown Av. DH1: Dur 1F **167**
Ashdown Cl. NE12: Longb 5K **45**
Ashdown Gro. DH7: Lan 5J **137**
Ashdown Rd. SR3: E Her 1K **131**
Ashdown Way NE12: Longb 5K **45**
Asher St. NE10: Fell 5A **84**
Ashfield DH8: Shot B 3F **121**
NE32: Jar 5D **86**
Ashfield Av. NE16: Whi 6J **81**
Ashfield Cl. NE4: Elsw 8A **4** (2C **82**)
Ashfield Ct. DH8: Shot B 3E **120**
NE12: Kil 3C **46**
NE39: H Spen 3E **94**
Ashfield Gdns. NE28: W'snd 2D **64**
Ashfield Gro. NE26: Whit B 5G **39**
NE29: N Shi 6G **49**
Ashfield Lodge NE4: Elsw 8A **4** (2C **82**)
Ashfield M. NE13: Haz 6C **34**
NE28: W'snd 2F **65**
NE63: Ash 2C **12**
Ashfield Pk. NE16: Whi 6H **81**
Ashfield Ri. NE16: Whi 2H **97**
Ashfield Rd. NE3: Gos 1C **62**
NE16: Whi 2H **97**
Ashfield Ter. DH3: Ches S 7B **128**
NE9: Spri 6D **100**
NE10: Pel 5D **84**
NE40: Ryton 1G **79**
Ashford NE9: Low F 5J **99**
Ashford Cl. NE24: News 4J **23**
NE29: N Shi 3F **49**
Ashford Dr. DH7: Sac 6E **140**
Ashford Gro. DH6: Thor 1A **180**
NE5: Cha P 1B **60**
Ashford Rd. SR3: E Her 2K **131**
Ashgill NE37: Wash 2F **115**
Ash Gro. DH8: Cons 6J **121**
NE11: Dun 5A **82**
NE28: W'snd 4H **65**
NE40: Ryton 7G **59**
NE61: Mor 1E **14**
SR6: Whit 5J **89**
TS29: Trim S 7C **180**
Ashgrove DH2: Ches S 7H **127**
Ashgrove Av. NE34: S Shi 2B **88**
Ashgrove Ter. DH3: Bir 3K **113**
NE8: Gate 5G **83**
Ash Hill Ct. SR2: Sund 4F **119**
ASHINGTON 3A **12**
Ashington Dr.
NE62: Chop, Stake 1H **17**
Ashington Leisure Cen. 3K **11**
Ashington M. NE62: Chop 1H **17**
Ashkirk NE23: Dud 3J **35**
SR3: New S 1A **132**
Ashkirk Cl. DH2: Ches S 1J **141**
Ashkirk Way NE25: Sea D 1H **37**
Ashlea Ct. SR3: E Her 1K **131**
Ashlea Pk. SR3: E Her 1K **131**
Ashleigh DH2: Ches S 4J **127**
Ashleigh Av. DH1: Dur 6K **153**
Ashleigh Cl. NE21: Blay 5E **80**
Ashleigh Cres. NE5: Den M 5F **61**
Ashleigh Gdns. SR6: Clead 4C **88**
Ashleigh Gro. DH7: Lan 6H **137**
NE2: Jes 3F **63**
NE12: Longb 5B **46**
NE30: Tyne 4J **49**
SR6: Ful 3G **105**
Ashleigh Rd. NE5: Den M 5G **61**
Ashleigh Ter. SR6: Ful 3G **105**
Ashleigh Vs. NE36: E Bol 7K **87**
Ashley Cl. NE12: Kil 7D **36**
NE38: Wash 5J **115**
Ashley Ct. DH9: Tan L 1C **124**
Ashley Gdns. NE62: Stake 7J **11**
Ashley Ho. TS29: Trim S 7B **180**
Ashley Rd. NE34: S Shi 7J **67**
Ashley Ter. DH3: Ches S 5A **128**
Ashmead Cl. NE12: Kil 7C **36**
Ash Mdws. NE38: Wash 2C **128**
Ash M. NE4: Fen 5K **61**
Ashmore St. SR2: Sund 7J **7** (3F **119**)
Ashmore Ter. DH6: Whe H 2B **180**
SR2: Sund 7J **7** (3F **119**)
Asholme NE5: W Dent 4E **60**
Ashover Rd. NE3: Ken 2K **61**
Ashridge Cl. NE34: S Shi 1D **88**
Ashridge Ct. NE10: Ward 7F **85**
Ash Sq. NE38: Wash 4J **115**
Ash St. DH7: Lang P 5J **151**
DH8: Cons 7H **121**
NE8: Gate 5D **82**
NE21: Blay 5C **80**
NE43: Mic 6A **76**
Ash Ter. DH6: Bowb 5H **177**
DH8: Lead 5B **122**
DH9: Ann P 4J **123**
DH9: Stly 6H **125**
DH9: Tant 6B **110**
NE13: Haz 6C **34**
SR7: Mur 7F **147**
Ashton Cl. NE5: Cha P 1B **60**
Ashton Ct. NE40: Ryton 2H **79**
Ashton Downe DH2: Ches S 7A **128**
Ashton Ri. DH2: Ches S 7A **128**
SR8: Pet 5C **172**
Ashton St. SR8: Eas C 7D **160**
Ashton Way NE26: Whit B 4E **38**
SR3: E Her 3J **131**
Ashtree Cl. NE4: Elsw 2B **82**
NE39: Row G 4K **95**
Ashtree Dr. NE22: Bed 6H **17**
Ashtree Gdns. NE25: Monks 1E **48**
Ashtree La. NE21: Barl 3E **94**
NE39: H Spen, Row G 3E **94**
Ashtrees Gdns. NE9: Low F 7H **83**
Ash Tree Ter. DH7: Edm 3K **139**
Ashvale Av. NE11: Kib 2E **112**
Ash Way DH4: Hou S 1A **144**
Ashwell Rd. SR3: E Her 2K **131**
Ashwood DH1: Dur 2C **166**
DH3: Ches S *7B 128*
(off George St.)
DH6: S Het 5C **158**
Ashwood Av. SR5: S'wck 5B **104**
Ashwood Bus. Pk. NE63: N Sea 6E **12**
Ashwood Cl. DH7: Sac 7E **140**
NE12: Longb 4C **46**
NE13: W Op 1B **44**
NE23: Cra 7K **21**
Ashwood Cres. NE6: Walk 4D **64**
Ashwood Cft. NE31: Heb 6H **65**
Ashwood Dr. NE63: N Sea 6F **13**
Ashwood Gdns. NE9: Low F 4J **99**
Ashwood Grange DH6: Thor 2J **179**
Ashwood Gro. NE13: W Op 6D **34**
SR5: Sund 6H **103**
Ashwood Ho. NE7: H Hea 1J **63**
Ashwood Mdw. SR8: Hord 5D **172**
Ashwood Rd. NE46: Hex 2E **70**
Ashwood St. SR2: Sund 7F **7** (3D **118**)
Ashwood Ter. NE40: G'sde 5D **78**
SR2: Sund 7F **7** (3D **118**)
Askern Av. SR2: Sund 7J **119**
Askerton Dr. SR8: Pet 2J **181**
Askew Rd. NE8: Gate 6D **82**
(Derwentwater Rd.)
NE8: Gate 10F **4** (4F **83**)
(St Cuthbert's Rd.)
Askew Rd. W. NE8: Gate 5E **82**
(not continuous)
Askrigg Av. NE28: W'snd 5H **47**
SR2: Sund 7H **119**
Askrigg Cl. DH2: Ous 6G **113**
DH8: Cons 2J **135**
Askrigg Wlk. NE5: Cha P 4C **60**
Aspatria Av. TS27: B Col 2H **183**
Aspen Av. SR8: Hord 6F **173**
Aspen Cl. DH1: Dur 1E **166**
DH4: S Row 4K **129**
Aspen Ct. DH3: Gt Lum 3E **142**
DH8: B'hill 5G **121**
SR3: Silk 3A **132**
Aspen Gro. SR7: S'hm 4A **148**
Aspenlaw NE9: Low F 3A **100**
Aspen Pl. NE34: S Shi 1B **88**
Aspen Ter. NE5: Fen 4A **62**
Aspen Way NE24: News 5G **23**
Aspers Casino
Newcastle upon Tyne 5E **4**
Aspley Cl. SR3: Silk 3C **132**
Asquith St. DH6: Thor 1K **179**
Asquith Ter. DH9: Ann P 4J **123**
Assembly Rooms-Durham Student
Theatre, The 4C **6** (3A **166**)
Association Rd. SR6: Roker 5G **105**
Astbury Cl. NE38: Wash 1F **129**
Aster Pl. NE4: Fen 6J **61**
Aster Ter. DH4: S Row 5B **130**
Astley Ct. NE12: Kil 1B **46**
Astley Dr. NE26: Whit B 2E **38**
Astley Gdns. NE25: Sea D 7G **27**
NE26: Sea S 3B **28**
Astley Gro. NE26: Sea S 3B **28**
Astley Rd. NE25: Sea D 6G **27**
Astley St. NE23: E Har 6K **21**

Astley Vs. NE26: Sea S ... 3B 28
Aston Sq. SR3: E Her ... 2K 131
Aston St. NE33: S Shi ... 6K 67
Aston Wlk. NE6: Walk ... 7E 64
Aston Way NE16: Whi ... 2F 97
Astral Ho. SR1: Sund ... 3J 7
Athelhampton NE38: Wash ... 4A 116
Athelstan Rigg SR2: Ryh ... 2J 133
Athenaeum St. SR1: Sund ... 4K 7 (2F 119)
Atherton Dr. DH4: Hou S ... 3A 144
NE4: Benw ... 2A 82
Atherton St. DH1: Dur ... 3A 6 (3K 165)
Athlone Ct. NE24: Bly ... 1J 23
Athlone Pl. DH3: Bir ... 7B 114
Athol Gdns. NE9: Low F ... 7K 83
NE25: Monks ... 1D 48
SR2: Ryh ... 4J 133
Athol Grn. NE11: Dun ... 5C 82
Athol Gro. SR3: New S ... 2C 132
Athol Ho. *NE20: Pon* ... *5K 31*
(off Callerton La.)
Atholl DH2: Ous ... 6H 113
Athol Pk. SR2: Sund ... 3G 119
Athol Rd. SR2: Sund ... 3G 119
Athol St. NE11: Dun ... 5C 82
Athol Ter. SR2: Sund ... 3G 119
Atkinson Gdns. DH8: Cons ... 1H 135
NE29: N Shi ... 2G 67
Atkinson Gro. DH6: Shot C ... 5D 170
Atkinson Rd. DH3: Ches S ... 4B 128
NE4: Benw ... 2K 81
SR6: Ful ... 3F 105
Atkinson's Bldgs. SR4: Sund ... 2F 7
Atkinson St. NE28: W'snd ... 4F 65
Atkinson Ter. NE4: Benw ... 1K 81
NE28: W'snd ... 4F 65
Atkin St. NE12: Kil ... 7K 35
Atlantis Fitness Cen. ... *6B 84*
(off Coldwell St.)
Atlantis Rd. SR3: E Her ... 1J 131
Atlas Gym ... *7H 101*
(off Front St.)
Atley Bus. Pk. NE23: Nel V ... 7G 21
Atley Way NE23: Nel V ... 7G 21
Atmel Way NE28: W'snd ... 5K 47
Attlee Av. TS27: B Col ... 4K 183
Attlee Cl. NE23: Dud ... 6K 35
Attlee Cotts. NE64: Newb S ... 2K 13
Attlee Cres. DH6: Has ... 3A 170
Attlee Gro. SR2: Ryh ... 1G 133
Attlee Sq. DH6: S'burn ... 2K 167
Attlee Ter. NE64: Newb S ... 2K 13
Attwood Gro. SR5: S'wck ... 5D 104
Aubone Av. NE15: Benw ... 7J 61
Auburn Cl. NE28: W'snd ... 3B 66
Auburn Ct. *NE28: W'snd* ... *3B 66*
(off Auburn Cl.)
Auburn Gdns. NE4: Fen ... 5A 62
Auburn Pl. NE61: Mor ... 7E 8
Auckland DH2: Ches S ... 7H 127
Auckland Av. NE34: S Shi ... 7D 68
Auckland Rd. DH1: Dur ... 4B 154
NE31: Heb ... 6K 65
Auckland Ter. NE32: Jar ... 2E 86
Auden Gro. NE4: Fen ... 7A 62
Audland Wlk. NE5: Cha P ... 4C 60
Audley Ct. NE2: Jes ... 3H 63
Audley Gdns. SR3: Sund ... 5D 118
Audley Rd. NE3: Gos ... 1G 63
Audouins Row NE8: Gate ... 6F 83
Augusta Cl. NE13: Bru V ... 5C 34
Augusta Ct. NE28: W'snd ... 6J 47
Augusta Sq. SR3: E Her ... 2K 131
(not continuous)
Augusta Ter. SR6: Whit ... 5H 89
August Courtyard *NE8: Gate* ... *4D 82*
(off North Side)
Augustine Cl. DH1: Dur ... 5J 153
August Pl. NE33: S Shi ... 4K 67
Augustus Dr. NE22: Bed ... 6G 17
Austen Av. NE34: S Shi ... 3H 87
Austen Pl. DH9: Stly ... 5H 125
Austerfield Pk. DH5: Hett H ... 7H 145
Austin Blvd. SR5: S'wck ... 7C 104
Australia Gro. NE34: S Shi ... 3F 87
Australia Twr. SR3: New S ... 1A 132
Austral Pl. NE13: W Op ... 6C 34
Austwick Wlk. NE5: Cha P ... 4C 60
Auton Cl. DH7: Bearp ... 1D 164
Auton Ct. DH7: Bearp ... 1E 164
Auton Fld. DH7: Bearp ... 1E 164
Auton Fld. Ter. DH7: Bearp ... 1E 164
Auton Stile DH7: Bearp ... 1D 164
Autumn Cl. NE38: Wash ... 2H 115
Autumn Dr. NE8: Gate ... 4D 82
Avalon Dr. NE15: Lem ... 5E 60
Avalon Rd. SR3: E Her ... 1K 131
Avebury Av. NE62: Chop ... 1J 17
Avebury Dr. NE38: Wash ... 3J 115
Avebury Pl. NE23: Cra ... 1A 26
Avenue, The DH1: Dur ... 3A 6 (3J 165)
DH1: P Me ... 4J 153
DH2: Ches S ... 6K 127
DH2: Pelt ... 2G 127
DH3: Bir ... 4A 114
DH3: Lam P ... 4J 129
DH5: Hett H ... 6H 145
DH6: Whe H ... 2A 180
DH7: B'hpe ... 5E 138
DH8: Cons ... 7J 121
DH9: Ann P ... 6J 123
DH9: Ann P, Dip ... 2H 123
NE6: W'snd ... 4F 65
NE9: Low F ... 7J 83
NE10: Fell ... 5B 84
Avenue, The NE20: Medb ... 3C 40
NE21: Blay ... 4E 80
NE25: Sea D ... 6H 27
NE26: Sea D, Sea S ... 6H 27
NE26: Sea S ... 4B 28
NE26: Whit B ... 6G 39
NE28: W'snd ... 4F 65
NE38: Wash ... 3J 115
NE39: Row G ... 6K 95
NE45: Corb ... 7D 52
NE61: Loan ... 3F 15
SR2: Sund ... 7H 7 (3F 119)
SR7: Mur ... 7F 147
SR7: S'hm ... 4H 147
Avenue Cres. NE25: Sea D ... 6G 27
Avenue Rd. NE8: Gate ... 6H 83
NE25: Sea D ... 7G 27
Avenues, The NE11: T Vall ... 4G 99
Avenue St. DH1: H Shin ... 1F 177
Avenue Ter. NE25: Sea D ... 7H 27
SR2: Sund ... 7J 7 (4E 118)
Avenue Vivian DH4: Hou S ... 1K 143
Aviemore Rd. NE36: W Bol ... 7H 87
Avis Av. NE64: Newb S ... 4G 13
Avison Ct. NE4: Newc T ... 5A 4 (7D 62)
Avison Pl. NE4: Newc T ... 4A 4 (7D 62)
Avison St. NE4: Newc T ... 5A 4 (1D 82)
Avocet Cl. NE24: News ... 6J 23
Avolon Ct. NE4: Newc T ... 4A 4 (7D 62)
Avolon Pl. NE4: Newc T ... 4A 4 (7D 62)
Avolon Wlk. NE4: Newc T ... 5A 4 (1D 82)
Avon Av. NE29: N Shi ... 1E 66
NE32: Jar ... 4C 86
Avon Cl. NE28: W'snd ... 6H 47
NE39: Row G ... 4K 95
Avon Ct. NE25: New Hart ... 4H 27
Avon Cres. DH4: Hou S ... 3A 144
Avoncroft Cl. SR7: Seat ... 2F 147
Avondale SR4: Sund ... 3G 117
Avondale Av. DH4: Pen ... 2B 130
NE12: Longb ... 4B 46
NE24: Cow ... 1C 22
Avondale Cl. NE24: Cow ... 1D 22
Avondale Ct. NE3: Gos ... 1F 63
Avondale Gdns. NE36: W Bol ... 1G 103
NE63: N Sea ... 5E 12
Avondale Ho. NE6: Byke ... 5P 5 (1A 84)
Avondale Ri. NE6: Byke ... 1A 84
Avondale Rd. DH8: Cons ... 6H 121
NE6: Byke ... 1A 84
NE20: Darr H ... 1E 40
Avondale Ter. DH3: Ches S ... 6A 128
NE8: Gate ... 5G 83
NE36: W Bol ... 7G 87
Avonlea Way NE5: Blak ... 2J 61
Avonmouth Rd. SR3: E Her ... 2K 131
Avonmouth Sq. SR3: E Her ... 2K 131
Avon Rd. DH9: Stly ... 4F 125
NE31: Heb ... 2J 85
SR8: Pet ... 7A 172
Avon St. NE8: Gate ... 5J 83
SR1: Sund ... 2H 119
SR8: Eas C ... 7C 160
Avon Ter. NE38: Wash ... 4J 115
Awnless Ct. NE34: S Shi ... 1J 87
Axbridge Cl. NE62: Chop ... 1J 17
Axbridge Gdns. NE4: Benw ... 1A 82
Axford Ter. NE17: Ham ... 3K 107
Axminster Cl. NE23: Cra ... 1A 26
Axwell Dr. NE24: Cow ... 2F 23
Axwell Hall NE21: Blay ... 5E 80
AXWELL PARK ... 5E 80
Axwell Park ... 5E 80
Axwell Pk. Cl. NE16: Whi ... 7G 81
Axwell Pk. Rd. NE21: Blay ... 5E 80
Axwell Pk. School Ho's. NE21: Blay ... 5E 80
Axwell Pk. Vw. NE15: Scot ... 1H 81
Axwell Ter. NE16: Swa ... 5G 81
Axwell Vw. NE16: Whi ... 7G 81
NE21: Winl ... 5C 80
Aycliffe Av. NE9: Wrek ... 3B 100
Aycliffe Cres. NE9: Wrek ... 3B 100
Aycliffe Pl. NE9: Wrek ... 3C 100
Ayden Gro. DH1: Dur ... 5A 154
AYDON ... 4H 53
Aydon Av. NE45: Corb ... 7E 52
Aydon Castle ... 4G 53
Aydon Cl. NE45: Corb ... 7F 53
Aydon Cres. NE45: Corb ... 7F 53
Aydon Dr. NE45: Corb ... 7E 53
Aydon Gdns. NE12: Longb ... 6H 45
NE45: Corb ... 7E 52
Aydon Gro. NE32: Jar ... 3B 86
NE45: Corb ... 7E 52
Aydon Ho. SR3: E Her ... 2A 132
Aydon Rd. NE30: Cull ... 3J 49
NE45: Ayd, Corb ... 7E 52
SR5: Sund ... 6J 103
Aydon Wlk. NE5: W Dent ... 4E 60
Aydon Way NE45: Corb ... 7E 52
Aykley Ct. DH1: Dur ... 7J 153
Aykley Grn. DH1: Dur ... 7J 153
AYKLEY HEADS ... 7K 153
Aykley Heads Bus. Cen. DH1: Dur ... 7K 153
Aykley Rd. DH1: Dur ... 5K 153
Aykley Va. DH1: Dur ... 6J 153
Ayle Cl. NE25: Monks ... 6B 38
Aylesbury Dr. SR3: Dox P ... 4C 132
Aylesbury Pl. NE12: Longb ... 5K 45
Aylesford M. SR2: Sund ... 6G 119
Aylesford Sq. NE24: News ... 4J 23
Aylsham Cl. NE5: Cha P ... 1B 60
Aylsham Ct. SR3: Dox P ... 5C 132
Aylward Pl. DH9: Stly ... 4H 125
Aylyth Pl. NE3: Ken ... 2B 62
Aynsley M. DH8: Cons ... 6H 121
Aynsley Ter. DH8: Cons ... 5H 121
Ayr Dr. NE32: Jar ... 3D 86
AYRE'S QUAY ... 1F 7 (7D 104)
Ayre's Ter. NE29: N Shi ... 6G 49
Ayrey Av. NE34: S Shi ... 2F 87
Aysgarth NE23: E Har ... 6K 21
Aysgarth Av. NE28: W'snd ... 5H 47
SR2: Sund ... 6H 119
Aysgarth Grn. NE3: Ken ... 1B 62
AYTON ... 5D 114
Ayton Av. SR2: Sund ... 7H 119
Ayton Cl. NE5: West ... 2E 60
NE43: Pains ... 1K 91
Ayton Ct. NE22: Bed ... 6F 17
Ayton Ri. NE6: Byke ... 1A 84
Ayton Rd. NE38: Wash ... 4D 114
Ayton St. NE6: Byke ... 1A 84
Azalea Av. SR2: Sund ... 7H 7 (3E 118)
Azalea Ter. SR8: Hord ... 6F 173
Azalea Ter. Nth. SR2: Sund ... 6H 7 (3E 118)
Azalea Ter. Sth. SR2: Sund ... 7H 7 (3E 118)
Azalea Way NE15: Newb ... 5J 59
Azure Ct. SR3: Dox P ... 5K 131

B

Bk. Albion Rd. NE30: N Shi ... 6G 49
Bk. Albion St. SR4: Sund ... 2G 117
Bk. Beach Rd. NE33: S Shi ... 3K 67
Bk. Beaumont Ter. NE3: Gos ... 7F 45
Bk. Bridge St. SR1: Sund ... 3J 7 (1F 119)
Bk. Buttsfield Ter. *DH4: Pen* ... *1B 130*
(off Buttsfield Ter.)
Bk. Chapman St. NE6: Walk ... 6A 64
Bk. Coronation Ter. *DH5: Hett H* ... *1G 157*
(off Coronation Ter.)
Back Cft. Rd. NE24: Bly ... 2J 23
Bk. Durham Rd. DH7: Esh W ... 4E 162
Bk. East Pde. DH8: Cons ... 7J 121
Bk. Ecclestone Rd. *NE33: S Shi* ... *4A 68*
(off Mowbray Rd.)
Bk. Eccleston Rd. *NE33: S Shi* ... *3A 68*
(off Ecclestone Rd.)
Bk. Ellison Rd. NE11: Dun ... 6C 82
Bk. Frederick St. Nth. DH7: B'don ... 1C 174
DH7: Mead ... 2E 174
Bk. Frederick St. Sth. DH7: Mead ... 2E 174
Bk. Front St. DH7: Sac ... 7E 140
Bk. George St. NE4: Newc T ... 8C 4 (2E 82)
Bk. Goldspink La.
NE2: Newc T ... 1K 5 (6H 63)
Bk. Grove Av. NE3: Gos ... 1E 62
Bk. Hawthorn Rd. W. NE3: Gos ... 1E 62
Bk. Heaton Pk. Rd. NE6: Byke ... 3N 5 (7K 63)
Bk. High Mkt. NE63: Ash ... 3J 11
Bk. High St. NE3: Gos ... 1E 62
Bk. Hylton Rd. SR4: Sund ... 3F 7 (1D 118)
Bk. Jesmond Rd. *NE2: Jes* ... *5H 63*
(off Deuchar St.)
Bk. John St. Nth. DH7: Mead ... 1F 175
Back La. DH3: Gt Lum ... 1E 142
DH4: Pen ... 1B 130
DH7: Lan ... 4K 137
DH8: Cons ... 1D 136
NE21: Winl ... 4B 80
NE25: Monks ... 6E 38
Bk. Lodge Ter. SR1: Sund ... 2H 119
Bk. Loud Ter. DH9: Ann P ... 5H 123
Bk. Main St. *NE40: Craw* ... *2D 78*
(off Kepier Chare)
Bk. Maling St. NE6: Byke ... 6M 5
Bk. Middle St. TS27: B Col ... 2H 183
Bk. Mount Joy DH1: Dur ... 6E 6 (4B 166)
Bk. Mowbray Ter. NE62: Chop ... 1H 17
Bk. New Bri. St. NE1: Newc T ... 4J 5 (7H 63)
Back Nth. Bri. St.
SR5: Monkw ... 1J 7 (7F 105)
Back Nth. Railway St. SR7: S'hm ... 2B 148
Back Nth. Ter. SR7: S'hm ... 2B 148
Bk. Osborne Ter. NE2: Jes ... 1H 5
Bk. Palmerston St. DH8: Cons ... 7H 121
Bk. Percy Gdns. NE30: Tyne ... 4K 49
Bk. Prudhoe Ter. *NE30: Tyne* ... *4K 49*
(off Prudhoe Ter.)
Bk. Rothesay Ter. NE22: Bed ... 6K 17
Back Row NE16: Whi ... 7G 81
NE46: Hex ... 1D 70
Bk. Ryhope St. SR2: Ryh ... 2G 133
Back St George's Ter. NE2: Jes ... 4G 63
Bk. Seaburn Ter. SR6: Seab ... 2G 105
Bk. Shipley Rd. NE30: Tyne ... 5K 49
Bk. Silver St. DH1: Dur ... 2C 6
Back Sth. Railway St. SR7: S'hm ... 3B 148
Bk. Station Rd. NE63: Ash ... 3A 12
Bk. Stephen St. NE6: Byke ... 4M 5 (7J 63)
Backstone Burn DH8: Shot B ... 4E 120
Backstone Rd. DH8: Shot B ... 5E 120
Back St. NE21: Winl ... 5B 80
Bk. Victoria Ter. DH9: Ann P ... 4K 123
Backview Ct. SR5: Ful ... 4E 104
Bk. Western Hill DH1: Dur ... 1A 6 (1K 165)
Bk. Westoe Rd. *NE33: S Shi* ... *3K 67*
(off Halstead Pl.)
Bk. Woodbine St. NE8: Gate ... 5G 83
BACKWORTH ... 6G 37
Backworth Bus. Pk. NE27: Back ... 7G 37
Backworth Ct. NE27: Back ... 1H 47
Backworth La. NE23: Seg ... 2D 36
NE27: Back ... 5D 36
Backworth Ter. *NE27: Shir* ... *3H 47*
(off West St.)
Backworth Workshops NE27: Back ... 7G 37
Baden Cres. SR5: Sund ... 4G 103
Baden Powell St. NE9: Low F ... 7J 83
Baden St. DH3: Ches S ... 7A 128
Bader Ct. NE24: Bly ... 3K 23
Badger Cl. SR3: Dox P ... 4C 132
Badger M. NE9: Spri ... 5D 100
Badgers Grn. NE61: Mor ... 5D 8
Badger's Wood DH9: Stly ... 7G 111
Badminton Cl. NE35: Bol C ... 5D 86
Baildon Cl. NE28: W'snd ... 1G 65
Bailey Ct. DH1: Dur ... 3C 6
Bailey Ind. Est. NE32: Jar ... 5B 66
Bailey Ri. SR8: Pet ... 4B 172
Bailey Sq. SR5: Sund ... 3G 103
Bailey St. DH9: Tant ... 6B 110
Bailey Way DH5: Hett H ... 2H 157
Bainbridge Av. NE34: S Shi ... 2F 87
SR3: Sund ... 5D 118
Bainbridge Bldgs. NE9: Eigh B ... 5A 100
Bainbridge Cl. DH8: Cons ... 2K 135
Bainbridge Holme Cl. SR3: Sund ... 5D 118
Bainbridge Holme Rd. SR3: Sund ... 5E 118
Bainbridge St. DH1: Carr ... 6H 155
Bainford Av. NE15: Den M ... 7G 61
Baird Av. NE28: W'snd ... 3C 66
Baird Cl. NE37: Wash ... 5J 101
Baird Ct. NE10: Gate ... 5A 84
Baird St. SR5: Sund ... 4G 103
Bakehouse La. DH1: Dur ... 1E 6 (2B 166)
Baker Gdns. NE10: Ward ... 6F 85
NE11: Dun ... 5B 82
Baker Rd. NE23: Nel V ... 1F 25
Baker Sq. SR5: Sund ... 4G 103
Baker St. DH5: Hou S ... 1E 144
DH8: Lead ... 5A 122
SR5: Sund ... 4G 103
Bakewell Ter. NE6: Walk ... 2B 84
Baldersdale Gdns. SR3: Sund ... 6D 118
Baldwin Av. NE4: Fen ... 6B 62
NE36: E Bol ... 7A 88
Baldwin St. SR8: Eas C ... 7D 160
Balfour Gdns. DH8: Cons ... 5H 121
Balfour Rd. NE15: Benw ... 1G 81
(not continuous)
Balfour St. DH5: Hou S ... 1E 144
DH8: Cons ... 5H 121
NE8: Gate ... 5F 83
NE24: Bly ... 7H 19
Balfour Ter. NE17: C'wl ... 6K 93
(Beaconsfield Ter.)
NE17: C'wl ... 7K 93
(Frederick St.)
Balgonie Cotts. NE40: Ryton ... 1G 79
Baliol Rd. NE43: Pains ... 7J 75
Baliol Sq. DH1: Dur ... 5J 165
Balkwell Av. NE29: N Shi ... 6D 48
Balkwell Grn. NE29: N Shi ... 6E 48
Ballast Hill NE24: Bly ... 1K 23
Ballast Hill Rd. NE29: N Shi ... 2G 67
Ballater Cl. DH9: Stly ... 3H 125
Balliol Av. NE12: Longb ... 3A 46
Balliol Bus. Pk. NE12: Longb ... 4J 45
Balliol Cl. SR8: Pet ... 7K 171
Balliol Gdns. NE7: Longb ... 7K 45
Balliol M. NE12: Longb ... 5A 46
Ballston Cl. NE38: Wash ... 5J 115
Balmain Rd. NE3: Ken ... 1A 62
Balmlaw NE9: Low F ... 3B 100
Balmoral DH3: Gt Lum ... 2E 142
Balmoral Av. DH9: Ann P ... 4J 123
NE3: Gos ... 1G 63
NE32: Jar ... 3E 86
Balmoral Cl. NE22: Bed ... 6A 18
Balmoral Ct. SR5: Sund ... 4G 103
Balmoral Cres. DH5: Hou S ... 3F 145
Balmoral Dr. DH9: Ann P ... 4J 123
NE10: Fell ... 6A 84
NE24: News ... 5G 23
SR8: Pet ... 2J 181
Balmoral Gdns. NE26: Whit B ... 5F 39
NE29: N Shi ... 5F 49
Balmoral Gro. DH8: Cons ... 5J 121
Balmoral St. NE28: W'snd ... 3F 65
Balmoral Ter. NE3: Gos ... 1G 63
NE6: Heat ... 1P 5 (6K 63)
SR2: Sund ... 6H 119
SR3: E Her ... 2J 131
Balmoral Way NE10: Fell ... 7A 84
Balmore SR3: Silk ... 3B 132
Balroy Ct. NE12: Longb ... 5C 46
Baltic Bus. Cen. NE8: Gate ... 10P 5 (3K 83)
Baltic Bus. Quarter NE8: Gate ... 8L 5 (2J 83)
BALTIC Cen. for Contemporary Art
... 7K 5 (2H 83)
Baltic Ct. NE33: S Shi ... 3A 68
Baltic Ind. Pk. NE29: N Shi ... 2E 66
Baltic Pl. NE8: Gate ... 7L 5 (2J 83)
Baltic Quay NE8: Gate ... 7K 5 (2H 83)
Baltic Rd. NE10: Fell ... 3B 84
Baltimore Av. SR5: Sund ... 4E 102
Baltimore Ct. NE37: Wash ... 7G 101
Baltimore Sq. SR5: Sund ... 4F 103
(not continuous)
Bamborough Ct. NE23: Dud ... 3J 35
Bamborough Ter. NE30: N Shi ... 5G 49
Bambro St. SR2: Sund ... 3G 119
Bamburgh Av. NE33: S Shi ... 4B 68
NE34: S Shi ... 4B 68
SR8: Hord ... 4D 172
Bamburgh Cl. NE24: Bly ... 2G 23
NE38: Wash ... 3E 114
Bamburgh Ct. NE4: Benw ... 3A 82
NE7: Longb ... 7H 45
NE11: T Vall ... 7E 82
Bamburgh Cres. DH4: S Row ... 4B 130
NE27: Shir ... 1K 47

Bamburgh Dr. NE10: Bill Q 4F 85
NE28: W'snd 3K 65
NE61: Peg 4B 10
SR7: S'hm 1A 148
Bamburgh Gdns. SR3: Sund 5D 118
Bamburgh Gro. NE32: Jar 3A 86
NE34: S Shi 5D 68
Bamburgh Ho. NE5: West 2E 60
Bamburgh Rd. DH1: Dur 4A 154
NE5: West 2E 60
NE12: Longb 4D 46
Bamburgh Ter. NE6: Byke 7A 64
NE63: Ash 4A 12
Bamburgh Wlk. NE3: Gos 6C 44
Bamford Ter. NE12: Longb 3D 46
Bamford Wlk. NE34: S Shi 1K 87
Bampton Av. SR6: Seab 2E 104
Banbury NE37: Wash 7J 101
Banbury Av. SR5: Sund 3G 103
Banbury Gdns. NE28: W'snd 7H 47
Banbury Rd. NE3: Ken 7B 44
Banbury Ter. NE33: S Shi 5K 67
NE34: S Shi 5K 67
Banbury Way NE24: News 4J 23
NE29: N Shi 1D 66
Bancroft Ter. SR4: Sund 2B 118
Banesley La. NE11: Kib, Rave 7C 98
Banff St. SR5: Sund 3G 103
Bangor Sq. NE32: Jar 5A 86
Bank, The NE1: Newc T 3G 4
SR6: Whit 6H 89
Bank Av. NE16: Whi 7G 81
Bank Cotts. NE22: E Sle 5D 18
Bank Ct. NE21: Blay 2F 81
NE30: N Shi 7H 49
Bankdale Gdns. NE24: Cow 2E 22
Bank Foot DH1: H Shin, Shin 6E 166
Bank Foot (Park & Tram) 6H 43
Bank Foot Station (Metro) 6H 43
Bankhead NE46: Hex 1D 70
Bankhead Rd. NE15: Walb 4K 59
Bankhead Ter. DH4: Hou S 1A 144
Banks, The DH1: Dur 4B 6 (3A 166)
Banks Bldgs. DH4: New H 3C 130
Banks Holt DH2: Ches S 7H 127
Bankside NE11: Dun 3J 81
NE61: Mor 7G 9
TS27: Cas E 6B 182
Bankside Cl. SR2: Ryh 2G 133
Bankside La. NE34: S Shi 1J 87
Bankside Rd. NE15: Scot 1F 81
Bankside Wlk. NE62: Stake 7K 11
BANK TOP 3G 59
Bank Top DH3: Gt Lum 3D 142
NE25: Ears 5A 38
NE30: Cull 1J 49
NE40: Craw 3C 78
NE40: G'sde 3F 79
Bank Top Hamlet NE16: Whi 7G 81
Bannatyne's Health Club
Durham 1F 167
Chester-le-Street 7C 128
Bannerman Ter. DH6: S Hil 3C 168
DH7: Ush M 2B 164
Bannister Dr. NE12: Longb 4D 46
Bannockburn NE12: Kil 7A 36
Bar, The NE4: Newc T 8D 4
Barbara St. SR2: Sund 6H 119
Barbary Cl. DH2: Pelt 2G 127
Barbary Dr. SR6: Roker 5H 105
Barbondale Lonnen NE5: Cha P 3C 60
Barbour Av. NE34: S Shi 6C 68
Barclay Pl. NE5: Blak 4H 61
Barclay St. SR6: Monkw 1J 7 (7F 105)
Barcusclose La. DH9: Tanf 2C 110
NE16: Burn 2C 110
Bardolph Cl. NE24: Bly 5K 23
Bardolph Dr. SR5: S'wck 4D 104
Bardolph Rd. NE29: N Shi 6D 48
Bardon Cl. NE5: West 1F 61
Bardon Ct. NE34: S Shi 1A 88
Bardon Cres. NE25: H'wll 1K 37
Bardsey Pl. NE12: Longb 5K 45
Barehirst St. NE33: S Shi 6H 67
Barents Cl. NE5: West 3F 61
Baret Rd. NE6: Walk 5C 64
Barford Ct. NE9: Low F 5J 99
Barford Dr. DH2: Ches S 1J 141
Baring St. NE33: S Shi 1J 67
Barker Ho. NE2: Newc T 2J 5 (6H 63)
Barkers Haugh DH1: Dur 1B 166
Barker St. NE2: Newc T 3J 5 (7H 63)
Barking Cres. SR5: Sund 4F 103
Barking Sq. SR5: Sund 4F 103
Barkwood Rd. NE39: Row G 5G 95
Barleycorn Pl. SR1: Sund 5K 7 (2G 119)
Barley Mill Cres. DH8: Shot B 5D 120
Barley Mill Rd. DH8: Cons, Shot B 5D 120
BARLEY MOW 7B 114
Barley Ri. DH7: New B 4B 164
BARLOW 1G 95
Barlow Cres. NE21: Barl 1G 95
Barlow Fell Rd. NE21: Barl 2G 95
Barlowfield Cl. NE21: Winl 6A 80
Barlow La. NE21: Barl, Winl 7J 79
Barlow La. End NE40: G'sde 5F 79
Barlow Rd. NE21: Barl 1G 95
Barlow Vw. *NE40: G'sde* *5F 79*
(off Dyke Heads La.)
BAR MOOR 1F 79
BARMOOR 3K 15
Barmoor Bank NE61: Hep 3K 15
Barmoor Dr. NE3: Gos 3B 44
Barmoor La. NE40: Ryton 1F 79
Barmoor Pl. NE40: Ryton 1F 79
Barmoor Ter. NE40: Ryton 1E 78
Barmouth Cl. NE28: W'snd 7H 47
Barmouth Rd. NE29: N Shi 7C 48
BARMSTON 2K 115
Barmston Cen. NE38: Wash 2K 115
Barmston Cl. NE38: Wash 4K 115
Barmston Ct. NE38: Wash 4K 115
Barmston Ferry NE38: Wash 5B 116
Barmston La. NE37: Wash 6A 102
NE38: Wash 4B 116
(not continuous)
SR5: Sund 1B 116
Barmston Mere Training Cen.
SR5: Sund 1B 116
Barmston Pond Local Nature Reserve
1A 116
Barmston Rd. NE38: Wash 4A 116
Barmston Way NE38: Wash 2K 115
Barnabas Pl. SR2: Sund 3H 119
Barnard Av. DH6: Ludw 5J 169
Barnard Cl. DH1: Dur 4B 154
NE22: Bed 7G 17
Barnard Ct. DH4: Hou S 1H 143
Barnard Cres. NE31: Heb 6J 65
Barnard Grn. NE3: Fawd 5A 44
Barnard Gro. NE32: Jar 2D 86
Barnard Pk. DH5: Hett H 6G 145
Barnard St. NE24: Bly 2J 23
SR4: Sund 3B 118
Barnard Wynd SR8: Pet 2K 181
Barnehurst Dr. NE24: Bly 4K 23
Barnesbury Rd. NE4: Benw 1A 82
Barnes Ct. SR4: Sund 3B 118
Barnes Pk. Rd. SR4: Sund 4C 118
Barnes Rd. NE33: S Shi 6H 67
SR7: Mur 7D 146
Barnes St. DH5: Hett H 6G 145
Barnes Vw. SR4: Sund 4B 118
Barnett Ct. SR5: S'wck 5D 104
Barnett Sq. DH6: Has 2A 170
Barnham Cl. SR5: Sund 4G 103
Barn Hill DH9: Stly 2E 124
Barn Hollows SR7: Hawt 3A 160
Barningham NE38: Wash 3A 116
Barningham Cl. SR3: Sund 6D 118
Barns, The DH9: Stly 1E 124
Barns Cl. NE32: Jar 2A 86
Barnsett Grange DH6: Sun B 5K 175
Barnstaple Cl. NE28: W'snd 7G 47
Barnstaple Rd. NE29: N Shi 3C 48
Barnston NE63: N Sea 4F 13
Barnstones DH2: Plaw 6J 141
Barnton Rd. NE10: Wind N 1C 100
BARNWELL 1B 130
Barnwell Vw. DH4: Pen, S Row 3C 130
Barnwood Cl. NE28: W'snd 7G 47
Baroness Dr. NE15: Den M 6G 61
Barons Quay Rd. SR5: Sund 7H 103
Baronswood NE3: Gos 1D 62
Barrack Ct. NE4: Newc T 4C 4 (7E 62)
Barrack Rd. NE2: Newc T 2A 4 (6C 62)
(not continuous)
NE4: Newc T 2A 4 (7E 62)
Barrack Row DH4: S Row 3A 130
Barrack St. SR1: Sund 7H 105
Barrack Ter. NE11: Kib 2F 113
Barras Av. NE23: Dud 2K 35
NE24: News 4H 23
Barras Av. W. NE24: News 5H 23
Barras Bri. NE1: Newc T 3F 4 (7F 63)
Barras Dr. SR3: Sund 5D 118
Barrasford Cl. NE3: Gos 1C 62
NE63: Ash 5J 11
Barrasford Dr. NE13: W Op 6E 34
Barrasford Rd. DH1: Dur 5B 154
NE23: Cra 5A 26
Barrasford St. NE28: W'snd 4C 66
Barras Gdns. NE23: Dud 2K 35
Barras M. NE23: Seg 2D 36
Barrass Av. NE23: Seg 2C 36
Barr Cl. NE28: W'snd 7J 47
Barr Hills DH8: Cons 6H 121
Barr Ho. Av. DH8: Cons 6H 121
Barr Ho. Ct. DH8: Cons 6H 121
Barrington Av. NE30: Cull 2F 49
Barrington Bus. Pk. NE12: Kil 6K 35
Barrington Cl. DH1: Dur 6J 153
Barrington Ct. DH5: Hett H 6G 145
NE22: Bed 1J 21
Barrington Dr. NE38: Wash 3H 115
Barrington Ind. Est. NE22: Bed 4J 17
Barrington Pk. NE22: E Sle 5D 18
Barrington Pl. NE4: Newc T 3A 4 (7D 62)
NE8: Gate 4F 83
Barrington Rd. NE22: Bed, Sco G 4H 17
Barrington St. NE33: S Shi 2J 67
Barrington Way DH6: Bowb 4H 177
Barrons Way DH7: B'hpe 5D 138
Barrowburn Pl. NE23: Seg 2E 36
Barrow St. SR5: Sund 3G 103
Barry St. NE8: Gate 7F 83
NE11: Dun 5B 82
Barsloan Gro. SR8: Pet 4K 171
Barton Cl. NE28: W'snd 7H 47
NE30: Cull 3H 49
NE37: Wash 5K 101
Barton Ct. SR6: Seab 2E 104
Barton Pk. SR2: Ryh 2F 133
Bartram Gdns. NE8: Gate 7G 83
Bartram St. SR5: Ful 4E 104
Barwell Cl. NE28: W'snd 7H 47
Barwell Ct. NE7: H Hea 3C 64
Barwick St. SR7: Mur 2F 159
SR8: Eas C 7D 160
Basildon Ct. NE10: Hew 2E 100
Basildon Gdns. NE28: W'snd 7G 47
Basil Way NE34: S Shi 3A 88
Basingstoke Pl. NE12: Longb 5A 46
Basingstoke Rd. SR8: Pet 5A 172
Baslow Gdns. SR3: Sund 5D 118
Bassenfell Ct. NE37: Wash 2F 115
Bassenthwaite Av. DH2: Ches S 1K 141
Bassington Av. NE23: Cra 3G 25
Bassington Cl.
NE4: Newc T 3B 4 (7D 62)
Bassington Dr. NE23: Cra 2F 25
Bassington Ind. Est. NE23: Cra 3G 25
Bassington La. NE23: Cra 2F 25
Bassington La. Ind. Est.
NE23: Cra 2F 25
Bates Av. NE24: Cow 7G 19
Bates Ho's. NE21: Blay 5F 81
Bates La. NE21: Blay 4F 81
Batey St. DH9: Ann P 4J 123
Bath Cl. NE28: W'snd 7J 47
Bathgate Av. SR5: Sund 3F 103
Bathgate Cl. NE28: W'snd 7J 47
Bathgate Sq. SR5: Sund 4F 103
Bath La. DH8: Cons 6H 121
NE1: Newc T 1E 82
NE4: Newc T 5C 4 (1E 82)
NE24: Bly 2K 23
Bath Rd. NE10: Fell 4B 84
NE31: Heb 3J 85
Bath Sq. NE32: Jar 5A 86
Bath St. NE6: Walk 7F 65
Bath St. Ind. Est. NE6: Walk 7F 65
Bath Ter. NE3: Gos 7F 45
NE24: Bly 2K 23
NE30: Tyne 5K 49
SR7: S'hm 2B 148
Batley St. SR5: Sund 4F 103
Batt Ho. Rd. NE43: Pains 2H 91
BATTLE FIELD 5L 5 (1J 83)
Battle Grn. DH2: P Fel 4G 127
BATTLE HILL 7H 47
Battle Hill NE46: Hex 2D 70
Battle Hill Dr. NE28: W'snd 1G 65
Battle Hill Est. NE28: W'snd 6K 47
Battleship Wharf NE24: Bly 6H 19
Battle Vw. NE21: Blay 1A 80
Baugh Cl. NE37: Wash 1E 114
Baulkham Hills DH4: Pen 3B 130
Bavington NE10: Hew 2E 100
Bavington Dr. NE5: Fen 4J 61
Bavington Gdns. NE30: Cull 3G 49
Bavington Rd. NE25: Sea D 7H 27
Bawtry Ct. NE28: W'snd 7G 47
Bawtry Gro. NE29: N Shi 7E 48
Baxter Av. NE4: Fen 7A 62
SR5: Sund 3F 103
Baxter Pl. NE25: Sea D 7H 27
Baxter Rd. SR5: Sund 3F 103
Baxter's Bldgs. NE25: Sea D 7H 27
Baxter Sq. SR5: Sund 3F 103
Baxterwood Ct. NE4: Newc T 4A 4 (7C 62)
Baxterwood Gro.
NE4: Newc T 4A 4 (7C 62)
Bay Av. SR8: Hord 6F 173
Baybridge Rd. NE5: West 2E 60
Bay Ct. DH7: Ush M 3D 164
SR6: Seab 1H 105
Bayfield NE27: Shir 2J 47
Bayfield Gdns. NE8: Gate 5K 83
Baysdale DH4: Pen 1J 129
Bayswater Av. SR5: Sund 4G 103
Bayswater Rd. NE2: Jes 3G 63
NE8: Gate 6K 83
Bayswater Sq. SR5: Sund 4G 103
Bay Tree Dr. NE34: S Shi 1B 88
Baytree Gdns. NE25: Monks 1E 48
Baytree Ter. DH2: Pelt 2D 126
Bay Vw. E. NE64: Newb S 2J 13
Bay Vw. W. NE64: Newb S 3J 13
Baywood Gro. NE28: W'snd 7G 47
Beach Av. NE26: Whit B 6G 39
Beachborough Cl. NE29: N Shi 3F 49
Beach Cft. Av. NE30: Cull 2H 49
Beachcross Rd. SR4: Sund 3D 118
Beachdale Cl. TS28: Sta T 7H 181
Beach Gro. SR8: Hord 5F 173
Beach Rd. NE29: N Shi 5E 48
NE30: Tyne 4G 49
NE33: S Shi 3K 67
Beach St. SR4: Sund 1F 7 (7D 104)
Beach Ter. NE64: Newb S 4H 13
Beachville St. SR4: Sund 3D 118
Beach Way NE30: Cull 3G 49
Beachway NE24: Bly 5K 23
Beacon Ct. NE9: Low F 2K 99
NE13: W Op 5C 34
Beacon Dr. NE13: W Op 5C 34
SR6: Roker 6H 105
Beacon Glade NE34: S Shi 1E 88
BEACON HILL 5D 178
Beacon Ho. NE26: Whit B 3F 39
Beacon La. NE23: Cra, Dud 4F 25
BEACON LOUGH 2K 99
Beacon Lough Rd. NE9: Low F 3H 99
Beacon M. NE23: Cra 4G 25
Beacon Ri. NE9: Low F 2K 99
Beacons, The NE25: Sea D 6G 27
Beaconsfield Av. NE9: Low F 2J 99
Beaconsfield Cl. NE25: Monks 4D 38
Beaconsfield Cres. NE9: Low F 2J 99
Beaconsfield Rd. NE9: Low F 2H 99
Beaconsfield St. DH8: Cons 5H 121
DH9: Stly 2F 125
NE4: Newc T 3A 4 (1C 82)
NE24: Bly 2K 23
Beaconsfield Ter. DH3: Bir 4K 113
NE17: C'wl 6K 93
Beacon Shop. Cen. NE29: N Shi 7H 49
Beaconside NE34: S Shi 7E 68
Beacon St. NE9: Low F 2H 99
NE30: N Shi 6J 49
NE33: S Shi 1J 67
Beadling Gdns. NE4: Fen 7A 62
Beadnell Av. NE29: N Shi 1D 66
Beadnell Cl. DH2: Ches S 1J 141
NE21: Winl 6A 80
Beadnell Ct. NE28: W'snd 7J 47
Beadnell Dr. SR7: S'hm 1A 148
Beadnell Gdns. NE27: Shir 1K 47
Beadnell Gro. NE63: Ash 3H 11
Beadnell Pl. NE2: Newc T 4J 5 (7H 63)
Beadnell Rd. NE24: Bly 4F 23
Beadnell Way NE3: Gos 7C 44
Beagle Sq. SR3: New S 2C 132
Beal Cl. NE24: Bly 2G 23
Beal Dr. NE12: Longb 3D 46
Beal Gdns. NE28: W'snd 7K 47
Beal Grn. NE3: Ken 1J 61
Beal Rd. NE27: Shir 1K 47
Beal Ter. NE6: Walk 2D 84
Beal Wlk. DH1: H Shin 7F 167
Beal Way NE3: Gos 7D 44
Beaminster Way NE3: Ki Pk 7J 43
Beaminster Way E. NE3: Ki Pk 7J 43
BEAMISH 1A 126
Beamishburn Rd. DH9: Beam, Stly 7G 111
NE16: Marl H 7G 111
Beamish Cl. DH7: Lang P 5H 151
NE28: W'snd 7G 47
Beamish Ct. DH2: Pelt 3E 126
DH9: Stly 3E 124
NE25: Monks 1E 48
Beamish Gdns. NE9: Wrek 3B 100
Beamish Hills DH9: Beam 2K 125
Beamish Mus. 6K 111
Beamish Pl. NE15: Benw 7H 61
Beamish Red Row DH9: Beam 5H 111
Beamish Ri. DH9: Stly 2J 125
Beamish St. DH9: Stly 3E 124
Beamish Vw. DH3: Bir 3B 114
DH9: Stly 2H 125
Beamish Wild Adventure Pk. 6J 111
Beamsley Ter. NE63: Ash 4B 12
Beaney La. DH2: Ches M, Plaw 3H 141
Beanley Av. *NE15: Lem* *7C 60*
(off Loraine Ter.)
NE31: Heb 2H 85
Beanley Cres. NE30: Tyne 5K 49
Beanley Pl. NE7: H Hea 2J 63
BEARL 1H 75
Bearl Vw. NE43: Mic 6A 76
BEARPARK 1D 164
Bear Pk. Cl. DH4: S Row 5K 129
Beatrice Av. NE24: News 5F 23
Beatrice Gdns. NE34: S Shi 7B 68
NE36: E Bol 7K 87
Beatrice Ho. SR2: Sund 6G 7
Beatrice Rd. NE6: Heat 4K 63
Beatrice St. NE63: Ash 3C 12
SR6: Roker 5G 105
Beatrice Ter. DH4: Pen 7J 115
DH4: S Row 3B 130
Beattie St. NE34: S Shi 1H 87
Beatty Av. NE2: Jes 2G 63
SR5: Sund 4F 103
Beatty Rd. NE22: Bed 1K 21
Beatty St. SR8: Eas C 7D 160
Beaufort Cl. DH4: S Row 4B 130
NE5: Ken 2K 61
Beaufort Gdns. NE28: W'snd 7H 47
Beaufront Av. NE46: Hex 2E 70
Beaufront Bus. Pk. NE46: B End 6F 51
Beaufront Cl. NE10: Ward 1F 101
Beaufront Gdns. NE5: Fen 4J 61
NE8: Gate 5K 83
Beaufront Ter. NE32: Jar 3B 86
NE33: S Shi 5J 67
NE36: W Bol 7H 87
Beaufront Wlk. NE24: Cow 3D 22
Beauly NE38: Wash 5H 115
Beaumaris DH4: Bour 6H 129
Beaumaris Ct. NE12: Longb 6J 45
Beaumaris Gdns. SR3: E Her 2J 131
Beaumaris Way NE5: Blak 1H 61
Beaumont Cl. DH1: Dur 4J 153
DH6: Bowb 4H 177
Beaumont Ct. NE25: Monks 5D 38
NE42: Pru 4D 76
NE61: Peg 3C 10
Beaumont Cres. SR8: Hord 3C 172
Beaumont Dr. NE25: Monks 4C 38
NE38: Wash 3H 115
Beaumont Grange NE23: Seg 2C 36
Beaumont Ho. NE5: Blak 3J 61
Beaumont Mnr. NE24: Cow 2D 22
Beaumont Pl. SR8: Pet 6C 172
Beaumont St. NE4: Elsw 3B 82
NE24: Bly 1H 23
NE29: N Shi 7G 49
NE46: Hex 2C 70
SR2: Sund 4G 119
SR5: S'wck 4C 104
SR7: S'hm 4B 148
Beaumont Ter. NE3: Gos 7F 45
NE5: West 3F 61
NE13: Bru V 5C 34
NE32: Jar 1A 86
NE42: Pru 4C 76
Beaumont Way NE42: Pru 5D 76
Beaurepaire DH7: Bearp 1C 164

Beaver Cl. DH1: P Me 3A **154**
Bebdon Ct. NE24: Bly 4G **23**
BEBSIDE 2B 22
Bebside NE24: Cow 1B **22**
Bebside Rd. NE24: Cow 2A **22**
Beckenham Av. NE36: E Bol 6K **87**
Beckenham Cl. NE36: E Bol 6A **88**
Beckenham Gdns. NE28: W'snd 1G **65**
Beckfoot Cl. NE5: Den M 4H **61**
Beckford NE38: Wash 4A **116**
Beckford Cl. NE28: W'snd 7G **47**
Beck Pl. SR8: Pet 5B **172**
Beckside Gdns. NE5: Cha P 4B **60**
Beckwith Cl. DH4: Hou S 7C **130**
Beckwith M. SR3: New S 2C **132**
Beckwith Rd. SR3: E Her 1J **131**
Beda Cotts. DH9: Tant 6A **110**
Beda Hill NE21: Blay 3C **80**
Bedale Cl. DH1: Carr 7H **155**
NE28: W'snd 7G **47**
Bedale Ct. NE9: Low F 5K **99**
NE34: S Shi 1G **87**
Bedale Cres. SR5: Sund 4G **103**
Bedale Dr. NE25: Whit B 1F **49**
Bedale Grn. NE5: Ken 2K **61**
Bedale St. DH5: Hett H 1G **157**
Bedburn NE38: Wash 7D **114**
Bedburn Av. SR5: Sund 5J **103**
Bede Av. DH1: Dur 3E **166**
Bede Brook SR3: Sund 5C **118**
Bedeburn Foot NE5: West 7F **43**
Bede Burn Rd. NE32: Jar 7B **66**
Bedeburn Rd. NE5: West 7F **43**
Bede Burn Vw. NE32: Jar 1B **86**
Bede Cl. DH9: Stly 2H **125**
NE12: Longb 4G **47**
Bede Ct. DH3: Ches S 6A **128**
NE8: Gate 4J **83**
NE30: Cull 1J **49**
Bede Courtyard NE8: Gate 4C **82**
Bede Cres. NE28: W'snd 1H **65**
NE38: Wash 2G **115**
Bede Gdns. NE8: Gate 5K **83**
(not continuous)
Bede Ho. NE8: Gate 4H **83**
SR3: E Her 2K 131
(off Castle Grn.)
Bede Ind. Est. NE32: Jar 7E **66**
Bede Pct. NE32: Jar 6B **66**
Bede Station (Metro) 7E 66
Bede St. SR6: Roker 5G **105**
SR8: Eas C 7D **160**
Bedesway NE32: Jar 7E **66**
Bedeswell Dr. DH5: Hou S 2F **145**
Bede's World 6D 66
Bede Ter. DH2: Ches S 6K **127**
DH6: Bowb 3H **177**
NE32: Jar 1C **86**
NE36: E Bol 7A **88**
Bede Twr. SR2: Sund 7K **7** (3F **119**)
Bede Trade Pk. NE32: Jar 7E **66**
Bede Trad. Est. NE32: Jar 7E **66**
Bede Wlk. NE3: Gos 7G **45**
NE31: Heb 1K **85**
Bede Way DH1: Dur 5A **154**
SR8: Pet 6B **172**
Bedewell Ind. Pk. NE31: Heb 1A **86**
Bedford Av. DH3: Bir 1A **128**
(not continuous)
NE28: W'snd 2E **64**
NE33: S Shi 4J **67**
Bedford Ct. NE30: N Shi 7H **49**
Bedford Ho. *NE29: N Shi 7H 49*
(off Saville St.)
Bedford Pl. NE5: Cha P 4C **60**
NE8: Gate 10G **4** (4G **83**)
SR3: New S 1C **132**
SR8: Pet 4A **172**
Bedfordshire Dr. DH1: Carr 1H **167**
Bedford St. DH5: Hett H 6F **145**
NE29: N Shi 6G **49**
SR1: Sund 3K **7** (1F **119**)
Bedford Ter. *NE29: N Shi 7G 49*
(off Bedford St.)
Bedford Way NE29: N Shi 7G **49**
BEDLINGTON 1H 21
Bedlington Bank NE22: Bed 1J **21**
Bedlington Country Pk. 3K 21
BEDLINGTON STATION 6A 18
Beech Av. DH4: Hou S 1D **144**
NE3: Fawd 6B **44**
NE13: Din 4H **33**
NE16: Whi 6J **81**
NE23: E Cram 5B **26**
NE46: Hex 1A **70**
NE61: Mor 1J **15**
SR6: Whit 5H **89**
SR7: Mur 7F **147**
TS27: B Col 3J **183**
Beechbrooke SR2: Ryh 3H **133**
Beechburn Wlk. NE4: Newc T 4A **4** (1D **82**)
(not continuous)
Beech Cl. DH1: Bras 3C **154**
NE3: Gos 3F **45**
Beech Ct. DH7: Lang P 5J **151**
NE20: Darr H 3E **40**
NE29: N Shi 6F **49**
(Brightman Rd.)
NE29: N Shi 3E **48**
(Cedar Ct.)
SR6: Whit 6G **89**
Beech Cres. SR7: S'hm 5A **148**
Beech Crest DH1: Dur 4A **6** (3K **165**)
Beechcroft NE3: Gos 3D **62**
NE37: Wash 5F **101**
Beechcroft Av. DH7: B'don 2B **174**
NE3: Ken 2C **62**
Beechcroft Cl. DH1: Dur 1E **166**
Beechdale Rd. DH1: Carr 7H **155**
DH8: Cons 6J **121**
Beech Dr. NE11: Dun 5A **82**
NE45: Corb 7F **53**
Beecher St. NE24: Cow 1F **23**
Beeches, The DH9: Stly 2G **125**
NE4: Elsw 3C **82**
NE12: Longb 6B **46**
NE20: Pon 5H **31**
NE24: Cow 1F 23
(off Edendale Av.)
Beeches La. DH8: C'sde 4B **134**
Beechfield Gdns. NE28: W'snd 2E **64**
Beechfield Rd. NE3: Gos 1D **62**
Beech Gdns. NE9: Low F 1H **99**
Beech Gro. DH7: B'hpe 6D **138**
DH7: Ush M 3D **164**
DH9: Dip 2G **123**
NE9: Spri 6D **100**
NE12: Longb 6A **46**
NE17: C'wl 2K **107**
NE22: Bed 7J **17**
NE26: Whit B 6F **39**
NE28: W'snd 3F **65**
NE40: Craw 2D 78
(off Grove Cotts.)
NE42: Pru 4D **76**
TS29: Trim S 7C **180**
Beech Gro. Ct. NE40: Craw 2D **78**
Beechgrove La. DH7: Edm 7B **126**
DH9: Crag 7B **126**
Beech Gro. Rd. NE4: Elsw 2C **82**
Beech Gro. Sth. NE42: Pru 4E **76**
Beech Gro. Ter. NE40: Craw 2D **78**
Beechgrove Ter. DH7: Edm 1A **140**
Beech Gro. Ter. Sth. NE40: Craw 2D **78**
Beech Hill NE46: Hex 1A **70**
Beech Ho. DH8: Shot B 2E **120**
Beech M. NE3: Fawd 4B **44**
Beecholm Ct. SR2: Sund 5F **119**
Beech Pk. DH7: B'don 2C **174**
Beech Rd. DH1: Dur 6K **153**
DH6: S'burn 2K **167**
DH8: Lead 6B **122**
Beech Sq. NE38: Wash 4J **115**
Beech St. NE4: Benw 2A **82**
NE8: Gate 5K **83**
NE16: Sun 5H **97**
NE32: Jar 6A **66**
NE43: Mic 6A **76**
Beech Ter. DH9: Ann P 4J **123**
DH9: Stly 6H **125**
(Ash Ter.)
DH9: Stly 5E **124**
(Sth. Moor Rd.)
NE16: Burn 2C **110**
NE63: Ash 5C **12**
SR8: Hord 6E **172**
Beech Vw. DH1: S Hou 5H **167**
Beechville DH7: Edm 2B **140**
Beech Way NE12: Kil 7A **36**
Beechway NE10: Hew 2D **100**
NE63: N Sea 4E **12**
Beechways DH1: Dur 1H **165**
Beechwood NE39: H Spen 4E **94**
TS27: Cas E 4J **181**
Beechwood Av. NE3: Gos 6G **45**
NE9: Low F 4J **99**
NE25: Monks 7D **38**
NE40: Ryton 1G **79**
NE62: Stake 7J **11**
Beechwood Cl. DH7: Sac 7E **140**
NE32: Jar 7D **66**
Beechwood Cres. SR5: S'wck 4B **104**
Beechwood Dr. NE42: Pru 6G **77**
Beechwood Gdns. NE11: Lob H 1D **98**
Beechwood Ho. NE7: H Hea 1J **63**
Beechwood Pl. NE20: Pon 4J **31**
Beechwoods DH2: Ches S 4K **127**
Beechwood St. SR2: Sund 6F **7** (3D **118**)
Beechwood Ter. SR2: Sund 6F **7** (3D **118**)
Beehive, The *NE23: Seg 1D 36*
(off Pit La.)
Beehive Workshops DH1: Dur 2F **167**
Beeston Av. SR5: Sund 4F **103**
Beetham Cres. NE5: Den M 5G **61**
Beethoven St. NE33: S Shi 3K **67**
Beggar La. NE61: Mor 6F **9**
Begonia Cl. NE31: Heb 3J **85**
Bek Rd. DH1: Dur 5A **154**
Beldene Dr. SR4: Sund 4A **118**
Beldon Dr. DH9: Stly 6D **124**
Belford Av. NE27: Shir 1K **47**
Belford Cl. NE28: W'snd 7H **47**
SR2: Sund 5F **119**
Belford Ct. NE24: Cow 2F **23**
Belford Gdns. NE11: Lob H 2C **98**
Belford Rd. SR2: Sund 5G **119**
Belford St. SR8: Hord 3D **172**
Belford Ter. NE6: Walk 1C **84**
NE30: N Shi 5G **49**
Belford Ter. E. SR2: Sund 5G **119**
Belfry, The DH4: S Row 5A **130**
Belgrade Cres. SR5: Sund 3F **103**
Belgrade Sq. SR5: Sund 4F **103**
Belgrave Ct. NE10: Fell 6B **84**
Belgrave Cres. NE24: Bly 3K **23**
Belgrave Gdns. NE34: S Shi 7B **68**
NE63: N Sea 5E **12**
Belgrave Pde. NE4: Newc T 8A **4** (2D **82**)
Belgrave Ter. NE10: Fell 6B **84**
NE33: S Shi 2K **67**
Belgravia Ct. SR2: Sund 4G **119**
Bellamy Cres. SR5: Sund 4F **103**
Bell Av. DH6: Bowb 3G **177**
Bellburn Ct. NE23: Cra 2B **26**
Belle Gro. Pl. NE2: Newc T 2A **4** (6D **62**)
Belle Gro. Ter. NE2: Newc T 1B **4** (6D **62**)
Belle Gro. Vs. NE2: Newc T 1B **4** (6D **62**)
Belle Gro. W. NE2: Newc T 1A **4** (6D **62**)
Bellerby Dr. DH2: Ous 5G **113**
Bellerbys Bldgs. DH9: Tant 6A **110**
Belle St. DH9: Stly 3F **125**
Belle Vw. Dr. DH8: C'sde 4C **134**
Belle Vue DH6: Quar H 5D **178**
DH8: M'sly 1H **121**
DH9: Tanf 3E **110**
NE39: H Spen 2D **94**
Belle Vue Av. NE3: Gos 7F **45**
Belle Vue Bank NE9: Low F 2G **99**
Belle Vue Cotts. NE9: Low F 2G **99**
Belle Vue Ct. DH1: Dur 1F **167**
Belle Vue Cres. NE33: S Shi 7H **67**
SR2: Sund 4E **118**
Bellevue Cres. NE23: Cra 7K **21**
Belle Vue Dr. SR2: Sund 4E **118**
Belle Vue Gdns. DH8: Cons 6H **121**
Belle Vue Gro. NE9: Low F 2H **99**
Belle Vue La. NE36: E Bol 1J **103**
Belle Vue Pk. SR2: Sund 4E **118**
Belle Vue Pk. W. SR2: Sund 4E **118**
Belle Vue Rd. SR2: Sund 4E **118**
Belle Vue St. NE30: Cull 1J **49**
Belle Vue Swimming Cen. 6J 121
Belle Vue Ter. DH1: Dur 1F **167**
NE9: Low F 2G **99**
NE9: Spri 6D **100**
NE22: E Sle 5D **18**
NE29: N Shi 7G **49**
NE40: Craw 2C **78**
Belle Vue Vs. NE36: E Bol 7J **87**
Bellfield Av. NE3: Fawd 6B **44**
Bellgreen Av. NE3: Gos 3F **45**
Bell Gro. NE12: Kil 7K **35**
Bell Ho. Rd. SR5: Ful, S'wck 2C **104**
Bellingham Cl. NE28: W'snd 1H **65**
Bellingham Ct. NE3: Ken 7K **43**
NE22: Bed 7J **17**
Bellingham Dr. NE12: Longb 5D **46**
Bellingham Ho. SR4: Sund 4H **117**
Bellister Ct. NE24: Cow 3E **22**
Bellister Gro. NE5: Fen 6J **61**
Bellister Pk. SR8: Pet 1C **182**
Bellister Rd. NE29: N Shi 6D **48**
Bell Mdw. DH7: B'don 2C **174**
Belloc Av. NE34: S Shi 3H **87**
Bellona Cl. NE31: Heb 7H **65**
Bellows Burn La. TS27: Cas E 7C **182**
Bell Rd. NE41: Wylam 7K **57**
Bells Bldgs. DH2: Nett 6G **141**
DH9: Ann P 4K **123**
Bellsburn Ct. NE63: Ash 5K **11**
BELL'S CLOSE 7E 60
Bells Cl. NE15: Lem 1E **80**
NE24: Cow 1D **22**
Bells Cl. Ind. Est. NE15: Lem 1E **80**
Bell's Cotts. NE40: G'sde 5E **78**
Bell's Ct. NE1: Newc T 5G **4** (1G **83**)
Bell's Folly DH1: Dur 5J **165**
Bellshiel Gro. NE15: Benw 2H **81**
Bellshill Cl. NE28: W'snd 6J **47**
Bells Lonnen NE42: Pru 2F **77**
Bells Pl. DH9: Ann P 4K **123**
NE22: Bed 1J **21**
Bell St. DH4: Pen 1B **130**
NE30: N Shi 7H **49**
NE31: Heb 7H **65**
NE38: Wash 4K **115**
SR4: Sund 2B **118**
Bell's Ville DH1: Dur 2E **166**
Bells Wood Ct. DH8: B'hill 5F **121**
Bell Ter. *NE46: Hex 7C 50*
(off Tyne Grn. Rd.)
Bell Vw. NE42: Pru 3H **77**
Bell Vs. NE20: Pon 5K **31**
Bellway Ind. Est. NE12: Longb 5D **46**
Bellwood Ter. DH8: Lead 6B **122**
BELMONT 1H 167
Belmont NE10: Hew 2E **100**
Belmont (Park & Ride) 5H 155
Belmont Av. NE25: Monks 7D **38**
SR7: Hawt 3K **159**
Belmont Bus. Pk. DH1: Dur 7F **155**
Belmont Cl. NE28: W'snd 7H **47**
Belmont Cotts. NE5: West 2F **61**
Belmont Ct. DH1: Carr 1G **167**
Belmonte Av. TS27: B Col 3K **183**
Belmont Ind. Est. DH1: Dur 6F **155**
Belmont Ri. DH5: Hett H 2G **157**
Belmont Rd. DH1: Carr, Dur 7E **154**
SR4: Sund 3B **118**
Belmont St. NE6: Walk 3D **84**
Belmont Ter. NE9: Spri 6C **100**
Belmont Wlk. NE6: Walk 3D **84**
Belmount Av. NE3: Gos 3F **45**
Belper Cl. NE28: W'snd 7G **47**
Belsay NE38: Wash 4D **114**
Belsay Av. NE13: Haz 7C **34**
NE25: Whit B 7H **39**
NE34: S Shi 6C **68**
SR8: Hord 4D **172**
Belsay Cl. NE28: W'snd 7G **47**
NE61: Peg 4B **10**
Belsay Ct. NE24: Cow 2G **23**
Belsay Gdns. NE3: Fawd 4B **44**
NE11: Lob H 2C **98**
SR4: Sund 3B **118**
Belsay Gro. NE22: Bed 5A **18**
Belsay Pl. NE4: Fen 7C **62**
Belsfield Gdns. NE32: Jar 2B **86**
Belsize Pl. NE6: Walk 5D **64**
Belstone Ct. SR3: New S 1C **132**
Beltingham NE5: W Dent 4E **60**
Belton Cl. NE38: Wash 4A **116**
SR2: Ryh 3F **133**
Belvedere NE29: N Shi 5F **49**
Belvedere Av. NE25: Monks 7F **39**
Belvedere Ct. NE6: Byke 6A **64**
Belvedere Gdns. DH6: Shot C 5D **170**
NE12: Longb 6B **46**
Belvedere Ho. NE6: Byke 3P **5**
Belvedere Parkway NE3: Ki Pk 6K **43**
Belvedere Retail Pk. NE3: Ki Pk 6J **43**
Belvedere Rd. SR2: Sund 7H **7** (3E **118**)
Belvoir Cl. NE38: Wash 4A **116**
Bemersyde Dr. NE2: Jes 2G **63**
Benbrake Av. NE29: N Shi 3E **48**
Bendigo Av. NE34: S Shi 3F **87**
Benedict Ct. SR1: Sund 6J **7** (3F **119**)
Benedict Rd. SR6: Roker 5H **105**
Benevente St. SR7: S'hm 4B **148**
Benfield Bus. Pk. NE6: Walk 5C **64**
Benfield Cl. DH8: Shot B 3E **120**
Benfield Gro. NE26: Sea S 3B **28**
Benfield Rd. NE6: Heat, Walk 3B **64**
BENFIELDSIDE 3E 120
Benfieldside Rd. DH8: Shot B 3E **120**
Benfleet Av. SR5: Sund 4F **103**
Benjamin Rd. NE28: W'snd 2A **66**
Benjamin St. NE40: Craw 3D **78**
Bennett Ct. NE15: Lem 7C **60**
SR2: Sund 5G **119**
Bennett Gdns. NE10: Fell 4B **84**
Bennett's Wlk. NE61: Mor 7G **9**
Benridge Bank DH4: W Rai 1A **156**
Benridge Pk. NE24: News 6F **23**
BENSHAM 5G 83
Bensham Av. NE8: Gate 5F **83**
Bensham Ct. NE8: Gate 5F **83**
NE34: S Shi 1J **87**
Bensham Cres. NE8: Gate 5E **82**
Bensham Rd. NE8: Gate 10G **4** (6F **83**)
(not continuous)
Bensham St. NE35: Bol C 5F **87**
Bensham Trad. Est. NE8: Gate 6E **82**
Benson Cl. NE46: Hex 2A **70**
Benson Pl. NE6: Byke 7A **64**
Benson Rd. NE6: Walk 7B **64**
Benson St. DH3: Ches S 7A **128**
DH9: Stly 2E **124**
Benson Ter. NE10: Fell 6B **84**
Bentall Bus. Pk. NE37: Wash 1K **115**
Bentham Cl. SR5: Sund 3G **103**
Bent Ho. La. DH1: Dur 3F **167**
Bentinck Cres. NE4: Elsw 2B **82**
NE61: Peg 4A **10**
Bentinck Pl. NE4: Elsw 2B **82**
Bentinck Rd. NE4: Elsw 2B **82**
Bentinck St. NE4: Elsw 2B **82**
Bentinck Ter. NE4: Elsw 1B **82**
Bentinck Vs. NE4: Elsw 1B **82**
Bentley Ct. NE24: Cow 7F **19**
BENTON 6B 46
Benton Av. SR5: Sund 3F **103**
Benton Bank NE7: H Hea 4J **63**
(not continuous)
Benton Bus. Pk. NE12: Longb 5D **46**
Benton Cl. NE7: Longb 7K **45**
Benton Hall Wlk. NE7: H Hea 3B **64**
Benton La. NE12: Longb 3K **45**
Benton Lodge Av. NE7: Longb 7K **45**
Benton Pk. Rd. NE7: Longb, Newc T 7H **45**
Benton Pk. Vw. NE7: Longb 1J **63**
Benton Rd. NE7: H Hea, Longb 7A **46**
NE27: Shir 2H **47**
NE34: S Shi 4J **87**
BENTON SQUARE 3F 47
Benton Sq. Ind. Est. NE12: Kil 3F **47**
Benton Station (Metro) 6B 46
Benton Ter. DH9: Stly 2F **125**
NE2: Newc T 1J **5** (6H **63**)
Benton Vw. NE12: Longb 4B **46**
Benton Way NE28: W'snd 4F **65**
(Brussels Rd.)
NE28: W'snd 5F **65**
(Neptune Rd.)
Bents, The SR6: Seab 7H **89**
Bents Cotts. NE33: S Shi 3A **68**
Bents Cotts. App. NE33: S Shi 3A **68**
Bents Pk. Rd. NE33: S Shi 2A **68**
Benville Ter. DH7: New B 4A **164**
BENWELL 2A 82
Benwell Cl. NE15: Benw 1K **81**
Benwell Dene Ter. NE15: Benw 1J **81**
Benwell Grange NE15: Benw 1K **81**
Benwell Grange Av. NE15: Benw 1K **81**
Benwell Grange Rd. NE15: Benw 1J **81**
Benwell Grange Ter. NE15: Benw 1J **81**
Benwell Gro. NE4: Benw 1A **82**
Benwell Hall Dr. NE15: Benw 7H **61**
Benwell Hill Gdns. NE5: Fen 6J **61**
Benwell Hill Rd. NE5: Fen 6H **61**
Benwell La. NE15: Benw 1H **81**
(not continuous)
Benwell Roman Temple 7K 61
Benwell Vallum Crossing 7K 61
Benwell Village NE15: Benw 7H **61**
Benwell Village M. NE15: Benw 7J **61**
Berberis Way *NE15: Newb 5J 59*
(off Lovaine St.)
Beresford Av. NE31: Heb 3H **85**
Beresford Ct. NE26: Sea S 4D **28**

Beresford Gdns. NE6: Byke 1A 84
Beresford Pk. SR2: Sund 6F 7 (3D 118)
Beresford Rd. NE26: Sea S 4D 28
NE30: Cull 1G 49
Beresford St. NE11: Dun 5C 82
Bergen Cl. NE29: N Shi 1B 66
Bergen Sq. SR5: Sund 3F 103
Bergen St. SR5: Sund 3F 103
(not continuous)
Berkdale Rd. NE9: Low F 4G 99
Berkeley Cl. NE12: Kil 7C 36
NE35: Bol C 4F 87
SR3: E Her 2J 131
Berkeley Sq. NE3: Gos 5D 44
Berkeley St. NE33: S Shi 3K 67
Berkhampstead Ct. NE10: Ward 7G 85
Berkley Av. NE21: Blay 4E 80
Berkley Cl. NE28: W'snd 7H 47
Berkley Rd. NE29: N Shi 6D 48
Berkley St. NE15: Newb 5K 59
Berkley Ter. NE15: Newb 5K 59
Berkley Way NE31: Heb 5K 65
Berkshire Cl. DH1: Carr 1G 167
NE5: West 3F 61
Berkshire Rd. SR8: Pet 4A 172
Berksyde DH8: Cons 1J 135
Bermondsey St. NE2: Newc T 4K 5 (7H 63)
Bernard Shaw St. DH4: Hou S 2D 144
Bernard St. DH4: Hou S 2D 144
Bernard Ter. DH2: P Fel 3G 127
Berrington Dr. NE5: Blak 2H 61
Berrishill Gro. NE25: Monks 5C 38
Berry Cl. NE6: Walk 1E 84
NE28: W'snd 7G 47
Berry Edge Rd. DH8: Cons 7G 121
Berry Edge Vw. DH8: Cons 6G 121
Berryfield Cl. SR3: Dox P 4C 132
Berry Hill NE40: G'sde 5F 79
Berryhill Cl. NE21: Blay 5D 80
Berrymoor NE63: Ash 3C 12
Berrymoor Ct. NE23: Dud 1K 35
Bertha St. DH8: Cons 6H 121
Bertha Ter. DH4: Nbot 5D 130
Bertram Cres. NE15: Benw 7J 61
Bertram Pl. NE27: Shir 7K 37
NE61: Peg 3B 10
Bertram St. DH3: Bir 4A 114
NE33: S Shi 5J 67
Bertram Ter. *NE61: Peg 3B 10*
(off Mortimer Ter.)
NE63: Ash 4B 12
Bertram Yd. NE25: Ears 6A 38
Berwick NE38: Wash 4D 114
Berwick Av. SR5: Sund 3F 103
Berwick Chase SR8: Pet 2K 181
Berwick Cl. NE15: Lem 6A 60
Berwick Ct. NE20: Pon 4K 31
NE24: Bly 4G 23
Berwick Dr. NE28: W'snd 7H 47
Berwick Hill Rd. NE20: Pon, Wool 3K 31
Berwick Sq. SR5: Sund 3F 103
Berwick St. NE31: Heb 7H 65
Berwick Ter. NE29: N Shi 1D 66
Besford Gro. SR1: Sund 2G 119
Bessemer Rd. DH6: S Het 4B 158
Bessemer St. DH8: B'hill 6G 121
Bessie Surtees House 7G 4
Bessie Ter. NE21: Winl 4A 80
Bests Yd. DH7: Wit G 3C 152
Best Vw. DH4: S Row 3B 130
Bethany Gdns. DH9: Ann P 4K 123
Bethany Ter. DH9: Ann P 4K 123
Bethel Av. NE6: Walk 6B 64
Bethune Av. SR7: S'hm 3J 147
(not continuous)
Betjeman Cl. DH9: Stly 3G 125
Betjeman M. NE8: Gate 5H 83
Betsey Pl. NE21: Blay 4C 80
Bet's La. NE61: Tra W 7D 14
Betts Av. NE15: Benw 1H 81
Bevan Av. SR2: Ryh 2G 133
Bevan Cres. DH6: Whe H 4A 180
Bevan Dr. NE12: Longb 6H 45
Bevan Gdns. NE10: Ward 6E 84
Bevan Gro. DH1: Dur 2F 167
DH6: Shot C 6E 170
Bevan Sq. SR7: Mur 6E 146
Beverley Cl. DH6: Coxh 7J 177
NE3: Gos 2D 44
Beverley Ct. NE9: Low F 1J 99
NE32: Jar 6B 66
NE37: Wash 1H 115
Beverley Cres. NE9: Low F 1J 99
Beverley Dr. NE16: Swa, Whi 5J 81
NE21: Winl 6K 79
NE62: Stake 7H 11
Beverley Gdns. DH3: Ches S 7B 128
DH8: B'hill 4F 121
DH8: Cons 6H 121
(off Beverley Ter.)
NE30: Cull 1J 49
NE40: Ryton 1E 78
Beverley Pk. NE25: Monks 7E 38
Beverley Pl. NE28: W'snd 2K 65
Beverley Rd. NE9: Low F 1J 99
NE25: Monks 7E 38
SR2: Sund 6H 119
Beverley Ter. DH8: Cons 6H 121
DH9: Ann P 4J 123
NE6: Walk 1E 84
NE15: Walb 3A 60
NE30: Cull 1J 49
Beverley Vs. NE30: Cull 1J 49
Beverley Way SR8: Pet 5A 172
Bevin Gro. TS27: B Col 3K 183
Bevin Sq. DH6: S Het 4D 158
Beweshill Cres. NE21: Winl 5A 80
Beweshill La. NE21: Blay 4K 79
(not continuous)
Bewick Cl. DH2: Ches S 2J 141
Bewick Ct. NE1: Newc T 4G 4
Bewick Cres. NE15: Lem 6D 60
Bewicke Lodge NE28: W'snd 3A 66
Bewicke Rd. NE28: W'snd 4A 66
(not continuous)
Bewicke Rd. Ind. Est. NE28: W'snd 4A 66
Bewicke St. NE28: W'snd 4B 66
Bewicke Vw. DH3: Bir 3B 114
Bewick Gth. NE43: Mic 5A 76
Bewick La. NE42: O'ham 2D 76
Bewick Main Cvn. Pk. DH2: Bir 3G 113
Bewick Pk. NE28: W'snd 6K 47
Bewick Rd. NE8: Gate 5G 83
Bewick St. NE1: Newc T 7D 4 (2E 82)
NE33: S Shi 5J 67
Bewley Gro. SR8: Pet 2J 181
Bewley Ter. DH7: New B 4A 164
Bexhill Rd. SR5: Sund 4F 103
Bexhill Sq. NE24: News 4J 23
SR5: Sund 3F 103
Bexley Av. NE15: Den M 7G 61
Bexley Gdns. NE28: W'snd 7H 47
Bexley Pl. NE16: Whi 2G 97
Bexley St. SR4: Sund 2B 118
Bicester Gro. NE31: Heb 7H 65
Bickerton Wlk. NE5: W Dent 4E 60
Bickington Ct. DH4: Nbot 6C 130
BIDDICK 4H 115
BIDDICK HALL 4H 87
Biddick Hall Dr. NE34: S Shi 2H 87
Biddick La. NE38: Wash 1H 129
Biddick Ter. NE38: Wash 5J 115
Biddick Vw. NE38: Wash 5J 115
Biddick Village Cen.
NE38: Wash 5H 115
Biddick Vs. NE38: Wash 5J 115
Biddlestone Cres. NE29: N Shi 7D 48
Biddlestone Rd. NE6: Heat 4A 64
Bideford Gdns. NE9: Low F 4H 99
NE26: Whit B 5F 39
NE32: Jar 1E 86
NE34: S Shi 4C 68
Bideford Gro. NE16: Whi 2G 97
Bideford Rd. NE3: Ken 1A 62
Bideford St. SR2: Sund 6H 119
Bigbury Cl. DH4: Nbot 5C 130
Bigges Gdns. NE28: W'snd 1D 64
BIGGES MAIN 3D 64
Bigg Mkt. NE1: Newc T 6F 4 (1F 83)
Big Waters Cl. NE13: Bru V 5C 34
Big Waters Nature Reserve 4C 34
Bilbrough Gdns. NE4: Benw 2K 81
Billingside Cl. DH8: Lead 3A 122
BILL QUAY 4F 85
Bill Quay Farm 4E 84
Bill Quay Ind. Est. NE10: Bill Q 3F 85
BILLY MILL 5D 48
Billy Mill Av. NE29: N Shi 6E 48
Billy Mill La. NE29: N Shi 4C 48
Bilsdale SR6: Seab 7H 89
Bilsdale Pl. NE12: Longb 6H 45
Bilsmoor Av. NE7: H Hea 3K 63
Bilton Hall Rd. NE32: Jar 7D 66
Bilton's Ct. NE61: Mor 6F 9
Binchester St. NE34: S Shi 2G 87
Bingfield Gdns. NE5: Fen 4J 61
Bingley Cl. NE28: W'snd 7J 47
Bingley St. SR5: Sund 4F 103
Bink Moss NE37: Wash 2E 114
Binsby Gdns. NE9: Low F 5K 99
Binswood Av. NE5: Blak 4H 61
Bircham Dr. NE21: Blay 4D 80
Bircham St. DH9: Stly 4D 124
Birch Av. NE10: Hew 7E 84
SR6: Whit 5H 89
Birch Cl. NE46: Hex 3A 70
Birch Ct. NE42: Pru 4C 76
SR3: Silk 3A 132
Birch Cres. NE16: Burn 2K 109
Birches, The DH5: Eas L 2J 157
DH9: Stly 1F 125
(not continuous)
NE16: Sun 5J 97
SR4: Sund 2H 117
BIRCHES NOOK 7J 75
Birches Nook Cotts.
NE43: Pains 7J 75
Birches Nook Rd. NE43: Pains 7J 75
Birchfield NE16: Whi 1H 97
NE38: Wash 6J 115
Birchfield Gdns. NE9: Low F 5J 99
NE15: Lem 6E 60
Birchfield Rd. SR2: Sund 7F 7 (4D 118)
Birchgate Cl. NE21: Winl 5A 80
Birch Gro. DH8: Cons 3A 136
NE28: W'snd 7G 47
NE32: Jar 4A 66
Birchgrove Av. DH1: Dur 1F 167
Birchington Av. NE33: S Shi 6J 67
Birch M. NE16: Burn 2K 109
Birch Pl. DH7: Esh W 4D 162
Birch Rd. NE21: Blay 4D 80
Birch St. DH8: Cons 7H 121
NE32: Jar 6A 66
Birch Ter. DH3: Bir 3K 113
NE6: Walk 1E 84
Birchtree Gdns. NE25: Monks 1F 49
Birchvale Av. NE5: Den M 4H 61
Birch Vw. DH2: Ches S 7H 127
Birchwood SR4: Sund 1H 117
Birchwood Av. NE7: H Hea 2A 64
NE13: W Op 6D 34
NE16: Whi 2G 97
Birchwood Chase NE13: W Op 1B 44
Birchwood Cl. DH9: Beam 1A 126
NE23: Seg 2D 36
Birchwood Dr. SR8: Pet 7H 171
Birchwood Way NE63: N Sea 6E 12
Birdhill Pl. NE34: S Shi 1J 87
Birdhope Cl. NE15: Benw 2H 81
Birds Nest Rd. NE6: Byke, Walk 2B 84
(not continuous)
Birds Ter. DH4: Pen 1C 130
Bird St. NE30: N Shi 6J 49
Birkdale NE25: Monks 6D 38
NE33: S Shi 4A 68
Birkdale Av. SR6: Seab 7G 89
Birkdale Cl. NE7: H Hea 1A 64
NE28: W'snd 1F 65
NE37: Wash 5F 101
Birkdale Dr. DH4: S Row 5A 130
Birkdale Gdns. DH1: Carr 1H 167
Birkdene NE43: Pains 1K 91
BIRKHEADS 2K 111
Birkheads La. NE11: Kib, Marl H 2K 111
Birkheads Secret Gardens & Nursery
2K 111
Birkland La. NE11: Kib 2A 112
NE16: Marl H 6J 97
Birkshaw Wlk. NE5: W Dent 4E 60
Birks Rd. NE15: Hed W, Thro 7F 41
Birling Pl. NE5: Fen 3K 61
Birnam Gro. NE32: Jar 4E 86
Birney Edge NE20: Darr H 3G 41
Birnham Pl. NE3: Ken 2B 62
Birnie Cl. NE4: Benw 2A 82
Birrell Sq. SR5: Sund 3F 103
Birrell St. SR5: Sund 3F 103
BIRTLEY 4A 114
Birtley Av. NE30: Tyne 4K 49
SR5: Sund 3F 103
Birtley By-Pass DH3: Bir 1A 114
Birtley Cl. NE3: Gos 1C 62
Birtley Crematorium DH3: Bir 2K 113
Birtley La. DH3: Bir 3A 114
Birtley Leisure Cen. 6A 114
Birtley Rd. NE38: Wash 7D 114
Birtley Swimming Centre 5A 114
Birtley Vs. DH3: Bir 3A 114
Birtwhistle Av. NE31: Heb 3H 85
Biscop Ter. NE32: Jar 1C 86
Biscuit Gallery, The 7H 63
Bishopbourne Ct. NE29: N Shi 3F 49
Bishop Cres. NE32: Jar 5C 66
Bishopdale DH4: Pen 1J 129
(not continuous)
NE28: W'snd 7D 46
Bishopdale Av. NE24: Cow 3E 22
Bishop Morton Gro. SR1: Sund 2G 119
Bishop Ramsey Ct. NE34: S Shi 7C 68
Bishop Rock Dr. NE12: Longb 6J 45
Bishop's Av. NE4: Fen 1C 82
Bishops Cl. DH1: Carr 7H 155
NE28: W'snd 3J 65
Bishops Ct. DH1: Shin 6D 166
NE5: Den M 5F 61
NE29: N Shi 7G 49
Bishops Dr. NE40: Ryton 2H 79
Bishops Ga. DH1: Dur 1J 165
Bishops Hill NE46: Acomb 3C 50
(not continuous)
Bishops Mdw. DH7: Lan 5J 137
NE22: Bed 7G 17
Bishops Pk. Rd. NE8: Gate 5K 83
Bishop's Rd. NE15: Benw 2K 81
Bishops Way DH1: P Me 4K 153
SR3: Dox P 4A 132
Bishops Wynd DH5: Hou S 3E 144
Bishopton St. NE24: Bly 3J 23
SR2: Sund 2G 119
Bishopton Way NE46: Hex 3A 70
BISHOPWEARMOUTH 2G 7 (1E 118)
Bisley Ct. NE28: W'snd 7H 47
Bisley Dr. NE34: S Shi 6K 67
Bittern Cl. NE11: Dun 4B 82
NE28: W'snd 6A 48
Biverfield Rd. NE42: Pru 3G 77
Blackberry Cotts. NE9: Spri 6D 100
Black Boy Rd. DH4: Hou S 4H 143
Black Boy Yd. NE1: Newc T 6F 4 (1F 83)
Blackburn Cl. DH7: Bearp 7C 152
Blackburn Grn. NE10: Fell 7A 84
BLACK CALLERTON 4B 42
Blackcap Cl. NE38: Wash 5D 114
Blackcliffe Way DH7: Bearp 7C 152
Blackclose Bank NE63: Ash 7A 12
Blackclose Est. NE63: Ash 7B 12
Blackdene NE63: Ash 5K 11
Blackdown Cl. SR8: Pet 7K 171
Black Dr. DH3: Lam P 4F 129
Blackettbridge NE1: Newc T 4E 4
Blackett Cotts. NE41: Wylam 7J 57
Blackett Ct. NE41: Wylam 7J 57
Blackett Pl. NE1: Newc T 5F 4 (1F 83)
Blackett St. DH9: Ann P 5J 123
NE1: Newc T 5E 4 (1F 83)
NE32: Jar 5K 65
Blackett Ter. SR4: Sund 2C 118
BLACKFELL 2E 114
Blackfell NE37: Bir 1C 114
Blackfell Rd. NE37: Wash 2D 114
Blackfell Village Cen. NE37: Wash 2E 114
Blackfell Way DH3: Bir 3B 114
Blackfriars 6D 4 (1E 82)
Blackfriars NE1: Newc T 6D 4
Blackfriars Ct. NE1: Newc T 6D 4
Blackfriars Way NE12: Longb 6J 45
BLACKFYNE 5G 121
BLACKHALL COLLIERY 2H 183
Blackhall Colliery Ind. Est.
TS27: B Col 1H 183
BLACKHALL MILL 2K 107
BLACKHALL ROCKS 3J 183
Blackhaugh Dr. NE25: Sea D 6F 27
Blackheath Cl. NE37: Wash 5G 101
Blackheath Ct. NE3: Ki Pk 7H 43
BLACKHILL 5F 121
Blackhill Av. NE28: W'snd 5J 47
Blackhill Cres. NE9: Wrek 3B 100
Blackhills Rd. SR8: Hord 4E 172
Blackhills Ter. SR8: Hord 5E 172
BLACKHOUSE 1A 140
Black Ho. La. DH7: Edm 2A 140
Blackhouse La. NE40: Ryton 1F 79
Black La. DH6: Whe H 2A 180
NE5: Call, West, Wool 6F 43
NE9: Eigh B 6K 99
NE9: Low F 5K 99
NE13: Wool 6F 43
NE20: Mil 1A 30
NE21: Winl 5A 80
Blacklock Cl. NE9: Low F 2K 99
Blackpool Pde. NE31: Heb 3A 86
Black Rd. DH7: Lang M 6G 165
NE31: Heb 6K 65
SR2: Ryh 2H 133
Blackrow La. NE9: Low F 4J 99
NE15: Hed W, Thro 2D 58
Blackstone Ct. NE21: Winl 4A 80
Black Thorn Cl. DH7: B'don 2C 174
Blackthorn Cl. NE16: Sun 5G 97
Blackthorn Dr. NE24: News 5G 23
NE28: W'snd 7G 47
Blackthorne NE10: Hew 2D 100
Blackthorne Av. SR8: Hord 6F 173
Blackthorn Pl. NE4: Newc T 9A 4 (3D 82)
Blackthorn Way DH4: Hou S 7A 130
NE63: Ash 5K 11
Blackwell Av. NE6: Walk 7D 64
Blackwood Rd. SR5: Sund 4F 103
Bladen St. NE32: Jar 6A 66
Bladen St. Ind. Est. NE32: Jar 6A 66
Blagdon Av. NE34: S Shi 5A 68
Blagdon Cl. NE1: Newc T 5J 5 (1H 83)
NE61: Mor 7E 8
Blagdon Ct. NE22: Bed 6A 18
Blagdon Cres. NE23: Nel V 2G 25
Blagdon Dr. NE24: News 6G 23
Blagdon La. NE13: Sea B 4C 24
NE23: Cra, Sea B 4C 24
Blagdon St. NE1: Newc T 5J 5 (1H 83)
Blagdon Ter. NE13: Sea B 3D 34
NE23: Cra 4K 25
Blaidwood Dr. DH1: Dur 7J 165
Blair Cl. DH6: S'burn 3K 167
Blair Ct. DH7: Lang M 7G 165
Blair Way SR7: S'hm 6C 148
Blake Av. NE16: Whi 7H 81
Blake Cl. DH9: Stly 3G 125
BLAKELAW 3J 61
Blakelaw Rd. NE5: Blak 3H 61
(Bonnington Way)
NE5: Blak 3J 61
(Cragston Cl.)
Blakemoor Pl. NE5: Fen 4J 61
Blake St. SR8: Eas C 7D 160
Blaketown NE23: Seg 1E 36
Blake Wlk. NE8: Gate 4J 83
Blanche Gro. SR8: Pet 7B 172
Blanche Ter. DH9: Tant 6B 110
Blanchland NE38: Wash 7J 115
Blanchland Av. DH1: Dur 5C 154
NE13: W Op 5D 34
NE15: Lem 6C 60
Blanchland Ct. NE63: Ash 2H 11
Blanchland Dr. NE25: H'wll 1K 37
SR5: S'wck 4E 104
Blanchland Ter. NE30: N Shi 5H 49
Blandford Ct. NE4: Newc T 7C 4 (2E 82)
Blandford Pl. SR7: S'hm 3B 148
Blandford Rd. NE29: N Shi 3D 48
Blandford Sq. NE1: Newc T 7C 4 (2E 82)
(not continuous)
Blandford St. NE1: Newc T 8C 4 (2E 82)
SR1: Sund 4J 7 (2F 119)
Blandford Way NE28: W'snd 7H 47
Bland's Opening DH3: Ches S 6A 128
Blaxton Pl. NE16: Whi 2F 97
BLAYDON 3D 80
Blaydon Av. SR5: Sund 3G 103
Blaydon Bank NE21: Blay, Winl 5B 80
BLAYDON BURN 4A 80
Blaydon Bus. Cen. NE21: Blay 3E 80
Blaydon Bus. Pk. NE21: Blay 2F 81
BLAYDON HAUGHS 2E 80
Blaydon Haughs Ind. Est.
NE21: Blay 2E 80
Blaydon Highway NE21: Blay 3C 80
Blaydon Ind. Pk. NE21: Blay 3D 80
Blaydon Leisure Cen. 4F 81
Blaydon Rugby Club 5F 81
Blaydon Station (Rail) 2C 80
Blaydon Trade Pk. NE21: Blay 3E 80
Blaykeston Cl. SR7: S'hm 1G 147
Blayney Row NE15: Thro 5G 59
Bleachery, The TS27: Cas E 6C 182
Bleachfeld NE10: Hew 1D 100
BLEACH GREEN 5C 80
Bleach Grn. DH5: Hett H 7G 145
Bleasdale Cres. DH4: Pen 2B 130

Blencathra NE30: Cull 2G 49
NE37: Wash 2G 115
Blencathra Way NE21: Winl 6C 80
Blenheim NE12: Kil 7B 36
Blenheim Ct. NE10: Wind N 1B 100
NE24: News 6H 23
Blenheim Dr. NE22: Bed 5A 18
Blenheim Gdns. NE61: Peg 3A 10
Blenheim Pl. NE11: Dun 5A 82
Blenheim Wlk. NE33: S Shi 2K 67
Blenkinsop Ct. NE34: S Shi 3H 87
Blenkinsop Gro. NE32: Jar 3B 86
Blenkinsop M. NE3: Gos 3C 44
Blenkinsopp Ct. SR8: Pet 2K 181
Blenkinsop St. NE28: W'snd 3F 65
Bletchley Av. SR5: Sund 3F 103
Blezard Bus. Pk. NE13: Sea B 2D 34
Blezard Ct. NE21: Blay 2E 80
Blind La. DH1: Dur 4A 6 (3K 165)
DH3: Ches S 3A 128
DH4: Hou S 5A 130
SR3: New S 1C 132
SR8: Eas 5A 160
Blindy Burn Ct. DH2: P Fel 6G 127
Blindy La. DH5: Eas L 2J 157
Bloemfontein Pl. DH9: Stly 6H 125
(off Middles Rd.)
Bloom Av. DH9: Stly 3E 124
Bloomfield Ct. SR6: Roker 5H 105
Bloomfield Dr. DH5: E Rain 7D 144
Bloomsbury Ct. NE3: Gos 1D 62
Blossomfield Way DH6: Has 1B 170
Blossom Gro. DH4: S Row 5B 130
Blossom St. DH5: Hett H 5H 145
Blount St. NE6: Walk 7B 64
Blucher Colliery Rd. NE15: Walb 4B 60
Blucher Rd. NE12: Kil 3A 46
NE29: N Shi 2F 67
Blucher Ter. NE15: Walb 4B 60
BLUCHER VILLAGE 4B 60
Blue Anchor Ct. NE1: Newc T 7H 5
Bluebell Cl. DH8: Lead 6A 122
NE9: Low F 2K 99
NE41: Wylam 6J 57
TS27: B Col 2H 183
Bluebell Ct. NE61: Mor 5G 9
Bluebell Dene NE5: West 7G 43
Bluebell Ri. NE61: Mor 1F 15
Bluebell Way NE34: S Shi 1H 87
Blueburn Dr. NE12: Kil 7D 36
Blue Carpet 5G 4 (1G 83)
Blue Coat Bldgs. DH1: Dur 2D 6 (2B 166)
Blue Coat Ct. DH1: Dur 2D 6 (2B 166)
Blue Ho. Bank DH2: P Fel 6B 126
DH9: Crag 6B 126
Blue Ho. Bldgs. DH1: Carr 7G 155
Blue Ho. Bungs. DH6: Has 4C 170
Blue Ho. Ct. NE37: Wash 7F 101
TS27: B Col 2H 183
Blue Ho. La. NE37: Wash 7F 101
SR6: Clead, S'wck 7B 88
Blue Ho. Rd. NE31: Heb 3H 85
Blue Quarries Rd. NE9: Low F 1K 99
Blue Reef Aquarium
Tynemouth 2J 49
Blue Row NE15: Hed W 3D 58
(off Marius Av.)
Blue Sky Way NE31: Heb 5K 85
Blue Star Sq. NE4: Newc T 5C 4 (1E 82)
Blue Top Cotts. NE23: Cra 4B 26
Blumer St. DH4: Hou S 2A 144
BLYTH 1J 23
Blyth Ct. NE15: Lem 6C 60
NE34: S Shi 1J 87
Blyth Crematorium NE24: Cow 1G 23
Blyth Dr. NE61: Hep 7A 16
Blythe Ter. DH3: Bir 4K 113
Blyth Riverside Bus. Pk. NE24: Cow 7F 19
(Cowley Rd.)
NE24: Cow 7D 18
(Loweswater Cl.)
Blyth Rd. NE26: Sea S, Whit B 6E 28
Blyth Spartans AFC 3J 23
Blyth Sports Cen. 2H 23
Blyth Sq. SR5: Sund 4G 103
Blyth St. NE17: C'wl 6A 94
NE25: Sea D 6G 27
SR5: Sund 4G 103
Blythswood NE2: Jes 5G 63
Blyth Ter. NE63: Ash 3C 12
Blyth Valley Retail Pk. NE24: Cow 7F 19
Blyton Av. NE34: S Shi 1F 87
SR2: Ryh 2G 133
Boat Ho's. NE38: Wash 5B 116
Bobby Shafto Cvn. Pk. DH9: Beam 7C 112
Bodium Rd. SR5: Sund 6J 103
Bodlewell Ho. SR1: Sund 1G 119
(off High St. E.)
Bodlewell La. SR1: Sund 1G 119
Bodley Cl. NE3: Ken 7K 43
Bodmin Cl. NE28: W'snd 7J 47
Bodmin Ct. NE9: Low F 5J 99
Bodmin Rd. NE29: N Shi 4C 48
Bodmin Sq. SR5: Sund 3G 103
Bodmin Way NE3: Ken 6B 44
Body Zone Health & Fitness Club 5G 4
Boghouse La. DH9: Stly 6G 111
Bog Houses NE23: E Har 7A 22
Bognor St. SR5: Sund 3F 103
Bog Row DH5: Hett H 7G 145
Bohemia Ter. NE24: Bly 3J 23
Boker La. NE36: E Bol 6H 87
Bolam NE38: Wash 4D 114
Bolam Av. NE24: Bly, Cow 2H 23
NE30: Cull 3G 49
Bolam Bus. Cen. NE23: Cra 2G 25
Bolam Ct. NE15: Thro 4H 59
Bolam Coyne NE6: Byke 6P 5 (1A 84)
Bolam Dr. NE63: Ash 5C 12
Bolam Gdns. NE28: W'snd 2B 66
Bolam Gro. NE30: Cull 3G 49
Bolam Ho. NE4: Newc T 4B 4 (1D 82)
Bolam Pl. NE22: Bed 6A 18
Bolam Rd. NE12: Kil 1A 46
Bolams Bldgs. DH9: Tant 7A 110
Bolam St. NE6: Byke 1A 84
NE8: Gate 6D 82
SR8: Eas C 7D 160
Bolam Way NE6: Byke 6P 5 (1A 84)
NE25: Sea D 7G 27
Bolbec Rd. NE4: Fen 6A 62
Bolburn NE10: Hew 7E 84
BOLDON 6J 87
Boldon Bus. Pk. NE35: Bol C 6E 86
(Brooklands Way)
NE35: Bol C 7E 86
(Didcot Way)
Boldon Business Pk. Lake Nature Reserve 7E 86
Boldon Cl. NE28: W'snd 7H 47
BOLDON COLLIERY 5E 86
Boldon Colliery Workshops
NE35: Bol C 5F 87
Boldon Dr. NE36: W Bol 7F 87
Boldon Gdns. NE9: Wrek 4A 100
Boldon Ho. DH1: P Me 2A 154
Boldon La. NE33: S Shi 7H 67
NE34: S Shi 7H 67
(not continuous)
NE36: E Bol 5J 87
SR6: Clead 5A 88
Boldon Lea NE35: Bol C 6H 87
Bolingbroke Rd. NE29: N Shi 6D 48
Bolingbroke St. NE6: Heat 3M 5 (7J 63)
NE33: S Shi 3K 67
Bollihope Dr. SR3: Sund 6D 118
Bolsover St. NE63: Ash 4B 12
Bolsover Ter. NE61: Peg 3B 10
NE63: Ash 4B 12
Bolton Cl. DH1: Dur 4A 154
Bolton's Bungs. NE17: C'wl 7K 93
BOMARSUND 3A 18
Bonaventure DH4: Pen 1C 130
Bonchester Cl. NE22: Bed 6H 17
Bonchester Ct. NE28: W'snd 7J 47
Bonchester Pl. NE23: Cra 2B 26
Bond Cl. SR5: Monkw 6E 104
Bond Ct. NE4: Benw 1A 82
Bondene Av. NE10: Hew 6C 84
Bondene Av. W. NE10: Fell 6B 84
Bondene Way NE23: Cra 7K 21
Bondfield Cl. NE28: W'snd 2K 65
Bondfield Gdns. NE10: Ward 6E 84
Bondgate Cl. NE46: Hex 3D 70
Bondgate Ct. NE46: Hex 2D 70
Bondicarr Pl. NE5: Fen 4K 61
Bondicar Ter. NE24: Bly 2H 23
Bond St. NE4: Benw 1K 81
Bone La. DH9: Dip 7H 109
Bonemill La. NE38: Wash 1C 128
Bonnar Ct. NE31: Heb 7K 65
Bonner's Fld. SR6: Monkw 1J 7 (7F 105)
Bonners Raft SR6: Monkw 1K 7 (7F 105)
Bonnington Way NE5: Blak 3H 61
Bonnivard Gdns. NE23: Seg 2E 36
Bonsall Ct. NE34: S Shi 1K 87
Booth Ct. NE27: Shir 2J 47
Booths Rd. NE63: Ash 3J 11
Booth St. NE10: Fell 6B 84
SR4: Sund 2C 118
Bootle St. SR5: Sund 4G 103
Bordeaux Cl. SR3: Silk 3A 132
Border Rd. NE28: W'snd 4F 65
Boreham Cl. NE28: W'snd 7H 47
Borehole Cotts. NE61: Mor 6H 9
Borehole La. NE61: Mor 6G 9
Borodin Av. SR5: Sund 4F 103
Borough & Scotch Gills Nature Reserve 7C 8
Borough Ct. SR1: Sund 1G 119
(off Coronation St.)
Borough Rd. NE29: N Shi 7G 49
NE32: Jar 7B 66
NE34: S Shi 1B 88
SR1: Sund 4K 7 (2F 119)
Borrowdale DH3: Bir 7B 114
DH8: Lead 5B 122
NE16: Whi 7K 81
NE37: Wash 7G 101
Borrowdale Av. NE6: Walk 6D 64
NE24: Cow 1E 22
SR6: Seab 2E 104
Borrowdale Cl. NE36: E Bol 6J 87
Borrowdale Cres. DH4: Pen 1A 130
NE21: Winl 6B 80
Borrowdale Dr. DH1: Carr 7G 155
Borrowdale Gdns. NE9: Low F 4K 99
Borrowdale Ho. NE34: S Shi 1J 87
Borrowdale St. DH5: Hett H 1G 157
Boscobel Cl. NE12: Longb 6H 45
Boscombe Dr. NE28: W'snd 1G 65
Boste Cres. DH1: Dur 7K 153
Boston Av. NE7: Longb 7K 45
NE38: Wash 2G 115
(not continuous)
Boston Cl. NE28: W'snd 7H 47
Boston Ct. NE12: Longb 4D 46
Boston Cres. SR5: Sund 3E 102
Boston St. SR5: Sund 3E 102
SR8: Eas C 7D 160
Boswell Av. NE34: S Shi 3H 87
Bosworth NE12: Kil 7B 36
Bosworth Gdns. NE6: Heat 3A 64
BOTHAL 5D 10
Bothal Av. NE62: Chop 1G 17
Bothal Bank NE61: Both 5D 10
Bothal Cl. NE24: Bly 2G 23
NE61: Peg 4A 10
Bothal Cotts. NE63: Ash 3H 11
BOTHALHAUGH 6D 10
Bothal Rd. NE61: Peg 4B 10
Bothal St. NE6: Byke 7B 64
Bothal Ter. NE62: Stake 7K 11
NE63: Ash 3H 11
Botham Ho. NE29: N Shi 2D 66
Bottle Bank NE8: Gate 8H 5 (2G 83)
Bottlehouse St. NE6: Byke 2A 84
Bottle Works Rd. SR7: S'hm 3C 148
Boulby Cl. SR3: Tuns 2E 132
Boulevard, The NE11: Dun 5J 81
NE12: Longb 6J 45
Boulmer Av. NE23: Cra 7K 21
Boulmer Cl. NE3: Fawd 4B 44
Boulmer Ct. DH2: Ches S 7A 128
Boulmer Gdns. NE13: W Op 5D 34
Boulmer Lea SR7: S'hm 2A 148
Boulsworth Rd. NE29: N Shi 3E 48
Boult Ter. DH4: S Row 3B 130
Boundary Cl. DH7: Ush M 3C 164
Boundary Dr. NE61: Mor 1G 15
Boundary Gdns. NE7: H Hea 2J 63
BOUNDARY HOUSES 5A 130
Boundary Ho's. DH4: S Row 4K 129
Boundary La. DH8: Shot B, W'stll 5A 106
Boundary Mill Stores NE27: Shir 2K 47
Boundary St. SR5: S'wck 5E 104
Boundary Way NE26: Sea S 4D 28
Bourdon Ho. SR1: Sund 5K 7 (2F 119)
Bourne Av. NE4: Fen 6A 62
Bourne Ct. DH9: Stly 2G 125
(not continuous)
Bournemouth Ct. NE28: W'snd 7H 47
Bournemouth Dr. SR7: Dalt D 4H 147
Bournemouth Gdns. NE5: West 2F 61
NE26: Whit B 5F 39
Bournemouth Pde. NE31: Heb 3A 86
(not continuous)
Bournemouth Rd. NE29: N Shi 7C 48
Bourne St. SR8: Eas C 7D 160
Bourne Ter. DH9: Ann P 5K 123
Bourn Lea DH4: S Row 4A 130
BOURNMOOR 6J 129
Bournmoor DH4: Bour 6J 129
Bourtree Cl. NE28: W'snd 1G 65
Bowbank Cl. SR3: Sund 6D 118
BOWBURN 5H 177
Bowburn Av. SR5: Sund 5J 103
Bowburn Cl. NE10: Ward 7G 85
Bowburn Nth. Ind. Est. DH6: Bowb 4G 177
Bowburn Sth. Ind. Est. DH6: Bowb 5G 177
Bowden Cl. NE13: Haz 2A 44
Bowden Ct. DH7: Mead 3G 175
Bowden Pl. DH7: Mead 3G 175
Bower, The NE32: Jar 6B 86
Bower Ct. DH6: Coxh 7K 177
Bower St. SR6: Ful 3F 105
Bowes Av. DH5: Eas L 2H 157
SR7: Dalt D 4G 147
Bowes Cl. NE16: Sun 5H 97
Bowes Ct. DH1: Dur 4B 154
NE3: Gos 7G 45
NE22: Bed 4J 17
NE24: Bly 2J 23
Bowes Cres. NE16: Burn 7D 96
Bowes Gdns. NE9: Spri 5D 100
Bowes Ho. SR3: E Her 2K 131
(off Castle Grn.)
Bowes Lea DH4: S Row 5K 129
Bowes Lyon Cl. NE39: Row G 7H 95
Bowes Lyon Ct. NE9: Low F 6H 83
Bowes Manor Equestrian Cen. 1B 114
Bowes Offices DH3: Lam P 4J 129
Bowes Railway Cen. 4C 100
Bowes St. NE3: Gos 7G 45
NE24: Bly 2H 23
(not continuous)
Bowes Ter. DH9: Dip 1H 123
Bowes Vw. DH3: Bir 2B 114
Bowesville NE16: Burn 3B 110
Bowes Wlk. NE12: Longb 5A 46
Bowfell Av. NE5: Ken 1K 61
Bowfell Cl. NE5: Ken 2K 61
Bowfell Gdns. NE62: Stake 7J 11
Bowfield Av. NE3: Gos 3E 44
Bowick Courtyard NE8: Gate 4D 82
Bowland Cres. NE21: Blay 4C 80
Bowland Ter. NE21: Blay 3C 80
Bow La. DH1: Dur 4C 6 (3A 166)
Bowler's Hill NE43: Mic 7B 76
Bowlynn Cl. SR3: Silk 3A 132
Bowman Dr. NE23: Dud 3K 35
NE46: Hex 1B 70
Bowman Pl. NE33: S Shi 4J 67
Bowman Sq. NE63: Ash 5H 11
Bowman St. SR6: Whit 5H 89
Bowmont Dr. DH9: Tan L 1C 124
NE23: Cra 2B 26
Bowmont Ho. NE13: Haz 2B 44
Bowmont Wlk. DH2: Ches S 1J 141
Bowness Av. NE28: W'snd 6J 47
Bowness Cl. NE36: E Bol 7J 87
SR8: Pet 5C 172
Bowness Pl. NE9: Low F 3K 99
Bowness Rd. NE5: Den M 4G 61
NE16: Whi 7J 81
Bowness St. SR5: Sund 3G 103
Bowness Ter. NE28: W'snd 7J 47
Bowood Cl. SR2: Ryh 3F 133
Bowsden Ct. NE3: Gos 7G 45
Bowsden Ter. NE3: Gos 7G 45
Bow St. DH6: Bowb 4H 177
DH6: Thor 1K 179
Bow St. E. DH6: Thor 1K 179
Bow St. W. DH6: Thor 1K 179
Bowtrees SR2: Sund 5F 119
Boxlaw NE9: Low F 2A 100
Boyd Cres. NE28: W'snd 3G 65
Boyd Rd. NE28: W'snd 3G 65
Boyd St. DH1: Dur 5D 6 (4B 166)
DH8: Cons 1J 135
NE2: Newc T 3K 5 (7H 63)
NE15: Newb 5J 59
SR8: Eas C 7D 160
Boyd Ter. DH9: Stly 4E 124
NE5: West 2F 61
NE15: Walb 4B 60
Boyne Ct. DH7: Lang M 7F 165
NE24: Bly 1J 23
Boyne Gdns. NE27: Shir 1J 47
Boyne Ter. NE37: Wash 7G 101
Boyntons DH2: Nett 6H 141
Boystones Ct. NE37: Wash 2F 115
Brabant Gdns. SR5: Sund 6H 103
Brabourne Gdns. NE29: N Shi 3F 49
Brabourne St. NE34: S Shi 7J 67
Bracken Av. NE28: W'snd 7G 47
Brackenbeds Cl. DH2: Pelt 3G 127
Brackenbeds La. DH2: Ous, Pelt 2H 127
Brackenburn Cl. DH4: Hou S 1C 144
Brackenbury DH1: Dur 7J 153
Bracken Cl. DH9: Stly 3E 124
NE13: Din 5H 33
Bracken Ct. DH7: Ush M 1C 164
(not continuous)
Brackendale Ct. TS28: Sta T 7H 181
Brackendale Rd. DH1: Carr 1H 167
Brackendene Dr. NE9: Low F 2G 99
Brackendene Pk. NE9: Low F 2G 99
Bracken Dr. NE11: Dun 1B 98
Bracken Fld. Rd. DH1: Dur 6K 153
Brackenfield Rd. NE3: Gos 1D 62
Bracken Hill SR8: Pet 7H 171
Brackenhill Av. DH6: Shot C 6G 171
Bracken Hill Bus. Pk. SR8: Pet 7H 171
Brackenlaw NE9: Low F 3A 100
Brackenpeth M. NE3: Gos 3D 44
Bracken Pl. NE4: Fen 6K 61
Bracken Ridge NE61: Mor 5C 8
Brackenridge DH6: Shot C 6F 171
NE16: Burn 2J 109
Brackenrigg DH8: Lead 5B 122
Brackenside NE3: Gos 3E 44
Bracken Way NE40: Craw 3E 78
Brackenway NE37: Wash 7F 101
Brackenwood Gro. SR2: Sund 6E 118
Brackley NE37: Wash 6J 101
Brackley Gro. NE29: N Shi 1D 66
Bracknell Cl. SR3: Tuns 1E 132
Bracknell Gdns. NE5: Cha P 4B 60
Brack Ter. NE10: Bill Q 4F 85
Bradbury Cl. DH9: Tan L 1C 124
NE10: Ward 7G 85
Bradbury Ct. NE20: Pon 5K 31
(off Thornhill Rd.)
NE25: New Hart 4H 27
Bradbury Pl. NE25: New Hart 4H 27
Braddyll Sq. DH6: S Het 3B 158
Bradford Av. NE28: W'snd 7H 47
SR5: Sund 3G 103
Bradford Cres. DH1: Dur 1D 166
Bradley Av. DH5: Hou S 4E 144
NE34: S Shi 7C 68
Bradley Bungs. DH8: Lead 3A 122
Bradley Cl. DH2: Ous 6F 113
Bradley Cotts. DH8: Lead 3A 122
Bradley Fell La. NE41: Wylam 4A 78
Bradley Fell Rd. NE40: G'sde 6J 77
NE42: Pru 6J 77
Bradley Gdns. NE41: Wylam 2B 78
Bradley Lodge Dr. DH9: Dip 1J 123
Bradley Rd. NE42: Pru 3H 77
Bradley St. DH8: Lead 5A 122
SR8: Eas C 7D 160
Bradley Ter. DH5: Eas L 2J 157
DH9: Dip 2J 123
Bradley Vw. NE40: Craw 3D 78
Bradley Workshops Ind. Est.
DH8: Lead 5K 121
Bradman Dr. DH3: Ches S 7C 128
Bradman Sq. SR5: Sund 3G 103
Bradman St. SR5: Sund 3G 103
Bradshaw Sq. SR5: Sund 3G 103
Bradshaw St. SR5: Sund 4G 103
Bradwell Rd. NE3: Ken 7A 44
Bradwell Way DH4: S Row 4C 130
Brady & Martin Ct.
NE1: Newc T 3G 4 (7G 63)
Brady Sq. NE38: Wash 4K 115
Brady St. SR4: Sund 1B 118
Brae, The SR2: Sund 2D 118
Braebridge Pl. NE3: Ken 2B 62
Braeburn Ct. NE15: Walb 3A 60
Braefell Ct. NE37: Wash 2F 115
Braemar Ct. DH8: B'hill 6E 120
NE10: Bill Q 4F 85
Braemar Dr. NE34: S Shi 5C 68
Braemar Gdns. NE25: Monks 7C 38
SR3: E Her 3J 131
SR3: Sund 5D 118
Braemar Ter. SR8: Hord 6F 173

Braes, The DH8: C'sde . . . 1E **134**
Braeside DH7: B'hpe . . . 6D **138**
DH7: Edm . . . 3D **140**
NE11: Dun . . . 7B **82**
SR2: Sund . . . 4D **118**
Braeside Cl. NE30: Cull . . . 1G **49**
Braeside Ter. NE26: Whit B . . . 7J **39**
Brahman Av. NE29: N Shi . . . 1D **66**
Braidwood M. DH9: Stly . . . 3E **124**
Braintree Gdns. NE3: Ken . . . 1B **62**
Braithwaite Rd. SR8: Pet . . . 6D **172**
Brakespeare Pl. SR8: Pet . . . 7C **172**
Brama Teams Ind. Pk. NE8: Gate . . . 5D **82**
Bramble Cl. NE24: News . . . 5G **23**
Bramble Ct. NE34: S Shi . . . 6D **68**
Bramble Dykes NE15: Benw . . . 1H **81**
Bramblelaw NE9: Low F . . . 3A **100**
Brambles, The DH3: Bir . . . 2B **114**
NE25: New Hart . . . 5G **27**
NE40: Ryton . . . 1F **79**
Brambling Lea NE22: Bed . . . 6A **18**
Bramhall Dr. NE38: Wash . . . 1E **128**
Bramham Ct. NE34: S Shi . . . 1A **88**
Bramhope Grn. NE9: Low F . . . 5K **99**
Bramley Cl. SR4: Sund . . . 5G **117**
Bramley Ct. NE7: H Hea . . . 2C **64**
Brampton Av. NE6: Walk . . . 2D **84**
Brampton Ct. NE23: Cra . . . 2A **26**
SR8: Eas . . . 1K **171**
Brampton Gdns. NE9: Low F . . . 4J **99**
NE15: Thro . . . 3H **59**
NE28: W'snd . . . 1A **66**
Brampton Pl. NE29: N Shi . . . 7D **48**
Brampton Rd. NE34: S Shi . . . 1G **87**
Bramwell Ct. NE3: Gos . . . 7F **45**
NE8: Gate . . . 5E **82**
Bramwell Rd. SR2: Sund . . . 3G **119**
Bramwell Ter. DH8: Cons . . . 5J **121**
BRANCEPETH . . . 4A **174**
Brancepeth Av. DH4: Hou S . . . 1A **144**
NE4: Benw . . . 2A **82**
Brancepeth Castle . . . 5A **174**
Brancepeth Chare SR8: Pet . . . 2K **181**
Brancepeth Cl. DH1: Dur . . . 5B **154**
DH7: Ush M . . . 3E **164**
NE15: Lem . . . 6C **60**
Brancepeth Rd. NE31: Heb . . . 6K **65**
NE38: Wash . . . 4E **114**
Brancepeth Ter. NE32: Jar . . . 3B **86**
Brancepeth Vw. DH7: B'don . . . 2B **174**
BRANCH END . . . 7K **75**
Branch End Ter. NE43: Pains . . . 7K **75**
Branch St. NE21: Winl . . . 5B **80**
Brand Av. NE4: Fen . . . 6A **62**
Brandling Ct. DH6: Shot C . . . 7F **171**
NE2: Jes . . . 1J **5** (5H **63**)
NE10: Fell . . . 5B 84
(off John Hodgson Cl.)
NE29: N Shi . . . 2F **67**
NE34: S Shi . . . 2C **88**
Brandling Dr. NE3: Gos . . . 3F **45**
Brandling La. *NE10: Fell . . . 5B 84*
(off Carlisle St.)
Brandling M. NE3: Gos . . . 3F **45**
Brandling Pk. NE2: Jes . . . 1F **4** (5F **63**)
Brandling Pl. Sth. NE2: Jes . . . 1F **4** (5G **63**)
Brandling St. NE8: Gate . . . 8J **5** (2G **83**)
SR6: Roker . . . 5G **105**
(not continuous)
Brandling St. Sth. SR6: Roker . . . 6G **105**
Brandlings Way SR8: Pet . . . 5B **172**
Brandling Ter. NE30: N Shi . . . 6H **49**
BRANDLING VILLAGE . . . 1G **4** (5G **63**)
BRANDON . . . 1D **174**
Brandon Av. NE27: Shir . . . 1J **47**
Brandon Cl. DH2: Ches S . . . 1H **141**
DH4: Hou S . . . 3D **144**
NE21: Winl . . . 6A **80**
NE24: Cow . . . 1F **23**
Brandon Gdns. NE9: Wrek . . . 4B **100**
Brandon Gro. NE2: Newc T . . . 1K **5** (6H **63**)
Brandon Ho. DH7: B'don . . . 2C **174**
Brandon La. DH7: B'don, Lang M . . . 1C **174**
DH7: Bran . . . 7F **163**
DL15: Crook . . . 7F **163**
Brandon Rd. DH7: Esh W . . . 4E **162**
NE3: Fawd . . . 6B **44**
NE29: N Shi . . . 6D **48**
Brandon Vw. DH7: Bro . . . 4E **164**
BRANDON VILLAGE . . . 7C **164**
Brandy La. NE37: Wash . . . 1F **115**
Brandywell NE10: Hew . . . 1D **100**
Brannen St. NE29: N Shi . . . 7G **49**
Bransdale DH4: Pen . . . 1J **129**
Bransdale Av. SR6: Seab . . . 7G **89**
Branston St. SR5: S'wck . . . 5D **104**
Branton Av. NE31: Heb . . . 3H **85**
Brantwood DH2: Ches S . . . 6H **127**
Brantwood Av. NE25: Monks . . . 7D **38**
Brantwood Ct. NE21: Blay . . . 4D **80**
Branxton Cres. NE6: Walk . . . 1D **84**
BRASSIDE . . . 3D **154**
Brass Thill DH1: Dur . . . 3A **6** (3K **165**)
Brass Thill Way NE33: S Shi . . . 3A **68**
(not continuous)
Braunespath Est. DH7: New B . . . 4B **164**
Bray Cl. NE28: W'snd . . . 7H **47**
Braydon Dr. NE29: N Shi . . . 2E **66**
Brayside NE32: Jar . . . 5D **86**
Breakespear Cl. DH1: Dur . . . 2J **165**
Breakneck Stairs NE1: Newc T . . . 8F **4**
Breamish Dr. NE38: Wash . . . 7D **114**
Breamish Ho. NE1: Newc T . . . 5L **5** (1J **83**)
Breamish Quays
NE1: Newc T . . . 5L **5** (1J **83**)
Breamish St. NE1: Newc T . . . 5K **5** (1J **83**)
NE32: Jar . . . 1A **86**
Brearley Way NE10: Fell . . . 6A **84**
Breckenbeds Rd. NE9: Low F . . . 3G **99**
Brecken Ct. NE9: Low F . . . 3G **99**
Brecken Way DH7: Mead . . . 1E **174**
Brecon Cl. NE5: Blak . . . 1H **61**
NE63: N Sea . . . 6C **12**
SR8: Pet . . . 7K **171**
Brecon Pl. DH2: Ous . . . 1H **127**
Brecon Rd. DH1: Dur . . . 4C **154**
Bredon Cl. NE38: Wash . . . 5F **115**
Brendale Av. NE5: West . . . 2D **60**
Brendon Pl. SR8: Pet . . . 5K **171**
BRENKLEY . . . 7A **24**
Brenkley Av. NE27: Shir . . . 2J **47**
Brenkley Cl. NE13: Din . . . 4H **33**
Brenkley Ct. NE13: Sea B . . . 3D **34**
Brenkley La. NE13: Sea B . . . 1J **33**
Brenkley Way NE13: Sea B . . . 2D **34**
Brenlynn Cl. SR3: Silk . . . 3A **132**
Brennan Cl. NE15: Benw . . . 7H **61**
NE63: N Sea . . . 4E **12**
Brentford Av. SR5: Sund . . . 4G **103**
(not continuous)
Brentford Ho. SR5: Sund . . . 4G **103**
Brentford Sq. SR5: Sund . . . 4G **103**
Brentwood Av. NE2: Jes . . . 3F **63**
NE64: Newb S . . . 2H **13**
Brentwood Cl. NE25: Sea D . . . 1J **37**
Brentwood Ct. DH9: Stly . . . 3J **125**
Brentwood Gdns. NE2: Jes . . . 3F **63**
NE16: Whi . . . 2H **97**
SR3: Sund . . . 5D **118**
Brentwood Gro. NE28: W'snd . . . 4H **65**
Brentwood M. *NE2: Jes . . . 4G 63*
(off Brentwood Av.)
Brentwood Pl. NE33: S Shi . . . 3K **67**
Brentwood Rd. DH4: S Row . . . 4A **130**
Brettanby Gdns. NE40: Ryton . . . 7G **59**
Brettanby Rd. NE10: Wind N . . . 7A **84**
Brett Cl. NE7: H Hea . . . 2B **64**
Brettonby Av. NE43: Pains . . . 7K **75**
Bretton Cl. NE38: Wash . . . 5B **116**
Bretton Gdns. NE7: H Hea . . . 3A **64**
Brewers La. NE29: N Shi . . . 3C **66**
Brewery Bank NE16: Swa . . . 5G **81**
Brewery Bond NE29: N Shi . . . 1H **67**
Brewery La. NE10: Fell . . . 4B **84**
NE16: Swa . . . 5G 81
(off Brewery Bank)
NE20: Pon . . . 5J **31**
NE33: S Shi . . . 3H **67**
Brewery Sq. DH9: Stly . . . 2F **125**
Brewery Stables *NE4: Newc T . . . 6C 4*
(off Blandford Sq.)
Brewery St. *NE24: Bly . . . 1K 23*
(off Sussex St.)
Brewery Yd. NE64: Newb S . . . 3H **13**
Brewhouse Bank NE30: N Shi . . . 6J **49**
Brian Ct. NE26: Whit B . . . 6F **39**
Briar Av. DH4: Hou S . . . 2D **144**
DH7: B'don . . . 2C **174**
NE26: Whit B . . . 4F **39**
Briar Bank DH1: P Me . . . 3K **153**
Briar Cl. DH2: Kim . . . 7H **141**
DH4: Hou S . . . 1J **143**
DH4: S Row . . . 5K **129**
NE21: Winl . . . 4A **80**
NE28: W'snd . . . 7G **47**
NE62: Sco G . . . 3G **17**
Briar Dale DH8: Cons . . . 3K **135**
Briardale NE13: Din . . . 4H **33**
NE22: Bed . . . 7G **17**
Briardale Rd. NE24: Cow . . . 2E **22**
Briardene DH1: Dur . . . 4A **6** (3K **165**)
DH7: Esh W . . . 3C **162**
DH7: Lan . . . 7J **137**
NE16: Burn . . . 2J **109**
NE63: Ash . . . 5K **11**
Briardene Cl. SR3: E Her . . . 3J **131**
Briardene Cres. NE3: Ken . . . 2C **62**
Briardene Dr. NE10: Ward . . . 6H **85**
Briardene Way SR8: Eas C . . . 7C **160**
Briar Edge NE12: Longb . . . 4B **46**
Briarfield NE38: Wash . . . 7H **115**
Briarfield Rd. NE3: Gos . . . 1D **62**
Briar Glen SR7: Mur . . . 7B **146**
Briarhill DH2: Ches S . . . 4J **127**
Briar La. NE15: Thro . . . 4J **59**
Briar Lea DH4: S Row . . . 5K **129**
DH7: Wit G . . . 2D **152**
Briarlea NE61: Hep . . . 4A **16**
Briar M. DH8: B'hill . . . 4F **121**
Briar Pl. NE15: Scot . . . 1G **81**
Briar Rd. DH1: Carr . . . 7H **155**
NE39: Row G . . . 5H **95**
Briars, The SR5: Sund . . . 6H **103**
Briarside DH8: B'hill . . . 4F **121**
NE5: West . . . 2G **61**
Briarsyde NE12: Longb . . . 6C **46**
Briarsyde Cl. NE16: Whi . . . 2E **96**
Briar Ter. NE16: Burn . . . 2C **110**
Briar Va. NE25: Monks . . . 1D **48**
Briarwood NE23: Dud . . . 3K **35**
Briarwood Av. DH2: P Fel . . . 6G **127**
NE3: Gos . . . 6G **45**
Briarwood Cres. NE6: Walk . . . 4D **64**
NE11: Dun . . . 6B **82**
Briarwood Rd. NE24: Bly . . . 3K **23**
Briarwood St. DH4: Hou S . . . 1J **143**
Briary, The DH8: Shot B . . . 3E **120**
NE15: Thro . . . 3G **59**
Briary Gdns. DH8: Shot B . . . 3E **120**
Brick Gth. DH5: Eas L . . . 3H **157**
Brick Row SR2: Ryh . . . 2G **133**
Bridekirk NE37: Wash . . . 1G **115**
(not continuous)
Bridge, The DH4: New H . . . 3D **130**
Bridge App. SR5: S'wck . . . 6C **104**
Bridge Cotts. NE23: Dud . . . 3K **35**
Bridge Ct. DH6: Shad . . . 5E **168**
NE1: Newc T . . . 8F **4** (2F **83**)
Bridge Cres. SR1: Sund . . . 2J **7** (1F **119**)
BRIDGE END . . . 7E **50**
Bridge End DH3: Ches S . . . 5A **128**
DH6: Coxh . . . 7K **177**
Bridge End Ind. Est.
NE46: B End . . . 7E **50**
BRIDGEHILL . . . 5E **120**
Bridgehill Farm Ct.
DH8: B'hill . . . 6E **120**
Bridge Ho. SR1: Sund . . . 3J **7**
Bridge Island DH8: Shot B . . . 3E **120**
Bridgemere Dr. DH1: Dur . . . 5J **153**
Bridge Pk. NE3: Gos . . . 4E **44**
Bridge Rd. DH6: Shot C . . . 7E **170**
Bridge Rd. Bungs.
DH6: Shot C . . . 7F **171**
Bridge Rd. Sth. NE29: N Shi . . . 1E **66**
Bridges, The *SR1: Sund . . . 3H 7*
(off West St.)
Bridges Shop. Cen., The
SR1: Sund . . . 4H **7** (2E **118**)
Bridge St. DH1: Dur . . . 2A **6** (2K **165**)
DH7: Lang P . . . 4J **151**
DH8: B'hill . . . 6F **121**
DH9: Stly . . . 5E **124**
NE8: Gate . . . 8H **5** (2G **83**)
NE13: Sea B . . . 3D **34**
NE21: Blay . . . 2B **80**
NE24: Bly . . . 1J **23**
(not continuous)
NE61: Mor . . . 7F **9**
NE64: Newb S . . . 3J **13**
SR1: Sund . . . 3J **7** (1F **119**)
Bridges Vw. NE8: Gate . . . 4F **83**
Bridge Ter. NE22: Bed . . . 5A **18**
NE27: Shir . . . 7K **37**
NE62: Stake . . . 7K **11**
Bridget Gdns. NE13: Haz . . . 3A **44**
Bridge Vw. NE1: Newc T . . . 5J **5** (1H **83**)
Bridgewater Cl. NE15: Lem . . . 6C **60**
NE28: W'snd . . . 1G **65**
Bridgewater Rd. NE37: Wash . . . 1J **115**
Bridge Way DH7: Lang P . . . 5K **151**
Bridle, The NE27: Mur . . . 2B **48**
Bridle Path NE3: Gos . . . 5G **45**
NE36: E Bol . . . 7J **87**
SR3: E Her . . . 1J **131**
Bridle Way DH5: Hou S . . . 3D **144**
Bridlington Av. NE9: Low F . . . 4H **99**
Bridlington Cl. NE28: W'snd . . . 7H **47**
Bridlington Pde. NE31: Heb . . . 3A **86**
Bridport Rd. NE29: N Shi . . . 3D **48**
Brier Av. SR8: Hord . . . 4D **172**
Brierdene Cl. NE26: Whit B . . . 3F **39**
Brierdene Ct. NE26: Whit B . . . 3E **38**
Brierdene Cres. NE26: Whit B . . . 3E **38**
Brierdene Rd. NE26: Whit B . . . 2F **39**
Brierdene Vw. NE26: Whit B . . . 3E **38**
Brierfield Gro. SR4: Sund . . . 4K **117**
Brierley Cl. NE24: Cow . . . 2F **23**
Brierley Rd. NE24: Cow . . . 2F **23**
Briermede Av. NE9: Low F . . . 3H **99**
Briermede Pk. NE9: Low F . . . 3H **99**
Brierville DH1: Dur . . . 4A **6** (3K **165**)
Brieryside NE5: Fen . . . 4K **61**
Briery Va. Cl. SR2: Sund . . . 7H **7** (3E **118**)
Briery Va. Rd. SR2: Sund . . . 7H **7** (3E **118**)
Brigham Av. NE3: Ken . . . 2A **62**
Brigham Pl. NE33: S Shi . . . 2J **67**
Brightlea DH3: Bir . . . 3C **114**
Brightman Rd. NE29: N Shi . . . 6G **49**
Brighton Cl. NE28: W'snd . . . 7J **47**
Brighton Gdns. NE8: Gate . . . 7G **83**
Brighton Gro. NE4: Fen . . . 2A **4** (7C **62**)
NE26: Whit B . . . 5F **39**
NE29: N Shi . . . 6F **49**
Brighton Pde. NE31: Heb . . . 3A **86**
Brighton Rd. NE8: Gate . . . 5F **83**
Brighton Ter. DH6: S Hil . . . 3D **168**
Bright St. DH8: Cons . . . 5H **121**
NE33: S Shi . . . 3K **67**
SR6: Roker . . . 6F **105**
Brignall Cl. DH3: Gt Lum . . . 3F **143**
Brignall Gdns. NE15: Den M . . . 6G **61**
Brignall Ri. SR3: Sund . . . 6D **118**
Brigside Cotts. NE13: Sea B . . . 3E **34**
(not continuous)
Brindley Rd. NE37: Wash . . . 2H **115**
SR8: Pet . . . 6H **171**
Brinkburn DH2: Ches S . . . 6J **127**
NE38: Wash . . . 6J **115**
Brinkburn Av. NE3: Gos . . . 6D **44**
NE8: Gate . . . 6G **83**
NE16: Swa . . . 6G **81**
NE23: Cra . . . 4A **26**
NE24: Bly . . . 3K **23**
Brinkburn Cl. NE6: Byke . . . 4P **5** (1K **83**)
NE21: Winl . . . 6A **80**
Brinkburn Ct. NE6: Byke . . . 4P **5**
NE30: N Shi . . . 6H **49**
Brinkburn Cres. DH4: Hou S . . . 7C **130**
NE63: Ash . . . 3D **12**
Brinkburn Gdns. NE62: Stake . . . 7H **11**
Brinkburn La. NE6: Byke . . . 4P **5**
Brinkburn Pl. NE6: Byke . . . 4P **5** (7K **63**)
Brinkburn Sq. NE6: Byke . . . 5P **5** (1K **83**)
Brinkburn St. NE6: Byke . . . 3P **5** (7K **63**)
NE28: W'snd . . . 4C **66**
NE34: S Shi . . . 1H **87**
SR4: Sund . . . 3C **118**
Brinkburn St. Sth. NE6: Byke . . . 6P **5** (1K **83**)
Brisbane Av. NE34: S Shi . . . 3F **87**
Brisbane Ct. NE8: Gate . . . 10H **5** (3G **83**)
Brisbane St. SR5: Sund . . . 4G **103**
Brislee Av. NE30: Tyne . . . 5J **49**
(not continuous)
Brislee Gdns. NE3: Ken . . . 1A **62**
Bristlecone SR3: Dox P . . . 4A **132**
Bristol Av. NE37: Wash . . . 7F **101**
SR5: Sund . . . 4F **103**
Bristol Dr. NE28: W'snd . . . 7H **47**
Bristol St. NE25: New Hart . . . 5G **27**
Bristol Ter. NE4: Elsw . . . 2C **82**
Bristol Wlk. NE25: New Hart . . . 4H **27**
Bristol Way NE32: Jar . . . 5C **86**
Britannia Ct. NE4: Elsw . . . 2C **82**
Britannia Pl. NE4: Elsw . . . 1C **82**
Britannia Rd. SR3: New S . . . 2C **132**
Britannia Ter. DH4: Hou S . . . 2A **144**
British Legion Ho's. *NE42: Pru . . . 4F 77*
(off South Rd.)
Briton Ter. DH8: Cons . . . 6G **121**
Britten Cl. DH9: Stly . . . 4G **125**
Brixham Av. NE9: Low F . . . 4H **99**
Brixham Cl. SR7: Dalt D . . . 4J **147**
Brixham Cres. NE32: Jar . . . 1D **86**
Brixham Gdns. SR3: Sund . . . 5D **118**
Broadacre NE10: Ward . . . 6F **85**
Broad Ash NE2: Jes . . . 1L **5** (5J **63**)
Broadbank NE10: Ward . . . 6F **85**
Broad Chare NE1: Newc T . . . 6H **5** (2G **83**)
(not continuous)
Broad Cl., The SR8: Pet . . . 6B **172**
Broadfield Pl. NE34: S Shi . . . 1K **87**
Broadfield Wlk. NE5: West . . . 1G **61**
Broad Garth NE1: Newc T . . . 7H **5** (2G **83**)
Broadgate Rd. DH7: Esh . . . 1J **163**
Broadgates NE46: Hex . . . 2D **70**
Broad Landing NE33: S Shi . . . 2H **67**
Broadlands SR6: Clead . . . 7C **88**
Broad Law NE23: Dud . . . 1J **35**
Broadlea NE10: Ward . . . 6F **85**
Broadmayne Av. SR4: Sund . . . 4K **117**
Broadmayne Gdns. SR4: Sund . . . 4K **117**
Broad Mdws. NE3: Ken . . . 2C **62**
SR2: Sund . . . 7F **7** (4D **118**)
Broadmeadows DH6: Bowb . . . 5J **177**
NE38: Wash . . . 6J **115**
SR3: E Her . . . 3H **131**
Broadmeadows Cl. NE16: Swa . . . 5G **81**
Broadmead Way NE15: Scot . . . 1F **81**
Broadmires Ter. DH2: Nett . . . 6H **141**
Broadoak NE10: Ward . . . 5F **85**
Broadoak Dr. DH7: Lan . . . 7J **137**
Broadoak M. NE17: Ham . . . 3H **107**
Broadoaks SR7: Mur . . . 1C **158**
Broadoak Ter. NE17: C'wl . . . 6K **93**
Broadpark NE10: Ward . . . 6F **85**
Broadpool Grn. NE16: Whi . . . 1J **97**
Broadpool Ter. NE16: Whi . . . 1J **97**
(Broom Ter.)
NE16: Whi . . . 1J **97**
(Southfield Ter.)
Broad Rd. TS27: B Col . . . 3K **183**
Broadsheath Ter. SR5: S'wck . . . 6B **104**
(not continuous)
Broadside NE10: Ward . . . 6F **85**
Broadstairs Ct. SR4: Sund . . . 4K **117**
Broadstone Gro. NE5: Cha P . . . 4C **60**
Broadstone Way NE28: W'snd . . . 1G **65**
Broadviews DH3: Gt Lum . . . 2E **142**
Broadview Vs. DH6: S'burn . . . 3A **168**
Broadwater NE10: Ward . . . 5F **85**
Broadway DH3: Ches S . . . 4B **128**
DH8: Cons . . . 3K **135**
NE9: Low F . . . 1K **99**
NE15: Lem . . . 6D **60**
NE16: Whi . . . 2F **97**
NE20: Darr H . . . 1G **41**
NE24: Bly . . . 3J **23**
NE62: Chop . . . 1H **17**
Broadway, The DH4: Hou S . . . 2E **144**
NE30: Cull, Tyne . . . 1H **49**
NE33: S Shi . . . 3B **68**
SR4: Sund . . . 5H **117**
(not continuous)
SR5: Sund . . . 7G **103**
Broadway Circ. NE24: Bly . . . 2H **23**
Broadway Cl. NE30: Cull . . . 1H **49**
Broadway Ct. NE3: Gos . . . 5E **44**
NE28: W'snd . . . 6J **47**
Broadway Cres. NE24: Bly . . . 3J **23**
Broadway E. NE3: Gos . . . 5E **44**
Broadway Gdns. NE46: Hex . . . 1B **70**
Broadway Vs. NE15: Benw . . . 1H **81**
Broadway W. NE3: Gos . . . 5D **44**
Broadwell Ct. NE3: Gos . . . 1H **63**
Broadwood Rd. NE15: Den M . . . 6F **61**
Broadwood Vw. DH3: Ches S . . . 7B **128**
DH8: Shot B . . . 4E **120**
Brockdale NE22: E Sle . . . 4D **18**
Brockenhurst Dr. SR4: Sund . . . 6G **117**
Brock Farm Ct. NE30: N Shi . . . 6G **49**
Brockhampton Cl. NE35: Bol C . . . 4E **86**
Brock La. NE22: E Sle, W Sle . . . 2D **18**
Brockley Av. NE34: S Shi . . . 2H **87**
Brockley St. SR5: Sund . . . 4G **103**
Brockley Ter. NE35: Bol C . . . 5E **86**
BROCKLEY WHINS . . . 3F **87**
Brockley Whins Station (Metro) . . . 4F **87**
Brock Sq. NE6: Byke . . . 5P **5** (1K **83**)

Brock St. NE6: Byke 5P 5 (1K 83)
Brockwade NE10: Hew 2D 100
Brockwell TS27: B Col 2G 183
Brockwell Cen. NE23: Cra 2K 25
Brockwell Cl. NE21: Winl 5A 80
Brockwell Ct. DH7: B'don 1D 174
NE24: Bly 4G 23
Brockwell Dr. NE39: Row G 4J 95
Brockwell Gro. NE25: Ears 6B 38
Brockwell Ho. NE5: Blak 3J 61
Brockwell La. DH8: B'hill 5G 121
Brockwell M. NE27: Back 6F 37
Brockwell Rd. NE38: Wash 3D 114
Brockwell St. DH6: Bowb 3G 177
NE24: Bly 5G 23
Brockwood Cl. NE63: Ash 6K 11
Broderick Ter. DH4: Nbot 6D 130
Brodie Cl. NE34: S Shi 2J 87
Brodrick Cl. NE3: Ken 7K 43
Brodrick St. NE33: S Shi 2K 67
Brokenheugh NE5: W Dent 4F 61
Bromarsh Ct. SR6: Roker 6H 105
Bromford Rd. NE3: Ken 7K 43
Bromley Av. NE25: Monks 1E 48
Bromley Cl. DH1: H Shin 1F 177
Bromley Ct. NE3: Ki Pk 5K 43
Bromley Gdns. NE24: News 4J 23
NE28: W'snd 7H 47
Brompton Cl. DH2: Ous 6G 113
Brompton Pl. NE11: Dun 6C 82
Brompton Ter. DH4: Nbot 5D 130
Bromsgrove Cl. NE28: W'snd 7H 47
Bronte Pl. DH9: Stly 5H 125
Brookbank Cl. SR3: Dox P 4B 132
Brook Ct. NE22: Bed 7J 17
Brookdale DH1: Carr 7J 155
Brooke Av. NE16: Swa, Whi 6G 81
NE35: Bol C 6H 87
Brooke Cl. DH9: Stly 3G 125
Brooke Ho. DH5: Hou S 3E 144
Brookes Ri. DH7: Lang M 7F 165
Brooke St. SR5: Monkw 1H 7 (7E 104)
Brookes Wlk. NE34: S Shi 4G 87
Brookfield NE3: Gos 3D 62
NE27: Shir 2J 47
Brookfield Cres. NE5: Cha P 4C 60
Brookfield Gdns. SR2: Sund 4F 119
Brookfield Ter. *NE10: Pel 5E 84*
(off Shields Rd.)
Brook Gdns. NE26: Whit B 5H 39
Brookland Dr. NE12: Kil 1C 46
Brookland Rd. SR4: Sund 2B 118
Brooklands NE20: Darr H 1E 40
Brooklands Way NE35: Bol C 6D 86
Brookland Ter. NE29: N Shi 3B 48
(not continuous)
Brooklyn St. SR7: Mur 1F 159
Brooklyn Ter. SR7: Mur 1F 159
Brooklyn Ter. Nth. *SR7: Mur 1F 159*
(off Johnson St.)
Brook Rd. SR4: Sund 3D 118
Brookside DH5: Hou S 4D 144
DH7: Sac 6E 140
DH7: Wit G 3D 152
NE23: Dud 4J 35
Brookside Av. NE13: Bru V 6C 34
NE24: Cow 2F 23
Brookside Cotts. SR2: Sund 4E 118
Brookside Cres. NE5: Fen 4K 61
Brookside Gdns. SR2: Sund 7G 7 (4E 118)
Brookside Ter. SR2: Sund 7H 7 (4E 118)
Brookside Wood NE38: Wash 7H 115
Brooksmead NE28: W'snd 1D 64
Brook St. NE6: Byke 1B 84
NE26: Whit B 6H 39
Brookvale Av. NE3: Ken 1B 62
Brook Vw. DH7: Lan 7J 137
SR7: S'hm 2H 147
Brookville Cres. NE5: Den M 3H 61
Brook Wlk. SR3: Dox P 4B 132
Broom Cl. DH9: Stly 2H 125
NE16: Whi 1J 97
NE21: Winl 6B 80
NE61: Mor 1J 15
Broom Ct. NE9: Spri 7D 100
Broom Cres. DH7: Ush M 2C 164
Broome Cl. NE3: Fawd 6B 44
Broome Ct. DH7: Bro 4F 165
Broome Rd. DH1: Carr 7H 155
Broom Farm W. DH7: Bro 4E 164
Broomfield NE32: Jar 4C 86
Broomfield Av. NE6: Walk 4C 64
NE28: W'snd 7G 47
Broomfield Cres. NE17: C'wl 7K 93
Broomfield Rd. NE3: Gos 1D 62
Broomfield Ter. NE40: Craw 3C 78
Broom Grn. NE16: Whi 1J 97
Broom Hall Dr. DH7: Ush M 3D 164
BROOMHAUGH 7A 74
Broomhaugh Cl. NE46: Hex 2E 70
BROOM HILL 4F 145
6H 107
Broom Hill DH9: Stly 2E 124
Broomhill DH5: Hett H 4F 145
Broomhill Est. DH5: Hett H 4F 145
Broomhill Gdns. NE5: Fen 4K 61
Broomhill Rd. NE42: Pru 3F 77
Broomhill Ter. DH5: Hett H 5F 145
DH8: M'sly 1J 121
Broomhouse Farm Ct. NE42: Pru 3F 77
Broomhouse La. NE42: Pru 3G 77
Broomhouse Rd. NE42: Pru 3G 77
Broom La. DH1: Dur 4E 164
DH7: Bro, Ush M 3C 164
NE16: Whi 2H 97
Broomlaw NE9: Low F 3A 100
Broomlea NE29: N Shi 3B 48
Broomlea Ct. NE21: Blay 3C 80
Broomlee NE63: Ash 5C 12
Broomlee Cl. NE7: H Hea 2B 64
Broomlee Rd. NE12: Kil 1A 46
BROOMLEY 2D 90
Broomley Ct. NE3: Fawd 5B 44
Broomley Wlk. NE3: Fawd 5B 44
BROOMPARK 4E 164
Broomridge Av. NE15: Benw 7K 61
Brooms, The DH2: Ous 6H 113
Broomshields Av. SR5: Ful 4D 104
Broomshields Cl. SR5: Ful 4D 104
BROOMSIDE 7J 155
Broomside Ct. DH1: Carr 7H 155
Broomside La. DH1: Carr 7G 155
Broomside Pk. DH1: Dur 7E 154
Brooms La. DH8: Cons, Lead 5C 122
Broom Ter. NE16: Burn 2B 110
NE16: Whi 1J 97
Broom Wood Ct. NE42: Pru 5D 76
Broomy Hill Rd. NE15: Thro 3G 59
Broomylinn Pl. NE23: Cra 2A 26
Brotherlee Rd. NE3: Fawd 5B 44
Brougham Ct. SR8: Pet 2J 181
Brougham St. SR1: Sund 4J 7 (2F 119)
Brough Ct. NE6: Byke 6A 64
Brough Gdns. NE28: W'snd 1A 66
Brough Pk. Way NE6: Walk 7B 64
Brough St. NE6: Byke 6A 64
Broughton Cl. NE5: West 1G 61
Broughton Rd. NE33: S Shi 3K 67
Brough Way NE6: Byke 6A 64
Brow, The NE6: Byke 1A 84
Browbank DH7: Sac 1F 153
Brown Cres. NE9: Eigh B 6A 100
Browne Rd. SR6: Ful 4F 105
BROWNEY 2F 175
Browney Ct. DH7: Lang P 4J 151
Browney La. DH6: Crox, Sun B 2E 174
DH7: Mead 2E 174
Browning Cl. DH9: Stly 3H 125
NE34: S Shi 4H 87
(not continuous)
Browning Ct. NE4: Fen 5A 62
Browning Sq. NE8: Gate 4J 83
Browning St. SR8: Eas C 7D 160
Brownlow Cl. NE7: H Hea 2C 64
Brownlow Rd. NE34: S Shi 7J 67
Brownrigg Dr. NE23: Cra 5A 26
Brownriggs Ct. NE37: Wash 2F 115
Browns Bldgs. DH3: Bir 7A 114
DH9: Dip 1G 123
NE22: Bed 1G 21
Brownsea Pl. NE9: Low F 7J 83
Brown's Ter. DH7: Lang P 5J 151
Browntop Pl. NE34: S Shi 1J 87
Broxbourne Ter. SR4: Sund 2C 118
Broxburn Cl. NE28: W'snd 7J 47
Broxburn Ct. NE5: Blak 2J 61
Broxholm Rd. NE6: Heat 4K 63
Bruce Cl. NE5: West 3F 61
NE34: S Shi 2J 87
Bruce Cres. TS28: Win 5F 181
Bruce Gdns. NE5: Fen 6J 61
Bruce Glasier Ter. DH6: Shot C 7E 170
Bruce Kirkup Rd. SR8: Hord 4D 172
Bruce Pl. SR8: Pet 4A 172
Bruce St. DH7: Sac 4D 140
SR5: S'wck 5E 104
Brumell Dr. NE61: Mor 6D 8
Brumwell Ct. NE43: Stoc 7H 75
Brundon Av. NE26: Whit B 4F 39
Brunel Dr. SR6: Roker 5H 105
Brunel Lodge *NE4: Elsw 3C 82*
(off Brunel St.)
Brunel St. NE4: Newc T 9B 4 (3D 82)
NE8: Gate 6F 83
Brunel Ter. NE4: Elsw 3C 82
Brunel Wlk. NE4: Elsw 3C 82
Brunswick Gro. NE13: Bru V 5C 34
Brunswick Ind. Est. NE13: Bru V 5B 34
Brunswick Pk. Ind. Est. NE13: Bru V 5C 34
Brunswick Pl. NE1: Newc T 4F 4 (1F 83)
Brunswick Rd. NE27: Shir 2K 47
SR5: Sund 3G 103
Brunswick Sq. NE27: Shir 2K 47
Brunswick St. NE33: S Shi 4J 67
BRUNSWICK VILLAGE 5C 34
Brunton Av. NE3: Fawd 6B 44
NE28: W'snd 2B 66
Brunton Cl. NE27: Shir 2K 47
Brunton Gro. NE3: Fawd 6B 44
Brunton La. NE3: Gos 2K 43
NE3: Ki Pk 7J 43
NE13: Haz, W Op 2K 43
(not continuous)
NE13: K Bank, Wool 2K 43
Brunton M. NE13: Haz 2B 44
Brunton Quarry NE13: W Op 1D 44
Brunton Rd. NE13: K Bank 5H 43
Brunton St. NE29: N Shi 2D 66
Brunton Ter. SR4: Sund 2C 118
Brunton Wlk. NE3: Ki Pk 6J 43
(not continuous)
Brunton Way NE10: Bill Q 4F 85
NE23: Cra 7K 21
Brussels Rd. NE28: W'snd 4F 65
SR4: Sund 1K 117
Bryan Roycroft Ct. NE6: Byke 4N 5
BRYANS LEAP 1A 110
Bryans Leap NE16: Burn 1A 110
Bryden Ct. NE34: S Shi 1K 87
Brydon Cres. DH6: S Het 5D 158
Bryers St. SR6: Whit 5H 89
Buchanan Grn. NE11: Dun 5C 82
Buchanan St. NE31: Heb 1H 85
Buckham Ct. DH7: Lan 3F 151
Buckham St. DH8: B'hill 5G 121
Buckingham SR3: New S 1A 132
Buckingham Cl. SR6: Whit 6H 89
Buckingham Rd. SR8: Pet 4K 171
Buckinghamshire Rd. DH1: Carr 1G 167
Buckingham St. NE4: Newc T 6B 4 (1D 82)
Buckland Cl. DH4: Hou S 7C 130
NE38: Wash 5H 115
Buck's Hill DH1: Dur 6A 166
Buck's Hill Vw. NE16: Whi 1J 97
Buck's Nook La. NE40: G'sde, Pru 7K 77
Buckthorne Gro. NE7: H Hea 2A 64
Buddle Cl. SR8: Pet 4B 172
Buddle Ct. NE4: Benw 2A 82
Buddle Gdns. NE40: G'sde 5D 78
Buddle Ind. Est. NE28: W'snd 5G 65
Buddle Rd. NE4: Benw 2K 81
Buddle St. DH8: Cons 1J 135
NE28: W'snd 4G 65
Buddle Ter. NE27: Shir 3J 47
SR2: Sund 3G 119
Bude Ct. NE28: W'snd 7G 47
Bude Gdns. NE9: Low F 4H 99
Bude Gro. NE29: N Shi 3D 48
Bude Sq. SR7: Mur 6F 147
Budle Cl. NE3: Gos 6D 44
NE24: Bly 2G 23
Budleigh Rd. NE3: Ken 7B 44
Budworth Av. NE26: Sea S 5D 28
Bugatti Ind. Pk. NE29: N Shi 7C 48
Buller's Grn. NE61: Mor 6E 8
Bullfinch Dr. NE16: Whi 7G 81
Bullfinch Rd. DH5: Eas L 2J 157
Bullion La. DH2: Ches S 6K 127
Bull La. SR1: Sund 1G 119
Bulman Ho. NE3: Gos 7E 44
Bulman's La. NE29: N Shi 4G 49
Bulmer Ho. NE34: S Shi 6C 68
Bulmer Rd. NE34: S Shi 6C 68
Bungalows, The DH3: Bir 2K 113
DH6: S Het 5D 158
DH6: Thor 2J 179
DH7: Esh W 4E 162
DH7: New B 4B 164
DH8: Ebc 4G 107
DH9: Tan L 1C 124
NE10: Hew 6C 84
NE11: Lame 7G 99
NE17: Ham 4K 107
NE21: Winl 4A 80
NE28: W'snd 2K 65
SR8: Hord 4D 172
TS27: Hes 4H 183
Bunker Hill DH4: S Row 4C 130
Bunny Hill Wellness Cen. 4H 103
Bunyan Av. NE34: S Shi 3G 87
Burdale Av. NE5: Den M 4G 61
Burden Ct. SR8: Hord 6E 172
BURDON 6D 132
Burdon Av. DH5: Hou S 2G 145
NE23: Nel V 3H 25
Burdon Cl. SR6: Clead 5A 88
Burdon Cres. SR2: Ryh 3G 133
SR6: Clead 5A 88
SR7: S'hm 1H 147
TS28: Win 4G 181
Burdon Dr. SR8: Pet 5G 171
Burdon Hall Pk. SR3: Bur 6D 132
Burdon La. SR2: New S, Ryh 4E 132
SR3: Bur 6B 132
Burdon Lodge NE16: Sun 5J 97
Burdon Main Row NE29: N Shi 1G 67
Burdon Pk. NE16: Sun 5J 97
Burdon Pl. NE2: Jes 5G 63
SR8: Pet 6C 172
(not continuous)
Burdon Plain NE16: Marl H 2H 111
Burdon Rd. SR1: Sund 6K 7 (3F 119)
SR2: Sund 7K 7 (3F 119)
SR3: Dox P, Silk, Tuns 4D 132
SR6: Clead 5A 88
Burdon St. NE29: N Shi 2D 66
Burdon Ter. NE2: Jes 5F 63
NE22: Bed 7G 17
Burdon Village Rd. SR3: Bur 5D 132
Burdon Wlk. TS27: Cas E 4J 181
Burford Ct. NE3: Gos 1J 63
Burford Gdns. SR3: Sund 6D 118
Burford Way NE35: Bol C 7E 86
Burghley Gdns. NE61: Peg 3B 10
Burghley Rd. NE10: Wind N 1A 100
Burgoyne Ct. NE37: Wash 7H 101
Burgoyne Ter. NE41: Wylam 7J 57
Burke St. SR5: Sund 4G 103
Burlawn Cl. SR2: Ryh 1A 133
Burleigh Cl. SR2: Ryh 3F 133
Burleigh St. NE33: S Shi 4K 67
Burlington Cl. SR2: Sund 3G 119
Burlington Ct. NE2: Jes 3H 63
NE28: W'snd 5J 47
Burlington Gdns. NE6: Heat 5K 63
Burlison Gdns. NE10: Fell 4A 84
Burnaby Dr. NE40: Ryton 2F 79
Burnaby St. SR4: Sund 3C 118
Burn Av. NE12: Longb 4B 46
(not continuous)
NE28: W'snd 3F 65
Burnbank NE10: Hew 1E 100
NE13: Sea B 3D 34
SR5: S'wck 5D 104
Burnbank Av. NE25: Well 6B 38
Burnbridge NE13: Sea B 3D 34
Burn Closes Cres. NE28: W'snd 2J 65
Burncroft NE46: Hex 2C 70
Burn Crook DH5: Hou S 4D 144
Burnden Gro. DH4: S Row 4K 129
Burnell Rd. DH7: Esh W 4E 162
Burnet Cl. NE28: W'snd 7G 47
Burnet Ct. NE63: Ash 6K 11
Burnett Cres. DH6: Kel 7E 178
Burney Vs. NE8: Gate 5J 83
Burneze Pl. NE16: Hob 5A 110
Burnfoot NE42: O'ham 2C 76
Burnfoot Ter. NE26: Whit B 7H 39
Burnfoot Way NE3: Ken 2A 62
Burn Gdns. SR8: Eas 7A 160
Burnhall Dr. SR7: S'hm 1J 147
Burnham Av. NE15: Lem 6A 60
Burnham Cl. DH4: Pen 3B 130
NE24: News 4J 23
NE36: E Bol 7K 87
Burnham Gro. NE6: Walk 2C 84
Burnham St. NE34: S Shi 7J 67
Burn Haugh NE46: Hex 7C 50
Burn Heads Rd. NE31: Heb 2H 85
Burnhills Gdns. NE40: G'sde 5E 78
Burnhills La. NE40: G'sde 6F 79
BURNHOPE 5D 138
Burnhope Ct. DH7: B'hpe 5D 138
Burnhope Dr. SR5: Ful 4D 104
Burnhope Gdns. NE9: Wrek 4B 100
Burnhope Rd. DH7: Maid L 2A 138
NE38: Wash 2J 115
Burnhopeside Av. DH7: Lan 7A 138
Burnhope Way SR8: Pet 5K 171
Burnigill DH7: Mead 2E 174
Burnip Cl. SR8: Eas C 7C 160
Burnip Rd. SR7: Mur 6E 146
Burnland Ter. NE46: Hex 1B 70
Burnland Vs. *NE46: Hex 1B 70*
(off Leazes Ter.)
Burn La. DH5: Hett H 7G 145
NE46: Hex 1C 70
Burn Lea DH4: Hou S 2C 144
Burnlea Gdns. NE23: Seg 1F 37
Burnley St. NE21: Blay 4C 80
Burnmill Bank DH8: Shot B 3A 120
Burnmoor Gdns. NE9: Wrek 4B 100
BURNOPFIELD 2K 109
Burnopfield Gdns. NE15: Den M 7G 61
Burnopfield Rd. NE39: Row G 6K 95
Burnop Ter. NE39: Row G 5E 94
Burn Pk. Rd. DH4: Hou S 2C 144
SR2: Sund 6F 7 (3D 118)
Burn Prom. DH4: Hou S 1D 144
Burn Rd. NE21: Winl 5K 79
Burns Av. NE24: Bly 4G 23
NE35: Bol C 6H 87
TS27: B Col 1G 183
Burns Av. Nth. DH5: Hou S 3E 144
(not continuous)
Burns Av. Sth. DH5: Hou S 3E 144
Burns Cl. DH4: W Rai 1A 156
DH9: Stly 3G 125
NE16: Whi 2H 97
NE34: S Shi 3H 87
Burns Cres. NE16: Swa 6G 81
BURNSIDE 1C 144
Burnside DH4: Hou S 1J 143
DH7: Esh W 3C 162
DH7: Lan 6J 137
DH7: Wit G 3D 152
NE2: Newc T 1B 4
NE10: Hew 7C 84
NE20: Darr H 1F 41
NE22: Bed 5B 18
NE25: H'wll 2K 37
NE32: Jar 2C 86
NE36: E Bol 7A 88
NE42: Oving 2K 75
NE46: Hex 3B 70
NE61: Mor 6G 9
NE63: N Sea 4E 12
SR8: Pet 6B 172
Burnside, The NE5: W Dent 4E 60
Burnside Av. DH4: Hou S 1C 144
NE23: Dud 3K 35
SR8: Hord 6E 172
Burnside Cl. NE16: Whi 3G 97
NE23: Seg 2C 36
NE24: Cow 1F 23
NE35: Bol C 6H 87
NE42: O'ham 2C 76
Burnside Cotts. NE23: Dud 3K 35
NE43: Mic 5A 76
NE43: Stoc 7H 75
SR7: Dalt D 5J 147
Burnside Rd. NE3: Gos 5E 44
NE25: Whit B 1H 49
NE30: Cull 1H 49
NE39: Row G 5H 95
Burnside Vw. NE23: Seg 2C 36
Burns St. DH6: Whe H 3A 180
NE32: Jar 6B 66
Burn's Ter. DH6: Shot C 6F 171
Burnstones NE5: W Dent 4E 60
Burn St. DH6: Bowb 4H 177
Burn Ter. DH4: S Row 3C 130
NE28: W'snd 3K 65
NE31: Heb 4G 85
Burnthouse Bank DH2: Ches S, P Fel 5H 127
Burnthouse Cl. NE21: Winl 6A 80
Burnthouse La. NE16: Sun, Whi 3G 97
NE16: Whi 2G 97
Burnt Ho. Rd. NE25: Monks 1E 48
Burnt Houses NE40: G'sde 5F 79

Burntland Av. SR5: S'wck .5B **104**
Burn Vw. NE23: Dud .3K **35**
NE32: Jar .6C **86**
Burnville NE6: Heat .1M **5** (6J **63**)
Burnville Rd. SR4: Sund .3D **118**
Burnville Rd. Sth. SR4: Sund .3D **118**
Burnway NE37: Wash .7F **101**
SR7: S'hm .2J **147**
Burnwood Cl. NE17: C'wl .6K **93**
BURRADON .5A **36**
Burradon Rd. NE23: Dud .5A **36**
(Cheviot Grange)
NE23: Dud .3A **36**
(Seaton Cft.)
Burrow St. NE33: S Shi .2J **67**
Burscough Cres. SR6: Ful .5F **105**
Burstow Av. NE6: Walk .3C **84**
Burswell Av. NE46: Hex .1B **70**
Burswell Vs. NE46: Hex .1B **70**
Burt Av. NE29: N Shi .7E **48**
Burt Cl. DH6: Has .1A **170**
SR8: Pet .4B **172**
Burt Cres. NE23: Dud .3K **35**
Burt Memorial Homes NE62: Sco G .3G **17**
Burtree NE38: Wash .6F **115**
Burt Rd. NE22: Bed .5C **18**
Burt St. NE24: Bly .1J **23**
Burt Ter. NE15: Walb .3A **60**
NE61: Mor .7G **9**
Burwell Av. NE5: W Dent .5F **61**
Burwood Cl. NE6: Walk .3E **84**
Burwood Rd. NE6: Walk .3D **84**
NE29: N Shi .4C **48**
Bushblades La. DH9: Tant .1J **123**
Bushblades M. DH9: Tant .2K **123**
Business & Innovation Cen.
SR5: Sund .6B **104**
Bus Station
Blaydon .3C **80**
Concord .7H **101**
Consett .7H **121**
Eldon Sq. .4E **4**
Gateshead .10H **5** (3G **83**)
Haymarket .4E **4** (7F **63**)
Hexham .2D **70**
Metrocentre .4K **81**
Park La. .5J **7** (2F **119**)
Peterlee .6B **172**
Stanley .3E **124**
Wallsend .4F **65**
Washington Galleries .4F **65**
Winlaton .5B **80**
Buston Ter. NE2: Jes .4H **63**
Busty Bank NE16: Burn .6K **95**
Busty Vw. DH2: Newf .4F **127**
Butcher's Bri. Rd. NE32: Jar .1B **86**
Butcher's La. NE61: Lngh, Peg .1B **10**
Butchers Lonnen NE61: Mor .6F **9**
Bute Cotts. NE11: Dun .5A **82**
Bute Ct. SR3: Silk .3C **132**
Bute Dr. NE39: H Spen .3D **94**
Buteland Rd. NE15: Den M .6F **61**
Buteland Ter. NE64: Newb S .3H **13**
Bute Rd. Nth. NE39: H Spen .3D **94**
Bute Rd. Sth. NE39: H Spen .4D **94**
Bute St. DH9: Tant .6A **110**
Butler St. SR8: Eas C .7D **160**
Butsfield Gdns. SR3: Sund .6D **118**
Butsfield La. DH8: Cons .7K **135**
Butterburn Cl. NE7: H Hea .1C **64**
Butterfield Cl. NE40: Craw .3D **78**
Buttermere NE10: Pel .6E **84**
NE37: Wash .2F **115**
SR6: Clead .5C **88**
SR8: Pet .2J **181**
Buttermere Av. DH5: Eas L .3J **157**
NE16: Whi .7J **81**
Buttermere Cl. DH2: Ches S .7A **128**
NE5: Den M .4H **61**
NE12: Kil .1A **46**
Buttermere Cres. DH6: S Het .3A **158**
NE21: Winl .6B **80**
Buttermere Gdns. NE9: Low F .2J **99**
NE34: S Shi .7A **68**
Buttermere Rd. NE30: Cull .2G **49**
Buttermere St. SR2: Sund .6G **119**
Buttermere Way NE24: Cow .7F **19**
Butterwell Dr. NE61: Peg .4K **9**
Button's Bank DH7: Wat .7B **162**
DL15: S Cro .7B **162**
Buttons Pl. DH7: Wat .6C **162**
Buttsfield Ter. DH4: Pen .1B **130**
Buxton Cl. NE28: W'snd .7H **47**
NE32: Jar .1C **86**
Buxton Gdns. NE5: West .2F **61**
SR3: Sund .5D **118**
Buxton Grn. NE5: West .2F **61**
Buxton St. NE1: Newc T .5J **5** (1H **83**)
Bye, The DH8: C'sde .2E **134**
Byer Bank DH5: Hou S .3G **145**
Byerhope DH4: Pen .2K **129**
BYERMOOR .1D **110**
Byermoor Ind. Est. NE16: Burn .1D **110**
Byers Ct. SR3: New S .1D **132**
BYERS GARTH .5K **167**
Byers Gth. DH1: S Hou .5K **167**
Byer Sq. DH5: Hett H .4G **145**
Byer St. DH5: Hett H .4G **145**
Byeways, The NE12: Longb .6K **45**
Bygate Cl. NE3: Ken .2A **62**
Bygate Ct. NE25: Monks .7E **38**
Bygate Rd. NE25: Monks .7E **38**
BYKER .5P **5** (7A **64**)
Byker Bank NE1: Byke .5M **5** (1J **83**)
NE6: Byke .5M **5** (1J **83**)
Byker Bri. NE1: Newc T .4K **5** (7H **63**)
NE6: Byke .4M **5** (7H **63**)
Byker Bus. Development Cen.
NE6: Byke .5N **5** (1K **83**)
Byker Cres. NE6: Byke .7A **64**
Byker Lodge NE6: Byke .6P **5** (1A **84**)
Byker Pier NE1: Newc T .4M **5**
Byker Station (Metro) .4P **5** (7K **63**)
Byker St. NE6: Walk .7D **64**
Byker Ter. NE6: Walk .7D **64**
Byland Cl. DH4: Hou S .7C **130**
Byland Ct. DH7: Bearp .1D **164**
NE38: Wash .3G **115**
Byland Rd. NE12: Longb .6H **45**
Bylands Gdns. SR3: Sund .5D **118**
Byland Way DH1: Dur .3K **165**
Byony Toft SR2: Ryh .2J **133**
Byrewood Wlk. NE3: Ken .6K **43**
Byrness NE5: W Dent .4E **60**
Byrness Cl. NE3: Ken .1J **61**
Byrness Ct. NE28: W'snd .7J **47**
Byrness Row NE23: Cra .2A **26**
Byrne Ter. W. SR3: New S .2D **132**
Byron Av. NE24: Bly .3G **23**
NE28: W'snd .4A **66**
NE31: Heb .7K **65**
NE35: Bol C .6G **87**
TS27: B Col .1G **183**
Byron Cl. DH2: Ous .7H **113**
DH9: Stly .3G **125**
NE62: Chop .1G **17**
Byron Ct. NE5: Cha P .3C **60**
NE16: Swa .6G **81**
Byron Lodge Est. SR7: S'hm .2G **147**
Byron M. NE2: Newc T .3H **5** (7G **63**)
Byron Pl. NE63: Ash .5D **12**
Byron Pl. Shop. Cen. SR7: S'hm .3C **148**
Byron Rd. SR5: S'wck .5C **104**
Byrons Ct. SR7: S'hm .7K **133**
Byron St. DH2: Ous .7H **113**
DH6: Whe H .3B **180**
NE2: Newc T .3H **5** (7G **63**)
NE33: S Shi .5K **67**
SR5: Monkw .6E **104**
SR8: Eas C .7D **160**
Byron Ter. DH5: Hou S .3E **144**
DH6: Shot C .6F **171**
SR7: S'hm .1H **147**
Byron Wlk. NE8: Gate .4J **83**
By-Way, The NE15: Thro .4H **59**
BYWELL .6F **75**
Bywell Av. NE3: Fawd .4B **44**
NE15: Lem .6E **60**
NE34: S Shi .6C **68**
NE46: Hex .2F **71**
SR5: S'wck .4E **104**
Bywell Castle (remains of) .6G **75**
Bywell Cl. NE40: Craw .3C **78**
Bywell Dr. SR8: Pet .2A **182**
Bywell Gdns. NE10: Wind N .1K **99**
NE11: Lob H .2C **98**
Bywell Gro. NE27: Shir .1A **48**
Bywell Rd. NE63: Ash .5B **12**
SR6: Clead .6B **88**
Bywell St. NE6: Byke .1B **84**
(not continuous)
Bywell Ter. NE26: Sea S .4D **28**
NE32: Jar .3B **86**
Bywell Vw. NE43: Pains .7K **75**

C

Caddy Cl. DH3: Bir .2B **114**
Cadehill Rd. NE43: Pains .1H **91**
Cadger Bank DH7: Lan .7J **137**
Cadlestone Ct. NE23: Cra .2B **26**
Cadwell La. SR8: Eas .7K **159**
Caedmon Hall .6H **83**
Caernarvon Cl. NE5: Blak .1H **61**
Caernarvon Dr. SR3: E Her .3J **131**
Caer Urfa Cl. NE33: S Shi .1J **67**
Caesar's Wlk. NE33: S Shi .1J **67**
Caesar Way NE28: W'snd .1J **65**
Cain Ter. DH6: Whe H .3A **180**
Caircross SR5: Sund .6G **103**
Cairnglass Grn. NE23: Cra .2B **26**
Cairngorm Av. NE38: Wash .5E **114**
Cairnhill Ter. DH4: Nbot .5D **130**
Cairnside SR3: E Her .2J **131**
SR7: Seat .1F **147**
Cairnside Sth. SR3: E Her .2H **131**
Cairnsmore Cl. NE6: Walk .5F **65**
NE23: Cra .6K **25**
Cairnsmore Dr. NE38: Wash .5F **115**
Cairns Rd. SR5: Ful .3E **104**
SR7: Mur .7C **146**
Cairns Sq. SR5: Ful .3E **104**
Cairns Way NE3: Fawd .5B **44**
Cairo St. SR2: Sund .4G **119**
Caister Cl. SR7: S'hm .2A **148**
Caithness Rd. SR5: Sund .5F **103**
Caithness Sq. SR5: Sund .5F **103**
Calais Rd. SR5: Sund .6F **103**
Calandra Chase NE2: Newc T .1B **4** (5D **62**)
Caldbeck Av. NE6: Walk .3D **84**
Caldbeck Cl. NE6: Walk .3D **84**
Calderbourne Av. SR6: Seab .3G **105**
Calder Ct. SR3: Silk .3B **132**
Calderdale NE28: W'snd .7D **46**
Calderdale Av. NE6: Walk .6D **64**
Calder Grn. NE32: Jar .4C **86**
Calder's Cres. NE38: Wash .7H **115**
Calder Wlk. NE16: Sun .5G **97**
Calderwood Cres. NE9: Low F .4J **99**
Calderwood Pk. NE9: Low F .4J **99**
Caldew Ct. DH5: Eas L .1H **157**
Caldew Cres. NE5: Den M .5G **61**
Caldwell Rd. NE3: Fawd .4B **44**
Caleb Dr. NE28: W'snd .7H **47**
Cale Cross Ho. NE1: Newc T .7G **4**
Caledonia DH3: Gt Lum .2E **142**
NE21: Winl .6A **80**
Caledonian Rd. SR5: Sund .4F **103**
Caledonian St. NE31: Heb .6H **65**
Caledonia St. NE6: Walk .2E **84**
Calf Cl. Dr. NE32: Jar .4B **86**
Calf Cl. La. NE32: Jar .4B **86**
Calf Cl. Wlk. NE32: Jar .3C **86**
California NE21: Winl .5B **80**
California Gdns. NE61: Mor .7H **9**
Callaley Av. NE16: Whi .1F **97**
Callaly Av. NE23: Cra .4A **26**
Callaly Cl. NE61: Peg .4B **10**
Callaly Way NE6: Walk .2B **84**
Callander DH2: Ous .6J **113**
Callaurie Ct. NE9: Low F .2H **99**
Callendar Ct. NE9: Low F .2K **99**
Callerdale Rd. NE24: Cow .1E **22**
CALLERTON .6B **42**
Callerton NE12: Kil .6B **36**
Callerton Av. NE29: N Shi .6C **48**
Callerton Cl. NE23: Cra .4A **26**
NE63: Ash .5D **12**
Callerton Ct. NE5: West .2G **61**
NE20: Darr H .7J **31**
Callerton Ga. DH9: Crag .7J **125**
Callerton La. NE5: H Cal .3J **41**
NE13: Wool .3C **42**
NE20: H Cal, Pon .2J **41**
CALLERTON LANE END .5J **41**
Callerton La. End Cotts. NE5: Call .5J **41**
Callerton Parkway (Park & Tram) .3E **42**
Callerton Parkway Station (Metro) .3E **42**
Callerton Pl. DH9: Crag .7K **125**
NE4: Fen .1C **82**
Callerton Rd. NE15: Thro .3H **59**
Callerton Vw. NE5: Cha P .1B **60**
Calley Cl. SR8: Pet .2A **182**
Callington Cl. DH4: Bour .7J **129**
Callington Dr. SR2: Ryh .2H **133**
Callum Dr. NE34: S Shi .5C **68**
Calow Way NE16: Whi .2F **97**
Calshot Rd. SR5: Sund .6J **103**
Calstock Cl. SR7: Mur .1F **159**
Calthwaite Cl. SR5: Sund .5G **103**
Calver Ct. NE34: S Shi .1A **88**
(not continuous)
Calvert Ter. SR7: Mur .7D **146**
Calvus Dr. NE15: Hed W .3D **58**
Camberley Cl. SR3: Tuns .1E **132**
Camberley Dr. DH7: B'don .2B **174**
Camberley Rd. NE28: W'snd .1A **66**
Camberwell Cl. NE11: Fest P .1D **98**
Camberwell Way SR3: Dox P .3K **131**
Cambo Av. NE22: Bed .7A **18**
NE25: Monks .1D **48**
Cambo Cl. NE3: Gos .7F **45**
NE24: Bly .2G **23**
NE28: W'snd .6H **47**
Cambo Dr. NE23: Cra .5A **26**
Cambo Grn. NE5: Blak .3J **61**
CAMBOIS .4H **19**
Cambo Pl. NE30: Cull .3G **49**
Camborne Gro. NE8: Gate .5H **83**
Camborne Pl. NE8: Gate .5H **83**
Cambourne Av. SR6: Seab .3G **105**
Cambria Grn. SR4: Sund .2G **117**
Cambrian Cl. NE38: Wash .5F **115**
Cambrian St. NE32: Jar .6C **66**
Cambrian Way NE38: Wash .4F **115**
Cambria St. SR4: Sund .2G **117**
Cambridge Av. DH8: C'sde .3C **134**
NE12: Longb .4B **46**
NE26: Whit B .6G **39**
NE28: W'snd .2E **64**
NE31: Heb .7K **65**
NE37: Wash .7F **101**
Cambridge Cres. DH4: S Row .3A **130**
Cambridge Dr. DH3: Gt Lum .3E **142**
Cambridge Pl. DH3: Bir .7A **114**
Cambridge Rd. NE62: Stake .1J **17**
SR3: New S .2C **132**
SR8: Pet .4A **172**
Cambridgeshire Dr. DH1: Carr .2G **167**
Cambridge St. NE4: Newc T .9A **4** (3D **82**)
Cambridge Ter. DH6: Bowb .5H **177**
NE8: Gate .5G **83**
Camden Ct. NE1: Newc T .3H **5**
Camden Sq. NE30: N Shi .7H **49**
SR7: S'hm .4A **148**
Camden St. NE2: Newc T .3H **5** (7G **63**)
NE30: N Shi .7H **49**
SR5: S'wck, Sund .6C **104**
Camelford Ct. NE15: Lem .5C **60**
Camelot Cl. SR7: S'hm .2A **148**
Cameron Cl. NE34: S Shi .3J **87**
Cameronian Sq. NE8: Gate .9G **4**
Cameron Rd. NE42: Pru .4F **77**
Camerons Bldgs. DH9: Dip .1G **123**
Cameron Wlk. NE11: Dun .4J **81**
Camerton Pl. NE28: W'snd .5J **47**
Camilla Rd. NE15: Hed W .3D **58**
Camilla St. NE8: Gate .5H **83**
Cam Mead SR3: Dox P .5C **132**
CAMPBELL PARK .1K **85**
Campbell Pk. Rd. NE31: Heb .7J **65**
Campbell Pl. NE4: Elsw .5A **4** (1C **82**)
Campbell Rd. SR5: Sund .5F **103**
Campbell Sq. SR5: Sund .5F **103**
Campbell St. NE31: Heb .6J **65**
SR8: Eas C .7D **160**
Campbell Ter. DH5: Eas L .2H **157**
CAMPERDOWN .6K **35**
Camperdown NE5: W Dent .4F **61**
Camperdown Av. DH3: Ches S .4B **128**
NE12: Kil .7K **35**
Camperdown Ind. Est. NE12: Kil .6K **35**
Campion Dr. DH9: Tan L .1D **124**
Campion Gdns. NE10: Wind N .2B **100**
Campion Way NE63: Ash .5A **12**
Campsie Cl. NE38: Wash .5F **115**
Campsie Cres. NE30: Cull .3G **49**
Camp St. SR8: Eas C .7D **160**
Camp Ter. NE29: N Shi .6G **49**
Campus Martius NE15: Hed W .3B **58**
Campville NE29: N Shi .6G **49**
Camsell Ct. DH1: Dur .6J **153**
Camsey Cl. NE12: Longb .6H **45**
Camsey Pl. NE12: Longb .6H **45**
CANADA .5A **128**
Canberra Av. NE25: Monks .1D **48**
Canberra Dr. NE34: S Shi .2E **86**
Canberra Rd. SR4: Sund .4K **117**
Candelford Cl. NE7: H Hea .2B **64**
Candlish St. NE33: S Shi .3K **67**
Candlish Ter. SR7: S'hm .4C **148**
Canmore SR3: Silk .4C **132**
Canning St. NE4: Benw .1A **82**
(Farndale Rd.)
NE4: Benw .1A **82**
(Strathmore Cres.)
NE31: Heb .1H **85**
Cannock DH2: Ous .6H **113**
NE12: Kil .7B **36**
Cannock Dr. NE7: H Hea .1J **63**
Cannon St. NE8: Gate .8H **5** (2G **83**)
Cann Rd. SR8: Pet .4B **172**
Cann St. SR8: Eas .7A **160**
Canonbie Sq. NE23: Cra .2B **26**
Canon Cockin St. SR2: Sund .4G **119**
Canon Ct. NE46: Hex .1D **70**
Canon Gro. NE32: Jar .6C **66**
Canon Savage Dr. NE46: Hex .2A **70**
Canonsfield Cl. NE15: Walb .2B **60**
SR3: Dox P .4B **132**
Canterbury Av. NE28: W'snd .6H **47**
Canterbury Cl. DH3: Gt Lum .4E **142**
NE12: Longb .6J **45**
NE63: N Sea .5D **12**
Canterbury Ho. SR5: Sund .3G **103**
Canterbury Rd. DH1: Dur .3B **154**
SR5: Sund .5G **103**
Canterbury St. NE6: Walk .7B **64**
(not continuous)
NE33: S Shi .5K **67**
Canterbury Way NE13: W Op .5D **34**
NE32: Jar .5A **86**
Capercaillie Lodge NE23: Dud .2A **36**
Capetown Rd. SR5: Sund .5F **103**
Capetown Sq. SR5: Sund .5F **103**
Capheaton Way NE25: Sea D .6F **27**
Caplestone Cl. NE38: Wash .5F **115**
Capstan Ct. *NE9: Wrek* .*5A* ***100***
(off Capstan La.)
Capstan La. NE9: Wrek .5A **100**
Captains Row, The NE33: S Shi .5H **67**
Captains Wharf NE33: S Shi .2J **67**
Capulet Gro. NE34: S Shi .1G **87**
Capulet Ter. SR2: Sund .4G **119**
Caradoc Cl. NE38: Wash .5F **115**
Caragh Rd. DH2: Ches S .1K **141**
Caraway Wlk. NE34: S Shi .4A **88**
Carden Av. NE34: S Shi .1D **88**
Cardiff Sq. SR5: Sund .6F **103**
Cardiff St. SR8: Eas C .7D **160**
Cardigan Gro. NE30: Cull .1G **49**
Cardigan Rd. SR5: Sund .5F **103**
Cardigan Ter. NE6: Heat .2N **5** (6K **63**)
Cardinal Cl. NE12: Longb .6J **45**
NE15: Walb .2B **60**
Cardinals Cl. SR3: Dox P .4B **132**
Cardonnel St. NE29: N Shi .1G **67**
Cardoon Rd. DH8: Cons .7J **121**
Cardwell St. SR6: Roker .6F **105**
(not continuous)
Careen Cres. SR3: E Her .2H **131**
Carew Ct. NE23: Cra .5K **25**
Carey Cl. DH6: Bowb .5H **177**
Cargodurham Distribution Cen.
SR7: S'hm .4C **148**
Carham Av. NE23: Cra .4A **26**
Carham Cl. NE3: Gos .6F **45**
NE45: Corb .1E **72**
Caribees DH8: Cons .3A **136**
Carisbrooke NE22: Bed .6H **17**
Carisbrooke Cl. NE37: Wash .7H **101**
Carisbrooke Ct. SR1: Sund .4F **7** (2D **118**)
Caris St. NE8: Gate .6J **83**
Carlby Way NE23: Cra .7H **21**
Carlcroft SR6: Roker .6G **105**
Carlcroft Pl. NE23: Cra .5A **26**
CARLEY HILL .3C **104**
Carley Hill Rd. SR5: S'wck .4D **104**
Carley Rd. SR5: S'wck .5D **104**
Carley Sq. SR5: S'wck .5D **104**
Carlile Ho. NE4: Newc T .5A **4**
Carlingford Rd. DH2: Ches S .1K **141**
Carlington Wlk. NE13: Ki Pk .4K **43**
Carliol Pl. NE1: Newc T .5G **4** (1G **83**)
Carliol Sq. NE1: Newc T .5G **4** (1G **83**)
(not continuous)
Carliol St. NE1: Newc T .5G **4** (1G **83**)
Carlisle Cl. NE27: Longb .4G **47**
Carlisle Ct. NE10: Fell .5B **84**

Carlisle Cres. DH4: Pen 2A 130
Carlisle Ho. *SR3: E Her* *2K 131*
(off Ashford Rd.)
Carlisle Pl. NE9: Low F 3K 99
Carlisle Rd. DH1: Dur 4C 154
Carlisle St. NE10: Fell 5B 84
Carlisle Ter. NE27: Shir 3J 47
NE46: Hex 1B 70
SR5: S'wck 5C 104
Carlisle Vw. *NE61: Mor* *7F 9*
(off Waterside)
Carlisle Way NE27: Longb 3G 47
Carlow Dr. NE62: W Sle 7B 12
Carlton Av. NE24: News 6G 23
Carlton Cl. DH2: Ous 6G 113
NE3: Ken 2C 62
Carlton Ct. NE11: T Vall 2E 98
NE29: N Shi 7F 49
Carlton Cres. SR3: E Her 2J 131
Carlton Gdns. NE15: Lem 6E 60
Carlton Grange NE3: Ken 2C 62
Carlton Gro. NE63: N Sea 6D 12
Carlton Ho. NE22: Bed 7H 17
Carlton Rd. NE12: Longb 6B 46
Carlton St. NE24: Bly 2K 23
Carlton Ter. NE2: Jes 2G 4 (6G 63)
NE9: Low F 2G 99
NE9: Spri 6D 100
NE24: Bly 1H 23
NE29: N Shi 7F 49
SR2: Sund 7K 7
SR8: Eas 1K 171
Carlyle Ct. NE28: W'snd 4A 66
Carlyle Cres. DH6: Shot C 6F 171
NE16: Swa 6G 81
Carlyle St. NE28: W'snd 4A 66
Carlyon St. SR2: Sund 7J 7 (3F 119)
Carmel Gro. NE23: Cra 1J 25
Carmel Rd. DH9: Stly 3D 124
Carnaby Cl. NE42: Pru 3F 77
Carnaby Rd. NE6: Walk 2D 84
Carnation Av. DH4: Bour 6J 129
Carnation Ter. NE16: Whi 7H 81
Carnegie Cl. NE34: S Shi 2J 87
Carnegie St. SR2: Sund 6H 119
Carnforth Cl. NE28: W'snd 5J 47
Carnforth Gdns. NE9: Low F 3K 99
NE39: Row G 4J 95
Carnforth Grn. NE3: Ken 1A 62
Carnoustie DH2: Ous 7J 113
NE37: Wash 4G 101
Carnoustie Cl. DH8: B'hill 4G 121
NE7: H Hea 1A 64
NE63: N Sea 4E 12
Carnoustie Ct. NE10: Ward 1F 101
NE25: Monks 6C 38
Carnoustie Dr. NE34: S Shi 3B 88
Carodoc Rd. TS28: Win 5G 181
Carole Dunes DH6: Quar H 6D 178
Carol Gdns. NE7: H Hea 2K 63
Caroline Cotts. NE5: Den M 5H 61
Caroline Gdns. NE28: W'snd 2A 66
Caroline Pit Cotts. NE5: Den M 5G 61
Caroline St. DH5: Hett H 6G 145
NE4: Benw 2A 82
NE32: Jar 4A 66
SR7: S'hm 3B 148
Caroline Ter. NE21: Blay 2B 80
Carol St. SR4: Sund 1D 118
Carolyn Cl. NE12: Longb 6A 46
Carolyn Cres. NE26: Whit B 4E 38
Carolyn Way NE26: Whit B 4E 38
Carpenter St. NE33: S Shi 3H 67
Carradale SR3: Silk 4B 132
Carr Av. DH7: B'don 1D 174
Carr-Ellison Ho. NE4: Elsw 3B 82
Carr Ellison Pk. 1J 85
Carr Fld. NE20: Pon 4K 31
Carrfield Rd. NE3: Ken 7B 44
CARR HILL 7K 83
Carr Hill Rd. NE9: Low F 6J 83
NE10: Wind N 6J 83
Carr Ho. Dr. DH1: Dur 5A 154
(not continuous)
Carrhouse La. SR7: Mur 5A 146
Carr Ho. M. DH8: Cons 6K 121
Carrick Ct. NE24: News 5H 23
Carrick Dr. NE24: News 4H 23
Carrigill Dr. NE12: Longb 6J 45
Carrington Cl. NE23: Seg 2D 36
Carrmere Rd. SR2: Sund 7G 119
Carrmyers DH9: Ann P 3J 123
Carrock Cl. SR8: Pet 2B 182
Carrock Ct. SR3: Silk 3B 132
Carroll Wlk. NE34: S Shi 4G 87
Carrowmore Rd. DH2: Ches S 1A 142
Carr Row DH4: Leam 7J 143
Carrs, The DH1: Dur 4A 154
Carrs Cl. NE42: Pru 3H 77
Carrsdale DH1: Carr 6H 155
Carrsfield NE45: Corb 1E 72
Carrside DH1: Dur 5K 153
Carrside M. NE24: Bly 5G 23
Carr St. NE24: Bly 5G 23
NE31: Heb 6H 65
(not continuous)
Carrsway DH1: Carr 6H 155
Carrsyde Cl. NE16: Whi 2F 97
Carr Vw. NE20: Pres 6C 32
CARRVILLE 7H 155
Carrville Link Rd. DH1: Dur 2C 166
Carsdale Rd. NE3: Ken 7K 43
Carter Av. NE31: Heb 7J 65
Cartington Av. NE27: Shir 2J 47
Cartington Cl. SR8: Pet 2B 182
Cartington Ct. NE3: Fawd 5A 44
Cartington Rd. DH1: Dur 6A 154
NE29: N Shi 7E 48
Cartington Ter. NE6: Heat 4K 63
Cartmel Bus. Cen. NE10: Pel 5E 84
Cartmel Ct. DH2: Ches S 7J 127
Cartmel Grn. NE5: Den M 4G 61
Cartmel Gro. NE8: Gate 7F 83
Cartmel Pk. NE10: Pel 5E 84
Cartmel Ter. DH2: Pelt 2D 126
Cartwright Rd. SR5: Sund 6H 103
Carville Gdns. NE28: W'snd 5F 65
Carville Ri. NE6: Byke 4P 5 (7A 64)
Carville Rd. NE28: W'snd 4F 65
(not continuous)
Carville Sta. Cotts. NE28: W'snd 4G 65
Carvis Cl. DH7: B'don 2C 174
Carwarding Pl. NE5: Blak 4J 61
Caseton Cl. NE25: Monks 5C 38
Casey Ct. NE63: N Sea 3E 12
Caspian Cl. NE32: Jar 1C 86
Caspian Rd. SR5: Sund 6F 103
Caspian Sq. SR5: Sund 6F 103
CASSOP 4F 179
Castellian Rd. SR5: Sund 6J 103
Casterton Gro. NE5: Cha P 2B 60
Castle Bank NE61: Mor 7G 9
Castle Chare DH1: Dur 2B 6 (2A 166)
(not continuous)
Castle Cl. DH3: Ches S 7B 128
DH5: Hett H 1H 157
NE3: Ken 7K 43
NE16: Whi 7G 81
NE42: Pru 3E 76
NE61: Mor 7F 9
Castle Ct. DH8: C'sde 4B 134
DH9: Ann P 5K 123
NE20: Pon 5J 31
Castledale Av. NE24: Cow 3E 22
CASTLE DENE 1F 143
Castledene Ct. NE3: Gos 1H 63
SR5: Sund 5G 103
Castle Dene Gro. DH4: Hou S 2D 144
Castledene Rd. DH8: Cons 1K 135
CASTLE EDEN 5A 182
Castle Eden Dene National Nature Reserve 1C 182
Castle Farm M. NE2: Jes 2H 63
Castlefields DH4: Bour 6H 129
DH7: Esh W 3F 163
Castlefields Dr. NE42: Pru 3F 77
Castleford Rd. SR5: Sund 5F 103
Castle Gth. NE1: Newc T 7G 4 (2G 83)
Castlegate Gdns. NE8: Dun 5C 82
Castle Grn. SR3: E Her 2K 131
Castle Hill Ho. NE41: Wylam 1A 78
Castlehills DH8: C'sde 4B 134
Castle Island Way NE63: N Sea 7D 12
Castle Keep 7G 4 (2G 83)
Castle Lea NE42: Pru 3E 76
Castle Leazes NE2: Newc T 1B 4 (6D 62)
Castlemain Cl. DH4: Bour 6H 129
Castle Mdws. NE61: Mor 1E 14
Castle M. SR3: E Her 2K 131
Castlenook Pl. NE15: Den M 6F 61
Castlereagh Homes, The
SR7: S'hm 1B 148
Castlereagh Rd. SR7: S'hm 3B 148
Castlereagh St. SR3: New S 2C 132
Castlereigh Cl. DH4: Bour 6H 129
Castle Riggs DH2: Ches S 6K 127
Castle Rd. NE38: Wash 3E 114
NE42: Pru 4D 76
Castles Farm Rd. NE2: Jes 2G 63
NE3: Gos 2G 63
Castles Grn. NE12: Kil 1C 46
CASTLESIDE 4B 134
Castleside Ind. Est. DH8: C'sde 3D 134
Castleside Rd. NE15: Den M 7G 61
Castle Sq. NE27: Back 6F 37
NE61: Mor 7G 9
Castle Stairs NE1: Newc T 7G 4 (2G 83)
Castle St. DH6: Bowb 4G 177
NE13: Haz 7C 34
NE61: Mor 7G 9
SR8: Eas C 7D 160
Castle Ter. NE63: Ash 3B 12
Castleton Cl. NE2: Jes 3H 63
NE23: Cra 1J 25
Castleton Gro. NE2: Jes 3H 63
Castleton Lodge NE4: Elsw 1B 82
Castleton Rd. NE32: Jar 1C 86
CASTLETOWN 6H 103
Castletown Rd. SR5: Sund 6J 103
Castletown Way SR5: Sund 5K 103
Castle Vw. DH3: Ches S 5A 128
DH3: Gt Lum 3D 142
DH4: Pen 1B 130
DH7: Esh W 3D 162
DH7: Ush M 3E 164
NE15: Hor 5E 56
NE42: O'ham 2D 76
NE42: Pru 3D 76
SR5: Sund 6H 103
Castle Wlk. NE61: Mor 1F 15
Castle Way NE61: Peg 4B 10
Castleway NE13: Din 5H 33
Castlewood Cl. NE5: W Dent 3D 60
CATCHBURN 3G 15
Catcheside Cl. NE16: Whi 2G 97
CATCHGATE 4J 123
Catchwell Rd. DH9: Dip 1H 123
Catcleugh Wlk. NE63: Ash 3D 12
Cateran Way NE23: Cra 5K 25
Caterhouse Rd. DH1: Dur 5K 153
Catharine St. W. SR4: Sund 2C 118
Cathedral Ct. NE8: Gate 10L 5 (3J 83)
Cathedral Pk. DH1: Dur 7F 155
Cathedral Stairs NE1: Newc T 6G 4
Cathedral Vw. DH4: Nbot 6D 130
DH7: Sac 1F 153
Catherine Cookson Ct.
NE33: S Shi 4A 68
Catherine Rd. DH4: New H 3D 130
Catherine St. NE33: S Shi 2K 67
Catherine Ter. DH9: Ann P 5B 124
DH9: Stly 1F 125
NE10: Fell 6A 84
NE40: Craw *3C 78*
(off Broomfield Ter.)
Catherine Vw. *NE40: Craw* *3D 78*
(off Westfield Av.)
Catholic Row NE22: Bed 1G 21
Catkin Wlk. NE40: Craw 3E 78
Cato St. SR5: S'wck 5C 104
(not continuous)
Catrail Pl. NE23: Cra 2A 26
Cattle Mkt. NE46: Hex 2D 70
Catton Gro. NE16: Sun 4H 97
Catton Pl. NE28: W'snd 6J 47
CAULDWELL 5A 68
Cauldwell Av. NE25: Monks 1D 48
NE34: S Shi 6A 68
Cauldwell Cl. NE25: Monks 7E 38
Cauldwell La. NE25: Monks 7D 38
Cauldwell Pl. NE34: S Shi 6A 68
Cauldwell Vs. NE34: S Shi 6A 68
Causeway NE9: Low F 7K 83
Causeway, The NE9: Low F 6J 83
NE15: Thro 4H 59
SR6: Monkw 7F 105
CAUSEY 3H 111
Causey Arch 4G 111
Causey Arch Station
Tanfield Railway 3H 111
Causey Bank NE1: Newc T 6H 5 (1H 83)
Causey Brae NE46: Hex 3B 70
Causey Bldgs. NE3: Gos 1E 62
Causey Dr. DH9: Stly 1G 125
CAUSEY HILL 3B 70
Causey Hill Cvn. Pk. NE46: Hex 4A 70
Causey Hill Rd. NE46: Hex 5B 70
Causey Hill Way NE46: Hex 3A 70
Causey Pk. NE46: Hex 2B 70
Causey Rd. DH9: Stly 7G 111
NE16: Marl H 7G 111
Causey Row NE16: Marl H 3H 111
Causey St. NE3: Gos 1E 62
Causey Vw. DH9: Stly 2H 125
Causey Way DH9: Stly 7G 111
NE46: Hex 3B 70
Cavalier Vw. NE31: Heb 6H 65
Cavalier Way SR3: New S 2B 132
Cavel Burrs SR2: Ryh 3J 133
Cavell Dr. DH6: Bowb 3H 177
Cavell Pl. DH9: Stly 4G 125
Cavell Rd. SR5: Sund 5G 103
Cavel Sq. SR8: Eas C 6B 160
Cavendish Ct. DH7: B'don 2C 174
Cavendish Gdns. NE63: Ash 4B 12
Cavendish Pl. NE2: Jes 4H 63
NE16: Hob 4A 110
SR3: New S 2B 132
Cavendish Rd. NE2: Jes 4H 63
Cavendish Sq. NE61: Peg 4A 10
Cavendish Ter. NE63: Ash 4B 12
Caversham Rd. NE5: Cha P 2B 60
Cawburn Cl. NE7: H Hea 2C 64
Cawdell Ct. NE30: N Shi 7H 49
Cawfields Cl. NE28: W'snd 4A 66
Cawfields Ct. NE12: Longb 6H 45
Cawnpore Sq. SR4: Sund 1A 118
Cawthorne Ter. *NE16: Hob* *4A 110*
(off Cragleas)
NE29: N Shi *4G 49*
(off Front St.)
Caxton Wlk. NE34: S Shi 4G 87
Caxton Way DH3: Ches S 1B 128
Caynham Cl. NE29: N Shi 4E 48
Cayton Gro. NE5: Cha P 3B 60
Cecil Ct. NE20: Pon 5K 31
NE28: W'snd 5F 65
Cecil Cres. DH7: Lan 7K 137
Cecil St. NE29: N Shi 7G 49
Cecil Ter. NE46: Hex 1D 70
Cedar Av. DH2: Kim 6H 141
Cedar Cl. DH1: Dur 1E 166
NE22: Bed 6H 17
NE25: Monks 1F 49
Cedar Ct. DH6: S Het 4B 158
DH6: Thor 1J 179
DH7: Lang P 5G 151
DH9: Ann P 5J 123
NE29: N Shi 3E 48
Cedar Cres. DH5: Eas L 3K 157
NE9: Low F 3H 99
NE11: Dun 7B 82
NE16: Burn 2K 109
SR7: Mur 7F 147
Cedar Dr. DH1: Dur 7K 165
NE32: Jar 6C 86
Cedar Gdns. DH8: C'sde 1E 134
Cedar Gro. NE24: News 5G 23
NE28: W'snd 3H 65
NE31: Heb 3J 85
NE34: S Shi 1B 88
NE40: Ryton 7F 59
SR6: Whit 4H 89
Cedar Rd. NE4: Fen 6K 61
Cedars DH2: Ches S 4K 127
Cedars, The DH4: Pen 1B 130
NE4: Elsw 9A 4 (3D 82)
NE9: Eigh B 5A 100
NE16: Whi 3H 97
SR2: Sund 5F 119
Cedars Ct. SR2: Sund 4F 119
Cedars Cres. SR2: Sund 5G 119
Cedars Grn. NE9: Low F 4J 99
Cedars Pk. SR2: Sund 5G 119
Cedar St. DH2: Wald 1G 141
SR8: Hord 6F 173
Cedar Ter. DH4: Hou S 2A 144
(not continuous)
NE38: Wash 7F 115
NE63: Ash 5C 12
Cedartree Gdns. NE25: Monks 1E 48
Cedar Way NE12: Longb 4C 46
Cedarway NE10: Hew 2C 100
Cedarwood DH4: Hou S 1J 143
Cedarwood Av. NE6: Walk 4E 64
Cedarwood Gro. SR2: Sund 6E 118
Cedric Cres. SR2: Sund 4D 118
Celadon Cl. NE15: Lem 5C 60
Celandine Cl. NE3: Gos 5F 45
Celandine Ct. NE63: Ash 6K 11
Celandine Way NE10: Wind N 1B 100
Cellar Hill Cl. DH4: Nbot 6D 130
Cellar Hill Ter. DH4: Hou S 7D 130
Celtic Cl. SR6: Clead 5A 88
Celtic Cres. SR6: Clead 5A 88
Cemetery App. NE34: S Shi 5A 68
Cemetery Rd. DH6: Trim S, Whe H 4B 180
DH9: Stly 2F 125
NE8: Gate 5H 83
NE32: Jar 7C 66
TS27: B Col 3J 183
Cemetery Wlk. NE8: Gate 5J 83
Centenary Av. NE34: S Shi 1C 88
Centenary Cotts. NE22: Bed 1H 21
Centenary Ct. NE4: Elsw 2B 82
Central Arc. NE1: Newc T 5F 4
Central Av. DH7: Mead 2E 174
NE29: N Shi 6D 48
NE34: S Shi 7B 68
NE62: Chop 1G 17
SR6: Whit 6G 89
Central Bus. & Techology Pk.
NE1: Newc T 5H 5 (1G 83)
Central Ct. NE26: Whit B 6G 39
Central Exchange DH3: Ches S 6A 128
Central Gdns. NE34: S Shi 7B 68
Central Link NE4: Newc T 5C 4
Central Lower Prom. NE26: Whit B 5H 39
Centralofts NE1: Newc T 7D 4
Central Parkway NE1: Newc T 7D 4
NE64: Newb S 3G 13
Central St James
NE4: Newc T 5C 4 (1E 82)
Central Sq. NE1: Newc T 7F 4 (2F 83)
Central Station (Metro) 7E 4 (2F 83)
Central Way SR4: Sund 1A 118
Centralway NE11: T Vall 3E 98
Centre for Sport 7K 61
Centurian Way NE22: Bed 6G 17
Centurion Rd. NE15: Lem 5F 61
Centurion Way NE9: Low F 1K 99
NE15: Hed W 3C 58
Century Ter. DH9: Ann P 4J 123
Ceolfrid Ter. NE32: Jar 2C 86
Cestrian Cl. DH3: Ches S 5A 128
Cestrium Ct. NE28: W'snd 1J 65
Chacombe NE38: Wash 5G 115
Chadderton Dr. NE5: Cha P 3B 60
Chad Ho. NE8: Gate 4H 83
Chadwick St. NE28: W'snd 4F 65
Chadwick Wlk. NE8: Gate 4E 82
Chaffinch Ct. NE63: Ash 5K 11
Chaffinch Rd. DH5: Eas L 2J 157
Chaffinch Way NE12: Kil 7A 36
Chainbridge Rd. NE21: Blay 3D 80
(Cowen Rd.)
NE21: Blay 2D 80
(Factory Rd.)
Chainbridge Rd. Ind. Est. NE21: Blay 2F 81
Chain Locker, The NE29: N Shi 1H 67
Chains, The DH1: Dur 2E 6 (2B 166)
NE45: Corb 7D 52
Chains Dr. NE45: Corb 7D 52
Chair La. DL16: Tudh 7J 175
Chalfont Gro. SR4: Sund 6G 117
Chalfont Rd. NE6: Walk 2D 84
Chalfont Way DH7: Mead 1E 174
Chalford Rd. SR5: S'wck 5D 104
Challoner Pl. *NE61: Mor* *7F 9*
(off Oldgate)
Challoner's Gdns. NE61: Mor 6E 8
Chamberlain St. NE24: Bly 3K 23
NE40: Craw 2D 78
Chambers Cres. NE9: Eigh B 6A 100
Chancery La. NE24: Bly 2H 23
Chandler Cl. DH1: Dur 3E 166
Chandler Ct. NE2: Jes 3H 63
SR8: Eas C 7D 160
Chandlers Ford DH4: Pen 1J 129
Chandlers Quay NE6: Byke 3A 84
Chandlers Rd. SR6: Monkw 1K 7 (7F 105)
Chandless St. NE8: Gate 10J 5
Chandos SR3: Dox P 5C 132
Chandos St. NE8: Gate 6H 83
Chandra Pl. NE5: Blak 3H 61
Chantry Cl. SR3: Dox P 4A 132
Chantry Dr. NE13: W Op 4D 34
Chantry Est. NE45: Corb 7D 52
Chantry M. *NE61: Mor* *7G 9*
(off Bridge St.)

Chantry Pl. DH4: W Rai 1A **156**
NE61: Mor 7G **9**
Chapel Av. NE16: Burn 2B **110**
Chapel Bank DH5: E Rain 6D **144**
Chapel Cl. NE3: Gos 3F **45**
NE11: Kib 2F **113**
NE46: Acomb 4B **50**
Chapel Ct. DH6: S'burn 3A **168**
DH7: Wit G 3C **152**
NE13: Sea B 3D **34**
NE15: Newb 5J **59**
NE39: H Spen 2D **94**
Chapel Dr. DH8: Cons 2K **135**
Chapel Grange NE5: West 2E **60**
Chapel Hill Rd. SR8: Pet 5C **172**
Chapel Ho. Dr. NE5: Cha P 3C **60**
Chapel Ho. Gro. NE5: Cha P 4C **60**
Chapel Ho. Rd. NE5: Cha P 4C **60**
Chapel La. DH6: Has 1B **170**
NE25: Monks 7E **38**
NE41: Wylam 7J **57**
Chapel M. DH1: Dur 2D **166**
CHAPEL PARK 3C **60**
Chapel Pl. DH1: H Shin 7F **167**
NE13: Sea B 3D **34**
SR5: Monkw 6E **104**
Chapel Rd. NE32: Jar 6B **66**
Chapel Row DH3: Bir 5C **114**
DH4: Bour 5J **129**
DH4: S Row 4C **130**
NE43: Mic 5A **76**
Chapel St. DH5: Hett H 6H **145**
DH9: Tant 6B **110**
NE29: N Shi 7E **48**
TS28: Win 7G **181**
Chapel Vw. DH4: W Rai 2K **155**
NE13: Bru V 5C **34**
NE39: Row G 4J **95**
Chapelville NE13: Sea B 3D **34**
Chaplin St. SR7: S'hm 5B **148**
Chapman St. SR6: Ful 3G **105**
Chapter Row NE33: S Shi 2J **67**
Chare, The NE1: Newc T 4E **4** (7F **63**)
SR8: Pet 6B **172**
Chare La. DH6: Shad 5E **168**
Chareway NE46: Hex 7C **50**
Chareway La. NE46: Hex 7C **50**
CHARLAW 6D **140**
Charlaw Cl. DH7: Sac 6D **140**
Charlaw La. DH7: Edm, Wit G 5K **139**
DH7: Sac, Wit G 6A **140**
Charlaw Ter. DH7: Sac 7D **140**
Charlbury Cl. NE9: Spri 6D **100**
Charlcote Cres. NE36: E Bol 7K **87**
Charles Av. NE3: Fawd 6A **44**
NE12: Longb 4B **46**
NE26: Whit B 6H **39**
NE27: Shir 7K **37**
Charles Baker Wlk. NE34: S Shi 6D **68**
Charles Ct. *NE6: Byke* *2P* ***5***
(off North Cl.)
Charles Dr. NE23: Dud 3K **35**
Charles Perkins Memorial Cott. Homes
DH3: Bir 5A **114**
Charles St. DH4: Nbot 5D **130**
DH9: Stly 5E **124**
NE8: Gate 10J **5** (4H **83**)
NE13: Haz 7C **34**
NE35: Bol C 6F **87**
NE61: Peg 4B **10**
SR1: Sund 2K **7** (1F **119**)
SR2: Ryh 3J **133**
SR3: New S 1C **132**
SR6: Monkw 1K **7** (7F **105**)
SR7: S'hm 3B **148**
SR8: Eas C 7D **160**
Charles Ter. DH2: P Fel 4G **127**
Charleswood NE3: Gos 4F **45**
Charlesworth Cl. DH6: Bowb 5H **177**
Charlie St. NE40: G'sde 5D **78**
Charlotte Cl. NE4: Newc T 9A **4** (3D **82**)
NE30: N Shi 6H **49**
Charlotte Ho. NE1: Newc T 6D **4**
Charlotte M. NE1: Newc T 6D **4**
Charlotte Sq. NE1: Newc T 6D **4** (1E **82**)
Charlotte St. DH9: Stly 5E **124**
NE28: W'snd 3G **65**
(not continuous)
NE30: N Shi 7H **49**
NE33: S Shi 3J **67**
NE40: Craw 3C **78**
Charlotte Ter. NE33: S Shi 3K **67**
Charlton Cl. NE46: Hex 4B **70**
Charlton Ct. DH6: Bowb 4J **177**
NE7: H Hea 1A **64**
NE25: Monks 1E **48**
Charlton Gdns. NE61: Mor 1H **15**
Charlton Gro. SR6: Clead 6C **88**
Charlton M. *NE15: Lem* *7D* ***60***
(off Charlton St.)
Charlton Rd. SR5: Ful 4E **104**
Charlton St. NE15: Lem 7D **60**
NE24: Bly 2H **23**
NE63: Ash 3A **12**
Charlton Vs. *NE40: G'sde* *5F* ***79***
(off Lead Rd.)
Charlton Wlk. NE8: Gate 5E **82**
Charman St. SR1: Sund 3J **7** (1F **119**)
Charminster Gdns. NE6: Heat 3A **64**
Charnwood DH9: Stly 1E **124**
Charnwood Av. NE12: Longb 6J **45**
Charnwood Ct. *NE33: S Shi* *3A* ***68***
(off Leighton St.)
Charnwood Gdns. NE9: Low F 1K **99**
Charter Dr. SR3: E Her 2J **131**
Charters Cres. DH6: S Het 5B **158**
Chartwell Pl. DH8: Cons 5H **121**
Chase, The NE12: Kil 2J **45**
NE22: Bed 7G **17**
NE29: N Shi 6G **49**
NE38: Wash 7D **114**
NE46: Hex 3B **70**
Chase Ct. DH6: S'burn 3A **168**
NE16: Whi 7H **81**
Chasedale Cres. NE24: Cow 2E **22**
CHASE FARM 2D **22**
Chase Farm Dr. NE24: Cow 1D **22**
Chase Mdws. NE24: Cow 3D **22**
Chase M. NE24: Cow 2D **22**
NE32: Jar 2D **86**
Chatham Cl. NE25: Sea D 2H **37**
Chatham Rd. SR5: Sund 5G **103**
Chathill Cl. NE25: Monks 6D **38**
NE61: Mor 3G **15**
Chathill Ter. NE6: Walk 1D **84**
Chatsworth NE3: Gos 3E **62**
Chatsworth Cl. NE42: Pru 3E **76**
Chatsworth Ct. NE33: S Shi 2K **67**
Chatsworth Cres. SR4: Sund 4C **118**
Chatsworth Dr. NE22: Bed 5A **18**
Chatsworth Gdns. NE5: West 2F **61**
NE6: Byke 2B **84**
NE25: Monks 1E **48**
Chatsworth Pl. NE16: Whi 2G **97**
Chatsworth Rd. NE32: Jar 1C **86**
Chatsworth St. SR4: Sund 3C **118**
Chatsworth St. Sth. SR4: Sund 4C **118**
Chatterton St. SR5: S'wck 5C **104**
Chatton Av. NE23: Cra 5A **26**
NE34: S Shi 5D **68**
Chatton Cl. DH2: Ches S 1J **141**
NE61: Hep 3J **15**
Chatton St. NE28: W'snd 4C **66**
Chatton Wynd NE3: Gos 5C **44**
NE62: W Sle 1B **18**
Chaucer Av. NE34: S Shi 3G **87**
TS27: B Col 1G **183**
Chaucer Cl. DH9: Stly 3G **125**
NE8: Gate 10L **5** (4J **83**)
Chaucer Rd. NE16: Whi 6H **81**
Chaucer St. DH4: Hou S 2D **144**
Chaytor Gro. SR1: Sund 2G **119**
Chaytor Rd. DH8: Shot B 4D **120**
Chaytor St. NE32: Jar 5B **66**
Chaytor Ter. Nth. DH9: Stly 6H **125**
Chaytor Ter. Sth. DH9: Stly 6J **125**
Cheadle Av. NE23: Cra 7J **21**
NE28: W'snd 6H **47**
Cheadle Rd. SR5: Sund 5G **103**
Cheam Cl. NE16: Whi 2H **97**
Cheam Rd. SR5: Sund 5G **103**
Cheddar Gdns. NE9: Low F 4H **99**
Chedder Ct. DH9: Ann P 6K **123**
Cheeseburn Gdns. NE5: Fen 5K **61**
Cheldon Cl. NE25: Monks 5C **38**
Chelford Cl. NE28: W'snd 5J **47**
Chelmsford Gro. NE2: Newc T 2L **5** (6J **63**)
Chelmsford Rd. SR5: Sund 5G **103**
Chelmsford Sq. SR5: Sund 4G **103**
Chelmsford St. SR3: New S 1C **132**
Chelsea Gdns. NE8: Gate 6K **83**
Chelsea Gro. NE4: Fen 1C **82**
Chelsea Ho. *DH9: Stly* *2F* ***125***
(off Quarry Rd.)
Cheltenham Ct. NE63: Ash 5A **12**
Cheltenham Dr. NE35: Bol C 4E **86**
Cheltenham Rd. SR5: Sund 5G **103**
Cheltenham Sq. SR5: Sund 5G **103**
Cheltenham Ter. NE6: Heat 1P **5** (6K **63**)
Chelton Cl. NE13: Haz 7D **34**
Chepstow Cl. DH8: Shot B 2F **121**
Chepstow Gdns. NE8: Gate 7F **83**
Chepstow St. SR4: Sund 2D **118**
Chequers, The DH8: Cons 1H **135**
Cherribank SR2: Ryh 3G **133**
Cherry Av. SR8: Hord 6F **173**
Cherry Banks DH3: Ches S 4B **128**
Cherry Blossom Way SR5: Sund 6B **102**
Cherryburn Gdns. NE4: Fen 5A **62**
Cherryburn (Thomas Bewick Birthplace Mus.)
4B **76**
Cherry Cotts. DH9: Tant 6B **110**
Cherry Dr. DH6: Has 1B **170**
Cherry Gro. NE12: Kil 7A **36**
NE42: Pru 3D **76**
SR7: S'hm 4A **148**
Cherry Knowle SR2: Ryh 4G **133**
Cherry La. NE46: Hex 6B **50**
Cherry Pk. DH7: B'don 2C **174**
Cherrytree Cl. NE12: Kil 2D **46**
Cherrytree Ct. NE22: Bed 6B **18**
Cherry Tree Dr. NE22: Bed 7H **17**
Cherrytree Dr. DH7: Lang P 5H **151**
NE16: Whi 6J **81**
Cherry Tree Gdns. DH5: Hou S 2F **145**
NE15: Hor 5E **56**
Cherrytree Gdns. NE9: Low F 3J **99**
NE25: Monks 1F **49**
Cherry Tree La. NE41: Wylam 7J **57**
Cherry Tree M. NE28: W'snd 7H **47**
Cherrytree Rd. DH2: Ches S 4J **127**
Cherry Trees NE24: Bly 3H **23**
Cherrytree Sq. SR2: Ryh 1G **133**
Cherry Tree Wlk. NE31: Heb 2J **85**
NE34: S Shi 2B **88**
Cherry Way DH4: Hou S 1B **144**
NE12: Kil 7A **36**
Cherrywood NE6: Walk 4C **64**
Cherrywood Gdns. SR3: Tuns 2D **132**
Cherwell NE37: Wash 7K **101**
Cherwell Rd. SR8: Pet 7K **171**
Cherwell Sq. NE12: Longb 3A **46**
Chesham Gdns. NE5: Cha P 3B **60**
Chesham Grn. NE3: Ken 7B **44**
Cheshire Av. DH3: Bir 7A **114**
Cheshire Cl. NE63: Ash 3J **11**
Cheshire Ct. NE31: Heb 1H **85**
Cheshire Dr. DH1: Carr 2G **167**
Cheshire Gdns. NE28: W'snd 2E **64**
Cheshire Gro. NE34: S Shi 6D **68**
Chesils, The NE12: Longb 7J **45**
Chesmond Dr. NE21: Blay 3C **80**
Chessar Av. NE5: Blak 3H **61**
Chester Av. NE28: W'snd 2K **65**
Chester Burn Cl. DH2: P Fel 6G **127**
Chester Cl. NE20: Darr H 7F **31**
Chester Cres. NE2: Newc T 2J **5** (6H **63**)
SR1: Sund 4F **7** (2D **118**)
Chesterfield Rd. NE4: Elsw 2B **82**
Chester Gdns. DH7: Wit G 2D **152**
NE34: S Shi 6A **68**
Chester Gro. NE23: Seg 2C **36**
NE24: Bly 3G **23**
Chesterhill NE23: Cra 6K **25**
CHESTER-LE-STREET 6A **128**
Chester-le-Street Leisure Cen. 6B **128**
Chester-le-Street Station (Rail) 6A **128**
Chester M. SR4: Sund 3D **118**
CHESTER MOOR 3J **141**
Chester Oval SR1: Sund 5F **7**
Chester Pike NE15: Scot 2H **81**
Chester Pl. NE8: Gate 4G **83**
SR8: Pet 5K **171**
Chester Rd. DH3: Gt Lum, Lam P 4C **128**
DH4: Bour, Pen, S Row 6F **129**
DH8: C'sde 3C **134**
DH9: Stly 2G **125**
SR1: Sund 5F **7** (2D **118**)
SR2: Sund 2D **118**
SR4: Sund 5G **117**
(Best Vw.)
SR4: Sund 3A **118**
(West Mt.)
Chester Rd. Est. DH9: Stly 2G **125**
Chesters, The DH8: Ebc 5G **107**
NE5: Cha P 4C **60**
NE25: Monks 5D **38**
Chesters Av. NE12: Longb 6H **45**
Chesters Cl. NE9: Low F 1H **99**
Chesters Ct. NE12: Longb 6K **45**
Chesters Dene DH8: Ebc 5G **107**
Chesters Gdns. NE40: Craw 2C **78**
Chesters Pk. NE9: Low F 1H **99**
Chester St. DH2: Wald 1G **141**
DH4: Hou S 7D **130**
NE2: Newc T 2J **5** (6H **63**)
SR4: Sund 2C **118**
Chester St. E. SR4: Sund 2D **118**
Chester St. W. SR4: Sund 2C **118**
Chester Ter. SR1: Sund 4F **7** (2D **118**)
SR8: Eas 7B **160**
Chester Ter. Nth. SR4: Sund 2D **118**
Chesterton Rd. NE34: S Shi 2H **87**
Chester Way NE32: Jar 5A **86**
Chesterwood Dr. NE28: W'snd 3E **64**
Chesterwood Ter. NE10: Bill Q 4F **85**
Chestnut Av. NE5: Fen 3K **61**
NE16: Whi 2H **97**
NE24: Bly 7H **19**
NE25: Monks 7F **39**
NE38: Wash 7F **115**
Chestnut Cl. NE12: Kil 7K **35**
NE32: Jar 5D **86**
Chestnut Cres. SR5: S'wck 4B **104**
Chestnut Dr. DH6: Has 1C **170**
Chestnut Gdns. NE8: Gate 6E **82**
Chestnut Gro. DH7: Ush M 3C **164**
NE34: S Shi 2B **88**
Chestnut St. NE28: W'snd 4G **65**
NE63: Ash 3B **12**
Chestnut Ter. DH4: Hou S 7C **130**
Chestnut Way SR7: S'hm 4A **148**
Cheswick Dr. NE3: Gos 6F **45**
Cheswick Rd. NE25: Sea D 1J **37**
Cheveley Ct. DH1: Carr 7H **155**
Cheveley Pk. Shop. Cen.
DH1: Carr 7H **155**
Cheveley Wlk. DH1: Carr 1H **167**
Chevin Cl. NE6: Walk 4E **64**
Chevington NE10: Hew 2E **100**
Chevington Cl. NE61: Peg 4K **9**
Chevington Gdns. NE5: Fen 4K **61**
Chevington Gro. NE25: Monks 4D **38**
Cheviot Cl. DH2: Ches S 2J **141**
NE21: Blay 5C **80**
(not continuous)
NE29: N Shi 2F **49**
NE37: Wash 2E **114**
Cheviot Ct. DH9: Ann P 6K **123**
NE7: H Hea 1J **63**
NE21: Blay 3C **80**
NE26: Whit B 7J **39**
NE61: Mor 2G **15**
SR7: S'hm 2J **147**
Cheviot Gdns. NE11: Lob H 7C **82**
SR7: S'hm 2J **147**
Cheviot Grange NE23: Dud 5A **36**
Cheviot Gro. NE61: Peg 4A **10**
Cheviot Ho. NE36: W Bol 7H **87**
NE38: Wash 4G **115**
Cheviot La. SR2: Ryh 2F **133**
Cheviot Mt. DH9: Dip 7J **109**
Cheviot M. NE6: Byke 7A **64**
Cheviot Pl. SR8: Pet 5K **171**
(not continuous)
Cheviot Rd. DH2: Ches S 1K **141**
(not continuous)
NE32: Jar 2A **86**
NE34: S Shi 5C **68**
Cheviot St. SR4: Sund 1B **118**
Cheviot Ter. DH9: Stly 4G **125**
Cheviot Vw. DH9: Dip 2G **123**
NE10: Wind N 1B **100**
NE12: Longb 6B **46**
NE13: Bru V 5C **34**
NE20: Pon 5A **32**
NE23: Seg 2D **36**
NE26: Whit B 7H **39**
NE27: Shir 3H **47**
NE42: Pru 4G **77**
NE63: Ash 2C **12**
Cheviot Way NE46: Hex 2C **70**
NE62: Stake 7K **11**
Chevron, The NE6: Byke 5P **5**
Chevy Chase NE1: Newc T 4E **4**
Chevychase Ct. SR7: Seat 7H **133**
Cheyne, The SR3: Dox P 4C **132**
Cheyne Rd. NE42: Pru 3E **76**
Chichester Av. NE23: Nel V 2H **25**
Chichester Cl. NE3: Ki Pk 5K **43**
NE8: Gate 4G **83**
NE63: N Sea 5E **12**
Chichester Gro. NE22: Bed 6H **17**
Chichester Pl. NE33: S Shi 5J **67**
Chichester Rd. DH1: Dur 4B **154**
NE33: S Shi 5K **67**
SR6: Seab 3G **105**
Chichester Rd. E. NE33: S Shi 4K **67**
Chichester Station (Metro) 5J **67**
Chichester Way NE32: Jar 5B **86**
Chicken Rd. NE28: W'snd 2E **64**
Chicks La. SR6: Whit 6H **89**
Chigwell Cl. DH4: Pen 2B **130**
Chilcote NE10: Fell 7B **84**
Chilcrosse NE10: Hew 1D **100**
(not continuous)
Childhood Memories Toy Mus. 3K **49**
Chilham Ct. NE29: N Shi 4B **48**
NE38: Wash 4F **115**
Chillerton Way TS28: Win 6G **181**
Chillingham Cl. NE24: Bly 4F **23**
Chillingham Ct. NE6: Byke 6A **64**
Chillingham Cres. NE63: Ash 4A **12**
Chillingham Dr. DH2: Ches S 2J **141**
NE29: N Shi 1D **66**
Chillingham Gro. SR8: Pet 2J **181**
Chillingham Ho. *SR6: Roker* *7G* ***105***
(off Mulgrave Dr.)
Chillingham Ind. Est. NE6: Walk 6A **64**
Chillingham Rd. DH1: Dur 5B **154**
NE6: Heat, Walk 4A **64**
Chillingham Road Station (Metro) 6B **64**
Chillingham Ter. NE32: Jar 2D **86**
Chilside Rd. NE10: Fell 7B **84**
Chiltern Av. DH2: Ches S 7K **127**
(not continuous)
Chiltern Cl. NE38: Wash 5F **115**
NE63: N Sea 6D **12**
Chiltern Dr. NE12: Longb 3K **45**
Chiltern Gdns. DH9: Stly 4H **125**
NE11: Lob H 7C **82**
Chiltern Rd. NE29: N Shi 3E **48**
Chilton Av. DH4: Hou S 1K **143**
Chilton Gdns. DH4: Hou S 2A **144**
(not continuous)
Chilton Gth. SR8: Pet 7D **172**
CHILTON MOOR 3A **144**
Chilton St. SR5: Monkw 6E **104**
Chimney Mills NE2: Newc T 1C **4** (5E **62**)
China St. SR2: Sund 4G **119**
Chingford Cl. DH4: Pen 2C **130**
Chip, The NE61: Loan 3F **15**
Chipchase NE38: Wash 4D **114**
Chipchase Av. NE23: Cra 4K **25**
Chipchase Cl. NE22: Bed 7F **17**
NE61: Peg 4B **10**
Chipchase Ct. DH4: Hou S 1H **143**
NE25: New Hart 4G **27**
SR7: Seat 7H **133**
Chipchase Cres. NE5: West 2E **60**
Chipchase M. NE3: Gos 3C **44**
Chipchase Ter. NE32: Jar 3B **86**
Chippendale Pl. NE2: Newc T 1B **4** (6D **62**)
Chirdon Cres. NE46: Hex 2E **70**
Chirnside NE23: Cra 6K **25**
Chirnside Ter. DH9: Ann P 6J **123**
CHIRTON 7F **49**
Chirton Av. NE29: N Shi 7F **49**
NE34: S Shi 7E **68**
Chirton Dene Quays NE29: N Shi 3F **67**
Chirton Dene Way NE29: N Shi 3F **67**
Chirton Grn. NE24: Bly 4F **23**
NE29: N Shi 7F **49**
Chirton Gro. NE34: S Shi 7E **68**
Chirton Hill Dr. NE29: N Shi 5C **48**
Chirton La. NE29: N Shi 6E **48**
Chirton Lodge NE29: N Shi 7E **48**
Chirton West Vw. NE29: N Shi 7F **49**
Chirton Wynd NE6: Byke 1A **84**
Chisholm Pl. NE46: Hex 1D **70**
Chislehurst Rd. DH4: Pen 2B **130**
Chiswick Gdns. NE8: Gate 6J **83**
Chiswick Rd. SR5: Sund 5G **103**
Chiswick Sq. SR5: Sund 5G **103**
Chollerford Av. NE25: Whit B 7H **39**
NE29: N Shi 6C **48**
Chollerford Cl. NE3: Gos 1C **62**
Chollerford M. NE25: H'wll 1K **37**
Chollerton Dr. NE12: Longb 4E **46**
NE22: Bed 7J **17**

CHOPPINGTON 1G 17
Choppington Rd. NE22: Bed 7H 17
NE61: Mor 2H 15
NE62: Sco G 7H 17
CHOPWELL 6K 93
Chopwell Gdns. NE9: Wrek 5B 100
Chopwell Rd. NE17: C'wl 1A 108
Chopwell Vw. *DH9: Dip* *2F 123*
(off Front St.)
Chopwell Wood 6C 94
Chopwell Woods Rd. NE39: H Spen 5D 94
Chorley Pl. NE6: Walk 1C 84
CHOWDENE 5G 99
Chowdene Bank NE9: Low F 5G 99
NE11: T Vall 5G 99
Chowdene Ter. NE9: Low F 3H 99
Christal Ter. SR6: Ful 4F 105
Christchurch Ct. SR7: S'hm 2J 147
Christchurch Pl. SR8: Pet 7A 172
Christie Ter. NE6: Walk 1D 84
Christmas Pl. NE8: Gate 4D 82
Christon Cl. NE3: Gos 7G 45
Christon Rd. NE3: Gos 7E 44
Christon Way NE10: Bill Q 4F 85
Christopher Rd. NE6: Walk 6C 64
Chudleigh Gdns. NE5: Cha P 3B 60
Chudleigh Ter. NE21: Blay 4C 80
Church Av. NE3: Gos 7F 45
NE62: Sco G 3G 17
NE62: W Sle 1B 18
Church Bank DH8: Shot B 3E 120
DH9: Stly 2F 125
NE15: Newb 6K 59
NE28: W'snd 3H 65
SR5: S'wck 6C 104
Churchburn Dr. NE61: Loan 3F 15
Church Chare DH3: Ches S 6B 128
NE16: Whi 7H 81
NE20: Pon 4K 31
Church Cl. DH4: Bour 5J 129
DH8: Ebc 5G 107
NE13: Din 4H 33
NE22: Bed 1H 21
NE25: Monks 7C 38
NE44: Rid M 7K 73
SR7: S'hm 2A 148
SR8: Pet 7C 172
Church Ct. *NE13: Haz* *7C 34*
(off Coach La.)
NE22: Bed 1H 21
Churchdown Cl. NE35: Bol C 4E 86
Church Dr. NE9: Low F 1J 99
Churcher Gdns. NE28: W'snd 1E 64
Church Flatt NE20: Pon 4K 31
Church Grn. NE16: Whi 7H 81
NE33: S Shi *6K 67*
(off Hepscott Ter.)
SR7: S'hm 2A 148
Churchill Av. DH1: Dur 2D 166
NE25: Monks 1E 48
SR5: S'wck 5C 104
Churchill Cl. DH8: Shot B 3E 120
Churchill Ct. NE25: Monks 7E 38
Churchill Gdns. NE2: Jes 4J 63
Churchill M. NE6: Byke 2A 84
Churchill Rd. NE8: Gate 5K 83
Churchill Sq. DH1: Dur 1D 166
DH4: Hou S 2B 144
Churchill St. NE1: Newc T 8C 4 (2E 82)
NE28: W'snd 7K 47
SR1: Sund 2G 119
Churchill Ter. DH6: S Hil 4E 168
CHURCH KELLOE 7F 179
Churchlands NE46: Hex 2F 71
Church La. DH1: Dur 2C 166
(Gilesgate)
DH1: Dur 5D 6 (4B 166)
(Oswald Ct.)
DH6: Shad 5E 168
NE3: Gos 7F 45
NE9: Low F 1K 99
NE22: Bed 1J 21
NE44: Rid M 7J 73
SR1: Sund 4H 7 (2E 118)
SR6: Whit 6H 89
SR7: Mur 7D 146
Church La. Nth. SR7: Mur 7D 146
Church Mdw. DH7: Mead 7F 165
Church M. DH2: Nett 6H 141
NE27: Back 6G 37
Church Pde. DH7: Sac 6D 140
Church Pk. DH6: Whe H 2B 180
Church Pl. NE10: Fell 5B 84
Church Point NE64: Newb S 3K 13
Church Point Cvn. Pk.
NE64: Newb S 2K 13
Church Ri. NE16: Whi 7H 81
NE40: Ryton 1J 79
(not continuous)
Church Rd. DH2: Pelt 3F 127
DH5: Hett H 4G 145
DH8: B'hill 5F 121
NE3: Gos 7E 44
NE9: Low F 2J 99
NE15: Newb 6K 59
NE27: Back, W Holy 6G 37
NE41: Wylam 7J 57
Church Row DH4: W Rai 1A 156
NE10: Wind N *1A 100*
(off Windy Nook Rd.)
NE46: Hex 1D 70
Churchside DH3: Gt Lum 3E 142
NE13: Din 4H 33
Churchside Gdns. DH5: Eas L 2J 157
Church Sq. DH7: B'don 7E 164
Church St. DH1: Dur 5D 6 (4B 166)
DH3: Bir 4A 114
DH4: Hou S 2E 144
DH4: S Row 3B 130
DH5: Hou S 2E 144
DH6: Has 1A 170
DH6: Quar H 5D 178
DH6: Whe H 2B 180
DH7: Lang P 5H 151
DH7: Sac 7D 140
DH8: Cons 7H 121
DH8: C'sde 5B 134
DH8: Lead 5A 122
DH9: Ann P 5K 123
DH9: Stly 2F 125
NE6: Walk 2E 84
(Caledonia St.)
NE6: Walk 1E 84
(Church Wlk.)
NE8: Gate 8H 5 (2G 83)
NE10: Fell 6B 84
NE11: Dun 5C 82
NE16: Marl H 7G 97
NE21: Winl 5B 80
NE23: Cra 4K 25
NE24: Bly 1J 23
NE30: N Shi 6H 49
NE31: Heb 6H 65
NE32: Jar 6B 66
SR4: Sund 2G 117
SR5: S'wck 5D 104
SR7: Mur 1E 158
SR7: S'hm 3B 148
TS27: Hes 4E 182
TS28: Sta T 7H 181
Church St. E. SR1: Sund 1G 119
Church St. Head DH1: Dur 6D 6 (4B 166)
(not continuous)
Church St. Nth. SR6: Roker 6G 105
Church St. Vs. DH1: Dur 6D 6 (4B 166)
Church Ter. NE21: Blay 3C 80
Church Va. DH6: H Pitt 7C 156
Church Vw. DH1: Carr 7H 155
DH2: Kim 7J 141
DH3: Bir 4A 114
DH6: Has 1A 170
DH6: Shot C 5E 170
DH6: Thor 1K 179
DH7: Esh W 3D 162
DH7: Lan 7K 137
DH7: Queb 7B 150
DH8: Cons 7G 121
NE25: Ears 6K 37
NE28: W'snd 3H 65
NE35: Bol C 5E 86
NE37: Wash 1H 115
SR3: New S 2C 132
Church Vw. Vs. DH5: Hett H 5G 145
Church Vs. DH6: Shad 5E 168
Church Wlk. DH6: Thor 1J 179
(not continuous)
NE6: Walk 1E 84
(not continuous)
NE8: Gate 8H 5 (2G 83)
NE61: Mor 7E 8
SR1: Sund 1H 119
SR8: Eas 1J 171
Churchwalk Ho. NE6: Walk 1E 84
Church Ward SR2: Ryh 3J 133
Church Way NE25: Ears 5A 38
NE29: N Shi 6G 49
NE33: S Shi 2J 67
Church Wood *NE23: Cra* *4K 25*
(off Church St.)
Church Wynd DH6: S'burn 3K 167
Churston Cl. DH4: Nbot 5C 130
Cicero Ct. NE6: Walk 2E 84
Cicero Ter. SR5: S'wck 5C 104
Cinderford Cl. NE35: Bol C 4E 86
Cineworld Cinema
Boldon Colliery 6E 86
Cinnamon Dr. *TS29: Trim S* *7C 180*
(off Margaret Ter.)
Circle, The NE32: Jar 2B 86
Circle Pl. NE46: Hex 1C 70
Circus Casino
Newcastle 7F 4 (2F 83)
Cirencester St. SR4: Sund 1D 118
Cirus Ho. SR3: Silk 3C 132
Citadel E. NE12: Kil 1B 46
Citadel W. NE12: Kil 1B 46
Citygate NE1: Newc T 5D 4 (1E 82)
City Grn. SR1: Sund 6J 7 (3F 119)
City Library 4K 7
City Quadrant NE1: Newc T 7D 4 (2E 82)
City Rd. NE1: Newc T 6H 5 (1G 83)
City Stadium 3L 5 (7J 63)
City Theatre 3C 6 (3A 166)
City Way SR3: Dox P 4H 131
City W. Bus. Pk. DH7: Mead 2F 175
Civic Cen.
Sunderland 6J 7 (3F 119)
Civic Ct. NE31: Heb 1K 85
Clacton Rd. SR5: Sund 6F 103
Clanfield Ct. NE3: Gos 1H 63
Clanny Ho. SR4: Sund 2B 118
Clanny St. SR1: Sund 4G 7 (2E 118)
(Hind St.)
SR1: Sund 5F 7 (2D 118)
(Westbourne Rd.)
Clapham Av. NE6: Byke 1B 84
Clapham Ho. NE1: Newc T 4G 4
Clappersgate SR8: Eas 1J 171
Clara Av. NE27: Shir 7K 37
Clarabad Ter. NE12: Longb 3E 46
Clara St. NE4: Benw 2K 81
NE21: Winl 5B 80
SR7: S'hm 2K 147
CLARA VALE 7C 58
Clara Va. Complex NE40: C Vale 7C 58
Clare Lea NE43: Hed 4C 92
Claremont Av. NE15: Lem 5D 60
SR6: Seab 4G 105
Claremont Ct. *NE26: Whit B* *3E 38*
(off Claremont Cres.)
Claremont Cres. NE26: Whit B 4E 38
Claremont Dr. DH4: S Row 3A 130
Claremont Gdns. NE26: Whit B 5F 39
NE36: E Bol 7K 87
Claremont Nth. Av. NE8: Gate 4G 83
Claremont Pl. NE2: Newc T 1D 4 (6E 62)
NE8: Gate 5G 83
Claremont Rd. NE1: Newc T 6F 63
NE2: Newc T 1B 4 (5C 62)
NE26: Whit B 3E 38
SR6: Seab 4G 105
Claremont Sth. Av. NE8: Gate 5G 83
Claremont St. NE2: Newc T 1C 4 (6E 62)
NE8: Gate 5G 83
Claremont Ter. NE2: Newc T 1C 4 (6E 62)
NE9: Spri 6D 100
NE10: Bill Q 4F 85
NE24: Bly 2H 23
SR2: Sund 6H 7 (3E 118)
Claremont Wlk. NE8: Gate 5G 83
(Bk. Woodbine St.)
NE8: Gate 5F 83
(St Cuthbert's Pl.)
Claremount Ct. NE36: W Bol 7H 87
Clarence Cres. NE26: Whit B 7H 39
Clarence Gdns. DH8: B'hill 5G 121
Clarence Ga. DH6: S Het 4C 158
Clarence Ho. NE2: Newc T 3J 5 (7H 63)
NE28: W'snd 3F 65
Clarence Pl. NE3: Gos 7G 45
Clarence St. DH6: Bowb 5H 177
DH6: Coxh 7K 177
DH9: Tant 6B 110
NE2: Newc T 4J 5 (7H 63)
NE26: Sea S 5D 28
SR5: S'wck 5B 104
(not continuous)
SR7: S'hm 3B 148
Clarence Ter. DH3: Ches S 6A 128
Clarence Vs. DH6: Coxh 7K 177
Clarence Wlk. NE2: Newc T 3J 5 (7H 63)
Clarendon M. NE3: Gos 2E 44
Clarendon Rd. NE6: Heat 4A 64
Clarendon Sq. SR5: S'wck 4D 104
Clarendon St. *DH8: Cons* *6H 121*
(off Green St.)
Clare Rd. SR8: Pet 7K 171
Clarewood Av. NE34: S Shi 5C 68
Clarewood Ct. NE4: Newc T 4A 4 (7D 62)
Clarewood Grn. NE4: Newc T 4A 4 (7C 62)
Clarewood Pl. NE5: Fen 5J 61
Clarke Ct. DH8: Cons 7G 121
Clarke's Ter. NE23: Dud 4J 35
Clarke Ter. NE10: Fell 6A 84
SR7: Mur 7E 146
Clarks Fld. NE61: Mor 7E 8
Clarks Hill Wlk. NE15: Newb 6K 59
Clark's Ter. SR7: S'hm 1G 147
Clark Ter. DH8: Lead 3K 121
DH9: Stly 1F 125
Clarty La. NE11: Kib 4F 113
NE46: Anic, Sand 4H 51
Clasper Ct. NE33: S Shi 1J 67
Clasper St. NE4: Newc T 10A 4 (3D 82)
Clasper Way NE16: Swa 3G 81
Claude Gibb Hall
NE1: Newc T 2H 5 (6G 63)
Claude St. DH5: Hett H 7G 145
NE40: Craw 3D 78
Claude Ter. SR7: Mur 7F 147
Claudius Ct. NE33: S Shi 1J 67
Claverdon St. NE5: Cha P 1B 60
Clavering Cen., The NE16: Whi 2F 97
Clavering Pl. DH9: Ann P 6K 123
NE1: Newc T 7F 4 (2F 83)
Clavering Rd. NE16: Swa 6G 81
NE21: Blay *5C 80*
(off Shibdon Bank)
Clavering Sq. NE11: Dun 6B 82
Clavering St. NE28: W'snd 4B 66
(not continuous)
Clavering Way NE21: Blay 5E 80
Claverley Dr. NE27: Back 6G 37
Claxheugh Cotts. SR4: Sund 1H 117
Claxheugh Rd. SR4: Sund 1H 117
Claxton St. SR8: Hord 5E 172
Clay La. DH1: Dur 5A 6 (4J 165)
Claymere Rd. SR2: Sund 7G 119
Claypath DH1: Dur 2C 6 (2B 166)
NE10: Hew 3D 100
Claypath Ct. DH1: Dur 2D 6 (2B 166)
Claypath La. NE33: S Shi 3J 67
(not continuous)
Claypath Rd. DH5: Hett H 1G 157
Claypath St. NE6: Byke 4M 5 (7J 63)
Claypit Cl. NE33: S Shi 1J 67
Claypool Ct. NE34: S Shi 1J 87
Clayside Ho. NE33: S Shi 4K 67
Clayton Pk. Sq. NE2: Jes 5G 63
Clayton Rd. NE2: Jes 5F 63
Clayton St. NE1: Newc T 6E 4 (1F 83)
NE22: Bed 6B 18
NE23: Dud 3H 35
NE32: Jar 6B 66
Clayton St. W. NE1: Newc T 7D 4 (2E 82)
Clayton Ter. NE10: Fell 5A 84
NE15: Hed W *3D 58*
(off Calvus Dr.)
Clayton Ter. Rd. NE17: C'wl 5A 94
NE39: H Spen 5A 94
Claytonville DH7: Edm 2B 140
Clayworth Rd. NE3: Gos 3D 44
CLEADON 5C 88
Cleadon Gdns. NE9: Wrek 4B 100
NE28: W'snd 7A 48
Cleadon Hill 2D 88
Cleadon Hill Dr. NE34: S Shi 2C 88
Cleadon Hill Rd. NE34: S Shi 2D 88
Cleadon La. NE36: E Bol 5A 88
SR6: Clead, Whit 5D 88
Cleadon La. Ind. Est. NE36: E Bol 6K 87
Cleadon Lea SR6: Clead 5B 88
Cleadon Mdws. SR6: Clead 5C 88
CLEADON PARK 1B 88
Cleadon St. DH8: Cons 6H 121
NE6: Walk 7C 64
Cleadon Towers NE34: S Shi 2D 88
Cleasby Gdns. NE9: Low F 1H 99
Cleasewell Hill NE62: Chop 1H 17
Cleasewell Ter. NE62: Stake 1J 17
Cleaside Av. NE34: S Shi 2C 88
Cleehill Dr. NE29: N Shi 3F 49
Cleeve Ct. NE38: Wash 3H 115
Cleghorn St. NE6: Heat 5A 64
Clegwell Ter. NE31: Heb 7K 65
Clematis Cres. NE9: Eigh B 5B 100
Clement Av. NE22: Bed 7A 18
Clementhorpe NE29: N Shi 5G 49
Clementina Cl. SR2: Sund 3G 119
Clement St. NE9: Low F 2H 99
Clennel Ho. NE4: Benw 1A 82
Clennell Av. NE31: Heb 1H 85
Clent Way NE12: Longb 6J 45
Clephan St. NE11: Dun 5B 82
Clervaux Ter. NE32: Jar 7C 66
Cleveland Av. DH2: Ches S 7K 127
NE29: N Shi 6F 49
NE64: Newb S 3H 13
Cleveland Cl. DH8: C'sde 2D 134
Cleveland Ct. NE32: Jar 6A 66
NE33: S Shi 1J 67
Cleveland Cres. NE29: N Shi 6G 49
Cleveland Dr. NE38: Wash 5F 115
Cleveland Gdns. NE7: H Hea 2J 63
NE28: W'snd 2B 66
Cleveland M. NE11: Dun 5C 82
Cleveland Pl. SR8: Pet 6K 171
Cleveland Rd. NE29: N Shi 6F 49
SR4: Sund 4B 118
Cleveland St. NE33: S Shi 1K 67
Cleveland Ter. DH9: Stly 4G 125
NE29: N Shi 6G 49
NE64: Newb S 3H 13
SR4: Sund 3C 118
Cleveland Vw. SR6: Seab 1G 105
Clickemin NE20: Pon 5A 32
Cliffe Ct. SR6: Seab 3H 105
Cliffe Pk. SR6: Seab 3H 105
Clifford Gdns. NE30: N Shi 6H 49
NE40: Craw 3D 78
Clifford Rd. DH9: Stly 3E 124
NE6: Byke 1B 84
Clifford's Bank DH7: Queb 1B 162
Clifford's Fort Moat NE30: N Shi 7J 49
(not continuous)
Cliffords Ga. DH7: Esh W 3C 162
Clifford St. DH3: Ches S 1A 142
DH7: Lang P 5H 151
NE6: Byke 4N 5 (7K 63)
NE21: Blay 3C 80
NE30: N Shi 6J 49
SR4: Sund 2C 118
Clifford Ter. DH3: Ches S 7A 128
NE40: Craw 2D 78
Cliff Rd. SR2: Ryh 3J 133
Cliff Row NE30: Whit B 7J 39
Cliffside NE34: S Shi 7E 68
Cliff Ter. SR2: Ryh 3J 133
SR8: Eas 1K 171
Cliff Vw. SR2: Ryh 3J 133
CLIFTON 6G 15
Clifton Av. NE28: W'snd 3F 65
NE34: S Shi 6A 68
Cliftonbourne Av. SR6: Seab 3G 105
Clifton Cl. NE40: Ryton 2J 79
NE62: Stake 7J 11
Clifton Ct. NE3: Ki Pk 5K 43
NE9: Spri 6C 100
Clifton Gdns. NE9: Low F 7H 83
NE24: News 5H 23
NE29: N Shi 2E 66
(not continuous)
Clifton Gro. NE25: Monks 5E 38
Clifton La. NE61: Tra W 7H 15
Clifton Rd. NE4: Benw 1A 82
NE23: Cra 5K 25
SR6: Seab 4G 105
Clifton Sq. SR8: Pet 5B 172
Clifton Ter. NE12: Longb 5B 46
NE26: Whit B 6H 39
NE33: S Shi 6J 67
Cliftonville Av. NE4: Benw 1A 82
Cliftonville Gdns. NE26: Whit B 5G 39
Clifton Wlk. NE5: Cha P 3B 60
NE25: Monks 4E 38
Climbing Tree Wlk. NE61: Peg 4A 10
Climb Newcastle 4P 5 (7K 63)
Clintburn Ct. NE23: Cra 2A 26
Clinton Pl. NE3: Gos 2D 44
SR3: E Her 3J 131

Clipsham Cl. NE12: Longb 6K 45
Clipstone Av. NE6: Walk 3C 84
Clipstone Cl. NE15: Thro 3G 59
Clitheroe Gdns. NE22: Bed 6F 17
Clive Pl. NE6: Byke 4N 5 (1K 83)
Clive St. NE29: N Shi 7H 49
NE34: S Shi 2G 87
Clockburn Lonnen NE16: Whi 2D 96
Clockburnsyde Cl. NE16: Whi 2E 96
Clockmill Rd. NE8: Dun, Gate 5C 82
Clockstand Cl. SR6: Roker 5G 105
Clock Twr. Flats NE61: Mor 6F 9
Clockwell St. SR5: S'wck 6B 104
Cloggs, The NE20: Pon 4K 31
Cloister Av. NE34: S Shi 1G 87
Cloister Ct. NE8: Gate 10K 5 (3H 83)
Cloister Gth. NE7: Longb 7H 45
Cloisters, The NE7: Longb 7H 45
NE34: S Shi 6B 68
SR2: Sund 7J 7 (3F 119)
TS28: Win 4G 181
Cloister Wlk. NE32: Jar 6C 66
Close NE1: Newc T 8F 4 (2F 83)
Close, The DH1: Carr 1H 167
DH2: Ches S 4A 128
DH7: Bran 4A 174
DH7: Lan 6J 137
DH8: Shot B 3F 121
NE5: W Dent 5E 60
NE16: Burn 1C 110
NE20: Pon 6J 31
NE21: Winl 5A 80
NE23: Seg 2D 36
NE24: Bly 7J 19
NE42: Oving 2B 76
NE42: Pru 3G 77
SR6: Clead 5B 88
Closeburn Sq. SR3: Silk 3D 132
Close East, The DH2: Ches S 4A 128
Closefield Gro. NE25: Monks 7E 38
Close Ho. Est. NE15: Hed W 4B 58
Close House Riverside Nature Reserve 6B 58
Close St. SR4: Sund 1C 118
SR5: S'wck 6D 104
Cloth Mkt. NE1: Newc T 6F 4 (1F 83)
CLOUGH DENE 5A 110
Clough Dene DH9: Tant 5A 110
NE16: Hob 5A 110
Clough La. NE1: Newc T 6F 4
Clousden Dr. NE12: Longb 3C 46
Clousden Grange NE12: Kil 3C 46
Clousden Hill NE12: Longb 3C 46
Clovelly Av. NE4: Benw 1A 82
Clovelly Gdns. NE22: Bed 1H 21
NE26: Whit B 5G 39
Clovelly Pl. NE20: Darr H 2G 41
NE32: Jar 1E 86
Clovelly Rd. SR5: Sund 4F 103
Clovelly Sq. SR5: Sund 4G 103
Clover Av. DH4: S Row 4B 130
NE21: W Mill 1C 96
Cloverdale NE22: Bed 7G 17
Cloverdale Ct. NE6: Walk 6E 64
Cloverdale Gdns. NE7: H Hea 2K 63
NE16: Whi 2H 97
Cloverfield NE27: Back, Shir 2H 47
Cloverfield Av. NE3: Fawd 6B 44
Clover Hill NE16: Sun 5H 97
(not continuous)
Cloverhill DH2: Ches S 7H 127
NE32: Jar 5C 86
Cloverhill Av. NE31: Heb 3H 85
Cloverhill Cl. NE23: Dud 2J 35
Cloverhill Ct. DH9: Stly 5H 125
Cloverhill Dr. NE40: Craw 2E 78
Clover Laid DH7: B'don 2C 174
Clover Way NE34: S Shi 2B 88
Clowes Ter. DH9: Ann P 5K 123
Clowes Wlk. DH9: Stly 2H 125
Club La. DH1: Dur 1H 165
Clumber St. NE4: Elsw 3C 82
Clumber St. Nth. NE4: Elsw 3C 82
(not continuous)
Cluny Gallery, The 4L 5 (7J 63)
Clyde Av. NE31: Heb 3J 85
Clyde Ct. SR3: Silk 3B 132
Clydedale Av. NE12: Longb 5A 46
Clydesdale Av. DH4: Pen 2B 130
Clydesdale Gth. DH1: P Me 3A 154
Clydesdale Mt. NE6: Byke 1A 84
Clydesdale Rd. NE6: Byke 1A 84
Clydesdale St. DH5: Hett H 1G 157
Clyde St. DH9: Stly 2H 125
NE8: Gate 6J 83
NE17: C'wl 6A 94
Clyvedon Ri. NE34: S Shi 3C 88
Coach Ho. Ct. NE9: Low F 1K 99
Coach Ho. La. *NE2: Jes* *4G 63*
(off Tankerville Ter.)
Coach La. DH7: Wit G 3C 152
NE7: Longb 7A 46
NE12: Longb 7A 46
NE13: Haz 7J 33
NE29: N Shi 7G 49
Coach Open NE28: W'snd 4B 66
Coach Rd. NE11: Lob H, Rave 2D 98
NE15: Thro 3G 59
NE28: W'snd 4G 65
NE37: Wash 6F 101
Coach Rd. Est. NE37: Wash 6G 101
Coach Rd. Grn. NE10: Fell 4A 84
Coalbank Rd. DH5: Hett H 1F 157
Coalbank Sq. DH5: Hett H 1F 157
COALBURNS 7B 78
Coalburn Ter. NE61: Hep 4K 15
Coaley La. DH4: Hou S, Nbot 6C 130
Coalford La. DH6: H Pitt, Litt 6C 156
Coalford Rd. DH6: S'burn 2K 167
Coal La. NE42: Oving 2K 75
Coalway Dr. NE16: Whi 6H 81
Coalway La. NE16: Swa, Whi 6H 81
NE16: Whi 6H 81
NE40: G'sde 4B 78
NE41: Wylam 4B 78
Coalway La. Nth. NE16: Swa 5H 81
Coanwood Bungs. NE23: Cra 5K 25
Coanwood Dr. NE23: Cra 5K 25
NE25: Monks 6B 38
Coanwood Gdns. NE11: Lob H 2D 98
Coanwood Way NE16: Sun 4H 97
Coast Rd. NE7: H Hea 3A 64
NE28: W'snd 2F 65
NE29: N Shi 6D 48
NE34: S Shi 4C 68
SR6: Whit 6F 69
SR8: Hord 6E 172
TS27: B Col 6E 172
TS27: B Col, H'pool 2J 183
Coast Vw. TS27: B Col 3K 183
Coastway Shop. Forum NE28: W'snd 1H 65
Coates Cl. DH9: Stly 4G 125
Coatsworth Ct. NE8: Gate 4G 83
Coatsworth Rd. NE8: Gate 4G 83
Cobalt Bus. Cen. NE27: Shir 4J 47
Cobalt Cl. NE15: Lem 5C 60
Cobalt Pk. Way NE27: Shir 4K 47
NE28: W'snd 4K 47
Cobbett Cres. NE34: S Shi 3H 87
Cobbler's La. NE18: Welt 2H 55
NE43: Newt 2H 55
Cobblestone Ct. NE6: Byke 6P 5 (1K 83)
Cobden Rd. NE23: Cra 6A 26
Cobden St. DH8: Cons 6J 121
NE8: Gate 5J 83
NE28: W'snd 3F 65
Cobden Ter. NE8: Gate 5J 83
Cobham Pl. NE6: Walk 1E 84
Coble Dene NE29: N Shi 2E 66
Coblehouse NE26: Whit B 7J 39
Coble Landing NE33: S Shi 2H 67
Coburg St. NE8: Gate 4H 83
NE24: Bly 2K 23
NE30: N Shi 6H 49
Coburn Cl. NE23: Dud 6A 36
Cochrane Ct. NE4: Benw 1A 82
Cochrane M. DH7: Ush M 3C 164
Cochrane Pk. Av. NE7: H Hea 2A 64
Cochrane St. NE4: Benw 1A 82
Cochrane Ter. DH7: Ush M 3C 164
NE13: Din 4H 33
Cochran St. NE21: Blay 3C 80
Cockburn Ter. NE29: N Shi 2D 66
Cocken La. DH3: Gt Lum 3F 143
Cocken Rd. DH3: Gt Lum, Plaw 7B 142
DH4: Leam 7F 143
Cockermouth Grn. NE5: Den M 5G 61
Cockermouth Rd. SR5: Sund 4F 103
Cockhouse La. DH7: Ush M 2J 163
Cockshaw NE46: Hex 1C 70
Cockshaw Ct. NE46: Hex 1C 70
Cockshott Dean NE42: Pru 3E 76
Cohen Ct. NE8: Gate 6G 83
Cohort Cl. DH8: Ebc 5G 107
Cohort Pl. NE15: Den M 6G 61
Colbeck Av. NE16: Swa 5H 81
Colbeck Ter. NE30: Tyne 5K 49
Colbourne Av. NE23: Nel V 1G 25
Colbourne Cres. NE23: Nel V 1G 25
Colbury Cl. NE23: Cra 7J 21
Colby Ct. NE4: Newc T 7A 4 (2D 82)
Colchester St. NE34: S Shi 2G 87
Colchester Ter. SR4: Sund 3B 118
Coldbeck Ct. NE23: Cra 5A 26
COLD HESLEDON 1J 159
Cold Hesledon Ind. Est. SR7: Cold H 7H 147
Coldingham Ct. DH7: Sac 7D 140
Coldingham Gdns. NE5: Fen 3K 61
Coldside Gdns. NE5: Cha P 2B 60
Coldstream DH2: Ous 6J 113
Coldstream Av. SR5: S'wck 5D 104
Coldstream Cl. DH4: S Row 4B 130
Coldstream Dr. NE21: Winl 6A 80
Coldstream Gdns. NE28: W'snd 2K 65
Coldstream Rd. NE15: Benw 7H 61
Coldstream Way NE29: N Shi 4C 48
Coldwell Cl. DH6: S Het 4A 158
Coldwell La. NE10: Fell, Wind N 7A 84
Coldwell Pk. Av. NE10: Fell 7A 84
Coldwell Pk. Dr. NE10: Fell 7A 84
Coldwell Rd. NE42: Pru 3H 77
Coldwell St. NE10: Fell 6B 84
Coldwell Ter. NE10: Fell 7A 84
Colebridge Cl. NE5: Blak 2J 61
Colebrooke DH3: Bir 6B 114
Cole Gdns. NE10: Ward 6E 84
Colegate NE10: Hew 7D 84
Colegate W. NE10: Hew 7D 84
Colepeth NE10: Fell 7C 84
Colepike Rd. DH7: Lan 7J 137
Coleridge Av. NE9: Low F 3G 99
NE33: S Shi 4A 68
TS27: B Col 7G 173
Coleridge Dr. NE62: Chop 1H 17
Coleridge Gdns. DH9: Dip 1H 123
Coleridge Pl. DH2: P Fel 6G 127
Coleridge Rd. SR5: Sund 5H 103
Coleridge Sq. NE31: Heb 7J 65
Coley Grn. NE5: Cha P 1B 60
Coley Hill Cl. NE5: Cha P 1C 60
Coley Ter. SR6: Ful 4G 105
Colgrove Pl. NE3: Ken 7A 44
Colgrove Way NE3: Ken 7B 44
Colima Av. SR5: Sund 7H 103
Colin Ct. NE21: Blay 2E 80
Colin Ter. SR2: Ryh 3H 133
Coliseum Bldgs., The NE26: Whit B 6H 39
College, The DH1: Dur 4B 6 (3A 166)
College Burn Rd. SR3: Dox P 4A 132
College Dr. NE33: S Shi 5A 68
College La. NE1: Newc T 3G 4 (7G 63)
NE12: Longb 6A 46
College Pl. NE63: Ash 5C 12
College Rd. DH7: Esh 7J 151
NE31: Heb 3H 85
NE63: Ash 5C 12
College St. NE1: Newc T 3G 4 (7G 63)
College Vw. DH7: Bearp 7C 152
DH7: Esh W 5D 162
DH8: Cons 2A 136
SR5: Monkw 6E 104
Collier Cl. NE15: Thro 4H 59
Collierley La. DH9: Dip 7G 109
Colliers, The NE23: Dud 6A 36
Colliers Cl. NE63: Ash 4C 12
Colliery Cl. NE12: Longb 7C 46
Colliery La. DH5: Hett H 1H 157
Colliery Rd. DH7: Bearp 7D 152
NE11: Dun 4B 82
NE46: Acomb 4B 50
COLLIERY ROW 3B 144
Collin Av. NE34: S Shi 1D 88
Collin Dr. NE34: S Shi 1G 87
Colling Av. SR7: S'hm 3J 147
(not continuous)
Collingdon Grn. NE39: H Spen 3D 94
Collingdon Rd. NE39: H Spen 3E 94
Collingwood Av. NE28: W'snd 1F 65
Collingwood Bldgs. *NE1: Newc T* *6F 4*
(off Collingwood St.)
Collingwood Cen. NE29: N Shi 3F 49
Collingwood Cl. NE23: Nel V 2G 25
Collingwood Cotts. NE20: Pon 4F 31
Collingwood Ct. *NE20: Pon* *5J 31*
(off Meadowfield)
NE29: N Shi 7F 49
NE37: Wash 7K 101
Collingwood Courtyard NE8: Gate 4D 82
Collingwood Cres. NE20: Darr H 7H 31
Collingwood Dr. DH4: S Row 3A 130
NE46: Hex 3B 70
Collingwood Gdns. NE10: Fell 4B 84
Collingwood Mans. NE29: N Shi 1H 67
Collingwood M. NE3: Gos 7E 44
Collingwood Pl. NE62: Stake 1J 17
Collingwood Rd. NE25: Well 6A 38
NE64: Newb S 2G 13
Collingwood St. DH5: Hett H 4G 145
NE1: Newc T 7F 4 (2F 83)
NE10: Fell 5B 84
NE31: Heb 7A 66
NE33: S Shi 5J 67
SR5: S'wck 5D 104
(not continuous)
Collingwood Ter. NE2: Jes 4H 63
NE11: Dun 5C 82
NE24: Bly 2J 23
NE26: Whit B 7J 39
NE30: Tyne 5K 49
NE61: Mor 6F 9
Collingwood Vw. NE29: N Shi 7F 49
Collingwood Wlk. *NE37: Wash* *7K 101*
(off Collingwood Ct.)
Collison St. DH8: Cons 6H 121
Collywell Bay Rd. NE26: Sea S 4D 28
Collywell Ct. NE26: Sea S 4D 28
Colman Av. NE34: S Shi 7G 67
Colmet Ct. NE11: T Vall 3F 99
Colnbrook Cl. NE3: Ki Pk 5K 43
Colombo Rd. SR5: Sund 6F 103
Colpitts' Ter. DH1: Dur 3A 6 (3K 165)
Colston Pl. NE12: Longb 5B 46
Colston Ri. SR8: Pet 5A 172
Colston St. NE4: Benw 1K 81
Colston Way NE25: Monks 4D 38
Coltere Av. NE36: E Bol 7A 88
Colton Gdns. NE9: Low F 4J 99
Colt Pk. NE17: Ham 3K 107
Coltpark NE5: W Dent 4F 61
Coltpark Pl. NE23: Cra 5K 25
Coltpark Woods NE17: Ham 2K 107
Coltsfoot Gdns. NE10: Wind N 2A 100
Coltspool NE11: Kib 2F 113
Columba St. SR5: S'wck 5D 104
Columba Wlk. NE3: Gos 7F 45
(not continuous)
COLUMBIA 4K 115
Columbia Grange NE3: Ken 7A 44
Columbia Ter. NE24: Bly 3J 23
Columbo Sq. NE8: Gate 9G 4
Column of Liberty 4B 96
Colville Ct. DH9: Stly 3H 125
Colwell Pl. NE5: Fen 6J 61
Colwell Rd. NE27: Shir 2K 47
NE29: N Shi 3F 49
NE63: Ash 6D 12
Colwyne Pl. NE5: Blak 3H 61
Colwyn Pde. NE31: Heb 4A 86
Combe Dr. NE15: Lem 6B 60
Combined Court Cen.
Newcastle upon Tyne (The Law Courts) 6H 5 (1G 83)
Comet Dr. SR8: Eas 7A 160
Comet Row NE12: Kil 2A 46
Comet Sq. SR3: New S 2C 132
Comma Ct. NE11: Fest P 7D 82
Commerce Way DH4: Hou S 3C 144
Commercial Bldgs. *NE24: Bly* *1J 23*
(off Commercial Rd.)
Commercial Pl. *NE46: Hex* *2D 70*
(off Priestpopple)
Commercial Rd. NE3: Gos 7G 45
NE6: Byke 5P 5 (1A 84)
NE24: Bly 1J 23
NE32: Jar 5C 66
(not continuous)
NE33: S Shi 4H 67
SR2: Sund 3H 119
Commercial Sq. DH7: B'don 1E 174
Commercial St. DH7: B'don 7E 164
DH7: Corn C 7A 150
NE21: Winl 5B 80
Commercial Way NE23: Cra 4J 25
Commissioners Wharf
NE29: N Shi 3G 67
Community North Sports Complex 3J 103
Community Recreation Cen. 1D 60
Complete Football 1G 45
Compton Av. NE34: S Shi 6K 67
Compton Ct. NE38: Wash 3F 115
Compton Rd. NE29: N Shi 7F 49
CONCORD 6H 101
Concorde Ho. NE25: H'wll 2J 37
Concorde Sq. SR3: New S 2C 132
Concorde Way NE32: Jar 7B 66
Concord Ho. NE37: Wash 7H 101
Concordia Leisure Cen. 4J 25
Condercum Ct. NE15: Benw 1J 81
Condercum Ind. Est. NE4: Benw 1K 81
Condercum Rd. NE4: Benw 1K 81
Condercum Rd. Bk. NE4: Benw 1K 81
Cone St. NE33: S Shi 3H 67
Cone Ter. DH3: Ches S 6B 128
Conewood Ho. NE3: Fawd 6B 44
Coney Gth. Pl. NE63: Ash 2D 12
Congburn Bank DH7: Edm 2C 140
Cong Burn Vw. DH2: P Fel 6G 127
Conhope La. NE4: Benw 1K 81
Conifer Cl. DH1: Dur 1E 166
NE21: Winl 6B 80
Conifer Ct. NE12: Longb 4D 46
NE40: G'sde 5F 79
Coningsby Cl. NE3: Gos 4F 45
Coningsby Gdns. NE61: Mor 7H 9
Coniscliffe Av. NE3: Ken 2B 62
Coniscliffe Pl. SR6: Roker 6G 105
Coniscliffe Rd. DH9: Stly 3D 124
Coniscliffe Ter. *SR8: Eas* *1K 171*
(off Thorpe Rd.)
Conishead Ter. DH6: S Het 3B 158
Coniston DH3: Bir 6B 114
NE10: Pel 6E 84
Coniston Av. DH5: Eas L 3J 157
NE2: Jes 3G 63
NE16: Whi 7K 81
NE31: Heb 1K 85
NE64: Newb S 4G 13
SR5: Ful 3E 104
Coniston Cl. DH1: Carr 7J 155
DH2: Ches S 7A 128
NE12: Kil 1A 46
NE15: Newb 6J 59
SR8: Pet 6C 172
Coniston Ct. NE5: Den M 5H 61
NE24: Cow 7E 18
Coniston Cres. NE21: Winl 6B 80
Coniston Dr. DH7: Sac 6D 140
NE32: Jar 3D 86
NE37: Wash 2G 115
Coniston Gdns. NE9: Low F 2K 99
Coniston Grange NE36: E Bol 6H 87
Coniston Pl. NE9: Low F 2K 99
Coniston Rd. NE24: Cow 7D 18
NE28: W'snd 1K 65
NE30: Cull 2F 49
Coniston Way DH8: Lead 5B 122
Connaught Cl. DH4: S Row 4C 130
Connaught Gdns. NE12: Longb 5B 46
Connaught M. *NE2: Jes* *4G 63*
(off Bk. St George's Ter.)
Connaught Ter. NE32: Jar 7B 66
Conniscliffe Ct. NE46: Hex 3A 70
Conniscliffe Rd. NE46: Hex 3B 70
Connolly Ho. NE34: S Shi 3K 87
Connolly Ter. NE17: C'wl 2A 108
CONSETT 7H 121
Consett Bus. Pk. DH8: Cons 5K 121
Consett La. DH8: C'sde 7D 120
Consett Pk. 6G 121
Consett Pk. Ter. DH8: C'sde 3D 134
Consett Rd. DH7: Lan 5J 137
DH8: C'sde 4B 134
NE11: Lob H 2B 98
Consett Ter. DH7: Esh 6G 151
Consort Pl. NE12: Longb 6J 45
Constable Cl. DH9: Stly 3F 125
NE40: Ryton 2G 79
Constable Gdns. NE34: S Shi 3J 87
Constables Gth. DH3: Bir 4A 114
Constance St. DH2: Pelt 2G 127
DH8: Cons 7H 121
Constitutional Hill DH1: Dur 2C 166
Content St. NE21: Blay 5C 80
Convent Rd. NE4: Fen 6K 61
(not continuous)
Conway Cl. NE22: Bed 7F 17
NE40: Ryton 2H 79
Conway Dr. NE7: H Hea 1J 63
Conway Gdns. NE28: W'snd 1E 64
SR3: E Her 2K 131

Conway Gro. NE26: Sea S .3B 28
Conway Pl. DH2: Ous .1H 127
Conway Rd. SR5: Sund .5F 103
Conway Sq. NE9: Low F .6J 83
SR5: Sund .5F 103
Conyers DH2: Nett .6H 141
Conyers Av. DH2: Ches S .4K 127
Conyers Cl. SR5: Sund .6H 103
Conyers Cres. SR8: Hord .3C 172
Conyers Gdns. DH2: Ches S .4K 127
Conyers Pl. DH2: Ches S .4K 127
Conyers Rd. DH2: Ches S .4K 127
NE6: Byke .4P 5 (7K 63)
Cook Av. DH7: Bearp .1C 164
Cook Cl. NE33: S Shi .5H 67
Cook Cres. SR7: Mur .7D 146
Cooke's Wood DH7: Bro .4E 164
Cook Gdns. NE10: Ward .6F 85
Cook Gro. SR8: Hord .3C 172
Cook's Cotts. DH7: Ush M .2B 164
Cookshold La. DH6: H Pitt, S'burn .3A 168
Cookson Cl. NE4: Newc T .5A 4 (1D 82)
NE45: Corb .7D 52
Cookson Ho. NE33: S Shi .2J 67
Cookson Pl. DH9: Stly .4H 125
Cookson's La. NE1: Newc T .8E 4 (3F 83)
Cookson St. NE4: Newc T .5A 4 (1C 82)
Cookson Ter. DH2: Ches S .6K 127
SR7: Mur .1F 159
Cook Sq. SR5: Sund .5G 103
Cooks Wood NE38: Wash .5H 115
Cook Way SR8: Pet .4G 171
Coomassie Rd. NE24: Bly .2J 23
Coomside NE23: Cra .6A 26
Coop Bldgs. DH3: Bir .4A 114
Co-operative Bldgs. DH9: Dip .1G 123
NE25: Sea D .7H 27
Co-operative Cres. NE10: Wind N .7A 84
Cooperative St. DH3: Ches S .5A 128
Cooperative Ter. DH4: Hou S .1K 143
NE61: Peg .4B 10
Co-operative Ter. DH2: Gra V .5C 126
DH2: Pelt .2C 126
DH5: Hett H .6G 145
DH6: Shot C .6E 170
DH7: B'hpe .5E 138
DH7: New B .4A 164
DH8: M'sly .7K 107
DH8: Shot B .2E 120
DH9: Dip .1G 123
NE10: Wind N .7A 84
NE12: Longb .3E 46
NE13: Bru V .5C 34
NE16: Burn .2B 110
NE27: Shir .3J 47
(Cramlington Ter.)
NE27: Shir .1J 47
(St Mark's Ct.)
NE37: Wash .7J 101
NE39: H Spen .2D 94
SR4: Sund .3C 118
Co-operative Ter. E. DH9: Dip .1H 123
Co-operative Ter. W. DH9: Dip .1G 123
Cooperative Vs. DH6: S Hil .3D 168
Co-operative Vs. *DH6: Whe H .2A 180*
(off Thornley Rd.)
DH7: Lang M .7G 165
DH9: Dip .1G 123
(off Front St.)
Cooperative Workshops *DH7: Sac .7E 140*
(off Plawsworth Rd.)
Cooper Pl. DH7: Wit G .3C 152
Coopers Cl. DH6: Thor .1K 179
Coopers Ct. *NE45: Corb .7D 52*
(off Orchard Vw.)
Cooper Sq. DH1: Dur .1D 166
Cooper's Ter. DH6: Thor .1J 179
Cooper St. SR6: Roker .5G 105
Coopies Fld. NE61: Mor .1H 15
Coopies Haugh NE61: Mor .1J 15
Coopies La. NE61: Mor .1G 15
Coopies La. Ind. Est. NE61: Mor .1J 15
Coopies Way NE61: Mor .1J 15
Copeland Ct. DH1: Dur .4J 165
Copland Ter. NE2: Newc T .4J 5 (7H 63)
Copley Av. NE34: S Shi .4J 87
Copley Dr. SR3: Sund .6D 118
Copperas La. NE15: Den M .6F 61
Copper Chare NE61: Mor .6F 9
Copperfield DH1: Dur .5J 165
Coppergate Ct. NE31: Heb .6K 65
Coppers Cl. NE11: Fest P .7D 82
Coppersmiths Sq.
NE1: Newc T .8E 4 (2F 83)
Coppice, The NE26: Sea S .4C 28
SR8: Eas, Eas C .7B 160
Coppice Hill DH7: Esh W .4F 163
Coppice Pl. NE12: Kil .3E 46
Coppice Way NE2: Newc T .3J 5 (7H 63)
Coppy La. DH9: Beam .3H 111
NE16: Marl H .3H 111
Copse, The NE3: Gos .4F 45
NE12: Longb .3C 46
NE16: Burn .2K 109
NE21: Blay .4F 81
NE37: Wash .5F 101
NE42: Pru .4H 77
Coptleigh DH5: Hou S .3G 145
Coquet NE38: Wash .7D 114
Coquet Av. NE3: Gos .6D 44
NE24: News .4J 23
NE26: Whit B .6G 39
NE34: S Shi .5C 68
Coquet Bldgs. NE15: Walb .4B 60
Coquet Cl. SR8: Pet .7A 172
Coquetdale Av. NE6: Walk .7E 64
Coquetdale Cl. NE61: Peg .4A 10
Coquetdale Pl. NE22: Bed .7A 18
Coquetdale Vs. SR6: Roker .5G 105
Coquet Dr. DH2: Ous .1G 127
Coquet Gdns. DH9: Stly .5E 124
NE28: W'snd .3J 65
Coquet Gro. NE15: Thro .3G 59
Coquet St. NE1: Newc T .5K 5 (1H 83)
NE17: C'wl .6A 94
NE31: Heb .7H 65
NE32: Jar .1A 86
NE63: Ash .3C 12
Coquet Ter. NE6: Heat .4A 64
NE23: Dud .3H 35
Corbett St. SR7: S'hm .2K 147
(not continuous)
SR8: Eas C .7D 160
Corbiere Cl. SR3: Silk .3A 132
Corbitt St. NE8: Gate .5E 82
CORBRIDGE .1D 72
Corbridge Av. NE13: W Op .5D 34
Corbridge Cl. NE28: W'snd .6J 47
CORBRIDGE COMMON .7C 72
Corbridge Ct. NE12: Longb .6H 45
Corbridge Rd. DH8: Cons, M'sly .1J 121
NE6: Byke .7A 64
NE45: Corb .2D 70
NE46: Hex .2D 70
Corbridge Roman Town Hadrian's Wall .7C 52
Corbridge Station (Rail) .2D 72
Corbridge St. NE6: Byke .4P 5 (7K 63)
Corby Gdns. NE6: Walk .7D 64
Corby Ga. SR2: Sund .4F 119
Corby Gro. SR8: Pet .2J 181
Corby Hall Dr. SR2: Sund .4F 119
Corby M. SR2: Sund .4F 119
Corchester Av. NE45: Corb .7D 52
Corchester La. NE45: Ayd, Corb .6J 51
NE46: Ayd, B End .6J 51
Corchester Rd. NE22: Bed .6G 17
Corchester Ter. NE45: Corb .7D 52
Corchester Towers NE45: Corb .6D 52
Corchester Wlk. NE7: Longb .1K 63
Corcyra St. SR7: S'hm .4B 148
Corfu Rd. SR5: Sund .5G 103
Corinthian Sq. SR5: Sund .5G 103
Cork St. SR1: Sund .1G 119
Cormorant Cl. NE24: News .5K 23
NE38: Wash .5D 114
NE63: Ash .6C 12
Cormorant Dr. NE11: Dun .4C 82
Cornbank Cl. SR3: Dox P .4C 132
Corndean NE38: Wash .4A 116
Cornelia Cl. SR3: New S .2C 132
Cornelia St. SR3: New S .2C 132
Cornelia Ter. SR7: S'hm .3A 148
Cornel M. NE7: H Hea .2A 64
Cornel Rd. NE7: H Hea .2K 63
Cornerstone M. *NE40: Craw .2C 78*
(off Greenside Rd.)
Corney St. NE33: S Shi .6H 67
Cornfield Gth. SR8: Pet .7D 172
Cornfields, The NE31: Heb .7J 65
Cornforth Cl. NE10: Ward .1G 101
NE63: Ash .5K 11
Cornhill NE5: W Dent .4F 61
NE32: Jar .5C 86
Cornhill Av. NE3: Fawd .5B 44
Cornhill Cen., The *SR5: S'wck .5D 104*
(off Goschen St.)
Cornhill Cl. NE29: N Shi .5D 48
Cornhill Cres. NE29: N Shi .5D 48
(not continuous)
Cornhill Rd. NE23: Cra .4A 26
SR5: S'wck .5D 104
Corning Rd. SR4: Sund .1C 118
Corn Mill Dr. DH5: Hou S .4D 144
Cornmoor DH2: Ches S .7H 127
Cornmoor Gdns. NE16: Whi .2H 97
Cornmoor Rd. NE16: Whi .1H 97
CORNSAY COLLIERY .1A 162
Cornthwaite Dr. SR6: Whit .5G 89
Cornwall Ct. SR7: Mur .7F 147
Cornwall Est. SR7: Mur .7F 147
Cornwallis NE37: Wash .6J 101
Cornwallis Sq. NE33: S Shi .4H 67
Cornwallis St. NE33: S Shi .2J 67
Cornwall Rd. NE31: Heb .3K 85
Cornwall St. SR8: Eas C .7D 160
Cornwall Wlk. DH1: Carr .1H 167
Cornwell Ct. NE3: Gos .1H 63
Cornwell Cres. NE22: Bed .1K 21
Coronation Av. DH1: Carr .7H 155
NE16: Sun .5H 97
SR2: Ryh .3H 133
SR8: Hord .6E 172
TS27: B Col .2J 183
Coronation Bldgs. *SR5: S'wck .5B 104*
(off Park Ter.)
Coronation Bungs. NE3: Gos .7F 45
Coronation Cl. SR1: Sund .1G 119
Coronation Cotts. DH6: Shot C .6E 170
NE10: Hew .6D 84
Coronation Cres. DH4: Hou S .7C 130
DH6: Low P .5B 156
NE25: Monks .6F 39
Coronation Grn. DH5: Eas L .3K 157
Coronation Homes DH7: Esh W .4F 163
Coronation Rd. NE5: Cha P .2B 60
NE16: Sun .5H 97
NE25: Sea D .7G 27
TS28: Win .4F 181
Coronation Sq. DH6: S Het .4D 158
Coronation St. *DH2: Pelt .3E 126*
(off Holyoake St.)
DH3: Ches S .1B 142
NE23: Dud .2K 35
NE24: Bly .3J 23
NE28: W'snd .3G 65
NE29: N Shi .1G 67
NE33: S Shi .3J 67
NE40: Ryton .2J 79
NE64: Newb S .2J 13
SR1: Sund .3K 7 (1G 119)
(not continuous)
Coronation Ter. DH1: Dur .3G 167
DH2: Gra V .5D 126
DH3: Ches S .1A 142
DH5: Hett H .1G 157
DH9: Ann P .5B 124
NE9: Spri .6D 100
NE11: Kib .2E 112
NE29: N Shi .3B 48
NE35: Bol C .5E 86
NE63: Ash .6B 12
TS29: Trim S .7B 180
Corporation Quay .7H 105
Corporation Rd. SR2: Sund .4H 119
Corporation St. NE4: Newc T .6B 4 (1D 82)
Corporation Yd. NE15: Newb .5K 59
NE61: Mor .6F 9
Corriedale Cl. DH1: P Me .3A 154
Corrighan Ter. DH5: E Rain .6C 144
Corrofell Gdns. NE10: Fell .4C 84
Corry Cl. TS27: B Col .2J 183
(not continuous)
Corry Ct. SR4: Sund .4A 118
Corsair NE16: Whi .1F 97
Corsenside NE5: W Dent .4F 61
Corstorphine Town NE33: S Shi .5H 67
Cortina Av. SR4: Sund .4K 117
Cortland Rd. DH8: Shot B .5E 120
Cort St. DH8: B'hill .6G 121
Corvan Ter. DH9: Tant .6A 110
Corver Way NE12: Longb .6B 46
Cosford Ct. NE3: K Bank .5J 43
Cosgrove Ct. NE7: Longb .7J 45
Cossack Ter. SR4: Sund .1A 118
Cosserat Pl. NE31: Heb .6H 65
Cosser St. NE24: News .5F 23
Coston Dr. NE33: S Shi .2J 67
(not continuous)
Cosyn St. NE6: Byke .5M 5 (1J 83)
Cotehill Dr. NE20: Darr H .7F 31
Cotehill Rd. NE5: Den M .4H 61
Cotemede NE10: Hew .1E 100
Cotemede Ct. NE10: Hew .1E 100
Cotfield Wlk. NE8: Gate .5F 83
Cotgarth, The NE10: Fell .7C 84
Cotherstone Cl. DH8: Cons .1H 135
Cotherstone Ct. DH5: Eas L .3K 157
SR3: Sund .6D 118
Cotherstone Rd. DH1: Dur .5B 154
Cotman Gdns. NE34: S Shi .4K 87
Cotsford Cres. SR8: Hord .6E 172
Cotsford Grange SR8: Hord .6F 173
Cotsford La. SR8: Hord .6E 172
Cotsford Pk. Est. SR8: Hord .6F 173
Cotswold Av. DH2: Ches S .7J 127
(not continuous)
NE12: Longb .3K 45
Cotswold Cl. NE38: Wash .4F 115
Cotswold Dr. NE25: Whit B .1F 49
NE63: N Sea .6C 12
Cotswold Gdns. NE7: H Hea .2J 63
NE11: Lob H .7C 82
Cotswold Pl. SR8: Pet .5K 171
Cotswold Rd. NE29: N Shi .2E 48
SR5: Sund .5G 103
Cotswolds La. NE35: Bol C .5E 86
Cotswold Sq. SR5: Sund .4G 103
Cotswold Ter. DH9: Stly .4G 125
Cottage Farm NE7: H Hea .2B 64
Cottage Gdns. SR6: Clead .5C 88
Cottage La. NE5: Fen .4K 61
Cottages, The NE11: Lame .6G 99
SR8: Hord .3C 172
Cottages Rd. SR7: S'hm .4B 148
Cottenham Chare
NE4: Newc T .5B 4 (1D 82)
Cottenham St. NE4: Newc T .6B 4 (1D 82)
Cotterdale NE28: W'snd .7D 46
Cotterdale Av. *NE8: Gate .6H 83*
(off Silverdale Ter.)
Cotter Riggs Pl. NE5: Cha P .3B 60
Cotter Riggs Wlk. NE5: Cha P .3B 60
Cottersdale Gdns. NE5: Cha P .2B 60
Cottingham Cl. SR8: Pet .5K 171
Cottingham Gro. DH6: Thor .1H 179
Cottinglea NE61: Mor .5F 9
Cottingvale NE61: Mor .5F 9
Cottingwood Ct. NE4: Newc T .4A 4 (7D 62)
Cottingwood Gdns.
NE4: Newc T .4A 4 (7D 62)
NE61: Mor .6F 9
Cottingwood Grn. NE24: News .6G 23
Cottingwood La. NE61: Mor .5F 9
Cottonwood DH4: S Row .3K 129
SR3: Dox P .4A 132
Coulson Cl. NE46: Hex .4B 70
Coulthards La. NE8: Gate .9K 5 (3H 83)
Coulton Dr. NE36: E Bol .7K 87
Council Av. DH4: S Row .3B 130
Council Rd. NE63: Ash .3A 12
Council Ter. NE37: Wash .1H 115
Counden Rd. NE5: West .2E 60
Countess Av. NE26: Whit B .6G 39
Countess Cl. SR7: S'hm .2A 148
Countess Dr. NE15: Den M .6G 61
Countess Way NE27: Shir .7J 37
Count's House .5C 6 (4A 166)
County Court
Consett .7H 121
Durham .3C 166
Gateshead .4H 83
North Shields .2E 66
South Shields .3J 67
Sunderland .4K 7 (2F 119)
County Ground
Northumberland County Cricket Club .5H 63
County Hall Bldgs. DH1: Dur .1K 165
County M. NE33: S Shi .4K 67
County Mills *NE46: Hex .2D 70*
(off Priestpopple)
Coupland Gro. NE32: Jar .3B 86
Coupland Rd. NE63: Ash .4A 12
Court, The NE16: Whi .1J 97
Courtfield Rd. NE6: Walk .5D 64
Court La. DH1: Dur .4D 6 (3B 166)
Courtney Ct. NE3: K Bank .5J 43
Courtney Dr. DH2: Ous .2H 127
SR3: New S .1B 132
Court Rd. NE22: Bed .7H 17
Court St. SR8: Eas C .7D 160
Courtyard, The DH9: Tan L .1C 124
NE11: Lame .6G 99
NE21: Blay .5E 80
NE27: Back .6G 37
Cousin St. SR1: Sund .1G 119
Coutts Rd. NE6: Walk .5C 64
Cove, The DH4: S Row .3B 130
Covent Gdn. NE64: Newb S .2J 13
Coventry Gdns. NE4: Benw .2A 82
NE29: N Shi .1E 66
Coventry Rd. DH1: Dur .4C 154
Coventry Way NE32: Jar .4B 86
Coverdale NE10: Hew .1E 100
NE28: W'snd .7D 46
Coverdale Av. NE24: Cow .2E 22
NE37: Wash .7G 101
Coverdale Wlk. NE33: S Shi .6H 67
Coverley DH3: Gt Lum .2E 142
Coverley Rd. SR5: Sund .5H 103
Covers, The NE12: Longb .6C 46
NE16: Swa .5F 81
NE28: W'snd .2F 65
NE61: Mor .1G 15
Cowan Cl. NE21: Blay .2A 80
Cowans Av. NE12: Kil .7A 36
Cowan Ter. SR1: Sund .5J 7 (2F 119)
Cowdray Ct. NE3: K Bank .5J 43
Cowdray Rd. SR5: Sund .5H 103
Cowdrey Ho. *NE29: N Shi .2D 66*
(off St John's Grn.)
Cowell Gro. NE39: Row G .5G 95
Cowell St. SR8: Hord .5D 172
Cowen Gdns. NE9: Low F .6J 99
Cowen Rd. NE21: Blay .3D 80
Cowen's Monument .6E 4
Cowen St. NE6: Walk .7D 64
NE21: Winl .6B 80
Cowen Ter. NE39: Row G .4K 95
Cowgarth NE46: Hex .1C 70
COWGATE .4K 61
Cowgate NE1: Newc T .6H 5 (1G 83)
Cow La. NE45: Ayd, Corb .7D 52
(not continuous)
Cowley Cres. DH5: E Rain .6C 144
Cowley Pl. NE24: Cow .1F 23
Cowley Rd. NE24: Cow .7F 19
Cowley St. DH6: Shot C .6F 171
Cowpath Gdns. NE10: Pel .5E 84
COWPEN .1E 22
Cowpen Hall Rd. NE24: Cow .1E 22
COWPEN NEW TOWN .7E 18
Cowpen Rd. NE24: Bly, Cow .1D 22
(not continuous)
Cowpen Sq. NE24: Bly .7H 19
Cowper Ter. NE12: Longb .3A 46
Cox Chare NE1: Newc T .6J 5 (1H 83)
Coxfoot Cl. NE34: S Shi .1J 87
COX GREEN .5B 116
Coxgreen Rd. DH4: Pen .1A 130
SR4: Cox G .1A 130
COXLODGE .7C 44
Coxlodge Rd. NE3: Gos .7C 44
Coxlodge Ter. NE3: Gos .7C 44
Coxon St. NE10: Bill Q .4F 85
SR2: Sund .3G 119
Coxon Ter. NE10: Fell .5A 84
Crabtree Rd. NE43: Pains .7J 75
Cradock Av. NE31: Heb .2H 85
Cragdale Gdns. DH5: Hett H .1F 157
Cragdale Vs. SR7: Dalt D .5J 147
Craggs Rd. NE38: Wash .4B 116
Craggyknowe NE37: Wash .2D 114
Craghall Dene NE3: Gos .1G 63
Craghall Dene Av. NE3: Gos .1G 63
CRAGHEAD .7J 125
Craghead La. DH9: Crag .7J 125
Craghead Rd. DH2: P Fel .5G 127
Cragleas NE16: Hob .4A 110
Cragmead Ind. Est. DH9: Crag .7J 125
Cragside DH2: Ches S .5J 127
DH7: Wit G .3D 152
NE7: H Hea .2K 63
NE13: Bru V .5D 34
NE23: Cra .6K 25
NE26: Whit B .4E 38
NE34: S Shi .1D 88
NE37: Wash .1E 114
NE45: Corb .6F 53

Cragside Av. NE29: N Shi 4D **48**
Cragside Ct. DH5: Hou S 2F **145**
DH8: B'hill 5E **120**
DH9: Ann P 6K **123**
NE4: Benw 3A **82**
NE11: Lob H 2C **98**
Cragside Gdns. NE11: Lob H 2C **98**
NE12: Kil 7D **36**
NE22: Bed 5K **17**
NE28: W'snd 2K **65**
Cragston Av. NE5: Blak 2J **61**
Cragston Cl. NE5: Blak 3J **61**
Cragston Ct. NE5: Blak 3J **61**
Cragston Way NE5: Blak 3J **61**
Cragton Gdns. NE24: Cow 2F **23**
Crag Works DH8: Lead 3A **122**
Craigavon Rd. SR5: Sund 6H **103**
Craig Ct. NE61: Mor 7H **9**
Craig Cres. NE23: Dud 3J **35**
Craigend NE23: Cra 5A **26**
Craighill DH4: S Row 3A **130**
Craiglands, The *SR2: Sund* *5E 118*
(off Tunstall)
Craigland Vs. DH7: Sac 1E **152**
Craigmillar Av. NE5: Blak 2J **61**
Craigmillar Cl. NE5: Blak 2H **61**
Craigmill Pk. NE24: Cow 1E **22**
Craigmont Ct. *NE12: Longb* *6B 46*
(off West Av.)
Craigshaw Rd. SR5: Sund 4F **103**
Craigshaw Sq. SR5: Sund 4F **103**
Craig St. DH3: Bir 4A **114**
Craig Ter. SR8: Eas 1K **171**
Craigwell Dr. SR3: Dox P 5C **132**
Crake Way NE38: Wash 6D **114**
Cramer St. NE8: Gate 5H **83**
CRAMLINGTON 4J 25
Cramlington Rd. NE23: Dud 2J **35**
SR5: Sund 6F **103**
Cramlington Sq. SR5: Sund 5F **103**
Cramlington Station (Rail) 3H 25
Cramlington Ter. NE24: News 5G **23**
NE27: Shir 3J **47**
CRAMLINGTON VILLAGE 4K 25
Cramond Ct. NE9: Low F 4G **99**
Cramond Way NE23: Cra 6K **25**
Cranberry Dr. NE38: Wash 5J **115**
Cranberry Rd. SR5: Sund 5G **103**
Cranberry Sq. SR5: Sund 5G **103**
Cranborne SR3: E Her 3J **131**
Cranbourne Gro. NE30: Cull 1H **49**
Cranbrook SR3: Sund 5C **118**
Cranbrook Av. NE3: Gos 5E **44**
Cranbrook Ct. NE3: Ki Pk 5A **44**
Cranbrook Dr. NE42: Pru 4D **76**
Cranemarsh Cl. NE63: Ash 6A **12**
Craneshaugh Cl. NE46: Hex 2G **71**
Cranesville NE9: Low F 2A **100**
(not continuous)
Craneswater Av. NE26: Whit B 2F **39**
Cranfield Pl. NE15: Lem 6C **60**
Cranford Gdns. NE15: Lem 6E **60**
Cranford St. NE34: S Shi 7J **67**
Cranford Ter. SR4: Sund 3C **118**
SR8: Eas 7K **159**
Cranham Cl. NE12: Kil 7D **36**
Cranlea NE3: Ki Pk 6J **43**
Cranleigh DH3: Gt Lum 3E **142**
Cranleigh Av. NE3: K Bank 5J **43**
Cranleigh Gro. NE42: Pru 3F **77**
Cranleigh Pl. NE25: Monks 5D **38**
Cranleigh Rd. SR5: Sund 5G **103**
Cranshaw Pl. NE23: Cra 5K **25**
Cranston Pl. SR2: Ryh 3J **133**
Crantock Rd. NE3: Ken 7B **44**
Cranwell Ct. NE3: K Bank 5J **43**
Cranwell Dr. NE13: W Op 5D **34**
Craster Av. NE12: Longb 3D **46**
NE27: Shir 1J **47**
NE34: S Shi 5D **68**
Craster Cl. DH2: Ches S 1H **141**
NE24: Bly 2G **23**
NE25: Monks 5D **38**
Craster Ct. NE11: T Vall 1E **98**
NE23: Cra 4J **25**
Craster Gdns. NE28: W'snd 2K **65**
Craster Point SR7: S'hm 1A **148**
Craster Rd. NE29: N Shi 7D **48**
Craster Sq. NE3: Gos 6C **44**
Craster Ter. NE7: H Hea 3K **63**
Craster Wlk. NE63: Ash 3H **11**
Crathie DH3: Bir 1A **114**
Crathorne Ct. NE16: Burn 2K **109**
Craven Ct. SR6: Roker 6H **105**
CRAWCROOK 3C 78
Crawcrook Ho's. *NE40: Craw* *3C 78*
(off Old Main St.)
Crawcrook La.
NE40: Craw, Wylam 2A **78**
NE41: Wylam 2A **78**
Crawcrook Ter. NE40: Craw 3C **78**
Crawford Av. SR8: Pet 4B **172**
Crawford Av. W. SR8: Pet 4A **172**
Crawford Cl. DH6: S'burn 3K **167**
Crawford Cotts. NE61: Mor 6G **9**
Crawford Gdns. NE40: Craw 2E **78**
Crawford Pl. NE25: Monks 7E **38**
Crawford St. NE24: Bly 7H **19**
Crawford Ter. NE6: Walk 1D **84**
NE61: Mor 6G **9**
Crawhall Cres. NE61: Mor 1E **14**
Crawhall Rd. NE1: Newc T 5K **5** (1H **83**)
Crawlaw Bungs. SR8: Eas C 6C **160**
Crawlaw Rd. SR8: Eas C 6B **160**
Crawley Av. NE31: Heb 3H **85**
Crawley Gdns. NE16: Whi 7J **81**
Crawley Rd. NE28: W'snd 4F **65**
Crawley Sq. NE31: Heb 3H **85**
Craythorne Gdns. NE6: Heat 3A **64**
Creevelea NE38: Wash 5G **115**
Creighton Av. NE3: Ken 2A **62**
Creland Way NE5: Blak 2J **61**
Crescent, The DH2: Ches M 3J **141**
DH2: Ches S 6K **127**
DH2: Nett 6H **141**
DH2: Ous 1H **127**
DH4: Nbot 5D **130**
DH4: S Row 4A **130**
DH4: W Rai 1K **155**
DH5: Hett H 7G **145**
DH6: S'burn 3K **167**
DH7: Lang P 5G **151**
DH7: Maid L 2A **138**
DH7: Wit G 2D **152**
DH8: Cons 5H **121**
DH8: Shot B 5D **120**
(Barley Mill Cres.)
DH8: Shot B 4E **120**
(Cutlers Av.)
DH9: Tan L 7D **110**
NE7: Longb 7K **45**
NE11: Dun 6B **82**
NE11: Kib 2E **112**
NE13: K Bank 6H **43**
NE15: Thro 3H **59**
NE16: Sun 5H **97**
NE16: Whi 1J **97**
NE20: Darr H 1E **40**
NE23: Seg 2D **36**
NE26: Whit B 7H **39**
NE28: W'snd 2F **65**
NE30: Tyne 4J **49**
NE32: Jar 2A **86**
NE34: S Shi 1B **88**
NE39: H Spen 4D **94**
NE39: Row G 5K **95**
NE40: Ryton 1H **79**
NE41: Wylam 1K **77**
NE61: Loan 2F **15**
SR3: New S 7C **118**
SR6: Clead 6B **88**
SR8: Eas C 6C **160**
TS27: B Col 2H **183**
Crescent Av. NE46: Hex 1B **70**
Crescent Cl. DH6: S'burn 3K **167**
Crescent Va. *NE26: Whit B* *7G 39*
(off Jesmond Ter.)
Crescent Way NE12: Longb 4C **46**
Crescent Way Nth. NE12: Longb 4C **46**
Crescent Way Sth. NE12: Longb 4C **46**
Creslow NE10: Hew 1D **100**
Cressbourne Av. SR6: Seab 3G **105**
Cressida Gdns. NE31: Heb 7J **65**
Cresswell Av. NE12: Longb 3C **46**
NE26: Sea S 4C **28**
NE29: N Shi 5F **49**
SR8: Hord 6E **172**
Cresswell Cl. NE21: Winl 6A **80**
NE25: Monks 1E **48**
Cresswell Ct. SR2: Sund 6H **7** (3E **118**)
Cresswell Dr. NE3: Fawd 5A **44**
NE24: Bly 4G **23**
Cresswell Rd. NE28: W'snd 4E **64**
Cresswell St. NE6: Walk 7B **64**
(not continuous)
Cresswell Ter. NE63: Ash 3A **12**
SR2: Sund 6H **7** (3E **118**)
Crest, The NE13: Din 4H **33**
NE22: Bed 7G **17**
NE26: Sea S 6D **28**
Cresthaven NE10: Hew 1C **100**
Crewe Av. DH1: Dur 3F **167**
Crichton Av. DH3: Ches S 1B **142**
Cricket Ter. NE16: Burn 2A **110**
Cricklewood Dr. DH4: Pen 2B **130**
Cricklewood Rd. SR5: Sund 6F **103**
Crieff Gro. NE32: Jar 3D **86**
Crieff Sq. SR5: Sund 5F **103**
Crigdon Hill NE5: W Dent 4F **61**
Crighton NE38: Wash 3E **114**
Crimdon Gro. DH4: Hou S 3C **144**
Crimea Rd. SR5: Sund 5F **103**
Crime Rigg Bank DH6: Shad 4D **168**
Crindledykes NE38: Wash 6J **115**
Cripps Av. NE10: Ward 6F **85**
Crispin Ct. NE5: West 2F **61**
Crocus Cl. NE21: Winl 4A **80**
Croft, The DH6: S Hil 3D **168**
DH9: Ann P 6J **123**
NE3: Ken 1C **62**
NE12: Kil 7C **36**
NE22: Nedd 1C **20**
NE40: Ryton 2H **79**
NE46: Hex 1B **70**
Croft Av. NE12: Longb 5C **46**
NE28: W'snd 3G **65**
SR4: Sund 2C **118**
Croft Cl. DH9: Ann P 6J **123**
NE40: Ryton 2H **79**
Croft Ct. DH7: Lan 6J **137**
Croftdale Rd. NE21: Blay 4C **80**
Crofters Cl. NE23: Dud 2J **35**
Crofthead Cl. NE24: Bly 2K **23**
Crofthead Dr. NE23: Cra 6K **25**
Crofton St. NE24: Bly 2J **23**
NE34: S Shi 7J **67**
Crofton Way NE15: Lem 6B **60**
Croft Pk. 3J 23
Croft Pl. DH8: Cons 2K **135**
Croft Rigg DH7: B'don 2C **174**
Croft Rd. NE24: Bly 2J **23**
Crofts, The NE20: Pon 5K **31**
NE45: Corb 1F **73**
SR7: Mur *1F 159*
(off East Vw.)
Crofts Av. NE45: Corb 1E **72**
Crofts Cl. NE45: Corb 1E **72**
Croftside DH3: Bir 3A **114**
Croftside Av. SR6: Whit 5H **89**
Croftside Ho. SR3: Dox P 4B **132**
Crofts La. NE15: Hor 5E **56**
Crofts Pk. NE61: Hep 3A **16**
Croft Stairs NE1: Newc T 6H **5** (1G **83**)
Croft St. DH7: Sac 7E **140**
NE1: Newc T 5G **4** (1G **83**)
Crofts Way NE45: Corb 1E **72**
Croftsway NE4: Elsw 2B **82**
Croft Ter. DH9: Ann P 5A **124**
NE15: Hor 5E **56**
NE32: Jar 7B **66**
NE46: Hex 2C **70**
Croft Vw. DH7: Lan 6J **137**
NE12: Kil 2C **46**
NE40: Craw 3C **78**
NE42: O'ham 2D **76**
Croft Vs. NE40: Craw 3C **78**
NE40: G'sde 4D **78**
Croftwell Cl. NE21: Blay 5D **80**
Cromarty DH2: Ous 6H **113**
Cromarty St. SR6: Ful 5F **105**
Cromdale Pl. NE5: Den M 4H **61**
Cromer Av. NE9: Low F 4H **99**
Cromer Ct. NE9: Low F 4J **99**
Cromer Gdns. NE2: Jes 2G **63**
NE26: Whit B 5G **39**
Crompton Rd. NE6: Heat 4K **63**
Cromwell Av. NE21: Winl 4B **80**
Cromwell Ct. *NE10: Bill Q* *4G 85*
(off Hartforth Cres.)
NE21: Blay 2A **80**
NE24: Bly 2H **23**
Cromwell Ford Way NE21: Blay 1A **80**
Cromwell Pl. NE21: Winl 5A **80**
Cromwell Rd. NE10: Bill Q 4F **85**
NE16: Whi 6J **81**
Cromwell St. NE8: Gate 5J **83**
NE21: Blay 2A **80**
SR4: Sund 1C **118**
Cromwell Ter. NE10: Bill Q 4F **85**
NE29: N Shi 6F **49**
Crondall St. NE33: S Shi 6K **67**
Cronin Av. NE34: S Shi 2H **87**
Cronniewell NE17: Ham 3K **107**
CROOKGATE BANK 2C 110
CROOKHALL 1K 135
Crook Hall & Gardens 1A 166
Crookhall La. DH8: Cons, Lead 7A **122**
(not continuous)
Crookhall Rd. DH8: Cons 6J **121**
Crookham Gro. NE61: Mor 3H **15**
Crookham Way NE23: Cra 6A **26**
CROOKHILL 2J 79
Crookhill Ter. NE40: Ryton 2J **79**
Croome Gdns. NE61: Peg 3B **10**
Cropthorne NE10: Hew 1F **101**
Crosby Gdns. NE9: Low F 4K **99**
Crosland Pk. NE23: Nel V 1H **25**
Crosland Way NE23: Nel V 7H **21**
Cross Av. NE28: W'snd 1D **64**
Cross Bank NE46: Acomb 3A **50**
Crossbank Rd. NE5: Ken 2K **61**
Crossbank Vw. NE46: Acomb 4B **50**
Crossbrook Rd. NE5: Blak 3K **61**
Crossby Ct. SR2: Sund 3H **119**
Cross Carliol St.
NE1: Newc T 5G **4** (1G **83**)
Cross Dr. NE40: Ryton 7G **59**
Crossfell NE20: Darr H 7G **31**
Crossfell Gdns. NE62: Stake 7J **11**
Crossfield DH7: Sac 1E **152**
Crossfield Cres. DH6: Shot C 5E **170**
Crossfield Pk. NE10: Wind N 1A **100**
Crossfield Ter. NE6: Walk 2E **84**
Crossgate DH1: Dur 3A **6** (3K **165**)
NE33: S Shi 3J **67**
CROSSGATE MOOR 2J 165
Crossgate Moor Gdns.
DH1: Dur 1H **165**
Crossgate Peth DH1: Dur 3A **6** (3J **165**)
Crossgate Rd. DH5: Hett H 1G **157**
Crossgill NE37: Wash 1F **115**
Cross Keys La. NE9: Low F 2H **99**
Cross La. DH7: Sac 6D **140**
NE11: Dun 5K **81**
NE11: Rave 4C **98**
NE16: Dun, Swa, Whi 6J **81**
Cross Lane Meadows Nature Reserve
. . . . 5J 81
Crosslaw NE5: W Dent 4F **61**
Crosslea Av. SR3: Sund 5D **118**
Crossleas DH7: Sac 7E **140**
Crossley Ter. NE4: Fen 7B **62**
NE12: Longb 3D **46**
Cross Morpeth St.
NE2: Newc T 1B **4** (5D **62**)
Cross Pde.
NE4: Elsw, Newc T 7A **4** (2C **82**)
(not continuous)
Cross Pl. SR1: Sund 1G **119**
Cross Rigg Cl. DH4: Pen 2K **129**
Cross Roads DH7: Sac 7E **140**
Crossroads DH8: M'sly 7K **107**
Cross Row DH1: Dur 4A **154**
NE10: Gate 5K **83**
NE40: Ryton 2J **79**
Cross Sheraton St. NE2: Newc T 1B **4**
Cross St. DH4: Hou S 2A **144**
(Front St.)
DH4: Hou S 1D **144**
(Station Rd.)
DH6: Crox 6K **175**
DH6: Litt 7D **156**
DH8: B'hill 5F **121**
NE1: Newc T 6D **4** (1E **82**)
NE6: Byke 5M **5** (1J **83**)
NE8: Gate 5H **83**
NE42: Pru 3F **77**
SR8: Eas C 7D **160**
Cross Ter. NE39: Row G 6H **95**
NE40: Ryton 7G **59**
Cross Va. Rd. SR2: Sund 7H **7** (4E **118**)
Cross Valley Ct. DH1: Dur 3J **165**
Cross Vw. Ter. DH1: Dur 4J **165**
Cross Villa Pl. No. 1
NE4: Newc T 6C **4**
Cross Villa Pl. No. 2
NE4: Newc T 6C **4** (1E **82**)
Cross Villa Pl. No. 3
NE4: Newc T 6C **4** (1E **82**)
Cross Villa Pl. No. 4
NE4: Newc T 6B **4** (1D **82**)
Cross Villa Pl. No. 5
NE4: Newc T 6B **4** (1D **82**)
Cross Way NE34: S Shi 1C **88**
Cross Way, The NE3: Ken 1B **62**
NE61: Loan 2F **15**
Crossway NE2: Jes 2G **63**
NE9: Low F 1J **99**
(Crossway Vs.)
NE9: Low F 1K **99**
(Tribune Pl.)
NE30: Tyne 4J **49**
NE62: Chop 1H **17**
Crossway, The NE15: Lem 6D **60**
Crossway Ct. NE3: Ken 2B **62**
Crossways DH3: Gt Lum 3F **143**
DH7: Lang P 5J **151**
DH7: Sac 1E **152**
NE32: Jar 5C **86**
NE36: E Bol 7A **88**
SR3: New S 2B **132**
Crossways, The NE13: Haz 7C **34**
Crossways Ct. DH6: Thor 2G **179**
Crossway Vs. NE9: Low F 1J **99**
Crosthwaite Gro. SR5: Sund 6G **103**
Croudace Row NE10: Fell 6B **84**
Crow Bank NE28: W'snd 3G **65**
Crowgill Ct. DH7: Esh W 4E **162**
Crow Hall DH7: Lan 5K **137**
Crow Hall La.
NE23: Cra, Nel V 7H **21**
Crowhall La. NE10: Fell 6B **84**
Crow Hall Rd. NE23: Nel V 1H **25**
Crowhall Towers NE10: Fell 6B **84**
Crow La. SR3: E Her 2H **131**
Crowley Av. NE16: Whi 6J **81**
Crowley Gdns. NE21: Blay 4C **80**
Crowley Rd. NE16: Swa 5G **81**
Crowley Vs. *NE16: Swa* *5G 81*
(off Crowley Rd.)
Crown & Anchor Cotts. NE15: Hor 5E **56**
Crown Court
Durham 4E 6 (3B 166)
Crown Rd. SR5: S'wck 7C **104**
Crown St. NE24: Bly 2K **23**
NE61: Mor *7G 9*
(off Castle St.)
Crown Ter. NE40: G'sde 5F **79**
Crowther Ind. Est. NE38: Wash 3D **114**
Crowther Rd. NE38: Wash 3D **114**
Crowtree Rd. SR1: Sund 3H **7** (2E **118**)
(not continuous)
Crowtrees La. DH6: Bowb 5H **177**
CROXDALE 6K 175
Croxdale Ct. NE34: S Shi 1G **87**
Croxdale Gdns. NE10: Pel 5E **84**
Croxdale Ter. NE10: Pel 5E **84**
NE40: G'sde 5G **79**
Croydon Rd. NE4: Fen 7C **62**
Crozier St. SR5: Monkw 6E **104**
Cruddas Pk. NE4: Elsw 2C **82**
Cruddas Pk. Shop. Cen.
NE4: Elsw 8A **4** (3C **82**)
Crudwell Cl. NE35: Bol C 4E **86**
Crummock Av. SR6: Seab 3E **104**
Crummock Ct. NE28: W'snd 1A **66**
Crummock Rd. NE5: Den M 5H **61**
Crumstone Ct. NE12: Kil 7C **36**
Crusade Wlk. NE32: Jar 1B **86**
Cuba St. SR2: Sund 4G **119**
Cuddy's La. *NE46: Hex* *2C 70*
(off Priestlands La.)
Cuillin Cl. NE38: Wash 5F **115**
Culford Pl. NE28: W'snd 6J **47**
Cullen Dr. DH3: Bir 2B **114**
CULLERCOATS 1J 49
Cullercoats Rd. SR5: Sund 6F **103**
Cullercoats Sq. SR5: Sund 6F **103**
Cullercoats Station (Metro) 1J 49
Cullercoats St. NE6: Walk 7C **64**
(not continuous)
Culloden Ter. SR8: Eas C 1D **172**
Culloden Wlk. NE12: Kil 7B **36**
Culzean Ct. DH8: B'hill 5F **121**
Cumberland Av. NE22: Bed 7G **17**
Cumberland Pl. DH3: Bir 7B **114**
NE34: S Shi 6D **68**
Cumberland Rd. DH8: C'sde 3C **134**
NE29: N Shi 5B **48**
SR3: New S 1C **132**

Cumberland St. NE28: W'snd 4B **66** (George St.)
NE28: W'snd 3G **65** (Richardson St.)
SR1: Sund 2J **7** (1F **119**) (not continuous)
Cumberland Wlk. NE7: H Hea 1K **63** (not continuous)
Cumberland Way NE37: Wash 5H **101**
Cumbrian Av. DH2: Ches S 7A **128** (not continuous)
SR6: Seab 2E **104**
Cumbrian Gdns. NE11: Lob H 1C **98**
Cumbrian Rd. NE23: Cra 3K **25**
Cumbrian Way SR8: Pet 6C **172**
Cumbria Pl. DH9: Stly 2G **125**
Cumbria Wlk.
NE4: Elsw, Newc T 6A **4** (1C **82**)
Cummings Av. DH6: S'burn 2K **167**
Cummings Sq. TS28: Win 5F **181**
Cummings St. NE24: Bly 1J **23**
Cunningham Pl. DH1: Dur 1D **166**
Curlew Cl. NE12: Longb 5J **45**
NE38: Wash 6E **114**
NE40: Ryton 2J **79**
NE63: Ash 7B **12**
Curlew Hill NE61: Mor 5D **8**
Curlew Rd. NE32: Jar 5C **66** (not continuous)
Curlew Way NE24: News 5J **23**
Curly Kews NE61: Mor 7E **8**
Curran Ho. M. NE32: Jar 5C **66**
Curren Gdns. NE10: Fell 4A **84**
Currys Bldgs. DH4: Leam 1J **155**
NE61: Mor 6E 8 (off Buller's Grn.)
Curtis Rd. NE4: Fen 6B **62**
Curzon Pl. NE5: Blak 3H **61**
NE8: Gate 8H **5** (2G **83**)
Curzon Rd. W. NE28: W'snd 4F **65**
Curzon St. NE8: Gate 6G **83**
Cushat Cl. NE6: Byke 6P **5** (1A **84**)
Cushycow La. NE40: Ryton 2H **79**
Customs House, The 3H **67**
Cut Bank NE1: Newc T 5L **5** (1J **83**)
Cuthbert Av. DH1: Dur 3F **167**
Cuthbert Cl. DH1: Dur 3F **167** (Crewe Av.)
DH1: Dur 3F **167** (Dragon Ville)
Cuthbertson Ct. SR6: Seab 2G **105**
Cuthbert St. NE8: Gate 4F **83**
NE16: Marl H 6G **97**
NE31: Heb 7H **65** (not continuous)
Cuthbert Wlk. NE3: Gos 7G **45**
Cutlers Av. DH8: Shot B 4E **120**
Cutlers Hall Rd. DH8: Shot B 3E **120**
Cut Throat La. NE17: Ham 4K **107**
Cutting St. SR7: S'hm 1H **147**
Cygnet Cl. NE5: Cha P 1D **60**
NE63: Ash 7B **12**
Cygnet Way DH4: W Rai 4C **144**
Cyncopa Way NE5: Blak 3K **61**
Cypress, The *NE23: Cra 4B 26 (off Evergreen Ct.)*
Cypress Av. NE4: Fen 5K **61**
Cypress Ct. DH7: B'don 2D **174**
Cypress Cres. NE11: Dun 6B **82**
NE24: Bly 2J **23**
Cypress Dr. NE24: Bly 2J **23**
Cypress Gdns. NE12: Kil 7A **36**
NE24: Bly 2J **23**
Cypress Gro. DH1: Dur 1E **166**
NE40: Ryton 7F **59**
Cypress Pk. DH7: Esh W 4D **162**
Cypress Rd. NE9: Eigh B 5B **100**
Cypress Sq. SR3: New S 1C **132**
Cypress Vw. DH6: Whe H 2A **180**
Cyprus Gdns. NE9: Low F 1J **99**
Cyril St. DH8: Cons 5H **121**

D

Dachet Rd. NE25: Monks 4D **38**
Dacre Gdns. DH8: Cons 7J **121**
Dacre Rd. SR6: Ful 3F **105**
Dacre St. NE33: S Shi 5J **67** (not continuous)
NE61: Mor 6F **9**
Daffodil Av. SR8: Hord 5D **172**
Daffodil Cl. NE21: Winl 4B **80**
TS27: B Col 2H **183**
Dahlia Ct. SR4: Sund 3F **7** (1D **118**)
Dahlia Cres. SR8: Eas 1B **172**
Dahlia Pl. NE4: Fen 6K **61**
Dahlia Way NE31: Heb 2J **85** (not continuous)
Dainton Cl. DH4: Nbot 5C **130**
Dairnbrook NE37: Wash 2E **114**
Dairy Gdns. NE28: W'snd 2J **65**
Dairy La. DH4: Hou S 2C **144**
NE2: Newc T 1B **4** (5D **62**)
Dairy Wlk. DH3: Lam P 3F **129**
Daisy Cotts. DH3: Bir 4A **114**
DAISY HILL 4D **140**
Dalamere Cl. NE38: Wash 2F **129**
Dalby Gro. SR7: Mur 7G **147**
Dalden Gro. SR7: S'hm 2B **148**
Dale Ct. DH8: Cons 7G **121**
NE46: Hex 2E **70**
Dalegarth Gro. SR6: Seab 2E **104**
Dale Rd. NE25: Monks 7D **38**
Dales, The NE5: Fen 3A **62**
Daleside DH7: Sac 5E **140**
Daleside Works DH9: Crag 7J **125**
Dale St. DH7: Lang P 4J **151**
DH7: Ush M 2B **164**
DH8: B'hill 6F **121**
NE24: Bly 7J **19**
NE33: S Shi 2K **67**
NE40: Craw 2D **78**
Dale Ter. SR6: Ful 4G **105**
SR7: Dalt D 5J **147**
Dale Top NE25: H'wll 2J **37**
Dale Vw. Gdns. NE40: Craw 3C **78**
Dale Vw. Ter. NE43: Pains 7K **75**
Dalla St. SR4: Sund 1G **117**
Dally M. NE3: Gos 3D **44**
Dallymore Dr. DH6: Bowb 3G **177**
Dalmahoy NE37: Wash 4H **101**
Dalmatia Ter. NE24: Bly 3J **23**
Dalston Pl. NE24: News 5J **23**
Dalton Av. SR7: S'hm 3K **147**
Dalton Cl. NE23: Cra 4K **25**
Dalton Ct. NE28: W'snd 7D **46**
Dalton Cres. DH1: Dur 4J **165**
NE6: Byke 4P **5** (7K **63**)
Dalton Hgts. SR7: Dalt D 4G **147** (not continuous)
DALTON-LE-DALE 5H **147**
Dalton Pk. SR7: Mur 1G **159**
Dalton Pl. NE5: Cha P 2C **60**
SR4: Sund 2D **118**
Daltons La. NE33: S Shi 3H **67**
Dalton St. NE6: Byke 4P **5** (7K **63**) (not continuous)
Dalton Ter. DH6: Whe H 4A **180**
NE17: C'wl 7K **93**
SR7: Mur 1F **159**
Dalton Way DH4: Pen 2A **130**
Dame Dorothy Cres. *SR6: Roker 6G 105 (off Dame Dorothy St.)*
Dame Dorothy St.
SR6: Monkw, Roker 1J **7** (7F **105**)
Dame Flora Robson Av. NE34: S Shi 2F **87**
Damside NE61: Mor 6G **9**
Damson Way DH1: Dur 2F **167**
Danby Cl. NE38: Wash 1D **128**
SR3: Tuns 3D **132**
Danby Gdns. NE6: Heat 3B **64**
Dance City 7D **4**
Danelaw DH3: Gt Lum 2E **142**
Daniel Pk. DH6: S Het 4C **158**
Danville Rd. SR6: Ful 3F **105**
Daphne Cres. SR7: S'hm 5A **148** (not continuous)
D'Arcy Ct. SR1: Sund 2G **119**
D'Arcy Sq. SR7: Mur 6G **147**
D'Arcy St. DH7: Lang P 4J **151**
SR1: Sund 2G **119**
Darden Cl. NE12: Kil 7D **36**
Darden Lough NE5: W Dent 4F **61**
Darenth St. NE34: S Shi 7J **67**
Darien Av. SR6: Ful 3F **105**
Dark La. NE61: Mor 6G **9**
Darley Ct. DH2: Plaw 6J **141**
Darley Pl. NE15: Scot 1G **81**
Darling Pl. DH9: Stly 4H **125**
Darlington Av. SR8: Hord 4D **172**
Darlington Railway Museum 3D **154**
Darlington Rd. DH1: Dur 4J **165**
Darnell Pl. NE4: Newc T 4A **4** (7D **62**)
Darnley Rd. NE63: Ash 4A **12**
Darras Ct. NE33: S Shi 4K **67**
Darras Dr. NE29: N Shi 5C **48**
DARRAS HALL 1G **41**
Darras M. NE20: Darr H 1G **41**
Darras Rd. NE20: Darr H, Pon 1E **40**
Darras Station NE20: Darr H 1G **41**
Darrell St. NE13: Bru V, W Op 5C **34**
Dartford Cl. NE25: Sea D 7J **27**
Dartford Rd. NE33: S Shi 3B **68**
SR6: Ful 3F **105**
Dartington Cl. SR4: Sund 4G **117**
Dartmouth Av. NE9: Low F 4H **99**
Dartmouth Cl. SR7: Dalt D 4J **147**
Darvall Cl. NE25: Monks 4D **38**
Darwin Cres. NE3: Ken 2B **62**
Darwin St. SR5: S'wck 6B **104**
Daryl Cl. NE21: Winl 5A **80**
Daryl Way NE10: Ward 6H **85**
Davenport Dr. NE3: Gos 3D **44**
David Gdns. SR6: Seab 4H **105**
David Lloyd Leisure
Newcastle upon Tyne 2H **63**
Davidson Cotts. NE2: Jes 2G **63**
Davidson Rd. NE10: Bill Q 4F **85**
Davidson St. NE10: Fell 6B **84**
David St. NE28: W'snd 4F **65**
David Ter. DH6: Bowb 4H **177**
DH6: Quar H 6D **178**
NE40: Craw 3D **78**
Davies Hall NE31: Heb 6H **65**
Davies Wlk. SR8: Hord 4C **172**
Davis Cres. DH7: Lang P 4G **151**
Davison Av. NE26: Whit B 5F **39**
SR3: New S 2D **132**
Davison Courtyard NE8: Gate 4D **82**
Davison Cres. SR7: Mur 6D **146**
Davison Sq. DH8: C'sde 4B **134**
Davison St. NE15: Newb 6J **59**
NE24: Bly 1J **23**
NE35: Bol C 5E **86**
Davison Ter. DH7: Sac 6D **140**
SR5: S'wck 5C 104 (off Nth. Hylton Rd.)
Davis Ter. SR8: Eas 7B **160**
Davy Bank NE28: W'snd 4H **65**
Davy Cl. NE31: Heb 6J **65**
Davy Dr. SR8: Pet 5H **171**
DAWDON 5B **148**
Dawdon Bus. Pk. SR7: S'hm 6C **148**
Dawdon Cres. SR7: S'hm 4B **148**
Dawlish Cl. NE29: N Shi 4D **48**
SR7: S'hm 4H **147**
Dawlish Gdns. NE9: Low F 4H **99**
Dawlish Pl. NE5: Cha P 2C **60**
Dawson Pl. NE61: Mor 6F **9**
Dawson Rd. TS28: Win 5G **181**
Dawson Sq. NE30: Tyne 5K **49**
Dawson St. NE6: Walk 7E **64**
Dawson Ter. SR4: Sund 1G **117**
Daylesford Dr. NE3: Gos 1H **63**
Daylesford Rd. NE23: Cra 7J **21**
Dayshield NE5: W Dent 4F **61**
Day St. NE1: Newc T 2G **4** (6G **63**)
Deacon Cl. NE15: Walb 3B **60**
Deacon Ct. NE12: Longb 6J **45**
Deaconsfield Cl. SR3: Dox P 4B **132**
Deadridge La. NE45: Corb 7F **53**
DEAF HILL 7B **180**
Deaf Hill Ter. TS29: Trim S 7B **180**
Deal Cl. NE24: News 5J **23**
Dean Cl. SR8: Pet 7D **172**
Dean Ct. NE24: Cow 1H **23**
Deanery St. NE22: Bed 7H **17**
Deanery Vw. DH7: Lan 6K **137** (not continuous)
Deanham Gdns. NE5: Fen 5J **61**
Dean Ho. NE6: Walk 5E **64**
Dean Rd. NE33: S Shi 6H **67** (Sth. Eldon St.)
NE33: S Shi 6H **67** (West Way, not continuous)
DEANS 6J **67**
Deans Av. NE64: Newb S 2G **13**
Deans Cl. NE16: Whi 6H **81**
Deansfield Cl. SR3: Dox P 4B **132**
Deansfield Gro. NE15: Walb 2B **60**
Deansgate Ho. DH1: Dur 4E **6** (3B **166**)
Dean St. DH7: Lang P 4K **151**
NE1: Newc T 6G **4** (1G **83**)
NE9: Low F 2H **99**
NE46: Hex 1E **70**
Deans Wlk. DH1: Dur 1D **166**
Dean Ter. NE33: S Shi 6H **67**
NE40: Ryton 1G **79**
SR5: S'wck 6B **104**
Dearham Gro. NE23: Cra 7J **21**
Debdon Gdns. NE6: Heat 4A **64**
Debdon Pl. NE23: Cra 4K **25**
Debdon Rd. NE63: Ash 5D **12**
Debussy Ct. NE32: Jar 7C **66**
December Courtyard *NE8: Gate 4D 82 (off Christmas Pl.)*
DECKHAM 6J **83**
Deckham St. NE8: Gate 6J **83**
Deckham Ter. NE8: Gate 6J **83**
Deepbrook Rd. NE5: Blak 4J **61**
Deepdale NE28: W'snd 7D **46**
NE38: Wash 7E **114**
Deepdale Cl. NE16: Whi 3F **97**
Deepdale Cres. NE5: Fen 3K **61**
Deepdale Dr. DH8: Cons 2J **135**
Deepdale Gdns. NE12: Kil 1A **46**
Deepdale Grn. NE5: Fen 3A **62**
Deepdale Rd. NE30: Cull 2H **49**
Deepdale St. DH5: Hett H 1G **157**
Deepdene Gro. SR6: Seab 2G **105**
Deepdene Rd. SR6: Seab 2F **105**
Deerbolt Pl. NE12: Longb 5A **46**
Deerbush NE5: W Dent 4F **61**
Deerfell Cl. NE63: Ash 5K **11**
Deerness Ct. DH7: B'don 1E **174**
Deerness Gro. DH7: Esh W 2D **162**
Deerness Hgts. DH7: B'don 7D **164**
Deerness Leisure Cen. 3D **164**
Deerness Pl. DH7: Wat 6C **162**
Deerness Rd. SR2: Sund 3G **119**
DEERNESS VIEW 2K **163**
Deerness Vw. DH7: Ush M 2K **163**
Dee Rd. NE31: Heb 3K **85**
Deer Pk. Way NE21: Blay 5E **80**
Dees Av. NE28: W'snd 2F **65**
Dee St. NE32: Jar 6C **66**
Defender Ct. SR5: Sund 7J **103**
Defoe Av. NE34: S Shi 3J **87**
De Grey St. NE4: Elsw 3C **82**
Deighton Wlk. NE5: W Dent 4F **61**
Delacour Rd. NE21: Blay 3C **80**
Delamere Ct. SR3: Silk 3C **132**
Delamere Cres. NE23: Cra 7J **21**
Delamere Gdns. SR8: Eas 7A **160**
Delamere Rd. NE3: Ken 7B **44**
DELAVAL 2H **81**
Delaval DH2: Ches S 6J **127**
Delaval Av. NE25: Sea D 7G **27**
NE29: N Shi 6E **48**
Delaval Ct. NE22: Bed 6A **18**
NE33: S Shi 4K **67**
Delaval Cres. NE24: News 5F **23**
Delavale Cl. SR8: Pet 6D **172**
Delaval Gdns. NE24: News 5F **23**
Delaval Rd. NE12: Longb 4B **46**
NE15: Benw, Scot 1H **81**
NE26: Whit B 7J **39**
Delaval St. NE24: News 5F **23**
Delaval Ter. NE3: Gos 1C **62**
NE24: Bly 1H **23** (not continuous)
Delaval Trad. Est. NE25: Sea D 5G **27**
Deleval Ct. *NE12: Longb 3C 46 (off Deleval Rd.)*
Deleval Cres. NE27: Back 7H **37**
Delhi Cres. NE40: G'sde 3E **78**
Delhi Gdns. NE40: G'sde 3E **78**
Delhi Vw. NE40: G'sde 3E **78**
Delight Bank DH9: Dip 2H **123**
Delight Ct. DH9: Dip 1H **123**
Delight Row DH9: Dip 1H **123**
Dell, The DH4: Nbot 6D **130**
NE61: Mor 4E **8**
Dellfield Dr. SR4: Sund 4G **117**
Delta Bank Rd. NE11: Dun 3J **81**
Delta Pk. NE11: Dun 3J **81**
Delton Cl. NE38: Wash 5J **115**
Delvedere DH8: Cons 1K **135**
DELVES 2K **135**
Delves La. DH8: Cons 7J **121**
Delves La. Ind. Est. DH8: Cons 3K **135**
Delves Ter. DH8: Cons 1J **135**
De Merley Rd. NE61: Mor 5F **9**
Demesne, The NE63: N Sea 5F **13**
Demesne Dr. NE22: Bed 1H **21**
De Mowbray Way NE61: Mor 5D **8**
Dempsey Rd. NE13: Haz 7D **34**
Denbeigh Pl. NE12: Longb 5A **46**
Denbigh Av. NE28: W'snd 1A **66**
SR6: Ful 3F **105**
Denby Cl. NE23: Cra 7J **21**
Denby Wlk. NE5: Cha P 2C **60**
DENE, THE 6J **107**
Dene, The DH2: Ches M 3K **141**
DH4: W Rai 7A **144**
DH8: M'sly 6J **107**
NE25: Monks 6E **38**
NE41: Wylam 7K **57**
SR7: Dalt D 5J **147**
Dene Av. DH5: Hou S 3G **145**
DH6: Shot C 6F **171**
NE3: Gos 1G **63**
NE12: Kil 2J **45**
NE13: Bru V 5C **34**
NE15: Lem 7D **60**
NE39: Row G 6H **95**
NE46: Hex 2E **70**
SR8: Eas C 5C **160**
Dene Bank DH7: Wit G 3C **152**
Denebank NE25: Monks 6E **38**
Dene Bank Av. SR8: Hord 6E **172**
Dene Bank Vw. NE3: Ken 2A **62**
Deneburn NE10: Hew 7E **84**
Deneburn Ter. DH8: C'sde 2E **134**
Dene Cl. NE7: H Hea 4J **63**
NE40: Ryton 1H **79**
NE42: O'ham 1D **76**
NE44: Rid M 6K **73**
Dene Cotts. DH2: Wald 1F **141**
Dene Ct. DH3: Bir 2A **114**
DH6: Shad 6E **168**
DH7: Wit G 2D **152**
NE7: H Hea 4K **63**
NE15: Lem 5E **60**
NE17: Ham 2K **107**
NE38: Wash 2G **115**
Dene Cres. DH6: Shot C 6F **171**
DH7: Sac 7F **141**
NE3: Gos 1G **63**
NE26: Monks 5F **39**
NE28: W'snd 3H **65**
NE39: Row G 6H **95**
NE40: Ryton 1H **79**
Denecrest DH8: M'sly 6J **107**
Denecroft NE41: Wylam 7J **57**
Dene Dr. DH1: Carr 6H **155**
Deneford NE9: Low F 6J **99**
Dene Gdns. DH5: Hou S 3F **145**
NE10: Bill Q 5F **85**
NE15: Lem 7D **60**
NE25: Monks 6E **38**
Dene Gth. NE42: O'ham 1C **76**
Dene Gro. NE3: Gos 1G **63**
NE23: Seg 1E **36**
NE42: Pru 3D **76**
Deneholm NE25: Monks 5E **38**
NE28: W'snd 2H **65**
Deneholme Ter. DH7: Edm 3K **139**
Dene Ho. Rd. SR7: S'hm 2A **148**
Denelands NE46: Hex 1E **70**
Dene La. DH6: Shad 6F **169**
SR6: Ful 3F **105**
SR6: Monkw, Whit 7E **88**
Dene M. SR5: Sund 6J **103**
Dene Pk. DH7: Esh W 4D **162**
NE20: Darr H 1F **41**
NE46: Hex 2E **70**
SR5: Sund 6J **103**
Dene Rd. NE21: Blay 3C **80**
NE30: Tyne 4J **49**
NE39: Row G 6H **95**
NE41: Wylam 7K **57**
NE62: Chop 1G **17**
SR5: Sund 6J **103**
SR7: Dalt D, S'hm 5H **147**
TS27: B Col 2J **183**
DENESIDE 4J **147**
Dene Side NE21: Blay 4D **80**
Deneside DH7: Lan 7K **137**
DH7: Sac 6E **140**
DH7: Wit G 3D **152**
NE5: West 1F **61**
NE11: Dun 7B **82**
NE15: Den M 6G **61**
NE17: Ham 2K **107**
NE23: Seg 1E **36**
NE32: Jar 5C **86**
NE34: S Shi 7E **68**
Deneside Av. NE9: Low F 3G **99**

Deneside Cl. NE15: Thro .3H 59
Deneside Ct. NE2: Jes .1L 5 (5J 63)
NE26: Whit B .3E 38
Dene St. DH5: Hett H .4G 145
DH9: Stly .4D 124
NE25: H'wll .1K 37
NE42: Pru .3G 77
SR3: New S .7C 118
SR4: Sund .1B 118
SR8: Hord .5E 172
Denesyde DH8: M'sly .6J 107
Dene Ter. DH6: Shot C .6F 171
DH7: Wit G .3D 152
NE3: Gos .1G 63
NE15: Walb .4K 59
NE21: Winl .4B 80
(off Park Av.)
NE32: Jar .2A 86
NE42: Oving .2K 75
NE42: Pru .4C 76
NE44: Rid M .6K 73
(off Dene Cl.)
SR6: Ful .3F 105
SR7: S'hm .2B 148
SR8: Hord .6E 172
Dene Ter. E. NE41: Wylam .7J 57
(off Algernon Ter.)
Dene Ter. W. NE41: Wylam .7J 57
(off Algernon Ter.)
Dene Vw. DH4: W Rai .1A 156
DH6: Cass .3F 179
DH9: Stly .2J 125
NE3: Gos .1G 63
NE16: Burn .2A 110
NE22: Bed .7A 18
NE25: H'wll .1K 37
NE39: H Spen .4E 94
NE39: Row G .5G 95
NE42: Oving .2K 75
NE63: Ash .4J 11
TS27: Cas E .6B 182
TS27: Hes .4G 183
Dene Vw. Ct. NE24: Cow .1F 23
Dene Vw. Cres. SR4: Sund .2H 117
Dene Vw. Dr. NE24: Cow .1F 23
Dene Vw. E. NE22: Bed .1A 22
Dene Vw. W. NE22: Bed .1K 21
Dene Vs. DH3: Ches S .1B 142
SR8: Hord .6F 173
Dene Wlk. NE29: N Shi .3E 66
Dene Way SR7: S'hm .2A 148
Deneway NE39: Row G .3A 96
Denewell Av. NE7: H Hea .2J 63
NE9: Low F .2H 99
Denewood NE12: Kil .2B 46
SR7: Mur .7E 146
Denewood Ct. DH9: Stly .5H 125
NE28: W'snd .3A 66
Dene Wood (Nature Reserve) .5H 125
Denham Av. SR6: Ful .3F 105
Denham Dr. NE25: Sea D .1H 37
Denham Gro. NE21: Winl .6K 79
Denham Wlk. NE5: Cha P .2B 60
Denhill Pk. NE15: Benw .7K 61
Denholm Av. NE23: Cra .7J 21
Denholme Lodge NE11: Dun .5B 82
Denmark Cen. NE33: S Shi .2J 67
Denmark Ct. NE6: Byke .2P 5 (6A 64)
Denmark St. NE6: Byke .2P 5 (6A 64)
(not continuous)
NE8: Gate .4H 83
Dennison Cres. DH3: Bir .2A 114
Dennis St. DH6: Whe H .2B 180
Denshaw Cl. NE23: Cra .7J 21
Dent Cl. DH6: Has .1A 170
Dentdale DH4: Pen .1J 129
Denton Av. NE15: Lem .7D 60
NE29: N Shi .6C 48
DENTON BURN .5F 61
Denton Chare NE1: Newc T .7F 4 (2F 83)
Denton Ct. NE5: Den M .6G 61
Denton Gdns. NE15: Benw .1J 81
Denton Ga. NE5: West .2G 61
Denton Gro. NE5: West .2G 61
Denton Hall Turret .6F 61
Denton Pk. Ho. NE5: W Dent .3E 60
Denton Pk. Shop. Cen. NE5: W Dent .3E 60
Denton Rd. NE15: Den M, Scot .7F 61
Denton Vw. NE21: Winl .4B 80
Dent St. NE24: Bly .3K 23
SR6: Ful .3F 105
Denver Gdns. NE6: Walk .1C 84
Denway Gro. NE26: Sea S .3B 28
Denwick Av. NE15: Lem .7C 60
(off Loraine Ter.)
Denwick Cl. DH2: Ches S .2J 141
Denwick Ter. NE30: Tyne .5J 49
Deodar, The NE23: Cra .4B 26
(off Evergreen Ct.)
Depot Rd. NE6: Walk .6B 64
DEPTFORD .7D 104
Deptford Rd. NE8: Gate .7M 5 (2J 83)
SR4: Sund .2F 7 (1D 118)
Deptford Ter. SR4: Sund .7C 104
Derby Ct. NE4: Newc T .4B 4 (7D 62)
Derby Cres. DH8: C'sde .3C 134
NE31: Heb .1H 85
Derby Dr. DH8: C'sde .3C 134
Derby Gdns. NE28: W'snd .2E 64
Derby Rd. DH9: Stly .4E 124
Derbyshire Dr. DH1: Carr .2H 167
Derby St. NE4: Newc T .4B 4 (7D 62)
NE32: Jar .6C 66
NE33: S Shi .3J 67
SR2: Sund .5G 7 (2E 118)

Derby Ter. NE33: S Shi .3K 67
Dereham Cl. NE26: Sea S .5D 28
Dereham Ct. NE5: Blak .1H 61
Dereham Rd. NE26: Sea S .6D 28
Dereham Ter. NE62: Stake .7A 12
Dereham Way NE29: N Shi .4B 48
Derek Armstrong Ct. SR8: Hord .5D 172
Dere Pk. DH8: Lead .5A 122
Dere Rd. DH8: Cons .1K 135
Dere St. DH7: Esh W, Queb .7C 150
Derry Av. SR6: Ful .3G 105
Derwent Av. NE11: T Vall .2F 99
NE15: Newb .6J 59
NE31: Heb .3J 85
NE39: Row G .6J 95
Derwent Cen., The DH8: Cons .7H 121
(off Trafalgar St.)
Derwent Cl. DH7: Sac .7D 140
SR7: S'hm .2A 148
Derwent Cote NE17: Ham .3K 107
Derwentcote Steel Furnace .2C 108
DERWENT COTTAGES .3J 121
Derwent Ct. NE11: T Vall .2F 99
Derwent Cres. DH3: Gt Lum .3F 143
DH8: Lead .4B 122
NE16: Swa .6G 81
NE17: Ham .3K 107
Derwent Crook Dr. NE9: Low F .2G 99
Derwent Crookfoot Rd. NE9: Low F .2G 99
Derwent Dale DH8: Shot B .4E 120
Derwentdale Ct. DH8: B'hill .6F 121
(off Meadowfield)
Derwentdale Gdns. NE7: H Hea .2K 63
Derwentdale Ind. Est. DH8: B'hill .6F 121
Derwent Dr. DH9: Ann P .5A 124
Derwent Gdns. NE9: Low F .2J 99
NE28: W'snd .1A 66
DERWENTHAUGH .3G 81
Derwenthaugh Ind. Est. NE16: Swa .3F 81
Derwenthaugh Marina NE21: Blay .3G 81
Derwenthaugh Riverside Pk.
NE16: Swa .4G 81
Derwenthaugh Rd. NE16: Blay, Swa .4G 81
NE21: Blay .3G 81
Derwent Haven NE17: Ham .3K 107
Derwent Ho. NE38: Wash .4F 115
Derwent M. DH8: B'hill .5F 121
Derwent Pk. NE39: Row G .5K 95
Derwent Pl. DH8: Shot B .3E 120
NE21: Winl .5B 80
Derwent Ri. DH9: Stly .6D 124
Derwent Rd. NE26: Sea S .4B 28
NE30: Cull .2H 49
NE46: Hex .2E 70
SR8: Pet .5C 172
Derwentside NE16: Swa .6G 81
Derwentside Retail Pk. DH8: Cons .1G 135
Derwent St. DH4: S Row .3B 130
DH5: Eas L .1H 157
DH8: B'hill .5F 121
DH9: Stly .1E 124
NE15: Scot .1H 81
NE17: C'wl .2K 107
(Mill Ct.)
NE17: C'wl .6K 93
(South Rd.)
SR1: Sund .5H 7 (2E 118)
Derwent Ter. DH6: S Het .3A 158
DH9: Ann P .6J 123
NE16: Burn .1B 110
(not continuous)
NE38: Wash .4J 115
Derwent Valley Cotts.
NE39: Row G .6K 95
Derwent Valley Vs. NE17: Ham .2J 107
Derwent Vw. DH8: Cons .3K 121
DH9: Dip .2G 123
NE16: Burn .2B 110
NE17: C'wl .4A 94
NE21: Winl .5B 80
Derwent Vw. Ter. DH9: Dip .7H 109
Derwent Wlk. DH9: Stly .4F 125
Derwent Walk Country Park
Lockhaugh .4A 96
Whickham .7E 80
Derwentwater Av. DH2: Ches S .1K 141
Derwentwater Ct. NE8: Gate .5F 83
Derwent Water Dr. NE21: Blay .1A 80
Derwentwater Gdns. NE16: Whi .7K 81
Derwentwater Rd. NE8: Gate .6D 82
NE64: Newb S .3G 13
Derwentwater Ter. NE33: S Shi .5J 67
Derwent Way NE12: Kil .1A 46
NE21: Blay .5E 80
NE28: W'snd .4J 65
Deuchar Ho. NE2: Newc T .1J 5
Deuchar St. NE2: Jes .5H 63
Devon Av. NE16: Whi .7J 81
Devon Cl. NE63: Ash .3H 11
Devon Cres. DH3: Bir .2K 113
Devon Dr. SR3: New S .1C 132
Devon Gdns. NE9: Low F .7H 83
NE34: S Shi .6D 68
Devonport DH4: Nbot .6C 130
Devon Rd. NE29: N Shi .3D 48
NE31: Heb .3K 85
Devonshire Dr. NE27: Kil .3G 47
Devonshire Gdns. NE28: W'snd .2E 64
Devonshire Pl. NE2: Jes .4H 63
Devonshire Rd. DH1: Carr .1G 167
Devonshire St. NE33: S Shi .6H 67
SR5: Monkw .6E 104
Devonshire Ter. NE2: Newc T .1F 4 (6F 63)
NE26: Whit B .7H 39
Devonshire Twr. SR5: Monkw .6F 105

Devon St. DH4: S Row .3C 130
DH5: Hett H .6F 145
Devon Wlk. NE37: Wash .6H 101
Devonworth Pl. NE24: Cow .2E 22
De Walden Sq. NE61: Peg .4A 10
De Walden Ter. NE61: Peg .4B 10
Dewberry Cl. NE24: News .5G 23
Dewhurst Ter. NE16: Sun .5H 97
Dewley NE23: Cra .5K 25
Dewley Ct. NE15: Thro .2J 59
NE23: Cra .5K 25
Dewley Pl. NE5: West .2E 60
Dewley Rd. NE5: Den M .4G 61
Dewsgreen NE23: Cra .4K 25
Dexter Ho. NE29: N Shi .2E 66
Dexter Way NE10: Fell .6A 84
Deyncourt DH1: Dur .6J 165
NE20: Darr H .2H 41
Deyncourt Cl. NE20: Darr H .3H 41
Diamond Ct. NE3: Ki Pk .7J 43
Diamond Sq. NE46: Hex .2D 70
Diamond St. NE28: W'snd .3F 65
Diamond Ter. DH1: Dur .1B 6 (2A 166)
Diana St. NE4: Newc T .5B 4 (1D 82)
Dibley Sq. NE6: Byke .5P 5 (1K 83)
Dibley St. NE6: Byke .5P 5 (1K 83)
Dickens Av. NE16: Swa .6G 81
NE34: S Shi .3H 87
Dickens St. DH4: Hou S .2D 144
SR5: S'wck .6C 104
Dickens Wlk. NE5: Cha P .2C 60
Dickens Wynd DH1: Dur .5J 165
Dickins Wlk. SR8: Pet .7C 172
Dickson Dr. NE46: Hex .3A 70
Dick St. NE40: Craw .3D 78
Didcot Av. NE29: N Shi .1E 66
Didcot Way NE35: Bol C, W Bol .7E 86
Diggerland
Durham .4H 151
Dillon St. NE32: Jar .1A 86
SR7: S'hm .3B 148
DILSTON .3B 72
Dilston Av. NE25: Whit B .7H 39
NE46: Hex .2E 70
Dilston Castle .3B 72
Dilston Cl. NE27: Shir .2K 47
NE38: Wash .4E 114
NE61: Peg .4C 10
SR8: Pet .2A 182
Dilston Dr. NE5: West .2E 60
NE63: Ash .5B 12
Dilston Gdns. SR4: Sund .3B 118
Dilston Grange NE28: W'snd .3A 66
Dilston Rd. DH1: Dur .5B 154
NE4: Fen .1C 82
(not continuous)
Dilston Ter. NE3: Gos .1G 63
NE32: Jar .3B 86
Dimbula Gdns. NE7: H Hea .3B 64
Dinmont Pl. NE23: Cra .5K 25
DINNINGTON .4H 33
Dinnington Rd. NE13: Din .5J 33
NE29: N Shi .6C 48
Dinsdale Av. NE28: W'snd .1G 65
Dinsdale Cotts. SR2: Ryh .3H 133
Dinsdale Dr. DH1: Carr .7H 155
Dinsdale Pl. NE2: Newc T .2K 5 (6H 63)
Dinsdale Rd. NE2: Newc T .2K 5 (6H 63)
SR6: Roker .5G 105
Dinsdale St. SR2: Ryh .3H 133
Dinsdale St. Sth. SR2: Ryh .3H 133
Dinsley Dr. TS29: Trim S .7C 180
(off Margaret Ter.)
Dinting Cl. SR8: Pet .7K 171
Dipe La. NE36: E Bol, W Bol .1G 103
DIPTON .1H 123
Dipton Av. NE4: Benw .2A 82
Dipton Cl. NE46: Hex .2G 71
Dipton Gdns. SR3: Sund .6D 118
Dipton Gro. NE23: Cra .4K 25
DIPTONMILL .7B 70
Dipton Mill Rd. NE46: Hex .7B 70
Dipton Rd. NE25: Monks .4D 38
Dipwood Rd. NE39: Row G .7H 95
Dipwood Way NE39: Row G .7H 95
Discovery Ct. SR3: Silk .3B 132
Discovery Mus. .7C 4 (2E 82)
Dishforth Grn. NE9: Low F .6K 99
Dispensary La.
NE1: Newc T .6D 4 (1E 82)
Disraeli St. DH4: Hou S .2B 144
NE24: Bly .1H 23
(not continuous)
Disraeli Ter. NE17: C'wl .6K 93
DISSINGTON .7A 30
Dissington La. NE15: Hed W .5B 40
DISSINGTON MARCH .4F 41
Dissington Pl. NE5: Fen .5J 61
NE16: Whi .2G 97
District Probate Registry
Newcastle upon Tyne .7D 4 (2E 82)
Ditchburn Ter. SR4: Sund .7B 104
Dixon Av. DH8: Ebc .5H 107
Dixon Est. DH6: Shot C .7E 170
Dixon Est. Bungs. DH6: Shot C .1E 180
Dixon Pl. NE11: Dun .6B 82
Dixon Ri. SR8: Hord .6F 173
Dixon Rd. DH5: Hou S .4D 144
Dixons Sq. SR6: Monkw .6F 105
Dixon St. DH8: B'hill .5G 121
NE8: Gate .5E 82
NE33: S Shi .4J 67
Dobson Cl. NE4: Newc T .9A 4 (3D 82)
NE39: H Spen .2D 94
Dobson Courtyard NE8: Gate .4D 82

Dobson Cres. NE6: Byke .2A 84
Dobson Ho. NE3: Gos .6E 44
NE12: Kil .2K 45
Dobson Ter. SR7: Mur .7E 146
TS28: Win .4F 181
Dockendale La. NE16: Whi .7J 81
Dockendale M. NE16: Whi .7J 81
Dockendale Pl. NE21: Blay .4D 80
Dock Rd. NE29: N Shi .1G 67
Dock Rd. Sth. NE29: N Shi .2G 67
Dock St. NE33: S Shi .7H 67
SR6: Roker .7G 105
Dockwray Cl. NE30: N Shi .7H 49
Dockwray Sq. NE30: N Shi .7H 49
Doctor Pit Cotts. NE22: Bed .7H 17
Doctor Ryan Ho. NE6: Walk .1E 84
Doctor Winterbottom Hall
NE33: S Shi .4A 68
Doddfell Cl. NE37: Wash .2E 114
Doddington Cl. NE15: Lem .6B 60
Doddington Dr. NE23: Cra .4K 25
Doddington Vs. NE10: Wind N .7A 84
Dodd's Bldgs. NE35: Bol C .5E 86
Dodds Cl. DH6: Whe H .2C 180
Dodd's Ct. SR5: Sund .4G 103
Dodds Farm NE3: Gos .7C 44
Dodds Ter. DH3: Bir .2A 114
TS28: Win .4F 181
Dodd Ter. DH9: Ann P .6K 123
Dodsworth Nth. NE40: G'sde .5F 79
Dodsworth Ter. NE40: G'sde .5F 79
Dodsworth Vs. NE40: G'sde .5F 79
Dog Bank NE1: Newc T .7H 5 (2G 83)
Dogger Bank NE61: Mor .6E 8
Dog Leap Stairs NE1: Newc T .7G 4
Dolphin Ct. NE4: Benw .1K 81
Dolphin Gro. NE24: Bly .5K 23
Dolphin Quay NE29: N Shi .7H 49
Dolphin St. NE4: Benw .1K 81
Dolphin Vs. NE13: Haz .7D 34
Dominies Cl. NE39: Row G .4K 95
Dominion Rd. DH7: B'don .2D 174
Donald Av. DH6: S Het .3A 158
Donald St. NE3: Gos .7G 45
Doncaster Rd.
NE2: Newc T .2K 5 (6H 63)
Don Cres. DH3: Gt Lum .3F 143
Doncrest Rd. NE37: Wash .6F 101
Don Dixon Dr. NE32: Jar .5B 86
Donerston Gro. SR8: Pet .1J 181
Don Gdns. NE36: W Bol .7F 87
NE37: Wash .6H 101
Donington Cl. SR5: Sund .6G 103
Donkin Rd. NE37: Wash .1E 114
Donkins St. NE35: Bol C .5E 86
Donkin Ter. NE30: N Shi .5J 49
NE40: Craw .3C 78
Donnington Ct. NE3: Gos .1H 63
Donnington Pl. DH8: C'sde .3D 134
Donnini Ho. SR8: Eas .7A 160
Donnini Pl. DH1: Dur .1D 166
Donnison Gdns. SR1: Sund .1G 119
Donridge NE37: Wash .6F 101
Don Rd. NE32: Jar .6D 66
Donside NE10: Hew .3D 100
Donside Cl. NE35: Bol C .6H 87
Don St. NE11: T Vall .3E 98
Donvale Rd. NE37: Wash .6E 100
Don Vw. NE36: W Bol .7F 87
DONWELL .6F 101
Donwell Village NE37: Wash .6F 101
Dorcas Av. NE15: Benw .1J 81
Dorcas Ter. NE37: Wash .7H 101
Dorchester Cl. NE5: Cha P .2B 60
Dorchester Ct. NE25: New Hart .4G 27
Dorchester Gdns. NE9: Low F .5H 99
Doreen Av. SR7: Dalt D .4H 147
Doric Rd. DH7: New B .5B 164
Dorking Av. NE29: N Shi .1E 66
Dorking Cl. NE24: News .5J 23
Dorking Rd. SR6: Ful .3G 105
Dorlonco Vs. DH7: Mead .2E 174
Dormand Ct. TS28: Sta T .7H 181
Dormand Dr. SR8: Pet .2B 182
Dornoch Cres. NE10: Wind N .1C 100
Dorothy Ter. DH7: Sac .1E 152
Dorrington Rd. NE3: Fawd .6A 44
Dorset Av. DH3: Bir .7B 114
NE28: W'snd .3E 64
NE31: Heb .1K 85
NE34: S Shi .6D 68
SR6: Ful .3G 105
Dorset Cl. NE63: Ash .3H 11
Dorset Cres. DH8: C'sde .2D 134
Dorset Gro. NE29: N Shi .3D 48
Dorset Rd. NE15: Den M .7F 61
Dorset St. DH5: Eas L .3J 157
Dotland Cl. NE46: Hex .2G 71
Douai Dr. DH8: Cons .2A 136
Double Row NE25: Sea D .6F 27
Douglas Av. NE3: Gos .2C 62
SR8: Hord .5D 172
Douglas Bader Ho. NE24: Bly .3K 23
(off Twizell St.)
Douglas Cl. NE34: S Shi .2J 87
Douglas Ct. DH9: Ann P .6J 123
NE11: T Vall .5G 99
Douglas Gdns. DH1: Dur .5J 165
(not continuous)
NE11: Dun .7C 82
Douglas Pde. NE31: Heb .4A 86
Douglas Rd. SR6: Seab .3G 105
Douglas Sq. SR1: Sund .2K 7 (1G 119)
Douglass St. NE28: W'snd .3F 65
Douglas St. NE28: W'snd .4A 66

Douglas Ter. DH4: Pen 1C 130
DH9: Dip 3E 122
NE4: Newc T 5A 4 (1D 82)
NE37: Wash 5H 101
Douglas Vs. DH1: Dur 2C 166
Douglas Way NE1: Newc T 4E 4
SR7: Mur 7F 147
Doulting Cl. NE12: Longb 6K 45
Doulton Dr. SR4: Sund 4G 117
Douro Ter. SR2: Sund 6J 7 (3F 119)
Dove Av. NE32: Jar 3C 86
Dove Cl. DH7: B'don 1C 174
NE12: Kil 7A 36
Dovecote Cl. NE25: Monks 5C 38
Dovecote Dr. DH2: P Fel 5G 127
Dovecote Farm DH2: Ches S 7H 127
Dovecote Rd. NE12: Longb 5C 46
Dove Ct. DH3: Bir 3A 114
NE30: Cull 1J 49
Dovecrest Ct. NE28: W'snd 1K 65
Dovedale Av. NE24: Cow 2E 22
Dovedale Ct. NE34: S Shi 1G 87
SR7: S'hm 2H 147
Dovedale Gdns. NE7: H Hea 2J 63
NE9: Low F 3J 99
Dovedale Rd. SR6: Seab 2E 104
Dover Cl. NE5: Cha P 2C 60
NE22: Bed 7F 17
Dovercourt Rd. NE6: Walk 2E 84
Dove Row NE30: Cull 1J 49
Dovestone Cl. NE38: Wash 5B 116
Dowding La. NE3: Ken 2K 61
Dowling Av. NE25: Monks 7F 39
Down at the Farm 6H 131
Downe Cl. NE24: News 5J 23
Downend Rd. NE5: West 2D 60
Downfield NE37: Wash 4H 101
Downham NE5: W Dent 4F 61
Downham Ct. NE33: S Shi 4J 67
DOWNHILL 4H 103
Downhill La. NE36: W Bol 3C 102
Downies Bldgs. NE64: Newb S 2K 13
Downing Dr. NE61: Mor 1E 14
Downing Plaza
NE4: Newc T 5C 4 (1E 82)
Downs La. DH5: Hett H 5H 145
Downs Pit La. DH5: Hett H 6H 145
Downswood NE12: Kil 1D 46
Dowsey Rd. DH6: S'burn 2K 167
Dowson Sq. SR7: Mur 7C 146
Doxford Av. DH5: Hett H 4F 145
Doxford Cotts. DH5: Hett H 4F 145
Doxford Dr. SR8: Pet 6H 171
Doxford Gdns. NE5: Fen 4K 61
Doxford Intl. Bus. Pk. SR3: Dox P 4J 131
DOXFORD PARK 4B 132
Doxford Pk. Way SR3: Dox P 3K 131
Doxford Pl. NE23: Cra 5K 25
Doxford Ter. DH5: Hett H 4F 145
Doxford Ter. Nth. SR7: Mur 7C 146
Doxford Ter. Sth. SR7: Mur 7C 146
Dragon La. DH1: Dur 1F 167
Dragon Ville DH1: Dur 3F 167
Dragonville Ct. DH1: Dur 3F 167
Dragonville Ind. Est. DH1: Dur 2F 167
Dragonville Ind. Pk. DH1: Dur 2F 167
Dragonville Retail Pk. DH1: Dur 2F 167
Drake Cl. NE33: S Shi 5H 67
Drake's Cotts. NE40: Craw 3D 78
Drawback NE42: Pru 4F 77
Drawback Cl. NE42: Pru 4F 77
Draymans Way
NE4: Newc T 5C 4 (1E 82)
Drayton Rd. NE3: Ken 1A 62
SR6: Ful 3F 105
Dreswick Ct. SR7: Mur 7F 147
Drey, The NE20: Darr H 1F 41
Drive, The DH3: Bir 6B 114
DH8: Shot B 3F 121
NE3: Gos 2E 62
NE5: Den M 5F 61
NE7: Longb 1K 63
NE9: Low F 7H 83
NE10: Fell, Hew 6C 84
NE16: Whi 1J 97
NE28: W'snd 3F 65
NE30: Tyne 4K 49
NE37: Wash 6F 101
NE61: Tra W 7D 14
Drivecote NE10: Fell 6C 84
Dronfield Cl. DH2: Ches S 1H 141
Drove Rd. NE15: Thro 1F 59
Drover Rd. DH8: C'sde 4C 134
Drover Ter. DH8: C'sde 4C 134
Drumaldrace NE37: Wash 2E 114
(not continuous)
Drum Ind. Est. DH2: Ches S 2J 127
Drummond Cres. NE34: S Shi 1F 87
Drummond Rd. NE3: Ken 2B 62
Drummond Sq. NE2: Newc T 1F 4 (6F 63)
Drummond Ter. NE30: N Shi 5H 49
Drumoyne Cl. SR3: E Her 3H 131
Drumoyne Gdns. NE25: Monks 1D 48
Drum Pk. DH2: Ches S 2K 127
Drum Rd. DH2: Ches S 1K 127
DH3: Bir, Ches S 1K 127
Drumsheugh Pl. NE5: Blak 3H 61
Druridge Av. SR6: Seab 2F 105
Druridge Cres. NE24: Bly 3F 23
NE34: S Shi 5D 68
Druridge Dr. NE5: Fen 4J 61
NE24: Bly 3F 23
Druridge Ho. NE29: N Shi 1D 66
Drury Bldgs. *NE11: Dun 4C 82*
(off Cormorant Dr.)
Drury La. DH1: Dur 3C 6 (3A 166)
NE1: Newc T 6F 4 (1F 83)
NE29: N Shi 5C 48
SR1: Sund 1G 119
Drybeck Ct. NE4: Newc T 6A 4 (1D 82)
NE23: Cra 2B 26
Drybeck Sq. SR3: Silk 3D 132
Drybeck Wlk. NE23: Cra 2B 26
Dryborough St. SR4: Sund 1D 118
Dryburgh NE38: Wash 3H 115
Dryburgh Cl. NE29: N Shi 4E 48
Dryburn Hill DH1: Dur 7J 153
Dryburn Pk. DH1: Dur 6J 153
Dryburn Rd. DH1: Dur 7J 153
Dryburn Vw. DH1: Dur 6J 153
Dryden Cl. DH9: Stly 3G 125
NE34: S Shi 4H 87
Dryden Ct. NE9: Low F 6H 83
Dryden Rd. NE9: Low F 6H 83
Drysdale Ct. NE13: Bru V 5C 34
Drysdale Cres. NE13: Bru V 5C 34
Dubmire Cotts. DH4: Hou S 2A 144
Dubmire Ct. DH4: Hou S 2A 144
Dubmire Ind. Est. DH4: Hou S 1B 144
Duchess Cres. E. NE32: Jar 3B 86
Duchess Cres. W. NE32: Jar 3B 86
Duchess Dr. NE15: Den M 6G 61
Duchess St. NE26: Whit B 6G 39
Duckets Dean NE42: Pru 3F 77
Duckpool La. NE16: Whi 7J 81
Duckpool La. Nth. NE16: Whi 6J 81
Duddon Cl. SR8: Pet 6C 172
Duddon Pl. NE9: Low F 3K 99
DUDLEY 3J 35
Dudley Av. SR6: Ful 3F 105
Dudley Bus. Cen. NE23: Dud 1H 35
Dudley Ct. NE23: Cra 4J 25
Dudley Dr. NE23: Dud 3J 35
Dudley Gdns. SR3: E Her 2J 131
Dudley Ho. NE4: Newc T 3B 4
Dudley La. NE13: Sea B 3E 34
NE23: Cra, Dud 1J 35
NE23: Dud 3E 34
Dudley La. Cotts. NE13: Sea B 3D 34
Dudley Ter. DH9: Ann P 5B 124
Duffy Ter. DH9: Ann P 6A 124
Dugdale Ct. NE3: Ken 7K 43
Dugdale Rd. NE3: Ken 7K 43
Duke of Northumberland Ct.
NE28: W'snd 7H 47
Duke's Av. NE31: Heb 2H 85
Dukes Cotts. NE15: Hor 4E 56
NE15: Newb 6K 59
NE27: Back 6G 37
Dukes Ct. NE42: Pru 2G 77
Dukes Dr. NE3: Gos 3D 44
Dukesfield NE23: Cra 4K 25
NE27: Shir 7J 37
Duke's Gdns. NE24: Cow 1G 23
Dukes Mdw. NE13: Wool 4E 42
NE27: Back 6F 37
Dukes Rd. NE46: Hex 1A 70
Duke St. DH9: Ann P 4J 123
NE1: Newc T 8C 4 (2E 82)
NE10: Pel 5E 84
NE26: Whit B 6G 39
NE29: N Shi 1H 67
NE63: Ash 3A 12
SR4: Sund 2C 118
SR7: S'hm 2K 147
Duke St. Nth. SR6: Ful 5F 105
Dukes Wlk. NE12: Longb 4K 45
NE26: Whit B 4G 39
Dukes Way NE42: Pru 2G 77
Dukesway NE11: T Vall 2D 98
Dukesway Ct. NE11: T Vall 4E 98
Dukesway W. NE11: T Vall 5E 98
Duke Wlk. NE8: Gate 5E 82
Dulcie Ho. NE1: Newc T 5J 5 (1H 83)
Dulverston Cl. NE5: Cha P 2C 60
Dulverton Av. NE33: S Shi 6K 67
Dulverton Ct. NE2: Jes 2H 63
Dumas Wlk. NE5: Cha P 2C 60
Dumbarton Cl. SR4: Sund 5K 117
Dumfries Cl. SR4: Sund 5J 117
Dumfries Cres. NE32: Jar 3E 86
Dunbar Cl. NE5: Cha P 2C 60
Dunbar Ct. NE24: Bly 5K 23
Dunbar Gdns. NE28: W'snd 1A 66
Dunbar St. SR4: Sund 3B 118
Dunblane Cres. NE5: W Dent 5F 61
Dunblane Dr. NE24: News 5J 23
Dunblane Rd. SR6: Ful 2G 105
Dunbreck Gro. SR4: Sund 4C 118
Duncairn *DH9: Stly 2F 125*
(off View La.)
Duncan Gdns. NE61: Mor 1F 15
Duncan St. NE6: Walk 7E 64
NE8: Gate 5K 83
SR4: Sund 1B 118
Duncombe Ct. DH9: Stly 1F 125
Duncombe Cres. DH9: Stly 1F 125
Dun Cow La. DH1: Dur 4C 6 (3A 166)
Dun Cow St. SR1: Sund 3H 7 (1E 118)
Dundas St. SR6: Monkw 1J 7 (7F 105)
Dundas Way NE10: Fell 6A 84
Dundee Cl. NE5: Cha P 2C 60
Dundee Ct. NE32: Jar 3E 86
Dundrennan NE38: Wash 5G 115
Dunedin Cl. DH9: Ann P 4K 123
Dunelm DH7: Sac 1E 152
SR2: Sund 4C 118
(not continuous)
Dunelm Cl. DH3: Bir 4A 114
DH8: Lead 6B 122
Dunelm Ct. DH1: Dur 3B 6 (3A 166)
DH7: B'don 2C 174
NE31: Heb 1H 85
Dunelm Cres. DH8: C'sde 3D 134
Dunelm Dr. DH4: Hou S 2C 144
NE36: W Bol 7H 87
Dunelm Grange NE35: Bol C 6E 86
Dunelm Pl. DH6: Shot C 6F 171
Dunelm Rd. DH5: Hett H 6F 145
DH6: Thor 2G 179
DH8: C'sde 2C 134
Dunelm Sth. SR2: Sund 4D 118
Dunelm St. NE33: S Shi 3K 67
Dunelm Ter. SR7: Dalt D 6H 147
Dunelm Wlk. DH8: Lead 6B 122
SR8: Pet 5B 172
Dunelm Way DH8: Lead 6B 122
Dunes Adventure Island 1A 68
Dunes Bowl 1A 68
Dunford Gdns. NE5: Cha P 1D 60
Dunholm Cl. DH5: Hou S 3E 144
Dunholme Cl. DH1: Dur 6K 153
Dunholme Rd. NE4: Elsw 1B 82
Dunira Cl. NE2: Jes 3H 63
Dunkeld Cl. DH4: S Row 4K 129
NE10: Ward 6F 85
NE24: News 5J 23
Dunkirk Av. DH5: Hou S 3F 145
Dunkirk Ter. NE45: Corb 7D 52
Dunlin Cl. NE40: Ryton 2J 79
Dunlin Dr. NE24: News 5J 23
NE38: Wash 5D 114
Dunlop Cl. NE7: H Hea 1A 64
Dunlop Cres. NE34: S Shi 7C 68
Dunmoor Cl. NE3: Gos 1C 62
Dunmoor Ct. DH2: Ches S 1J 141
Dunmore Av. SR6: Ful 2G 105
Dunmorlie St. NE6: Byke 7B 64
Dunn Av. SR3: New S 7C 118
Dunne Rd. NE21: Blay 2E 80
Dunnlynn Cl. SR3: Silk 3A 132
Dunnock Ct. NE15: Lem 7D 60
Dunnock Dr. NE16: Sun 4G 97
NE38: Wash 6D 114
Dunnock Pl. NE13: W Op 6E 34
Dunn Rd. SR8: Pet 5B 172
Dunns Bldgs. DH9: Ann P 4A 124
Dunn's Ter. NE2: Newc T 1A 4 (5D 62)
Dunn St. DH9: Ann P 5K 123
NE4: Newc T 9A 4 (3D 82)
Dunns Way NE21: Blay 5C 80
Dunns Yd. DH9: Ann P 4A 124
Dunn Ter. NE6: Byke 4N 5 (7K 63)
Dunnykirk Av. NE3: Ken 7K 43
Dunraven Cl. DH4: S Row 4C 130
Dunsany Ter. DH2: P Fel 5G 127
Dunscar DH4: Hou S 1B 144
Dunsdale Dr. NE23: Cra 2B 26
Dunsdale Rd. NE25: H'wll 1J 37
Dunsgreen NE20: Pon 6J 31
Dunsgreen Ct. NE20: Pon 6J 31
Dunslaw Cft. NE15: Hor 4E 56
Dunsley Gdns. NE13: Din 4H 33
Dunsmuir Gro. NE8: Gate 6F 83
Dunstable Pl. NE5: Cha P 2B 60
Dunstanburgh Cl. NE6: Byke 1B 84
NE22: Bed 7F 17
NE38: Wash 4F 115
Dunstanburgh Ct. DH4: Hou S 1H 143
NE10: Ward 7F 85
NE32: Jar 1E 86
Dunstanburgh Rd. NE6: Byke, Walk 1B 84
Dunstan Cl. DH2: Ches S 1J 141
Dunstan Wlk. NE5: W Dent 4F 61
DUNSTON 5C 82
Dunston Activity Cen. 6C 82
Dunston Bank NE11: Dun 7A 82
Dunston Ent. Pk. NE11: Dun 4A 82
DUNSTON HILL 7B 82
Dunston Leisure Centre 7A 82
Dunston Pl. NE24: Cow 2F 23
Dunston Rd. NE11: Dun 4B 82
(not continuous)
Dunston Station (Rail) 6C 82
Dunston Workshops *NE11: Dun 4B 82*
(off Flour Mill Rd.)
Dunswell Grange TS29: Trim S 7C 180
Dunvegan DH3: Bir 6C 114
Dunvegan Av. DH2: Ches S 1K 141
Dunwood SR4: Sund 1H 117
Dunwoodie Ter. *NE46: Hex 1C 70*
(off Cockshaw)
Durant Rd. NE1: Newc T 4G 4 (7G 63)
Durban St. NE24: Bly 1H 23
DURHAM 4C 6 (3A 166)
Durham Amateur Rowing Club 3D 166
Durham Av. NE37: Wash 7F 101
SR8: Hord 4D 172
Durham Bus Station 2K 165
Durham Castle 3C 6 (3A 166)
Durham Cathedral 4C 6 (3A 166)
Durham City Retail Pk. DH1: Dur 1F 167
Durham Climbing Cen. 1F 175
Durham Cl. NE22: Bed 6F 17
Durham County Cricket Club 7C 128
Durham Ct. DH7: Sac 1F 153
NE31: Heb 1H 85
Durham Crematorium DH1: Dur 7K 165
Durham Dr. NE32: Jar 5A 86
Durham Gdns. DH7: Wit G 2D 152
Durham Gro. NE32: Jar 4A 86
Durham Heritage Centre & Museum
4D 6 (3A 166)
Durham Ho. SR5: Sund 3F 103
Durham Indoor Bowling Cen. 3B 154
Durham La. DH6: Has 4E 168
DH6: Has, Ludw, S Hil 4E 168
SR8: Eas, Pet 3F 171
(not continuous)
Durham Light Infantry Mus.
& Durham Art Gallery 1K 165
Durham Moor DH1: Dur 6J 153
Durham Moor Cres. DH1: Dur 6J 153
Durham Pl. DH3: Bir 7A 114
DH4: Nbot 6D 130
(off Front St.)
NE8: Gate 5H 83
SR7: Mur 1F 159
DURHAM RIDING 7F 77
Durham Rd. DH1: Dur 6J 153
(Aykley Va.)
DH1: Dur 1E 164
(Toll Ho. Rd.)
DH2: Ches M 2A 142
DH3: Bir, Ches S 2A 114
DH3: Ches M, Ches S 1A 142
DH4: Hou S 7F 131
(Houghton Cut)
DH4: Hou S 2E 144
(The Broadway)
DH4: Ston 7F 131
DH5: E Rain 6C 144
DH5: E Rain, Hou S 5D 144
DH6: Bowb 4G 177
DH6: Whe H 4B 180
DH7: Bearp 1E 164
DH7: Bran 5A 174
DH7: Esh W 4E 162
DH7: Lan 7K 137
DH7: Sac 1E 152
DH7: Ush M 2B 164
DH8: B'hill, Cons 5F 121
DH8: Lead 5B 122
DH9: Ann P 6A 124
DH9: Stly 4G 125
NE8: Gate 5H 83
NE9: Low F 3H 99
NE23: Cra 1A 26
SR2: Sund 5F 7 (2D 118)
(New Durham Rd.)
SR2: Sund 4D 118
(Stapylton Dr.)
SR3: E Her, Sund 3H 131
TS28: Win 4E 180
Durham Rd. Nth. DH3: Bir 4A 114
DH6: Bowb 4H 177
(off Durham Rd.)
Durham Rd. Trad. Est. DH3: Bir 1A 128
Durham Rd. W. DH6: Bowb 5H 177
DURHAM SERVICE AREA 6H 177
Durham Station (Rail) 1A 6 (2K 165)
Durham St. DH4: Hou S 2A 144
DH7: Lang P 4J 151
NE4: Elsw 2B 82
(not continuous)
NE10: Pel 5D 84
NE28: W'snd 3G 65
SR7: S'hm 2K 147
Durham St. W. NE28: W'snd 3G 65
Durham Ter. DH1: Dur 5J 153
SR3: New S 7C 118
Durham University
Hatfield College 3B 166
New Elvet 3B 166
Old Elvet 3E 6 (3B 166)
Palace Green 3C 6 (3A 166)
Stockton Road 7D 6 (5B 166)
Durham University Mus. of Archaeology
3C 6 (3A 166)
Durham University Oriental Mus.
7A 6 (5K 165)
Durham University Rowing Club 4C 166
Durham Vw. DH3: Gt Lum 3E 142
Durham Way SR8: Pet 1K 181
Durham World Heritage Site Vis. Cen. 3C 6
Durken Bus. Pk. NE23: Seg 1D 36
Dutton Ct. NE21: Blay 2F 81
Duxbury Pk. NE38: Wash 1H 129
Duxfield Rd. NE7: H Hea 2K 63
DW Fitness
Newcastle upon Tyne 6A 64
North Shields 3E 66
Dwyer Cres. SR2: Ryh 3H 133
Dykefield Av. NE3: Fawd 5A 44
DYKE HEADS 4F 79
Dyke Heads La. NE40: G'sde 4F 79
Dykelands Rd. SR6: Ful, Seab 3F 105
Dykelands Way NE34: S Shi 3F 87
Dykenook Cl. NE16: Whi 3G 97
Dykes Way NE10: Wind N 2B 100
Dykewood DH9: Beam 2K 125
Dymock Ct. NE3: Ki Pk 7H 43
Dyrham Cl. SR2: Ryh 3F 133
Dysons Bldgs. DH7: Edm 2A 140

E

EACHWICK 1A 40
Eaglescliffe SR2: Ryh 3G 133
Eaglescliffe Dr. NE7: H Hea 3B 64
Eaglesdene DH5: Hett H 6G 145
Ealing Ct. NE3: K Bank 6H 43
Ealing Dr. NE30: Cull 3J 49
Ealing Sq. NE23: Cra 4F 25
SR5: S'wck 4C 104
Eames Ct. SR5: S'wck 4C 104
Eardulph Av. DH3: Ches S 6B 128
Earl Grey's Monument 5F 4 (1F 83)
Earl Grey Way NE29: N Shi 2F 67

Earlington Ct. NE12: Longb 3C 46
Earls Cl. NE13: Wool 4F 43
Earls Ct. NE11: T Vall 2F 99
NE42: Pru 2G 77
SR5: S'wck 3C 104
Earls Court Health Club 4J 7
(off Blandford St.)
Earls Dene NE9: Low F 3H 99
Earls Dr. NE9: Low F 3H 99
NE15: Den M 6G 61
Earl's Gdns. NE24: Cow 1G 23
Earls Grn. DH5: E Rain 7D 144
Earlsmeadow NE27: Shir 7K 37
Earls Pk. Nth. NE11: T Vall 7E 82
Earlston St. SR5: S'wck 3C 104
Earlston Way NE23: Cra 7A 22
Earl St. DH9: Ann P 4K 123
SR4: Sund 2D 118
SR7: S'hm 2J 147
Earls Way NE1: Newc T 4F 4
Earlsway NE11: T Vall 7E 82
Earlswood Av. NE9: Low F 3H 99
Earlswood Gro. NE24: News 6H 23
Earlswood Pk. NE9: Low F 3H 99
Earnshaw Way NE25: Monks 4D 38
EARSDON 6A 38
Earsdon Cl. NE5: W Dent 4G 61
Earsdon Ct. NE25: Monks 7D 38
Earsdon Grange Rd. DH5: Hou S 1F 145
Earsdon Rd. DH5: Hou S 2F 145
NE3: Ken 2A 62
NE25: Ears, H'wll 2K 37
NE25: Ears, Monks, Well 6A 38
NE27: Back, Shir 2H 47
Earsdon Ter. NE27: Shir 3J 47
SR2: Ryh 3H 133
Earsdon Vw. NE27: Shir 7K 37
Easby Cl. NE3: Gos 4F 45
Easby Rd. NE38: Wash 4H 115
Easedale NE26: Sea S 4C 28
Easedale Av. NE3: Gos 3E 44
Easedale Gdns. NE9: Low F, Wrek 3J 99
EASINGTON 7K 159
Easington Av. NE9: Wrek 4A 100
NE23: Cra 7A 22
EASINGTON COLLIERY 7B 160
Easington Greyhound Stadium 6J 159
EASINGTON LANE 2J 157
EASINGTON LEA 5B 160
Easington Rd. DH6: S Het 5E 158
EASINGTON SERVICE AREA 3J 159
Easington St. SR5: Monkw 1H 7 (7E 104)
SR8: Eas C 7B 160
Easington St. Nth. SR5: Monkw 1H 7
East Acres NE13: Din 3J 33
NE21: Blay 4D 80
E. Atherton St. DH1: Dur 3A 6 (3K 165)
East Av. DH2: Ches M 3J 141
NE12: Longb 6B 46
NE25: Monks 6E 38
NE34: S Shi 7C 68
(not continuous)
NE38: Wash 7F 115
SR8: Eas C 5C 160
East Bk. Pde. SR2: Sund 3H 119
East Bailey NE12: Kil 7B 36
East Block DH7: Wit G 3C 152
EAST BOLDON 7K 87
East Boldon (Park & Tram) 7A 88
E. Boldon Rd. SR6: Clead 6A 88
East Boldon Station (Metro) 7A 88
Eastbourne Av. NE6: Walk 7E 64
NE8: Gate 6G 83
Eastbourne Ct. NE6: Walk 7E 64
Eastbourne Gdns. NE6: Walk 7E 64
NE23: Cra 4F 25
NE26: Whit B 5F 39
Eastbourne Gro. NE33: S Shi 2K 67
Eastbourne Pde. NE31: Heb 4A 86
Eastbourne Sq. SR5: S'wck 3C 104
East Bri. St. DH4: Pen 7J 115
E. Brunton Wynd NE13: Gos 2D 44
Eastburn Gdns. NE10: Pel 4E 84
Eastbury Av. NE5: W Dent 5F 61
Eastcheap NE6: Heat 4A 64
E. Cleft Rd. SR1: Sund 5F 7 (2D 118)
East Clere DH7: Lang P 5J 151
Eastcliffe NE26: Whit B 6J 39
Eastcliffe Av. NE3: Ken 2C 62
Eastcliffe M. NE3: Gos 1F 63
E. Cliff Rd. SR7: S'hm 5C 148
East Cl. NE34: S Shi 7C 68
Eastcombe Cl. NE35: Bol C 4E 86
E. Coronation St. SR7: Mur 7F 147
Eastcote Ter. NE6: Walk 2D 84
EAST CRAMLINGTON 5B 26
E. Cramlington Ind. Est.
NE23: E Cram 6C 26
East Cramlington Pond (Nature Reserve) 6E 26
East Cres. NE22: Bed 6C 18
Eastcroft NE26: Sea S 6E 28
E. Cross St. SR1: Sund 2K 7
Eastdene Rd. SR7: S'hm 3H 147
Eastdene Way SR8: Pet 7D 172
EAST DENTON 5G 61
East Dr. NE24: News 5G 23
SR6: Clead 6B 88
E. Durham Link Rd. SR7: Hawt, Mur 3F 159
E. Ellen St. SR7: Mur 1F 159
(off W. Ellen St.)
East End NE26: Sea S 6E 28
East End Pool 3P 5 (7A 64)
Easten Gdns. NE10: Fell 5B 84
Easten Ter. NE28: W'snd 4C 66
Easterfield Ct. NE61: Mor 6G 9
Eastern Av. DH7: Lang P 5J 151
NE9: Low F 3F 99
NE11: T Vall 3F 99
Eastern Av. Trade Pk. NE11: T Vall 3F 99
Eastern Ct. NE10: Gate 4A 84
Eastern Way NE5: Blak 3K 61
NE20: Darr H 6H 31
SR4: Sund 7A 104
Easter Pk. NE23: Nel V 1F 25
Easter St. NE8: Gate 5D 82
East Farm Ct. NE16: Sun 4J 97
NE23: Cra 4K 25
E. Farm M. DH8: M'sly 6A 108
NE27: Back 6G 37
E. Farm Pk. NE62: Chop 1F 17
E. Farm Ter. NE23: Cra 4K 25
Eastfield SR8: Pet 7D 172
Eastfield Av. NE6: Walk 5E 64
NE25: Monks 7D 38
Eastfield Ho. NE6: Walk 5E 64
Eastfield Rd. NE12: Longb 6A 46
NE34: S Shi 5B 68
East Flds. SR6: Whit 6H 89
Eastfields DH9: Stly 4E 124
NE46: Hex 2F 71
Eastfield St. SR4: Sund 3B 118
Eastfield Ter. NE12: Longb 6B 46
East Ford Rd. NE62: Stake 7A 12
E. Forest Hall Rd. NE12: Longb 4C 46
East Front NE2: Jes 1G 4 (5G 63)
Eastgarth NE5: West 7G 43
Eastgate NE8: Gate 8J 5 (2H 83)
NE46: Hex 2D 70
NE61: Mor 1G 15
NE62: Sco G 3G 17
Eastgate Bank NE43: Mic 5B 76
Eastgate Gdns. NE4: Benw 2B 82
EAST GATESHEAD 10L 5 (4J 83)
E. George Potts St. NE33: S Shi 4K 67
E. George St. NE30: N Shi 6J 49
East Grange NE25: H'wll 1K 37
SR5: S'wck 4E 104
E. Grange Ct. SR8: Eas 1K 171
East Grn. DH6: Shot C 6F 171
Eastgreen NE62: Sco G 3H 17
East Gro. SR4: Sund 3H 117
EAST HARTFORD 6K 21
E. Hendon Rd. SR1: Sund 2H 119
EAST HERRINGTON 2J 131
E. Hetton Aged Workmen's Homes
DH6: Kel 7E 178
East Hill Rd. NE8: Gate 5K 83
East Holburn NE33: S Shi 3H 67
EAST HOLYWELL 4H 37
EAST HOWDON 3C 66
E. Howdon By-Pass NE28: W'snd 4C 66
NE29: N Shi, W'snd 3C 66
EAST JARROW 7D 66
EAST KYO 3B 124
Eastlands DH5: Hett H 7F 145
NE7: H Hea 2J 63
NE21: Winl 5B 80
NE38: Wash 2C 128
East Law DH8: Ebc 7F 107
East Lea DH6: Thor 7J 169
NE21: Winl 6C 80
NE64: Newb S 1J 13
Eastlea Cres. SR7: S'hm 3J 147
Eastlea Rd. SR7: S'hm 3H 147
Eastleigh Cl. NE35: Bol C 6E 86
East Loan NE61: Mor 5G 9
E. Moffett St. NE33: S Shi 4K 67
East Moor Rd. SR4: Sund 1B 118
Eastmoor Rd. SR7: Mur 1G 159
E. Norfolk St. NE30: N Shi 7H 49
E. Oakwood NE46: Oakw 5G 51
Easton Hall NE2: Jes 1H 5 (5G 63)
Easton Homes NE22: Bed 6A 18
Easton Ho. NE1: Newc T 5J 5 (1H 83)
East Pde. DH2: Kim 7H 141
DH8: Cons 7J 121
DH9: Stly 2G 125
NE26: Whit B 5H 39
East Pk. Gdns. NE21: Winl 5C 80
East Pk. Rd. NE9: Low F 1G 99
East Pk. Vw. NE24: Bly 2K 23
E. Pastures NE63: Ash 5K 11
E. Percy St. NE30: N Shi 6J 49
EAST RAINTON 6C 144
East Riggs NE22: Bed 1H 21
E. Sea Vw. NE64: Newb S 2K 13
E. Shore Dr. SR7: S'hm 1A 148
EAST SHORE VILLAGE 1A 148
E. Side Av. DH7: Bearp 1C 164
EAST SLEEKBURN 5D 18
E. Smithy St. NE33: S Shi 2J 67
East Sq. NE23: Cra 4J 25
E. Stainton St. NE33: S Shi 4K 67
EAST STANLEY 2F 125
E. Stanley By-Pass
DH9: Beam, Stly 2H 125
E. Stevenson St. NE33: S Shi 4K 67
East St. DH2: Gra V 4C 126
DH6: Hett 7C 176
DH6: Shot C 6F 171
DH7: Sac 6D 140
DH8: Cons 7J 121
(Meadow Ri.)
DH8: Cons 7K 121
(North St.)
DH9: Stly 2H 125
NE8: Gate 9J 5 (3H 83)
NE17: C'wl 6B 94
NE30: Tyne 4K 49
East St. NE31: Heb 6K 65
(not continuous)
NE33: S Shi 2J 67
NE39: H Spen 3D 94
NE43: Mic 5B 76
SR6: Whit 6H 89
TS27: B Col 1H 183
East Tanfield Station
Tanfield Railway 6E 110
East Ter. NE17: C'wl 1A 108
NE62: Stake 1A 18
TS27: Hes 5E 182
TS28: Sta T 7H 181
East Thorp NE5: West 7F 43
East Vw. DH2: Kim 1H 153
DH6: Ludw 5J 169
DH6: S Hil 3D 168
DH6: Whe H 4B 180
DH7: Mead 2E 174
DH8: Cons 5H 121
DH9: Dip 1H 123
DH9: Stly 6E 124
NE10: Hew 1D 100
NE13: W Op 4D 34
NE16: Burn 2A 110
NE21: Blay 3D 80
NE22: Bed 5B 18
NE23: Seg 2D 36
NE25: Sea D 5G 27
NE31: Heb 2H 85
NE35: Bol C 6F 87
NE36: W Bol 7G 87
NE39: Row G 5G 95
NE40: C Vale 7C 58
NE44: Rid M 7A 74
NE61: Mor 7G 9
NE62: Stake 1A 18
SR2: Ryh 3G 133
SR5: Sund 6J 103
SR6: Ful 4G 105
SR7: Mur 1F 159
SR7: S'hm 1H 147
SR8: Hord 5E 172
East Vw. Av. NE23: Cra 4K 25
East Vw. Ter. NE10: Hew 1D 100
NE16: Swa 6H 81
NE23: Dud 3J 35
NE42: Pru 5G 77
East Vs. DH6: Has 7B 158
East Vines SR1: Sund 1H 119
Eastward Grn. NE25: Monks 7D 38
Eastway NE34: S Shi 1D 88
Eastwood DH7: Sac 1E 152
Eastwood Av. NE24: News 6H 23
Eastwood Cl. NE23: Dud 6A 36
Eastwood Ct. NE12: Longb 5B 46
Eastwood Gdns. NE3: Ken 1B 62
NE9: Low F 1J 99
NE10: Fell 5A 84
Eastwood Grange Ct. NE46: Hex 2G 71
Eastwood Grange Rd. NE46: Hex 2G 71
East Woodlands NE46: Hex 2F 71
Eastwood Pl. NE23: Cra 7A 22
Eastwoods Rd. NE42: Pru 3H 77
Eastwood Ter. NE42: Pru 4H 77
Eastwood Vs. NE42: Pru 2H 77
Eaton Cl. NE38: Wash 1F 129
Eaton Pl. NE4: Elsw 1B 82
Eavers Ct. NE34: S Shi 1J 87
Ebba Wlk. NE3: Gos 7F 45
EBCHESTER 5G 107
Ebchester Av. NE9: Wrek 4B 100
Ebchester Ct. NE3: Ki Pk 7J 43
Ebchester Hill DH8: Ebc, M'sly 5G 107
Ebchester St. NE34: S Shi 1G 87
Ebdon La. SR6: Ful 3F 105
Ebor St. NE6: Heat 5A 64
NE34: S Shi 2G 87
Eccles Grange NE27: Back 6G 37
Eccles Ter. NE27: Shir 3J 47
Eccleston Cl. NE27: Back 7G 37
Eccleston Rd. NE33: S Shi 3A 68
Ecgfrid Ter. NE32: Jar 1C 86
Eco Centre, The NE31: Heb 5K 65
Edale Cl. NE38: Wash 4B 116
Eddison Rd. NE38: Wash 4K 115
Eddleston NE38: Wash 7E 114
Eddleston Av. NE3: Ken 2C 62
Eddrington Gro. NE5: Cha P 2C 60
Ede Av. NE11: Dun 6B 82
NE34: S Shi 7D 68
Eden Av. DH8: Lead 4B 122
NE16: Burn 2A 110
Edenbridge Cres. NE12: Longb 5K 45
Eden Cl. NE5: Cha P 3C 60
Eden Cotts. TS27: Hes 4E 182
Eden Ct. NE22: Bed 1J 21
NE28: W'snd 4F 65
SR8: Hord 5E 172
Edencroft DH9: W Pelt 3C 126
Eden Dale NE40: Craw 2D 78
Edendale Av. NE6: Walk 7E 64
NE12: Longb 5A 46
NE24: Cow 1F 23
Edendale Ct. NE24: Cow 1F 23
NE34: S Shi 2G 87
Edendale Ter. NE8: Gate 6H 83
SR8: Hord 6D 172
Edenfield DH9: W Pelt 2C 126
Edengarth NE30: Cull 2F 49
Eden Gro. NE61: Mor 2G 15
Edenhill Rd. SR8: Pet 5C 172
Eden Ho. Rd. SR4: Sund 3D 118
Eden La. SR8: Pet 4B 172
Eden Pl. NE30: Cull 3G 49
Eden Rd. DH1: Dur 5A 154
Eden St. NE28: W'snd 4F 65
SR8: Hord 5E 172
Eden St. West
SR1: Sund 3G 7 (1E 118)
Eden Ter. DH1: Dur 1G 167
DH4: S Row 3B 130
DH9: Stly 4D 124
SR2: Sund 3D 118
EDEN VALE 6B 182
Eden Va. SR2: Sund 3D 118
Edenvale Est. SR8: Hord 6D 172
Eden Va. M. DH8: Lead 5A 122
(off Front St.)
Eden Vw. DH6: Shot C 6F 171
Eden Vs. DH9: Beam 2K 125
NE38: Wash 4J 115
Eden Wlk. NE32: Jar 3C 86
Edgar St. NE3: Gos 7H 45
Edgecote NE37: Wash 7K 101
Edge Ct. DH1: Dur 2D 166
(not continuous)
Edgefield NE27: Shir 1J 47
Edgefield Av. NE3: Ken 7B 44
Edgefield Dr. NE23: Cra 7A 22
Edge Hill NE20: Darr H 3F 41
Edgehill NE61: Mor 2H 15
Edgehill Cl. NE20: Darr H 3G 41
Edgehill Vs. NE9: Spri 6E 100
Edge La. DH7: B'hpe, Maid L 2A 138
Edgemount NE12: Kil 6B 36
Edgeware Ct. SR5: S'wck 3C 104
Edgeware Rd. NE8: Gate 6J 83
Edgeware Wlk. NE4: Benw 3A 82
Edgewell Av. NE42: Pru 5D 76
Edgewell Ct. NE42: Pru 5D 76
(off Edgewell Rd.)
Edgewell Grange NE42: Pru 4E 76
Edgewell Ho. Rd. NE42: Pru 7C 76
Edgewell Rd. NE42: Pru 4D 76
Edgewell Rd. W. NE42: Pru 4D 76
(off Edgewell Rd.)
Edgewood NE20: Darr H 2H 41
NE46: Hex 2F 71
Edgewood Av. NE22: Bed 7A 18
Edgewood Ct. DH7: Sac 6D 140
Edgeworth Cl. NE35: Bol C 4E 86
Edgeworth Cres. SR6: Ful 5F 105
Edgmond Ct. SR2: Ryh 1G 133
Edhill Av. NE34: S Shi 1F 87
Edhill Gdns. NE34: S Shi 2F 87
Edinburgh Ct. NE3: Ki Pk 4K 43
Edinburgh Dr. NE22: Bed 6F 17
Edinburgh Rd. NE32: Jar 2E 86
Edinburgh Sq. SR5: S'wck 4C 104
Edington Gdns. NE40: C Vale 7C 58
Edington Gro. NE30: Cull 3G 49
Edington Rd. NE30: Cull 3G 49
Edison Ct. SR5: S'wck 4C 104
Edison Gdns. NE8: Gate 7G 83
Edison St. SR7: Mur 7E 146
Edith Av. NE21: Blay 4C 80
Edith Moffat Ho. NE29: N Shi 6G 49
(off Albion Rd.)
Edith St. DH8: Cons 7H 121
NE30: Tyne 4J 49
NE32: Jar 6A 66
SR2: Sund 4G 119
SR7: S'hm 5C 148
Edith Ter. DH4: Nbot 5D 130
NE16: Whi 7G 81
(off Swalwell Bank)
Edlingham Cl. NE3: Gos 1H 63
Edlingham Ct. DH5: Hou S 2F 145
Edlingham Rd. DH1: Dur 6A 154
EDMONDSLEY 3D 140
Edmondsley La. DH7: Sac 4D 140
Edmondsley Rd. DH2: Wald 3D 140
DH7: Edm 3D 140
Edmonton Sq. SR5: S'wck 4C 104
E D Morel Ter. NE17: C'wl 7A 94
Edmund Ct. DH7: Bearp 7C 152
Edmund Pl. NE9: Low F 2H 99
Edmund Rd. NE27: Longb 3H 47
Edna St. DH6: Bowb 5H 177
Edna Ter. NE5: West 2G 61
Edrich Ho. NE29: N Shi 2E 66
Edtech Bus. Pk. NE12: Kil 6K 35
Edward Av. DH6: Bowb 4H 177
SR8: Hord 5D 172
Edward Burdis St. SR5: S'wck 5D 104
Edward Cain Ct. SR8: Hord 5E 172
Edward Ho. SR2: Sund 5G 7
Edwardia Ct. DH8: Cons 7G 121
Edward Pl. NE4: Newc T 5A 4 (1D 82)
Edward Rd. DH3: Bir 3K 113
NE22: Bed 6B 18
NE28: W'snd 2K 65
Edwardson Rd. DH7: Mead 2F 175
Edwards Rd. NE26: Whit B 7J 39
Edward St. DH1: Dur 2D 166
DH3: Ches S 6A 128
DH5: Hett H 6G 145
DH7: Esh W 4E 162
DH7: Sac 7D 140
DH9: Crag 7J 125
NE3: Gos 7E 44
NE16: Hob 4A 110
NE24: Bly 1H 23
NE31: Heb 7G 65
NE40: Craw 3C 78
NE61: Mor 7G 9
NE61: Peg 4B 10
SR3: New S 2C 132
SR7: S'hm 4B 148

Edwards Wlk. DH7: B'hpe 4E 138
NE1: Newc T 3E 4 (7F 63)
Edward Ter. DH2: Pelt 3E 126
DH7: New B 4B 164
DH9: Ann P 5B 124
Edwina Gdns. NE29: N Shi 5E 48
Edwin Gro. NE28: W'snd 2A 66
Edwin's Av. NE12: Longb 4C 46
Edwin's Av. Sth. NE12: Longb 4C 46
Edwin St. DH5: Hou S 1E 144
NE6: Byke 3P 5 (7K 63)
NE13: Bru V 5C 34
SR4: Sund 1A 118
Edwin Ter. NE40: G'sde 4G 79
Egerton Rd. NE34: S Shi 7J 67
Egerton St. NE4: Benw 2K 81
(not continuous)
SR2: Sund 6K 7 (3G 119)
Eggleston Cl. DH1: Dur 5C 154
DH3: Gt Lum 3F 143
Eggleston Dr. DH8: Cons 1H 135
SR3: Sund 6C 118
Egham Rd. NE5: Cha P 3C 60
Eglesfield Rd. NE33: S Shi 5J 67
Eglingham Av. NE30: Cull 3J 49
Eglingham Cl. NE61: Hep, Mor 2H 15
Eglingham Way NE61: Hep 2H 15
Eglinton St. SR5: Monkw 6E 104
Eglinton St. Nth. SR5: Monkw 6E 104
Eglinton Twr. SR5: Monkw 6F 105
Egremont Dr. NE9: Low F 1J 99
Egremont Gdns. NE9: Low F 1J 99
Egremont Gro. SR8: Pet 2J 181
Egremont Pl. NE26: Whit B 7H 39
Egremont Way NE23: Cra 7A 22
Egton Ter. DH3: Bir 3A 114
Eider Cl. NE24: News 6J 23
Eider Wlk. NE12: Kil 7A 36
Eighteenth Av. NE24: Bly 4G 23
(not continuous)
Eighth Av. DH2: Ches S 6K 127
NE6: Heat 1P 5 (5A 64)
NE11: T Vall 4E 98
NE24: Bly 4H 23
NE61: Mor 1H 15
NE63: Ash 5C 12
Eighth Row NE63: Ash 3K 11
Eighth St. SR8: Hord 5E 172
TS27: B Col 1H 183
EIGHTON BANKS 5B 100
Eighton Ter. NE9: Wrek 4C 100
Eilansgate NE46: Hex 1B 70
Eilansgate Ter. NE46: Hex 1C 70
Eilanville NE46: Hex 1C 70
Eishort Way NE12: Longb 6K 45
Eland Cl. NE3: Ken 7K 43
Eland Edge NE20: Pon 4K 31
Eland Grange NE20: Pon 4J 31
Eland La. NE20: Pon 5K 31
Eland Vw. NE20: Pon 5K 31
Elberfeld Ct. NE32: Jar 7B 66
Elder Cl. DH7: Ush M 3D 164
Elder Dr. NE4: Fen 5K 61
Elder Gdns. NE9: Eigh B 6A 100
Elder Gro. NE9: Low F 2H 99
Elder Sq. NE63: Ash 5C 12
Elders Wlk. SR6: Whit 6H 89
Elderwood Gdns. NE11: Lob H 2D 98
Eldon Cl. DH7: Lang P 5G 151
Eldon Ct. NE1: Newc T 4E 4 (7F 63)
NE28: W'snd 4B 66
(off Eldon St.)
Eldon Gdn. NE1: Newc T 4E 4 (7F 63)
Eldon Ho. NE3: Gos 6E 44
Eldon La. NE1: Newc T 5F 4 (1F 83)
Eldon Leisure 5E 4
Eldon Pl. NE1: Newc T 2F 4 (6F 63)
NE15: Lem 6D 60
NE33: S Shi 6H 67
Eldon Rd. NE15: Lem 6D 60
NE46: Hex 2F 71
Eldon Sq. NE1: Newc T 4F 4 (7F 63)
Eldon St. NE8: Gate 10L 5 (4J 83)
NE28: W'snd 3A 66
NE33: S Shi 4H 67
SR4: Sund 2C 118
Eldon Wlk. NE1: Newc T 4E 4
Eldon Way NE1: Newc T 4F 4 (7F 63)
Eleanor St. NE30: Cull 7J 39
NE33: S Shi 2K 67
Eleanor Ter. *NE16: Whi 7G 81*
(off Swalwell Bank)
NE40: Craw 2E 78
Electric Cres. DH4: Nbot 5C 130
Elemore Cl. DH7: Lang P 5H 151
NE13: Haz 2A 44
Elemore La. DH5: Eas L 4F 157
(Lorne St.)
DH5: Eas L 3H 157
(Vale St.)
DH6: Litt 6C 156
Elemore St. DH6: H Pitt 6B 156
ELEMORE VALE 3H 157
Elemore Vw. DH6: S Het 4B 158
Elenbel Av. NE22: Bed 7A 18
Eleventh Av. DH2: Ches S 6K 127
NE11: T Vall 5F 99
NE24: Bly 3J 23
NE61: Mor 1H 15
Eleventh Av. Nth.
NE11: T Vall 4G 99
Eleventh Row NE63: Ash 3K 11
Eleventh St. SR8: Hord 5D 172
TS27: B Col 1G 183
(not continuous)
Elfin Way NE24: Bly 5K 23
Elford Av. NE13: Ki Pk 4A 44
Elford Cl. NE25: Monks 6D 38
Elfordleigh DH4: Nbot 5C 130
Elgar Av. NE5: Cha P 3C 60
Elgar Cl. DH9: Stly 4G 125
Elgen Vs. NE39: Row G 6H 95
Elgin SR3: Silk 3C 132
Elgin Av. NE28: W'snd 1K 65
SR7: S'hm 3H 147
Elgin Cen. 6K 83
Elgin Cl. NE22: Bed 6B 18
NE23: Cra 4F 25
NE29: N Shi 4C 48
Elgin Ct. NE10: Bill Q 4F 85
Elgin Gdns. NE6: Walk 7D 64
Elgin Gro. DH9: Stly 3H 125
Elgin Pl. DH3: Bir 6B 114
Elgin Rd. NE9: Low F 7K 83
Elgin St. NE32: Jar 2E 86
Elgy Rd. NE3: Gos 2D 62
Elisabeth Av. DH3: Bir 2K 113
Elite Bldgs. DH9: Stly 2F 125
Elizabeth Ct. DH6: H Pitt 6C 156
NE12: Longb 4E 46
Elizabeth Cres. NE23: Dud 3J 35
Elizabeth Diamond Gdns.
NE33: S Shi 5H 67
Elizabeth Dr. NE12: Longb 4E 46
Elizabeth Pl. *DH6: Shot C 6F 171*
(off East St.)
Elizabeth Rd. NE28: W'snd 2A 66
Elizabeth St. DH5: Hou S 1E 144
DH9: Ann P 5A 124
NE6: Byke 3M 5 (7J 63)
NE17: C'wl 6K 93
NE23: E Cram 5D 26
NE33: S Shi 3K 67
SR5: Ful 4E 104
SR5: Sund 6H 103
SR7: S'hm 3A 148
TS27: B Col 3J 183
Elizabeth Va. DH6: Cass 4F 179
Elizabeth Woodcock Maritime
Almshouses, The SR2: Sund 7J 7
Eliza St. DH7: Sac 1D 152
Ella McCambridge Ho.
NE6: Walk 1E 84
Ellam Av. DH1: Dur 4J 165
Ell-Dene Cres. NE10: Fell 7C 84
Ellen Ct. NE32: Jar 6B 66
Ellen Ter. NE37: Wash 7K 101
Ellerbeck Cl. NE10: Fell 6A 84
Ellerby M. DH6: Thor 1H 179
Ellersmere Gdns. NE30: Cull 2H 49
Ellerton Way NE10: Fell 6A 84
NE23: Cra 7A 22
Ellesmere DH4: Bour 6H 129
(not continuous)
Ellesmere Av. NE3: Gos 1G 63
NE5: West 3G 61
NE6: Walk 6C 64
Ellesmere Cl. DH4: Hou S 1A 144
Ellesmere Ct. SR2: Sund 7G 119
Ellesmere Dr. SR7: S'hm 3H 147
Ellesmere Gdns. NE62: Stake 7A 12
Ellesmere Rd. NE4: Benw 1A 82
Ellesmere Ter. SR6: Ful 4G 105
Ellie Bldgs. *DH9: Stly 2E 124*
(off Royal Rd.)
Ellington Cl. DH2: Ous 6G 113
NE15: Lem 6B 60
SR2: Ryh 4H 133
Ellington Rd. NE63: Ash 3H 11
Ellington Ter. NE63: Ash 3H 11
Elliot Rd. NE10: Gate 4K 83
(not continuous)
Elliot St. DH6: Thor 1K 179
Elliott Cl. DH4: Pen 2B 130
Elliott Ct. DH7: Mead 1F 175
NE61: Mor 2H 15
Elliott Dr. NE10: Fell 6B 84
Elliott Gdns. NE28: W'snd 1E 64
NE34: S Shi 4K 87
Elliott Rd. SR8: Pet 5B 172
Elliott St. DH7: Sac 7E 140
NE24: Bly 5F 23
Elliott Ter. DH9: Ann P 6A 124
NE4: Elsw 1B 82
NE37: Wash 7J 101
Elliott Wlk. NE13: Haz 7B 34
Elliott Way DH8: Cons 7F 121
Ellis Leazes DH1: Dur 2C 166
Ellison Mdw. SR8: Hord 5D 172
Ellison Pl. NE1: Newc T 4G 4 (7G 63)
NE9: Low F 3H 99
NE32: Jar 5B 66
Ellison Rd. NE8: Dun 6B 82
NE11: Dun 6B 82
SR8: Pet 5C 172
Ellison St. NE31: Heb 6G 65
(not continuous)
NE32: Jar 5B 66
(not continuous)
Ellison Ter. NE40: G'sde 5D 78
Ellison Vs. NE8: Gate 5J 83
(not continuous)
Ellison Wlk. NE8: Gate 10J 5 (3H 83)
Ellis Sq. NE61: Peg 4B 10
Ellwood Gdns. NE9: Low F 6H 83
Ellwoods Gym 6F 173
(off Windsor Cnr.)
Elm Av. DH2: Pelt 3E 126
DH7: B'don 2D 174
NE11: Dun 6B 82
Elm Av. NE13: Din 4H 33
NE16: Whi 6J 81
TS27: B Col 3K 183
Elm Bank Rd. NE41: Wylam 1K 77
Elm Cl. NE23: Cra 7A 22
NE46: Hex 3A 70
Elm Ct. DH7: Sac 7E 140
NE16: Whi 2H 97
NE63: Ash 3E 12
Elm Cres. DH2: Kim 7H 141
DH3: Bir 2K 113
Elmcroft Rd. NE12: Longb 5C 46
Elmdale Rd. DH8: Cons 6J 121
Elm Dr. NE22: Bed 1H 21
SR6: Whit 5J 89
Elmfield DH5: Hett H 4G 145
DH7: Lan 6J 137
Elmfield App. NE3: Gos 2E 62
Elmfield Av. DH1: Dur 1F 167
Elmfield Cl. SR3: E Her 3J 131
Elmfield Ct. *NE22: Bed 6B 18*
(off Palace Rd.)
Elmfield Gdns. NE3: Gos 1D 62
NE25: Monks 1D 48
NE28: W'snd 2D 64
Elmfield Gro. NE3: Gos 1D 62
Elmfield Pk. NE3: Gos 2D 62
Elmfield Rd. DH8: Cons 5H 121
NE3: Gos 2D 62
NE15: Thro 3J 59
NE31: Heb 3K 85
Elmfield Sq. NE3: Gos 2D 62
Elmfield Ter. NE10: Pel 5E 84
NE31: Heb 2K 85
Elm Gro. DH4: S Row 4C 130
DH7: Ush M 3D 164
NE3: Fawd 5B 44
NE12: Kil 3B 46
NE16: Burn 2K 109
NE34: S Shi 2B 88
Elmont Cl. NE5: Den M 3G 61
Elm Pk. Rd. DH8: Cons, Shot B 2H 121
Elm Pk. Ter. DH8: Shot B 2G 121
Elm Pl. DH4: Nbot 6D 130
Elm Rd. NE20: Pon 6A 32
NE21: Blay 4D 80
NE29: N Shi 5B 48
Elms, The DH5: Eas L 3K 157
DH8: Shot B 2G 121
NE3: Gos 2D 62
SR2: Sund 7J 7 (3F 119)
SR4: Sund 2G 117
TS27: Hes 4H 183
Elmsford Gro. NE12: Longb 6K 45
Elmsleigh Gdns. SR6: Clead 4C 88
Elm St. DH3: Ches S 6A 128
DH7: Lang P 4J 151
(not continuous)
DH8: Cons 5H 121
DH9: Stly 5D 124
NE13: Sea B 3E 34
NE16: Sun 5H 97
NE32: Jar 6A 66
NE43: Mic 6A 76
Elm St. W. NE16: Sun 5H 97
Elms West SR2: Sund 7J 7 (3F 119)
Elm Ter. DH3: Bir 3K 113
DH8: Lead 5B 122
DH9: Ann P 5J 123
DH9: Stly 6H 125
DH9: Tant 6B 110
NE28: W'snd 3G 65
SR8: Hord 6E 172
Elmtree Ct. SR7: S'hm 5A 148
Elmtree Dr. NE40: G'sde 5F 79
Elm Tree Gdns. SR8: Pet 6D 172
Elmtree Gdns. NE25: Monks 1E 48
Elmtree Gro. NE3: Gos 2D 62
Elm Trees NE24: Bly 3H 23
Elm Vs. NE13: Haz 6C 34
Elmway DH2: Ches S 4J 127
Elmwood DH2: Ches S 7H 127
NE15: Lem 5C 60
Elmwood Av. NE13: W Op 6E 34
NE28: W'snd 3K 65
(not continuous)
SR5: S'wck 4B 104
Elmwood Cres. NE6: Walk 4D 64
Elmwood Dr. NE20: Pon 4J 31
Elmwood Gdns. NE11: Lob H 1D 98
Elmwood Gro. NE26: Whit B 5G 39
Elmwood M. NE13: W Op 7D 34
Elmwood Pk. Ct. NE13: W Op 1C 44
Elmwood Rd. NE25: Monks 7E 38
Elmwood Sq. SR5: S'wck 5B 104
Elmwood St. DH4: Hou S 1J 143
SR2: Sund 6F 7 (3D 118)
Eloise Cl. SR7: S'hm 4B 148
Elrick Cl. NE5: Cha P 3C 60
Elrington Gdns. NE5: Den M 5H 61
Elsdon Av. NE25: Sea D 7G 27
Elsdonburn Rd. SR3: Dox P 4A 132
Elsdon Cl. DH2: Ches S 1H 141
NE24: Bly 2G 23
SR8: Pet 2A 182
Elsdon Ct. NE16: Whi 2G 97
Elsdon Dr. NE12: Longb 4D 46
NE63: Ash 4A 12
Elsdon Gdns. DH8: Cons 4H 121
NE11: Dun 6C 82
Elsdon M. NE31: Heb 6K 65
Elsdon Pl. NE29: N Shi 1G 67
Elsdon Rd. DH1: Dur 5B 154
NE3: Gos 7E 44
NE16: Whi 1G 97
Elsdon St. NE29: N Shi 1G 67
Elsdon Ter. NE28: W'snd 4F 65
NE29: N Shi 1D 66
Elsham Grn. NE3: Fawd 6A 44
Elsing Cl. NE5: Blak 1H 61
Elstob Cotts. SR3: Sund 6C 118
Elstob Farm Caravans SR3: Sund 6D 118
Elstob Pl. NE6: Walk 2C 84
SR3: Sund 6C 118
Elston Cl. NE5: Cha P 3C 60
Elstree Ct. NE3: K Bank 5H 43
Elstree Gdns. NE24: News 6H 23
Elstree Sq. SR5: S'wck 3C 104
(not continuous)
ELSWICK 2C 82
Elswick Ct. NE1: Newc T 4F 4 (7F 63)
Elswick Dene NE4: Elsw 3C 82
Elswick E. Ter. NE4: Newc T 7B 4 (2D 82)
Elswick Rd.
NE4: Benw, Elsw, Newc T 7A 4 (2A 82)
NE37: Wash 1E 114
Elswick Row NE4: Newc T 6A 4 (1D 82)
Elswick St. NE4: Newc T 6A 4 (1D 82)
Elswick Swimming Pool 2C 82
Elswick Way NE34: S Shi 7G 67
Elswick Way Ind. Est. NE34: S Shi 7G 67
Elsworth Grn. NE5: Blak 2J 61
Elterwater NE37: Wash 2G 115
Elterwater Rd. DH2: Ches S 1K 141
Eltham Rd. SR2: Ryh 3E 132
Eltham St. NE33: S Shi 5H 67
Elton St. E. NE28: W'snd 4F 65
Elton St. W. NE28: W'snd 4F 65
ELTRINGHAM 4C 76
Eltringham Cl. NE28: W'snd 3E 64
Eltringham Rd. NE42: Pru 4C 76
Elvaston Cres. NE3: Ken 2K 61
Elvaston Dr. NE46: Hex 3C 70
Elvaston Gro. NE46: Hex 3D 70
Elvaston Pk. Rd. NE46: Hex 3C 70
Elvaston Rd. NE40: Ryton 7G 59
NE46: Hex 2C 70
Elvet Bri. DH1: Dur 3C 6 (3A 166)
Elvet Cl. NE6: Byke 2P 5 (6A 64)
NE13: W Op 5D 34
Elvet Ct. NE6: Byke 2P 5 (6A 64)
Elvet Cres. DH1: Dur 4D 6 (3B 166)
Elvet Grn. DH2: Ches S 7A 128
DH5: Hett H 2G 157
Elvet Hill Rd. DH1: Dur 7B 6 (5A 166)
Elvet Moor DH1: Dur 5J 165
Elvet Waterside DH1: Dur 3D 6 (3B 166)
Elvet Way NE6: Byke 2P 5 (6A 64)
Elvington St. SR6: Ful 4G 105
Elwin Cl. NE26: Sea S 5D 28
Elwin Pl. DH2: Pelt 3G 127
NE26: Sea S 5D 28
Elwin St. DH2: Pelt 2G 127
Elwin Ter. SR2: Sund 5G 7 (2E 118)
Ely Cl. NE7: H Hea 1B 64
Ely Rd. DH1: Dur 3B 154
Elysium La. NE8: Gate 5E 82
Ely St. NE8: Gate 5G 83
Ely Ter. DH9: Ann P 4C 124
Ely Way NE32: Jar 5B 86
Embankment Rd. SR7: S'hm 4B 148
(Cottages Rd.)
SR7: S'hm 2K 147
(Stockton St.)
Embassy Gdns. NE15: Den M 7H 61
Emblehope NE37: Wash 2E 114
Emblehope Dr. NE3: Gos 1C 62
Emblehope Ho. SR3: E Her 1A 132
Embleton Av. NE3: Gos 6C 44
NE28: W'snd 7J 47
NE34: S Shi 5D 68
Embleton Cl. DH1: Dur 5B 154
Embleton Cres. NE29: N Shi 4C 48
Embleton Dr. DH2: Ches S 1H 141
NE24: Bly 4G 23
Embleton Gdns. NE5: Fen 4K 61
NE10: Fell 5B 84
Embleton M. SR7: S'hm 5B 148
Embleton Rd. NE10: Bill Q 4F 85
NE29: N Shi 4C 48
Embleton St. SR7: S'hm 5B 148
Embleton Wlk. NE63: Ash 2H 11
Emden Rd. NE3: Ken 6B 44
EMERSON 6D 114
Emerson Chambers *NE1: Newc T 5F 4*
(off Blackett St.)
Emerson Ct. NE27: Shir 1J 47
SR8: Hord 5E 172
TS27: B Col 2J 183
Emerson Rd. NE37: Wash 4D 114
NE64: Newb S 2H 13
Emery Ct. NE23: Dud 3J 35
Emily Davison Av. NE61: Mor 7E 8
Emily St. DH4: Nbot 5D 130
NE6: Walk 7C 64
Emily St. E. SR7: S'hm 3B 148
(not continuous)
Emirates Durham International
Cricket Ground 7C 128
Emlyn Rd. NE34: S Shi 7J 67
Emma Ct. SR2: Sund 3G 119
Emma St. DH8: Cons 5H 121
Emma Vw. NE40: Craw 3D 78
Emmaville NE40: Craw 2E 78
Emmbrook Cl. DH5: E Rain 6D 144
Emmerson Pl. NE27: Shir 1J 47
Emmerson Sq. DH6: Thor 7J 169
Emmerson Ter. NE38: Wash 3J 115
Emmerson Ter. W. SR3: New S 2D 132
Emperor Way SR3: Dox P 4H 131

Empire Bldgs. DH1: Dur 2E 166
Empire Cinema
Newcastle 5E 4
Sunderland 3K 7 (1F 119)
Empire Theatre
Consett 7H 121
Sunderland 3G 7 (1E 118)
Empress Rd. NE6: Walk 2F 85
Empress St. SR5: Monkw 6E 104
Emsworth Rd. SR5: S'wck 4C 104
Emsworth Sq. SR5: S'wck 4C 104
Enderby Dr. NE46: Hex 2A 70
Enderby Rd. SR4: Sund 1D 118
Enfield Av. NE16: Swa 5H 81
Enfield Gdns. NE16: Whi 2H 97
Enfield Rd. NE8: Gate 6H 83
SR7: S'hm 3H 147
Enfield St. SR4: Sund 1B 118
Engels Ter. DH9: Stly 4G 125
Engel St. NE39: Row G 5F 95
Engine Inn Rd. NE28: W'snd 1K 65
Engine La. NE9: Low F 3H 99
Engine Rd. NE17: C'wl 3G 93
NE42: C'wl, Pru 2H 93
Engleby Ho. NE61: Mor 7F 9
(off Oldgate)
Englefeld NE10: Hew 3D 100
Englefield Cl. NE3: Ki Pk 5K 43
Englemann Way SR3: Dox P 4A 132
Enid Av. SR6: Ful 4F 105
Enid Gdns. TS27: B Col 2J 183
Enid St. NE13: Haz 7C 34
Ennerdale DH3: Bir 6C 114
NE10: Pel 6E 84
NE37: Wash 1G 115
SR2: Sund 7H 7 (4E 118)
Ennerdale Cl. DH1: Carr 7J 155
SR7: S'hm 3H 147
SR8: Pet 5B 172
Ennerdale Cres. DH4: Pen 1A 130
NE21: Winl 6B 80
Ennerdale Gdns. NE9: Low F 2J 99
NE28: W'snd 1A 66
Ennerdale Pl. DH2: Ches S 1A 142
Ennerdale Rd. NE6: Walk 7D 64
NE24: Cow 7D 18
NE30: Cull 2G 49
Ennerdale St. DH5: Hett H 1F 157
Ennerdale Ter. NE17: Ham 3J 107
Ennerdale Wlk. NE16: Whi 3F 97
Ennis Cl. NE62: W Sle 7B 12
Ennismore Ct. NE12: Longb 6B 46
Ensign Ho. NE30: Tyne 5K 49
Enslin Gdns. NE6: Walk 3D 84
Enslin St. NE6: Walk 3D 84
Enterprise Ct. NE23: Nel V 1H 25
SR7: Seat 7G 133
Enterprise Ho. NE11: T Vall 3F 99
Eothen Rest Home NE26: Whit B 7G 39
Epinay Wlk. NE32: Jar 7C 66
Epping Cl. SR7: S'hm 4H 147
Epping Ct. NE23: Cra 4F 25
Epping Sq. SR5: S'wck 4C 104
EPPLETON 5G 145
Eppleton Cl. DH7: Lang P 5H 151
Eppleton Est. DH5: Hett H 5H 145
Eppleton Hall Cl. SR7: S'hm 2G 147
Eppleton Row DH5: Hett H 6H 145
Eppleton Ter. DH2: Pelt 2D 126
Eppleton Ter. E. DH5: Hett H 6H 145
Eppleton Ter. W. DH5: Hett H 6H 145
Epsom Cl. DH8: Shot B 2G 121
NE29: N Shi 1F 67
Epsom Ct. NE3: K Bank 5J 43
Epsom Dr. NE63: Ash 5A 12
Epsom Sq. SR5: S'wck 4C 104
Epsom Way NE24: News 6H 23
Epwell Gro. NE23: Cra 7A 22
Epworth DH9: Tan L 1C 124
Epworth Gro. NE8: Gate 5F 83
Equitable St. NE28: W'snd 4F 65
Erick St. NE1: Newc T 5G 4 (1G 83)
(not continuous)
Erin Sq. SR5: S'wck 4D 104
Erith Ter. SR4: Sund 2B 118
Ermine Cres. NE9: Low F 1K 99
Ernest Pl. DH1: Dur 2F 167
Ernest St. DH2: Pelt 2G 127
NE35: Bol C 6G 87
SR2: Sund 4G 119
Ernest Ter. DH3: Ches S 7A 128
DH9: Stly 1F 125
SR2: Ryh 3J 133
Ernwill Av. SR5: Sund 6H 103
Errington Bungs. DH7: Sac 7D 140
Errington Cl. NE20: Darr H 3G 41
Errington Dr. DH9: Tan L 1C 124
Errington Pl. NE42: Pru 4E 76
Errington Rd. NE20: Darr H 2F 41
Errington St. NE24: Cow 2C 22
Errington Ter. NE12: Longb 3C 46
Errol Pl. DH3: Bir 6B 114
Erskine Ct. NE2: Jes 3H 63
Erskine Rd. NE33: S Shi 3K 67
Erskine Way NE33: S Shi 3K 67
Escallond Dr. SR7: Dalt D 4H 147
Esdale SR2: Ryh 3G 133
ESH 6F 151
Esh Bank DH7: Esh 6D 150
Esh Cl. Vw. DH7: Esh 6F 151
Esher Ct. NE3: K Bank 5J 43
Esher Gdns. NE24: News 6H 23
Esher Pl. NE23: Cra 4F 25
Esh Hillside DH7: Lang P 5K 151
Esh Laude DH7: Esh 7E 150
Eshmere Cres. NE5: Cha P 2C 60
Eshott Cl. NE3: Gos 6C 44
NE5: W Dent 4G 61
Eshott Ct. NE5: W Dent 4G 61
Esh Plaza Bus. Pk. NE13: W Op 1C 44
Esh Rd. DH7: Esh W 2H 163
Esh Ter. DH7: Lang P 5J 151
ESH WINNING 4E 162
Esh Winning Ind. Est. DH7: Esh W 3E 162
Esh Wood Vw. DH7: Ush M 2B 164
Esk Av. DH3: Gt Lum 3F 143
Esk Ct. SR3: Silk 3B 132
Eskdale DH3: Bir 7C 114
DH4: Pen 1A 130
Eskdale Av. NE24: Cow 1E 22
NE28: W'snd 7G 47
Eskdale Cl. DH1: Carr 7J 155
SR7: S'hm 3H 147
Eskdale Ct. NE34: S Shi 7J 67
Eskdale Cres. NE37: Wash 7F 101
Eskdale Dr. NE32: Jar 3D 86
Eskdale Gdns. NE9: Low F 3J 99
Eskdale Mans. NE2: Jes 1G 4
Eskdale Rd. SR6: Seab 1H 105
Eskdale St. DH5: Hett H 1F 157
NE34: S Shi 1J 87
Eskdale Ter. NE2: Jes 1G 4 (5G 63)
NE26: Whit B 7J 39
NE30: Cull 7J 39
Eskdale Wlk. SR8: Pet 6C 172
Esk St. NE9: Low F 7K 83
Esk Ter. DH3: Bir 3A 114
Eslington Ct. NE8: Gate 6D 82
Eslington M. NE63: Ash 3D 12
Eslington Park 6D 82
Eslington Rd. NE2: Jes 1H 5 (6G 63)
Eslington Ter. NE2: Jes 1H 5 (5G 63)
Esmeralda Gdns. NE23: Seg 2E 36
Esperley Av. NE13: Haz 2A 44
Esplanade NE26: Whit B 6H 39
Esplanade, The SR2: Sund 6J 7
Esplanade Av. NE26: Whit B 6H 39
Esplanade Mews SR2: Sund 6J 7 (3F 119)
Esplanade Pl. NE26: Whit B 6H 39
Esplanade West SR2: Sund 7J 7 (3F 119)
Espley Cl. NE12: Longb 4E 46
Espley Ct. NE3: Fawd 5A 44
Essen Way SR3: Sund 5D 118
Essex Av. DH8: C'sde 4C 134
Essex Cl. NE4: Newc T 9A 4 (3D 82)
NE63: Ash 3J 11
Essex Cres. SR7: S'hm 3H 147
Essex Dr. NE37: Wash 5H 101
Essex Gdns. NE9: Low F 7H 83
NE28: W'snd 2J 65
NE34: S Shi 6E 68
Essex Gro. SR3: New S 1C 132
Essex Pl. SR8: Pet 4A 172
Essex St. DH5: Hett H 6F 145
Essington Way SR8: Pet 3A 172
Essyn Ct. SR8: Eas 7J 159
Estate Ho's. DH4: Bour 5J 129
Esther Campbell Ct.
NE2: Newc T 1C 4 (6E 62)
Esther Ct. NE63: Ash 2K 11
Esther Sq. NE38: Wash 4J 115
Esthwaite NE37: Wash 2F 115
Esthwaite Av. DH2: Ches S 1K 141
Eston Ct. NE24: Cow 1F 23
NE28: W'snd 7D 46
Eston Gro. SR5: Ful 4E 104
Estuary Way SR4: Sund 1H 117
Etal Av. NE25: Whit B 7H 39
NE29: N Shi 1D 66
Etal Cl. NE27: Shir 1K 47
Etal Ct. NE29: N Shi 6G 49
Etal Cres. NE27: Shir 1K 47
NE32: Jar 2E 86
Etal Ho. NE63: Ash 3D 12
Etal La. NE5: Blak, West 2G 61
Etal Pl. NE3: Gos 5C 44
Etal Rd. NE24: News 6F 23
Etal Way NE5: Blak 1H 61
Ethel Av. NE21: Blay 4C 80
SR2: Ryh 3J 133
Ethel St. NE4: Benw 2K 81
NE23: Dud 5J 35
Ethel Ter. NE34: S Shi 1H 87
NE39: H Spen 4D 94
NE46: Hex 2C 70
SR5: Sund 6H 103
Etherley Cl. DH1: Dur 4B 154
Etherley Rd. NE6: Walk 6B 64
Etherstone Av. NE7: H Hea 3A 64
Eton Cl. NE23: Cra 7A 22
Eton Sq. NE31: Heb 7K 65
Ettrick Cl. NE12: Kil 7A 36
Ettrick Gdns. NE8: Gate 6K 83
SR4: Sund 4B 118
Ettrick Gro. SR3: Sund 4B 118
SR4: Sund 3A 118
Ettrick Lodge NE3: Gos 1F 63
Ettrick Rd. NE32: Jar 1A 86
Ettrick Ter. Nth. DH9: Stly 6H 125
Ettrick Ter. Sth. DH9: Stly 6H 125
Eureka M. DH2: Nett 6H 141
European Way SR4: Sund 1K 117
Euryalus Ct. NE33: S Shi 4B 68
Eustace Av. NE29: N Shi 7E 48
Euston Ct. SR5: S'wck 3C 104
Evanlade NE10: Hew 1F 101
Evans Bus. Cen. DH1: Dur 6F 155
NE29: N Shi 7B 48
Evansleigh Rd. DH8: C'sde 2E 134
Eva St. NE15: Lem 7C 60
Evelyn St. SR2: Sund 7F 7 (3D 118)
Evelyn Ter. DH9: Stly 3E 124
NE21: Blay 3C 80
SR2: Ryh 3H 133
Evenwood Gdns. NE9: Low F 2K 99
Evenwood Rd. DH7: Esh W 4E 162
Everard St. NE23: E Har 6K 21
Everest Gro. NE36: W Bol 7H 87
Everest Sq. SR5: S'wck 3C 104
Evergreen Ct. NE23: Cra 4B 26
Ever Ready Ind. Est. DH9: Tan L 6E 110
Eversleigh Pl. NE15: Thro 3J 59
Eversley Cres. SR5: S'wck 4C 104
Eversley Pl. NE6: Heat 1N 5 (6K 63)
NE28: W'snd 2K 65
Everton Dr. SR7: S'hm 3H 147
Everton La. SR5: S'wck 4C 104
Evesham SR4: Sund 2G 117
Evesham Av. NE26: Whit B 5F 39
Evesham Cl. NE35: Bol C 5F 87
Evesham Gth. NE3: Ken 2A 62
Evesham Pl. NE23: Cra 3F 25
Evesham Rd. SR7: S'hm 3H 147
Eve St. SR8: Hord 6F 173
Evistones Gdns. NE6: Walk 3C 84
Evistones Rd. NE9: Low F 1H 99
Ewart Ct. NE3: Gos 5C 44
Ewart Cres. NE34: S Shi 2E 86
Ewbank Av. NE4: Fen 6A 62
Ewe Hill Cotts. DH4: Hou S 1K 143
Ewe Hill Ter. DH4: Hou S 1K 143
Ewe Hill Ter. W. DH4: Hou S 1K 143
Ewehurst Cres. DH9: Dip 7J 109
Ewehurst Gdns. DH9: Dip 7J 109
Ewehurst Rd. DH9: Dip 7J 109
(not continuous)
Ewen Ct. NE29: N Shi 4B 48
Ewesley NE38: Wash 1E 128
Ewesley Cl. NE5: W Dent 4G 61
Ewesley Gdns. NE13: W Op 5D 34
Ewesley Rd. SR4: Sund 3B 118
Ewing Rd. SR4: Sund 3C 118
(not continuous)
Exchange Bldgs. NE26: Whit B 6H 39
Exelby Cl. NE3: Gos 4F 45
Exeter Av. SR7: S'hm 3K 147
Exeter Cl. DH3: Gt Lum 4E 142
NE23: Cra 3G 25
NE63: N Sea 5E 12
Exeter Ct. NE31: Heb 1H 85
Exeter Rd. NE28: W'snd 7E 46
NE29: N Shi 3C 48
Exeter St. NE6: Walk 2E 84
NE8: Gate 5G 83
SR4: Sund 1B 118
Exeter Way NE32: Jar 4B 86
Exhibition Pk. 1E 4 (5F 63)
Exmouth Cl. SR7: S'hm 4J 147
Exmouth Rd. NE29: N Shi 7C 48
Exmouth Sq. SR5: S'wck 4C 104
Exmouth St. SR5: S'wck 4C 104
Extension Rd. SR1: Sund 2H 119
Eyemouth Ct. NE34: S Shi 1G 87
Eyemouth La. SR5: S'wck 4C 104
Eyemouth Rd. NE29: N Shi 7C 48
Eyre St. DH9: Stly 4D 124

F

Faber Rd. SR5: S'wck 4C 104
Factory, The TS27: Cas E 4K 181
Factory Rd. NE21: Blay 2D 80
Fairacres DH5: Hett H 7H 145
Fair Av. NE62: Stake 2K 17
Fairbairn Dr. DH4: Hou S 7C 130
Fairbairn Rd. SR8: Pet 4B 172
Fairburn Av. DH5: Hou S 4E 144
NE7: H Hea 1A 64
Fairclough Ct. SR8: Pet 7K 171
Fairdale Av. NE7: H Hea 1A 64
Fairfalls Ter. DH7: New B 4A 164
Fairfield DH2: Pelt 2F 127
DH4: Hou S 1B 144
DH8: Cons 1K 135
DH9: Ann P 4K 123
NE12: Longb 6H 45
NE46: Hex 2B 70
Fairfield Av. NE12: Longb 4B 46
NE16: Whi 2G 97
NE24: News 5H 23
Fairfield Cl. NE11: Dun 5B 82
Fairfield Cres. NE46: Oakw 5G 51
Fairfield Dr. NE25: Monks 7C 38
NE30: Cull 2H 49
NE63: N Sea 5E 12
SR6: Whit 4G 89
Fairfield Grn. NE25: Monks 7C 38
Fairfield Gro. SR7: Mur 1F 159
Fairfield Ind. Pk. NE10: Bill Q 4E 84
Fairfield Pl. NE21: Winl 5B 80
(off Mt. Pleasant)
Fairfield Rd. NE2: Jes 4F 63
Fairfields NE40: Ryton 2F 79
Fairfield Ter. NE10: Pel 5E 84
Fair Grn. NE25: Monks 7C 38
Fairgreen Cl. SR3: Dox P 4B 132
Fairhaven NE9: Spri 5D 100
Fairhaven Av. NE6: Walk 7E 64
Fairhill Cl. NE7: H Hea 1A 64
Fairhills Av. DH9: Dip 2G 123
Fairholme Av. NE34: S Shi 7B 68
Fairholme Rd. SR3: Sund 5E 118
Fairholm Rd. NE4: Benw 1A 82
Fairisle DH2: Ous 7J 113
Fairlands E. SR6: Ful 5F 105
Fairlands W. SR6: Ful 5F 105
Fairlawn Gdns. SR4: Sund 4A 118
Fairlawns Cl. TS29: Trim S 7B 180
Fairless Gdn. NE6: Byke 7A 64
(off Grace St.)
Fairles St. NE33: S Shi 1K 67
Fairmead Way SR4: Sund 3G 117
Fairmile Dr. SR3: Dox P 4C 132
Fairmont Way NE7: H Hea 1A 64
FAIR MOOR 3C 8
Fairney Cl. NE20: Pon 5K 31
Fairney Edge NE20: Pon 5K 31
Fairnley Wlk. NE5: West 3G 61
Fairport Ter. SR8: Eas C 1D 172
Fairspring NE5: West 3G 61
Fair Vw. DH4: W Rai 1K 155
DH7: B'hpe 7D 138
DH7: Esh W 3E 162
DH7: Wit G 2C 152
NE16: Burn 2J 109
NE42: Pru 4E 76
(not continuous)
Fairview DH6: Thor 1K 179
NE62: Stake 2A 18
Fairview Av. NE34: S Shi 6B 68
Fairview Dr. DH8: Cons 1J 121
Fairview Grn. NE7: H Hea 1A 64
Fairview Pk. DH5: Hett H 7H 145
Fairview Ter. DH9: Ann P 6J 123
Fairville Cl. NE23: Cra 7K 21
Fairville Cres. NE7: H Hea 1A 64
Fairway NE21: Blay 2A 80
NE62: Stake 7J 11
Fairway, The NE3: Gos 4D 44
NE37: Wash 4G 101
NE61: Loan 3F 15
Fairway Cl. NE3: Gos 4D 44
Fairway Ct. NE8: Gate 9G 4
Fairways DH8: Cons 4H 121
NE25: Monks 6C 38
SR3: Tuns 2D 132
Fairways, The DH9: Stly 7E 124
DH9: W Pelt 3C 126
NE36: W Bol 7G 87
Fairways Av. NE7: H Hea 1A 64
Fairwood Rd. NE46: Hex 2F 71
Fairy St. DH5: Hett H 6G 145
Falconars Ct. NE1: Newc T 6E 4 (1F 83)
Falconar St. NE1: Newc T 4H 5 (7G 63)
NE2: Newc T 4H 5 (7G 63)
Falcon Ct. NE63: Ash 6K 11
Falcon Hill NE61: Mor 7D 8
Falcon Pl. NE12: Longb 5J 45
Falcon Ter. NE41: Wylam 7K 57
Falcon Way DH7: Esh W 3C 162
NE34: S Shi 2H 87
Faldo Dr. NE63: N Sea 3D 12
Faldonside NE6: Heat 3B 64
Falkirk NE12: Kil 7B 36
Falkland Av. NE3: Ken 2B 62
NE31: Heb 7J 65
Falkland Rd. SR4: Sund 2A 118
Falkous Ter. DH7: Wit G 3C 152
Falla Pk. Cres. NE10: Fell 6A 84
Falla Pk. Rd. NE10: Fell 6A 84
Falloden Av. NE3: Fawd 4B 44
Fallodon Gdns. NE5: Fen 3K 61
Fallodon Rd. NE29: N Shi 7D 48
Fallowfeld NE10: Hew 1E 100
Fallowfield Av. NE3: Fawd 6B 44
Fallowfield Dene Cvn. Pk.
NE46: Acomb 1D 50
Fallowfield Ter. DH6: S Het 4C 158
Fallowfield Way NE38: Wash 6J 115
NE63: Ash 5K 11
Fallow Pk. Av. NE24: Bly 3G 23
Fallow Rd. NE34: S Shi 7F 69
Fall Pass NE8: Gate 4D 82
Fallsway DH1: Carr 6H 155
Falmouth Cl. SR7: Dalt D 4J 147
Falmouth Dr. NE32: Jar 1D 86
Falmouth Rd. NE6: Heat 2N 5 (6K 63)
NE29: N Shi 3D 48
SR4: Sund 1A 118
Falmouth Sq. SR4: Sund 2A 118
Falmouth Wlk. NE23: Cra 2J 25
Falsgrave Pl. NE16: Whi 2F 97
Falstaff Rd. NE29: N Shi 6D 48
Falston Cl. NE12: Longb 4E 46
Falstone NE10: Hew 2D 100
NE38: Wash 6J 115
Falstone Av. NE15: Lem 5E 60
NE34: S Shi 7C 68
Falstone Ct. NE46: Hex 3B 70
Falstone Cres. NE63: Ash 6C 12
Falstone Dr. DH2: Ches S 1H 141
Falstone Sq. NE3: Gos 6C 44
Falstone Way NE46: Hex 3B 70
Falston Rd. NE24: Bly 4G 23
Faraday Cl. NE38: Wash 3B 116
Faraday Ct. DH1: Dur 4J 165
Faraday Gro. NE8: Gate 7F 83
SR4: Sund 2A 118
Faraday Rd. SR8: Pet 3C 172
Faraday St. SR7: Mur 7E 146
Faraday Ter. DH6: Has 1A 170
Farbridge Cres. DH8: Ebc 5H 107
Farding Lake Ct. NE34: S Shi 7E 68
Farding Sq. NE34: S Shi 7E 68
Fareham Gro. NE35: Bol C 6D 86
Fareham Way NE23: Cra 3K 25
FAREWELL HALL 7K 165
Farewell Vw. DH7: Lang M 6G 165
Farlam Av. NE30: Cull 3G 49

Farlam Rd. NE5: Den M .5H 61
Farleigh Ct. NE29: N Shi .4B 48
Farm Cl. NE16: Sun .5H 97
NE37: Wash .6F 101
Farm Cotts. DH6: Shot C .5F 171
Farmer Cres. SR7: Mur .7D 146
Farm Hill Rd. SR6: Clead .4C 88
Farm La. DH5: E Rain .6D 144
Farm Rd. DH1: Dur .6B 166
NE23: E Har .6K 21
Farmstead, The NE13: Sea B .3E 34
Farmstead Ct. NE22: H Bri .4F 21
Farm St. SR5: Monkw .6D 104
Farm Wlk. SR3: Dox P .4C 132
Farm Well Pl. NE42: Pru .3F 77
Farnborough Cl. NE23: Cra .2K 25
Farnborough Dr. SR3: Tuns .1D 132
Farn Ct. NE3: Ki Pk .4K 43
Farndale NE28: W'snd .7D 46
Farndale Av. NE62: Stake .6J 11
SR6: Seab .1H 105
Farndale Cl. NE13: Din .4H 33
NE21: Winl .6K 79
Farndale Ct. NE24: News .5H 23
Farndale Rd. NE4: Benw .1A 82
Farne Av. NE3: Fawd .5C 44
NE34: S Shi .6D 68
NE63: Ash .5B 12
Farne Rd. NE12: Longb .3C 46
NE27: Shir .1K 47
Farne Sq. SR4: Sund .1K 117
Farne Ter. NE6: Walk .7C 64
Farnham Cl. DH1: Dur .6A 154
NE15: Lem .7D 60
Farnham Gro. NE24: News .5H 23
Farnham Lodge NE12: Longb .5K 45
Farnham Rd. DH1: Dur .5A 154
NE34: S Shi .7J 67
Farnham St. NE15: Lem .7D 60
Farnham Ter. SR4: Sund .3B 118
Farnley NE45: Corb .3E 72
Farnley Hey Rd. DH1: Dur .3J 165
Farnley Mt. DH1: Dur .3J 165
Farnley Ridge DH1: Dur .3J 165
Farnley Rd. NE6: Heat .4A 64
Farnon Rd. NE3: Gos .7C 44
Farnsworth Ct. NE2: Jes .3H 63
Farquhar St. NE2: Jes .5H 63
Farrfeld NE10: Hew .3D 100
Farrier Cl. DH1: P Me .3K 153
NE38: Wash .6J 115
Farrier Ct. NE22: Bed .3A 18
Farriers Way DH8: Shot B .3E 120
FARRINGDON .2K 131
Farringdon Rd. NE30: Cull .2F 49
Farringdon Row
SR1: Sund .1F 7 (7D 104)
Farrington Av. SR3: E Her .1J 131
Farrington Ct. NE1: Newc T .6F 4 (1F 83)
Farrow Dr. SR6: Whit .5G 89
Farthings, The NE37: Wash .5F 101
FATFIELD .7H 115
Fatfield Pk. NE38: Wash .6H 115
Fatfield Rd. NE38: Wash .4J 115
Fatherly Ter. DH4: Hou S .2B 144
Faversham Ct. NE3: Ki Pk .5K 43
Faversham Pl. NE23: Cra .2K 25
Fawcett Hill Ter. DH9: Crag .7J 125
Fawcett St. SR1: Sund .3J 7 (1F 119)
Fawcett Ter. *SR5: Sund* .*6H 103*
(off West Vw.)
Fawcett Way NE33: S Shi .2J 67
FAWDON .6B 44
Fawdon Cl. NE3: Fawd .4B 44
Fawdon Gro. NE61: Peg .4K 9
Fawdon Ho. NE3: Fawd .4B 44
Fawdon La. NE3: Fawd .5B 44
Fawdon Pk. Cen. NE3: Fawd .6B 44
Fawdon Pk. Cl. NE3: Fawd .5A 44
Fawdon Pk. Ct. NE3: Fawd .5A 44
Fawdon Pk. Ho. *NE3: Fawd* .*6B 44*
(off Fawdon Pk. Rd.)
Fawdon Pk. Rd. NE3: Fawd .5A 44
Fawdon Pl. NE29: N Shi .6C 48
Fawdon Station (Metro) .6B 44
Fawdon Wlk. NE13: Ki Pk .5K 43
Fawlee Grn. NE3: Ken .1J 61
Fawley Cl. NE35: Bol C .5E 86
Fearon Wlk. DH1: Dur .3D 6 (3B 166)
Featherbed Ct. SR7: S'hm .1B 148
Featherbed La. SR2: Ryh .3J 133
(not continuous)
Featherstone DH3: Gt Lum .2F 143
NE38: Wash .3D 114
Featherstone Gro. NE3: Gos .4B 44
NE22: Bed .6G 17
NE32: Jar .3A 86
Featherstone Rd. DH1: Dur .6B 154
Featherstone St. SR6: Roker .5H 105
Featherstone Vs. SR6: Roker .5H 105
Featherwood Av. NE15: Scot .2H 81
February Courtyard *NE8: Gate* .*5D 82*
(off North Side)
Federation Sq. SR7: Mur .1E 158
Federation Ter. DH9: Tant .6B 110
Federation Way NE11: Dun .5A 82
Fee Ter. SR2: Ryh .3G 133
Feetham Av. NE12: Longb .4D 46
Feetham Ct. NE12: Longb .3E 46
Felixstowe Dr. NE7: H Hea .2A 64
Fell, The NE16: Burn .2B 110
Fell Bank DH3: Bir .4A 114
Fell Cl. DH3: Bir .5C 114
NE16: Sun .5H 97
NE37: Wash .1F 115
Fell Cotts. *NE9: Spri* .*6D 100*
(off Fell Rd.)
Fell Ct. NE9: Low F .2K 99
Fellcross DH3: Bir .3A 114
Fell Dyke NE10: Wind N .1A 100
Felldyke NE10: Hew .2C 100
FELLGATE .5B 86
Fellgate Av. NE32: Jar .5C 86
Fellgate Gdns. NE10: Ward .6G 85
Fellgate Station (Metro) .4C 86
Fell Ho. Farm Rd. NE5: Cha P .1A 60
FELLING .6B 84
Felling Bus. Cen. NE10: Fell .4B 84
Felling By-Pass
NE10: Fell, Hew, Ward .4A 84
(not continuous)
Felling Dene Gdns. NE10: Fell .5C 84
Felling Ga. NE10: Fell .5A 84
Felling Ho. Gdns. NE10: Fell .5B 84
Felling Ind. Est. NE10: Fell .4A 84
Felling Shore Ind. Est. NE10: Fell .3B 84
Felling Station (Metro) .5B 84
Felling Vw. NE6: Walk .3D 84
Fellmere Av. NE10: Pel .6E 84
Fell Pl. NE9: Spri .6D 100
Fell Rd. DH2: P Fel .6G 127
NE9: Spri .6D 100
SR4: Sund .1K 117
Fellrose Ct. DH2: P Fel .5G 127
Fells, The NE9: Low F .1J 99
Fellsdyke Ct. NE10: Wind N .1A 100
FELLSIDE .5E 96
Fell Side DH8: Cons .2K 135
Fellside DH3: Bir .5B 114
NE20: Darr H .3F 41
NE34: S Shi .1D 88
Fellside, The NE3: Ken .1B 62
Fellside Av. NE16: Sun .4H 97
Fellside Cl. DH9: Stly .2H 125
NE20: Darr H .3F 41
Fellside Ct. DH9: Dip .6J 109
NE16: Whi .7G 81
NE37: Wash .2F 115
Fellside Gdns. DH1: Carr .7G 155
Fellside M. NE16: Whi .2F 97
FELLSIDE PARK .1F 97
Fellside Rd. NE16: Burn, Whi .1C 110
Fellside Ter. DH9: Stly .7D 124
Fellside Vw. DH7: B'hpe .5E 138
Fell Sq. SR4: Sund .1J 117
Fells Rd. NE11: T Vall .7F 83
Fell Ter. NE16: Burn .2B 110
Felltop DH8: B'hill .6F 121
Fell Vw. DH8: C'sde .1E 134
DH9: Stly .4E 124
NE37: Wash .1G 115
NE39: H Spen .4E 94
NE40: Craw .3D 78
Fell Vw. W. NE40: Craw .3D 78
Fellway DH2: P Fel .6G 127
Felsham Sq. SR4: Sund .2A 118
Felstead Cres. SR4: Sund .1K 117
Felstead Pl. NE24: News .5H 23
Felstead Sq. SR4: Sund .2K 117
Felthorpe Ct. NE5: Blak .1H 61
Felton Av. NE3: Gos .6C 44
NE25: Whit B .7H 39
NE34: S Shi .7C 68
Felton Cl. NE27: Shir .1K 47
NE61: Mor .2H 15
Felton Cres. NE8: Gate .7G 83
Felton Dr. NE12: Longb .3C 46
Felton Grn. NE6: Byke .7A 64
Felton Ter. *NE30: Tyne* .*4K 49*
(off Hotspur St.)
NE63: Ash .5B 12
Felton Wlk. NE6: Byke .7A 64
FENCE HOUSES .1A 144
Fencer Ct. NE3: Gos .4E 44
Fencer Hill Pk. NE3: Gos .4E 44
Fencer Hill Sq. NE3: Gos .4E 44
Fence Rd. DH3: Lam P .3J 129
Fenchurch Cl. NE13: W Op .6F 35
FENHALL .5J 137
Fenhall Pk. DH7: Lan .6J 137
FENHAM .5K 61
Fenham Chase NE4: Fen .5K 61
Fenham Ct. NE4: Fen .5A 62
Fenham Hall Dr. NE4: Fen .5K 61
Fenham Rd. NE4: Fen .7C 62
(not continuous)
Fenham Swimming Pool .5K 61
Fenkle St. NE1: Newc T .6D 4 (1F 83)
Fennel NE9: Low F .3A 100
Fennel Gro. NE34: S Shi .3A 88
SR8: Eas .7K 159
Fenning Pl. NE6: Byke .2A 84
Fenside Rd. SR2: Ryh .1H 133
Fenton Cl. DH2: Ches S .7J 127
Fenton Sq. SR4: Sund .2K 117
Fenton Ter. DH4: New H .3D 130
Fenton Wlk. NE5: West .3G 61
Fenton Well La. DH3: Gt Lum .3C 142
Fenwick Av. NE24: News .4H 23
NE34: S Shi .1G 87
Fenwick Cl. DH2: Ches S .1H 141
DH4: Pen .2B 130
NE2: Jes .4H 63
NE27: Back .1H 47
SR5: S'wck .4D 104
Fenwick Dr. NE24: Cow .1E 22
Fenwick Gro. NE46: Hex .1C 70
NE61: Mor .6G 9
Fenwick Row SR7: S'hm .4C 148
Fenwick St. DH4: Pen .1B 130
NE35: Bol C .5E 86
Fenwick Ter. DH1: Dur .4H 165
NE2: Jes .4H 63
NE29: N Shi .6G 49
Fenwick Way DH8: Cons .6F 121
Ferens Cl. DH1: Dur .1E 6 (1B 166)
Ferens Pk. DH1: Dur .1E 6 (1B 166)
Ferguson Cres. NE13: Haz .7C 34
Fergusons Bus. Pk. W.
NE22: W Sle .2D 18
Ferguson's La. NE15: Benw .7G 61
Ferguson St. SR2: Sund .2H 119
Fern Av. DH9: Stly .4D 124
NE2: Jes .4G 63
NE3: Fawd .5B 44
NE23: Cra .7K 21
NE26: Whit B .6H 39
NE29: N Shi .6F 49
SR5: S'wck .5C 104
SR6: Whit .4H 89
Fernbank NE26: Sea S .4C 28
Fern Cl. NE42: Pru .6G 77
Fern Ct. NE62: Chop .1G 17
SR8: Pet .1H 181
Fern Cres. SR7: S'hm .6A 148
Ferndale DH1: Carr .1H 167
NE34: S Shi .1B 88
Ferndale Av. NE3: Gos .3F 45
NE28: W'snd .3G 65
NE36: E Bol .7K 87
Ferndale Cl. NE24: Cow .1E 22
TS28: Sta T .7H 181
Ferndale Ct. DH8: Cons .6J 121
Ferndale Gro. NE36: E Bol .7K 87
Ferndale La. NE36: E Bol .7K 87
Ferndale Rd. DH4: Pen .1A 130
Ferndale Ter. NE9: Spri .6D 100
SR4: Sund .7A 104
Fern Dene NE28: W'snd .1J 65
Ferndene Av. DH2: P Fel .6G 127
Ferndene Ct. NE3: Gos .1F 63
Ferndene Cres. SR4: Sund .2B 118
Ferndene Gro. NE7: H Hea .2K 63
NE40: Ryton .7H 59
Fern Dene Rd. NE8: Gate .6G 83
Ferndown Ct. NE10: Ward .7F 85
NE40: Ryton .2H 79
Fern Dr. NE23: Dud .3J 35
SR6: Clead .5B 88
Fern Gdns. NE9: Low F .1H 99
Ferngrove NE32: Jar .6C 86
Fernhill Av. NE16: Whi .7G 81
Fernlea Cl. NE38: Wash .6J 115
Fernlea Dr. NE62: Sco G .3G 17
Fernlea Gdns. NE40: Craw .2E 78
Fernlea Grn. NE3: Ken .7B 44
Fernleigh DH3: Gt Lum .3E 142
Fernley Vs. NE23: Cra .4A 26
Fernlough NE9: Low F .2A 100
Fern Mdws. DH2: Wald .1G 141
Fern Rd. DH7: Sac .7F 141
Fern St. DH8: Cons .6H 121
SR4: Sund .2F 7 (1D 118)
Fernsway SR3: Sund .5D 118
Fern Ter. DH9: Tant .6K 109
Fernville Av. NE16: Sun .5H 97
Fernville Rd. NE3: Gos .2D 62
Fernville St. SR4: Sund .3D 118
Fernway NE61: Mor .7H 9
Fernwood DH7: Sac .1D 152
NE2: Jes .5G 63
Fernwood Av. NE3: Gos .6F 45
Fernwood Cl. SR3: Dox P .4C 132
Fernwood Gro. NE39: Ham M .3D 108
Fernwood Rd. NE2: Jes .1H 5 (5G 63)
NE15: Lem .7D 60
Ferrand Dr. DH4: Hou S .2D 144
Ferriby Cl. NE3: Gos .4F 45
Ferrisdale Way NE3: Fawd .5B 44
Ferry App. NE33: S Shi .2H 67
Ferryboat La. SR5: Sund .4F 103
Ferrydene Av. NE3: Ken .1B 62
Ferry M. NE29: N Shi .1H 67
Ferry Rd. NE46: B End .7E 50
Ferry St. NE32: Jar .5B 66
NE33: S Shi .2H 67
Festival Cotts. NE12: Kil .6K 35
FESTIVAL PARK .7D 82
Festival Pk. Dr. NE11: Fest P .7D 82
Festival Way NE11: Dun .5C 82
Fetcham Ct. NE3: K Bank .5J 43
Fewster Sq. NE10: Hew .1E 100
Field Cl. NE2: Newc T .4K 5 (7H 63)
Fieldfare Cl. NE38: Wash .5D 114
Fieldfare Ct. NE16: Burn .3C 110
Field Ho. NE33: S Shi .4B 68
Fieldhouse Cl. NE61: Hep .3A 16
Field Ho. Farm SR7: S'hm .1G 147
Fieldhouse La. DH1: Dur .1J 165
NE61: Hep .3A 16
Field Ho. Rd. NE8: Gate .7G 83
Field Ho's. DH9: Ann P .6A 124
Field Ho. Ter. DH6: Has .1B 170
Fieldhouse Ter. DH1: Dur .1K 165
Fielding Ct. NE5: West .1G 61
NE34: S Shi .3G 87
Fielding Pl. NE9: Low F .6K 83
Field La. NE10: Hew .6D 84
Fieldside DH2: Pelt .2G 127
DH5: E Rain .7C 144
SR6: Whit .5G 89
Field St. NE3: Gos .7G 45
NE10: Fell .5B 84
Fields Vw. DH5: E Rain .6C 144
Field Ter. NE15: Thro .3H 59
NE32: Jar .1B 86
Field Vw. DH7: Bearp .1D 164
Fieldway NE32: Jar .5C 86
Fiennes Rd. SR8: Pet .5H 171
Fife Av. DH2: Ches S .6K 127
NE32: Jar .3E 86
Fife St. NE8: Gate .5J 83
SR7: Mur .1F 159
Fife Ter. NE17: C'wl .2K 107
Fifteenth Av. NE24: Bly .3H 23
Fifth Av. DH2: Ches S .6K 127
NE6: Heat .1P 5 (6A 64)
NE11: T Vall .2F 99
(Earlsway)
NE11: T Vall .2E 98
(Kingsway Nth.)
NE24: Bly .3H 23
NE61: Mor .1H 15
NE63: Ash .5B 12
Fifth Av. Bus. Pk. NE11: T Vall .3F 99
Fifth Av. E. NE11: T Vall .2F 99
Fifth St. DH8: Cons .7K 121
SR8: Hord .5E 172
(not continuous)
TS27: B Col .1H 183
Filby Dr. DH1: Carr .6H 155
Filey Cl. NE23: Cra .2K 25
Filton Cl. NE23: Cra .2K 25
Finchale NE38: Wash .5G 115
Finchale Abbey Village DH1: Bras .1E 154
Finchale Av. DH1: Bras .3C 154
Finchale Cl. DH4: Hou S .2C 144
NE11: Dun .1B 98
SR2: Sund .3G 119
Finchale Ct. DH4: W Rai .1K 155
Finchale Gdns. NE9: Wrek .5A 100
NE15: Thro .2H 59
Finchale Priory (remains of) .7F 143
Finchale Rd. DH1: Dur .3B 154
(Canterbury Rd.)
DH1: Dur .6J 153
(Durham Moor)
NE31: Heb .4J 85
Finchale Ter. DH4: Hou S .1J 143
NE6: Byke .1A 84
NE32: Jar .2D 86
Finchale Vw. DH1: P Me .3K 153
DH4: W Rai .1J 155
Finchdale Cl. NE29: N Shi .1F 67
Finchdale Ter. DH3: Ches S .6A 128
Finchley Ct. NE6: Walk .5E 64
Finchley Cres. NE6: Walk .5E 64
Findon Av. DH7: Sac .7E 140
DH7: Wit G .2D 152
Findon Gro. NE29: N Shi .1E 66
Findon Hill DH7: Sac .1E 152
Fine La. DH8: Ebc, Shot B .4E 106
Fines Pk. DH9: Ann P .5K 123
(not continuous)
Fines Pk. Ct. DH9: Ann P .5K 123
Fines Rd. DH8: M'sly .1K 121
Fines Ter. DH9: Ann P .5K 123
Finings Av. DH7: Lang P .5G 151
Finings St. DH7: Lang P .5H 151
Finlay Ct. NE34: S Shi .1F 87
Finney Ct. DH1: Dur .1D 6 (2B 166)
Finney Ter. DH1: Dur .1D 6 (2B 166)
Finsbury Av. NE6: Walk .7C 64
Finsbury St. SR5: Monkw .6E 104
Finsmere Pl. NE5: Den M .4H 61
Finstock Ct. NE3: Gos .1H 63
Fir Av. DH1: Dur .3E 166
DH7: B'don .2D 174
Firbank Av. NE30: Cull .2H 49
Firbanks NE32: Jar .5D 86
Firebrick Av. NE4: Newc T .6C 4 (1E 82)
Fire Station Cotts. SR6: Ful .3F 105
Fire Station Ho's.
NE31: Heb .3G 85
Firfield Rd. NE5: Blak .3J 61
Fir Gro. NE34: S Shi .1B 88
Fir Pk. DH7: Ush M .2D 164
Firs, The DH2: Kim .7H 141
NE3: Gos .1D 62
First Av. DH2: Ches S .1K 127
NE6: Heat .1P 5 (6A 64)
NE11: T Vall .1E 98
NE24: Bly .3H 23
NE29: N Shi .1B 66
NE61: Mor .1H 15
NE63: Ash .3B 12
Firs Ter. DH7: Lang P .4K 151
Fir St. NE32: Jar .6A 66
First Row NE63: Ash .3J 11
First St. DH6: Whe H .2B 180
DH8: Cons .7K 121
DH8: Lead .3A 122
(Bradley Bungs.)
DH8: Lead .4A 122
(Second St., not continuous)
NE8: Gate .5F 83
SR8: Hord .5E 172
TS27: B Col .2H 183
Fir Ter. NE16: Burn .2B 110
Fir Terraces DH7: Esh W .3D 162
Firtree Av. NE6: Walk .4E 64
NE12: Longb .3B 46
NE38: Wash .7F 115
Fir Tree Cl. DH1: Dur .7E 154
Fir Tree Copse NE61: Hep .4A 16
Firtree Cres. NE12: Longb .3A 46
Firtree Gdns. NE25: Monks .1F 49
Fir Tree La. DH5: Eas L .1H 157
Firtree Rd. NE16: Whi .1G 97

Firtrees DH2: Ches S 4K 127
NE10: Hew 2C 100
Firtrees Av. NE28: W'snd 2B 66
Firwood Cres. NE39: H Spen 4E 94
Firwood Gdns. NE11: Lob H 2D 98
Fisher Ind. Est. NE6: Walk 7F 65
Fisher La. NE13: Sea B 1D 34
NE23: Cra, Dud, Nel V 5D 24
Fisher Rd. NE27: Back 6F 37
Fisher St. NE6: Walk 6F 65
Fisherwell Rd. NE10: Pel 4E 84
Fish Quay NE30: N Shi 7J 49
Fitzpatrick Pl. NE33: S Shi 3A 68
Fitzroy Ter. SR5: S'wck 5B 104
Fitzsimmons Av. NE28: W'snd 2F 65
Flag Chare NE1: Newc T 6J 5
Flagg Ct. NE33: S Shi 2K 67
Flagg Ct. Ho. NE33: S Shi 2K 67
Flake Cotts. DH3: Ches S 5B 128
Flambard Rd. DH1: Dur 6K 153
Flamborough Wlk. SR7: S'hm 1A 148
Flanders Ct. DH3: Bir 2K 113
Flass Av. DH7: Ush M 2B 164
Flassburn Rd. DH1: Dur 1J 165
Flasshall La. DH7: Esh W 2H 163
Flass St. DH1: Dur 2A 6 (2K 165)
Flass Ter. DH7: Esh W 2G 163
DH7: Ush M 2B 164
Flass Va. DH1: Dur 2K 165
Flaunden Cl. NE34: S Shi 1D 88
Flaxby Cl. NE3: Gos 4F 45
Flax Cotts. NE62: Sco G 3G 17
Flax Sq. SR4: Sund 1J 117
Fleece Cotts. DH7: Edm 4D 140
Fleece Ter. DH7: Edm 4D 140
Fleetham Cl. DH2: Ches S 1H 141
Fleet St. SR1: Sund 2H 119
Fleetwood Way NE8: Gate 5K 83
Fleming Bus. Cen., The NE2: Jes 5F 63
Fleming Ct. DH6: Shot C 5D 170
NE8: Gate 4E 82
FLEMING FIELD 5D 170
Fleming Fld. Farm Rd. DH6: Shot C 5D 170
Fleming Gdns. NE10: Wind N 7A 84
Fleming Pl. SR8: Pet 6B 172
Fletcher Cres. DH4: New H 3E 130
Fletcher Rd. NE8: Gate 9G 4 (3G 83)
Fletcher Ter. DH4: Nbot 5D 130
Fleurs, The *NE9: Eigh B* 5A 100
(off Rockcliffe Way)
Flexbury Gdns. NE9: Low F 5J 99
NE10: Fell 6A 84
NE15: Lem 6E 60
Flight, The NE21: Winl 5A 80
Flighters Pl. *DH4: New H* 3D 130
(off West Lea)
FLINT HILL 7J 109
Flint Hill Bank DH9: Dip 7J 109
Flint Rd. SR4: Sund 1C 118
Flixton DH4: Hou S 1B 144
Flodden NE12: Kil 7B 36
Flodden Cl. DH2: Ches S 1H 141
Flodden Rd. SR4: Sund 2K 117
Flodden St. NE6: Newc T, Walk 1B 84
Floral Dene SR4: Sund 2G 117
Floralia Av. SR2: Ryh 3J 133
Flora St. NE6: Byke 3P 5 (7K 63)
Florence Av. NE9: Low F 1J 99
Florence Cres. SR5: S'wck 5B 104
Florence St. NE21: Winl 5B 80
Florence Ter. DH5: Hett H 1G 157
Florian M. SR4: Sund 4K 117
Florida St. SR4: Sund 7B 104
Florin Ct. NE22: H Bri 4F 21
Flotterton Gdns. NE5: Fen 6J 61
Flour Mill Rd. NE11: Dun 4B 82
Fold, The DH7: Queb 7C 150
NE6: Walk 5E 64
NE16: Burn 1A 110
NE25: Monks 6E 38
SR3: Dox P 4D 132
Folds, The DH4: Hou S 2B 144
DH5: E Rain 6D 144
(off North St.)
Folds Cl. DH7: New B 5A 164
Folldon Av. SR6: Ful 4F 105
FOLLINGSBY 2H 101
Follingsby Av. NE10: Ward 2H 101
Follingsby Cl. NE10: Ward 1H 101
Follingsby Dr. NE10: Ward 7G 85
Follingsby La. NE10: Ward 2G 101
NE36: W Bol 3C 102
NE37: Ward 2K 101
Follingsby Pk. NE10: Ward 1H 101
(not continuous)
Follonsby Ter. NE36: W Bol 7J 85
FOLLY, THE 4G 79
Folly, The NE36: W Bol 7G 87
NE40: G'sde 5F 79
Folly Cotts. NE40: G'sde 5F 79
Folly La. NE40: G'sde 4E 78
Folly Ter. DH1: P Me 4J 153
Folly Yd. NE40: G'sde 4G 79
Fondlyset La. DH9: Ann P, Dip 2H 123
Fontburn Ct. NE29: N Shi 1E 66
SR5: S'wck 3B 104
Fontburn Cres. NE63: Ash 4D 12
Fontburn Gdns. NE61: Mor 1E 14
Fontburn Pl. NE7: Longb 7J 45
Fontburn Rd. NE22: Bed 7A 18
NE25: Sea D 7H 27
Fontburn Ter. NE30: N Shi 6H 49
Fonteyn Pl. DH9: Stly 4H 125
NE23: Cra 7K 21
Fontside NE61: Mit 6A 8
Fontwell Dr. NE8: Gate 7F 83
Forber Av. NE34: S Shi 7D 68
Forbes Ter. SR2: Ryh 3G 133
Ford, The NE42: Pru 3E 76
Ford Av. NE29: N Shi 1D 66
NE63: Ash 5B 12
SR4: Sund 2G 117
Ford Cres. DH7: Lan 7K 137
NE27: Shir 1J 47
NE32: Jar 3B 86
SR4: Sund 2G 117
Ford Dr. NE24: Bly 2G 23
Fordenbridge Cres. SR4: Sund 2K 117
Fordenbridge Rd. SR4: Sund 2K 117
Fordenbridge Sq. SR4: Sund 2A 118
FORD ESTATE 2A 118
Fordfield Rd. SR4: Sund 2J 117
Ford Gro. NE3: Gos 5D 44
Ford Hall Dr. SR4: Sund 2A 118
Fordham Dr. DH7: Sac 6D 140
Fordham Rd. DH1: Dur 5A 154
SR4: Sund 1K 117
Fordham Sq. SR4: Sund 2A 118
Fordland Pl. SR4: Sund 2B 118
FORDLEY 3K 35
Ford Lodge SR4: Sund 2G 117
Fordmoss Wlk. NE5: West 3G 61
Ford Pk. NE62: Stake 7K 11
Ford Rd. DH1: Dur 4B 154
DH7: Lan 7K 137
Ford St. DH7: Lan 7K 137
DH8: Cons 2K 135
NE6: Byke 5M 5 (1J 83)
Ford Ter. NE28: W'snd 3K 65
NE44: Rid M 6A 74
NE62: Chop 1H 17
SR4: Sund 2B 118
Ford Vw. NE23: Dud 2J 35
Forest Av. NE12: Longb 4C 46
Forestborn Ct. NE5: West 3F 61
Forest Dr. NE38: Wash 1D 128
Forest Ga. NE12: Kil 3E 46
TS28: Win 5F 181
FOREST HALL 4B 46
Forest Hall Rd. NE12: Longb 4C 46
Fore St. NE2: Newc T 1M 5 (5J 63)
NE46: Hex 1D 70
Forest Rd. NE33: S Shi 3J 67
SR4: Sund 2K 117
(Fordfield Rd.)
SR4: Sund 1K 117
(St Luke's Rd.)
Forest Rd. Ind. Est. NE33: S Shi 3J 67
Forest Vw. DH7: B'don 2B 174
Forest Way NE23: Seg 2D 36
Forfar St. SR6: Ful 5F 105
Forge, The DH1: P Me 3J 153
DH7: Bran 4A 174
NE46: Acomb 4B 50
SR4: Sund 1B 118
Forge Cl. NE17: C'wl 2K 107
Forge La. DH3: Gt Lum 1F 143
NE17: Ham 2B 108
Forge Rd. NE8: Gate 6C 82
Forge Wlk. NE15: Walb 4K 59
Formula 1 Karting 6C 82
Forres Ct. DH9: Stly 3H 125
Forres Pl. NE23: Cra 2K 25
Forrest Rd. NE28: W'snd 4E 64
Forster Av. DH6: S'burn 2K 167
NE22: Bed 7G 17
NE34: S Shi 6A 68
SR7: Mur 2G 159
Forster Ct. NE9: Low F 3H 99
Forster Cres. DH6: S Het 5D 158
Forster Sq. TS28: Win 5F 181
Forster St. DH8: Cons 7J 121
NE1: Newc T 6J 5 (1H 83)
NE24: Bly 2K 23
SR6: Roker 5G 105
Forsyth Rd. NE2: Jes 4F 63
Forsyth St. NE29: N Shi 3B 48
Forth Banks NE1: Newc T 8E 4 (2F 83)
Forth Banks Twr. NE1: Newc T 9E 4
Forth Cl. SR8: Pet 7B 172
Forth Ct. NE34: S Shi 1J 87
SR3: Silk 3B 132
Forth Goods Yd. NE1: Newc T 8D 4 (2E 82)
Forth La. NE1: Newc T 7E 4 (2F 83)
Forth Pl. NE1: Newc T 7D 4 (2E 82)
Forth St. NE1: Newc T 8D 4 (2E 82)
NE17: C'wl 6A 94
Fortrose Av. SR3: Sund 5C 118
Fort Sq. NE33: S Shi 1J 67
Fort St. NE33: S Shi 1K 67
Forum, The NE15: Den M 6F 61
NE28: W'snd 4F 65
Forum Cinema, The 1D 70
Forum Ct. NE22: Bed 7H 17
Forum Shop. Cen., The NE28: W'snd 4F 65
Forum Way NE23: Cra 4J 25
Fossdyke NE10: Hew 2D 100
Fossefeld NE10: Hew 7E 84
Fosse Law NE15: Thro 4J 59
Fosse Ter. NE9: Low F 1J 99
Foss Way DH8: Ebc 5G 107
NE34: S Shi 1H 87
Fossway NE6: Walk 6B 64
Foster Ct. NE11: T Vall 4E 98
Foster Dr. NE8: Gate 10N 5 (4K 83)
Foster Memorial Homes NE24: Bly 2H 23
Foster St. NE6: Walk 7F 65
(not continuous)
Foster Ter. DH6: Crox 7K 175
NE24: Camb 2G 19
Foundry, The TS27: Cas E 5A 182
Foundry Cotts. NE46: Hex 1C 70
Foundry Ct. NE6: Byke 2A 84
Foundry Ind. Est. NE46: B End 7E 50
Foundry La. NE6: Byke 4M 5 (7J 63)
NE16: Swa 5G 81
Foundry La. Ind. Est.
NE1: Byke 5M 5 (1J 83)
Foundry M. TS29: Trim S 7C 180
Foundry Rd. SR7: S'hm 3C 148
Fountain Cl. NE22: Bed 7H 17
Fountain Ct. NE8: Gate 7F 83
Fountain Gro. NE34: S Shi 5B 68
Fountain Head Bank NE26: Sea S 4B 28
Fountain La. NE21: Blay 3C 80
(not continuous)
Fountain Row NE2: Newc T 1A 4 (6D 62)
Fountains Cl. NE11: Dun 1B 98
NE38: Wash 4H 115
Fountains Cres. DH4: Hou S 7C 130
NE31: Heb 3J 85
Fouracres Rd. NE5: Fen 3A 62
Four La. Ends DH5: Hett H 1H 157
Four Lane Ends (Park & Tram) 6A 46
Four Lane Ends Station (Metro) 7A 46
Fourstones NE5: West 3G 61
Fourstones Cl. NE3: Ken 7K 43
Fourstones Rd. SR4: Sund 1A 118
Fourteenth Av. NE24: Bly 3H 23
Fourth Av. DH2: Ches S 6K 127
NE6: Heat 6A 64
NE11: T Vall 2E 98
NE24: Bly 3H 23
NE61: Mor 1H 15
NE63: Ash 4B 12
Fourth St. DH8: Cons 7K 121
DH8: Lead 3A 122
(not continuous)
DH9: Stly 7D 124
NE8: Gate 5F 83
SR8: Hord 6E 172
(Cotsford La.)
SR8: Hord 5E 172
(Edward Cain Ct.)
TS27: B Col 2H 183
Fourways Ct. TS28: Win 4G 181
Fowberry Cres. NE4: Fen 6A 62
Fowberry Rd. NE15: Scot 2F 81
Fowler Cl. DH4: S Row 5C 130
Fowler Gdns. NE11: Dun 5B 82
Fowler St. NE33: S Shi 2J 67
Fowlers Yd. DH1: Dur 2C 6
Fox & Hounds La. NE15: Benw 7J 61
Fox & Hounds Rd. NE5: Fen 6J 61
Fox Av. NE34: S Shi 2F 87
Fox Cover NE63: Ash 6D 12
Foxcover Ct. SR7: S'hm 5A 148
Fox Cover Ind. Pk. SR7: S'hm 6B 148
Foxcover La. SR3: E Her 2H 131
Foxcover Rd. SR3: E Her 6F 117
SR4: Sund 6F 117
Fox Covert La. NE20: Pon 5H 31
Foxdale Ct. SR7: Mur 7G 147
Fox Dene Vw. NE40: G'sde 6D 78
Foxes Covert DH9: Dip 7H 109
Foxes Row DH7: Bran 5A 174
Foxglove DH2: Ches S 7H 127
DH4: S Row 4K 129
Foxglove Cl. NE24: News 5G 23
Foxglove Ct. NE34: S Shi 2H 87
Foxhill Cl. NE63: Ash 6K 11
Foxhills, The NE16: Whi 1E 96
Foxhills Cl. NE38: Wash 6J 115
Foxhills Covert NE16: Whi 2E 96
Foxhills Cres. DH7: Lan 6J 137
Foxhomes NE32: Jar 6D 86
Foxhunters Rd. NE25: Whit B 1F 49
Foxhunters Trad. Est. NE25: Whit B 1F 49
Foxlair Cl. SR3: Dox P 5C 132
Fox Lea Wlk. NE23: Seg 2C 36
Foxley NE37: Wash 7J 101
Foxley Cl. NE12: Kil 7D 36
Foxpit La. DH9: Stly 5G 111
Fox St. NE10: Fell 5A 84
SR2: Sund 7F 7 (3D 118)
SR7: S'hm 4B 148
Foxton Av. NE3: Fawd 5B 44
NE30: Cull 1H 49
Foxton Cl. NE29: N Shi 2E 66
Foxton Ct. DH6: Kel 7E 178
SR6: Clead 5C 88
Foxton Grn. NE3: Ken 7A 44
Foxton Hall NE37: Wash 4H 101
Foxton Way DH1: H Shin 7F 167
NE10: Bill Q 4F 85
Foxwood Ct. DH7: Lan 5J 137
Foyle St. SR1: Sund 4K 7 (2F 119)
Framlington Ho. NE2: Newc T 1C 4 (6E 62)
Framlington Pl. NE2: Newc T 1C 4 (6E 62)
Framwelgate DH1: Dur 1B 6 (2A 166)
Framwelgate Bri. DH1: Dur 3B 6 (3A 166)
Framwelgate Peth DH1: Dur 1A 6 (1K 165)
Framwelgate Waterside
DH1: Dur 2C 6 (2A 166)
FRAMWELLGATE MOOR 6J 153
Framwellgate School Sports Cen. 5K 153
Francesca Ter. *NE5: Den M* 5H 61
(off Pooley Rd.)
Frances St. NE21: Winl 4A 80
SR3: New S 2C 132
Frances Ville NE62: Sco G 3G 17
Francis St. SR6: Ful 5F 105
Francis Way DH5: Hett H 6G 145
NE27: Longb 3H 47
Frank Av. SR7: S'hm 3K 147
Frankham St. NE5: West 3F 61
Frankland Dr. NE25: Monks 1E 48
Frankland La.
DH1: Bras, Dur 1C 6 (1A 166)
Frankland Mt. NE25: Monks 1E 48
Frankland Rd. DH1: Dur 6K 153
Franklin Ct. NE37: Wash 7H 101
Franklin St. NE33: S Shi 3J 67
SR4: Sund 1C 118
Franklin Trad. Est. NE21: Blay 2E 80
Franklyn Av. NE26: Sea S 3B 28
Franklyn Rd. SR8: Pet 5K 171
Frank Pl. DH3: Bir 5A 114
NE29: N Shi 6G 49
Frank St. DH1: Dur 2E 166
NE28: W'snd 4F 65
NE40: G'sde 5D 78
SR5: S'wck 5D 104
Fraser Cl. NE33: S Shi 5H 67
Frater Ter. NE28: W'snd 3C 66
Frazer Rd. DH8: Shot B 3G 121
Frazer Ter. NE10: Pel 5E 84
Freda St. SR5: S'wck 6B 104
Frederick Gdns. DH4: Pen 2A 130
Frederick Pl. DH4: Hou S 2E 144
Frederick Rd. SR1: Sund 3K 7 (1F 119)
Frederick St. NE17: C'wl 7K 93
NE33: S Shi 4J 67
SR1: Sund 3K 7 (1F 119)
SR4: Sund 2G 117
SR7: S'hm 3B 148
Frederick St. Nth. DH7: Mead 2E 174
Frederick St. Sth. DH7: Mead 2E 174
Frederick Ter. DH5: Eas L 2H 157
DH6: S Het 5B 158
SR6: Whit 5H 89
Fred Peart Sq. DH6: Whe H 3B 180
Freehold Av. NE62: Chop 1H 17
Freehold St. NE24: Bly 1K 23
Freeman Ct. NE63: N Sea 6D 12
Freeman Rd. NE3: Gos 1H 63
NE7: H Hea 1H 63
Freemans Pl. DH1: Dur 2C 6 (2A 166)
Freeman's Quay DH1: Dur 1C 6 (2A 166)
Freeman's Quay Leisure Cen.
1C 6 (2A 166)
Freeman Way NE26: Whit B 4E 38
NE63: N Sea 6D 12
Freesia Gdns. SR5: Ful 4E 104
Freesia Grange NE38: Wash 5J 115
Freezemoor Rd. DH4: New H 3D 130
Freight Village NE13: Wool 2E 42
Freik's Bldgs. DH9: Dip 6J 109
Fremantle Rd. NE34: S Shi 1D 88
French Gdn. Ind. Est. NE46: B End 7E 50
Frenchmans Row NE15: Thro 3F 59
Frenchmans Way NE34: S Shi 6D 68
French St. NE24: Bly 1J 23
Frensham NE38: Wash 4A 116
Frensham Way DH7: Mead 1E 174
Frenton Cl. NE5: Cha P 3C 60
Friarage Av. SR6: Ful 4F 105
Friar Rd. SR4: Sund 2K 117
Friars NE1: Newc T 6D 4
Friars Dene Rd. NE10: Gate 4A 84
Friarsfield Cl. SR3: Dox P 4A 132
Friars Ga. NE61: Mor 1D 14
FRIARS GOOSE 3B 84
Friars Goose Water Sports Club 3B 84
Friarside DH7: Wit G 3D 152
Friarside Cres. NE39: Row G 7H 95
Friarside Gdns. NE16: Burn 2K 109
NE16: Whi 1G 97
Friarside Rd. NE4: Fen 5A 62
Friar Sq. SR4: Sund 2K 117
Friars Ri. NE25: Monks 1D 48
Friars Row DH1: Dur 1D 166
NE16: Burn 3K 109
Friars St. NE1: Newc T 6D 4 (1E 82)
Friar St. DH6: Shot C 6F 171
Friars Way NE5: Fen 5H 61
Friars Wharf Apartments NE10: Gate 3B 84
Friar Way NE32: Jar 6C 66
Friary Gdns. NE10: Fell 4A 84
Friday Flds. La. NE2: Jes 2G 63
Friendly Bldgs. NE13: Din 4H 33
Frinton Pk. SR3: Sund 5C 118
Frobisher St. NE31: Heb 7K 65
Frome Gdns. NE9: Low F 5H 99
Frome Pl. NE23: Cra 2K 25
Front Rd. SR4: Sund 1K 117
Front St. DH1: Dur, P Me 5J 153
DH1: Dur, S Hou 3E 166
DH2: Gra V 5C 126
DH2: Newf, P Fel 4F 127
DH2: Ous 1H 127
DH2: Pelt 2F 127
DH2: Plaw 6J 141
DH3: Ches S 5A 128
DH3: Gt Lum 3E 142
DH4: Hou S 2A 144
DH4: Nbot 6D 130
DH4: Pen 1C 130
DH5: Hett H 6G 145
(Caroline St.)
DH5: Hett H 2E 156
(York St.)
DH6: Crox 7K 175
DH6: Has 3A 170
(Gloucester Ter.)
DH6: Has 1B 170
(Station St.)
DH6: Kel 7E 178
DH6: Low P 5A 156
DH6: S Het 3A 158

Front St. DH6: S Hil .3C 168
DH6: S'burn .3G 167
DH6: Shot C .5F 171
DH6: Whe H .2B 180
DH7: B'hpe .6D 138
DH7: Corn, Queb .7A 150
DH7: Edm .3D 140
DH7: Esh, Lang P .6F 151
DH7: Lan .6J 137
DH7: Lang M .6G 165
DH7: Lang P .4J 151
DH7: Sac .6D 140
DH7: Wit G .3B 152
DH8: Cons .7H 121
DH8: C'sde .3B 134
DH8: Ebc .5G 107
DH8: Lead .5A 122
DH8: Shot B .3E 120
DH9: Ann P .5K 123
DH9: Crag .6J 125
DH9: Dip .2G 123
(not continuous)
DH9: Stly .3E 124
(Braidwood M.)
DH9: Stly .2G 125
(Chester Rd.)
DH9: Tanf .4D 110
DH9: Tant .6B 110
DL16: Tudh .7K 175
NE7: Longb, Newc T .7A 46
NE12: Kil .6K 35
NE12: Longb, Newc T .7A 46
NE13: Din .4H 33
NE13: Sea B .2D 34
NE15: Lem .1E 80
NE16: Burn .2J 109
(Briardene)
NE16: Burn .2B 110
(Derwent Vw.)
NE16: Burn, Hob .5K 109
NE16: Swa .5G 81
NE16: Whi .7G 81
NE21: Winl .5B 80
NE23: Cra .5B 26
(High Pit Rd.)
NE23: Cra .4K 25
(Station Rd.)
NE23: Dud .2K 35
NE23: Seg .2C 36
NE24: Cow .2B 22
NE25: Ears .6A 38
NE25: Monks .7E 38
NE29: N Shi .4G 49
(Argyle Pl.)
NE29: N Shi .7E 48
(The Quadrant)
NE30: Cull .1J 49
NE30: Tyne .5K 49
NE35: Bol C .5E 86
NE36: E Bol .7J 87
NE37: Wash .7H 101
NE39: H Spen .2D 94
NE41: Wylam .7H 57
NE42: Pru .4F 77
NE45: Corb .1D 72
NE61: Peg .4B 10
NE62: Chop .1G 17
NE64: Newb S .3H 13
SR6: Clead .5C 88
SR6: Whit .6G 89
TS27: Hes .4D 182
TS27: Hutt .7B 182
TS28: Sta T .7H 181
TS28: Win .6F 181
Front St. E. DH4: Pen .1B 130
DH6: Crox .7K 175
DH6: Has .1B 170
(off Front St.)
NE22: Bed .1J 21
TS28: Win .6F 181
Front St. Ind. Est. DH6: Whe H .2B 180
Front St. Nth. DH6: Cass, Quar H .6D 178
Front St. Sth. DH6: Cass, Quar H .6D 178
Front St. W. DH4: Pen .1B 130
DH6: Has .7B 158
NE22: Bed .1H 21
TS28: Win .6F 181
Front Ter. NE29: N Shi .7E 48

Frosterley Cl. DH1: Dur .5B 154
DH5: Eas L .3K 157
Frosterley Dr. DH3: Gt Lum .3F 143
Frosterley Gdns. DH9: Ann P .5K 123
SR3: Sund .6D 118
Frosterley Pl.
NE4: Newc T .4A 4 (7C 62)
Frosterley Wlk. NE16: Sun .4H 97
Frost M. NE33: S Shi .4J 67
Froude Av. NE34: S Shi .3J 87
Fuchsia Pl. NE5: Blak .3K 61
FULBECK .4E 8
Fulbroke Cl. SR2: Ryh .4H 133
Fulbrook Cl. NE23: Cra .7K 21
Fulbrook Rd. NE3: Ken .7B 44
Fulforth Cl. DH7: Bearp .7C 152
Fulforth Way DH7: Sac .6D 140
Fuller Rd. SR2: Sund .4G 119
Fullerton Pl. NE9: Low F .6J 83
Fulmar Dr. NE24: News .5J 23
NE38: Wash .4D 114
Fulmar Lodge NE33: S Shi .3B 68
Fulmar Wlk. SR6: Whit .4H 89
FULWELL .3F 105
Fulwell Av. NE34: S Shi .6D 68
Fulwell Grn. NE5: Blak .4H 61
Fulwell Quarry Local Nature Reserve .3C 104
Fulwell Rd. SR6: Ful, Roker .3F 105
SR8: Pet .6C 172
Fulwell Windmill .3E 104
Fun Shack .1G 147
Furnace Bank NE22: Bed .7B 18
Furnace Rd. NE24: Cow .1B 22
Furness Cl. SR8: Pet .6K 171
Furness Ct. SR3: Silk .3B 132
Furrowfield NE10: Wind N .2A 100
Furzefield Rd. NE3: Gos .1D 62
Fuschia Gdns. NE31: Heb .3J 85
Fylingdale Dr. SR3: Tuns .2E 132
Fyndoune DH7: Sac .1E 152
Fyndoune Community College Sports Cen. .1E 152
Fyndoune Way DH7: Wit G .2D 152
Fynes Cl. SR8: Pet .4B 172
Fynes St. NE24: Bly .1J 23
Fynway DH7: Sac .1E 152

G

Gables, The DH6: Thor .1J 179
DH7: B'hpe .6D 138
DH9: Dip .1G 123
NE13: K Bank .6H 43
NE24: Bly .7H 19
NE38: Wash .4J 115
(off Fatfield Rd.)
Gables Ct. SR4: Sund .5J 117
Gable Ter. DH6: Whe H .2B 180
Gadwall Rd. DH4: W Rai .4B 144
Gainers Ter. NE28: W'snd .5G 65
Gainford DH2: Ches S .6J 127
NE9: Low F .5H 99
Gainsborough Av. NE34: S Shi .3K 87
NE38: Wash .4J 115
Gainsborough Cl. NE25: Monks .4C 38
Gainsborough Cres. DH4: S Row .4K 129
NE9: Low F .7K 83
Gainsborough Gro. NE4: Fen .7B 62
Gainsborough Pl. NE23: Cra .7K 25
Gainsborough Rd. DH9: Stly .4F 125
SR4: Sund .6J 117
Gainsborough Sq. SR4: Sund .6J 117
Gainsford Av. NE9: Low F .3G 99
Gair Ct. DH2: Nett .6H 141
Gairloch Cl. NE23: Cra .1K 25
Gairloch Dr. DH2: Ous .2H 127
NE38: Wash .5E 114
Gairloch Rd. SR4: Sund .5J 117
Gairsay Cl. SR2: Ryh .1G 133
Gala Bingo
Gateshead, Metro Cen. .3H 81
Newcastle .4N 5 (7K 63)
Sunderland .1C 118
Wallsend .7K 47
Washington .3G 115
Galashiels Gro. DH4: S Row .4B 130
Galashiels Rd. SR4: Sund .5H 117
Galashiels Sq. SR4: Sund .5J 117
Gala Theatre & Cinema .2C 6
Galen Ho. NE1: Newc T .6D 4
Gale St. DH9: Stly .4D 124
Galfrid Cl. SR7: Dalt D .4H 147
Gallagher Cres. SR8: Hord .6D 172
Gallalaw Ter. NE3: Gos .7H 45
Gallant Ter. NE28: W'snd .4C 66
Galleria, The NE11: Dun .5J 81
Galleries, The NE38: Wash .3G 115
Galleries Retail Pk., The
NE38: Wash .2G 115
Galley's Gill Rd. SR1: Sund .3G 7 (1E 118)
Galloping Grn. Cotts. NE9: Eigh B .5B 100
Galloping Grn. Farm Cl.
NE9: Eigh B .5B 100
Galloping Grn. Rd.
NE9: Eigh B, Wrek .4B 100
Galloway Rd. NE10: Pel .5F 85
SR8: Pet .5B 172
Gallowgate NE1: Newc T .5D 4 (1E 82)
Gallowhill La. NE15: Hor .1C 76
NE42: O'ham .1C 76
Gallows Bank NE46: Hex .3D 70
Galsworthy Rd. NE34: S Shi .3G 87
SR4: Sund .5J 117
Galt St. DH6: Thor .1K 179
Galway Rd. SR4: Sund .5H 117
Galway Sq. SR4: Sund .5H 117
Gambia Rd. SR4: Sund .6H 117
Gambia Sq. SR4: Sund .6H 117
Ganton Av. NE23: Cra .6K 25
Ganton Cl. NE37: Wash .5G 101
Ganton Ct. NE34: S Shi .3B 88
Gaprigg Ct. NE46: Hex .2D 70
Gaprigg La. NE46: Hex .2C 70
Gaps, The NE46: Acomb .3C 50
Garasdale Cl. NE24: News .5H 23
Garcia Dr. NE63: N Sea .4D 12
Garcia Ter. SR6: Ful .3G 105
(not continuous)
Garden Av. DH1: Dur .5J 153
DH7: Lang P .5H 151
Garden City Vs. NE63: Ash .4B 12
Garden Cl. DH8: Cons .6H 121
NE13: Sea B .3D 34
Garden Cotts. NE9: Low F .2J 99
Garden Ct. DH6: S'burn .2A 168
Garden Cres. DH8: Ebc .4H 107
Garden Cft. NE12: Longb .4C 46
Garden Dr. NE31: Heb .2H 85
Garden Est. DH5: Hett H .6H 145
Garden Ho. Bank NE46: Acomb .5B 50
Garden Ho. Cres. NE16: Whi .6J 81
Garden Ho. Dr. NE46: Acomb .4B 50
Garden Ho. Est. NE40: Craw .2C 78
Garden Ho's. NE21: Winl .5B 80
(off May St.)
Garden La. NE33: S Shi .2J 67
SR6: Clead .6B 88
Garden Pk. NE28: W'snd .1K 65
Garden Pl. DH4: Pen .2B 130
DH8: Cons .6H 121
(off Cleadon St.)
DH8: Lead .5A 122
SR1: Sund .3H 7 (1E 118)
Gardens, The DH2: Ches S .6K 127
NE21: Blay .5E 80
NE25: Monks .7F 39
NE38: Wash .4J 115
Garden St. DH4: Nbot .5D 130
NE3: Gos .7E 44
NE21: Blay .3C 80
Garden Ter. DH4: Nbot .6D 130
DH6: Thor .1K 179
DH8: Lead .5A 122
DH9: Stly .6H 125
(Middles Rd.)
DH9: Stly .4E 124
(Spen St.)
NE21: Winl .5B 80
(off Florence St.)
NE25: Ears .6A 38
NE40: Craw .2D 78
NE40: G'sde .3E 78
NE45: Corb .1D 72
(off Hill St.)
NE46: Hex .1C 70
Garden Vs. DH9: Ann P .4K 123
Garden Wlk. NE11: Dun .4J 81
Gardiner Cres. DH2: P Fel .5G 127
Gardiner Rd. SR4: Sund .5G 117
Gardiner Sq. NE11: Kib .3E 112
SR4: Sund .5H 117
Gardner Ct. SR8: Eas C .6D 160
Gardner Pk. NE29: N Shi .7F 49
Gardner Pl. NE29: N Shi .7H 49
Gardners Pl. DH7: Lang M .7F 165
Garesfield Gdns. NE16: Burn .2K 109
NE39: Row G .4J 95
Garesfield La. NE21: Winl .2J 95
Gareston Cl. NE24: Cow .2F 23
Garfield St. SR4: Sund .1B 118
Garforth Cl. NE23: Cra .6J 25
Garland Pl. NE46: Hex .1C 70
(off Alexander Pl.)
Garland Ter. DH4: Hou S .2A 144
Garleigh Cl. NE12: Kil .1D 46
Garmondsway NE6: Byke .1A 84
Garner Cl. NE5: Cha P .2D 60
Garnet St. SR4: Sund .1B 118
Garrett Cl. NE28: W'snd .2K 65
Garrick Cl. NE29: N Shi .5C 48
Garrick St. NE33: S Shi .5J 67
Garrigill NE38: Wash .7K 115
Garron St. SR7: S'hm .4B 148
Garsdale DH3: Bir .7C 114
Garsdale Av. NE37: Wash .7G 101
Garsdale Rd. NE26: Whit B .2E 38
Garside Av. DH3: Bir .2A 114
Garside Gro. SR8: Pet .4K 171
Garstin Cl. NE7: H Hea .2C 64
Garth, The DH2: Pelt .2G 127
DH8: M'sly .6A 108
NE3: Ken .1B 62
NE5: W Dent .4E 60
NE21: Winl .5B 80
Garth Cotts. NE46: Hex .2C 70
Garth Cres. NE21: Winl .5B 80
NE34: S Shi .4C 68
Garth Farm Rd. NE21: Winl .5B 80
Garthfield Cl. NE5: West .2G 61
Garthfield Cnr. NE5: West .2G 61
Garthfield Cres. NE5: West .2G 61
Garth Heads NE1: Newc T .6J 5 (1H 83)
Garths, The DH7: Lan .7K 137
Garth Sixteen NE12: Kil .7B 36
Garth Thirteen NE12: Kil .7A 36
Garth Thirty Three NE12: Kil .1B 46
Garth Thirty Two NE12: Kil .1C 46
Garth Twenty NE12: Kil .1C 46
Garth Twenty Five NE12: Kil .1D 46
Garth Twenty Four NE12: Kil .1C 46
Garth Twenty One NE12: Kil .7C 36
Garth Twenty Seven NE12: Kil .1D 46
Garth Twenty Two NE12: Kil .1C 46
Gartland Rd. SR4: Sund .5G 117
Garvey Vs. NE10: Wind N .1K 99
Garwood St. NE33: S Shi .5H 67
Gashouse Dr. DH3: Lam P .3G 129
Gas Ho. La. NE61: Mor .7G 9
Gaskell Av. NE34: S Shi .3H 87
Gas La. NE21: Blay .2C 80
Gas Works Rd. SR7: S'hm .4C 148
Gatacre St. NE24: Bly .1J 23
Gate, The .5E 4 (1F 83)
Gateley Av. NE24: News .5H 23
Gatesgarth NE9: Low F .2J 99
Gatesgarth Gro. SR6: Seab .2F 105
GATESHEAD .10J 5 (4H 83)
Gateshead NE36: W Bol .1G 103
(off Addison Rd.)
Gateshead FC .10P 5 (3A 84)
Gateshead Heritage @ St Mary's .8H 5
Gateshead Highway
NE8: Gate .9J 5 (3H 83)
Gateshead Indoor Bowling Cen. .5H 83
Gateshead Intl. Bus. Cen. NE8: Gate .9H 5
Gateshead International Stadium .10P 5 (3A 84)
Gateshead Leisure Cen. .6H 83
Gateshead Rd. NE16: Marl H, Sun .6H 97
Gateshead Stadium Station (Metro) .4J 83
Gateshead Station (Metro) .10H 5 (3G 83)
Gateshead Ter. NE36: W Bol .7G 87
(off Addison Rd.)
Gateshead Western By-Pass
NE9: Lame, Low F .6H 99
NE11: Fest P, Lob H, Rave, T Vall .5J 81
NE16: Dun, Swa .5J 81
Gates Shop. Centre, The
DH1: Dur .2B 6 (2A 166)
Gattis Bldgs. DH9: Ann P .4A 124
Gatwick Ct. NE3: K Bank .5H 43
Gatwick Rd. SR4: Sund .5H 117
Gaughan Cl. NE6: Walk .3D 84
Gaweswell Ter. DH4: Nbot .5D 130
(off North St.)
Gayfield Ter. SR8: Eas C .1D 172
Gayhurst Cres. SR3: Silk .3C 132
Gayle Ct. DH8: Cons .2J 135
Gayton Rd. NE37: Wash .6J 101
Geantree Cotts. NE61: Mor .5F 9
Geddes Rd. SR4: Sund .5H 117
Gellesfield Chare NE16: Whi .3H 97
Gelt Cres. DH5: Eas L .1H 157
General Graham St. SR4: Sund .3B 118
General Havelock Rd. SR4: Sund .1A 118
General's Wood, The NE38: Wash .1F 129
Generation Pl. DH8: Cons .7G 121
Genesis Way DH8: Cons .6G 121
Geneva Rd. SR4: Sund .5H 117
Genister Pl. NE4: Fen .5K 61
Geoffrey Av. DH1: Dur .4J 165
Geoffrey St. NE34: S Shi .3J 87
SR6: Whit .5H 89
Geoffrey Ter. DH9: Stly .4D 124
George Av. SR8: Eas C .6C 160
George Parkinson Ct. DH6: S'burn .3K 167
George Pit La. DH3: Gt Lum .4F 143
George Pl. NE1: Newc T .3E 4 (7F 63)
George Rd. NE22: Bed .6B 18
NE28: W'snd .5F 65
George Scott St. NE33: S Shi .1K 67
George Smith Gdns. NE10: Fell .4A 84
George Sq. DH6: Shad .6E 168
DH6: Shot C .6F 171
Georges Rd. NE4: Elsw .2B 82
(not continuous)
George Stephenson's Birthplace .7B 58
George Stephenson Way NE29: N Shi .2F 67
George St. DH1: Dur .3J 165
DH3: Bir .4K 113
DH3: Ches S .7B 128
DH5: Hett H .5G 145
DH6: Bowb .3G 177
DH6: Has .1B 170
DH6: S Hil .4E 168
DH6: S'burn .3K 167
DH7: Esh W .4E 162
DH7: Lang P .4J 151
DH8: B'hill .5F 121
DH8: Cons .6H 121
DH9: Crag .7J 125
DH9: Dip .1H 123
NE3: Gos .7C 44
NE4: Newc T .7B 4 (2E 82)
NE10: Pel .5D 84
NE13: Bru V .5C 34
NE15: Walb .3K 59
NE16: Whi .7G 81
NE21: Blay .3D 80
NE24: Bly .3J 23
NE28: W'snd .4B 66
NE30: N Shi .6H 49
NE40: Craw .3D 78
NE63: Ash .3C 12
SR2: Ryh .3J 133
SR3: New S .1C 132
SR7: Mur .1F 159
SR7: S'hm .3A 148
George St. E. SR3: New S .1C 132
George St. Ind. Est. SR7: S'hm .3A 148
George St. Nth. SR6: Monkw .7F 105
George St. West SR3: New S .1C 132
George's Vw. NE23: Dud .4J 35
George Ter. DH7: Bearp .1E 164
George Way NE4: Newc T .8C 4 (2E 82)
Georgia Ct. DH8: Cons .7G 121
Georgian Ct. NE12: Longb .3K 45
SR4: Sund .4C 118
Gerald St. NE4: Benw .2K 81
NE34: S Shi .3J 87
Gerrard Cl. NE23: Cra .6K 25
NE26: Whit B .2E 38
Gerrard Rd. NE26: Whit B .2E 38
SR4: Sund .5H 117
Gertrude St. DH4: Hou S .7D 130
Ghyll Edge NE61: Mor .6D 8
Ghyll Fld. Rd. DH1: Dur .6K 153
Gibbons Wlk. NE34: S Shi .4G 87
Gibbs Ct. DH2: Ches S .7A 128
GIBSIDE .6C 96
Gibside .5B 96
Gibside DH2: Ches S .6J 127
Gibside Cl. DH9: Stly .2H 125
Gibside Ct. NE11: Dun .1B 98
Gibside Cres. NE16: Burn .7D 96
Gibside Gdns. NE15: Benw .7H 61
Gibside Ter. NE16: Burn .2B 110
Gibside Vw. NE21: Winl .5B 80
Gibside Way NE11: Dun, Swa .4H 81

Gibson Bldgs. *NE40: Craw* 2E 78
(off Main St.)
Gibson Ct. NE35: Bol C 6F 87
(not continuous)
Gibson Flds. NE46: Hex 2D 70
Gibson Ho. *NE46: Hex* 2C 70
(off Battle Hill)
Gibson Pl. NE46: Hex 1C 70
Gibsons Ct. NE21: Blay 4C 80
Gibson St. DH8: Cons 6H 121
NE1: Newc T 5J 5 (1H 83)
NE28: W'snd 7K 47
NE64: Newb S 4H 13
Gibson Street Cen. 5K 5 (1H 83)
Gibson Ter. *NE40: Craw* 2E 78
(off Main St.)
Gifford Sq. SR4: Sund 4J 117
Gilberdyke NE10: Hew 2E 100
Gilbert Rd. SR4: Sund 5H 117
SR8: Pet 5A 172
Gilbert Sq. SR4: Sund 6H 117
Gilbert St. NE33: S Shi 5J 67
Gilderdale DH4: Pen 1J 129
Gilderdale Way NE23: Cra 7J 25
GILESGATE 1E 166
Gilesgate DH1: Dur 2E 6 (2B 166)
NE46: Hex 1C 70
Gilesgate Cl. DH1: Dur 1E 6 (2B 166)
GILESGATE MOOR 2F 167
Gilesgate Rd. DH5: Eas L 1H 157
Giles Pl. NE46: Hex 1C 70
Gilhurst Grange SR1: Sund 4F 7 (2D 118)
Gilhurst Ho. SR1: Sund 3F 7 (1D 118)
Gill, The SR4: Sund 2G 117
Gillas La. DH5: Hou S 3G 145
Gillas La. E. DH5: Hou S 3F 145
Gillas La. W. DH5: Hou S 4E 144
Gillbridge Av. SR1: Sund 3H 7
Gill Burn NE39: Row G 4J 95
Gill Ct. NE13: Bru V 5C 34
Gill Cres. Nth. DH4: Hou S 7J 129
Gill Cres. Sth. DH4: Hou S 7J 129
Gill Cft. DH2: Ches S 7H 127
GILLEY LAW 1A 132
Gillies St. NE6: Byke 7B 64
Gilliland Cres. DH3: Bir 2A 114
Gillingham Rd. SR4: Sund 5H 117
Gillside Ct. NE34: S Shi 1G 87
Gill Side Gro. SR6: Roker 5G 105
Gillside Vw. DH8: Shot B 5E 120
Gill St. DH8: Cons 1H 135
NE4: Benw 1A 82
Gill Ter. *SR4: Sund* 1G 117
(off Pottery La.)
Gill Vw. DH8: C'sde 2E 134
Gilmore Cl. NE5: Cha P 2D 60
Gilmore Ho. *NE8: Gate* 6G 83
(off Whitehall Rd.)
Gilpin Ho. DH4: Hou S 7C 130
Gilpin St. DH4: Hou S 2D 144
Gilsland Av. NE28: W'snd 2K 65
Gilsland Gro. NE23: Cra 1K 25
Gilsland St. SR4: Sund 2C 118
Gilwell Way NE3: Gos 3D 44
Gilwood Ct. DH4: Pen 3A 130
Gingler La. NE40: G'sde 4E 78
Girtin Rd. NE34: S Shi 4K 87
Girton Cl. SR8: Pet 7K 171
Girvan Cl. DH9: Stly 3H 125
Girven Ter. DH5: Eas L 2J 157
Girven Ter. W. DH5: Eas L 2H 157
Gisburn Ct. NE23: Cra 1K 25
Gishford Way NE5: Blak 3H 61
Givens St. SR6: Roker 5G 105
Glade, The NE15: Walb 3A 60
NE32: Jar 5B 86
Gladeley Way NE16: Sun 5G 97
Gladewell Ct. NE62: Chop 2G 17
Gladstonbury Pl. NE12: Longb 6A 46
Gladstone Av. NE26: Whit B 5F 39
Gladstone Gdns. DH8: Cons 6J 121
Gladstone M. NE24: Bly 1H 23
Gladstone Pl. NE2: Newc T 2H 5 (6G 63)
Gladstone St. DH4: Hou S 2B 144
DH8: Cons 6J 121
DH9: Beam 2K 125
DH9: Stly 4D 124
NE15: Lem 7C 60
NE24: Bly 1H 23
NE28: W'snd 4B 66
NE31: Heb 7A 66
NE61: Mor 7H 9
SR6: Roker 6F 105
Gladstone Ter. DH3: Bir 4K 113
DH4: Pen 1K 129
NE2: Newc T 2H 5 (6G 63)
NE8: Gate 5H 83
NE22: Bed 1J 21
NE26: Whit B 7H 39
NE35: Bol C 4E 86
NE37: Wash 7K 101
TS28: Sta T 7G 181
Gladstone Ter. W. NE8: Gate 5G 83
Gladstone Vs. DH1: Dur 6D 6 (4B 166)
Gladwyn Rd. SR4: Sund 6H 117
Gladwyn Sq. SR4: Sund 6H 117
Glaholm Rd. SR1: Sund 2H 119
Glaisdale Ct. NE34: S Shi 2G 87
Glaisdale Dr. SR6: Seab 1G 105
Glaisdale Rd. NE7: Longb 7J 45
Glamis Av. NE3: Gos 2E 44
SR4: Sund 4J 117
Glamis Ct. DH4: Hou S 1H 143
NE34: S Shi 3B 88
Glamis Cres. NE39: Row G 3A 96
Glamis Ter. NE16: Marl H 6G 97
Glamis Vs. DH3: Bir 2A 114
Glanmore Rd. SR4: Sund 5H 117
Glantlees NE5: West 3G 61
Glanton Av. NE25: Sea D 7G 27
Glanton Cl. DH2: Ches S 7J 127
NE6: Byke 2A 84
NE10: Ward 7G 85
NE28: W'snd 2J 65
NE61: Hep 3H 15
Glanton Ct. NE11: Dun 5C 82
Glanton Rd. NE29: N Shi 5D 48
NE46: Hex 2F 71
Glanton Sq. SR4: Sund 5J 117
Glanton Ter. SR8: Hord 6F 173
Glanton Wynd NE3: Gos 5D 44
Glanville Cl. NE11: Fest P 7D 82
Glanville Rd. SR3: Dox P 4K 131
Glasbury Av. SR4: Sund 4J 117
Glasgow Rd. NE32: Jar 2E 86
Glassey Ter. NE22: Bed 7B 18
Glasshouse Bri. NE1: Newc T 6M 5 (1J 83)
NE6: Byke 6M 5 (1J 83)
Glasshouse St. NE6: Byke 2A 84
Glastonbury NE38: Wash 4H 115
Glastonbury Gro. NE2: Jes 3H 63
Glaston Ho. NE24: Cow 1F 23
Glazebury Way NE23: Cra 1K 25
Gleaston Ct. SR8: Pet 2K 181
GLEBE 3H 115
Glebe Av. NE12: Longb 5B 46
NE16: Whi 7H 81
SR8: Eas 7B 160
Glebe Cl. NE5: Cha P 2D 60
NE20: Pon 4J 31
Glebe Ct. NE22: Bed 7H 17
Glebe Cres. NE12: Longb 3B 46
NE38: Wash 2J 115
SR8: Eas 7B 160
Glebe Dr. SR7: S'hm 7H 133
Glebe Est. SR7: S'hm 7H 133
Glebe Farm NE62: Chop 7G 11
Glebe Farm Ct. NE36: W Bol 7F 87
Glebelands NE45: Corb 7E 52
Glebe M. NE22: Bed 7H 17
Glebe Mt. NE38: Wash 2J 115
Glebe Ri. NE16: Whi 7G 81
Glebe Rd. NE12: Longb 3B 46
NE22: Bed 7H 17
Glebeside DH5: Hett H 5G 145
DH7: Wit G 3D 152
Glebe St. NE4: Benw 7K 61
Glebe Ter. DH4: Hou S 1D 144
NE11: Dun 6B 82
NE12: Longb 3B 46
NE62: Sco G 4G 17
SR8: Eas 7A 160
(not continuous)
Glebe Vw. SR7: Mur 6G 147
(not continuous)
Glebe Vs. NE12: Longb 3A 46
Glebe Wlk. NE16: Whi 7H 81
Glen, The SR2: Sund 5F 119
Glenallen Gdns. NE30: Cull 3J 49
Glenamara Ho. NE2: Newc T 3H 5
Glen Av. NE43: Pains 7J 75
Glenavon Av. DH2: Ches S 5K 127
Glen Barr DH2: Ches S 5K 127
Glenbrooke Ter. NE9: Low F 3H 99
Glenburn Cl. NE38: Wash 5D 114
Glencarron Cl. NE38: Wash 5E 114
Glen Cl. NE39: Row G 4J 95
Glencoe NE12: Kil 7B 36
Glencoe Av. DH2: Ches S 5K 127
NE23: Cra 7K 25
Glencoe Ri. NE39: Row G 6G 95
Glencoe Rd. SR4: Sund 6H 117
Glencoe Sq. SR4: Sund 5H 117
Glencoe Ter. NE39: Row G 6G 95
Glencot Gro. SR7: Hawt 4J 159
Glencourse NE36: E Bol 7A 88
Glen Ct. NE31: Heb 7H 65
Glencrest Ct. DH2: P Fel 6G 127
Glendale Av. NE3: Gos 1C 62
NE16: Whi 1G 97
NE24: Cow 1C 22
NE26: Whit B 4G 39
NE28: W'snd 1F 65
NE29: N Shi 6E 48
NE37: Wash 7G 101
NE62: Stake 7J 11
Glendale Cl. NE5: Cha P 2D 60
NE21: Winl 6K 79
SR3: E Her 3J 131
Glendale Gdns. NE9: Low F 2K 99
NE62: Stake 7J 11
Glendale Gro. NE29: N Shi 6F 49
Glendale Rd. NE27: Shir 1A 48
NE63: N Sea 5E 12
Glendale Ter. NE6: Byke 7A 64
Glendford Pl. NE24: News 5H 23
Glendower Av. NE29: N Shi 6D 48
Glendyn Cl. NE7: H Hea 4J 63
Gleneagle Cl. NE5: Cha P 2D 60
Gleneagles NE25: Monks 6D 38
NE33: S Shi 4B 68
Gleneagles Cl. NE7: Longb 7A 46
Gleneagles Ct. NE25: Monks 6D 38
Gleneagles Dr. NE37: Wash 5F 101
Gleneagles Rd. NE9: Low F 4G 99
SR4: Sund 6H 117
Gleneagles Sq. SR4: Sund 6H 117
Glenesk Gdns. SR2: Sund 6E 118
Glenesk Rd. SR2: Sund 5E 118
Glenfield Av. NE23: Cra 1K 25
Glenfield Rd. NE12: Longb 5A 46
(not continuous)
Glengarvan Cl. NE38: Wash 5E 114
Glenholme Cl. NE38: Wash 5D 114
Glenholme Ter. TS27: B Col 2J 183
Glenhurst Cotts. SR8: Eas 7B 160
Glenhurst Dr. NE5: Cha P 2D 60
NE16: Whi 3F 97
Glenhurst Gro. NE34: S Shi 7B 68
Glenhurst Rd. SR8: Eas 7B 160
Glenhurst Ter. SR7: Mur 7F 147
Glenkerry Cl. NE38: Wash 5E 114
Glenleigh Dr. SR4: Sund 4J 117
Glenluce DH3: Bir 5C 114
(not continuous)
Glenluce Ct. DH8: B'hill 6E 120
NE23: Cra 6K 25
Glen Luce Dr. SR2: Sund 6H 119
Glenluce Dr. NE23: Cra 7J 25
Glenmeads DH2: Nett 6H 141
Glenmoor NE31: Heb 6H 65
Glenmore DH8: Cons 2A 136
Glenmore Av. DH2: Ches S 5A 128
Glenmuir Av. NE23: Cra 7J 25
Glenorrin Cl. NE38: Wash 5E 114
Glen Path SR2: Sund 5F 119
Glenridge Av. NE6: Heat 4K 63
Glenroy Gdns. DH2: Ches S 5K 127
Glens Flats DH6: H Pitt 6B 156
Glenshiel Cl. NE38: Wash 5E 114
Glenside DH8: Shot B 3F 121
NE32: Jar 4C 86
Glenside Ct. NE9: Low F 3G 99
Glenside Ter. DH2: P Fel 5H 127
Glen St. NE31: Heb 1H 85
Glen Ter. DH2: Ches S 5J 127
DH4: Pen 1B 130
(off Rainton St.)
NE38: Wash 4J 115
NE46: Hex 1B 70
Glenthorne Rd. SR6: Roker 5G 105
Glenthorn Rd. NE2: Jes 3G 63
Glen Thorpe Av. SR6: Roker 5G 105
Glenthorpe Ho. NE33: S Shi 4K 67
Glenview Cl. DH2: P Fel 5G 127
Glenwood NE63: Ash 5A 12
Glenwood Wlk. NE5: Cha P 2D 60
Globe, The NE2: Newc T 3J 5
Gloria Av. NE25: New Hart 4H 27
Glossop St. NE39: H Spen 3D 94
Gloucester Av. SR6: Ful 3G 105
Gloucester Cl. DH3: Gt Lum 4E 142
Gloucester Ct. NE3: Ki Pk 4J 43
Gloucester Pl. NE34: S Shi 1B 88
SR8: Pet 5K 171
Gloucester Rd. DH8: Cons 1J 135
NE4: Elsw 6A 4 (1C 82)
NE29: N Shi 5B 48
Gloucestershire Dr. DH1: Carr 1G 167
Gloucester St. NE25: New Hart 5H 27
Gloucester Ter. DH6: Has 3A 170
NE4: Elsw 7A 4 (2C 82)
Gloucester Way NE4: Newc T 8A 4 (2D 82)
NE32: Jar 5B 86
Glover Ind. Est. NE37: Wash 1J 115
Glover Network Cen. NE37: Wash 1A 116
Glover Rd. NE37: Wash 7K 101
SR4: Sund 6H 117
Glovers Pl. NE46: Hex 1C 70
Glover Sq. SR4: Sund 6H 117
Glue Gth. DH1: Dur 2D 166
Glynfellis NE10: Hew 2D 100
Glynfellis Ct. NE10: Hew 2D 100
Glynwood Cl. NE23: Cra 1K 25
Glynwood Gdns. NE9: Low F 2J 99
Goalmouth Cl. SR6: Roker 5G 105
Goatbeck Ter. DH7: Lang M 7F 165
Goathland Av. NE12: Longb 6K 45
Goathland Dr. SR3: Tuns 2D 132
Godfrey Rd. SR4: Sund 5H 117
Gofton Wlk. NE5: West 3G 61
Goldcrest Rd. NE38: Wash 5D 114
Goldcrest Way NE15: Lem 1C 80
Golden Acre DH8: Shot B 3F 121
Goldfinch Cl. NE4: Elsw 3B 82
Goldfinch Rd. DH5: Eas L 2J 157
Goldlynn Dr. SR3: Silk 3A 132
Goldsborough Ct. TS28: Win 4G 181
Goldsbrough Ct. NE2: Newc T 1C 4 (6E 62)
Goldsmith Rd. SR4: Sund 6H 117
Goldspink La. NE2: Newc T 1K 5 (6H 63)
Goldstone NE9: Low F 3H 99
Goldstone Ct. NE12: Kil 7C 36
Goldthorpe Cl. NE23: Cra 1K 25
Golf Course Rd. DH4: S Row 5K 129
Gompertz Gdns. NE33: S Shi 5H 67
Gooch Av. NE22: Bed 4J 17
Goodrich Cl. DH4: S Row 4C 130
Good St. DH9: Stly 1E 124
Goodwell Lea DH7: Bran 4A 174
Goodwood NE12: Kil 1C 46
Goodwood Av. NE8: Gate 6E 82
Goodwood Cl. DH8: Shot B 3F 121
NE5: Cha P 2D 60
Goodwood Ct. NE63: Ash 5B 12
Goodwood Rd. SR4: Sund 5G 117
Goodwood Sq. SR4: Sund 5G 117
Goodyear Cres. DH1: Dur 3E 166
Goole Rd. SR4: Sund 5J 117
Goose Hill NE61: Mor 7G 9
Gordon Av. NE3: Gos 1E 62
SR5: Sund 7G 103
SR8: Hord 5D 172
Gordon Dr. NE36: E Bol 7K 87
Gordon Ho. NE6: Byke 5P 5
Gordon Rd. NE6: Byke 5P 5 (1K 83)
NE24: Bly 4K 23
NE34: S Shi 7J 67
SR4: Sund 6H 117
Gordon Sq. NE6: Byke 5P 5 (1K 83)
NE26: Whit B 7J 39
Gordon St. NE33: S Shi 5J 67
Gordon Ter. DH4: Pen 1C 130
DH9: Stly 1F 125
NE22: Bed 1J 21
NE26: Whit B 6J 39
NE42: Pru 4F 77
NE62: Stake 1A 18
SR2: Ryh 3J 133
SR5: S'wck 5C 104
Gordon Ter. W. NE62: Stake 1A 18
Gorecock La. DH8: Cons 2F 137
DH9: Ann P, Cons, Lan 2F 137
Gore Hill Est. DH6: Thor 1J 179
Gore La. DH6: Thor 1J 179
Gorleston Way SR3: Dox P 5C 132
Gorse Av. NE34: S Shi 1B 88
Gorsedale Gro. DH1: Carr 1H 167
Gorsedene Av. NE26: Whit B 2F 39
Gorsedene Rd. NE26: Whit B 2E 38
Gorsehill NE9: Low F 2A 100
Gorse Hill Way NE5: Blak 2J 61
Gorse Rd. SR2: Sund 7J 7 (3F 119)
Gorseway NE61: Mor 1D 14
Gort Pl. DH1: Dur 1D 166
Goschen St. NE8: Gate 6F 83
NE24: Bly 1H 23
(not continuous)
SR5: S'wck 5C 104
GOSFORTH 1E 62
Gosforth Av. NE34: S Shi 2J 87
Gosforth Bowling Club 1E 62
Gosforth Bus. Pk. NE12: Longb 5H 45
Gosforth Cen., The NE3: Gos 1E 62
Gosforth Ind. Est. NE3: Gos 7G 45
Gosforth Pk. Av. NE12: Longb 5J 45
Gosforth Pk. Vs. NE13: W Op 7E 34
Gosforth Pk. Way NE12: Longb 5H 45
Gosforth St. NE2: Newc T 3J 5 (7H 63)
(not continuous)
NE10: Fell 5B 84
Gosforth Swimming Pool 6E 44
Gosforth Ter. NE3: Gos 7G 45
NE10: Pel 5D 84
Gosport Way NE24: News 5H 23
Gossington NE38: Wash 3A 116
Goswick Av. NE7: H Hea 3K 63
Goswick Dr. NE3: Fawd 4B 44
Goswick Way SR7: S'hm 2A 148
Gourock Sq. SR4: Sund 5G 117
Gowanburn NE23: Cra 7J 25
NE38: Wash 6K 115
Gowan Ct. *NE32: Jar* 5B 66
(off Walter St.)
Gowan Ter. NE2: Jes 4H 63
Gower Wlk. NE8: Gate 6A 84
Gowland Av. NE4: Fen 7A 62
Gowland Sq. SR7: Mur 7D 146
Gowland Ter. DH6: Whe H 2C 180
Grace Ct. DH9: Ann P 6J 123
NE33: S Shi 5J 67
Gracefield Cl. NE5: Cha P 2D 60
Grace Gdns. NE28: W'snd 1E 64
Grace Ho. NE29: N Shi 2E 66
Grace St. NE6: Byke 7A 64
NE6: Byke, Walk 7B 64
NE11: Dun 6B 82
Gradys Yd. NE15: Thro 2H 59
Grafton Cl. NE6: Byke 3P 5 (7K 63)
Grafton Ho. NE6: Byke 3N 5 (7K 63)
Grafton Pl. NE6: Byke 3P 5 (7K 63)
Grafton Rd. NE26: Whit B 7J 39
Grafton St. NE6: Byke 3P 5 (7K 63)
SR4: Sund 1D 118
Gragareth Way NE37: Wash 2E 114
Graham Av. NE16: Whi 6G 81
Graham Ct. DH7: Sac 7E 140
Graham Pk. Rd. NE3: Gos 2E 62
Graham Rd. NE31: Heb 1H 85
Grahamsley St. NE8: Gate 10J 5 (4H 83)
Graham Sports Centre, The
(University of Durham) 5D 166
Graham St. NE33: S Shi 3K 67
Graham Ter. DH6: H Pitt 6B 156
SR7: Mur 7F 147
Graham Way, The SR7: Dalt D, S'hm 4H 147
Grainger, The NE8: Gate 4D 82
Grainger Arc. NE1: Newc T 5E 4 (1F 83)
Grainger Mkt. NE1: Newc T 5E 4 (1F 83)
Grainger Pk. Rd. NE4: Benw 2B 82
Grainger St. NE1: Newc T 7E 4 (2F 83)
Graingerville Nth. *NE4: Fen* 1C 82
(off Westgate Rd.)
Graingerville Sth. *NE4: Elsw* 1C 82
(off Westgate Rd.)
Grampian Av. DH2: Ches S 7K 127
Grampian Cl. NE29: N Shi 3F 49
Grampian Ct. DH9: Ann P 6J 123
Grampian Dr. SR8: Pet 7K 171
Grampian Gdns. NE11: Lob H 1D 98
Grampian Gro. NE36: W Bol 7H 87
Grampian Pl. NE12: Longb 3K 45
Granaries, The NE39: H Spen 3D 94
Granary, The DH4: Hou S 2B 144
Granary Ct. DH8: Cons 5K 121
Granby Cl. NE16: Sun 4H 97
SR3: Sund 5D 118
Granby Ter. NE16: Sun 5H 97
TS28: Win 4G 181
Grand Pde. NE30: Cull, Tyne 2J 49

Grandstand, The NE61: Mor 2D 14
Grandstand Rd. NE2: Gos, Newc T 5B 62
Grand Vw. DH6: S'burn 5K 167
Grange, The DH9: Tan L 1C 124
NE22: Nedd 1C 20
NE23: Seg .7D 26
NE25: Monks 7C 38
NE36: E Bol 7K 87
Grange Av. DH4: Hou S 1A 144
NE12: Longb 6C 46
NE22: Bed .5C 18
NE27: Shir 7K 37
SR8: Eas .1K 171
Grange Cl. NE24: News 5H 23
NE25: Monks 7D 38
NE28: W'snd 3G 65
NE30: Cull .2H 49
SR8: Pet 4A 172
Grange Ct. DH1: Carr 6H 155
DH2: Gra V 4D 126
DH6: Shot C 6F 171
NE10: Hew .6E 84
NE40: Ryton 2G 79
NE42: Pru .4F 77
NE61: Mor .1G 15
Grange Cres. NE10: Hew 7E 84
NE40: Ryton 2G 79
SR2: Sund 6J 7 (3F 119)
Grange Dr. NE40: Ryton 2G 79
Grange Est. NE11: Kib 2E 112
Grange Farm DH1: H Shin 1F 177
DH8: M'sly 7K 107
Grange Farm Dr. NE16: Whi 2G 97
Grange La. NE16: Whi 2G 97
Grange Lonnen NE40: Ryton 1F 79
Grange Mnr. NE16: Whi 2H 97
Grangemere Cl. SR2: Sund 7G 119
Grange Nook NE16: Whi 2G 97
GRANGE PARK 5C 18
Grange Pk. NE25: Monks 1C 48
Grange Pk. Av. NE22: Bed 5B 18
SR5: S'wck 4E 104
Grange Pk. Cres. DH6: Bowb 5J 177
Grange Pl. NE32: Jar 6B 66
Grange Rd. DH1: Carr 7G 155
(not continuous)
DH9: Stly .3D 124
NE3: Gos 5E 44
NE4: Fen 7J 61
NE10: Hew .7E 84
NE15: Newb 5J 59
NE20: Pon .4J 31
NE32: Jar .6B 66
NE40: Ryton 1G 79
NE61: Mor .1G 15
SR5: Sund .7G 103
Grange Rd. W. NE32: Jar 6A 66
Grangeside Ct. *NE29: N Shi 3F 49*
(off Brabourne Gdns.)
Grange St. DH2: Pelt 2G 127
DH8: Cons 2K 135
Grange St. Sth. SR2: Sund 6H 119
Grange Ter. DH2: P Fel 5F 127
DH6: Shot C 5E 170
DH8: M'sly 7K 107
NE9: Low F .6J 83
NE11: Kib .2E 112
NE36: E Bol 7K 87
NE42: Pru .4F 77
SR2: Sund 6H 7 (3E 118)
SR5: S'wck 5D 104
GRANGETOWN 6H 119
Grange Vw. DH4: Nbot 6D 130
DH5: E Rain 5D 144
NE40: Ryton 2G 79
SR5: S'wck 4E 104
GRANGE VILLA 4C 126
Grange Villa Rd. DH2: Gra V, Newf 4D 126
Grange Vs. NE28: W'snd 3G 65
Grange Wlk. NE16: Whi 2G 97
Grange Way DH6: Bowb 3G 177
Grangeway NE29: N Shi 3F 49
Grangewood Cl. DH4: S Row 4A 130
Grangewood Ct. DH4: S Row 3A 130
Grantham Av. SR7: S'hm 4K 147
Grantham Dr. NE9: Low F 3G 99
Grantham Pl. NE23: Cra 6J 25
(not continuous)
Grantham Rd. NE2: Newc T 2J 5 (6H 63)
SR6: Roker 5G 105
Grantham St. NE24: Bly 3K 23
Grants Cres. SR7: S'hm 3A 148
Grant St. NE32: Jar 6A 66
SR8: Hord .5E 172
Granville Av. DH9: Ann P 5K 123
NE12: Longb 3C 46
NE26: Sea S 5D 28
Granville Ct. NE2: Jes 1H 5 (5G 63)
Granville Cres. NE12: Longb 5C 46
Granville Dr. DH4: S Row 4C 130
NE5: Cha P .2D 60
NE12: Longb 5C 46
Granville Gdns. NE2: Jes 5J 63
NE62: Stake 7J 11
Granville Lodge NE12: Longb 4C 46
Granville Rd. NE2: Jes 1J 5 (5H 63)
NE3: Gos 5F 45
SR8: Pet 7D 172
Granville St. NE8: Gate 5H 83
SR4: Sund .1D 118
Granville Ter. DH6: Whe H 2B 180
Grape La. DH1: Dur 3B 6 (3A 166)
(not continuous)
Grasmere DH3: Bir 6C 114
SR6: Clead 5C 88
Grasmere Av. DH5: Eas L 3J 157
NE6: Walk .1C 84
NE10: Pel .6D 84
NE15: Newb 6J 59
NE32: Jar .3D 86
Grasmere Ct. NE12: Kil 1A 46
NE15: Newb 6J 59
Grasmere Cres. DH4: S Row 3B 130
NE21: Winl .6B 80
NE26: Whit B 4F 39
SR5: Ful 4E 104
Grasmere Gdns. NE34: S Shi 7A 68
NE38: Wash 4J 115
Grasmere Ho. NE6: Walk 1C 84
Grasmere M. DH8: Lead 5B 122
Grasmere Pl. NE3: Gos 5E 44
Grasmere Rd. DH2: Ches S 1K 141
NE16: Whi .7J 81
NE28: W'snd 4E 64
NE31: Heb .1K 85
SR8: Pet 5C 172
Grasmere St. NE8: Gate 5G 83
Grasmere St. W. NE8: Gate 5G 83
Grasmere Ter. DH6: S Het 4D 158
DH9: Stly .5D 124
NE29: N Shi 6F 49
NE38: Wash 4J 115
NE64: Newb S 3H 13
SR7: Mur .1F 159
Grasmere Way NE24: Cow 1E 22
Grasmoor Pl. NE15: Lem 6B 60
Grassbanks NE10: Hew 1F 101
Grassdale DH1: Carr 1H 167
Grassholme Cl. DH8: Cons 1J 135
Grassholm Mdws. SR3: Sund 6D 118
Grassholm Pl. NE12: Longb 5J 45
Grassington Dr. NE23: Cra 6J 25
Grasslees NE38: Wash 1D 128
GRASSWELL .7D 130
Grasswell Cvn. Pk.
DH4: Hou S 7D 130
Grasswell Dr. NE5: Ken 2K 61
Grasswell Ter. DH4: Hou S 7D 130
Gravel Walks DH5: Hou S 1E 144
Gravesend Rd. SR4: Sund 6H 117
Gravesend Sq. SR4: Sund 6J 117
Gray Av. DH1: Dur 6K 153
DH2: Ches S 7K 127
DH6: S'burn 2K 167
NE13: W Op 4E 34
SR7: Mur 7E 146
TS27: Hes .4D 182
Gray Ct. SR2: Sund 7K 7 (4F 119)
SR8: Eas C 7B 160
Graylands NE38: Wash 1C 128
Grayling Ct. SR3: Dox P 4J 131
Grayling Rd. NE11: Fest P 7D 82
Gray Rd. SR2: Sund 7K 7 (4F 119)
SR7: Mur 7F 147
Grays Cross *SR1: Sund 1G 119*
(off High St. E.)
Gray Sq. TS28: Win 5G 181
Grays Ter. DH1: Dur 3J 165
NE35: Bol C 5E 86
Graystones NE10: Hew 7F 85
Gray St. DH8: Cons 6G 121
NE24: Bly .7J 19
NE32: Jar .6C 66
Gray's Wlk. NE34: S Shi 4G 87
Gray Ter. DH9: Ann P 4C 124
Graythwaite DH2: Ches S 6H 127
Gray Towers SR2: Sund 7K 7 (4F 119)
GREAT EPPLETON 5K 145
Greathead St. NE33: S Shi 6H 67
Gt. Lime Rd.
NE12: Dud, Gos, Kil, Longb 1J 45
(not continuous)
Great Lime Rd. NE23: Kil 7J 35
GREAT LUMLEY 3E 142
Great North Mus: Hancock
. . . . .2F 4 (6F 63)
Great Nth. Rd. DH1: Dur 5J 153
(Bridgemere Dr.)
DH1: Dur .2H 165
(Toll Ho. Rd.)
NE2: Gos, Newc T 1F 4 (2F 63)
NE3: Gos 3E 44
NE13: W Op 5E 34
NE61: Tra W 6G 15
Great Pk. NE13: W Op 1C 44
Great Pk. Way
NE13: Haz, W Op 1B 44
Grebe Cl. NE11: Dun 4C 82
NE24: News 4J 23
NE63: Ash .6C 12
Grebe Ct. NE2: Jes 4H 63
Greely Rd. NE5: West 3F 61
Green, The DH1: H Shin 1F 177
DH2: Ches S 6K 127
DH2: Nett .6H 141
DH5: Hou S 1F 145
DH6: Hett .7C 176
DH6: Thor .2J 179
DH8: Cons .7H 121
NE3: Ken 2B 62
NE10: Fell .6C 84
NE11: Kib .2F 113
NE15: Walb 4K 59
NE17: C'wl 7K 93
NE20: Pon .3K 31
NE25: Monks 5E 38
NE28: W'snd 3F 65
NE38: Wash 2J 115
NE39: Row G 5G 95
NE42: Oving 2J 75
Green, The NE46: Acomb 4C 50
SR5: S'wck 6C 104
SR7: Hawt .4K 159
SR8: Pet 1J 181
Greenacre Pk. NE9: Low F 4H 99
Green Acres NE61: Mor 1E 14
Greenacres DH2: Pelt 2F 127
NE20: Darr H 2G 41
Greenacres Cl. NE12: Kil 7C 36
NE40: Craw 3E 78
Greenacres Rd. DH8: B'hill 4F 121
Green Av. DH4: Nbot 5D 130
Green Bank NE46: Hex 2E 70
Greenbank NE21: Blay 4C 80
NE32: Jar .6B 66
Greenbank Dr. SR4: Sund 3G 117
Greenbank St. DH3: Ches S 5B 128
Greenbank Ter. DH3: Ches S 5A 128
Greenbank Vs. NE32: Jar 7B 66
Greenbourne Gdns. NE10: Wind N 7A 84
Green Cl. NE25: Monks 7D 38
NE30: Cull .3H 49
Green Ct. DH1: Dur 2D 166
DH7: Esh .7F 151
Green Cres. NE23: Dud 3H 35
GREENCROFT 6J 123
Greencroft DH6: S Het 4C 158
NE63: Ash .5A 12
Greencroft Av. NE6: Walk 5E 64
NE45: Corb 7E 52
Greencroft Ind. Est. DH9: Ann P 7J 123
Greencroft Ind. Pk. DH9: Ann P 7J 123
GREENCROFT PARK 2J 137
Greencroft Parkway DH9: Ann P 1J 137
Greencroft Rd. DH8: Cons 2A 136
Greencroft Ter. DH9: Ann P 6H 123
Greendale Cl. NE24: Cow 1E 22
Greendale Gdns. DH5: Hett H 1F 157
Green Dr. SR7: S'hm 5B 148
Greendyke Ct. NE5: West 7G 43
Greener Ct. NE42: Pru 5D 76
Greener Rd. SR4: Sund 1C 118
GREENESFIELD 9G 4 (3G 83)
Greenesfield Bus. Cen.
NE8: Gate 10G 4 (3G 83)
Greenfield Av. NE5: West 3G 61
Greenfield Dr. NE62: Chop 2G 17
Greenfield Pl. NE4: Newc T 6C 4 (1E 82)
NE40: Ryton 1G 79
Greenfield Rd. NE3: Gos 2D 44
Greenfields DH2: Ous 6J 113
NE40: Ryton 1F 79
Greenfield Ter. DH9: Ann P 5K 123
NE10: Pel .5D 84
Greenfield Way DH3: Bir 2B 114
Greenfinch Cl. NE38: Wash 5D 114
Greenfinch Rd. DH5: Eas L 2J 157
Greenfinch Way NE15: Lem 1D 80
Greenford NE11: Kib 2F 113
Greenford La. DH2: Bir, Kib 2H 113
NE11: Lame 7G 99
Greenford Rd. NE6: Walk 3D 84
Green Gro. NE40: G'sde 3F 79
Greenhall Vw. NE5: Fen 3A 62
Greenhaugh NE12: Longb 3K 45
Greenhaugh Rd. NE25: Well 6B 38
Greenhead NE38: Wash 4D 114
Greenhead Rd. NE17: C'wl 4J 93
Greenhead Ter. NE17: C'wl 5K 93
Greenhill SR7: Mur 7F 147
Greenhills DH9: Stly 6E 124
NE12: Kil 6A 36
Greenhills Est. TS28: Win 4G 181
Greenhills Ter. DH6: Whe H 2B 180
Greenhill Vw. NE5: Fen 3A 62
Green Hill Wlk. NE34: S Shi 7E 68
Greenholme Cl. NE23: Cra 1K 25
Greenhouse, The DH9: Ann P 7K 123
Greenhow Cl. SR2: Ryh 4H 133
Greenland Rd. DH7: Esh, Queb 7C 150
Greenlands DH9: Stly 5D 124
NE32: Jar .4C 86
Greenlands Ct. NE25: Sea D 6H 27
Green La. DH1: Dur 2D 166
(McNally Pl.)
DH1: Dur .3C 166
(Old Elvet)
DH1: S Hou 3J 167
DH6: Has, Litt 7G 157
DH7: B'hpe, Stly 2E 138
NE10: Fell .5A 84
(not continuous)
NE10: Pel .5E 84
NE12: Kil 7C 36
NE13: Wool 4F 43
NE23: Dud .3H 35
NE34: S Shi 2G 87
NE36: E Bol 1K 103
NE61: Lngh 3J 9
NE61: Mor .1H 15
(Charlton Gdns.)
NE61: Mor .7H 9
(Salisbury St.)
NE63: Ash .4K 11
SR7: Seat .4A 146
TS29: Trim S 5K 179
Green La. Gdns. NE10: Fell 4A 84
Green La. Ind. Est. NE10: Pel 6E 84
Greenlaw NE5: W Dent 5E 60
Greenlaw Rd. NE23: Cra 7J 25
Green Lea DH7: Wit G 2D 152
Greenlea NE29: N Shi 3B 48
Greenlea Cl. NE39: H Spen 4E 94
SR4: Sund .5J 117
Greenlee NE63: Ash 5C 12
Greenlee Dr. NE7: H Hea 2B 64
Greenmount DH4: Hou S 1B 144
Greenock Cl. NE24: Bly 4K 23
Greenock Rd. SR4: Sund 6H 117
Green Pk. NE28: W'snd 2C 64
Greenrigg NE21: Blay 5D 80
(not continuous)
NE26: Sea S 4C 28
Greenrigg Gdns. SR3: Sund 5D 118
Greenrigg Pl. NE27: Shir 7K 37
Greenriggs Av. NE3: Gos 3F 45
Greenrising NE42: Oving 2K 75
Green's Bank DH9: W Pelt 2C 126
Greenshields Rd. SR4: Sund 6H 117
Greenshields Sq. SR4: Sund 6H 117
GREENSIDE 5D 78
Greenside NE34: S Shi 7D 68
NE63: Ash .3A 12
Greenside Av. NE13: Bru V 5C 34
NE28: W'snd 2K 65
SR8: Hord .5D 172
Greenside Ct. SR3: Sund 6J 117
Greenside Cres. NE15: Den M 6G 61
Greenside Drift NE33: S Shi 3B 68
Greenside Rd. NE40: Craw 3C 78
NE40: G'sde 4D 78
Green's Pl. NE33: S Shi 1J 67
Green Sq. NE25: Monks 7D 38
Green St. DH8: Cons 6H 121
DH8: Lead .5A 122
DH8: Shot B 2E 120
SR1: Sund 3J 7 (1F 119)
SR7: S'hm .3B 148
Green Ter. SR1: Sund 4H 7 (2E 118)
Green Tree Ct. *NE15: Benw 7H 61*
(off Beamish Pl.)
Greentree La. DH9: Ann P 4J 123
Greentree Sq. NE5: Den M 3H 61
Greenvale Av. NE5: Den M 3G 61
Greenway NE4: Fen 5K 61
NE5: Cha P .1C 60
NE25: Monks 7D 38
Greenway, The SR4: Sund 4J 117
Greenway Ct. DH8: Cons 2A 136
Greenways DH8: Cons 3A 136
Greenwell Cl. NE21: Winl 5A 80
Greenwell Dr. NE42: Pru 2F 77
Greenwell Pk. DH7: Lan 7K 137
Greenwell Ter. NE40: Craw 2C 78
Greenwood NE12: Kil 1D 46
Greenwood Av. DH4: Hou S 2C 144
DH7: B'hpe 6D 138
NE6: Walk .4E 64
NE22: Bed .5B 18
Greenwood Cl. DH6: Whe H 2C 180
NE38: Wash 5K 115
Greenwood Cotts. DH6: Thor 1J 179
Greenwood Gdns. NE10: Fell 5B 84
NE11: Lob H 2C 98
Greenwood Rd. SR4: Sund 5H 117
Greenwood Sq. SR4: Sund 6H 117
Greetlands Rd. SR2: Sund 6E 118
Gregory Rd. SR4: Sund 6H 117
Gregory Ter. DH4: Hou S 1A 144
Gregson St. DH7: Sac 7E 140
NE15: Scot .2G 81
Gregson Ter. DH6: S Het 5D 158
SR7: S'hm .1H 147
Gregson Ter. W. SR7: S'hm 2H 147
Grenaby Way SR7: Mur 7G 147
Grenada Cl. NE26: Whit B 3F 39
Grenada Dr. NE26: Whit B 3F 39
Grenada Pl. NE26: Whit B 3F 39
Grenfell Sq. SR4: Sund 6H 117
Grenville Ct. NE20: Darr H 7E 30
NE23: Cra .5J 25
Grenville Dr. NE3: Gos 3D 44
Grenville Ter. NE1: Newc T 6J 5 (1H 83)
Grenville Way NE26: Whit B 4E 38
Gresford St. NE33: S Shi 7J 67
Gresham Cl. NE23: Cra 6K 25
Gresley Rd. SR8: Pet 6J 171
Greta Av. DH4: Pen 3A 130
Greta Gdns. NE33: S Shi 5K 67
Greta Pl. DH7: Lan 7K 137
Greta St. Nth. DH2: Pelt 3E 126
Greta St. Sth. DH2: Pelt 3E 126
Greta Ter. SR4: Sund 3C 118
Gretna Dr. NE32: Jar 4F 87
Gretna Rd. NE15: Benw 6H 61
Gretna Ter. NE10: Fell 6A 84
Gretton Pl. NE7: H Hea 2J 63
Greville Gdns. NE13: Haz 2B 44
Grey Av. NE23: Cra 7J 25
Greybourne Gdns. SR2: Sund 6E 118
Greyfriars La. NE12: Longb 6J 45
Grey Gables DH7: B'don 1E 174
Grey Lady Wlk. NE42: Pru 3F 77
Greylingstadt Ter. DH9: Stly 6G 125
Grey Pl. *NE61: Mor 7G 9*
(off Jackson Ter.)
Grey Ridges DH7: B'don 1E 174
Grey's Ct. NE1: Newc T 6F 4 (1F 83)
Greystead Cl. NE5: Cha P 2D 60
Greystead Rd. NE25: Well 6B 38
Greystoke Av. NE2: Newc T 1L 5 (6J 63)
NE16: Whi .1H 97
SR2: Sund .6E 118
Greystoke Gdns. NE2: Newc T 1L 5 (5J 63)
NE9: Low F 5K 99
NE16: Whi .2H 97
NE61: Mor 6F 9
(off Howard Ter.)
SR2: Sund .5E 118
Greystoke Pk. NE3: Gos 4D 44

Greystoke Pl. NE23: Cra 7J 25
(not continuous)
Greystoke Wlk. NE16: Whi 2G 97
Greystone Pl. SR5: S'wck 5C 104
Greystones DH6: Ludw 5J 169
Grey St. DH4: Hou S 1D 144
NE1: Newc T 5F 4 (1F 83)
NE13: Bru V 5C 34
NE28: W'snd 3G 65
NE30: N Shi 6H 49
Grey Ter. SR2: Ryh 3H 133
Greywood Av. NE4: Fen 6A 62
Grieves Bldgs. DH4: New H 3C 130
Grieves' Row NE23: Dud 2J 35
Grieve's Stairs *NE29: N Shi 7H 49*
(off Bedford St.)
Grieve St. NE24: Bly 7H 19
Griffiths Ct. DH6: Bowb 3H 177
Griffith Ter. NE27: Shir 3H 47
Grimsby St. NE24: Bly 3J 23
Grindleford Ct. NE34: S Shi 1A 88
GRINDON 5H 117
Grindon Av. SR4: Sund 3H 117
Grindon Cl. NE23: Cra 7J 25
NE25: Monks 2E 48
Grindon Ct. SR4: Sund 5J 117
Grindon Gdns. SR4: Sund 5J 117
Grindon La. SR3: Sund 5J 117
SR4: Sund 5J 117
(Grindon Pk.)
SR4: Sund 3H 117
(Rowan Cl.)
Grindon Pk. SR4: Sund 5J 117
Grindon Ter. SR4: Sund 3C 118
Grinstead Cl. NE34: S Shi 6B 68
Grinstead Way DH1: Carr 6H 155
Grisedale Gdns. NE9: Low F 3J 99
Grisedale Rd. SR8: Pet 6C 172
Grizedale NE37: Wash 2F 115
Grizedale Ct. SR6: Seab 1E 104
Groat Mkt. NE1: Newc T 6F 4 (1F 83)
Grosmont DH3: Gt Lum 2E 142
Grosvenor Av. NE2: Jes 4H 63
NE16: Swa 6H 81
Grosvenor Casino
Newcastle 8C 4 (2E 82)
Grosvenor Cl. NE23: Cra 7J 25
Grosvenor Ct. NE5: Cha P 2D 60
Grosvenor Cres. NE31: Heb 2K 85
Grosvenor Dr. NE26: Whit B 7G 39
NE34: S Shi 5B 68
SR6: Clead 5A 88
Grosvenor Gdns. NE2: Jes 5J 63
NE28: W'snd 2A 66
NE34: S Shi 7B 68
Grosvenor M. NE29: N Shi 6G 49
NE33: S Shi 5A 68
Grosvenor Pl. NE2: Jes 4G 63
NE24: Cow 3D 22
NE29: N Shi 6G 49
Grosvenor Rd. NE2: Jes 4H 63
NE33: S Shi 5A 68
Grosvenor St. SR5: S'wck 5B 104
Grosvenor Ter. DH8: Cons 6J 121
Grosvenor Vs. NE2: Jes 4G 63
Grosvenor Way NE5: Cha P 3D 60
Grotto Gdns. NE34: S Shi 6F 69
Grotto Rd. NE34: S Shi 7F 69
Grousemoor DH6: Has 1B 170
NE37: Wash 1E 114
Grousemoor Dr. NE63: Ash 5A 12
GROVE, THE 1E 134
Grove, The DH1: Dur 1J 165
DH5: Hou S 4D 144
DH7: B'hpe 6D 138
NE2: Jes 3H 63
NE3: Gos 1F 63
NE5: W Dent 4D 60
NE12: Longb 6B 46
NE16: Whi 1J 97
NE20: Pon 6H 31
NE25: Monks 7F 39
NE32: Jar 5B 86
NE39: Row G 6K 95
NE43: B'ley 4J 91
NE61: Mor 6F 9
SR2: Ryh 2H 133
SR2: Sund 7J 7 (4F 119)
SR5: Sund 6H 103
SR8: Eas 7J 159
TS27: B Col 2H 183
(off Hesleden Rd.)
Grove Av. NE3: Gos 1F 63
Grove Cotts. DH3: Bir 4A 114
NE40: Craw 2D 78
Grove Ct. DH6: Hett 7C 176
DH6: Shot C 7E 170
Grove Ho. Dr. DH1: Dur 2C 166
Grove Ind. Est., The
DH8: C'sde 1F 135
Grove Pk. Av. NE3: Gos 1F 63
Grove Pk. Cres. NE3: Gos 1F 63
Grove Pk. Oval *NE3: Gos 1F 63*
(off Grove Pk. Cres.)
Grove Pk. Sq. NE3: Gos 1F 63
Grove Rd. DH7: B'don 2C 174
NE9: Low F 1J 99
NE15: Walb 4K 59
Grove Rd. Shop. Units
DH7: B'don 2D 174
Grove St. DH1: Dur 4A 6 (3K 165)
Grove Ter. DH7: Lang M 6G 165
NE16: Burn 2B 110
NE16: Marl H 6J 97
Grove Vw. DH3: Bir 3B 114
Guardian Ct. *NE26: Whit B 7J 39*
(off Rockcliffe Av.)
Guardians Ct. NE20: Pon 4K 31
Guardswood Cl. NE42: Pru 6G 77
Gubeon Wood NE61: Tra W 6B 14
Guelder Rd. NE7: H Hea 2A 64
Guernsey Rd. SR4: Sund 6H 117
Guernsey Sq. SR4: Sund 6H 117
Guessburn NE43: Stoc 7G 75
GUIDE POST 1H 17
Guildford Pl. NE6: Heat 2P 5 (6K 63)
Guildford St. SR2: Sund 4G 119
Guillemot Cl. NE24: News 4J 23
Guillemot Row NE12: Kil 7A 36
Guisborough Dr.
NE29: N Shi 4B 48
Guisborough St. SR4: Sund 3B 118
Gullane NE37: Wash 4H 101
Gullane Cl. DH9: Stly 3H 125
NE10: Bill Q 4G 85
Gully Rd. TS28: Win 5G 181
Gunnerston Gro. NE3: Ken 7K 43
Gunnerton Cl. NE23: Cra 7K 25
Gunnerton Pl. NE29: N Shi 6D 48
Gunn St. NE11: Dun 6B 82
Gut Rd. NE28: W'snd 3K 65
Guyzance Av. NE3: Gos 6C 44
Gym Newcastle East, The 2A 64
Gypsies Green Sports Ground
3B 68

H

Habgood Dr. DH1: Dur 3E 166
Hackwood Glade NE46: Hex 3D 70
Hackwood Pk. NE46: Hex 3D 70
Hackworth Gdns. NE41: Wylam 7K 57
Hackworth Rd. SR8: Eas, Pet 3H 171
TS27: B Col 1H 183
Hackworth Way NE29: N Shi 2F 67
Haddington Rd. NE25: Monks 4C 38
Haddon Cl. NE25: Monks 6B 38
Haddon Grn. NE25: Monks 6B 38
Haddon Rd. SR2: Sund 6H 119
Haddricks Mill Ct. NE3: Gos 1G 63
Haddricks Mill Rd. NE3: Gos 1G 63
Hadleigh Ct. DH4: S Row 3B 130
Hadleigh Rd. SR4: Sund 3K 117
Hadrian Av. DH3: Ches S 4B 128
Hadrian Ct. NE12: Kil 1C 46
NE15: Lem 5E 60
NE20: Darr H 3F 41
TS28: Win 7G 181
Hadrian Dr. NE21: Blay 1A 80
Hadrian Gdns. NE21: Blay 5D 80
Hadrian Ho. NE1: Newc T 4G 4
NE15: Thro 3H 59
Hadrian Lodge NE34: S Shi 1F 87
Hadrian M. NE62: Chop 2G 17
Hadrian Pl. NE9: Low F 7J 83
NE15: Thro 3H 59
Hadrian Rd. NE4: Fen 6K 61
NE24: News 6G 23
NE28: W'snd 4G 65
NE32: Jar 3D 86
(not continuous)
Hadrian Road Station (Metro) 4J 65
Hadrians Ct. NE11: T Vall 3F 99
Hadrian's Leisure Cen. 3H 65
Hadrian Sq. NE6: Byke 3P 5 (7A 64)
Hadrian St. SR4: Sund 1C 118
Hadrians Way DH8: Ebc 5G 107
Hadrian Way NE28: W'snd 4J 65
Hadrian Wynd NE28: W'snd 5J 47
Hadstone Pl. NE5: Fen 4J 61
Hagan Hall NE32: Jar 5C 86
Hagg Bank NE41: Wylam 1H 77
Haggerston Cl. NE5: Blak 1H 61
Haggerston Ct. NE5: Blak 1H 61
Haggerston Cres. NE5: Blak 2H 61
Haggerstone Dr. SR5: Sund 6G 103
Haggerstone M. NE21: Blay 5C 80
Haggerston Rd. NE24: Cow 3E 22
Haggerston Ter. NE32: Jar 2E 86
Haggie Av. NE28: W'snd 2H 65
Haggs La. NE11: Kib, Lame 7C 98
Hahnemann Ct. SR5: S'wck 5D 104
Haig Av. NE25: Monks 7C 38
Haig Cres. DH1: Dur 3E 166
NE15: Scot 1G 81
Haigh Ter. DH1: Dur 3E 166
NE9: Eigh B 6A 100
Haig Rd. NE22: Bed 1K 21
Haig St. NE11: Dun 6B 82
Hailsham Av. NE12: Longb 5A 46
Hailsham Pl. SR8: Pet 6B 172
Hainford Cl. SR4: Sund 3J 117
HAINING 6H 131
Haining Ct. NE46: Hex 2D 70
Haining Cft. NE46: Hex 2C 70
Haining Cft. Ho. *NE46: Hex 2C 70*
(off Haining Cft.)
Haininghead NE38: Wash 6J 115
Hainingwood Ter.
NE10: Bill Q 4F 85
Halcyon Pl. NE9: Low F 7K 83
Haldane Ct. NE2: Jes 5G 63
Haldane St. NE63: Ash 3A 12
Haldane Ter. NE2: Jes 5G 63
Haldon Pl. SR8: Pet 7K 171
Hale Ri. SR8: Pet 6C 172
Halesworth Dr. SR4: Sund 3J 117
Halewood Av. NE3: Ken 7A 44
Half Flds. Rd. NE21: Winl 5B 80
Half Moon La. NE8: Gate 9H 5 (3G 83)
(Hudson St.)
NE8: Gate 10H 5 (3G 83)
(Mulgrave Ter.)
NE30: Tyne 5K 49
(off Front St.)
Half Moon St. NE62: Stake 7K 11
Half Moon Yd. NE1: Newc T 6F 4 (1F 83)
Halidon Rd. SR2: Sund 7F 119
Halidon Sq. SR2: Sund 7F 119
Halifax Ct. NE11: Dun 5A 82
Halifax Pl. NE11: Dun 5A 82
SR2: Ryh 3H 133
Halifax Rd. NE11: Dun 5A 82
Halkirk Way NE23: Cra 1J 25
Hallam Rd. SR8: Pet 5B 172
Hall Av. DH7: Ush M 2B 164
NE4: Fen 7A 62
Hall Cl. DH4: W Rai 1A 156
SR7: Seat 1F 147
TS27: B Col 2H 183
Hall Cres. SR8: Hord 3D 172
Hall Dene Way SR7: Seat 1G 147
Hall Dr. NE12: Kil 6A 36
Halleypike Cl. NE7: H Hea 2B 64
Hall Farm DH1: Shin 6D 166
Hall Farm Cl. NE43: Stoc 6H 75
Hall Farm Rd. SR3: Dox P 4B 132
Hallfield Cl. SR3: Dox P 4C 132
Hallfield Dr. SR8: Eas 1J 171
Hall Gdns. DH6: S'burn 3A 168
NE10: Wind N 7B 84
NE36: W Bol 7G 87
HALLGARTH 7B 156
Hall Gth. NE3: Gos 4E 44
Hallgarth DH8: C'sde, Cons 1E 134
NE10: Hew 7E 84
(not continuous)
Hallgarth, The DH1: Dur 5E 6 (4B 166)
Hallgarth Bungs. DH5: Hett H 1G 157
Hallgarth Cl. NE45: Corb 7E 52
Hallgarth Ct. SR6: Roker 6H 105
Hallgarth Ho. NE33: S Shi 5J 67
Hallgarth La. DH6: H Pitt 7B 156
Hallgarth Mnr. Farm DH6: H Pitt 7B 156
Hallgarth Rd. NE21: Winl 4B 80
Hallgarth St. DH1: Dur 4D 6 (3B 166)
DH6: S'burn 3K 167
Hallgarth Ter. DH7: Lan 7K 137
Hallgarth Vw. DH1: Dur 5E 6 (4B 166)
DH6: H Pitt 6C 156
Hallgarth Vs. DH6: S'burn 3A 168
Hallgate NE46: Hex 1D 70
Hall Grn. NE24: Cow 2F 23
Hall Grn. Mnr. NE36: W Bol 1G 103
Halliday Gro. DH7: Lang M 7F 165
Halling Cl. NE6: Walk 2E 84
Hallington Dr. NE25: Sea D 7H 27
Hallington M. NE12: Kil 1A 46
Halliwell St. DH4: Hou S 1D 144
Hall La. DH1: Shin 7D 166
DH4: W Rai 1A 156
DH5: Hou S 2E 144
DH6: Has 1B 170
Hallorchard Rd. NE46: Hex 1D 70
Hallow Dr. NE15: Thro 4G 59
Hall Pk. NE21: Blay 2A 80
Hall Rd. DH7: Esh 7F 151
DH8: C'sde 7E 120
NE17: C'wl 6A 94
NE31: Heb 1J 85
NE37: Wash 7J 101
Hall Rd. Bungs. NE17: C'wl 5K 93
Hallside Rd. NE24: Cow 3F 23
Hallstile Bank NE46: Hex 1D 70
Hallstile Cotts. NE46: Hex 1D 70
Hall St. DH6: S Het 4B 158
Hall Ter. NE10: Bill Q 4F 85
NE24: Bly 1J 23
Hall Vw. SR6: Whit 6H 89
Hall Wlk. SR8: Eas 7J 159
Hall Walks SR8: Eas 7H 159
Hallwood Cl. NE22: Nedd 1C 20
Halstead Pl. NE33: S Shi 3K 67
(not continuous)
Halstead Sq. SR4: Sund 3K 117
Halterburn Cl. NE3: Gos 1C 62
HALTON 1F 53
Halton Castle (remains of) 1F 53
Halton Cl. NE43: Pains 1K 91
Halton Dr. NE13: W Op 5D 34
NE27: Back 1H 47
Halton Rd. DH1: Dur 6B 154
Halton Way NE3: Gos 3C 44
Halvergate Cl. SR4: Sund 3J 117
Hamar Cl. NE29: N Shi 1C 66
Hambard Way NE38: Wash 3H 115
Hambledon Av. DH2: Ches S 7K 127
NE30: Cull 1G 49
Hambledon Cl. NE35: Bol C 6E 86
Hambledon Gdns. NE7: H Hea 2J 63
Hambledon Pl. SR8: Pet 7J 171
Hambledon St. NE24: Bly 1H 23
Hambleton Ct. NE63: N Sea 6D 12
Hambleton Dr. SR7: S'hm 2K 147
Hambleton Grn. NE9: Low F 6K 99
Hambleton Rd. NE38: Wash 5F 115
Hamilton Cl. DH7: Esh W 5D 162
Hamilton Ct. DH6: Shot C 6E 170
NE8: Gate 6J 83
SR6: Roker 5H 105
Hamilton Cres. NE4: Newc T 4A 4 (7D 62)
NE29: N Shi 4C 48
Hamilton Dr. NE26: Whit B 3F 39
Hamilton Pl. NE4: Newc T 4A 4 (7D 62)
HAMILTON ROW 6B 162
Hamilton Row DH7: Wat 6B 162
Hamilton Row St. DH7: Wat 6B 162
Hamilton St. SR8: Hord 5D 172
Hamilton Ter. DH7: Sac 4D 140
NE36: W Bol 1G 103
NE61: Mor 7G 9
(off Noble Ter.)
Hamilton Way NE26: Whit B 3F 39
Hammermill La. DH8: Shot B 2A 120
Hammer Sq. Bank DH9: Beam 1A 126
Hammerton Ct. *NE28: W'snd 4E 64*
(off Grasmere Rd.)
Hampden Rd. SR6: Roker 5G 105
Hampden St. NE33: S Shi 5J 67
Hampshire Ct. NE4: Newc T 10A 4 (4C 82)
Hampshire Gdns. NE28: W'snd 1J 65
Hampshire Pl. NE37: Wash 6H 101
SR8: Pet 5K 171
Hampshire Rd. DH1: Carr 1G 167
Hampshire Way NE34: S Shi 6E 68
Hampstead Cl. NE24: News 6G 23
Hampstead Gdns. NE32: Jar 4D 86
Hampstead Rd. NE4: Benw 1A 82
SR4: Sund 4K 117
Hampstead Sq. SR4: Sund 4J 117
Hampton Cl. DH9: Ann P 5J 123
NE23: Cra 3B 26
Hampton Ct. DH3: Ches S 2B 128
NE16: Swa 5H 81
Hampton Dr. NE10: Fell 6A 84
NE25: Monks 7C 38
Hampton Gdns. NE1: Newc T 6E 4
Hampton Rd. NE30: Cull 2F 49
Hamsteels Bank DH7: Queb 5A 150
Hamsteels La. DH7: Queb 5B 150
(Hamsteels Bank)
DH7: Queb 5A 150
(Hedleyhill La.)
HAMSTERLEY 3K 107
Hamsterley Cl. DH3: Gt Lum 3F 143
Hamsterley Ct. SR3: Silk 3C 132
Hamsterley Cres. DH1: Dur 5B 154
NE9: Wrek 4A 100
NE15: Lem 6B 60
Hamsterley Dr. NE12: Kil 7A 36
Hamsterley Gdns. DH9: Ann P 5J 123
HAMSTERLEY MILL 3E 108
Hanby Gdns. SR3: Sund 5C 118
Hancock St. NE2: Newc T 2F 4 (6F 63)
Handel St. NE33: S Shi 3K 67
Handel Ter. DH6: Whe H 3A 180
Handley Cres. DH5: E Rain 6C 144
Handley Cross DH8: M'sly 6A 108
Handley St. SR8: Hord 5D 172
Handy Dr. NE11: Dun 4K 81
Handyside Pl. NE1: Newc T 4E 4 (7F 63)
Hangingstone La. DH9: Ann P 6F 123
Hangmans La. DH5: Hou S 7A 132
SR3: Bur 7A 132
Hanlon Ct. NE32: Jar 5K 65
Hannington Pl. NE6: Byke 3M 5 (7J 63)
Hannington St. NE6: Byke 3M 5 (7J 63)
Hann Ter. NE37: Wash 7K 101
Hanover Cl. NE5: Cha P 3C 60
Hanover Ct. DH1: Dur 3A 6 (3K 165)
(not continuous)
NE9: Low F 5J 99
NE23: Dud 2K 35
Hanover Dr. NE21: Winl 5A 80
Hanover Gdns. *NE28: W'snd 4A 66*
(off Station Rd.)
Hanover Ho. NE32: Jar 2B 86
Hanover Mill NE1: Newc T 8F 4 (2F 83)
Hanover Pl. NE23: Cra 7J 21
SR4: Sund 1F 7 (7D 104)
Hanover Sq. NE1: Newc T 7F 4 (2F 83)
NE21: Winl 5A 80
(off Waterloo St.)
Hanover Stairs NE1: Newc T 8F 4
Hanover St. NE1: Newc T 8F 4 (2F 83)
Hanover Wlk. NE5: Cha P 3C 60
NE21: Winl 6A 80
Ha'Penny Ga. NE22: H Bri 4F 21
Harbord Ter. NE26: Sea D 5K 27
Harbottle Av. NE3: Gos 6C 44
NE27: Shir 2K 47
Harbottle Ct. NE6: Byke 2A 84
Harbottle Cres. NE32: Jar 4B 86
Harbottle St. NE6: Byke 2A 84
Harbour, The DH4: S Row 3B 130
Harbour Lodge SR7: S'hm 1A 148
Harbour Vw. NE22: E Sle 5F 19
NE29: N Shi 7H 49
(off Lit. Bedford St.)
NE33: S Shi 7J 49
SR6: Roker 5H 105
Harbour Wlk. SR7: S'hm 2A 148
Harcourt Pk. NE9: Low F 2J 99
Harcourt Rd. SR2: Sund 7F 119
Harcourt St. NE9: Low F 2J 99
Hardgate Rd. SR2: Sund 7F 119
Hardie Av. NE16: Whi 6G 81
Hardie Dr. NE36: E Bol, W Bol 7G 87
Hardman Cl. NE40: Ryton 1H 79
Hardman Gdns. NE40: Ryton 1H 79
Hardwick Ct. NE8: Gate 2H 83
TS27: B Col 2H 183
(off Middle St.)
Hardwick Pl. NE3: Ken 2C 62
Hardwick Ri. SR6: Roker 7G 105
Hardwick St. SR8: Hord 6E 172
TS27: B Col 2G 183
Hardyards Ct. NE34: S Shi 1J 87
Hardy Av. NE34: S Shi 3H 87

Hardy Ct. NE30: N Shi . . . 6H 49
Hardy Gro. NE28: W'snd . . . 7E 46
Hardy St. SR7: S'hm . . . 3B 148
Hardy Ter. DH9: Ann P . . . 5C 124
Harebell Rd. NE9: Low F . . . 2A 100
Harehills Av. NE5: Ken . . . 2K 61
Harehills Twr. NE3: Ken . . . 2A 62
Hareholme Ct. DH7: New B . . . 3J 163
Harehope Ct. NE25: Sea D . . . 6F 27
HARELAW . . . 3J 123
Harelaw Cl. DH2: Pelt . . . 3F 127
Harelaw Dr. NE63: Ash . . . 6K 11
SR6: Roker . . . 6G 105
Harelaw Gdns. DH9: Ann P . . . 3J 123
Harelaw Gro. NE5: W Dent . . . 4D 60
Harelaw Ind. Est. DH9: Ann P . . . 2J 123
Hares Bldgs. DH2: Newf . . . 4E 126
Hareshaw Rd. NE25: Well . . . 6B 38
Hareside NE23: Cra . . . 5J 25
Hareside Cl. NE15: Newb . . . 5K 59
Hareside Ct. NE15: Newb . . . 5K 59
Hareside Foot Path
NE15: Newb . . . 6K 59
Hareside Wlk. NE15: Newb . . . 5K 59
Harewood Cl. NE16: Whi . . . 3G 97
NE25: Monks . . . 7B 38
Harewood Ct. NE25: Monks . . . 7B 38
Harewood Cres. NE25: Monks . . . 7B 38
Harewood Dr. NE22: Bed . . . 6A 18
Harewood Gdns. NE61: Peg . . . 3A 10
SR3: Sund . . . 5C 118
Harewood Grn. NE9: Low F . . . 5K 99
Harewood Rd. NE3: Gos . . . 6E 44
Hareydene NE5: West . . . 6F 43
Hargill Dr. NE38: Wash . . . 7E 114
Hargrave Ct. NE24: Bly . . . 3G 23
Harland Way NE38: Wash . . . 3H 115
Harlaur Pl. DH5: Hett H . . . 7G 145
Harlebury NE27: Back . . . 6F 37
Harle Cl. DH4: Hou S . . . 7C 130
NE5: W Dent . . . 4E 60
Harle Oval DH6: Bowb . . . 3G 177
Harlequin Lodge NE10: Fell . . . 6B 84
Harle Rd. NE27: Back . . . 1H 47
Harleston Way NE10: Hew . . . 1C 100
Harle St. DH7: Mead . . . 2F 175
NE28: W'snd . . . 3F 65
Harley Ter. DH6: S'burn . . . 2K 167
NE3: Gos . . . 7F 45
Harleyville DH5: Hett H . . . 7G 145
Harlow Av. NE3: Fawd . . . 5B 44
NE27: Back . . . 1H 47
Harlow Cl. NE23: Cra . . . 1K 25
HARLOW GREEN . . . 5J 99
Harlow Grn. La. NE9: Low F . . . 5J 99
Harlow Pl. NE7: H Hea . . . 2K 63
Harlow St. SR4: Sund . . . 2D 118
Harnham Av. NE29: N Shi . . . 7D 48
Harnham Gdns. NE5: Fen . . . 5J 61
Harnham Gro. NE23: Cra . . . 5J 25
Harold Sq. SR2: Sund . . . 3G 119
Harold St. NE32: Jar . . . 6C 66
Harold Wilson Dr. TS27: Hes . . . 4D 182
Harper Bungs. DH6: Whe H . . . 4A 180
(off Bevan Cres.)
HARPERLEY . . . 3A 124
Harperley Dr. SR3: Sund . . . 6D 118
Harperley Gdns. DH9: Ann P . . . 4J 123
Harperley La. DH9: Harp, Tant . . . 7B 110
Harperley Rd. DH9: Ann P . . . 4K 123
Harper St. NE24: Bly . . . 2H 23
Harraby Gdns. NE9: Low F . . . 4J 99
Harras Bank DH3: Bir . . . 5A 114
HARRATON . . . 7G 115
Harraton Skills Cen. . . . 7F 115
Harraton Ter. DH3: Bir . . . 4A 114
DH3: Lam P . . . 2G 129
Harriet Pl. NE6: Byke . . . 7A 64
Harriet St. NE6: Byke . . . 7B 64
NE21: Blay . . . 4C 80
Harrington Gdns. NE62: Stake . . . 7K 11
Harrington St. NE28: W'snd . . . 3F 65
(off Blenkinsop St.)
Harrington Way NE63: N Sea . . . 3D 12
Harriot Dr. NE12: Kil . . . 2J 45
Harrison Cl. SR8: Pet . . . 7C 172
Harrison Ct. DH3: Bir . . . 5A 114
NE23: Dud . . . 3K 35
Harrison Gdns. NE8: Gate . . . 7F 83
Harrison Gth. DH6: S'burn . . . 2K 167
Harrison Pl. NE2: Newc T . . . 2H 5 (6G 63)
Harrison Rd. NE28: W'snd . . . 2A 66
Harrison Ter. SR8: Eas . . . 7B 160
Harrogate Ct. NE63: Ash . . . 2D 12
Harrogate St. SR2: Sund . . . 3G 119
Harrogate Ter. SR7: Mur . . . 7E 146
Harrow Cres. DH4: S Row . . . 3A 130
Harrow Gdns. NE13: W Op . . . 6E 34
Harrow Sq. SR4: Sund . . . 3K 117
Harrow St. NE27: Shir . . . 7J 37
Harry Letch M. DH3: Bir . . . 3K 113
Hartburn NE10: Hew . . . 2E 100
Hartburn Cl. NE5: Cha P . . . 1D 60
Hartburn Dr. NE5: Cha P . . . 2D 60
Hartburn Pl. NE4: Fen . . . 6B 62
Hartburn Rd. NE30: Cull . . . 3G 49
Hartburn Ter. NE25: Sea D . . . 7H 27
Hartburn Wlk. NE3: Ken . . . 7K 43
Hart Ct. SR1: Sund . . . 2K 7 (1F 119)
Hart Cres. TS27: B Col . . . 4K 183
Hartford NE12: Kil . . . 6B 36
Hartford Bank NE22: H Bri . . . 5E 20
NE23: Nel V . . . 5E 20
HARTFORD BRIDGE . . . 4E 20
Hartford Bri. Farm NE22: H Bri . . . 4D 20
Hartford Cvn. Site NE22: H Bri . . . 3D 20
Hartford Ct. NE6: Heat . . . 6A 64
NE22: Bed . . . 1G 21
NE23: Cra . . . 3K 25
Hartford Cres. NE22: Bed . . . 1G 21
NE63: Ash . . . 5B 12
Hartford Dr. NE22: H Bri . . . 4E 20
Hartford Gdns. NE23: E Har . . . 6K 21
Hartford Hall Est. NE22: H Bri . . . 4F 21
Hartford Ho. NE4: Newc T . . . 3B 4
Hartford Rd. NE3: Gos . . . 5F 45
NE22: Bed, H Bri . . . 4E 20
NE34: S Shi . . . 1G 87
SR4: Sund . . . 3K 117
Hartford Rd. E. NE22: Bed . . . 1H 21
Hartford Rd. W. NE22: Bed . . . 1H 21
Hartford St. NE6: Heat . . . 5A 64
Hartforth Cres. NE10: Bill Q . . . 4F 85
Harthope Av. SR5: Sund . . . 4J 103
Harthope Cl. NE38: Wash . . . 1D 128
Harthope Dr. NE29: N Shi . . . 2E 66
Hartington Rd. NE30: Cull . . . 3G 49
Hartington St. DH8: Cons . . . 6H 121
NE4: Elsw . . . 1C 82
NE8: Gate . . . 5H 83
SR6: Roker . . . 5G 105
Hartington Ter. NE33: S Shi . . . 5K 67
Hartland Dr. DH3: Bir . . . 5B 114
Hartlands NE22: Bed . . . 1G 21
Hartleigh Pl. NE24: Cow . . . 2E 22
Hartlepool Av. SR8: Hord . . . 4D 172
Hartlepool St. DH6: Thor . . . 1K 179
Hartlepool St. Nth. DH6: Thor . . . 1K 179
Hartlepool St. Sth. DH6: Thor . . . 1K 179
HARTLEY . . . 6D 28
Hartley Av. NE26: Monks . . . 6E 38
Hartleyburn Av. NE31: Heb . . . 3H 85
HARTLEYBURN ESTATE . . . 3J 85
Hartley Ct. NE13: Bru V . . . 5B 34
NE25: New Hart . . . 4H 27
Hartley Gdns. NE25: Sea D . . . 7G 27
SR5: Ful . . . 4E 104
Hartley La. NE25: Ears, Monks . . . 5A 38
NE26: Sea S, Whit B . . . 1C 38
Hartley Sq. NE26: Sea S . . . 6D 28
Hartley St. NE25: Sea D . . . 7G 27
SR1: Sund . . . 1H 119
Hartley St. Nth. NE25: Sea D . . . 7G 27
Hartley Ter. NE24: News . . . 5G 23
Hartoft Cl. DH4: Nbot . . . 6D 130
HARTON . . . 7B 68
Harton Gro. NE34: S Shi . . . 6A 68
Harton Ho. Rd. NE34: S Shi . . . 6A 68
Harton Ho. Rd. E.
NE34: S Shi . . . 6C 68
Harton La. NE34: S Shi . . . 1J 87
HARTON NOOK . . . 1B 88
Harton Quay NE33: S Shi . . . 3H 67
Harton Ri. NE34: S Shi . . . 6B 68
Harton Vw. NE36: W Bol . . . 7G 87
HARTSIDE . . . 3F 153
Hartside DH3: Bir . . . 7B 114
NE15: Lem . . . 6C 60
Hartside Cotts. DH9: Ann P . . . 5K 123
Hartside Cres. NE21: Winl . . . 6A 80
NE23: Cra . . . 7J 21
NE27: Back . . . 7H 37
Hartside Gdns. DH5: Eas L . . . 2J 157
NE2: Jes . . . 4H 63
Hartside Pl. NE3: Gos . . . 3E 44
Hartside Rd. SR4: Sund . . . 4K 117
Hartside Sq. SR4: Sund . . . 4K 117
Hartside Vw. DH1: P Me . . . 4J 153
DH7: Bearp . . . 7C 152
Hart Sq. SR4: Sund . . . 3A 118
Hartswood NE9: Low F . . . 6J 99
Hart Ter. SR6: Seab . . . 1H 105
Harvard Rd. NE3: Ken . . . 7A 44
Harvest Cl. SR3: Dox P . . . 4B 132
Harvest Vw. DH1: P Me . . . 2A 154
Harvey Av. DH1: Dur . . . 4K 153
Harvey Cl. NE33: S Shi . . . 5H 67
NE38: Wash . . . 3D 114
NE63: N Sea . . . 4E 12
SR8: Pet . . . 5B 172
Harvey Combe NE12: Kil . . . 1K 45
Harvey Ct. DH8: Cons . . . 6J 121
Harvey Cres. NE10: Ward . . . 6F 85
Harvey Gdn. NE6: Byke . . . 7A 64
(off Grace St.)
Harwood Cl. DH8: Cons . . . 2J 135
NE23: Cra . . . 5J 25
NE38: Wash . . . 7E 114
Harwood Ct. NE23: Cra . . . 5J 25
SR6: Roker . . . 6G 105
Harwood Dr. DH4: Hou S . . . 1B 144
NE12: Kil . . . 1D 46
Harwood Grn. NE3: Ken . . . 6A 44
Hascombe Cl. NE25: Monks . . . 6A 38
Haslemere Dr. SR3: Sund . . . 5C 118
Hassop Way NE22: Bed . . . 6H 17
Hastings Av. DH1: Dur . . . 5J 165
NE3: Ki Pk . . . 5K 43
NE12: Longb . . . 5B 46
NE26: Sea S . . . 3B 28
NE26: Whit B . . . 3E 38
Hastings Ct. NE22: Bed . . . 6A 18
NE25: New Hart . . . 4H 27
Hastings Dr. NE27: Shir . . . 7J 37
NE30: Tyne . . . 4J 49
Hastings Gdns. NE25: New Hart . . . 4H 27
HASTINGS HILL . . . 6G 117
Hastings Pde. NE31: Heb . . . 3A 86
Hastings St. NE23: Cra . . . 5A 26
SR2: Sund . . . 4G 119
Hastings Ter. NE23: Cra . . . 7B 22
NE25: New Hart . . . 3H 27
SR2: Sund . . . 5H 119
Hastings Wlk. NE37: Wash . . . 7K 101
(off Thomas St.)
HASWELL . . . 1B 170
Haswell Cl. NE10: Ward . . . 7H 85
Haswell Ct. SR5: S'wck . . . 7C 104
Haswell Gdns. NE30: N Shi . . . 6G 49
Haswell Ho. NE30: Tyne . . . 5K 49
HASWELL PLOUGH . . . 3A 170
Haswell Rd. SR8: Win . . . 4F 181
TS28: Win . . . 4F 181
Hatfield Av. NE31: Heb . . . 7K 65
Hatfield Chase NE22: Bed . . . 7K 17
Hatfield Cl. DH1: Dur . . . 5J 153
Hatfield Dr. NE23: Seg . . . 1D 36
Hatfield Gdns. NE25: Monks . . . 6B 38
SR3: Sund . . . 5C 118
Hatfield Ho. NE29: N Shi . . . 7G 49
Hatfield Pl. SR8: Pet . . . 7C 172
Hatfield Sq. NE33: S Shi . . . 2K 67
(not continuous)
Hatfield Vw. DH1: Dur . . . 4D 6 (3B 166)
Hathaway Gdns. SR3: Sund . . . 5C 118
Hatherley Sq. TS27: B Col . . . 2H 183
Hathersage Gdns. NE34: S Shi . . . 1K 87
Hatherton Av. NE30: Cull . . . 1H 49
Hathery La. NE24: Bly, Cow . . . 2B 22
Hattam Cl. DH3: Bir . . . 2B 114
Hatton Gallery . . . 2E 4 (6F 63)
Haugh La. NE21: Blay . . . 1A 80
NE40: Blay . . . 7J 59
NE46: Hex . . . 1C 70
Haugh La. Ind. Est. NE46: Hex . . . 7C 50
Haughs, The NE42: Pru . . . 3F 77
Haughton Ct. NE4: Elsw . . . 3C 82
Haughton Cres. NE5: W Dent . . . 4E 60
NE32: Jar . . . 4B 86
Haughton Ter. NE24: Bly . . . 2J 23
Hautmont Rd. NE31: Heb . . . 2K 85
Hauxley NE12: Kil . . . 6B 36
Hauxley Dr. DH2: Ches S . . . 2H 141
NE3: Fawd . . . 5A 44
NE23: Cra . . . 7H 21
NE25: Monks . . . 5B 38
Hauxley Gdns. NE5: Fen . . . 3K 61
Havanna NE12: Kil . . . 6A 36
Havannah Cres. NE13: Din . . . 4H 33
Havannah Dr. NE13: W Op . . . 6E 34
Havannah Nature Reserve . . . 7A 34
Havannah Rd. NE37: Wash . . . 1F 115
Havant Gdns. NE13: W Op . . . 4D 34
Havelock Cl. NE8: Gate . . . 4G 83
Havelock Ct. SR4: Sund . . . 2K 117
Havelock Cres. NE22: E Sle . . . 5D 18
Havelock Ho. SR2: Sund . . . 7K 7
SR4: Sund . . . 2K 117
Havelock M. NE22: E Sle . . . 4D 18
Havelock Pl. NE4: Newc T . . . 6A 4 (1D 82)
Havelock Rd. NE27: Back . . . 1H 47
SR4: Sund . . . 2A 118
Havelock St. NE24: Bly . . . 1J 23
NE33: S Shi . . . 4H 67
(not continuous)
SR1: Sund . . . 1H 119
Havelock Ter. DH9: Stly . . . 2F 125
(off High St.)
DH9: Tant . . . 6B 110
NE8: Gate . . . 4G 83
NE17: C'wl . . . 6K 93
NE32: Jar . . . 1B 86
SR2: Sund . . . 6F 7 (3D 118)
Havelock Vs. NE22: E Sle . . . 5D 18
Haven, The DH4: S Row . . . 3B 130
DH7: B'hpe . . . 6D 138
DH7: Lang P . . . 4G 151
DH8: Lead . . . 5A 122
NE29: N Shi . . . 2G 67
NE42: Pru . . . 4F 77
NE64: Newb S . . . 3J 13
Haven Ct. DH1: P Me . . . 3A 154
NE24: Bly . . . 3G 23
SR6: Roker . . . 6H 105
Haven Ho. DH8: Lead . . . 6A 122
Haven Point . . . 1A 68
Haven Vw. NE64: Newb S . . . 3J 13
Havercroft NE10: Hew . . . 7F 85
Haverley Dr. SR7: S'hm . . . 1G 147
Haversham Cl. NE7: Longb . . . 7J 45
Haversham Pk. SR5: Ful . . . 2E 104
Hawarden Cres. SR4: Sund . . . 3C 118
Hawes Av. DH2: Ches S . . . 1A 142
Hawes Ct. SR6: Seab . . . 2E 104
Hawesdale Cres. NE21: Winl . . . 6B 80
Hawes Rd. SR8: Pet . . . 5B 172
Haweswater Cl. NE34: S Shi . . . 7K 67
Haweswater Cres. NE64: Newb S . . . 3G 13
Hawick Ct. DH9: Stly . . . 3H 125
Hawick Cres. NE6: Byke . . . 7P 5 (2K 83)
Hawick Cres. Ind. Est.
NE6: Byke . . . 7P 5 (2K 83)
Hawkesley Rd. SR4: Sund . . . 3K 117
Hawkey's La. NE29: N Shi . . . 6F 49
Hawkhill Cl. DH2: Ches S . . . 2J 141
Hawkhills Ter. DH3: Bir . . . 3A 114
Hawkhurst NE38: Wash . . . 6J 115
Hawkins Rd. SR7: Mur . . . 2G 159
Hawksbury NE16: Whi . . . 7G 81
Hawks Edge NE12: Longb . . . 3J 45
Hawksfeld NE10: Hew . . . 3C 100
Hawkshead Ct. NE3: Ki Pk . . . 5K 43
Hawkshead Pl. NE9: Low F . . . 2K 99
Hawkshill Ter. DH7: Corn C . . . 1A 162
Hawksley NE5: West . . . 3F 61
Hawksmoor Cl. NE63: Ash . . . 6A 12
Hawks Rd. NE8: Gate . . . 8K 5 (2H 83)
Hawk Ter. DH3: Bir . . . 5C 114
Hawkwell Cl. NE15: Thro . . . 4H 59
Hawkwell Ri. NE15: Thro . . . 4H 59
Hawsker Cl. SR3: Tuns . . . 2E 132
HAWTHORN . . . 3K 159
Hawthorn Av. NE13: Bru V . . . 6C 34
SR3: Tuns . . . 1D 132
Hawthorn Bus. Pk. SR7: Hawt . . . 3E 158
Hawthorn Cl. DH2: Kim . . . 7H 141
NE15: Benw . . . 1J 81
NE16: Whi . . . 2H 97
SR7: Mur . . . 1F 159
Hawthorn Cotts. DH6: S Het . . . 4D 158
DH8: B'hill . . . 5F 121
Hawthorn Ct. NE1: Newc T . . . 8E 4 (2F 83)
NE46: Hex . . . 2E 70
NE61: Mor . . . 7E 8
Hawthorn Cres. DH1: Dur . . . 1E 166
DH6: Quar H . . . 6C 178
NE38: Wash . . . 7F 115
SR8: Hord . . . 6E 172
Hawthorn Dene Nature Reserve . . . 3C 160
Hawthorn Dr. NE11: Dun . . . 6B 82
NE32: Jar . . . 4D 86
Hawthorne Av. NE31: Heb . . . 7K 65
NE34: S Shi . . . 2B 88
TS27: B Col . . . 2J 183
Hawthorne Cl. DH7: Lang P . . . 5H 151
Hawthorne Rd. NE24: Bly . . . 3K 23
Hawthorne Ter. DH6: Shot C . . . 6E 170
DH7: Lang P . . . 4K 151
DH9: Tanf . . . 5C 110
DH9: Tant . . . 7A 110
Hawthorn Gdns. NE3: Ken . . . 1B 62
NE9: Low F . . . 1H 99
NE10: Fell . . . 5B 84
NE26: Whit B . . . 6F 39
NE29: N Shi . . . 5F 49
NE40: Ryton . . . 2J 79
Hawthorn Grange NE13: Haz . . . 2A 44
Hawthorn Gro. NE28: W'snd . . . 3F 65
Hawthorn M. NE3: Gos . . . 1E 62
SR2: Sund . . . 6G 119
Hawthorn Pk. DH7: B'don . . . 1D 174
Hawthorn Pl. DH1: P Me . . . 3J 153
NE4: Newc T . . . 8A 4 (2D 82)
NE12: Kil . . . 7A 36
Hawthorn Rd. DH1: Carr . . . 6H 155
DH6: S Het . . . 4E 158
NE3: Gos . . . 1E 62
NE21: Blay . . . 5C 80
NE63: Ash . . . 3B 12
Hawthorn Rd. W. NE3: Gos . . . 1E 62
Hawthorns, The DH9: Ann P . . . 4K 123
NE3: Gos . . . 1E 62
NE4: Elsw . . . 9A 4 (3C 82)
NE9: Eigh B . . . 6B 100
NE36: E Bol . . . 7K 87
Hawthorn Sq. NE1: Newc T . . . 8E 4 (2F 83)
SR7: S'hm . . . 2B 148
Hawthorn St. DH4: Hou S, Nbot . . . 7C 130
DH8: B'hill . . . 5F 121
NE15: Walb . . . 3K 59
NE32: Jar . . . 6A 66
SR4: Sund . . . 2C 118
SR8: Eas C . . . 6B 160
Hawthorn Ter. DH1: Dur . . . 3A 6 (3K 165)
DH2: P Fel . . . 4G 127
DH3: Ches S . . . 7B 128
DH7: New B . . . 4A 164
DH8: B'hill . . . 5F 121
DH9: Ann P . . . 5B 124
NE4: Elsw . . . 8A 4 (2C 82)
NE9: Eigh B . . . 6B 100
NE9: Spri . . . 6D 100
NE11: Dun . . . 6B 82
NE15: Walb . . . 3K 59
NE40: Craw . . . 3C 78
(off Mitchell St.)
SR6: Seab . . . 1G 105
Hawthorn Vw. DH6: Thor . . . 2J 179
Hawthorn Vs. NE23: Cra . . . 4A 26
NE28: W'snd . . . 3F 65
Hawthorn Wlk. NE4: Newc T . . . 8A 4 (2D 82)
Hawthorn Way NE20: Darr H . . . 1H 41
Haydn St. NE8: Gate . . . 6H 83
Haydock Dr. NE10: Ward . . . 7F 85
Haydon NE38: Wash . . . 7J 115
Haydon Cl. NE3: Fawd . . . 4B 44
Haydon Dr. NE25: Whit B . . . 1F 49
NE28: W'snd . . . 3A 66
Haydon Gdns. NE27: Back . . . 1H 47
Haydon Pl. NE5: Den M . . . 5G 61
Haydon Rd. NE63: Ash . . . 5B 12
Haydon Sq. SR4: Sund . . . 3K 117
Hayes Wlk. NE13: W Op . . . 5D 34
Hayfield La. NE16: Whi . . . 1H 97
Hayhole Rd. NE29: N Shi . . . 3E 66
Haylands Sq. NE34: S Shi . . . 1A 88
Hayleazes Rd. NE15: Den M . . . 6F 61
Haymarket NE1: Newc T . . . 3F 4 (7F 63)
Haymarket La.
NE1: Newc T . . . 3E 4 (7F 63)
Haymarket Station (Metro) . . . 3F 4 (7F 63)
Haynyng, The NE10: Fell . . . 7C 84
Hayricks, The DH9: Tanf . . . 4D 110
Hay St. SR5: Monkw . . . 1H 7 (7E 104)
Hayton Av. NE34: S Shi . . . 1C 88
Hayton Cl. NE23: Cra . . . 3A 26
SR5: S'wck . . . 5C 104
Hayton Rd. NE30: Cull . . . 3F 49
Hayward Av. NE25: Sea D . . . 7H 27
Hazard La. DH5: E Rain, Hett H . . . 7D 144

Hazel Av. DH4: Hou S .2C 144
DH6: Quar H .6D 178
DH7: B'don .2C 174
NE29: N Shi .5F 49
SR3: Tuns .1D 132
Hazel Ct. DH6: Has .1B 170
Hazel Cres. SR8: Eas .1B 172
Hazeldene NE25: Monks .6D 38
NE32: Jar .6C 86
Hazeldene Av. NE3: Ken .1J 61
Hazeldene Ct. NE30: Tyne .5J 49
Hazel Dene Way SR7: S'hm .5C 148
Hazel Dr. TS27: Hes .4D 182
Hazeley Gro. NE3: Ken .7K 43
Hazeley Way NE3: Ken .7K 43
Hazel Gro. NE12: Kil .2K 45
NE16: Burn .2C 110
Hazelgrove DH2: Ches S .4J 127
NE10: Hew .7F 85
Hazel Leigh DH3: Gt Lum .3E 142
Hazelmere Av. NE3: Gos .3F 45
NE22: Bed .7G 17
Hazelmere Cres. NE23: Cra .2A 26
Hazelmere Dene NE23: Seg .2C 36
Hazelmoor NE31: Heb .6H 65
Hazel Rd. NE8: Gate .6E 82
NE21: Blay .4D 80
Hazel St. NE32: Jar .6A 66
Hazel Ter. DH4: Hou S .7C 130
DH6: Shot C .6E 170
DH9: Stly .6H 125
Hazelwood NE12: Kil .1D 46
NE32: Jar .7D 66
Hazelwood Av. NE2: Jes .3G 63
NE64: Newb S .2H 13
SR5: S'wck .5B 104
Hazelwood Cl. NE9: Eigh B .5B 100
Hazelwood Ct. DH7: Lang P .5J 151
Hazelwood Gdns. NE38: Wash .7F 115
Hazelwood Rd. NE13: W Op .1B 44
Hazelwood Ter. NE28: W'snd .2A 66
Hazledene Ter. SR4: Sund .2B 118
HAZLERIGG .7C 34
Hazlitt Av. NE34: S Shi .3H 87
Hazlitt Pl. NE23: Seg .2E 36
Headlam Gdn. NE6: Byke .7A 64
(off Grace St.)
Headlam Grn. NE6: Byke .1A 84
(off Headlam St.)
Headlam St. NE6: Byke .3P 5 (7A 64)
Headlam Vw. NE28: W'snd .3A 66
Heads Hope TS27: Cas E .5J 181
Healey Dr. SR3: Sund .6D 118
HEALEYFIELD .5A 134
Healeyfield La. DH8: C'sde .5A 134
Health Connection, The .7A 44
Healthlands Ladies Leisure Cen.
Whitley Bay .4E 38
(off Claremont Cres.)
Heartsbourne Dr. NE34: S Shi .3B 88
Heath Cl. DH6: Bowb .5H 177
NE11: Fest P .7D 82
SR8: Pet .7D 172
(not continuous)
Heathcote Grn. NE5: Blak .2H 61
Heath Ct. NE1: Newc T .6G 4 (1G 83)
Heathdale Gdns. NE7: H Hea .2K 63
Heather Cl. SR6: Clead .4C 88
Heatherdale Cres. DH1: Carr .7H 155
Heatherdale Ter. NE9: Wrek .4K 99
Heather Dr. DH5: Hett H .5G 145
Heatherfield M. NE23: Dud .2K 35
Heather Hill NE9: Spri .6D 100
Heatherlaw NE9: Low F .2A 100
NE37: Wash .2D 114
Heather Lea DH9: Dip .6J 109
NE24: Cow .2C 22
Heatherlea Gdns. NE62: Stake .7J 11
SR3: Sund .5D 118
Heather Lea La. NE42: Pru .3F 77
Heatherlea Pl. NE37: Wash .6H 101
Heather Pl. NE4: Fen .5A 62
NE40: Craw .2E 78
Heatherslaw Rd. NE5: Fen .5J 61
Heather Ter. NE16: Burn .2B 110
Heather Way DH9: Stly .3D 124
Heatherwell Grn. NE10: Fell .7A 84
Heathery La. NE3: Gos .5G 45
Heathfield DH2: Ches S .7H 127
NE27: Back .2H 47
NE61: Mor .2G 15
SR2: Sund .6E 118
Heathfield Cres. NE5: Blak .2K 61
Heathfield Farm NE40: G'sde .5E 78
Heathfield Gdns. NE40: G'sde .5E 78
Heathfield Pl. NE3: Gos .3F 45
NE9: Low F .1H 99
Heathfield Rd. NE9: Low F .1H 99
Heath Grange DH5: Hou S .1E 144
Heath Hill NE15: Hed W .3C 58
Heathlands Fitness & Leisure Cen.
Chester-le-Street .7B 128
(off Front St.)
Heathmeads DH2: Pelt .3F 127
Heath Sq. SR4: Sund .3A 118
Heath Vw. TS28: Sta T .7J 181
Heathway NE32: Jar .4C 86
SR7: S'hm .6A 148
Heathways DH1: H Shin .7F 167
Heathwell Gdns. NE16: Swa .6H 81
Heathwell Rd. NE15: Den M .6F 61
Heathwood Av. NE16: Whi .7G 81
HEATON .4A 64
Heaton Bingo .2P 5 (6K 63)
Heaton Cl. NE6: Byke .2P 5 (6K 63)
Heaton Gdns. NE34: S Shi .4J 87
Heaton Gro. NE6: Heat .2N 5 (6K 63)
Heaton Hall Rd. NE6: Heat .2P 5 (6K 63)
Heaton Pk. Ct. NE6: Heat .3N 5 (7K 63)
Heaton Pk. Rd.
NE6: Byke, Heat .2N 5 (6K 63)
Heaton Pk. Vw. NE6: Heat .1N 5 (6K 63)
Heaton Pl. NE6: Byke .2P 5 (6K 63)
Heaton Rd. NE6: Byke, Heat .1P 5 (4K 63)
Heaton Ter. NE6: Byke .3M 5 (7J 63)
NE29: N Shi .6E 48
Heaton Wlk. NE6: Byke .3P 5 (7K 63)
Heaviside Pl. DH1: Dur .2C 166
HEBBURN .1H 85
HEBBURN COLLIERY .6K 65
HEBBURN NEW TOWN .1G 85
Hebburn Station (Metro) .7H 65
Hebburn St. SR8: Eas .7A 160
Hebburn Swimming Pool .7K 65
Heber St. NE4: Newc T .5C 4 (1E 82)
Hebron Av. NE61: Peg .3K 9
Hebron Pl. NE63: Ash .4D 12
Hebron Ter. NE46: Hex .7C 50
Hebron Way NE23: Cra .4J 25
Hector St. NE27: Shir .7K 37
Heddon Av. NE13: Haz .7C 34
Heddon Banks NE15: Hed W .4B 58
Heddon Cl. NE3: Gos .6C 44
NE40: Ryton .1H 79
HEDDON-ON-THE-WALL .3C 58
Heddon Steads NE15: Hed W .6A 40
Heddon Vw. NE21: Winl .4B 80
NE40: Ryton .1H 79
Heddon Way NE34: S Shi .7G 67
Hedge Cl. NE11: Fest P .7D 82
HEDGEFIELD .1K 79
Hedgefield Av. NE21: Blay .1K 79
Hedgefield Cotts. NE21: Blay .1K 79
Hedgefield Ct. NE21: Blay .1K 79
Hedgefield Gro. NE24: News .6G 23
Hedgefield Vw. NE23: Dud .2J 35
Hedgehope NE9: Low F .2A 100
NE37: Wash .2E 114
Hedgehope Rd. NE5: West .1G 61
Hedgehope Wlk. NE24: Cow .3E 22
Hedgelea NE40: Ryton .1F 79
Hedgelea Rd. DH5: E Rain .7C 144
Hedgeley Rd. NE5: W Dent .5E 60
NE29: N Shi .5D 48
NE31: Heb .7H 65
Hedgeley Ter. NE6: Walk .7D 64
Hedgerow M. NE63: Ash .5K 11
Hedley Av. NE24: Bly .3J 23
Hedley Cl. NE33: S Shi .1J 67
Hedley Ct. DH7: Bearp .7C 152
NE24: Bly .3K 23
NE29: N Shi .7B 48
Hedleyhill La. DH7: Corn C .2A 162
Hedley Hill Rd. DH7: Wat .6A 162
Hedley Hill Ter. DH7: Wat .6A 162
Hedley La. NE16: Marl H .2H 111
HEDLEY ON THE HILL .4B 92
Hedley Pl. NE28: W'snd .4F 65
(not continuous)
Hedley Rd. NE25: H'wll .1J 37
NE29: N Shi .2F 67
NE41: Wylam .7K 57
Hedleys Bldgs. DH7: Wit G .3D 152
Hedley St. NE3: Gos .7E 44
NE8: Gate .6F 83
NE33: S Shi .1J 67
Hedley Ter. DH6: S Het .4B 158
DH7: Lang P .4J 151
(off Front St.)
DH9: Dip .3E 122
NE3: Gos .7E 44
SR2: Ryh .3J 133
Hedley Way NE63: N Sea .6D 12
HEDWORTH .5D 86
Hedworth Av. NE34: S Shi .2G 87
Hedworth Ct. SR1: Sund .2G 119
Hedworth La. NE32: Jar .3C 86
NE35: Bol C .5D 86
Hedworth Pl. NE9: Wrek .4A 100
Hedworth Sq. SR1: Sund .2G 119
Hedworth St. DH3: Ches S .5A 128
Hedworth Ter. DH4: S Row .3B 130
SR6: Whit .6H 89
(off North Guards)
Hedworth Vw. NE32: Jar .3D 86
Heighley St. NE15: Scot .1F 81
Heightley Ct. NE24: Camb .1G 19
Helena Av. NE26: Whit B .6H 39
Helena Ho. SR2: Sund .6F 7
Helen St. NE21: Winl .4A 80
NE23: E Cram .5D 26
SR6: Ful .3G 105
Helford Rd. SR8: Pet .1A 182
Hellpool La. NE46: Hex .1B 70
Hellvellyn Ct. DH9: Ann P .6K 123
Helmdon NE37: Wash .7J 101
Helmsdale Av. NE10: Fell .5B 84
Helmsdale Rd. SR4: Sund .3K 117
Helmsley Cl. DH4: Pen .3A 130
Helmsley Ct. SR5: S'wck .4A 104
Helmsley Dr. NE28: W'snd .3K 65
Helmsley Grn. NE9: Low F .5K 99
Helmsley M. NE2: Newc T .2K 5 (6H 63)
Helmsley Rd. DH1: Dur .4A 154
NE2: Newc T .2J 5 (6H 63)
Helston Ct. NE15: Lem .6B 60
Helvellyn Av. NE38: Wash .5E 114
Helvellyn Cl. NE21: Winl .6C 80
Helvellyn Rd. SR2: Sund .7F 119
Hemel St. DH3: Ches S .7A 128
Hemlington Cl. SR2: Ryh .3H 133
Hemmel Courts DH7: B'don .7E 164
Hemming St. SR2: Sund .6H 119
Hemsby Cl. SR4: Sund .3K 117
Hemsley Rd. NE34: S Shi .4B 68
Hencotes NE46: Hex .2C 70
Hencote's Ct. NE46: Hex .2C 70
(off St Cuthbert's Ter.)
Hencotes M. NE46: Hex .2C 70
Henderson Av. DH6: Whe H .3A 180
NE16: Whi .6G 81
Henderson Cl. NE46: Hex .3B 70
Henderson Ct. NE20: Pon .4J 31
NE29: N Shi .2F 67
Henderson Gdns. NE10: Ward .6F 85
Henderson Rd. NE28: W'snd .1F 65
NE34: S Shi .2F 87
SR4: Sund .2B 118
Hendersons Bldgs. NE64: Newb S .2J 13
(off Vernon Pl.)
Hendersyde Cl. NE5: Blak .2H 61
HENDON .4G 119
Hendon Burn Av. SR2: Sund .3G 119
Hendon Burn Av. W. SR2: Sund .4G 119
Hendon Cl. NE29: N Shi .2G 67
SR1: Sund .2G 119
Hendon Dock .2J 119
Hendon Gdns. NE32: Jar .4D 86
Hendon Rd. NE8: Gate .6K 83
SR1: Sund .1G 119
SR2: Sund .1G 119
Hendon St. SR1: Sund .2H 119
Hendon Valley Ct. SR2: Sund .4G 119
Hendon Valley Rd. SR2: Sund .3G 119
Henley Av. DH2: P Fel .6G 127
Henley Cl. NE23: Cra .3B 26
Henley Gdns. DH8: Cons .7J 121
NE28: W'snd .1B 66
Henley Rd. NE30: Cull .3J 49
SR4: Sund .3K 117
Henley St. NE6: Walk .6A 64
Henley Way NE35: Bol C .6E 86
Henlow Rd. NE15: Lem .6C 60
Henry Av. DH6: Bowb .3G 177
(not continuous)
Henry Nelson St. NE33: S Shi .1K 67
Henry Robson Way NE33: S Shi .1J 67
Henry Sq. NE2: Newc T .4J 5 (7H 63)
Henry St. DH4: S Row .3B 130
DH5: Hett H .4G 145
DH5: Hou S .1E 144
DH6: Thor .1A 180
DH8: B'hill .6G 121
NE3: Gos .7E 44
NE15: Walb .3A 60
NE29: N Shi .7G 49
NE33: S Shi .1K 67
SR7: S'hm .2B 148
Henry St. E. SR2: Sund .2H 119
Henry St. Nth. SR7: Mur .7F 147
Henry St. Sth. SR7: Mur .7F 147
Henry Ter. DH4: Hou S .7K 129
Hensby Ct. NE5: Blak .1H 61
Henshaw Ct. NE63: Ash .5K 11
Henshaw Gro. NE25: H'wll .1K 37
Henshaw Pl. NE5: Den M .6H 61
Henshelwood Ter. NE2: Jes .4G 63
Henson Cl. NE38: Wash .4H 115
Hepburn Av. NE13: Ki Pk .4K 43
Hepburn Gdns. NE10: Fell .5A 84
Hepburn Gro. SR5: Sund .6F 103
Hepple Ct. NE24: Bly .3G 23
Hepple Rd. NE64: Newb S .4G 13
Hepple Way NE3: Gos .6C 44
HEPSCOTT .3A 16
Hepscott Av. TS27: B Col .2J 183
Hepscott Dr. NE25: Monks .5D 38
HEPSCOTT PARK .7A 16
Hepscott Ter. NE33: S Shi .6K 67
Hepscott Wlk. NE61: Peg .4A 10
Hepworth Rd. SR5: S'wck .5A 104
Herbert St. DH8: Cons .6H 121
NE8: Gate .5J 83
Herbert Ter. SR5: Ful .2D 104
SR7: S'hm .3B 148
Herd Cl. NE21: Winl .5A 80
Herd Ho. La. NE21: Blay .4K 79
Herdinghill NE37: Wash .2D 114
Herdlaw NE23: Cra .4J 25
Hereford Ct. NE3: Ki Pk .4K 43
SR2: Sund .7F 119
Hereford Rd. SR2: Sund .7F 119
Herefordshire Dr. DH1: Carr .1G 167
Hereford Sq. SR2: Sund .7F 119
Hereford Way NE32: Jar .4B 86
(not continuous)
Heritage Cl. NE8: Gate .5E 82
Hermiston NE25: Monks .6E 38
Hermiston Retail Pk. DH8: Cons .1H 135
Hermitage, The DH2: Ches S .2K 141
DH3: Ches S .1A 142
Hermitage Gdns. DH2: Ches S .1K 141
Hermitage Pk. DH3: Ches S .1A 142
Heron Cl. NE24: News .5J 23
NE38: Wash .6E 114
NE63: Ash .6C 12
Heron Cres. NE13: Haz .2A 44
Heron Dr. NE33: S Shi .1J 67
Heron Pl. NE12: Longb .5J 45
Herons Ct. DH1: Dur .2E 166
Heron Vs. NE34: S Shi .2H 87
Heron Way NE16: Whi .7H 81
Herrick St. NE5: West .2G 61
Herring Gull Cl. NE24: News .6J 23
HERRINGTON .3H 131
Herrington Cl. DH7: Lang P .5H 151
Herrington Country Pk. .1D 130
Herrington M. DH4: New H .3E 130
Herrington Rd. DH4: W Herr .3F 131
SR3: E Her .2H 131
Hersham Cl. NE3: Ki Pk .5K 43
Hertburn Gdns. NE37: Wash .1H 115
Hertburn Ind. Est. NE37: Wash .1J 115
Hertford NE9: Low F .5H 99
Hertford Av. NE34: S Shi .6E 68
Hertford Cl. NE25: Monks .5C 38
Hertford Cres. DH5: Hett H .6F 145
Hertford Gro. NE23: Cra .3A 26
Hertford Pl. SR8: Pet .4A 172
Herton Cl. SR8: Pet .5A 172
(not continuous)
Hesket Ct. NE3: Ki Pk .5A 44
HESLEDEN .4E 182
Hesleden Rd. TS27: B Col, Hes .3E 182
Hesledon La. SR7: Hawt .2K 159
Hesledon Wlk. SR7: Mur .6G 147
Hesleyside NE63: Ash .5D 12
Hesleyside Dr. NE5: Fen .5H 61
Hesleyside Rd. NE25: Well .6B 38
Hessewelle Cres. DH6: Has .3A 170
Hester Av. NE25: New Hart .4H 27
Hester Bungs. NE25: New Hart .4H 27
(off Hester Av.)
Hester Gdns. NE25: New Hart .4J 27
Heswall Rd. NE23: Cra .7J 21
Hetherset Cl. SR4: Sund .3K 117
Hethpool Ct. NE13: Ki Pk .4A 44
HETT .7C 176
Hett La. DH6: Crox, Hett, Sun B .5K 175
Hetton Bogs Local Nature Reserve .5F 145
Hetton Cen. DH5: Hett H .6G 145
Hetton Community Pool & Wellness Cen.
.6G 145
(within Hetton Sports Complex)
HETTON DOWNS .4H 145
HETTON-LE-HOLE .6G 145
Hetton Lyons Country Pk. .6J 145
Hetton Lyons Ind. Est. DH5: Hett H .7H 145
Hetton Moor Ter. DH5: Hett H .1H 157
Hetton Rd. DH5: Hou S .3E 144
Hetton Sports Complex .6G 145
Heugh Edge DH7: Sac .5D 140
Heugh Hall Row DH6: Old Q .5K 177
Heugh Hill NE9: Spri .5E 100
Hevingham Cl. SR4: Sund .3K 117
Hewitson Ter. NE10: Fell .7A 84
Hewitt Av. SR2: Ryh .1G 133
Hewley Cres. NE15: Thro .4H 59
HEWORTH .6C 84
Heworth (Park & Tram) .6D 84
Heworth Av. NE10: Pel .5E 84
Heworth Burn Cres. NE10: Hew .6C 84
Heworth Ct. NE34: S Shi .1G 87
Heworth Cres. NE37: Wash .7H 101
Heworth Dene Gdns. NE10: Fell .5C 84
Heworth Gro. NE37: Wash .7G 101
Heworth Leisure Cen. .7D 84
Heworth Rd. NE37: Wash .5H 101
Heworth Station (Metro) .5D 84
Heworth Station (Rail) .6D 84
Heworth Way NE10: Pel .6E 84
Hewson Pl. NE9: Low F .1K 99
HEXHAM .1D 70
Hexham NE38: Wash .4D 114
Hexham Abbey .1C 70
Hexham Av. NE6: Walk .1D 84
NE23: Cra .3B 26
NE31: Heb .4J 85
SR7: S'hm .4K 147
Hexham Bus. Pk. NE46: Hex .7C 50
Hexham Cl. NE29: N Shi .5C 48
Hexham Ct. DH7: Sac .7D 140
NE6: Walk .7E 64
NE11: Dun .1B 98
Hexham Dr. DH9: Ann P .4K 123
Hexham Gdns. DH8: C'sde .2D 134
Hexham Ho. NE6: Walk .7E 64
NE46: Hex .1C 70
(off Market St.)
Hexham Moothall & Gallery .1D 70
Hexham Old Rd. NE21: Blay .2K 79
NE40: Ryton .1G 79
Hexham Racecourse .6A 70
Hexham Race Course Cvn. Site
NE46: Hex .5A 70
Hexham Rd.
NE15: Hed W, Thro, Walb .3C 58
NE16: Swa .5F 81
SR4: Sund .3K 117
Hexham Station (Rail) .1E 70
Hextol Ct. NE46: Hex .2B 70
Hextol Cres. NE46: Hex .2C 70
Hextol Gdns. NE15: Den M .6F 61
Hextol Ter. NE46: Hex .2B 70
Heybrook Av. NE29: N Shi .4F 49
Heyburn Gdns. NE15: Benw .1K 81
Heywood's Ct. NE1: Newc T .6F 4
Hezlett Ct. DH7: Lang P .5K 151
Hibernian Rd. NE32: Jar .6B 66
Hickling Ct. NE5: Blak .1J 61
Hickstead Cl. NE28: W'snd .5J 47
Hickstead Gro. NE23: Cra .3B 26
Hiddleston Av. NE7: Longb .7K 45
HIGHAM DYKES .1C 30
Higham Pl. NE1: Newc T .4G 4 (7G 63)
High Axwell NE21: Blay .4D 80
High Back Cl. NE32: Jar .2A 86
HIGH BARNES .3B 118
High Barnes DH3: Gt Lum .3E 142
High Barnes Ter. SR4: Sund .2C 118

High Beacon Stairs *NE30: N Shi* *7J* ***49***
(off Union Quay)
High Bri. NE1: Newc T 6F **4** (1F **83**)
Highbridge NE3: Gos 5E **44**
Highburn NE23: Cra 5J **25**
High Burn Ter. NE10: Hew 7C **84**
High Burswell NE46: Hex 1B **70**
Highbury NE2: Jes 4F **63**
NE10: Fell 6C **84**
NE25: Monks 6E **38**
Highbury Av. NE9: Spri 5E **100**
Highbury Cl. NE9: Spri 5E **100**
Highbury Pl. NE29: N Shi 7E **48**
HIGH CALLERTON 2J 41
High Carr Cl. DH1: Dur 6K **153**
High Carr Rd. DH1: Dur 6J **153**
High Chare DH3: Ches S 6A **128**
HIGH CHURCH 1F 15
Highclere DH4: S Row 4K **129**
Highclere Dr. SR2: Ryh 3F **133**
Highcliffe Gdns. NE8: Gate 6J **83**
HIGH CLIFTON 7H 15
High Cl. NE42: Pru 3H **77**
High Cft. DH7: B'don 7D **164**
NE37: Wash 6F **101**
High Cft. Cl. NE31: Heb 2H **85**
Highcroft Dr. SR6: Whit 5G **89**
Highcroft Pk. SR6: Whit 5H **89**
(not continuous)
Highcrofts NE15: Hor 5E **56**
Highcross Rd. NE30: Cull 1G **49**
High Cross St. DH6: Cass 4F **179**
High Dene NE7: H Hea 4J **63**
NE34: S Shi 1H **87**
High Dewley Burn NE15: Thro 2H **59**
High Downs Sq. DH5: Hett H 5G **145**
HIGH DUBMIRE 2A 144
High Dubmire DH4: Hou S 2K **143**
High Elm Pk. DH8: Cons 3J **121**
High Elms SR4: Sund 1H **117**
HIGH FELL 1J 99
HIGHFIELD 5G 95
Highfield DH3: Bir 2A **114**
DH7: Sac 7E **140**
NE16: Sun 4H **97**
NE24: Cow 2D **22**
NE42: Pru 4E **76**
Highfield Av. NE12: Longb 4B **46**
Highfield Cl. NE5: West 2F **61**
Highfield Ct. NE10: Hew 7C **84**
Highfield Cres. DH3: Ches S 4A **128**
Highfield Dr. DH4: Hou S 2B **144**
NE34: S Shi 5B **68**
NE63: N Sea 5D **12**
Highfield Gdns. DH3: Ches S 4A **128**
Highfield Grange DH4: Hou S 3B **144**
Highfield La. NE42: Pru 5E **76**
Highfield Pl. NE13: W Op 6C **34**
SR4: Sund 2B **118**
Highfield Ri. DH3: Ches S 4A **128**
Highfield Rd. DH4: S Row 3A **130**
NE5: West 3F **61**
NE8: Gate 5J **83**
NE33: S Shi 4B **68**
NE34: S Shi 4B **68**
NE39: Row G 5G **95**
Highfield Ter. DH7: Ush M 3B **164**
NE6: Walk 2D **84**
NE42: Pru 4D **76**
High Flatworth NE29: N Shi 6B **48**
Highford Gdns. NE61: Mor 1E **14**
Highford La. NE46: Hex 3A **70**
High Friar La. NE1: Newc T 5F **4** (1F **83**)
High Friars NE1: Newc T 5E **4**
HIGH FRIARSIDE 2J 109
High Garth *SR1: Sund* *1G* ***119***
(off High St. E.)
High Gate, The NE3: Ken 1A **62**
Highgate DH1: Dur 1B **6** (2A **166**)
Highgate Gdns. NE32: Jar 4D **86**
Highgate M. DH8: Shot B 5E **120**
Highgate Rd. SR4: Sund 3K **117**
Highgate Ter. NE29: N Shi 1G **67**
High Gosforth Pk. 2G 45
High Graham St. DH7: Sac 1E **152**
Highgreen Chase NE16: Whi 3G **97**
High Grindon Ho. SR4: Sund 5J **117**
High Gro. NE40: Ryton 2H **79**
Highgrove NE5: Cha P 3D **60**
Highgrove Ct. SR8: Eas 2A **172**
High Hamsterley Rd.
NE39: Ham M 3E **108**
HIGH HANDENHOLD 2D 126
HIGH HASWELL 7K 157
Highheath NE37: Wash 2D **114**
HIGH HEATON 3K 63
High Hedgefield Ter. NE21: Blay 1J **79**
High Hermitage Cvn. Pk.
NE42: O'ham 1F **77**
HIGH HESLEDEN 4H 183
HIGH HEWORTH 7C 84
High Heworth La. NE10: Hew 7C **84**
High Hold Bungs. DH2: Pelt 2D **126**
High Horse Cl. NE39: Row G 3A **96**
High Horse Cl. Wood
NE39: Row G 3A **96**
High Ho. Cl. NE61: Mor 7D **8**
High Ho. Gdns. NE10: Fell 6C **84**
High Ho. La. DH8: Cons 7G **135**
High Ho. Rd. NE61: Mor 7C **8**
Highland Rd. NE5: Ken 2K **61**
High La. DH4: Nbot 5E **130**
DH6: Has 7A **158**
High La. Row NE31: Heb 5K **65**
High Lanes NE10: Hew 7D **84**
High Laws NE3: Gos 1H **63**
Highlaws Gdns. NE9: Low F 5K **99**
High Level Rd. NE8: Gate 9G **4** (3G **83**)
High Ling Cl. DH6: Has 2E **170**
High Mkt. NE63: Ash 3H **11**
High Mdw. NE34: S Shi 5B **68**
High Mdws. DH7: B'don 7C **164**
NE3: Ken 2A **62**
HIGH MICKLEY 7B 76
High Mill Rd. NE39: Ham M 3E **108**
Highmoor NE61: Mor 1D **14**
High Moor Ct. NE5: Fen 3A **62**
High Moor Pl. NE34: S Shi 1J **87**
HIGH MOORSLEY 3D 156
HIGH NEWPORT 1C 132
HIGH ONSTEAD 4K 9
High Pk. NE2: Newc T 5J **63**
NE61: Mor 1F **15**
High Pk. La. NE61: Mor 1G **15**
High Pasture NE38: Wash 7J **115**
High Pit Rd. NE23: Cra 5B **26**
HIGH PITTINGTON 6B 156
High Primrose Hill DH4: Bour 6H **129**
High Quay NE1: Newc T 6L **5** (1J **83**)
NE24: Bly 1K **23**
High Reach NE10: Bill Q 4E **84**
High Ridge DH8: B'hill 6E **120**
NE13: Haz 7D **34**
NE22: Bed 7G **17**
Highridge DH3: Bir 3A **114**
High Road, The NE34: S Shi 7B **68**
High Row DH4: Hou S 1J **143**
NE15: Lem 7C **60**
NE37: Wash 6H **101**
NE40: Ryton 2J **79**
High St Cuthberts La. NE46: Hex 2C **70**
High Sandgrove SR6: Clead 5C **88**
High Shaw NE42: Pru 5D **76**
High Shaws DH7: B'don 7E **164**
HIGH SHIELDS 4J 67
HIGH SHINCLIFFE 7F 167
Highside Dr. SR3: Sund 5C **118**
HIGH SOUTHWICK 4C 104
HIGH SPEN 3D 94
High Spen Ct. NE39: H Spen 3E **94**
High Spen Ind. Est. NE39: H Spen 2D **94**
HIGH STANNERS 6E 8
High Stanners NE61: Mor 6E **8**
Highstead Av. NE23: Cra 1J **25**
Highsteads DH8: M'sly 7K **107**
High Stobhill NE61: Mor 2G **15**
High St. DH1: Carr 7G **155**
DH1: Dur 2C **6** (2A **166**)
DH1: H Shin 7F **167**
DH1: Shin 6D **166**
DH5: Eas L 2J **157**
DH6: Low P 5B **156**
DH6: Thor 1J **179**
DH7: Lang M 7G **165**
DH9: Stly 2F **125**
NE3: Gos 7E **44**
NE8: Gate 8H **5** (2G **83**)
(Bottle Bank)
NE8: Gate 9J **5** (3H **83**)
(Lambton St.)
NE9: Wrek 4A **100**
NE10: Fell 6B **84**
NE15: Newb 6K **59**
NE24: Bly 2H **23**
(Edward St.)
NE24: Bly 2J **23**
(Thoroton St.)
NE32: Jar 6C **66**
(not continuous)
NE62: Chop 2G **17**
NE64: Newb S 2J **13**
SR4: Sund 2G **117**
High St. East NE28: W'snd 4G **65**
SR1: Sund 1G **119**
High St. Nth. DH1: Shin 6E **166**
DH7: Lang M 6G **165**
(Black Rd.)
DH7: Lang M 7F **165**
(Brookes Ri.)
High St. Sth. DH1: Shin 6E **166**
DH7: Lang M 7G **165**
High St. Sth. Bk. DH7: Lang M 7G **165**
High St. West NE6: W'snd 4E **64**
NE28: W'snd 4F **65**
SR1: Sund 4G **7** (2E **118**)
(not continuous)
High Swinburne Pl.
NE4: Newc T 6C **4** (1E **82**)
High Tree Cl. SR3: Dox P 4B **132**
High Trees NE34: S Shi 2C **88**
HIGH URPETH 1D 126
High Vw. DH7: Ush M 2B **164**
NE20: Darr H 2H **41**
NE28: W'snd 2F **65**
NE43: Hed 4B **92**
Highview Ct. DH9: Dip 7J **109**
High Vw. Nth. NE28: W'snd 1E **64**
High Wlk. DH3: Lam P 3G **129**
High Well Gdns. NE10: Fell 5C **84**
Highwell La. NE5: W Dent 4E **60**
High West La. SR7: Hawt 4J **159**
High West St. NE8: Gate 10J **5** (4H **83**)
HIGH WESTWOOD 4K 107
High Winning Cotts. *TS27: Win* *4H* ***181***
(off Wellfield Rd.)
Highwood Rd. NE15: Den M 6F **61**
High Wood Ter. DH1: Dur 6D **6**
High Wood Vw. DH1: Dur 6D **6** (4B **166**)
Highworth Dr. NE7: H Hea 2B **64**
NE9: Spri 6D **100**
High Yd. DH1: Dur 4D **6** (3B **166**)
Hilary St. NE8: Gate 5C **82**
Hilda Av. DH1: Dur 3E **166**
Hilda Cl. DH1: Dur 3F **167**
Hilda Pk. DH2: Ches S 4J **127**
Hilda St. DH9: Ann P 4J **123**
NE8: Gate 5F **83**
SR6: Ful 4F **105**
(not continuous)
Hilda Ter. DH2: Ches S 4K **127**
NE15: Thro 3H **59**
Hilden Bldgs. NE7: H Hea 3A **64**
Hilden Gdns. NE7: H Hea 3A **64**
Hill, The NE42: O'ham 2D **76**
Hillary Av. NE12: Longb 4C **46**
Hillary Pl. NE5: West 2G **61**
Hill Av. NE23: Seg 1E **36**
Hill Brow SR3: Tuns 3D **132**
Hill Cotts. NE9: Spri 6D **100**
Hill Cres. SR7: Mur 7D **146**
SR7: S'hm 5C **148**
Hill Crest DH7: Esh 7F **151**
DH7: Sac 1F **153**
NE10: Hew 1C **100**
NE16: Burn 2B **110**
Hillcrest DH1: Dur 1E **6** (2B **166**)
DH1: H Shin 7F **167**
DH7: B'hpe 6D **138**
DH8: C'sde 4B **134**
NE25: Monks 6E **38**
NE32: Jar 4C **86**
NE34: S Shi 1D **88**
NE42: Pru 4F **77**
NE63: N Sea 5E **12**
SR3: E Her 2H **131**
Hillcrest Av. NE62: Chop 7H **11**
Hillcrest Ct. NE42: Pru 4F **77**
Hillcrest Dr. NE11: Dun 7A **82**
NE46: Hex 2E **70**
Hill Crest Gdns. NE2: Jes 1G **63**
Hillcrest M. DH1: Dur 1D **6** (2B **166**)
SR7: Cold H 2J **159**
Hillcrest Pl. TS27: Hes 4D **182**
Hill Cft. NE15: Hor 4E **56**
Hillcroft DH3: Bir 3A **114**
NE9: Low F 1J **99**
NE39: Row G 5G **95**
Hilldyke NE9: Wrek 5A **100**
Hillfield DH8: B'hill 6F **121**
NE25: Monks 6D **38**
Hillfield Gdns. SR3: Sund 5D **118**
Hillfield St. NE8: Gate 4G **83**
Hillford Ter. NE17: C'wl 6K **93**
Hillgarth DH8: C'sde 4D **134**
Hillgate NE8: Gate 8H **5** (2G **83**)
NE61: Mor 7F **9**
Hillhead Dr. NE5: W Dent 4D **60**
Hillhead Gdns. NE11: Dun 1C **98**
Hillhead La. NE16: Burn 6D **96**
Hillhead Parkway NE5: Cha P 3C **60**
Hillhead Rd.
NE5: W Dent, West 4D **60**
Hillheads Ct. NE25: Whit B 7G **39**
Hillheads Rd. NE25: Whit B 1F **49**
Hillhead Way NE5: West 2E **60**
Hill Ho. Rd. NE15: Thro 3G **59**
Hillingdon Gro. SR4: Sund 6G **117**
Hill La. DH4: Pen 7C **116**
Hill Mdws. DH1: H Shin 7E **166**
Hillmeads DH2: Nett 6H **141**
Hill Pk. NE20: Darr H 2H **41**
HILL PARK ESTATE 1C 86
Hill Pk. Rd. NE32: Jar 1C **86**
Hill Ri. NE38: Wash 2H **115**
NE40: Craw 3D **78**
Hillrise Cres. SR7: Seat 2F **147**
Hill Rd. NE46: Hex 7D **70**
Hills Ct. NE21: Blay 2E **80**
Hillsden Rd. NE25: Monks 4D **38**
Hillside DH3: Bir 4B **114**
DH3: Ches S 5A **128**
DH7: Wit G 2D **152**
NE11: Dun 7A **82**
NE12: Kil 2C **46**
NE20: Darr H 3G **41**
NE21: Winl 4B **80**
NE34: S Shi 2D **88**
NE36: W Bol 7G **87**
NE61: Mor 1F **15**
NE63: Ash 3A **12**
SR3: Sund 5E **118**
Hillside Av. NE15: Lem 6E **60**
Hillside Cl. NE39: Row G 4J **95**
TS27: B Col 3J **183**
Hillside Dr. SR6: Whit 5G **89**
Hillside Gdns. DH9: Stly 1G **125**
(not continuous)
SR2: Sund 5E **118**
Hillside Gro. DH6: H Pitt 6B **156**
Hillside Pl. NE9: Low F 1J **99**
Hillside Rd. NE46: Hex 2F **71**
Hillside Vw. DH6: S'burn 2K **167**
Hillside Vs. SR8: Hord 5D **172**
Hillside Way DH4: Hou S 1E **144**
Hillsleigh Rd. NE5: Blak 2K **61**
Hills St. NE8: Gate 9H **5** (3G **83**)
Hill St. NE32: Jar 6A **66**
NE33: S Shi 4H **67**
NE45: Corb 1D **72**
SR3: New S 2C **132**
SR7: S'hm 4B **148**
Hillsview Av. NE3: Ken 7A **44**
Hillsyde Cres. DH6: Thor 1J **179**
Hill Ter. DH4: New H 3E **130**
Hillthorne Cl. NE38: Wash 4J **115**
HILL TOP
DH7 6J 151
DH9 6J 109
Hill Top DH3: Bir 4B **114**
DH7: Esh 6K **151**
DH9: Stly 2H **125**
NE21: Winl 5B **80**
Hill Top Av. NE9: Low F 2J **99**
Hilltop Bungs. DH6: Thor 2H **179**
Hill Top Cl. NE62: Chop 7H **11**
Hill Top Gdns. NE9: Low F 2J **99**
Hilltop Gdns. SR3: Tuns 2E **132**
Hilltop Ho. NE5: W Dent 3G **61**
Hilltop Rd. DH7: Bearp 7C **152**
Hilltop Vw. DH7: Lang P 5K **151**
SR6: Whit 4G **89**
Hilltop Wlk. DH7: Lang P 5K **151**
Hill Vw. DH7: Bro 4E **164**
DH7: Esh W 4E **162**
DH9: Beam 2K **125**
Hillview SR3: E Her 2H **131**
Hillview Cres. DH4: Nbot 6D **130**
Hill Vw. Gdns. SR3: Sund 5D **118**
Hillview Gro. DH4: Nbot 6D **130**
SR8: Eas C 7C **160**
Hill Vw. Rd. SR2: Sund 6F **119**
Hillview Rd. DH4: Nbot 6D **130**
Hill Vw. Sq. SR2: Sund 6F **119**
Hilton Av. NE5: Blak 3H **61**
Hilton Cl. NE23: Cra 7J **21**
Hilton Dr. SR8: Pet 7B **172**
HINDLEY 4F 91
Hindley Cl. NE40: Craw 3C **78**
Hindley Gdns. NE4: Fen 6K **61**
Hindmarch Dr. NE35: Bol C 7G **87**
NE36: W Bol 7G **87**
Hindmarsh Dr. NE63: Ash 2D **12**
Hindson's Cres. Nth.
DH4: S Row 4A **130**
Hindson's Cres. Sth. DH4: S Row 4A **130**
Hind St. SR1: Sund 4G **7** (2E **118**)
Hinkley Cl. SR3: Silk 3D **132**
Hippingstones La. NE45: Corb 7D **52**
Hipsburn Dr. SR3: Sund 5C **118**
Hiram Dr. NE36: E Bol 7K **87**
HIRST 4C 12
Hirst Castle M. NE63: Ash 3C **12**
Hirst Head NE22: Bed 7J **17**
Hirst Ter. Nth. NE22: Bed 7J **17**
Hirst Vs. NE22: Bed 7J **17**
Hirst Yd. NE63: Ash 3B **12**
Histon Ct. NE5: Blak 2H **61**
Histon Way NE5: Blak 2H **61**
Hi-Tec Village NE35: Bol C 7D **86**
Hither Grn. NE32: Jar 4D **86**
HMP & YOI Low Newton
DH1: Bras 3D **154**
HMP Durham DH1: Dur 4E **6** (3B **166**)
HMP Frankland DH1: Bras 3D **154**
Hobart NE26: Whit B 4F **39**
Hobart Av. NE34: S Shi 3F **87**
Hobart Gdns. NE7: Longb 7K **45**
HOBSON 3A 110
Hobson Ind. Est. NE16: Hob 3A **110**
Hobson's Bldgs. *DH9: Ann P* *4J* ***123***
(off North Rd.)
Hobson Way NE34: S Shi 7G **67**
Hodgkin Pk. Cres. NE15: Benw 1J **81**
Hodgkin Pk. Rd. NE15: Benw 1H **81**
Hodgson's Rd. NE24: Bly 1H **23**
Hodgson Ter. NE37: Wash 7K **101**
Hodkin Gdns. NE9: Low F 1K **99**
Hogarth Cotts. NE22: Bed 1J **21**
Hogarth Dr. NE38: Wash 5J **115**
Hogarth Rd. NE34: S Shi 4J **87**
Holbein Rd. NE34: S Shi 3J **87**
Holborn Cl. DH7: Esh W 4E **162**
Holborn Pl. NE5: W Dent 4E **60**
Holborn Rd. SR4: Sund 4K **117**
Holborn Sq. SR4: Sund 4K **117**
Holburn Av. NE24: Cow 3E **22**
Holburn Cl. NE40: Ryton 1H **79**
Holburn Ct. DH7: Ush M 3D **164**
Holburn Cres. NE40: Ryton 1J **79**
Holburn Gdns. NE40: Ryton 1J **79**
Holburn La. NE40: Ryton 7H **59**
Holburn La. Ct. NE40: Ryton 7G **59**
Holburn Ter. NE40: Ryton 1J **79**
Holburn Wlk. NE13: Haz 2B **44**
NE40: Ryton 1J **79**
Holburn Way NE40: Ryton 1H **79**
Holden Pl. NE5: Blak 3K **61**
Holder Ho. Way NE34: S Shi 3A **88**
Holderness Rd. NE6: Heat 4K **63**
NE28: W'snd 2A **66**
Hole La. NE16: Sun, Whi 3F **97**
Holeyn Hall Rd. NE41: Wylam 4H **57**
Holeyn Rd. NE15: Thro 4G **59**
Holland Dr. NE2: Newc T 2A **4** (6D **62**)
Holland Pk. NE2: Newc T 1A **4** (6D **62**)
NE28: W'snd 2C **64**
Holland Pk. Dr. NE32: Jar 4D **86**
Hollinghill Rd. NE25: H'wll 1J **37**
Hollings Cres. NE28: W'snd 1F **65**
Hollingside La. DH1: Dur 5A **166**
Hollingside Way NE34: S Shi 1K **87**
Hollings Ter. NE17: C'wl 6J **93**
Hollington Av. NE12: Longb 6K **45**
Hollington Cl. NE12: Longb 6K **45**
Hollinhill NE39: Row G 3A **96**
Hollinhill La. NE39: Row G 2K **95**
Hollin Hill Rd. NE37: Wash 1J **115**
Hollinhill Ter. NE44: Rid M 6K **73**
Hollinside Cl. NE16: Whi 2G **97**
Hollinside Gdns. NE15: Benw 7H **61**

Hollinside Rd. NE11: Dun 5H 81
NE16: Dun, Swa 5H 81
SR4: Sund 3K 117
Hollinside Sq. SR4: Sund 3J 117
Hollinside Ter. NE39: Row G 5H 95
Hollon St. NE61: Mor 6E 8
Hollow, The NE32: Jar 5B 86
NE63: N Sea 5F 13
Hollowdene DH5: Hett H 7G 145
Hollow Mdws. NE46: Hex 1E 70
Holly Av. NE2: Jes 4G 63
NE3: Fawd 6B 44
NE11: Dun 7B 82
NE12: Longb 3B 46
NE21: W Mill 1C 96
NE25: Well 6B 38
NE26: Whit B 6G 39
NE28: W'snd 4G 65
NE34: S Shi 1C 88
NE40: Ryton 7G 59
NE61: Mor 1E 14
SR3: Tuns 1D 132
SR6: Whit 5H 89
Holly Av. W. NE2: Jes 4G 63
Hollybush Gdns. NE40: Ryton 2J 79
Hollybush Rd. NE10: Fell 6A 84
Hollybush Vs. NE40: Ryton 1J 79
Hollycarrside Rd. SR2: Ryh 1G 133
Holly Cl. NE12: Kil 7K 35
NE46: Hex 3A 70
Holly Ct. NE5: Blak 3H 61
NE26: Whit B 6F 39
SR4: Sund 2C 118
Holly Cres. DH7: Sac 7E 140
NE38: Wash 7G 115
Hollycrest DH2: Ches S 4K 127
Hollydene NE11: Kib 2F 113
NE39: Row G 5K 95
Holly Gdns. DH8: C'sde 2E 134
NE9: Low F 1H 99
Holly Gro. NE42: Pru 3D 76
Hollyhaven DH5: E Rain 6D 144
Holly Hill NE10: Fell 6B 84
Holly Hill Gdns. DH9: Stly 4F 125
Holly Hill Gdns. E. DH9: Stly 4G 125
Holly Hill Gdns. W. DH9: Stly 5F 125
Hollyhock NE38: Wash 6J 115
Hollyhock Gdns. NE31: Heb 3J 85
Hollyhock Ter. DH6: Coxh 7J 177
Holly Ho. DH8: Shot B 2E 120
Holly M. NE26: Whit B 6G 39
Hollymount Av. NE22: Bed 1J 21
Hollymount Sq. NE22: Bed 1J 21
Hollymount Ter. NE22: Bed 1J 21
Hollyoak Ho. NE24: Bly 4F 23
Holly Pk. DH7: B'don 1D 174
DH7: Ush M 2C 164
Holly Pk. Vw. NE10: Fell 6B 84
Holly Rd. NE29: N Shi 5F 49
Hollys, The DH3: Bir 1K 113
Hollyside Cl. DH7: Bearp 7C 152
Hollystone Dr. NE31: Heb 6K 65
Holly St. DH1: Dur 3A 6 (3K 165)
NE32: Jar 6A 66
NE63: Ash 4B 12
Holly Ter. DH9: Ann P 4J 123
DH9: Stly 4D 124
NE16: Burn 2C 110
Holly Vw. NE10: Fell 6A 84
Hollywell Ct. DH7: Ush M 3D 164
Hollywell Gro. NE13: Wool 4F 43
Hollywell La. NE16: Sun 4H 97
Hollywell Rd. NE29: N Shi 6D 48
Hollywood Av. NE3: Gos 6F 45
NE6: Walk 4E 64
SR5: S'wck 5B 104
Hollywood Cres. NE3: Gos 6F 45
Hollywood Gdns. NE11: Lob H 2D 98
Holman Ct. NE33: S Shi 3J 67
Holmcroft NE64: Newb S 2J 13
Holmdale NE46: Hex 2E 70
NE63: Ash 5A 12
Holme Av. NE6: Walk 4D 64
NE16: Whi 7G 81
Holme Dr. NE10: Gate 10P 5 (4K 83)
Holme Gdns. NE28: W'snd 3A 66
SR3: Sund 5D 118
Holme Ri. NE16: Whi 7H 81
Holmesdale Rd. NE5: Fen 4K 61
Holmeside SR1: Sund 4J 7 (2F 119)
Holmeside Ter. NE16: Sun 5J 97
Holmesland Vs. DH7: Sac 1E 152
Holmewood Dr. NE39: Row G 7H 95
Holmfield Av. NE34: S Shi 6A 68
Holmfield Vs. DH6: Coxh 7J 177
Holm Grn. NE25: Monks 7C 38
Holm Hill Gdns. SR8: Eas 7B 160
Holmhill La. DH2: Ches M 2K 141
DH3: Ches M, Plaw 2K 141
SR8: Eas C 6B 160
Holmlands NE25: Monks 6E 38
Holmlands Cl. NE25: Monks 6E 38
Holmlands Cres. DH1: Dur 6J 153
Holmlands Pk. DH3: Ches S 7B 128
Holmlands Pk. Nth. SR2: Sund 4E 118
Holmlands Pk. Sth. SR2: Sund 4E 118
Holmlea DH7: B'hpe 6D 138
HOLMSIDE 3K 139
Holmside Av. DH7: Lan 7K 137
NE11: Dun 6C 82
Holmside Hall Rd. DH7: B'hpe, Edm 1G 139
DH9: B'hpe, Edm, Stly 1G 139
Holmside La. DH7: B'hpe, Edm 6C 138
Holmside Pl. NE6: Heat 1N 5 (6K 63)
Holmside Ter. DH9: Crag 7J 125
Holmwood Av. NE25: Monks 7D 38
NE64: Newb S 2H 13
Holmwood Gro. NE2: Jes 3F 63
Holwick Cl. DH8: Cons 1J 135
NE38: Wash 6E 114
HOLY CROSS 2H 65
Holy Cross Cemetery NE28: W'snd 2H 65
Holy Cross Church (remains of) 2G 65
Holyfields NE27: Shir 2H 47
Holyhead Cl. SR7: S'hm 4H 147
Holy Ho. *SR1: Sund* *1H 119*
(off Adelaide Pl.)
Holy Island NE46: Hex 1C 70
Holy Jesus Bungs.
NE2: Newc T 1A 4 (5D 62)
Holy Jesus Hospital 6H 5 (1G 83)
Holylake Sq. SR4: Sund 3K 117
Holyoake DH9: Stly 5E 124
Holyoake Gdns. DH3: Bir 4A 114
NE9: Low F 6H 83
Holyoake St. DH2: Pelt 3E 126
NE42: Pru 3F 77
Holyoake Ter. DH9: Stly 5E 124
NE37: Wash 7H 101
SR6: Ful 4G 105
Holyrood DH3: Gt Lum 2E 142
Holyrood Rd. SR2: Sund 6H 119
HOLYSTONE 3G 47
Holystone Av. NE3: Gos 6D 44
NE24: Bly 4G 23
NE25: Whit B 7H 39
Holystone Cl. DH4: Hou S 7B 130
NE24: Bly 4F 23
Holystone Ct. NE8: Gate 5F 83
Holystone Cres. NE7: H Hea 2K 63
Holystone Dr. NE27: Kil 2G 47
Holystone Gdns. NE29: N Shi 4D 48
Holystone Grange NE27: Longb 3G 47
Holystone St. NE31: Heb 7H 65
Holystone Trad. Est. NE31: Heb 7H 65
Holystone Way NE12: Longb 4F 47
NE27: Longb 4F 47
HOLYWELL 1K 37
Holywell Av. NE6: Walk 3C 84
NE25: H'wll 1K 37
NE26: Monks 5E 38
Holywell Cl. NE4: Newc T 3B 4 (7D 62)
NE21: Blay 5D 80
NE25: H'wll 1K 37
Holywell Dene 1B 38
Holywell Dene Rd. NE25: H'wll 1K 37
Holywell M. NE26: Monks 5F 39
Holywell Pond Nature Reserve 7K 27
Holywell Rd. DH5: Hou S 2F 145
Holywell Ter. NE27: Shir 3H 47
Home Av. NE9: Low F 3H 99
Homedale NE42: Pru 4G 77
Homedale Ct. NE46: Hex 2E 70
Homedale Pl. NE42: Pru 5G 77
Homedale Ter. *NE42: Pru* *4G 77*
(off Homedale)
Homedowne Ho. NE3: Gos 7E 44
Home Farm Cl. NE63: Ash 3H 11
Homeforth Ho. NE3: Gos 7E 44
Homelea DH4: Bour 5J 129
Home Pk. NE28: W'snd 2C 64
Homeprior Ho. NE25: Monks 7E 38
Homer Ter. DH1: Dur 4J 165
Homestall Cl. NE34: S Shi 1K 87
Home Vw. NE38: Wash 3J 115
Honeycomb Cl. SR3: Dox P 4B 132
Honeycrook Dr. NE7: H Hea 2C 64
Honeysuckle Av. NE34: S Shi 2H 87
Honeysuckle Cl. SR3: Dox P 4C 132
Honeysuckle Ter. DH5: Eas L 3J 157
Honister Av. NE2: Jes 2G 63
Honister Cl. NE15: Lem 6D 60
Honister Dr. SR5: Ful 4E 104
Honister Pl. NE15: Lem 6D 60
Honister Rd. NE30: Cull 2H 49
Honister Way NE24: News 6G 23
Honiton Cl. DH4: Nbot 5C 130
Honiton Ct. NE3: Ki Pk 6H 43
Honiton Way NE29: N Shi 4B 48
Hood Cl. SR5: Monkw 6E 104
Hood Sq. NE21: Winl 5A 80
Hood St. NE1: Newc T 5F 4 (1F 83)
NE16: Swa 5G 81
NE61: Mor 6F 9
HOOKER GATE 5E 94
Hookergate La. NE39: H Spen, Row G 3D 94
(not continuous)
Hope Av. SR8: Hord 6E 172
Hopedene NE10: Hew 2E 100
Hope La. DH6: S'burn 3A 168
Hope Shield NE38: Wash 7D 114
Hope St. DH6: S'burn 3K 167
DH8: B'hill 5G 121
NE32: Jar 6C 66
SR1: Sund 4G 7 (2E 118)
Hope Vw. SR2: Ryh 2H 133
Hopgarth Ct. DH3: Ches S 5B 128
Hopgarth Gdns. DH3: Ches S 5B 128
Hopkins Ct. SR4: Sund 1B 118
Hopkins Wlk. NE34: S Shi 4G 87
Hopper Pl. DH1: Dur 6A 154
NE8: Gate 10J 5 (3H 83)
Hopper Rd. NE10: Wind N 7A 84
Hoppers Ct. *NE16: Swa* *5G 81*
(off Front St.)
Hopper St. NE8: Gate 10J 5 (3H 83)
NE28: W'snd 3E 64
NE29: N Shi 7G 49
SR8: Eas 7K 159
Hopper St. W. NE29: N Shi 7F 49
Hopper Ter. DH6: Shot C 6E 170
Hopton Ct. NE5: West 7G 43
Hopton Dr. SR2: Ryh 4H 133
Horatio Ho. NE30: Tyne 5K 49
Horatio St. NE1: Newc T 6L 5 (1J 83)
SR6: Roker 6G 105
HORDEN 5E 172
Horden Dene SR8: Eas C 1D 172
Hornbeam DH4: S Row 4K 129
Hornbeam Pl. NE4: Elsw 9A 4 (3D 82)
Horncliffe Gdns. NE16: Swa 6J 81
Horncliffe Pl. NE15: Thro 3F 59
Horncliffe Wlk. NE15: Lem 6A 60
Horning Ct. NE5: Blak 1H 61
Hornsby Ct. NE28: W'snd 2J 65
Hornsea Cl. NE13: W Op 6D 34
Hornsey Cres. DH5: Eas L 2H 157
Hornsey Ter. DH5: Eas L 2H 157
Horse Crofts NE21: Blay 3C 80
Horsegate Bank NE17: C'wl 3B 94
NE40: Coal 3B 94
Horsham Gdns. SR3: Sund 5C 118
Horsham Gro. NE29: N Shi 1E 66
Horsham Ho. NE29: N Shi 1E 66
HORSLEY 5E 56
Horsley Av. NE27: Shir 2K 47
NE40: Craw 3C 78
Horsley Bldgs. NE61: Mor 7G 9
Horsley Bus. Cen. NE15: Hor 5F 57
Horsley Cl. NE62: Stake 7H 11
Horsley Ct. NE3: Fawd 6A 44
Horsley Gdns. NE11: Dun 6C 82
NE25: H'wll 1K 37
SR3: Sund 5C 118
HORSLEY HILL 6D 68
Horsley Hill Rd. NE33: S Shi 4A 68
Horsley Hill Sq. NE34: S Shi 6D 68
(not continuous)
Horsley Ho. NE3: Gos 6E 44
Horsley Rd. NE7: H Hea 4K 63
NE38: Wash 2A 116
NE42: O'ham 1C 76
Horsley Ter. NE6: Walk 1D 84
NE30: Tyne 5K 49
Horsley Va. NE34: S Shi 6B 68
Horsley Vw. NE28: W'snd 3A 66
NE42: Pru 3H 77
Horsley Wood Cotts. NE15: Hor 6F 57
Horton Av. NE22: Bed 1H 21
NE27: Shir 2K 47
NE34: S Shi 3K 87
Horton Cl. DH8: Cons 2K 135
Horton Cres. DH6: Bowb 3H 177
NE13: Din 4H 33
Hortondale Gro. NE24: Cow 2F 23
Horton Dr. NE23: Cra 1J 25
Horton Grange Rd. NE13: Din 1G 33
Horton Mnr. NE24: Cow 2B 22
Horton Pk. NE24: Cow 2D 22
Horton Pl. NE24: News 5F 23
Horton Rd. NE24: Bed, Bly, Cow 2K 21
Horton St. NE24: Bly 2K 23
Horwood Av. NE5: West 2D 60
Hospital Dr. NE31: Heb 2H 85
Hospital La. NE15: Lem, Newb 6A 60
Hospital of St Mary the Virgin, The
NE4: Newc T 8B 4 (2D 82)
Hospital Rd. DH7: Lang P 5H 151
Hotch Pudding Pl. NE5: W Dent 5F 61
Hotspur Av. NE22: Bed 1H 21
NE25: Whit B 7G 39
NE34: S Shi 6A 68
Hotspur Nth. NE27: Back 1G 47
Hotspur Rd. NE28: W'snd 7E 46
Hotspur Sth. NE27: Back 1H 47
Hotspur St. NE6: Heat 2L 5 (6J 63)
NE30: Tyne 4K 49
Hotspur Way NE1: Newc T 4F 4 (7F 63)
HOUGHALL 7B 166
HOUGHTON 3B 58
Houghton Av. NE5: Blak 2A 62
NE30: Cull 1H 49
Houghton Cut DH4: Hou S 1E 144
Houghton Ent. Cen. DH5: Hou S 2E 144
Houghton Ga. DH3: Gt Lum 6F 129
HOUGHTON-LE-SPRING 2E 144
Houghton Rd. DH4: Hou S, Nbot 6D 130
DH5: Hett H 4F 145
Houghton Rd. Nth. DH5: Hett H 4F 145
Houghton Rd. W. DH5: Hett H 6G 145
Houghtonside DH4: Hou S 1E 144
Houghton Sports Cen. 1D 144
Houghton St. SR4: Sund 2C 118
Houghton Wheeled Sports Pk. 1D 144
Houghwell Gdns. DH9: Stly, Tan L 1D 124
Houlet Gth. NE6: Byke 6P 5 (1A 84)
Houlsyke Cl. SR3: Tuns 2E 132
Hoults Estates NE6: Byke 6P 5 (1K 83)
Houndelee Pl. NE5: Fen 4J 61
Houndslow Dr. NE63: Ash 5K 11
Hounslow Gdns. NE32: Jar 4D 86
Housesteads Cl. NE28: W'snd 3A 66
Housesteads Gdns. NE12: Longb 6H 45
House Ter. NE37: Wash 7H 101
Housing La. DH8: M'sly 7A 108
Houston Ct. NE4: Newc T 7B 4 (2D 82)
Houston St. NE4: Newc T 7B 4 (2D 82)
Houxty Rd. NE25: Well 6B 38
Hovingham Cl. SR8: Pet 7C 172
Hovingham Gdns. SR3: Sund 5C 118
Howard Cl. NE27: Longb 3G 47
Howard Ct. NE30: N Shi 7H 49
Howard Gro. NE61: Peg 4A 10
Howardian Cl. NE38: Wash 5F 115
Howard Pl. NE3: Gos 7E 44
Howard Rd. NE61: Mor 6G 9
Howards Bldgs. DH8: C'sde 4D 134
Howard St. NE1: Newc T 5K 5 (1H 83)
NE8: Gate 5K 83
NE10: Wind N 1A 100
NE30: N Shi 7H 49
NE32: Jar 6C 66
SR5: Monkw 6F 105
Howard Ter. NE39: H Spen 3D 94
NE61: Mor 6F 9
Howard Wlk. NE63: Ash 2D 12
Howarth St. SR4: Sund 2C 118
Howarth Ter. DH6: Has 1B 170
Howat Av. NE5: Fen 4A 62
Howburn Ct. NE61: Mor 5G 9
Howburn Cres. NE61: Peg 4A 10
Howden DH8: B'hill 6F 121
Howden Bank DH7: Lan 5J 137
Howden Bank Cotts. DH7: Lan 3A 138
Howden Cl. NE45: Corb 1F 73
Howdene Rd. NE15: Den M 7F 61
Howden Gdns. TS28: Win 5G 181
HOWDON 2A 66
Howdon Grn. NE28: W'snd 3B 66
Howdon La. NE28: W'snd 2A 66
HOWDON PANS 4C 66
Howdon Rd. NE28: W'snd 3C 66
NE29: N Shi, W'snd 3C 66
Howdon Station (Metro) 3A 66
Howe Sq. SR4: Sund 3J 117
Howe St. NE8: Gate 5K 83
NE31: Heb 7A 66
Howford La. NE46: Acomb 4A 50
Howford Quarry NE46: Acomb 4A 50
Howick Av. NE3: Gos 5C 44
Howick Pk. SR6: Monkw 1K 7 (7F 105)
Howick Rd. SR6: Monkw 1K 7 (7F 105)
Howlands (Park & Ride) 6A 166
Howlcroft Vs. DH1: Dur 4J 165
Howletch La. SR8: Pet 6A 172
Howlett DH2: P Fel 5G 127
Howlett Hall Rd. NE15: Den M 6F 61
Howley Av. SR5: Sund 5J 103
Hownam Cl. NE3: Gos 1C 62
Hownham Cl. NE25: Sea D 6G 27
Hownsgill Dr. DH8: Cons 3K 135
Hownsgill Ind. Pk. DH8: Cons 2H 135
Hoy Cres. SR7: S'hm 1H 147
Hoylake Av. NE7: Longb 7A 46
Hoyle Av. NE4: Fen 7A 62
Hoyle Fold SR3: Dox P 5C 132
Hoyson Vs. NE10: Bill Q 4F 85
Hubbway Bus. Cen. NE23: Cra 3F 25
Hubert St. NE35: Bol C 6F 87
Hucklow Gdns. NE34: S Shi 1K 87
Huddart Ter. DH3: Bir 3A 114
Huddleston Rd. NE6: Walk 6B 64
Hudleston NE30: Cull 7J 39
Hudleston Ri. SR6: Roker 7G 105
Hudshaw NE46: Hex 2F 71
Hudshaw Gdns. NE46: Hex 2F 71
Hudson Av. NE22: Bed 7K 17
NE23: Dud 3K 35
SR8: Hord 5D 172
Hudson Dock 1J 119
Hudson Pl. NE61: Mor 6F 9
Hudson Rd. SR1: Sund 2G 119
Hudson St. NE8: Gate 9H 5 (3G 83)
NE30: N Shi 6H 49
NE34: S Shi 7H 67
(not continuous)
Hudson Wlk. NE63: Ash 2D 12
Hudspeth Cres. DH1: P Me 4J 153
Hugar Rd. NE39: H Spen 4D 94
Hugh Av. NE27: Shir 7K 37
Hugh Gdns. NE4: Benw 2A 82
Hugh St. NE28: W'snd 4F 65
NE38: Wash 4K 115
SR6: Ful 3G 105
Hull St. NE4: Elsw 1B 82
Hulme Ct. SR8: Pet 7A 172
Hulne Av. NE30: Tyne 5K 49
Hulne Ter. NE15: Lem 7C 60
Humber Ct. SR3: Silk 3B 132
Humber Gdns. NE8: Gate 5K 83
Humber Hill DH9: Stly 4G 125
Humberhill Dr. DH7: Lan 7J 137
Humberhill La. DH7: Lan 5C 136
Humber St. NE17: C'wl 6A 94
Humbert St. NE32: Jar 7B 66
Humber Vw. DH9: Ann P 7H 123
Humbleburn La. DH7: Edm 1A 140
Humbledon Pk. SR3: Sund 5C 118
Humbledon Vw. SR2: Sund 7H 7 (4E 118)
Humbleton Rd. NE13: Ki Pk 4A 44
Hume St. NE6: Byke 5M 5 (1J 83)
SR4: Sund 2C 118
Humford Grn. NE24: Cow 2D 22
Humford Way NE22: Bed 2J 21
Humsford Gro. NE23: Cra 2A 26
Humshaugh Cl. NE12: Longb 4E 46
Humshaugh Rd. NE29: N Shi 6C 48
Hunns Bldgs. NE62: Sco G 3G 17
Hunstanton SR7: S'hm 2A 148
Hunstanton Ct. NE9: Low F 4G 99
Huntcliffe Av. SR6: Seab 1G 105
Huntcliffe Gdns. NE6: Heat 4A 64
Hunter Av. DH7: Ush M 2B 164
NE24: Bly 3K 23
Hunter Cl. NE36: E Bol 1K 103
Hunter Ho. NE6: Walk 2E 84
Hunter Memorial Homes *NE61: Mor* *7F 9*
(off Oldgate)
Hunter Pl. SR8: Eas C 7B 160
Hunter Rd. SR8: Pet 7J 171

Hunters Cl. DH8: M'sly . . . 7A **108**
Hunters Ct. NE3: Gos . . . 7G **45**
NE28: W'snd . . . 3G **65**
Hunters Hall Rd. SR4: Sund . . . 3D **118**
Hunters Lodge NE28: W'snd . . . 3G **65**
Hunters Moor Cl.
NE2: Newc T . . . 1A **4** (6D **62**)
Hunters Pl. NE2: Newc T . . . 1A **4** (5D **62**)
Hunters Rd. NE2: Newc T . . . 1A **4** (6C **62**)
NE3: Gos . . . 7H **45**
Hunter's Ter. *NE9: Spri . . . 6E **100***
(off Peareth Hall Rd.)
NE33: S Shi . . . 4K **67**
Hunter St. DH4: S Row . . . 4A **130**
NE33: S Shi . . . 4K **67**
Hunter Ter. SR2: Sund . . . 4G **119**
Huntingdon Cl. NE3: Ki Pk . . . 4J **43**
Huntingdon Dr. NE23: Cra . . . 3A **26**
Huntingdon Gdns. SR3: Sund . . . 5C **118**
Huntingdon Pl. NE30: Tyne . . . 5K **49**
Huntingdon Rd. SR8: Pet . . . 4A **172**
Huntingdonshire Dr. DH1: Carr . . . 1H **167**
Hunt Lea NE16: Whi . . . 2E **96**
Huntley Av. SR7: Mur . . . 7D **146**
Huntley Cres. NE21: Winl . . . 6A **80**
Huntley Sq. SR4: Sund . . . 3K **117**
Huntley Ter. SR2: Ryh . . . 3H **133**
Huntly Rd. NE25: Monks . . . 4C **38**
Huntscliffe Ho. NE34: S Shi . . . 3J **87**
Hunworth Cl. SR4: Sund . . . 3K **117**
Hurbuck Cotts. DH7: Lan . . . 4D **136**
Hursley Wlk. NE6: Walk . . . 3C **84**
Hurst Ter. NE6: Walk . . . 7C **64**
Hurstwood Rd. SR4: Sund . . . 4C **118**
Hurworth Av. NE34: S Shi . . . 7C **68**
Hurworth Pl. NE32: Jar . . . 7B **66**
Hustledown Gdns. DH9: Stly . . . 5F **125**
Hustledown Ho. DH9: Stly . . . 3F **125**
Hustledown Rd. DH9: Stly . . . 5E **124**
Hutchinson Av. DH8: Cons . . . 6H **121**
Hutton Cl. DH3: Ches S . . . 1C **142**
DH4: Hou S . . . 2C **144**
NE38: Wash . . . 3D **114**
Hutton Ct. DH6: S Het . . . 4B **158**
DH9: Ann P . . . 5K **123**
Hutton Gro. DH6: Has . . . 7A **158**
HUTTON HENRY . . . 7A **182**
Hutton Ho. NE29: N Shi . . . 2E **66**
Hutton Row NE33: S Shi . . . 3A **68**
Hutton St. NE3: Gos . . . 7C **44**
NE35: Bol C . . . 5F **87**
SR4: Sund . . . 3D **118**
Hutton Ter. NE2: Jes . . . 1J **5** (6H **63**)
NE9: Low F . . . 3H **99**
Hutton Way DH1: Dur . . . 4A **154**
Huxley Cl. NE34: S Shi . . . 4H **87**
Huxley Cres. NE8: Gate . . . 7F **83**
Hyacinth Ct. SR4: Sund . . . 1D **118**
Hybrid Cl. DH4: S Row . . . 4K **129**
Hydenside DH8: C'sde . . . 2E **134**
Hyde Pk. NE28: W'snd . . . 2D **64**
Hyde Pk. St. NE8: Gate . . . 6F **83**
Hyde St. NE33: S Shi . . . 3K **67**
SR2: Sund . . . 4H **119**
Hyde Ter. NE3: Gos . . . 7F **45**
Hylton Av. NE34: S Shi . . . 7D **68**
Hylton Bank SR4: Sund . . . 2H **117**
HYLTON CASTLE . . . 5G **103**
Hylton Castle (remains of) . . . 5H **103**
Hylton Castle Rd. SR5: Sund . . . 6H **103**
Hylton Cl. DH7: Lang P . . . 5H **151**
NE22: Bed . . . 7F **17**
Hylton Ct. DH1: Dur . . . 5B **154**
NE38: Wash . . . 3F **115**
Hylton Dene Local Nature Reserve . . . 5H **103**
Hylton Grange SR5: Sund . . . 1F **117**
Hylton La. NE36: W Bol . . . 1G **103**
SR5: Sund . . . 3G **103**
Hylton Pk. SR5: Sund . . . 6A **104**
Hylton Pk. Rd. SR5: Sund . . . 6K **103**
HYLTON RED HOUSE . . . 5J **103**
Hylton Riverside Retail Pk.
SR5: Sund . . . 6K **103**
Hylton Rd. DH1: Dur . . . 5A **154**
NE32: Jar . . . 2B **86**
SR4: Sund . . . 3F **7** (4G **117**)
Hylton St. DH4: Hou S . . . 7D **130**
NE8: Gate . . . 5K **83**
NE29: N Shi . . . 1G **67**
SR4: Sund . . . 2C **118**
Hylton Ter. DH2: Pelt . . . 2G **127**
NE10: Bill Q . . . 4F **85**
NE29: N Shi . . . 7G **49**
SR2: Ryh . . . 3G **133**
Hylton Wlk. SR4: Sund . . . 3G **117**
Hymers Av. NE34: S Shi . . . 2F **87**
Hyperion Av. NE34: S Shi . . . 1G **87**
Hyperion Way NE6: Walk . . . 2E **84**
Hysehope Ter. *DH8: Cons . . . 7J **121***
(off Cobden St.)

I

Ilchester St. SR7: S'hm . . . 4B **148**
Ilderton Cres. NE25: Sea D . . . 6G **27**
Ilderton Pl. NE5: W Dent . . . 5E **60**
Ilford Av. NE23: Cra . . . 1J **25**
Ilford Pl. NE8: Gate . . . 6J **83**
Ilford Rd. NE2: Jes . . . 2F **63**
NE28: W'snd . . . 2K **65**
Ilford Road Station (Metro) . . . 2F **63**
Ilfracombe Av. NE4: Benw . . . 1A **82**
Ilfracombe Gdns. NE9: Low F . . . 4H **99**
NE26: Whit B . . . 5F **39**
Illingworth Ho. NE29: N Shi . . . 2E **66**
Ilminster Ct. NE3: Ki Pk . . . 6J **43**
Imeary Gro. NE33: S Shi . . . 4K **67**
Imeary St. NE33: S Shi . . . 4K **67**
Imex Bus. Cen. DH3: Bir . . . 4K **113**
Imperial Bldgs. DH4: Hou S . . . 2E **144**
Inchberry Cl. NE4: Benw . . . 2A **82**
Inchcape Ter. SR8: Eas C . . . 1D **172**
Inchcliffe Cres. NE5: Blak . . . 3J **61**
Independence Sq. NE38: Wash . . . 3G **115**
Industrial Rd. NE37: Wash . . . 7J **101**
(not continuous)
Industrial St. DH2: Pelt . . . 3E **126**
Industry Rd. NE6: Heat . . . 3B **64**
Ingham Grange NE33: S Shi . . . 4K **67**
Ingham Gro. NE23: Cra . . . 1J **25**
Ingham Pl. NE2: Newc T . . . 4K **5** (7H **63**)
Ingham Ter. NE41: Wylam . . . 7K **57**
Ingleborough Cl. NE37: Wash . . . 2E **114**
Ingleby Ter. SR4: Sund . . . 3C **118**
Ingleby Way NE24: News . . . 6G **23**
Ingleside NE16: Whi . . . 1F **97**
NE34: S Shi . . . 7D **68**
Ingleside Rd. NE29: N Shi . . . 5F **49**
Ingleton Ct. SR4: Sund . . . 3C **118**
Ingleton Dr. NE15: Thro . . . 3F **59**
Ingleton Gdns. NE24: News . . . 6G **23**
Inglewood Cl. NE24: Cow . . . 2D **22**
Inglewood Pl. NE3: Gos . . . 3E **44**
Ingoe Av. NE3: Fawd . . . 5B **44**
Ingoe Cl. NE24: Bly . . . 2G **23**
Ingoe St. NE15: Lem . . . 7C **60**
NE28: W'snd . . . 3C **66**
Ingoldsby Ct. SR4: Sund . . . 4A **118**
Ingram Av. NE3: Fawd . . . 4B **44**
Ingram Cl. DH2: Ches S . . . 1J **141**
NE28: W'snd . . . 7K **47**
Ingram Dr. NE5: Cha P . . . 1D **60**
NE24: Bly . . . 2F **23**
Ingram Ter. NE6: Walk . . . 7E **64**
Ingram Way TS28: Win . . . 4G **181**
Inkerman Rd. NE37: Wash . . . 6H **101**
Inkerman St. SR5: S'wck . . . 6C **104**
Inleborough Dr. NE40: Ryton . . . 2H **79**
Innesmoor NE31: Heb . . . 6H **65**
Inskip Ho. NE34: S Shi . . . 1J **87**
Inskip Ter. NE8: Gate . . . 6H **83**
Institute Rd. NE63: Ash . . . 3K **11**
Institute Ter. DH7: Bearp . . . 1E **164**
Institute Ter. E. DH2: Ous . . . 1H **127**
Institute Ter. W. DH2: Ous . . . 1H **127**
Interchange Cen.
NE8: Gate . . . 10H **5** (3G **83**)
Inverness Rd. NE32: Jar . . . 3E **86**
Inverness St. SR6: Ful . . . 5F **105**
Invertay NE3: Gos . . . 7F **45**
Invincible Dr. NE4: Newc T . . . 10A **4** (3C **82**)
Iolanthe Cres. NE6: Walk . . . 6C **64**
Iolanthe Ter. NE33: S Shi . . . 3A **68**
Iona Ct. NE28: W'snd . . . 1K **65**
Iona Pl. NE6: Walk . . . 7E **64**
Iona Rd. NE10: Wind N . . . 7K **83**
NE32: Jar . . . 3E **86**
Irene Av. SR2: Sund . . . 7H **119**
Irene Ter. DH7: Lang P . . . 5J **151**
Iris Cl. NE21: Winl . . . 4A **80**
Iris Cres. DH2: Ous . . . 6H **113**
Iris Pl. NE4: Fen . . . 6K **61**
Iris Steadman Ho. NE4: Newc T . . . 4A **4**
Iris Ter. DH4: Bour . . . 6J **129**
NE40: Craw . . . 3D **78**
Ironside St. DH5: Hou S . . . 1E **144**
Irthing Av. NE6: Byke . . . 2B **84**
Irton St. NE3: Gos . . . 7E **44**
Irvin Bldgs. NE30: N Shi . . . 6J **49**
Irvine Ho. NE12: Longb . . . 4B **46**
Irving Pl. NE42: O'ham . . . 2D **76**
Irwin Av. NE28: W'snd . . . 2G **65**
Isabella Cl. NE4: Benw . . . 3A **82**
Isabella Colliery Rd.
NE24: Bly . . . 3G **23**
ISABELLA PIT . . . 3G **23**
Isabella Rd. NE24: Bly . . . 3G **23**
Isabella Wlk. NE15: Thro . . . 4H **59**
Isis Rd. SR8: Pet . . . 7A **172**
Islay Ho. SR3: Silk . . . 3C **132**
Islestone NE9: Low F . . . 3H **99**
Ivanhoe NE25: Monks . . . 6E **38**
Ivanhoe Cres. SR2: Sund . . . 4D **118**
Ivanhoe Ter. DH3: Ches S . . . 7B **128**
DH9: Dip . . . 7J **109**
Ivanhoe Vw. NE9: Low F . . . 5K **99**
Iveagh Cl. NE4: Benw . . . 2K **81**
Ivesley Cotts. DH7: Wat . . . 6A **162**
Ivesley La. DH7: Wat . . . 4A **162**
Ivesley Vs. DH7: Wat . . . 6B **162**
Iveson Rd. NE46: Hex . . . 3A **70**
Iveson Ter. DH7: Sac . . . 7D **140**
IVESTON . . . 1D **136**
Iveston Av. NE13: Haz . . . 2A **44**
Iveston La. DH8: Cons . . . 1D **136**
Iveston Rd. DH8: Cons . . . 2K **135**
Iveston Ter. DH9: Stly . . . 2F **125**
Ivy Av. NE40: Ryton . . . 7G **59**
SR7: S'hm . . . 4K **147**
Ivy Cl. NE4: Newc T . . . 9B **4** (3D **82**)
NE40: Ryton . . . 7G **59**
Ivy Farm Ct. NE13: K Bank . . . 5H **43**
Ivy La. NE9: Low F . . . 3J **99**
Ivymount Rd. NE6: Heat . . . 4K **63**
Ivy Pl. DH9: Tant . . . 5C **110**
Ivy Rd. NE3: Gos . . . 7E **44**
NE6: Walk . . . 5D **64**
NE12: Longb . . . 4C **46**
Ivy St. NE13: Sea B . . . 3E **34**
Ivy Ter. DH4: S Row . . . 3B **130**
DH7: Lang P . . . 5J **151**
DH9: Stly . . . 6H **125**
(Hazel Ter.)
DH9: Stly . . . 5D **124**
(Pine St.)
NE40: Craw . . . 3C **78**
Ivyway DH2: Pelt . . . 2G **127**

J

Jack Comn. Ho. NE6: Heat . . . 1P **5** (6K **63**)
Jack Crawford Ho. SR2: Sund . . . 4H **119**
Jack Lawson Ter. DH6: Whe H . . . 3A **180**
Jackson Av. NE20: Pon . . . 4K **31**
Jackson Cl. DH8: Cons . . . 7G **121**
Jackson Rd. NE41: Wylam . . . 7K **57**
Jacksons Pl. DH3: Bir . . . 3A **114**
Jackson St. NE6: Walk . . . 7D **64**
NE8: Gate . . . 10J **5** (3H **83**)
NE30: N Shi . . . 6H **49**
SR4: Sund . . . 3C **118**
Jackson St. W. NE30: N Shi . . . 6H **49**
Jackson Ter. NE61: Mor . . . 7G **9**
SR8: Eas . . . 7J **159**
Jack's Ter. NE34: S Shi . . . 1H **87**
Jacobins Chare NE1: Newc T . . . 5D **4** (1E **82**)
Jacques St. SR4: Sund . . . 1B **118**
Jacques Ter. DH2: Ches S . . . 5K **127**
Jade Cl. NE15: Lem . . . 5C **60**
James Armitage St. SR5: S'wck . . . 5D **104**
James Av. NE27: Shir . . . 1K **47**
James Bowman Ho. NE12: Kil . . . 1C **46**
James Mather St. NE33: S Shi . . . 2J **67**
Jameson Dr. NE45: Corb . . . 6F **53**
Jameson St. DH8: Cons . . . 6H **121**
James Pl. St. NE6: Byke . . . 4M **5** (7J **63**)
James St. DH9: Ann P . . . 5A **124**
DH9: Dip . . . 2F **123**
DH9: Stly . . . 7F **111**
NE4: Elsw . . . 2B **82**
NE5: West . . . 3F **61**
NE16: Whi . . . 7G **81**
SR5: S'wck . . . 5C **104**
SR7: S'hm . . . 4B **148**
SR8: Eas C . . . 6B **160**
James St. Nth. *SR7: Mur . . . 7F **147***
(off Nth. Coronation St.)
James St. Sth. SR7: Mur . . . 7F **147**
James Ter. DH4: Hou S . . . 2A **144**
DH5: Eas L . . . 3H **157**
NE28: W'snd . . . 4F **65**
James Williams St. SR1: Sund . . . 1G **119**
Jamieson Ter. DH6: S Het . . . 5D **158**
Jam Jar Cinema . . . 6H **39**
Jane St. DH5: Hett H . . . 4G **145**
DH9: Stly . . . 5D **124**
NE6: Byke . . . 7A **64**
Jane Ter. NE6: Walk . . . 1E **84**
Janet Sq. NE6: Byke . . . 1A **84**
Janet St. NE6: Byke . . . 6P **5** (1A **84**)
(Kirk St.)
NE6: Byke . . . 2A **84**
(St Peter's Rd., not continuous)
January Courtyard *NE8: Gate . . . 5D **82***
(off Teemers Dr.)
Janus Cl. NE5: Cha P . . . 1C **60**
JARROW . . . 6B **66**
Jarrow Bus Station . . . 6B **66**
Jarrow Community Pool . . . 1B **86**
Jarrow Rd. NE34: Jar, S Shi . . . 7F **67**
Jarrow Slake . . . 6E **66**
Jarrow Station (Metro) . . . 6B **66**
Jarvis Rd. SR8: Pet . . . 4B **172**
Jasmin Av. NE5: Cha P . . . 1C **60**
Jasmine Cl. NE6: Walk . . . 4C **64**
Jasmine Ct. NE63: Ash . . . 6A **12**
SR4: Sund . . . 3F **7** (1D **118**)
Jasmine Cres. SR7: S'hm . . . 5A **148**
Jasmine Ter. DH3: Bir . . . 4B **114**
Jasmine Vs. *NE16: Whi . . . 7G **81***
(off Front St.)
Jasper Av. NE40: G'sde . . . 5F **79**
SR7: S'hm . . . 4K **147**
Jaycroft Ct. *NE30: N Shi . . . 7H **49***
(off Stephenson St.)
Jays Ct. NE22: Bed . . . 7H **17**
Jedburgh Cl. NE5: Cha P . . . 1C **60**
NE8: Gate . . . 5H **83**
NE29: N Shi . . . 4E **48**
SR7: Mur . . . 1C **158**
Jedburgh Ct. NE11: T Vall . . . 5G **99**
Jedburgh Gdns. NE15: Benw . . . 7H **61**
Jedburgh Rd. DH4: S Row . . . 3B **130**
NE2: Newc T . . . 1C **4** (4A **62**)
NE4: Fen, Newc T . . . 4A **62**
Jedmoor NE31: Heb . . . 6H **65**
Jefferson Cl. SR5: Ful . . . 3E **104**
Jefferson Pl. NE4: Newc T . . . 4B **4** (7D **62**)
Jellico Ter. DH4: Leam . . . 7H **143**
Jenifer Gro. NE7: H Hea . . . 2J **63**
Jenison Av. NE15: Benw . . . 1J **81**
Jennifer Av. SR5: Sund . . . 6H **103**
Jervis St. NE31: Heb . . . 7K **65**
JESMOND . . . 4H **63**
Jesmond Dene . . . 2H **63**
Jesmond Dene Rd. NE2: Jes . . . 3F **63**
Jesmond Dene Ter. NE2: Jes . . . 4J **63**
Jesmond Gdns. NE2: Jes . . . 4H **63**
NE34: S Shi . . . 3J **87**
Jesmond Pk. Ct. NE7: H Hea . . . 4K **63**
Jesmond Pk. E. NE7: H Hea . . . 3K **63**
Jesmond Pk. M. NE7: H Hea . . . 4J **63**
Jesmond Pk. W. NE7: H Hea . . . 3J **63**
Jesmond Pl. NE2: Jes . . . 4G **63**
Jesmond Rd. NE2: Jes . . . 1H **5** (6H **63**)
Jesmond Rd. W. NE2: Jes . . . 2F **4** (6F **63**)
Jesmond Station (Metro) . . . 1H **5** (6G **63**)
Jesmond Swimming Pool . . . 3G **63**
Jesmond Ter. NE26: Whit B . . . 7H **39**
JESMOND VALE . . . 1M **5** (6J **63**)
Jesmond Va. NE2: Newc T . . . 1L **5** (6J **63**)
Jesmond Va. La. NE6: Heat . . . 1N **5** (5K **63**)
Jesmond Va. Ter. NE6: Heat . . . 5K **63**
(not continuous)
Jessel St. NE9: Low F . . . 3H **99**
Jetty, The NE10: Bill Q . . . 4E **84**
Joan Av. SR2: Sund . . . 7H **119**
Joannah St. SR5: Ful . . . 4E **104**
Joan St. NE4: Benw . . . 2K **81**
(not continuous)
Jobling Av. NE21: Winl . . . 4A **80**
Jobling Cres. NE61: Mor . . . 1H **15**
Joel Ter. NE10: Bill Q . . . 4F **85**
Joe's Pond Nature Reserve . . . 4B **144**
John Av. NE40: G'sde . . . 5F **79**
John Brown Ct. NE22: Bed . . . 7H **17**
John Candlish Rd. SR4: Sund . . . 1C **118**
John Clay St. NE33: S Shi . . . 5K **67**
(Dean Rd.)
NE33: S Shi . . . 4K **67**
(Halstead Pl.)
John Dobson St. NE1: Newc T . . . 3F **4** (7F **63**)
John F Kennedy Est. NE38: Wash . . . 2J **115**
(not continuous)
John Reid Rd. NE34: S Shi . . . 2E **86**
(not continuous)
Johnson Cl. SR8: Pet . . . 4B **172**
Johnson Est. DH6: Whe H . . . 3B **180**
Johnson's Bldgs. DH8: Cons . . . 1C **136**
Johnson's St. TS28: Win . . . 7G **181**
Johnson St. NE8: Gate . . . 5D **82**
NE11: Dun . . . 5B **82**
NE15: Lem . . . 7C **60**
NE33: S Shi . . . 6J **67**
SR1: Sund . . . 3F **7** (1D **118**)
Johnson Ter. DH6: Crox . . . 6K **175**
DH9: Ann P . . . 6A **124**
NE37: Wash . . . 7K **101**
NE39: H Spen . . . 3D **94**
Johnson Vs. NE62: Chop . . . 1D **16**
Johnston Av. NE31: Heb . . . 3H **85**
Johnstone Vs. SR5: Monkw . . . 6D **104**
John St. DH1: Dur . . . 3A **6** (3K **165**)
DH4: Hou S . . . 2A **144**
DH5: Hett H . . . 6G **145**
DH5: Hou S . . . 2F **145**
DH7: Sac . . . 7E **140**
DH8: B'hill . . . 5F **121**
DH8: Cons . . . 7H **121**
DH9: Beam . . . 2K **125**
DH9: Crag . . . 7J **125**
DH9: Stly . . . 5D **124**
NE3: Gos . . . 7G **45**
(Bowes St.)
NE3: Gos . . . 7C **44**
(Hutton St.)
NE10: Pel . . . 5D **84**
NE24: Cow . . . 1F **23**
NE25: Ears . . . 6A **38**
NE28: W'snd . . . 3F **65**
NE30: Cull . . . 7J **39**
NE35: Bol C . . . 6F **87**
NE42: Pru . . . 3G **77**
NE61: Peg . . . 4B **10**
NE63: Ash . . . 3A **12**
SR1: Sund . . . 3K **7** (1F **119**)
SR2: Ryh . . . 3J **133**
SR4: Sund . . . 1G **117**
SR8: Eas C . . . 6C **160**
John St. Nth. DH7: Mead . . . 1F **175**
John St. Sth. DH7: Mead . . . 1F **175**
John St. Sq. DH8: Cons . . . 6H **121**
John Taylor Ct. SR5: S'wck . . . 4C **104**
John Wesley Ct. NE42: Pru . . . 4F **77**
John Williamson St. NE33: S Shi . . . 6H **67**
John Wilson Ct. SR8: Hord . . . 5E **172**
Joicey Aged Miners' Homes
*DH4: S Row . . . 3B **130***
(off Philadelphia La.)
Joicey Gdns. DH9: Stly . . . 2F **125**
Joicey Pl. NE9: Low F . . . 1J **99**
Joicey Rd. NE9: Low F . . . 1H **99**
Joicey St. NE10: Pel . . . 5E **84**
Joicey Ter. DH9: Tan L . . . 1D **124**
Jolliffe St. DH3: Ches S . . . 1B **142**
Jonadab Rd. NE10: Bill Q . . . 4E **84**
Jonadab St. NE10: Pel . . . 5E **84**
Jones Ct. DH6: Bowb . . . 4H **177**
Jones St. DH3: Bir . . . 4A **114**
Jonquil Cl. NE5: Cha P . . . 1C **60**
Joseph Cl. NE4: Benw . . . 2A **82**
Joseph Hopper Aged Miners Homes
DH3: Bir . . . 1A **114**
Joseph Hopper Memorial Homes
NE10: Wind N . . . 1K **99**
Joseph St. DH9: Stly . . . 4E **124**
Joseph Ter. NE17: C'wl . . . 6K **93**
Joyce Cl. NE10: Ward . . . 6G **85**
Joyce Gro. SR8: Pet . . . 2J **181**
Joyce Ter. DH7: Ush M . . . 2K **163**
SR5: Sund . . . 6H **103**
Jubilee Av. NE9: Eigh B . . . 6A **100**
SR7: Dalt D . . . 4H **147**
Jubilee Bldgs. *NE46: Hex . . . 2D **70***
(off Cattle Mkt.)
Jubilee Cen. SR7: S'hm . . . 3B **148**
Jubilee Cl. DH7: Edm . . . 3D **140**
DH7: New B . . . 5B **164**

Jubilee Cotts. DH4: Hou S 2D **144**
NE40: Coal .7B **78**
Jubilee Ct. DH8: C'sde 3C **134**
NE8: Gate 6E **82**
NE23: Dud .2K **35**
NE24: Bly 3H **23**
NE31: Heb .7A **66**
Jubilee Cres. DH6: S Hil 3D **168**
(not continuous)
NE3: Gos 7C **44**
Jubilee Est. NE63: Ash 6B **12**
Jubilee Ho. DH5: Eas L 2J **157**
Jubilee Ind. Est. NE63: Ash 5A **12**
Jubilee Lodge NE23: Cra 6K **25**
Jubilee M. NE3: Gos 7D **44**
NE22: Bed .6B **18**
Jubilee Pl. DH1: Shin 6D **166**
DH6: Shot C 5E **170**
Jubilee Rd. NE1: Newc T 5J **5** (1H **83**)
NE3: Gos 6C **44**
NE24: Bly 3J **23**
NE42: Oving 2J **75**
Jubilee Sq. DH5: Eas L 3J **157**
DH6: S Het 4B **158**
NE38: Wash 3G **115**
Jubilee St. NE28: W'snd 3F **65**
Jubilee Ter. DH9: Ann P 5B **124**
DH9: Tant .6A **110**
NE13: Sea B 3D **34**
NE16: Swa .5G **81**
NE22: Bed .6B **18**
NE38: Wash 6A **116**
NE40: Craw 3C 78
(off Greenside Rd.)
NE64: Newb S 3J **13**
Jubilee Terraces NE6: Byke 7B **64**
Jude Pl. SR8: Pet 4A **172**
Jude St. SR8: Eas 7A **160**
Judson Rd. SR8: Pet 5H **171**
Julian Av. NE6: Walk 6C **64**
NE33: S Shi 1K **67**
Julian Rd. NE10: Ward 6H **85**
Julian St. NE33: S Shi 1K **67**
Juliet Av. NE29: N Shi 6D **48**
Juliet St. NE63: Ash 3C **12**
Julius Caesar St. SR5: S'wck 5C **104**
July Courtyard *NE8: Gate 5D 82*
(off Summers Pass)
Jumbo Jungle 5K **121**
June Av. NE21: W Mill 1C **96**
June Courtyard *NE8: Gate 4D 82*
(off North Side)
Juniper Cl. NE3: Gos 3E **44**
NE24: News 5G **23**
SR2: Sund .4G **119**
Juniper Ct. NE21: Blay 3C **80**
Juniper Wlk. NE5: Cha P 1D **60**
Juniper Way DH1: Dur 3K **165**
Jupiter Ct. NE29: N Shi 7B **48**
SR8: Eas 7A **160**
Jupiter Health & Fitness Cen. 7K **159**
Jutland Av. NE31: Heb 1J **85**
Jutland Ter. DH9: Tan L 1D **124**

K

Kane Gdns. NE10: Wind N 1A **100**
Karting North East (Go-Kart Track)
. . . . .7A **132**
Kateregina DH3: Bir 4B **114**
Katherine St. NE63: Ash 3C **12**
Kathleen Ct. *NE28: W'snd 4F 65*
(off Frank St.)
Katrine Cl. DH2: Ches S 7K **127**
Kayll Rd. SR4: Sund 2B **118**
KAYSBURN .3A **152**
Kay's Cotts. NE10: Wind N 7A **84**
Kay St. DH9: Stly 2F **125**
Kearsley Cl. NE25: Sea D 7H **27**
Kearton Av. NE5: Cha P 2C **60**
Keating Cl. TS27: B Col 2H **183**
Keats Av. NE24: Bly 4G **23**
NE35: Bol C 6H **87**
SR5: S'wck .5C **104**
Keats Cl. DH9: Stly 3G **125**
Keats Gro. NE63: Ash 4D **12**
Keats Rd. NE15: Lem 7A **60**
Keats Wlk. NE8: Gate 4J **83**
NE34: S Shi 3G **87**
Kedleston Cl. SR2: Ryh 3F **133**
Keeble Ct. NE63: N Sea 4F **13**
Keebledale Av. NE6: Walk 6D **64**
Keele Dr. NE23: Cra 4F **25**
Keel Ho. NE1: Newc T 6J **5**
Keelman's Ho. *NE24: Bly 1J 23*
(off Maddison St.)
Keelman's La. SR4: Sund 1J **117**
Keelman Sq. NE1: Newc T 6J **5**
Keelman's Rd. SR4: Sund 1H **117**
Keelmans Ter. NE24: Bly 1J **23**
Keelman's Way NE8: Gate 4E **82**
Keelmen's Hospital
NE1: Newc T 6J **5** (1H **83**)
Keel Row NE11: Swa 3H **81**
NE24: Bly 1J **23**
Keighley Av. SR5: Sund 3H **103**
Keighley Sq. SR5: Sund 3G **103**
Keilder Dr. DH9: Stly 5F **125**
Keir Hardie Av. DH9: Stly 4F **125**
(not continuous)
NE10: Ward 6E **84**
Keir Hardie Ct. NE64: Newb S 2J **13**
Keir Hardie St. DH4: Hou S 2B **144**
NE39: Row G 5F **95**
Keir Hardie Ter. DH3: Bir 2K **113**
DH6: Shot C 7E **170**
Keir Hardie Way SR5: Monkw 6D **104**
Keith Cl. NE4: Benw 2A **82**
Keith Sq. SR5: Sund 3H **103**
Keldane Gdns. NE4: Benw 1A **82**
Kelfield Gro. NE23: Cra 7K **21**
Kelham Sq. SR5: Sund 3G **103**
Kell Cres. DH6: S Hil 3C **168**
Kellett Cl. NE37: Wash 6F **101**
Kellfield Av. NE9: Low F 1J **99**
Kellfield Rd. NE9: Low F 2J **99**
KELLOE 7E **178**
Kell Rd. SR8: Hord 6D **172**
Kells Bldgs. DH1: Dur 4H **165**
Kells Gdns. NE9: Low F 2J **99**
Kells La. NE9: Low F 3H **99**
Kell's Way NE39: Row G 6J **95**
Kellsway NE10: Hew 2D **100**
Kellsway Ct. NE10: Hew 2D **100**
Kelly Cl. DH8: B'hill 5F **121**
Kelly Rd. NE31: Heb 3J **85**
Kelpie Gdns. SR6: Roker 6G **105**
Kelsey Way NE23: Cra 7K **21**
Kelso Cl. NE5: Cha P 1C **60**
Kelso Dr. NE29: N Shi 4E **48**
Kelso Gdns. NE15: Benw 7H **61**
NE22: Bed .7A **18**
NE28: W'snd 1A **66**
Kelso Gro. DH4: S Row 3A **130**
Kelson Way NE5: Cha P 1C **60**
Kelso Pl. NE8: Gate 5D **82**
Kelston Way NE5: Blak 3J **61**
Kelvedon Av. NE3: Ken 2K **61**
Kelvin Gdns. *DH8: Cons 7H 121*
(off Palmerston St.)
NE11: Dun .5B **82**
Kelvin Gro. NE2: Newc T 1K **5** (6H **63**)
NE8: Gate .6F **83**
NE29: N Shi 4G **49**
NE33: S Shi 4B **68**
SR6: Clead .5A **88**
SR6: Roker 5G **105**
Kelvin Pl. NE12: Longb 3E **46**
Kemble Cl. NE23: Cra 7K **21**
Kemble Sq. SR5: Sund 3H **103**
Kemp Rd. SR8: Pet 5A **172**
Kempton Cl. DH8: Shot B 2F **121**
Kempton Gdns. NE8: Gate 7E **82**
Kenber Dr. TS27: B Col 2H **183**
Kendal DH3: Bir 6C **114**
(not continuous)
Kendal Av. NE24: Bly 3H **23**
NE30: Cull .2H **49**
Kendal Cl. SR8: Pet 2J **181**
Kendal Cres. NE9: Low F 3K **99**
Kendal Dr. NE23: Cra 2A **26**
NE36: E Bol 7J **87**
Kendale Wlk. NE5: West 2E **60**
Kendal Gdns. DH8: C'sde 3D **134**
NE28: W'snd 7A **48**
Kendal Grn. *NE6: Byke 5P 5*
(off Kendal St.)
Kendal Ho. NE6: Byke 4P **5**
Kendal Pl. NE6: Byke 4P **5** (1K **83**)
Kendal Ri. NE22: Bed 6F **17**
Kendal St. NE6: Byke 4P **5** (1K **83**)
Kendor Gro. NE61: Mor 2F **15**
Kenilworth DH3: Gt Lum 2E **142**
NE12: Kil .7B **36**
Kenilworth Ct. NE4: Elsw 2C **82**
NE37: Wash 7K **101**
Kenilworth Ho. NE8: Gate 9G **4**
Kenilworth Rd. NE4: Elsw 2C **82**
NE25: Monks 6F **39**
NE63: Ash .3A **12**
Kenilworth Sq. SR5: Sund 3J **103**
Kenilworth Vw. NE9: Low F 5J **99**
Kenley Rd. NE5: Den M 5G **61**
SR5: Sund .3J **103**
Kenmoor Way NE5: Cha P 2C **60**
Kenmore Cl. NE10: Ward 6F **85**
Kenmore Cres. NE40: G'sde 4F **79**
Kennersdene NE30: Tyne 3J **49**
Kennet Av. NE32: Jar 3C **86**
Kennet Sq. SR5: Sund 3H **103**
Kennford NE9: Low F 5J **99**
Kennington Gro. NE6: Walk 1C **84**
Kenny Pl. DH1: Dur 1D **166**
Kenny Sq. TS28: Win 5F **181**
Kensington Av. NE3: Gos 5E **44**
Kensington Cl. NE25: Monks 6F **39**
Kensington Cotts. NE61: Mor 7H **9**
Kensington Ct. NE10: Fell 6A **84**
NE31: Heb .1H **85**
NE33: S Shi 5A **68**
Kensington Gdns. NE25: Monks 6F **39**
NE28: W'snd 2C **64**
NE30: N Shi 6H **49**
Kensington Gro. NE30: N Shi 5H **49**
Kensington Ho. SR2: Sund 4G **119**
Kensington Ter. NE2: Newc T 1F **4** (6F **63**)
NE11: Dun .6B **82**
Kensington Vs. NE5: West 2E **60**
Kensington Way DH2: Newf 4F **127**
Kent Av. NE11: Dun 6C **82**
NE28: W'snd 3K **65**
NE31: Heb .1H **85**
Kentchester Rd. SR5: Sund 3J **103**
Kent Cl. NE63: Ash 3J **11**
Kent Ct. NE3: Ki Pk 4K **43**
Kent Gdns. DH5: Hett H 6F **145**
DH8: C'sde 2D **134**
Kentmere DH3: Bir 7B **114**
NE37: Wash 2F **115**
Kentmere Av. NE6: Walk 7D **64**
SR6: Seab .2E **104**
Kentmere Cl. NE23: Seg 1E **36**
Kentmere Ho. DH4: Hou S 7C **130**
Kentmere Pl. SR8: Pet 6C **172**
Kentmore SR3: Silk 3B **132**
KENTON 1A **62**
Kenton Av. NE3: Ken 2C **62**
KENTON BANKFOOT 6H **43**
KENTON BAR 1K **61**
Kenton Ct. NE33: S Shi 4K **67**
Kenton Cres. DH6: Thor 2J **179**
NE3: Ken 7B **44**
Kenton Gro. SR6: Ful 6F **105**
Kenton La. NE3: Ken, Newc T 1K **61**
Kenton Pk. Shop. Cen. NE3: Ken 1C **62**
Kenton Pk. Sports Cen. 7A **44**
Kenton Rd. NE3: Gos, Ken 7C **44**
NE29: N Shi 5C **48**
Kent Pl. NE34: S Shi 7B **68**
Kent Rd. DH8: C'sde 2D **134**
Kent St. NE32: Jar 7A **66**
Kent Ter. DH6: Has 3A **170**
Kentucky Rd. SR5: Sund 3G **103**
Kent Vs. NE32: Jar 7A **66**
Kent Wlk. SR8: Pet 4A **172**
Kenwood Gdns. NE9: Low F 5J **99**
(not continuous)
Kenya Rd. SR5: Sund 3J **103**
Kepier Chare NE40: Craw 2D **78**
Kepier Ct. DH1: Dur 1E **6** (2B **166**)
Kepier Cres. DH1: Dur 1E **166**
(not continuous)
Kepier Gdns. SR4: Sund 2G **117**
Kepier Hgts. DH1: Dur 1E **6** (2B **166**)
Kepier La. DH1: Dur 1C **166**
(not continuous)
Kepier Ter. DH1: Dur 1E **6** (2B **166**)
Kepier Vs. DH1: Dur 1E **6**
Keppel St. NE11: Dun 5B **82**
NE33: S Shi 2J **67**
Kepwell Bank Top NE42: Pru 3E **76**
Kepwell Ct. NE42: Pru 3F **77**
Kepwell Rd. NE42: Pru 4E **76**
Kerry Cl. NE24: Bly 1J **23**
Kerryhill Dr. DH1: P Me 3A **154**
Kerry Sq. SR5: Sund 3H **103**
Kestel Cl. NE40: Craw 2E **78**
Kesteven Sq. SR5: Sund 3H **103**
Keston Dr. NE23: Cra 7K **21**
Kestrel Cl. DH5: Eas L 2J **157**
NE38: Wash 6E **114**
Kestrel Ct. DH3: Bir 4A **114**
Kestrel Dr. NE63: Ash 6K **11**
Kestrel Lodge Flats NE33: S Shi 2K **67**
Kestrel M. NE16: Whi 7G **81**
Kestrel Pl. NE12: Longb 5J **45**
Kestrel Sq. SR5: Sund 3H **103**
Kestrel Way DH6: Has 1B **170**
NE29: N Shi 2G **67**
NE34: S Shi 2H **87**
Keswick Av. SR6: Seab 3E **104**
Keswick Dr. NE30: Cull 2H **49**
Keswick Gdns. DH8: C'sde 3D **134**
NE28: W'snd 2A **66**
Keswick Gro. NE5: Den M 5G **61**
Keswick Rd. DH9: Stly 5D **124**
SR8: Pet 5C **172**
Keswick St. NE8: Gate 5G **83**
Keswick Ter. DH6: S Het 3A **158**
Kettering Pl. NE23: Cra 2A **26**
Kettering Sq. SR5: Sund 3H **103**
Kettlewell Ter. NE30: N Shi 6H **49**
Ketton Cl. NE12: Longb 6K **45**
Kew Gdns. NE26: Whit B 5F **39**
Kew Sq. SR5: Sund 3G **103**
Keyes Gdns. NE2: Jes 2G **63**
KIBBLESWORTH 2E **112**
Kibblesworth Bank NE11: Kib 3C **112**
Kicks Leisure Club *4F 65*
(off Warwick Rd.)
Kidd Av. DH6: S'burn 3K **167**
Kidderminster Dr. NE5: Cha P 2C **60**
Kidderminster Rd. SR5: Sund 4H **103**
Kidderminster Sq. SR5: Sund 4H **103**
Kidd Sq. SR5: Sund 3H **103**
Kidland Cl. NE63: Ash 3D **12**
Kidlandlee Grn. NE5: West 1G **61**
Kidlandlee Pl. NE5: West 1G **61**
Kidsgrove Sq. SR5: Sund 4H **103**
Kielder NE38: Wash 4D **114**
Kielder Av. NE23: Cra 4F **25**
Kielder Cl. NE5: West 2G **61**
NE12: Kil .7A **36**
NE24: Bly .4F **23**
Kielder Dr. NE63: Ash 4A **12**
Kielder Gdns. NE32: Jar 3B **86**
NE62: Stake 6J **11**
Kielder Ho. NE2: Jes 4G **63**
Kielder Pl. NE25: Well 6B **38**
Kielder Rd. NE15: Lem 6B **60**
NE25: Well 6B **38**
Kielder Ter. NE30: N Shi 6H **49**
Kielder Way NE3: Gos 5D **44**
Kilburn Cl. SR2: Ryh 3J **133**
Kilburn Dr. SR8: Hord 3D **172**
Kilburne Cl. NE7: H Hea 2C **64**
Kilburn Gdns. NE29: N Shi 2D **66**
Kilburn Grn. NE9: Low F 6K **99**
(not continuous)
Kilchurn DH8: B'hill 6F **121**
Kildale DH4: Pen 1J **129**
Kildare Sq. SR5: Sund 3H **103**
Killarney Av. SR5: Sund 3H **103**
Killarney Sq. SR5: Sund 3H **103**
Killiebrigs NE15: Hed W 3B **58**
Killin Cl. NE5: Cha P 1C **60**
KILLINGWORTH 1B **46**
Killingworth Av. NE27: Back 7E **36**
Killingworth Cen., The NE12: Kil 1B **46**
Killingworth Dr. NE12: Kil 2K **45**
SR4: Sund .4K **117**
Killingworth Ind. Area NE12: Kil 1K **45**
Killingworth La. NE12: Kil 2C **46**
NE27: Back .7E **36**
Killingworth Pl.
NE1: Newc T 4E **4** (7F **63**)
Killingworth Rd. NE3: Gos, Newc T 7H **45**
NE12: Kil .3C **46**
KILLINGWORTH VILLAGE 2C **46**
Killingworth Way NE12: Kil 7J **35**
NE27: Back .7J **35**
Killowen St. NE9: Low F 3G **99**
Kilnhill Wlk. SR8: Pet 6C **172**
Kiln Ri. NE16: Whi 3G **97**
Kilnshaw Pl. NE3: Gos 3F **45**
Kilsyth Av. NE29: N Shi 2E **48**
Kilsyth Sq. SR5: Sund 4H **103**
Kimberley NE38: Wash 3A **116**
Kimberley Av. NE29: N Shi 6E **48**
Kimberley Ct. DH9: Stly 6J **125**
Kimberley Gdns. DH9: Stly 6J **125**
NE2: Jes 5J **63**
NE43: Pains 7J **75**
Kimberley St. NE24: Bly 1H **23**
SR4: Sund .2B **118**
Kimberley Ter. NE24: Bly 1J **23**
KIMBLESWORTH 7H **141**
Kimblesworth Ind. Est. DH2: Kim 1J **153**
Kimmerstone Rd. NE13: Ki Pk 4A **44**
Kincross Cl. SR4: Sund 5J **117**
Kineton Way SR2: Ryh 4H **133**
Kinfauns Ter. NE9: Low F 2J **99**
Kingarth Av. SR6: Seab 2G **105**
King Charles Ct. SR5: Sund 3G **103**
King Charles Twr.
NE2: Newc T 3J **5** (7H **63**)
Kingdom Pl. NE29: N Shi 2G **67**
King Edward VIII Ter. DH9: Stly 1G **125**
King Edward Bri. Arches
NE1: Newc T 9E **4** (3F **83**)
King Edward Pl. NE8: Gate 5K **83**
King Edward Rd. NE6: Heat 4K **63**
NE30: Tyne 5J **49**
NE40: Ryton 2J **79**
SR4: Sund .1H **117**
SR7: S'hm .4B **148**
King Edward St. NE8: Gate 5K **83**
King Edward Ter. DH9: Tan L 7C **110**
Kingfisher Blvd. NE15: Lem 1C **80**
Kingfisher Cl. DH7: Esh W 3D **162**
NE63: Ash .7C **12**
Kingfisher Ct. NE11: Dun 4C **82**
Kingfisher Dr. DH5: Eas L 2J **157**
(not continuous)
Kingfisher Ind. Est. SR7: S'hm 2J **147**
Kingfisher Lodge NE32: Jar 7A **66**
Kingfisher Rd. NE12: Longb 5J **45**
Kingfisher Way NE24: News 5K **23**
NE28: W'snd 6A **48**
King George Av. NE11: Dun 7B **82**
King George Rd. NE3: Fawd 6A **44**
NE34: S Shi 6A **68**
King George's Rd. NE64: Newb S 2G **13**
Kingham Ct. NE3: Gos 1H **63**
King Henry Ct. SR5: Sund 3G **103**
Kinghorn Sq. SR5: Sund 3H **103**
King James Ct. SR5: Sund 3G **103**
King James Hospital Bungs.
NE8: Gate .4K **83**
King James St. NE8: Gate 5H **83**
King John's Ct. NE20: Darr H 7E **30**
King John's Palace (remains of)
. . . . .1N **5** (5K **63**)
King John St. NE6: Heat 1P **5** (5K **63**)
King John Ter. NE6: Heat 1P **5** (5K **63**)
King Oswald Dr. NE21: Blay 1A **80**
Kings Av. DH7: Lang P 5J **151**
NE31: Heb .1K **85**
NE61: Mor .5F **9**
SR6: Seab .2G **105**
Kingsbridge NE12: Longb 5H **45**
Kingsbridge Cl. NE29: N Shi 1E **66**
Kingsbury Cl. SR5: Sund 3H **103**
Kingsbury Ct. NE12: Longb 6J **45**
Kingsclere Av. SR5: Sund 3H **103**
Kingsclere Sq. SR5: Sund 4H **103**
Kings Cl. NE8: Gate 5K **83**
Kings Ct. NE11: T Vall 4F **99**
NE32: Jar .6A **66**
Kingsdale Av. NE24: Cow 2E **22**
NE37: Wash 7F **101**
Kingsdale Cl. DH9: Ann P 4K **123**
Kingsdale Rd. NE12: Longb 5H **45**
Kings Dr. NE26: Whit B 6G **39**
NE40: G'sde 5F **79**
King's Gdns. NE24: Cow 1G **23**
Kingsgate NE46: Hex 1C **70**
Kingsgate Ter. NE46: Hex 1C **70**
Kings Gro. DH1: Dur 5J **165**
Kings Ho. NE1: Newc T 8E **4** (2F **83**)
Kingsland NE2: Jes 5G **63**
Kingsland Sq. SR5: Sund 4H **103**
King's La. DH2: Pelt 2F **127**
(not continuous)
Kingsley Av. NE3: Gos 3E **44**
NE25: Monks 7F **39**
NE34: S Shi 3G **87**
Kingsley Cl. DH9: Stly 2H **125**
SR5: S'wck .6C **104**

Kingsley Pl. NE6: Heat 1N 5 (6K 63)
NE11: Dun 5B 82
NE16: Whi 6H 81
NE28: W'snd 2K 65
Kingsley Ter. NE4: Elsw 1C 82
NE40: Craw 2C 78
Kingsley Vs. NE40: Craw 2C 78
King's Mnr. NE1: Newc T 5H 5 (1G 83)
Kings Mdw. NE32: Jar 5C 86
Kings Mdws. NE4: Elsw 3C 82
Kingsmere DH3: Ches S 2A 128
Kingsmere Gdns. NE6: Walk 2E 84
Kings M. NE46: Hex 2D 70
Kings Pk. NE62: Sco G 3G 17
King's Pl. SR4: Sund 1C 118
Kings Rd. DH8: B'hill 4F 121
NE1: Newc T 3E 4 (7F 63)
NE12: Longb 3A 46
NE22: Bed 6B 18
NE26: Whit B 5F 39
TS28: Win 4F 181
King's Rd., The SR5: S'wck 5C 104
Kings Rd. Nth. NE28: W'snd 1F 65
Kings Rd. Sth. NE28: W'snd 2F 65
Kings Ter. NE9: Spri 6D 100
SR4: Sund 1B 118
Kingston Av. DH7: Bearp 1C 164
NE6: Newc T, Walk 1B 84
SR7: S'hm 4K 147
Kingston Cl. NE26: Whit B 3F 39
Kingston Ct. NE26: Whit B 3F 39
(off Kingston Dr.)
Kingston Cres. DH6: Has 1A 170
Kingston Dr. NE26: Whit B 3F 39
Kingston Grn. NE6: Walk 1B 84
Kingston M. DH4: S Row 4C 130
KINGSTON PARK 6J 43
Kingston Pk. 5H 43
Kingston Park (Park & Tram) 6J 43
Kingston Pk. Av. NE3: Ki Pk 6J 43
Kingston Park Cen. NE3: Ki Pk 6J 43
Kingston Pk. Rd.
NE3: Fawd, Gos, Ki Pk 4J 43
Kingston Park Station (Metro) 6J 43
Kingston Pl. NE8: Gate 6J 83
Kingston Retail Pk. NE3: Ki Pk 6J 43
Kingston Rd. NE8: Gate 6J 83
Kingston Ter. SR6: Roker 5F 105
Kingston Way NE26: Whit B 3F 39
King St. DH3: Bir 4K 113
DH6: S'burn 3K 167
DH6: Shot C 6F 171
NE1: Newc T 7H 5 (2G 83)
NE8: Gate 6E 82
NE10: Pel 4E 84
NE24: Bly 1J 23
NE30: N Shi 6H 49
NE33: S Shi 2J 67
NE64: Newb S 2J 13
SR1: Sund 3J 7 (1F 119)
SR6: Ful 3F 105
Kings Va. NE28: W'snd 1G 65
Kings Wlk. NE1: Newc T 2E 4 (6F 63)
NE5: Cha P 1B 60
Kingsway DH5: Hou S 2F 145
DH7: Lang P 5J 151
NE4: Fen 5A 62
NE16: Sun 4G 97
NE20: Pon 5J 31
NE24: Bly 3J 23
NE30: Tyne 4J 49
NE33: S Shi 3B 68
Kingsway Av. NE3: Gos 5E 44
Kingsway Ho. NE11: T Vall 3F 99
Kingsway Nth. NE11: T Vall 1E 98
Kingsway Rd. SR5: Sund 3G 103
Kingsway Sth. NE11: T Vall 3F 99
Kingsway Sq. SR5: Sund 3H 103
Kingsway Vs. DH2: Pelt 2F 127
Kingswell NE61: Mor 1G 15
Kingswood DH4: Pen 2A 130
DH7: Lang P 5H 151
Kingswood Av. NE2: Jes 2F 63
Kingswood Cl. NE35: Bol C 5E 86
Kingswood Ct. NE30: Tyne 5K 49
Kingswood Dr. NE20: Darr H 7G 31
Kingswood Gro. SR4: Sund 6F 117
Kingswood Rd. NE23: Cra 2A 26
Kingswood Sq. SR5: Sund 4H 103
King Ter. DH9: Stly 4D 124
Kinlet NE38: Wash 3A 116
Kinley Rd. DH1: Carr 6H 155
Kinloch Ct. DH2: Ches S 1K 141
Kinloss Sq. NE23: Cra 2A 26
Kinnaird Av. NE15: Den M 7G 61
Kinnock Cl. DH6: S'burn 3A 168
Kinross Cl. DH3: Bir 6B 114
Kinross Ct. NE10: Bill Q 4F 85
Kinross Dr. DH9: Stly 3H 125
NE3: Ken 7A 44
Kinsale Sq. SR5: Sund 3H 103
Kinver Dr. NE5: Cha P 2C 60
KIP HILL 7G 111
Kip Hill Ct. DH9: Stly 1G 125
Kipling Av. NE16: Swa, Whi 6H 81
NE31: Heb 7K 65
NE35: Bol C 6H 87
TS27: B Col 7G 173
Kipling Cl. DH9: Stly 3G 125
Kipling Ct. NE16: Swa 6H 81
Kiplings Ter. DH1: Dur 5H 165
Kipling St. SR5: S'wck 6C 104
Kipling Wlk. NE8: Gate 4J 83
Kira Dr. DH1: P Me 3A 154
Kirby Av. DH1: Dur 6J 153
Kirby Cl. NE34: S Shi 2F 87
Kirbys Dr. DH6: Bowb 4H 177
Kirkbride Pl. NE23: Cra 2A 26
Kirkdale Ct. NE23: Dud 6A 36
NE34: S Shi 2G 87
Kirkdale Grn. NE4: Newc T 7A 4 (2D 82)
Kirkdale Sq. SR5: Sund 4H 103
Kirkdale St. DH5: Hett H 1F 157
Kirkfield Gdns. DH9: Ann P 4J 123
Kirkham NE38: Wash 4H 115
Kirkham Av. NE3: K Bank 5J 43
Kirkham Ct. NE21: Winl 5A 80
Kirkham Rd. DH1: Dur 5B 154
Kirkharle Dr. NE61: Peg 3A 10
Kirkheaton Pl. NE5: Fen 5J 61
Kirkhill SR3: Silk 4C 132
Kirkland Hill SR8: Pet 5C 172
Kirklands NE23: Dud 6A 36
Kirkland Wlk. NE27: Shir 1J 47
Kirklea Rd. DH5: Hou S 2F 145
Kirkleatham Gdns. NE6: Heat 3B 64
Kirkley Av. NE34: S Shi 7C 68
Kirkley Cl. NE3: Gos 6D 44
Kirkley Dr. NE20: Pon 4J 31
NE63: Ash 5C 12
Kirkley Lodge NE3: Gos 6D 44
Kirkley Rd. NE27: Shir 2K 47
Kirklinton Rd. NE30: Cull 2G 49
Kirknewton Cl. DH5: Hou S 2F 145
Kirkside DH4: New H 3E 130
Kirkston Av. NE15: Lem 6D 60
Kirkstone DH3: Bir 6B 114
Kirkstone Av. NE30: Cull 2G 49
NE32: Jar 3D 86
SR5: Ful 4E 104
SR8: Pet 6C 172
Kirkstone Cl. DH5: Hou S 2F 145
NE21: Winl 6C 80
Kirkstone Dr. DH1: Carr 6G 155
Kirkstone Gdns. NE7: H Hea 2J 63
Kirkstone Rd. NE10: Pel 5D 84
Kirk St. DH8: B'hill 6G 121
NE6: Byke 1B 84
(Clifford Rd.)
NE6: Byke 6P 5 (1A 84)
(Janet St.)
Kirk Vw. DH4: Nbot 6D 130
Kirkwall Cl. SR5: Sund 6G 103
Kirkwood DH7: Sac 7D 140
NE23: Dud 6A 36
Kirkwood Av. SR4: Sund 6G 117
Kirkwood Dr. DH1: Dur 4J 165
NE3: Ken 7A 44
Kirkwood Gdns. NE10: Ward 5F 85
Kirkwood Pl. NE3: Gos 3D 44
Kirton Av. NE4: Fen 7A 62
Kirton Pk. Ter. NE29: N Shi 5G 49
NE30: N Shi 5G 49
Kirton Way NE23: Cra 2A 26
Kismet St. SR5: S'wck 5C 104
Kitchener Rd. SR6: Whit 2G 89
Kitchener St. NE9: Low F 7J 83
SR4: Sund 4B 118
Kitchener Ter. DH4: New H 3D 130
NE30: N Shi 5J 49
NE32: Jar 1B 86
SR2: Sund 7H 119
Kitching Rd. SR8: Eas 3H 171
Kitswell Bungs. DH7: Lan 5J 137
Kitswell Rd. DH7: Lan 5G 137
Kittiwake Cl. NE24: News 6J 23
NE28: W'snd 5A 48
Kittiwake Dr. NE38: Wash 5D 114
Kittiwake Ho. NE26: Whit B 6H 39
Kitty Brewster Rd. NE24: Cow 1D 22
Klok Way NE10: Gate 4A 84
Klondyke Wlk. NE21: Blay 1A 80
(not continuous)
Knaresborough Cl. NE22: Bed 6F 17
Knaresborough Rd. SR7: Mur 7E 146
Knaresborough Sq. SR5: Sund 3H 103
Knaresdale DH3: Bir 7B 114
Knarsdale Av. NE29: N Shi 6D 48
Knarsdale Pl. NE5: W Dent 4E 60
Kneller Cl. DH9: Stly 3F 125
Knightsbridge NE3: Gos 6E 44
SR3: New S 1A 132
Knightsbridge Ct. NE3: Gos 6E 44
(off Knightsbridge)
Knightside Gdns. NE11: Dun 1B 98
Knightside Wlk. NE5: Cha P 2C 60
KNITSLEY 4J 135
Knitsley Gdns. DH8: Cons 1H 135
Knitsley La. DH8: Cons 6F 135
(Longedge La.)
DH8: Cons 7H 121
(Palmerston St.)
Knitsley Nook DH8: Cons 4A 136
Knivestone Ct. NE12: Kil 7C 36
Knobbyends La. NE21: Winl 6K 79
Knoll, The SR2: Sund 3D 118
Knoll Ct. NE1: Newc T 5J 5
Knoll Ri. NE11: Dun 7B 82
Knollside Cl. SR3: Dox P 4B 132
Knott Flats NE30: Tyne 6K 49
Knott Pl. NE15: Scot 1H 81
Knoulberry NE37: Wash 2E 114
Knoulberry Rd. NE37: Wash 2D 114
Knowledge Hill NE21: Winl 5B 80
Knowle Pl. NE12: Longb 7K 45
Knowles, The NE16: Whi 7J 81
Knowsley Ct. NE3: Ki Pk 7H 43
Knox Cl. NE22: Bed 6B 18
Knox La. DH7: Corn C 1A 162
Knox Rd. NE22: Bed 1K 21
Knutsford Wlk. NE23: Cra 2A 26
Koppers Way NE31: Heb 5K 85
Kristin Av. NE32: Jar 2C 86
Kyffin Vw. NE34: S Shi 1D 88
Kyle Cl. NE4: Newc T 8B 4 (2D 82)
Kyle Rd. NE8: Gate 6E 82
Kylins, The NE61: Mor 2F 15
Kyloe Av. NE25: Sea D 1H 37
Kyloe Cl. NE3: Fawd 5A 44
Kyloe Pl. NE5: West 2G 61
NE22: Bed 7H 17
Kyloe Vs. NE5: West 2G 61
Kyo Bog La. NE41: Wylam 6J 77
NE42: Pru 6J 77
Kyo Cl. NE41: Wylam 5K 77
Kyo Heugh Rd. DH9: Ann P, Harp 3A 124
Kyo La. DH9: Ann P, Harp 3B 124
NE40: Coal, G'sde 7B 78
Kyo Rd. DH9: Ann P 4K 123

L

Laburnum Av. DH1: Dur 3K 165
DH8: B'hill 5G 121
NE6: Walk 5D 64
NE10: Hew 7E 84
NE24: Bly 1H 23
NE26: Whit B 6G 39
NE28: W'snd 3F 65
NE38: Wash 7F 115
Laburnum Cl. SR4: Sund 2G 117
Laburnum Ct. DH7: Sac 7D 140
DH7: Ush M 2D 164
NE12: Kil 7A 36
NE62: Chop 1G 17
(off Sheepwash Bank)
Laburnum Cres. NE11: Kib 2E 112
SR7: S'hm 6A 148
SR8: Eas 7A 160
Laburnum Gdns. NE9: Low F 1H 99
NE10: Fell 5B 84
NE32: Jar 2A 86
Laburnum Gro. NE16: Sun 4H 97
NE16: Whi 7G 81
NE31: Heb 3J 85
NE34: S Shi 1B 88
SR5: Sund 7G 103
SR6: Clead 5C 88
Laburnum Ho. NE28: W'snd 4G 65
Laburnum Pk. DH7: B'don 2B 174
Laburnum Rd. SR6: Ful 4F 105
Laburnum Sq. TS29: Trim S 7D 180
Laburnum Ter. DH6: Shot C 6E 170
DH9: Ann P 4J 123
NE41: Wylam 7J 57
(off Main Rd.)
NE63: Ash 3B 12
Lacebark DH4: S Row 3K 129
SR3: Dox P 5A 132
Ladock Cl. SR2: Ryh 1J 133
Lady Anne Rd. DH6: S'burn 2K 167
Ladybank NE5: Cha P 1B 60
SR3: Silk 3B 132
Lady Beatrice Ter. DH4: New H 2E 130
Ladycutters La. NE45: Corb 3C 72
Lady Durham Cl. DH6: S'burn 3J 167
Ladyhaugh Dr. NE16: Whi 3G 97
Ladykirk Rd. NE4: Benw 1A 82
Ladykirk Way NE23: Cra 4G 25
LADY PARK 5E 98
Ladyrigg NE20: Darr H 7H 31
Ladysmith Ct. DH9: Stly 4G 125
(not continuous)
Ladysmith St. NE33: S Shi 3K 67
Ladysmith Ter. DH7: Ush M 2B 164
Lady's Piece La. DH6: H Pitt, Low P 5A 156
Lady St. DH5: Hett H 5G 145
Lady's Wlk. NE33: S Shi 1J 67
NE61: Mor 6E 8
Ladywell NE43: Pains 1K 91
Ladywell Rd. DH8: Cons 2A 136
Ladywell Way NE20: Pon 4H 31
Ladywood Pk. DH4: Pen 1K 129
Laet St. NE29: N Shi 7H 49
Laidler Cl. TS27: B Col 2H 183
Laindon Av. SR6: Ful 3F 105
Laing Art Gallery 4G 4 (7G 63)
Laing Gro. NE28: W'snd 2A 66
Laing Ho. NE38: Wash 4F 115
Laing Sq. TS28: Win 4F 181
Laing St. DH8: Cons 5H 121
Lairage, The NE20: Pon 5J 31
Laith Rd. NE3: Ken 7A 44
Lake App. NE21: Blay 5E 80
Lake Av. NE34: S Shi 7E 68
Lake Bank Ter. TS28: Sta T 7G 181
Lake Ct. SR3: Silk 3C 132
Lakeland Dr. SR8: Pet 5C 172
Lakemore SR8: Pet 7A 172
Lake Rd. DH5: Hou S 2E 144
Lakeside NE21: Blay 5F 81
NE34: S Shi 7F 69
Lakeside Cen. 2B 46
Lakeside Ct. NE11: T Vall 2F 99
Lakeside Gdns. NE38: Wash 4K 115
Lake Vw. NE31: Heb 2H 85
TS28: Sta T 7G 181
Laleham Ct. NE3: Ki Pk 5K 43
Lamara Dr. SR5: Ful 4E 104
Lambden Cl. NE29: N Shi 2E 66
Lambert Rd. NE37: Wash 1D 114
Lambert Sq. NE3: Gos 7C 44
Lambeth Pl. NE8: Gate 6J 83
Lamb Farm Cl. NE12: Kil 3C 46
Lambley Av. NE30: Cull 2H 49
Lambley Cl. NE16: Sun 5G 97
Lambley Cres. NE25: Sea D 5G 27
NE31: Heb 3H 85
Lambley Way NE13: Haz 2A 44
Lambourn Av. NE29: N Shi 1D 66
Lambourne Av. NE12: Longb 5A 46
Lambourne Cl. DH4: Bour 6J 129
Lambourne Rd. SR2: Sund 5E 118
Lambs Arms Bldgs. NE40: Craw 3C 78
(off Greenside Rd.)
Lamb's Cl. TS27: Hutt 7C 182
Lamb's Pl. DH6: Bowb 5H 177
Lamb St. NE6: Walk 1E 84
NE23: Cra 5B 26
NE23: E Cram 5D 26
Lamb Ter. NE27: Shir 3J 47
LAMBTON 5F 115
Lambton Av. DH8: Cons 2K 135
NE16: Whi 6J 81
Lambton Cen. NE38: Wash 5F 115
Lambton Cl. NE40: Craw 3D 78
Lambton Ct. NE22: Bed 6A 18
NE38: Wash 1C 128
SR3: E Her 2J 131
SR8: Pet 2A 182
Lambton Dr. DH5: Hett H 1G 157
Lambton Fld. DH6: S'burn 2K 167
Lambton Gdns. NE16: Burn 3J 109
(not continuous)
Lambton La. DH4: Hou S 7K 129
Lambton Lea DH4: S Row 5A 130
Lambton Pk. 3F 129
Lambton Pl. DH4: Pen 1B 130
Lambton Rd. NE2: Jes 1F 4 (5G 63)
NE31: Heb 6K 65
Lambton St. DH1: Dur 2A 6 (2K 165)
DH3: Ches S 7B 128
DH7: Lang P 4H 151
NE8: Gate 9J 5 (3H 83)
SR1: Sund 2K 7 (1F 119)
Lambton Ter. DH4: Pen 1K 129
DH9: Crag 6K 125
NE32: Jar 2B 86
Lambton Twr. SR1: Sund 1G 119
(off High St. E.)
Lambton Vw. DH4: W Rai 2K 155
Lambton Wlk. DH1: Dur 3B 6
Lamedon Mill Ct. NE15: Lem 6B 60
Lamerton Av. NE6: Walk 3C 84
LAMESLEY 7G 99
Lamesley Rd. DH3: Bir 6G 99
NE11: Lame 6G 99
Lamonby Way NE23: Cra 6J 25
Lampeter Cl. NE5: Blak 2H 61
Lamplight Arts Cen. 3E 124
Lamport St. NE31: Heb 6G 65
Lanark Cl. NE29: N Shi 4C 48
SR4: Sund 5J 117
Lanark Dr. NE32: Jar 3E 86
Lancashire Dr. DH1: Carr 1H 167
Lancaster Ct. NE3: Ki Pk 5K 43
Lancaster Dr. NE28: W'snd 5H 47
Lancaster Hill SR8: Pet 4K 171
Lancaster Ho. NE4: Newc T 10A 4 (3C 82)
NE23: Cra 5B 26
Lancaster Pl. NE11: Dun 5A 82
Lancaster Rd. DH8: C'sde 3C 134
NE11: Dun 5A 82
Lancaster St. NE4: Newc T 6B 4 (1D 82)
Lancaster Ter. DH3: Ches S 7B 128
NE61: Mor 6G 9
(off Bennett's Wlk.)
Lancaster Way NE32: Jar 5A 86
Lancastrian Rd. NE23: Cra 5J 25
Lancefield Av. NE6: Walk 2D 84
Lancet Ct. NE8: Gate 10K 5 (4H 83)
LANCHESTER 6J 137
Lanchester NE38: Wash 6J 115
Lanchester Av. NE9: Wrek 4B 100
Lanchester Cl. NE10: Ward 1G 101
Lanchester Grn. NE22: Bed 6H 17
Lanchester Rd. DH1: Dur 4F 153
DH7: Maid L 3A 138
DH9: Ann P 7A 124
Lancing Ct. NE3: K Bank 5J 43
Landfall Dr. NE31: Heb 7H 65
Land of Green Ginger NE30: Tyne 5K 49
(off Front St.)
Landsale Cotts. NE40: G'sde 5E 78
Landscape Ter. NE40: G'sde 5F 79
Landsdowne Gdns. NE62: Stake 7J 11
Landseer Cl. DH9: Stly 3F 125
Landseer Gdns. NE9: Low F 6K 83
NE34: S Shi 4K 87
Landswood Ter. NE21: W Mill 7D 80
Lane, The NE42: Pru 4F 77
Lane7 2E 82
Lane Cnr. NE34: S Shi 1J 87
Lane Head NE40: Ryton 1G 79
Lanercost NE38: Wash 3G 115
Lanercost Av. NE21: Winl 4B 80
Lanercost Dr. NE5: Fen 5H 61
Lanercost Gdns. NE10: Wind N 1A 100
NE15: Thro 3H 59
Lanercost Pk. NE23: E Cram 5B 26
Lanercost Rd. NE29: N Shi 7E 48
Lanesborough Ct. NE3: Gos 1C 62
Langdale DH3: Bir 7C 114
NE25: Monks 6E 38
NE37: Wash 1G 115
Langdale Cl. DH8: Lead 5B 122
NE12: Longb 6J 45
Langdale Cres. DH1: Carr 6G 155
NE21: Winl 6B 80

Langdale Dr. NE23: Cra 3G 25
Langdale Gdns. NE6: Walk 7E 64
NE28: W'snd 7A 48
Langdale Pl. SR8: Pet 6C 172
Langdale Rd. DH4: Pen 1A 130
NE9: Low F 2J 99
Langdale St. DH5: Hett H 1F 157
Langdale Ter. NE17: Ham 3J 107
Langdale Way NE36: E Bol 6J 87
Langdon Cl. DH8: Cons 2J 135
NE29: N Shi 3F 49
Langdon Gdns. DH9: Ann P 4J 123
Langdon M. DH8: Cons 2J 135
Langdon Rd. NE5: West 2D 60
Langeeford Pl. SR6: Roker 6G 105
Langford Dr. NE35: Bol C 4F 87
Langham Rd. NE15: Scot 1F 81
Langholm Av. NE29: N Shi 4C 48
Langholm Ct. *NE36: E Bol* *7A 88*
(off Station Rd.)
Langholm Rd. NE3: Gos 5E 44
NE36: E Bol 6K 87
Langhope DH4: Pen 2K 129
Langhorn Cl. NE6: Byke 2P 5 (6K 63)
Langhurst SR2: Ryh 1G 133
Langleeford Rd. NE5: West 1G 61
Langley Av. DH7: B'hpe 5D 138
NE10: Ward 1F 101
NE24: Cow 1F 23
NE25: Monks 1D 48
NE27: Shir 2A 48
NE46: Hex 2F 71
Langley Cl. DH7: Maid L 3A 138
NE38: Wash 4F 115
Langley Cres. DH7: Lang M 7F 165
Langley Gro. SR8: Pet 1J 181
Langley La. DH7: B'hpe, Wit G 6C 138
Langley Mere NE12: Longb 4B 46
LANGLEY MOOR 7G 165
Langley Moor Ind. Est. DH7: Lang M 7G 165
(not continuous)
LANGLEY PARK 5J 151
Langley Pk. Ind. Est. DH7: Lang P 4J 151
Langley Pk. Nth. Ind. Est.
DH7: Lang P 3J 151
Langley Rd. DH1: Dur 5A 154
NE5: W Dent 5F 61
NE6: Walk 7D 64
NE29: N Shi 6C 48
NE63: Ash 4A 12
SR3: Sund 6D 118
Langley St. DH4: New H 3D 130
DH7: Lang P 4J 151
Langley Tarn NE29: N Shi 1G 67
Langley Ter. DH7: B'hpe 5D 138
DH9: Ann P 5A 124
NE32: Jar 3B 86
Langley Vw. DH9: Ann P 6C 124
Langport Rd. SR2: Sund 5F 119
Langthorne Av. SR8: Hord 6F 173
Langton Cl. SR4: Sund 2D 118
Langton Ct. NE20: Darr H 7F 31
Langton Dr. NE23: Cra 7A 22
Langton Lea DH1: H Shin 7F 167
Langton Ter. DH4: New L 7J 129
NE7: H Hea 3K 63
Langwell Cres. NE63: Ash 3A 12
Langwell Ter. NE61: Peg 3B 10
Lanivet Cl. SR2: Ryh 1H 133
Lannerwood *NE29: N Shi* *1G 67*
(off Coach La.)
Lansbury Cl. DH3: Bir 2K 113
Lansbury Ct. NE12: Longb 7J 45
Lansbury Dr. DH3: Bir 2K 113
SR7: Mur 7E 146
Lansbury Gdns. NE10: Ward 6E 84
Lansbury Rd. NE16: Whi 1J 97
Lansbury Way SR5: Sund 6H 103
Lansdowne SR2: Ryh 2G 133
Lansdowne Ct. NE3: Gos 7E 44
NE46: Hex 3B 70
Lansdowne Cres. DH6: Bowb 5J 177
NE3: Gos 6E 44
Lansdowne Gdns. NE2: Jes 5J 63
Lansdowne Pl. NE3: Gos 7E 44
Lansdowne Pl. W. NE3: Gos 7E 44
Lansdowne Rd. NE12: Longb 4B 46
Lansdowne St. SR4: Sund 1D 118
Lansdowne Ter. NE3: Gos 7E 44
NE29: N Shi 6F 49
Lansdowne Ter. E. NE3: Gos 7E 44
Lansdowne Ter. W. NE29: N Shi 6E 48
Lantern Ct. DH1: Dur 2E 166
Lanthwaite Rd. NE9: Low F 2J 99
Lanton St. DH4: New H 3D 130
Lapford Dr. NE23: Cra 1A 26
Lapwing Cl. NE24: News 5J 23
NE38: Wash 5D 114
Lapwing Ct. DH6: Has 1B 170
NE16: Burn 3C 110
NE34: S Shi 1A 88
L'Arbre Cres. NE16: Whi 7F 81
Larch Av. DH4: Hou S 1C 144
NE34: S Shi 1C 88
SR6: Whit 5J 89
Larch Cl. NE9: Eigh B 5B 100
Larches, The DH1: Carr 7H 155
DH7: Esh W 4D 162
NE4: Elsw 9A 4 (3C 82)
NE16: Burn 1B 110
Larches Rd. DH1: Dur 1J 165
Larch Gro. NE24: News 5G 23
Larchlea NE20: Darr H 2G 41
Larchlea Sth. NE20: Darr H 2G 41
Larch Rd. NE21: Blay 3D 80
Larch St. DH8: Cons 6H 121
NE16: Sun 5H 97
Larch Ter. DH7: Lang P 5J 151
DH9: Stly 6H 125
DH9: Tant 7A 110
Larchwood NE38: Wash 7F 115
Larchwood Av. NE3: Fawd 5B 44
(not continuous)
NE6: Walk 5C 64
NE13: W Op 6E 34
Larchwood Dr. NE63: Ash 6A 12
Larchwood Gdns. NE11: Lob H 2D 98
Larchwood Gro. SR2: Sund 6E 118
Larkfield Cres. DH4: S Row 4A 130
Larkfield Rd. SR2: Sund 5E 118
Larkhill SR2: Ryh 2H 133
Larkrise Cl. NE7: H Hea 2B 64
Larkspur NE9: Low F 2A 100
Larkspur Cl. DH9: Tan L 1D 124
Larkspur Rd. NE16: Whi 7H 81
Larkspur Ter. NE2: Jes 4G 63
Larkswood NE34: S Shi 6D 68
Larne Cres. NE9: Low F 2J 99
Larriston *NE42: Pru* *5D 76*
(off Simonside)
Larriston Pl. NE23: Cra 4H 25
Lartington Ct. DH3: Gt Lum 4F 143
Lartington Gdns. NE3: Gos 7H 45
Larwood Ct. DH3: Ches S 1C 142
DH9: Ann P 6J 123
La Sagesse NE2: Jes 2G 63
Lascelles Av. NE34: S Shi 1A 88
Laski Gdns. NE10: Ward 6F 85
Lassells Rigg NE42: Pru 3F 77
Latimer St. NE30: Tyne 4K 49
Latimer Way NE64: Newb S 2G 13
Latton Cl. NE23: Cra 6J 25
Laude Bank DH7: Esh 7C 150
Lauderdale Av. NE28: W'snd 1F 65
Lauder Way NE10: Pel 5F 85
Launceston DH3: Gt Lum 3E 142
Launceston Cl. NE3: Ki Pk 4K 43
Launceston Ct. SR3: E Her 2J 131
Launceston Dr. SR3: E Her 2J 131
Laura St. SR1: Sund 5K 7 (2F 119)
SR7: S'hm 4B 148
Laurel, The *NE23: Cra* *4B 26*
(off Evergreen Ct.)
Laurel Av. DH1: Dur 2E 166
NE3: Fawd 6C 44
NE12: Kil 3E 46
SR7: S'hm 3K 147
Laurel Ct. DH2: Ches S 4K 127
DH7: Esh W 5D 162
NE30: N Shi 7H 49
Laurel Cres. DH2: Pelt 2D 126
DH6: Thor 2J 179
NE6: Walk 4D 64
Laurel Dr. DH8: Lead 6B 122
NE63: Ash 6A 12
Laurel End NE12: Kil 3E 46
Laurel Gro. NE34: S Shi 2B 88
SR2: Sund 6E 118
Laurel Hgts. NE29: N Shi 7G 49
Laurel Pl. NE12: Kil 3D 46
NE23: Cra 3K 25
Laurel Rd. NE21: Blay 4D 80
Laurels, The *SR3: New S* *1C 132*
(off Chelmsford St.)
Laurel St. NE15: Thro 2H 59
NE28: W'snd 4G 65
Laurel Ter. DH7: Lang P 5K 151
NE16: Burn 2K 109
NE25: H'wll 1J 37
Laurel Wlk. NE3: Gos 7E 44
Laurel Way NE40: Craw 3E 78
Laurelwood Gdns. NE11: Lob H 2D 98
Lauren Ct. SR8: Eas 7A 160
Laurens Ct. NE37: Wash 7H 101
Lavender Ct. NE63: Ash 6A 12
Lavender Gdns. DH7: Sac 7F 141
NE2: Jes 4F 63
NE9: Low F 1H 99
Lavender Gro. NE32: Jar 6C 86
SR5: Sund 6G 103
Lavender La. NE34: S Shi 1H 87
Lavender Rd. NE16: Whi 1G 97
Lavender Row NE9: Low F 2K 99
Lavender St. SR4: Sund 2G 117
Lavender Wlk. NE31: Heb 3J 85
Lavendon Cl. NE23: Cra 6J 25
Laverick NE10: Hew 1D 100
Laverick La. NE36: W Bol 7K 85
Laverick Ter. DH9: Ann P 6A 124
Laverock Ct. NE6: Byke 6P 5 (1A 84)
Laverock Hall Rd. NE24: Bly, News 7C 22
Laverock Pl. NE3: Ken 7K 43
NE24: News 6F 23
Lavers Rd. DH3: Bir 3A 114
Lavington Rd. NE34: S Shi 5A 68
Law Courts, The
Newcastle upon Tyne Combined
Court Cen. 6H 5 (1G 83)
LAWE, THE 1K 67
Lawe Rd. NE33: S Shi 1K 67
Lawn, The NE40: Ryton 7G 59
Lawn Cotts. SR3: Silk 3B 132
Lawn Ct. NE63: Ash 4K 11
Lawn Dr. NE36: W Bol 1F 103
Lawnhead Sq. SR3: Silk 3D 132
Lawns, The DH5: Eas L 2J 157
SR3: Silk 3B 132
SR6: Whit 6H 89
SR7: S'hm 4J 147
Lawnside SR7: S'hm 4J 147
Lawnsway NE32: Jar 5C 86
Lawnswood DH5: Hou S 3F 145
Lawrence Av. NE21: Blay 3C 80
NE34: S Shi 3K 87
Lawrence Ct. NE21: Blay 3C 80
Lawrence Hill Ct. NE10: Ward 6F 85
Lawrence St. SR1: Sund 2G 119
Lawson Av. NE32: Jar 3C 86
Lawson Ct. DH2: Ches S 7A 128
DH9: W Pelt 3C 126
NE35: Bol C 7F 87
Lawson Cres. SR6: Ful 3F 105
Lawson Rd. DH6: Bowb 4H 177
Lawson St. NE28: W'snd 4G 65
NE29: N Shi 1G 67
Lawson St. W. NE29: N Shi 1G 67
Lawson Ter. DH1: Dur 3K 165
DH5: Eas L 2H 157
NE4: Benw 2A 82
Laws St. SR6: Ful 3F 105
Laxey St. DH9: Stly 3E 124
Laxford DH3: Bir 6B 114
Laybourn Gdns. NE34: S Shi 2G 87
Layburn Gdns. NE15: Lem 5E 60
Layburn Pl. SR8: Pet 5A 172
Laycock Gdns. NE23: Seg 2C 36
Layfield Rd. NE3: Gos 3E 44
Laygate NE33: S Shi 4H 67
Laygate Pl. NE33: S Shi 4J 67
Laygate St. NE33: S Shi 4H 67
Lea Av. NE32: Jar 4C 86
Leabank NE15: Lem 5D 60
Leaburn Ter. NE42: Pru 4D 76
LEADGATE 5B 122
3J 93
Leadgate Cotts. NE17: C'wl 3J 93
Leadgate Ind. Est. DH8: Cons 7C 122
Leadgate Rd. DH8: Cons, Lead 6J 121
(not continuous)
Lead La. DH8: Ebc, W'stll 3E 106
NE15: Hor 4E 56
NE43: Hed 7E 92
Lead Rd. NE17: C'wl 4G 93
NE21: Blay 4G 79
NE40: Coal, G'sde 3K 93
NE43: B'ley 4H 91
Leafield NE63: Ash 3D 12
Leafield Cl. DH3: Bir 2B 114
Leafield Cres. NE34: S Shi 5C 68
Leafield Glade DH3: Bir 5B 114
Lea Grn. DH3: Ches S 7C 114
Leagreen Ct. NE3: Gos 7C 44
Leaholme Cres. NE24: Bly 3G 23
Leaholme Ter. TS27: B Col 3K 183
Lea La. SR8: Eas 5K 159
Lealholm Rd. NE7: Longb 7J 45
Leam Gdns. NE10: Ward 6G 85
Leamington Cen., The 7D 60
Leamington Ct. NE15: Lem 6D 60
Leamington St. SR4: Sund 2D 118
Leam La. NE10: Ward 6J 85
NE10: Wrek, Hew, Ward 4C 100
NE32: Jar 4B 86
LEAM LANE ESTATE 2E 100
LEAMSIDE 1J 155
Leamside NE10: Hew 1D 100
NE32: Jar 2C 86
Leander Av. DH3: Ches S 1B 128
NE62: Stake 7J 11
Leander Ct. NE62: Stake 7K 11
Leander Dr. NE35: Bol C 6E 86
Leander M. NE62: Stake 7K 11
Leaplish NE38: Wash 6K 115
Leap Mill 1B 110
Lea Rigg DH4: W Rai 1A 156
(not continuous)
Learmouth Way NE13: Ki Pk 4K 43
Leas, The DH4: Nbot 6D 130
NE25: Monks 7D 38
Lea Side DH8: Cons 2K 135
Leasingthorne Way NE13: Haz 2A 44
Leasyde Wlk. NE16: Whi 2E 96
Leatham SR2: Ryh 1G 133
Leat Ho. NE38: Wash 4B 116
Lea Vw. NE34: S Shi 5D 68
Leaway NE42: Pru 4D 76
LEAZES 2K 109
Leazes, The DH6: Bowb 4H 177
NE15: Thro 4G 59
NE16: Burn 2K 109
NE34: S Shi 7B 68
SR1: Sund 4F 7 (2D 118)
Leazes Arc. NE1: Newc T 4E 4
Leazes Ct. DH1: Dur 2D 6 (2B 166)
NE4: Newc T 3A 4 (7D 62)
Leazes Cres. NE1: Newc T 4D 4 (7E 62)
NE46: Hex 1B 70
Leazes La. DH1: Dur 2C 166
NE1: Newc T 4E 4 (7F 63)
(not continuous)
NE45: Ayd 5E 52
NE46: Hex 1A 70
Leazes Pde. NE2: Newc T 3A 4 (6D 62)
Leazes Pk. NE46: Hex 1A 70
Leazes Pk. Rd. NE1: Newc T 3D 4 (7F 63)
(not continuous)
Leazes Parkway NE15: Thro 4G 59
Leazes Pl. DH1: Dur 2D 6 (2B 166)
Leazes Ri. SR8: Pet 6D 172
Leazes Rd. DH1: Dur 2B 6 (2A 166)
Leazes Sq. NE1: Newc T 4E 4 (7F 63)
Leazes Ter. NE1: Newc T 3D 4 (7E 62)
NE45: Corb 7D 52
NE46: Hex 1B 70
Leazes Vw. NE39: Row G 5H 95
NE42: Oving 2K 75
Leazes Vs. NE16: Burn 2A 110
Lecondale NE10: Hew 3D 100
Lecondale Ct. NE10: Hew 3D 100
Ledbury Rd. SR2: Sund 5F 119
Leech Ct. SR8: Eas C 7D 160
Leechmere Cres. SR7: S'hm 1G 147
Leechmere Ind. Est. SR2: Sund 7G 119
Leechmere Rd. SR2: Sund 6E 118
Leechmere Vw. SR2: Ryh 1H 133
Leechmere Way SR2: Ryh 1G 133
(not continuous)
Lee Cl. NE38: Wash 3B 116
Leeds St. SR6: Ful 5F 105
Lee Hill Ct. DH7: Lan 6J 137
Leeholme DH5: Hou S 3F 145
Leeholme Ct. DH9: Ann P 6A 124
Leeman's La. DH6: Hett 7C 176
Leeming Gdns. NE9: Low F 1K 99
Leesfield Dr. DH7: Mead 2E 174
Leesfield Gdns. DH7: Mead 2E 174
Leesfield Rd. DH7: Mead 2E 174
Lees St. DH9: Stly 2F 125
Lee St. NE23: Dud 2K 35
SR5: S'wck 6D 104
SR6: Ful 3F 105
Lee Ter. DH5: Hett H 1H 157
DH6: Shot C 6E 170
SR8: Eas 7A 160
Legg Av. NE22: Bed 5C 18
Legion Gro. NE15: Den M 6F 61
Legion Rd. NE15: Den M 6F 61
Leicester Cl. NE28: W'snd 7E 46
Leicestershire Dr. DH1: Carr 1H 167
Leicester St. NE6: Walk 1C 84
Leicester Wlk. SR8: Pet 4A 172
Leicester Way NE32: Jar 5A 86
Leighton Rd. SR2: Sund 6F 119
Leighton St. NE6: Byke 4M 5 (7J 63)
NE33: S Shi 3A 68
Leighton Ter. DH3: Bir 3K 113
Leith Ct. NE34: S Shi 1J 87
Leith Gdns. DH9: Tan L 7D 110
Leland Pl. NE61: Mor 1D 14
LEMINGTON 7C 60
Lemington Gdns. NE5: Fen 6J 61
Lemington Rd. NE15: Lem 6A 60
Lemon St. NE33: S Shi 7H 67
Lena Av. NE25: Monks 7E 38
Lenin Ter. DH9: Stly 5F 125
NE17: C'wl 7A 94
Lennep Way NE63: Ash 6B 12
Lenore Ter. NE40: G'sde 4F 79
Leominster Rd. SR2: Sund 6F 119
Leopold Ho. SR2: Sund 6G 7
Leopold St. NE32: Jar 7B 66
Lepidina Cl. NE15: Lem 5D 60
Lesbury Av. NE27: Shir 1J 47
NE28: W'snd 2K 65
NE62: Stake 6J 11
NE63: Ash 5B 12
Lesbury Chase NE3: Gos 5D 44
Lesbury Cl. DH2: Ches S 1H 141
Lesbury Gdns. NE13: W Op 5E 34
Lesbury Rd. NE6: Heat 4K 63
Lesbury St. NE15: Lem 7C 60
NE28: W'snd 4C 66
Lesbury Ter. NE17: C'wl 7K 93
Lesley Ct. *NE3: Gos* *7E 44*
(off Regent Rd.)
Leslie Av. NE31: Heb 1J 85
Leslie Cl. NE40: Ryton 2J 79
Leslie Cres. NE3: Gos 2E 62
Leslies Vw. NE61: Mor 5E 8
Letch, The NE12: Longb 3B 46
Letch Av. SR7: Hawt 3J 159
Letch Path NE15: Lem 6C 60
Letch Way NE15: Lem 6C 60
Letchwell Vs. NE12: Longb 3C 46
Leuchars Ct. DH3: Bir 5A 114
Leven Av. DH2: Ches S 1K 141
Levens Wlk. NE23: Cra 3G 25
Leven Wlk. SR8: Pet 1A 182
Levisham Cl. SR3: Tuns 2E 132
Lewis Cres. SR2: Sund 3H 119
Lewis Dr. NE4: Fen 7B 62
Lewis Gdns. NE34: S Shi 3J 87
Lexington Ct. DH7: B'don 3C 174
Leybourne Av. NE12: Kil 3B 46
Leybourne Dene NE12: Kil 2B 46
Leybourne Hold DH3: Bir 2A 114
Leyburn Cl. DH2: Ous 7F 113
DH4: Hou S 1D 144
Leyburn Ct. NE23: Cra 6J 25
Leyburn Dr. NE7: H Hea 2J 63
Leyburn Gro. DH4: Hou S 1C 144
Leyburn Pl. DH3: Bir 2K 113
Leyfield Cl. SR3: Dox P 4D 132
Leyland Cl. DH6: Bowb 3J 177
Leyton Pl. NE8: Gate 6J 83
Liberty Ct. NE4: Newc T 6A 4 (2C 82)
Liberty Grn. NE38: Wash 2H 115
Liberty Ter. DH9: Tant 6B 110
Liberty Way SR6: Roker 7G 105
Library Ct. NE42: Pru 3F 77
Library Stairs NE30: N Shi 7H 49
Library Ter. DH9: Ann P 5K 123
Library Wlk. DH9: Ann P 4K 123
Lichfield Av. NE6: Walk 2C 84
Lichfield Cl. DH3: Gt Lum 4E 142
NE3: Ki Pk 5A 44
NE63: N Sea 5D 12
Lichfield Rd. DH1: Dur 3B 154
SR5: S'wck 4C 104

Lichfield Way NE32: Jar . . . 5A 86
Lidcombe Cl. SR3: Tuns . . . 2D 132
Liddell Ct. SR6: Roker . . . 5H 105
Liddells Fell Rd. NE21: Blay . . . 4K 79
Liddell St. NE29: N Shi . . . 7H 49
NE30: N Shi . . . 7H 49
SR6: Monkw . . . 1K 7 (7F 105)
Liddell Ter. DH6: Whe H . . . 4A 180
NE8: Gate . . . 5F 83
NE11: Kib . . . 2E 112
Liddle Av. DH6: S'burn . . . 3K 167
Liddle Cl. SR8: Pet . . . 4K 171
Liddle Ct. NE4: Newc T . . . 5A 4 (1C 82)
Liddle Rd. NE4: Newc T . . . 5A 4 (1C 82)
Liddles St. NE22: Bed . . . 5B 18
Lieven St. NE13: Haz . . . 7C 34
Lievers Cl. DH8: Shot B . . . 2G 121
Life . . . 8D 4 (2E 82)
Lifeboat Station
Cullercoats . . . 1J 49
Newbiggin-by-theSea . . . 2K 13
Tynemouth . . . 7J 49
Lifespan Ladies Fitness . . . 7H 101
Liffey Rd. NE31: Heb . . . 3K 85
Lightbourne Rd. NE6: Walk . . . 7E 64
Lighthouse Vw. SR6: Whit . . . 1H 89
SR7: S'hm . . . 6C 148
Lilac Av. DH1: Dur . . . 6K 153
DH7: Sac . . . 1E 152
NE12: Longb . . . 4D 46
NE24: Bly . . . 1H 23
NE34: S Shi . . . 1B 88
SR3: Tuns . . . 1D 132
SR6: Whit . . . 3H 89
TS27: B Col . . . 3K 183
Lilac Cl. NE5: Cha P . . . 1B 60
Lilac Ct. NE63: Ash . . . 6A 12
Lilac Cres. NE16: Burn . . . 2A 110
Lilac Gdns. DH2: Pelt . . . 2D 126
NE9: Low F . . . 1H 99
NE16: Whi . . . 7G 81
NE38: Wash . . . 7G 115
SR6: Clead . . . 4C 88
Lilac Gro. DH2: Ches S . . . 4J 127
SR6: Ful . . . 4F 105
Lilac Pk. DH7: Ush M . . . 3C 164
Lilac Pl. DH8: Lead . . . 6B 122
Lilac Rd. NE6: Walk . . . 4E 64
Lilac Sq. DH4: Bour . . . 6J 129
Lilac St. SR4: Sund . . . 2G 117
Lilac Ter. DH6: Shot C . . . 6E 170
DH9: Ann P . . . 4J 123
Lilac Wlk. NE31: Heb . . . 3J 85
Lilburn Cl. DH2: Ches S . . . 2J 141
NE6: Byke . . . 2A 84
NE36: E Bol . . . 6J 87
Lilburne Cl. SR1: Sund . . . 1G 119
Lilburn Gdns. NE3: Gos . . . 1H 63
Lilburn Pl. SR5: S'wck . . . 6C 104
Lilburn Rd. NE27: Shir . . . 2J 47
Lilburn St. NE29: N Shi . . . 7F 49
Lilian Av. NE28: W'snd . . . 4E 64
SR2: Ryh . . . 1G 133
Lilian Ter. DH7: Lang P . . . 5J 151
Lilleycroft NE39: Row G . . . 5K 95
Lilley Ter. NE39: Row G . . . 4K 95
Lillico Ho. NE2: Jes . . . 1J 5 (6H 63)
Lily Av. NE2: Jes . . . 4G 63
NE22: Bed . . . 1K 21
Lily Bank NE28: W'snd . . . 3F 65
Lily Cl. NE21: Winl . . . 4A 80
Lily Ct. DH9: Dip . . . 1J 123
Lily Cres. NE2: Jes . . . 4G 63
SR6: Whit . . . 3H 89
Lily Est. NE15: Thro . . . 2H 59
Lily Gdns. DH9: Dip . . . 1J 123
Lily St. SR4: Sund . . . 2F 7 (1D 118)
Lily Ter. DH4: Nbot . . . 5D 130
NE5: West . . . 2G 61
Lilywhite Ter. DH5: Eas L . . . 1H 157
Lime Av. DH4: Hou S . . . 1C 144
TS27: B Col . . . 2J 183
Limecrag Av. DH1: Dur . . . 1F 167
Limecroft NE32: Jar . . . 5C 86
Lime Gro. NE40: Ryton . . . 1F 79
NE42: Pru . . . 3D 76
Limekiln Ct. NE28: W'snd . . . 3H 65
Limekiln Rd. NE28: W'snd . . . 3H 65
Lime Pk. DH7: B'don . . . 1D 174
Limes, The DH4: Pen . . . 1B 130
NE12: Longb . . . 3A 46
NE61: Mor . . . 6F 9
(off Cottingwood La.)
SR2: Sund . . . 7J 7 (4F 119)
SR6: Whit . . . 6G 89
(off Front St.)
Limes Av. NE24: Bly . . . 7H 19
Lime Sq. NE1: Newc T . . . 5L 5 (1J 83)
Limestone La. NE18: Diss . . . 5C 30
NE20: Pon . . . 5C 30
Lime St. DH2: Wald . . . 1G 141
DH9: Stly . . . 6D 124
NE1: Newc T . . . 4L 5 (7J 63)
NE15: Thro . . . 2H 59
NE21: Blay . . . 5D 80
SR4: Sund . . . 1D 118
Lime Ter. DH7: Lang P . . . 5K 151
Limetree NE38: Wash . . . 6J 115
Limetrees Gdns. NE9: Low F . . . 7H 83
Limewood Ct.
NE2: Newc T . . . 1B 4 (5D 62)
Limewood Gro. NE13: W Op . . . 6D 34
Linacre Cl. NE3: Ki Pk . . . 6H 43
Linacre Ct. SR8: Pet . . . 7K 171
Linbridge Dr. NE5: W Dent . . . 4D 60
Linburn NE38: Wash . . . 1F 129
Lincoln Av. NE28: W'snd . . . 2E 64
SR3: New S . . . 1C 132
Lincoln Ct. NE31: Heb . . . 1H 85
Lincoln Cres. DH5: Hett H . . . 6F 145
Lincoln Grn. NE3: Gos . . . 3E 44
Lincoln Pl. DH8: C'sde . . . 3C 134
Lincoln Rd. DH1: Dur . . . 4B 154
DH8: C'sde . . . 3C 134
NE23: Cra . . . 7A 22
NE34: S Shi . . . 6D 68
Lincolnshire Cl. DH1: Carr . . . 1G 167
Lincoln St. NE8: Gate . . . 5G 83
SR4: Sund . . . 1B 118
Lincoln Ter. NE46: Hex . . . 2B 70
Lincoln Wlk. DH3: Gt Lum . . . 3E 142
SR8: Pet . . . 4A 172
Lincoln Way NE32: Jar . . . 5B 86
Lincrest Ct. NE5: West . . . 3F 61
Lindale Av. NE16: Whi . . . 2G 97
Lindale Rd. NE4: Fen . . . 5A 62
Lindean Pl. NE23: Cra . . . 4H 25
Linden NE9: Low F . . . 3B 100
Linden Av. NE3: Gos . . . 1E 62
NE4: Fen . . . 6K 61
Linden Cl. NE62: Stake . . . 7J 11
Linden Gdns. SR2: Sund . . . 5E 118
Linden Gro. DH4: Hou S . . . 2D 144
DH8: Lead . . . 6B 122
NE11: Dun . . . 6C 82
Linden M. DH7: Lang P . . . 5J 151
Linden Pk. DH7: B'don . . . 1D 174
DH8: Cons . . . 4K 121
Linden Rd. DH7: Bearp . . . 1D 164
NE3: Gos . . . 1E 62
NE12: Longb . . . 6B 46
NE21: Blay . . . 4D 80
NE25: Sea D . . . 7F 27
SR2: Sund . . . 5E 118
Linden Ter. NE9: Spri . . . 6D 100
NE12: Longb . . . 5B 46
NE26: Whit B . . . 6H 39
Linden Way DH8: B'hill . . . 5G 121
NE9: Eigh B . . . 5A 100
(not continuous)
NE20: Darr H . . . 1G 41
Lindfield Av. NE5: Blak . . . 4H 61
Lindisfarne DH1: H Shin . . . 7F 167
NE38: Wash . . . 4G 115
SR2: Ryh . . . 3G 133
SR8: Pet . . . 1A 182
Lindisfarne Av. DH3: Ches S . . . 6B 128
Lindisfarne Cl. DH2: Ches S . . . 1J 141
DH4: Hou S . . . 7C 130
NE2: Jes . . . 3H 63
NE5: W Dent . . . 4F 61
NE61: Mor . . . 2G 15
NE61: Peg . . . 3C 10
Lindisfarne Ct. NE32: Jar . . . 7F 67
Lindisfarne Dr. NE8: Gate . . . 10K 5 (4H 83)
Lindisfarne Ho. SR7: S'hm . . . 4B 148
Lindisfarne La. NE61: Mor . . . 2G 15
Lindisfarne Nursing Home
DH2: Ches S . . . 6J 127
Lindisfarne Pl. NE28: W'snd . . . 2H 65
Lindisfarne Recess NE32: Jar . . . 2D 86
Lindisfarne Ri. DH1: Dur . . . 6B 154
Lindisfarne Rd. DH1: Dur . . . 6B 154
NE2: Jes . . . 3H 63
NE31: Heb . . . 3J 85
NE32: Jar . . . 2D 86
Lindisfarne Ter. NE30: N Shi . . . 5G 49
Lindisfarne Wlk. NE62: Chop . . . 1G 17
(off Morpeth Rd.)
Lindom Av. DH3: Ches S . . . 6B 128
Lindon Mnr. NE12: Kil . . . 7A 36
Lindon Rd. DH9: Stly . . . 4E 124
Lindrick Ct. NE10: Ward . . . 7G 85
Lindrick Pk. DH5: Hett H . . . 7H 145
Lindsay Av. NE24: Cow . . . 1G 23
Lindsay Cl. SR2: Sund . . . 3G 119
Lindsay Ct. SR6: Whit . . . 4H 89
Lindsay Rd. SR1: Sund . . . 2G 119
SR2: Sund . . . 2G 119
Lindsay St. DH5: Hett H . . . 4H 145
Lindsey Cl. NE23: Cra . . . 4G 25
Lindum Rd. NE9: Low F . . . 6H 83
Linfield SR2: Ryh . . . 2G 133
Lingcrest NE9: Low F . . . 2A 100
Lingdale DH1: Carr . . . 1H 167
Lingdale Av. SR6: Seab . . . 1G 105
Lingey Cl. DH7: Sac . . . 6D 140
Lingey Gdns. NE10: Ward . . . 6G 85
Lingey La. NE10: Ward . . . 7F 85
Lingfield DH5: Hou S . . . 3F 145
Lingfield Rd. DH8: Cons . . . 6H 121
Lingholme DH2: Ches S . . . 5J 127
Lingmell NE37: Wash . . . 2F 115
Lingshaw NE10: Hew . . . 7F 85
Lingside NE32: Jar . . . 4C 86
Linhope Av. NE3: Fawd . . . 5B 44
Linhope Rd. NE5: West . . . 3F 61
Link, The NE46: Hex . . . 1B 70
Link Av. NE22: Bed . . . 7F 17
Link Rd. NE2: Jes, Newc T . . . 2G 4 (6G 63)
NE5: Fen . . . 3A 62
NE13: Haz . . . 7C 34
Links, The DH1: Carr . . . 7H 155
NE26: Sea S . . . 4C 28
NE26: Whit B . . . 2F 39
Links Av. NE26: Whit B . . . 4F 39
NE30: Cull . . . 2J 49
Links Ct. NE26: Whit B . . . 4G 39
Links Dr. DH8: B'hill . . . 4G 121
Links Grn. NE3: Gos . . . 6F 45
Links Grn. Wlk. NE3: Gos . . . 6F 45
LINKS QUARRY . . . 5H 13
Links Rd. NE24: Bly . . . 5K 23
NE24: Bly . . . 7K 23
NE26: Sea S . . . 7K 23
NE30: Cull . . . 1J 49
Links Vw. NE24: News . . . 5G 23
NE63: N Sea . . . 7E 12
Links Wlk. NE5: West . . . 3F 61
Linkway DH7: Sac . . . 7E 140
NE32: Jar . . . 5D 86
Linley Hill NE16: Whi . . . 2E 96
Linnel Dr. NE15: Lem . . . 6E 60
Linnels Bank NE46: Hex . . . 6H 71
Linnet Cl. NE38: Wash . . . 5E 114
Linnet Ct. NE63: Ash . . . 5K 11
Linnetsfield NE6: Walk . . . 5D 64
(off Northmoor Rd.)
Linney Gdns. NE34: S Shi . . . 2G 87
Linnheads NE42: Pru . . . 5D 76
Linshiels Gdns. NE63: Ash . . . 5D 12
Linskell SR2: Ryh . . . 1G 133
Linskill Pk. NE30: N Shi . . . 5H 49
Linskill Pl. NE3: Ken . . . 2B 62
NE30: N Shi . . . 5H 49
Linskill St. NE30: N Shi . . . 7H 49
Linskill Ter. NE30: N Shi . . . 6H 49
Linslade Wlk. NE23: Cra . . . 4H 25
Lintfort NE38: Wash . . . 2C 128
Linthorpe Av. SR7: S'hm . . . 3C 148
Linthorpe Ct. NE34: S Shi . . . 1G 87
Linthorpe Rd. NE3: Gos . . . 5E 44
NE30: Cull . . . 3H 49
Linton NE12: Kil . . . 6B 36
Linton Rd. NE9: Low F . . . 4H 99
NE26: Whit B . . . 2E 38
Lintonville Ent. Cen. NE63: Wood . . . 2B 12
Lintonville Parkway NE63: Wood . . . 2A 12
Lintonville Ter. NE63: Ash . . . 3A 12
NE63: Wood . . . 2A 12
LINTZ . . . 2K 109
LINTZFORD . . . 1G 109
Lintzford Cl. NE39: Row G . . . 7H 95
Lintzford Gdns. NE15: Lem . . . 6E 60
NE39: Row G . . . 7H 95
Lintzford Grange NE39: Ham M . . . 1G 109
Lintzford La. NE39: C'wl, Row G . . . 5E 94
Lintzford M. SR8: Eas C . . . 7C 160
Lintzford Rd.
NE39: Ham M, Row G . . . 3D 108
LINTZ GREEN . . . 3G 109
Lintz Grn. La. NE39: Ham M . . . 2G 109
Lintz La. NE16: Burn . . . 3G 109
Lintz Ter. DH9: Stly . . . 4C 124
NE16: Burn . . . 2K 109
Linum Pl. NE4: Fen . . . 5A 62
Linwood Pl. NE3: Gos . . . 3E 44
Lion Pl. SR4: Sund . . . 2G 117
Lion Wlk. NE29: N Shi . . . 2F 67
Lisa Av. SR4: Sund . . . 3G 117
Lisburn Ter. SR4: Sund . . . 1C 118
Lish Av. NE26: Whit B . . . 7J 39
Lishman Cotts. NE40: Craw . . . 2C 78
(off Main St.)
Lishman Ter. NE40: Craw . . . 2E 78
Lisle Ct. NE28: W'snd . . . 3F 65
Lisle Gro. NE28: W'snd . . . 2A 66
Lisle Rd. NE34: S Shi . . . 6B 68
Lisle St. NE1: Newc T . . . 4F 4 (7F 63)
NE28: W'snd . . . 3F 65
Lismore Av. NE33: S Shi . . . 6K 67
Lismore Pl. NE15: Benw . . . 7K 61
Lismore Ter. NE9: Spri . . . 6D 100
Lister Av. NE11: Dun . . . 5B 82
NE40: G'sde . . . 6D 78
Lister Cl. DH5: Hou S . . . 4D 144
Lister Rd. SR8: Pet . . . 4J 171
Listers La. NE9: Low F . . . 6J 83
Litchfield Cres. NE21: Winl . . . 5B 80
Litchfield La. NE21: Winl . . . 5B 80
Litchfield St. NE21: Winl . . . 5B 80
Litchfield Ter. NE21: Winl . . . 5B 80
Lit. Bedford St. NE29: N Shi . . . 7G 49
Littlebridge Ct. DH1: Dur . . . 4J 153
Little Bldgs. NE42: Oving . . . 2K 75
LITTLEBURN . . . 7G 165
Littleburn Cl. DH4: Hou S . . . 7C 130
Littleburn Ind. Est. DH7: Lang M . . . 1H 175
Littleburn La. DH7: Lang M . . . 7G 165
Littleburn Rd. DH7: Lang M . . . 7G 165
Little Burn Way DH2: P Fel . . . 6G 127
Little Dene NE2: Jes . . . 2F 63
Littledene NE9: Low F . . . 7H 83
Little Eden SR8: Pet . . . 5B 172
Little Theatre, The
Gateshead . . . 6H 83
LITTLE THORPE . . . 2A 172
LITTLETOWN . . . 1D 168
Littletown La. DH6: Litt . . . 2D 168
Lit. Villiers St. SR1: Sund . . . 3K 7 (1G 119)
(not continuous)
Littondale NE28: W'snd . . . 1D 64
Liverpool St. NE1: Newc T . . . 4E 4 (7F 63)
Live Theatre . . . 7H 5
Livingstone Pl. NE33: S Shi . . . 1J 67
Livingstone St. DH8: Cons . . . 6H 121
NE33: S Shi . . . 1K 67
Livingstone Vw. NE30: Tyne . . . 5J 49
LivingWell Health Club
Newcastle, Gateshead . . . 8H 5
Lizard La. NE34: S Shi . . . 7F 69
SR6: Whit . . . 3G 89
Lizard La. Caravan & Camping Site
NE34: S Shi . . . 7F 69
Lizard Vw. SR6: Whit . . . 3G 89
Lloyd Ct. NE11: Dun . . . 4A 82
Lloyds Av. DH5: E Rain . . . 6C 144
Lloyds Ter. DH7: Lang P . . . 5J 151
Lloyd St. NE40: Craw . . . 3D 78
LOANING BURN . . . 7H 159
LOANSDEAN . . . 3F 15
Loansdean Wood NE61: Mor . . . 2F 15
Lobban Av. NE31: Heb . . . 3H 85
Lobelia Av. NE10: Gate . . . 4K 83
Lobelia Cl. NE5: Cha P . . . 2B 60
Lobley Gdns. NE11: Dun . . . 1C 98
LOBLEY HILL . . . 1C 98
Lobley Hill DH7: Mead . . . 1F 175
Lobley Hill Rd. NE8: Gate . . . 1D 98
NE11: Fest P, Lob H . . . 1C 98
NE16: Burn, Marl H . . . 1C 110
Local Av. DH6: S Hil . . . 3C 168
Locarno Ct. NE64: Newb S . . . 2J 13
(off Locarno Pl.)
Locarno Pl. NE64: Newb S . . . 2J 13
Lochcraig Pl. NE23: Cra . . . 4G 25
Lochfield Gdns. NE11: Kib . . . 2E 112
Loch Lomond NE37: Wash . . . 5F 101
Lochmaben Ter. SR5: Monkw . . . 5F 105
Lockerbie Gdns. NE15: Lem . . . 6E 60
Lockerbie Rd. NE23: Cra . . . 4H 25
LOCKHAUGH . . . 3A 96
Lockhaugh Rd. NE39: Row G . . . 4K 95
Locksley Cl. NE29: N Shi . . . 3B 48
Lockwood Av. DH3: Bir . . . 2B 114
Locomotion Way NE12: Kil . . . 6K 35
NE29: N Shi . . . 2G 67
Locomotive Ct. NE42: Pru . . . 4E 76
Lodge Cl. NE39: Ham M . . . 3E 108
Lodge Ct. NE26: Whit B . . . 3E 38
Lodgeside Mdw. SR3: Dox P . . . 4D 132
Lodges Rd., The NE9: Low F . . . 4G 99
Lodge Ter. NE28: W'snd . . . 3H 65
Lodore Ct. SR3: Silk . . . 3B 132
Lodore Gro. NE32: Jar . . . 3D 86
Lodore Rd. NE2: Jes . . . 2F 63
Lodsworth Dr. NE23: Cra . . . 6J 25
Loefield DH3: Gt Lum . . . 2E 142
Lofthill SR3: Dox P . . . 4A 132
Logan Rd. NE6: Walk . . . 4D 64
Logan St. DH5: Hett H . . . 7G 145
DH7: Lang P . . . 4J 151
Logan Ter. DH6: S Het . . . 3A 158
(off Front St.)
Lola St. NE13: Haz . . . 7B 34
Lombard Dr. DH3: Ches S . . . 2A 128
Lombard Pl. DH3: Gt Lum . . . 3E 142
Lombard St. NE1: Newc T . . . 7H 5 (2G 83)
SR1: Sund . . . 1G 119
Lomond Cl. NE38: Wash . . . 5F 115
Lomond Pl. DH2: Ches S . . . 1K 141
London Av. NE37: Wash . . . 6F 101
Londonderry Bungs.
SR8: Eas C . . . 7B 160
Londonderry Ct. SR7: S'hm . . . 2B 148
Londonderry St. SR3: New S . . . 2C 132
SR7: S'hm . . . 5C 148
Londonderry Ter. SR3: New S . . . 2D 132
SR8: Eas C . . . 7B 160
Londonderry Way DH4: Pen . . . 2A 130
Longacre DH4: Hou S . . . 2C 144
NE38: Wash . . . 7J 115
Long Acres DH1: Dur . . . 1D 166
Long Bank DH3: Bir . . . 1A 114
NE9: Eigh B, Wrek . . . 7K 99
LONGBENTON . . . 6J 45
Longbenton Station (Metro) . . . 7J 45
Longborough Ct. NE3: Gos . . . 1J 63
Long Burn Dr. DH2: Ches S . . . 7H 127
Long Cl. NE46: Hex . . . 2D 70
Longclose Bank DH8: M'sly . . . 6B 108
NE17: Ham . . . 6B 108
NE39: Ham M . . . 6B 108
Long Cl. Rd. NE39: Ham M . . . 3D 108
Long Crag NE37: Wash . . . 3E 114
Long Dale DH2: Ches S . . . 7H 127
Longdean Cl. NE31: Heb . . . 1G 85
Longdean Pk. DH3: Ches S . . . 3A 128
Long Dr. NE61: Loan . . . 3F 15
Long Edge DH7: B'hpe, Wit G . . . 7E 138
Longedge La. DH8: Cons . . . 6D 134
Longfellow St. DH5: Hou S . . . 3E 144
Longfield Cl. NE34: S Shi . . . 2K 87
Longfield Rd. SR6: Ful . . . 4F 105
Longfield Ter. NE6: Walk . . . 2E 84
Long Gair NE21: Winl . . . 6A 80
Long Gth. DH1: Dur . . . 7H 153
Long Headlam NE6: Byke . . . 7A 64
LONGHIRST . . . 1B 10
Longhirst NE5: West . . . 3F 61
NE10: Hew . . . 7E 84
NE12: Kil . . . 6B 36
Longhirst Ct. NE61: Peg . . . 3B 10
Longhirst Dr. NE13: W Op . . . 6D 34
NE23: Cra . . . 6J 25
Longhirst Rd. NE61: Peg . . . 3B 10
Longhirst Village NE61: Lngh . . . 1A 10
Longlands NE46: Hex . . . 2C 70
Longlands Dr. DH5: Hou S . . . 3E 144
Longleat Gdns. NE33: S Shi . . . 2K 67
NE61: Peg . . . 3A 10
Longley St. NE4: Newc T . . . 4A 4 (7C 62)
Long Meadow Cl. NE40: Craw . . . 3D 78
Longmeadows NE20: Darr H . . . 1F 41
SR3: E Her . . . 3J 131
Longnewton St. SR7: S'hm . . . 5B 148
Longniddry NE37: Wash . . . 4G 101
Longniddry Ct. NE9: Low F . . . 4G 99
Long Pk. NE64: Newb S . . . 3H 13
Longridge NE21: Winl . . . 5A 80

Longridge Av. NE7: H Hea 2B 64
NE38: Wash 5E 114
Longridge Ct. NE22: Bed 4J 17
Longridge Dr. NE26: Whit B 4E 38
Longridge Rd. NE21: Blay 4G 79
Longridge Sq. SR2: Sund 6F 119
Longridge Way NE22: Bed 4J 17
NE23: Cra 4H 25
Longrigg NE10: Hew 7D 84
NE16: Swa 4G 81
Longriggs, The NE44: Rid M 7J 73
Long Row NE33: S Shi 1H 67
Long Row Cl. NE40: G'sde 6D 78
LONG SANDS 3K 49
Longshank La. DH3: Bir 2J 113
Longstaff Gdns. NE34: S Shi 2F 87
Long Stairs NE1: Newc T 7G 4 (2G 83)
Longston Av. NE30: Cull 1H 49
Longstone NE9: Low F 3H 99
Longstone Ct. NE12: Kil 7C 36
Longstone Sq. NE5: W Dent 4D 60
Longthorpe Cl. NE30: Cull 3G 49
Longwood Cl. NE16: Sun 4H 97
Lonnen, The NE34: S Shi 1D 88
NE40: Ryton 1J 79
Lonnen Av. NE4: Fen 5K 61
Lonnen Dr. NE16: Swa 6G 81
Lonsdale DH3: Bir 7C 114
Lonsdale Av. NE24: Cow 1C 22
SR6: Seab 1G 105
Lonsdale Ct. NE2: Jes 3G 63
NE17: Ham 4K 107
NE34: S Shi 2G 87
Lonsdale Gdns. NE28: W'snd 1A 66
Lonsdale Rd. SR6: Roker 5G 105
Lonsdale Ter. NE2: Jes 3G 63
Lookout Farm NE26: Sea S 4B 28
Lope Hill Rd. DH8: Cons 7C 122
Loraine Ter. NE15: Lem 7C 60
Lord Byrons Wlk. SR7: S'hm 1H 147
Lordenshaw NE5: West 3F 61
Lord Gort Cl. SR5: S'wck 6C 104
Lord Nelson St. NE33: S Shi 7H 67
Lord St. NE1: Newc T 7C 4 (2E 82)
NE33: S Shi 4A 68
SR3: New S 2D 132
SR7: S'hm 3B 148
Lorimers Cl. SR8: Pet 1K 181
Lorne St. DH5: Eas L 4H 157
Lorne Ter. SR2: Sund 7H 7 (3E 118)
Lorrain Rd. NE34: S Shi 4K 87
Lort Ho. NE2: Newc T 3J 5 (7H 63)
Lorton Av. NE30: Cull 2G 49
Lorton Rd. NE9: Low F 3J 99
Losh Ter. NE6: Walk 1D 84
Lossiemouth Rd. NE29: N Shi 7C 48
Lothian Cl. DH3: Bir 7B 114
SR4: Sund 5K 117
Lothian Ct. NE5: Blak 2J 61
Lotus Cl. NE5: Cha P 2B 60
Lotus Pl. NE4: Fen 6K 61
LOUD HILL 5H 123
Loudon St. NE34: S Shi 1J 87
Loud Ter. DH9: Ann P 5H 123
Loud Vw. Ter. DH9: Ann P 6J 123
Loughborough Av. NE30: Tyne 3J 49
SR2: Sund 5E 118
Loughbrow Pk. NE46: Hex 4D 70
Lough Ct. NE9: Low F 2K 99
Loughrigg Av. NE23: Cra 4G 25
Louie Ter. NE9: Low F 2J 99
Louisa Centre, The 3E 124
Louisa Ter. DH7: Wit G 3D 152
DH9: Stly 3E 124
Louis Av. SR6: Ful 4F 105
Louise Ho. SR2: Sund 6G 7
Louise Ter. DH3: Ches S 6A 128
Louisville NE20: Pon 4K 31
Loup St. NE21: Blay 3C 80
Loup Ter. NE21: Blay 3C 80
Louvaine Ter. DH7: Wit G 3D 152
Louvain Ter. DH5: Hett H 5G 145
NE62: Chop 1H 17
Louvain Ter. W. DH5: Hett H 5G 145
Lovaine Av. NE25: Whit B 7G 39
NE29: N Shi 7G 49
Lovaine Flats NE1: Newc T 2H 5 (7G 63)
Lovaine Hall NE1: Newc T 2H 5 (6G 63)
Lovaine Pl. NE29: N Shi 7G 49
Lovaine Pl. W. NE29: N Shi 7F 49
Lovaine Row NE30: Tyne 4K 49
Lovaine St. DH2: Pelt 3E 126
NE15: Newb 5J 59
Lovaine Ter. NE29: N Shi 6G 49
Love Av. NE23: Dud 4K 35
Love Av. Cotts. NE23: Dud 3K 35
Lovelady Ct. *NE30: Tyne* *5K 49*
(off St Oswin's Pl.)
Love La. NE1: Newc T 6J 5 (1H 83)
NE21: Winl 5B 80
Loveless Gdns. NE10: Ward 6F 85
Lovett Wlk. NE8: Gate 10D 4 (4E 82)
Lowbiggin NE5: West 7E 42
Low Burswell NE46: Hex 1B 70
Low Carrs Pk. DH1: Dur 4K 153
Low Chare DH3: Ches S 6A 128
Low Chu. St. DH9: Ann P 4K 123
Low Cl. NE42: Pru 3G 77
Lowdham Av. NE29: N Shi 1E 66
Lowdon Ct. NE2: Newc T 1C 4 (6E 62)
Low Downs Rd. DH5: Hett H 4G 145
Low Downs Sq. DH5: Hett H 4H 145
Lwr. Crone St. NE27: Shir 7K 37
Lwr. Dundas St. SR6: Monkw 7F 105
Lower Promenade NE30: Tyne 4K 49
Lwr. Rudyerd St. NE29: N Shi 7H 49
Lowerson Av. DH4: S Row 4A 130
Lowery La. DH9: Crag 7K 125
Lowery Pl. NE2: Newc T 3K 5 (7H 63)
LOWE'S BARN 5H 165
Lowe's Barn Bank DH1: Dur 5H 165
Lowes Ct. DH1: Dur 4J 165
Lowes Fall DH1: Dur 4J 165
Lowes Ri. DH1: Dur 4J 165
Loweswater NE37: Wash 2G 115
Loweswater Av. DH2: Ches S 1K 141
DH5: Eas L 3J 157
Loweswater Cl. NE24: Cow 7D 18
Loweswater Rd. NE5: Den M 5H 61
NE9: Low F 3J 99
Loweswood Cl. NE7: H Hea 4J 63
Lowes Wynd DH1: Dur 4J 165
LOW FELL 2H 99
Lowfield Ter. NE6: Walk 2D 84
Lowfield Wlk. NE16: Whi 7G 81
Low Flatts Rd. DH3: Ches S 3A 128
Low Fold NE6: Byke 4N 5 (1K 83)
LOW FRIARSIDE 1H 109
Low Friar St. NE1: Newc T 6E 4 (1F 83)
Low Gosforth Ct. NE3: Gos 3F 45
Low Graham St. *DH7: Sac* *7E 140*
(off Front St.)
Low Green DH1: Shin 6D 166
LOW GREENSIDE 4E 78
Low Haugh NE20: Pon 4K 31
Low Heighley NE61: Fair M 1A 8
Low Heighley Dr. NE61: Fair M 1B 8
Low Heworth La. NE10: Hew 4D 84
Lowhills Rd. SR8: Pet 4K 171
Lowick Cl. DH3: Bir 7B 114
Lowick Ct. NE3: Gos 1G 63
Lowland Cl. SR3: Dox P 4C 132
Lowland Rd. DH7: B'don 1D 174
Low La. NE34: S Shi 1J 87
Lowlean Ct. NE5: West 3F 61
Low Level Bri. NE1: Newc T 6M 5 (1J 83)
NE6: Byke 6M 5 (1J 83)
LOW LIGHTS 6J 49
Low Main Pl. NE23: Cra 4K 25
Low Mdws. DH7: Wit G 3C 152
SR6: Clead 5C 88
Low Mill Vs. NE21: Blay 4C 80
Low Moor Cotts. DH1: P Me 2B 154
Low Moor Rd. DH7: Esh, Lang P 6D 150
LOW MOORSLEY 2E 156
Lownds Ter. NE6: Walk 7C 64
Low Newton Local Nature Reserve 4C 154
LOW PITTINGTON 5B 156
LOW PRUDHOE 2G 77
Low Prudhoe Ind. Est. NE42: Pru 2F 77
(Princess Ct.)
NE42: Pru 1H 77
(Regents Dr.)
Lowrey's La. NE9: Low F 2H 99
Low Rd. DH1: Shin 6D 166
Low Rd. E. DH1: Shin 6D 166
Low Rd. W. DH1: Shin 6D 166
Low Row NE40: Ryton 3J 79
SR1: Sund 4G 7 (2E 118)
SR8: Eas 7K 159
Lowry Gdns. NE34: S Shi 4K 87
Lowry Rd. SR6: Seab 2G 105
LOW SOUTHWICK 6D 104
Low Sta. Rd. DH4: Leam 1J 155
Low Stobhill NE61: Mor 1G 15
Low St. SR1: Sund 1G 119
Lowther Av. DH2: Ches S 7K 127
Lowther Cl. NE63: N Sea 6D 12
SR8: Pet 5B 172
Lowther Ct. SR8: Pet 3K 181
Lowther Sq. NE23: Cra 4G 25
Lowthian Cres. NE6: Walk 1C 84
Lowthian Ter. NE38: Wash 4K 115
LOW WALKER 7F 65
Low Waskerley DH8: Shot B 2D 120
Low Well Gdns. NE10: Fell 5C 84
Low West Av. NE39: Row G 6G 95
LOW WESTWOOD 3J 107
Loxton Sq. NE23: Cra 7J 25
Lucknow St. SR1: Sund 1H 119
Lucock St. NE34: S Shi 1H 87
Lucombe Cl. DH4: S Row 4K 129
Lucy St. DH3: Ches S 5A 128
NE21: Blay 3D 80
Ludlow Av. NE29: N Shi 4E 48
Ludlow Ct. NE3: Ki Pk 5A 44
Ludlow Dr. NE25: Monks 6B 38
Ludlow Rd. SR2: Sund 6F 119
LUDWORTH 5J 169
Luffness Dr. NE34: S Shi 3B 88
Luke Av. DH6: Cass 4E 178
Luke Ct. SR8: Pet 1B 182
Luke Cres. SR7: Mur 7D 146
Luke's La. NE31: Gate, Heb 4K 85
Lukes La. Est. NE31: Heb 4A 86
Luke Ter. DH6: Whe H 3A 180
Lulsgate SR5: Sund 6G 103
Lulworth Av. NE32: Jar 1D 86
Lulworth Ct. SR3: E Her 2J 131
Lulworth Gdns. SR2: Sund 5E 118
Lumley Av. NE16: Swa 5H 81
NE34: S Shi 7D 68
Lumley Cl. DH2: Ches S 6K 127
NE38: Wash 3F 115
Lumley Ct. DH2: Ches S 2J 127
NE22: Bed 6A 18
NE31: Heb 5K 65
SR3: E Her 2J 131
Lumley Cres. DH4: Nbot 5C 130
Lumley Dr. DH8: Cons 2A 136
SR8: Pet 2B 182
Lumley Gdns. NE8: Gate 5K 83
NE16: Burn 3J 109
(not continuous)
Lumley New Rd.
DH3: Ches S, Gt Lum 7D 128
DH4: Hou S 1F 143
Lumley Rd. DH1: Dur 4A 154
Lumley Sixth Pit DH4: Hou S 7H 129
Lumley's La. NE42: Pru 7C 76
Lumley St. DH4: Hou S 7D 130
SR4: Sund 2C 118
Lumley Ter. DH3: Ches S 7B 128
NE32: Jar 3B 86
SR2: Ryh 3H 133
LUMLEY THICKS 1G 143
Lumley Twr. SR1: Sund 1G 119
Lumley Wlk. NE11: Dun 5C 82
Lumley Way NE3: Gos 3C 44
Lumsden's La. NE61: Mor 6F 9
Lumsden Sq. SR7: Mur 7D 146
Lumsden Ter. DH9: Ann P 4J 123
Lund Av. DH1: Dur 5K 153
Lund Ct. DH1: Dur 5K 153
Lund's La. DH8: Cons 1E 136
Lunedale Av. SR6: Seab 2E 104
Lunedale Cl. DH3: Gt Lum 4F 143
Lune Grn. NE32: Jar 4C 86
Lunesdale St. DH5: Hett H 1G 157
Lupin Cl. NE5: Cha P 1C 60
Luss Av. NE32: Jar 3E 86
Lutterworth Cl. NE12: Longb 7K 45
Lutterworth Pl. NE12: Longb 7K 45
Lutterworth Rd. NE12: Longb 7K 45
SR2: Sund 5E 118
Luxembourg Rd. SR4: Sund 1K 117
Lyall Ho. NE23: Seg 2D 36
Lycaon Gdns. NE31: Heb 7H 65
Lychgate Ct. NE8: Gate 10K 5 (3H 83)
Lydbury Cl. NE23: Cra 1A 26
Lydcott NE38: Wash 3B 116
Lydford Ct. DH4: Nbot 6C 130
NE3: Ki Pk 6J 43
Lydford Way DH3: Bir 5B 114
Lydney Ct. NE15: Thro 4G 59
Lymington DH7: Esh W 5E 162
Lyncroft NE63: Ash 5A 12
Lyncroft Rd. NE29: N Shi 6E 48
Lyndale NE23: Cra 1A 26
Lynden Gdns. NE5: West 2G 61
Lynden Ga. NE9: Low F 4J 99
Lynden Rd. SR2: Ryh 1H 133
LYNDHURST 3H 99
Lyndhurst Av. DH3: Ches S 3A 128
NE2: Jes 3G 63
NE9: Low F 3H 99
Lyndhurst Cl. NE21: Winl 6A 80
Lyndhurst Cres. NE9: Low F 3J 99
Lyndhurst Dr. DH1: Dur 3J 165
NE9: Low F 3J 99
Lyndhurst Gdns. NE2: Jes 3F 63
Lyndhurst Grn. NE9: Low F 3H 99
Lyndhurst Gro. NE9: Low F 3J 99
Lyndhurst Rd. DH9: Stly 3D 124
NE12: Longb 5B 46
NE25: Monks 6E 38
NE63: N Sea 6D 12
Lyndhurst St. NE33: S Shi 3K 67
Lyndhurst Ter. NE16: Swa 5G 81
SR4: Sund 7A 104
Lyndon Cl. NE36: E Bol 7H 87
Lyndon Dr. NE36: E Bol 7H 87
Lyndon Gro. NE36: E Bol 7H 87
Lyndon Wlk. NE24: Cow 1D 22
Lyne Cl. DH2: Ous 1H 127
Lynes Dr. DH7: Lang M 7F 165
Lynfield NE26: Whit B 4E 38
Lynfield Ct. NE5: Blak 2H 61
Lynfield Pl. NE5: Blak 2H 61
Lynford Gdns. SR2: Sund 5E 118
Lyngrove SR2: Ryh 1H 133
Lynholm Gro. NE12: Longb 4B 46
Lynmouth Pl. NE7: H Hea 2K 63
Lynmouth Rd. NE9: Low F 4H 99
NE29: N Shi 7C 48
Lynmouth Way NE13: Haz 2A 44
Lynn Cres. DH6: Cass 4F 179
Lynndale Av. NE24: Cow 2E 22
Lynneholm Ct. NE8: Gate 6J 83
Lynnholm Cl. NE7: H Hea 3K 63
Lynnholme Gdns. NE9: Low F 6H 83
(not continuous)
Lynn Rd. NE28: W'snd 4E 64
NE29: N Shi 5D 48
Lynn St. DH3: Ches S 7A 128
NE24: Bly 2H 23
Lynn Ter. DH6: Whe H 1C 180
Lynnwood Av. NE4: Elsw 1B 82
Lynnwood Bus. Development Cen.
NE4: Elsw 1B 82
Lynnwood Ter. NE4: Elsw 1B 82
Lynthorpe SR2: Ryh 1H 133
Lynthorpe Gro. SR6: Ful 3G 105
Lynton Av. NE32: Jar 1E 86
Lynton Ct. DH4: Nbot 6C 130
NE5: Blak 2H 61
Lynton Pl. NE5: Blak 2H 61
Lynton Way NE5: Blak 2H 61
Lynwood Av. NE21: Blay 3C 80
NE64: Newb S 2H 13
SR4: Sund 6G 117
Lynwood Cl. NE20: Darr H 2G 41
Lynwood Way NE34: S Shi 1B 88
(not continuous)
LYONS 1H 157
Lyons, The DH5: Eas L 1H 157
Lyons Av. DH5: Eas L 1H 157
Lyons Ct. NE10: Pel 5E 84
Lyons Gdns. DH5: Eas L 1J 157
Lyons La. DH5: Eas L 2J 157
Lyon St. NE31: Heb 7H 65
Lyric Cl. NE29: N Shi 4C 48
Lysander Dr. NE6: Walk 2E 84
Lysdon Av. NE25: New Hart 4H 27
Lyster Cl. SR7: S'hm 1G 147
Lytchfeld NE10: Hew 7F 85
Lytham Cl. DH8: B'hill 3G 121
NE23: Cra 4G 25
NE28: W'snd 5J 47
NE37: Wash 5G 101
Lytham Dr. NE25: Monks 6D 38
Lytham Grange DH4: S Row 5A 130
Lytham Grn. NE10: Bill Q 4F 85
Lytham Pl. NE6: Walk 1C 84
Lythe Way NE12: Longb 6A 46

M

Mabel St. NE21: Blay 3C 80
Macadam St. NE8: Gate 7F 83
McAnany Av. NE34: S Shi 1K 87
McAteer Ct. DH6: Has 3A 170
Macbeth Wlk. SR8: Hord 6F 173
McClaren Way DH4: W Herr 2F 131
McCormick Cl. DH6: Bowb 3H 177
McCracken Cl. NE3: Gos 4E 44
McCracken Dr. NE13: W Op 4E 34
McCutcheon St. SR7: S'hm 1G 147
Macdonald Rd. NE4: Benw 2K 81
McErlane Sq. NE10: Pel 5E 84
McEwan Gdns. NE4: Elsw 1B 82
McGowen Ct. NE6: Byke 1A 84
McGuinness Av. SR8: Hord 3C 172
(not continuous)
McIlvenna Gdns. NE28: W'snd 1E 64
McIntyre Hall NE31: Heb 6K 65
McIntyre Rd. NE31: Heb 6K 65
McIntyre Way DH1: Dur 2F 167
McKendrick Vs. NE5: Fen 4K 61
Mackintosh Ct. DH1: Dur 2D 166
Mackley Cl. NE34: S Shi 2J 87
McLennan Ct. NE38: Wash 2H 115
Maclynn Cl. SR3: Silk 3A 132
Macmerry Cl. SR5: Sund 7F 103
McMillan Ct. NE9: Low F 1H 99
Macmillan Gdns. NE10: Ward 6E 84
McNally Pl. DH1: Dur 2D 166
McNamara Rd. NE28: W'snd 2J 65
McNulty Ct. NE23: Dud 3H 35
Maddison Ct. SR1: Sund 1H 119
Maddison Gdns. DH3: Bir 2B 114
NE23: Seg 2C 36
Maddison St. NE24: Bly 1J 23
Maddox Rd. NE12: Longb 6B 46
Madeira Av. NE26: Whit B 4F 39
Madeira Cl. NE5: Cha P 1C 60
Madeira Ter. NE33: S Shi 4K 67
Madras St. NE34: S Shi 2G 87
Madrona Cl. DH4: S Row 4K 129
Madron Cl. NE3: Ken 7A 44
Mafeking Pl. NE29: N Shi 3B 48
Mafeking St. NE6: Walk 3D 84
NE9: Low F 6J 83
SR4: Sund 1B 118
Mafeking Ter. DH7: Sac 1D 152
Magdalene Av. DH1: Carr 7G 155
Magdalene Ct. *DH1: Dur* *2C 166*
(off Leazes La.)
DH8: M'sly *7K 107*
(off North Magdalene)
NE2: Newc T 1B 4 (6D 62)
SR7: S'hm 2B 148
Magdalene Hgts. *DH1: Dur* *2C 166*
(off Leazes La.)
Magdalene Pl. SR4: Sund 1B 118
Magdalene St. DH1: Dur 2C 166
Magenta Cres. NE5: Cha P 7C 42
Magistrates' Court
Chester-le-Street 5B 128
Consett 6H 121
Gateshead 4H 83
Gosforth 1E 62
Houghton-le-Spring 2D 144
Newcastle upon Tyne 5G 4 (1G 83)
North Tyneside 6H 49
Peterlee 7B 172
South East Northumberland 7H 17
South Tyneside 3J 67
Sunderland 3H 7 (1E 118)
Tynedale 1C 70
Maglona St. SR7: S'hm 4B 148
Magnet Ct. NE1: Newc T 4E 4
Magnolia Cl. NE4: Fen 6K 61
Magnolia Ct. DH7: Esh W 5D 162
Magnolia Dr. NE63: Ash 6A 12
Magnolia Gro. NE16: Burn 2B 110
Magpie Ct. NE63: Ash 5K 11
Mahogany Row DH9: Beam 7K 111
Maidenhair DH4: S Row 4K 129
Maiden La. NE40: G'sde 4E 78
MAIDEN LAW 2A 138
Maiden Law DH4: Hou S 3A 144
Maidens Cft. NE46: Hex 2B 70
Maiden St. NE4: Newc T 9B 4 (3D 82)
Maidens Wlk. NE8: Gate 8J 5 (2H 83)
NE46: Hex 2D 70
Maidstone Cl. SR3: Dox P 3K 131
Maidstone Ter. DH4: Nbot 5D 130

Main Cres. NE28: W'snd 1D 64
Maingate NE11: T Vall 1E 98
Main Rd. NE13: Din 4H 33
NE13: K Bank 5H 43
NE40: Ryton 1E 78
NE41: Wylam 7J 57
NE42: O'ham, Pru 2D 76
NE43: Mic, Pains, Stoc 7G 75
Mains Ct. DH1: Dur 6J 153
Mainsforth Ter. SR2: Sund 3H 119
Mainsforth Ter. W. SR2: Sund 4G 119
Mains Pk. Rd. DH3: Ches S 6B 128
Mains Pl. NE61: Mor 6F 9
Mainstone Cl. NE23: Cra 4J 25
Main St. DH8: Cons 7K 121
NE20: Pon 5J 31
NE40: Craw 2D 78
NE45: Corb 1D 72
NE46: Acomb 4B 50
Main St. Nth. NE23: Seg 2D 36
Main St. Sth. NE23: Seg 2D 36
Maitland Ter. NE64: Newb S 3H 13
Makendon St. NE31: Heb 6J 65
Makepeace Ter. NE9: Spri 6D 100
Malaburn Way SR5: S'wck 6C 104
Malaga Cl. NE5: Cha P 1B 60
Malaya Dr. NE6: Walk 1F 85
Malcolm Av. DH6: Quar H 6D 178
Malcolm Ct. NE25: Monks 7D 38
Malcolm St. NE6: Heat 3M 5 (7J 63)
SR7: S'hm 4B 148
Malden Cl. NE23: Cra 4H 25
Maling Ct. NE2: Newc T 4K 5
Maling Pk. SR4: Sund 1H 117
Malings Cl. SR1: Sund 2H 119
Maling St. NE6: Byke 5M 5 (1J 83)
Mallard Cl. NE38: Wash 4D 114
NE63: Ash 7B 12
Mallard Ct. NE12: Kil 7A 36
Mallard Lodge NE10: Fell 6B 84
Mallard Way DH4: W Rai 4B 144
NE24: News 6K 23
NE28: W'snd 6A 48
Mallowburn Cres. NE3: Ken 1J 61
Malmo Cl. NE29: N Shi 7B 48
Malone Gdns. DH3: Bir 2A 114
Malory Pl. NE8: Gate 4H 83
Maltby Cl. NE38: Wash 4H 115
SR3: Dox P 4A 132
Malt Cres. SR8: Hord 5D 172
Malthouse Way NE5: Blak 1H 61
Maltings, The DH1: Dur 3B 6
SR3: Tuns 2E 132
TS28: Win 4G 181
Maltkiln NE46: Hex 2C 70
Malton Cl. NE15: Lem 7E 60
NE24: Cow 2F 23
Malton Ct. NE32: Jar 6A 66
Malton Cres. NE29: N Shi 1E 66
Malton Gdns. NE28: W'snd 1F 65
Malton Grn. NE9: Low F 6K 99
Malvern Av. DH2: Ches S 7K 127
Malvern Cl. NE63: N Sea 6D 12
SR8: Pet 7K 171
Malvern Ct. NE11: Lob H 1C 98
NE15: Lem 6B 60
SR6: Clead 5B 88
Malvern Cres. SR7: S'hm 3J 147
TS29: Trim S 7C 180
Malvern Gdns. NE11: Lob H 1C 98
(not continuous)
SR6: Roker 4G 105
Malvern Rd. NE26: Sea S 5D 28
NE28: W'snd 2K 65
NE29: N Shi 4E 48
NE38: Wash 5F 115
Malvern St. NE4: Elsw 2C 82
NE33: S Shi 6J 67
Malvern Ter. DH9: Stly 4G 125
Malvern Vs. DH1: Dur 2D 166
Malvins Cl. Rd. NE24: Cow 2G 23
Malvins Rd. NE24: Cow 1F 23
Manchester St. NE61: Mor 6F 9
Mandale Cres. NE30: Cull 1G 49
Mandale Pk. DH1: Dur 7F 155
Mandarin Cl. NE5: Cha P 1B 60
Mandarin Lodge *NE10: Fell* *6B 84*
(off St Oswald's Ct.)
Mandarin Rd. DH4: W Rai 4C 144
Mandarin Way NE38: Wash 2B 116
Mandela Cl. DH9: Stly 4D 124
SR1: Sund 1H 119
Mandela Way NE11: Dun 3J 81
Mandeville NE37: Wash 7K 101
Mandleston Cl. SR2: Ryh 3F 133
Manet Gdns. NE34: S Shi 2K 87
Mangrove Cl. NE5: Cha P 1B 60
Manila St. SR2: Sund 4G 119
Manisty Ho. NE4: Benw 2A 82
Manisty Ter. SR8: Eas 7A 160
Manley Vw. NE63: N Sea 5E 12
Mann Cres. SR7: Mur 6F 147
Manners Gdns. NE25: Sea D 6G 27
Manningford Cl. NE23: Cra 5J 25
Manningford Dr. SR3: Dox P 4A 132
Manor Av. NE7: Longb 7A 46
NE15: Newb 5K 59
Manor Chare NE1: Newc T 6H 5 (1G 83)
Mnr. Chare Apartments
NE1: Newc T 6H 5
Manor Cl. DH1: Shin 6E 166
DH8: C'sde 1E 134
NE3: Gos 7F 45
NE44: Rid M 7K 73
Manor Cotts. NE45: Corb 7D 52
Manor Ct. DH3: Bir 4K 113
DH9: Ann P 4K 123
NE2: Jes *4H 63*
(off Manor Ho. Rd.)
NE33: S Shi 4B 68
NE45: Corb 7D 52
NE64: Newb S 2J 13
Manor Dr. DH9: Ann P 4K 123
NE7: Longb 7A 46
NE64: Newb S 2J 13
Manor Farm NE23: Dud 1J 35
Manorfields NE12: Longb 6B 46
Manor Gdns. NE7: Longb 7A 46
NE10: Ward 6F 85
Manor Grange DH7: Lan 7A 138
Manor Gro. DH4: W Herr 2F 131
NE7: Longb 7A 46
NE15: Newb 6K 59
Manor Hall Cl. SR7: S'hm 2G 147
Manor Ho. Cl. NE6: Byke 1A 84
Manor Ho. Est. TS27: Hutt 7K 181
(No's 5-18)
TS27: Hutt 7B 182
(Numbers 19-30)
Manor Ho. Farm Cotts. NE3: Ken 1K 61
Manor Ho. Rd. NE2: Jes 4H 63
Manor Pk. NE7: H Hea 1A 64
NE37: Wash 7H 101
NE45: Corb 7D 52
Manor Pl. NE7: Longb 7A 46
Manor Rd. DH8: M'sly 7K 107
DH9: Stly 2F 125
NE7: Longb 1A 64
NE30: Tyne 4K 49
NE37: Wash 7H 101
Manors, The NE42: Pru 3G 77
Manors Station (Metro) 5H 5 (1G 83)
Manors Station (Rail) 5H 5 (1G 83)
Manor Ter. NE21: W Mill 7C 80
NE21: Winl 5A 80
Manor Vw. DH6: H Pitt 7B 156
NE37: Wash 7J 101
NE64: Newb S 2J 13
Manor Vw. E. NE37: Wash 7J 101
Manor Wlk. NE7: Longb 7A 46
Mnr. Walks Shop. Cen. NE23: Cra 4J 25
Manor Way SR8: Pet 7C 172
Manorway NE30: Tyne 4K 49
NE32: Jar 5C 86
Manse, The DH3: Ches S 5A 128
Mansell Cres. SR8: Pet 5C 172
Mansell Pl. NE3: Ken 2A 62
Mansel Ter. NE24: Cow 2C 22
Manse St. DH8: B'hill 5G 121
Mansfield Ct. NE36: W Bol 7G 87
Mansfield Cres. SR6: Roker 4G 105
Mansfield Pl. NE4: Newc T 5B 4 (1D 82)
Mansfield St. NE4: Newc T 5A 4 (1D 82)
Mansion Ct. NE22: Bed 7B 18
Mansion Hgts. NE11: Dun 7A 82
Mansion Ho. NE11: Dun 7A 82
NE36: W Bol 7G 87
Manston Cl. SR3: Dox P 3K 131
Manx Sq. SR5: S'wck 4D 104
Maple Av. DH1: Dur 2E 166
NE11: Dun 7C 82
NE25: Monks 1F 49
SR3: Tuns 1D 132
Maplebeck Cl. SR3: Dox P 4K 131
Maple Cl. NE15: Lem 7E 60
NE22: Bed 7H 17
Maple Ct. DH7: B'don 2B 174
NE12: Kil 7A 36
NE25: New Hart 4H 27
NE34: S Shi 2B 88
NE63: Ash 2E 12
Maple Cres. NE24: Cow 1D 22
SR7: S'hm 6A 148
Mapledene NE38: Wash 6J 115
Mapledene Rd. NE3: Fawd 6B 44
Maple Gdns. DH8: Shot B 5E 120
DH9: Stly 5E 124
Maple Gro. DH9: Stly 5D 124
NE8: Gate 7G 83
NE10: Fell 6C 84
NE42: Pru 4D 76
SR6: Whit 5H 89
Maple Pk. DH7: Ush M 3D 164
Maple Rd. NE21: Blay 4C 80
Maple Row NE11: Dun 4H 81
Maple St. DH8: Cons 6H 121
DH9: Stly 5D 124
NE4: Newc T 8B 4 (2D 82)
NE32: Jar 6A 66
NE63: Ash 3B 12
Maple Ter. DH4: S Row 4A 130
DH9: Ann P *4J 123*
(off Pine Ter.)
NE4: Newc T 8A 4 (2D 82)
NE16: Burn 2K 109
Maplewood DH2: Ches S 4J 127
NE6: Walk 5C 64
Maplewood Av. SR5: S'wck 4B 104
Maplewood Ct. DH7: Lang P 5H 151
Maplewood Cres. NE38: Wash 7F 115
Maplewood Dr. DH6: Has 1B 170
Maplewood St. DH4: Hou S 1J 143
Mapperley Dr. NE15: Lem 6E 60
Mappleton Dr. SR7: S'hm 1A 148
Marblet Ct. NE11: Fest P 7D 82
Marbury Cl. SR3: Dox P 3K 131
Marchburn La. NE44: Rid M 7J 73
March Courtyard *NE8: Gate* *5D 82*
(off Ash St.)
March Rd. NE23: Dud 3K 35
March Ter. NE13: Din 4G 33
Marcia Av. DH6: Shot C 5E 170
SR6: Ful 4F 105
Marconi Ho. *NE1: Newc T* *6H 5*
(off Melbourne St.)
Marconi Way NE11: Dun, Swa 5H 81
Marcross Cl. NE15: Walb 3B 60
Marcross Dr. SR3: Dox P 4K 131
Mardale NE37: Wash 1F 115
Mardale Gdns. NE9: Low F 4J 99
Mardale Rd. NE5: Den M 4H 61
Mardale St. DH5: Hett H 1G 157
MARDEN 7G 39
Marden Av. NE30: Cull 1J 49
Marden Bridge Sports Cen. 7G 39
Marden Cl. NE26: Whit B 7G 39
NE61: Mor 1D 14
Marden Ct. NE26: Sea S 3B 28
Marden Cres. NE26: Whit B 7J 39
Marden Farm Dr. NE30: Cull 1H 49
Marden Quarry Nature Reserve 1G 49
Marden Rd. NE26: Whit B 6G 39
(not continuous)
Marden Rd. Sth. NE25: Whit B 7G 39
(not continuous)
Marden Ter. NE30: Cull 1J 49
Mareburn Cres. NE10: Hew 6C 84
Mare Cl. NE23: Seg 7E 26
Maree Cl. SR3: Dox P 4A 132
Margaret Alice St. SR4: Sund 1A 118
Margaret Collins Ho. NE6: Walk 7C 64
Margaret Cotts. NE25: Cull 2F 49
Margaret Ct. DH6: Bowb 4H 177
DH9: Ann P 6J 123
Margaret Dr. NE12: Longb 4E 46
Margaret Gro. NE34: S Shi 1G 87
Margaret Rd. NE26: Whit B 7J 39
Margaret St. DH6: Ludw 5J 169
SR2: Sund 6J 119
SR7: S'hm 4B 148
Margaret Ter. DH4: New H 3C 130
DH9: Tan L 7C 110
NE39: Row G 6G 95
TS29: Trim S 7C 180
Margate St. SR3: New S 1C 132
Margery La. DH1: Dur 4A 6 (3K 165)
Marguerite Ct. SR4: Sund 3F 7 (1D 118)
Maria Cl. NE15: Thro 4H 59
Marian Ct. NE8: Gate 5F 83
Marian Dr. NE10: Bill Q 4F 85
Marian Way NE20: Darr H 2F 41
NE34: S Shi 3B 88
Maria St. NE4: Benw 2A 82
SR3: New S 2C 132
SR7: S'hm 3B 148
Marie Curie Dr. NE4: Elsw 2B 82
Marigold Av. NE10: Gate 4K 83
Marigold Ct. NE10: Gate 10P 5 (4K 83)
SR4: Sund 1D 118
Marigold Cres. DH4: Bour 6J 129
Marigold Wlk. NE34: S Shi 1H 87
Marina Av. SR6: Ful 3E 104
Marina Ct. SR6: Ful 4F 105
Marina Dr. NE25: Monks 7B 38
NE33: S Shi 2A 68
Marina Gro. SR6: Ful 4F 105
Marina Ter. SR2: Ryh 3H 133
SR6: Whit 5H 89
Marina Vw. NE28: W'snd 3K 65
NE31: Heb 7G 65
Marine App. NE33: S Shi 3K 67
Marine Av. NE26: Monks, Whit B 6F 39
Marine Cotts. NE64: Newb S 3H 13
Marine Ct. E. NE26: Whit B 5G 39
Marine Ct. W. NE26: Whit B 5G 39
Marine Cres. TS27: B Col 3K 183
Marine Dr. NE31: Heb, Jar 3A 86
SR2: Ryh 1H 133
Marine Gdns. NE26: Whit B 6G 39
Mariner's Cotts. NE33: S Shi 2A 68
(not continuous)
Mariners' La. NE30: Tyne 5J 49
Mariners Point NE30: Tyne 5K 49
Mariner Sq. SR1: Sund 7H 105
Mariners Way SR7: S'hm 2A 148
Mariners Wharf NE1: Newc T 6L 5 (1J 83)
Marine St. NE64: Newb S 2J 13
Marine Ter. NE24: Bly 2J 23
Marine Ter. E. NE24: Bly 2J 23
Marine Vw. NE26: Sea S 3B 28
Marine Wlk. SR6: Roker 4H 105
Marion St. SR2: Sund 4G 119
Maritime Cres. SR8: Eas C 2D 172
Maritime Pl. NE61: Mor 6F 9
Maritime St. SR1: Sund 4J 7 (2F 119)
Maritime Ter. SR1: Sund 4H 7 (2F 119)
Marius Av. NE15: Hed W 3D 58
Mariville E. SR2: Ryh 4J 133
Mariville W. SR2: Ryh 4J 133
Marjorie St. NE23: E Cram 5D 26
Markby Cl. SR3: Dox P 4A 132
Market Cres. DH4: New H 3C 130
TS28: Win 7G 181
Market Hall DH9: Stly 2E 124
Market La. NE1: Newc T 6G 4 (1G 83)
NE11: Dun 6A 82
NE16: Swa, Whi 5G 81
Market Pl. DH1: Dur 2C 6
DH3: Ches S 5A 128
DH5: Hou S 2F 145
DH7: B'don 7E 164
DH7: Esh W 4E 162
NE22: Bed 1H 21
NE24: Bly 1J 23
NE33: S Shi 2J 67
Market Pl. NE45: Corb 1D 72
NE46: Hex 1D 70
NE61: Mor 6F 9
Market Pl. Ind. Est. DH5: Hou S 1F 145
Market Pl. W. NE61: Mor 7F 9
Market Sq. NE32: Jar 6B 66
SR1: Sund 4J 7 (2F 119)
Market St. DH5: Hett H 5H 145
DH8: B'hill *5F 121*
(off Queen's Rd.)
NE1: Newc T 5F 4 (1F 83)
NE23: Dud 3H 35
NE24: Bly 1J 23
NE46: Hex 1D 70
Market St. E. NE1: Newc T 5G 4 (1G 83)
Market Wlk. NE32: Jar 6B 66
Market Way NE11: T Vall 1F 99
Markham Av. SR6: Whit 6J 89
Markham St. SR2: Sund 6H 119
Markington Dr. SR2: Ryh 3H 133
Markle Gro. DH5: E Rain 5D 144
Mark Ri. DH5: Hett H 5G 145
Mark's La. DH4: Leam, W Rai 6J 143
Marlboro Av. NE16: Swa 6H 81
Marlborough SR7: S'hm 3B 148
Marlborough App. NE3: Gos 5E 44
Marlborough Av. NE3: Gos 5D 44
Marlborough Ct. DH5: Hou S 4E 144
NE3: Ki Pk 5K 43
NE32: Jar 1B 86
Marlborough Cres.
NE1: Newc T 7D 4 (2E 82)
NE9: Wrek 4A 100
SR8: Hord 6F 173
Marlborough Ho. NE26: Monks 5F 39
Marlborough Rd. NE37: Wash 6J 101
SR4: Sund 5F 117
Marlborough St. Nth. NE33: S Shi 5K 67
Marlborough St. Sth. NE33: S Shi 5K 67
Marlborough Ter. NE62: Sco G 4H 17
Marleen Av. NE6: Heat 5B 64
Marleen Ct. NE6: Heat 5A 64
Marlene Av. DH6: Bowb 3G 177
Marlesford Cl. SR3: Dox P 3K 131
Marley Cres. SR5: S'wck 4B 104
MARLEY HILL 6G 97
MARLEY POTS 4B 104
Marleys Ho's. DH7: Queb 7A 150
Marlfield Ct. NE5: Blak 2H 61
Marlow Dr. SR3: Dox P 4K 131
Marlowe Gdns. NE8: Gate 5H 83
Marlowe Pl. DH5: Hou S 3E 144
Marlowe Wlk. NE34: S Shi 3G 87
Marlow Pl. NE12: Longb 6A 46
Marlow St. NE24: Bly 2H 23
Marlow Way NE16: Whi 2F 97
Marmion Rd. NE6: Walk 5D 64
Marmion Ter. NE25: Monks 7F 39
Marne St. DH4: S Row 3C 130
Marondale Av. NE6: Walk 6D 64
Marquess Point SR7: S'hm 2C 148
Marquis Av. NE5: Cha P 7C 42
Marquis Cl. NE12: Longb 7B 46
Marquis Ct. NE11: T Vall 4F 99
NE42: Pru 2G 77
SR3: Tuns 2D 132
Marquisway NE11: T Vall 4F 99
Marquisway Cen. NE11: T Vall 4E 98
Marris Ho. NE2: Newc T 1C 4 (6E 62)
Marr Rd. NE31: Heb 1K 85
MARSDEN 1D 88
Marsden Av. SR6: Whit 3H 89
Marsden Cl. DH4: Hou S 2C 144
Marsden Gro. NE9: Wrek 4B 100
Marsden Ho. SR6: Whit 5H 89
Marsden La. NE5: West 2G 61
NE34: S Shi 6D 68
Marsden Old Quarry Local Nature Reserve
. . . . . 1E 88
Marsden Rd. NE34: S Shi 6B 68
SR6: Clead 6B 88
Marsden St. NE33: S Shi 5K 67
Marsden Vw. SR6: Whit 3H 89
Marsdon Way SR7: S'hm 1A 148
Marshall Cl. NE63: Ash 2D 12
Marshall Grn. Way NE25: Monks 5B 38
Marshall's Ct. NE1: Newc T 6E 4 (1F 83)
Marshall St. SR6: Ful 3F 105
Marshall Ter. DH1: Dur 2E 166
(not continuous)
Marshall Wallis Rd. NE33: S Shi 5J 67
(not continuous)
Marsham Cl. NE15: Lem 6E 60
SR6: Clead 4C 88
Marsham Rd. NE5: West 2E 60
Marsh Ct. NE11: Fest P 7D 82
Marshes Ho's. NE62: W Sle 1B 18
Marshmont Av. NE30: Tyne 3J 49
Marske Ter. NE6: Walk 7C 64
Marston NE12: Kil 7B 36
Marston Wlk. NE16: Whi 2F 97
Martello Gdns. NE7: H Hea 3B 64
Martha St. DH9: Tant 6B 110
Martin Ct. NE38: Wash 6D 114
Martindale Av. SR6: Seab 3E 104
Martindale Pk. DH5: Hou S 3E 144
Martindale Pl. NE25: Sea D 7J 27
Martindale Wlk. NE12: Kil 1A 46
TS28: Win 4G 181
Martin Hall NE32: Jar 7C 66
Martin Rd. NE28: W'snd 3K 65
Martin Ter. SR4: Sund 1B 118
Martin Way NE13: Bru V 5C 34
Marwell Dr. NE37: Wash 5J 101
Marwood Ct. NE25: Monks 5D 38

Marwood Gro. SR8: Pet 2A 182
Marwood Pk. DH1: Dur 1J 165
Marx Cres. DH9: Stly 4F 125
(not continuous)
Marx Ter. NE17: C'wl 7A 94
Mary Agnes St. NE3: Gos 7C 44
Mary Av. DH3: Bir 2K 113
Mary Cres. DH6: Kel 7E 178
Maryhill Cl. NE4: Benw 2A 82
Mary Magdalene Bungs.
NE2: Newc T 1A 4 (5D 62)
Maryside Pl. NE40: C Vale 6D 58
Mary's Pl. NE6: Walk 7F 65
Mary St. DH9: Ann P 5A 124
DH9: Stly 3E 124
NE21: Blay 3C 80
NE21: Winl 4A 80
SR1: Sund 5H 7 (2E 118)
SR3: New S 1C 132
SR7: S'hm 3C 148
Mary Ter. DH6: Bowb 4G 177
NE5: West 3G 61
Masefield Av. NE16: Swa 5H 81
Masefield Cl. DH9: Stly 2H 125
Masefield Dr. NE34: S Shi 3G 87
Masefield Pl. NE8: Gate 4H 83
Masefields DH2: P Fel 6G 127
Maslin Gro. SR8: Pet 2J 181
MASON 3H 33
Mason Av. NE26: Whit B 6H 39
Mason Cres. SR8: Hord 6D 172
Mason Rd. NE28: W'snd 1E 64
Mason St. DH8: Cons 7H 121
NE6: Byke 5P 5 (1A 84)
NE13: Bru V 5C 34
Mason Vw. NE13: Sea B 3D 34
Masseys Vw. NE21: Blay 4C 80
Massingham Way NE34: S Shi 1H 87
Master Mariners' Homes NE30: Tyne . . . 5J 49
Master's Cres. NE42: Pru 4D 76
Mast La. NE30: Cull 1H 49
Matamba Ter. SR4: Sund 2D 118
Matanzas St. SR2: Sund 5G 119
Matfen Av. NE13: Haz 7C 34
NE27: Shir 2A 48
Matfen Cl. NE15: Lem 7E 60
NE24: Bly 2G 23
Matfen Ct. DH2: Ches S 6J 127
Matfen Dr. SR3: Dox P 3K 131
Matfen Gdns. NE28: W'snd 7K 47
Matfen Pl. NE3: Gos 6C 44
NE4: Fen 6B 62
Matfen Ter. NE64: Newb S 4H 13
Mather Rd. NE4: Newc T 8A 4 (2D 82)
Mathesons Gdns. NE61: Mor 7F 9
Matlock Av. NE3: Ken 2K 61
Matlock Gdns. NE5: West 2F 61
Matlock Rd. NE32: Jar 1C 86
Matlock St. SR1: Sund 2J 7 (1F 119)
Matterdale Rd. SR8: Pet 6D 172
Matthew Bank NE2: Jes 2G 63
Matthew Cl. NE6: Byke 3P 5 (7K 63)
Matthew Rd. NE24: Bly 4K 23
Matthews Cres. DH6: S Het 5D 158
Matthews Rd. SR7: Mur 2G 159
Matthew St. NE6: Byke 3P 5 (7K 63)
Maude Gdns. NE28: W'snd 4F 65
Maudlin Pl. NE5: Fen 4K 61
Maudlin Row NE33: S Shi 3A 68
Maudlin St. DH5: Hett H 4H 145
Mauds La. SR1: Sund 1G 119
Mauds Ter. NE64: Newb S 2J 13
Maud St. NE15: Lem 7C 60
SR6: Ful 3G 105
Maud Ter. DH9: Tanf 5D 110
NE27: Shir 3J 47
Maudville DH8: C'sde 4C 134
Maughan St. NE24: Bly 2K 23
Maureen Av. TS27: B Col 3J 183
Maureen Ter. DH1: Dur 5G 155
SR7: S'hm 3A 148
Maurice Rd. NE28: W'snd 5F 65
Maurice Rd. Ind. Est. NE28: Walk 5F 65
Mautland Sq. DH4: Hou S 1E 144
Mautland St. DH4: Hou S 1E 144
Mavin St. DH1: Dur 5E 6 (4B 166)
Maxton Cl. SR3: Dox P 4K 131
Maxwell Ct. *NE15: Benw* *7J 61*
(off Beamish Pl.)
Maxwell St. NE8: Gate 7F 83
NE33: S Shi 3J 67
SR4: Sund 1B 118
May Av. NE21: W Mill 7C 80
NE40: Ryton 7G 59
Maybury Vs. NE12: Longb 7J 45
May Cl. NE31: Heb 7H 65
May Courtyard *NE8: Gate* *5D 82*
(off Shrove Pass)
May Cres. TS29: Trim S 7D 180
Maydown Cl. SR5: Sund 7F 103
Mayfair Ct. NE31: Heb 1H 85
Mayfair Gdns. NE8: Gate 6J 83
NE20: Pon 5K 31
NE34: S Shi 6A 68
Mayfair Rd. NE2: Jes 3F 63
Mayfield NE16: Whi 2H 97
NE61: Mor 1E 14
Mayfield Av. NE15: Thro 4J 59
NE23: Cra 4A 26
Mayfield Ct. SR6: Ful 4F 105
Mayfield Dr. SR6: Clead 6D 88
Mayfield Gdns. NE15: Thro 4J 59
NE28: W'snd 2D 64
NE32: Jar 7A 66
Mayfield Gro. SR4: Sund 6G 117
Mayfield Pl. NE13: W Op 6C 34
Mayfield Rd. NE3: Gos 1D 62
SR4: Sund 2G 117
Mayfield Ter. NE5: Fen 4A 62
May Gro. SR6: Whit 3H 89
May Lea DH7: Wit G 2D 152
Maynard Rd. NE13: Haz 2B 44
Maynards Row DH1: Dur 2D 166
Maynes Way DH9: Stly 2H 125
Mayo Dr. SR3: Dox P 4A 132
Mayoral Way NE11: T Vall 4F 99
Mayorswell Cl. DH1: Dur 1E 6 (2B 166)
Mayorswell Fld. DH1: Dur 1E 6 (2C 166)
Mayorswell St. DH1: Dur 1E 6 (2B 166)
Maypole Cl. SR5: S'wck 5D 104
May St. DH1: Dur 3K 165
DH3: Bir 4A 114
NE21: Winl 5B 80
NE33: S Shi 4K 67
SR4: Sund 3F 7 (1D 118)
Mayswood Rd. SR6: Ful 4F 105
May Ter. DH7: Lang P 5J 151
Maythorne Dr. DH6: S Het 5D 158
Maytree Ho. NE4: Elsw 8A 4 (2C 82)
Maywood Cl. NE3: Ken 1A 62
Mazine Ter. DH6: Has 3A 170
Meaburn St. SR1: Sund 2G 119
Meaburn Ter. SR1: Sund 2G 119
Meacham Way NE16: Whi 2G 97
Mead Av. NE12: Longb 4C 46
Mead Ct. NE12: Longb 4D 46
Mead Cres. NE12: Longb 4C 46
Meadow Av. TS27: B Col 3J 183
Meadowbank DH7: Lang P 5H 151
NE23: Dud 3J 35
Meadowbank Dr. NE62: Chop 1G 17
Meadowbrook Dr. NE10: Ward 7G 85
NE17: C'wl 5A 94
Meadow Cl. DH5: Hou S 3F 145
NE11: Dun 5A 82
NE12: Longb 5K 45
NE21: Winl 5K 79
NE23: Seg 1D 36
NE40: Ryton 1H 79
Meadow Ct. NE20: Darr H 6J 31
NE22: Bed 7G 17
Meadowcroft M. NE8: Gate 5F 83
Meadowdale Cres. NE5: Blak 2K 61
NE22: Bed 7F 17
Meadow Dr. DH2: Ches S 7H 127
NE13: Sea B 3E 34
SR3: E Her 3H 131
SR4: Sund 3H 117
Meadow Edge DH6: S'burn 2A 168
MEADOWFIELD 1F 175
Meadowfield DH7: B'hpe 6D 138
DH8: B'hill 6F 121
NE9: Spri 6D 100
NE20: Pon 4J 31
NE25: Monks 6D 38
NE63: N Sea 5E 12
Meadowfield Av. NE3: Fawd 6C 44
Meadowfield Ct. NE20: Pon 4H 31
Meadowfield Cres. NE40: Craw 2E 78
Meadowfield Dr. SR6: Clead 5C 88
Meadowfield Est. DH7: Mead 2G 175
Meadowfield Gdns. NE6: Walk 4E 64
Meadowfield Ind. Est. DH7: Mead 2F 175
(not continuous)
NE20: Pon 5J 31
Meadowfield Leisure Cen. 1F 175
Meadowfield Pk. *NE20: Pon* *5J 31*
(off Meadowfield)
Meadowfield Pk. Sth. NE43: Pains 2J 91
Meadowfield Pl. DH7: Mead 1F 175
Meadowfield Rd. DH7: B'hpe 6D 138
NE3: Gos 1D 62
NE43: Pains 1H 91
Meadowfield Ter. NE12: Longb 3D 46
NE43: Pains 7K 75
Meadowfield Way DH9: Tan L 1C 124
Meadow Gdns. SR3: Sund 5D 118
Meadow Grange DH4: New L 7J 129
Meadow Gro. SR4: Sund 3H 117
Meadow La. DH1: Dur 6G 155
NE11: Dun 5A 82
NE40: Craw 2E 78
SR3: E Her 3H 131
Meadow Laws NE34: S Shi 2C 88
Meadow Pk. NE44: Rid M 7K 73
Meadow Rise DH7: Mead 1F 175
DH8: Cons 7J 121
NE5: Blak 1H 61
NE9: Low F 2A 100
Meadow Rd. NE15: Lem 5D 60
NE25: Monks 7D 38
NE26: Sea S 4B 28
NE28: W'snd 3K 65
Meadows, The DH4: Bour 6H 129
DH4: W Rai 1A 156
NE3: Fawd 6B 44
NE16: Hob 4A 110
NE28: W'snd 2G 65
NE40: Ryton 1H 79
SR7: Seat 1F 147
Meadows Crest NE43: Hed 4C 92
Meadowside SR2: Sund 4D 118
Meadows La. DH4: W Rai 6B 144
Meadow St. DH5: E Rain 7C 144
Meadowsweet Cl. DH8: Cons 7J 121
NE24: News 5G 23
Meadow Ter. DH4: S Row 3C 130
Meadow Va. NE27: Back 1H 47
SR2: Sund 4E 118
Meadowvale NE20: Darr H 2E 40
Meadow Vw. DH6: Whe H 2B 180
DH7: Sac 7E 140
DH8: Cons 3A 136
DH9: Dip 7J 109
NE25: New Hart 4H 27
NE29: N Shi 1E 66
NE32: Jar 6D 86
NE40: G'sde 4E 78
SR3: E Her 3H 131
Meadow Wlk. NE40: Ryton 1H 79
SR3: Dox P 4B 132
Meadow Way DH7: Lan 7J 137
Meadow Well Station (Metro) 1E 66
Meadow Well Way
NE29: N Shi 1E 66
Mead Wlk. NE6: Walk 7D 64
Mead Way NE12: Longb 4D 46
Meadway NE12: Longb 4C 46
Meadway Dr. NE12: Longb 5D 46
MEA Ho. NE1: Newc T 4G 4 (7G 63)
Meal Mkt. *NE46: Hex* *1D 70*
(off Fore St.)
Means Ct. NE23: Dud 5K 35
Means Dr. NE23: Dud 5K 35
Mecca Bingo
Blyth 1K 23
Gateshead 9K 5 (3H 83)
South Shields 5K 67
Sunderland 4J 7 (2F 119)
MEDBURN 2C 40
Medburn Av. NE30: Cull 2J 49
Medburn Rd. NE15: Lem 6B 60
NE25: H'wll 1J 37
Medina Cl. SR3: Dox P 4A 132
Mediterranean Village *NE11: Dun* *4J 81*
(off Metro Cen.)
Medlar NE9: Low F 3A 100
Medlar Cl. DH4: S Row 3K 129
MEDOMSLEY 7K 107
Medomsley Gdns. NE9: Wrek 3C 100
Medomsley Rd. DH8: Cons 6H 121
Medomsly St. SR4: Sund 1C 118
Medway DH3: Gt Lum 3E 142
NE32: Jar 4C 86
Medway Av. NE31: Heb 3J 85
Medway Cl. DH4: Hou S 3A 144
SR8: Pet 1A 182
Medway Cres. NE8: Gate 5K 83
Medway Gdns. DH9: Stly 5E 124
NE30: N Shi 5G 49
SR4: Sund 4K 117
Medway Pl. NE23: Cra 1A 26
Medwood Ct. NE3: Ken 7A 44
Medwyn Cl. DH4: Bour 6J 129
NE24: News 4H 23
Megan Ri. *NE40: Craw* *3D 78*
(off Greenside Rd.)
Megstone NE9: Low F 3H 99
Megstone Av. NE23: Cra 5J 25
Megstone Ct. NE12: Kil 7C 36
Melbeck Ct. DH3: Gt Lum 3E 142
Melbeck Dr. DH2: Ous 6G 113
Melbourne Ct. NE1: Newc T 5K 5 (1H 83)
NE8: Gate 9H 5 (3G 83)
Melbourne Cres. NE25: Monks 1E 48
Melbourne Gdns. NE34: S Shi 3F 87
Melbourne Pl. SR4: Sund 4A 118
Melbourne St. NE1: Newc T 6H 5 (1G 83)
Melbourne Ter. DH7: Sac 5D 140
NE61: Mor *7G 9*
(off Bennett's Wlk.)
Melbourne Vs. DH7: Sac 5D 140
Melbury NE25: Monks 5C 38
Melbury Ct. SR6: Ful 4F 105
Melbury Rd. NE7: H Hea 4J 63
Melbury St. SR7: S'hm 5B 148
Meldon Av. DH6: S'burn 3A 168
NE3: Fawd 5B 44
NE34: S Shi 7A 68
Meldon Cl. NE28: W'snd 2J 65
NE38: Wash 4A 116
Meldon Ct. NE40: Craw 3C 78
Meldon Gdns. NE11: Lob H 2C 98
NE62: Stake 7H 11
Meldon Ho. NE24: Cow 1F 23
Meldon Rd. SR4: Sund 1B 118
Meldon St. NE4: Elsw 2C 82
NE28: W'snd 4C 66
Meldon Ter. NE6: Heat 5K 63
NE40: G'sde 5D 78
NE64: Newb S 4H 13
Meldon Way DH1: H Shin 7F 167
DH9: Ann P 5B 124
NE21: Winl 6K 79
Melford Pl. NE29: N Shi 3D 48
Melgarve Dr. SR3: Dox P 4A 132
Melkington Ct. NE5: Blak 2H 61
Melkridge Gdns. NE7: H Hea 2B 64
Melkridge Pl. NE23: Cra 5H 25
Mellendean Cl. NE5: Blak 2H 61
Melling Rd. NE23: Cra 4H 25
Melmerby Cl. NE3: Gos 5F 45
Melness Rd. NE13: Haz 6C 34
Melock Ct. NE13: Haz 6C 34
Melrose NE38: Wash 5H 115
Melrose Av. NE9: Low F 2J 99
NE22: Bed 7B 18
NE25: Monks 7F 39
NE25: Sea D 1H 37
NE27: Back 6G 37
NE30: Cull 2G 49
NE31: Heb 3J 85
SR7: Mur 1C 158
Melrose Cl. NE3: Gos 2D 44
NE15: Lem 7E 60
Melrose Ct. DH8: B'hill 5E 120
NE22: Bed 6B 18
Melrose Cres. SR7: S'hm 2H 147
Melrose Gdns. DH4: Nbot 6C 130
NE28: W'snd 7A 48
SR6: Roker 4G 105
Melrose Gro. NE32: Jar 2E 86
Melrose Ter. NE22: Bed 6B 18
NE64: Newb S 4H 13
Melrose Vs. NE22: Bed 6B 18
Melsonby Cl. SR3: Dox P 3K 131
Meltham Ct. NE15: Walb 3B 60
Meltham Dr. SR3: Dox P 4A 132
Melton Av. NE6: Walk 1D 84
Melton Cres. NE26: Sea S 6D 28
Melton Dr. NE25: New Hart 4H 27
Melton Ter. NE25: New Hart 4H 27
Melvaig Cl. SR3: Dox P 4A 132
Melville Av. NE24: News 4H 23
Melville Gdns. NE25: Monks 7C 38
Melville Gro. NE7: H Hea 2J 63
Melville St. DH3: Ches S 7A 128
Melvin Pl. NE5: Blak 3H 61
Melvyn Gdns. SR6: Roker 4G 105
Membury Cl. SR3: Dox P 4A 132
Memorial Av. SR8: Eas C 7C 160
Memorial Homes DH9: Tan L 1D 124
Memorial Sq. NE64: Newb S 2H 13
Menai Ct. SR3: Silk 3B 132
Menceforth Cotts.
DH2: Ches S 5K 127
Mendham Cl. NE10: Hew 1C 100
Mendip Av. DH2: Ches S 7K 127
(not continuous)
Mendip Cl. NE29: N Shi 3F 49
NE63: N Sea 6C 12
SR8: Pet 6K 171
Mendip Dr. NE38: Wash 5F 115
Mendip Gdns. NE11: Lob H 1D 98
Mendip Ho. DH2: Ches S 7A 128
Mendip Ter. DH9: Stly 4G 125
Mendip Way NE12: Longb 6H 45
Mentieth Cl. NE38: Wash 5F 115
Menvill Pl. SR1: Sund 2G 119
Mercantile Rd. DH4: Hou S 3C 144
Merchant Ct. NE31: Heb 5K 85
NE63: N Sea 6D 12
Merchants Quay NE1: Newc T 7F 4
Merchants Wharf NE6: Byke 3A 84
Mercia Retail Pk. DH1: P Me 3A 154
Mercia Way NE15: Lem 1E 80
Meredith Ct. *NE8: Gate* *5H 83*
(off Cemetery Rd.)
Meredith Gdns. NE8: Gate 5H 83
Mere Dr. DH1: P Me 4K 153
Mere Knolls Rd. SR6: Seab 2G 105
Meresyde NE10: Hew 1E 100
Meresyde Ct. NE10: Hew 7E 84
Merevale Cl. NE37: Wash 5J 101
Merganser Lodge *NE10: Fell* *6B 84*
(off Crowhall La.)
Meridian Ct. SR8: Pet 5G 171
Meridian Way NE7: H Hea 2B 64
Merlay Dr. NE13: Din 5H 33
Merlay Hall NE6: Walk 2E 84
Merle Gdns. NE6: Byke 6P 5 (1A 84)
NE61: Mor 5D 8
Merle Ter. SR4: Sund 7B 104
Merley Cft. NE61: Mor 2G 15
Merley Ga. NE61: Mor 2G 15
Merlin Cl. SR7: S'hm 2A 148
Merlin Ct. DH7: Esh W 4C 162
NE10: Fell *6B 84*
(off High St.)
Merlin Cres. NE28: W'snd 2K 65
Merlin Dr. DH3: Ches S 2B 128
Merlin Pl. NE12: Longb 5J 45
Merlin Way NE27: Shir 3A 48
Merrington Cl. NE25: New Hart 3H 27
SR3: Dox P 3K 131
Merrion Cl. SR3: Dox P 3K 131
Merryfield Gdns. SR6: Roker 4G 105
Merryleazes NE46: Hex 2A 70
MERRYOAKS 5J 165
Merryshields Ter. NE43: Stoc 6J 75
Merryweather Ri. SR3: Tuns 2E 132
Mersey Pl. NE8: Gate 6K 83
Mersey Rd. NE8: Gate 6K 83
NE31: Heb 3J 85
Mersey St. DH8: Lead 4B 122
NE17: C'wl 6A 94
Merton Ct. NE4: Benw 2A 82
Merton Rd. NE6: Walk 3D 84
NE20: Pon 5J 31
Merton Sq. NE24: Bly 1J 23
Merton Way NE20: Pon 5J 31
Messenger Bank
DH8: Shot B 3E 120
Messenger M. *DH8: Shot B* *3E 120*
(off Messenger Bank)
Metcalfe Cres. SR7: Mur 7D 146
Metcalfe Ho. DH1: Dur 2A 6 (2K 165)
Metcalfe Rd. DH8: Cons 1K 135
Methold Ho's. DH9: Beam 1A 126
Methuen St. NE9: Low F 6J 83
Methven Way NE23: Cra 7A 22
Metroasis NE11: Dun 4H 81
Metrocentre NE11: Dun 4J 81
Metrocentre E. Bus. Pk.
NE11: Dun 4A 82
Metro Centre Station (Rail) 4K 81
Metro Pk. W. NE11: Dun 4H 81
Metro Radio Arena Newcastle
. . . . . 9C 4 (3E 82)
Metro Retail Pk. NE11: Dun 4H 81

Mews, The DH1: Shin .6D 166
DH4: Hou S .3A 144
NE1: Newc T .3E 4 (7F 63)
NE3: Gos .3F 45
NE10: Ward .6F 85
NE21: Blay .4E 80
NE30: Tyne .4K 49
SR3: E Her .2H 131
Mews Ct. DH5: Hou S .2E 144
Mews Gdns. NE1: Newc T .6H 5
MFA Bowl
Sunderland .3K 7 (1F 119)
MFA Bowling
Newcastle .1B 82
MFA Bowl (Starbowl) .2E 66
Michaelgate NE6: Byke .1A 84
Michaelmas St. NE8: Gate .5C 82
Mickle Cl. NE37: Wash .2E 114
Mickle Hill Rd. TS27: B Col, Hes .4E 182
Mickleton Cl. DH3: Gt Lum .3F 143
DH8: Cons .1H 135
Mickleton Gdns. SR3: Sund .6D 118
Micklewood Cl. NE61: Lngh .1A 10
Mickley Cl. NE28: W'snd .3A 66
MICKLEY SQUARE .5B 76
Mid Cross St. NE4: Newc T .9B 4 (3D 82)
Middlebrook NE20: Darr H .1F 41
Middle Chare DH3: Ches S .6A 128
Middle Cl. NE38: Wash .7F 115
Middle Ct. DH8: Cons .7H 121
Middle Dr. NE13: Wool .2F 43
NE20: Darr H .2E 40
Middle Engine La.
NE28: N Shi, W'snd .7K 47
NE29: N Shi, Shir .5A 48
Middle Engine La. Retail Pk.
NE28: W'snd .7K 47
Middle Farm NE23: Seg .7D 26
Middle Farm Ct. NE23: Cra .3K 25
Middle Farm Sq. NE23: Cra .3K 25
Middlefield DH2: Pelt .2G 127
Middlefields Ind. Est.
NE34: S Shi .7H 67
Middlefield Ter. DH7: Ush M .3B 164
Middle Gth. NE5: Blak .3K 61
Middle Ga. NE61: Loan .2F 15
Middlegate NE5: W Dent .4D 60
Middle Grn. NE25: Monks .7C 38
Middle Gro. DH7: B'don .2C 174
Middleham Cl. DH2: Ous .7F 113
Middleham Ct. SR5: S'wck .4A 104
Middleham Rd. DH1: Dur .4B 154
MIDDLE HERRINGTON .2H 131
MIDDLE RAINTON .7B 144
Middle Row DH4: Hou S .1J 143
NE40: Ryton .3J 79
MIDDLES, THE .6H 125
Middles Rd. DH9: Crag, Stly .5F 125
Middle St. DH8: Cons .7H 121
NE6: Walk .7D 64
NE24: News .5F 23
NE30: Tyne .5K 49
NE45: Corb .1D 72
SR1: Sund .3H 7 (1E 118)
(not continuous)
TS27: B Col .1H 183
Middle St. E. NE6: Walk .7E 64
Middleton Av. NE4: Fen .7A 62
NE39: Row G .6K 95
Middleton Cl. DH8: Cons .1J 135
SR7: S'hm .1G 147
Middleton Ct. NE2: Jes .1J 5 (6H 63)
Middleton Nth. NE13: Haz .2A 44
Middleton Sth. NE13: Haz .2A 44
Middleton St. NE24: Bly .2J 23
Middlewood DH7: Ush M .2C 164
Middlewood Pk. NE4: Fen .6A 62
Middlewood Rd. DH7: Lan .7J 137
Middridge Rd. DH7: Lang P .5G 151
Midfield Dr. SR6: Roker .5G 105
Midgley Dr. SR3: Dox P .4A 132
Midhill Cl. DH7: B'don .1D 174
DH7: Lang P .5J 151
Midhurst Av. NE34: S Shi .5B 68
Midhurst Cl. SR3: Dox P .3K 131
Midhurst Rd. NE12: Longb .5B 46
Midlothian Cl. SR4: Sund .4K 117
Midmoor Rd. SR4: Sund .1A 118
Midsomer Cl. SR3: Dox P .4K 131
Mid Summer Way NE8: Gate .4D 82
Midway NE6: Walk .7E 64
Milbanke Cl. DH2: Ous .7H 113
Milbanke St. DH2: Ous .7H 113
Milbank Ter. DH6: Shot C .6E 170
TS28: Sta T .7H 181
MILBOURNE .1A 30
Milburn Cl. DH3: Ches S .7C 128
NE46: Hex .4B 70
Milburn Dr. NE15: Benw .7H 61
Milburn Ho. NE1: Newc T .7G 4
Milburn M. *NE63: Ash .4B 12*
(off Milburn Rd.)
Milburn Rd. NE63: Ash .4B 12
Milburn St. SR4: Sund .1D 118
Milburn Ter. NE62: Stake .2A 18
Milcombe Cl. SR3: Dox P .3K 131
Mildmay Rd. NE2: Jes .3F 63
Mildred St. DH5: Hou S .1E 144
Milecastle Ct. NE5: W Dent .3D 60
Mile End Rd. NE33: S Shi .1J 67
(not continuous)
Milfield Av. NE27: Shir .1K 47
NE28: W'snd .1G 65
Milford Gdns. NE3: Gos .3D 44
Milford Rd. NE15: Benw .1J 81
Military Rd. NE15: Hed W .1J 57
NE30: N Shi .6H 49
Milk Mkt. NE1: Newc T .6J 5
Milkwell NE45: Corb .7E 52
Milkwell Cl. DH9: Stly .6D 124
Milkwell La. NE45: Ayd, Corb .5E 52
Mill, The DH7: Lan .6J 137
NE8: Gate .5F 83
Millais Gdns. NE34: S Shi .4J 87
Mill Bank SR5: Ful .3E 104
Millbank NE33: S Shi .3J 67
Millbank Ct. DH1: Dur .2K 165
Millbank Cres. NE22: Bed .7J 17
Millbank Ho. SR7: S'hm .2H 147
Millbank Ind. Est. NE33: S Shi .3J 67
Millbank Pl. NE22: Bed .1K 21
Millbank Rd. NE6: Walk .2E 84
NE22: Bed .7K 17
Millbank Ter. NE22: Bed .7J 17
Millbeck Gdns. NE9: Low F .4K 99
Millbeck Gro. DH5: Hou S .4D 144
Millbrook NE10: Hew .7C 84
NE29: N Shi .7E 48
Millbrook Rd. NE23: Cra .1A 26
Millburn DH4: S Row .3B 130
Millburngate DH1: Dur .2B 6 (2A 166)
Millburn Ho. NE5: Fen .3A 62
Mill Cl. NE29: N Shi .7E 48
NE44: Rid M .7K 73
Mill Cotts. *DH7: Lan .6J 137*
(off Victoria St.)
Mill Ct. DH4: Bour .7J 129
NE17: C'wl .2K 107
Mill Cres. DH4: S Row .3B 130
NE31: Heb .4G 85
Millcroft Ct. NE24: Bly .3K 23
Milldale SR7: S'hm .2H 147
Milldale Av. NE24: Cow .2E 22
MILL DAM .3H 67
Mill Dam NE33: S Shi .3H 67
Milldene Av. NE30: Tyne .4J 49
Mill Dene Vw. NE32: Jar .1C 86
Mill Dyke Cl. NE25: Monks .5C 38
Millennium Ct. NE40: G'sde .5D 78
Millennium Place .2C 6 (2A 166)
Millennium Pl. *DH1: Dur .2C 6*
(off Claypath)
Millennium Way
SR5: Monkw .1H 7 (7E 104)
Miller Cl. NE12: Longb .4E 46
Miller Gdns. DH2: P Fel .5F 127
Millers Bank NE28: W'snd .3K 65
Millers Dene NE6: Walk .5D 64
Millersfield NE46: Acomb .3B 50
(not continuous)
Millersfield Cl. NE46: Acomb .3B 50
Millers Hill DH4: S Row .3C 130
Millershill La. DH8: C'sde, Cons .7F 135
Miller's La. NE16: Swa .5H 81
Millers Rd. NE6: Walk .6A 64
Miller St. NE8: Gate .6F 83
Miller Ter. SR3: New S .1C 132
Mill Farm Cl. NE4: Newc T .6A 4 (1D 82)
Mill Farm Rd. NE39: Ham M .2E 108
MILLFIELD .1C 118
Millfield DH7: Lan .6J 137
DH8: Cons .2H 135
NE22: Bed .2J 21
NE26: Sea S .5D 28
Millfield Av. NE3: Ken .2A 62
Millfield Cl. DH2: Ches S .1J 141
NE15: Newb .6K 59
Millfield Ct. DH8: B'hill .6E 120
NE16: Whi .7J 81
NE22: Bed .1J 21
NE26: Sea S .5D 28
NE46: Hex .1B 70
Millfield E. NE22: Bed .2J 21
Millfield Gdns. NE10: Fell .6A 84
NE24: Bly .7H 19
NE30: Tyne .4J 49
NE46: Hex .1B 70
Millfield Gro. NE30: Tyne .3J 49
Millfield La. NE15: Newb .5K 59
Millfield Nth. NE22: Bed .1J 21
Millfield Rd. NE16: Whi .1H 97
NE44: Rid M .7K 73
Millfield Sth. NE22: Bed .2J 21
Millfield Station (Metro) .1C 118
Millfield Ter. NE17: C'wl .6K 93
NE46: Hex .1B 70
SR6: Whit .3H 89
Millfield W. NE22: Bed .1J 21
Millford NE10: Hew .7F 85
Millford Ct. NE10: Hew .1F 101
Millford Way DH6: Bowb .4J 177
Mill Grange NE44: Rid M .6A 74
Mill Gro. NE30: Tyne .4J 49
NE34: S Shi .2D 88
Millgrove Vw. NE3: Ken .2B 62
Mill Hill DH5: Hou S .4D 144
SR8: Eas, Pet .4H 171
Mill Hill La. DH1: Dur .5J 165
Mill Hill Rd. NE5: W Dent .5F 61
SR3: Silk .3B 132
Mill Hill Wlk. SR3: Silk .3C 132
Mill Ho. NE2: Newc T .1B 4 (5D 62)
Mill Ho. Ct. DH1: Dur .2E 166
Milling Ct. NE8: Gate .4E 82
Mill La. DH1: Dur .2E 166
DH1: Dur, Shin .5E 166
DH2: Plaw .6J 141
DH3: Plaw .6J 141
DH6: S'burn .3A 168
DH7: New B .4C 164
Mill La. DH8: Ebc .4G 107
DH9: Beam .6F 113
NE4: Elsw .2C 82
NE15: Hed W .2D 58
NE21: Winl, W Mill .7B 80
NE23: Seg .2A 36
NE29: N Shi .1H 67
NE31: Heb .3H 85
SR6: Whit .2H 89
Mill La. Nth. NE4: Elsw .1C 82
Millne Ct. NE22: Bed .7H 17
Millom Ct. SR8: Pet .2J 181
Millom Pl. NE9: Low F .3K 99
Mill Pit DH4: S Row .3B 130
Millport SR3: Silk .3B 132
Mill Race Cl. NE17: C'wl .2K 107
Mill Race Ct. NE61: Mor .7G 9
Mill Ri. NE3: Gos .1G 63
Mill Rd. DH7: Lang M .7G 165
NE8: Gate .8K 5 (2H 83)
NE17: C'wl .6K 93
SR7: S'hm .2H 147
Mills, The DH9: Dip .6J 109
Mills Gdns. NE28: W'snd .2F 65
Millside NE61: Mor .7F 9
Mill St. DH8: Cons .2K 135
SR4: Sund .2D 118
Mill Ter. DH4: S Row .3B 130
DH5: Hou S .4D 144
SR8: Eas .7J 159
Millthorp Cl. SR2: Sund .7J 119
Millum Ter. SR6: Roker .6G 105
Mill Va. NE15: Newb .5K 59
Mill Vw. NE10: Wind N .7A 84
NE36: W Bol .7G 87
Mill Vw. Av. SR6: Ful .4F 105
Millview Dr. NE30: Tyne .3H 49
Mill Vw. Ri. NE42: Pru .2F 77
Mill Vs. NE36: W Bol .7G 87
Mill Volvo Tyne Theatre, The .6D 4 (1E 82)
Mill Way NE15: Hor, O'ham .5F 57
Millway NE9: Low F .7J 83
NE26: Sea S .5D 28
Millway Cl. NE9: Low F .7J 83
Millway Gro. NE26: Sea S .5D 28
Millwood Grn. NE21: W Mill .1C 96
Milner Cres. NE21: Winl .5A 80
Milner St. NE33: S Shi .3A 68
Milne Way NE3: Ken .7B 44
Milrig Cl. SR3: Dox P .4A 132
Milsted Cl. SR3: Dox P .4K 131
Milsted Ct. NE15: Walb .3B 60
Milton Av. DH5: Hou S .3E 144
(not continuous)
NE31: Heb .7J 65
TS27: B Col .7G 173
Milton Cl. DH9: Stly .3H 125
NE2: Newc T .2J 5 (6H 63)
SR7: S'hm .3J 147
Milton Grn. NE2: Newc T .2J 5 (6H 63)
Milton Gro. DH6: Shot C .6F 171
NE29: N Shi .6F 49
NE42: Pru .5D 76
NE63: Ash .4D 12
(not continuous)
Milton La. SR8: Eas .7A 160
Milton Pl. NE2: Newc T .2J 5 (6H 63)
NE9: Spri .6D 100
NE29: N Shi .6F 49
Milton Rd. NE16: Swa, Whi .6G 81
Milton Sq. NE8: Gate .4J 83
(not continuous)
Milton St. NE32: Jar .5B 66
NE33: S Shi .5K 67
(not continuous)
NE40: G'sde .5C 78
SR4: Sund .1C 118
Milton Ter. NE29: N Shi .6F 49
Milvain Av. NE4: Fen .7A 62
Milvain Cl. NE8: Gate .5H 83
Milvain St. NE8: Gate .5H 83
Milverton Ct. NE3: Ki Pk .6J 43
Mimosa Dr. NE31: Heb .3J 85
Mimosa Pl. NE4: Fen .5K 61
Minden St. NE1: Newc T .5H 5 (1G 83)
Mindrum Ter. NE6: Walk .2D 84
NE29: N Shi .1D 66
Mindrum Way NE25: Sea D .7H 27
Minehead Gdns. SR3: New S .1C 132
Miners Cotts. NE15: Den M .6G 61
Miners' Vs. DH6: Whe H .2C 180
Minerva Cl. NE5: Cha P .1C 60
Mingarry DH3: Bir .6C 114
Mingary Cl. DH5: E Rain .6C 144
Ministry Cl. NE7: Longb .7K 45
Minorca Cl. SR1: Sund .2G 119
Minorca Pl. NE3: Ken .2B 62
Minories, The NE2: Jes .5J 63
Minskip Cl. SR3: Dox P .4A 132
Minster Ct. DH1: Carr .1G 167
NE8: Gate .10K 5 (3H 83)
Minster Gro. NE15: Walb .2B 60
Minsterley DH3: Gt Lum .3E 142
Minster Pde. NE32: Jar .6C 66
Minting Pl. NE23: Cra .4H 25
Minton Ct. NE29: N Shi .1F 67
Minton La. NE29: N Shi .1F 67
Minton Sq. SR4: Sund .1A 118
Mirk La. NE8: Gate .8H 5 (2G 83)
Mirlaw Rd. NE23: Cra .5H 25
Mistletoe Rd. NE2: Jes .4G 63
Mistletoe St. DH1: Dur .3A 6 (3K 165)
Mitcham Cres. NE7: H Hea .2K 63
Mitchell Av. NE2: Jes .2G 63
NE25: Monks .7D 38
Mitchell Bldgs. NE9: Spri .6E 100
Mitchell Cl. SR8: Pet .4K 171
Mitchell Dr. NE63: N Sea .4F 13
Mitchell Gdns. NE34: S Shi .6B 68
Mitchell St. DH1: Dur .2A 6 (2K 165)
DH3: Bir .4K 113
DH9: Ann P .5A 124
DH9: Stly .5D 124
NE6: Walk .7E 64
(not continuous)
NE40: Craw .3C 78
Mitchell Ter. DH9: Tant .6B 110
MITFORD .6A 8
Mitford Av. NE24: Bly .3G 23
NE25: Sea D .7G 27
NE61: Peg .3A 10
Mitford Cl. DH1: H Shin .7F 167
DH3: Ches S .1B 128
NE38: Wash .4F 115
Mitford Ct. SR8: Pet .1B 182
Mitford Dr. DH6: S'burn .3A 168
NE5: West .2E 60
NE63: Ash .5B 12
Mitford Gdns. NE11: Lob H .2C 98
NE13: W Op .4E 34
NE28: W'snd .7K 47
NE62: Stake .7H 11
(not continuous)
Mitford Pl. NE3: Gos .6C 44
Mitford Rd. NE34: S Shi .7A 68
NE61: Mor .6E 8
Mitford St. NE28: W'snd .3C 66
SR6: Ful .3G 105
Mitford Ter. NE32: Jar .4B 86
Mitford Way NE13: Din .5H 33
Mithras Gdns. NE15: Hed W .3C 58
Mitre Pl. NE33: S Shi .5H 67
Moat Gdns. NE10: Ward .6G 85
Moatside Ct. DH1: Dur .3C 6 (3A 166)
Moatside La. DH1: Dur .3C 6 (3A 166)
Moatside M. DH1: Dur .3C 6
Modder St. NE6: Walk .3D 84
Model Dwellings NE38: Wash .4J 115
Model Ter. DH4: Pen .1A 130
Modigars La. NE43: Pains .3A 92
Moffat Av. NE32: Jar .2E 86
Moffat Cl. NE29: N Shi .4C 48
Moffett Vs. NE33: S Shi .4K 67
Moine Gdns. SR6: Roker .4G 105
Moir Ter. *SR2: Ryh .3J 133*
(off Robson Pl.)
Molesdon Cl. NE30: Cull .3G 49
Molineux Cl. NE6: Byke .3N 5 (7K 63)
Molineux Ct. NE6: Byke .3N 5 (7K 63)
Molineux St. NE6: Byke .3N 5 (7K 63)
Mollyfair Cl. NE40: Craw .2D 78
Monarch Av. SR3: Dox P .4J 131
Monarch Ct. NE12: Longb .4E 46
Monarch Rd. NE4: Newc T .10A 4 (3C 82)
Monarch Ter. NE21: Blay .4C 80
Monastery Ct. NE32: Jar .6B 66
Mona St. DH9: Stly .2F 125
Moncrieff Ter. SR8: Eas .7B 160
Monday Cres. NE4: Newc T .3A 4 (7D 62)
(not continuous)
Monday Pl. NE4: Newc T .3A 4 (7D 62)
MONEY HILL .7C 112
Money Slack DH1: Dur .7K 165
Monkchester Grn.
NE6: Walk .1C 84
Monkchester Rd. NE6: Walk .1C 84
Monk Ct. NE8: Gate .10K 5 (4H 83)
SR8: Pet .2K 181
Monkdale Av. NE24: Cow .3E 22
MONK HESLEDEN .6H 183
Monkhouse Av. NE30: Cull .3G 49
Monkridge NE15: Walb .3B 60
NE26: Whit B .4E 38
Monkridge Ct. NE3: Gos .1G 63
Monkridge Gdns.
NE11: Dun .7B 82
Monks Av. NE25: Monks .1D 48
Monks Cres. DH1: Dur .1D 166
Monks Dormitory
& Treasures of Durham University
.4C 6
MONKSEATON .6F 39
Monkseaton Dr. NE25: Monks .6C 38
NE26: Whit B .4F 39
Monkseaton Rd. NE25: Well .6A 38
Monkseaton Station (Metro) .6F 39
Monkseaton Ter. NE63: Ash .6C 12
Monksfeld NE10: Fell .7C 84
Monksfield Cl. SR3: Dox P .4B 132
Monkside NE6: Heat .5B 64
NE23: Cra .5H 25
Monkside Cl. NE38: Wash .6E 114
Monks Mdws. NE46: Hex .2F 71
Monks Pk. Ct. NE12: Longb .6J 45
Monks Pk. Way NE12: Longb .6J 45
Monks Ridge NE61: Mor .1D 14
Monks Rd. NE25: Monks .1C 48
Monk's Ter. NE46: Hex .2F 71
Monkstone Av. NE30: Tyne .4J 49
Monkstone Cl. NE30: Tyne .4J 49
Monkstone Cres. NE30: Tyne .4J 49
Monk St. NE1: Newc T .6D 4 (1E 82)
SR6: Roker .6F 105
Monks Way NE30: Tyne .3J 49
Monksway NE32: Jar .1E 86
Monks Wood NE30: N Shi .4E 48
Monkswood Sq. SR3: Silk .3D 132
Monk Ter. NE32: Jar .7C 66
MONKTON .3B 86
Monkton NE10: Hew .1D 100

Monkton Av. NE34: S Shi 2F 87
Monkton Bus. Pk. Nth. NE31: Heb 4J 85
Monkton Bus. Pk. Sth. NE31: Heb 5K 85
Monkton Dene NE32: Jar 2A 86
Monkton Dene Pk. 2B 86
Monkton Hall NE31: Heb 2K 85
Monkton La. NE31: Heb 4J 85
NE32: Jar 3K 85
Monkton Rd. NE32: Jar 6B 66
(not continuous)
Monkton Stadium 2A 86
Monkton Ter. NE32: Jar 6C 66
MONKWEARMOUTH 7F 105
Monkwearmouth Station Mus. 1J 7 (7F 105)
Monmouth Gdns. NE28: W'snd 1A 66
Monroe Pl. NE5: Blak 3K 61
Mons Av. NE31: Heb 7J 65
Mons Cres. DH4: S Row 3C 130
Montagu Av. NE3: Ken 2C 62
Montagu Ct. NE3: Ken 3C 62
Montague Ct. NE9: Low F 6H 83
Montague St. NE15: Lem 7D 60
SR6: Ful 4F 105
Monteigne Dr. DH6: Bowb 4H 177
Monterey NE37: Wash 6H 101
SR3: Dox P 4A 132
Montfalcon Cl. SR8: Pet 6A 172
Montford Cl. SR3: Dox P 4K 131
Montgomerie Ct. NE63: N Sea 3D 12
Montgomery Rd. DH1: Dur 1D 166
Montorosso NE20: Pres 6C 32
Montpelier Ter. SR2: Sund 5G 119
Montpellier Pl. NE3: Ken 2B 62
Montrose Cl. NE25: New Hart 4H 27
Montrose Cres. NE9: Low F 7K 83
NE31: Heb 6J 65
Montrose Dr. NE10: Ward 7F 85
Montrose Gdns. NE61: Mor 1F 15
SR3: Sund 5C 118
Monument Ct. DH1: Dur 4J 165
NE17: C'wl 6A 94
Monument Mall
NE1: Newc T 5F 4 (1F 83)
Monument Pk. NE38: Wash 3B 116
Monument Station (Metro) 5F 4 (1F 83)
Monument Ter. DH3: Bir 4A 114
DH4: Pen 1A 130
Monument Vw. DH4: Pen 1B 130
DH7: Sac 6E 140
Moonfield NE46: Hex 2D 70
MOOR 4D 46
Moor Cl. NE29: N Shi 4C 48
SR1: Sund 1H 119
Moor Ct. DH4: Bour 6J 129
NE3: Gos 3D 62
SR6: Whit 6G 89
Moor Cres. DH1: Dur 1E 166
DH6: Ludw 5H 169
NE3: Gos 3E 62
Moor Crest Ter. *NE29: N Shi* *4F 49*
(off Walton Av.)
Moor Cft. NE64: Newb S 2J 13
Moorcroft NE23: Dud 3K 35
Moorcroft Cl. NE15: Lem 6D 60
Moorcroft Rd. NE15: Lem 6E 60
Moor Cft. Vw. NE64: Newb S 2J 13
Moordale Av. NE24: Cow 3E 22
Moore Av. NE11: Dun 6B 82
NE34: S Shi 7A 68
Moore Ct. NE15: Thro 6G 59
Moore Cres. DH3: Bir 2A 114
Moore Cres. Nth. DH5: Hou S 3E 144
Moore Cres. Sth. DH5: Hou S 3E 144
Moor Edge DH1: Dur 2H 165
DH7: B'don 2D 174
Moor Edge Rd. NE27: Shir 7J 37
MOOR END 7G 155
Moor End Ter. DH1: Carr 7G 155
Moor End Vs. NE64: Newb S 2K 13
Moore Pk. NE8: Gate 5J 83
Moore Sq. TS28: Win 4F 181
Moore St. DH6: Whe H 3B 180
DH9: Stly 4E 124
NE8: Gate 5J 83
Moore St. Vs. *NE8: Gate* *5J 83*
(off Moore St.)
Moore Ter. DH6: Shot C 6F 171
Moorfield NE2: Jes 2F 63
Moorfield Gdns. SR6: Clead 7C 88
Moorfields NE61: Mor 2G 15
Moorfoot Av. DH2: Ches S 7A 128
Moorfoot Gdns. NE11: Lob H 7C 82
Moor Gdns. NE29: N Shi 4C 48
Moor Grange NE42: Pru 5F 77
Moorhead NE5: Fen 4A 62
Moorhead Ct. NE5: Fen 4A 62
Moorhead M. NE5: Fen 4A 62
Moorhill Ct. SR2: Sund 6G 119
Moor Ho. NE4: Newc T 4B 4 (7D 62)
Moorhouse DH7: Queb 1C 162
Moorhouse Cl. NE34: S Shi 1K 87
Moorhouse Est. NE63: Ash 3C 12
Moorhouse Gdns. DH5: Hett H 1G 157
(not continuous)
Moorhouse La. NE63: Ash 4D 12
Moorhouses Rd. NE29: N Shi 4C 48
Moorings, The NE6: Byke 2A 84
Moorland Av. NE22: Bed 5C 18
Moorland Cotts. NE22: Bed 5B 18
Moorland Ct. NE22: Bed 5C 18
Moorland Cres. DH8: C'sde 4B 134
NE6: Walk 6C 64
NE22: Bed 5C 18
Moorland Dr. NE22: Bed 6C 18
Moorlands DH8: B'hill 4E 120
DH9: Dip 7J 109
NE32: Jar 5D 86
NE42: Pru 5G 77
Moorlands, The DH1: Dur 2E 166
Moorlands Cres. DH8: B'hill 5F 121
Moorland Sq. SR4: Sund 7B 104
Moorland Vw. DH8: C'sde 4B 134
NE17: C'wl 7K 93
Moorland Vs. NE22: Bed 5C 18
Moorland Way NE23: Nel V 1G 25
Moor La. NE3: Ken 1K 61
NE20: Darr H 7F 31
NE34: S Shi 7A 68
NE36: Clead, E Bol 6A 88
SR6: Clead, Whit 7C 88
TS28: Win 6G 181
Moor La. E. NE34: S Shi 7B 68
Moormill NE11: Kib 2E 112
Moormill Ct. NE11: Kib 2E 112
Moormill La. NE11: Kib 2F 113
Moor Pk. Ct. NE29: N Shi 5C 48
Moor Pk. Ho. NE29: N Shi 5C 48
Moor Pk. Rd. NE29: N Shi 5B 48
(not continuous)
Moor Pl. NE3: Gos 2E 62
Moor Rd. NE42: Pru 5F 77
Moor Rd. Nth. NE3: Gos 7F 45
Moor Rd. Sth. NE3: Gos 2F 63
Moorsburn Dr. DH4: Hou S 1C 144
Moors Cl. DH4: Hou S 2B 144
Moorsfield DH4: Hou S 2B 144
MOORSIDE
DH8 3D 134
SR3 4A 132
Moorside NE12: Longb 2K 45
NE32: Jar 5C 86
NE37: Wash 1F 115
Moorside Ct. NE5: Fen 4A 62
Moorside Nth. NE4: Fen 4A 62
Moorside Pl. NE4: Fen 5B 62
Moorside Rd. SR3: Dox P 3K 131
Moorside Sth. NE4: Fen 6B 62
Moorsley Rd. DH5: Hett H 2E 156
DH6: Low P 4B 156
Moor St. SR1: Sund 1G 119
(Coronation St.)
SR1: Sund 2H 119
(Woodbine St.)
Moor Ter. SR1: Sund 1H 119
Moorvale La. NE5: Fen 3A 62
Moor Vw. DH6: Thor 1A 180
DH6: Whe H 2B 180
DH8: B'hill 5G 121
NE3: Ken 1K 61
NE12: Kil 6A 36
NE40: Craw 2E 78
NE64: Newb S 2J 13
SR6: Whit 6G 89
Moor Vw. Cl. NE61: Peg 4K 9
Moorview Cres. NE5: Fen 3A 62
Moor Vw. Ter. DH9: Ann P 6J 123
Moor Vw. Wlk. NE12: Kil 7A 36
Moorway NE37: Wash 1F 115
Moorway Dr. NE15: Lem 6E 60
Moot Hall
Newcastle upon Tyne 7G 4 (2G 83)
Moraine Cres. NE17: C'wl 2K 107
Moralee Cl. NE7: H Hea 2B 64
Moran St. SR6: Ful 3F 105
Moray Cl. DH3: Bir 7B 114
SR8: Pet 7A 172
Moray St. SR6: Ful 5F 105
Morcott Gdns. NE29: N Shi 1E 66
Morden St. NE1: Newc T 4E 4 (7F 63)
Mordey Cl. SR2: Sund 3G 119
Mordue Ter. DH9: Ann P 6A 124
Morecambe Pde. NE31: Heb 4A 86
Moreland Rd. NE34: S Shi 3K 87
Moreland St. SR6: Roker 5F 105
Moresby Rd. NE23: Cra 7A 22
Morgan Bus. Cen. NE12: Kil 6K 35
Morgan St. SR5: S'wck 5D 104
Morgans Way NE21: Winl 4A 80
Morgan Vs. *NE28: W'snd* *3G 65*
(off North Vw.)
Morgy Hill E. NE40: Craw 3D 78
Morgy Hill Sth. NE40: Craw 3D 78
Morgy Hill W. NE40: Craw 2C 78
Morinda Cl. DH4: S Row 4K 129
Morland Av. NE38: Wash 5J 115
Morland Gdns. NE9: Low F 7K 83
Morley Av. NE10: Bill Q 4F 85
Morley Ct. NE6: Byke 6A 64
Morley Cres. DH6: Kel 7E 178
Morley Gdns. DH8: Cons 5H 121
Morley Hill Rd. NE5: W Dent 5F 61
Morley La. DH7: Bran 7K 163
Morley Pl. NE27: Shir 7K 37
Morley Ter. DH4: Hou S 1A 144
NE10: Fell 6B 84
Morningside DH7: Sac 6E 140
NE38: Wash 1C 128
Morningside Ct. DH3: Ches S 5A 128
Mornington Av. NE3: Ken 2B 62
MORPETH 7F 9
Morpeth Av. NE13: W Op 4E 34
NE32: Jar 3B 86
NE34: S Shi 6K 67
NE61: Peg 3K 9
Morpeth Castle 7G 9
Morpeth Chantry Bagpipe Mus. *7G 9*
(off Bridge St.)
Morpeth Clocktower *7F 9*
(off Oldgate)
Morpeth Cl. NE38: Wash 4E 114
NE62: Chop 2G 17
Morpeth Cricket, Hockey and Tennis Club 1K 9
Morpeth Dr. SR3: Dox P 3K 131
Morpeth Rd. NE62: Chop 1C 16
(not continuous)
NE63: Ash 3H 11
Morpeth Station (Rail) 1G 15
Morpeth St. NE2: Newc T 1B 4 (5D 62)
SR8: Hord 4D 172
Morpeth Ter. NE29: N Shi 1D 66
Morris Av. NE34: S Shi 3H 87
Morris Ct. NE23: Dud 3K 35
Morris Cres. DH6: Thor 1J 179
NE35: Bol C 6G 87
Morris Gdns. NE10: Ward 6F 85
Morrison Ind. Est. DH9: Ann P 6B 124
Morrison Rd. NE61: Mor 6F 9
Morrison Rd. Nth. Ind. Est.
DH9: Ann P 6A 124
Morrison St. NE8: Gate 4E 82
Morrison Ter. NE46: Acomb 4B 50
Morris Rd. NE16: Whi 6H 81
Morris Sq. SR8: Eas 1A 172
Morris St. DH3: Bir 4K 113
NE8: Gate 6E 82
NE37: Wash 7G 101
Morris Ter. DH5: Hou S 3F 145
Morrit Ct. NE7: Longb 7A 46
Morston Dr. NE15: Lem 7E 60
Mortimer Av. NE5: West 2F 61
NE29: N Shi 6D 48
Mortimer Chase NE23: E Har 6K 21
(not continuous)
Mortimer Rd. NE33: S Shi 5K 67
NE34: S Shi 5K 67
Mortimer St. DH8: B'hill 6F 121
SR4: Sund 1B 118
Mortimer Ter. *NE25: H'wll* *1J 37*
(off Laurel Ter.)
NE61: Peg 3B 10
Morton Cl. NE38: Wash 4H 115
SR7: Mur 7F 147
Morton Cres. DH4: Hou S 1K 143
NE5: Call 6B 42
Morton Grange Ter. DH4: Hou S 1J 143
Morton M. DH4: Hou S 1J 143
Morton Sq. SR8: Pet 5A 172
Morton St. NE6: Byke 7B 64
NE33: S Shi 1J 67
Morton Wlk. NE33: S Shi 1J 67
Morval Cl. SR3: Dox P 4K 131
Morven Dr. NE10: Bill Q 5F 85
Morven Lea NE21: Winl 4B 80
Morven Pl. NE63: Ash 3K 11
Morven Ter. NE63: Ash 3K 11
Morwick Cl. NE23: Cra 5J 25
Morwick Pl. NE5: Fen 4K 61
Morwick Rd. NE29: N Shi 4D 48
Mosley St. NE1: Newc T 6G 4 (1G 83)
Moss Cl. NE15: Lem 5C 60
Moss Cres. NE40: Craw 2E 78
Mossdale DH1: Carr 7J 155
Moss Heaps NE9: Low F 4K 99
Mosspool NE21: Winl 4A 80
Moss Side NE9: Wrek 4K 99
Mossway DH2: Pelt 2F 127
MOSSWOOD 1A 134
Mostyn Grn. NE3: Ken 7B 44
Motcombe Way NE23: Cra 7A 22
Moulton Ct. NE5: Blak 3J 61
Moulton Pl. NE5: Blak 3J 61
MOUNT, THE 7C 100
Mount, The DH8: Shot B 3F 121
NE15: Thro 3G 59
NE40: Ryton 1G 79
Mountbatten Av. NE31: Heb 2J 85
Mount Cl. NE12: Kil 7B 36
NE25: Monks 1D 48
SR4: Sund 2H 117
Mount Cott. NE9: Spri 7C 100
Mount Ct. DH3: Bir 3B 114
Mountfield Gdns. NE3: Ken 7B 44
Mountford Rd. NE25: New Hart 3H 27
Mount Gro. NE11: Dun 7B 82
SR4: Sund 4C 118
Mount Ho. Dr. NE9: Spri 6D 100
Mt. Joy Cres. DH1: Dur 6E 6 (4B 166)
Mount La. NE9: Spri 7C 100
Mt. Lonnen NE9: Spri 7C 100
Mount Pk. Dr. DH7: Lan 6J 137
MOUNT PLEASANT
DH4 1J 129
NE8 5J 83
NE43 6A 76
Mt. Pleasant DH3: Bir 3A 114
DH5: Hou S 2F 145
DH7: B'hpe 6D 138
DH7: Lan 6J 137
DH7: Sac 6D 140
DH9: Dip 7J 109
NE21: Winl 5B 80
SR5: S'wck 6C 104
Mt. Pleasant Bungs. DH3: Bir 3A 114
Mt. Pleasant Ct. NE15: Thro 3H 59
Mt. Pleasant Gdns. NE8: Gate 5J 83
Mt. Pleasant Rd. DH3: Bir 3A 114
Mount Ridge DH3: Bir 3B 114
Mount Rd. DH3: Bir 3A 114
NE9: Spri 7C 100
SR4: Sund 4B 118
Mountsett Cl. DH9: Dip 6J 109
Mountsett Crematorium
DH9: Dip 6J 109
Mountside DH8: Shot B 3F 121
Mountside Gdns. NE11: Dun 7B 82
Mt. Stewart St. SR7: S'hm 5B 148
Mount Ter. NE33: S Shi 3J 67
Mount Vw. DH2: Ous 1H 127
DH7: Lan 6J 137
NE16: Swa 6H 81
NE40: Craw 3D 78
Mount Vw. Ter. NE43: Stoc 7G 75
Mountwood NE2: Jes 1L 5 (5J 63)
Mourne Gdns. NE11: Lob H 1C 98
Moutter Cl. SR8: Hord 4C 172
Mowbray Almshouses
SR1: Sund 4H 7
Mowbray Cl. SR2: Sund 7K 7 (3F 119)
Mowbray Ct. NE62: Chop 1H 17
Mowbray M. NE33: S Shi 3A 68
Mowbray Rd. NE12: Longb 4B 46
NE29: N Shi 6D 48
NE33: S Shi 4K 67
SR2: Sund 7J 7 (4F 119)
Mowbray St. DH1: Dur 2A 6 (2K 165)
NE6: Heat 3L 5 (7J 63)
Mowbray Ter. DH4: Hou S 7D 130
NE62: Chop 1H 17
Mowbray Vs. NE33: S Shi 4B 68
Mowlam Dr. DH9: Stly 3G 125
Moyle Ter. NE16: Hob 4A 110
Mozart St. NE33: S Shi 3K 67
Muirfield NE25: Monks 6D 38
NE33: S Shi 4B 68
Muirfield Cl. DH8: B'hill 4G 121
Muirfield Dr. NE10: Wind N 1B 100
NE37: Wash 5G 101
Muirfield Rd. NE7: Longb 7A 46
Mulben Cl. NE4: Benw 2A 82
Mulberry Av. SR5: S'wck 4B 104
Mulberry Cl. NE24: News 5H 23
Mulberry Cres. NE34: S Shi 2B 88
Mulberry Gdns. NE10: Fell 4A 84
Mulberry Gro. NE16: Hob 4A 110
Mulberry Pk. NE9: Low F 2H 99
Mulberry Pl. NE4: Newc T 9A 4 (3D 82)
Mulberry St. NE10: Fell 5A 84
Mulberry Ter. DH9: Ann P 5B 124
Mulberry Way DH4: Hou S 1A 144
Mulcaster Gdns. NE28: W'snd 2E 64
Mulgrave Dr. SR6: Roker 7G 105
Mulgrave Ter. NE8: Gate 10H 5 (3G 83)
Mulgrave Vs. NE8: Gate 10H 5 (4G 83)
Mullen Dr. NE40: Ryton 2G 79
Mullen Gdns. NE28: W'snd 1E 64
Mullen Rd. NE28: W'snd 1E 64
Mull Gro. NE32: Jar 3E 86
Mullin Cl. DH7: Bearp 1D 164
Muncaster M. SR8: Pet 2J 181
Mundella Ter. NE6: Heat 1P 5 (6K 63)
Mundell St. DH9: Stly 5E 124
Mundle Av. NE21: W Mill 1C 96
Mundles La. NE36: E Bol 7K 87
Municipal Ter. NE37: Wash 2H 115
Munslow Rd. SR3: E Her 1J 131
Muriel St. DH9: Stly 6E 124
Murphy Gro. SR2: Ryh 2G 133
Murray Av. DH4: Hou S 1A 144
Murray Ct. DH2: Ches S 6K 127
DH8: B'hill 4F 121
Murrayfield NE23: Seg 1D 36
SR3: Silk 3B 132
Murrayfield Dr. DH7: B'don 2C 174
Murrayfield Rd. NE5: Blak 3K 61
Murrayfields NE27: Shir 3H 47
Murray Gdns. NE11: Dun 7C 82
Murray Pk. DH9: Stly 2F 125
Murray Pl. DH2: Ches S 6K 127
Murray Rd. DH2: Ches S 6K 127
NE28: W'snd 2K 65
Murray St. NE21: Blay 3C 80
SR8: Hord 6E 172
Murray Ter. DH9: Dip 1G 123
Murston Av. NE23: Cra 7A 22
Murtagh Diamond Ho.
NE34: S Shi 1J 87
MURTON
NE27 2B 48
SR7 7F 147
Murton Ho. NE1: Newc T 6F 4
NE29: N Shi 3C 48
Murton La. DH5: Eas L 2J 157
NE27: Mur, Shir 3A 48
NE29: N Shi 2C 48
Murton M. SR7: Mur 7D 146
Murton St. NE13: Ki Pk 4K 43
SR1: Sund 5K 7 (2G 119)
SR7: Mur 1F 159
Muscott Gro. NE15: Scot 7G 61
Musgrave Gdns. DH1: Dur 2E 166
(not continuous)
Musgrave Rd. NE9: Low F 1H 99
Musgrave Ter. NE6: Walk 7C 64
NE10: Pel 5E 84
NE38: Wash 2H 115
Muswell Hill NE15: Scot 1G 81
Mutual St. NE28: W'snd 4F 65
Mylord Cres. NE12: Kil 6K 35
Myra Av. TS27: Hes 4E 182
Myre Hall DH5: Hou S 2E 144
Myrella Cres. SR2: Sund 6E 118
Myreside Pl. NE12: Longb 5K 45
Myrtle Av. NE11: Dun 6B 82
NE9: Whit 5H 89
Myrtle Cres. NE12: Longb 3B 46
Myrtle Gro. NE2: Jes 3G 63
NE9: Low F 2H 99
NE16: Burn 2K 109

Myrtle Gro. NE28: W'snd 4H 65
NE34: S Shi 2B 88
Myrtles DH2: Ches S 4K 127
Myrtle St. NE63: Ash 3B 12

N

Nafferton Pl. NE5: Fen 5J 61
Nailor's Bank NE8: Gate 7L 5 (2J 83)
Nailsworth Cl. NE35: Bol C 4E 86
Nairn Cl. DH3: Bir 7B 114
NE37: Wash 5G 101
SR4: Sund 4K 117
Nairn Rd. NE23: Cra 3K 25
Nairn St. NE32: Jar 3E 86
Naisbitt Av. SR8: Hord 4C 172
Namco Fun Scape 4J 81
Nansen Cl. NE5: West 3F 61
Nansen St. DH8: Cons 6J 121
Napier Cl. DH3: Ches S 1B 128
Napier Ct. NE16: Whi 3H 97
Napier Rd. NE16: Swa 5G 81
SR7: S'hm 2J 147
Napier St. NE2: Newc T 3J 5 (7H 63)
NE32: Jar 6B 66
(not continuous)
NE33: S Shi 7H 67
Napier Way NE21: Blay 4E 80
Napoleon Cl. SR2: Ryh 2H 133
Narvik Way NE29: N Shi 7B 48
Nash Av. NE34: S Shi 3K 87
Nater's Bank *NE30: N Shi 7J 49*
(off Union Quay)
Naters St. NE26: Whit B 7J 39
National Glass Cen. 7G 105
Natley Av. NE36: E Bol 7A 88
Nattress Ter. TS28: Win 5F 181
Navan Cl. NE62: W Sle 7B 12
Navenby Cl. NE3: Gos 4F 45
SR7: S'hm 1J 147
Naworth Av. NE30: Cull 3G 49
Naworth Ct. SR8: Pet 2K 181
Naworth Dr. NE5: West 2E 60
Naworth Ter. NE32: Jar 2D 86
Nawton Av. SR5: Monkw 5E 104
Nayland Rd. NE23: Cra 3J 25
Naylor Av. NE21: W Mill 1C 96
Naylor Ct. NE21: Blay 2E 80
Naylor Pl. NE26: Sea S 3B 28
Nazareth M. NE2: Newc T 1K 5 (5H 63)
Neale St. DH9: Ann P 5A 124
DH9: Tant 6B 110
NE42: Pru 3F 77
SR6: Ful 4F 105
Neale Ter. DH3: Bir 4A 114
Neale Wlk. NE3: Ken 2A 62
Nearlane Cl. NE13: Sea B 3E 34
Neasdon Cres. NE30: Cull 3H 49
Neasham Rd. SR7: S'hm 1J 147
NEDDERTON 1C 20
Nedderton Cl. NE5: Cha P 1B 60
Needham Pl. NE23: Cra 3K 25
Neighbourhood Cen., The NE5: West 1G 61
Neil Cres. DH6: Quar H 6D 178
Neill Dr. NE16: Sun 5H 97
Neilson Rd. NE10: Gate 10P 5 (4K 83)
Neil St. DH5: Eas L 2J 157
Nellie Gormley Ho. NE12: Kil 2K 45
Nell Ter. NE39: Row G 6G 95
Nelson Av. NE3: Gos 7C 44
NE23: Nel V 2G 25
NE33: S Shi 2A 68
Nelson Cl. NE63: Ash 5C 12
SR2: Sund 6K 7 (3G 119)
SR8: Hord 5E 172
(not continuous)
Nelson Cres. NE29: N Shi 2D 66
Nelson Dr. NE23: Cra, Nel V 3F 25
Nelson Ho. NE30: Tyne 5K 49
Nelson Ind. Est. NE23: Nel V 1G 25
Nelson Pk. NE23: Nel V 1G 25
Nelson Pk. E. NE23: Nel V 1H 25
Nelson Pk. Networkcentre
NE23: Nel V 1G 25
Nelson Pk. W. NE23: Nel V 1F 25
Nelson Rd. NE6: Walk 2F 85
NE23: Nel V 1F 25
NE25: Well 6B 38
NE62: Stake 1J 17
Nelson St. DH3: Ches S 7A 128
DH5: Hett H 7G 145
DH8: Cons 7H 121
DH8: Lead 5A 122
NE1: Newc T 5F 4 (1F 83)
NE8: Gate 9H 5 (3G 83)
NE29: N Shi 7G 49
NE33: S Shi 2J 67
NE38: Wash 4J 115
NE40: G'sde 5D 78
SR2: Ryh 2H 133
SR7: S'hm 2K 147
Nelson Ter. DH6: S'burn 3A 168
NE17: C'wl 7K 93
NE29: N Shi 2D 66
NELSON VILLAGE 2G 25
Nelson Way NE23: Nel V 7F 21
Nene Ct. NE37: Wash 7J 101
Nent Gro. NE46: Hex 2E 70
Nenthead Cl. DH3: Gt Lum 3F 143
Nep Bus. Pk. NE38: Wash 5A 116
Neptune Ct. NE29: N Shi 7B 48
Neptune Rd. NE15: Lem 6E 60
NE28: W'snd 5F 65
Neptune Way SR8: Eas 7A 160
Nesbit Rd. SR8: Pet 7C 172
Nesburn Rd. SR4: Sund 4C 118
Nesham Pl. DH5: Hou S 2E 144
Nesham St. NE4: Elsw 3C 82
Nesham Ter. SR1: Sund 1H 119
Ness Ct. NE21: Winl 4A 80
Neston Ct. NE3: Ken 2K 61
Nest Rd. NE10: Fell 4B 84
Netherburn Rd. SR5: Monkw 5E 104
Netherby Ct. NE5: Fen 5K 61
Netherby Dr. NE5: Fen 5J 61
Netherdale NE22: Bed 7F 17
Nether Farm Rd. NE10: Pel 5D 84
Nether Riggs NE22: Bed 1H 21
Netherton NE12: Kil 6A 36
Netherton Av. NE29: N Shi 4D 48
Netherton Cl. DH2: Ches S 7H 127
DH7: Lang P 5H 151
Netherton Gdns. NE13: W Op 5D 34
Netherton Gro. NE29: N Shi 5D 48
Netherton La. NE22: Bed 6E 16
NETHERTON PARK 3A 20
Netherwitton Way NE3: Gos 3D 44
Nettleham Rd. SR5: Monkw 5E 104
Nettles La. SR3: Silk 3D 132
NETTLESWORTH 6H 141
Nettlesworth Av. NE13: Haz 2A 44
Network Bus. Cen. NE63: Ash 2K 11
Neville Ct. NE37: Wash 7J 101
Neville Cres. DH3: Bir 2A 114
Nevilledale Ter. DH1: Dur 4A 6
Neville Dene DH1: Dur 3H 165
Neville Ho. DH1: Dur 4J 165
Neville Rd. NE15: Lem 6D 60
SR4: Sund 1B 118
SR8: Pet 5A 172
Nevilles Ct. DH1: Dur 3J 165
NEVILLE'S CROSS 4J 165
Neville's Cross Bank DH1: Dur 5G 165
Neville's Cross Rd. NE31: Heb 1K 85
Neville's Cross Vs. DH1: Dur 4J 165
Neville Sq. DH1: Dur 5J 165
Neville St. DH1: Dur 3B 6 (3A 166)
NE1: Newc T 7E 4 (2E 82)
Neville Ter. *DH1: Dur 2J 165*
(off Redhills La.)
DH6: Bowb 5J 177
Neville Wlk. *NE37: Wash 6K 101*
(off Marlborough Rd.)
Nevill Rd. NE43: Pains 7K 75
Nevinson Av. NE34: S Shi 3K 87
Nevis Cl. NE26: Whit B 3E 38
Nevis Ct. NE26: Whit B 3E 38
Nevis Gro. NE36: W Bol 7H 87
Nevis Way NE26: Whit B 4E 38
New Acres DH7: Ush M 2C 164
New Acres Rd. DH9: Stly 7E 124
Newark Cl. NE22: Bed 6F 17
SR8: Pet 5A 172
(not continuous)
Newark Cres. SR7: S'hm 1J 147
Newark Dr. SR6: Whit 6H 89
Newark Sq. NE29: N Shi 1F 67
Newarth Cl. NE15: Lem 6E 60
Newbank Wlk. NE21: Winl 5A 80
Newbell Ct. DH8: Cons 6K 121
Newbiggen La. DH7: Lan 6D 136
NEWBIGGIN
DH7 6F 137
NE46 7F 71
NEWBIGGIN-BY-THE-SEA 2J 13
Newbiggin-by-the-Sea Heritage Vis. Cen.
Newbiggin-by-the-Sea 3J 13
Newbiggin Hall Cen. *NE5: West 2G 61*
(off Trevelyan Dr.)
NEWBIGGIN HALL ESTATE 7G 43
Newbiggin La. NE5: West 1F 61
Newbiggin Maritime Cen. 2K 13
Newbiggin Rd. NE63: Ash, N Sea 6B 12
Newbiggin Sports & Community Cen.
2H 13
New Blackett St. DH9: Ann P 4J 123
Newbold Av. SR5: Monkw 5E 104
Newbold St. NE6: Walk 1B 84
Newbolt Ct. NE8: Gate 4J 83
NEWBOTTLE 6D 130
Newbottle La. DH4: Hou S 3K 143
Newbottle St. DH4: Hou S 7D 130
NEW BRANCEPETH 5B 164
Newbridge Av. SR5: Monkw 5E 104
Newbridge Bank DH3: Lam P 4D 128
Newbridge Banks DH2: Gra V 5C 126
New Bridge St. NE1: Newc T 5H 5 (1G 83)
New Bridge St. W.
NE1: Newc T 5F 4 (1F 83)
Newbrough Cres. NE2: Jes 3G 63
Newburgh Av. NE25: Sea D 1G 37
NEWBURN 6K 59
Newburn Activity Cen. 5J 59
Newburn Av. DH6: Bowb 4H 177
SR5: Monkw 5E 104
Newburn Bri. Rd. NE15: Blay 7J 59
NE21: Blay 7J 59
Newburn Ct. NE33: S Shi 4K 67
Newburn Cres. DH4: Hou S 1D 144
Newburn Hall Motor Mus. 5K 59
Newburn Haugh Ind. Est.
NE15: Lem 7B 60
Newburn Ind. Est. NE15: Lem 7A 60
Newburn La. End NE15: Thro 3H 59
Newburn Riverside Ind. Pk.
NE15: Lem 2C 80
Newburn Rd. DH9: Stly 1F 125
NE15: Newb, Thro 3H 59
Newbury NE12: Kil 7B 36
Newbury Av. NE8: Gate 6F 83
(not continuous)
Newbury Cl. NE15: Lem 6D 60
Newbury Dr. DH8: Shot B 2G 121
Newbury St. NE33: S Shi 6K 67
SR5: Ful 4E 104
Newby Cl. NE22: Bed 5A 18
Newby La. DH6: H Pitt 6C 156
Newby Pl. NE9: Low F 3K 99
Newcastle Arts Cen. 7E 4 (1F 83)
Newcastle Av. SR8: Hord 4D 172
Newcastle Bank DH3: Bir 1K 113
Newcastle Bus. Pk.
NE4: Elsw 10A 4 (3B 82)
NE4: Newc T 3C 82
Newcastle City Hall 3G 4 (7G 63)
Newcastle City Heliport 10B 4 (3D 82)
Newcastle Climbing Cen. 7A 64
Newcastle Falcons RUFC 5H 43
Newcastle Football Academy 1C 64
Newcastle Football Cen. 7H 61
Newcastle Great Park (Park & Ride) 1B 44
NEWCASTLE INTERNATIONAL AIRPORT
7D 32
Newcastle Racecourse 2F 45
Newcastle Racecourse Exhibition Cen.
1F 45
Newcastle RC Cathedral Church of St Mary
7D 4 (2F 83)
Newcastle Rd. DH1: Dur 7H 153
DH3: Bir 2A 114
DH3: Ches S 5A 128
DH4: Hou S 2C 144
NE24: News 5G 23
NE34: S Shi 2E 86
(not continuous)
NE36: W Bol 7J 85
NE45: Corb 1F 73
SR5: Ful, Monkw 2C 104
Newcastle Shop. Pk. NE6: Walk 6A 64
Newcastle Stadium (Speedway) 7B 64
Newcastle Station (Rail) 7E 4 (2F 83)
Newcastle St. NE29: N Shi 7G 49
Newcastle Ter. DH1: Dur 5J 153
NE30: Tyne 5K 49
Newcastle United FC 4C 4 (7E 62)
Newcastle University
Campus for Ageing & Vitality 7B 62
Claremont Road 1D 4 (6E 62)
Gallowgate 5C 4 (1E 82)
Queen Victoria Road 2E 4 (6F 63)
NEWCASTLE UPON TYNE 5E 4 (1F 83)
Newcastle Western By-Pass
NE3: Haz, Ken 3B 44
NE5: Blak 1J 61
NE15: Den M, Lem, Scot 7E 60
New Cotts. NE62: Chop 1E 16
New Cross Row TS28: Win 5F 181
NEW DELAVAL 6F 23
Newdene Wlk. NE15: Lem 6D 60
New Dr. SR7: S'hm 1K 147
New Durham Courtyard DH1: Dur 2E 166
New Durham Rd. DH9: Ann P 6A 124
SR2: Sund 5F 7 (2D 118)
New Elvet DH1: Dur 2D 6 (3B 166)
NEWFIELD 4E 126
Newfield Rd. DH2: Newf 4E 126
Newfield Ter. DH2: Newf 4E 126
Newfield Wlk. NE16: Whi 1G 97
New Front St. DH9: Ann P 5K 123
DH9: Tan L 7D 110
Newgate Shopping Cen.
NE1: Newc T 6E 4 (1F 83)
Newgate St. NE1: Newc T 5E 4 (1F 83)
NE61: Mor 6F 9
New George St. NE33: S Shi 4J 67
New Grange Ter. DH2: P Fel 5F 127
New Green St. NE33: S Shi 4J 67
Newham Av. NE13: Haz 7C 34
NEW HARTLEY 4H 27
Newhaven Av. SR5: Monkw 5E 104
NEW HERRINGTON 3D 130
New Herrington Ind. Est. DH4: New H 3D 130
Newhouse Av. DH7: Esh W 3D 162
Newhouse Rd. DH7: Esh W 3D 162
Newington Ct. NE37: Wash 7G 101
SR5: Monkw 6E 104
Newington Dr. NE29: N Shi 3F 49
Newington Rd. NE2: Newc T 2K 5 (6H 63)
(not continuous)
NE6: Heat 2L 5 (6J 63)
New King St. NE64: Newb S 2K 13
NEW KYO 5B 124
NEW LAMBTON 7J 129
Newland Ct. NE34: S Shi 1J 87
NEWLANDS 5E 106
Newlands DH8: B'hill 4F 121
NE30: Cull 2G 49
Newlands Av. NE3: Gos 3E 44
NE24: Bly 4H 23
NE25: Monks 1D 48
SR3: Sund 5D 118
Newlands Pl. NE24: Bly 4H 23
Newlands Rd. DH1: Carr 7G 155
NE2: Jes 2F 63
NE24: Bly 4H 23
Newlands Rd. E. SR7: S'hm 2K 147
Newlands Rd. W. SR7: S'hm 2J 147
Newlyn Cres. NE29: N Shi 7E 48
Newlyn Dr. NE23: Cra 3J 25
NE32: Jar 7D 66
Newlyn Rd. NE3: Ken 7A 44
Newman La. NE38: Wash 5J 115
Newman Pl. NE8: Gate 6J 83
Newman Ter. NE8: Gate 6J 83
Newmarch St. NE32: Jar 6A 66
New Market NE61: Mor 7F 9
Newmarket St. DH8: Cons 6H 121
Newmarket Wlk. NE33: S Shi 3J 67
New Mill, The NE4: Elsw 1C 82
New Mills NE4: Newc T 3A 4 (7D 62)
New Mills Ho. NE4: Newc T 3A 4
Newminster Abbey (remains of) 7D 8
Newminster Cl. DH4: Hou S 7B 130
Newminster Pl. NE61: Mor 5F 9
Newminster Rd. NE4: Fen 7J 61
Newminster Ter. NE61: Mor 6E 8
Newmin Way NE16: Whi 2F 97
New Moor Cl. NE63: Ash 3H 11
New Phoenix Yd. NE61: Mor 7G 9
Newport Gro. SR3: New S 1C 132
New Quay NE29: N Shi 1H 67
Newquay Gdns. NE9: Low F 5H 99
New Queen St. NE64: Newb S 2J 13
New Rainton St. *DH4: Pen 1B 130*
(off Rainton St.)
New Redheugh Bri. Rd.
NE1: Newc T 9D 4 (3E 82)
NE8: Gate 9D 4 (3F 83)
NEW RIDLEY 4H 91
New Ridley Rd. NE43: B'ley, Pains 7K 75
Newriggs NE38: Wash 6H 115
(not continuous)
New Rd. DH6: Ludw, Thor 5J 169
DH9: Beam 2B 126
NE10: Ward 1F 101
NE11: T Vall 1D 98
NE16: Burn 1A 110
NE35: Bol C 6F 87
NE36: E Bol 6F 87
NE38: Wash 1G 129
(not continuous)
New Row TS28: Win 6F 181
New Sandridge *NE64: Newb S 2K 13*
(off Sandridge)
NEWSHAM 5F 23
Newsham Cl. NE5: Cha P 1B 60
Newsham Rd. NE24: Bly 4G 23
NEW SILKSWORTH 2B 132
New South Ter. DH3: Bir 4B 114
Newstead Ct. NE38: Wash 3G 115
Newstead Ri. DH8: Shot B 4E 120
Newstead Rd. DH4: Hou S 7C 130
NE13: Ki Pk 4A 44
Newsteads Cl. NE25: Monks 6D 38
Newsteads Dr. NE25: Monks 6C 38
Newsteads Farm Cotts. NE25: Monks 7C 38
Newstead Sq. SR3: Silk 3C 132
New Strangford Rd. SR7: S'hm 2K 147
New St. DH1: Dur 2A 6 (2K 165)
DH6: S'burn 3A 168
SR4: Sund 2G 117
NEWTON 7D 54
Newton Av. NE28: W'snd 2K 65
NE30: Cull 1H 49
Newton Cl. NE15: Lem 6E 60
Newton Dr. DH1: Dur 6K 153
Newton Gth. DH7: Wit G 3C 152
Newton Gro. NE34: S Shi 1G 87
NEWTON HALL
DH1 4A 154
NE43 6D 54
Newton Hall NE7: H Hea 3K 63
Newton Ho. NE4: Newc T 3B 4
Newtonmore SR3: Silk 4C 132
Newton Pl. NE7: H Hea 3K 63
Newton Rd. NE7: H Hea 2J 63
Newton St. DH7: Wit G 3C 152
NE8: Gate 6F 83
NE11: Dun 5B 82
Newton Ter. NE43: Mic 5A 76
Newton Vs. DH6: Coxh 7J 177
NEW TOWN
DH5 2F 145
NE35 6F 87
Newtown Ind. Est. DH3: Bir 6A 114
Newtown Vs. DH7: Sac 7E 140
New Villas NE2: Newc T 1A 4
New Watling St. DH8: Lead 5A 122
NEW YORK 3B 48
New York By-Pass NE29: N Shi 3B 48
New York Ind. Pk. NE27: Shir 3A 48
(not continuous)
New York Rd. NE27: Back, Shir 1J 47
NE27: Shir 2J 47
(not continuous)
NE29: N Shi, Shir 3A 48
New York Way NE27: Shir 4A 48
Nicholas Av. SR6: Whit 6H 89
Nicholas St. DH5: Hett H 5H 145
Nichol Ct. NE4: Benw 1K 81
Nicholson Cl. SR1: Sund 2G 119
Nicholsons Bldgs. DH9: Dip 6J 109
Nicholson's Ter. DH9: Beam 1B 126
Nicholson Ter. NE12: Kil 3C 46
Nichol St. NE4: Benw 1K 81
Nichol St. E. *NE4: Benw 1K 81*
(off Adelaide Ter.)
Nickleby Chare DH1: Dur 5K 165
Nidderdale Av. DH5: Hett H 1F 157
Nidderdale Cl. NE24: Cow 1E 22
Nidsdale Av. NE6: Walk 6E 64
Nightingale Pl. DH9: Stly 4H 125
Nile Cl. NE15: Lem 5C 60
Nile Ct. NE8: Gate 5J 83
Nile St. DH8: Cons 7H 121
NE29: N Shi 6G 49
NE33: S Shi 3H 67
SR1: Sund 3K 7 (1G 119)
Nilverton Av. SR2: Sund 5F 119

Nimbus Ct. SR3: Silk 3C 132
Nine Lands DH4: Hou S 2C 144
Nine Pins NE8: Gate 7F 83
NE9: Low F 1G 99
Ninian Ter. DH9: Dip 1G 123
Ninth Av. DH2: Ches S 6K 127
NE6: Heat 1P 5 (5A 64)
NE11: T Vall 4F 99
NE24: Bly 3H 23
NE61: Mor 1H 15
Ninth Av. E. NE11: T Vall 4F 99
Ninth Row NE63: Ash 3J 11
Ninth St. SR8: Hord 5E 172
TS27: B Col 1H 183
Nissan Way SR5: Sund 1B 116
Nithdale Cl. NE6: Walk 5F 65
Nixon Ter. NE21: Winl 5B 80
NE24: Bly 3K 23
Noble Gdns. NE34: S Shi 2F 87
Noble's Bank Rd. SR2: Sund 3H 119
Noble St. NE4: Elsw 3B 82
NE10: Fell 5B 84
SR2: Sund 3H 119
SR8: Eas C 6C 160
Noble St. Ind. Est. NE4: Elsw 3B 82
Noble Ter. NE61: Mor 7G 9
SR2: Sund 3H 119
Noel Av. NE21: W Mill 1C 96
Noel St. DH9: Stly 2H 125
Noel Ter. NE10: Fell 5A 84
NE21: W Mill 7D 80
Noirmont Way SR3: Silk 3A 132
Nook, The NE25: Monks 7F 39
NE29: N Shi 7F 49
Nookside SR4: Sund 4J 117
Nookside Ct. SR4: Sund 4J 117
NO PLACE 2K 125
Nora St. NE34: S Shi 1J 87
SR4: Sund 4B 118
Norburn La. DH7: Wit G 7B 140
Norburn Pk. DH7: Wit G 2C 152
Norbury Gro. NE6: Byke, Walk 1B 84
Nordale Way NE24: Cow 1E 22
Norfolk Av. DH3: Bir 7A 114
SR3: New S 1B 132
Norfolk Cl. NE63: Ash 3J 11
SR7: S'hm 1J 147
Norfolk Dr. NE37: Wash 5H 101
Norfolk Gdns. NE28: W'snd 1J 65
Norfolk M. NE30: N Shi 6G 49
Norfolk Pl. DH3: Bir 7B 114
Norfolk Rd. DH8: C'sde 3D 134
NE34: S Shi 6E 68
Norfolk Sq. NE6: Byke 4P 5 (7K 63)
Norfolk St. DH5: Hett H 6F 145
NE30: N Shi 6H 49
SR1: Sund 3K 7 (1F 119)
Norfolk Wlk. SR8: Pet 4A 172
Norfolk Way NE15: Lem 6E 60
Norham Av. Nth. NE34: S Shi 5C 68
Norham Av. Sth. NE34: S Shi 5C 68
Norham Cl. NE13: W Op 6C 34
NE24: Bly 2G 23
Norham Ct. DH4: Hou S 1H 143
NE38: Wash 4F 115
Norham Dr. NE5: West 2E 60
NE61: Hep, Mor 2H 15
SR8: Pet 2A 182
Norham Gdns. NE62: Stake 6J 11
Norham Pl. NE2: Jes 4G 63
Norham Rd. DH1: Dur 4B 154
NE3: Gos 6D 44
NE26: Whit B 6F 39
NE29: N Shi 6C 48
NE63: Ash 5B 12
Norham Rd. Nth. NE29: N Shi 4A 48
Norham Ter. NE21: Winl 4B 80
NE32: Jar 2B 86
Norhurst NE16: Whi 2E 96
Norley Av. SR5: Monkw 5E 104
Norma Cres. NE26: Whit B 7J 39
Norman Av. SR3: New S 2D 132
Normanby Cl. SR7: S'hm 1J 147
Normanby Ct. SR6: Roker 6H 105
Normandy Cres. DH5: Hou S 2F 145
Norman Rd. NE39: Row G 6J 95
Norman Ter. DH6: H Pitt 6C 156
DH8: Cons 6G 121
NE28: W'snd 3B 66
NE61: Mor 7G 9
Normanton Ter. NE4: Elsw 1C 82
Normount Av. NE4: Benw 1A 82
Normount Gdns. NE4: Benw 1A 82
Normount Rd. NE4: Benw 1A 82
Northampton Rd. SR8: Pet 4A 172
Northamptonshire Dr. DH1: Carr 1H 167
North App. DH2: Ches S 5K 127
North Av. NE3: Gos 1D 62
NE5: West 3F 61
NE12: Longb 6B 46
NE34: S Shi 7B 68
NE37: Wash 6G 101
NE62: Chop 1G 17
SR8: Hord 5D 172
North Bailey DH1: Dur 4C 6 (3A 166)
Nth. Balkwell Farm Ind. Est.
NE29: N Shi 5B 48
Nth. Bank Ct. SR5: S'wck 5D 104
NORTH BLYTH 7J 19
Northbourne Av. NE61: Mor 5F 9
Northbourne Rd. NE32: Jar 7A 66
Northbourne St. NE4: Elsw 2B 82
NE8: Gate 6H 83
Nth. Brancepeth Cl.
DH7: Lang M 6G 165
Nth. Brancepeth Ter.
DH7: Lang M 6G 165
North Bri. St. SR5: Monkw 1J 7 (7F 105)
North Burns DH3: Ches S 5A 128
Northburn Sports & Community Cen. 1H 25
Nth. Church St. NE30: N Shi 6H 49
North Cliff SR6: Roker 4H 105
North Cl. NE6: Byke 2P 5 (6A 64)
NE34: S Shi 7B 68
NE40: Ryton 1G 79
NORTH COMMON 2D 14
Nth. Coronation St. SR7: Mur 7F 147
Northcote NE16: Whi 2G 97
Northcote Av. NE5: Cha P 4C 60
NE25: Monks 7D 38
SR1: Sund 2G 119
Northcote St. NE4: Newc T 5A 4 (1C 82)
NE33: S Shi 5K 67
Northcott Gdns. NE23: Seg 2C 36
North Cres. DH1: Dur 1J 165
NE38: Wash 7F 115
NE62: Stake 7K 11
SR8: Eas 1K 171
North Cft. NE12: Longb 5C 46
Nth. Cross St. DH8: Lead 5A 122
NE3: Gos 7E 44
North Dene DH3: Bir 1A 114
Northdene Av. SR7: S'hm 2B 148
North Dock SR6: Roker 6H 105
North Dr. NE31: Heb 1G 85
NE38: Ches S, Wash 2B 128
SR6: Clead 5A 88
Nth. Durham St. SR1: Sund 1G 119
Nth. Eastern Ct. NE11: Dun 7A 82
North East Fruit & Vegetable Mkt.
NE11: T Vall 1F 99
North E. Ind. Est. SR8: Pet 3B 172
North East Land, Air & Sea Museums
4E 102
NORTH END 1J 165
North End DH1: Dur 1J 165
DH7: B'don 7C 164
Northern Gallery for Contemporay Art
4K 7
Northern Prom. NE26: Whit B 3G 39
Northern Rock Foundation Gallery 4K 63
Northern Stage 2F 4 (6F 63)
Northern Ter. NE23: Dud 2J 35
Northern Way SR5: S'wck 5C 104
North Farm NE11: Lame 6G 99
NE22: Nedd 1C 20
NE61: Peg 4A 10
Nth. Farm Av. SR4: Sund 6H 117
Nth. Farm Ct. NE15: Thro 3G 59
Nth. Farm Est. NE22: Nedd 7C 16
Nth. Farm Rd. NE31: Heb 1H 85
Northfield NE22: E Sle 4F 19
Northfield Cl. NE16: Whi 2F 97
Northfield Dr. NE12: Kil 2K 45
SR4: Sund 6H 117
Northfield Gdns. NE34: S Shi 5B 68
Northfield Rd. NE3: Gos 1D 62
NE33: S Shi 4B 68
Northfields Cl. NE6: Byke 6A 64
Northfields Ho. *NE6: Byke 6A 64*
(off North Vw.)
Northfield Vw. DH8: Cons 6J 121
Northgate DH9: Ann P 6K 123
NE12: Kil 7B 36
North Grange NE20: Pon 3J 31
North Gro. NE40: Ryton 1H 79
SR6: Roker 4G 105
North Guards SR6: Whit 6G 89
North Hall Rd. SR4: Sund 4K 117
North Haven SR7: S'hm 2K 147
North Holm DH8: Lead 5A 122
NORTH HYLTON 1G 117
Nth. Hylton Rd. SR5: S'wck, Sund 5K 103
Nth. Hylton Rd. Ind. Est.
SR5: Sund 5K 103
Nth. Jesmond Av. NE2: Jes 2G 63
Nth. King St. NE30: N Shi 6H 49
Northland Cl. SR4: Sund 6H 117
Northlands DH3: Ches S 4A 128
NE21: Winl 5B 80
NE30: Cull 3H 49
Northlands Rd. NE61: Mor 5F 9
North La. DH5: Hett H 4A 146
NE36: E Bol 7J 87
NORTHLEA 2J 147
Northlea NE15: Lem 5E 60
Northlea Rd. SR7: S'hm 2J 147
North Leech NE61: Mor 5D 8
North Leigh DH9: Tan L 7D 110
NORTH LODGE 2A 128
North Lodge DH3: Ches S 2A 128
North Magdalene DH8: M'sly 7K 107
Nth. Main Ct. NE33: S Shi 2A 68
Nth. Mason Lodge NE13: Din 3H 33
North Mdw. NE42: O'ham 1D 76
Nth. Milburn St. SR4: Sund 1D 118
Nth. Moor Cotts. SR3: Sund 7A 118
Nth. Moor La.
SR3: E Her, New S, Sund 7A 118
Nth. Moor Rd. SR3: Sund 7A 118
Northmoor Rd. NE6: Walk 5C 64
Nth. Moor St. SR1: Sund 7H 105
Nth. Nelson Ind. Est. NE23: Nel V 7G 21
Northolt Av. NE23: Cra 3K 25
North Pde. NE26: Whit B 6H 39
NE29: N Shi 3E 66
NE62: Chop 2G 17
North Pk. Av. NE13: Haz 1A 44
Nth. Railway St. SR7: S'hm 3B 148
Nth. Ravensworth St. SR4: Sund 1D 118
North Ridge NE22: Bed 7G 17
(Forster Av.)
NE22: Bed 7F 17
(Meadowdale Cres.)
NE25: Monks 6C 38
North Rd. DH1: Dur 1A 6 (1K 165)
DH3: Ches S 2A 128
DH5: Hett H, Hou S 4D 144
DH9: Ann P, Dip 2J 123
NE13: W Op 5E 34
NE20: Pon 2J 31
NE28: W'snd 3F 65
NE29: N Shi 4F 49
NE35: Bol C 5E 86
NE35: Bol C, W Bol 6F 87
NE36: E Bol 7J 87
(not continuous)
NE36: W Bol 6F 87
SR7: S'hm 1B 148
TS28: Win 4F 181
North Rd. E. TS28: Win 6F 181
North Rd. Head DH1: Dur 2A 6
North Rd. W. TS28: Win 6F 181
North Row NE42: Pru 4C 76
Nth. Sands Bus. Cen. SR6: Roker 7G 105
NORTH SEATON 5E 12
NORTH SEATON COLLIERY 7E 12
Nth. Seaton Ind. Est.
NE63: N Sea 6D 12
Nth. Seaton Rd. NE63: Ash 3B 12
NE64: Newb S 4H 13
NORTH SHIELDS 7G 49
North Shields Station (Metro) 7G 49
North Side DH6: Shad 6E 168
NE8: Gate 5D 82
Northside DH3: Bir 2B 114
(not continuous)
Northside Pl. NE25: H'wll 1J 37
Nth. Stead Dr. DH8: Shot B 4E 120
North St. DH3: Bir 5C 114
DH4: Nbot 5D 130
DH4: W Rai 1K 155
DH5: E Rain 6D 144
DH6: Hett 7C 176
DH8: Cons 7K 121
NE1: Newc T 4F 4 (7F 63)
NE21: Winl 4A 80
NE32: Jar 6B 66
NE33: S Shi 2J 67
SR3: New S 1C 132
SR5: Monkw 6E 104
SR6: Clead 5C 88
TS27: B Col 2H 183
North St. Ct. NE1: Newc T 4G 4
North St. E. NE1: Newc T 4G 4 (7G 63)
North Ter. DH1: Dur 5J 153
DH7: Wit G 3C 152
DH8: Lead 5A 122
DH9: Ann P 4C 124
NE2: Newc T 1D 4 (6E 62)
NE17: C'wl 5K 93
NE27: Shir 3J 47
NE28: W'snd 3H 65
NE46: Hex 2D 70
SR3: New S 1D 132
SR7: S'hm 2B 148
SR8: Eas 1K 171
North Thorn DH9: Stly 2F 125
Nth. Tyne Ind. Est. NE12: Longb 4E 46
North Tyneside Steam Railway 7B 48
Northumberland Av. NE3: Gos 1C 62
NE12: Longb 5B 46
NE22: Bed 7G 17
NE28: W'snd 3K 65
(off Northumberland Ter.)
NE64: Newb S 4H 13
Northumberland Bus. Pk. NE23: Dud 1J 35
Northumberland Bus. Pk. W.
NE23: Dud 1H 35
Northumberland Cl. NE63: Ash 3J 11
Northumberland Club, The 3G 63
Northumberland County Cricket Club
(County Ground) 5H 63
Northumberland Ct. *NE24: Bly 7J 19*
(off Argyle St.)
NE42: Pru 2G 77
NE46: Acomb 3C 50
Northumberland Dock Rd.
NE28: N Shi, W'snd 4C 66
NE29: N Shi 4C 66
Northumberland Gdns. NE2: Jes 5J 63
NE5: Cha P 2B 60
Northumberlandia (Lady of the North, The)
3D 24
NORTHUMBERLAND PARK 1H 47
Northumberland Park Station (Metro)
1H 47
Northumberland Pk. Way NE27: Back 2H 47
Northumberland Pl. DH3: Bir 7B 114
NE1: Newc T 4F 4 (7F 63)
NE30: N Shi 6G 49
SR8: Pet 4K 171
Northumberland Retail Pk.
NE27: Back 1H 47
Northumberland Rd.
NE1: Newc T 4F 4 (7F 63)
NE15: Lem 7C 60
NE40: Ryton 7G 59
Northumberland Sq. NE30: N Shi 6G 49
Northumberland St.
NE1: Newc T 3F 4 (7F 63)
NE8: Gate 5E 82
NE28: W'snd 3G 65
NE30: N Shi 6J 49
SR8: Hord 4D 172
Northumberland Ter.
NE6: Byke 4N 5 (1K 83)
NE28: W'snd 3K 65
NE30: Tyne 5K 49
Northumberland Vs. NE28: W'snd 3J 65
Northumberland Way NE37: Wash 3G 101
NE38: Wash 2J 115
Northumbria Cen. for Enterprise
NE63: Wood 2B 12
Northumbria Ho. NE3: Gos 6E 44
Northumbria Lodge NE5: Fen 4A 62
Northumbrian Rd. NE23: Cra 2J 25
Northumbrian Way NE12: Kil 1K 45
NE29: N Shi 2G 67
Northumbria Pl. DH9: Stly 2H 125
Northumbria University
Coach Lane Campus 7B 46
Falconar Street 4H 5 (7G 63)
Newcastle City Campus 2G 4 (6G 63)
Pandon Building 3H 5 (7G 63)
Northumbria Wlk. NE5: W Dent 4F 61
North Vw. DH1: Dur 2E 166
DH2: Newf 4F 127
DH2: Ous 7G 113
DH4: New L 7J 129
DH5: Eas L 2J 157
DH6: Has 3A 170
(Gloucester Ter.)
DH6: Has 1B 170
(Kestrel La.)
DH6: Ludw 5J 169
DH6: S Hil 3D 168
DH7: Bearp 1C 164
DH7: Lang P 5H 151
DH7: Mead 2E 174
DH8: B'hill 5F 121
DH8: M'sly 7K 107
DH9: Stly 6H 125
NE6: Byke 3N 5 (7K 63)
(not continuous)
NE9: Wrek 4K 99
NE12: Longb 4B 46
NE13: Din 4H 33
NE13: Haz 7C 34
NE16: Whi 7G 81
NE22: Bed 5B 18
NE24: Camb 2G 19
NE26: Whit B 7J 39
NE28: W'snd 3G 65
NE29: N Shi 4F 49
NE30: Cull 7J 39
NE32: Jar 7A 66
NE34: S Shi 5B 68
NE37: Wash 7H 101
NE39: H Spen 4D 94
NE40: C Vale 6C 58
NE40: Ryton 1E 78
NE43: Mic 5A 76
NE46: Hex 2E 70
NE62: Stake 7A 12
NE63: Ash 3A 12
NE64: Newb S 4H 13
SR2: Ryh 3H 133
(off Stockton Rd.)
SR4: Sund 3H 117
SR5: Sund 6J 103
SR6: Ful 4F 105
SR7: Mur 1E 158
SR8: Eas C 6C 160
TS27: Cas E 4K 181
North Vw. Bungs. NE39: H Spen 4D 94
North Vw. E. NE39: Row G 5G 95
North Vw. Ter. DH4: Hou S 2B 144
NE10: Fell 5A 84
NE42: Pru 4D 76
NE43: Pains 7J 75
North Vw. W. NE39: Row G 5F 95
North Vs. NE23: Dud 2J 35
NORTH WALBOTTLE 2B 60
Nth. Walbottle Rd. NE5: Cha P 2A 60
NE15: Walb 3A 60
(not continuous)
Northway NE9: Low F 7K 83
NE15: Thro 2H 59
NE62: Chop 1H 17
North W. Ind. Est. SR8: Pet 5J 171
North W. Radial NE2: Newc T 5D 62
North W. Side NE8: Gate 4D 82
Northwood Ct. SR5: Monkw 5E 104
Northwood Grange DH8: B'hill 4F 121
Northwood Rd. SR7: S'hm 2K 147
Nth. Wylam Vw. NE42: Pru 2G 77
Norton Av. DH6: Bowb 4H 177
SR7: S'hm 1J 147
Norton Cl. DH2: Ches S 1H 141
Norton Rd. SR5: S'wck 4C 104
Norton Way NE15: Lem 7E 60
Norway Av. SR4: Sund 4A 118
Norwich Av. NE13: W Op 6D 34
Norwich Cl. DH3: Gt Lum 3F 143
NE63: N Sea 5E 12
Norwich Rd. DH1: Dur 4B 154
Norwich Way NE23: Cra 3J 25
(not continuous)
NE32: Jar 5B 86
Norwood Av. NE3: Gos 3E 44
NE6: Heat 4K 63
Norwood Ct. NE9: Eigh B 5A 100
NE12: Longb 6B 46
Norwood Cres. NE39: Row G 5K 95
Norwood Gdns. NE9: Low F 6J 83
Norwood Rd. NE11: Fest P 7D 82
NE15: Lem 5D 60
Nottingham Ct. NE22: Bed 6F 17
Nottingham Pl. SR8: Pet 4K 171

Nottinghamshire Rd. DH1: Carr 1G **167**
November Courtyard *NE8: Gate 4D 82*
(off Fall Pass)
Nuffield, Fitness
& Wellbeing Cen. (Gosforth)
Longbenton 5J 45
Number One Ind. Est.
DH8: Cons 5J **121**
Numbers Gth. SR1: Sund 1G **119**
Nuneaton Way NE5: Cha P 1B **60**
Nunn Gdns. NE16: Whi 7G **81**
Nunn St. DH4: S Row 4A **130**
Nunns Way NE21: Blay 1A **80**
Nunnykirk Cl. NE42: O'ham 2C **76**
Nunnywick Way NE13: Ki Pk 4A **44**
Nuns La. NE1: Newc T 6E **4** (1F **83**)
NE8: Gate 10J **5** (3H **83**)
NUNS MOOR 4A **62**
Nuns Moor Cres. NE4: Fen 6A **62**
Nuns Moor Rd. NE4: Fen 6A **62**
Nuns' Row DH1: Dur 1D **166**
Nun St. NE1: Newc T 5E **4** (1F **83**)
Nunthorpe Av. SR2: Sund 7H **119**
Nunwick Gdns. NE29: N Shi 6C **48**
Nunwick Way NE7: H Hea 2B **64**
Nurseries, The SR6: Clead 5C **88**
Nursery, The NE20: Medb 3C **40**
Nursery Cl. SR3: Sund 6C **118**
Nursery Cotts. DH1: Dur 3K **165**
Nursery Ct. NE17: C'wl 2K **107**
Nursery Gdns. NE5: Fen 5H **61**
NE25: Sea D 7H **27**
SR8: Eas 1K **171**
Nursery Grange NE46: Hex 3B **70**
Nursery La. NE10: Fell, Wind N 7A **84**
SR6: Clead 5C **88**
(not continuous)
Nursery M. NE61: Mor 1G **15**
Nursery Pk. NE63: Ash 7C **12**
Nursery Rd. SR3: Sund 6C **118**
Nutley Pl. NE15: Scot 1G **81**
Nye Bevan Ho. NE24: Bly 3K **63**
Nye Dene SR5: Sund 6H **103**

O

O2 Academy Newcastle 6D **4**
Oakapple Cl. NE22: Bed 7H **17**
Oak Av. DH1: Dur 3E **166**
DH4: Hou S 1D **144**
NE11: Dun 7B **82**
NE13: Din 4J **33**
NE34: S Shi 1C **88**
TS27: B Col 2J **183**
Oak Cl. NE46: Hex 3A **70**
Oak Ct. DH7: Sac 7E **140**
Oak Cres. DH2: Kim 6J **141**
SR6: Whit 5J **89**
Oakdale NE22: Nedd 1D **20**
Oakdale Cl. NE15: Lem 7D **60**
Oakdale Rd. DH8: Cons 6J **121**
Oakdale Ter. DH2: Newf 4E **126**
DH3: Ches S 7A **128**
Oakenshaw NE15: Lem 7E **60**
Oakerside Dr. SR8: Pet 7A **172**
OAKERSIDE PARK 1A **182**
Oakey's Rd. DH9: Tan L 1F **125**
Oakfield DH2: Ches S 7H **127**
Oakfield Av. NE16: Whi 1H **97**
Oakfield Cl. NE16: Whi 1H **97**
SR3: E Her 3J **131**
Oakfield Ct. SR3: E Her 3J **131**
Oakfield Cres. DH6: Bowb 4J **177**
Oakfield Dr. NE12: Kil 1D **46**
NE16: Whi 1H **97**
Oakfield Gdns. NE15: Benw 1K **81**
NE28: W'snd 2D **64**
Oakfield Grange NE13: Din 4H **33**
Oakfield Ho. NE24: News 6H **23**
Oakfield La. DH8: C'sde 1E **134**
Oakfield Nth. NE40: Ryton 1F **79**
Oakfield Pk. NE42: Pru 4F **77**
Oakfield Rd. NE3: Gos 2D **62**
NE11: Lob H 1C **98**
NE16: Whi 2F **97**
Oakfields NE16: Burn 1B **110**
Oakfield Ter. NE3: Gos 1D **62**
NE10: Pel 5E **84**
NE12: Kil 3C **46**
NE42: Pru 4F **77**
Oakfield Way NE23: Seg 2D **36**
Oak Grn. Flats DH7: B'don 1D **174**
Oak Gro. NE12: Longb 4B **46**
NE28: W'snd 4H **65**
Oakham Av. NE16: Whi 1F **97**
Oakham Dr. DH1: Carr 6H **155**
Oakham Gdns. NE29: N Shi 1E **66**
Oakhurst Dr. NE3: Ken 2C **62**
Oakhurst Ter. NE12: Longb 6B **46**
Oakland Rd. NE2: Jes 3F **63**
NE25: Monks 7D **38**
Oaklands DH9: Ann P 4K **123**
NE3: Gos 2E **62**
NE16: Swa 5H **81**
NE20: Darr H 7H **31**
NE44: Rid M 7K **73**
(not continuous)
NE46: B End 7F **51**
Oaklands, The *DH6: Whe H 2A 180*
(off Thornley Rd.)
Oaklands Av. NE3: Gos 2E **62**
Oaklands Ct. NE20: Darr H 7H **31**
Oaklands Cres. SR5: S'wck 5B **104**
Oaklands Pl. NE42: Pru 4G **77**
Oaklands Ri. NE44: Rid M 7K **73**
Oaklands Ter. SR4: Sund 3C **118**
Oakland Ter. NE63: Ash 3A **12**
Oak La. DH8: Shot B 2E **120**
Oak Lea DH7: Wit G 2D **152**
Oaklea DH2: Ches S 4J **127**
DH4: S Row 5K **129**
Oak Lea Ter. DH7: Bearp 2E **164**
Oakleigh Gdns. SR6: Clead 4C **88**
Oakley Cl. NE23: Dud 3K **35**
Oakley Dr. NE23: Cra 3A **26**
Oakmere Cl. DH4: Pen 3A **130**
Oakmont Ri. NE63: N Sea 3E **12**
Oakridge NE16: Whi 1F **97**
Oakridge Rd. DH7: Ush M 2C **164**
Oak Rd. NE29: N Shi 5B **48**
SR8: Eas 7A **160**
Oaks, The DH4: Pen 1B **130**
DH7: Esh W 5D **162**
NE24: Cow 1F 23
(off Edendale Av.)
NE40: G'sde 5F **79**
NE46: Hex 3B **70**
SR2: Sund 7K **7** (3G **119**)
Oak Sq. NE8: Gate 5E **82**
Oak St. DH2: Wald 1G **141**
DH4: Hou S 1J **143**
DH7: Lang P 4J **151**
DH8: Cons 7H **121**
NE13: Sea B 3E **34**
NE15: Thro 3H **59**
NE32: Jar 6A **66**
NE38: Wash 4K **115**
NE43: Mic 6A **76**
SR1: Sund 2H **119**
Oaks West, The
SR2: Sund 7K **7** (3F **119**)
Oak Ter. DH2: Pelt 2E **126**
DH7: Edm 3K **139**
DH8: Lead 5B **122**
DH9: Ann P 4J **123**
DH9: Stly 6H **125**
DH9: Tant 6B **110**
NE16: Burn 1C **110**
NE21: Blay 5C **80**
SR7: Mur 7F **147**
SR8: Hord 6E **172**
Oaktree Av. NE6: Walk 4E **64**
Oak Tree Dr. SR3: Silk 2B **132**
Oaktree Gdns. NE25: Monks 1E **48**
(not continuous)
Oak Tree M. DH7: B'don 1D **174**
Oaktree Ter. NE42: Pru 4F **77**
Oakville NE63: N Sea 5E **12**
(not continuous)
Oakway Ct. DH7: Lang M 1G **175**
Oakwell Ct. NE17: Ham 3A **108**
Oakwellgate NE8: Gate 8J **5** (2H **83**)
Oakwell Ter. NE42: Pru 4F **77**
OAKWOOD 5G **51**
Oakwood DH6: S Het 5D **158**
DH7: Lan 1A **150**
DH9: Ann P 5J **123**
NE2: Newc T 1L **5** (5J **63**)
NE10: Hew 2C **100**
(not continuous)
NE31: Heb 6G **65**
NE46: Oakw 5F **51**
Oakwood Av. NE9: Low F 4J **99**
NE13: W Op 6E **34**
NE64: Newb S 2H **13**
Oakwood Bank NE46: B End 6E **50**
Oakwood Cl. DH7: Sac 7E **140**
NE9: Spri 6D **100**
Oakwood Ct. DH9: Ann P 5J **123**
Oakwood Dr. NE13: W Op 1B **44**
Oakwood Gdns. DH8: B'hill 4G **121**
NE11: Lob H 1D **98**
Oakwood Pl. NE5: Blak 4J **61**
Oakwood St. SR2: Sund 6F **7** (3D **118**)
Oakwood Way NE63: N Sea 6F **13**
Oasis Health Club 3B **12**
Oatens Bank NE15: Hor, Welt 1B **56**
Oates St. SR4: Sund 2C **118**
Oatfield Cl. NE63: Ash 5K **11**
Oatlands Rd. SR4: Sund 4A **118**
Oatlands Way DH1: P Me 3A **154**
Oban Av. NE28: W'snd 1K **65**
Oban Ct. NE6: Byke 1A **84**
Oban Gdns. NE6: Byke 1A **84**
Oban St. NE32: Jar 3E **86**
Oban Ter. NE10: Fell 5A **84**
Obelisk La. DH1: Dur 1A **6** (2K **165**)
Oberon Way NE24: Bly 5K **23**
Occupation Rd. NE34: S Shi 3B **88**
(not continuous)
Oceana Bus. Pk. NE28: W'snd 4H **65**
Ocean Beach Pleasure Pk. 1A **68**
Ocean Rd. NE33: S Shi 2J **67**
(not continuous)
SR2: Sund 6H **119**
Ocean Rd. E. SR2: Sund 6J **119**
Ocean Rd. Nth. *SR2: Sund 6H 119*
(off Ocean Rd.)
Ocean Rd. Sth. *SR2: Sund 6H 119*
(off Ocean Rd.)
Ocean Vw. NE26: Whit B 6H **39**
NE64: Newb S 3J **13**
SR2: Ryh 2H **133**
SR8: Hord 5E **172**
TS27: B Col 3J **183**
(not continuous)
Ochiltree Ct. NE26: Sea S 4D **28**
Octavia Cl. NE22: Bed 6G **17**
Octavia Ct. NE28: W'snd 1J **65**
Octavian Way NE11: T Vall 4E **98**
October Courtyard *NE8: Gate 4D 82*
(off Fall Pass)
Odeon Cinema
Gateshead, Metrocentre 4J **81**
Newcastle upon Tyne 6A **48**
Odinel Ct. NE42: Pru 3F **77**
OFFERTON 5E **116**
Offerton Cl. SR4: Sund 2G **117**
Offerton La. SR4: Cox G, Sund 6C **116**
SR4: Sund 2F **117**
Offerton St. SR4: Sund 2C **118**
Office Pl. DH5: Hett H 7G **145**
Office Row DH4: New H 2E **130**
NE23: Dud 6A **36**
NE38: Wash 7E **114**
Office St. DH6: Whe H 2D **180**
SR8: Eas C 7D **160**
Official Ter. DH7: Lan 2B **150**
Off Quay Building, The
NE1: Byke 5M **5** (7J **63**)
Ogden St. SR4: Sund 2C **118**
Ogle Av. NE13: Haz 7C **34**
NE61: Mor 7E **8**
Ogle Dr. NE24: Bly 3G **23**
Ogle Gro. NE32: Jar 3A **86**
O'Hanlon Cres. NE28: W'snd 1E **64**
Oil Mill Rd. NE6: Walk 6F **65**
Okehampton Ct. NE9: Low F 5J **99**
Okehampton Dr. DH4: Nbot 5C **130**
Okehampton Sq. SR5: S'wck 4C **104**
Olaman Wlk. SR8: Pet 4K **171**
OLD BENWELL 1H **81**
Old Blackett St. DH9: Ann P 4J **123**
Old Brewery, The DH4: Hou S 2E **144**
Old Brewery Ct.
NE2: Newc T 1J **5** (6H **63**)
Old Brewery Sq. NE42: Oving 2J **75**
OLD BURDON 7C **132**
OLD CASSOP 1D **178**
Old Course Rd. SR6: Clead 6C **88**
Old Crow Hall La.
NE23: Nel V 3H **25**
Old Customs Ho. NE29: N Shi 1H **67**
Old Dryburn Way DH1: Dur 7J **153**
OLD DURHAM 4D **166**
Old Durham Rd. NE8: Gate 5H **83**
NE9: Low F 5H **83**
Old Eldon Sq.
NE1: Newc T 5E **4** (7F **63**)
Old Eltringham Ct. NE42: Pru 4C **76**
Old Elvet DH1: Dur 3D **6** (3B **166**)
Old Farm Ct. NE16: Sun 5H **97**
Oldfield Cl. SR5: S'wck 4C **104**
Oldfield Rd. NE6: Walk 3D **84**
OLD FOLD 4K **83**
Old Fold Rd. NE10: Gate 10P **5** (4K **83**)
Old Forge, The NE43: Newt 1C **74**
Old Gaol & Border History Mus., The
1D **70**
Old Gardens DH7: B'don 7C **164**
Oldgate NE61: Mor 7F **9**
Oldgate Ct. NE61: Mor 7F **9**
Old George Yd. NE1: Newc T 6F **4**
Old Great Nth. Rd. NE13: Sea B 4A **24**
Old Hall Rd. DH8: Cons 1K **135**
OLD HARTLEY 6E **28**
Old Hartley Cvn. Site NE26: Sea S 6E **28**
Old Main St. NE40: Craw 3C **78**
Old Mill La. DH3: Gt Lum 5D **142**
Old Mill Rd. SR2: Sund 3H **119**
SR5: S'wck 4C **104**
Old Newbiggin La. NE5: West 7F **43**
Old Orchard, The NE20: Pon 4K **31**
NE44: Rid M 6A **74**
Old Pit La. DH1: Dur 4A **154**
Old Pit Ter. DH1: Dur 4A **154**
OLD QUARRINGTON 5A **178**
Old Rectory Cl. DH9: Tanf 4D **110**
Old Sawmill NE61: Mit 7A **8**
Old School Dr. NE15: Lem 5D **60**
Old Station Ct. NE20: Darr H 1G **41**
Oldstead Gdns. SR4: Sund 4A **118**
Oldstone Rd. NE23: E Cram 5C **26**
OLD THORNLEY 4J **179**
Old Vicarage Wlk. NE6: Byke 7A **64**
Old Village Way SR7: Mur 7D **146**
Oldwell Av. NE21: Winl 5B **80**
Old Well La. NE21: Winl 5B **80**
OLD WINGATE 5A **180**
Oley Mdws. DH8: Shot B 2E **120**
Olga Ter. NE39: Row G 6G **95**
Olive Gdns. NE9: Low F 1J **99**
Olive Pl. NE4: Fen 6K **61**
Oliver Av. NE4: Fen 7A **62**
Oliver Ct. NE6: Walk 3D **84**
Oliver Cres. DH3: Bir 2A **114**
DH6: Shad 6E **168**
Oliver Pl. DH1: Dur 5J **165**
Olivers Mill *NE61: Mor 7F 9*
(off Waterside)
Oliver St. DH9: Stly 5E **124**
NE38: Wash 4J **115**
SR7: Mur 2G **159**
SR7: S'hm 2K **147**
Olive St. DH2: Wald 1G **141**
NE33: S Shi 7H **67**
SR1: Sund 5H **7** (2E **118**)
Ollerton Dr. NE15: Thro 3F **59**
Ollerton Gdns. NE10: Wind N 1A **100**
Olney Cl. NE23: Cra 3B **26**
Olwen Dr. NE31: Heb 6H **65**
Olympia Av. NE62: Chop 1G **17**
Olympia Beauty & Fitness
Sunderland 3H **7** (1E **118**)
Olympia Gdns. NE61: Mor 6F **9**
Olympia Hill NE61: Mor 5F **9**
Olympic Fitness Cen.
South Shields 2J 67
(off Fowler St.)
O'Neil Dr. SR8: Pet 7C **172**
Ongar Way NE12: Longb 5K **45**
Onix Ind. Est. NE29: N Shi 6C **48**
Onslow Gdns. NE9: Low F 2H **99**
Onslow St. SR4: Sund 1A **118**
Onslow Ter. DH7: Lang M 7G **165**
Open, The NE1: Newc T 4E **4** (7F **63**)
Oram Cl. NE61: Mor 7H **9**
Orange Gro. NE16: Whi 7J **81**
NE23: Dud 2K **35**
Orchard, The DH1: P Me 4K **153**
DH3: Ches S 5B **128**
NE15: Lem 7D **60**
NE16: Whi 7J **81**
(not continuous)
NE29: N Shi 6G **49**
NE36: E Bol 7J **87**
NE41: Wylam 7J **57**
NE45: Corb 1E **72**
NE46: Acomb 4B **50**
NE61: Hep 3A **16**
Orchard Av. NE39: Row G 6H **95**
NE46: Acomb 4B **50**
Orchard Cl. DH9: W Pelt 3C **126**
NE12: Kil 2D **46**
NE16: Sun 4H **97**
NE39: Row G 7H **95**
NE42: Pru 4F **77**
NE61: Mor 7H **9**
Orchard Ct. NE29: N Shi 4G **49**
NE40: G'sde 5D **78**
NE40: Ryton 1G **79**
SR6: Ful 3E **104**
Orchard Cres. NE45: Corb 1E **72**
Orchard Dene NE39: Row G 6H **95**
Orchard Dr. DH1: Dur 1C **166**
Orchard Gdns. DH3: Ches S 1A **142**
NE9: Low F 3J **99**
NE28: W'snd 2E **64**
SR6: Whit 6G **89**
Orchard Grn. NE5: Ken 1K **61**
Orchard Gro. DH9: Stly 1E **124**
Orchard Hill NE42: Pru 3E **76**
Orchard Holiday Home Pk.
NE45: Corb 2E **72**
Orchard Ho. DH1: Dur 4D **6**
SR2: Sund 5F **119**
Orchardleigh NE15: Lem 7E **60**
Orchard M. NE61: Mor 6F **9**
Orchard Pk. DH3: Bir 4A **114**
Orchard Pl. DH5: Hou S 2E **144**
NE2: Jes 4H **63**
Orchard Ri. NE15: Lem 6B **60**
Orchard Rd. NE16: Whi 7J **81**
NE39: Row G 6H **95**
Orchards, The DH7: B'don 2C **174**
NE24: Cow 1F **23**
Orchard St. DH2: Pelt 2G **127**
DH3: Bir 4A **114**
NE1: Newc T 7F **4** (2F **83**)
SR4: Sund 1B **118**
Orchard Ter. DH3: Ches S 1A **142**
NE15: Lem 7C **60**
NE15: Thro 3H **59**
NE39: Row G 6H **95**
NE46: Acomb 4B **50**
Orchard Vw. NE45: Corb 7D **52**
Orchid Cl. NE34: S Shi 1H **87**
NE63: Ash 5A **12**
Orchid Ct. TS27: B Col 2H **183**
Orchid Gdns. NE34: S Shi 1B **88**
(not continuous)
Orchid M. NE25: Monks 7B **38**
Ord Ct. NE4: Fen 6K **61**
Orde Av. NE28: W'snd 2J **65**
Ordley Cl. NE15: Lem 7E **60**
Ord St. NE4: Newc T 9C **4** (3E **82**)
Ord Ter. NE62: Stake 7K **11**
Oriole Ho. NE12: Longb 5B **46**
Orion Bus. Pk. NE29: N Shi 7B **48**
Orion Way NE29: N Shi 7B **48**
Orkney Dr. SR2: Ryh 1F **133**
Orlando Rd. NE29: N Shi 6E **48**
Ormesby Rd. SR6: Ful 4F **105**
Ormiscraig NE15: Lem 7E **60**
Ormiston NE15: Lem 7E **60**
Ormonde Av. NE15: Den M 7G **61**
Ormonde St. NE32: Jar 6B **66**
SR4: Sund 3B **118**
Ormsby Grn. NE5: Den M 5G **61**
Ormskirk Cl. NE15: Lem 7D **60**
Ormskirk Gro. NE23: Cra 3A **26**
Ormston St. NE23: E Har 6K **21**
ORNSBY HILL 5K **137**
Orpen Av. NE34: S Shi 3J **87**
Orpine Ct. NE63: Ash 5A **12**
Orpington Av. NE6: Walk 6C **64**
Orpington Rd. NE23: Cra 3A **26**
Orr Av. SR3: New S 3D **132**
Orton Cl. NE4: Benw 2A **82**
Orwell Cl. NE34: S Shi 4H **87**
SR8: Pet 1K **181**
Orwell Gdns. DH9: Stly 5E **124**
Orwell Grn. NE3: Ken 2A **62**
Osbaldeston Gdns. NE3: Ken 2D **62**
Osborne Av. NE2: Jes 5G **63**
NE33: S Shi 4K **67**
NE46: Hex 1B **70**
Osborne Bldgs. DH9: Stly 5D **124**
Osborne Cl. NE22: Bed 6A **18**

Osborne Ct. DH2: Newf 4E **126**
NE2: Jes 5H **63**
Osborne Gdns. NE26: Whit B 6F **39**
NE29: N Shi 5G **49**
Osborne Ho. NE28: W'snd 3J **65**
Osborne Pl. NE12: Longb 3D **46**
Osborne Rd. DH3: Ches S 6A **128**
NE2: Jes 1H **5** (2F **63**)
SR5: Sund 1G **117**
Osbornes Cotts. *NE17: C'wl 2A **108***
(off Peartree Ct.)
Osborne St. SR6: Ful 5F **105**
Osborne Ter. NE2: Jes 1H **5** (6G **63**)
NE8: Gate 5F **83**
NE23: Cra 3J **25**
SR8: Eas 7K **159**
Osborne Vs. DH9: Stly 1E **124**
NE2: Jes 5G **63**
Osier Ct. NE62: Stake 1A **18**
Oslo Cl. NE29: N Shi 1B **66**
Osman Cl. SR2: Sund 3G **119**
Osman Ter. DH4: Hou S 7A **130**
Osmund Ter. DH4: S Row 3A **130**
Osprey Cl. DH7: Esh W 4C **162**
Osprey Dr. NE24: News 4J **23**
NE28: W'snd 6A **48**
Osprey Ho. NE2: Jes 4G **63**
Osprey Way NE34: S Shi 2G **87**
Oswald Av. DH1: Dur 3E **166**
Oswald Cl. DH1: Dur 3E **166**
NE35: Bol C 6F **87**
Oswald Cotts. NE9: Wrek 4A **100**
Oswald Ct. DH1: Dur 5D **6** (4B **166**)
Oswald Rd. DH5: Hett H 5G **145**
NE61: Mor 5G **9**
NE64: Newb S 2H **13**
Oswald St. DH9: Crag 7K **125**
NE34: S Shi 3J **87**
SR4: Sund 1C **118**
Oswald Ter. DH9: Stly 6E **124**
NE8: Gate 5F **83**
SR2: Sund 6H **119**
SR8: Eas C 7B **160**
Oswald Ter. Sth. SR5: Sund 6J **103**
Oswald Ter. W. SR5: Sund 6J **103**
Oswald Wlk. NE3: Gos 7F **45**
Oswestry Pl. NE23: Cra 3A **26**
Oswin Av. NE12: Longb 4B **46**
Oswin Ct. NE12: Longb 3C **46**
Oswin Rd. NE12: Longb 3B **46**
Oswin Ter. NE29: N Shi 7D **48**
Otley Cl. NE23: Cra 3B **26**
Otterburn Av. NE3: Gos 1C **62**
NE25: Monks, Well 7B **38**
Otterburn Cl. NE12: Longb 4D **46**
Otterburn Ct. NE8: Gate 5F **83**
NE25: Monks 7B **38**
Otterburn Cres. DH4: Hou S 1C **144**
Otterburn Dr. NE63: Ash 6K **11**
Otterburn Gdns. NE9: Low F 2G **99**
NE11: Dun 7C **82**
NE16: Whi 7H **81**
NE34: S Shi 7A **68**
Otterburn Gro. NE24: Bly 4F **23**
Otterburn Rd. NE29: N Shi 5F **49**
Otterburn Ter. NE2: Jes 4G **63**
Otterburn Vs. *NE2: Jes 4G **63***
(off Otterburn Ter.)
Otterburn Vs. Nth. *NE2: Jes 4G **63***
(off Otterburn Ter.)
Otterburn Vs. Sth. *NE2: Jes 4G **63***
(off Otterburn Ter.)
Otter Burn Way NE42: Pru 5C **76**
Ottercap Cl. NE15: Lem 7D **60**
Ottercops NE42: Pru 5D **76**
Otterington NE38: Wash 4B **116**
Ottershaw NE15: Lem 7E **60**
Otto Ter. SR2: Sund 7F **7** (3D **118**)
Ottovale Cres. NE21: Winl 5A **80**
Ottringham Cl. NE15: Lem 7D **60**
Otus Gro. NE24: Bly 5K **23**
Otway Gro. NE24: Bly 5K **23**
Oulton Cl. NE5: Blak 1H **61**
NE23: Cra 3A **26**
Ousby Ct. NE3: Ki Pk 5K **43**
Ouseburn Cl. DH9: Stly 4F **125**
SR2: Sund 1H **133**
Ouseburn Farm *4M **5***
(off Lime St.)
Ouseburn Rd. NE1: Newc T 4L **5** (7J **63**)
NE6: Heat 1M **5** (6J **63**)
Ouseburn Wharf NE6: Byke 7N **5** (2K **83**)
Ouse Cres. DH3: Gt Lum 3F **143**
Ouselaw NE11: Kib 2F **113**
Ouse St. NE1: Newc T 5M **5** (1J **83**)
Ouslaw La. NE11: Kib 7C **98**
Ousterley Ter. DH9: Crag 7J **125**
OUSTON 6H **113**
Ouston Cl. NE10: Ward 7G **85**
Ouston La. DH2: Ous, Pelt 2H **127**
(not continuous)
Ouston St. NE15: Scot 1F **81**
Outer West Pool 3E **60**
Outlet Rd. NE46: Hex 1E **70**
Outputs La. DH8: Cons 6G **135**
Outram St. DH5: Hou S 1E **144**
Oval, The DH2: Ches M 3K **141**
DH2: Ous 6H **113**
DH4: Hou S 2D **144**
NE6: Walk 3B **84**
NE12: Longb 6C **46**
NE13: Wool 4F **43**
NE22: Bed 7A **18**
NE24: News 6F **23**
NE37: Wash 7H **101**
Oval, The NE40: Ryton 1G **79**
*SR5: S'wck 5D **104***
(off Branston St.)
Oval Pk. Vw. NE10: Fell 7B **84**
Overdale Ct. NE62: Chop 2G **17**
Overdene NE15: Den M 6F **61**
NE42: Oving 7J **55**
SR7: Dalt D 5H **147**
Overfield Rd. NE3: Ken 7B **44**
Overhill NE15: Hed W 3C **58**
Overhill Ter. NE8: Gate 5F **83**
Overman St. DH1: H Shin 1F **177**
Override Skate Park 1E **86**
Overstone Av. NE40: G'sde 4D **78**
Over the Hill Farm Steadings
DH4: Hou S 6F **131**
Overton Cl. NE15: Lem 7D **60**
Overton Rd. NE29: N Shi 4E **48**
Ovett Gdns. NE8: Gate 4K **83**
OVINGHAM 2C **76**
Ovingham Cl. NE38: Wash 3K **115**
Ovingham Gdns. NE13: W Op 5D **34**
Ovingham Rd. NE41: Wylam 7J **57**
Ovingham Way NE25: Sea D 6G **27**
OVINGTON 2K **75**
Ovington Cl. DH8: Cons 2H **135**
Ovington Gro. NE5: Fen 6J **61**
Ovington Vw. NE42: Pru 5D **76**
Owen Brannigan Dr. NE23: Dud 4K **35**
Owen Ct. NE2: Newc T 1C **4** (6E **62**)
Owen Dr. NE35: Bol C, W Bol 6H **87**
NE36: W Bol 6H **87**
Owengate DH1: Dur 3C **6** (3A **166**)
Owen Ter. DH9: Tant 6B **110**
NE17: C'wl 7A **94**
Owlet Cl. NE21: Winl 5A **80**
Owlet Grange NE39: Ham M 3C **108**
Oxberry Gdns. NE10: Wind N 7A **84**
Oxbridge St. SR2: Sund 6H **119**
OXCLOSE 4E **114**
Ox Cl. NE41: Wylam 5K **57**
Oxclose Rd. NE38: Wash 4J **115**
Oxclose Village NE38: Wash 3D **114**
Oxclose Village Cen. NE38: Wash 4E **114**
Oxford Av. NE23: Cra 3A **26**
NE28: W'snd 2E **64**
NE33: S Shi 5K **67**
NE37: Wash 7F **101**
Oxford Centre 6J **45**
Oxford Cl. NE12: Longb 6K **45**
SR3: New S 1B **132**
Oxford Cres. DH5: Hett H 6F **145**
NE31: Heb 7K **65**
Oxford Pl. DH3: Bir 7A **114**
DH8: C'sde 3D **134**
Oxford Rd. NE62: Stake 1J **17**
Oxfordshire Dr. DH1: Carr 1G **167**
Oxford Sq. SR4: Sund 1A **118**
Oxford St. DH9: Ann P 4K **123**
NE1: Newc T 4G **4** (7G **63**)
NE24: Bly 2K **23**
NE26: Whit B 6G **39**
NE30: Tyne 5K **49**
NE33: S Shi 5K **67**
SR4: Sund 1A **118**
SR7: S'hm 3J **147**
Oxford Ter. DH4: S Row 3A **130**
DH6: Bowb 5H **177**
NE8: Gate 5G **83**
Oxford Way NE32: Jar 5B **86**
OXHILL 3D **124**
Oxhill Vs. DH9: Ann P 4B **124**
Oxley M. NE35: Bol C 5E **86**
Oxley St. DH8: B'hill 5F **121**
Oxley Ter. DH1: P Me 4J **153**
Oxnam Cres. NE2: Newc T 1A **4** (6D **62**)
Oxted Cl. NE23: Cra 3B **26**
Oxted Pl. NE6: Walk 3C **84**
Oystershell La. NE4: Newc T 6B **4** (1D **82**)
Oyston St. NE33: S Shi 3J **67**
Ozanan Cl. NE23: Dud 4K **35**

P

Pacha Way NE8: Gate 5C **82**
Pacific Hall Cl. SR7: S'hm 2G **147**
Packham Rd. SR4: Sund 3J **117**
Paddock, The DH1: Dur 7E **154**
DH4: W Herr 2F **131**
DH7: Lan 7J **137**
DH7: Wat 6B **162**
DH9: Tan L 1C **124**
NE10: Hew 1D **100**
NE12: Kil 1C **46**
NE13: Wool 4F **43**
NE15: Walb 4K **59**
NE23: E Cram 5B **26**
NE24: Cow 2G **23**
NE25: Sea D 7J **27**
NE39: H Spen 3D **94**
NE43: Pains 2J **91**
Paddock Cl. DH4: S Row 4K **129**
NE42: Pru 4G **77**
SR6: Clead 5A **88**
Paddock Hill NE20: Pon 4K **31**
Paddock La. NE18: Diss 6A **30**
SR3: Tuns 2D **132**
Paddock M. NE24: Camb 2G **19**
Paddock Ri. NE63: Ash 5K **11**
Paddocks, The SR7: Hawt 3K **159**
Paddock Wood NE42: Pru 4G **77**
Pader Cl. NE13: Haz 6C **34**
Padgate Rd. SR4: Sund 2J **117**
Padonhill SR3: Dox P 4A **132**
Padstow Cl. SR2: Ryh 1H **133**
Padstow Gdns. NE9: Low F 5H **99**
Padstow Rd. NE29: N Shi 1E **66**
Page Av. NE34: S Shi 6A **68**
Page's Bldgs. NE35: Bol C 6E **86**
Page St. NE31: Heb 6K **65**
Paignton Av. NE4: Benw 1A **82**
NE25: Monks 7D **38**
Paignton Sq. SR3: Sund 6A **118**
PAINSHAWFIELD 1J **91**
Painshawfield Rd. NE43: Pains 2H **91**
Painter Heugh
NE1: Newc T 7G **4** (1G **83**)
Paisley Sq. SR3: Sund 6A **118**
Palace Grn. DH1: Dur 3C **6** (3A **166**)
Palace Rd. NE22: Bed 6B **18**
Palace St. NE4: Newc T 7B **4** (2D **82**)
Palatine Pl. NE11: Dun 6C **82**
Palatine St. NE33: S Shi 1J **67**
Palatine Vw. *DH1: Dur 3A **6***
(off Margery La.)
DH6: S Hil 3C **168**
Palermo St. SR4: Sund 7B **104**
Paley St. SR1: Sund 3G **7** (1E **118**)
Palgrove Rd. SR4: Sund 3J **117**
Palgrove Sq. SR4: Sund 3J **117**
Palladian Chapel 6A **96**
Pallinsburn Ct. NE5: Blak 2H **61**
PALLION 7B **104**
Pallion Ind. Est. SR4: Sund 1K **117**
Pallion New Rd. SR4: Sund 7B **104**
Pallion Pk. SR4: Sund 1B **118**
Pallion Quay SR4: Sund 7B **104**
Pallion Retail Pk. SR4: Sund 7K **103**
Pallion Rd. SR4: Sund 2B **118**
Pallion Station (Metro) 7A **104**
Pallion Subway SR4: Sund 7A **104**
Pallion Way SR4: Sund 1K **117**
Pallion West Ind. Est. SR4: Sund 7K **103**
Palm Av. NE4: Fen 6A **62**
NE34: S Shi 1C **88**
Palm Ct. NE12: Kil 3D **46**
Palmer Cres. NE31: Heb 7K **65**
Palmer Gdns. NE10: Ward 6G **85**
Palmer Rd. DH9: Dip 7J **109**
SR8: Pet 7J **171**
Palmers Gth. DH1: Dur 4D **6** (3B **166**)
Palmers Grn. NE12: Kil 3D **46**
Palmer's Hill Rd. SR6: Monkw 1K **7**
Palmerston Av. NE6: Walk 6C **64**
Palmerstone Rd. SR4: Sund 4J **117**
Palmerston Rd. SR4: Sund 5G **117**
Palmerston Sq. SR4: Sund 4J **117**
Palmerston St. DH8: Cons 7H **121**
NE33: S Shi 5J **67**
Palmerston Wlk. NE8: Gate 4E **82**
Palmer St. DH6: S Het 5D **158**
DH9: Stly 4D **124**
NE32: Jar 6A **66**
PALMERSVILLE 3D **46**
Palmersville NE12: Kil 3D **46**
(not continuous)
Palmersville Station (Metro) 4E **46**
Palmer Wlk. NE32: Jar 6B **66**
Palm Lea DH7: B'don 1C **174**
Palmstead Rd. SR4: Sund 3H **117**
Palmstead Sq. SR4: Sund 3J **117**
Palm St. DH7: Lang P 4K **151**
DH8: Cons 6H **121**
Palm Ter. DH9: Stly 6H **125**
DH9: Tant 5C **110**
Pancras Rd. SR3: Sund 6A **118**
Pandon NE1: Newc T 6H **5** (1G **83**)
Pandon Bank NE1: Newc T 6H **5** (1G **83**)
Pandon Ct. NE2: Newc T 3J **5** (7H **63**)
Pandongate Ho. *NE1: Newc T 6H **5***
(off City Rd.)
Panfield Ter. DH4: New L 7J **129**
Pangbourne Cl. NE15: Lem 5C **60**
Pankhurst Gdns. NE10: Ward 6E **84**
Pankhurst Pl. DH9: Stly 4H **125**
Pann La. SR1: Sund 3J **7** (1F **119**)
Panns Bank SR1: Sund 2J **7** (1F **119**)
Pantiles, The NE37: Wash 5H **101**
Parade, The DH2: Pelt 3E **126**
(not continuous)
DH3: Ches S 1B **142**
NE6: Walk 1E **84**
NE11: Dun 4J **81**
NE28: W'snd 7H **47**
NE38: Wash 4H **115**
SR2: Sund 2H **119**
Parade Cl. NE6: Walk 1E **84**
PARADISE 2J **81**
Paradise Cres. SR8: Eas 7B **160**
Paradise Gdns. SR8: Eas C 7C **160**
Paradise La. SR8: Eas 7B **160**
Paradise Row NE23: Cra 4K **25**
Paradise St. SR8: Hord 5F **173**
Paramount Fitness Cen. 7H **17**
Park & Ride
Belmont 5H **155**
Howlands 6A **166**
Newcastle Great Park 1B **44**
Sniperley 6H **153**
Stadium of Light 6F **105**
Park & Tram
(Bank Foot) 6H **43**
Callerton Parkway 3E **42**
East Boldon 7A **88**
Four Lane Ends 6A **46**
Heworth 6D **84**
Kingston Park 6J **43**
Regent Centre 6E **44**
Walkergate 5C **64**
Park Av. DH6: Coxh 7J **177**
DH8: Cons 6J **121**
DH9: Stly 2F **125**
NE3: Fawd 5B **44**
NE3: Gos 6C **44**
(not continuous)
NE11: Dun 7A **82**
NE21: Blay 4C **80**
NE21: Winl 4B **80**
NE22: Bed 5C **18**
NE26: Whit B 6G **39**
NE27: Shir 1K **47**
NE28: W'snd 3F **65**
NE30: N Shi 5J **49**
NE37: Wash 6H **101**
NE42: Pru 5F **77**
NE46: Hex 1B **70**
SR3: New S 2D **132**
SR6: Seab 4G **105**
TS27: B Col 2H **183**
Park Chare NE38: Wash 3H **115**
Park Cl. DH7: Lang P 5K **151**
DH9: Ann P 6A **124**
NE4: Elsw 2C **82**
Park Cotts. NE17: C'wl 2K **107**
Park Ct. NE6: Walk 4E **64**
NE8: Gate 10J **5**
NE11: T Vall 4F **99**
Park Cres. NE27: Shir 1K **47**
NE30: N Shi 5H **49**
Park Cres. E. NE30: N Shi 5J **49**
Parkdale Ri. NE16: Whi 7F **81**
Park Dr. DH7: Lang P 4J **151**
NE3: Gos 3E **44**
NE12: Longb 4C **46**
NE16: Whi 7J **81**
NE24: News 5F **23**
NE61: Hep 7K **15**
NE61: Mor 1F **15**
Parker Av. NE3: Gos 1D **62**
Parker Ct. NE11: Dun 4A **82**
Parker's Bldgs. DH8: Cons 1C **136**
Park Farm NE24: News 6G **23**
Park Farm Vs. NE24: News 7G **23**
Park Fld. NE40: Ryton 1F **79**
Parkfield DH6: Coxh 7J **177**
NE26: Sea S 4C **28**
NE32: Jar 5C **86**
Parkfield Ter. DH9: Ann P 3J **123**
Park Gdns. NE26: Whit B 6G **39**
Park Ga. SR6: Roker 4G **105**
Parkgate DH5: Hett H 7J **145**
Parkgate La. NE21: Winl 6B **80**
Park Gro. NE27: Shir 1K **47**
NE37: Wash 6H **101**
Parkham Cl. NE23: Cra 1K **25**
Parkhead DH9: Ann P 7J **123**
Parkhead Gdns. NE21: Winl 6B **80**
Park Head Rd. NE7: H Hea 3J **63**
Parkhead Sq. NE21: Winl 5C **80**
Park Hill DH6: Coxh 7J **177**
Parkhouse Av. SR5: Sund 7H **103**
Park Ho. Cl. DH6: S'burn 2K **167**
Park Ho. Ct. DH7: Lan 7K **137**
Park Ho. Gdns. DH6: S'burn 2K **167**
(not continuous)
Park Ho. Rd. DH1: Dur 5J **165**
Parkhurst Rd. SR4: Sund 4H **117**
Parkin Gdns. NE10: Hew 7C **84**
Parkinson Cotts. NE40: Ryton 2J **79**
Parkland NE12: Longb 6B **46**
NE21: Blay 2A **80**
Parkland Av. NE21: Winl 6B **80**
Parkland Ct. SR7: S'hm 2K **147**
Parkland Gro. DH6: S Het 5D **158**
Parklands NE10: Ward 6G **85**
NE20: Darr H 2F **41**
NE39: Ham M 3D **108**
Parklands Ct. NE10: Ward 5G **85**
TS27: Cas E 4K **181**
Parklands Dr. TS27: Cas E 4K **181**
Parklands Way NE10: Ward 6G **85**
Parkland Ter. SR7: S'hm 2K **147**
Park La. NE8: Gate 10K **5** (3H **83**)
NE21: Winl 6B **80**
NE27: Shir 1K **47**
NE42: Pru 5F **77**
(not continuous)
SR1: Sund 4H **7** (2E **118**)
SR7: Mur 7D **146**
SR8: Hord 5E **172**
Park La. Interchange SR1: Sund 5H **7**
Park Lane Station (Metro) 5J **7** (2F **119**)
Park Lea DH8: B'hill 6G **121**
SR3: E Her 3G **131**
Parklea NE26: Sea S 4C **28**
Park Lea Rd. SR6: Roker 4G **105**
Parkmore Rd. SR4: Sund 4G **117**
Park Pde. NE26: Whit B 6G **39**
SR6: Roker 5G **105**
Park Pl. DH3: Ches S 4B **128**
DH5: Hett H 7G **145**
*DH8: B'hill 6G **121***
(off Park Rd.)
Park Pl. E. SR2: Sund 6K **7** (3F **119**)
Park Pl. W. SR2: Sund 6K **7** (3F **119**)
Park Ri. NE15: Lem 6C **60**
Park Rd. DH5: Hett H 6G **145**
DH6: S'burn 2K **167**
DH8: B'hill, Cons 6F **121**
DH9: Stly 4D **124**
NE4: Elsw 8A **4** (2C **82**)
NE8: Gate 10M **5** (3J **83**)
NE10: Gate 10M **5** (3J **83**)
NE12: Longb 5J **45**

Park Rd. NE15: Newb 5K 59
NE22: Bed 7J 17
NE24: Bly 2K 23
NE25: Sea D 7G 27
NE26: Whit B 5G 39
NE27: Shir 1K 47
NE28: W'snd 3F 65
NE31: Heb 1J 85
NE32: Jar 7A 66
NE39: Row G 5H 95
NE63: Ash 4K 11
SR2: Sund 6J 7 (3F 119)
SR8: Hord 4D 172
Park Rd. Central DH3: Ches S 6B 128
Park Rd. E. NE63: Ash 4A 12
Park Rd. Ind. Est. DH8: B'hill 6F 121
Park Rd. Nth. DH3: Ches S 3A 128
Park Rd. Nth. Ind. Est. DH8: B'hill 6F 121
Park Rd. Sth. DH3: Ches S 1A 142
Park Row NE10: Fell 6B 84
SR5: S'wck 6B 104
Parks, The DH3: Ches S 1C 142
Parkshiel NE34: S Shi 2C 88
PARKSIDE 5A 148
Park Side NE61: Hep 3B 16
Parkside DH1: Dur 2A 6 (2K 165)
DH7: B'hpe 5D 138
DH7: Sac 7E 140
DH8: Cons 6G 121
DH9: Tan L 7C 110
NE11: Dun 6B 82
NE12: Kil 2J 45
NE15: Thro 4J 59
NE22: Bed 5C 18
NE28: W'snd 2H 65
NE30: Tyne 3K 49
NE31: Heb 2G 85
SR3: E Her 3H 131
Parkside, The NE42: Pru 3G 77
Parkside Av. NE7: Longb 7K 45
NE21: Winl 5C 80
Parkside Cotts. DH9: Tan L 7C 110
Parkside Ct. NE13: W Op 5E 34
NE17: C'wl 6A 94
NE63: Ash 5C 12
Parkside Cres. NE30: Tyne 4K 49
SR7: S'hm 5A 148
Parkside Rd. SR7: S'hm 4A 148
Parkside Sth. SR3: E Her 3H 131
Parkside Ter. NE28: W'snd 1E 64
Parks Leisure Centre, The 1F 67
Parkstone Cl. SR4: Sund 6G 117
Park St. DH8: B'hill 5G 121
SR7: S'hm 4B 148
Park St. Sth. SR5: Sund 6J 103
Park Ter. DH8: C'sde 4C 134
DH8: Lead 5B 122
NE2: Newc T 1E 4 (6F 63)
NE11: Dun 6B 82
NE12: Kil 2K 45
NE16: Burn 2A 110
NE16: Swa 5G 81
NE21: Blay 5D 80
NE22: Bed 5B 18
NE26: Whit B 5G 39
NE28: W'snd 3F 65
NE30: N Shi 5J 49
NE37: Wash 6H 101
SR5: S'wck 5B 104
SR8: Hord 6E 172
Park Vw. DH2: Ches S 4K 127
DH2: Nett 6H 141
DH3: Ches S 1A 128
DH4: Bour 5H 129
DH4: S Row 3B 130
DH5: Hett H 7G 145
DH7: Lang M 6G 165
DH7: Wit G 3B 152
DH8: B'hill 5G 121
DH8: Cons 5H 121
NE6: Walk 1E 84
NE9: Spri 6D 100
(off Windsor Rd.)
NE10: Fell 6B 84
NE12: Longb 4B 46
NE13: W Op 5E 34
NE16: Burn 2B 110
NE16: Swa 5F 81
NE21: Winl 6C 80
NE23: Cra 4K 25
(off Station Rd.)
NE23: Dud 5A 36
NE24: Bly 2K 23
NE25: Sea D 7H 27
(not continuous)
NE26: Whit B 6G 39
NE28: W'snd 3F 65
NE32: Jar 2B 86
NE63: Ash 3K 11
SR7: S'hm 2H 147
SR8: Hord 5E 172
Park Vw. Av. NE9: Low F 7H 83
Park Vw. Cl. NE40: Ryton 1H 79
Park Vw. Ct. NE3: Ken 7A 44
NE12: Longb 2K 45
NE26: Whit B 6G 39
Park Vw. Gdns. NE40: Ryton 1H 79
Park Vw. Grange NE5: Blak 2H 61
Park Vw. Shop. Cen. NE26: Whit B 6G 39
Park Vs. *DH8: Lead 5B 122*
(off Dunelm Way)
DH9: Dip 2G 123
NE3: Gos 3D 62
NE28: W'snd 3F 65
NE63: Ash 3K 11
Parkville NE6: Heat 1M 5 (6J 63)
Park Wlk. SR3: Dox P 4C 132
Parkway NE16: Whi 1F 97
NE38: Wash 3G 115
NE62: Chop 1H 17
Parkwood Av. DH7: Bearp 1C 164
NE42: Pru 3H 77
Parliament St. DH8: Cons 7G 121
NE31: Heb 6G 65
Parmeter St. DH9: Stly 5E 124
Parmontley St. NE15: Scot 1F 81
Parnaby St. DH8: Cons 7H 121
Parnell St. DH4: Hou S 2B 144
Parrish Ct. NE6: Byke 3P 5
Parrish Vw. NE1: Newc T 6F 4
Parry Dr. SR6: Whit 5G 89
Parson Rd. NE41: Wylam 7K 57
Parson's Av. NE6: Walk 1D 84
Parsons Courtyard NE8: Gate 4C 82
Parsons Dr. NE40: Ryton 1G 79
Parsons Gdns. NE11: Dun 5B 82
Parsons Ind. Est. NE37: Wash 1F 115
Parsons Rd. NE37: Wash 1F 115
SR8: Pet 3B 172
Parsons St. *NE24: Bly 1J 23*
(off Bridge St.)
Partick Rd. SR4: Sund 4H 117
Partick Sq. SR4: Sund 4J 117
Partnership Ct. SR7: Seat 7G 133
Partridge Cl. NE38: Wash 5D 114
Partridge Ter. TS28: Win 5F 181
Passfield Sq. DH6: Thor 1J 179
SR8: Eas 1A 172
Passfield Way SR8: Pet 1J 181
Pasteur Rd. DH6: S Het 4B 158
Paston Rd. NE25: Sea D 1H 37
Pastures, The DH5: E Rain 6D 144
NE24: News 5H 23
NE43: Stoc 6H 75
NE61: Mor 1D 14
Path, The NE9: Low F 3J 99
PATH HEAD 3A 80
Path Head Water Mill 2A 80
Pathside NE32: Jar 4C 86
Patience Av. NE13: Sea B 3E 34
Patina Cl. NE15: Lem 5C 60
Paton Rd. SR3: Sund 6B 118
Paton Sq. SR3: Sund 6B 118
Patrick Cain Ho. NE33: S Shi 5H 67
Patrick Cres. DH6: S Het 3A 158
Patrick Ter. NE23: Dud 4K 35
Patterdale Cl. DH1: Carr 7J 155
NE36: E Bol 7J 87
Patterdale Gdns. NE7: H Hea 2K 63
Patterdale Gro. SR5: Ful 3E 104
Patterdale M. DH8: Lead 5B 122
Patterdale Rd. NE24: Cow 1E 22
Patterdale St. DH5: Hett H 1G 157
Patterdale Ter. NE8: Gate 6H 83
Patterson Cl. NE46: Hex 3A 70
Patterson Ho. NE24: Bly 3J 23
Patterson St. NE21: Blay 2E 80
Patterson Way NE63: Ash 2D 12
Pattinson Dr. NE40: Craw 3D 78
Pattinson Gdns. NE9: Low F 7K 83
NE10: Fell 4A 84
Pattinson Ind. Est. NE38: Wash 2B 116
(Mandarin Way)
NE38: Wash 4A 116
(Station Rd.)
Pattinson Nth. Ind. Est. NE38: Wash 3B 116
Pattinson Rd. NE38: Wash 5K 115
Pattinson Sth. Ind. Est. NE38: Wash 5K 115
Pattison Cres. TS27: B Col 3K 183
Pattison Gdns. TS27: B Col 3K 183
Patton Wlk. DH6: Whe H 2C 180
Patton Way NE61: Peg 4A 10
Pauline Av. SR6: Ful 4F 105
Pauline Gdns. NE15: Den M 6G 61
Paul Lea DH9: Beam 1A 126
Pauls Grn. DH5: Hett H 4G 145
Paul's Rd. SR1: Sund 2G 119
Paulsway NE32: Jar 7E 66
Pavilion, The NE16: Swa 5F 81
Pavilion Ct. DH7: Esh W 4E 162
Pavilion M. NE2: Jes 5H 63
Pavilion Ter. DH5: Hett H 7G 145
DH7: B'hpe 5D 138
Pavillion Ct. SR1: Sund 5K 7
Pawston Rd. NE21: Barl 2E 94
NE39: H Spen 2E 94
Paxford Cl. NE7: Longb 7H 45
Paxton M. DH1: P Me 3K 153
Paxton Ter. SR4: Sund 1C 118
Peacehaven Ct. NE37: Wash 5G 101
Peacock Ct. NE11: Fest P 7D 82
Peacock La. NE61: Mor 5D 8
Peacock St. W. SR4: Sund 2B 118
Pea Flatts La. DH3: Gt Lum 3G 143
Peareth Ct. NE8: Gate 10J 5
Peareth Edge NE9: Spri 6D 100
Peareth Gro. SR6: Seab 4H 105
Peareth Hall Rd. NE9: Spri 6D 100
NE37: Wash 5F 101
Peareth Rd. SR6: Seab 3G 105
Peareth Ter. DH3: Bir 4A 114
Pear Lea DH7: B'don 1C 174
Pearl Rd. SR3: Sund 6B 118
Pea Rd. DH9: Stly 3D 124
Pearson Ct. NE21: Blay 2E 80
Pearson Pl. NE30: N Shi 6H 49
NE32: Jar 5C 66
Pearson's Ter. NE46: Hex 1C 70
Pearson St. DH9: Stly 1F 125
NE33: S Shi 1K 67
Peart Cl. DH6: S'burn 3A 168
Peartree Bungs. NE17: C'wl 2A 108
Peartree Cotts. DH1: Dur 6D 6
Peartree Ct. NE17: C'wl 2A 108
Peartree Gdns. NE6: Walk 4E 64
Peartree M. SR2: Sund 4E 118
Pear Tree Pl. DH4: Hou S 1D 144
Pear Tree Ri. SR7: Seat 1F 147
Pear Tree Ter. DH3: Gt Lum 1F 143
NE17: C'wl 7K 93
Peartree Ter. DH7: B'hpe 4H 139
Peary Cl. NE5: West 3F 61
Pease Av. NE15: Benw 7J 61
Peasemore Rd. SR4: Sund 3H 117
Pease Rd. SR8: Pet 4H 171
Pebble Beach SR6: Seab 7H 89
Pecket Cl. NE24: Bly 4E 22
Peddars Way NE34: S Shi 1H 87
Peebles Cl. NE29: N Shi 4C 48
Peebles Rd. SR3: Sund 6A 118
Peel Av. DH1: Dur 2F 167
Peel Centre, The NE37: Wash 1K 115
Peel Ct. NE13: Sea B 3D 34
Peel Gdns. NE34: S Shi 2E 86
Peel Ho. NE1: Newc T 6D 4
Peel La. NE1: Newc T 7D 4 (2E 82)
Peel Retail Pk. NE37: Wash 1K 115
Peel St. NE1: Newc T 7D 4 (1E 82)
SR2: Sund 6K 7 (3G 119)
Peggy's Wicket DH9: Beam 1B 126
PEGSWOOD 4B 10
Pegswood By-Pass NE61: Mor, Peg 4J 9
Pegswood Ho. NE4: Newc T 3B 4
Pegswood Ind. Est. NE61: Peg 3B 10
Pegswood Station (Rail) 4B 10
PEGSWOOD VILLAGE 3A 10
Pegwood Rd. SR4: Sund 3J 117
Peile Ct. DH8: Shot B 3E 120
Peile Pk. DH8: Shot B 3E 120
PELAW 5E 84
Pelaw Av. DH2: Ches S 4K 127
DH9: Stly 1G 125
NE64: Newb S 2H 13
Pelaw Bank DH3: Ches S 5A 128
Pelaw Ct. DH9: Stly 2G 125
Pelaw Cres. DH2: Ches S 4K 127
(not continuous)
Pelaw Grange Ct. DH3: Ches S 1A 128
Pelaw Grange Stadium 1A 128
Pelaw Ind. Est. NE10: Pel 5E 84
Pelaw Leazes La. DH1: Dur 2E 6 (2B 166)
Pelaw M. DH9: Stly 2G 125
Pelaw Pl. DH2: Ches S 4A 128
Pelaw Rd. DH2: Ches S 4A 128
Pelaw Sq. DH2: Ches S 4K 127
SR4: Sund 1J 117
Pelaw Station (Metro) 5E 84
Pelaw Ter. DH2: Ches S 4K 127
Pelaw Way NE10: Pel 6E 84
Peldon Cl. NE7: Longb 7H 45
Pelham Ct. NE3: Ki Pk 5K 43
PELTON 2G 127
Peltondale Av. NE24: Cow 3E 22
PELTON FELL 5G 127
Pelton Fell Rd. DH2: Ches S, P Fel 5G 127
Pelton Ho. Farm Est. DH2: P Fel 3G 127
Pelton La. DH2: Ches S, Pelt 2G 127
DH2: Gra V 5C 126
DH2: Pelt 2E 126
PELTON LANE ENDS 3E 126
Pelton M. DH2: Pelt 3E 126
Pelton Rd. SR4: Sund 4J 117
Pemberton Av. DH8: C'sde 2E 134
Pemberton Bank DH5: Eas L 2H 157
Pemberton Cl. SR5: Monkw 6D 104
Pemberton Gdns. SR3: Sund 5D 118
Pemberton Rd. DH8: Allen, B'hill 1B 134
Pemberton St. DH5: Hett H 6G 145
Pemberton Ter. Nth. DH9: Stly 6H 125
Pemberton Ter. Sth. DH9: Stly 6H 125
Pembridge NE38: Wash 3E 114
Pembroke Av. DH3: Bir 7B 114
NE6: Walk 5C 64
SR3: New S 3D 132
Pembroke Ct. NE3: Ki Pk 5K 43
NE24: Bly 2K 23
NE64: Newb S 2J 13
SR5: Sund 3H 103
Pembroke Dr. NE20: Darr H 6E 30
Pembroke Gdns. NE28: W'snd 1A 66
NE63: N Sea 6E 12
Pembroke Pl. SR8: Pet 4K 171
Pembroke Ter. NE33: S Shi 6J 67
Pendeford NE38: Wash 4A 116
Pendle Cl. NE38: Wash 5F 115
SR8: Pet 7K 171
Pendle Grn. SR4: Sund 3C 118
Pendleton Dr. NE23: Cra 1J 25
Pendower Way NE15: Benw 7J 61
Pendragon DH3: Gt Lum 2F 143
Penfold Cl. NE7: H Hea 1A 64
Penhale Dr. SR2: Ryh 2H 133
Penhill Cl. DH2: Ous 7H 113
Penistone Rd. SR4: Sund 4G 117
Penman Pl. NE29: N Shi 1G 67
Penman Sq. SR4: Sund 4H 117
Pennant Sq. SR4: Sund 2J 117
Pennine Av. DH2: Ches S 7K 127
Pennine Ct. DH9: Ann P 6K 123
Pennine Dr. NE63: N Sea 6C 12
SR8: Pet 7J 171
Pennine Gdns. DH9: Stly 4G 125
NE11: Lob H 7C 82
Pennine Gro. NE36: W Bol 7H 87
Pennine Ho. NE38: Wash 4F 115
Pennine Vw. DH6: S Hil 3D 168
DH8: Cons 6G 121
NE17: C'wl 7K 93
Pennine Way NE12: Longb 6J 45
Pennon Pl. NE1: Newc T 4F 4
Penn Sq. SR4: Sund 2J 117
Penn St. NE4: Newc T 10A 4 (3D 82)
Pennycross Rd. SR4: Sund 4G 117
Pennycross Sq. SR4: Sund 3G 117
Pennyfine Cl. NE29: N Shi 4G 49
Pennyfine Ct. NE29: N Shi 3B 48
Pennyfine Rd. NE16: Sun 4J 97
Pennygate Sq. SR4: Sund 3G 117
Pennygreen Sq. SR4: Sund 3G 117
Penny La. NE22: H Bri 4F 21
Pennymore Sq. SR4: Sund 3G 117
PENNYWELL 4J 117
Pennywell Bus. Cen. SR4: Sund 3H 117
Pennywell Ind. Est. SR4: Sund 4G 117
Pennywell Rd. SR4: Sund 4J 117
Pennywell Shop. Pct. SR4: Sund 4H 117
Penrith Av. NE30: Cull 2G 49
Penrith Ct. NE22: Bed 6F 17
Penrith Gdns. NE9: Low F 3K 99
Penrith Gro. NE9: Low F 3K 99
Penrith Pl. DH8: C'sde 3D 134
Penrith Rd. NE31: Heb 2K 85
SR5: Ful 3E 104
Penrose Grn. NE3: Ken 7B 44
Penrose Rd. SR4: Sund 4H 117
Penryn Av. SR7: Mur 7F 147
Penryn Way DH7: Mead 1E 174
Pensford Ct. NE3: Ki Pk 6J 43
PENSHAW 1B 130
Penshaw Cl. DH7: Lang P 5H 151
Penshaw Gdns. DH9: Stly 2H 125
(not continuous)
Penshaw Grn. NE5: Blak 2K 61
Penshaw La. DH4: Pen 1B 130
Penshaw Monument 7C 116
Penshaw Vw. DH3: Bir 5C 114
DH7: Sac 1F 153
NE9: Spri 6E 100
NE10: Ward 6G 85
NE31: Heb 2H 85
NE32: Jar 2B 86
Penshaw Way DH3: Bir 4C 114
DH4: Hou S 7A 130
Pensher St. NE10: Gate 5A 84
SR4: Sund 2D 118
Pensher St. E. NE10: Fell 5A 84
Pensher Vw. NE37: Wash 6K 101
Pent Ct. NE40: G'sde 5E 78
Pentland Cl. NE23: Cra 1K 25
NE29: N Shi 3F 49
NE38: Wash 5F 115
NE63: N Sea 7C 12
SR8: Pet 7J 171
Pentland Ct. DH2: Ches S 7A 128
Pentland Gdns. NE11: Lob H 7C 82
Pentland Gro. NE12: Longb 3K 45
Pentlands Ter. DH9: Stly 4G 125
Pentridge Cl. NE23: Cra 3A 26
Penwood Rd. SR4: Sund 3J 117
Penyghent Way NE37: Wash 2E 114
Penzance Bungs. SR7: Mur 6F 147
Penzance Ct. SR7: Mur 6F 147
Penzance Pde. NE31: Heb 4A 86
Penzance Rd. SR4: Sund 4H 117
Peoples Theatre 4K 63
Peplow Sq. SR4: Sund 1J 117
Peppercorn Ct. NE1: Newc T 7H 5
Peppermires DH7: Bran 4C 174
Percival St. SR4: Sund 1B 118
Percy Av. DH9: Ann P 4J 123
NE26: Whit B 6F 39
NE30: Cull 7J 39
Percy Cl. NE46: Hex 4B 70
Percy Cotts. NE25: Sea D 7J 27
(not continuous)
NE42: Pru 3E 76
Percy Ct. NE29: N Shi 2D 66
Percy Cres. DH7: Lan 7K 137
NE29: N Shi 2D 66
Percy Gdns. DH8: Cons 1K 135
(not continuous)
NE11: Dun 7C 82
NE12: Longb 4B 46
NE25: Whit B 7G 39
NE30: Tyne 4K 49
NE62: Stake 7J 11
Percy Gdns. Cotts. *NE30: Tyne 4K 49*
(off Percy Gdns.)
Percy La. DH1: Dur 3J 165
Percy Lonnen NE42: Pru 3F 77
PERCY MAIN 2D 66
Percy Main Station
North tyneside Steam Railway 2C 66
Percy Main Station (Metro) 2D 66
Percy Pk. NE30: Tyne 4K 49
Percy Pk. Rd. NE30: Tyne 4K 49
Percy Pl. *DH7: Lan 7K 137*
(off Percy Cres.)
Percy Rd. NE26: Whit B 6H 39
Percy Scott St. NE34: S Shi 3J 87
Percy Sq. DH1: Dur 5J 165
Percy St. DH5: Hett H 6H 145
DH6: Thor 1K 179
DH6: Whe H 2B 180
DH9: Stly 4D 124
NE1: Newc T 4E 4 (7F 63)
NE12: Longb 3E 46
NE15: Lem 7C 60
NE23: Cra 5A 26
NE24: Bly 1K 23

Percy St. NE28: W'snd .3G **65**
NE30: Tyne .5K **49**
(not continuous)
NE32: Jar .6C **66**
NE33: S Shi .3K **67**
NE63: Ash .3C **12**
Percy St. Sth. NE24: Bly .2K **23**
Percy St. W. DH6: Thor .1K **179**
Percy Ter. DH1: Dur .3J **165**
DH4: Pen .1A **130**
DH8: Cons .1K **135**
DH9: Ann P .5B **124**
NE3: Gos .7G **45**
NE15: Newb .6K **59**
NE25: Monks .6E **38**
SR2: Sund .4G **119**
SR6: Whit .5H **89**
Percy Ter. Sth. SR2: Sund .5G **119**
Percy Way NE15: Walb .4A **60**
Peregrine Ct. NE29: N Shi .6F **49**
Peregrine Pl. NE12: Longb .5J **45**
Perivale Rd. SR4: Sund .4H **117**
PERKINSVILLE .1H **127**
Perrycrofts SR3: Dox P .5C **132**
Perrystone M. NE22: Bed .1J **21**
Perry St. NE9: Low F .6H **83**
Perth Av. NE32: Jar .3E **86**
NE34: S Shi .3E **86**
Perth Cl. NE28: W'snd .1K **65**
NE29: N Shi .4C **48**
Perth Ct. NE11: T Vall .5G **99**
SR3: Sund .7A **118**
Perth Gdns. NE28: W'snd .1K **65**
Perth Grn. NE32: Jar .3E **86**
Perth Rd. SR3: Sund .7A **118**
Perth Sq. SR3: Sund .6B **118**
Pescott Ct. NE46: Hex .2D **70**
Pesspool Av. DH6: Has .1B **170**
Pesspool Bungs. DH6: Has .1B **170**
Pesspool La. DH6: Has, S Het .1B **170**
SR8: Eas .1B **170**
Pesspool Ter. DH6: Has .1B **170**
Peterborough Cl. NE8: Gate .4G **83**
Peterborough Rd. DH1: Dur .4C **154**
Peterborough Way NE32: Jar .5B **86**
PETERLEE .6B **172**
Peterlee Cl. SR8: Pet .5A **172**
Peter Lee Cotts. DH6: Whe H .3A **180**
Peterlee Leisure Cen. .7B **172**
Peter's Bank DH9: Harp .2A **124**
Petersfield Rd. SR4: Sund .4H **117**
Petersham Rd. SR4: Sund .2J **117**
Peter Stracey Ho. SR6: Ful .3F **105**
Peth Bank DH7: Lan .7K **137**
Petherton Ct. NE3: Ki Pk .6J **43**
Peth Grn. DH5: Eas L .2H **157**
PETH HEAD .1E **70**
Peth Head NE46: Hex .1E **70**
Peth La. DH7: B'hpe, Lan .6A **138**
NE40: Ryton, Thro .7H **59**
Pethside DH7: Lan .7A **138**
Petrel Cl. NE33: S Shi .2J **67**
Petrel Way NE24: News .5K **23**
Petteril NE38: Wash .7E **114**
Petwell Cres. SR8: Eas .7A **160**
Petwell La. SR8: Eas, Eas C .7K **159**
Petworth Cl. NE33: S Shi .2K **67**
Petworth Gdns. NE61: Peg .3A **10**
Pevensey Cl. NE29: N Shi .3F **49**
Pexton Way NE5: Den M .5G **61**
Phalp St. DH6: S Het .5D **158**
Pheasantmoor NE37: Wash .1E **114**
PHILADELPHIA .4D **130**
Philadelphia Complex DH4: Nbot .4D **130**
Philadelphia La. DH4: Nbot, S Row .3B **130**
Philip Av. DH6: Bowb .3H **177**
Philip Ct. NE9: Low F .2K **99**
Philiphaugh NE28: Walk, W'snd .5F **65**
Philip Pl. NE4: Newc T .3A **4** (7C **62**)
Philipson St. NE6: Walk .7D **64**
Philip Sq. SR3: Sund .6A **118**
Philip St. NE4: Newc T .7C **62**
Phillips Av. NE16: Whi .6G **81**
Phillips Cl. DH6: Has .1A **170**
Phoebe Grange Cotts. NE42: Pru .4F **77**
Phoenix Chase NE29: N Shi .4B **48**
Phoenix Cl. DH7: Lang P .5H **151**
Phoenix Ct. DH8: B'hill .6E **120**
NE29: N Shi .4C **48**
NE61: Mor .7F 9
(off Whalebone La.)
Phoenix Ho. SR1: Sund .3J **7**
Phoenix Rd. NE38: Wash .2C **114**
SR4: Sund .2J **117**
Phoenix St. NE24: Bly .5F **23**
Phoenix Theatre, The .2K **23**
Phoenix Way DH4: Hou S .3C **144**
Phoenix Workshops SR8: Hord .4E **172**
Piccadilly SR3: New S .1A **132**
Picherwell NE10: Fell .7B **84**
Pickard Cl. SR8: Pet .5C **172**
Pickard St. SR4: Sund .1C **118**
Pickering Cl. NE23: Cra .5A **26**
Pickering Ct. NE32: Jar .3C **66**
Pickering Dr. NE21: Blay .4C **80**
Pickering Grn. NE9: Low F .5K **99**
PICKERING NOOK .4A **110**
Pickering Pl. DH1: Carr .7G **155**
Pickering Rd. SR4: Sund .5G **117**
Pickering Sq. SR4: Sund .4H **117**
Pickering St. TS28: Win .7F **181**
Pickersgill Ct. SR5: S'wck .7C **104**
Pickersgill Ho. SR5: Sund .4J **103**
Pickhurst Rd. SR4: Sund .5G **117**
Pickhurst Sq. SR4: Sund .4H **117**
PICKTREE .2C **128**
Picktree Cotts. DH3: Ches S .5B **128**
Picktree Cotts. E. DH3: Ches S .5B **128**
Picktree Farm Cotts.
NE38: Ches S, Wash .2C **128**
Picktree La. DH3: Ches S .5B **128**
DH3: Ches S, Lam P .3C **128**
NE38: Wash .1C **128**
Picktree Lodge DH3: Ches S .1B **128**
Picktree M. DH3: Ches S .5B **128**
Picktree Ter. DH3: Ches S .5B **128**
Pickwick Cl. DH1: Dur .5K **165**
Pier Pde. NE33: S Shi .1A **68**
Pier Rd. NE30: Tyne .5K **49**
Pier Vw. SR6: Roker .5H **105**
Pike Hill DH8: Shot B .7A **106**
Pikestone Cl. NE38: Wash .5E **114**
Pikesyde DH9: Dip .2F **123**
Pilgrim Cl. SR5: Monkw .6E **104**
Pilgrims Ct. NE2: Jes .5G **63**
Pilgrim St. NE1: Newc T .5F **4** (1F **83**)
(New Bridge St. W.)
NE1: Newc T .7G **4** (2G **83**)
(Tyne Bri.)
Pilgrims Way DH1: Dur .1D **166**
NE61: Mor .1D **14**
Pilgrimsway NE9: Low F .7J **83**
NE32: Jar .7E **66**
Pilton Rd. NE5: West .2F **61**
Pilton Wlk. NE5: West .2F **61**
Pimlico DH1: Dur .5B **6** (4A **166**)
Pimlico Ct. NE9: Low F .3H **99**
Pimlico Rd. DH5: Hett H .2H **157**
SR4: Sund .4H **117**
Pinders Way DH6: S Hil .3D **168**
Pine Av. DH1: Dur .3E **166**
DH4: Hou S .2D **144**
NE3: Fawd .5B **44**
NE13: Din .4J **33**
NE16: Burn .2K **109**
NE34: S Shi .1C **88**
NE62: Chop .1F **17**
Pinedale Dr. DH6: S Het .4B **158**
Pinegarth NE20: Darr H .2G **41**
Pine Lea DH7: B'don .1C **174**
Pine Pk. DH7: Ush M .3D **164**
Pines, The NE4: Elsw .9A **4** (3C **82**)
NE37: Wash .5J **101**
NE40: G'sde .5F **79**
Pine St. DH2: Gra V .4C **126**
DH2: Pelt .2D **126**
DH2: Wald .1G **141**
DH3: Bir .3A **114**
DH3: Ches S .6A **128**
DH7: Lang P .4J **151**
DH9: Stly .5D **124**
NE13: Sea B .3E **34**
NE15: Thro .2H **59**
NE32: Jar .7A **66**
NE40: G'sde .5F **79**
SR4: Sund .1B **118**
Pinesway SR3: Sund .5D **118**
Pine Ter. DH9: Ann P .4J **123**
Pine Tree DH7: Esh W .4D **162**
Pinetree Cen. DH3: Bir .5A **114**
Pinetree Gdns. NE25: Monks .1E **48**
Pinetree Health & Fitness .5J 63
(off Jesmond Rd.)
Pinetree Way NE11: Dun .4H **81**
Pine Vw. DH9: Stly .5D **124**
Pine Vw. Vs. DH7: Esh W .4F **163**
Pinewood NE31: Heb .6G **65**
Pinewood Av. NE13: W Op .6E **34**
NE23: Cra .1K **25**
NE38: Wash .7G **115**
Pinewood Cl. NE3: K Bank .5H **43**
NE6: Walk .4C **64**
NE38: Wash .5K **115**
Pinewood Dr. NE61: Mor .6C **8**
Pinewood Gdns. NE11: Lob H .2C **98**
Pinewood Rd. SR5: S'wck .5B **104**
Pinewoods NE21: Winl .1K **95**
Pinewood Sq. SR5: S'wck .5B **104**
Pinewood St. DH4: Hou S .1J **143**
Pinewood Vs. NE34: S Shi .7C **68**
Pink La. NE1: Newc T .6D **4** (1E **82**)
(not continuous)
Pinner Pl. NE6: Walk .2C **84**
Pinner Rd. SR4: Sund .3J **117**
Pintail Ct. NE34: S Shi .2G **87**
Pioneer Ter. NE22: Bed .6A **18**
Piper Ct. NE3: Ken .7K **43**
Piper Rd. NE42: O'ham .1D **76**
Pipershaw NE37: Wash .2D **114**
Pipe Track La. NE4: Benw .2K **81**
Pipewellgate NE8: Gate .9F **4** (3F **83**)
Pitcairn Rd. SR4: Sund .3H **117**
Pit Ho. La. DH4: Leam .6J **143**
Pithouse Rd. DH8: Cons .1K **121**
Pit La. DH1: Dur .5K **153**
DH7: B'don .7K **163**
Pit Row SR3: New S .1B **132**
PITTINGTON .4A **156**
Pittington Crossing DH6: Low P .5A **156**
Pittington La. DH1: Carr .6J **155**
DH6: Low P .6J **155**
Pittington Rd. DH5: E Rain .3K **155**
DH6: Low P .3K **155**
Pitt St. DH8: Cons .7H **121**
NE4: Newc T .4B **4** (7D **62**)
PITY ME .4J **153**
Pity Me By-Pass DH1: Dur, P Me .6H **153**
Pity Me Local Nature Reserve .4K **153**
Pixley Dell DH8: Cons .3A **136**
PLAINS FARM .6B **118**
Plains Rd. SR3: Sund .6B **118**
Plaistow Sq. SR4: Sund .2J **117**
Plaistow Way NE23: Cra .1K **25**
Plane St. DH8: Cons .7J **121**
Planesway NE10: Hew .2C **100**
Planet Ho. SR1: Sund .3J **7**
Planet Pl. NE12: Kil .2A **46**
Planetree Av. NE4: Fen .5K **61**
Plane Tree Ct. SR3: Silk .3A **132**
Plantagenet Av. DH3: Ches S .7B **128**
Plantation, The NE9: Low F .2J **99**
Plantation Av. DH6: Litt .1D **168**
NE16: Swa .6G **81**
Plantation Ct. *NE40: G'sde .6C 78*
(off Rockwood Hill Rd.)
Plantation Gro. NE10: Bill Q .4F **85**
Plantation Rd. SR4: Sund .1A **118**
Plantation Sq. SR4: Sund .1A **118**
Plantation St. DH8: Lead .5B **122**
NE28: W'snd .5F **65**
Plantation Vw. DH9: W Pelt .3B **126**
Plantation Wlk. DH6: S Het .4B **158**
PLAWSWORTH .6J **141**
Plawsworth Gdns. NE9: Wrek .4B **100**
Plawsworth M. DH2: Plaw .5J **141**
Plawsworth Rd. DH7: Sac .7E **140**
Pleasant Pl. DH3: Bir .3A **114**
Pleasant Vw. DH7: B'hpe .6D **138**
DH8: Cons .3K **121**
DH8: Shot B .5D **120**
Plenmeller Pl. NE16: Sun .4G **97**
Plessey Av. NE24: Bly .3K **23**
Plessey Ct. NE24: News .5F **23**
Plessey Cres. NE25: Whit B .7H **39**
Plessey Gdns. NE29: N Shi .7D **48**
Plessey Old Wagonway NE24: Bly .6C **22**
Plessey Rd. NE24: Bly, News .5F **23**
Plessey Rd. Workshops NE24: News .5F **23**
Plessey St. NE23: E Har .6K **21**
Plessey Ter. NE7: H Hea .3K **63**
Plessey Woods Country Pk. .5D **20**
Plessey Woods Country Pk. Vis. Cen.
.4D **20**
Plessy Rd. NE24: Bly .1K **23**
Plough Rd. SR3: Dox P .4B **132**
Plover Cl. NE24: News .5J **23**
NE38: Wash .5D **114**
Plover Dr. NE16: Burn .3C **110**
Ploverfield Cl. NE63: Ash .5A **12**
Plover Lodge DH3: Bir .2A **114**
Plummer Chare NE1: Newc T .7H **5** (2G **83**)
Plummer St. NE4: Newc T .9C **4** (3E **82**)
Plumtree Av. SR5: Sund .5J **103**
(not continuous)
Plunkett Rd. DH9: Dip .7J **109**
Plunkett Ter. DH2: P Fel .5F **127**
Plymouth Cl. SR7: Dalt D .4H **147**
Plymouth Sq. SR3: Sund .6A **118**
Pockerley Waggonway .7A **112**
Poets Dr. DH2: P Fel .6G **127**
Point, The NE8: Gate .9G **4** (3G **83**)
Point 5 NE8: Gate .9G **4** (3G **83**)
POINT PLEASANT .4J **65**
Point Pleasant Ind. Est.
NE28: W'snd .3K **65**
Point Pleasant Ter. NE28: W'snd .3J **65**
Polden Cl. SR8: Pet .7J **171**
Polden Cres. NE29: N Shi .3F **49**
Polebrook Rd. SR4: Sund .2J **117**
Polemarch St. SR7: S'hm .4B **148**
Police Ho's. NE64: Newb S .2H **13**
SR8: Pet .6A **172**
Pollard St. NE33: S Shi .2K **67**
Polmaise St. NE21: Blay .4C **80**
Polmuir Rd. SR3: Sund .6A **118**
Polmuir Sq. SR3: Sund .6A **118**
Polpero Cl. DH3: Bir .5B **114**
Polperro Cl. SR2: Ryh .2H **133**
Polton Sq. SR4: Sund .2J **117**
Polwarth Cres. NE3: Gos .4E **44**
Polwarth Dr. NE3: Gos .3D **44**
Polwarth Pl. NE3: Gos .4E **44**
Polwarth Rd. NE3: Gos .3E **44**
Polworth Sq. SR3: Sund .6B **118**
Ponds Cotts. NE40: G'sde .5D **78**
Ponds Ct. DH8: Cons .7G **121**
Ponds Ct. Bus. Pk. DH8: Cons .7G **121**
Pond St. DH1: H Shin .1F **177**
PONT .3A **122**
Pont Bungs. DH8: Lead .3K **121**
Pontdyke NE10: Hew .3D **100**
Pontefract Rd. SR4: Sund .5H **117**
PONTELAND .5J **31**
Ponteland Cl. NE29: N Shi .5C **48**
NE38: Wash .4D **114**
Ponteland Leisure Cen. .5K **31**
Ponteland Rd. NE2: Newc T .1A **4** (4B **62**)
NE3: Ki Pk .6H **43**
NE5: Blak, Fen .1J **61**
NE5: Fen .4A **62**
NE13: K Bank, Wool .1D **42**
NE15: Thro .1H **59**
NE20: Pon .5K **31**
Pont Haugh NE20: Pon .4K **31**
Ponthaugh NE39: Row G .4K **95**
Ponthead M. DH8: Lead .5B **122**
Pont La. DH8: Cons, Lead .2K **121**
PONTOP .3E **122**
Pontop Ct. DH9: Ann P .5K **123**
Pontop Pike DH9: Dip .3G **123**
Pontop Pike La. DH9: Ann P, Dip .4F **123**
Pontop Sq. SR4: Sund .1J **117**
Pontop St. DH5: E Rain .6C **144**
Pontopsyde DH9: Dip .2G **123**
Pontop Ter. DH9: Ann P .6J **123**
Pontop Vw. DH8: Cons .2K **135**
DH9: Dip .2F **123**
NE39: Row G .5H **95**
Pont Pk. NE20: Pon .1A **32**
Pont Rd. DH8: Lead .4B **122**
Pont St. NE63: Ash .4B **12**
Pont Ter. DH8: Lead .5A **122**
Pont Vw. DH8: Lead .3K **121**
NE20: Pon .4K **31**
Pool Bri. NE10: Ward .7J **85**
Poole Cl. NE23: Cra .3A **26**
Poole Rd. SR4: Sund .2J **117**
Pooley Cl. NE5: Den M .4H **61**
Pooley Rd. NE5: Den M .5H **61**
Poplar Av. DH4: Hou S .2D **144**
NE6: Walk .4D **64**
NE13: Din .4J **33**
NE16: Burn .2K **109**
NE24: Bly .7H **19**
TS27: B Col .3J **183**
Poplar Cl. NE31: Heb .3J **85**
Poplar Ct. DH3: Ches S .6A **128**
NE23: Nel V .7G **21**
Poplar Cres. DH3: Bir .3K **113**
NE8: Gate .5G **83**
NE11: Dun .7B **82**
Poplar Dr. DH1: Dur .1E **166**
SR6: Whit .5H **89**
Poplar Gro. DH9: Dip .1J **123**
NE22: Bed .7K **17**
SR2: Ryh .1G **133**
Poplar Lea DH7: B'don .1C **174**
Poplar Pl. NE3: Gos .7E **44**
Poplar Rd. DH1: Carr .7H **155**
Poplars, The DH1: Dur .4H **165**
DH3: Ches S .7B **128**
DH4: Pen .1B **130**
DH5: Eas L .2J **157**
NE3: Gos .2E **62**
NE4: Elsw .3C **82**
NE38: Wash .4H **115**
SR4: Sund .2G **117**
SR5: S'wck .5B **104**
Poplar St. DH2: Pelt .2D **126**
DH2: Wald .1G **141**
DH3: Ches S .6A **128**
DH7: Sac .7E **140**
DH9: Stly .5D **124**
NE15: Thro .3H **59**
NE63: Ash .3B **12**
Poplar Ter. *DH1: Shin .6E 166*
(off High St.)
DH3: Ches S .5B **128**
Popplewell Gdns. NE9: Low F .3J **99**
Popplewell Ter. NE29: N Shi .4G **49**
Poppyfields DH2: Ches S .7H **127**
Porchester Dr. NE23: Cra .2A **26**
Porchester St. NE33: S Shi .6H **67**
Porlock Ct. NE23: Cra .1J **25**
Porlock Ho. NE32: Jar .1D **86**
Porlock Rd. NE32: Jar .1D **86**
Portadown Rd. SR4: Sund .5H **117**
Portberry St. NE33: S Shi .5H **67**
Portberry St. Ind. Est. NE33: S Shi .4H **67**
Portberry Way NE33: S Shi .4H **67**
(not continuous)
Portchester Gro. NE35: Bol C .6E **86**
Portchester Rd. SR4: Sund .3J **117**
Portchester Sq. SR4: Sund .4J **117**
Porter Ter. SR7: Mur .7E **146**
Porthcawl Dr. NE37: Wash .5G **101**
Portia St. NE63: Ash .3C **12**
Portland Av. SR7: S'hm .3J **147**
Portland Cl. DH2: Ches S .1J **141**
NE28: W'snd .7A **48**
Portland Gdns. NE9: Low F .5H **99**
NE23: Cra .3A **26**
NE30: N Shi .5G **49**
NE46: Hex .1B **70**
Portland M. NE2: Newc T .2J **5** (6H **63**)
Portland Rd. NE2: Newc T .7H **63**
(Gosforth St.)
NE2: Newc T .2J **5** (6H **63**)
(Sandyford Rd.)
NE15: Thro .3J **59**
SR3: Sund .6B **118**
Portland Sq. SR3: Sund .5B **118**
Portland St. NE4: Elsw .2B **82**
NE10: Pel .5E **84**
NE24: Bly .7H **19**
Portland Ter. NE2: Jes .1H **5** (6H **63**)
NE46: Hex .1B **70**
NE63: Ash .2H **11**
Portman M. NE2: Newc T .3K **5**
Portman Pl. NE6: Walk .3C **84**
Portman Sq. SR4: Sund .3J **117**
Portmarnock NE37: Wash .5F **101**
PORTMEADS .5B **114**
Portmeads Ri. DH3: Bir .4B **114**
Portmeads Rd. DH3: Bir .3B **114**
PORTOBELLO .5C **114**
Portobello Ind. Est. DH3: Bir .4C **114**
Portobello La. SR6: Roker .6F **105**
(not continuous)
Portobello Rd. DH3: Bir .3C **114**
Portobello Ter. DH3: Bir .5C **114**
Portobello Way DH3: Bir .4B **114**
Portree Cl. DH3: Bir .7B **114**
Portree Sq. SR3: Sund .6A **118**
Portrush Cl. NE37: Wash .5G **101**
Portrush Rd. SR4: Sund .2J **117**
Portrush Way NE7: Longb .7A **46**
Portslade Rd. SR4: Sund .4H **117**
Portsmouth Rd. NE29: N Shi .7C **48**
SR4: Sund .3H **117**

Portsmouth Sq. SR4: Sund . . . 3H 117
Portugal Pl. NE28: W'snd . . . 4F 65
Postern Cres. NE61: Mor . . . 1F 15
Post Office La. *NE29: N Shi . . . 4G 49*
(off Front St.)
Post Office Sq. *NE24: Bly . . . 1K 23*
(off Post Office St.)
Post Office St. NE24: Bly . . . 1K 23
Potterburn Cl. DH9: Stly . . . 6D 124
Potterhouse La. DH1: P Me . . . 3G 153
Potterhouse Ter. DH1: P Me . . . 3J 153
Potteries, The NE33: S Shi . . . 4A 68
Potter Pl. DH9: Stly . . . 4H 125
Potters Bank DH1: Dur . . . 7A 6 (5J 165)
Potters Cl. DH1: Dur . . . 5K 165
Potter Sq. SR3: Sund . . . 6B 118
Potter St. NE28: W'snd . . . 4A 66
NE32: Jar . . . 6A 66
Pottersway NE9: Low F . . . 7J 83
Pottery Bank NE6: Walk . . . 3D 84
NE61: Mor . . . 5E 8
SR1: Sund . . . 7H 105
Pottery Bank Ct. NE61: Mor . . . 5E 8
Pottery La. NE1: Newc T . . . 9D 4 (3E 82)
SR4: Sund . . . 2G 117
Pottery Rd. SR5: S'wck . . . 6C 104
Pottery Vs. *SR4: Sund . . . 2G 117*
(off Pottery La.)
Pottery Yd. DH4: Hou S . . . 2E 144
Potto St. DH6: Shot C . . . 6F 171
Potts St. NE6: Byke . . . 7A 64
Poulton Cl. NE38: Wash . . . 1F 129
Powburn Cl. DH2: Ches S . . . 1J 141
Powburn Gdns. NE4: Fen . . . 5A 62
Pow Dene Ct. NE30: N Shi . . . 6J 49
Powerleague
Gateshead . . . 5D 82
Powis Rd. SR3: Sund . . . 6B 118
Powis Sq. SR3: Sund . . . 6B 118
Powys Pl. NE4: Newc T . . . 3A 4 (7C 62)
Poynings Cl. NE3: Ki Pk . . . 7J 43
Praetorian Dr. NE28: W'snd . . . 4F 65
Prebend Row DH2: Pelt . . . 3F 127
Prebends Fld. DH1: Dur . . . 7D 154
Prebends' Wlk. DH1: Dur . . . 5B 6
Precinct, The NE21: Blay . . . 3D 80
SR2: Sund . . . 5F 7 (2D 118)
(Chester Rd.)
SR2: Sund . . . 6E 118
(Leechmere Rd.)
Prefect Pl. NE9: Low F . . . 7J 83
Premier Rd. SR3: Sund . . . 6A 118
Prendwick Av. NE13: Haz . . . 2C 44
(not continuous)
NE31: Heb . . . 3H 85
Prendwick Cl. DH2: Ches S . . . 2J 141
Prendwick Ct. NE31: Heb . . . 3H 85
Prengarth Av. SR6: Ful . . . 4F 105
Prensgarth Way NE34: S Shi . . . 3F 87
Prescot Rd. SR4: Sund . . . 2J 117
Press La. SR1: Sund . . . 3K 7 (1F 119)
Prestbury Av. NE23: Cra . . . 1J 25
Prestbury Rd. SR4: Sund . . . 4G 117
Prestdale Av. NE24: Cow . . . 2E 22
Presthope Rd. SR4: Sund . . . 4G 117
Prestmede NE10: Fell . . . 7C 84
PRESTON . . . 5G 49
Preston Av. NE30: N Shi . . . 5G 49
Preston Ct. *NE29: N Shi . . . 4G 49*
(off Rosebery Av.)
Preston Ga. NE29: N Shi . . . 3F 49
PRESTON GRANGE . . . 3F 49
Preston Hill SR3: Dox P . . . 4A 132
Preston M. NE29: N Shi . . . 6G 49
Preston Nth. Rd. NE29: N Shi . . . 2F 49
Preston Pk. NE29: N Shi . . . 5G 49
Preston Rd. NE29: N Shi . . . 4G 49
SR2: Sund . . . 4H 119
Preston Ter. NE27: Shir . . . 3J 47
NE29: N Shi . . . 4F 49
Preston Towers NE29: N Shi . . . 5G 49
Preston Wood NE30: Cull . . . 3G 49
PRESTWICK . . . 6C 32
Prestwick NE10: Hew . . . 2C 100
Prestwick Av. NE29: N Shi . . . 5C 48
Prestwick Carr Rd. NE13: Din . . . 4G 33
Prestwick Cl. NE37: Wash . . . 5G 101
Prestwick Dr. NE10: Ward . . . 7G 85
Prestwick Gdns. NE3: Ken . . . 1B 62
Prestwick Ho. NE4: Newc T . . . 3B 4
Prestwick Ind. Est. NE20: Pon . . . 1C 42
Prestwick Pk. Bus. Cen. NE20: Pres . . . 6C 32
Prestwick Pit Ho's. NE20: Pon . . . 7C 32
Prestwick Rd. NE13: Din . . . 4G 33
SR4: Sund . . . 2J 117
PRESTWICK ROAD END . . . 7C 32
Prestwick Ter. NE20: Pon . . . 1D 42
Pretoria Av. NE61: Mor . . . 7F 9
Pretoria Sq. SR3: Sund . . . 6A 118
Price St. NE31: Heb . . . 6G 65
NE61: Mor . . . 6E 8
Priestburn Cl. DH7: Esh W . . . 3D 162
Priestclose Cotts. NE42: Pru . . . 4H 77
Priestclose Rd. NE42: Pru . . . 4F 77
Priestclose Wood Nature Reserve . . . 4H 77
Priestfield Gdns. NE16: Burn . . . 2K 109
Priestlands Av. NE46: Hex . . . 2C 70
Priestlands Cl. NE46: Hex . . . 3C 70
Priestlands Cres. NE46: Hex . . . 2C 70
Priestlands Dr. NE46: Hex . . . 2C 70
Priestlands Gro. NE46: Hex . . . 3C 70
Priestlands La. NE46: Hex . . . 2C 70
Priestlands Rd. NE46: Hex . . . 2C 70
Priestley Ct. NE34: S Shi . . . 3G 87
Priestley Gdns. NE10: Ward . . . 6F 85
Priestly Cres. SR4: Sund . . . 1F 7 (7D 104)
Priestman Av. DH8: C'sde . . . 1E 134
Priestman Ct. SR4: Sund . . . 2K 117
Priestpopple NE46: Hex . . . 2D 70
Priestsfield Cl. SR3: Dox P . . . 4B 132
Primary Gdns. SR2: Sund . . . 3H 119
Primate Rd. SR3: Sund . . . 7A 118
PRIMROSE . . . 2C 86
Primrose Av. NE34: S Shi . . . 1H 87
SR8: Hord . . . 5D 172
Primrose Cl. NE23: Dud . . . 3J 35
Primrose Cotts. SR6: Ful . . . 4F 105
Primrose Ct. NE63: Ash . . . 6K 11
TS27: B Col . . . 2H 183
Primrose Cres. DH4: Bour . . . 6J 129
SR6: Ful . . . 4F 105
Primrose Gdns. DH2: Ous . . . 6H 113
NE21: Blay . . . 1J 79
NE28: W'snd . . . 1E 64
Primrose Hill DH4: Bour . . . 7J 129
NE9: Low F . . . 2J 99
NE32: Jar . . . 3C 86
Primrose Hill Ter. NE32: Jar . . . 3C 86
Primrose Pl. NE9: Low F . . . 2H 99
Primrose Pct. SR6: Ful . . . 4F 105
Primrose St. SR4: Sund . . . 2G 117
Primrose Ter. DH3: Bir . . . 4B 114
NE32: Jar . . . 2B 86
Prince Albert Ter.
NE2: Newc T . . . 4J 5 (7H 63)
Prince Bishop M. DH7: Ush M . . . 2B 164
Prince Bishop River Cruiser . . . 3D 6 (3B 166)
Prince Bishop Shop. Cen.
DH1: Dur . . . 2C 6 (3A 166)
Prince Charles Av. DH6: Bowb . . . 3H 177
Prince Consort Ind. Est. NE31: Heb . . . 6G 65
Prince Consort La. NE31: Heb . . . 7H 65
(not continuous)
Prince Consort Rd.
NE8: Gate . . . 10H 5 (4G 83)
NE31: Heb . . . 7G 65
NE32: Jar . . . 7C 66
Prince Consort Way NE29: N Shi . . . 2G 67
Prince Edward Ct. NE34: S Shi . . . 1C 88
Prince Edward Gro. NE34: S Shi . . . 7E 68
Prince Edward Rd. NE34: S Shi . . . 1B 88
Prince George Av. SR6: Ful . . . 3F 105
Prince Georg Sq. NE33: S Shi . . . 2K 67
Prince of Wales Cl. NE34: S Shi . . . 1B 88
Prince Philip Cl. NE15: Benw . . . 1J 81
Prince Rd. NE28: W'snd . . . 2F 65
Princes Av. NE3: Gos . . . 6D 44
SR6: Seab . . . 2G 105
Princes Cl. NE3: Gos . . . 4D 44
Princes Ct. NE45: Corb . . . 1E 72
Princes Gdns. NE24: Cow . . . 1G 23
NE25: Monks . . . 6E 38
SR6: Seab . . . 2G 105
Princes Mdw. NE3: Gos . . . 7C 44
Princes Pk. NE11: T Vall . . . 2D 98
(not continuous)
Princes Rd. NE3: Gos . . . 3D 44
Princess Av. DH8: B'hill . . . 4F 121
Princess Cl. TS27: B Col . . . 3J 183
Princess Ct. NE29: N Shi . . . 2F 67
NE42: Pru . . . 2F 77
Princess Dr. NE8: Dun . . . 5C 82
Princess Gdns. DH5: Hett H . . . 5G 145
Princess Louise Rd. NE24: Bly . . . 2H 23
Princess Mary Ct. NE2: Jes . . . 4F 63
Princess Rd. SR7: S'hm . . . 3A 148
Princess Sq. NE1: Newc T . . . 4G 4 (7G 63)
Princess St. NE10: Pel . . . 5E 84
NE16: Sun . . . 5H 97
SR2: Sund . . . 6H 7 (3E 118)
Princes St. DH1: Dur . . . 1A 6 (2K 165)
DH4: S Row . . . 4A 130
DH9: Ann P . . . 4J 123
NE30: N Shi . . . 5H 49
NE45: Corb . . . 1D 72
Princes St. Vw. NE45: Corb . . . 1E 72
Princess Way NE42: Pru . . . 3D 76
Prince St. NE17: C'wl . . . 6K 93
SR1: Sund . . . 3J 7 (1F 119)
Princesway NE11: T Vall . . . 3E 98
Princesway Central NE11: T Vall . . . 3E 98
Princesway Nth. NE11: T Vall . . . 1E 98
Princesway Sth. NE11: T Vall . . . 3E 98
(not continuous)
Princetown Ter. SR3: Sund . . . 6A 118
Princeway NE30: Tyne . . . 4K 49
Pringle Cl. DH7: New B . . . 5A 164
Pringle Gro. DH7: New B . . . 5B 164
Pringle Pl. DH7: New B . . . 5B 164
Prinn Pl. NE16: Sun . . . 5H 97
Priors Cl. DH1: Dur . . . 2J 165
Priors Grange DH6: H Pitt . . . 6B 156
Prior's Ho. NE30: Tyne . . . 5K 49
Priors Path DH1: Dur . . . 2K 165
Prior's Ter. NE30: Tyne . . . 5K 49
Priors Wlk. NE61: Mor . . . 1E 14
Priors Way NE28: W'snd . . . 3J 65
Prior Ter. *NE45: Corb . . . 7D 52*
(off Cookson Cl.)
NE46: Hex . . . 7C 50
Priory Av. NE25: Monks . . . 7F 39
Priory Cl. DH8: Shot B . . . 4E 120
Priory Ct. DH7: Sac . . . 1E 152
NE8: Gate . . . 9J 5
NE10: Ward . . . 6F 85
NE30: Tyne . . . 4K 49
NE33: S Shi . . . 7K 49
Priory Dr. NE46: B End . . . 6E 50
Priory Gdns. NE45: Corb . . . 6D 52
Priory Grange NE24: Cow . . . 2G 23
Priory Grn. NE6: Byke . . . 4P 5 (7K 63)
Priory Gro. SR4: Sund . . . 3B 118
Priory M. NE30: Tyne . . . 5K 49
Priory Orchard DH1: Dur . . . 4A 6 (3K 165)
Priory Pl. NE6: Byke . . . 5P 5 (1A 84)
NE13: W Op . . . 6C 34
NE62: Stake . . . 7J 11
Priory Rd. DH1: Dur . . . 6K 153
NE32: Jar . . . 5C 66
Priory Rd. Flats DH1: Dur . . . 6K 153
Priory Way NE5: West . . . 1F 61
Proctor Ct. NE6: Walk . . . 1E 84
Proctor Sq. SR3: Sund . . . 6B 118
Proctor St. NE6: Walk . . . 1E 84
Promenade NE26: Whit B . . . 5G 39
NE33: S Shi . . . 1A 68
(not continuous)
NE64: Newb S . . . 4H 13
SR6: Seab . . . 3H 105
Promenade, The DH8: Cons . . . 5H 121
Promenade Ter. NE30: Tyne . . . 5K 49
Promontory Ter. NE26: Whit B . . . 7J 39
Promotion Cl. SR6: Roker . . . 5G 105
Prospect Av. NE25: Sea D . . . 7G 27
NE28: W'snd . . . 2F 65
Prospect Av. Nth. NE28: W'snd . . . 1F 65
Prospect Bus. Pk. DH8: Lead . . . 6A 122
Prospect Cotts. NE9: Spri . . . 6D 100
NE22: Bed . . . 3A 18
Prospect Ct. NE4: Newc T . . . 5A 4 (1C 82)
Prospect Cres. DH5: Eas L . . . 3J 157
Prospect Gdns. NE36: W Bol . . . 7G 87
Prospect Pl. DH6: Coxh . . . 7K 177
DH7: New B . . . 4A 164
DH8: Cons . . . 6H 121
NE4: Newc T . . . 5A 4 (1C 82)
NE64: Newb S . . . 2K 13
Prospect Row SR1: Sund . . . 1H 119
Prospect St. DH3: Ches S . . . 5A 128
DH8: Cons . . . 6H 121
Prospect Ter. DH1: Dur . . . 4H 165
DH1: Shin . . . 6E 166
DH2: Plaw . . . 6J 141
DH3: Ches S . . . 5A 128
DH7: Lan . . . 7J 137
DH7: New B . . . 4B 164
DH9: Ann P . . . 5B 124
NE9: Eigh B . . . 6B 100
NE9: Spri . . . 5D 100
NE11: Kib . . . 2E 112
NE16: Hob . . . 4A 110
NE30: N Shi . . . 6J 49
NE36: E Bol . . . 7J 87
NE42: Pru . . . 4D 76
Prospect Vw. DH4: W Rai . . . 1K 155
Providence Cl. DH1: Dur . . . 1D 6
Providence Pl. DH1: Dur . . . 1D 6 (1F 167)
NE10: Fell . . . 5B 84
Providence Row DH1: Dur . . . 2D 6 (2B 166)
Providence Ter. *DH9: Ann P . . . 5K 123*
(off Front St.)
Provident St. DH2: Pelt . . . 3E 126
Provident Ter. DH9: Crag . . . 6K 125
NE28: W'snd . . . 3E 64
Provost Gdns. NE15: Benw . . . 2K 81
PRUDHOE . . . 4F 77
Prudhoe Castle . . . 3E 76
Prudhoe Chare NE1: Newc T . . . 4F 4 (7F 63)
Prudhoe Ct. NE3: Fawd . . . 5A 44
Prudhoe Football & Sports Cen. . . . 5F 77
Prudhoe Gro. NE32: Jar . . . 3A 86
Prudhoe Pl. NE1: Newc T . . . 4E 4 (7F 63)
Prudhoe Station (Rail) . . . 2D 76
Prudhoe St. NE1: Newc T . . . 4E 4 (7F 63)
NE29: N Shi . . . 7G 49
SR4: Sund . . . 1B 118
Prudhoe Ter. NE29: N Shi . . . 7G 49
NE30: Tyne . . . 4K 49
Prudoe St. Bk. NE29: N Shi . . . 7G 49
Pudding Chare NE1: Newc T . . . 6F 4 (1F 83)
Pudding M. NE46: Hex . . . 1D 70
Puddlers Dr. NE22: Bed . . . 7K 17
Pudsey Ct. DH1: Dur . . . 5A 154
Puffin Cl. NE24: News . . . 6K 23
Pullman Ct. NE9: Low F . . . 2G 99
Pump La. NE6: Byke . . . 5N 5 (1K 83)
Purbeck Cl. NE29: N Shi . . . 2F 49
Purbeck Gdns. NE23: Cra . . . 3A 26
Purbeck Rd. NE12: Longb . . . 6K 45
Purley NE38: Wash . . . 4A 116
Purley Cl. NE28: W'snd . . . 1K 65
Purley Gdns. NE3: Ken . . . 1B 62
Purley Rd. SR3: Sund . . . 6A 118
Purley Sq. SR3: Sund . . . 6A 118
Putney Sq. SR4: Sund . . . 4H 117
Pykerley M. NE25: Monks . . . 7E 38
Pykerley Rd. NE25: Monks . . . 6E 38

Q

Quadrant, The NE29: N Shi . . . 7E 48
SR1: Sund . . . 1H 119
Quadrus Cen., The NE35: Bol C . . . 7D 86
QUAKING HOUSES . . . 7D 124
Quality Row DH6: Cass . . . 4E 178
NE6: Byke . . . 5M 5 (1J 83)
NE16: Swa . . . 5G 81
Quality Row Rd. NE16: Swa . . . 5G 81
Quality St. DH1: H Shin . . . 7F 167
Quantock Av. DH2: Ches S . . . 7J 127
Quantock Cl. NE12: Longb . . . 6J 45
NE29: N Shi . . . 2E 48
Quantock Pl. SR8: Pet . . . 6J 171
Quarries La. NE21: Blay . . . 4C 80
Quarrington Hgts. DH6: Quar H . . . 5D 178
QUARRINGTON HILL . . . 6D 178
Quarrington Hill Ind. Est.
DH6: Quar H . . . 6D 178
Quarry, The NE23: Seg . . . 2C 36
Quarry Bank Ct. NE4: Newc T . . . 6A 4 (1D 82)
Quarry Cotts. NE13: Din . . . 4H 33
NE23: Dud . . . 5A 36
NE63: Wood . . . 1F 13
Quarry Cres. DH7: Bearp . . . 1C 164
Quarry Edge NE46: Hex . . . 3E 70
Quarryfield Rd. NE8: Gate . . . 8K 5 (2H 83)
Quarryheads La. DH1: Dur . . . 5A 6 (4K 165)
Quarry Ho. Gdns. DH5: E Rain . . . 6C 144
Quarry Ho. La. DH1: Dur . . . 3H 165
DH5: E Rain . . . 6D 144
Quarry La. NE34: S Shi . . . 1C 88
(not continuous)
Quarry Rd. DH9: Stly . . . 2F 125
NE15: Lem . . . 7C 60
NE31: Heb . . . 1J 85
SR3: New S . . . 2D 132
Quarry Row DH4: Hou S . . . 1D 144
NE10: Fell . . . 5B 84
Quarry Sq. DH9: Tant . . . 6B 110
Quarry St. SR3: New S . . . 2C 132
Quasar (South Shields) . . . 1A 68
Quatre Bras NE46: Hex . . . 1B 70
Quay, The DH5: Hett H . . . 7G 145
Quay Corner . . . 6D 66
Quay Cnr. Av. NE32: Jar . . . 5D 66
Quay Point NE1: Newc T . . . 5J 5 (1H 83)
Quay Rd. NE24: Bly . . . 1K 23
(Sussex St.)
NE24: Bly . . . 1K 23
(Wellington St. E.)
Quaysgate NE8: Gate . . . 8J 5 (2H 83)
QUAYSIDE . . . 7H 5 (2G 83)
Quayside NE1: Newc T . . . 7H 5 (2G 83)
NE6: Byke . . . 7N 5 (2K 83)
NE24: Bly . . . 1K 23
Quayside Bus. Development Cen.
NE6: Byke . . . 5N 5 (1K 83)
Quayside Ct. NE24: Bly . . . 1K 23
NE30: N Shi . . . 7H 49
Quayside Ho. *NE1: Newc T . . . 6K 5*
(off Quayside)
NE24: Bly . . . 1K 23
(off Sussex St.)
Quay Vw. NE28: W'snd . . . 3A 66
QUEBEC . . . 7C 150
Quebec St. DH7: Lang P . . . 5H 151
Queen Alexandra Bri. SR5: Sund . . . 7C 104
Queen Alexandra Rd. NE29: N Shi . . . 5F 49
SR2: Sund . . . 5E 118
SR3: Sund . . . 4C 118
SR7: S'hm . . . 4B 148
Queen Alexandra Rd. W. NE29: N Shi . . . 5E 48
Queen Anne Ct. NE6: Byke . . . 6A 64
Queen Anne St. *NE6: Byke . . . 6A 64*
(off Queen Anne Ct.)
Queen Elizabeth II Country Pk. . . . 1D 12
Queen Elizabeth Av. NE9: Low F . . . 2K 99
Queen Elizabeth Ct. NE34: S Shi . . . 3F 87
Queen Elizabeth Dr. DH5: Eas L . . . 3K 157
Queen's Av. SR6: Seab . . . 2G 105
SR7: Dalt D . . . 4H 147
Queensberry St.
SR4: Sund . . . 3F 7 (1D 118)
Queensbridge NE12: Longb . . . 5H 45
Queensbury Dr. NE15: Walb . . . 2A 60
Queensbury Ga. NE12: Longb . . . 6J 45
Queensbury Rd. SR7: S'hm . . . 3J 147
Queens Cl. NE46: Acomb . . . 4C 50
Queens Ct. NE3: Gos . . . 2E 44
NE4: Newc T . . . 4B 4 (7D 62)
NE8: Gate . . . 5E 82
NE15: Walb . . . 4A 60
NE25: Sea D . . . 7H 27
(off Sinclair Gdns.)
Queens Ct. Nth. NE11: T Vall . . . 1F 99
Queen's Cres. NE28: W'snd . . . 2E 64
NE31: Heb . . . 2H 85
SR4: Sund . . . 3C 118
Queens Dr. NE16: Sun . . . 5H 97
NE16: Whi . . . 2J 97
NE26: Whit B . . . 6G 39
Queens Gdns. NE12: Longb . . . 6B 46
NE23: Dud . . . 2K 35
NE24: Cow . . . 1G 23
NE61: Mor . . . 1E 14
Queens Gth. DH6: Crox . . . 6K 175
Queens Gate DH8: Cons . . . 6H 121
Queens Gro. DH1: Dur . . . 5J 165
Queens Hall Bldgs. *NE25: Sea D . . . 7H 27*
(off Hayward Av.)
Queensland Av. NE34: S Shi . . . 2E 86
Queens La. NE1: Newc T . . . 7F 4 (2G 83)
Queensmere DH3: Ches S . . . 2A 128
Queens Pde. DH9: Ann P . . . 5K 123
SR6: Seab . . . 2H 105
Queens Pk. DH3: Ches S . . . 7B 128
NE11: T Vall . . . 1E 98
Queens Pl. NE64: Newb S . . . 2J 13
Queens Rd. DH8: B'hill . . . 5G 121
NE2: Jes . . . 4G 63
(not continuous)
NE5: West . . . 2G 61
NE15: Walb . . . 4A 60
NE22: Bed . . . 6B 18
NE23: Dud . . . 2K 35
NE26: Monks . . . 5F 39
NE26: Sea S . . . 4D 28
SR5: S'wck . . . 6C 104
TS28: Win . . . 5F 181

Queens Sq. NE1: Newc T 4F **4** (7F **63**)
NE10: Gate 6K **83**
Queens Ter. NE2: Jes 4H **63**
NE28: W'snd 2F **65**
Queen St. DH2: Gra V 4C **126**
DH3: Bir 4K **113**
DH5: Hett H 5G **145**
DH6: Shot C 6F **171**
DH8: Cons 7H **121**
NE1: Newc T 7H **5** (2G **83**)
NE8: Gate 6E **82**
NE30: N Shi 6H **49**
NE33: S Shi 2J **67**
NE61: Mor 7G **9**
NE63: Ash 3C **12**
NE64: Newb S 2J **13**
(not continuous)
SR1: Sund 3J **7** (1F **119**)
SR2: Ryh 1H **133**
SR7: S'hm 3A **148**
(not continuous)
Queen St. E. SR1: Sund 1G **119**
Queens Va. NE28: W'snd 1G **65**
Queensway DH5: Hou S 3F **145**
DH8: Shot B 4E **120**
NE3: Gos 3D **44**
NE4: Fen 5K **61**
NE20: Darr H 1H **41**
NE30: Tyne 4K **49**
NE38: Wash 4J **115**
NE46: Hex 1A **70**
NE61: Mor 1D **14**
Queensway Ct. NE11: T Vall 1E **98**
Queensway Nth. NE11: T Vall 7E **82**
Queensway Sth. NE11: T Vall 3F **99**
Queen Victoria Rd.
NE1: Newc T 3E **4** (7F **63**)
Queen Victoria St. NE10: Pel 5D **84**
Quentin Av. NE3: Ken 7K **43**
Que Sera DH5: Hett H 7G **145**
Quetlaw Rd. DH6: Whe H 3A **180**
Quick Silver Way NE27: Shir 4J **47**
Quigley Ter. DH3: Bir 2K **113**
Quilstyle Rd. DH6: Whe H 3A **180**
Quinn Cl. SR8: Pet 7B **172**
Quinn Cres. TS28: Win 5F **181**
Quinn's Ter. DH1: Dur 4J **165**
Quin Sq. DH6: S Het 4C **158**
Quorum Bus. Pk. NE12: Longb 4K **45**

R

Rabbit Banks Rd.
NE8: Gate 10F **4** (3F **83**)
Raby Av. SR8: Eas C 6C **160**
Raby Cl. DH4: Hou S 1A **144**
NE22: Bed 7F **17**
Raby Cres. NE6: Byke 4P **5** (7A **64**)
Raby Cross NE6: Byke 6P **5** (1A **84**)
Raby Dr. SR3: E Her 2J **131**
Raby Gdns. NE16: Burn 2J **109**
NE32: Jar 2B **86**
Raby Ga. NE6: Byke 7A **64**
Raby Rd. DH1: Dur 4A **154**
NE38: Wash 3D **114**
Raby St. NE6: Byke 3P **5** (7K **63**)
(Corbridge St.)
NE6: Byke 4P **5** (7A **64**)
(Raby Way)
NE8: Gate 6H **83**
SR4: Sund 2D **118**
Raby Wlk. NE6: Byke 3P **5** (7A **64**)
Raby Way NE6: Byke 4P **5** (7A **64**)
Rachel Cl. SR2: Ryh 2E **132**
Rackly Way SR6: Whit 6H **89**
(not continuous)
Radcliffe Cl. NE8: Gate 4K **83**
Radcliffe Pl. NE5: Fen 3K **61**
Radcliffe Rd. NE46: Hex 2E **70**
SR5: Sund 5A **104**
Radcliffe St. DH3: Bir 5A **114**
Radial Pk. Rd. NE37: Wash 7E **114**
Radlett Rd. SR5: Sund 5K **103**
Radlig Ct. NE10: Gate 4A **84**
Radnor Gdns. NE28: W'snd 2A **66**
Radnor St. NE1: Newc T 3H **5** (7G **63**)
Radstock Pl. NE12: Longb 5A **46**
Radstock Wlk. NE6: Walk 3C **84**
Rae Av. NE28: W'snd 1F **65**
Raeburn Av. NE38: Wash 4J **115**
Raeburn Gdns. NE9: Low F 7K **83**
Raeburn Rd. NE34: S Shi 4K **87**
SR5: Sund 4J **103**
Raglan NE38: Wash 3E **114**
Raglan Av. SR2: Sund 5G **119**
Raglan Pl. NE16: Burn 1B **110**
Raglan Row DH4: S Row 4C **130**
Raglan St. DH8: Cons 7H **121**
NE32: Jar 6C **66**
Raich Carter Sports Cen. 4H **119**
Railton Gdns. NE9: Low F 1K **99**
Railway Cl. DH6: S'burn 3J **167**
DH7: Lang P 4J **151**
Railway Cotts. DH1: Dur 3H **165**
DH2: Ches S 4J **127**
DH3: Bir 4K **113**
DH4: Hou S 2K **143**
DH4: Pen 1A **130**
DH6: Shot C 6E **170**
NE24: Cow 1C **22**
NE24: News 7G **23**
NE41: Wylam 1J **77**
NE44: Rid M 6A **74**
NE46: Hex 7C **50**
Railway Cotts. SR4: Cox G 6C **116**
TS27: B Col 3K **183**
TS27: Win 4H 181
(off Wellfield Rd.)
Railway Gdns. DH9: Ann P 5K **123**
Railway Pl. DH8: B'hill 6F **121**
Railway Row SR1: Sund 4F **7** (2D **118**)
Railway St. DH4: Hou S 7D **130**
DH5: Hett H 6G **145**
DH7: Lan 7K **137**
DH7: Lang P 4J **151**
DH8: Cons 7H **121**
DH8: Lead 5B **122**
DH9: Ann P 6A **124**
DH9: Crag 7J **125**
NE4: Newc T 10B **4** (3D **82**)
NE11: Dun 5C **82**
(Clockmill Rd.)
NE11: Dun 4B **82**
(St Omers Rd.)
NE29: N Shi 7G **49**
NE31: Heb 6K **65**
NE32: Jar 6A **66**
SR1: Sund 2H **119**
SR4: Sund 1B **118**
Railway Ter. DH4: New H 3D **130**
DH4: Pen 1A **130**
DH5: Hett H 5G **145**
NE4: Newc T 10A **4** (3D **82**)
NE24: Bly 2H **23**
NE28: W'snd 4H **65**
NE29: N Shi 7G **49**
NE38: Wash 4K **115**
SR4: Sund 2G **117**
Railway Ter. Nth. DH4: New H 2D **130**
Raine Gro. SR1: Sund 2G **119**
Rainford Av. SR2: Sund 5G **119**
Rainhill Cl. NE37: Wash 6K **101**
Rainhill Rd. NE37: Wash 6J **101**
Rainton Bank DH5: Hou S 4F **145**
Rainton Bri. Ind. Est. DH4: Hou S 3C **144**
Rainton Bri. Sth. Ind. Est.
DH4: W Rai 4B **144**
Rainton Cl. NE10: Ward 1G **101**
RAINTON GATE 2K **155**
Rainton Gro. DH5: Hou S 4E **144**
Rainton Meadows Arena 4D **144**
Rainton Meadows Nature Reserve 5B **144**
Rainton Meadows Vis. Cen. 4A **144**
Rainton St. DH4: Pen 1B **130**
SR4: Sund 2C **118**
SR7: S'hm 4B **148**
Rainton Vw. DH4: W Rai 1K **155**
DH5: Hett H 5G **145**
Rake La. NE29: N Shi 3C **48**
Raleigh Cl. NE33: S Shi 5H **67**
Raleigh Rd. SR5: Sund 5K **103**
Raleigh Sq. SR5: Sund 5K **103**
Ralph Av. SR2: Ryh 1G **133**
Ralph St. NE31: Heb 6K **65**
Ramilies SR2: Ryh 3F **133**
Ramillies Rd. SR5: Sund 4J **103**
Ramillies Sq. SR5: Sund 4J **103**
Ramona Av. DH6: Kel 7C **178**
Ramparts, The NE15: Lem 5E **60**
Ramsay Rd. NE17: C'wl 5K **93**
Ramsay Sq. SR5: Sund 4A **104**
Ramsay St. NE21: Winl 5B **80**
NE39: H Spen 2E **94**
Ramsay Ter. DH8: Cons 2K **135**
Ramsey Cl. DH1: Dur 2E **166**
SR8: Pet 4B **172**
Ramsey Gro. SR7: Mur 1F **159**
Ramsey St. DH3: Ches S 7A **128**
Ramsgate Rd. SR5: Sund 4A **104**
Ramshaw Cl. DH7: Lang P 5G **151**
NE7: H Hea 2C **64**
Ramside Vw. DH1: Carr 6H **155**
Randolph St. NE32: Jar 6C **66**
Range Vs. SR6: Whit 5H **89**
Rangoon Rd. SR5: Sund 4J **103**
Ranksborough St. SR7: S'hm 2K **147**
Ranmere Rd. NE15: Scot 1H **81**
Ranmore Cl. NE23: Cra 3K **25**
Rannoch Av. DH2: Ches S 1K **141**
Rannoch Cl. NE10: Ward 6G **85**
Rannoch Rd. SR5: Sund 4J **103**
Ranson Cres. NE34: S Shi 1F **87**
Ranson St. SR2: Sund 4D **118**
SR4: Sund 4D **118**
Raphael Av. NE34: S Shi 3J **87**
Rapperton Ct. NE5: West 2F **61**
Rathmore Gdns. NE30: N Shi 5G **49**
Ratho Ct. NE10: Wind N 1C **100**
Ravel Ct. NE32: Jar 7C **66**
Ravelston Cl. SR3: Silk 4C **132**
Ravenburn Gdns. NE15: Den M 7F **61**
Raven Ct. DH7: Esh W 4C **162**
Ravenna Rd. SR5: Sund 4H **103**
Raven Rd. NE8: Gate 9F **4** (3G **83**)
Ravensbourne Av. NE36: E Bol 6K **87**
Ravensburn Wlk. NE15: Thro 3G **59**
Ravenscar Cl. NE16: Whi 2E **96**
Ravenscourt Pl. NE8: Gate 5F **83**
Ravenscourt Rd. SR5: Sund 4J **103**
Ravensdale Cres. NE9: Low F 1J **99**
Ravensdale Gro. NE24: Cow 2E **22**
Ravens Hill Dr. NE63: Ash 5J **11**
Ravenshill Rd. NE5: W Dent 4D **60**
Ravenside Rd. NE4: Fen 5A **62**
Ravenside Ter. DH8: B'hill 5F **121**
NE17: C'wl 6J **93**
Ravenstone NE37: Wash 1F **115**
Ravenswood Cl. NE12: Longb 4C **46**
Ravenswood Gdns. NE9: Low F 4H **99**
Ravenswood Rd. NE6: Heat 4A **64**
SR5: Sund 4H **103**
Ravenswood Sq. SR5: Sund 4H **103**
RAVENSWORTH 3A **98**
Ravensworth SR2: Ryh 3E **132**
Ravensworth Av. DH4: Hou S 1A **144**
NE9: Eigh B 5A **100**
Ravensworth Castle 4C **98**
Ravensworth Cl. NE28: W'snd 3K **65**
Ravensworth Ct. DH6: S Het 3B **158**
NE3: Ki Pk 5K **43**
NE11: Dun 5C **82**
NE22: Bed 5B **18**
Ravensworth Cres.
NE16: Burn 7D **96**
Ravensworth Gdns. DH3: Bir 3K **113**
Ravensworth Pk. DH4: S Row 5K **129**
Ravensworth Pk. Est.
NE11: Rave 3B **98**
Ravensworth Rd. DH3: Bir 3K **113**
NE11: Dun 6C **82**
Ravensworth St. NE22: Bed 5B **18**
NE28: W'snd 3K **65**
SR4: Sund 1D **118**
Ravensworth Ter. DH1: Dur 2E **6** (2B **166**)
DH3: Bir 4A **114**
NE4: Newc T 6B **4** (1D **82**)
NE11: Dun 6C **82**
NE16: Sun 5J **97**
NE22: Bed 5B **18**
NE32: Jar 3B **86**
NE33: S Shi 5J **67**
Ravensworth Vw. NE11: Dun 4C **82**
Ravensworth Vs. NE9: Wrek 4A **100**
Raven Ter. DH3: Bir 3A **114**
Ravine Ter. SR6: Roker 4H **105**
Rawdon Rd. SR5: Sund 4A **104**
Rawling Rd. NE8: Gate 6F **83**
Rawlston Way NE5: Blak 2J **61**
Rawmarsh Rd. SR5: Sund 4J **103**
Rayburn Ct. NE24: News 6G **23**
Raydale SR5: Sund 4A **104**
Raydale Av. NE37: Wash 7F **101**
Raylees Gdns. NE11: Dun 7C **82**
Rayleigh Dr. NE13: W Op 4D **34**
Rayleigh Gro. NE8: Gate 7F **83**
Raynes Cl. NE61: Mor 1D **14**
Raynham Cl. NE23: Cra 7H **25**
Raynham Ct. NE33: S Shi 3J **67**
Reader Ct. NE28: W'snd 4F **65**
Readhead Av. NE33: S Shi 4A **68**
Readhead Dr. NE6: Walk 2D **84**
Readhead Rd. NE34: S Shi 5A **68**
Reading Rd. NE33: S Shi 6K **67**
SR5: Sund 4K **103**
Reading Sq. SR5: Sund 4J **103**
Rear Mkt. Cres. DH4: New H 3C **130**
Rear Woodbine St. *NE8: Gate 5G 83*
(off Woodbine St.)
Reasby Gdns. NE40: Ryton 1F **79**
Reasby Vs. NE40: Ryton 1F **79**
Reavley Av. NE22: Bed 5C **18**
Reay Ct. DH2: Ches S 7A **128**
Reay Cres. NE35: Bol C 6H **87**
Reay Gdns. NE5: West 2G **61**
Reay Pl. NE3: Gos 7C **44**
NE34: S Shi 1H **87**
Reay St. NE10: Bill Q 4F **85**
Rectory Av. NE3: Gos 1F **63**
Rectory Bank NE36: W Bol 7F **87**
Rectory Cotts. NE40: Ryton 7G **59**
Rectory Ct. NE16: Whi 7H **81**
Rectory Dene NE61: Mor 1F **15**
Rectory Dr. NE3: Gos 1G **63**
Rectory Grn. NE36: W Bol 7F **87**
Rectory Gro. NE3: Gos 7F **45**
Rectory La. DH8: Ebc 5G **107**
NE16: Whi 1H **97**
NE21: Winl 5B **80**
Rectory Pk. NE61: Mor 1F **15**
Rectory Pl. NE8: Gate 5F **83**
Rectory Rd. DH5: Hett H 7G **145**
NE3: Gos 2F **63**
NE8: Gate 5F **83**
NE10: Wind N 7A **84**
Rectory Rd. E. NE10: Fell 7B **84**
(not continuous)
Rectory Ter. *DH1: Shin 6E 166*
(off High St.)
NE3: Gos 1G **63**
NE36: W Bol 1F **103**
Rectory Vw. DH6: Shad 5E **168**
Red Admiral Ct. NE11: Fest P 7D **82**
Red Banks DH2: Ches S 7H **127**
Red Barns NE1: Newc T 5K **5** (1H **83**)
Redberry Way NE34: S Shi 2H **87**
Red Briar Wlk. DH1: P Me 4J **153**
Red Bungs. NE9: Spri 6C **100**
Redburn Cl. DH4: Hou S 2C **144**
Redburn Cres. NE46: Acomb 4B **50**
Redburn Est. NE46: Acomb 4B **50**
Redburn Rd. DH4: Hou S, W Rai 3B **144**
NE5: West 1F **61**
Redburn Row DH4: Hou S 3B **144**
Redburn Vs. NE46: Acomb 4B **50**
Redby Cl. SR6: Ful 5F **105**
Redcar Rd. NE6: Heat 4B **64**
NE28: W'snd 2A **66**
SR5: S'wck, Sund 5K **103**
Redcar Sq. SR5: Sund 5A **104**
Redcar Ter. NE36: W Bol 1G **103**
Redcliffe Way NE5: Blak 2H **61**
Red Courts DH7: B'don 1E **174**
Redcroft Grn. NE5: Blak 2H **61**
Redditch Sq. SR5: Sund 4K **103**
Rede Av. NE31: Heb 7J **65**
NE46: Hex 2E **70**
Redemarsh NE10: Hew 1D **100**
Redesdale Av. NE3: Gos 6C **44**
NE21: Winl 6K **79**
Redesdale Cl. NE12: Longb 4A **46**
NE15: Lem 6E **60**
Redesdale Ct. NE29: N Shi 3E **48**
SR8: Pet 7A **172**
Redesdale Gdns. NE11: Dun 7B **82**
Redesdale Gro. NE29: N Shi 6D **48**
Redesdale Pl. NE24: Cow 2F **23**
Redesdale Rd. DH2: Ches S 1J **141**
NE29: N Shi 6C **48**
SR5: Sund 4J **103**
Rede St. NE11: T Vall 2E **98**
NE32: Jar 1A **86**
Rede Ter. *NE46: Hex 2E 70*
(off Rede Av.)
Redewater Gdns. NE16: Whi 1G **97**
Redewater Rd. NE4: Fen 5A **62**
Redewood Cl. NE5: Den M 4G **61**
Red Firs DH7: B'don 1D **174**
Redford Pl. NE23: Dud 6A **36**
Redgrave Cl. NE8: Gate 10N **5** (4K **83**)
Red Hall Dr. NE7: H Hea 2B **64**
REDHEUGH 4E **82**
Redheugh Bri. Rd.
NE4: Newc T 9D **4** (3E **82**)
Redheugh Ct. NE8: Gate 6D **82**
Redheugh Rd. NE25: Well 6B **38**
Redhill SR6: Whit 6G **89**
Redhill Dr. NE16: Whi 3E **96**
Redhill Rd. SR5: Sund 4K **103**
Redhills La. DH1: Dur 2A **6** (2J **165**)
Red Hills Ter. DH1: Dur 3J **165**
Redhills Way DH5: Hett H 1G **157**
Red Hill Vs. DH1: Dur 2K **165**
Redhill Wlk. NE23: Cra 3K **25**
Redhouse Cl. DH7: Sac 1F **153**
Red Ho. Dr. NE25: Monks 5C **38**
Red Ho. Farm Est. NE22: Bed 1F **21**
Red Ho. Gdns. NE22: Bed 7F **17**
Red Ho. Rd. NE31: Heb 7K **65**
Red Kite Way NE39: Row G 5G **95**
Redland Av. NE3: Ken 6K **43**
Redlands DH4: Pen 2A **130**
NE16: Marl H 7G **97**
Red Lion Bldg. NE9: Eigh B 6B **100**
Red Lion La. NE37: Wash 5G **101**
Redmayne Ct. NE10: Fell 6B **84**
Redmire Dr. DH8: Cons 2J **135**
Redmires Cl. DH2: Ous 7G **113**
Redmond Rd. SR5: Sund 4A **104**
Redmond Sq. SR5: Sund 4A **104**
Rednam Pl. NE5: Blak 3H **61**
Redpath Way NE11: Dun 4J **81**
Red Ridges DH7: B'don 7E **164**
Red Rose Ter. DH3: Ches S 7B **128**
Red Row NE22: Bed 4A **18**
Red Row Ct. NE22: Bed 4A **18**
Red Row Dr. NE22: Bed 5A **18**
Redruth Gdns. NE9: Low F 5H **99**
Redruth Sq. SR5: Sund 5K **103**
Redshank Cl. NE38: Wash 6D **114**
Redshank Dr. NE24: News 5J **23**
Redstart Ct. NE39: Row G 6H **95**
Red Wlk. NE2: Jes 2H **63**
NE7: H Hea 2H **63**
Redwell Ct. NE34: S Shi 6E **68**
NE42: Pru 4F **77**
Redwell Hills DH8: Lead 5C **122**
Redwell La. NE34: S Shi 6F **69**
Redwell Rd. NE42: Pru 4F **77**
Redwing Cl. DH5: Eas L 2J **157**
NE38: Wash 5D **114**
Redwing Ct. NE6: Walk 6C **64**
Redwood DH7: Esh W 5D **162**
SR7: S'hm 4A **148**
Redwood Av. NE34: S Shi 2B **88**
Redwood Cl. DH5: Hett H 7F **145**
NE12: Kil 7A **36**
Redwood Ct. DH8: B'hill 5G **121**
NE63: Ash 5C **12**
Redwood Cres. NE24: Cow 1H **23**
Redwood Flats DH7: B'don 1D **174**
Redwood Gdns. NE11: Lob H 2D **98**
Redwood Gro. SR3: Tuns 2D **132**
Redworth M. NE63: Ash 5C **12**
Reed Av. NE12: Kil 6A **36**
Reedham Ct. NE5: Blak 1H **61**
Reedling Ct. SR5: Sund 3J **103**
Reedside NE40: Ryton 1H **79**
Reedsmouth Pl. NE5: Fen 5H **61**
Reed St. NE30: N Shi 6H **49**
NE33: S Shi 5H **67**
Reedswood Cres. NE23: E Cram 5B **26**
Reestones Pl. NE3: Ken 7K **43**
Reeth Rd. SR5: Sund 5K **103**
Reeth Sq. SR5: Sund 5K **103**
Reeth Way NE15: Thro 4G **59**
Reform Pl. DH1: Dur 2B **6**
Regal Bus. Cen. NE4: Elsw 2B **82**
Regal Rd. SR4: Sund 1C **118**
Regency Apartments NE12: Kil 1B **46**
Regency Ct. NE2: Jes 5H **63**
SR7: S'hm 3B **148**
Regency Dr. NE16: Whi 1F **97**
SR3: Tuns 1D **132**
Regency Gdns. NE29: N Shi 6E **48**
Regency Way NE20: Darr H 6E **30**
Regent Av. NE3: Gos 7D **44**
Regent Cen. NE3: Gos 6E **44**
Regent Centre (Park & Tram) 6E **44**
Regent Centre Station (Metro) 6E **44**

Regent Ct. DH6: S Het 4B 158
NE8: Gate 10J 5 (4H 83)
NE24: Bly 2H 23
NE31: Heb 1H 85
NE33: S Shi 4J 67
Regent Dr. NE16: Whi 3F 97
Regent Farm Ct. NE3: Gos 7E 44
Regent Farm Rd. NE3: Gos 6C 44
Regent Rd. NE3: Gos 7E 44
NE28: W'snd 2E 64
NE32: Jar 7C 66
SR2: Ryh 4J 133
Regent Rd. Nth. NE3: Gos 7E 44
Regents Ct. DH1: Dur 3F 167
NE12: Longb 3K 45
NE28: W'snd 1C 64
Regents Dr. NE30: Tyne 3J 49
NE42: Pru 2G 77
Regents Pk. NE28: W'snd 2C 64
Regent St. DH5: Hett H 5G 145
DH9: Ann P 4K 123
NE8: Gate 10H 5 (4G 83)
NE24: Bly 7J 19
NE33: S Shi 4H 67
Regent Ter. NE8: Gate 10H 5 (4G 83)
NE29: N Shi 5E 48
SR2: Sund 6H 119
Reginald St. NE10: Fell 5K 83
NE35: Bol C 6F 87
SR4: Sund 1B 118
Regina Sq. SR5: Sund 4K 103
Reid Av. NE28: W'snd 2F 65
Reid Pk. Cl. NE2: Jes 3H 63
Reid Pk. Ct. NE2: Jes 3H 63
Reid Pk. Rd. NE2: Jes 3H 63
Reid's La. NE23: Seg 2C 36
Reid St. NE61: Mor 6G 9
Reigate Sq. NE23: Cra 3K 25
Reins Ct. NE46: Hex 1A 70
Reiver Ct. NE28: W'snd 3F 65
Reiverdale Rd. NE63: Ash 2B 12
Rekendyke Ind. Est. NE33: S Shi 4H 67
Rekendyke La. NE33: S Shi 4H 67
Relley Gth. DH7: Lang M 7F 165
Relly Cl. DH7: Ush M 3D 164
Relly Path DH1: Dur 4J 165
Relton Av. NE6: Byke 2B 84
Relton Cl. DH4: Hou S 3A 144
Relton Ct. NE25: Monks 6E 38
Relton Pl. NE25: Monks 6E 38
Relton Ter. DH3: Ches S 7A 128
NE25: Monks 6E 38
Rembrandt Av. NE34: S Shi 3J 87
Remscheid Way NE63: Ash 5A 12
Remus Av. NE15: Hed W 3B 58
Remus Cl. NE13: W Op 6D 34
Renaissance Point NE30: N Shi 6J 49
Rendel St. NE11: Dun 5B 82
Rendle Rd. NE6: Walk 2F 85
Renforth Cl. NE8: Gate 10N 5 (4K 83)
Renforth St. NE11: Dun 6B 82
Renfrew Cl. NE29: N Shi 4C 48
Renfrew Grn. NE5: Blak 2H 61
Renfrew Pl. DH3: Bir 6B 114
Renfrew Rd. SR5: Sund 4K 103
Rennie Rd. SR5: Sund 4H 103
Rennie Sq. SR5: Sund 4H 103
Rennington NE10: Hew 2D 100
Rennington Av. NE30: Cull 3J 49
Rennington Cl. NE30: Cull 3J 49
NE61: Mor 3H 15
Rennington Pl. NE5: Fen 3K 61
Rennison M. NE21: Blay 5C 80
Renny's La. DH1: Carr, Dur 2E 166
Renny St. DH1: Dur 2C 166
Renoir Gdns. NE34: S Shi 4K 87
Renwick Av. NE3: Fawd 6A 44
Renwick Rd. NE24: Bly 2H 23
Renwick St. NE6: Walk 7B 64
Renwick Ter. NE8: Gate 6E 82
Renwick Wlk. NE61: Mor 7E 8
Rescue Sta. Cotts. DH5: Hou S 4F 145
Resida Cl. NE15: Lem 5C 60
Retail World NE11: T Vall 5F 99
Retford Rd. SR5: Sund 4K 103
Retford Sq. SR5: Sund 4K 103
Retreat, The NE15: Newb 6K 59
SR2: Sund 5F 7 (2D 118)
Revell Ter. NE5: Fen 4A 62
Revelstoke Rd. SR5: Sund 4H 103
Revesby St. NE33: S Shi 7J 67
Rewcastle Chare NE1: Newc T 7H 5
Reynolds Av. NE12: Kil 2K 45
NE34: S Shi 3K 87
NE38: Wash 4J 115
Reynolds Cl. DH9: Stly 3F 125
Reynolds Ct. SR8: Hord 6F 173
Reyrolle Ct. NE31: Heb 1H 85
Rheims Ct. SR4: Sund 1K 117
Rheims Ct. Factories SR4: Sund 1K 117
Rheydt Av. NE28: W'snd 3D 64
Rhoda Ter. SR2: Sund 7H 119
Rhodes Ct. NE23: Nel V 2H 25
Rhodesia Rd. SR5: Sund 4K 103
Rhodes St. NE6: Walk 1E 84
Rhodes Ter. DH1: Dur 4H 165
Rhondda Rd. SR5: Sund 4H 103
Rhuddlan Ct. NE5: Blak 1H 61
Rhyl Pde. NE31: Heb 4A 86
Rhyl Sq. SR5: Sund 4A 104
Rialto NE1: Newc T 5H 5
Ribbledale Gdns. NE7: H Hea 2K 63
Ribble Rd. SR5: Sund 5J 103
Ribblesdale DH4: Pen 2B 130
NE28: W'snd 1D 64
Ribblesdale Av. NE24: Cow 1E 22
(Grasmere Way)
NE24: Cow 1E 22
(Patterdale Rd.)
Ribble Wlk. NE32: Jar 3C 86
Richard Ashley Cl. NE64: Newb S 1J 13
Richard Av. SR4: Sund 4C 118
Richard Browell Rd. NE15: Thro 4H 59
Richard Hollon Ct. NE61: Mor 7F 9
Richardson Av. NE34: S Shi 2F 87
Richardson Gdns. NE27: Back, Shir 7H 37
Richardson Rd. NE2: Newc T 1B 4 (6D 62)
Richardsons Bldgs. NE62: Sco G 3G 17
Richardson St. NE6: Heat 5A 64
NE28: W'snd 3G 65
NE63: Ash 5C 12
Richardson Ter. NE17: C'wl 6J 93
NE37: Wash 7H 101
(not continuous)
SR2: Ryh 3J 133
Richardson Way DH8: Cons 7G 121
Richard St. DH5: Hett H 7G 145
NE24: Bly 2J 23
Richmond SR2: Ryh 2E 132
Richmond Av. NE10: Bill Q 5G 85
NE16: Swa 5H 81
NE38: Wash 2H 115
Richmond Cl. NE22: Bed 6G 17
Richmond Ct. DH1: Dur 4B 154
NE8: Gate 5H 83
NE9: Low F 3H 99
NE24: Bly 1J 23
(off Wright St.)
NE32: Jar 6A 66
Richmond Dr. DH4: Hou S 1H 143
Richmond Flds. NE20: Darr H 6E 30
Richmond Gdns. NE28: W'snd 2J 65
Richmond Gro. NE29: N Shi 7E 48
Richmond Ho. NE28: W'snd 3H 65
Richmond M. NE3: Gos 2D 62
Richmond Pk. NE28: W'snd 1C 64
Richmond Pl. DH3: Bir 6A 114
Richmond Rd. DH1: Dur 4B 154
NE34: S Shi 7J 67
Richmond St. SR5: Monkw 1H 7 (7E 104)
Richmond Ter. DH6: Has 1A 170
NE8: Gate 5G 83
NE10: Fell 6B 84
NE15: Walb 4K 59
NE26: Whit B 4F 39
Richmond Way NE20: Darr H 6E 30
NE23: Cra 7H 25
Rickaby St. SR1: Sund 7H 105
Rickgarth NE10: Hew 2D 100
(not continuous)
RICKLETON 1C 128
Rickleton Av. DH3: Ches S 4B 128
Rickleton Village Cen. NE38: Wash 1D 128
Rickleton Way NE38: Wash 7D 114
Riddell Av. NE15: Benw 1J 81
Riddell Ct. DH2: Ches S 7A 128
Riddell Ter. NE3: Gos 7C 44
Ridding Ct. DH7: Esh W 4D 162
Ridding Rd. DH7: Esh W 5D 162
Riddings Rd. SR5: Sund 4K 103
Riddings Sq. SR5: Sund 4K 103
Ridge, The NE40: Ryton 2G 79
Ridge Ct. NE13: Haz 7D 34
Ridgely Cl. NE20: Pon 5A 32
Ridgely Dr. NE20: Pon 5A 32
Ridges, The TS28: Sta T 7H 181
Ridge Ter. NE22: Bed 7G 17
Ridge Vs. NE22: Bed 7G 17
Ridge Way, The NE3: Ken 1B 62
Ridgeway DH3: Bir 2A 114
DH7: Lan 6J 137
NE4: Fen 5A 62
NE10: Hew 7F 85
NE25: H'wll 2J 37
NE62: Stake 7J 11
NE63: N Sea 5E 12
SR2: Ryh 3E 132
Ridgeway, The DH5: Hett H 7G 145
NE34: S Shi 3B 88
Ridgeway Cres. SR3: Sund 5D 118
Ridgewood Cres. NE3: Gos 7H 45
Ridgewood Gdns. NE3: Gos 7G 45
Ridgewood Vs. NE3: Gos 7G 45
Riding, The NE3: Ken 2A 62
Riding Bank NE46: Acomb 4C 50
Riding Barns Way NE16: Sun 5G 97
Riding Cl. NE40: Craw 3C 78
NE44: Rid M 6K 73
Riding Dene NE43: Mic 5B 76
Riding Grange NE44: Rid M 6J 73
Riding Hill DH3: Gt Lum 3E 142
Riding Hill Rd. DH9: Ann P 4A 124
Riding La. NE11: Beam, Kib 3C 112
NE61: Chop 6F 11
RIDING LEA 6H 73
Riding Lea NE21: Winl 5A 80
RIDING MILL 7K 73
Riding Mill Station (Rail) 6K 73
Ridings, The DH9: Ann P 4J 123
NE25: Monks 5C 38
Ridings Ct. NE40: Craw 3C 78
Riding Ter. *NE43: Mic 5A 76*
(off Station Bank)
Ridley Av. DH2: Ches S 7K 127
NE24: Bly 2K 23
NE28: W'snd 1A 66
SR2: Ryh 2H 133
Ridley Cl. NE3: Fawd 4B 44
NE46: Hex 3B 70
NE61: Mor 7E 8
Ridley Ct. NE1: Newc T 6F 4 (1F 83)
Ridley Gdns. NE16: Swa 5G 81
NE27: Shir 7J 37
Ridley Gro. NE34: S Shi 6C 68
Ridley Ho. NE3: Gos 7E 44
Ridley Mill Cotts. NE43: Pains 1H 91
Ridley Mill Rd. NE43: Pains 1H 91
Ridley Pl. NE1: Newc T 3F 4 (7F 63)
Ridley St. DH8: B'hill 6F 121
DH9: Stly 2F 125
NE8: Gate 6F 83
NE23: Cra 5A 26
NE24: Bly 1K 23
SR5: S'wck 5C 104
Ridley Ter. DH8: Lead 5B 122
NE10: Hew 6C 84
NE24: Camb 4H 19
NE46: Hex 7C 50
(off Tyne Grn. Rd.)
SR2: Sund 3H 119
Ridsdale NE42: Pru 4D 76
Ridsdale Av. NE5: W Dent 4D 60
Ridsdale Cl. NE25: Sea D 7G 27
NE28: W'snd 1G 65
Ridsdale Ct. NE8: Gate 5F 83
Ridsdale Sq. NE63: Ash 4A 12
Rievaulx NE38: Wash 5G 115
Riga Sq. SR5: Sund 4J 103
Riggs, The DH7: B'don 7E 164
NE45: Corb 6D 52
Rignall NE38: Wash 3A 116
Riley St. NE32: Jar 6A 66
Ringlet Cl. NE11: Fest P 7D 82
Ringmore Ct. SR2: Sund 6E 118
Ringway NE62: Stake 6H 11
SR5: Sund 7F 103
Ringwood Dr. NE23: Cra 3K 25
Ringwood Grn. NE12: Longb 5A 46
Ringwood Rd. SR5: Sund 4K 103
Ringwood Sq. SR5: Sund 4K 103
Rink St. NE24: Bly 1K 23
Rink Way NE25: Whit B 1F 49
Ripley Av. NE29: N Shi 7E 48
(not continuous)
Ripley Cl. NE22: Bed 6F 17
Ripley Ct. DH7: Sac 7E 140
NE9: Low F 6K 99
Ripley Dr. NE23: Cra 7H 25
Ripley Ter. NE6: Walk 7C 64
Ripon Cl. NE23: Cra 7H 25
Ripon Ct. DH7: Sac 7D 140
Ripon Gdns. NE2: Jes 5J 63
NE28: W'snd 2J 65
Ripon Rd. DH1: Dur 3B 154
Ripon Sq. NE32: Jar 5B 86
Ripon St. DH3: Ches S 1A 142
NE8: Gate 5G 83
SR6: Roker 5G 105
Ripon Ter. DH2: Plaw 7J 141
SR7: Mur 7E 146
Rise, The DH8: C'sde 4C 134
NE3: Ken 1A 62
NE8: Gate 5K 83
(off Duncan St.)
NE20: Darr H 1F 41
NE21: Blay 2A 80
NE26: Sea S 6D 28
Rishton Sq. SR5: Sund 4J 103
Rising Sun NE28: W'snd 6G 47
Rising Sun Cotts. NE28: W'snd 7F 47
Rising Sun Country Pk. 5F 47
Rising Sun Countryside Cen. 4G 47
Rising Sun Vs. NE28: W'snd 7F 47
Ritson Av. DH7: Bearp 1C 164
Ritson Cl. NE29: N Shi 5E 48
Ritsons Ct. DH8: B'hill 5F 121
Ritson's Rd. DH8: B'hill 4F 121
Ritson St. DH8: B'hill 5F 121
DH9: Stly 3F 125
SR6: Ful 3G 105
Ritz Bingo
Forest Hall 4C 46
Walker 7D 64
River Bank NE62: Stake 7A 12
River Bank E. NE62: Stake 7A 12
Riverbank Rd. SR5: Sund 5K 103
Riverdale SR5: Sund 7H 103
River Dr. NE33: S Shi 2J 67
River Gth. *SR1: Sund 1G 119*
(off High St. E.)
Rivergreen Cen. DH1: Dur 7A 154
Rivergreen Ind. Est.
SR4: Sund 1A 118
River La. NE40: Ryton 7G 59
Rivermead NE38: Wash 7J 115
Rivermede NE20: Pon 4K 31
Riversdale Av. NE62: Stake 7J 11
Riversdale Cl. NE17: C'wl 2K 107
Riversdale Ct. NE15: Lem 7C 60
NE62: Stake 1J 17
Riversdale Ho. *NE62: Stake 1J 17*
(off Riversdale Av.)
Riversdale Rd. NE8: Gate 10F 4 (3F 83)
Riversdale Ter. SR2: Sund 3D 118
Riversdale Way NE15: Lem 7B 60
Riverside DH3: Ches S 7C 128
DH8: Shot B 3E 120
NE20: Pon 5J 31
NE61: Mor 7F 9
(off Waterside)
SR4: Sund 2F 117
Riverside, The NE31: Heb 6G 65
Riverside Apartments NE62: Stake 7K 11
Riverside Av. NE62: Chop 1F 17
Riverside Bowling 6J 103
Riverside Bus. Pk. NE28: W'snd 4A 66
Riverside Cen., The DH1: Dur 1B 166
Riverside Ct. NE11: Dun 5C 82
NE21: Blay 2D 80
NE24: Cow 7E 18
NE33: S Shi 3H 67
RIVERSIDE DENE 9A 4 (3C 82)
Riverside E. Ind. Est.
NE6: Byke 7P 5 (2A 84)
Riverside Ind. Est. DH7: Lang P 4H 151
Riverside Leisure Cen.
Morpeth 7F 9
Riverside Leisure Complex 7C 128
Riverside Leisure Pk. NE46: Hex 7B 50
Riverside Park 3F 83
Riverside Pk. 6C 128
Riverside Pk. SR4: Sund 1H 117
Riverside Rd. SR5: S'wck 5K 103
Riverside Row NE8: Gate 4D 82
Riverside Sth. DH3: Ches S 7C 128
SR4: Sund 7A 104
Riverside Studios NE4: Newc T 3B 82
Riverside Way NE11: Dun, Swa 3G 81
NE16: Swa 3G 81
NE39: Row G 7H 95
Riverslea NE34: S Shi 7C 68
River St. NE33: S Shi 5G 67
River Ter. DH3: Ches S 5B 128
River Vw. NE4: Benw 2K 81
NE17: C'wl 2K 107
NE21: Winl 4B 80
NE22: Bed 7B 18
NE30: Tyne 6J 49
NE40: Ryton 1J 79
NE42: O'ham 2C 76
NE42: Pru 4E 76
NE46: Hex 1C 70
(off Circle Pl.)
NE61: Mor 6G 9
(off Howard Rd.)
Riverview NE38: Wash 7H 115
River Vw. Cl. NE22: Bed 7B 18
Riverview Lodge NE4: Benw 2K 81
Roachburn Rd. NE5: West 3E 60
Roadside Cotts. NE21: Blay 1K 79
Robert Allen Ct. NE13: Bru V 5C 34
Robert Moore Cl. DH6: Bowb 3G 177
Robert Owen Gdns. NE10: Wind N 7A 84
Robertson Ct. DH3: Ches S 7A 128
Robertson Rd. SR5: Sund 4H 103
Robertson Sq. SR5: Sund 4H 103
Robert Sq. SR7: S'hm 4C 148
Roberts Ter. NE32: Jar 1B 86
Robert St. NE24: Bly 2J 23
NE33: S Shi 4K 67
SR3: New S 2D 132
SR4: Sund 1C 118
SR7: S'hm 4C 148
Robert Ter. DH6: Bowb 3H 177
DH9: Stly 1F 125
NE39: H Spen 3D 94
Robert Ter. Cotts. *NE39: H Spen 3D 94*
(off North Vw. Bungs.)
Robert Westall Way NE29: N Shi 2G 67
Robert Wheatman Ct. SR2: Sund 6G 119
Robin Ct. DH5: E Rain 7C 144
Robin La. DH5: E Rain 2A 156
Robinson Gdns. NE28: W'snd 2A 66
SR6: Whit 5H 89
Robinson Ho. SR8: Hord 5E 172
Robinsons Dr. NE21: Blay 4C 80
Robinson Sq. *NE64: Newb S 2J 13*
(off High St.)
Robinson St. DH8: B'hill 5G 121
NE6: Byke 7A 64
NE33: S Shi 4K 67
Robinson Ter. NE16: Hob 4A 110
NE38: Wash 4K 115
SR2: Sund 4H 119
Robinswood NE9: Low F 2H 99
Robsheugh Pl. NE5: Fen 5J 61
Robson Av. SR8: Pet 5B 172
Robson Cl. NE34: S Shi 1G 87
NE40: Craw 3D 78
(off Greenside Rd.)
Robson Cres. DH6: Bowb 3H 177
Robson Dr. NE46: Hex 3B 70
Robson Pl. SR2: Ryh 3J 133
Robson St. DH8: Cons 6J 121
NE6: Byke 3N 5 (7K 63)
NE9: Low F 2H 99
Robsons Way DH3: Bir 2B 114
(not continuous)
Robson Ter. DH1: Shin 6D 166
DH9: Dip 6K 109
NE9: Eigh B 6B 100
NE39: Row G 4E 94
Rochdale Rd. SR5: Sund 4K 103
Rochdale St. DH5: Hett H 1G 157
NE28: W'snd 4E 64
Rochdale Way SR5: Sund 4K 103
Roche Ct. NE38: Wash 4G 115
(not continuous)
Rochester Cl. NE63: N Sea 5E 12
Rochester Gdns. NE11: Dun 6C 82
Rochester Rd. DH1: Dur 4B 154
Rochester Sq. NE32: Jar 5B 86
Rochester St. NE6: Walk 2E 84
Rochester Ter. NE10: Fell 6C 84
Rochford Gro. NE23: Cra 7J 25
Rochford Rd. SR5: Sund 4J 103
Rockcliffe *NE26: Whit B 6J 39*
(off Cheviot Vw.)
NE33: S Shi 4B 68
Rockcliffe Av. NE26: Whit B 7J 39

Rockcliffe Gdns. NE15: Den M 6G 61
NE26: Whit B 6J 39
Rockcliffe St. NE26: Whit B 6J 39
Rockcliffe Way NE9: Eigh B 5A 100
Rocket Way NE12: Longb 4D 46
Rock Farm M. DH6: Whe H 2B 180
Rock Gro. NE9: Low F 2H 99
Rockingham Cl. SR7: S'hm 1A 148
Rockingham Dr. NE38: Wash 4A 116
Rockingham Rd. SR5: Sund 4J 103
Rockingham Sq. SR5: Sund 4J 103
Rock Lodge Gdns. SR6: Seab 4G 105
Rock Lodge Rd. SR6: Seab 4H 105
Rockmore Rd. NE21: Blay 5C 80
Rock Ter. DH7: New B 4B 164
NE2: Newc T 3J 5 (7H 63)
NE37: Wash 7J 101
Rockville SR6: Ful 3G 105
(not continuous)
Rock Wlk. DH3: Lam P 3F 129
Rockwood Gdns. NE40: G'sde 5C 78
Rockwood Hill Est. NE40: G'sde 6C 78
Rockwood Hill Rd. NE40: G'sde 6C 78
Rockwood Ter. NE40: G'sde 5D 78
Rocky Island NE26: Sea S 4D 28
Rodham Ter. DH9: Stly 1F 125
Rodin Av. NE34: S Shi 4K 87
Rodney Cl. NE30: Tyne 5K 49
SR2: Ryh 3E 132
Rodney Ct. *NE26: Whit B 4D 38*
(off Woodburn Sq.)
Rodney St. NE6: Byke 6N 5 (1K 83)
Rodney Way NE26: Whit B 4D 38
Rodridge Pk. TS28: Sta T 7G 181
Rodsley Av. NE8: Gate 6G 83
Roeburn Way NE3: Ken 2B 62
Roedean Rd. SR5: Sund 4A 104
Roehedge NE10: Hew 1F 101
Rogan Av. *NE37: Wash 2E 114*
(off Thirlmoor)
Rogerley Ter. DH9: Ann P 4J 123
Rogers Cl. SR8: Hord 6E 172
Rogerson Cl. DH6: Crox 6K 175
Rogerson Ter. DH6: Crox 6K 175
NE5: West 3E 60
Roger St. DH8: B'hill 6G 121
NE6: Byke 3N 5 (7K 63)
Rogues La. NE39: H Spen 1E 94
Rokeby Av. NE15: Lem 7D 60
Rokeby Dr. NE3: Ken 1B 62
Rokeby Sq. DH1: Dur 5J 165
Rokeby St. NE15: Lem 7D 60
SR4: Sund 2D 118
Rokeby Ter. NE6: Heat 4A 64
(not continuous)
Rokeby Vw. NE9: Low F 5J 99
Rokeby Vs. NE15: Lem 7D 60
ROKER 4G 105
Roker Av. NE25: Monks 7E 38
SR6: Roker 7F 105
Roker Baths Rd. SR6: Roker 5F 105
Rokerby Av. NE16: Whi 1J 97
Roker Pk. Cl. SR6: Roker 5G 105
Roker Pk. Rd. SR6: Roker 5G 105
Roker Pk. Ter. SR6: Roker 5H 105
Roker Ter. SR6: Roker 4H 105
Roland Rd. NE28: W'snd 3J 65
Roland St. NE38: Wash 4J 115
Rollesby Ct. NE5: Blak 1H 61
Rolley Way NE42: Pru 3G 77
Rolling Mill DH8: Cons 6J 121
Rolling Mill Rd. NE32: Jar 5A 66
Romaine Sq. *DH6: Bowb 4H 177*
(off Bede Ter.)
Romaldkirk Cl. DH8: Cons 1H 135
SR4: Sund 3H 117
Roman Av. DH3: Ches S 6B 128
NE6: Walk 6C 64
Roman Ct. NE28: W'snd 1J 65
Roman Forum *NE11: Dun 4J 81*
(off Metro Cen.)
Roman Rd. DH7: B'don 3C 174
NE32: Jar 4B 86
(not continuous)
NE33: S Shi 1K 67
Roman Rd. Nth. NE33: S Shi 7J 49
Roman Way NE45: Corb 7D 52
Roman Way, The NE5: W Dent 4D 60
Romany Dr. DH8: Cons 7G 121
Romford Cl. NE23: Cra 7J 25
Romford Pl. NE9: Low F 6J 83
Romford St. SR4: Sund 2B 118
Romiley Gro. NE10: Ward 7H 85
Romilly St. NE33: S Shi 3K 67
Romney Av. NE34: S Shi 3K 87
NE38: Wash 4J 115
SR2: Sund 5G 119
Romney Cl. DH4: S Row 4C 130
NE26: Whit B 7J 39
Romney Dr. DH1: Carr 6H 155
Romney Gdns. NE9: Low F 7K 83
Romney Vs. NE38: Wash 4J 115
Romsey Cl. NE23: Cra 3K 25
Romsey Dr. NE35: Bol C 6D 86
Romsey Gro. NE15: Lem 5C 60
Romulus Ct. NE4: Fen 7B 62
Ronald Dr. NE15: Den M 7G 61
Ronald Gdns. NE31: Heb 2H 85
Ronaldsay Cl. SR2: Ryh 1G 133
Ronald Sq. SR6: Ful 5F 105
Ronan M. DH4: W Rai 1A 156
Ronsdorf Ct. NE32: Jar 7B 66
Rookery, The NE16: Burn 2K 109
Rookery Cl. NE24: Cow 2F 23
Rookery La. NE16: Whi 3E 96
Rookhope NE38: Wash 1D 128
Rookland Pl. NE23: Dud 1J 35
Rooksleigh NE21: Winl 5B 80
Rookswood NE61: Mor 2G 15
Rookswood Gdns. NE39: Row G 4J 95
Rookwood Dr. NE13: Sea B 3E 34
Rookwood Rd. NE5: Den M 5G 61
Roosevelt Rd. DH1: Dur 1D 166
Ropery, The NE6: Byke 2B 84
Ropery La. DH3: Ches S, Gt Lum 7B 128
NE28: W'snd 3J 65
NE31: Heb 7H 65
Ropery Rd. NE8: Gate 6D 82
SR4: Sund 7C 104
Ropery Stairs NE30: N Shi 7H 49
Ropery Wlk. SR7: S'hm 4B 148
Rosalie Ter. SR2: Sund 4H 119
Rosalind Av. NE22: Bed 1J 21
Rosalind St. NE63: Ash 3B 12
(not continuous)
Rosamond Pl. NE24: Bly 2K 23
Rosa St. NE33: S Shi 3K 67
Rose Acre DH1: Shin 6E 166
Rose Av. DH4: Hou S 1K 143
DH9: Stly 4D 124
NE16: Whi 7H 81
NE23: Nel V 2H 25
Rosebank Cl. SR2: Ryh 1G 133
Rosebank Cotts. *NE9: Spri 6E 100*
(off Peareth Hall Rd.)
Rosebank Hall NE28: W'snd 3J 65
Rosebay Rd. DH7: Lang M 7G 165
Roseberry Ct. NE37: Wash 7J 101
Roseberry Cres. DH6: Thor 1J 179
Roseberry Grange NE12: Longb 3E 46
Roseberry M. DH9: W Pelt 3C 126
Roseberry St. DH9: Beam 2K 125
Roseberry Ter. DH8: Cons 7H 121
NE35: Bol C 5E 86
Roseberry Vs. DH2: Newf 4E 126
Rosebery Av. NE8: Gate 6J 83
NE24: Bly 2H 23
NE29: N Shi 4G 49
NE33: S Shi 4A 68
Rosebery Ct. NE25: Monks 6E 38
Rosebery Cres. NE2: Jes 5J 63
Rosebery Pl. NE2: Jes 5H 63
Rosebery St. SR5: Monkw 6F 105
Rosebrough Rd. NE13: Ki Pk 4K 43
Rosebud Cl. NE16: Swa 5G 81
Rosebury Dr. NE12: Longb 7J 45
Roseby Rd. SR8: Hord 5D 172
Rose Cotts. DH6: S Het 4C 158
NE16: Burn 3J 109
NE37: Wash 1G 115
Rose Ct. DH7: Esh W 2C 162
DH9: Ann P 4J 123
NE31: Heb 1H 85
SR8: Pet 2K 181
Rose Cres. DH4: Bour 6H 129
DH7: Sac 7F 141
SR6: Whit 4H 89
(not continuous)
Rosecroft DH2: Pelt 3E 126
Rosedale DH3: Bir 2B 114
NE22: Bed 7G 17
NE28: W'snd 1D 64
Rosedale Av. DH8: Shot B 4F 121
SR6: Seab 1G 105
Rosedale Ct. NE5: W Dent 3D 60
Rosedale Cres. DH4: Hou S 7B 130
Rosedale Gdns. *DH7: Edm 3D 140*
(off Tyzack St.)
Rosedale Rd. DH1: Carr 7H 155
NE40: Craw 3D 78
Rosedale St. DH5: Hett H 2E 156
SR1: Sund 4F 7 (2D 118)
Rosedale Ter. DH4: Nbot 6E 130
NE2: Newc T 2J 5 (6H 63)
NE30: N Shi 5H 49
SR6: Ful 3G 105
SR8: Hord 5D 172
Roseden Ct. NE12: Longb 5A 46
Rosedene Vs. NE23: Cra 4B 26
Roseden Way NE13: Haz 2A 44
Rosefinch Lodge NE9: Low F 2H 99
Rose Gdns. NE11: Kib 2E 112
NE28: W'snd 1F 65
Rosegill NE37: Wash 2F 115
ROSEHILL 3K 65
Rosehill Bank NE28: W'snd 3J 65
Rosehill Rd. NE28: W'snd 3K 65
Rosehill Ter. *NE28: W'snd 3J 65*
(off Willington Ter.)
Rosehill Way NE5: Blak 4J 61
Rosehip Ct. NE38: Wash 3H 115
Rose Lea DH7: Wit G 2D 152
Roselea DH6: Thor 1J 179
NE32: Jar 5C 86
Roselea Av. SR2: Ryh 2H 133
Rosella Pl. *NE29: N Shi 6G 49*
(off Brightman Rd.)
Rosemary Cl. DH8: Cons 7J 121
Rosemary Gdns. NE9: Eigh B 5B 100
Rosemary La. NE1: Newc T 6F 4 (1F 83)
SR8: Eas 7K 159
Rosemary Rd. SR5: Sund 4K 103
Rosemary Ter. NE24: Bly 3K 23
Rosemount DH1: P Me 3B 154
DH6: Has 7B 158
(off Pesspool La.)
DH9: W Pelt 2C 126
NE5: West 3F 61
NE61: Mor 1G 15
SR4: Sund 3G 117
Rosemount Av. NE10: Ward 7F 85
Rosemount Cl. NE37: Wash 5G 101
Rosemount Ct. NE36: W Bol 7H 87
Rosemount Way NE7: Longb 7A 46
NE25: Monks 6C 38
Roseneath Ct. NE63: Ash 4B 12
Rose Pk. NE23: Seg 2C 36
Rose St. DH4: Hou S 2D 144
NE8: Gate 4E 82
NE31: Heb 1H 85
SR4: Sund 3F 7 (1D 118)
Rose St. E. DH4: Pen 1B 130
Rose St. W. DH4: Pen 1B 130
Rose Ter. DH2: P Fel 4G 127
DH7: Lang P 5J 151
DH8: M'sly 1H 121
NE5: Fen 4A 62
NE40: G'sde 5G 79
Rosetown Av. SR8: Hord 6E 172
Rose Villa La. NE16: Whi 7H 81
Rose Vs. NE4: Elsw 1B 82
Roseville St. SR4: Sund 3D 118
Rosewell Pl. NE16: Whi 2G 97
Rosewood NE12: Kil 1D 46
Rosewood Av. NE3: Gos 6F 45
Rosewood Cl. DH7: Sac 7E 140
Rosewood Cres. NE6: Walk 4D 64
NE26: Sea S 6D 28
Rosewood Dr. NE20: Pon 2H 31
Rosewood Gdns. DH2: Ches S 4K 127
NE3: Ken 1B 62
NE9: Low F 2K 99
Rosewood Sq. SR4: Sund 6G 117
Rosewood Ter. DH3: Bir 3K 113
NE28: W'snd 3A 66
Rosewood Wlk. DH7: Ush M 2B 164
Roseworth Av. NE3: Gos 2E 62
Roseworth Cl. NE3: Gos 1F 63
Roseworth Cres. NE3: Gos 2F 63
Roseworth Ter. NE3: Gos 1E 62
NE16: Whi 7H 81
Roslin Pk. NE22: Bed 7A 18
Roslin Way NE23: Cra 7J 25
Roslyn M. NE5: Den M 3H 61
Ross DH2: Ous 6J 113
(not continuous)
Ross Av. NE11: Dun 5B 82
Rossdale *NE40: Craw 3C 78*
(off Bank Top)
Rosse Cl. NE37: Wash 7F 101
Rossendale Pl.
NE12: Longb 6H 45
Ross Gth. DH5: Hou S 3E 144
Ross Gro. NE23: Nel V 3H 25
Ross Lea DH4: S Row 5A 130
Rosslyn Av. NE3: Ken 7A 44
NE9: Low F 1J 99
SR2: Ryh 2H 133
Rosslyn M. SR4: Sund 2C 118
(not continuous)
Rosslyn Pl. DH3: Bir 6B 114
Rosslyn St. SR4: Sund 2C 118
Rosslyn Ter. SR4: Sund 2C 118
Ross St. SR5: Monkw 6E 104
SR7: S'hm 3B 148
Ross Way NE3: Fawd 4B 44
NE26: Whit B 4E 38
Rosyth Rd. SR5: Sund 4A 104
Rosyth Sq. SR5: Sund 4A 104
Rotary Parkway NE63: Ash 3K 11
Rotary Rd. NE27: Back, Shir 7H 37
Rotary Way DH1: P Me 3K 153
DH8: Cons 7J 121
NE3: Gos 1D 44
NE20: Pon 7J 31
NE24: Bly, News 3J 23
NE29: N Shi 2E 66
NE46: B End, Hex 7E 50
Rotha Ct. *NE24: Bly 5K 23*
(off Elfin Way)
Rothay Pl. NE5: Blak 3J 61
Rothbury SR2: Ryh 3F 133
Rothbury Av. NE3: Gos 6D 44
NE10: Pel 5E 84
NE24: Bly 3F 23
NE32: Jar 2A 86
SR8: Hord 4D 172
Rothbury Cl. DH2: Ches S 1J 141
NE12: Kil 1A 46
Rothbury Dr. NE63: Ash 2H 11
Rothbury Gdns. NE11: Lob H 2C 98
NE13: W Op 5E 34
NE28: W'snd 2K 65
Rothbury Rd. DH1: Dur 4A 154
SR5: Sund 4K 103
Rothbury Ter. NE6: Heat 5K 63
NE29: N Shi 1C 66
Rotherdale Ct. NE6: Walk 6E 64
Rotherfield Cl. NE23: Cra 3K 25
Rotherfield Gdns. NE9: Low F 5J 99
Rotherfield Rd. SR5: Sund 5J 103
Rotherfield Sq. SR5: Sund 4J 103
Rotherham Cl. DH5: Hou S 4D 144
Rotherham Rd. SR5: Sund 4J 103
Rothesay DH2: Ous 7H 113
Rothesay M. NE22: Bed 7K 17
Rothesay Ter. NE22: Bed 7K 17
Rothesay Ter. Bk. NE22: Bed 6A 18
Rothlea Gdns. NE62: Stake 7J 11
Rothley NE38: Wash 6K 115
Rothley Av. NE5: Fen 6J 61
NE63: Ash 5B 12
SR8: Hord 4D 172
Rothley Cl. NE3: Gos 7F 45
NE20: Pon 4H 31
Rothley Ct. NE12: Kil 1A 46
SR5: S'wck 3B 104
Rothley Gdns. NE30: Cull 3H 49
Rothley Gro. NE25: Sea D 7G 27
Rothley Ter. DH8: M'sly 7K 107
Rothley Way NE26: Whit B 4E 38
Rothsay Ter. NE64: Newb S 4H 13
Rothwell Rd. NE3: Gos 7E 44
SR5: Sund 5J 103
Rotterdam Ho. NE1: Newc T 6K 5
Roundhaven DH1: Dur 7J 165
ROUND HILL 6C 54
Roundhill NE32: Jar 5D 86
Roundhill Av. NE5: Blak 3J 61
Roundstone Cl. NE7: H Hea 1B 64
Roundway, The NE12: Longb 5K 45
Routledge's Bldgs. NE22: Bed 5K 17
Rowan Av. NE38: Wash 7G 115
Rowanberry Rd. NE12: Longb 6K 45
Rowan Cl. NE22: Bed 6H 17
SR4: Sund 3H 117
Rowan Ct. DH7: Esh W 5C 162
NE12: Longb 4D 46
NE16: Burn 2B 110
NE24: Bly 3H 23
NE34: S Shi 2G 87
(off Tennant St.)
Rowan Dr. DH1: Bras 3C 154
DH5: Hett H 7F 145
NE3: Ken 6A 44
NE20: Pon 4J 31
NE34: S Shi 3B 88
Rowan Gro. NE23: E Cram 5B 26
NE42: Pru 4D 76
Rowan Lea DH7: B'don 1D 174
Rowans, The NE9: Eigh B 5B 100
Rowan Tree Av. DH1: Dur 7E 154
Rowantree Rd. NE6: Walk 4E 64
Rowan Vw. SR8: Eas 1A 172
Rowanwood Gdns. NE11: Lob H 2C 98
Rowedge Wlk. NE5: West 3G 61
Rowell Cl. SR2: Ryh 3E 132
Rowes M. NE6: Byke 2A 84
Rowland Burn Way NE39: Row G 5J 95
Rowland Cres. TS27: Cas E 4J 181
Rowlands Bldgs. NE23: Dud 2J 35
ROWLANDS GILL 6K 95
Rowlandson Cres. NE10: Fell 6B 84
Rowlandson Ter. *NE10: Fell 6B 84*
(off Rowlandson Cres.)
SR2: Sund 4G 119
Rowlands Ter. TS28: Win 7G 181
ROWLEY 5D 134
Rowley Bank DH8: C'sde 4B 134
Rowley Cl. DH7: New B 5A 164
Rowley Cres. DH7: Esh W 3D 162
Rowley Dr. DH7: Ush M 3D 164
Rowley Link DH7: Esh W 3D 162
Rowley St. NE24: Bly 2J 23
Rowlington Ter. NE63: Ash 5B 12
Rowlington Way NE25: Monks 5B 38
Rowntree Way NE29: N Shi 2G 67
Rowsley Rd. NE32: Jar 1C 86
Row's Ter. NE3: Gos 7G 45
Roxborough Ho. NE26: Whit B 6G 39
Roxburgh Cl. NE21: Winl 6A 80
NE25: Sea D 6G 27
Roxburgh Pl. NE6: Heat 1P 5 (6K 63)
Roxburgh St. SR6: Ful 5F 105
Roxburgh Ter. NE26: Whit B 6G 39
Roxby Gdns. NE29: N Shi 7E 48
Roxby Wynd TS28: Win 4G 181
Royal Cres. NE4: Fen 5A 62
Royal Ind. Est. NE32: Jar 6K 65
Royal Northumberland Yacht Club 4K 23
Royal Quays Outlet Shopping
NE29: N Shi 3E 66
Royal Rd. DH9: Stly 2E 124
Royalty, The SR2: Sund 5F 7 (2D 118)
Royalty Theatre, The 5F 7
Roydon Av. SR2: Sund 5G 119
Royle Cl. NE13: Ki Pk 4K 43
Royle St. SR2: Sund 6H 119
Royston Ter. NE6: Walk 2E 84
Ruabon Cl. NE23: Cra 7J 25
Rubens Av. NE34: S Shi 3K 87
Rubicon Ho. NE1: Newc T 7D 4 (2E 82)
Ruby St. DH4: Hou S 7D 130
Rudby Cl. NE3: Gos 4F 45
Rudchester Pl. NE5: Fen 5J 61
Ruddock Sq. NE6: Byke 7P 5 (1A 84)
Rudyard Av. SR2: Sund 5G 119
Rudyerd Ct. NE29: N Shi 7H 49
Rudyerd St. NE29: N Shi 7G 49
Rugby Gdns. NE9: Wrek 4A 100
NE28: W'snd 2J 65
Ruislip Pl. NE23: Cra 7H 25
Ruislip Rd. SR4: Sund 3G 117
Runcie Rd. DH6: Bowb 5H 177
Runcorn SR2: Ryh 2E 132
Runcorn Rd. SR5: Sund 4J 103
Runhead Est. NE40: Ryton 2H 79
Runhead Gdns. NE40: Ryton 1H 79
Runhead Ter. NE40: Ryton 1J 79
RUNNING WATERS 7C 168
Runnymede DH3: Gt Lum 2E 142
SR2: Ryh 2F 133
Runnymede Gdns. NE17: C'wl 1K 107
Runnymede Rd. NE16: Whi 1G 97
NE20: Darr H, Pon 7E 30
SR5: Sund 4K 103
Runnymede Way NE3: Ken 1A 62
SR5: Sund 4K 103
Runswick Av. NE12: Longb 6H 45
Runswick Cl. SR3: Tuns 2E 132

Runswick Dr. SR7: S'hm 1B 148
Rupert Ct. NE15: Newb 5K 59
Rupert Ho. NE15: Newb 5K 59
Rupert Sq. SR5: Sund 4A 104
Rupert St. SR6: Whit 5H 89
Rupert Ter. NE15: Newb 5K 59
Rushall Pl. NE12: Longb 6K 45
Rushbury Ct. NE27: Back 6G 37
Rushcliffe SR6: Ful 4F 105
Rushey Gill DH7: B'don 1C 174
Rushford SR2: Ryh 2F 133
Rushie Av. NE15: Benw 1J 81
Rushley Cres. NE21: Blay 3C 80
Rushmore Grange NE38: Wash 2J 115
Rushsyde Cl. NE16: Whi 2E 96
Rushton Av. SR2: Sund 5G 119
Rushton Way NE38: Wash 4B 116
Rushyrig NE37: Wash 2E 114
Ruskin Av. DH2: P Fel 6G 127
(not continuous)
DH5: Eas L 3J 157
NE11: Dun 5B 82
NE12: Longb 3A 46
NE63: Ash 5D 12
Ruskin Cl. DH9: Stly 2H 125
Ruskin Ct. NE42: Pru 5D 76
Ruskin Cres. DH6: Thor 1J 179
NE34: S Shi 3H 87
Ruskin Dr. NE7: H Hea 3C 64
NE35: Bol C 6G 87
Ruskin Rd. DH3: Bir 4A 114
NE10: Wind N 7K 83
NE16: Swa 6G 81
Russel Ct. NE2: Jes 3H 63
Russell Av. NE34: S Shi 7C 68
Russell Cl. DH7: Bran 4A 174
DH8: Cons 6J 121
NE28: W'snd 7H 47
Russell Ct. NE8: Gate 5E 82
Russell Cres. TS29: Trim S 7D 180
Russell Foster Football Cen., The 6C 130
Russell Sq. NE13: Sea B 3D 34
Russell St. DH7: Wat, Esh W 6C 162
NE29: N Shi 7G 49
NE32: Jar 6C 66
NE33: S Shi 2J 67
NE37: Wash 7G 101
SR1: Sund 1G 119
Russell Ter. DH3: Bir 2K 113
(not continuous)
NE1: Newc T 4J 5 (7H 63)
NE22: Bed 1H 21
Russell Way NE11: Dun 4J 81
Rustic Ter. NE64: Newb S 2J 13
Ruswarp Dr. SR3: Silk 3D 132
Ruth Av. NE21: Blay 4C 80
Rutherford Av. SR7: S'hm 2H 147
Rutherford Cl. NE62: Chop 1G 17
Rutherford Ct. DH7: Lang P 4H 151
Rutherford Ho. SR8: Eas C 7B 160
Rutherford Pl. NE61: Mor 1F 15
Rutherford Rd. NE37: Wash 6J 101
SR5: Sund 4H 103
Rutherford Sq. SR5: Sund 4H 103
Rutherford St. NE4: Newc T 6D 4 (1E 82)
NE24: Bly 2H 23
NE28: W'snd 2B 66
Rutherford Vw. SR8: Eas C 7B 160
(off Seaside La.)
Rutherglen Rd. SR5: Sund 4A 104
Rutherglen Sq. SR5: Sund 4A 104
Rutland Av. SR3: New S 2B 132
Rutland Pl. DH8: C'sde 3D 134
NE29: N Shi 6E 48
NE37: Wash 5H 101
Rutland Rd. DH8: C'sde 3C 134
NE28: W'snd 4E 64
NE31: Heb 3K 85
Rutland Sq. DH3: Bir 3A 114
Rutland St. DH5: Hett H 6F 145
NE34: S Shi 7H 67
NE63: Ash 4A 12
SR4: Sund 1B 118
SR7: S'hm 2K 147
Rutland Ter. DH6: Has 3K 169
Rutland Wlk. SR8: Pet 4A 172
Rutter Sq. DH7: Esh 6G 151
Rutter St. DH7: Lang M 6G 165
Rutter Ter. NE46: Acomb 4C 50
Ryal Cl. NE24: Bly 2G 23
NE25: Sea D 7H 27
Ryall Av. NE13: Haz 7C 34
Ryal Ter. NE6: Walk 1D 84
Ryal Wlk. NE3: Ken 1K 61
Ryan Ter. DH6: Whe H 4A 180
Rydal NE10: Pel 6E 84
Rydal Av. DH5: Eas L 3J 157
DH9: Stly 4D 124
NE30: Cull 2G 49
Rydal Cl. DH7: Sac 7D 140
NE12: Kil 1D 46
NE36: E Bol 6J 87
Rydal Cres. NE21: Winl 6B 80
SR8: Pet 6C 172
Rydale Pk. SR2: Sund 7J 119
Rydal Gdns. NE34: S Shi 7A 68
Rydal M. DH8: Lead 5B 122
Rydal Mt. NE64: Newb S 4G 13
SR5: Ful 4E 104
SR5: Sund 7G 103
SR8: Eas 7B 160
Rydal Rd. DH2: Ches S 1K 141
NE3: Gos 7F 45
NE15: Lem 5D 60
Rydal St. NE8: Gate 5G 83
Rydal Ter. NE13: W Op 7D 34
Ryde Pl. NE23: Cra 3K 25
Ryder Ct. NE12: Kil 2A 46
Ryder Wlk. NE63: N Sea 3D 12
Ryde Ter. DH9: Ann P 5K 123
NE11: Dun 5C 82
Ryde Ter. Bungs. DH9: Ann P 4K 123
(off Lwr. Church St.)
Rye Cl. NE15: Thro 4J 59
NE46: Hex 1B 70
Ryedale DH1: Carr 1H 167
NE28: W'snd 7D 46
SR6: Seab 7H 89
Ryedale Cl. NE63: Ash 5K 11
Ryedale Ct. NE34: S Shi 2G 87
TS29: Trim S 7C 180
Ryehaugh NE20: Pon 5K 31
Rye Hill NE4: Newc T 6A 4 (2D 82)
Rye Hill Sports Cen. 7B 4 (2D 82)
Ryehill Vw. DH5: E Rain 6C 144
Ryelands Way DH1: P Me 3A 154
Ryemount Rd. SR2: Ryh 2F 133
Rye Ter. NE46: Hex 1B 70
Rye Vw. SR2: Ryh 2H 133
RYHOPE 3J 133
Ryhope Beach Rd. SR2: Ryh 3J 133
RYHOPE COLLIERY 1G 133
Ryhope Engines Mus. 4G 133
Ryhope Gdns. NE9: Wrek 3B 100
Ryhope Grange Ct. SR2: Sund 7H 119
Ryhope Rd. SR2: Ryh, Sund 7K 7 (3F 119)
Ryhope St. DH5: Hou S 2F 145
SR2: Sund 6H 119
Ryhope St. Nth. SR2: Ryh 2G 133
Ryhope St. Sth. SR2: Ryh 2H 133
Rymers Cl. SR8: Eas 1J 171
RYTON 1G 79
Ryton Ct. NE33: S Shi 4K 67
Ryton Crawcrook By-Pass NE21: Blay 4D 78
NE40: Craw, Ryton 4D 78
Ryton Cres. DH9: Stly 1G 125
SR7: S'hm 3J 147
Ryton Gdns. NE28: W'snd 1K 65
Ryton Hall Dr. NE40: Ryton 7G 59
Ryton Ind. Est. NE21: Blay 1K 79
Ryton Sq. SR2: Sund 5G 119
Ryton Ter. NE6: Walk 2D 84
NE27: Shir 3H 47
RYTON VILLAGE 7G 59
Ryton Village East NE40: Ryton 7G 59
Ryton Village West NE40: Ryton 7G 59
Ryton Willows NE40: Ryton 6F 59
RYTON WOODSIDE 4F 79

S

Sabin Ct. DH9: Ann P 5B 124
Sabin Ter. DH9: Ann P 5B 124
Sackville Rd. NE6: Heat 4A 64
SR3: Sund 5A 118
SACRISTON 7E 140
Sacriston Av. SR3: Sund 5B 118
Sacriston Gdns. NE9: Wrek 5A 100
Sacriston Ind. Est. DH7: Sac 7E 140
Sacriston La. DH7: Wit G 3C 152
Saddleback NE37: Wash 1F 115
Saddler's La. DH1: Dur 3C 6 (3A 166)
Saddler St. DH1: Dur 2C 6 (2A 166)
Saffron Pl. NE6: Walk 1E 84
Saga Ct. NE6: Walk 4D 64
Sage Cl. NE15: Lem 5C 60
Sage Gateshead, The 7J 5 (2H 83)
St Accas Ct. NE46: Hex 7B 50
St Agathas Cl. DH7: B'don 7E 164
St Agnes' Gdns. NE40: Craw 2C 78
St Agnes' Gdns. Nth. NE40: Craw 2C 78
St Agnes' Gdns. W. NE40: Craw 2C 78
St Agnes Ter. NE40: Craw 2C 78
St Agnes Vs. NE40: Craw 3C 78
(off Main St.)
St Aidan Cres. DH6: Thor 2J 179
St Aidans Av. DH1: Dur 6K 153
NE12: Longb 3G 47
SR2: Sund 7H 119
St Aidans Cl. NE29: N Shi 4D 48
St Aidan's Ct. DH4: New H 3E 130
NE30: Tyne 5J 49
St Aidan's Cres. DH1: Dur 2J 165
DH9: Ann P 6K 123
NE61: Mor 2G 15
St Aidan's Pl. DH8: B'hill 5G 121
St Aidan's Rd. NE28: W'snd 4E 64
NE33: S Shi 1K 67
St Aidan's Sq. NE12: Longb 3G 47
St Aidans St. DH8: B'hill 5G 121
NE8: Gate 5F 83
St Aidan's Ter. DH4: New H 3E 130
TS29: Trim S 7C 180
St Aidans Way SR8: Pet 7B 172
St Aiden's Apartments DH8: B'hill 5G 121
St Albans Cl. DH3: Gt Lum 4F 143
NE25: Ears 6A 38
NE63: N Sea 5E 12
St Albans Cres. NE6: Heat 3B 64
NE10: Wind N 7A 84
St Albans Pl. NE10: Wind N 7A 84
NE30: Tyne 5K 49
St Alban's St. SR2: Sund 5G 119
St Alban's Ter. NE8: Gate 5G 83
St Albans Vw. NE27: Shir 2J 47
St Aldate's Ct. SR4: Sund 5G 117
(off Gartland Rd.)
St Aldwyn Rd. SR7: S'hm 2K 147
St Aloysius Vw. NE31: Heb 1G 85
St Andrew's DH4: Hou S 2B 144
St Andrew's Av. NE37: Wash 7F 101
St Andrews Cl. DH8: B'hill 5F 121
NE25: Monks 6D 38
St Andrews Ct. DH1: Dur 3D 6 (3B 166)
DH6: Ludw 5H 169
NE7: Longb 7A 46
NE29: N Shi 4F 49
(off Walton Av.)
St Andrew's Cres. DH8: B'hill 5F 121
St Andrew's Dr. NE9: Low F 4G 99
St Andrew's Gdns. DH8: B'hill 5E 120
St Andrew's La. NE42: Oving 2K 75
St Andrew's Rd. DH8: B'hill 5E 120
DH9: Tan L 7F 111
NE46: Hex 2C 70
St Andrew's Sq. DH7: B'don 1D 174
SR7: Mur 6G 147
St Andrew's St. NE1: Newc T 5D 4 (1E 82)
NE31: Heb 6G 65
St Andrews Ter. NE45: Corb 7D 52
NE63: Ash 4C 12
SR6: Roker 5G 105
St Andrews Way
NE1: Newc T 5E 4 (1F 83)
St Annes Cl. NE21: Winl 5B 80
St Annes Ct. DH1: Dur 2B 6 (2A 166)
NE25: Monks 1E 48
ST ANN'S 6L 5 (1J 83)
St Ann's Cl. NE1: Newc T 5L 5 (1J 83)
St Ann's Quay NE1: Newc T 6K 5 (1H 83)
St Ann's Stairs NE1: Newc T 6L 5
St Ann's St. NE1: Newc T 6K 5 (1H 83)
St Ann's Wharf NE1: Newc T 6K 5
St Anselm Cres. NE29: N Shi 5C 48
St Anselm Rd. NE29: N Shi 5C 48
ST ANTHONY'S 3D 84
St Anthony's Ct. NE6: Walk 7D 64
St Anthony's Gdns. NE31: Heb 1G 85
St Anthony's Ho. NE6: Walk 3D 84
(off Yelverton Cres.)
St Anthony's Rd. NE6: Walk 1C 84
St Anthony's Wlk. NE6: Walk 3D 84
St Asaph Cl. NE7: H Hea 1B 64
St Aubyns Way DH9: Stly 2H 125
St Austell Cl. NE5: Blak 1J 61
St Austell Gdns. NE9: Low F 5H 99
St Barnabas DH4: Bour 6H 129
St Barnabas Way SR2: Sund 3H 119
St Bede Cres. DH6: Thor 2H 179
St Bede's NE36: E Bol 7K 87
St Bede's Cl. DH1: Dur 3J 165
DH5: Hett H 6G 145
St Bede's Ct. DH7: Lan 5J 137
St Bede's Dr. NE8: Gate 10J 5 (4H 83)
St Bede's Ho. NE9: Low F 7J 83
NE61: Mor 7F 9
(off Mathesons Gdns.)
St Bede's Pk. SR2: Sund 6K 7 (3F 119)
St Bedes Pl. NE24: News 5F 23
NE61: Mor 7F 9
(off Oldgate)
St Bedes Rd. NE24: News 5F 23
St Bede's Ter. SR2: Sund 6K 7 (3F 119)
St Bedes Wlk. NE27: Longb 3G 47
St Bedes Way DH7: Lang M 7G 165
St Benedicts Way SR2: Ryh 4H 133
St Benet's Ct. DH2: Ous 1H 127
St Brandon's Gro. DH7: B'don 1C 174
St Brelades Way DH9: Stly 2H 125
St Buryan Cres. NE5: Blak 1J 61
St Catherine's Chapel (remains of) 5H 103
St Catherines Ct.
NE2: Newc T 1K 5 (5H 63)
SR5: Sund 6K 103
St Catherines Gro.
NE2: Newc T 1L 5 (5J 63)
St Cecelias Cl. SR2: Sund 4H 119
St Chad's Cres. SR3: E Her 2H 131
St Chad Sq. DH6: Thor 2J 179
St Chad's Rd. SR3: E Her 2H 131
St Chad's Vs. NE36: E Bol 7K 87
St Christophers Cl. NE63: Ash 2D 12
St Christopher's Ho. NE61: Mor 7E 8
St Christopher's Rd. SR3: Sund 6C 118
St Christopher Way
NE29: N Shi 2C 66
St Clements Ct. NE3: Fawd 4B 44
NE12: Longb 6J 45
NE63: N Sea 5E 12
SR4: Sund 2K 117
St Columbas Ct. SR5: S'wck 5E 104
Saint Ct. SR3: Silk 3C 132
St Cuthbert Rd. DH6: Thor 2J 179
St Cuthberts Av. DH1: Dur 6J 153
DH3: Ches S 6B 128
DH8: B'hill 4E 120
NE34: S Shi 5C 68
St Cuthberts Cl. DH5: Hett H 6G 145
NE27: Longb 3G 47
NE42: Pru 4E 76
NE46: Hex 2C 70
St Cuthberts Ct. NE3: Gos 7C 44
NE8: Gate 10F 4 (4F 83)
NE24: Bly 2K 23
SR7: S'hm 2H 147
St Cuthberts Dr. DH7: Sac 7D 140
NE10: Hew 7D 84
(not continuous)
St Cuthbert's Grn. NE5: Fen 6J 61
St Cuthbert's La. NE46: Hex 2C 70
St Cuthberts Mdw. DH7: Sac 7D 140
St Cuthberts Pk. NE16: Marl H 7G 97
St Cuthbert's Pl. NE8: Gate 5F 83
St Cuthberts Rd. DH4: Nbot 6D 130
DH4: W Herr 2F 131
NE5: Fen 6H 61
(not continuous)
NE8: Gate 10F 4 (4F 83)
NE16: Marl H 6H 97
NE27: Kil 3G 47
NE28: W'snd 2H 65
SR8: Pet 7B 172
St Cuthbert's Ter. NE22: Bed 7K 17
(off Millbank Rd.)
NE46: Hex 2C 70
SR4: Sund 1D 118
SR7: Dalt D 5H 147
St Cuthberts Wlk. DH3: Ches S 6A 128
DH7: Lang M 7G 165
St Cuthberts Way DH6: S'burn 3K 167
NE21: Blay 3D 80
NE27: Longb 3G 47
SR8: Pet 7B 172
St David's Cl. NE26: Whit B 3E 38
St David's Ct. NE26: Whit B 3E 38
St David's Way NE26: Whit B 3F 39
NE32: Jar 5C 86
St Ebba's Way DH8: Ebc 5G 107
St Edmunds Cl. NE27: Back 1H 47
St Edmund's Ct. NE8: Gate 5J 83
St Edmund's Dr. NE10: Hew 7D 84
St Edmund's Rd. NE8: Gate 5H 83
St Edmund's Ter. DH9: Dip 2G 123
St Elvins Pl. DH3: Gt Lum 3F 143
St Gabriel Av. NE31: Heb 1G 85
St Gabriel's Av. NE6: Heat 4K 63
SR4: Sund 2B 118
St George's Av. NE33: S Shi 5A 68
NE34: S Shi 5A 68
St George's Cl. NE2: Jes 3G 63
St Georges Ct. NE10: Ward 7F 85
St Georges Cres. NE25: Monks 7F 39
NE29: N Shi 7F 49
St George's Est. NE38: Wash 7G 115
St Georges Ho. NE11: T Vall 3E 98
St Georges Pl. DH8: B'hill 6G 121
NE15: Lem 1E 80
St George's Rd. NE15: Lem 1D 80
NE30: Cull 1J 49
NE46: Hex 2C 70
St Georges Sq. NE61: Mor 7G 9
(off Bridge St.)
SR2: Sund 6J 7 (3F 119)
St George's Ter. NE2: Jes 4G 63
NE15: Lem 1E 80
NE36: E Bol 7K 87
SR6: Roker 5H 105
St George's Way NE1: Newc T 4E 4
SR2: Sund 6J 7 (3F 119)
St Giles Cl. DH1: Dur 2D 166
St Godric's Cl. DH1: Dur 4A 154
St Godrics Ct. DH1: Dur 2B 6
St Godric's Dr. DH4: W Rai 1A 156
St Gregorys Ct. NE34: S Shi 1B 88
St Helen's Cres. DH6: Quar H 6D 178
NE9: Low F 2G 99
St Helens Dr. SR7: S'hm 5C 148
St Helen's La. NE45: Corb 7D 52
St Helens Pl. NE45: Corb 1D 72
St Helen's St. NE45: Corb 7D 52
St Helen's Ter. NE9: Low F 2H 99
St Helen's Well DH1: Dur 3B 6 (3A 166)
St Heliers Way DH9: Stly 2H 125
St Hilda Ind. Est. NE33: S Shi 3J 67
St Hildas Av. NE28: W'snd 2J 65
St Hilda's La. NE33: S Shi 2J 67
(off Church St.)
St Hildas Pl. NE21: Blay 1A 80
St Hilda's Rd. NE46: Hex 2C 70
St Hilda St. NE33: S Shi 3J 67
St Hilds Ct. DH1: Dur 2E 166
St Hild's La. DH1: Dur 2C 166
St Ignatius Cl. SR2: Sund 3G 119
St Ives Ct. DH8: Lead 5C 122
St Ives Gdns. DH8: Lead 5B 122
St Ives Pl. SR7: Mur 6F 147
St Ives' Rd. DH8: Lead 5B 122
St Ives Way NE5: Blak 1J 61
St James Blvd. NE1: Newc T 8C 4 (2E 82)
NE4: Newc T 6C 4 (1E 82)
NE8: Gate 4K 83
NE10: Gate 10P 5
(off Old Fold Rd.)
St James Cl. NE44: Rid M 7K 73
St James Ct. NE10: Fell 5K 83
St James' Cres. NE15: Benw 2K 81
St James Flds. TS27: Cas E 5A 182
St James Gdns. NE15: Benw 1K 81
St James' Ga. NE4: Newc T 8D 4 (2E 82)
St James' Mall NE31: Heb 1H 85
St James' Park
Newcastle-upon-Tyne 4C 4 (7E 62)
St James Point NE4: Newc T 4C 4
St James Retail Pk.
NE5: Den M 4H 61
St James Rd. NE8: Gate 10M 5 (4J 83)
NE15: Benw 1K 81
St James Sq. NE8: Gate 10M 5 (3J 83)
St James St. NE1: Newc T 4D 4 (7E 62)
NE3: Gos 7F 45
St James Ter. NE1: Newc T 4D 4
NE29: N Shi 2D 66
NE44: Rid M 7A 74
NE61: Mor 6F 9
(off Copper Chare)
St Johns SR1: Sund 7H 105
St John's Av. NE31: Heb 1H 85
St John's Cl. NE26: Whit B 3F 39

St Johns Ct. DH7: Mead 1G 175
DH7: Sac 7D 140
NE4: Benw 2A 82
NE12: Kil 3B 46
NE27: Back 6G 37
St John's Cres. DH6: Bowb 4H 177
NE22: Bed 5B 18
St John's Grn. NE29: N Shi 2D 66
St John's Ho. *NE33: S Shi* *2K 67*
(off Beach Rd.)
St John's Mall NE31: Heb 1H 85
St Johns M. DH7: B'hpe 4E 138
St John's Pl. DH3: Bir 4A 114
(not continuous)
NE10: Fell 6B 84
NE22: Bed 5B 18
NE26: Whit B 3F 39
St John's Pct. *NE31: Heb* *1H 85*
(off St John's Mall)
St Johns Rd. DH1: Dur 3J 165
DH6: H Pitt, Low P 5B 156
DH7: Mead 1F 175
NE4: Benw, Elsw 2A 82
NE22: Bed 6B 18
NE46: Hex 3B 70
St John's Sq. SR7: S'hm 3B 148
St John's Ter. DH9: Dip 2G 123
NE29: N Shi 2D 66
NE32: Jar 6B 66
NE36: E Bol 7A 88
SR7: S'hm 1G 147
St John St. NE1: Newc T 6E 4 (1F 83)
NE29: N Shi 2D 66
(not continuous)
St Johns Va. SR4: Sund 4G 117
St John's Wlk. NE4: Benw 2A 82
(not continuous)
NE29: N Shi 2D 66
NE31: Heb 1J 85
St Johns Way *DH9: Ann P* *5K 123*
(off Front St.)
St John's W. NE22: Bed 5B 18
St Josephs Cl. DH1: Dur 2E 166
NE12: Kil 2B 46
St Josephs Ct. DH3: Bir 3A 114
DH9: Stly 3F 125
NE31: Heb 3H 85
St Joseph's Way NE32: Jar 5C 86
St Jude's Ter. NE33: S Shi 5J 67
St Julien Gdns. NE7: H Hea 2B 64
NE28: W'snd 2B 66
St Just Pl. NE5: Blak 1J 61
St Keverne Sq. NE5: Blak 1J 61
St Kitt's Cl. NE26: Whit B 3F 39
ST LAWRENCE 6N 5 (1K 83)
St Lawrence Cl. DH6: H Pitt 6C 156
St Lawrence Ct. *NE6: Byke* *7A 64*
(off Spires La.)
St Lawrence M. NE6: Byke 2A 84
St Lawrence Rd. DH6: H Pitt 6B 156
NE6: Byke 6N 5 (1K 83)
St Lawrence Sq. NE6: Byke 6N 5 (1K 83)
St Leonard Cres. DH6: Thor 2J 179
St Leonards DH1: Dur 1K 165
St Leonards Cl. SR8: Pet 7K 171
St Leonards Ct. NE30: N Shi 5H 49
St Leonard's La. NE61: Fair M, Mit 6A 8
St Leonard St. SR2: Sund 4G 119
St Leonard's Wlk. NE61: Mor 5C 8
St Lucia Cl. NE26: Whit B 3E 38
SR2: Sund 3G 119
St Lukes Cres. NE31: Heb 2H 85
St Luke's M. DH7: Ush M 2A 164
St Lukes Pl. NE31: Heb 7G 65
St Lukes Rd. NE29: N Shi 2D 66
NE46: Hex 2C 70
SR4: Sund 3H 117
St Luke's Ter. SR4: Sund 1B 118
St Margarets Av. NE12: Longb 6B 46
SR5: Sund 6G 103
St Margaret's Ct. DH1: Dur 3A 6 (3K 165)
NE26: Whit B *7J 39*
(off Margaret Rd.)
SR5: Sund 6G 103
St Margaret's Dr. DH9: Tanf 5D 110
St Margarets Gth. DH1: Dur 3A 6 (3K 165)
St Margarets M. DH1: Dur 3A 6 (3K 165)
St Mark's Cl. NE6: Byke 6A 64
St Marks Ct. NE5: West 1F 61
NE8: Gate *6J 83*
(off Split Crow Rd.)
NE27: Shir 1J 47
NE29: N Shi 3D 66
St Marks Cres. SR4: Sund 2D 118
St Marks Rd. NE46: Hex 2C 70
SR4: Sund 2C 118
St Mark's St. NE6: Byke 6A 64
NE61: Mor 6E 8
SR4: Sund 2D 118
St Mark's Ter. SR4: Sund 2D 118
St Mark's Way NE33: S Shi 4J 67
St Martin's Cl. NE26: Whit B 4E 38
St Martin's Ct. NE26: Whit B 4E 38
St Martin's Way NE26: Whit B 4E 38
St Mary's Av. NE26: Whit B 4F 39
(not continuous)
NE34: S Shi 7B 68
St Mary's Blvd. SR1: Sund 3G 7 (1E 118)
St Marys Chare NE45: Corb 1D 72
NE46: Hex 1D 70
St Marys Cl. DH1: Shin 6D 166
DH2: Ches S 1K 141
DH8: B'hill 5F 121
SR8: Eas 1J 171
(not continuous)
St Marys Ct. NE8: Gate 10K 5 (3H 83)
SR8: Hord 5E 172
St Mary's Cres. DH8: B'hill 5E 120
St Mary's Dr. DH4: W Rai 1A 156
DH6: S'burn 3K 167
NE24: Bly 3F 23
St Mary's Fld. NE61: Mor 1F 15
St Mary's Grn. NE16: Whi 7H 81
St Mary's Island Nature Reserve 1F 39
St Mary's Lighthouse 7G 29
St Mary's Pl. NE1: Newc T 3F 4 (7F 63)
NE15: Thro 3J 59
St Mary's Pl. E. NE1: Newc T 3F 4
St Mary's Rd. DH1: Carr 7G 155
St Mary's Sq. NE8: Gate 8J 5 (2H 83)
St Mary's St. DH8: B'hill 5F 121
St Mary's Ter. DH6: Coxh 7J 177
NE10: Hew 6D 84
NE33: S Shi 6H 67
NE36: E Bol 7K 87
NE40: Ryton 1F 79
St Mary's Vw. *NE26: Whit B* *5H 39*
(off Brook St.)
St Mary's Wynd NE26: Sea S 6E 28
NE46: Hex 1D 70
St Matthews La. NE42: Pru 4F 77
St Matthews Rd. NE46: Hex 3B 70
St Matthew's Ter. DH4: Nbot 5D 130
St Matthew's Vw. SR3: New S 2C 132
St Michael's DH4: Hou S 2B 144
St Michaels Av. NE25: New Hart 4H 27
NE26: New Hart 4H 27
NE33: S Shi 4K 67
St Michaels Av. Nth. NE33: S Shi 4K 67
St Michaels Cl. NE4: Elsw 2B 82
St Michaels Ct. SR2: Sund 7K 7 (4G 119)
St Michael's Mt. NE6: Byke 1A 84
St Michaels Ri. SR7: Hawt 3K 159
St Michael's Rd. NE6: Byke 5N 5 (1K 83)
St Michael's Va. NE31: Heb 1G 85
St Michael's Way NE11: Dun 5H 81
SR1: Sund 3G 7 (1E 118)
St Michaels Workshops NE6: Byke 5N 5
St Monica Gro. DH1: Dur 3J 165
Saint-Nazaire Way SR2: Ryh, Sund 6J 119
St Nicholas Av. NE3: Gos 1E 62
(not continuous)
SR3: Sund 5D 118
St Nicholas Bldg., The
NE1: Newc T 7F 4 (2F 83)
St Nicholas Cathedral 6G 4 (1G 83)
St Nicholas' Chambers *NE1: Newc T* *7G 4*
(off Amen Cnr.)
St Nicholas Chare *NE1: Newc T* *7F 4*
(off St Nicholas St.)
St Nicholas Chyd.
NE1: Newc T 6F 4 (1F 83)
St Nicholas Cl. NE63: Ash 2D 12
St Nicholas Dr. DH1: Dur 7H 153
St Nicholas Pk. Nature Reserve 7C 44
St Nicholas Pct. NE1: Newc T 6F 4
St Nicholas Rd. NE36: W Bol 7G 87
NE46: Hex 2C 70
St Nicholas Sq. NE1: Newc T 6F 4 (1F 83)
St Nicholas St. NE1: Newc T 7F 4 (2F 83)
St Nicholas Ter. NE36: W Bol 7G 87
SR8: Eas 7B 160
St Nicholas Vw. NE36: W Bol 7G 87
St Nicholas Vs. NE36: W Bol 7G 87
St Nicholas Way NE31: Heb 1G 85
St Omers Rd. NE11: Dun 5A 82
St Oswald Bungs. *DH6: Thor* *2J 179*
(off St Cuthbert Rd.)
St Oswald's Av. NE6: Walk 6C 64
St Oswalds Ct. NE10: Fell 6B 84
NE42: Pru 3G 77
St Oswald's Dr. DH1: Dur 7J 165
St Oswald's Grn. NE6: Walk 6C 64
St Oswald Sq. DH1: P Me 4J 153
St Oswalds Rd. NE28: W'snd 1H 65
NE31: Heb 6K 65
NE46: Hex 2C 70
St Oswald's Ter. DH4: S Row 3B 130
St Oswin's Av. NE30: Cull 1J 49
St Oswin's Pl. DH8: B'hill 5F 121
NE30: Tyne 4K 49
St Oswin's St. NE33: S Shi 6K 67
St Patricks Cl. NE10: Fell 6B 84
St Patricks M. NE10: Fell 5B 84
St Patrick's Ter. SR2: Ryh 3H 133
St Patrick's Wlk. NE10: Fell 6B 84
St Pauls Cl. NE63: Ash 2D 12
St Paul's Ct. NE8: Gate 5E 82
St Pauls Dr. DH4: Pen 1J 129
St Paul's Gdns. NE25: Whit B 7G 39
St Paul's Monastery (remains of) 6D 66
St Paul's Pl. NE4: Newc T 6A 4 (1D 82)
St Pauls Rd. NE32: Jar 6C 66
NE46: Hex 2B 70
St Paul's Ter. DH9: W Pelt 2C 126
SR2: Ryh 3H 133
ST PETER'S 7P 5 (2A 84)
St Peters Av. NE34: S Shi 7A 68
St Peters Basin Marina NE6: Byke 2A 84
St Peter's Church & Visitor Cen. *7G 105*
(off St Peter's Way)
St Peters Ct. NE6: Byke 2A 84
NE28: W'snd 3H 65
St Peter's Ga. SR6: Monkw 1K 7 (7F 105)
St Peter's Quayside W. NE6: Byke 2A 84
St Peter's Riverside Sculpture Trail 7H 105
St Peter's Rd. NE6: Byke 2A 84
NE28: W'snd 2H 65
St Peter's Stairs NE29: N Shi 1H 67
St Peter's Vw. SR6: Monkw 1K 7 (7F 105)
St Peters Way SR6: Roker 1K 7 (7G 105)
St Peter's Wharf NE6: Byke 2A 84
St Philips Cl. NE4: Newc T 4A 4 (7D 62)
St Philips Way NE4: Newc T 5A 4 (1D 82)
St Rollox St. NE31: Heb 1H 85
St Ronan's Dr. NE26: Sea S 3B 28
St Ronan's Rd. NE25: Monks 7F 39
St Ronans Vw. NE9: Low F 5J 99
St Simon St. NE34: S Shi 2G 87
St Stephen's Cl. NE25: Sea D 7F 27
St Stephen's Way NE29: N Shi 3C 66
St Stevens Cl. DH4: Pen 1J 129
St Thomas Cl. NE42: Pru 4F 77
SR8: Eas 1J 171
St Thomas Cres. NE1: Newc T 3E 4 (7F 63)
St Thomas M. NE42: Pru 4F 77
St Thomas' Sq. NE1: Newc T 3E 4 (7F 63)
St Thomas St. NE1: Newc T 3E 4 (7F 63)
NE9: Low F 2J 99
SR1: Sund 3K 7 (1F 119)
St Thomas St. Bus. Cen.
NE1: Newc T 3E 4 (7F 63)
St Thomas' Ter. NE1: Newc T 3E 4
St Vincent Ct. NE8: Gate 5J 83
St Vincent Ho. NE30: Tyne 5K 49
St Vincent's Cl. NE15: Lem 5E 60
St Vincents Pl. NE26: Whit B 3F 39
St Vincent St. NE8: Gate 5J 83
NE33: S Shi 4A 68
SR2: Sund 6K 7 (3G 119)
St Vincent's Way NE26: Whit B 3F 39
St Wilfred's Ct. NE45: Corb 7E 52
St Wilfred's Rd. NE45: Corb 7E 52
St Wilfred's Ter. *NE45: Corb* *7E 52*
(off St Wilfred's Rd.)
St Wilfrids Ct. *NE46: Hex* *2D 70*
(off St Wilfrids Rd.)
St Wilfrids Rd. NE46: Hex 2C 70
Saker Pl. *NE28: W'snd* *4F 65*
(off David St.)
Salcombe Av. NE32: Jar 1D 86
Salcombe Cl. SR7: S'hm 4J 147
Salcombe Gdns. NE9: Low F 5H 99
Salem Av. DH8: Cons 1K 135
Salem Hill SR2: Sund 3G 119
Salem Rd. SR2: Sund 3G 119
Salem St. NE32: Jar 6C 66
NE33: S Shi 2J 67
SR2: Sund 3G 119
Salem St. Sth. SR2: Sund 3G 119
Salem Ter. SR2: Sund 3G 119
Salisbury Av. DH3: Ches S 7A 128
NE29: N Shi 5F 49
Salisbury Cl. DH3: Gt Lum 4E 142
DH8: Shot B 2G 121
NE23: Cra 4G 25
NE63: N Sea 5D 12
Salisbury Gdns. NE2: Jes 5J 63
Salisbury Pl. NE33: S Shi 2A 68
Salisbury Rd. DH1: Dur 3C 154
Salisbury St. DH8: Cons 6J 121
DH9: Stly 4D 124
NE10: Pel 5E 84
NE24: Bly 1H 23
NE33: S Shi 3K 67
NE61: Mor 7H 9
SR1: Sund 5K 7 (2G 119)
SR4: Sund 1G 117
Salisbury Way NE32: Jar 5B 86
Salkeld Gdns. NE9: Low F 6J 83
Salkeld Rd. NE9: Low F 1J 99
Sallyport Cres. NE1: Newc T 6H 5 (1G 83)
Sallyport Ho. NE1: Newc T 6H 5 (1G 83)
Salmon St. NE33: S Shi 1K 67
Saltburn Cl. DH4: Hou S 1C 144
Saltburn Gdns. NE28: W'snd 2B 66
Saltburn Rd. SR3: Sund 5A 118
Saltburn Sq. SR3: Sund 5A 118
Salterfen La. SR2: Ryh 1J 133
Salterfen Rd. SR2: Sund 1J 133
Salter La. SR3: Sund 1H 131
Salters Cl. NE3: Gos 6G 45
Salters Ct. NE3: Gos 6G 45
Salter's La. DH5: Hou S 1A 146
DH6: Has 4A 158
DH6: Has, Shot C 1B 170
Salters' La. NE3: Longb 6H 45
NE12: Gos, Longb 6H 45
Salter's La. SR7: Mur, Seat 1A 158
SR8: Pet 4C 170
TS28: Win 5G 181
TS29: Trim G, Trim S 7K 179
Salters La. Ind. Est. NE12: Longb 3J 45
Salters Rd. NE3: Gos 1C 62
Saltford NE9: Low F 5J 99
SALTMEADOWS 7L 5 (2J 83)
Saltmeadows Ind. Pk.
NE8: Gate 9N 5 (3K 83)
Saltmeadows Rd. NE8: Gate 7M 5 (2J 83)
Saltmeadows Trade Pk.
NE10: Gate 10P 5 (3K 83)
SALTWELL 1G 99
Saltwell Bus. Pk. NE9: Low F 1H 99
Saltwell Crematorium NE9: Low F 1G 99
Saltwell Pk. 7G 83
Saltwell Pk. Mansion (Mus.) 1G 99
Saltwell Pl. NE8: Gate 6F 83
Saltwell Rd. NE8: Gate 6F 83
Saltwell Rd. Sth. NE9: Low F 2G 99
Saltwell St. NE8: Gate 6F 83
Saltwell Vw. NE8: Gate 7G 83
Saltwick Av. NE13: Ki Pk 4A 44
Saltwood Gdns. NE25: Monks 5C 38
Salvin St. DH6: Crox 7K 175
(not continuous)
Sams Ct. NE23: Dud 3H 35
Samson Cl. NE12: Kil 2A 46
Sancroft Dr. DH5: Hou S 3E 144
Sandalwood NE34: S Shi 3K 87
Sandalwood Sq. SR4: Sund 6G 117
Sandalwood Wlk. DH9: Stly 2G 125
Sandbach DH3: Gt Lum 2E 142
Sanderling Cl. NE40: Ryton 2J 79
Sanderlings NE28: W'snd 4F 65
Sanderlings, The SR2: Ryh 3J 133
Sanders Gdns. DH3: Bir 3A 114
Sanders Memorial Homes
DH2: Ches S 6A 128
Sanderson Arc. NE61: Mor 6F 9
Sanderson Rd. NE2: Jes 3G 63
NE26: Whit B 6F 39
Sanderson's Ter. NE23: Cra 7A 26
Sanderson St. NE4: Elsw 3B 82
Sanderson Vs. NE8: Gate 4K 83
Sandfield Rd. NE22: E Sle 4F 19
NE30: Cull 1H 49
Sandford Av. NE23: Cra 1K 25
Sandford Cl. TS28: Win 7G 181
Sandford M. NE13: W Op 6C 34
Sandford Rd. DH8: Shot B 5D 120
Sandgate DH6: Coxh 7K 177
DH6: Shot C 5F 171
DH9: Ann P 5B 124
NE1: Newc T 6J 5 (1H 83)
Sandgate Ho. NE1: Newc T 6J 5
Sandgrove SR6: Clead 5C 88
Sandhill NE1: Newc T 7G 4 (2G 83)
NE21: Winl 5B 80
Sandhill M. NE21: Winl 5B 80
Sandhill Sports Cen. 6K 117
SANDHOE 4K 51
Sandhoe Gdns. NE15: Scot 1H 81
Sandhoe Wlk. NE28: W'snd 3A 66
Sandholm Cl. NE28: W'snd 7K 47
Sandhurst Av. NE30: Cull 2H 49
Sandiacres NE32: Jar 5C 86
Sandison Ct. NE13: Bru V 6B 34
Sandmartin Cl. NE63: Ash 7C 12
Sandmere Pl. NE15: Scot 7G 61
Sandmere Rd. SR2: Sund 7F 119
Sandon Cl. NE27: Back 6G 37
Sandown NE25: Monks 6D 38
Sandown Cl. NE25: Sea D 1H 37
Sandown Ct. NE28: W'snd 1A 66
Sandown Gdns. NE8: Gate 6E 82
NE28: W'snd 1K 65
SR3: New S 1B 132
Sandpiper Cl. NE24: News 5K 23
NE38: Wash 6D 114
NE40: Ryton 2H 79
Sandpiper Ct. NE30: Tyne 4K 49
Sandpiper Pl. NE12: Longb 5J 45
Sandpiper Way NE63: Ash 6B 12
Sand Point Rd. SR6: Roker 6G 105
Sandray Cl. DH3: Bir 7B 114
Sandridge NE64: Newb S 2K 13
Sandrigg Sq. NE34: S Shi 1A 88
Sandringham Av. NE12: Longb 6A 46
Sandringham Cl. NE25: Monks 7B 38
Sandringham Ct. DH3: Ches S 5B 128
NE10: Fell 6A 84
NE12: Longb 6J 45
Sandringham Cres. SR3: E Her 3J 131
SR8: Hord 6F 173
Sandringham Dr. DH9: Ann P 4K 123
NE16: Whi 7G 81
NE24: News 6G 23
NE25: Monks 7B 38
Sandringham Gdns. NE29: N Shi 5G 49
Sandringham Mdws. NE24: News 6H 23
Sandringham M. NE28: W'snd 1K 65
Sandringham Rd. NE3: Gos 1G 63
NE5: W Dent 5E 60
SR6: Ful 5F 105
Sandringham Ter. SR6: Roker 5G 105
Sandringham Way DH2: Newf 4E 126
NE20: Darr H 7G 31
Sands, The DH1: Dur 1D 6 (2B 166)
Sandsay Cl. SR2: Ryh 1F 133
Sands Flats, The DH1: Dur 1D 6 (2B 166)
Sands Ind. Est. NE16: Swa 5G 81
Sands La. NE16: Swa 5G 81
Sands Rd. NE16: Swa 5G 81
Sandstone Cl. NE34: S Shi 3F 87
Sand St. DH9: Stly 2G 125
Sandwell Dr. DH4: Pen 1K 129
Sandwich Rd. NE29: N Shi 3F 49
Sandwich St. NE6: Walk 3D 84
Sandwick Ter. DH6: Whe H 4A 180
Sandy Bank NE44: Rid M 6J 73
Sandy Bay Caravan Pk. NE63: N Sea 7G 13
Sandy Chare SR6: Whit 6G 89
Sandy Cres. NE6: Walk 2C 84
Sandyford DH2: Pelt 2F 127
Sandyford Av. NE42: Pru 3H 77
Sandyford Ho. NE2: Jes 1H 5
Sandyford Pk. NE2: Newc T 1K 5 (5H 63)
Sandyford Pl. DH2: Pelt 2G 127
Sandyford Rd. NE1: Newc T 3G 4 (7G 63)
NE2: Newc T 1J 5 (7G 63)
Sandygate M. NE16: Marl H 6H 97
Sandy La. NE3: Gos 7F 35
NE9: Eigh B 6B 100
NE13: Bru V, Din 5J 33
NE13: W Op 7E 34
NE44: Rid M 6J 73
NE63: N Sea 5F 13
Sandy La. Ind. Area NE3: Gos 7G 35
Sandy Path La. NE16: Burn 1A 110
(not continuous)

Sandysykes NE42: Pru . . . 4D 76
Sanford Ct. SR2: Sund . . . 5E 118
Sans St. SR1: Sund . . . 1G 119
Sans St. Sth. SR1: Sund . . . 2G 119
Sarabel Av. NE62: Chop . . . 1G 17
Sargent Av. NE34: S Shi . . . 4K 87
Satley Gdns. NE9: Wrek . . . 5A 100
SR3: Sund . . . 6D 118
Saturn Cl. SR8: Eas . . . 7A 160
Saturn Ct. NE29: N Shi . . . 7B 48
Saturn St. SR7: S'hm . . . 3J 147
Saunton Ct. DH4: Nbot . . . 6C 130
Saville Ct. *NE33: S Shi* . . . *2K 67*
(off Saville St.)
Saville Gdns. NE3: Gos . . . 1F 63
Saville Pl. NE1: Newc T . . . 4G 4
SR1: Sund . . . *2G 119*
(off Borough Rd.)
Saville Row NE1: Newc T . . . 4F 4 (7F 63)
Saville St. NE29: N Shi . . . 7H 49
NE30: N Shi . . . 7H 49
NE33: S Shi . . . 2K 67
Saville St. W. NE29: N Shi . . . 7G 49
Savory Rd. NE28: W'snd . . . 2K 65
Sawmill Cotts. DH9: Dip . . . 7J 109
NE46: Hex . . . 1D 70
Sawmills La. DH7: B'don . . . 1C 174
Saxilby Dr. NE3: Gos . . . 4F 45
Saxon Cl. SR6: Clead . . . 5A 88
Saxon Ct. NE22: Bed . . . 1J 21
Saxon Cres. SR3: Sund . . . 5B 118
Saxondale Rd. NE3: Ken . . . 7A 44
Saxon Dr. NE30: Tyne . . . 3J 49
Saxon Ter. DH8: Cons . . . 6G 121
Saxon Way NE32: Jar . . . 5C 66
Saxton Gro. NE7: H Hea . . . 1J 63
Sayer Wlk. SR8: Pet . . . 7C 172
Scafell DH3: Bir . . . 7B 114
Scafell Ct. DH9: Ann P . . . 6J 123
Scafell Dr. NE5: Ken . . . 2K 61
Scafell Gdns. NE11: Lob H . . . 1C 98
Scaffold Hill NE12: Longb . . . 4G 47
Scalby Cl. NE3: Gos . . . 4F 45
Scales Cres. NE42: Pru . . . 4H 77
Scarborough Ct. NE6: Byke . . . 7B 64
NE23: Cra . . . 5K 25
Scarborough Pde. NE31: Heb . . . 4A 86
Scarborough Rd. NE6: Byke, Walk . . . 7B 64
(not continuous)
SR3: New S . . . 1B 132
Scardale Way DH1: Carr . . . 7J 155
Scarfell Cl. SR8: Pet . . . 6C 172
Sceptre Ct. NE4: Elsw . . . 2C 82
Sceptre Pl. NE4: Elsw . . . 1C 82
(not continuous)
Sceptre St. NE4: Elsw . . . 1C 82
Schalksmuhle Rd. NE22: Bed . . . 7H 17
Schimel St. SR5: S'wck . . . 5D 104
Scholars Ct. DH7: Ush M . . . 2B 164
School App. NE34: S Shi . . . 7C 68
School Av. DH4: W Rai . . . 2K 155
DH6: Kel . . . 7D 178
NE11: Dun . . . 6B 82
NE62: Chop . . . 1H 17
TS27: B Col . . . 2H 183
School Cl. NE10: Wind N . . . 1B 100
NE61: Mor . . . 6F 9
School Ct. DH6: S'burn . . . 3A 168
DH7: Bro . . . 4E 164
SR8: Hord . . . 5E 172
School Grn. DH6: Thor . . . 7K 169
Schoolhouse La. NE16: Marl H . . . 7E 96
School La. DH1: Dur . . . 5D 6 (4B 166)
DH9: Stly . . . 4D 124
NE16: Whi . . . 7J 81
NE39: H Spen . . . 4E 94
School Rd. DH5: E Rain . . . 6C 144
NE22: Bed . . . 5B 18
School Row NE42: Pru . . . 3G 77
NE43: Hed . . . 4B 92
School St. DH3: Bir . . . 4A 114
NE8: Gate . . . 4F 83
NE16: Whi . . . 7G 81
NE31: Heb . . . 6J 65
SR8: Eas C . . . 7C 160
School Ter. DH4: Hou S . . . 1J 143
DH9: Stly . . . 4D 124
School Vw. DH4: W Rai . . . 1K 155
DH5: Eas L . . . 3K 157
DH9: Dip . . . 1G 123
School Way DH1: Dur . . . 1E 166
Science Sq. NE4: Newc T . . . 5C 4 (1E 82)
Scorer's La. DH3: Gt Lum . . . 1F 143
Scorer St. NE29: N Shi . . . 7F 49
Scoresby Cl. SR5: S'wck . . . 5C 104
Scotby Gdns. NE9: Low F . . . 4K 99
Scotland Ct. NE21: Winl . . . 5A 80
SCOTLAND GATE . . . 3G 17
Scotland Head NE21: Winl . . . 7A 80
Scotland St. SR2: Ryh . . . 3J 133
SCOTSWOOD . . . 1G 81
Scotswood Bri. Works NE21: Blay . . . 3G 81
Scotswood Rd. NE1: Newc T . . . 2E 82
NE4: Elsw, Newc T . . . 10A 4 (3C 82)
NE15: Lem, Newc T . . . 7D 60
Scotswood Sports & Social Cen. . . . 7F 61
Scotswood Sta. App. NE15: Scot . . . 2G 81
Scotswood Vw. NE11: Dun . . . 3H 81
Scott Av. NE23: Nel V . . . 2H 25
Scott Cl. NE46: Hex . . . 4B 70
Scott Ct. DH3: Gt Lum . . . 3E 142
NE34: S Shi . . . 3G 87
Scott Ho. NE30: N Shi . . . 6G 49
Scott's Av. NE40: Craw . . . 3C 78
Scotts Bank SR5: S'wck . . . 6C 104
Scotts Cotts. DH1: Dur . . . 2H 165
Scotts Ct. NE10: Ward . . . 1F 101
Scott's Ter. DH5: Hett H . . . 6G 145
Scott St. DH4: Hou S . . . 2D 144
DH9: Stly . . . 3E 124
NE23: E Har . . . 6K 21
Scott Ter. NE17: C'wl . . . 6K 93
Scoular Dr. NE63: N Sea . . . 4E 12
Scripton Gill DH7: B'don . . . 1C 174
Scripton Gill Rd. DH7: B'don . . . 2B 174
Scripton La. DH7: Bran . . . 3C 174
Scrogg Rd. NE6: Walk . . . 6C 64
Scruton Av. SR3: Sund . . . 6A 118
Sea Bank NE64: Newb S . . . 3J 13
Sea Banks NE30: Tyne . . . 4K 49
SEABURN . . . 3G 105
Seaburn Av. NE25: New Hart . . . 4H 27
Seaburn Cen. . . . 2G 105
Seaburn Cl. SR6: Seab . . . 3G 105
Seaburn Ct. SR6: Seab . . . 3G 105
Seaburn Dr. DH4: Hou S . . . 2C 144
Seaburn Gdns. NE9: Wrek . . . 4B 100
SR6: Seab . . . 3G 105
Seaburn Gro. NE26: Sea S . . . 4C 28
Seaburn Hill SR6: Seab . . . 3G 105
Seaburn Station (Metro) . . . 3E 104
Seaburn Ter. SR6: Seab . . . 3H 105
Seaburn Vw. NE25: New Hart . . . 4H 27
Seacombe Av. NE30: Cull . . . 1H 49
Seacrest Av. NE30: Cull . . . 1H 49
Sea Crest Rd. NE64: Newb S . . . 1J 13
Seafield M. NE26: Sea S . . . 3B 28
Seafield Rd. NE24: News . . . 4J 23
Seafields SR6: Seab . . . 2G 105
Seafield Ter. NE33: S Shi . . . 2K 67
Seafield Vw. NE30: Tyne . . . 4K 49
Seaforth Rd. SR3: Sund . . . 5C 118
Seaforth St. NE24: Bly . . . 1J 23
Seagent Pl. DH8: Shot B . . . 3G 121
SEAHAM . . . 3B 148
Seaham Cl. NE34: S Shi . . . 7D 68
Seaham Gdns. NE9: Wrek . . . 5A 100
Seaham Grange Ind. Est. SR7: Seat . . . 6H 133
Seaham Harbour Marina SR7: S'hm . . . 2C 148
Seaham Leisure Cen. . . . 3K 147
Seaham Rd. DH5: Hou S . . . 2F 145
SR2: Ryh . . . 3J 133
Seaham Station (Rail) . . . 2A 148
Seaham St. SR3: New S . . . 2C 132
SR7: S'hm . . . 5C 148
SEAL, THE . . . 1C 70
Sea La. SR6: Seab . . . 3G 105
SR6: Whit . . . 7H 89
Seal Ter. NE46: Hex . . . 2C 70
Sea Rd. NE33: S Shi . . . 1K 67
SR6: Ful . . . 3F 105
Seascale Pl. NE9: Low F . . . 3K 99
Seaside La. SR8: Eas, Eas C . . . 7K 159
Seaside La. Sth. SR8: Eas C . . . 7C 160
Seasons Courtyard *NE8: Gate* . . . *5C 82*
(off Michaelmas St.)
Seasons Edge NE8: Gate . . . 5D 82
Seatoller Ct. SR3: Silk . . . 3B 132
SEATON . . . 5K 27
. . . 2F 147
Seaton Av. DH5: Hou S . . . 2F 145
NE22: Bed . . . 7K 17
NE23: Dud . . . 2K 35
NE24: News . . . 5G 23
NE64: Newb S . . . 3H 13
SEATON BURN . . . 3D 34
Seaton Cl. NE10: Ward . . . 1F 101
Seaton Cres. NE25: H'wll . . . 1K 37
NE25: Monks . . . 6E 38
SR7: S'hm . . . 1G 147
Seaton Cft. NE23: Dud . . . 3A 36
SEATON DELAVAL . . . 7G 27
Seaton Delaval Hall . . . 5A 28
Seaton Gdns. NE9: Wrek . . . 4A 100
Seaton Gro. SR7: Seat . . . 2F 147
Seaton Holme (Discovery / Exhibition Cen.)
. . . 7J 159
Seaton La. SR7: S'hm, Seat . . . 1F 147
Seaton Pk. SR7: S'hm . . . 2H 147
Seaton Pl. NE6: Walk . . . 3C 84
NE13: W Op . . . 6C 34
Seaton Rd. NE27: Shir . . . 7A 38
SR3: Sund . . . 5K 117
SEATON SLUICE . . . 4D 28
SEATON TERRACE . . . 7H 27
Seatonville Cres. NE25: Monks . . . 1E 48
Seatonville Gro. NE25: Monks . . . 1E 48
Seatonville Rd. NE25: Monks . . . 7D 38
Sea Vw. NE10: Wind N . . . 1A 100
NE63: N Sea . . . 7E 12
SR2: Ryh . . . 3J 133
(not continuous)
SR8: Eas . . . 1K 171
TS27: B Col . . . 3K 183
Sea Vw. Cotts. TS27: Hes . . . 4D 182
Sea Vw. Gdns. SR6: Roker . . . 4G 105
SR8: Hord . . . 4E 172
Seaview Ind. Est. SR8: Hord . . . 3E 172
Sea Vw. La. NE64: Newb S . . . 2J 13
Sea Vw. Pk. NE23: Cra . . . 4B 26
SR6: Whit . . . 6F 89
Sea Vw. Rd. SR2: Sund . . . 6G 119
Sea Vw. Rd. W. SR2: Sund . . . 6F 119
Sea Vw. St. SR2: Sund . . . 6H 119
Sea Vw. Ter. NE64: Newb S . . . 2J 13
Seaview Ter. NE33: S Shi . . . 2A 68
Sea Vw. Vs. NE23: Cra . . . 4B 26
Sea Vw. Wlk. SR7: Mur . . . 6G 147
Sea Way NE33: S Shi . . . 2A 68
Sea Winnings Way NE33: S Shi . . . 3A 68
Second Av. DH2: Ches S . . . 1K 127
(Drum Rd.)
DH2: Ches S . . . 7K 127
(Yetholm Av.)
NE6: Heat . . . 1P 5 (5A 64)
NE11: T Vall . . . 1D 98
NE24: Bly . . . 3H 23
NE29: N Shi . . . 1B 66
NE61: Mor . . . 1H 15
NE63: Ash . . . 4B 12
Seconds Out Sherburn ASET Cen. . . . 2K 167
Second St. DH8: Cons . . . 7K 121
DH8: Lead . . . 3A 122
(Bradley Bungs.)
DH8: Lead . . . 4A 122
(Fourth St.)
DH9: Stly . . . 7D 124
NE8: Gate . . . 5F 83
SR8: Hord . . . 4E 172
TS27: B Col . . . 2H 183
Secretan Way NE33: S Shi . . . 3J 67
Sedbergh Rd. NE30: Cull . . . 2G 49
Sedgefield Ct. NE12: Kil . . . 1A 46
SEDGELETCH . . . 7A 130
Sedgeletch Ind. Est. DH4: Hou S . . . 7A 130
Sedgeletch Rd. DH4: Hou S . . . 1A 144
Sedgemoor NE12: Kil . . . 7B 36
Sedgewick Pl. NE8: Gate . . . 5G 83
Sedley Rd. NE28: W'snd . . . 4F 65
Sedling Rd. NE38: Wash . . . 6F 115
Sefton Av. NE6: Heat . . . 4A 64
Sefton Ct. NE23: Cra . . . 1A 26
Sefton Sq. SR3: Sund . . . 5A 118
Segedunum Cres. NE28: W'snd . . . 1J 65
Segedunum Roman Fort, Baths & Museum
. . . 5G 65
Segedunum Way NE28: W'snd . . . 4F 65
SEGHILL . . . 2D 36
Seghill Rd. End NE23: Dud . . . 3A 36
Seine Ct. NE32: Jar . . . 7C 66
Selborne Av. NE9: Low F . . . 3G 99
Selborne Gdns. DH8: Shot B . . . 3F 121
NE2: Jes . . . 5J 63
Selbourne Cl. NE23: Cra . . . 4G 25
Selbourne St. NE33: S Shi . . . 3K 67
SR6: Roker . . . 6F 105
(not continuous)
Selbourne Ter. NE24: Camb . . . 5H 19
Selby Cl. NE23: Cra . . . 1K 25
Selby Ct. NE6: Walk . . . 2D 84
NE32: Jar . . . 6B 66
Selby Gdns. DH8: C'sde . . . 1E 134
NE6: Walk . . . 5D 64
NE28: W'snd . . . 2F 65
Selby Sq. SR3: Sund . . . 5A 118
Sele Ct. NE46: Hex . . . 2C 70
Selina Pl. SR6: Roker . . . 6G 105
Selkirk Cres. DH3: Bir . . . 2A 114
Selkirk Gro. NE23: Cra . . . 1A 26
Selkirk Sq. SR3: Sund . . . 5K 117
Selkirk St. NE32: Jar . . . 3E 86
Selkirk Way NE29: N Shi . . . 4C 48
Selsdon Av. SR4: Sund . . . 6G 117
Selsey Ct. NE10: Wind N . . . 1C 100
Selwood Ct. NE34: S Shi . . . 1B 88
Selwyn Av. NE25: Monks . . . 1D 48
Selwyn Cl. NE5: Ken . . . 2K 61
Senet Ent. Cen. NE63: Ash . . . 5B 12
September Courtyard *NE8: Gate* . . . *5D 82*
(off Fall Pass)
Serin Ho. NE5: West . . . 2G 61
Serlby Cl. NE37: Wash . . . 6G 101
Serlby Pk. DH5: Hett H . . . 7H 145
Seton Av. NE34: S Shi . . . 2F 87
Seton Wlk. NE34: S Shi . . . 2F 87
Setting Stones NE38: Wash . . . 1E 128
Settlingstone Cl. NE7: H Hea . . . 2B 64
Sevenacres DH3: Gt Lum . . . 2F 143
Sevenoaks Dr. SR4: Sund . . . 5G 117
Seven Stories . . . 4L 5 (7J 63)
Seventh Av. DH2: Ches S . . . 6K 127
NE6: Heat . . . 1P 5 (6A 64)
NE11: T Vall . . . 3F 99
NE24: Bly . . . 3H 23
(not continuous)
NE61: Mor . . . 1H 15
NE63: Ash . . . 5C 12
Seventh Row NE63: Ash . . . 3K 11
Seventh St. SR8: Hord . . . 5E 172
(not continuous)
TS27: B Col . . . 1H 183
Severn Av. NE31: Heb . . . 3J 85
Severn Cl. SR8: Pet . . . 1A 182
Severn Ct. SR3: Silk . . . 3B 132
Severn Cres. DH9: Stly . . . 4E 124
Severn Dr. NE32: Jar . . . 4C 86
Severn Gdns. NE8: Gate . . . 5K 83
Severn Ho's. NE37: Wash . . . 7A 102
Severn St. NE17: C'wl . . . 6A 94
Severs Ter. NE5: Call . . . 6B 42
Severus Rd. NE4: Fen . . . 6A 62
Seymour Ct. NE11: Dun . . . 5C 82
NE63: N Sea . . . 4F 13
Seymour Sq. SR3: Sund . . . 5A 118
Seymour St. DH8: Cons . . . 7H 121
NE11: Dun . . . 5C 82
NE29: N Shi . . . 1G 67
SR8: Hord . . . 6F 173
Seymour Ter. DH5: Eas L . . . 2H 157
NE40: Ryton . . . 1E 78
Shadfen Cres. NE61: Peg . . . 4A 10
Shadfen Pk. Rd. NE30: Cull . . . 1G 49
SHADFORTH . . . 5E 168
Shadforth Cl. SR8: Pet . . . 1J 181
Shadon Way DH3: Bir . . . 5C 114
Shaftesbury Av. NE26: Whit B . . . 4F 39
NE32: Jar . . . 7D 66
NE34: S Shi . . . 7D 66
SR2: Ryh . . . 2G 133
TS27: B Col . . . 1H 183
Shaftesbury Cres. NE30: Cull . . . 1G 49
SR3: Sund . . . 5B 118
TS27: B Col . . . 1G 183
Shaftesbury Gro. NE6: Heat . . . 1N 5 (6K 63)
Shaftesbury Rd. TS27: B Col . . . 7G 173
Shaftesbury Wlk. NE8: Gate . . . 4E 82
Shafto Bank DH9: Crag . . . 6J 125
Shafto Cl. DH8: Cons . . . 2K 135
Shafto Ct. NE15: Benw . . . 1H 81
Shaftoe Cl. NE40: Craw . . . 3D 78
Shaftoe Ct. NE3: Gos . . . 5C 44
NE12: Kil . . . 1B 46
Shaftoe Cres. NE46: Hex . . . 1C 70
Shaftoe Leazes NE46: Hex . . . 1B 70
Shaftoe Rd. SR3: Sund . . . 6K 117
Shaftoe Sq. SR3: Sund . . . 6K 117
Shaftoe Way NE13: Din . . . 4H 33
Shafto St. NE15: Scot . . . 1G 81
NE28: W'snd . . . 2J 65
Shafto St. Nth. NE28: W'snd . . . 2J 65
Shafto Ter. DH9: Crag . . . 6K 125
DH9: Stly . . . 1F 125
NE37: Wash . . . 1H 115
Shaftsbury Dr. DH7: B'don . . . 3C 174
Shaftsbury Pk. DH5: Hett H . . . 1H 157
Shakespeare Av. NE31: Heb . . . 7J 65
TS27: B Col . . . 7G 173
Shakespeare Cl. DH9: Stly . . . 2H 125
Shakespeare St. DH5: Hou S . . . 3E 144
DH6: Whe H . . . 3B 180
NE1: Newc T . . . 5F 4 (1F 83)
NE28: W'snd . . . 2K 65
NE32: Jar . . . 5B 66
NE33: S Shi . . . 4K 67
SR5: S'wck . . . 5D 104
SR7: S'hm . . . 3B 148
Shakespeare Ter. *DH2: P Fel* . . . *6G 127*
(off Fellway)
SR2: Sund . . . 6G 7 (3E 118)
SR8: Eas . . . 7A 160
Shalcombe Cl. SR3: Silk . . . 3C 132
Shallcross SR2: Sund . . . 4D 118
Shallon Ct. NE63: Ash . . . 5A 12
Shalstone NE37: Wash . . . 6K 101
Shamrock Cl. NE15: Lem . . . 5C 60
Shandon Way NE3: Ken . . . 7A 44
SHANKHOUSE . . . 7A 22
Shanklin Pl. NE23: Cra . . . 4G 25
Shannon Cl. SR5: Sund . . . 6G 103
Shannon Ct. NE3: K Bank . . . 5J 43
Shap Cl. NE38: Wash . . . 5H 115
Shap Ct. SR3: Silk . . . 3B 132
Shap La. NE5: Den M . . . 4G 61
Shap Rd. NE30: Cull . . . 2G 49
Sharnford Cl. NE27: Back . . . 6H 37
Sharon Cl. NE12: Kil . . . 2K 45
Sharp Cres. DH1: Dur . . . 1E 166
(not continuous)
Sharpendon St. NE31: Heb . . . 6J 65
Sharperton Dr. NE3: Gos . . . 3C 44
Sharperton Ho. NE2: Newc T . . . 3H 5
Sharpley Dr. SR7: S'hm . . . 1G 147
Shaw Av. NE34: S Shi . . . 2H 87
Shawbrow Cl. NE7: H Hea . . . 2C 64
Shawdon Cl. NE5: West . . . 1H 61
Shaw Gdns. NE10: Ward . . . 6F 85
Shaw La. DH8: Ebc . . . 5G 107
NE17: Ham . . . 5G 107
Shaws La. NE46: Hex . . . 2A 70
(Allendale Rd.)
NE46: Hex . . . 1A 70
(Leazes La.)
Shaws Pk. NE46: Hex . . . 7A 50
Shaw St. SR7: S'hm . . . 3B 148
Shaw Wood Cl. DH1: Dur . . . 1J 165
Shearlegs Rd. NE8: Gate . . . 9M 5 (3J 83)
Shearwater SR6: Whit . . . 3H 89
Shearwater Av. NE12: Longb . . . 5J 45
Shearwater Cl. NE5: Blak . . . 1H 61
Shearwater Way NE24: News . . . 5J 23
Shed Crossing, The NE36: E Bol . . . 5K 87
Sheelin Av. DH2: Ches S . . . 1A 142
Sheen Cl. DH4: W Rai . . . 1A 156
Sheen Ct. NE3: Ki Pk . . . 7H 43
Sheepfolds Nth.
SR5: Monkw . . . 1J 7 (7F 105)
Sheepfolds Rd. SR5: Monkw . . . 1J 7 (7F 105)
SHEEP HILL . . . 2B 110
Sheephill NE16: Burn . . . 2B 110
SHEEPWASH . . . 7G 11
Sheepwash Av. NE62: Chop . . . 1G 17
Sheepwash Bank NE62: Chop . . . 1G 17
Sheepwash Rd. NE61: Both, Chop . . . 4G 11
NE62: Chop . . . 4G 11
Sheldon Ct. NE12: Longb . . . 3A 46
Sheldon Gro. NE3: Ken . . . 3B 62
NE23: Cra . . . 1K 25
Sheldon Rd. NE34: S Shi . . . 4B 68
Sheldon St. NE32: Jar . . . 6B 66
Shelford Gdns. NE15: Lem . . . 6E 60
Shellbark DH4: S Row . . . 3K 129
Shelley Av. DH5: Eas L . . . 3K 157
NE9: Spri . . . 6D 100
NE34: S Shi . . . 1D 88
NE35: Bol C . . . 6G 87
Shelley Cl. DH9: Stly . . . 3G 125
Shelley Ct. DH2: P Fel . . . 6H 127
Shelley Cres. NE24: Bly . . . 4G 23
Shelley Dr. NE8: Gate . . . 4J 83
Shelley Gdns. DH2: P Fel . . . 6G 127

Shelley Rd. NE15: Newb 6K **59**
Shelley Sq. SR8: Eas 1A **172**
Shelley St. SR7: S'hm 3B **148**
Shepherd Cl. NE23: Dud 5A **36**
Shepherds Ct. DH1: Dur 2E **166**
Shepherd's Quay NE29: N Shi 1H **67**
Shepherd St. SR4: Sund 1C **118**
Shepherds Way NE36: W Bol 7G **87**
Shepherd Way NE38: Wash 6J **115**
Sheppard Ter. SR5: Sund 6H **103**
Sheppey Ct. SR3: Silk 3C **132**
Shepton Cotts. NE16: Sun 4J **97**
Sheraton NE10: Hew 2E **100**
Sheraton Ho. DH1: Dur 4J **165**
Sheraton St. NE2: Newc T 1B **4** (5D **62**)
Sherborne DH3: Gt Lum 2F **143**
Sherborne Av. NE29: N Shi 4D **48**
Sherbourne Rd. SR5: Sund 6J **103**
Sherbourne Vs. NE62: Chop 1H **17**
SHERBURN 3K 167
Sherburn Grange Nth. NE32: Jar 1A **86**
Sherburn Grange Sth. NE32: Jar 2A **86**
Sherburn Grn. NE39: Row G 4K **95**
Sherburn Gro. DH4: Hou S 1C **144**
SHERBURN HILL 3C 168
SHERBURN HOUSE 5H 167
Sherburn Pk. 6J 121
Sherburn Pk. Dr. NE39: Row G 4J **95**
Sherburn Rd. DH1: Dur 2D **166**
Sherburn Rd. Est. DH1: Dur 3E **166**
Sherburn Rd. Flats *DH1: Dur* *2D* ***166***
(off Sherburn Rd.)
Sherburn Sta. DH1: S Hou 3J **167**
Sherburn Ter. DH8: Cons 7J **121**
NE9: Wrek 5A **100**
NE17: Ham 3H **107**
Sherburn Vs. *DH8: Cons* *6H* ***121***
(off Hartington St.)
Sherburn Way NE10: Ward 1G **101**
Sherfield Dr. NE7: H Hea 3B **64**
Sheridan Dr. DH9: Stly 3G **125**
Sheridan Grn. NE38: Wash 7E **114**
Sheridan Rd. NE34: S Shi 3G **87**
Sheridan St. SR4: Sund 1B **118**
SHERIFF HILL 2J 99
SHERIFF MOUNT 7J 83
Sheriff Mt. Nth. NE9: Low F 7J **83**
Sheriff Mt. Sth. NE9: Low F 7J **83**
Sheriffs Cl. NE10: Fell 6K **83**
Sheriffs Hall Vs. NE9: Low F 1J **99**
Sheriff's Highway NE9: Low F 1J **99**
Sheriff's Moor Av. DH5: Eas L 3J **157**
Sheringham Av. NE29: N Shi 5D **48**
Sheringham Cl. SR3: Dox P 5C **132**
Sheringham Dr. NE23: Cra 4G **25**
Sheringham Gdns. NE15: Thro 3F **59**
Sheringham Ho. NE38: Wash 4K **115**
Sherringham Av. NE3: Ken 7A **44**
Sherwood NE27: Mur 2B **48**
Sherwood Cl. DH8: Shot B 2G **121**
NE27: Mur 2B **48**
NE38: Wash 3H **115**
Sherwood Ct. SR3: Silk 3C **132**
Sherwood Pl. NE3: Gos 2E **44**
Sherwood Vw. NE28: W'snd 1E **64**
Shetland Ct. SR3: Silk 3C **132**
Shibdon Bank NE21: Blay 5C **80**
Shibdon Bus. Pk. NE21: Blay 3E **80**
Shibdon Ct. *NE21: Blay* *3C* ***80***
(off Shibdon Rd.)
Shibdon Cres. NE21: Blay 4D **80**
Shibdon Pk. Vw. NE21: Blay 4D **80**
Shibdon Pond Local Nature Reserve 3E 80
Shibdon Rd. NE21: Blay 3C **80**
Shibdon Way NE21: Blay 4F **81**
Shield Av. NE16: Swa 5H **81**
Shieldclose NE37: Wash 2E **114**
Shieldclose Cotts. NE46: Hex 3E **70**
Shield Ct. NE2: Newc T 2J **5** (6H **63**)
NE46: Hex 3D **70**
SHIELDFIELD 4J 5 (7H 63)
Shieldfield Grn. *NE2: Newc T* *4J* ***5***
(off Simpson Ter.)
Shieldfield Ho. NE2: Newc T 3J **5** (7H **63**)
Shieldfield Ind. Est.
NE2: Newc T 4K **5** (7H **63**)
Shieldfield La. NE2: Newc T 4K **5** (7H **63**)
Shield Gro. NE3: Gos 6F **45**
SHIELD ROW 1G 125
Shield Row DH9: Stly 2F **125**
Shield Row Gdns. DH9: Stly 1F **125**
Shieldrow La. DH9: Ann P 6A **124**
Shields La. NE6: Byke 3P **5** (7A **64**)
Shields Pl. DH5: Hou S 1E **144**
Shields Rd. DH3: Ches S, Gt Lum 4B **128**
NE6: Byke 4N **5** (7K **63**)
NE6: Walk 6A **64**
NE10: Hew, Bill Q, Pel 6D **84**
(not continuous)
NE22: H Bri 4D **20**
NE25: Whit B 1F **49**
NE61: Mor 1G **15**
SR6: Clead, S Shi 3B **88**
SR6: Ful 1D **104**
Shields Rd. By-Pass
NE6: Byke 4N **5** (7K **63**)
Shields Rd. W. NE6: Byke 4M **5** (7J **63**)
Shield St. NE2: Newc T 4J **5** (7H **63**)
Shiel Gdns. NE23: Cra 4G **25**
Shillaw Pl. NE23: Dud 5K **35**
Shillmoor Cl. DH2: Ches S 1H **141**
Shilmore Rd. NE3: Ken 7B **44**
Shilton Cl. NE34: S Shi 1C **88**
SHINCLIFFE 6E 166
Shincliffe Av. SR5: Sund 5J **103**
Shincliffe Gdns. NE9: Wrek 4A **100**
Shincliffe La. DH1: S Hou, Shin 5F **167**
SHINEY ROW 4A 130
Shinwell Cres. DH6: Thor 1J **179**
(not continuous)
Shinwell Ter. DH6: Whe H 3A **180**
SR7: Mur 7D **146**
Shipby SR3: Silk 2B **132**
SHIPCOTE 6G 83
Shipcote La. NE8: Gate 6H **83**
Shipcote Ter. NE8: Gate 6H **83**
Shipley Art Gallery 6H 83
Shipley Av. NE4: Fen 7A **62**
SR6: Seab 3G **105**
Shipley Ct. NE8: Gate 5H **83**
Shipley Pl. NE6: Byke 4P **5** (7K **63**)
Shipley Ri. NE6: Byke 4P **5** (7A **64**)
Shipley Rd. NE30: Tyne 5J **49**
Shipley St. NE15: Lem 7C **60**
Shipley Wlk. NE6: Byke 4P **5** (7K **63**)
Shipton Cl. NE35: Bol C 5E **86**
Shipton La. NE3: Ken 2K **61**
Shire Chase DH1: P Me 3B **154**
Shire Farm Gro. NE63: Ash 5J **11**
SHIREMOOR 1K 47
Shiremoor Station (Metro) 1K 47
Shires, The NE61: Tra W 6G **15**
Shirlaw Cl. NE5: West 1F **61**
Shirley Gdns. SR3: Sund 5D **118**
Shirwood Av. NE16: Whi 2G **97**
Shop Row DH4: S Row 4C **130**
Shop Spouts NE21: Blay 3C **80**
Shoreham Ct. NE3: K Bank 6J **43**
Shoreham Sq. SR3: Sund 5A **118**
Shorestone Av. NE30: Cull 1H **49**
Shore St. SR6: Roker 6F **105**
Shoreswood Dr. SR3: Tuns 2D **132**
Shoreswood Way NE13: Ki Pk 4K **43**
Short Gro. SR7: Mur 7C **146**
Shortridge St. NE33: S Shi 2K **67**
Shortridge Ter. NE2: Jes 4H **63**
Short Row DH4: Bour 5J **129**
NE5: Call 6B **42**
Shot Factory La. NE4: Newc T 9D **4** (3E **82**)
Shotley Av. SR5: S'wck 4D **104**
SHOTLEY BRIDGE 2F 121
Shotley Ct. NE63: Ash 5J **11**
Shotleyfield Vw. DH8: Cons 6G **121**
Shotley Gdns. NE9: Low F 7J **83**
Shotley Gro. NE36: E Bol 7H **87**
Shotley Gro. Rd. DH8: Cons, Shot B 4D **120**
Shotley Pk. 2E 120
SHOTTON 1B 24
1J 181
Shotton Av. NE24: Bly 3J **23**
Shotton Bank SR8: Pet 3H **181**
SHOTTON COLLIERY 6F 171
Shotton Colliery Ind. Est.
DH6: Shot C 5F **171**
SHOTTON EDGE 4A 24
Shotton La. DH6: Shot C, Pet 6F **171**
NE23: Nel V 7D **20**
NE61: Cra, Stan 1A **24**
SR8: Pet 6F **171**
Shotton Rd. SR8: Hord 5D **172**
SR8: Pet, Shot C 5G **171**
Shotton St. NE23: E Har 6K **21**
Shotton Vw. NE13: Haz 3B **44**
Shotton Way NE10: Ward 1J **101**
Shrewsbury Cl. NE7: H Hea 1B **64**
SR8: Pet 7K **171**
Shrewsbury Cres. SR3: Sund 5A **118**
Shrewsbury Dr. NE27: Back 6G **37**
Shrewsbury St. NE11: Dun 6B **82**
SR7: S'hm 5B **148**
Shrewsbury Ter. NE33: S Shi 6J **67**
Shrigley Cl. NE38: Wash 1F **129**
Shrigley Gdns. NE3: Ken 7B **44**
Shropshire Dr. DH1: Carr 2G **167**
Shrove Pass NE8: Gate 5D **82**
Shummard Cl. DH4: S Row 4K **129**
Shunner Cl. NE37: Wash 2E **114**
Sibthorpe St. NE29: N Shi 7H **49**
Side NE1: Newc T 7G **4** (2G **83**)
(not continuous)
Side Cinema 7G 4
Side Cliff Rd. SR6: Ful, Roker 4F **105**
Side Gallery 7G 4
Sidegate DH1: Dur 1B **6** (2A **166**)
Side La. NE61: Hep 3A **16**
Sideriate NE1: Newc T 5F **4**
Sidings, The DH1: Dur 2C **166**
TS27: B Col 3K **183**
Sidings Pl. DH4: Hou S 1K **143**
Sidlaw Av. DH2: Ches S 7J **127**
NE29: N Shi 3F **49**
Sidlaw Ct. NE63: N Sea 6C **12**
Sidmouth Cl. DH4: Nbot 5C **130**
SR7: Dalt D 4H **147**
Sidmouth Rd. NE9: Low F 4H **99**
NE29: N Shi 6C **48**
Sidney Cl. DH9: Stly 3H **125**
Sidney Cres. NE64: Newb S 4H **13**
Sidney Gdns. NE24: Cow 1D **22**
Sidney Gro. NE4: Fen 7C **62**
NE8: Gate 5F **83**
Sidney St. NE24: Bly 2H **23**
NE29: N Shi 7G **49**
NE35: Bol C 6F **87**
Sidney Ter. DH9: Tan L 1D **124**
Signet Way NE24: Bly 5K **23**
Silent Bank DH6: Old C 1E **178**
Silkeys La. NE29: N Shi 7F **49**
Silkstun Ct. SR3: New S 2C **132**
SILKSWORTH 3A 132
Silksworth Cl. SR3: New S 1B **132**
Silksworth Community Pool, Tennis
& Wellness Cen. 7B 118
Silksworth Gdns. NE9: Wrek 5A **100**
SR3: Silk 3A **132**
Silksworth Hall Dr. SR3: Silk 3B **132**
Silksworth La. SR3: E Her 2J **131**
(not continuous)
SR3: New S, Sund 2A **132**
Silksworth Rd. SR3: E Her 2H **131**
SR3: Silk 3A **132**
Silksworth Row SR1: Sund 3G **7** (1E **118**)
(not continuous)
Silksworth Ski Slope 7B 118
Silksworth Sports Complex 7A 118
Silksworth Ter. SR3: New S 2C **132**
Silksworth Way SR3: Dox P 3A **132**
Silkwood Cl. NE23: Cra 1K **25**
Silloth Av. NE5: Den M 5G **61**
Silloth Dr. NE37: Wash 5G **101**
Silloth Pl. NE30: Cull 2H **49**
Silloth Rd. SR3: Sund 6K **117**
Silvas Ct. NE61: Mor 6G **9**
Silverbirch Ind. Est. NE12: Kil 7K **35**
Silverbriar SR5: Sund 6B **104**
Silver Ct. NE9: Low F 6J **83**
Silver Courts DH7: B'don 1D **174**
Silverdale SR3: Dox P 5C **132**
Silverdale Av. NE10: Ward 6H **85**
Silverdale Dr. NE21: Winl 5K **79**
Silverdale Rd. NE23: Cra 1K **25**
Silverdale Ter. NE8: Gate 6H **83**
Silverdale Way NE16: Whi 2F **97**
NE34: S Shi 3F **87**
Silver Fox Way NE27: N Shi, Shir 4J **47**
SILVER HILL 2F 51
Silverhill Dr. NE5: Den M, Fen 6G **61**
Silverlink, The NE28: W'snd 5A **48**
Silverlink Bus. Pk. NE27: Shir 4A **48**
NE28: W'snd 5K **47**
Silverlink Nth., The NE27: Shir 3J **47**
Silverlink Pk. 3K 47
Silverlink Retail Pk. NE28: W'snd 6A **48**
Silver Lonnen NE5: Den M, Fen 6G **61**
Silvermere Dr. NE40: Ryton 2H **79**
Silverstone NE12: Kil 1C **46**
Silverstone Way NE37: Wash 7J **101**
Silver St. DH1: Dur 3B **6** (3A **166**)
DH8: B'hill 5F **121**
NE30: Tyne 5K **49**
SR1: Sund 7H **105**
Silverton Ct. NE23: Dud 1K **35**
Silvertop Gdns. NE40: G'sde 3E **78**
Silvertop Ter. NE40: G'sde 5D **78**
Silverwood Gdns. NE11: Lob H 2D **98**
Simonburn NE38: Wash 4D **114**
Simonburn Av. NE4: Fen 5A **62**
NE29: N Shi 6C **48**
Simonburn La. NE63: Ash 5D **12**
Simon Pl. NE13: W Op 6C **34**
SIMONSIDE 1F 87
Simonside NE26: Sea S 6D **28**
NE34: S Shi 1G **87**
NE42: Pru 5D **76**
Simonside Av. NE28: W'snd 1K **65**
NE62: Stake 7J **11**
Simonside Cl. NE26: Sea S 6D **28**
NE61: Mor 1D **14**
Simonside Ct. NE34: S Shi 1G **87**
Simonside E. Ind. Est. NE34: S Shi 1E **86**
Simonside Hall NE34: S Shi 1F **87**
Simonside Ind. Est. NE32: Jar 1D **86**
Simonside Pl. NE9: Wrek 4A **100**
Simonside Rd. NE21: Blay 5C **80**
SR3: Sund 5K **117**
Simonside Station (Metro) 1F 87
Simonside Ter. NE6: Heat 5K **63**
NE64: Newb S 3J **13**
Simonside Vw. NE16: Whi 7G **81**
NE20: Pon 4H **31**
NE32: Jar 2C **86**
Simonside Wlk. NE11: Lob H 2C **98**
Simonside Way NE12: Kil 1D **46**
Simonside Youth Cen. 2G 87
Simpson Cl. NE35: Bol C 6E **86**
Simpson Ct. NE63: N Sea 4E **12**
Simpsons Memorial Homes
NE40: Craw 2E **78**
Simpson St. DH9: Stly 2F **125**
NE24: Bly 1J **23**
NE29: N Shi 7E **48**
NE30: Cull 7J **39**
NE40: Ryton 2J **79**
SR4: Sund 7D **104**
Simpson Ter. NE2: Newc T 4J **5** (7H **63**)
NE15: Walb 4B **60**
Sinclair Ct. NE13: Bru V 5C **34**
Sinclair Dr. DH3: Ches S 1B **128**
Sinclair Gdns. NE25: Sea D 7H **27**
Sinclair Mdws. NE33: S Shi 5J **67**
Sinderby Cl. NE3: Gos 4F **45**
Sir Bobby Robson Sports Cen., The 2C 164
Sir Bobby Robson Way NE13: W Op 1C **44**
Sir Godfrey Thomson Ct. NE10: Fell 6A **84**
Sitwell Rd. DH9: Stly 3G **125**
Sixth Av. DH2: Ches S 6K **127**
NE6: Heat 1P **5** (6A **64**)
NE11: T Vall 3E **98**
NE24: Bly 4H **23**
NE61: Mor 1H **15**
NE63: Ash 5B **12**
Sixth St. DH8: Cons 1K **135**
SR8: Hord 5E **172**
TS27: B Col 1H **183**
Skaylock Dr. NE38: Wash 5E **114**
Skegness Pde. NE31: Heb 4A **86**
Skelder Av. NE12: Longb 6K **45**
Skelton Ct. NE3: Ki Pk 4A **44**
Skendleby Dr. NE3: Ken 2K **61**
Skerne Cl. SR8: Pet 1A **182**
Skerne Gro. DH8: Lead 4B **122**
Skiddaw Cl. SR8: Pet 6C **172**
Skiddaw Ct. DH9: Ann P 6K **123**
Skiddaw Dr. SR6: Seab 2E **104**
Skiddaw Pl. NE9: Low F 3K **99**
Skinnerburn Rd.
NE1: Newc T 10A **4** (3E **82**)
NE4: Newc T 10A **4** (4D **82**)
Skipper Cl. NE11: Fest P 7D **82**
Skippers Mdw. DH7: Ush M 3D **164**
(not continuous)
Skipsea Vw. SR2: Ryh 2F **133**
(not continuous)
Skipsey Ct. NE29: N Shi 2D **66**
Skipton Cl. NE22: Bed 6F **17**
NE23: Cra 1A **26**
Skipton Grn. NE9: Low F 5K **99**
Skirlaw Cl. NE38: Wash 4H **115**
Ski Vw. SR3: New S 2B **132**
Skye Ct. SR3: Silk 3C **132**
Skye Gro. NE32: Jar 4E **86**
Skylark NE38: Wash 6D **114**
Slaidburn Rd. DH9: Stly 2F **125**
Slake Rd. NE32: Jar 5D **66**
Slake Ter. NE34: S Shi 6H **67**
Slaley NE38: Wash 7J **115**
Slaley Cl. NE10: Ward 7G **85**
Slaley Ct. NE22: Bed 7J **17**
SR3: Silk 3C **132**
Slaley Dr. NE63: N Sea 4E **12**
Slater Pl. DH6: Bowb 5H **177**
Slatyford La. NE5: Den M 5G **61**
Sled La. NE41: Wylam 2A **78**
Sledmere Cl. SR8: Pet 4B **172**
Sleekburn Av. NE22: Bed 5B **18**
Sleekburn Bus. Cen. NE22: W Sle 2E **18**
Sleekburn Bus. Pk. NE24: Camb 2E **18**
Sleekburn Ho. NE22: Bed 5B **18**
Sleetburn La. DH7: Lang M 6F **165**
Slingley Cl. SR7: S'hm 1G **147**
Slingsby Gdns. NE7: H Hea 2B **64**
Slipway, The NE10: Bill Q 4E **84**
Sloane Ct. NE2: Jes 2G **4** (6G **63**)
Smailes La. NE39: Row G 5G **95**
Smailes St. DH9: Stly 4E **124**
SMALLBURN 2H 31
Smallholdings NE64: Newb S 1G **13**
Smallhope Dr. DH7: Lan 7K **137**
Smeaton Ct. NE28: W'snd 4A **66**
Smeaton St. NE28: W'snd 4A **66**
Smillie Cl. SR8: Pet 5B **172**
Smillie Rd. SR8: Hord 3C **172**
Smithburn Rd. NE10: Fell 7B **84**
Smith Cl. DH6: S'burn 3K **167**
Smithfield DH1: P Me 3K **153**
Smith Gro. SR2: Ryh 3G **133**
Smith's Ter. DH5: Eas L 2H **157**
Smith St. NE33: S Shi 5H **67**
SR2: Ryh 3H **133**
Smith St. Sth. SR2: Ryh 3H **133**
Smithyford NE9: Low F 6J **99**
Smithy La. NE9: Lame, Low F 6G **99**
NE11: Lame 6G **99**
Smithy Sq. NE23: Cra 4K **25**
Smuggler's Cave 1K 49
Smyrna Pl. SR1: Sund 2G **119**
Snaith Ter. TS28: Win 5F **181**
Sniperley (Park & Ride) 6H 153
Sniperley Gro. DH1: Dur 6H **153**
Snipes Dene NE39: Row G 4J **95**
Snowberry Gro. NE34: S Shi 1B **88**
Snowdon Ct. DH9: Ann P 6J **123**
Snowdon Gdns. NE11: Lob H 1C **98**
Snowdon Gro. NE36: W Bol 7H **87**
Snowdon Pl. SR8: Pet 7J **171**
Snowdon Ter. NE39: H Spen 2D **94**
SR2: Ryh 2H **133**
Snowdrop Av. SR8: Hord 5D **172**
Snowdrop Cl. NE21: Winl 4A **80**
Snow's Grn. Rd. DH8: Shot B 3E **120**
Soane Gdns. NE34: S Shi 3K **87**
Softley Pl. NE15: Den M 6F **61**
Solar Ho. SR1: Sund 4J **7**
Solingen Est. NE24: Bly 3J **23**
Solway Av. NE30: Cull 2G **49**
Solway Rd. NE31: Heb 2K **85**
Solway Sq. SR3: Sund 5A **118**
Solway St. NE6: Byke 2A **84**
Somerford NE9: Spri 5D **100**
Somersby Dr. NE3: Ken 7A **44**
Somerset Cl. NE63: Ash 3J **11**
Somerset Cotts. SR3: New S 7C **118**
Somerset Gdns. NE28: W'snd 2E **64**
Somerset Gro. NE29: N Shi 4D **48**
Somerset Pl. NE4: Newc T 6A **4** (1C **82**)
Somerset Rd. DH8: C'sde 3C **134**
NE31: Heb 3K **85**
SR3: Sund 5K **117**
Somerset Sq. SR3: Sund 5K **117**
Somerset St. SR3: New S 1C **132**
Somerset Ter. NE36: E Bol 7K **87**
Somerton Ct. NE3: Ki Pk 6J **43**
Somervyl Av. NE12: Longb 6H **45**
Somervyl Ct. NE12: Longb 5H **45**
Sophia SR7: S'hm 3B **148**
Sophia St. SR7: S'hm 3B **148**
Sophy St. SR5: S'wck 5E **104**
Sorley St. SR4: Sund 2C **118**
Sorrel Cl. NE63: Ash 5A **12**
Sorrel Gdns. NE34: S Shi 3A **88**

Sorrell Cl. NE4: Fen 6K 61
Soulby Ct. NE3: Ki Pk 4K 43
Sourmilk Hill La. NE9: Low F 1J 99
Souter Dr. SR7: S'hm 1A 148
Souter Lighthouse 1H 89
Souter Rd. NE3: Gos 7C 44
Souter Vw. SR6: Whit 4H 89
South App. DH2: Ches S 6K 127
South Av. DH6: Shad 4E 168
NE16: Whi 2H 97
NE34: S Shi 1B 88
NE37: Wash 7G 101
NE40: Ryton 1G 79
South Bailey DH1: Dur 5C 6 (4A 166)
South Bend NE3: Gos 3D 44
SOUTH BENTS 1H 105
Sth. Bents Av. SR6: Seab 1G 105
SOUTH BENWELL 3A 82
Sth. Benwell Rd.
NE15: Benw 2J 81
SOUTH BOLDON 7H 87
Southburn Cl. DH4: Hou S 2C 144
South Burns DH3: Ches S 5A 128
Sth. Burn Ter. DH4: S Row 3C 130
South Cliff SR6: Roker 5H 105
Southcliff NE26: Whit B 7J 39
South Cl. DH5: Eas L 3K 157
NE34: S Shi 1B 88
NE40: Ryton 2G 79
SR2: Ryh 3H 133
(off Stockton Rd.)
Sth. Coronation St. *SR7: Mur 1F 159*
(off George St.)
Southcote NE16: Whi 2G 97
South Cres. DH1: Dur 1K 165
DH4: Hou S 1K 143
NE35: Bol C 6F 87
NE38: Wash 1F 129
SR7: S'hm 3C 148
SR8: Hord 3C 172
South Cft. NE12: Longb 5C 46
Southcroft NE38: Wash 7H 115
Sth. Cross St. DH8: Lead 5A 122
NE3: Gos 7E 44
South Dene NE34: S Shi 1H 87
South Docks 1J 119
Southdowns DH2: Ches S 7A 128
South Dr. NE13: Sea B 4A 24
NE13: Wool 4G 43
NE31: Heb 2G 85
NE43: Newt 6E 54
SR6: Clead 5B 88
Sth. Durham Ct. SR1: Sund 2G 119
South E. Vw. SR8: Hord 5F 173
Sth. Eldon St. NE33: S Shi 6H 67
South End DH6: H Pitt 7B 156
SR6: Clead 6A 88
Southend Av. NE24: Bly 3G 23
Southend Pde. NE31: Heb 4A 86
Southend Rd. NE9: Low F 3J 99
SR3: Sund 6A 118
Southend Ter. NE9: Low F 1K 99
Southern Cl. NE63: N Sea 4F 13
Southern Prom. NE26: Whit B 6J 39
Southern Rd. NE6: Walk 2D 84
Southern Way NE40: Ryton 2G 79
Southernwood DH8: Cons 7J 121
NE9: Low F 6J 99
Southey St. NE33: S Shi 5J 67
(not continuous)
South Farm NE22: Nedd 1D 20
SR2: Ryh 3J 133
Southfield DH2: Pelt 2G 127
NE61: Mor 2F 15
South Fld. Ct. DH9: Stly 4E 124
Southfield Gdns. NE16: Whi 7J 81
Southfield Grn. NE16: Whi 1J 97
Southfield La. NE17: Ham 5C 108
Southfield Rd. NE12: Longb 6A 46
NE16: Whi 1J 97
NE34: S Shi 5B 68
Southfields DH9: Stly 5E 124
NE23: Dud 4J 35
Southfields Ho. *NE6: Byke 3P 5*
(off Heaton Pl.)
Southfield Ter. NE6: Walk 2E 84
NE16: Whi 1J 97
Southfield Way DH1: Dur 7J 153
South Foreshore NE33: S Shi 3B 68
Southfork NE15: Lem 5C 60
Sth. Frederick St. NE33: S Shi 6H 67
South Front NE2: Jes 1G 4 (5G 63)
Southgate NE12: Kil 2A 46
Southgate Ct. NE12: Longb 6H 45
Southgate M. NE61: Mor 3G 15
(not continuous)
Southgate Wood NE61: Mor 3G 15
SOUTH GOSFORTH 1G 63
South Gosforth Station (Metro) 1G 63
Sth. Grange Pk. SR7: S'hm 1H 147
South Grn. DH6: Hett 7C 176
South Gro. NE40: Ryton 2H 79
South Harbour NE24: Bly 3K 23
SOUTH HETTON 4C 158
Sth. Hetton Ind. Est. DH6: S Het 4B 158
Sth. Hetton Rd.
DH5: Eas L, S Het 3K 157
DH6: S Het 6F 159
SR8: Eas 6F 159
South Hill Cres.
SR2: Sund 6F 7 (3D 118)
South Hill Rd. NE8: Gate 5E 82
SOUTH HYLTON 2G 117
South Hylton Station (Metro) 2H 117
Southill Rd. NE34: S Shi 7C 68
Southlands DH6: Coxh 6J 177
NE7: H Hea 3J 63
NE9: Eigh B 5A 100
(not continuous)
NE30: Tyne 4H 49
NE32: Jar 5D 86
SR2: Ryh 3H 133
South La. NE36: E Bol 7J 87
South Lea DH7: Wit G 2D 152
NE15: Hor 5E 56
NE21: Blay 5C 80
Sth. Leam Farm NE10: Hew 3E 100
South Leigh DH9: Tan L 7D 110
Southleigh NE26: Whit B 6H 39
Sth. Lodge Wood NE61: Hep 3A 16
South Magdalene DH8: M'sly 7K 107
South Mall NE23: Cra 4J 25
South Mkt. St. DH5: Hett H 6H 145
Southmayne Rd. SR4: Sund 4K 117
Southmead Av. NE5: Blak 4H 61
South Mdws. DH9: Dip 1H 123
South M. DH6: Shad 6E 168
SOUTH MOOR 5D 124
Sth. Moor Rd. DH9: Stly 5E 124
Southmoor Rd. NE6: Walk 6D 64
Sth. Nelson Ind. Est. NE23: Nel V 2G 25
Sth. Nelson Rd. NE23: Nel V 2G 25
SOUTH NEWSHAM 6G 23
South Newsham Nature Reserve 6G 23
Sth. Newsham Rd. NE24: News 6G 23
South Pde. DH6: Thor 1K 179
(not continuous)
NE10: Bill Q 4F 85
NE26: Whit B 6H 39
NE29: N Shi 3E 66
NE43: Stoc 7G 75
NE62: Chop 2G 17
South Pk. NE46: Hex 2D 70
SOUTH PELAW 4K 127
South Pier NE33: S Shi 1A 68
Southport Pde. NE31: Heb 3A 86
Sth. Preston Gro. NE29: N Shi 7G 49
Sth. Preston Ter. *NE29: N Shi 7G 49*
(off Albion Rd. W.)
South Prom. NE33: S Shi 2B 68
Sth. Railway St. SR7: S'hm 3B 148
South Ridge NE3: Gos 4D 44
NE63: N Sea 5F 13
South Rigg NE46: Hex 1B 70
South Riggs NE22: Bed 1H 21
South Rd. DH1: Dur 7C 6 (1K 175)
NE17: C'wl 6K 93
NE42: Pru 4F 77
South Row NE8: Gate 8N 5 (2J 83)
South Sherburn NE39: Row G 6H 95
SOUTH SHIELDS 2J 67
South Shields Bowls Cen. 4B 68
South Shields Mus. & Art Gallery 2J 67
South Shields Station (Metro) 2J 67
Sth. Shore Rd. NE8: Gate 7J 5 (2H 83)
(not continuous)
South Side DH6: Shad 6E 168
NE63: N Sea 5F 13
(not continuous)
SR8: Eas 1K 171
South Side Gdns. SR4: Sund 3G 117
SOUTH STANLEY 5E 124
South St. DH1: Dur 4B 6 (3A 166)
DH2: Ches S 5K 127
DH4: Hou S 2A 144
DH4: Nbot 6D 130
DH4: W Rai 1A 156
DH5: E Rain 6C 144
DH6: S'burn 3A 168
DH8: Cons 7K 121
NE1: Newc T 8E 4 (2F 83)
NE3: Gos 7C 44
NE8: Gate 5H 83
(not continuous)
NE27: Shir 7K 37
NE31: Heb 6K 65
NE39: H Spen 3D 94
SR1: Sund 3H 7 (1E 118)
(not continuous)
South St. Banks DH1: Dur 5B 6 (4A 166)
Southstreet Banks DH1: Dur 4B 6 (4A 166)
South Ter. DH1: Dur 6J 153
DH7: Corn C 2A 162
DH7: Esh W 3E 162
NE17: C'wl 7K 93
NE28: W'snd 3J 65
NE61: Hep 3A 16
NE61: Mor 6F 9
SR5: S'wck 6D 104
SR7: Mur 1F 159
(off Church St.)
SR7: S'hm 3C 148
SR8: Hord 5D 172
South Thorn DH9: Stly 2F 125
Sth. Tyneside Crematorium
NE34: S Shi 3G 87
South Vw. DH1: Dur 2D 166
DH2: Kim 7H 141
DH2: Newf 4E 126
DH2: Pelt 2G 127
(Fieldside)
DH2: Pelt 2C 126
(Victoria Ter.)
DH3: Bir 4B 114
DH4: S Row 3B 130
DH5: Eas L 3K 157
DH6: Has 1A 170
DH6: Hett 7C 176
DH6: S Hil 3D 168
DH6: Whe H 4A 180
South Vw. DH7: Bearp 1D 164
DH7: B'hpe 5D 138
DH7: Lang P 5J 151
DH7: Mead 2E 174
DH7: Sac 6D 140
DH7: Ush M 2B 164
DH8: Shot B 5E 120
DH9: Ann P 6A 124
DH9: Stly 6H 125
DH9: Tant 6B 110
NE5: W Dent 5E 60
NE7: Longb 7A 46
(off Front Vw.)
NE9: Spri 6E 100
NE13: Din 4G 33
NE13: Haz 7C 34
NE17: C'wl 7J 93
NE22: E Sle 4D 18
NE23: Dud 2K 35
NE24: Camb 2F 19
NE24: News 5G 23
NE32: Jar 7A 66
NE38: Wash 7J 115
NE40: C Vale 6C 58
NE40: Craw 2D 78
NE41: Wylam 7J 57
NE42: Pru 4D 76
NE43: Mic 5A 76
NE43: Stoc 7J 75
NE46: Acomb 4C 50
NE61: Peg 4B 10
NE62: Chop 1G 17
NE63: Ash 3A 12
SR4: Sund 3G 117
SR6: Ful 4F 105
SR6: Whit 3H 89
SR7: Dalt D 5H 147
SR7: Mur 7F 147
(off E. Coronation St.)
TS27: Cas E 4K 181
TS28: Win 5F 181
South Vw. Bungs. NE39: H Spen 4D 94
South Vw. E. NE39: Row G 5G 95
South Vw. Gdns. DH9: Ann P 6A 124
NE46: Hex 2C 70
South Vw. Pl. NE23: Cra 4K 25
South Vw. Rd. SR4: Sund 3G 117
South Vw. Ter. DH4: Hou S 2B 144
DH7: Bearp 1D 164
NE10: Fell 6B 84
NE16: Swa 6H 81
NE16: Whi 1H 97
South Vw. W. NE6: Heat 3M 5 (7J 63)
NE39: Row G 5F 95
Southward NE26: Sea S 5D 28
Southward Cl. NE26: Sea S 5D 28
Southward Way NE25: H'wll 2J 37
Southway DH7: Lan 6J 137
NE9: Low F 1K 99
NE15: Lem 6E 60
SR8: Pet 7A 172
SOUTH WELLFIELD 6A 38
South W. Ind. Est. SR8: Pet 6H 171
SOUTHWICK 6C 104
Southwick Goods Yd. SR5: S'wck 6C 104
Southwick Ind. Est. SR5: S'wck 5B 104
Southwick Rd. SR5: Monkw, S'wck 5D 104
(not continuous)
Southwold Gdns. SR3: New S 1B 132
(not continuous)
Southwold Pl. NE23: Cra 4G 25
Sth. Woodbine St. NE33: S Shi 3K 67
Southwood Cres. NE39: Row G 5K 95
Southwood Gdns. NE3: Ken 1A 62
Sovereign Ct. NE2: Jes 5H 63
NE4: Elsw 1C 82
Sovereign Ho. NE30: Tyne 5K 49
Sovereign Pl. NE4: Elsw 2C 82
Sowerby St. DH7: Sac 1D 152
Spa Dr. DH8: Shot B 1E 120
Spa Gdns., The DH8: Shot B 2E 120
Spalding Cl. NE7: H Hea 1A 64
Sparkwell Cl. DH4: Nbot 5D 130
Spartylea NE38: Wash 7K 115
Spa Well Cl. NE21: Winl 6B 80
Spa Well Dr. SR5: Sund 5J 103
Spa Well Rd. NE21: W Mill 1D 96
Spectrum Bus. Pk. SR7: S'hm 6C 148
Speculation Pl. NE37: Wash 7H 101
Speedwell NE9: Low F 2A 100
Speedwell Ct. NE63: Ash 6K 11
Spelter Works Rd. SR2: Sund 6H 119
(not continuous)
Spelvit La. NE61: Mor 1E 14
Spen Burn NE39: H Spen 4E 94
Spencer Cl. DH9: Stly 3H 125
Spencer Ct. NE15: Newb 5K 59
NE24: Cow 7F 19
Spencer Dr. NE61: Peg 4A 10
Spencer Gro. NE16: Whi 6H 81
Spencer Ind. Est. DH3: Bir 4K 113
Spencer Rd. NE24: Cow 7F 19
Spencers Bank NE16: Swa 5G 81
Spencer St. DH8: Cons 6H 121
NE6: Heat 5A 64
NE29: N Shi 7G 49
NE31: Heb 6K 65
NE32: Jar 5B 66
Spencers Vw. NE21: Blay 1A 80
Spencer Ter. NE15: Walb 4B 60
Spence Ter. NE29: N Shi 7F 49
Spenfield Rd. NE5: Ken 2K 61
Spen La. NE39: H Spen 7D 78
NE39: H Spen, Row G 3E 94
NE40: G'sde 7D 78
Spen Rd. NE39: H Spen 3D 94
Spenser Wlk. NE34: S Shi 3G 87
Spen St. DH9: Stly 4E 124
Spetchells NE42: Pru 3F 77
Spindlestone Vw. NE13: Ki Pk 3A 44
Spinney, The NE7: H Hea 3K 63
NE12: Kil 2C 46
NE23: Dud 3A 36
NE38: Wash 6H 115
NE61: Mor 2G 15
SR8: Eas 7J 159
Spinneyside Gdns. NE11: Dun 7B 82
Spinney Ter. NE6: Walk 7D 64
Spire Hollin SR8: Pet 6A 172
Spire Rd. NE37: Wash 2K 115
Spires La. NE6: Byke 7A 64
Spiro Ct. DH8: Cons 1H 135
Spital Cres. NE64: Newb S 4G 13
Spital La. NE46: Hex 7A 50
Spital Rd. NE64: Newb S 4G 13
Spital Ter. NE3: Gos 7E 44
SPITAL TONGUES 1A 4 (6D 62)
Spital Vs. NE15: Welt 2B 56
Spittal Ter. NE46: Hex 1C 70
Split Crow Rd. NE8: Gate 6J 83
NE10: Fell 6J 83
Spohr Ter. NE33: S Shi 4K 67
Spoors Cotts. NE16: Whi 1G 97
Spoor St. NE11: Dun 5B 82
Sporting Club, Blyth 2E 22
Sporting Club of Cramlington, The
6J 25
Sports Central 3H 5 (7G 63)
Sportsman's Pl. *DH9: Dip 1G 123*
(off Front St.)
Spout La. NE37: Wash 7H 101
(not continuous)
NE38: Wash 2H 115
Spoutwell La. NE45: Corb 1E 72
Springbank Ho. NE2: Newc T 1L 5
Springbank Rd. NE2: Newc T 1L 5 (6J 63)
SR3: Sund 5K 117
Springbank Sq. SR3: Sund 5K 117
Spring Cl. DH8: Ebc 6G 107
DH9: Ann P 6A 124
Spring Dr. DH5: Hou S 2F 145
Springfeld NE10: Hew 3D 100
Springfell DH3: Bir 5B 114
Springfield DH8: Shot B 3E 120
NE29: N Shi 6G 49
NE42: Oving 2K 75
Springfield Av. NE9: Eigh B 6A 100
Springfield Cl. NE42: Oving 2K 75
Springfield Cres. SR7: S'hm 4A 148
Springfield Gdns. DH3: Ches S 4A 128
NE28: W'snd 1D 64
Springfield Gro. NE25: Monks 1E 48
Springfield Mdw. DH6: Ludw 5J 169
Springfield Pk. DH1: Dur 1J 165
NE12: Longb 4B 46
Springfield Pl. NE9: Low F 1J 99
Springfield Rd. DH4: Nbot 6D 130
NE5: Blak 4J 61
NE21: Blay 4C 80
NE46: Hex 2E 70
Springfield Ter. DH2: P Fel 4G 127
NE10: Fell 7A 84
SR8: Eas C 1D 172
Spring Gdn. Cl. SR1: Sund 1G 119
Spring Gdn. La. NE4: Newc T 4B 4 (7D 62)
Spring Gdns. DH7: Lan 4K 137
NE29: N Shi 7F 49
Spring Gdns. Ct. NE29: N Shi 6G 49
SPRING HILL 1E 14
Springhill Gdns. NE15: Benw 7K 61
Springhill Wlk. NE61: Mor 1E 14
Springhouse La. DH8: Ebc 7G 107
Spring La. DH8: Shot B 2F 121
SpringLite Gym
Kingston Park 6J 43
Spring Pk. NE22: Bed 1J 21
Springs, The DH3: Bir 5B 114
(not continuous)
Springside DH7: Sac 7E 140
SpringsLite Gym 6H 5 (1G 83)
Spring St. NE4: Newc T 4C 4 (7D 62)
NE8: Gate 5D 82
Springsyde Cl. NE16: Whi 2E 96
Spring Ter. NE29: N Shi 6G 49
Spring Ville NE22: E Sle 4D 18
SPRINGWELL 6D 100
5K 117
Springwell Av. DH1: Dur 1J 165
DH7: Lang P 5J 151
NE6: Walk 2C 84
NE9: Wrek 4A 100
NE32: Jar 7C 66
Springwell Bldgs. SR8: Hord 5E 172
Springwell Cl. DH7: Lang P 5J 151
NE21: Blay 5D 80
SPRINGWELL ESTATE 3C 100
Springwell La.
NE9: Eigh B, Spri 4C 100
Springwell Rd. DH1: Dur 1J 165
NE9: Spri 5D 100
NE9: Wrek 4A 100
NE32: Jar 1B 86
SR3: Sund 4K 117
SR4: Sund 4K 117
Springwell Ter. DH5: Hett H 7G 145
NE9: Spri 6D 100
NE9: Wrek 4C 100
Springwood NE31: Heb 6G 65
Spruce, The *NE23: Cra 4B 26*
(off Evergreen Ct.)

Square, The DH7: Lan 7K 137
NE16: Whi 7H 81
NE20: Pres 6C 32
NE27: Shir 2H 47
NE44: Rid M 6A 74
NE62: Chop 1G 17
SR6: Ful 1D 104
Square Ho's. NE10: Wind N 7K 83
Squires Gdns. NE10: Fell 7B 84
Stable Cl. NE61: Lngh 1A 10
Stable Green NE61: Mit 7A 8
Stable La. NE3: Fawd 4B 44
Stables, The DH4: W Herr 2F 131
SR7: Seat 7C 132
Stack Gth. DH7: B'don 7E 164
Staddon Way DH4: Nbot 5C 130
Stadium Ind. Pk. NE10: Gate 10P 5 (3K 83)
Stadium of Light 1H 7 (7E 104)
Stadium of Light (Park & Ride) 6F 105
Stadium of Light Station (Metro) 6F 105
Stadium Rd. NE10: Gate 10N 5 (3K 83)
Stadium Vs. NE28: W'snd 3G 65
Stadium Way SR5: Monkw 6E 104
Stafford Gro. SR2: Ryh 3G 133
SR5: S'wck 5D 104
Stafford La. SR6: Whit 6H 89
Stafford Pl. SR8: Pet 5K 171
Staffordshire Dr. DH1: Carr 1H 167
Stafford St. DH5: Hett H 6F 145
SR1: Sund 7H 105
Stafford Vs. NE9: Spri 6D 100
Stagshaw NE12: Kil 6A 36
Stagshaw Rd. NE45: Corb 6D 52
(not continuous)
Staindrop NE10: Hew 2E 100
Staindrop Rd. DH1: Dur 5B 154
Staindrop Ter. DH9: Ann P 5K 123
Staines Rd. NE6: Newc T, Walk 2B 84
Stainmore Dr. DH3: Gt Lum 3F 143
Stainthorpe Ct. *NE46: Hex 2D 70*
(off Battle Hill)
Stainton Dr. NE10: Fell 6B 84
Stainton Gdns. NE9: Wrek 5A 100
Stainton Gro. SR6: Seab 2E 104
Stainton Way SR8: Pet 6A 172
Staithes NE11: Dun 3H 81
Staithes Av. NE12: Longb 6A 46
Staithes Ct. SR7: S'hm 1A 148
Staithes Ho. NE38: Wash 5A 116
Staithes La. NE61: Mor 6G 9
Staithes Quay NE22: E Sle 7C 18
Staithes Rd. NE11: Dun 4C 82
NE38: Wash 5A 116
Staithes St. NE6: Walk 7F 65
Staith La. NE21: Blay 2A 80
STAKEFORD 7J 11
Stakeford Cres. NE62: Stake 1K 17
Stakeford La. NE62: Chop, Stake 1H 17
Stakeford Rd. NE22: Bed 5A 18
Stakeford Ter. NE62: Stake 1J 17
Stalks Rd. NE13: W Op 5D 34
Stamford NE12: Kil 7B 36
Stamford Av. NE25: Sea D 1J 37
SR3: Sund 5B 118
Stamfordham Av. NE29: N Shi 7D 48
Stamfordham Cl. NE28: W'snd 3E 64
Stamfordham Ct. NE63: Ash 3H 11
Stamfordham M. NE5: Fen 4K 61
Stamfordham Rd.
NE5: Blak, Call, Cha P, Fen, West 5J 41
NE15: Darr H, Thro 4D 40
Stamp Exchange NE1: Newc T 7F 4
Stampley Cl. NE21: Winl 6A 80
Stamps La. SR1: Sund 1H 119
Stancley Rd. NE42: Pru 4G 77
Stand Comedy Club, The 1F 83
Standerton Ter. DH9: Stly 6H 125
Standish St. DH9: Stly 4D 124
Stanelaw Way DH9: Tan L 7F 111
Staneway NE10: Hew 2C 100
Stanfield Bus. Cen. SR2: Sund 3H 119
Stanfield Ct. NE7: H Hea 2C 64
Stanfield Gdns. NE10: Ward 6G 85
Stanfield Ho. SR2: Sund 7K 7
Stang Wlk. NE12: Longb 5A 46
Stanhope NE38: Wash 3D 114
Stanhope Chase SR8: Pet 2B 182
Stanhope Cl. DH1: Dur 4B 154
DH4: Hou S 3D 144
DH7: Mead 1E 174
Stanhope Gdns. DH9: Ann P 5K 123
Stanhope Pde. NE33: S Shi 5K 67
Stanhope Rd. NE32: Jar 1D 86
NE33: S Shi 7H 67
SR6: Seab 3G 105
Stanhope St. NE4: Newc T 4A 4 (7C 62)
NE33: S Shi 2J 67
NE40: G'sde 5D 78
Stanhope Way NE4: Newc T 4A 4 (7D 62)
Stank La. DH1: P Me 2J 153
STANLEY 3E 124
Stanleyburn Ct. DH9: Ann P 5B 124
Stanleyburn Vw. DH9: Ann P 5B 124
Stanley By-Pass DH9: Stly 4D 124
Stanley Cl. DH6: S'burn 3K 167
Stanley Ct. DH9: Stly 3G 125
Stanley Cres. *NE26: Whit B 7H 39*
(off Alma Pl.)
NE42: Pru 3G 77
Stanley Gdns. DH8: Cons 6H 121
NE9: Wrek 5A 100
NE23: Seg 2D 36
Stanley Gro. NE7: H Hea 2J 63
NE22: Bed 7K 17
Stanley Indoor Bowling Cen. 3E 124
Stanley St. DH5: Hou S 1E 144
DH8: Cons 6H 121
NE4: Elsw 2B 82
NE24: Bly 1K 23
NE28: W'snd 2K 65
NE29: N Shi 7G 49
NE32: Jar 6C 66
NE34: S Shi 1H 87
SR5: Sund 6H 103
SR7: S'hm 2K 147
Stanley St. W. NE29: N Shi 7G 49
Stanley Ter. DH3: Ches S 7B 128
DH4: S Row 3B 130
DH6: Thor 1J 179
NE61: Mor 6G 9
Stanmore Rd. NE6: Heat 4A 64
Stannerford Rd. NE40: C Vale, Craw 7C 58
Stanners, The NE45: Corb 1D 72
Stanners Vw. NE40: C Vale 6C 58
Stannington Av. NE6: Heat 1P 5 (6K 63)
Stannington Gdns. SR2: Sund 6E 118
Stannington Gro. NE6: Heat 1N 5 (6K 63)
SR2: Sund 5E 118
Stannington Pl. NE6: Heat 1P 5 (6A 64)
NE20: Pon 3J 31
Stannington Rd. NE29: N Shi 7C 48
Stannington Sta. Rd. NE22: Hep 1A 20
NE61: Hep 1A 20
Stannington St. NE24: Bly 2K 23
Stansfield St. SR6: Roker 6G 105
Stanstead Cl. SR5: Sund 7G 103
Stanton Av. NE24: Bly 4F 23
NE34: S Shi 6A 68
Stanton Cl. NE10: Ward 7H 85
Stanton Ct. NE30: Cull 3G 49
SR7: Mur 7F 147
Stanton Dr. NE61: Peg 4K 9
Stanton Rd. NE27: Shir 1J 47
NE30: Cull 3F 49
Stanton St. NE4: Newc T 7C 62
Stanway Dr. NE7: H Hea 2J 63
Stanwick St. NE30: Tyne 4K 49
Stapeley Ct. NE3: Ken 7K 43
Stapeley Vw. NE3: Ken 7K 43
Stapleford Cl. NE5: Den M 4H 61
Staple Rd. NE32: Jar 6C 66
Stapylton Dr. SR2: Sund 4D 118
SR8: Hord 6F 173
Star & Shadow Cinema 5K 5 (7H 63)
Starbeck Av. NE2: Newc T 1K 5 (6H 63)
Starbeck M. NE2: Newc T 1K 5 (6H 63)
Stardale Av. NE24: Cow 3E 22
STARGATE 2H 79
Stargate Cl. DH7: Lang P 5G 151
Stargate Gdns. NE9: Wrek 5A 100
Stargate Ind. Est. NE40: Ryton 3H 79
Stargate La. NE21: Blay 1J 79
NE40: Ryton 1J 79
Starlight Cres. NE25: Sea D 7G 27
Starling Wlk. NE16: Sun 5H 97
Startforth Cl. DH3: Gt Lum 3F 143
Stately Pk. DH5: Hett H 7H 145
Station App. DH1: Dur 2A 6 (2K 165)
NE11: T Vall 3F 99
NE12: Longb 6B 46
NE33: S Shi 2J 67
NE36: E Bol 6A 88
Station Av. DH5: Hett H 7G 145
DH7: B'don 1E 174
DH7: Esh W 4E 162
Station Av. Nth. DH4: Hou S 1K 143
Station Av. Sth. DH4: Hou S 1K 143
Station Bank DH1: Dur 2B 6 (2A 166)
DH8: Ebc 6H 107
NE40: Ryton 7G 59
NE43: Mic 4A 76
NE61: Mor 1G 15
Station Bri. NE63: Ash 3A 12
Station Cl. NE44: Rid M 6K 73
Station Cotts. DH9: Beam 1A 126
NE3: Fawd 6B 44
NE12: Longb 6B 46
NE20: Pon 5J 31
NE23: Seg 2E 36
NE34: S Shi 7H 67
NE39: Ham M 2G 109
NE46: Hex 1E 70
NE61: Mor 1G 15
SR8: Hord 6G 173
Station Ct. NE6: Walk 5D 64
Station Cres. SR7: S'hm 2K 147
Station Est. E. SR7: Mur 7C 146
Station Est. Nth. SR7: Mur 7C 146
(Cairns Rd.)
SR7: Mur 7C 146
(Station Rd.)
Station Est. Sth. SR7: Mur 7C 146
Station Fld. Rd. DH9: Tan L 7F 111
Station Ho's. DH2: P Fel 4G 127
DH8: Ebc 6H 107
Station Ind. Est. NE42: Pru 3D 76
Station La. DH1: Dur 2C 166
DH2: Bir 4K 113
DH2: Pelt, P Fel 2F 127
DH3: Bir 4K 113
TS28: Sta T 7G 181
Station M. NE22: Bed 5B 18
NE30: Tyne 5K 49
Station Rd. DH3: Ches S 6A 128
DH4: Hou S 1D 144
DH4: Leam, W Rai 1J 155
DH4: Pen 7J 115
DH5: Hett H 7G 145
DH6: Low P 5A 156
DH6: Shot C 5D 170
Station Rd. DH7: Lan 7K 137
DH7: Mead 1E 174
DH7: Ush M 3B 164
DH8: Cons 7J 121
DH9: Ann P 6K 123
DH9: Beam 1A 126
DH9: Stly 2F 125
NE3: Gos 7G 45
NE6: Walk 2E 84
NE9: Low F 2G 99
NE10: Bill Q 4F 85
(Reay St.)
NE10: Bill Q 4F 85
(South Pde.)
NE12: Kil 6K 35
NE12: Longb 4B 46
NE13: K Bank 6H 43
NE15: Hed W 3D 58
NE15: Newb 6K 59
NE22: Bed 6A 18
NE23: Cra 3H 25
NE23: Dud 3H 35
NE23: Seg 2D 36
NE24: News 5G 23
NE25: Sea D 6E 26
NE26: Whit B 7H 39
NE27: Back 7G 37
NE28: W'snd 4A 66
(Armstrong Rd.)
NE28: W'snd 2E 64
(Queen's Cres.)
NE29: N Shi 1D 66
NE30: Cull 1J 49
NE31: Heb 7H 65
NE33: S Shi 3J 67
NE35: Bol C 4E 86
NE36: E Bol 7K 87
NE38: Wash 3J 115
NE39: Row G 6J 95
NE41: Wylam 7K 57
NE42: Pru 3D 76
NE45: Corb 2D 72
NE46: Hex 1D 70
NE63: Ash 3K 11
SR2: Ryh 3J 133
SR6: Ful 3E 104
SR7: Mur 7C 146
SR7: S'hm 2H 147
SR8: Eas C 7D 160
TS27: B Col 3K 183
TS27: Hes 4E 182
TS28: Sta T 7G 181
TS29: Trim S 7B 180
Station Rd. Bungs. TS27: B Col 3K 183
Station Rd. E. TS29: Trim S 7B 180
Station Rd. Nth. DH5: Hett H 7G 145
NE12: Longb 4B 46
NE28: W'snd 6D 46
SR7: Mur 7C 146
Station Rd. Sth. SR7: Mur 7C 146
Station Rd. W. TS29: Trim S 7B 180
Station Sq. NE26: Whit B 7H 39
Station St. DH6: Has 1B 170
DH7: Wat 6C 162
NE22: Bed 5B 18
NE24: Bly 1J 23
NE32: Jar 6B 66
SR1: Sund 3J 7 (1F 119)
Station Ter. DH4: Hou S 1K 143
DH8: Cons 7J 121
NE30: Tyne 5K 49
NE36: E Bol 7A 88
NE37: Wash 7J 101
NE62: Sco G 5H 17
STATION TOWN 7G 181
Station Vw. DH2: Ches S 6A 128
DH5: Hett H 7G 145
DH7: Esh W 5E 162
Station Vs. DH9: Stly 1F 125
Station Yd. DH8: Cons 7J 121
NE45: Corb 3E 72
Staveley Rd. SR6: Seab 2E 104
SR8: Pet 6C 172
Stavordale St. SR7: S'hm 4B 148
(not continuous)
Stavordale St. W. SR7: S'hm 5B 148
Stavordale Ter. NE9: Low F 7J 83
Staward Av. NE25: Sea D 1H 37
Staward Ter. NE6: Walk 2D 84
Staynebrigg NE10: Hew 1D 100
Steading Ct. DH8: Cons 6J 121
Steadings, The DH1: Dur 5J 165
NE40: G'sde 5D 78
NE63: Ash 5J 11
Steadlands Sq. NE22: Bed 7A 18
Stead La. NE22: Bed 7K 17
Steadman's La. DH7: Corn C, Queb 7A 150
Steads, The NE61: Mor 2G 15
Stead St. NE28: W'snd 2A 66
Steavenson St. DH6: Bowb 5H 177
Stedham Cl. NE37: Wash 5J 101
Steel St. DH8: Cons 6H 121
Steephill SR3: E Her 1H 131
Steetley Ter. DH6: Quar H 6D 178
STELLA 2A 80
Stella Bank NE21: Blay 1K 79
Stella Cotts. NE21: Blay 2A 80
Stella Gill Ind. Est. DH2: P Fel 4H 127
Stella Hall Dr. NE21: Blay 2K 79
Stella La. NE21: Blay 2K 79
Stella Rd. NE21: Blay 1A 80
Stellas, The *DH2: Ches S 4J 127*
(off Elmway)
Stephen Ct. NE32: Jar 7C 66
Stephenson, The NE8: Gate 4D 82
Stephenson Bldg. NE2: Newc T 3K 5
Stephenson Cl. DH5: Hett H 6G 145
Stephenson Ct. NE22: Bed 4J 17
NE30: N Shi 7H 49
(off Stephenson St.)
NE41: Wylam 7A 58
Stephenson Ho. NE12: Kil 2A 46
NE46: Hex 1C 70
(off Haugh La.)
Stephenson Ind. Est. NE12: Kil 2A 46
NE37: Wash 5J 101
Stephenson Railway Mus. 5A 48
Stephenson Rd. NE6: H Hea 4K 63
NE7: H Hea 4K 63
NE37: Wash 5H 101
SR8: Pet 3A 172
Stephenson's La.
NE1: Newc T 8F 4 (2F 83)
Stephenson Sq. SR8: Eas 1A 172
Stephenson's Sq.
NE1: Newc T 8E 4 (2F 83)
Stephenson St. NE8: Gate 6F 83
NE28: W'snd 4A 66
NE30: N Shi 6H 49
(not continuous)
NE30: Tyne 5K 49
SR7: Mur 7E 146
Stephenson Ter. NE10: Fell 7B 84
NE15: Thro 3G 59
NE15: Walb 4B 60
NE41: Wylam 7K 57
Stephenson Trail, The NE12: Kil 3D 46
Stephenson Way NE21: Winl 6B 80
NE22: Bed 4J 17
Stephens Rd. SR7: Mur 7D 146
Stephen's Ter. DH6: Whe H 2B 180
Stephen St. DH8: Cons 6H 121
NE6: Byke 4M 5 (7J 63)
NE23: E Har 6K 21
NE24: Bly 1J 23
Stepney Bank NE1: Newc T 4K 5 (7H 63)
Stepney La. NE1: Newc T 5J 5 (1H 83)
Stepney Rd. NE1: Newc T 3K 5 (7H 63)
NE2: Newc T 3K 5 (7H 63)
Sterling Cotts. NE10: Wind N 7A 84
Sterling St. SR4: Sund 2C 118
Stevenson Rd. DH9: Stly 3G 125
Stevenson St. DH4: Hou S 2D 144
NE33: S Shi 4K 67
Steve Smiths Shooting Ground 1G 33
Steward Cres. NE34: S Shi 6D 68
Stewart Av. SR2: Ryh 3G 133
Stewart Ct. NE15: Newb 6A 60
Stewart Dr. NE36: W Bol 7H 87
TS28: Win 4G 181
Stewartsfield NE39: Row G 5H 95
Stewart St. SR3: New S 2C 132
SR4: Sund 3D 118
SR7: S'hm 4C 148
SR8: Eas C 7B 160
Stewart St. E. SR7: S'hm 4C 148
Stileford NE10: Hew 7E 84
Stillington Cl. SR2: Ryh 4H 133
Stirling Av. NE32: Jar 2E 86
NE39: Row G 6J 95
Stirling Cl. NE38: Wash 4A 116
SR4: Sund 5K 117
Stirling Ct. NE11: T Vall 5G 99
Stirling Dr. NE22: Bed 6A 18
NE29: N Shi 4C 48
Stirling La. NE39: Row G 6J 95
St James Station (Metro) 5D 4 (1E 82)
Stobart St. DH7: Edm 3D 140
SR5: Monkw 1H 7 (7E 104)
Stobb Ho. Vw. DH7: B'don 7C 164
STOBHILL 3H 15
STOBHILLGATE 1H 15
Stobhill Vs. NE61: Mor 1G 15
Stobswood Cl. NE25: Monks 6B 38
Stockbridge NE1: Newc T 6H 5 (1G 83)
Stockdale Gdns. *NE6: Walk 2E 84*
(off Rochester St.)
Stockerley La. DH8: Cons 4C 136
Stockerley Rd. DH8: Cons 1K 135
Stockfold NE38: Wash 6J 115
Stockholm Cl. NE29: N Shi 7B 48
Stockley Av. SR5: Sund 5J 103
Stockley Ct. DH7: Ush M 3E 164
Stockley Gro. DH7: Bran 6A 174
Stockley La. DH7: Bran 6A 174
Stockley Rd. NE38: Wash 2K 115
STOCKSFIELD 7G 75
Stocksfield Av. NE5: Fen 6J 61
Stocksfield Gdns. NE9: Low F 5J 99
Stocksfield Station (Rail) 7G 75
Stockton Av. SR8: Hord 4D 172
Stockton Rd. DH1: Dur 6D 6 (4B 166)
NE29: N Shi 2F 67
SR1: Sund 5H 7 (2E 118)
(not continuous)
SR2: Ryh 7J 7 (5H 133)
SR2: Sund 3F 119
SR7: Cold H, Dalt D, S'hm 7H 147
SR7: Dalt D, S'hm, Seat 5H 147
SR8: Eas 2J 171
TS27: Cas E 4K 181
Stockton Rd. E. SR7: Hawt 3K 159
Stockton Rd. W. SR7: Hawt 4K 159
Stockton St. SR7: S'hm 2K 147
Stockton Ter. SR2: Sund 6H 119
Stockwell Grn. NE6: Walk 5D 64
Stoddart Ho. NE2: Newc T 3J 5 (7H 63)
Stoddart St. NE2: Newc T 3K 5 (7H 63)
NE34: S Shi 7H 67
Stoker Av. NE34: S Shi 2F 87

Stoker Cres. DH6: Whe H 4A 180
Stoker Ter. NE39: H Spen 4E 94
Stokesley Gro. NE7: H Hea 2J 63
Stokoe Dr. NE63: N Sea 4E 12
Stokoe's Bldgs. *DH8: Lead* *5B 122*
(off Railway St.)
Stokoe St. DH8: B'hill 5G 121
Stone Cellar Rd. NE37: Wash 5F 101
Stone Cellars NE37: Wash 5F 101
Stonechat Cl. NE38: Wash 5D 114
Stonechat Mt. NE21: Blay 1A 80
Stonechat Pl. NE12: Longb 5J 45
Stonecroft NE15: Hor 4F 57
Stonecroft Gdns. NE7: H Hea 2B 64
Stonecrop NE9: Low F 2A 100
Stonecross NE63: Ash 5A 12
Stonefold Cl. NE5: Blak 2H 61
Stonehaugh Way NE20: Darr H 2F 41
Stonehills NE10: Pel 5F 85
Stonelea Ct. SR8: Eas 1K 171
Stoneleigh NE61: Hep 4A 16
Stoneleigh Av. NE12: Longb 6H 45
Stoneleigh Cl. DH4: Hou S 1C 144
Stoneleigh Pl. NE12: Longb 6H 45
Stone Row DH2: Gra V 4C 126
Stonesdale DH4: Pen 1J 129
Stone St. NE10: Wind N 1A 100
Stonethwaite NE29: N Shi 2D 66
Stoney Bank NE28: W'snd 3J 65
Stoneycroft E. NE12: Kil 2C 46
Stoneycroft Way SR7: S'hm 2A 148
Stoneycroft W. NE12: Kil 2C 46
STONEYGATE 5G 131
Stoneygate Cl. NE10: Fell 5C 84
Stoneygate Gdns. NE10: Fell 5C 84
Stoneygate La. NE10: Fell 6C 84
Stoneyhurst Av. NE15: Scot 1H 81
Stoneyhurst Rd. NE3: Gos 1G 63
Stoneyhurst Rd. W. NE3: Gos 1F 63
Stoney La. DH9: Beam 2C 126
NE9: Spri 6D 100
SR5: S'wck 6C 104
Stoneylea Cl. NE40: Craw 3C 78
Stoneylea Rd. NE5: W Dent 5F 61
Stoneywaites NE40: G'sde 6C 78
Stonybank Way NE43: Mic 6K 75
Stonycroft NE37: Wash 1G 115
Stonyflat Bank NE42: Pru 4G 77
STONY HEAP 6F 123
Stonyheap La. DH8: Cons 7F 123
DH9: Ann P 6F 123
Store Bldgs. NE35: Bol C 6E 86
TS29: Trim S 7C 180
Store Cotts. DH7: Sac 4D 140
Store Farm Rd. NE64: Newb S 2G 13
Store St. DH8: Cons 6H 121
NE15: Lem 7C 60
NE21: Winl 5B 80
Store Ter. DH5: Eas L 2H 157
Storey Ct. NE21: Blay 2E 80
Storey Cres. NE64: Newb S 2G 13
Storey La. NE21: Blay 2A 80
Storey St. NE23: Cra 5A 26
Stormont Grn. NE3: Ken 2B 62
Stormont St. NE29: N Shi 7G 49
Stotfold Cl. SR7: S'hm 2G 147
Stothard St. NE32: Jar 6C 66
Stotts Pastures DH4: S Row 5A 130
Stotts Rd. NE6: Walk 5E 64
Stowe Gdns. NE61: Peg 3A 10
Stowell Sq. NE1: Newc T 6D 4 (1E 82)
Stowell St. NE1: Newc T 6D 4 (1E 82)
Stowell Ter. NE10: Hew 6C 84
St Peters Station (Metro) 1J 7 (7F 105)
Straker Dr. NE46: Hex 3A 70
Straker St. NE32: Jar 7D 66
Straker Ter. NE34: S Shi 1H 87
NE61: Lngh 1D 10
Strand, The SR3: New S 1A 132
Strangford Av. DH2: Ches S 1K 141
Strangford Rd. SR7: S'hm 3K 147
Strangways St. SR7: S'hm 4B 148
Stranton Ter. SR6: Roker 5F 105
Stratfield St. SR4: Sund 1A 118
Stratford Av. SR2: Sund 5G 119
Stratford Cl. NE12: Kil 1C 46
NE23: Cra 3G 25
Stratford Gdns. DH8: Cons 5H 121
NE9: Low F 1H 99
Stratford Gro. NE6: Heat 2M 5 (6J 63)
Stratford Gro. Ter. NE6: Heat 2L 5 (6J 63)
Stratford Gro. W. NE6: Heat 2L 5 (6J 63)
Stratford Rd. NE6: Heat 2M 5 (6J 63)
(not continuous)
NE38: Wash 5A 116
Stratford Vs. NE6: Heat 2M 5 (6J 63)
Strathearn Way NE3: Fawd 6B 44
Strathmore DH3: Gt Lum 2E 142
Strathmore Av. NE39: Row G 6J 95
Strathmore Cl. DH9: Stly 2H 125
Strathmore Cres. NE4: Benw 1A 82
NE16: Burn 7D 96
Strathmore Gdns. NE34: S Shi 2J 87
Strathmore Rd. NE3: Gos 5E 44
NE9: Low F 7K 83
NE39: Row G 6H 95
SR3: Sund 6A 118
Strathmore Sq. SR3: Sund 6A 118
Stratton Cl. SR2: Ryh 1J 133
Stratus Ct. SR3: Silk 3C 132
Strawberry Ct. SR2: Sund 4E 118
Strawberry Gdns. NE28: W'snd 1E 64
Strawberry La. DH1: H Shin 1E 176
NE1: Newc T 4D 4 (7E 62)
Strawberry M. NE62: Stake 7K 11
Strawberry Pl. NE1: Newc T 5D 4 (1E 82)
Strawberry Ter. NE13: Haz 7B 34
NE23: Dud 6A 36
STREETGATE 4J 97
Streetgate Pk. NE16: Sun 4J 97
Street Ho's. NE20: Pon 7B 32
NE41: Wylam 6B 58
NE45: Ayd 2D 52
Stretford Ct. NE9: Low F 5J 99
Stretton Cl. DH4: Hou S 3A 144
Stretton Way NE27: Back 6G 37
Stridingedge NE37: Wash 2E 114
(not continuous)
Stringer Ter. DH7: Lang P 5G 151
Stronsay Cl. SR2: Ryh 1G 133
Strothers Rd. NE39: H Spen 2D 94
Strothers Ter. NE39: H Spen 3C 94
Struan Ter. NE36: E Bol 7A 88
Struddars Farm Ct. NE21: Blay 4F 81
Stuart Ct. TS27: B Col 2H 183
Stuart Ct. DH8: Cons 7G 121
NE3: Ki Pk 6H 43
Stuart Gdns. NE15: Thro 3G 59
Stuart Ter. NE10: Fell 5B 84
Stubbs Av. NE16: Whi 6G 81
Studdon Wlk. NE3: Ken 7K 43
Studios, The NE1: Newc T 5K 5 (1H 83)
Studland Cl. NE29: N Shi 3F 49
Studley Gdns. NE9: Low F 2H 99
NE25: Whit B 7G 39
Studley Ter. NE4: Fen 6C 62
Studley Vs. NE12: Longb 5C 46
Sturdee Gdns. NE2: Jes 2G 63
Styan Av. NE26: Whit B 6H 39
Styford Gdns. NE15: Lem 6E 60
SUCCESS 5B 130
Success Rd. DH4: S Row 5B 130
Sudbury Way NE23: Cra 3G 25
Suddick St. SR5: S'wck 6D 104
Suez St. NE30: N Shi 6H 49
Suffolk Cl. NE63: Ash 3J 11
Suffolk Gdns. NE28: W'snd 1J 65
NE34: S Shi 6E 68
Suffolk Pl. DH3: Bir 7B 114
Suffolk Rd. NE31: Heb 3K 85
Suffolk St. DH5: Hett H 6F 145
NE32: Jar 7B 66
SR2: Sund 3G 119
Suffolk Wlk. SR8: Pet 4A 172
Suffolk Way DH1: P Me 3B 154
Sugley Ct. NE15: Lem 5E 60
Sugley Dr. NE15: Lem 7D 60
Sugley St. NE15: Lem 7D 60
(not continuous)
Sugley Vs. NE15: Lem 7D 60
SULGRAVE 6J 101
Sulgrave Ind. Est. NE37: Wash 6J 101
Sulgrave Rd. NE37: Wash 6K 101
Sullivan Wlk. NE31: Heb 1J 85
Summerdale DH8: Shot B 2F 121
Summerfield DH9: W Pelt 3C 126
NE17: Ham 3J 107
Summerfield Rd. NE9: Low F 7H 83
Summerfields DH2: Ches S 7H 127
Summerhill DH8: M'sly, Shot B 2G 121
NE4: Elsw 8A 4 (2C 82)
NE21: Blay 3A 80
NE32: Jar 5D 86
SR2: Sund 5F 7 (2D 118)
SR3: E Her 2H 131
Summerhill Av. NE3: Gos 3F 45
Summerhill Gro.
NE4: Newc T 6B 4 (1D 82)
Summerhill Rd. NE34: S Shi 6B 68
Summerhill St. NE4: Newc T 6B 4 (1D 82)
Summerhill Ter. NE4: Newc T 7C 4 (2E 82)
Summerhouse NE63: N Sea 4F 13
Summerhouse Farm DH5: E Rain 5D 144
Summerhouse La.
NE63: N Sea, Wood 2F 13
(not continuous)
Summerson St. DH5: Hett H 6H 145
Summerson Way NE22: Bed 6B 18
Summers Pass NE8: Gate 5D 82
Summers St. NE24: Bly 1J 23
Summer St. NE10: Fell 5B 84
Summerville DH1: Dur 4A 6 (3K 165)
Sunbury Av. NE2: Jes 3G 63
SUNDERLAND 4J 7 (2F 119)
Sunderland AFC 1H 7 (7E 104)
Sunderland Aquatic Cen. & Wellness Cen.
6E 104
Sunderland Av. SR8: Hord 4D 172
SUNDERLAND BRIDGE 5K 175
Sunderland By-Pass NE36: W Bol 1D 102
SR3: Dox P, E Her 4H 131
SR4: Sund 1F 117
SR5: Sund 4E 102
SR7: Seat 7E 132
Sunderland Climbing Centre 5D 104
Sunderland Crematorium SR4: Sund 3A 118
Sunderland Ent. Pk. SR5: Sund 7J 103
(Defender Ct.)
SR5: Sund 6A 104
(Wearfield)
Sunderland Golf Centre 3D 104
Sunderland Greyhound Stadium 1B 104
Sunderland Highway
NE37: Bir, Wash 2C 114
SR5: Sund 2A 116
Sunderland Marine Activities Cen. 5H 105
Sunderland Minster 4H 7 (2E 118)
Sunderland Mus. & Winter Gdns.
4K 7 (2F 119)
Sunderland Retail Pk. SR6: Roker 6F 105
Sunderland Rd. DH1: Dur 2D 166
DH4: Nbot 6E 130
NE8: Gate 4H 83
NE10: Fell, Hew 5A 84
NE10: Ward 7F 85
NE33: S Shi 5A 68
NE34: S Shi 6A 68
NE36: E Bol 7K 87
SR5: Ful 7K 87
SR5: S'wck 5C 104
SR6: Clead 1B 88
SR6: Clead, Whit 5D 88
SR7: Hawt 4K 159
SR8: Eas 4K 159
SR8: Eas C, Hord 3D 172
Sunderland Rd. Vs. NE10: Hew 6D 84
Sunderland Station (Rail & Metro)
4J 7 (2F 119)
Sunderland St. DH4: Hou S 2E 144
DH5: Hou S 1E 144
DH8: Lead 5A 122
NE1: Newc T 6C 4 (1E 82)
SR1: Sund 2K 7 (1G 119)
Sunderland Technology Pk. SR1: Sund 5G 7
Sunderland Wall Climbing Centre 7B 104
Sunderland Yacht Club 6H 105
Sundew Rd. NE9: Low F 3A 100
NE10: Wind N 2A 100
Sundridge Dr. NE10: Ward 7G 85
Sungold Vs. NE4: Benw 1A 82
Sun Hill DH5: Hett H 7F 145
Sunhill NE16: Sun 5H 97
Sunholme Dr. NE28: W'snd 7E 46
Sunlea Av. NE30: Cull 1J 49
Sunley Ho. NE3: Gos 7E 44
Sunnidale NE16: Whi 2E 96
Sunnilaws NE34: S Shi 3C 88
Sunningdale DH8: Cons 3A 136
NE25: Monks 6C 38
NE33: S Shi 4A 68
Sunningdale Av. NE6: Walk 6E 64
NE28: W'snd 3G 65
Sunningdale Cl. NE10: Fell 7B 84
Sunningdale Dr. NE37: Wash 5G 101
Sunningdale Rd. NE63: N Sea 4E 12
SR3: Sund 5K 117
Sunnirise NE34: S Shi 2C 88
SUNNISIDE 7C 130
5H 97
Sunniside NE29: N Shi 7D 48
SR4: Sund 2G 117
Sunniside Ct. NE16: Sun 4H 97
Sunniside Dr. NE34: S Shi 2C 88
Sunniside Gdns. NE9: Wrek 5A 100
NE15: Benw 7H 61
Sunniside Ladies Fitness Cen. *3K 7*
(off High St. West)
Sunniside La. NE34: S Shi 3D 88
SR6: Clead 5D 88
Sunniside Rd. NE16: Sun, Whi 2H 97
Sunniside Station
Tanfield Railway 6H 97
Sunniside Ter. SR6: Clead 4C 88
Sunnybank Av. NE15: Benw 1K 81
Sunnybanks DH7: Lan 6J 137
Sunny Blunts SR8: Pet 1A 182
Sunny Brae NE40: G'sde 6D 78
Sunnybrow SR3: New S 1B 132
Sunnycrest Av. NE6: Walk 7D 64
Sunnycroft Ct. NE5: W Dent 5F 61
Sunnygill Ter. NE40: G'sde 4D 78
Sunnyside NE23: Cra 3J 25
Sunny Side Sth. NE8: Gate 5D 82
Sunny Ter. DH9: Dip 2G 123
DH9: Stly 2E 124
Sunnyway NE5: Blak 3J 61
Sunrise Ent. Pk. SR5: Sund 7G 103
Sunrise La. DH4: Hou S 1D 144
Sunset Vw. DH9: Dip 6J 109
Sun St. NE16: Sun 5H 97
Sun Vw. Ter. SR6: Clead 5A 88
Surrey Av. SR3: New S 3C 132
Surrey Cl. NE63: Ash 3J 11
Surrey Cres. DH8: C'sde 3D 134
Surrey Pl. DH4: S Row 3C 130
NE4: Elsw 6A 4 (1C 82)
Surrey Rd. NE29: N Shi 6D 48
NE31: Heb 3K 85
Surrey St. DH4: S Row 3C 130
DH5: Hett H 6F 145
NE32: Jar 7A 66
Surrey Ter. DH3: Bir 7A 114
Surtees Av. DH6: Bowb 4H 177
Surtees Dr. DH1: Dur 2J 165
Surtees Haugh NE21: Blay 1A 80
Surtees Pl. DH8: B'hill 4E 120
Surtees Rd. SR8: Pet 6B 172
Surtees St. SR2: Sund 3H 119
Surtees Ter. DH9: Crag 6K 125
Sussex Ct. SR1: Sund 1G 119
Sussex Gdns. NE28: W'snd 2J 65
Sussex Pl. NE37: Wash 6H 101
Sussex Rd. DH8: C'sde 3D 134
Sussex St. NE24: Bly 1K 23
NE32: Jar 7A 66
SR3: New S 1C 132
Sutherans Yd. *DH5: E Rain* *6D 144*
(off North St.)
Sutherland Av. NE4: Fen 6A 62
NE64: Newb S 3H 13
Sutherland Ct. NE34: S Shi 4K 87
Sutherland Dr. SR4: Sund 5J 117
Sutherland Grange
DH4: New H 3D 130
Sutherland Gro. DH6: Shot C 5E 170
Sutherland Pl. DH1: Dur 3E 166
Sutherland St. NE8: Gate 5H 83
SR6: Ful 5F 105
SR7: S'hm 2K 147
Sutton Cl. DH4: Pen 3B 130
Sutton Ct. NE28: W'snd 7D 46
Sutton Dwellings
NE4: Newc T 3A 4 (7D 62)
Sutton Est. NE4: Benw 2A 82
Sutton St. DH1: Dur 3A 6 (3K 165)
NE6: Walk 5C 64
Sutton Way NE34: S Shi 1D 88
Swainby Cl. NE3: Gos 4F 45
Swale Ct. DH7: Lang M 7F 165
Swale Cres. DH3: Gt Lum 3F 143
Swaledale NE28: W'snd 7D 46
SR6: Seab 7H 89
Swaledale Av. NE24: Cow 2E 22
Swaledale Cl. DH5: Hett H 2E 156
Swaledale Ct. NE24: Cow 2E 22
Swaledale Cres. DH4: Pen 1A 130
Swaledale Gdns. NE7: H Hea 2K 63
SR4: Sund 3B 118
Swallow Cl. DH7: Esh W 3C 162
NE63: Ash 7C 12
Swallow Ct. NE12: Kil 7K 35
Swallow Pond Nature Reserve 5G 47
Swallows, The NE28: W'snd 5J 47
Swallow St. SR7: S'hm 2K 147
Swallow Tail Ct. NE34: S Shi 2H 87
Swallow Tail Dr. NE11: Fest P 7D 82
SWALWELL 5G 81
Swalwell Bank NE16: Swa, Whi 5G 81
Swalwell Cl. NE42: Pru 4E 76
Swalwell Vis. Cen. 6F 81
Swan Av. NE28: W'snd 2H 65
Swan Cl. NE28: W'snd 3E 64
Swan Ct. NE8: Dun 5C 82
SR5: Sund 5H 103
Swan Dr. NE11: Dun 5C 82
Swan Ho. SR2: Sund 7K 7
Swan Ind. Est. (North) NE38: Wash 4K 115
Swan Ind. Est. (South) NE38: Wash 5K 115
Swan Rd. NE6: Walk 2F 85
NE38: Wash 5K 115
SR8: Pet 7H 171
Swansfield NE61: Mor 1E 14
Swan St. DH9: Ann P 4J 123
NE8: Gate 9J 5 (3H 83)
SR5: Monkw 5E 104
Swanton Cl. NE5: Blak 1H 61
Swanway NE9: Low F 7K 83
Swards Rd. NE10: Fell 7C 84
Swarland Av. NE7: Longb 7K 45
Swarland Rd. NE25: Sea D 1H 37
Swarth Cl. NE37: Wash 2E 114
Sweetbriar Cl. NE61: Mor 5D 8
Sweetbriar Way NE24: News 5G 23
Sweethope Av. NE24: Cow 1H 23
NE63: Ash 5C 12
Sweethope Dene NE61: Mor 2G 15
Swiftdale Cl. NE22: Bed 7H 17
Swinbourne Gdns. NE26: Whit B 5F 39
Swinbourne Ter. NE32: Jar 3B 86
Swinburne Pl. DH3: Bir 5A 114
NE4: Newc T 6C 4 (1E 82)
NE8: Gate 9H 5 (3G 83)
Swinburne St. NE8: Gate 9H 5 (3G 83)
NE32: Jar 7E 66
Swinburne Ter. DH9: Dip 2F 123
Swinburn Rd. NE25: Sea D 1H 37
Swindale Cl. NE21: Winl 6C 80
Swindale Cotts. *NE41: Wylam* *7K 57*
(off The Dene)
Swindale Dr. NE12: Kil 1A 46
Swindon Rd. SR3: Sund 5K 117
Swindon Sq. SR3: Sund 5A 118
Swindon St. NE31: Heb 7H 65
Swindon Ter. NE6: Heat 4K 63
Swinhoe Gdns. NE13: W Op 4D 34
Swinhoe Rd. NE13: Haz 2B 44
Swinhope NE38: Wash 1E 128
Swinley Gdns. NE15: Den M 7F 61
Swinside Dr. DH1: Carr 7G 155
Swinton Cl. NE61: Mor 2H 15
Swirle, The NE1: Newc T 6K 5 (1H 83)
Swirral Edge NE37: Wash 1G 115
Swiss Cotts. NE38: Wash 7G 115
Swordfish, The NE4: Newc T 3B 82
Swordmakers Ter. *DH8: Shot B* *3E 120*
(off Wood St.)
Swordsmiths La. DH8: Shot B 3E 120
Swyntoft NE10: Hew 7F 85
Sycamore Av. NE13: Din 4J 33
NE20: Darr H 7H 31
NE24: Bly 7H 19
NE25: Monks 7F 39
NE34: S Shi 2B 88
NE38: Wash 7F 115
NE62: Chop 1G 17
(not continuous)
TS27: B Col 2J 183
Sycamore Cl. DH5: Hou S 3F 145
DH6: S Het 4B 158
NE2: Jes 3H 63
Sycamore Cotts. SR4: Sund 4J 117
Sycamore Ct. NE39: H Spen 2D 94
Sycamore Dr. SR5: S'wck 4D 104
TS27: Hes 4D 182
Sycamore Gro. NE9: Spri 6D 100
NE10: Fell 6C 84
NE42: Pru 4C 76
Sycamore Pk. DH7: B'don 7D 164
Sycamore Pl. DH7: Lan 7J 137
NE12: Kil 7A 36

Sycamore Rd. DH2: Kim . . . 7H **141**
NE21: Blay . . . 4C **80**
SR6: Whit . . . 5H **89**
Sycamores DH2: Ches S . . . 4J **127**
Sycamores, The NE4: Elsw . . . 9A **4** (3C **82**)
NE16: Burn . . . 3C **110**
NE24: Cow . . . 1F 23
(off Edendale Av.)
NE62: Chop . . . 1G **17**
SR2: Sund . . . 5G **119**
Sycamore Sq. SR8: Eas . . . 1A **172**
Sycamore St. NE15: Thro . . . 2H **59**
NE17: Ham . . . 5K **107**
NE28: W'snd . . . 4G **65**
NE63: Ash . . . 3B **12**
Sycamore Ter. *DH6: Has . . . 1B 170*
(off Pesspool La.)
DH9: Ann P . . . 5B **124**
Sydenham Ter. NE33: S Shi . . . 2K **67**
SR4: Sund . . . 3C **118**
Sydney Ct. NE8: Gate . . . 10H **5** (3G **83**)
Sydney Gdns. DH8: Cons . . . 2K **135**
NE34: S Shi . . . 3F **87**
Sydney Gro. NE28: W'snd . . . 7E **46**
Sydney St. DH2: Pelt . . . 2C **126**
DH4: Hou S . . . 7J **129**
Syke Rd. NE16: Burn, Hob . . . 2K **109**
Syke Vw. DH9: Ann P . . . 5K **123**
Sylvan Cl. NE61: Mor . . . 1D **14**
Sylverton Gdns. NE33: S Shi . . . 4B **68**
Sylvia Ter. DH9: Stly . . . 1F **125**
Symington Gdns. SR3: New S . . . 1B **132**
Symon Ter. NE17: C'wl . . . 7K **93**
Symphony Ct. *NE8: Gate . . . 5H 83*
(off Durham Rd.)
Synclen Av. NE45: Corb . . . 7E **52**
Synclen Rd. NE45: Corb . . . 7E **52**
Synclen Ter. NE45: Corb . . . 7E **52**
Syon St. NE30: Tyne . . . 4K **49**
Syron NE16: Whi . . . 1F **97**
Syston Cl. DH4: Hou S . . . 3B **144**

T

Taberna Cl. NE15: Hed W . . . 3C **58**
Tadcaster Rd. SR3: Sund . . . 7J **117**
Tadema Rd. NE33: S Shi . . . 3B **68**
Tail-upon-End La. DH6: Bowb . . . 3G **177**
Taku Ct. NE24: Bly . . . 5K **23**
Talbot Cl. NE38: Wash . . . 4H **115**
Talbot Cotts. DH3: Bir . . . 4A **114**
Talbot Pl. SR7: S'hm . . . 3B **148**
Talbot Rd. NE34: S Shi . . . 7J **67**
SR6: Seab . . . 4G **105**
Talbot Row *NE5: W Dent . . . 5F 61*
(off Burwell Av.)
Talbot Ter. DH3: Bir . . . 4A **114**
Talgarth NE38: Wash . . . 3B **116**
Talisman Cl. DH6: S'burn . . . 3K **167**
Talisman Vw. NE9: Low F . . . 5J **99**
Talisman Way NE24: Bly . . . 5K **23**
Talley Ct. NE38: Wash . . . 3G **115**
Tamar Cl. NE29: N Shi . . . 4C **48**
SR8: Pet . . . 7A **172**
Tamar Ct. SR3: Silk . . . 3B **132**
Tamarisk Way NE9: Low F . . . 2A **100**
Tamar St. DH5: Eas L . . . 3J **157**
Tamerton Dr. DH3: Bir . . . 6B **114**
Tamerton St. SR4: Sund . . . 2B **118**
Tamworth Rd. NE4: Fen . . . 7C **62**
Tamworth Sq. SR3: Sund . . . 7J **117**
Tanbark DH4: S Row . . . 3K **129**
TANFIELD . . . 5D **110**
Tanfield Bus. Cen. DH9: Tan L . . . 7E **110**
Tanfield Comprehensive School Sports Cen. . . . 1D **124**
Tanfield Gdns. NE34: S Shi . . . 7D **68**
TANFIELD LEA . . . 1D **124**
Tanfield Lea Nth. Ind. Est.
DH9: Tan L . . . 7D **110**
Tanfield Lea Rd.
DH9: Stly, Tan L . . . 1D **124**
Tanfield Lea Sth. Ind. Est.
DH9: Tan L . . . 7F **111**
Tanfield Pl. NE9: Wrek . . . 5A **100**
Tanfield Railway
Andrews House Station . . . 1H **111**
Causey Arch Station . . . 3H **111**
East Tanfield Station . . . 6E **110**
Sunniside Station . . . 6H **97**
Tanfield Rd. NE9: Wrek . . . 5A **100**
NE15: Benw . . . 7G **61**
SR3: Sund . . . 6K **117**
Tanfield St. SR4: Sund . . . 1A **118**
Tanglewood M. DH9: Stly . . . 2F **125**
Tangmere Cl. NE23: Cra . . . 3A **26**
TAN HILLS . . . 6J **141**
Tankerville Pl. NE2: Jes . . . 4G **63**
Tankerville Ter. NE2: Jes . . . 5G **63**
Tanmeads DH2: Nett . . . 6H **141**
Tanners Bank NE30: N Shi . . . 6J **49**
Tanners Ct. *NE1: Newc T . . . 6D 4*
(off Friars)
Tanners Row NE46: Hex . . . 1C **70**
Tanners Yd. NE46: Hex . . . 1C **70**
Tantallon DH3: Bir . . . 6B **114**
(not continuous)
Tantallon Ct. DH4: Hou S . . . 1H **143**
TANTOBIE . . . 6B **110**
Tantobie Rd. NE15: Den M . . . 7G **61**
Tarlton Cres. NE10: Fell . . . 6A **84**
Tarn Cl. SR8: Pet . . . 6C **172**
Tarn Dr. SR2: Sund . . . 1H **133**
Tarragon Way NE34: S Shi . . . 3A **88**
Tarrington Cl. NE28: W'snd . . . 7K **47**
Tarset Dr. NE42: Pru . . . 4F **77**
Tarset Pl. NE3: Gos . . . 6C **44**
Tarset Rd. NE25: Well . . . 6B **38**
Tarset St. NE1: Newc T . . . 5L **5** (1J **83**)
Tarset Wlk. NE24: Cow . . . 3E **22**
Tasmania Rd. NE34: S Shi . . . 3F **87**
Tasman Rd. SR3: Sund . . . 1J **131**
Tate St. NE24: Bly . . . 1K **23**
Tatham St. SR1: Sund . . . 4K **7** (2G **119**)
Tatham St. Bk. SR1: Sund . . . 4K **7** (2G **119**)
Tattershall SR2: Sund . . . 4D **118**
Taunton Av. NE29: N Shi . . . 3D **48**
NE32: Jar . . . 1E **86**
Taunton Cl. NE28: W'snd . . . 7K **47**
Taunton Pl. NE23: Cra . . . 2K **25**
Taunton Rd. SR3: Sund . . . 7K **117**
Taunton Sq. SR3: Sund . . . 6K **117**
Tavistock Ct. DH4: Nbot . . . 6C **130**
Tavistock Pl. NE32: Jar . . . 1E **86**
SR1: Sund . . . 4K **7** (2F **119**)
Tavistock Rd. NE2: Jes . . . 3G **63**
Tavistock Sq. SR3: New S . . . 1C **132**
Tavistock Wlk. NE23: Cra . . . 2K **25**
Taylor Av. DH7: Bearp . . . 1D **164**
NE13: W Op . . . 5E **34**
NE39: Row G . . . 6K **95**
NE63: N Sea . . . 4F **13**
Taylor Ct. DH1: Carr . . . 6H **155**
Taylor Gdns. NE10: Pel . . . 5E **84**
NE26: Sea S . . . 4D **28**
SR2: Sund . . . 4G **119**
Taylor Gro. TS28: Win . . . 4F **181**
Taylor's Bldgs. NE22: Bed . . . 6B **18**
Taylors Ct. *NE1: Newc T . . . 6E 4*
(off Monk St.)
Taylors Ter. DH8: C'sde . . . 1E **134**
Taylor St. DH8: Cons . . . 7H **121**
DH9: Ann P . . . 4J **123**
NE24: Cow . . . 1E **22**
NE33: S Shi . . . 5H **67**
Taylor Ter. NE27: Shir . . . 3H **47**
NE34: S Shi . . . 2F **87**
Taynton Gro. NE23: Seg . . . 1D **36**
Tay Rd. SR3: Sund . . . 6J **117**
Tay St. DH5: Eas L . . . 3K **157**
NE17: C'wl . . . 6A **94**
Teal Av. NE24: News . . . 5K **23**
Teal Cl. NE7: Longb . . . 7A **46**
NE38: Wash . . . 5D **114**
Teal Farm Way NE38: Wash . . . 5A **116**
TEAMS . . . 6E **82**
Team St. NE8: Dun, Gate . . . 5C **82**
Team Va. Vs. NE11: Fest P . . . 1D **98**
TEAM VALLEY . . . 4F **99**
Team Valley Bus. Cen.
NE11: T Vall . . . 1F **99**
Team Valley Trad. Est.
NE11: T Vall . . . 1E **98**
(North)
NE11: T Vall . . . 4F **99**
(South)
Teasdale Ho. NE5: West . . . 2F **61**
(Mortimer Av.)
NE5: West . . . 7G **43**
(Trevelyan Dr.)
Teasdale St. DH8: Cons . . . 6J **121**
SR2: Sund . . . 3H **119**
Teasdale Ter. DH1: Dur . . . 2F **167**
Tebay Dr. NE5: Den M . . . 5F **61**
Tedco Bus. Cen. NE32: Jar . . . 5K **65**
Tedco Bus. Works
NE33: S Shi . . . 3J **67**
Teddington Cl. NE3: K Bank . . . 5H **43**
Teddington Rd. SR3: Sund . . . 6J **117**
Teddington Sq. SR3: Sund . . . 6J **117**
Tedham Rd. NE15: Lem . . . 6C **60**
Teemers Dr. NE8: Gate . . . 5D **82**
Tees Cl. SR8: Pet . . . 1A **182**
Tees Ct. NE34: S Shi . . . 7J **67**
Tees Cres. DH9: Stly . . . 4F **125**
Teesdale Av. DH4: Pen . . . 1A **130**
Teesdale Ct. DH9: Ann P . . . 5A **124**
Teesdale Gdns. NE7: H Hea . . . 2K **63**
Teesdale Gro. NE12: Longb . . . 4B **46**
Teesdale Pl. NE24: Cow . . . 1D **22**
Teesdale Ter. DH9: Ann P . . . 5A **124**
Tees Gro. DH8: Lead . . . 4B **122**
Tees Rd. NE31: Heb . . . 3J **85**
Tees St. DH5: Eas L . . . 3K **157**
NE17: C'wl . . . 6A **94**
SR7: S'hm . . . 2B **148**
SR8: Hord . . . 5E **172**
Tees Ter. NE37: Wash . . . 7H **101**
Teign Cl. SR8: Pet . . . 7A **172**
Teikyo University of Japan in Durham . . . 7B **6** (5A **166**)
Teindland Cl. NE4: Benw . . . 2A **82**
Tel-El-Kebir Rd. SR2: Sund . . . 4G **119**
Telford Cl. DH1: H Shin . . . 1F **177**
NE9: Low F . . . 1H **99**
NE27: Back . . . 6G **37**
Telford Ct. NE28: W'snd . . . 3C **66**
NE61: Mor . . . 2F **15**
Telford Rd. SR3: Sund . . . 6K **117**
Telford St. NE8: Gate . . . 7F **83**
NE28: W'snd . . . 3C **66**
Temperance Ter. DH7: Ush M . . . 2B **164**
Temperance Yd. DH8: Ebc . . . 5G **107**
Temperley Pl. NE46: Hex . . . 2C **70**
Tempest Rd. SR7: S'hm . . . 3A **148**
Tempest St. NE21: Blay . . . 2A **80**
SR3: New S . . . 2C **132**
Templar M. DH8: M'sly . . . 1J **121**
Templar St. DH8: B'hill . . . 5F **121**
Temple Av. NE24: Cow . . . 1G **23**
Temple Forge M. DH8: Cons . . . 1H **135**
Temple Gdns. DH8: Cons . . . 1H **135**
Temple Grn. NE8: Gate . . . 6E **82**
NE34: S Shi . . . 1A **88**
Temple Memorial Pk. . . . 2K **87**
Temple Pk. Leisure Cen. . . . 2A **88**
Temple Pk. Rd. NE33: S Shi . . . 7J **67**
NE34: S Shi . . . 7J **67**
Temples Lodge TS27: Hes . . . 4D **182**
Temple St. NE1: Newc T . . . 7D **4** (2E **82**)
NE10: Fell . . . 5B **84**
NE33: S Shi . . . 6H **67**
Temple St. W. NE33: S Shi . . . 6H **67**
TEMPLETOWN . . . 1H **135**
Templetown NE33: S Shi . . . 5H **67**
Tenbury Cres. NE12: Longb . . . 5A **46**
NE29: N Shi . . . 3E **48**
Tenby Rd. SR3: Sund . . . 1J **131**
Tenby Sq. NE23: Cra . . . 2A **26**
Ten Fields DH5: Hett H . . . 7F **145**
Tennant St. NE31: Heb . . . 1H **85**
NE34: S Shi . . . 2G **87**
Tennyson Av. NE31: Heb . . . 7K **65**
NE35: Bol C . . . 6H **87**
TS27: B Col . . . 7G **173**
Tennyson Ct. NE8: Gate . . . 4J **83**
NE42: Pru . . . 5D **76**
Tennyson Cres. NE16: Swa . . . 6G **81**
Tennyson Gdns. DH9: Dip . . . 2G **123**
Tennyson Grn. NE3: Ken . . . 2A **62**
Tennyson Rd. DH2: P Fel . . . 6G **127**
SR8: Eas . . . 7B **160**
Tennyson St. NE33: S Shi . . . 3K **67**
SR5: S'wck . . . 5C **104**
Tennyson Ter. NE29: N Shi . . . 1G **67**
Tenter Gth. NE15: Thro . . . 3G **59**
Tenter Ter. DH1: Dur . . . 2B **6** (2A **166**)
NE61: Mor . . . 7G **9**
Tenth Av. DH2: Ches S . . . 6K **127**
NE6: Heat . . . 1P **5** (5A **64**)
NE11: T Vall . . . 5F **99**
NE24: Bly . . . 4H **23**
NE61: Mor . . . 2H **15**
Tenth Av. Trade Pk.
NE11: T Vall . . . 5F **99**
Tenth Av. W. NE11: T Vall . . . 5E **98**
Tenth St. SR8: Hord . . . 5E **172**
TS27: B Col . . . 1G **183**
Tern Cl. NE24: News . . . 5K **23**
Terrace, The DH6: Shot C . . . 5F **171**
DH7: Mead . . . 1F **175**
DH8: Shot B . . . 3E **120**
NE35: Bol C . . . 5E **86**
NE36: E Bol . . . 7K **87**
NE42: O'ham . . . 2D **76**
NE46: Acomb . . . 4B **50**
SR4: Sund . . . 2G **117**
Terrace Pl. NE1: Newc T . . . 4D **4** (7E **62**)
Terraces, The NE38: Wash . . . 4J **115**
Terrier Cl. NE22: Bed . . . 7A **18**
Territorial La. DH1: Dur . . . 3D **6** (3B **166**)
Terry Cooney Pl. NE5: Fen . . . 5H **61**
Tesla St. DH4: Nbot . . . 5D **130**
Tetford Pl. NE12: Longb . . . 5A **46**
Teviot NE38: Wash . . . 7E **114**
Teviotdale Gdns. NE7: H Hea . . . 2K **63**
Teviot St. DH5: Eas L . . . 3J **157**
NE8: Gate . . . 6J **83**
Teviot Way NE32: Jar . . . 1A **86**
Tewkesbury NE12: Kil . . . 7B **36**
Tewkesbury Rd. NE15: Lem . . . 5C **60**
Thackeray Rd. SR3: Sund . . . 6K **117**
Thackeray St. DH4: Hou S . . . 2D **144**
Thames Av. NE32: Jar . . . 3C **86**
Thames Cres. DH4: Hou S . . . 2A **144**
DH9: Stly . . . 5F **125**
Thames Gdns. NE28: W'snd . . . 4F **65**
(not continuous)
Thames Rd. NE31: Heb . . . 2K **85**
SR3: Sund . . . 1J **131**
SR8: Pet . . . 7A **172**
Thames St. DH5: Eas L . . . 3J **157**
NE8: Gate . . . 6J **83**
NE17: C'wl . . . 6A **94**
Thanet Rd. SR3: Sund . . . 7K **117**
Tharsis Rd. NE31: Heb . . . 1H **85**
Thatcher Cl. NE16: Whi . . . 3G **97**
The . . .
Names prefixed with 'The' for example 'The Adelaide Cen.' are indexed under the main name such as 'Adelaide Cen., The'
Theatre Pl. NE29: N Shi . . . 7G **49**
Theatre Royal
Newcastle upon Tyne . . . 5F **4** (1F **83**)
Thelma St. SR4: Sund . . . 2D **118**
Theme Rd. SR3: Sund . . . 1J **131**
Theresa Russell Ho.
NE6: Byke . . . 3P **5** (7A **64**)
Theresa St. NE21: Blay . . . 3C **80**
(not continuous)
SR7: S'hm . . . 5C 148
(off Queen Alexandra St.)
Thetford NE38: Wash . . . 4H **115**
Thieves Bank NE62: Chop . . . 6G **11**
Third Av. DH2: Ches S . . . 6K **127**
(Bullion La.)
DH2: Ches S . . . 2K **127**
(Drum Rd.)
NE6: Heat . . . 1P **5** (6A **64**)
NE11: T Vall . . . 1E **98**
NE24: Bly . . . 3H **23**
NE29: N Shi . . . 7B **48**
NE61: Mor . . . 1H **15**
NE63: Ash . . . 4B **12**
Third St. DH8: Cons . . . 7K **121**
DH8: Lead . . . 3A **122**
(Fourth St.)
DH8: Lead . . . 4A **122**
(Second St.)
DH9: Stly . . . 7D **124**
NE28: W'snd . . . 4H **65**
SR8: Hord . . . 5E **172**
TS27: B Col . . . 2H **183**
Thirkeld Pl. DH4: Pen . . . 2A **130**
Thirlaway Ter. NE16: Sun . . . 5J **97**
Thirlington Cl. NE5: Blak . . . 2H **61**
Thirlmere DH3: Bir . . . 6C **114**
NE10: Pel . . . 6E **84**
SR6: Clead . . . 5C **88**
Thirlmere Av. DH2: Ches S . . . 1K **141**
DH5: Eas L . . . 3J **157**
NE30: Cull . . . 2G **49**
Thirlmere Cl. NE12: Kil . . . 1D **46**
Thirlmere Ct. NE31: Heb . . . 1K **85**
Thirlmere Cres. DH4: S Row . . . 3B **130**
NE21: Winl . . . 6B **80**
Thirlmere Rd. SR8: Pet . . . 5C **172**
Thirlmere Ter. NE64: Newb S . . . 3H **13**
Thirlmere Way NE5: Den M . . . 4H **61**
NE24: Cow . . . 7E **18**
Thirlmoor NE37: Wash . . . 2E **114**
Thirlmoor Pl. NE62: Stake . . . 7J **11**
Thirlwall Ct. NE12: Longb . . . 6H **45**
Thirlwell Gro. NE32: Jar . . . 3A **86**
Thirsk Rd. SR3: Sund . . . 6K **117**
Thirston Dr. NE23: Cra . . . 4A **26**
Thirston Pl. NE29: N Shi . . . 5D **48**
Thirston Way NE3: Ken . . . 7K **43**
Thirteenth St. SR8: Hord . . . 5D **172**
Thistle Av. NE40: Craw . . . 2E **78**
Thistle Ct. NE31: Heb . . . 1H **85**
Thistlecroft DH5: Hou S . . . 3E **144**
Thistledale SR2: Sund . . . 3H **119**
Thistledon Av. NE16: Whi . . . 1F **97**
Thistle Rd. DH7: Lang M . . . 1H **175**
SR3: Sund . . . 7J **117**
Thistley Cl. NE6: Walk . . . 5C **64**
Thistley Grn. NE10: Bill Q . . . 5F **85**
Thistly Cl. SR5: S'wck . . . 5C **104**
Thomas Bell Ho. NE34: S Shi . . . 2G **87**
Thomas Bewick Sq.
NE1: Newc T . . . 7E **4** (2F **83**)
Thomas Dr. NE31: Heb . . . 7H **65**
Thomas Ferguson Ct. NE30: N Shi . . . 6J **49**
Thomas Hawksley Pk. SR3: Sund . . . 5C **118**
Thomas Holiday Homes *NE22: Bed . . . 5B 18*
(off Burnside)
Thomas Horsley Ho. NE15: Benw . . . 1H **81**
Thomas St. DH3: Ches S . . . 7A **128**
DH5: Hett H . . . 5H **145**
(not continuous)
DH7: Lang P . . . 5J **151**
DH7: Sac . . . 1D **152**
DH8: B'hill . . . 5F **121**
DH8: Cons . . . 6H 121
(off Gibson St.)
DH9: Ann P . . . 5A **124**
DH9: Crag . . . 7J **125**
(not continuous)
NE5: West . . . 3F **61**
NE9: Eigh B . . . 6B **100**
NE16: Whi . . . 7G **81**
NE33: S Shi . . . 2J **67**
NE37: Wash . . . 7K **101**
SR2: Ryh . . . 3H **133**
SR8: Eas C . . . 6C **160**
Thomas St. Nth. SR6: Monkw . . . 7F **105**
Thomas St. Sth. SR2: Ryh . . . 3H **133**
SR5: S'wck . . . 6C **104**
Thomas Taylor Cotts. NE27: Back . . . 6G **37**
Thomaston Ct. NE5: Den M . . . 3H **61**
Thompson Av. NE12: Kil . . . 7A **36**
Thompson Gdns. NE28: W'snd . . . 3F **65**
Thompson Pl. NE10: Fell . . . 6B **84**
Thompson Rd. SR5: S'wck . . . 5D **104**
Thompson's Bldgs. DH4: S Row . . . 4C **130**
Thompson St. NE22: Bed . . . 5B **18**
NE24: Bly . . . 7H **19**
SR8: Hord . . . 5E **172**
Thompson Ter. SR2: Ryh . . . 3J **133**
Thorburn St. SR6: Ful . . . 3F **105**
Thornbank Cl. SR3: Dox P . . . 5C **132**
Thornborough Ho. *NE6: Byke . . . 7A 64*
(off Spires La.)
Thornbridge NE38: Wash . . . 3A **116**
Thornbury Av. NE23: Seg . . . 1E **36**
Thornbury Cl. NE3: Ki Pk . . . 7H **43**
NE35: Bol C . . . 5E **86**
Thornbury Dr. NE25: Monks . . . 5C **38**
Thornbury St. SR4: Sund . . . 1C **118**
Thorncliffe Cl. NE38: Wash . . . 5B **116**
Thorncliffe Pl. NE29: N Shi . . . 7E **48**
Thorn Cl. NE13: W Op . . . 6C **34**
Thorndale Pl. NE24: Cow . . . 1E **22**
Thorndale Rd. DH1: Carr . . . 7H **155**
NE15: Scot . . . 1F **81**
SR3: Sund . . . 6J **117**
Thorne Av. NE10: Ward . . . 6F **85**
Thornebrake NE10: Hew . . . 7E **84**
Thorne Rd. SR3: Sund . . . 7J **117**
Thornes Cl. SR8: Pet . . . 6D **172**
Thorne Sq. SR3: Sund . . . 7J **117**
Thorne Ter. NE6: Walk . . . 6C **64**
Thorneyburn Av. NE25: Well . . . 6B **38**
Thorneyburn Cl. DH4: Hou S . . . 7C **130**
Thorneyburn Way NE24: Cow . . . 1F **23**
THORNEY CLOSE . . . 7K **117**
Thorney Cl. Rd. SR3: Sund . . . 7K **117**
Thorneyfield Dr. NE12: Kil . . . 2K **45**

Thorneyford Pl. NE20: Pon .4J 31
Thorneyholme Ter. DH9: Stly .3F 125
NE21: Blay .3C 80
Thornfield Gro. SR2: Sund .6G 119
Thornfield Pl. NE39: Row G .4J 95
Thornfield Rd. DH8: C'sde .2E 134
NE3: Gos .1D 62
Thornhaugh Av. NE16: Whi .2F 97
Thornhill Cl. NE11: Gate .6C 82
NE25: Sea D .1H 37
Thornhill Cres. SR2: Sund .5H 7 (2E 118)
Thornhill Gdns. NE16: Burn .3K 109
NE62: Stake .7J 11
SR2: Sund .7G 7 (4E 118)
Thornhill Pk. NE20: Pon .4J 31
SR2: Sund .7G 7 (3E 118)
Thornhill Reach SR7: S'hm .2K 147
Thornhill Rd. DH6: Shot C .6E 170
NE12: Longb .6B 46
NE20: Pon .3J 31
Thornhill St. DH4: Hou S .2D 144
Thornhill Ter. SR2: Sund .6G 7 (3E 118)
Thornholme Av. NE34: S Shi .7D 68
Thornholme Rd. SR2: Sund .7F 7 (4D 118)
Thornhope Cl. NE38: Wash .2K 115
Thornlaw Nth. DH6: Thor .1H 179
Thornlea NE61: Hep .4A 16
Thornlea Gdns. NE9: Low F .1H 99
Thornlea Gro. DH7: Lan .6J 137
Thornleigh Gdns. SR6: Clead .4C 88
Thornleigh Rd. NE2: Jes .4G 63
THORNLEY .1J 179
Thornley Av. NE10: Ward .1F 101
NE23: Cra .4A 26
Thornley Cl. DH7: Ush M .3D 164
NE16: Whi .3G 97
Thornley La. NE21: Row G, Winl .1A 96
NE39: Row G .1A 96
Thornley Rd. DH6: Whe H .2A 180
NE5: W Dent .5F 61
TS29: Trim S .7B 180
Thornley Sta. Ind. Est.
DH6: Shot C .1F 181
Thornley Ter. NE22: Bed, Stake .3A 18
Thornley Vw. NE39: Row G .5K 95
Thornley Wood (Country Pk.) .1B 96
Thornley Woodlands Cen. .2B 96
Thornton Av. NE33: S Shi .6H 67
Thornton Cl. DH4: Pen .2B 130
DH6: Ludw .5J 169
NE61: Mor .2H 15
Thornton Cotts. NE40: Ryton .7G 59
(off Northumberland Rd.)
Thornton Ct. NE1: Newc T .7D 4
NE38: Wash .3G 115
Thornton Cres. NE21: Blay .3C 80
Thornton Lea DH2: Pelt .2F 127
Thorntons Cl. DH2: Pelt .2F 127
Thornton St. NE1: Newc T .7D 4 (1E 82)
Thornton Ter. NE12: Longb .3E 46
TS27: B Col .2J 183
Thorntree Av. NE13: Sea B .2D 34
Thorntree Cl. NE25: Monks .7B 38
Thorntree Cotts. NE13: Sea B .2D 34
Thorntree Ct. NE12: Longb .4D 46
Thorntree Dr. NE15: Den M .7G 61
NE22: Bed .6H 17
NE25: Monks .7B 38
Thorntree Gdns. NE63: N Sea .5E 12
Thorntree Gill SR8: Hord .7E 172
Thorntree M. SR3: Sund .6J 117
Thorntree Ter. DH9: Stly .2H 125
Thorntree Wlk. NE32: Jar .4D 86
Thorntree Way NE24: Cow .2D 22
Thornwood Gdns. NE11: Lob H .1D 98
Thornyford Ho. NE4: Newc T .3B 4
Thornygarth NE10: Fell .7C 84
Thoroton St. NE24: Bly .1J 23
Thorp Av. NE61: Mor .5G 9
Thorp Cl. NE24: Bly .4F 23
Thorp Cotts. NE40: Ryton .1E 78
Thorp Dr. NE40: Ryton .1H 79
Thorpe Cl. NE4: Newc T .4A 4 (7C 62)
Thorpe Cres. SR8: Hord .3D 172
Thorpeness Rd. SR3: Sund .7J 117
Thorpe Rd. SR8: Eas, Hord, Pet .1K 171
Thorpe St. NE4: Newc T .3A 4 (7C 62)
SR8: Eas C .6C 160
SR8: Hord .5E 172
Threap Gdns. NE28: W'snd .1J 65
Three Indian Kings Ho. NE1: Newc T .7H 5
(off Quayside)
Three Mile Ct. NE3: Gos .4E 44
Three Rivers Ct. NE36: W Bol .7G 87
Threlkeld Gro. SR6: Seab .2E 104
Thrift St. NE29: N Shi .1G 67
Thristley Gdns. SR2: Sund .5E 118
THROCKLEY .3H 59
Throckley Ind. Est. NE15: Thro .2H 59
Throckley Pond Nature Reserve .5F 59
Throckley Way NE34: S Shi .7H 67
Thropton Av. NE7: Longb .7K 45
NE24: Bly .4G 23
Thropton Cl. DH1: H Shin .7F 167
DH2: Ches S .1J 141
NE10: Ward .1G 101
Thropton Ct. NE24: Bly .2G 23
Thropton Cres. NE3: Gos .6D 44
Thropton Pl. NE29: N Shi .5D 48
Thropton Ter. NE7: H Hea .3K 63
Thrunton Ct. DH5: Hou S .2F 145
Thrunton Wlk. NE13: Haz .2C 44
Thrush Cross Pl. DH1: Dur .1F 167
Thurleston DH4: Nbot .5C 130
Thurlow Way DH5: Hou S .4D 144
Thursby DH3: Bir .6C 114
(not continuous)
Thursby Av. NE30: Cull .2H 49
Thursby Gdns. NE9: Low F .4K 99
Thurso Cl. SR3: Sund .7H 117
Tiberius Cl. NE28: W'snd .4F 65
Tidespring Row NE31: Heb .6H 65
Tiger Stairs NE29: N Shi .7H 49
(off Bedford St.)
Tilbeck Sq. SR3: Silk .4D 132
Tilbury Cl. DH4: S Row .4C 130
Tilbury Gdns. SR3: Sund .1J 131
Tilbury Gro. NE30: Cull .1G 49
Tilbury Rd. SR3: Sund .1J 131
Tileshed La. NE36: E Bol .5J 87
Till Av. NE21: Winl .4B 80
Tilley Cres. NE42: Pru .3F 77
Tilley Rd. NE38: Wash .3D 114
Tillmouth Av. NE25: H'wll, Sea D .1H 37
Tillmouth Gdns. NE4: Fen .7J 61
Tillmouth Pk. Rd. NE15: Thro .4H 59
Till St. NE6: Byke .2A 84
Tilson Way NE3: Ken .6B 44
Timber Beach Rd. SR5: Sund .6K 103
Timber Rd. SR8: Hord .3E 172
Time Central NE1: Newc T .4D 4
Times Sq. NE1: Newc T .8D 4 (2E 82)
Timlin Gdns. NE28: W'snd .2B 66
Timothy Duff Ct. NE30: Tyne .5K 49
(off Front St.)
Tindal Cl. NE4: Newc T .5B 4 (1D 82)
Tindale Av. DH1: Dur .6J 153
NE23: Cra .4A 26
Tindale Dr. NE16: Whi .1G 97
Tindale St. DH8: Lead .5A 122
Tindal St. NE4: Newc T .6B 4 (1D 82)
Tindle St. DH8: B'hill .5G 121
Tinkler's Bank NE45: Corb .2D 72
Tinklers La. DH1: Dur .2E 6 (2B 166)
Tinklers Yd. NE45: Corb .3D 72
Tinkler Ter. DH3: Gt Lum .1F 143
Tinmill Pl. DH8: B'hill .6F 121
Tinn St. NE8: Gate .5F 83
Tintagel DH3: Gt Lum .2F 143
Tintagel Cl. NE23: Cra .2K 25
SR3: Sund .7H 117
Tintagel Dr. SR7: S'hm .2A 148
Tintern NE38: Wash .5G 115
Tintern Cl. DH4: Hou S .7C 130
Tintern Cres. NE6: Heat .1P 5 (6K 63)
NE29: N Shi .4D 48
Tintern St. SR4: Sund .2D 118
Tiree Cl. DH7: B'don .7E 164
Tiree Ct. SR3: Silk .3C 132
Tirril Pl. NE5: Den M .4G 61
Titan Ho. NE6: Walk .7E 64
Titania Ct. NE24: Bly .5K 23
Titan Rd. NE6: Walk .7E 64
Titchfield Rd. NE38: Wash .4G 115
Titchfield Ter. NE61: Peg .4B 10
NE63: Ash .5B 12
Tithe Cotts. NE20: Pon .4J 31
(off Thornhill Rd.)
Titian Av. NE34: S Shi .4J 87
Titlington Gro. NE31: Heb .3H 85
Tiverton Av. NE4: Benw .1A 82
NE29: N Shi .3C 48
Tiverton Cl. DH4: Nbot .5D 130
NE28: W'snd .7K 47
Tiverton Gdns. NE9: Low F .4H 99
Tiverton Pl. NE23: Cra .2K 25
Tiverton Sq. SR3: Sund .7J 117
Tivoli Bldgs. DH4: S Row .3C 130
Tivoli Gdns. DH5: Hett H .7G 145
Toberty Gdns. NE10: Ward .6F 85
Tobin St. TS29: Trim S .7B 180
Todd's Nook NE4: Newc T .5A 4 (1D 82)
Toft Cres. SR7: Mur .6E 146
Togstone Pl. NE5: Fen .4J 61
Toll Bar Rd. SR2: Sund .7F 119
Toll Bri. Rd. NE21: Blay .3F 81
Tollerton Dr. SR5: Sund .7F 103
Tollgate Bungs. DH9: Ann P .4J 123
Tollgate Flds. DH4: W Rai .2K 155
Tollgate Rd. NE39: Ham M .3D 108
Tollgate Ter. DH9: Ann P .4J 123
Toll Ho. Rd. DH1: Dur .2H 165
Tolls Cl. NE25: Monks .6C 38
Toll Sq. NE30: N Shi .6J 49
Tomlea Av. NE22: Bed .7B 18
Tomlinson Ct. NE25: Monks .5D 38
Tom Urwin Ho. SR3: New S .2C 132
(off Silksworth Ter.)
Tonbridge Av. NE29: N Shi .7E 48
Toner Av. NE31: Heb .3H 85
Topaz St. SR7: S'hm .3J 147
Topcliff SR6: Roker .7G 105
Topcliffe Grn. NE9: Low F .5K 99
Top Gear Indoor Karting .2G 167
Toppings St. NE35: Bol C .5E 86
Torcross Way NE23: Cra .2K 25
Tor Mere Cl. NE37: Wash .2E 114
Toronto Rd. SR3: Sund .6K 117
Toronto Sq. SR3: Sund .6K 117
Torphin Hill Dr. SR3: Silk .4C 132
Torquay Gdns. NE9: Low F .4H 99
Torquay Pde. NE31: Heb .3A 86
Torquay Rd. SR3: Sund .6K 117
Torrance Cl. NE63: N Sea .3D 12
Torrens Rd. SR3: Sund .6K 117
Torrington Cl. DH4: Nbot .5C 130
Torver Cl. NE13: W Op .6D 34
SR8: Pet .6C 172
Torver Cres. SR6: Seab .2E 104
Torver Pl. NE9: Low F .3K 99
Torver Way NE30: Cull .2F 49
Torwood Ct. NE23: Cra .4A 26
Tosson Cl. NE22: Bed .7K 17
Tosson Pl. NE29: N Shi .7D 48
NE63: Ash .4C 12
Tosson Ter. NE6: Heat .4A 64
Total Fitness
South Shields .5K 67
(off Imeary St.)
Totnes Cl. SR3: Sund .7H 117
Totnes Dr. NE23: Cra .2K 25
Tourist Info. Cen.
Corbridge .1D 72
Gateshead .8H 5 (2G 83)
Hexham .1D 70
Morpeth .7G 9
Newcastle upon Tyne, Central Arc.
.5F 4 (1F 83)
North Shields .3E 66
Prudhoe .4G 77
Quayside .2G 83
Sunderland .4J 7 (2F 119)
Whitley Bay .5G 39
Toward Rd. SR1: Sund .4K 7 (2F 119)
SR2: Sund .6K 7 (2F 119)
Tower Ct. DH5: Eas L .2J 157
NE11: Dun .5C 82
Tower Gdns. NE40: Ryton .1G 79
Tower Ho. NE1: Newc T .6J 5 (1H 83)
Tower Pl. SR2: Sund .3G 119
Tower Rd. DH9: Ann P .7H 123
NE37: Wash .1J 115
Tower Rd. Cvn. Site DH9: Ann P .1K 137
Towers, The SR4: Sund .2H 117
Towers Av. NE2: Jes .2G 63
Towers Cl. NE22: Bed .1J 21
Towers Ho. DH8: Cons .7H 121
Towers Pl. NE34: S Shi .1E 86
Tower St. NE1: Newc T .5H 5 (1G 83)
SR2: Sund .3H 119
SR8: Eas C .6D 160
Tower St. W. SR2: Sund .4G 119
Tower Vw. NE15: Benw .7J 61
TOWN CENTRE .3G 115
Town Cen. NE23: Cra .4J 25
Towne Gate, The NE15: Hed W .3C 58
Towneley Ct. DH9: Stly .4E 124
NE42: Pru .3G 77
Towneley Flds. NE39: Row G .5K 95
Towneley Main Wagonway
NE40: Ryton .2G 79
Towneley St. DH9: Stly .3E 124
Towneley Ter. NE39: H Spen .3C 94
Townend Ct. NE34: S Shi .1J 87
TOWN END FARM .3G 103
Townfield Gdns. NE15: Newb .5K 59
Towngate Bus. Cen. DH7: Lang M .7G 165
TOWN KELLOE .7H 179
Townley Cotts. NE40: Ryton .2E 78
Townley Rd. NE39: Row G .5H 95
TOWN MOOR .5D 62
Townsend Ct. TS28: Sta T .7H 181
Townsend Cres. NE61: Mor .1D 14
Townsend Rd. SR3: Sund .1J 131
Townsend Sq. SR3: Sund .1J 131
Town Sq. NE28: W'snd .3F 65
Townsville Av. NE25: Monks .1D 48
Towton NE12: Kil .7B 36
Toynbee NE38: Wash .3A 116
Tracey Av. NE36: W Bol .6H 87
Trafalgar Ho. NE30: Tyne .5K 49
Trafalgar Rd. NE37: Wash .6J 101
Trafalgar Sq. SR1: Sund .1H 119
Trafalgar St. DH8: Cons .7H 121
NE1: Newc T .5H 5 (1G 83)
Trafford NE9: Low F .5J 99
Trafford Rd. SR5: S'wck .6C 104
Trafford Wlk. NE5: West .2E 60
Trajan Av. NE33: S Shi .1K 67
Trajan St. NE33: S Shi .1K 67
Trajan Wlk. NE15: Hed W .3B 58
Tranquil Ho. NE8: Gate .9G 4
Transbritannia Ct. NE21: Blay .2E 80
Transbritannia Ent. Pk. NE21: Blay .2E 80
TRANWELL .4D 14
Tranwell Cl. NE3: Fawd .4B 44
NE61: Peg .4A 10
Tranwell Cotts. NE61: Loan .4D 14
Tranwell Ct. NE61: Loan .5D 14
Tranwell Dr. NE25: Sea D .1J 37
TRANWELL WOODS .6B 14
Travers St. DH4: New H .3C 130
Traynor Way SR8: Pet .6G 171
Treby St. SR4: Sund .1C 118
(not continuous)
Tredegar Cl. NE5: Blak .1H 61
Treecone Cl. SR3: Dox P .4C 132
Treen Cres. SR7: Mur .7F 147
Tree Top M. NE28: W'snd .7H 47
Treetops, The NE32: Jar .2A 86
Trefoil Rd. DH9: Tan L .1D 124
Tregoney Av. SR7: Mur .6F 147
Treherne Rd. NE2: Jes .2F 63
Trent Av. NE31: Heb .3J 85
Trent Cres. DH3: Gt Lum .2F 143
Trent Dale DH8: Lead .4B 122
Trent Dr. NE32: Jar .4C 86
Trent Gdns. NE8: Gate .6K 83
Trentham Av. NE7: Longb .7K 45
Trentham Gdns. NE61: Peg .3A 10
Trenton Av. NE38: Wash .2H 115
Trent Rd. SR3: Sund .7J 117
Trent St. DH5: Eas L .3J 157
NE17: C'wl .6A 94
Trevarren Dr. SR2: Ryh .2H 133
Trevelyan Av. NE22: Bed .7K 17
NE24: Bly .3G 23
Trevelyan Cl. NE27: Shir .1J 47
SR3: Sund .7H 117
Trevelyan Dr. NE5: West .7G 43
Trevelyan Pl. SR8: Pet .7K 171
Trevethick St. NE8: Gate .6F 83
Trevone Pl. NE23: Seg .1E 36
Trevone Sq. SR7: Mur .7F 147
Trevor Gro. SR6: Clead .6C 88
Trevor Ter. NE30: N Shi .5G 49
Trewhitt Rd. NE6: Heat .5A 64
Trewitt Rd. NE26: Whit B .7H 39
Tribune Pl. NE9: Low F .1K 99
Trident Dr. NE24: Bly .5K 23
Trident Rd. SR3: New S .2C 132
Trimdon Gro. NE9: Wrek .4B 100
Trimdon St. SR4: Sund .2F 7 (1D 118)
Trimdon St. W. SR4: Sund .7D 104
Trinity Bldgs. NE30: N Shi .7J 49
Trinity Chare NE1: Newc T .7H 5 (2G 83)
Trinity Cl. NE29: N Shi .1G 67
Trinity Ct. NE8: Gate .10J 5 (3H 83)
NE29: N Shi .7G 49
NE45: Corb .7D 52
SR7: S'hm .2A 148
Trinity Courtyard NE6: Byke .2B 84
NE8: Gate .5C 82
(off Michaelmas St.)
Trinity Gdns. NE1: Newc T .6H 5 (1G 83)
Trinity Gro. NE23: Seg .1E 36
Trinity House .6H 5
Trinity Pk. DH4: S Row .4B 130
Trinity Pl. NE29: N Shi .1G 67
Trinity Sq. NE8: Gate .10J 5 (3H 83)
SR1: Sund .1G 119
Trinity St. NE29: N Shi .1G 67
SR5: S'wck .5B 104
Trinity Ter. NE29: N Shi .1G 67
NE45: Corb .7D 52
Trinity Wlk. NE33: S Shi .4H 67
Triumph Dr. NE31: Heb .7H 65
Troilus Gdns. NE31: Heb .7H 65
Trojan Av. NE6: Walk .6C 64
Tromso Cl. NE29: N Shi .7C 48
Troon Cl. DH8: B'hill .4G 121
NE37: Wash .5G 101
Tropicana Health & Fitness Club .6F 9
Trotter Gro. NE22: Bed .7A 18
Trotter Ter. DH6: Shot C .6E 170
SR2: Ryh .3H 133
Troutbeck Av. NE6: Walk .1D 84
Troutbeck Gdns. NE9: Low F .4J 99
Troutbeck Rd. SR6: Seab .2E 104
Troutbeck Way NE34: S Shi .3G 87
SR8: Pet .5C 172
Troutdale Pl. NE12: Longb .6H 45
Trout's La. DH1: Dur .4F 153
Troves Cl. NE4: Benw .2A 82
Trowbridge Way NE3: Ken .7B 44
Trowsdale St. DH9: Ann P .4J 123
Truro Av. SR7: Mur .6F 147
Truro Gro. NE29: N Shi .4D 48
Truro Rd. SR3: Sund .7K 117
Truro Way NE32: Jar .5C 86
Tuart St. DH3: Ches S .6A 128
Tube Ct. NE1: Newc T .5K 5 (1H 83)
Tudhoe Cl. DH4: S Row .5K 129
Tudor Av. NE29: N Shi .6E 48
Tudor Ct. DH6: Shot C .6F 171
NE20: Darr H .7G 31
Tudor Dr. DH9: Tanf .5D 110
Tudor Grange SR8: Eas .1J 171
Tudor Gro. SR3: Sund .5B 118
Tudor Rd. DH3: Ches S .4B 128
NE33: S Shi .3H 67
Tudor Ter. DH8: Cons .6G 121
Tudor Wlk. NE3: Ki Pk .7J 43
(Ebchester Ct.)
NE3: Ki Pk .5K 43
(Hersham Cl.)
NE3: Ki Pk .6J 43
(Petherton Ct.)
Tudor Way NE3: Ki Pk .6H 43
Tudor Wynd NE6: Heat .3B 64
Tulip Cl. NE21: Winl .4B 80
Tulip Ct. DH4: Pen .1B 130
Tulip St. NE10: Fell .5A 84
NE42: Pru .4D 76
Tumulus Av. NE6: Walk .5E 64
Tunbridge Rd. SR3: Sund .6K 117
Tundry Way NE21: Blay .2F 81
Tunis Rd. SR3: Sund .6K 117
TUNSTALL .2C 132
Tunstall SR2: Sund .5E 118
Tunstall Av. DH6: Bowb .4H 177
NE6: Byke, Walk .7B 64
(not continuous)
NE34: S Shi .7D 68
Tunstall Bank SR2: Ryh, Tuns .2E 132
Tunstall Gro. DH8: Lead .4B 122
Tunstall Hill Cl. SR2: Sund .6E 118
TUNSTALL HILLS .6D 118
Tunstall Hills Local Nature Reserve .7F 119
Tunstall Hope Rd. SR3: Tuns .7E 118
Tunstall Lodge Pk. SR3: Dox P .4D 132
Tunstall Pk. SR2: Sund .4E 118
Tunstall Rd. SR2: Sund .6H 7 (2E 118)
SR3: Sund, Tuns .6D 118
Tunstall Ter. SR2: Ryh .2F 133
SR2: Sund .5H 7 (2E 118)
SR3: New S .2C 132
Tunstall Ter. W. SR2: Sund .5G 7 (2E 118)
Tunstall Va. SR2: Sund .7H 7 (4E 118)
Tunstall Vw. SR3: New S .1D 132

Tunstall Village Grn. SR3: Tuns 2E **132**
Tunstall Village Rd. SR3: Tuns 2D **132**
Tunstall Vs. SR3: Tuns 2D **132**
Turbine Bus. Pk. SR5: Sund 1D **116**
Turbinia Gdns. NE7: H Hea 3A **64**
Turfside NE10: Hew 7E **84**
(not continuous)
NE32: Jar 5D **86**
Turn, The NE61: Loan 3F **15**
Turnberry DH2: Ous 6H **113**
NE25: Monks 6C **38**
NE33: S Shi 4A **68**
Turnberry Cl. DH8: B'hill 3G **121**
NE37: Wash 5G **101**
Turnberry Ct. NE10: Ward 7F **85**
Turnberry Way NE3: Gos 7G **45**
NE23: Cra 4A **26**
Turnbull Cl. DH1: Dur 2E **166**
Turnbull Cres. SR7: Mur 7E **146**
Turnbulls Bldgs. NE37: Wash 7H **101**
Turnbull St. SR1: Sund 7H **105**
Turner Av. NE34: S Shi 3K **87**
Turner Cl. NE40: Ryton 2H **79**
Turner Cres. NE3: Gos 7C **44**
Turners Bldgs. DH7: Wit G 3C **152**
Turner Sq. NE61: Mor 2H **15**
Turner St. DH8: B'hill 5F **121**
NE27: Shir .3J **47**
Turners Way NE61: Mor 1D **14**
Turnham Rd. SR3: Sund 7J **117**
Turn Pk. DH3: Ches S 6A **128**
Turnstile M. SR6: Roker 5G **105**
Turnstone Dr. NE38: Wash 5D **114**
Turret Rd. NE15: Den M 5F **61**
Tursdale Rd. DH6: Bowb 6H **177**
Tuscan Cl. DH7: New B 5A **164**
Tuscan Rd. SR3: Sund 7J **117**
Tuthill Stairs NE1: Newc T 8F **4** (2F **83**)
Tweddle, Childrens Animal Farm 5K **183**
Tweddle Cres. TS27: B Col 3K **183**
Tweddle Ter. DH6: Bowb 4G **177**
Tweed Av. DH8: Lead 4B **122**
Tweed Cl. DH2: Ous 1H **127**
SR2: Sund 1H **133**
SR8: Pet .7A **172**
Tweed Dr. NE61: Hep 7A **16**
Tweed Gro. NE15: Lem 6C **60**
Tweedmouth Ct. NE3: Gos 1G **63**
Tweed St. DH5: Eas L 3J **157**
NE4: Elsw .1B **82**
NE8: Gate .5J **83**
NE17: C'wl 6A **94**
NE31: Heb 7H **65**
NE32: Jar .1A **86**
NE38: Wash 4K **115**
NE63: Ash .2C **12**
(not continuous)
Tweed Ter. DH9: Stly 4F **125**
Tweedy's Bldgs. NE40: Ryton 1F **79**
Tweedy St. NE24: Cow 1E **22**
Tweedy Ter. NE6: Walk 1D **84**
Twelfth Av. DH2: Ches S 5K **127**
NE24: Bly .3H **23**
Twelfth St. SR8: Hord 5D **172**
Twentieth Av. NE24: Bly 4G **23**
Twentyfifth Av. NE24: Bly 4H **23**
Twentysecond Av. NE24: Bly 4G **23**
Twentysixth Av. NE24: Bly 4G **23**
Twentythird Av. NE24: Bly 4G **23**
Twickenham Ct. NE23: Seg 1D **36**
Twickenham Rd. SR3: Sund 6J **117**
Twizell Av. NE21: Winl 4B **80**
Twizell Burn DH4: S Row 5K **129**
Twizell Burn Wlk. DH2: P Fel 6G **127**
Twizell La. DH9: W Pelt 4B **126**
Twizell Pl. NE20: Pon 4J **31**
Twizell St. NE24: Bly 3K **23**
Two Ball Lonnen NE4: Fen 6J **61**
Twyford Cl. NE23: Cra 2K **25**
Tyldesley Sq. SR3: Sund 7J **117**
Tyndal Gdns. NE11: Dun 5B **82**
Tyne App. NE32: Jar 5A **66**
Tyne Av. DH8: Lead 4B **122**
Tynebank NE21: Winl 4B **80**
Tyne Bri. NE1: Newc T 7G **4** (2G **83**)
NE8: Gate 7G **4** (2G **83**)
Tyne Bri. Twr. NE8: Gate 8J **5**
Tyne Ct. NE46: Hex 7C **50**
Tynedale Av. NE26: Whit B 5F **39**
NE28: W'snd 1F **65**
Tynedale Cl. NE41: Wylam 7K **57**
Tynedale Ct. NE28: W'snd 1A **66**
Tynedale Cres. DH4: Pen 2B **130**
Tynedale Dr. NE24: Cow 1D **22**
Tynedale Gdns. NE43: Pains 1K **91**
Tynedale Ho. NE15: Benw 1H **81**
Tynedale Rd. NE34: S Shi 5A **68**
SR3: Sund .7J **117**
Tynedale St. DH5: Hett H 2E **156**
Tynedale Ter. DH9: Ann P 5A **124**
NE12: Longb 6B **46**
NE46: Acomb 4B **50**
NE46: Hex 2B **70**
Tynedale Vw. NE46: Hex 2B **70**
Tynedale Vs. NE46: Hex 2B **70**
TYNE DOCK 6H **67**
Tyne Dock Station (Metro) 7H **67**
Tyne Gdns. NE37: Wash 6H **101**
NE40: Ryton 2J **79**
NE42: O'ham 2D **76**
Tynegate Pct. NE8: Gate 4H **83**
Tyne Grn. NE46: Hex 7C **50**
Tyne Green Country Pk. 7D **50**
Tyne Grn. Rd. NE46: Hex 7C **50**
Tynell Wlk. NE3: Ki Pk 7H **43**
Tyne Main Rd. NE10: Gate 10P **5** (3A **84**)
Tyne Mills NE46: Hex 1E **70**
Tyne Mills Ind. Est. NE46: Hex 7E **50**
TYNEMOUTH 5K **49**
Tynemouth Castle 5K **49**
Tynemouth Cl. NE6: Byke 3P **5** (7K **63**)
Tynemouth Ct. NE6: Byke 2P **5**
NE29: N Shi 6F **49**
Tynemouth Crematorium NE29: N Shi . . .5F **49**
Tynemouth Gro. NE6: Byke 2P **5**
Tynemouth Park 3K **49**
Tynemouth Pass NE8: Gate 4E **82**
Tynemouth Pl. NE30: Tyne 5K **49**
Tynemouth Pool 4F **49**
Tynemouth Priory Theatre 4K **49**
Tynemouth Rd. NE6: Byke 2P **5** (6A **64**)
(not continuous)
NE28: W'snd 3K **65**
NE30: N Shi, Tyne 6H **49**
NE32: Jar .4B **86**
Tynemouth Sailing Club
(off Pier Rd.) 5K **49**
Tynemouth Sq. SR3: Sund 7K **117**
Tynemouth Squash Club 5D **48**
Tynemouth Station (Metro) 5K **49**
Tynemouth Ter. NE30: Tyne 5K **49**
Tynemouth Volunteer Life Brigade Mus.
(off Pier Rd.) 5K **49**
Tynemouth Way NE6: Byke 6A **64**
Tyne Point Ind. Est. NE32: Jar 1E **86**
Tyne Riverside Country Pk. 3C **76**
Tyne Rd. DH9: Stly 4E **124**
Tyne Rd. E. DH9: Stly 4F **125**
NE8: Gate 10E **4** (4E **82**)
Tyneside Cinema 5F **4** (1F **83**)
Tyneside Rd. NE4: Newc T 9B **4** (3D **82**)
Tyneside Works NE32: Jar 5B **66**
Tyne St. DH5: Eas L 3J **157**
DH8: Cons 7J **121**
NE1: Newc T 6M **5** (1J **83**)
NE10: Fell 4C **84**
NE17: C'wl 6K 93
(off Derwent St.)
NE21: Blay 2C **80**
NE21: Winl 5B **80**
NE30: N Shi 7H **49**
NE31: Heb 6H **65**
NE32: Jar .5C **66**
NE63: Ash .3C **12**
SR7: S'hm 3B **148**
Tyne Ter. NE34: S Shi 1H **87**
SR8: Eas .7B **160**
Tyne Tunnel Trade Pk. NE29: N Shi 1B **66**
Tyne Tunnel Trad. Est. NE29: N Shi 7B **48**
Tyne Va. DH9: Stly 4F **125**
Tynevale Av. NE21: Winl 5C **80**
Tynevale Ter. NE8: Gate 5E **82**
NE15: Lem 7C **60**
Tyne Valley Gdns. NE40: Ryton 1C **78**
Tyne Vw. NE15: Lem 7C **60**
NE21: Winl 5C **80**
NE31: Heb 7G **65**
NE40: C Vale 6D **58**
NE41: Wylam 7K **57**
Tyne Vw. Av. NE16: Whi 6J **81**
Tyne Vw. Gdns. NE10: Pel 5D **84**
Tyneview Pk. NE12: Longb 7B **46**
Tyne Vw. Pl. NE8: Gate 5E **82**
Tyne Vw. Ter. NE28: W'snd 4C **66**
NE42: Pru .3F **77**
NE45: Corb 7D **52**
Tyneview Ter. NE46: Hex 3E **70**
Tyne Wlk. NE15: Thro 4H **59**
Tynewold Cl. NE8: Gate 5E **82**
Tyzack Cres. SR6: Ful 5F **105**
Tyzack St. DH7: Edm 3D **140**

U

Ugly La. DH2: Nett 6H **141**
Uldale Ct. NE3: Ki Pk 5K **43**
Ullerdale Cl. DH1: Carr 7J **155**
Ullswater Av. DH5: Eas L 3J **157**
NE32: Jar .3D **86**
Ullswater Cl. NE24: Cow 1C **22**
Ullswater Cres. NE21: Winl 6B **80**
Ullswater Dr. NE12: Kil 1D **46**
NE37: Wash 2F **115**
Ullswater Gdns. NE34: S Shi 6K **67**
Ullswater Gro. SR5: Ful 3E **104**
Ullswater Rd. DH2: Ches S 1K **141**
NE64: Newb S 4G **13**
Ullswater Ter. DH6: S Het 3A **158**
Ullswater Way NE5: Den M 4H **61**
Ultor Ct. NE24: Bly 5K **23**
Ulverstone Ter. NE6: Walk 6C **64**
Ulverston Gdns. NE9: Low F 3K **99**
Umfraville Dene NE42: Pru 3F **77**
Underhill NE9: Low F 1J **99**
Underhill Dr. NE62: Chop 2G **17**
Underhill Rd. SR6: Clead 6B **88**
Underhill Ter. NE9: Spri 6E **100**
Underwood NE10: Hew 1E **100**
Underwood Gro. NE23: Cra 1J **25**
Unicorn Ho. NE30: N Shi 6H **49**
Union All. NE33: S Shi 2J **67**
Union Ct. DH3: Ches S 7A **128**
Union Hall Rd. NE15: Lem 7D **60**
Union La. DH2: Ches M 3K **141**
SR1: Sund 1G **119**
Union Pl. DH1: Dur 6D **6**
Union Quay NE30: N Shi 7J **49**
Union Rd. NE6: Byke 7A **64**
NE30: N Shi 6J **49**
Union Sq. NE2: Newc T 4K **5**
Union Stairs NE30: N Shi 7H **49**
Union St. DH5: Hett H 6G **145**
NE2: Newc T 4K **5** (7H **63**)
(not continuous)
NE24: Bly .1J **23**
NE28: W'snd 5F **65**
NE30: N Shi 7H **49**
NE32: Jar .5B **66**
NE33: S Shi 7H **67**
SR1: Sund 3J **7** (1F **119**)
SR4: Sund 2G **117**
SR7: S'hm 4B **148**
Unity Ter. DH9: Ann P 5B **124**
DH9: Dip .2J **123**
DH9: Tant 6B **110**
NE24: Camb 4H **19**
University Gallery 3G 4 (7G 63)
University of Durham Botanic Garden
. . . . .6B 166
University of Newcastle upon Tyne
Botanical Gdns. 5C 62
University of Sunderland
City Campus 4G 7 (2E 118)
Pallion New Road 1B 118
St Michael's Way 2E 118
Sir Tom Cowie Campus at St Peter's
. . . . .7G 105
University Sports Centre, The 1C 4
University Station (Metro) 5G 7 (2E 118)
Unsworth Gdns. *DH8: Cons 7H 121*
(off Unsworth St.)
Unsworth St. DH8: Cons 7H **121**
Uphill Dr. DH7: Sac 7F **141**
Uplands NE25: Monks 6D **38**
Uplands, The DH3: Bir 3B **114**
NE3: Ken .1B **62**
Uplands Way NE9: Spri 6D **100**
Up. Camden St. NE30: N Shi 6G **49**
Upper Chare SR8: Pet 6B **172**
Up. Claremont NE2: Newc T 1C **4** (6E **62**)
Up. Crone St. NE27: Shir 7K **37**
Up. Elsdon St. NE29: N Shi 1G **67**
Up. Fenwick Gro. NE61: Mor 5F **9**
Upper Mkt. Sq. SR1: Sund 4J **7** (1F **119**)
Up. Nile St. SR1: Sund 3K **7** (2G **119**)
Up. Norfolk St. NE30: N Shi 6H **49**
Up. Pearson St. NE30: N Shi 6H **49**
Up. Penman St. NE29: N Shi 1G **67**
Up. Precinct NE21: Blay 3D **80**
Up. Queen St. NE30: N Shi 6H **49**
Up. Sans St. SR1: Sund 1G **119**
Up. Walworth Way
SR1: Sund 3H **7** (1F **119**)
Up. Yoden Way SR8: Pet 6B **172**
Upton St. NE8: Gate 5D **82**
Urban Gdns. NE37: Wash 1H **115**
Urfa Ter. NE33: S Shi 1K **67**
URPETH 6G **113**
Urpeth Hill Top DH9: Beam 2C **126**
Urpeth Ter. DH2: Pelt 2C **126**
Urpeth Vs. DH9: Beam 2B **126**
Urswick Ct. NE3: Ki Pk 7H **43**
Urwin St. DH5: Hett H 7H **145**
USHAW MOOR .2B **164**
Ushaw Rd. NE31: Heb 7K **65**
Ushaw Ter. DH7: Ush M 2B **164**
Ushaw Vs. DH7: Ush M 2B **164**
(not continuous)
Usher Av. DH6: S'burn 2K **167**
Usher St. DH6: Ludw 5J **169**
SR5: S'wck 6D **104**
Usk Av. NE32: Jar 3C **86**
Usway Cl. NE31: Heb 6K **65**
USWORTH 5F **101**
Usworth Hall NE37: Wash 5J **101**
Usworth Sta. Rd. NE37: Wash 7K **101**
(Mandeville)
NE37: Wash 7J **101**
(Woodland Ter.)
Uxbridge Ter. NE10: Fell 5B **84**

V

Valebrook NE46: Hex 2B **70**
Valebrooke SR2: Sund 7H **7**
Valebrooke Av. SR2: Sund 7H **7** (3E **118**)
Valebrooke Gdns.
SR2: Sund 7H **7** (3E **118**)
Valehead NE25: Monks 6D **38**
Vale Ho. NE2: Newc T 1M **5** (5J **63**)
Valentia Av. NE6: Walk 6C **64**
Valentine Way NE8: Gate 5C **82**
Valeria Cl. NE28: W'snd 6H **47**
Valerian Av. NE15: Hed W 3D **58**
Valerian Ct. NE63: Ash 6K **11**
Valeshead Ho. NE28: W'snd 3G **65**
Valeside DH1: Dur 2K **165**
NE15: Thro 3G **59**
(not continuous)
Vale St. DH5: Eas L 3H **157**
SR4: Sund 3D **118**
Vale St. E. SR4: Sund 3D **118**
Vale Vw. DH7: B'hpe 5E **138**
Vale Wlk. NE2: Newc T 1M **5** (5J **63**)
Valiant Way DH9: Ann P 4J **123**
Valley Cl. DH9: Stly 4F **125**
Valley Ct. SR2: Sund 3G **119**
Valley Cres. NE21: Winl 4A **80**
Valley Dene NE17: C'wl 7K **93**
Valley Dr. DH7: Esh W 2C **162**
NE9: Low F 7H **83**
NE11: Dun 7B **82**
NE16: Swa 6G **81**
Valley Forge NE38: Wash 2H **115**
Valley Gdns. DH8: Shot B 5E **120**
NE9: Low F 7J **83**
NE25: Monks 6D **38**
NE28: W'snd 2H **65**
Valley Gth. DH7: Esh W 2C **162**
Valley Grn. NE40: Craw 3D **78**
Valley Gro. DH7: Lan 7K **137**
Valley La. NE34: S Shi 7E **68**
Valley Rd. DH2: P Fel 5G **127**
NE25: H'wll 1K **37**
Valley Shop. Village
NE11: T Vall 2E **98**
Valley Vw. DH3: Bir 2K **113**
DH5: Hett H 2D **156**
DH6: Crox 7K **175**
DH7: Sac .1D **152**
DH7: Ush M 3D **164**
DH8: Cons 4A **136**
DH8: Lead 6A **122**
DH8: Shot B 4D **120**
DH9: Ann P 4K **123**
DH9: Stly .5E **124**
NE2: Jes 4H **63**
NE11: Kib .2E **112**
NE15: Lem 6B **60**
NE16: Burn 1K **109**
NE32: Jar .2B **86**
NE38: Wash 7J **115**
NE39: Row G 5G **95**
NE42: Pru .5G **77**
NE46: Hex 2E **70**
Vallum Ct. NE4: Newc T 5A **4** (1D **82**)
Vallum Pl. NE9: Low F 1K **99**
Vallum Rd. NE6: Walk 7C **64**
NE15: Thro 3H **59**
Vallum Way
NE4: Newc T 5A **4** (1D **82**)
Vanburgh Ct. NE25: Sea D 1H **37**
Vanburgh Gdns. NE61: Mor 7D **8**
Vance Bus. Pk. NE11: Fest P 6D **82**
Vance Ct. NE21: Blay 2E **80**
Vancouver Dr. NE7: H Hea 3B **64**
Vane St. SR3: New S 2C **132**
(not continuous)
SR8: Eas C 7C **160**
Vane Ter. SR2: Sund 3H **119**
SR7: S'hm 2B **148**
Vanguard Ct. SR3: Silk 3B **132**
(not continuous)
Van Mildert Cl. SR8: Pet 1K **181**
Vardy Ter. DH4: New H 3E **130**
Vaux Brewery Way SR5: Monkw 6E **104**
Vauxhall Rd. NE6: Walk 5E **64**
Vedra St. SR5: S'wck 6D **104**
Velville Ct. NE3: Ki Pk 6H **43**
Ventnor Av. NE4: Benw 1B **82**
Ventnor Cres. NE9: Low F 2G **99**
Ventnor Gdns. NE9: Low F 1G **99**
NE26: Whit B 5G **39**
Vera St. NE40: G'sde 6D **78**
Verdun Av. NE31: Heb 7J **65**
Vermont NE37: Wash 7H **101**
Verne Rd. NE29: N Shi 7C **48**
Vernon Cl. NE33: S Shi 5H **67**
Vernon Dr. NE25: Monks 7E **38**
Vernon Pl. NE64: Newb S 2J **13**
Vernon St. NE37: Wash 7H **101**
Veryan Gdns. SR3: Sund 5D **118**
Vespasian Av. NE33: S Shi 1K **67**
Vespasian St. NE33: S Shi 1K **67**
Viador DH3: Ches S 5A **128**
Viaduct St. NE28: W'snd 3J **65**
Vicarage Av. NE34: S Shi 7A **68**
Vicarage Cl. DH2: Pelt 2G **127**
DH5: Hett H 6G **145**
DH6: S Het 5D **158**
SR3: New S 2B **132**
Vicarage Ct. NE10: Hew 6D **84**
SR5: Sund 6H **103**
Vicarage Est. TS28: Win 5G **181**
Vicarage Flats DH7: B'don 1D **174**
Vicarage Gdns. NE22: Bed 1J **21**
Vicarage La. SR4: Sund 2G **117**
Vicarage Rd. SR3: New S 2C **132**
Vicarage St. NE29: N Shi 7G **49**
Vicarage Ter. NE22: Bed 1J **21**
SR7: Mur .1E **158**
Vicarsholme Cl. SR3: Dox P 4A **132**
Vicars La. NE7: Longb 7J **45**
Vicars Pele 1D **72**
Viceroy St. SR7: S'hm 3B **148**
Victoria Apartments
NE6: Heat 1M **5** (6J **63**)
Victoria Av. DH7: B'don 1E **174**
NE10: Fell 6A **84**
NE12: Longb 5B **46**
NE26: Whit B 6H **39**
NE28: W'snd 3F **65**
SR2: Sund 6G **119**
SR4: Sund 2H **117**
Victoria Av. W. SR2: Sund 6G **119**
Victoria Bldgs. SR1: Sund 4G **7**
Victoria Cen. DH8: Cons 7H **121**
Victoria Cl. DH6: Bowb 3H **177**
NE25: Sea D 7H **27**
Victoria Ct. DH1: Dur 5J **153**
DH7: Ush M 2C **164**
DH8: Cons 7H **121**
NE8: Gate .5E **82**
NE12: Longb 3A **46**
NE25: Sea D 7H **27**
NE30: Cull 1J **49**
NE31: Heb 1H **85**
SR2: Sund 5G **7**

Victoria Cres. NE29: N Shi 7F 49
NE30: Cull 1J 49
(Beverley Ter.)
NE30: Cull 7J 39
(Promontory Ter.)
Victoria Gro. NE25: Monks 6B 38
NE42: Pru 2G 77
Victoria Hall NE2: Newc T 3H 5
Victoria Ho. NE4: Newc T 10A 4 (3D 82)
NE8: Gate 5E 82
Victoria Ind. Est. NE31: Heb 3G 85
Victoria M. NE2: Jes 5J 63
NE16: Whi 7G 81
(off Simonside Vw.)
NE24: Bly 2H 23
NE26: Whit B 6H 39
SR8: Eas 1K 171
Victoria Parkway NE7: H Hea 2C 64
Victoria Pl. DH3: Ches S 7A 128
DH7: Edm 1A 140
NE25: Monks 7E 38
NE37: Wash 7H 101
SR1: Sund 5K 7 (2G 119)
SR4: Sund 2D 118
Victoria Rd. DH8: Cons 7H 121
(not continuous)
NE8: Gate 6E 82
NE33: S Shi 4J 67
NE37: Wash 7H 101
Victoria Rd. E. NE31: Heb 1J 85
Victoria Rd. W. NE31: Heb 4G 85
Victoria Sq. NE2: Jes 1G 4 (6G 63)
NE10: Fell 6B 84
Victoria St. DH5: Hett H 6G 145
DH6: Shot C 6E 170
DH7: Lan 6J 137
DH7: Sac 7E 140
DH8: Cons 6G 121
NE4: Newc T 7B 4 (2D 82)
NE11: Dun 5C 82
NE29: N Shi 1G 67
NE31: Heb 6G 65
NE40: Craw 2D 78
SR7: S'hm 3A 148
Victoria Ter. DH1: Dur 1A 6 (2K 165)
DH2: P Fel 4G 127
DH2: Pelt 3E 126
(Beamish Ct.)
DH2: Pelt 2C 126
(Urpeth Ter.)
DH4: Pen 2C 130
DH7: Lan 6J 137
DH9: Ann P 5K 123
NE9: Spri 6D 100
NE9: Wrek 4A 100
NE10: Fell 6B 84
NE15: Thro 3H 59
NE17: Ham 2K 107
NE22: Bed 7K 17
(not continuous)
NE26: Whit B 6H 39
NE32: Jar 7A 66
NE36: E Bol 7J 87
NE39: Row G 6G 95
NE42: Pru 4F 77
NE64: Newb S 3J 13
SR7: Mur 1F 159
Victoria Ter. Bk. NE15: Thro 3H 59
Victoria Ter. Sth. SR5: Monkw 6F 105
(off Warwick St.)
Victoria Tunnel 5M 5 (1J 83)
Victoria Vs. NE22: Bed 7K 17
Victor Pasmore Apollo Pavilion 1A 182
Victor St. DH3: Ches S 6A 128
SR6: Roker 6G 105
(off Brandling St. Sth.)
Victor Ter. DH7: Bearp 1D 164
Victory Cotts. NE23: Dud 2J 35
Victory Ho. NE30: Tyne 5K 49
Victory St. SR4: Sund 7A 104
Victory St. E. DH5: Hett H 6H 145
Victory St. W. DH5: Hett H 6H 145
Victory Way SR3: Dox P 4J 131
View, The DH3: Ches S 5A 128
(off West Vw.)
Viewforth Dr. SR5: S'wck 4E 104
Viewforth Grn. NE5: Blak 4J 61
Viewforth Rd. SR2: Ryh 4H 133
Viewforth Ter. SR5: S'wck 4D 104
(not continuous)
Viewforth Vs. DH1: Dur 2H 165
Viewlands NE63: Ash 3B 12
View La. DH9: Stly 2F 125
View Tops DH9: Beam 1B 126
VIGO 6C 114
Vigodale DH3: Bir 7C 114
Vigo La. DH3: Bir, Ches S 1A 128
DH3: Ches S 7C 114
NE38: Wash 1D 128
Vigo Rd. NE38: Wash 7G 115
Viking Ct. NE24: Bly 5K 23
Viking Ind. Pk. NE32: Jar 5K 65
Viking Pct. NE32: Jar 6K 65
Viking Shop. Cen., The NE32: Jar 6B 66
Villa Cl. SR4: Sund 2B 118
VILLAGE, THE
SR7, HAWTHORN 4A 160
SR7, MURTON 7D 146
TS27 4B 182
Village, The DH7: Bran 5A 174
SR2: Ryh 3J 133
SR7: Seat 2F 147
SR8: Pet 1J 181
Village Ct. NE26: Whit B 6F 39
Village East NE40: Ryton 7G 59
Village Farm NE15: Walb 4A 60
Village Grn. DH8: Shot B 2E 120
Village Hgts. NE8: Gate 10G 4 (4F 83)
Village La. NE38: Wash 2G 115
Village Pl. NE6: Byke 1A 84
Village Rd. NE23: Cra 4A 26
Villa Pl. NE8: Gate 5G 83
Villa Real Bungs. DH8: Lead 5K 121
Villa Real Ct. DH8: Cons 5J 121
Villa Real Est. DH8: Cons 5J 121
Villa Real Rd. DH8: Cons 5J 121
Villas, The DH6: Thor 1J 179
DH7: B'hpe 5D 138
DH9: Ann P 6J 123
NE13: W Op 6E 34
NE23: E Har 6K 21
SR2: Ryh 4H 133
SR5: Sund 6J 103
Villa Vw. NE9: Low F 1J 99
Villette Brooke St. SR2: Sund 4G 119
Villette Path SR2: Sund 4G 119
Villette Rd. SR2: Sund 4G 119
Villettes, The DH4: Nbot 6D 130
Villiers Pl. DH3: Ches S 5A 128
Villiers St. SR1: Sund 3K 7 (1G 119)
Villiers St. Sth. SR1: Sund 2G 119
Vimy Av. NE31: Heb 7J 65
Vincent's Ct. DH6: Thor 1K 179
Vincent St. SR7: S'hm 4B 148
SR8: Eas C 7C 160
Vincent Ter. DH9: Ann P 6A 124
Vindomora Rd. DH8: Ebc 5G 107
Vindomora Roman Fort (Remains) 4G 107
Vindomora Vs. DH8: Ebc 4G 107
Vine Cl. NE8: Gate 4E 82
Vine Ct. NE46: Hex 2D 70
Vine La. NE1: Newc T 3F 4 (7F 63)
Vine La. E. NE1: Newc T 3G 4 (7G 63)
Vine Pl. DH4: Hou S 2E 144
SR1: Sund 5H 7 (2E 118)
Vine St. NE28: W'snd 4G 65
NE33: S Shi 7H 67
Vine Ter. NE46: Hex 2D 70
Viola Cres. DH2: Ous 6H 113
DH7: Sac 1E 152
Viola St. NE37: Wash 7H 101
Viola Ter. NE16: Whi 7H 81
Violet Cl. NE4: Benw 2K 81
Violet St. DH4: Hou S 2D 144
SR4: Sund 3F 7 (1D 118)
(Deptford Rd.)
SR4: Sund 2G 117
(Primrose St.)
Violet Ter. DH4: Bour 6H 129
Virgin Active (Wearside)
Silksworth 4K 131
Viscount Cl. DH9: Ann P 4K 123
(not continuous)
NE27: Shir 7J 37
Viscount Rd. SR3: New S 2C 132
Vivian Cres. DH2: Ches S 7A 128
Vivian Sq. SR6: Ful 5F 105
Volary Gro. NE24: Bly 5K 23
Voltage Ter. DH4: Nbot 5D 130
Vroom Car Retail Pk. NE29: N Shi 7A 48
Vue Cinema
Cramlington 4J 25
Gateshead 3H 83
Vulcan Pl. NE22: Bed 1J 21
SR6: Ful 6F 105
Vulcan Ter. NE12: Longb 3C 46

W

Waddington St. DH1: Dur 2A 6 (2K 165)
Wadham Cl. SR8: Pet 7K 171
Wadham Ct. SR2: Ryh 2G 133
Wadham Ter. NE34: S Shi 1H 87
Wadsley Sq. SR2: Sund 5G 119
Waggonway, The NE42: Pru 3E 76
Wagon Way NE28: W'snd 3H 65
Wagonway Dr. NE13: Haz 1A 44
Wagonway Ind. Est. NE31: Heb 5J 65
Wagonway Rd. NE31: Heb 6H 65
Wagtail Cl. NE21: Winl 6C 80
Wagtail La. DH9: Crag, Stly 1E 138
Wagtail Ter. DH9: Crag 7J 125
Wakefield Av. NE34: S Shi 1D 88
Wakenshaw Rd. DH1: Dur 1D 166
WALBOTTLE 4K 59
Walbottle Hall Gdns. NE15: Walb 4A 60
Walbottle Rd. NE15: Newb, Walb 4K 59
Walbridge Way NE34: S Shi 1F 87
Walcher Gro. NE8: Gate 5K 83
Walden Cl. DH2: Ous 6F 113
Waldo St. NE29: N Shi 7H 49
WALDRIDGE 1G 141
Waldridge Cl. NE37: Wash 2E 114
Waldridge Fell Country Pk. 2G 141
Waldridge Gdns. NE9: Wrek 4B 100
Waldridge Hall Ct. DH2: Ches S 2H 141
Waldridge La.
DH2: Ches M, Ches S, Wald 1G 141
Waldridge Rd. DH2: Ches S, Wald 1G 141
Waldron Sq. SR2: Sund 5G 119
WALKER 1E 84
Walker Activity Dome 2D 84
Walkerburn NE23: Cra 7K 25
Walker Ct. NE16: Whi 7G 81
(off Fellside Rd.)
Walkerdene Ho. NE6: Walk 5F 65
WALKERGATE 5C 64
Walkergate DH1: Dur 2C 6 (2A 166)
Walkergate (Park & Tram) 5C 64
Walker Ga. Ind. Est. NE6: Walk 7F 65
Walkergate Station (Metro) 5C 64
Walker Gro. NE6: Walk 5D 64
Walker Pk. Cl. NE6: Walk 2E 84
Walker Pk. Gdns. NE6: Walk 2E 84
Walker Pl. NE30: N Shi 6J 49
WALKER RIVERSIDE 2F 85
Walker Riverside Ind. Pk.
NE6: Walk 1F 85
Walker Rd. NE6: Byke 6N 5 (1K 83)
NE6: Walk 2B 84
Walker St. DH6: Bowb 5H 177
Walker Ter. NE8: Gate 10H 5 (4G 83)
Walker Vw. NE10: Fell 6B 84
WALKERVILLE 4E 64
Walkley Rd. NE24: Bly 4K 23
Wallace Av. NE16: Whi 6J 81
Wallace Gdns. NE9: Wrek 4C 100
Wallace St. DH4: Hou S 2D 144
NE2: Newc T 1B 4 (5E 62)
NE11: Dun 5C 82
SR5: Monkw 6E 104
Wallace Ter. NE25: Sea D 7J 27
(off Martindale Pl.)
NE40: Ryton 1G 79
Wall Cl. NE3: Gos 7C 44
Walled Gdn., The DH4: Hou S 2J 143
Waller Ter. DH5: Hou S 3E 144
(not continuous)
Wallflower Av. SR8: Hord 5D 172
Wallinfen NE10: Hew 2D 100
Wallingford Av. SR2: Sund 6G 119
Wallington Av. NE13: Bru V 5C 34
NE30: Cull 3G 49
Wallington Cl. NE21: Blay 4C 80
NE22: Bed 6A 18
Wallington Ct. NE3: Ki Pk 5K 43
NE12: Kil 1A 46
NE25: Sea D 7H 27
NE30: Cull 3H 49
Wallington Dr. NE15: Lem 5E 60
Wallington Gro. NE33: S Shi 2K 67
Wallington Rd. NE63: Ash 5D 12
Wallis St. DH4: Pen 1B 130
NE10: Fell 6B 84
NE33: S Shi 2J 67
Wallnook La. DH7: Lang P, Wit G 4K 151
WALL NOOK 4K 151
Wallnook La. DH7: Lang P 4K 151
Wallridge Dr. NE25: H'wll 1J 37
WALLSEND 4F 65
Wallsend Dene 2G 65
Wallsend Rd. NE29: N Shi 2C 66
(not continuous)
Wallsend Station (Metro) 4G 65
Wall St. NE3: Gos 7C 44
Wall Ter. NE6: Walk 6C 64
Walmer Ter. NE9: Eigh B 6B 100
Walnut Gdns. NE8: Gate 6E 82
Walnut Pl. NE3: Ken 2B 62
Walpole Cl. SR7: S'hm 4H 147
Walpole Cl. SR4: Sund 2B 118
Walpole St. NE6: Walk 5C 64
NE33: S Shi 4J 67
Walsham Cl. NE24: Bly 4F 23
Walsh Av. NE31: Heb 6J 65
Walsingham NE38: Wash 5G 115
Walter St. NE13: Bru V 5C 34
NE32: Jar 5B 66
Walter Ter. DH5: Eas L 2H 157
NE4: Newc T 3A 4 (7C 62)
Walter Thomas St. SR5: S'wck 5B 104
Waltham NE38: Wash 4H 115
Waltham Cl. NE28: W'snd 2D 64
Waltham Pl. NE5: Blak 3H 61
Walton Av. NE24: Cow 1G 23
NE29: N Shi 5F 49
SR7: S'hm 4H 147
Walton Cl. DH9: Stly 4G 125
Walton Dr. NE62: Chop 1H 17
Walton Gdns. NE28: W'snd 3A 66
Walton La. SR1: Sund 1G 119
Walton Pk. NE29: N Shi 4F 49
Walton Rd. NE5: Den M 4G 61
NE38: Wash 2A 116
Walton's Bldgs. DH7: Ush M 2B 164
(off Temperance Ter.)
Walton's Ter. DH7: New B 4B 164
Walton Ter. DH8: Cons 5J 121
DH8: C'sde 4C 134
TS28: Win 4F 181
Walwick Av. NE29: N Shi 6D 48
Walwick Fell NE15: Scot 2H 81
Walwick Rd. NE25: Well 6B 38
Walworth Av. NE34: S Shi 7E 68
Walworth Gro. NE32: Jar 3B 86
Walworth Rd. SR5: Sund 6J 103
Wandsworth Rd. NE6: Heat 2N 5 (6K 63)
Wanless La. NE46: Hex 2D 70
Wanless Ter. DH1: Dur 1D 6 (2B 166)
Wanley St. NE24: Bly 1J 23
Wanlock Cl. NE23: Cra 7A 26
Wanny Rd. NE22: Bed 7K 17
Wansbeck NE38: Wash 7E 114
Wansbeck Av. DH9: Stly 4F 125
NE24: News 3J 23
NE30: Cull 1J 49
NE62: Stake 7J 11
Wansbeck Bus. Cen. NE63: Ash 3K 11
Wansbeck Bus. Pk. NE63: Ash 2K 11
Wansbeck Cl. DH2: Ous 2H 127
NE16: Sun 4G 97
Wansbeck Ct. NE61: Mor 7G 9
(off Wansbeck St.)
SR8: Pet 1A 182
Wansbeck Cres. NE61: Peg 4A 10
Wansbeck Gro. DH8: Lead 4B 122
NE25: New Hart 4H 27
Wansbeck M. NE34: S Shi 1J 87
NE63: Ash 3K 11
Wansbeck Pl. NE61: Mor 6E 8
Wansbeck Riverside Cvn. Pk.
NE63: Ash 6H 11
Wansbeck Riverside Pk. 6J 11
Wansbeck Rd. NE3: Gos 6C 44
NE23: Dud 3H 35
NE32: Jar 1A 86
NE63: Ash 3J 11
Wansbeck Rd. Sth. NE3: Gos 6C 44
Wansbeck Road Station (Metro) 6C 44
Wansbeck Sq. NE63: Ash 3A 12
Wansbeck St. NE17: C'wl 6A 94
NE61: Mor 7G 9
NE63: N Sea 7E 12
Wansbeck Ter. NE23: Dud 3H 35
NE62: W Sle 1B 18
Wansbeck Vw. NE62: Stake 7K 11
Wansdyke NE61: Mor 6C 8
Wansdyke Grange NE61: Mor 5E 8
Wansfell Av. NE5: Ken 2K 61
Wansford Av. NE5: Den M 4H 61
Wansford Way NE16: Whi 3F 97
Wantage Av. NE29: N Shi 1D 66
Wantage Rd. DH1: Carr 6H 155
Wantage St. NE33: S Shi 6K 67
Wapping NE24: Bly 1K 23
Wapping St. NE33: S Shi 1H 67
Warbeck Cl. NE3: Ki Pk 6H 43
Warburton Cres. NE9: Low F 6J 83
Warcop Ct. NE3: Ki Pk 5A 44
Ward Ct. SR2: Sund 3G 119
Warden Gro. DH5: Hou S 3F 145
WARDEN LAW 1K 145
Wardenlaw NE10: Hew 2D 100
Warden Law La. SR3: Silk 3A 132
Wardill Gdns. NE9: Low F 7K 83
Ward La. NE43: Mic 7B 76
Wardle Av. NE33: S Shi 4A 68
Wardle Dr. NE23: Dud 3K 35
Wardle Gdns. NE10: Hew 7C 84
Wardles Ter. DH1: Dur 3A 6
Wardle St. DH9: Stly 6E 124
NE3: Gos 7G 45
Wardle Ter. NE40: Craw 2D 78
WARDLEY 6G 85
Wardley Ct. NE10: Ward 6H 85
Wardley Dr. NE10: Ward 6H 85
Wardley Grn. NE10: Bill Q, Heb 4G 85
Wardley Hall Cotts. NE10: Ward 6F 85
Wardley La. NE10: Ward 6H 85
Wardroper Ho. NE6: Walk 2E 84
Ward St. SR2: Sund 3G 119
Warenford Cl. NE23: Cra 6A 26
Warenford Pl. NE5: Fen 6J 61
Warenmill Cl. NE15: Lem 6B 60
Warennes St. SR4: Sund 1A 118
Warenton Pl. NE29: N Shi 3B 48
Warenton Way NE13: Ki Pk 4A 44
Waring Av. NE26: Sea S 3B 28
Waring Ter. SR7: Dalt D 4H 147
Wark Av. NE27: Shir 7K 37
NE29: N Shi 6C 48
Wark Ct. NE3: Gos 1G 63
Wark Cres. NE32: Jar 4B 86
Warkdale Av. NE24: Cow 2E 22
Wark St. DH3: Ches S 1A 142
Warkworth Av. NE24: News 4J 23
NE26: Whit B 6G 39
NE28: W'snd 1G 65
NE34: S Shi 6D 68
SR8: Hord 4D 172
Warkworth Cl. NE38: Wash 4F 115
Warkworth Cres. NE3: Gos 6D 44
NE15: Newb 6J 59
NE63: Ash 4A 12
SR7: S'hm 3G 147
Warkworth Dr. DH2: Ches S 1J 141
NE13: W Op 4E 34
NE61: Peg 4B 10
Warkworth Gdns. NE10: Fell 6A 84
Warkworth Rd. DH1: Dur 4A 154
Warkworth St. NE15: Lem 7C 60
Warkworth Ter. NE30: Tyne 4K 49
NE32: Jar 3B 86
Warkworth Woods
NE3: Gos, W Op 2D 44
Warnbrook Cres. TS27: B Col 3K 183
Warnebrook Av. SR7: Mur 1F 159
(off W. Coronation St.)
Warnham Av. SR2: Sund 6G 119
Warnhead Rd. NE22: Bed 7K 17
Warren Av. NE6: Walk 5E 64
Warren Cl. DH4: Nbot 5C 130
Warren Ct. NE63: Ash 5A 12
Warrenmor NE10: Hew 7E 84
Warren Sq. SR1: Sund 7H 105
SR8: Hord 6E 172
Warren St. SR8: Hord 5E 172
Warrens Wlk. NE21: Winl 5A 80
Warrington Gro. NE29: N Shi 1D 66
Warrington Rd. NE3: Fawd 6A 44
NE4: Elsw 2C 82
Warton Ter. NE6: Heat 5A 64
Warwick Av. DH8: C'sde 3C 134
NE16: Whi 2G 97
Warwick Cl. NE16: Whi 2G 97
NE23: Seg 2C 36
Warwick Ct. DH1: Dur 5J 165
NE3: Ki Pk 5K 43
NE8: Gate 4H 83

Warwick Dr. DH5: Hou S .4E **144**
NE16: Whi .2H **97**
NE37: Wash .5H **101**
SR3: E Her .2J **131**
Warwick Gro. NE22: Bed .7F **17**
Warwick Hall Wlk. NE7: H Hea .2B **64**
Warwick Pl. SR8: Pet .5K **171**
Warwick Rd. NE5: W Dent .5E **60**
NE28: W'snd .4F **65**
NE31: Heb .3K **85**
NE33: S Shi .5K **67**
NE34: S Shi .5K **67**
Warwickshire Dr. DH1: Carr .2G **167**
Warwick St.
NE2: Heat, Newc T .2K **5** (6H **63**)
NE6: Heat .2K **5** (6H **63**)
NE8: Gate .4H **83**
NE24: Bly .5G **23**
SR5: Monkw .6F **105**
Warwick Ter. SR3: New S .1C **132**
Warwick Ter. Nth. *SR3: New S* .*1C 132*
(off Warwick Ter.)
Warwick Ter. W. SR3: New S .1C **132**
Wasdale Cl. NE23: Cra .7A **26**
SR8: Pet .6C **172**
Wasdale Ct. SR6: Seab .2E **104**
Wasdale Cres. NE21: Winl .6B **80**
Wasdale Rd. NE5: Den M .5H **61**
WASHINGTON .7H **101**
Washington Arts Cen. .6H **115**
Washington 'F' Pit .1G **115**
Washington Gdns. NE9: Wrek .4A **100**
Washington Highway
DH4: Pen .5G **115**
NE37: Wash .7E **100**
NE38: Wash .5G **115**
Washington Leisure Cen. .4G **115**
Washington M. NE30: N Shi .5H **49**
Washington Old Hall .2J **115**
Washington Rd. NE36: W Bol .3E **102**
NE37: Wash, W Bol .7A **102**
SR5: Sund .5D **102**
WASHINGTON SERVICE AREA .5C **114**
Washington Sq. SR8: Eas .1K **171**
WASHINGTON STAITHES .5A **116**
Washington St. SR4: Sund .2B **118**
Washington Ter. NE30: N Shi .5H **49**
WASHINGTON VILLAGE .2H **115**
Washington Wetland Cen. .3C **116**
Washingwell La. NE16: Whi .7J **81**
Washingwell Pk. NE16: Whi .1J **97**
Waskerley Cl. NE16: Sun .4G **97**
Waskerley Dr. DH6: Shot C .5D **170**
Waskerley Gdns. NE9: Wrek .4B **100**
Waskerley Rd. NE38: Wash .3K **115**
Watch Ho. Cl. NE29: N Shi .2G **67**
Watch House Mus. .5H **105**
Watcombe Cl. NE37: Wash .5K **101**
Water Activities Cen. .7K **49**
Waterbeach Pl. NE5: Den M .3H **61**
Waterbeck Cl. NE23: Cra .7A **26**
Waterbury Cl. SR5: S'wck .4B **104**
Waterbury Rd. NE3: Gos .3D **44**
Waterfield Rd. NE22: E Sle .4F **19**
Waterford Cl. DH5: E Rain .6D **144**
NE26: Sea S .4D **28**
Waterford Cres. NE26: Whit B .7H **39**
Waterford Grn. NE63: Ash .7B **12**
SR4: Sund .4G **117**
Waterford Pk. NE13: Bru V .5B **34**
Watergate NE1: Newc T .7G **4** (2G **83**)
Watergate Bank NE11: Rave .3A **98**
WATERGATE ESTATE .1J **97**
Watergate Rd. DH8: C'sde .4B **134**
Water Ho. Rd. DL15: Crook .7E **162**
WATERHOUSES .6B **162**
Waterhouses DH4: S Row .5K **129**
Water La. NE15: Hor .5E **56**
Waterloo Ct. NE37: Wash .7J **101**
Waterloo Pl. NE29: N Shi .6G **49**
SR1: Sund .4J **7** (2F **119**)
Waterloo Rd. NE24: Bly .2H **23**
NE25: Well .6A **38**
NE37: Wash .5K **101**
(Barton Cl.)
NE37: Wash .6J **101**
(Brackley)
Waterloo Sq. NE1: Newc T .7D **4**
NE33: S Shi .2J **67**
Waterloo St. NE1: Newc T .7D **4** (2E **82**)
NE21: Winl .5A **80**
Waterloo Va. NE33: S Shi .2J **67**
Waterloo Wlk. *NE37: Wash* .*7J 101*
(off Waterloo Ct.)
Waterlow Cl. SR5: S'wck .3B **104**
Watermark, The
NE11: Dun, Swa .3H **81**
Watermill NE40: Ryton .1G **79**
Watermill La. NE10: Fell, Hew .6C **84**
Watermill Pk. NE10: Fell .7B **84**
Water Row NE15: Newb .6J **59**
Waterside NE61: Mor .7F **9**
SR4: Cox G .5B **116**
Waterside, The SR7: S'hm .2C **148**
Waterside Ct. NE63: N Sea .7E **12**
Waterside Dr. NE11: Dun .4A **82**
Waterside Gdns. NE38: Wash .7J **115**
Waterside Pk. NE31: Heb .7G **65**
Waterson Cres. DH7: Wit G .2D **152**
Water St. DH7: Sac .7E **140**
NE4: Newc T .10A **4** (3D **82**)
Waterview Pk. NE38: Wash .3C **116**
Waterville Pl. NE29: N Shi .7G **49**
Waterville Rd. NE29: N Shi .1D **66**
Waterville Ter. NE29: N Shi .7G **49**
Waterworks, The SR2: Ryh .4G **133**
SR7: Cold H .7J **147**
Waterworks Rd. SR1: Sund .4F **7** (2D **118**)
SR2: Ryh .4G **133**
Waterworld .4G **77**
Watford Cl. SR5: S'wck .3B **104**
Watkin Cres. SR7: Mur .7E **146**
Watling Av. SR7: S'hm .4G **147**
Watling Pl. NE9: Low F .1K **99**
Watling St. DH8: Lead .5B **122**
NE45: Corb .7D **52**
Watling St. Bungs. DH8: Lead .4A **122**
Watling Way DH7: Lan .7J **137**
Watson Av. NE23: Dud .3H **35**
NE34: S Shi .1D **88**
Watson Cl. DH6: Whe H .2C **180**
SR7: Dalt D .4H **147**
Watson Cres. TS29: Trim S .7C **180**
Watson Gdns. NE28: W'snd .2A **66**
Watson Pl. NE34: S Shi .1D **88**
Watson's Bldgs. DH7: Edm .3D **140**
Watson St. DH8: B'hill .5G **121**
DH9: Stly .1F **125**
NE8: Gate .5E **82**
NE16: Burn .2B **110**
NE32: Jar .5C **66**
NE39: H Spen .2E **94**
Watson Ter. NE35: Bol C .7F **87**
NE61: Mor .7G **9**
Watt's La. NE64: Newb S .2J **13**
Watts Moses Ho. *SR1: Sund* .*1H 119*
(off High St. E.)
Watt's Slope NE26: Whit B .5G **39**
Watt St. NE8: Gate .7F **83**
SR7: Mur .7E **146**
Wavendon Cres. SR4: Sund .4K **117**
Waveney Gdns. DH9: Stly .5E **124**
Waveney Rd. SR8: Pet .1K **181**
Waverdale Av. NE6: Walk .6E **64**
Waverdale Way NE33: S Shi .7H **67**
Waverley NE33: S Shi .2J **67**
Waverley Av. NE22: Bed .7A **18**
(not continuous)
NE25: Monks .7F **39**
Waverley Cl. DH6: Shot C .5D **170**
NE21: Winl .6K **79**
Waverley Ct. NE22: Bed .6A **18**
Waverley Cres. NE15: Lem .6D **60**
Waverley Dr. NE22: Bed .6A **18**
(not continuous)
Waverley Lodge NE2: Newc T .1J **5**
Waverley Pl. NE64: Newb S .2J **13**
Waverley Rd. NE4: Newc T .8A **4** (2D **82**)
NE9: Low F .5J **99**
Waverley Ter. DH9: Dip .7J **109**
SR4: Sund .1A **118**
Waverton Cl. NE23: Cra .7K **25**
Waves at Whitley Bay .4F **39**
Wawn St. NE33: S Shi .5K **67**
Waxwing NE38: Wash .6D **114**
Wayfarer Rd. SR5: S'wck .6C **104**
Wayland Sq. SR2: Sund .7G **119**
Wayman St. SR5: Monkw .6E **104**
Wayside DH6: Crox .7K **175**
DH6: Whe H .4A **180**
NE15: Scot .1H **81**
NE34: S Shi .7D **68**
SR2: Sund .4D **118**
Wayside Ct. DH7: Bearp .1D **164**
Wealcroft NE10: Hew .3D **100**
Wealcroft Ct. NE10: Hew .2D **100**
Wealleans Cl. NE63: N Sea .4F **13**
WEAR .6F **115**
Wear Av. DH8: Lead .4B **122**
Wear Ct. NE34: S Shi .1J **87**
Wear Cres. DH3: Gt Lum .3F **143**
Weardale Av. NE6: Walk .6E **64**
NE12: Longb .4A **46**
NE24: Cow .1D **22**
NE28: W'snd .1F **65**
NE37: Wash .7G **101**
SR6: Seab .1G **105**
Weardale Cres. DH4: Pen .2B **130**
Weardale Ho. NE38: Wash .4F **115**
Weardale Pk. DH6: Whe H .2C **180**
Weardale St. DH5: Hett H .2E **156**
Weardale Ter. DH3: Ches S .7B **128**
DH9: Ann P .5A **124**
Weardale Way DH3: Gt Lum .4E **142**
(not continuous)
Wearfield SR5: Sund .6A **104**
Wearhead Dr. SR4: Sund .4D **118**
Wear Ind. Est. NE37: Wash .6F **115**
NE38: Wash .6F **115**
Wear Lodge DH3: Ches S .2A **128**
Wearmouth Av. SR5: Monkw .5E **104**
Wearmouth Dr. SR5: Monkw .5E **104**
Wearmouth St. SR6: Roker .6F **105**
Wear Rd. DH9: Stly .3F **125**
NE31: Heb .2J **85**
Wearside Dr. DH1: Dur .1D **6** (2B **166**)
Wear St. DH3: Ches S .7B **128**
DH4: Hou S .3A **144**
DH5: Hett H .7G **145**
DH8: Cons .7J **121**
NE17: C'wl .6K **93**
NE32: Jar .6B **66**
SR1: Sund .2H **119**
SR4: Sund .1G **117**
SR5: S'wck .6C **104**
SR7: S'hm .3B **148**
Wear Ter. NE38: Wash .4K **115**
SR8: Eas .7B **160**
Wear Vw. DH1: Dur .1E **6** (2B **166**)
SR4: Sund .1H **117**
Weathercock La. NE9: Low F .2H **99**
Weatherside NE21: Winl .5B **80**
Webb Av. SR7: Mur .6E **146**
SR7: S'hm .3G **147**
Webb Gdns. NE10: Ward .6E **84**
Webb Sq. SR8: Hord .3C **172**
Websters Bank SR4: Sund .7D **104**
Wedderburn Sq. NE63: Ash .4A **12**
Wedder Law NE23: Cra .7K **25**
Wedgewood Cotts. NE15: Lem .7D **60**
Wedgewood Rd. SR7: S'hm .4H **147**
Wedmore Rd. NE5: West .3D **60**
Weetman St. NE33: S Shi .4H **67**
Weetslade Ct. NE13: W Op .6E **34**
Weetslade Cres. NE23: Dud .4J **35**
Weetslade Ind. Est. NE23: Dud .6H **35**
Weetslade Rd. NE23: Dud .3H **35**
Weetslade Ter. NE23: Dud .6K **35**
Weetwood Rd. NE23: Cra .6A **26**
Weidner Rd. NE15: Benw .7K **61**
Welbeck Grn. NE6: Walk .1C **84**
Welbeck Rd. NE6: Byke, Walk .1A **84**
NE62: Chop .1G **17**
Welbeck Ter. NE61: Peg .3B **10**
NE63: Ash .5B **12**
Welburn Cl. NE42: O'ham .1D **76**
Welbury Way NE23: Cra .7K **25**
Welby Dr. DH7: Ush M .2B **164**
Weldon Av. SR2: Sund .6G **119**
Weldon Cl. DH6: Shot C .5D **170**
Weldon Ct. NE29: N Shi .6D **48**
Weldon Cres. NE7: H Hea .3K **63**
Weldon Pl. NE29: N Shi .4D **48**
Weldon Rd. NE12: Longb .6K **45**
NE23: E Cram .5C **26**
Weldon Ter. DH3: Ches S .7B **128**
Weldon Way NE3: Gos .6D **44**
Welfare Cl. SR8: Eas C .7C **160**
Welfare Cres. DH6: S Het .5D **158**
NE63: Ash .3D **12**
NE64: Newb S .3G **13**
TS27: B Col .2G **183**
Welfare Pk.
Horden .5D **172**
Welfare Rd. DH5: Hett H .6F **145**
(not continuous)
Welford Av. NE3: Gos .7C **44**
Welford Rd. DH8: C'sde .2E **134**
Welland Cl. SR8: Pet .1A **182**
Wellands Cl. SR6: Whit .5G **89**
Wellands Ct. SR6: Whit .5G **89**
Wellands Dr. SR6: Whit .5G **89**
Wellands La. SR6: Whit .5G **89**
Well Bank NE45: Corb .7D **52**
Well Bank Rd. NE37: Wash .6F **101**
Wellburn Cl. DH6: Shot C .5D **170**
Wellburn Pk. NE2: Jes .4J **63**
Wellburn Rd. NE37: Wash .6F **101**
Well Cl. Wlk. NE16: Whi .1G **97**
Well Dean NE42: Pru .3F **77**
Wellesley Ct. NE33: S Shi .7J **49**
Wellesley St. NE32: Jar .1B **86**
Wellesley Ter. NE4: Fen .1C **82**
WELLFIELD .6B **38**
.4G **181**
Wellfield Cl. NE15: Thro .4G **59**
Wellfield Ct. NE40: Craw .3C **78**
SR7: Mur .7D **146**
Wellfield La. NE5: West .3G **61**
Wellfield M. SR2: Ryh .4G **133**
Wellfield Rd. NE4: Benw .1K **81**
(not continuous)
NE39: Row G .6G **95**
SR7: Mur .7D **146**
TS28: Win .4G **181**
Wellfield Rd. Nth. TS28: Win .4G **181**
Wellfield Rd. Sth. TS28: Win .4G **181**
Wellfield Ter. *NE10: Bill Q* .*5F 85*
(off Shields Rd.)
NE10: Wind N .7A **84**
TS27: Win .*4H 181*
(off Wellfield Rd.)
Wellgarth Rd. NE37: Wash .6F **101**
Wellhead Ct. NE63: Ash .3J **11**
Wellhead Dean Rd. NE61: Chop .5H **11**
NE63: Ash .5H **11**
Wellhead Ter. NE63: Ash .3J **11**
Wellhope NE38: Wash .1D **128**
Wellington Av. NE25: Well .6A **38**
Wellington Ct. NE10: Fell .6A **84**
NE37: Wash .7J **101**
Wellington Dr. NE33: S Shi .1J **67**
Wellington La. SR4: Sund .1F **7** (7D **104**)
Wellington Pl. NE32: Jar .6C **66**
Wellington Rd. NE11: Dun .5K **81**
(not continuous)
NE62: Stake .1J **17**
Wellington Row DH4: S Row .4C **130**
Wellington St. DH6: H Pitt .6B **156**
NE4: Newc T .4B **4** (7E **62**)
NE8: Gate .8H **5** (3G **83**)
NE10: Fell .6A **84**
NE15: Lem .7D **60**
NE24: Bly .2K **23**
(not continuous)
NE31: Heb .1H **85**
Wellington St. E. NE24: Bly .1K **23**
Wellington St. W. NE29: N Shi .7G **49**
Wellington Wlk. NE37: Wash .7J **101**
Well La. NE9: Low F .3H **99**
NE27: Mur .2B **48**
(not continuous)
Wellmere Rd. SR2: Sund .7H **119**
Well Ridge Cl. NE25: Monks .5C **38**
Well Ridge Pk. NE25: Monks .4C **38**
Well Rd. NE43: Pains .2H **91**
Wells Cl. NE7: H Hea .1B **64**
Wells Cres. SR7: S'hm .3H **147**
Wells Gdns. NE9: Low F .5H **99**
Wells Gro. DH1: Dur .4C **154**
NE34: S Shi .6C **68**
Wellshede NE10: Hew .7F **85**
Wells St. NE35: Bol C .5E **86**
Well St. SR4: Sund .2B **118**
Wellway NE32: Jar .4B **86**
NE61: Mor .6F **9**
Wellway Ct. NE61: Mor .6F **9**
Wellwood Gdns. NE61: Mor .7G **9**
Welsh Ter. DH9: Ann P .6A **124**
WELTON .2H **55**
Welton Cl. NE43: Pains .1K **91**
Welwyn Av. NE22: Bed .5B **18**
Welwyn Cl. NE28: W'snd .1D **64**
SR5: Sund .7G **103**
Wembley Av. NE25: Monks .7E **38**
Wembley Cl. SR5: S'wck .4B **104**
Wembley Gdns. NE24: Camb .2F **19**
Wembley Rd. SR5: S'wck .4B **104**
Wembley Ter. NE24: Camb .2F **19**
Wendover Cl. SR5: S'wck .3A **104**
Wendover Way SR5: S'wck .3A **104**
Wenham Sq. SR2: Sund .4D **118**
Wenlock NE38: Wash .4G **115**
Wenlock Dr. NE29: N Shi .4E **48**
Wenlock Pl. NE34: S Shi .2G **87**
Wenlock Rd. NE34: S Shi .1F **87**
Wensley Cl. DH2: Ous .7G **113**
NE5: Blak .1J **61**
Wensleydale NE28: W'snd .7D **46**
Wensleydale Av. DH4: Pen .2A **130**
NE37: Wash .7G **101**
Wensleydale Dr. NE12: Longb .4B **46**
Wensleydale Ter. NE24: Bly .3K **23**
Wentbridge SR5: S'wck .3B **104**
Wentworth NE33: S Shi .4A **68**
Wentworth Cl. NE10: Fell .7B **84**
Wentworth Ct. NE20: Darr H .7G **31**
Wentworth Dr. NE37: Wash .5G **101**
Wentworth Gdns. NE25: Monks .7C **38**
Wentworth Grange NE3: Gos .1F **63**
Wentworth Leisure Cen. .1D **70**
Wentworth Pl. NE46: Hex .1D **70**
Wentworth Ter. SR4: Sund .4F **7** (1D **118**)
Wentworth Way NE63: N Sea .4E **12**
Werdohl Bus. Pk. DH8: Cons .4J **121**
Werdohl Way DH8: Cons .4J **121**
Werhale Grn. NE10: Fell .6B **84**
Wesley Cl. DH7: Sac .7D **140**
DH9: Stly .2G **125**
Wesley Ct. DH7: Lang M .7G **165**
DH9: Ann P .4K **123**
NE10: Fell .5A **84**
NE12: Kil .3G **47**
NE21: Blay .3D **80**
Wesley Dr. NE12: Kil .3F **47**
Wesley Gdns. DH8: C'sde .4C **134**
Wesley Gro. NE40: Craw .3C **78**
Wesley Lea DH8: C'sde .4D **134**
Wesley Mt. NE40: Craw .3C **78**
Wesley Sq. NE1: Newc T .7J **5** (2H **83**)
Wesley St. DH8: B'hill .5F **121**
DH8: Cons .7H **121**
NE2: Newc T .3J **5** (7H **63**)
NE9: Low F .2H **99**
NE33: S Shi .2J **67**
NE42: Pru .4F **77**
Wesley Ter. DH2: P Fel .4G **127**
DH3: Ches S .6A **128**
DH6: S Hil .3C **168**
DH8: C'sde .4D **134**
DH9: Ann P .5K **123**
DH9: Dip .7H **109**
NE42: Pru .4F **77**
Wesley Way NE12: Kil .3F **47**
NE15: Thro .3H **59**
SR7: S'hm .3H **147**
Wessex Cl. SR5: S'wck .3B **104**
Wessington Ind. Est. SR5: Sund .6J **103**
Wessington Ter. NE37: Wash .1H **115**
Wessington Way SR5: Sund .1F **117**
West Acre DH8: Shot B .4E **120**
Westacre Gdns. NE5: Fen .6J **61**
West Acres NE13: Din .4H **33**
NE21: Blay .4D **80**
Westacres Av. NE16: Whi .2H **97**
Westacres Cres. NE15: Benw .7J **61**
WEST ALLOTMENT .3J **47**
W. Allotment By-Pass NE27: Shir .2H **47**
West Av. DH2: Ches M .3J **141**
NE3: Gos .1E **62**
NE5: West .3F **61**
NE12: Longb .6B **46**
(Thornhill Rd.)
NE12: Longb .3D **46**
(Young Rd.)
NE25: Monks .6E **38**
NE29: N Shi .7D **48**
NE34: S Shi .7A **68**
NE38: Wash .7F **115**
NE39: Row G .6H **95**
NE62: Chop .1F **17**
SR6: Whit .5G **89**
SR7: Mur .1E **158**
SR8: Eas C .6C **160**
TS27: B Col .1H **183**
West Bailey NE12: Kil .7A **36**
West Bank *NE40: Craw* .*3C 78*
(off Bank Top)
West Block DH7: Wit G .3C **152**
WEST BOLDON .7G **87**

Westbourne Av. NE3: Gos 5E 44
NE6: Walk 5D 64
NE8: Gate 6G 83
NE62: Stake 6J 11
Westbourne Cotts. DH4: S Row 3A 130
Westbourne Dr. DH4: S Row 3A 130
Westbourne Gdns. NE6: Walk 7E 64
Westbourne Gro. NE46: Hex 1B 70
Westbourne Rd. SR1: Sund 5F 7 (2D 118)
Westbourne Ter. DH4: S Row 3A 130
NE25: Sea D 7J 27
WEST BRANDON 7F 163
West Bri. St. DH4: Pen 1J 129
NE24: Camb 5H 19
Westbrooke Ho. SR2: Sund 4F 119
W. Brunton Farm Cotts. NE13: Haz 1K 43
Westburn NE40: Craw 3C 78
(not continuous)
Westburn Cotts. NE40: Craw 3C 78
Westburn Gdns. NE28: W'snd 1D 64
Westburn M. NE40: Craw 3C 78
Westburn Ter. SR6: Ful 5G 105
Westbury Av. NE6: Walk 5E 64
Westbury Ct. NE12: Longb 7J 45
Westbury Rd. NE29: N Shi 4F 49
Westbury St. SR4: Sund 1D 118
WEST CHIRTON 6C 48
W. Chirton Ind. Est. (South)
NE29: N Shi 6C 48
W. Chirton (Middle) Trad. Est.
NE29: N Shi 5B 48
W. Chirton Nth. Ind. Est. NE29: N Shi 5A 48
WEST CHOPWELL 5K 93
Westcliff Cl. SR8: Eas 1J 171
Westcliffe Rd. SR6: Seab 3H 105
Westcliffe Way NE34: S Shi 3F 87
West Clifton NE12: Kil 7A 36
West Copperas NE15: Lem 6E 60
W. Coronation St. SR7: Mur 7F 147
Westcott Av. NE33: S Shi 4A 68
Westcott Dr. DH1: Dur 6J 153
Westcott Rd. NE34: S Shi 1J 87
SR8: Pet 5B 172
Westcott Ter. DH4: Pen 1C 130
West Ct. DH1: Dur 7B 6 (5A 166)
NE24: Bly 3G 23
West Cres. NE10: Ward 6G 85
NE17: C'wl 1K 107
SR8: Eas 7A 160
Westcroft SR6: Whit 5G 89
Westcroft Rd. NE12: Longb 5C 46
W. Dene Dr. NE30: N Shi 4G 49
WEST DENTON 3D 60
W. Denton Cl. NE15: Lem 5D 60
W. Denton Retail Pk. NE5: W Dent 3G 61
W. Denton Rd. NE15: Lem 5D 60
W. Denton Way NE5: W Dent 3D 60
West Dr. DH2: Ches S 7H 127
DH7: Lan 7J 137
NE24: News 5G 23
SR6: Clead 5A 88
W. Durham Office Pk. DH7: Lang M 1G 175
W. Ellen St. SR7: Mur 1F 159
W. Ellimore Vw. DH8: Cons 1K 135
West End NE26: Sea S 6D 28
NE46: Hex 2B 70
West End Ter. NE45: Corb 7D 52
NE46: Hex 2C 70
West End Ter. M. NE45: Corb 7D 52
Westerdale DH4: Pen 1J 129
NE28: W'snd 1D 64
Westerdale Pl. NE6: Walk 7F 65
Westerham Cl. SR5: S'wck 3B 104
WESTERHOPE 3F 61
Westerhope Gdns. NE5: Fen 4K 61
Westerhope Rd. NE38: Wash 3K 115
Westerhope Small Bus. Pk.
NE5: West 1E 60
Westerkirk NE23: Cra 7A 26
Western App. NE33: S Shi 6H 67
Western App. Ind. Est. *NE33: S Shi 4J 67*
(off Western App.)
Western Av. DH7: Esh W 3D 162
NE4: Benw 1A 82
NE5: W Dent 4D 60
NE11: T Vall 3E 98
NE25: Sea D 7F 27
NE42: Pru 4D 76
Western Ct. *NE26: Whit B 3F 39*
(off Western Way)
Western Dr. NE4: Benw 1B 82
Western Highway NE38: Wash 6C 114
WESTERN HILL 1K 165
Western Hill DH8: B'hill 4E 120
SR2: Ryh 2G 133
SR2: Sund 5F 7 (2D 118)
Westernhope Homes NE5: West 2E 60
Westernmoor NE37: Wash 2D 114
Western Pk. SR7: Hawt 4J 159
Western Rd. NE28: W'snd 3K 65
NE32: Jar 6A 66
Western Ter. NE23: Dud 3H 35
NE36: E Bol, W Bol 7G 87
NE37: Wash 1H 115
Western Ter. Nth. SR7: Mur 7F 147
Western Ter. Sth. SR7: Mur 7F 147
Western Vw. NE9: Eigh B 6A 100
Western Way NE20: Darr H 7E 30
NE21: Blay 4E 80
NE26: Whit B 3F 39
NE40: Ryton 2G 79
Westerwood SR3: Silk 4C 132
West Farm DH2: Ches S 7H 127
DH8: M'sly 6A 108
NE36: E Bol 7J 87
W. Farm Av. NE12: Longb 6H 45
W. Farm Ct. DH7: Bro 4E 164
DH8: M'sly 6A 108
NE12: Kil 2C 46
NE23: Cra 3K 25
West Farm Dr. NE17: C'wl 5A 94
W. Farm Grange DH8: M'sly 6A 108
W. Farm La. DH8: M'sly 6A 108
W. Farm M. NE5: Blak 2J 61
W. Farm Rd. NE6: Walk 6C 64
NE28: W'snd 2J 65
SR6: Clead 6D 88
W. Farm Wynd NE12: Longb 6H 45
Westfield NE3: Gos 3D 62
NE10: Hew 1C 100
NE23: Dud 3H 35
NE32: Jar 5C 86
NE61: Mor 1E 14
Westfield Av. NE3: Gos 2E 62
NE13: Bru V 5C 34
NE25: Monks 7D 38
NE40: Craw 3D 78
Westfield Cl. NE46: Hex 1B 70
Westfield Ct. NE28: W'snd 5F 65
NE32: Jar 7B 66
SR4: Sund 4A 118
Westfield Cres. NE9: Spri 6D 100
NE40: Craw 3D 78
NE64: Newb S 3H 13
Westfield Dr. NE3: Gos 2D 62
Westfield Gro. NE3: Gos 2D 62
SR4: Sund 4A 118
Westfield La. NE40: Ryton 7F 59
Westfield Pk. NE3: Gos 2E 62
NE28: W'snd 3E 64
Westfield Rd. NE8: Gate 6G 83
NE15: Benw 1J 81
Westfields DH9: Stly 4D 124
Westfield Ter. NE8: Gate 6G 83
NE9: Spri 6D 100
(off Windsor Rd.)
NE46: Hex 1B 70
Westfield Vw. NE23: Dud 2J 35
Westford Rd. NE62: Stake 7K 11
Westgarth NE5: West 1E 60
Westgarth Gro. DH6: Shot C 5D 170
Westgarth Ter. NE37: Wash 7J 101
Westgate NE61: Mor 1D 14
Westgate Av. SR3: New S 1C 132
Westgate Cl. NE25: Monks 5C 38
Westgate Ct. NE4: Newc T 5A 4 (1D 82)
Westgate Gro. SR3: New S 1C 132
Westgate Hill Ter.
NE4: Newc T 6C 4 (1E 82)
Westgate Rd. NE1: Newc T 6D 4 (1E 82)
NE4: Benw, Elsw, Newc T 5A 4 (7B 62)
W. George Potts St. NE33: S Shi 4J 67
West Grange SR5: S'wck 4E 104
Westgreen NE62: Sco G 3G 17
West Greens NE61: Mor 7G 9
West Gro. SR4: Sund 3H 117
SR7: S'hm 3H 147
W. Hartford Bus. Pk. NE23: E Har 6H 21
WEST HARTON 1J 87
West Haven DH8: Cons 6G 121
Westheath Av. SR2: Sund 7F 119
WEST HERRINGTON 2F 131
W. Hextol NE46: Hex 2B 70
W. Hextol Cl. NE46: Hex 2B 70
W. High Horse Cl. NE39: Row G 3A 96
West Hill NE61: Mor 1E 14
SR4: Sund 4A 118
Westhills DH9: Tant 6A 110
Westhills Cl. DH7: Sac 5D 140
West Holborn NE33: S Shi 4H 67
Westholme Gdns. NE15: Benw 7K 61
Westholme Ter. *SR2: Sund 6H 119*
(off Ryhope Rd.)
WEST HOLYWELL 5H 37
Westhope Cl. NE34: S Shi 6C 68
Westhope Rd. NE34: S Shi 6C 68
Westhouse *NE25: Monks 7E 38*
(off Front St.)
Westhouse Av. DH1: Dur 5K 165
WEST JESMOND 3G 63
W. Jesmond Av. NE2: Jes 3G 63
West Jesmond Station (Metro) 3G 63
WEST KYO 4K 123
Westlands DH6: Coxh 7J 177
NE5: Cha P 4C 60
NE7: H Hea 3J 63
NE26: Sea S 4B 28
NE30: Cull 3H 49
NE32: Jar 5D 86
Westlands, The SR4: Sund 3B 118
West La. DH3: Ches S 7A 128
DH6: S Het 4D 158
NE12: Kil 3B 46
NE16: Burn 6C 96
NE17: Ham 4K 107
NE21: Winl 6A 80
SR7: Hawt 4H 159
West Lawn SR2: Sund 4F 119
W. Lawrence St. SR1: Sund 2G 119
West Law Rd. DH8: Shot B 2F 121
WESTLEA 3H 147
West Lea DH4: New H 3D 130
DH7: Wit G 3D 152
NE21: Winl 6C 80
Westlea NE22: Bed 1F 21
Westlea Ct. DH7: Esh W 4E 162
Westlea Rd. DH4: Nbot 6C 130
SR7: S'hm 3H 147
West Leigh DH9: Tan L 1D 124
Westley Av. NE26: Whit B 2E 38
Westley Cl. NE26: Whit B 2E 38
Westline Ind. Est. DH2: Bir 6K 113
Westlings DH5: Hett H 7G 145
Westloch Rd. NE23: Cra 7K 25
Westmacott St. NE15: Newb 5J 59
(not continuous)
West Mdws. NE5: Cha P 1D 60
NE17: C'wl 5A 94
West Mdws. Dr. SR6: Clead 7C 88
West Mdws. Rd. SR6: Clead 6C 88
WEST MICKLEY 6A 76
Westminster Av. NE29: N Shi 4B 48
Westminster Cl. NE26: Whit B 7J 39
Westminster Cres. NE31: Heb 4J 85
Westminster Dr. NE11: Dun 1B 98
Westminster St. NE8: Gate 6F 83
SR2: Sund 6H 119
Westminster Way NE7: H Hea 1B 64
W. Moffett St. NE33: S Shi 4K 67
WEST MONKSEATON 7D 38
West Monkseaton Station (Metro) 7D 38
WEST MOOR 3K 45
W. Moor Ct. NE12: Longb 3K 45
W. Moor Dr. SR6: Clead 7C 88
Westmoor Dr. NE12: Longb 3K 45
Westmoor Rd. SR4: Sund 1K 117
Westmorland Av. NE22: Bed 7G 17
NE28: W'snd 3B 66
NE37: Wash 6H 101
NE64: Newb S 3H 13
Westmorland Ct. NE31: Heb 1H 85
Westmorland Gdns. NE9: Low F 2H 99
Westmorland La.
NE1: Newc T 7D 4 (2E 82)
Westmorland Retail Pk.
NE23: Cra 4H 25
Westmorland Ri. SR8: Pet 4K 171
Westmorland Rd.
NE1: Newc T 7D 4 (2E 82)
NE4: Elsw, Newc T 8A 4 (2B 82)
NE29: N Shi 5B 48
NE34: S Shi 6E 68
Westmorland St. NE28: W'snd 3G 65
Westmorland Wlk. NE4: Elsw 3B 82
Westmorland Way NE23: Cra 4H 25
West Mt. NE12: Kil 1A 46
SR4: Sund 3A 118
WESTOE 4A 68
Westoe Av. NE33: S Shi 4A 68
Westoe Dr. NE33: S Shi 4A 68
Westoe Rd. NE33: S Shi 3K 67
Westoe Village NE33: S Shi 5A 68
Weston Av. NE16: Whi 2F 97
Weston Vw. SR8: Pet 5A 172
W. Ousterley Rd. DH9: Stly 5F 125
Westover Gdns. NE9: Low F 7H 83
Westovian Theatre 1A 68
West Pde. DH8: Cons 7J 121
DH8: Lead 5A 122
NE4: Newc T 7A 4 (2D 82)
NE31: Heb 1H 85
West Pk. *NE11: Dun 5B 82*
(off Meadow La.)
NE61: Mor 1E 14
SR3: E Her 3H 131
West Pk. Gdns. NE21: Winl 5C 80
West Pk. Rd. NE8: Gate 7G 83
NE33: S Shi 5J 67
SR6: Clead 5C 88
West Pk. Vw. NE23: Dud 3H 35
NE33: S Shi 6J 67
West Pastures NE36: W Bol 3C 102
NE63: Ash 5K 11
WEST PELTON 3C 126
W. Percy Rd. NE29: N Shi 1E 66
W. Percy St. NE29: N Shi 7G 49
Westport Cl. SR5: S'wck 3B 104
West Promenade DH8: Cons 5H 121
West Quarter NE46: Hex 1B 70
West Quay Rd. SR5: Sund 6B 104
WEST RAINTON 1A 156
Westray DH2: Ches S 1J 141
Westray Cl. SR2: Ryh 1F 133
West Rig, The NE3: Ken 1A 62
West Riggs NE22: Bed 1H 21
West Rd. DH8: Shot B 5E 120
DH9: Ann P 5K 123
DH9: Tant 7A 110
NE4: Fen 5F 61
NE5: Den M 5F 61
NE15: Den M 5F 61
NE20: Pon 5H 31
NE22: Bed 6B 18
NE42: O'ham 2C 76
NE42: Pru 5C 76
NE43: Mic 6A 76
NE46: Hex 7A 50
West Rd. Crematorium
NE5: Fen 6H 61
West Row DH3: Bir 5C 114
West Row Ho. DH8: B'hill 5F 121
W. Salisbury St. NE24: Bly 1H 23
W. Shield Row Vs. DH9: Stly 1E 124
WEST SLEEKBURN 1B 18
W. Sleekburn Ind. Est.
NE22: W Sle 2B 18
W. Sleekburn Rd. NE22: W Sle 2C 18
W. Spencer Ter. NE15: Walb 4B 60
W. Stainton St. NE33: S Shi 4K 67
(Darras Ct.)
NE33: S Shi 4J 67
(W. George Potts St.)
W. Stevenson St. NE33: S Shi 4K 67
West St. DH2: Gra V 4C 126
DH3: Bir 4A 114
DH6: Hett 7C 176
DH6: Shot C 6E 170
DH8: Lead 5A 122
West St. DH9: Tan L 1D 124
NE8: Gate 9H 5 (3G 83)
NE16: Whi 7G 81
NE27: Shir 3H 47
NE28: W'snd 2E 64
NE31: Heb 6K 65
NE39: H Spen 3D 94
SR1: Sund 3H 7 (1E 118)
SR3: New S 1C 132
SR7: S'hm 3B 148
TS27: B Col 1G 183
West St. Cotts. TS27: B Col 2G 183
West Sunniside SR1: Sund 3K 7 (1F 119)
Westsyde NE20: Darr H 1E 40
West Ter. DH1: Dur 1A 6 (2K 165)
DH6: Coxh 7K 177
DH7: B'hpe 5D 138
NE26: Sea S 4D 28
NE45: Corb 7D 52
NE62: Stake 1A 18
W. Thorns Wlk. NE16: Whi 1G 97
West Thorp NE5: West 7F 43
Westvale NE15: Thro 3F 59
West Vallum NE15: Den M 6F 61
W. Victoria St. DH8: Cons 6H 121
West Vw. DH1: Dur 2C 166
DH3: Ches S 5A 128
DH4: Bour 6J 129
DH4: Hou S 7D 130
DH4: Pen 1B 130
DH4: S Row 5B 130
DH6: Has 3A 170
DH6: S Hil 3C 168
DH7: Esh W 4E 162
DH7: Mead 2E 174
DH7: Sac 7D 140
DH8: B'hill 4F 121
DH8: M'sly 1J 121
DH9: Stly 6E 124
NE4: Elsw 2B 82
NE9: Low F 3A 100
NE9: Spri 6C 100
NE11: Kib 2F 113
NE12: Longb 4B 46
NE13: W Op 4D 34
NE15: Lem 7C 60
NE16: Burn 2A 110
NE17: C'wl 5A 94
NE21: Blay 3C 80
NE22: Bed 5A 18
NE23: Cra 5A 26
NE23: Dud 3J 35
NE23: Seg 2D 36
NE24: Camb 2G 19
NE25: Ears 6A 38
NE35: Bol C 5D 86
NE37: Wash 7H 101
NE40: C Vale 7C 58
NE41: Wylam 7K 57
NE46: Acomb 4C 50
NE61: Fair M 2C 8
NE61: Peg 4A 10
NE63: Ash 3A 12
NE64: Newb S 2J 13
SR2: Ryh 3G 133
SR5: Sund 6H 103
SR6: Ful 4F 105
SR7: Dalt D 5H 147
SR7: Mur 1E 158
SR8: Eas 1K 171
SR8: Hord 5E 172
West Vw. Bk. NE9: Spri 6D 100
West Vw. Bldgs. NE30: Cull 1J 49
West Vw. Gdns. DH9: Stly 2E 124
West Vw. Ter. NE11: Dun 4A 82
NE46: Hex 3E 70
Westview Ter. DH9: Ann P 6J 123
West Vs. DH9: W Pelt 3B 126
West Wlk. DH3: Lam P 3E 128
West Walls NE1: Newc T 6D 4 (1E 82)
W. Walpole St. NE33: S Shi 4H 67
Westward Ct. NE5: West 2E 60
Westward Grn. NE25: Monks 7C 38
Westward Pl. NE38: Wash 7F 115
West Way NE11: Dun 6C 82
NE33: S Shi 6H 67
Westway NE15: Thro 2H 59
NE21: Winl 4B 80
SR8: Pet 7A 172
Westway Ind. Pk. NE15: Thro 2H 59
W. Wear St. SR1: Sund 2K 7 (1F 119)
Westwell Ct. NE3: Gos 1H 63
Westwood Av. NE6: Heat 4K 63
Westwood Cl. NE16: Burn 1B 110
Westwood Gdns. NE3: Ken 1A 62
NE9: Wrek 4B 100
NE38: Wash 3J 115
NE62: Stake 6H 11
Westwood La. NE17: Ham 3J 107
Westwood Rd. NE3: Gos 3E 44
Westwood St. SR4: Sund 2B 118
Westwood Ter. DH3: Ches S 7A 128
Westwood Vw. DH3: Ches S 1A 142
DH7: Sac 1D 152
NE40: Craw 3C 78
WEST WYLAM 3G 77
W. Wylam Dr. NE42: Pru 4G 77
West Wynd NE12: Kil 1A 46
Wetheral Gdns. NE9: Low F 4J 99
Wetheral Ter. NE6: Walk 2D 84
Wetherburn Av. SR7: Mur 7D 146
Wetherby Cl. DH8: Shot B 2F 121
NE63: Ash 5A 12
Wetherby Gro. NE8: Gate 7F 83
Wetherby Rd. SR2: Sund 7J 119
Wet 'n' Wild Water Pk. 3F 67

Wettondale Av. NE24: Cow 2E 22
Weybourne Lea SR7: S'hm 1A 148
Weybourne Sq. SR2: Sund 6G 119
Weyhill Av. NE29: N Shi 1D 66
Weymouth Dr. DH4: S Row 4K 129
SR7: Dalt D, S'hm 4H 147
Weymouth Gdns. NE9: Low F 5H 99
Weymouth Ho. NE4: Newc T 4C 82
Weymouth Rd. NE29: N Shi 7C 48
SR3: Dox P 4A 132
Whaggs La. NE16: Whi 1H 97
Whalebone La. NE61: Mor 7F 9
Whalton Av. NE3: Gos 6C 44
Whalton Cl. DH6: S'burn 3A 168
NE10: Ward 7G 85
NE61: Hep 3H 15
Whalton Ct. NE3: Gos 6C 44
NE34: S Shi 7A 68
Whalton Gro. NE63: Ash 2H 11
Whalton Rd. NE61: Loan, Mor, Tra W 6A 14
Wharfedale DH4: Pen 1A 130
NE28: W'snd 7D 46
Wharfedale Av. NE37: Wash 7F 101
Wharfedale Dr. NE33: S Shi 6J 67
Wharfedale Gdns. NE24: Cow 1E 22
Wharfedale Grn. NE9: Low F 6K 99
Wharfedale Pl. NE6: Walk 7F 65
Wharmlands Gro. NE15: Den M 6F 61
Wharmlands Rd. NE15: Den M 6F 61
Wharncliffe St. SR1: Sund 4F 7 (2D 118)
Wharnley Way DH8: C'sde 4B 134
Wharrier Sq. DH6: Whe H 4A 180
Wharrier St. NE6: Walk 2D 84
Wharry Ct. NE7: H Hea 1A 64
Wharton Cl. DH5: E Rain 6D 144
Wharton St. NE24: Bly 4F 23
NE33: S Shi 3K 67
Wheatall Dr. SR6: Whit 3H 89
Wheatall Way SR6: Whit 4H 89
Wheat Cl. DH8: Shot B 2G 121
Wheatear Cl. NE38: Wash 5D 114
Wheatfield Cl. NE42: O'ham 1D 76
Wheatfield Gro. NE12: Longb 5K 45
Wheatfield Rd. NE5: West 2F 61
Wheatfields NE25: Sea D 6F 27
Wheatlands Way DH1: P Me 3A 154
Wheatley Gdns. NE36: W Bol 7G 87
Wheatley Grn. La. DH7: Edm 2K 139
WHEATLEY HILL 2B 180
Wheatley Ter. DH6: Whe H 3A 180
Wheatleywell La. DH2: Plaw 6J 141
DH3: Plaw 6J 141
Wheatridge NE25: Sea D 6F 27
Wheatridge Row NE25: Sea D 6F 27
Wheatsheaf Cnr. DH4: S Row 3B 130
Wheatsheaf Ct. SR6: Roker 6H 105
Wheatsheaf Yd. NE61: Mor 6F 9
(off Newgate St.)
Wheldon Ter. DH2: Pelt 2G 127
Wheler St. DH4: Hou S 1D 144
Whernside Cl. NE37: Wash 2E 114
Whernside Pl. NE23: Cra 7K 25
Whernside Wlk. NE40: Ryton 2H 79
Whetstone Bri. Rd. NE46: Hex 2B 70
Whetstone Grn. NE46: Hex 2B 70
WHICKHAM 7H 81
Whickham Av. NE11: Dun 6B 82
Whickham Bank NE16: Whi 7G 81
Whickham Cl. DH4: Hou S 2C 144
Whickham Gdns. NE6: Byke 1A 84
Whickham Glebe Sports Club 7H 81
Whickham Highway
NE11: Dun, Lob H 7A 82
NE16: Whi 7K 81
Whickham Ind. Est. NE16: Swa 6F 81
Whickham Lodge NE16: Whi 7J 81
Whickham Lodge Ri. NE16: Whi 7J 81
Whickham Pk. NE16: Whi 7J 81
(not continuous)
Whickham Rd. NE31: Heb 1H 85
Whickham St. SR6: Roker 6G 105
SR8: Eas 7B 160
Whickham St. E. SR6: Roker 6G 105
Whickham Thorns Outdoor Activity Cen. 6K 81
Whickham Vw. NE9: Low F 2J 99
NE15: Benw, Den M, Scot 6G 61
Whickhope NE38: Wash 6J 115
Whinbank NE20: Darr H 2H 41
Whinbrooke NE10: Hew 1E 100
Whindyke TS27: B Col 2G 183
Whinfell NE37: Wash 1F 115
Whinfell Cl. NE23: Cra 7A 26
Whinfell Ct. SR3: Silk 3B 132
Whinfell Rd. NE20: Darr H 1H 41
Whinfield Av. DH6: Shot C 6E 170
Whinfield Ind. Est. NE39: Row G 6G 95
Whinfield Ter. NE39: Row G 5H 95
Whinfield Way NE39: Row G 6G 95
Whingrove Cl. TS28: Win 4G 181
Whinham Way NE61: Mor 3G 15
Whinlatter Gdns. NE9: Low F 3J 99
Whinlaw NE9: Low F 3A 100
Whinmoor Pl. NE5: Fen 4A 62
Whinney Cl. NE21: Winl 6A 80
Whinneyfield Rd. NE6: Walk 6D 64
WHINNEY HILL 2G 17
Whinney Hill DH1: Dur 5E 6 (4B 166)
DH1: Dur 6E 6 (4B 166)
Whinney Leas NE17: C'wl 7J 93
Whinny La. DH8: Ebc, M'sly, Shot B 7G 107
Whinny Pl. DH8: C'sde 4C 134
Whinshaw NE10: Hew 7D 84
Whinside DH9: Stly 2D 124
Whinstone M. NE12: Longb 6B 46
Whinway NE37: Wash 1F 115
Whistler Gdns. NE34: S Shi 3K 87
Whitbeck Ct. NE5: Den M 4G 61
Whitbeck Rd. NE5: Den M 5F 61
Whitbourne Cl. NE37: Wash 5J 101
WHITBURN 6H 89
Whitburn Bents Rd. SR6: Seab 1H 105
Whitburn Cl. DH7: Lang P 5H 151
WHITBURN COLLIERY 4H 89
Whitburn Gdns. NE9: Wrek 4B 100
Whitburn Pl. NE23: Cra 7K 25
Whitburn Rd. NE36: E Bol 6A 88
SR6: Clead 6A 88
SR6: Seab 2H 105
Whitburn Rd. E. SR6: Clead 5D 88
Whitburn St. SR6: Monkw 1K 7 (7F 105)
Whitburn Ter. NE36: E Bol 7K 87
SR6: Ful 3F 105
Whitby Av. NE46: Hex 1B 70
SR6: Seab 1H 105
Whitby Cl. NE8: Gate 5H 83
Whitby Cres. NE12: Longb 6A 46
Whitby Dr. NE38: Wash 5H 115
Whitby Gdns. NE28: W'snd 1J 65
Whitby St. NE30: N Shi 6H 49
Whitchester Ho. NE4: Newc T 3A 4
Whitchurch Cl. NE35: Bol C 5E 86
SR5: S'wck 3B 104
Whitchurch Rd. SR5: S'wck 3B 104
Whitdale Av. NE24: Cow 3E 22
Whiteacres NE61: Mor 1G 15
Whitebark SR3: Dox P 5A 132
Whitebeam Pl. NE4: Elsw 9A 4 (3D 82)
Whitebridge Cl. NE3: Gos 4F 45
Whitebridge Ct. NE3: Gos 5E 44
Whitebridge Pk. NE3: Gos 4F 45
Whitebridge Parkway NE3: Gos 4F 45
Whitebridge Wlk. NE3: Gos 4F 45
Whiteburn NE42: Pru 5D 76
White Cedars DH7: B'don 2C 174
Whitecliff Cl. NE29: N Shi 4F 49
White Cotts. NE32: Jar 2A 86
White Cres. TS27: Hes 4E 182
Whitecroft Rd. NE12: Kil 2K 45
White Cross NE46: Hex 2E 70
Whitefield Cres. DH4: Pen 2A 130
NE61: Peg 4A 10
Whitefield Gdns. NE40: G'sde 6D 78
Whitefield Gro. NE10: Fell 6B 84
Whitefield Pit DH4: Pen 2A 130
Whitefield Ter. NE6: Heat 4B 64
Whiteford Pl. NE23: Seg 1E 36
Whitegate Cl. NE11: Dun 4B 82
White Gates Dr. DH5: Eas L 1H 157
Whitegates Rd. DH6: S'burn 1K 167
Whitehall La. DH8: Cons 1D 136
Whitehall Rd. NE8: Gate 6F 83
NE15: Walb 3K 59
Whitehall St. NE33: S Shi 7J 67
Whitehall Ter. SR4: Sund 2B 118
White Hart Yd. NE1: Newc T 6F 4
Whitehead St. NE33: S Shi 7H 67
(Hudson St., not continuous)
NE33: S Shi 6H 67
(Western App., not continuous)
WHITEHILL 6G 127
Whitehill NE10: Hew 2D 100
Whitehill Cres. DH2: P Fel 6G 127
(off Blindy Burn Ct.)
Whitehill Dr. NE10: Hew, Wind N 1A 100
Whitehill Hall Gdns. DH2: Ches S 5J 127
White Hill Rd. DH5: Eas L 3J 157
Whitehill Rd. NE23: Cra 1J 25
WHITEHILLS 2D 100
Whitehill Way DH2: Ches S 6H 127
White Horse Vw. NE34: S Shi 7E 68
Whitehouse Av. DH7: B'hpe 5D 138
DH7: Ush M 2B 164
Whitehouse Ct. DH7: Ush M 1C 164
(not continuous)
SR8: Eas 1K 171
SR8: Pet 4K 171
Whitehouse Cres. NE9: Wrek 3C 100
SR8: Pet 6H 171
Whitehouse Farm NE12: Kil 1J 45
Whitehouse Farm Centre 7E 14
Whitehouse Ind. Est. NE15: Benw 2J 81
Whitehouse Ind. Pk. SR8: Pet 6G 171
Whitehouse La. DH7: Ush M 2B 164
NE9: Low F 3A 100
NE9: Low F, Wrek 3B 100
NE29: N Shi 4D 48
Whitehouse M. NE28: W'snd 3G 65
White Ho. Pl. SR2: Sund 2H 119
White Ho. Rd. SR2: Sund 2G 119
(not continuous)
Whitehouse Rd. NE15: Benw, Scot 2H 81
Whitehouse Ter. DH7: B'hpe 5D 138
Whitehouse Vw. DH7: Bearp 1C 164
White Ho. Way NE10: Hew 2C 100
Whitehouse Way SR8: Pet 6H 171
White Ladies Cl. NE38: Wash 2H 115
Whitelaw Pl. NE23: Cra 6A 26
Whitelea Cl. SR8: Pet 7D 172
WHITELEAS 4K 87
Whiteleas Way NE34: S Shi 2J 87
WHITE-LE-HEAD 7A 110
White-le-Head Gdns. DH9: Tant 6A 110
Whiteley Cl. NE40: G'sde 5E 78
Whiteley Rd. NE21: Blay 2E 80
White Mare Pool NE10: Ward 7H 85
Whitemere Cl. SR2: Sund 7G 119
Whitemere Gdns. NE10: Ward 6G 85
Whiteoak Av. DH1: Dur 1F 167
White Oaks NE10: Hew 2C 100
White Rocks Gro. SR6: Whit 3H 89
White Rose Way NE10: Ward 2J 101
Whites Gdns. NE31: Heb 7H 65
Whiteside NE44: Rid M 7K 73
WHITESMOCKS 1H 165
Whitesmocks DH1: Dur 7J 153
Whitesmocks Av. DH1: Dur 1H 165
White St. NE6: Walk 1F 85
White Swan Cl. NE12: Kil 1B 46
Whitethorn Cres. NE5: Fen 3K 61
Whitethroat Cl. NE38: Wash 5D 114
Whitewell Cl. NE40: Ryton 1G 79
Whitewell La. NE40: Ryton 1G 79
Whitewell Rd. NE21: Blay 4C 80
Whitewell Ter. NE40: Ryton 7G 59
Whitfield Ct. DH1: Dur 5J 153
DH7: Mead 2G 175
Whitfield Dr. NE12: Longb 6A 46
Whitfield Rd. NE12: Longb 4B 46
NE15: Scot 1F 81
NE25: Sea D 7H 27
Whitfield St. DH8: Cons 6J 121
Whitfield Vs. NE33: S Shi 7H 67
Whitgrave Rd. NE5: Ken 2K 61
Whithorn Ct. NE24: Cow 2G 23
Whitlees Ct. NE3: Fawd 5A 44
WHITLEY BAY 6H 39
Whitley Bay Crematorium
NE26: Whit B 2E 38
Whitley Bay Holiday Pk. NE26: Whit B 1E 38
Whitley Bay Ice Rink 1F 49
Whitley Bay Playhouse 5G 39
Whitley Bay Station (Metro) 7H 39
Whitley Ct. NE9: Wrek 4B 100
Whitley Pl. NE25: H'wll 1J 37
Whitley Rd. NE12: Kil, Longb 5E 46
NE12: W'snd, Longb, Newc T 6B 46
NE25: Well 6A 38
NE26: Whit B 6G 39
NE27: Kil, Longb 3G 47
WHITLEY SANDS 4G 39
Whitley Ter. NE22: Bed 5B 18
NE25: H'wll 1J 37
Whitmore Rd. NE21: Blay 3C 80
Whitsun Av. NE22: Bed 7J 17
Whitsun Gdns. NE22: Bed 7J 17
Whitsun Gro. NE22: Bed 7J 17
Whitticks, The NE36: E Bol 7H 87
Whittingham Cl. NE30: Cull 2J 49
NE63: Ash 5J 11
Whittingham Ct. NE8: Gate 5F 83
(off Second St.)
Whittingham Rd. NE5: West 1F 61
NE30: Cull 2J 49
Whittingham Rd. Bungs. NE5: West 1G 61
Whittington Gro. NE5: Fen 6J 61
Whittleburn NE10: Hew 2D 100
Whittle Ri. NE24: Cow 3E 22
Whitton Av. NE24: Bly 4F 23
Whitton Gdns. NE29: N Shi 5D 48
Whitton Pl. NE7: H Hea 1K 63
NE25: Sea D 7H 27
WHITTONSTALL 1A 106
Whittonstall NE38: Wash 7K 115
Whittonstall Rd. NE17: C'wl 6J 93
Whittonstall Ter. NE17: C'wl 6J 93
Whitton Way NE3: Gos 6D 44
Whitwell Acres DH1: H Shin 7F 167
Whitwell Ct. DH1: Dur 1E 166
Whitworth Cl. NE6: Walk 1E 84
NE8: Gate 7F 83
Whitworth La. DH7: Bran 6A 174
DL16: Page B 6A 174
Whitworth Pk. Dr. DH4: S Row 5K 129
Whitworth Pl. NE6: Walk 1E 84
Whitworth Rd. NE37: Wash 1D 114
SR8: Pet 6H 171
WHORLTON 7D 42
Whorlton Grange NE5: West 1E 60
Whorlton Grange Cotts.
NE5: West 1E 60
Whorlton La. NE5: Call, West 5B 42
Whorlton Pl. NE5: West 2E 60
Whorlton Ter. NE5: Cha P 1B 60
Whorral Bank NE61: Mor 5H 9
Whyndyke NE10: Hew 2D 100
Whytrigg Cl. NE25: Sea D 6F 27
Wicklow Ct. NE62: W Sle 1B 18
Widdrington Av. NE34: S Shi 5D 68
Widdrington Gdns. NE13: W Op 5E 34
Widdrington Rd. NE21: Blay 4C 80
Widdrington Ter. NE21: Blay 2A 80
NE29: N Shi 7G 49
(not continuous)
WIDE OPEN 5E 34
Widnes Pl. NE12: Longb 5A 46
Wigeon Cl. NE38: Wash 6E 114
Wigham Chare NE2: Newc T 3J 5
Wigham Ter. DH4: Pen 2B 130
NE16: Hob 4A 110
Wigmore Av. NE6: Walk 2C 84
Wigton Pl. DH4: Pen 1C 130
Wilber Ct. SR4: Sund 1B 118
Wilberforce St. NE28: W'snd 5F 65
NE32: Jar 6C 66
Wilberforce Wlk. NE8: Gate 4E 82
Wilber St. SR4: Sund 2B 118
Wilbury Pl. NE5: Blak 3J 61
Wildbriar NE38: Wash 6H 115
Wilden Ct. SR3: Sund 6C 118
Wilden Rd. NE38: Wash 4K 115
Wildshaw Cl. NE23: Cra 7A 26
Wilfred St. DH3: Bir 5A 114
DH3: Ches S 7A 128
NE6: Byke 4M 5 (7J 63)
NE35: Bol C 7F 87
SR4: Sund 1A 118
Wilfrid Gdns. NE8: Gate 5K 83
Wilkes Cl. NE5: West 3F 61
Wilkinson Av. NE31: Heb 3H 85
Wilkinson Ct. NE32: Jar 6B 66
Wilkinson Pl. NE46: Hex 1C 70
(off Glovers Pl.)
Wilkinson Rd. SR8: Hord 3C 172
Wilkinson St. NE34: S Shi 1H 87
Wilkinson Ter. SR2: Ryh 3G 133
WILK'S HILL 6A 150
Wilkwood Cl. NE23: Cra 6A 26
Willans Bldgs. DH1: Dur 2D 166
Willbrook Ho. NE8: Gate 9G 4
Willerby Ct. NE9: Low F 6K 99
Willerby Dr. NE3: Gos 4F 45
Willerby Gro. SR8: Pet 5K 171
William Allan Homes
NE22: Bed 7F 17
William Armstrong Dr.
NE4: Benw, Elsw 3A 82
William Cl. NE12: Longb 4E 46
William Doxford Cen.
SR3: Silk 3B 132
William Hopkinson Way
NE64: Newb S 3H 13
William Johnson St. SR7: Mur 1F 159
William Morris Av. NE39: Row G 5F 95
William Morris Ter. DH6: Shot C 7E 170
William Pl. DH1: Dur 2D 166
William Roberts Ct. NE12: Kil 3B 46
Williams Cl. DH9: Stly 3G 125
Williamson Sq. TS28: Win 5F 181
Williamson Ter.
SR6: Monkw 1K 7 (7F 105)
Williams Pk. NE12: Longb 6A 46
Williams Rd. SR7: Mur 7E 146
William's Ter. SR2: Ryh 3G 133
William St. DH2: Newf 4F 127
DH3: Ches S 5A 128
DH6: Bowb 4H 177
DH9: Ann P 6A 124
DH9: Crag 7J 125
DH9: Stly 5D 124
NE3: Gos 7G 45
NE10: Fell 5B 84
NE16: Whi 7G 81
NE17: C'wl 6K 93
NE24: Bly 2J 23
NE29: N Shi 7G 49
NE31: Heb 6H 65
(not continuous)
NE33: S Shi 2J 67
NE61: Peg 4B 10
SR1: Sund 2K 7
SR4: Sund 2G 117
William St. W. NE29: N Shi 7G 49
NE31: Heb 7H 65
William Ter. DH4: Nbot 6D 130
NE31: Heb 7H 65
William Whiteley Homes
NE40: G'sde 5E 78
(off Whiteley Cl.)
WILLINGTON 1K 65
Willington M. NE28: W'snd 1K 65
WILLINGTON QUAY 4A 66
WILLINGTON SQUARE 7K 47
Willington Ter. NE28: W'snd 2J 65
Willis St. DH5: Hett H 5G 145
Williston Cl. NE5: Den M 3H 61
Willmore St. SR4: Sund 2C 118
Willoughby Dr. NE26: Whit B 4E 38
Willoughby Rd. NE29: N Shi 6D 48
Willoughby Way NE26: Whit B 4E 38
Willow Av. DH9: Ann P 6J 123
NE4: Fen 5K 61
NE11: Dun 6B 82
NE24: Bly 7H 19
Willow Bank Ct. NE36: E Bol 6A 88
Willowbank Gdns. NE2: Jes 1G 63
Willow Bank Rd. SR2: Sund 5E 118
WILLOW BRIDGE 4H 17
Willowbrook Cl. NE22: Bed 4A 18
Willow Cl. DH7: B'don 1D 174
NE16: Whi 1H 97
NE61: Mor 7H 9
Willow Ct. NE23: Dud 1J 35
NE29: N Shi 5F 49
NE40: Ryton 7H 59
NE62: Stake 1K 17
Willow Cres. DH5: Eas L 2J 157
DH8: Lead 6B 122
NE24: News 5G 23
Willowdene NE12: Kil 3C 46
NE23: Dud 4H 35
NE37: Wash 5F 101
Willow Dyke NE45: Corb 7E 52
Willowfield Av. NE3: Fawd 6B 44
Willow Gdns. NE12: Kil 7A 36
Willow Grange NE32: Jar 6A 66
Willow Grn. SR2: Sund 4E 118
Willow Gro. NE10: Fell 6B 84
NE28: W'snd 3H 65
NE34: S Shi 1B 88
SR8: Hord 6F 173
Willow Lodge NE29: N Shi 5G 49
Willow Pk. DH7: Lang P 5G 151
Willow Pl. NE20: Darr H 7J 31
Willow Rd. DH4: Hou S 2C 144
DH7: Esh W 3D 162
NE21: Blay 4D 80
Willows, The DH1: Carr 6H 155
DH7: Wit G 3C 152
NE4: Elsw 3C 82
NE10: Hew 2F 101
NE13: Sea B 2D 34
NE15: Thro 4H 59
NE22: Bed 4A 18

Willows, The NE27: Back 6G 37
NE31: Heb 2J 85
NE32: Jar 5C 86
NE38: Wash 4K 115
NE61: Mor 7G 9
Willows Bus. Cen., The NE21: Blay 1K 79
Willows Cl. NE13: W Op 6C 34
NE38: Wash 4K 115
Willow Tree Av. DH1: Shin 6E 166
Willowtree Av. DH1: Dur 7E 154
Willow Va. NE22: Bed 7H 17
Willowvale DH2: Ches S 4J 127
Willow Vw. NE16: Burn 2A 110
Willow Way NE20: Darr H 1J 41
Wills Bldg. NE7: H Hea 3C 64
Wills M. NE7: H Hea 3C 64
Wills Oval NE7: H Hea 3C 64
Wilmington Cl. NE3: Ki Pk 6H 43
Wilson Av. DH3: Bir 3A 114
NE22: E Sle 4F 19
Wilson Cl. DH6: Cass 4F 179
Wilson Ct. NE25: Monks 7E 38
Wilson Cres. DH1: Dur 1E 166
Wilson Dr. NE36: W Bol 6H 87
Wilson Gdns. NE3: Ken 2D 62
Wilson Pl. SR8: Pet 4B 172
Wilson's Ct. NE1: Newc T 6F 4 (1F 83)
Wilson's La. NE9: Low F 2H 99
Wilson St. NE11: Dun 6B 82
NE28: W'snd 3F 65
NE33: S Shi 4J 67
SR4: Sund 2B 118
Wilson St. Nth. SR5: Monkw 1H 7 (7E 104)
Wilson Ter. NE12: Longb 4B 46
SR3: New S 1C 132
Wilsway NE15: Thro 3G 59
Wilton Av. NE6: Walk 1C 84
Wilton Cl. NE23: Cra 7A 26
NE25: Monks 6C 38
Wilton Dr. NE25: Monks 7B 38
Wilton Gdns. Nth. NE35: Bol C 5E 86
Wilton Gdns. Sth. NE35: Bol C 5E 86
Wilton Manse NE25: Monks 7B 38
Wilton Sq. SR2: Sund 7G 119
Wiltshire Cl. DH1: Carr 1G 167
SR5: S'wck 3A 104
Wiltshire Dr. NE28: W'snd 1D 64
Wiltshire Gdns. NE28: W'snd 2D 64
Wiltshire Pl. NE37: Wash 5H 101
Wiltshire Rd. SR5: S'wck 4A 104
Wimbledon Cl. SR5: S'wck 4B 104
Wimborne Cl. NE35: Bol C 6E 86
Wimbourne Av. SR4: Sund 4A 118
Wimbourne Grn. NE5: West 2F 61
Wimbourne Quay NE24: Bly 7J 19
Wimpole Cl. NE37: Wash 5J 101
Wimslow Cl. NE28: W'snd 2D 64
Winalot Av. SR2: Sund 6G 119
Wincanton Pl. NE29: N Shi 1E 66
Winchcombe Pl. NE7: H Hea 2J 63
Winchester Av. NE24: Bly 2J 23
Winchester Cl. DH3: Gt Lum 3E 142
NE63: N Sea 5D 12
Winchester Ct. NE32: Jar 5B 86
Winchester Dr. DH7: B'don 3C 174
SR8: Pet 7H 171
Winchester Rd. DH1: Dur 4C 154
Winchester St. NE33: S Shi 2K 67
Winchester Ter. NE4: Newc T 6B 4 (1D 82)
Winchester Wlk. NE13: W Op 6D 34
Winchester Way NE22: Bed 6H 17
Wincomblee NE6: Walk 1E 84
Wincomblee Rd. NE6: Walk 3E 84
Wincomblee Workshops NE6: Walk 1F 85
(off White St.)
Windburgh Dr. NE23: Cra 7K 25
Windermere DH3: Bir 6B 114
SR6: Clead 5C 88
Windermere Av. DH2: Ches S 1A 142
DH5: Eas L 3J 157
NE10: Pel 6D 84
Windermere Cl. NE23: Cra 7K 25
NE28: W'snd 4E 64
Windermere Cres. DH4: S Row 3B 130
NE21: Winl 6B 80
NE31: Heb 1K 85
NE32: Jar 3D 86
NE34: S Shi 7A 68
Windermere Dr. NE12: Kil 1A 46
Windermere Gdns. NE16: Whi 7J 81
Windermere Rd. DH6: S Het 3D 158
NE5: Den M 5H 61
NE64: Newb S 4G 13
SR7: S'hm 3G 147
Windermere St. NE8: Gate 5G 83
SR2: Sund 6H 119
Windermere St. W. NE8: Gate 5G 83
Windermere Ter. DH9: Stly 5D 124
NE29: N Shi 6F 49
Windhill Rd. NE6: Walk 3D 84
Winding, The NE13: Din 4H 33
Windlass Ct. NE34: S Shi 1J 87
Windlass La. NE37: Wash 1G 115
Windmill Ct. NE2: Newc T 1C 4 (5E 62)
Windmill Gro. NE24: Cow 1E 22
Windmill Hill DH1: Dur 5K 165
NE33: S Shi 4H 67
NE46: Hex 1C 70
Windmill Ind. Est. NE23: Nel V 7E 20
Windmill Sq. SR5: Ful 3E 104
SR5: Ful 4E 104
Windmill Way NE8: Gate 4F 83
NE31: Heb 5J 65
NE61: Mor 7H 9
Winds La. SR7: Mur 1C 158
Winds Lonnen SR7: Mur 7C 146
Windsor Av. NE3: Gos 1G 63
NE8: Gate 6G 83
NE26: Whit B 7J 39
Windsor Cl. NE16: Whi 3G 97
NE28: W'snd 1A 66
Windsor Cnr. SR8: Hord 6F 173
Windsor Cotts. NE28: W'snd 1A 66
Windsor Ct. DH3: Ches S 7B 128
DH6: Crox 6K 175
NE3: Gos 1G 63
NE3: Ki Pk 5A 44
NE10: Fell 6A 84
NE22: Bed 1H 21
NE23: Cra 1J 25
NE39: Row G 5K 95
NE45: Corb 7E 52
SR8: Eas 1J 171
Windsor Cres. NE5: West 2G 61
NE26: Whit B 7J 39
NE31: Heb 7K 65
NE42: O'ham 1D 76
Windsor Dr. DH5: Hou S 4E 144
DH6: S Het 3B 158
DH9: Ann P 4K 123
NE24: News 6H 23
NE28: W'snd 2K 65
SR3: New S 2C 132
SR6: Clead 6A 88
Windsor Gdns. DH8: Cons 7J 121
NE10: Fell 6K 83
NE22: Bed 1H 21
NE26: Whit B 5F 39
NE29: N Shi 5G 49
NE34: S Shi 6A 68
NE64: Newb S 3H 13
Windsor Gdns. W. NE26: Monks 5F 39
Windsor M. DH9: Ann P 4K 123
Windsor Pk. NE28: W'snd 2D 64
Windsor Pl. DH6: Shot C 6F 171
NE2: Jes 1G 4 (6G 63)
NE20: Darr H 7F 31
NE27: Kil 3G 47
Windsor Rd. DH3: Bir 2K 113
(not continuous)
NE9: Spri 6C 100
NE25: Monks 6E 38
NE64: Newb S 3H 13
SR7: S'hm 3H 147
Windsor St. NE28: W'snd 3F 65
Windsor Ter. DH3: Gt Lum 3F 143
DH6: Crox 6K 175
DH6: Has 1A 170
DH8: Lead 5B 122
DH9: Ann P 5B 124
DH9: Dip 2F 123
NE2: Jes 1F 4 (6G 63)
NE3: Gos 1G 63
NE9: Spri 6D 100
NE26: Whit B 7J 39
NE40: Craw 2E 78
NE45: Corb 7E 52
NE46: Hex 1B 70
NE62: Sco G 4H 17
NE64: Newb S 3J 13
SR2: Sund 6H 119
SR3: E Her 3J 131
SR7: Mur 7F 147
SR8: Hord 6F 173
Windsor Ter. Sth. SR7: Mur 1F 159
(off Federation Sq.)
Windsor Vs. NE62: Chop 1J 17
Windsor Wlk. NE3: Ki Pk 5K 43
NE63: N Sea 5E 12
Windsor Way NE3: K Bank 5J 43
Windt St. NE13: Haz 6C 34
Windy Gyle NE63: Ash 3C 12
Windyhill Carr NE16: Whi 2F 97
WINDY NOOK 1A 100
Windy Nook Rd. NE9: Low F 1K 99
NE10: Wind N 1K 99
Windyridge NE10: Wind N 7A 84
Windy Ridge Vs. NE10: Wind N 7A 84
Winford Gro. TS28: Win 6G 181
WINGATE 5G 181
Wingate Cl. DH4: Hou S 2D 144
NE15: Lem 7E 60
Wingate Gdns. NE9: Wrek 4B 100
Wingate Grange Ind. Est. TS28: Win 6F 181
Wingate La. DH6: Whe H 3J 179
Wingate La. Sth. DH6: Whe H 4A 180
Wingate Quarry Local Nature Reserve 5K 179
Wingate Rd. TS29: Trim S 7B 180
Wingrove NE39: Row G 6H 95
Wingrove Av. NE4: Fen 7B 62
SR6: Ful 4G 105
Wingrove Gdns. NE4: Fen 7B 62
Wingrove Ho. NE5: Fen 4A 62
NE33: S Shi 7J 67
Wingrove Rd. NE4: Fen 7B 62
Wingrove Rd. Nth. NE4: Fen 4A 62
NE5: Fen 4A 62
(not continuous)
Wingrove Ter. DH8: Lead 5B 122
NE9: Spri 6D 100
NE10: Bill Q 5F 85
Winifred Gdns. NE28: W'snd 4G 65
Winifred St. SR6: Ful 3G 105
Winifred Ter. SR1: Sund 2G 119
WINLATON 5B 80
WINLATON MILL 1C 96
Winn Studios Residence NE2: Newc T 4K 5
Winsford Av. NE29: N Shi 3F 49
Winshields NE23: Cra 6A 26
Winshields Way NE15: Thro 4G 59
Winship Cl. NE34: S Shi 3J 87
Winship Gdn. NE6: Byke 7A 64
(off Grace St.)
Winship St. NE24: Bly 5G 23
Winship Ter. NE6: Byke 7A 64
Winskell Rd. NE34: S Shi 2F 87
Winslade Cl. SR3: Tuns 1D 132
Winslow Cl. NE6: Walk 7E 64
NE35: Bol C 4F 87
SR5: S'wck 3B 104
Winslow Ct. NE30: Cull 1J 49
Winslow Cres. SR7: S'hm 3G 147
Winslow Gdns. NE9: Low F 2G 99
Winslow Pl. NE6: Walk 7E 64
Winson Grn. DH4: Pen 1K 129
Winster NE38: Wash 7E 114
Winster Pl. NE23: Cra 7K 25
Winston Ct. NE9: Spri 6D 100
Winston Cres. SR4: Sund 4A 118
Winston Way NE43: B'ley 4J 91
Winters Bank DH4: Hou S 2B 144
Winters Pass NE8: Gate 4C 82
Winton Cl. NE23: Seg 1E 36
Winton Ct. NE21: Winl 6C 80
Winton Way NE3: Ken 7B 44
Wirralshir NE10: Hew 1E 100
Wiseton Ct. NE7: Longb 7H 45
Wishart Ho. NE4: Benw 2A 82
Wishart Ter. NE39: H Spen 3D 94
Wishaw Cl. NE23: Cra 6A 26
Wishaw Ri. NE15: Lem 6E 60
Wisteria Gdns. NE34: S Shi 2B 88
Witham Grn. NE32: Jar 4C 86
Witham Rd. NE31: Heb 3K 85
Witherington Cl. NE7: H Hea 2C 64
Withernsea Gro. SR2: Ryh 2F 133
WITHERWACK 3B 104
Witney Cl. SR5: S'wck 3A 104
Witney Way NE35: Bol C 7E 86
Witton Av. DH7: Sac 7E 140
NE34: S Shi 7C 68
Witton Ct. DH7: Sac 1D 152
NE3: Fawd 6A 44
NE38: Wash 4F 115
SR3: Sund 6D 118
Witton Dene Local Nature Reserve 4D 152
Witton Gdns. NE9: Wrek 5B 100
NE32: Jar 3B 86
Witton Gth. SR8: Pet 2A 182
WITTON GILBERT 3C 152
Witton Gro. DH1: Dur 6H 153
DH4: Hou S 3C 144
Witton Rd. DH7: Sac 1D 152
NE27: Shir 1K 47
NE31: Heb 5K 65
Witton Station Ct. DH7: Lang P 4K 151
Wittonstone Ho. NE4: Newc T 3A 4
Witton St. DH8: Cons 2K 135
Witton Vs. DH7: Sac 1D 152
(off Witton Rd.)
Witty Av. NE31: Heb 1K 85
Woburn NE38: Wash 4H 115
Woburn Cl. NE23: Cra 1J 25
NE28: W'snd 2D 64
Woburn Dr. NE22: Bed 6A 18
SR3: Silk 3C 132
Woburn Way NE5: West 3G 61
Wolmer Rd. NE24: Bly 4K 23
Wolseley Cl. NE8: Gate 5E 82
Wolseley Gdns. NE2: Jes 5J 63
Wolseley Ter. SR4: Sund 3C 118
Wolsey Cl. DH6: Bowb 4H 177
Wolsey Ct. NE34: S Shi 7J 67
Wolsey Rd. SR7: S'hm 4G 147
Wolsingham DH4: Hou S 1A 144
Wolsingham Ct. NE23: Nel V 3H 25
Wolsingham Dr. DH1: Dur 5B 154
Wolsingham Gdns. NE9: Wrek 4B 100
Wolsingham Rd. DH7: Bran 4A 174
DH7: Wat 6B 162
NE3: Gos 1D 62
Wolsingham Ter. DH9: Ann P 5K 123
Wolsington St. NE4: Elsw 3C 82
Wolsington Wlk. NE4: Elsw 3B 82
Wolsley Rd. NE24: Bly 2J 23
Wolveleigh Ter. NE3: Gos 7F 45
Wolviston Gdns. NE9: Wrek 4B 100
Woodbine Av. NE3: Gos 1E 62
NE28: W'snd 3F 65
SR8: Hord 4D 172
Woodbine Cl. NE4: Elsw 2B 82
Woodbine Cotts. DH2: Ches S 5J 127
NE40: Ryton 1F 79
Woodbine Pl. NE8: Gate 5G 83
Woodbine Rd. DH1: P Me 4J 153
NE3: Gos 1E 62
Woodbine St. NE8: Gate 5G 83
NE33: S Shi 2K 67
(Hatfield Sq.)
NE33: S Shi 2K 67
(Ocean Rd.)
SR1: Sund 2H 119
Woodbine Ter. DH3: Bir 4B 114
DH7: New B 4A 164
DH9: Ann P 5B 124
NE8: Gate 5G 83
Woodbine Ter. NE10: Gate 6K 83
NE10: Pel 5E 84
NE24: Bly 2K 23
NE45: Corb 7D 52
NE46: Hex 1B 70
NE63: Ash 3H 11
SR4: Sund 7A 104
Woodbine Vs. NE8: Gate 5G 83
(off Villa Pl.)
WOODBRIDGE 2D 12
Woodbridge DH7: Lang M 6F 165
Woodbrook Av. NE5: Den M 5G 61
Woodburn DH9: Tan L 1C 124
NE10: Hew 2C 100
Woodburn Av. NE4: Fen 4A 62
Woodburn Cl. DH4: Bour 7J 129
NE21: Winl 6A 80
Woodburn Dr. DH4: Hou S 1C 144
NE26: Whit B 4E 38
Woodburn Gdns. NE11: Dun 7C 82
Woodburn Gro. DH7: Lang M 6F 165
Woodburn Sq. NE26: Whit B 4D 38
Woodburn St. NE15: Lem 6C 60
Woodburn Ter. NE42: Pru 4D 76
Woodburn Way NE26: Whit B 4E 38
Woodchurch Cl. NE7: H Hea 1B 64
Woodcliff Cl. NE38: Wash 5J 115
Woodcock Rd. SR3: Dox P 4C 132
Woodcroft Cl. NE23: Dud 2K 35
Woodcroft Rd. NE41: Wylam 7J 57
Woodend NE20: Darr H 2H 41
Woodend Way NE13: Ki Pk 4J 43
Woodfield SR8: Pet 6A 172
Wood Flds. NE20: Pon 5K 31
Woodford NE9: Low F 5H 99
Woodford Cl. SR5: S'wck 3B 104
Woodgate Gdns. NE10: Bill Q 5F 85
Woodgate La. NE10: Bill Q 4F 85
Wood Grn. NE10: Bill Q 5G 85
Wood Gro. NE15: Den M 6F 61
Woodhall Cl. DH2: Ous 6G 113
Woodhall Ct. NE25: Sea D 7G 27
Woodhall Spa DH4: S Row 5A 130
Woodham Ct. DH7: Lan 6J 137
Woodham Dr. SR2: Ryh 3G 133
Woodhead Rd. NE6: Walk 5D 64
NE42: Pru 3H 77
Woodhill Dr. NE61: Mor 7E 8
Woodhill Rd. NE23: Cra 6A 26
WOODHORN 1F 13
Woodhorn Church Mus. 1G 13
Woodhorn Colliery Ho's.
NE63: Wood 2D 12
Woodhorn Ct. NE63: Ash 3C 12
Woodhorn Cres. NE64: Newb S 2H 13
(off Woodhorn Rd.)
WOODHORN DEMESNE 2H 13
Woodhorn Dr. NE62: Stake 7H 11
Woodhorn Farm NE64: Newb S 1H 13
Woodhorn Gdns. NE13: W Op 5D 34
Woodhorn La. NE63: Ash 2D 12
NE64: Newb S 2J 13
Woodhorn M. NE63: Wood 1F 13
Woodhorn Mus. & Northumberland Archives 2E 12
Woodhorn Pk. NE63: Ash 3B 12
Woodhorn Rd. NE63: Ash 3B 12
NE64: Newb S 2H 13
Woodhorn Vs. NE63: Ash 2D 12
(not continuous)
Woodhouse Ct. NE34: S Shi 6E 68
Woodhouse La. NE16: Swa, Whi 2E 96
Woodhurst Gro. SR4: Sund 6G 117
Woodkirk Cl. NE23: Seg 1E 36
Woodland Av. SR8: Hord 6E 172
Woodland Cl. DH7: Bearp 1C 164
NE25: Ears 6A 38
Woodland Ct. DH8: Shot B 3F 121
DH9: Ann P 7K 123
Woodland Cres. DH6: Kel 7D 178
Woodland Dr. SR4: Sund 4A 118
Woodland Grange DH4: Hou S 1K 143
Woodland M. NE2: Jes 3H 63
NE16: Burn 2B 110
Woodland Ri. SR3: Silk 3A 132
Woodland Rd. DH7: Bearp 1C 164
DH7: Esh W 3D 162
Woodland Rd. Flats DH7: Esh W 3D 162
Woodlands DH2: Ous 6H 113
DH3: Ches S 5A 128
DH7: Lan 7K 137
NE3: Gos 2E 62
NE15: Thro 3G 59
NE20: Darr H 1H 41
NE29: N Shi 5G 49
NE38: Wash 1C 128
NE46: Hex 2F 71
SR7: S'hm 1J 147
Woodlands, The DH4: Hou S 1J 143
DH7: Lang P 4K 151
NE11: Kib 2F 113
NE38: Wash 4J 115
Woodlands Av. DH6: Whe H 2B 180
(not continuous)
NE3: Gos 2E 62
Woodlands Cl. NE39: H Spen 4E 94
Woodlands Ct. NE11: Kib 2F 113
NE15: Thro 3G 59
Woodlands Cres. DH8: Shot B 3F 121
Woodlands Dr. SR6: Clead 6C 88
Woodlands Grange NE12: Kil 3C 46
Woodlands Pk. NE13: W Op 6E 34
Woodlands Pk. Dr. NE21: Blay 4D 80
Woodlands Pk. Vs. NE13: W Op 7E 34
Woodlands Pl. DH7: Esh W 5E 162
Woodlands Rd. DH8: Shot B 3F 121
NE15: Lem 6D 60
NE39: Row G 5H 95
NE63: N Sea 5E 12
SR6: Clead 6B 88
Woodlands Ter. DH7: Esh W 5E 162
DH9: Dip 2G 123
NE10: Fell 6A 84
NE12: Longb 3C 46
NE33: S Shi 1K 67
Woodlands Vw. DH8: Cons 3A 136
SR6: Clead 6C 88

Woodland Ter. DH2: Nett 6G **141**
DH4: Pen 1A **130**
DH7: Bearp 1C **164**
NE37: Wash 7J **101**
Woodland Vw. DH4: W Rai 1K **155**
(not continuous)
DH7: Sac 7E 140
(off Water St.)
TS28: Win 5F **181**
Wood La. NE22: Bed 7K **17**
Wood Lea DH5: Hou S 3G **145**
Woodlea DH7: Lan 7J **137**
NE12: Longb 3B **46**
NE64: Newb S 2J **13**
Woodlea Cl. DH5: Hett H 6G **145**
Woodlea Ct. NE29: N Shi 2E **66**
NE32: Jar 2A **86**
NE21: Newb S 2J **13**
Woodlea Cres. NE29: N Shi 2E **66**
NE46: Hex 2E **70**
Woodlea Gdns. NE3: Gos 6G **45**
Woodlea Rd. NE39: Row G 5F **95**
Woodlea Sq. NE29: N Shi 2E **66**
Woodleigh Rd.
NE25: Monks 6D **38**
Woodleigh Vw. NE3: Ken 2A **62**
Woodman Cl. NE61: Mor 1E **14**
Woodmansey Cl. SR8: Pet 5K **171**
Woodman St. NE28: W'snd 2B **66**
Woodmans Way NE16: Whi 3E **96**
Woodpack Av. NE16: Whi 1F **97**
WOOD SIDE 2J **155**
Woodside DH6: Shad 4E **168**
DH7: Sac 1D **152**
DH8: Cons 4D **136**
DH9: Beam 1B **126**
DH9: Stly 2F 125
(off Quarry Rd.)
NE20: Darr H 1G **41**
NE22: Bed 7A **18**
NE24: Bly 3K **23**
NE42: Pru 4G **77**
NE46: Hex 2F **71**
NE61: Mor 1D **14**
SR2: Sund 7H **7** (3E **118**)
SR3: E Her 3J **131**
Woodside Av. DH7: Bearp 1C **164**
NE6: Walk 6F **65**
NE15: Thro 4J **59**
NE25: Sea D 1H **37**
NE45: Corb 7F **53**
Woodside Bank DH8: Cons 2D **136**
Woodside Cl. NE32: Jar 2A **86**
NE40: Ryton 1F **79**
Woodside Ct. NE12: Longb 4C **46**
Woodside Cres. NE12: Longb 4C **46**
Woodside Dr. DH8: Cons 2K **135**
NE35: Bol C 6H **87**
Woodside Gdns. DH9: Stly 5H **125**
NE11: Dun 7B **82**
Woodside Gro. DH9: Tant 6C **110**
SR3: E Her 3J **131**
Woodside La. DH4: Leam 2J **155**
NE40: G'sde 5E **78**
NE40: Ryton 2F **79**
Woodside Rd. NE40: Ryton 1F **79**
Woodside Ter. DH9: Stly 7D **124**
NE17: C'wl 7K **93**
SR3: E Her 3J **131**
Woodside Vw. DH7: Sac 4D **140**
Woodside Vs. NE46: Hex 2F **71**
Woodside Wlk.
NE39: Row G 6G **95**
Woodside Way NE33: S Shi 6H **67**
NE40: Ryton 1G **79**
Woods Ter. NE8: Gate 5J **83**
SR7: Mur 7F **147**
Woods Ter. E. *SR7: Mur 7F 147*
(off Wood's Ter.)
Woods Ter. Nth. SR7: Mur 7F **147**
Woodstock Av. SR2: Sund 6G **119**
(not continuous)
Woodstock Rd. NE9: Low F 5J **99**
NE15: Scot 7F **61**
Woodstock Way NE35: Bol C 7E **86**
Woodstone Ter. DH4: Hou S 1H **143**
WOODSTONE VILLAGE 1J **143**
Woodstone Village Ind. Est.
DH4: Hou S 7H **129**
Wood St. DH2: Pelt 2G **127**
DH8: Shot B 3E **120**
NE11: Dun 6B **82**
NE16: Burn 2A **110**
SR4: Sund 1C **118**
Wood Ter. NE10: Bill Q 4F **85**
NE32: Jar 2A **86**
NE33: S Shi 5K **67**
NE37: Wash 7H **101**
NE39: Row G 5E **94**
Woodthorne Rd. NE2: Jes 2G **63**
Woodvale NE20: Darr H 2G **41**
Woodvale Dr. NE31: Heb 2G **85**
Woodvale Gdns. NE10: Wind N 1A **100**
NE15: Lem 6E **60**
NE41: Wylam 7J **57**
Woodvale Rd. NE12: Kil 7K **35**
NE21: Blay 4D **80**
Wood Vw. DH1: Shin 6D **166**
DH6: Crox 7K **175**
DH7: Esh W 3E **162**
DH7: Lang P 4J **151**
TS29: Trim S 7D **180**
Woodville Ct. SR4: Sund 4A **118**
Woodville Cres. SR4: Sund 4A **118**
Woodville Rd. NE15: Lem 5D **60**
Woodward Av. NE8: Gate 5K **83**
Woodwynd NE10: Hew 1D **100**
(not continuous)
Woody Cl. DH8: Cons 1A **136**
Wooler Av. NE29: N Shi 1D **66**
Wooler Cres. NE8: Gate 6D **82**
Wooler Dr. DH9: Stly 5F **125**
Wooler Grn. NE15: Lem 6B **60**
Wooler Sq. NE13: W Op 5E **34**
SR2: Sund 5G **119**
Woolerton Dr. NE10: Wind N 1K **99**
NE15: Lem 6E **60**
Wooler Wlk. NE32: Jar 2A **86**
Wooley Dr. DH7: Ush M 3E **164**
Wooley St. NE28: W'snd 4F **65**
Woolmer Ct. NE7: H Hea 2C **64**
WOOLSINGTON 4F **43**
Woolsington By-Pass NE3: Ki Pk 5F **43**
NE13: Ken, Wool 5F **43**
NE20: Pon 1C **42**
Woolsington Ct. NE22: Bed 7H **17**
Woolsington Gdns. NE13: Wool 4F **43**
Woolsington Pk. Sth. NE13: Wool 4F **43**
Woolsington Rd. NE29: N Shi 5C **48**
Woolwich Cl. SR5: S'wck 3B **104**
Woolwich Rd. SR5: S'wck 3B **104**
Wooperton Gdns. NE5: Fen 6J **61**
Worcester Cl. DH3: Gt Lum 4E **142**
Worcester Grn. NE8: Gate 4G **83**
Worcester Rd. DH1: Dur 4B **154**
Worcester St. SR2: Sund 6H **7** (3E **118**)
Worcester Ter. SR2: Sund 6H **7** (3E **118**)
Worcester Way NE13: W Op 6D **34**
Wordsworth Av. DH2: P Fel 6G **127**
DH5: Eas L 3K **157**
DH6: Whe H 3B **180**
NE16: Whi 6H **81**
NE24: Bly 4G **23**
NE31: Heb 7J **65**
SR7: S'hm 3G **147**
TS27: B Col 7G **173**
Wordsworth Av. E. DH5: Hou S 3E **144**
Wordsworth Av. W. DH5: Hou S 3E **144**
Wordsworth Cl. NE46: Hex 7C **50**
Wordsworth Cres. NE9: Spri 6C **100**
Wordsworth Gdns. DH9: Dip 1H **123**
Wordsworth Rd. SR8: Eas 7A **160**
Wordsworth St. NE8: Gate 4J **83**
Worley Av. NE9: Low F 3H **99**
Worley Cl. NE4: Newc T 5A **4** (1C **82**)
Worley M. NE9: Low F 3H **99**
Worley St. NE4: Newc T 5A **4** (1D **82**)
Worley Ter. DH9: Tant 7A **110**
NE9: Low F 2H **99**
Worm Hill Ter. NE38: Wash 7J **115**
Worsdell Dr. NE8: Gate 10G **4** (3G **83**)
Worsdell Ho. *NE8: Gate 9H 5*
(off Wellington St.)
Worsdell St. NE24: Bly 7J **19**
Worsley Cl. NE28: W'snd 2D **64**
Worswick St. NE1: Newc T 5G **4** (1G **83**)
Worthing Cl. NE28: W'snd 2D **64**
Worthington Ct. NE2: Newc T 1K **5** (5H **63**)
Worton Cl. DH6: Shot C 5E **170**
Wouldhave Ct. NE33: S Shi 2K **67**
Wouldhave St. NE33: S Shi 2A **68**
Wraith Ter. SR2: Ryh 3G **133**
SR8: Hord 4D **172**
Wranghams Entry NE1: Newc T 6J **5**
Wraysbury Ct. NE3: Ki Pk 5K **43**
Wreay Wlk. NE23: Cra 7A **26**
Wreigh St. NE31: Heb 7H **65**
Wreken Gdns. NE10: Ward 6G **85**
WREKENTON 4A **100**
Wrekenton Row NE9: Wrek 5A **100**
Wren Cl. NE38: Wash 5E **114**
Wrendale Ct. *NE3: Gos 7G 45*
(off William St.)
Wren's Cotts. NE40: Craw 2D **78**
Wretham Pl. NE2: Newc T 3J **5** (7H **63**)
Wright Dr. NE23: Dud 4J **35**
Wrightson St. NE23: E Har 6K **21**
Wright St. NE24: Bly 1H **23**
Wright Ter. DH4: S Row 4A **130**
Wroxham Ct. NE5: Blak 1H **61**
SR2: Sund 6G **119**
Wroxton NE38: Wash 5G **115**
Wuppertal Ct. NE32: Jar 7B **66**
Wychcroft Way NE5: Blak 3J **61**
Wych Elm Cres. NE7: H Hea 2A **64**
Wycliffe Av. NE3: Ken 2B **62**
Wycliffe Rd. SR4: Sund 4B **118**
SR7: S'hm 3G **147**
Wydon Grange NE46: Hex 3C **70**
(not continuous)
Wydon Pk. NE46: Hex 3B **70**
Wye Av. NE32: Jar 3C **86**
Wyedale Way NE6: Walk 6E **64**
Wye Rd. NE31: Heb 3J **85**
WYLAM 7K **57**
Wylam Av. NE25: H'wll 1K **37**
Wylam Cl. NE34: S Shi 1A **88**
NE37: Wash 6J **101**
Wylam Gdns. NE28: W'snd 1K **65**
Wylam Gro. SR1: Sund 2G **119**
Wylam Railway Mus. 7K **57**
Wylam Rd. DH9: Stly 2F **125**
NE29: N Shi 2F **67**
Wylam Station (Rail) 1A **78**
Wylam St. DH6: Bowb 5H **177**
DH9: Crag 7J **125**
NE32: Jar 6B **66**
Wylam Tennis Club 1K **77**
Wylam Ter. DH6: Coxh 7J **177**
DH9: Stly 1F **125**
Wylam Vw. NE21: Winl 4B **80**
Wylam Wharf SR1
: Sund 1G **119**
Wylam Wood Rd. NE41: Wylam 1K **77**
Wynbury Rd. NE9: Low F 2J **99**
Wyncote Ct. NE7: H Hea 3K **63**
Wynd, The DH2: Pelt 2G **127**
NE3: Ken 1C **62**
NE12: Longb 3C **46**
NE15: Thro 4H **59**
NE30: N Shi 4G **49**
Wynde, The NE20: Darr H 7H **31**
NE34: S Shi 1J **87**
Wyndfall Way NE3: Ken 2C **62**
Wyndham Av. NE3: Ken 2B **62**
Wyndham Way NE29: N Shi 4B **48**
Wynding, The NE22: Bed 7G **17**
NE23: Dud 3J **35**
Wyndley Cl. NE16: Whi 2F **97**
Wyndley Ho. NE3: Ken 3B **62**
Wyndley Pl. NE3: Ken 2B **62**
Wyndrow Pl. NE3: Ken 2C **62**
(not continuous)
Wynds, The DH7: Esh W 4D **162**
Wyndsail Pl. NE3: Ken 2C **62**
Wyndtop Pl. NE3: Ken 2C **62**
Wyndward Pl. NE3: Ken 2C **62**
Wyndways Dr. DH9: Dip 7J **109**
Wynn Gdns. NE10: Pel 5D **84**
Wynyard DH2: Ches S 6J **127**
Wynyard Dr. NE22: Bed 5A **18**
Wynyard Gdns. NE9: Wrek 5A **100**
Wynyard Gro. DH1: Dur 2D **166**
Wynyard Sq. SR2: Sund 5G **119**
Wynyard St. DH4: Hou S 2A **144**
NE11: Dun 6B **82**
SR3: New S 2C **132**
Wynyard St. SR7: S'hm 5B **148**
Wythburn Pl. NE9: Low F 3K **99**
Wyvern Sq. SR2: Sund 6G **119**

Y

Yardley Cl. SR3: Dox P 4D **132**
Yardley Gro. NE23: Cra 2J **25**
Yarmouth Cl. SR7: S'hm 4J **147**
Yarmouth Dr. NE23: Cra 2J **25**
Yarridge Rd. NE46: Hex 5A **70**
Yatesbury Av. NE5: Blak 3H **61**
Yeadon Ct. NE3: K Bank 5J **43**
Yeavering Cl. NE3: Gos 1D **62**
Yeckhouse La. DH7: Lan 7F **137**
Yeldon Cl. SR2: Ryh 4H **133**
Yellow Leas Farm NE36: E Bol 7J **87**
Yelverton Ct. NE23: Cra 2J **25**
Yelverton Cres. NE6: Walk 3D **84**
Yeoman St. NE29: N Shi 7H **49**
Yeovil Cl. NE23: Cra 2J **25**
Yetholm Av. DH2: Ches S 7K **127**
Yetholm Pl. NE5: West 1G **61**
Yetholm Rd. NE8: Gate 5D **82**
Yetlington Dr. NE3: Gos 1C **62**
Yewbank Av. DH1: Dur 1F **167**
Yewburn Way NE12: Longb 6A **46**
Yewcroft Av. NE15: Den M, Scot 7F **61**
(not continuous)
Yewdale Gdns. NE9: Low F 3J **99**
Yew Ter. DH7: Lang P 4J **151**
Yewtree Av. SR5: S'wck 5B **104**
Yewtree Dr. NE22: Bed 6H **17**
Yewtree Gdns. NE6: Walk 4E **64**
Yewtrees NE10: Hew 2C **100**
Yewvale Rd. NE5: Fen 4K **61**
Yoden Av. SR8: Hord 4D **172**
Yoden Rd. SR8: Pet 5B **172**
Yoden Way SR8: Hord, Pet 6B **172**
(not continuous)
Yohden Bungs. TS27: B Col 2G **183**
Yohden Cres. SR8: Hord 4D **172**
York Av. DH8: C'sde 3C **134**
NE32: Jar 2B **86**
SR8: Hord 5D **172**
York Cl. NE8: Gate 7E **82**
NE23: Cra 2J **25**
York Ct. DH3: Ches S 7B **128**
NE28: W'snd 4E **64**
York Cres. DH1: Dur 3B **154**
DH5: Hett H 6F **145**
Yorkdale Pl. NE6: Walk 7E **64**
York Dr. NE28: W'snd 4F **65**
York Gro. NE22: Bed 6F **17**
York Ho. SR5: Sund 3G **103**
York Pl. DH8: C'sde 3C **134**
York Rd. DH3: Bir 7A **114**
DH8: B'hill 4E **120**
NE26: Whit B 6H **39**
SR8: Pet 4A **172**
Yorkshire Dr. DH1: Carr 1H **167**
York St. DH3: Bir 7A **114**
DH5: Hett H 2E **156**
DH9: Ann P 4K **123**
NE4: Newc T 6A **4** (1D **82**)
NE10: Pel 5E **84**
NE24: Bly 1J **23**
NE32: Jar 7A **66**
SR1: Sund 3J **7** (1F **119**)
SR3: New S 1C **132**
York Ter. DH3: Ches S 7B **128**
NE10: Fell 6B **84**
NE29: N Shi 7G **49**
York Way NE34: S Shi 1C **88**
Yorkwood NE31: Heb 6G **65**
Youll's Pas. SR1: Sund 7H **105**
Younghall Cl. NE40: G'sde 5E **78**
Young Rd. NE12: Longb 3D **46**
Young St. DH1: Dur 2D **166**

Z

Zetland Dr. NE25: Whit B 2F **49**
Zetland Sq. SR6: Roker 6G **105**
Zetland St. SR6: Roker 6G **105**
Zion St. SR1: Sund 1G **119**
Zion Ter. NE21: Winl 5B **80**

MIX
Paper from responsible sources
FSC® C005461

The representation on the maps of a road, track or footpath is no evidence of the existence of a right of way.

SAFETY CAMERA INFORMATION

PocketGPSWorld.com's CamerAlert is a self-contained speed and red light camera warning system for SatNavs and Android or Apple iOS smartphones/tablets. Visit www.cameralert.com to download.

Safety camera locations are publicised by the Safer Roads Partnership which operates them in order to encourage drivers to comply with speed limits at these sites. It is the driver's absolute responsibility to be aware of and to adhere to speed limits at all times.

By showing this safety camera information it is the intention of Geographers' A-Z Map Company Ltd. to encourage safe driving and greater awareness of speed limits and vehicle speed. Data accurate at time of printing.

HOSPITALS, HOSPICES and selected HEALTHCARE FACILITIES covered by this atlas.

N.B. Where it is not possible to name these facilities on the map, the reference given is for the road in which they are situated.

BENSHAM HOSPITAL 7F **83**
Saltwell Road
GATESHEAD
NE8 4YL
Tel: 0191 482 0000

BLYTH COMMUNITY HOSPITAL 1H **23**
Thoroton Street
BLYTH
NE24 1DX
Tel: 0844 811 8111

CHESTER-LE-STREET HOSPITAL 7A **128**
Front Street
CHESTER LE STREET
DH3 3AT
Tel: 0191 333 2333

COBALT HOSPITAL 3J **47**
The Silverlink North
Cobalt Business Park
NEWCASTLE UPON TYNE
NE27 0BY
Tel: 0191 270 3250

DUNSTON HILL HOSPITAL 7K **81**
Whickham Highway
GATESHEAD
NE11 9QT
Tel: 0191 482 0000

EMERGENCY CARE CENTRE (ASHINGTON)
. . . . .3D **12**
Wansbeck General Hospital
Woodhorn Lane
ASHINGTON
NE63 9JJ
Tel: 0344 811 8111

EMERGENCY CARE CENTRE (NORTH SHIELDS)
. . . . .3E **48**
North Tyneside General Hospital
Rake Lane
NORTH SHIELDS
NE29 8NH
Tel: 0344 811 8111

EMMERGENCY CARE CENTRE (HEXHAM)
. . . . .2E **70**
Hexham General Hospital
Corbridge Road
HEXHAM
NE46 1QJ
Tel: 0344 811 8111

FERNDENE 6G **77**
Moor Road
PRUDHOE
NE42 5NT
Tel: 0166 183 8400

FLEMING NUFFIELD UNIT 5G **63**
Burdon Terrace
NEWCASTLE UPON TYNE
NE2 3AE
Tel: 0191 219 6432

FREEMAN HOSPITAL 1J **63**
Freeman Road
High Heaton
NEWCASTLE UPON TYNE
NE7 7DN
Tel: 0191 233 6161

GATESHEAD COMMUNITY TREATMENT CENTRE
. . . . .7J **83**
134 Dryden Road
GATESHEAD
NE9 5BY
Tel: 0191 441 6700

GRACE HOUSE HOSPICE 4D **104**
Bardolph Drive
southwick
SR5 2DE
Tel: 0191 5252800

GREAT NORTH CHILDREN'S HOSPITAL
. . . . .2D **4**
Queen Victoria Road
NEWCASTLE UPON TYNE
NEWCASTLE
NE1 4LP
Tel: 0191 233 6161

HEXHAM GENERAL HOSPITAL 2E **70**
Corbridge Road
HEXHAM
NE46 1QJ
Tel: 0844 811 8111

HOUGHTON PRIMARY CARE CENTRE
. . . . .1D **144**
Brinkburn Crescent
Houghton Le Spring
SUNDERLAND
DH4 5HB
Tel: 0191 502 5661

LANCHESTER ROAD HOSPITAL 4G **153**
Lanchester Road
DURHAM
DH1 5RD
Tel: 0191 441 5700

MARIE CURIE HOSPICE CENTRE 2B **82**
Marie Curie Drive
NEWCASTLE UPON TYNE
NE4 6SS
Tel: 0191 219 1000

MINOR INJURIES UNIT (BLAYDON) 4F **81**
Blaydon Primary Care Centre
Shibdon Road
Blaydon
NE21 5NW
Tel: 0191 283 4500

MINOR INJURIES UNIT (BLYTH) 1H **23**
Thoroton Street
BLYTH
NE24 1DX
Tel: 0344 811 8111

MINOR INJURIES UNIT (BRINKBURN CRESCENT)
. . . . .1D **144**
Brinkburn Crescent
Houghton Le Spring
SUNDERLAND
DH4 5HB
Tel: 0191 502 5661

MINOR INJURIES UNIT (CONSETT) 3G **121**
Shotley Bridge Hospital
Shotley Bridge
CONSETT
DH8 0NB
Tel: 0191 333 2333

MINOR INJURIES UNIT (DEERNESS PARK)
. . . . .3G **119**
Deerness Park Medical Group
Suffolk Street
SUNDERLAND
SR2 8AD
Tel: 0191 565 8849

MINOR INJURIES UNIT (GRINDON LANE)
. . . . .5K **117**
Grindon Lane Primary Care Centre
Grindon Lane
SUNDERLAND
SR2 4DE
Tel: 0191 525 2300

MINOR INJURIES UNIT (HYLTON LANE)
. . . . .4H **103**
Bunny Hill Primary Care Centre
Hylton Lane
SUNDERLAND
SR5 4BW
Tel: 0191 519 5800

MINOR INJURIES UNIT (JARROW) 6B **66**
Palmer Community Hospital
Wear Street
JARROW
NE32 3UX
Tel: 0191 404 1046

MINOR INJURIES UNIT (NEWCASTLE) 2D **4**
Royal Victoria Infirmary
Queen Victoria Road
NEWCASTLE UPON TYNE
NE1 4LP
Tel: 0191 282 0531

MINOR INJURIES UNIT (SOUTH SHIELDS)
. . . . .1K **87**
South Tyneside District Hospital
Harton Lane
SOUTH SHIELDS
NE34 0PL
Tel: 0191 404 1000

MONKWEARMOUTH HOSPITAL 5E **104**
Newcastle Road
SUNDERLAND
SR5 1NB
Tel: 0191 565 6256

MORPETH NHS CENTRE 6G **9**
Dark Lane
MORPETH
NE61 1JY
Tel: 0344 811 8111

NEWCASTLE DENTAL HOSPITAL . . .1C **4** (6E **62**)
Richardson Road
NEWCASTLE UPON TYNE
NE2 4AZ
Tel: 0191 233 6161

NEWCASTLE NUFFIELD HEALTH HOSPITAL
. . . . .5G **63**
Clayton Road
NEWCASTLE UPON TYNE
NE2 1JP
Tel: 0191 281 6131

NHS WALK-IN CENTRE (BATTLE HILL) 7H **47**
Belmont Close
WALLSEND
NE28 9DX
Tel: 0191 295 8520

NHS WALK-IN CENTRE (GATESHEAD) 2K **99**
Queen Elizabeth Hospital
Sheriff Hill
GATESHEAD
NE9 6SX
Tel: 0191 445 5454

NHS WALK-IN CENTRE (MOLINEUX STREET)
. . . . .3P **5**
Molineux Street
Byker
NEWCASTLE UPON TYNE
NE6 1SG
Tel: 0191 275 5862

NHS WALK-IN CENTRE (NEWCASTLE WESTGATE)
. . . . .7B **62**
Westgate Road
NEWCASTLE UPON TYNE
NE4 6BE
Tel: 0191 282 3000

NHS WALK-IN CENTRE (SUNDERLAND)
. . . . .2C **118**
Sunderland Royal Hospital
Kayll Road
SUNDERLAND
SR4 7TP
Tel: 0191 565 6256

NORTHGATE HOSPITAL 3D **8**
Fair Moor
MORPETH
NE61 3BP
Tel: 0191 213 0151

NORTH TYNESIDE GENERAL HOSPITAL . . .3E **48**
Rake Lane
NORTH SHIELDS
NE29 8NH
Tel: 0844 811 8111

PALMER COMMUNITY HOSPITAL 6B **66**
Wear Street
JARROW
NE32 3UX
Tel: 0191 451 6000

PETERLEE COMMUNITY HOSPITAL 7B **172**
O'Neil Drive
PETERLEE
SR8 5UQ
Tel: 0191 586 3474

PRIMROSE HILL HOSPITAL 2C **86**
Primrose Terrace
JARROW
NE32 5HA
Tel: 0191 451 6375

PRIORY DAY HOSPITAL 6F **49**
Hawkeys Lane
NORTH SHIELDS
NE29 0SF
Tel: 0191 219 6629

QE METRO RIVERSIDE 3J **81**
Unit 6
Delta Bank Road
Metro Riverside Park
GATESHEAD
NE11 9DJ
Tel: 0191 482 0000

QUEEN ELIZABETH HOSPITAL 2K **99**
Queen Elizabeth Avenue
GATESHEAD
NE9 6SX
Tel: 0191 482 0000

ROYAL VICTORIA INFIRMARY 2D **4** (6E **62**)
Queen Victoria Road
NEWCASTLE UPON TYNE
NE1 4LP
Tel: 0191 233 6161

RYHOPE GENERAL HOSPITAL 4H **133**
Stockton Road
Ryhope
SUNDERLAND
SR2 0LY
Tel: 0191 565 6256

ST BENEDICT'S HOSPICE 4H **133**
St. Benedicts Way
SUNDERLAND
SR2 0NY
Tel: 0191 512 8400

ST CLARE'S HOSPICE 2C **86**
within Primrose Hill Hospital
Primrose Terrace
JARROW
NE32 5HA
Tel: 0191 451 6378

ST CUTHBERT'S HOSPICE 5J **165**
Park House Road
DURHAM
DH1 3QF
Tel: 0191 386 1170

ST GEORGE'S PARK 4G **9**
Whorral Bank
MORPETH
NE61 2NU
Tel: 0191 213 0151

ST NICHOLAS HOSPITAL 7C **44**
Jubilee Road
Gosforth
NEWCASTLE UPON TYNE
NE3 3XT
Tel: 0191 213 0151

ST OSWALD'S HOSPICE 7E **44**
Regent Avenue
NEWCASTLE UPON TYNE
NE3 1EE
Tel: 0191 285 0063

SHOTLEY BRIDGE HOSPITAL 3G **121**
Woodlands Road
CONSETT
DH8 0NB
Tel: 0191 333 2333

SIR G.B. HUNTER MEMORIAL HOSPITAL
. . . . .3G **65**
The Green
WALLSEND
NE28 7PB
Tel: 0191 220 5953

SOUTH QUAY NEURODISABILITY SUITE
. . . . .1G **23**
Cowpen Road
BLYTH
NE24 5TT
Tel: 0167 054 6795

SOUTH TYNESIDE DISTRICT HOSPITAL
. . . . .1K **87**
Harton Lane
SOUTH SHIELDS
NE34 0PL
Tel: 0191 404 1000

ST. BEDE'S UNIT 2K **99**
Queen Elizabeth Hospital
Queen Elizabeth Avenue
GATESHEAD
NE10 9RW
Tel: 0191 445 5704

SUNDERLAND EYE INFIRMARY 5F **119**
Queen Alexandra Road
SUNDERLAND
SR2 9HP
Tel: 0191 565 6256

SUNDERLAND ROYAL HOSPITAL 2C **118**
Kayll Road
SUNDERLAND
SR4 7TP
Tel: 0191 565 6256

UNIVERSITY HOSPITAL OF NORTH DURHAM
. . . . .7J **153**
North Road
DURHAM
DH1 5TW
Tel: 0191 333 2333

WALKERGATE PARK 4C **64**
Benfield Road
NEWCASTLE UPON TYNE
NE6 4QD
Tel: 0191 287 5000

WANSBECK GENERAL HOSPITAL 3E **12**
Woodhorn Lane
ASHINGTON
NE63 9JJ
Tel: 0844 811 8111

WASHINGTON SPIRE HOSPITAL 1C **128**
Picktree Lane
WASHINGTON
NE38 9JZ
Tel: 0191 418 8687

WHALTON UNIT, THE 2F **15**
South Road
MORPETH
NE61 2BT
Tel: 0344 811 8111

WILLOW BURN HOSPICE 4K **137**
Howden Bank
Lanchester
DURHAM
DH7 0QS
Tel: 0120 752 9224

From the Helpline...

Featuring 50 commonly encountered electrical problems and their solutions

NICEIC

NICEIC

'NICEIC' is a trading name of NICEIC Group Limited, a wholly owned subsidiary of the Electrical Safety Council. Under licence from the Electrical Safety Council, NICEIC acts as the electrical contracting industry's independent voluntary regulatory body for electrical installation safety matters throughout the UK, and maintains and publishes registers of electrical contractors that it has assessed against particular scheme requirements (including the technical standard of electrical work).

The registers include the national Roll of Approved Contractors (established in 1956), and the register of NICEIC Domestic Installers that, since January 2005, have been authorised to self-certify their domestic electrical installation work as compliant with the Building Regulations for England and Wales.

The NICEIC Approved Contractor scheme is accredited by the United Kingdom Accreditation Service (UKAS) to *EN 45011 – General requirements for bodies operating product certification systems.*

The Electrical Safety Council

The Electrical Safety Council (formerly the National Inspection Council for Electrical Installation Contracting) is a charitable non-profit making organization set up in 1956 to protect users of electricity against the hazards of unsafe and unsound electrical installations.

The Electrical Safety Council is supported by all sectors of the electrical industry, approvals and research bodies, consumer interest organizations, the electricity distribution industry, professional institutes and institutions, regulatory bodies, trade and industry associations and federations, trade unions and local and central government.

Published by:

NICEIC Group Limited
Warwick House, Houghton Hall Park, Houghton Regis, Dunstable, Bedfordshire LU5 5ZX

Tel: 01582 531000 Fax: 01582 556024

Email: customerservice@niceic.com Website: www.niceicgroup.com

ISBN-10 0-9548791-7-1
ISBN-13 978-0-9548791-7-4
EAN 9780954879174

Foreword

The NICEIC technical helpline answers in excess of 30 000 telephone calls a year and receives an even larger number of emails.

Many of the telephone calls and emails are asking for information that can be found from current publications, such as the Electrical Safety Council *Technical Manual*[1] , the IEE *On-Site Guide*[2] and *Snags and Solutions*[3]. However, there are also many questions that relate to specific issues, or to common misconceptions. This handy, pocket-sized book aims to answer fifty of the most commonly asked questions.

The questions and answers in this book are arranged under four section headings:

Section 1	Assessment of general characteristics and verification
Section 2	Selection and erection
Section 3	Earthing and bonding
Section 4	Fire alarms and emergency lighting

The amounts of questions in the sections of the book differ, and reflect the numbers of questions coming into the helpline. Additionally, the answers in the book are commonly longer than would be provided by a telephone conversation with the helpline, requiring, as they do, to include material relating to the content of specific standards and/or reference documents.

Every question and corresponding answer is clearly illustrated, and concludes with reference to the relevant requirements of *BS 7671*, or other applicable regulations or standards.

This new edition is fully updated to reflect the requirements of *BS 7671: 2008* (IEE Wiring Regulations 17th edition).

---

1 Published by The Electrical Safety Council, London, UK

2 Published by The IEE, London, UK.

3 Published by NICEIC

Contents

Section 1

Assessment of general characteristics and verification

Question 1 **Designer of the electrical installation**

I have just completed a rewire of a house and am compiling the Electrical Installation Certificate. Who is the designer? **page 2**

Question 2 **Alterations and additions**

When I am adding a new circuit or making an alteration to an existing electrical installation, what are the main things I should consider? **page 4**

Question 3 **Maximum demand - calculation of**

How do I calculate the maximum demand of a domestic electrical installation? **page 8**

Question 4 ***Part P*** **- notifying**

What work needs notifying under the requirements of *Part P* of the *Building Regulations for England and Wales*? **page 10**

Question 5 ***Part P*** **– application of**

I am finding the requirements of *Part P* difficult to understand. What do they apply to? **page 14**

Question 6 **Types of certificates and reports**

I have added a new circuit to an existing electrical installation. What type of certificate should be filled in? **page 16**

Question 7 Record keeping

Why is it necessary to have so much form filling when electrical installation work or periodic inspection and testing of an installation has been carried out? **page 18**

Question 8 Insulation resistance tests – when current-using equipment is connected

How do I carry out an insulation resistance test on a fixed installation when current-using equipment is connected? **page 22**

Question 9 Insulation resistance tests – position for testing

At what positions should the insulation resistance be measured when testing a new electrical installation or an alteration or addition to an existing installation? **page 24**

Question 10 Time/current characteristics

What are time/current characteristics and how are they used? **page 26**

Question 11 Earth fault loop impedance – when not listed in *BS 7671*

If the maximum permitted value of earth fault loop impedance for a circuit is not given in Tables 41.2, 41.3 or 41.4 of *BS 7671*, how can it be determined? **page 30**

Question 12 Earth fault loop impedance – calculation of

How should the earth loop impedance of a circuit in an installation be calculated? **page 32**

Question 13 Earth fault loop impedance testing – operation of protective devices

Certain protective devices, such as RCDs, trip when an earth loop impedance test is carried out. Why is this and what should I do where this occurs? **page 36**

Contents

Question 14 Verification of steel conduit

Where an existing steel conduit system is used as the circuit protective conductor, how can I verify its suitability for continued use for this purpose when carrying out periodic inspection and testing on the installation? **page 40**

Section 2

Selection and erection

Question 15 Rewireable fuses

Does *BS 7671* require rewireable (semi-enclosed) fuses complying with *BS 3036* to be replaced with circuit-breakers or cartridge fuses? **page 44**

Question 16 Unswitched socket-outlets

If socket-outlets to *BS 1363* do not have a switch do they need replacing? **page 46**

Question 17 Switches in bathrooms

Is it permitted for a wall-mounted switch to be installed in a bathroom? **page 48**

Question 18 Socket-outlets near sinks

Is it permitted for a socket-outlet to be installed near to a kitchen sink? **page 50**

Question 19 Socket-outlets installed on or in wooden panels

I want to install a socket-outlet in a wooden panel. Do I need to use an accessory box? **page 52**

Question 20 Grommets for metal back boxes

Does a metal back box require a grommet where an insulated and sheathed cable enters it? **page 54**

Question 21 Cables installed within cavity walls

Is it permitted to install insulated and sheathed cables within a cavity wall? **page 56**

Question 22 Cables installed under a floor or above a ceiling - holes

Where an insulated and sheathed cable is to be installed through a hole in a timber joist under a floor or above a ceiling, at what depth in the joist should the hole be drilled? **page 58**

Question 23 Cables installed under a floor or above a ceiling - notches

When installing insulated and sheathed cables under a floor or above a ceiling, is it permissible to use a notch in a timber joist? **page 62**

Question 24 Dedicated circuit for an immersion heater

Must an immersion heater be supplied through its own dedicated circuit? **page 66**

Question 25 Fan control

Is it permitted to supply a fan fitted in a location containing a bath or shower or in a kitchen from a lighting circuit? **page 68**

Question 26 Fire hoods for downlighters

Do I need to install a fire hood behind a downlighter? **page 72**

Contents

Question 27 **Outside lighting fixed to a building**

I am planning to install an outside light on the external wall of a building. Are there any particular requirements of *BS 7671* that I need to take into account? **page 74**

Question 28 **Lighting circuit without a cpc**

I am thinking of extending and altering an existing lighting circuit wired in pvc-insulated and sheathed twin cable without a circuit protective conductor, by adding lighting points and switches and changing the existing lighting switches from the all-insulated type to the type having metal plates. Is it permissible to do this or must the existing circuit be rewired? **page 78**

Question 29 **Instantaneous electric showers installed in a bathroom or shower room**

Does the supply circuit to an electric shower installed in zone 1 of a bathroom or shower room have to be protected by a residual current device (RCD)? **page 82**

Question 30 **Length of meter tails**

Why do meter tails longer than 3 m require additional switchgear? **page 84**

Question 31 **Fixing heights of accessories**

When adding new accessories to an existing electrical installation in a dwelling that does not comply with the requirements of *Part M* of the *Building Regulations for England and Wales*, must I comply with the fixing heights recommended by *Approved Document M* of the *Building Regulations for England and Wales*? **page 88**

Section 3

Earthing and bonding

Question 32 **Earthing and bonding – what is the difference?**

What is the difference between earthing and bonding? **page 92**

Question 33 **Main and supplementary bonding – what is the difference**

What is the difference between main equipotential bonding and supplementary equipotential bonding? **page 96**

Question 34 **Extraneous-conductive-parts – metal staircase**

In a brick built industrial unit there is an internal staircase leading to an upper level. The staircase has an exposed structural metal frame bolted to the concrete ground floor slab of the building. Is there a requirement to carry out main equipotential bonding to the frame of the staircase? **page 98**

Question 35 **Extraneous-conductive-parts – plastic pipework**

A mains water service enters a building and connects to the supply side of a stopcock close to the point of entry. From the discharge side of the stopcock, plastic installation pipework within the building runs for a distance and then changes to copper pipework for the rest water installation. Is there a requirement to carry out main or supplementary bonding to the copper pipework? **page 100**

Contents

Question 36 Earthing or bonding to metal cable tray or cable basket

A number of multicore cables are grouped together on a length of cable tray or metal cable basket. Is it necessary to earth or bond the tray or basket? **page 102**

Question 37 Metal sink – bonding

Is it necessary to bond a metallic kitchen sink? **page 106**

Question 38 Earthing of metal back boxes

When installing a socket-outlet or a metallic wall-mounted switch, do I need to provide an earthing tail between the accessory and the accessory box? **page 108**

Question 39 Locations containing a bath or shower

What needs to be connected together when carrying out supplementary bonding within a room containing a bath or shower? **page 110**

Question 40 Lightning protection systems

What are the requirements for connecting a lightning protection system to an electrical installation's Main Earthing Terminal? **page 112**

Question 41 Supplies from a PME system – caravan pitches

Are there any special earthing requirements that must be taken into account where a caravan park is supplied from a Protective Multiple Earthing supply? **page 116**

Question 42 Cross-sectional area of an earthing conductor – TN system

How should I size a single-core green-yellow pvc-covered copper cable for use as the earthing conductor for an installation forming part of a TN system? **page 120**

Question 43 **Installing earth electrodes – types for a TT system**

What may be used as the installation earth electrode in a TT system? **page 124**

Question 44 **Installing earthing conductors – for a TT system**

In a TT system what cross-sectional area of green-yellow pvc-covered copper earthing conductor should be used to connect between a Main Earthing Terminal of the installation and the installation earth electrode? **page 126**

Section 4

Fire alarms and emergency lighting

Question 45 **Grades and Categories of fire detection and alarm systems in dwellings**

I am planning to install a fire alarm system in a dwelling. What are the meanings of the 'Grades' of system and 'Categories' of system? **page 130**

Question 46 **Wiring used in fire detection and alarm systems**

What type of wiring should be used for a fire alarm and detection system in a dwelling and what should be the sheath colour? **page 134**

Question 47 **Segregation requirements for fire alarm cables in a dwelling**

What requirements for segregation (or separation) apply to the wiring of a fire detection and alarm system in a dwelling? **page 136**

Contents

Question 48 Tests on emergency lighting systems

The model form of Emergency Lighting Periodic Inspection and Test Certificate in Annex D of *BS 5266-1: 2005* refers to daily, monthly and annual periodic tests.
What should be covered during these tests? **page 138**

Question 49 Test facility for emergency lighting luminaires

Is it a requirement of the emergency lighting standard or *BS 7671* to provide a test facility for an emergency lighting luminaire local to the luminaire's position? **page 142**

Question 50 Lighting levels of an emergency lighting system

When carrying out a periodic inspection and test on an emergency lighting system, how do I determine the lighting levels being achieved? **page 144**

Assessment of general characteristics and verification

Questions 1-14

FROM THE HELPLINE ...

Designer of the electrical installation

Question

I have just completed a rewire of a house and am compiling the Electrical Installation Certificate. Who is the designer?

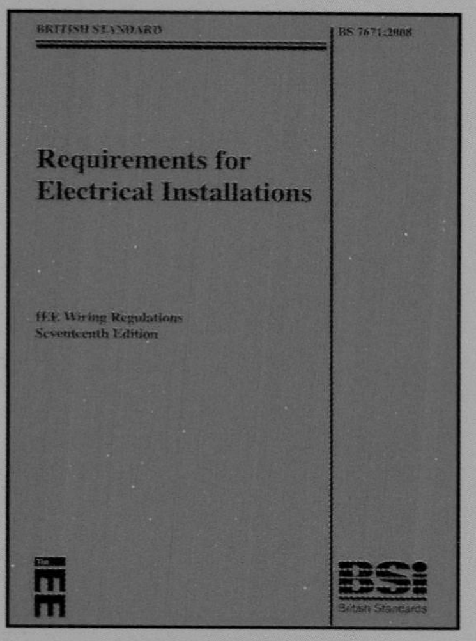

Answer

The designer is the person or organization responsible for all aspects of the installation design, such as the selection of protective devices, sizing of cables; and selection of the method of installation, suitable equipment, and precautions for special locations.

The positioning of socket-outlets, lights etc is considered to be layout detail and not electrical design. However, the electrical designer will need to know the proposed positions of the equipment before determining whether or not such positions will allow compliance with the requirements of *BS 7671* and completing the design calculations. The client or installation user may be able to decide where they require such items to be positioned, but the sizing and method of installing the cables and the selection of suitable equipment are matters for the designer.

Standard applied
BS 7671

Regulations referred to
None listed

Alterations and additions

Question

When I am adding a new circuit or making an alteration to an existing electrical installation, what are the main things I should consider?

Answer

Before any new circuit is added, or any existing circuit is altered, account must be taken of the requirement of Regulation 131.8:

"No addition or alteration, temporary or permanent, shall be made to an existing installation, unless it has been ascertained that the rating and the condition of any existing equipment, including that of the distributor, will be adequate for the altered circumstances. Furthermore, the earthing and bonding arrangements, if necessary for the protective measure applied for the safety of the addition or alteration, shall be adequate."

Therefore, prior to any installation work being carried out, an assessment must be made of the impact of the proposed addition or alteration. This should be carried out in accordance with the requirements of Part 3 of *BS 7671*.

1. Maximum demand

If the addition or alteration to the installation increases the load, the maximum demand of the installation should be assessed, in accordance with the requirements of Regulation 311.1, to establish whether the rating of switchgear and the cross-sectional area (csa) of distribution cables, such as meter tails, are adequate. (Any inadequacies would need to be corrected before the alteration or addition was made.)

2. Arrangement of live conductors and type of earthing

Section 312 requires that the characteristics of the live conductors and the type of earthing arrangement for the installation are determined. This is so that the designer of the installation, or of the alteration or addition to the installation, can, amongst other things, correctly assess whether the installation has the appropriate means of protection for safety required by Part 4 of *BS 7671*. The designer needs to assess whether:

- for a TN-S system, the cross-sectional area (csa) of the earthing conductor meets the requirements of both the distributor and Regulation 543.1, and that the main protective bonding conductors meet the requirements of Regulation 544.1

- for a TN-C-S system, the csa of the earthing conductor meets the requirements of both the distributor and Regulation 543.1 of *BS 7671*. Additionally, the csa of the main protective bonding conductors and the earthing conductor should meet the requirements of Table 54.8
- for a TT system, the csa of the earthing conductor, where buried in the ground, meets the requirements of Regulation 543.1 and Table 54.1. Additionally, the designer will need to satisfy himself or herself that the requirements of Regulation 411.5.3, or where applicable Regulation 411.5.4, are being met with regard to the resistance of the installation earth electrode and associated protective conductor(s)
- there is a need to carry out any additional bonding in order for the alterations and additions to comply with the requirements of *BS 7671*.

3. Supplies

The characteristics of the incoming supply listed in Regulation 313.1 must be determined. This is necessary so that the designer can check, amongst other things, that the voltage, current-carrying capacity and number of phases of the supply are adequate for the load of the installation. This requirement will include the proposed alterations and/or additions. Additionally, the external earth fault loop impedance (Z_e) should be of a suitably low value for the purposes of fault protection in the altered/extended installation.

4. Division of installation

Regulation 314.1, amongst other things, requires that every installation is divided into circuits to avoid danger and minimize inconvenience in the event of a fault, to facilitate safe inspection, testing and maintenance, and to take account of danger that may arise from the failure of a single circuit such as a lighting circuit.

Thus, for example, where a circuit is added to an installation, the designer will need to ensure that, should a fault occur on the new circuit, this will not cause any other circuit to lose its supply.

5. Compatibility

The designer will need to make an assessment in accordance with Regulation 331.1 as to whether any proposed additional electrical equipment will not have harmful effects on other electrical equipment or services, or be harmfully affected by them, or impair the supply.

6. Maintainability

Chapter 34 requires that:

> *"An assessment shall be made of the frequency and quality of maintenance that the installation can reasonably be expected to receive during its intended life."*

The information from the assessment will need to be used by the designer to help in the choice of equipment and protective measures for the addition and/or alteration to the installation.

Standard applied
BS 7671

Regulations referred to
131.8, 311.1, 312, 313.1, 314.1, 331.1, Chapter 34, 411.5.3, 411.5.4, 543.1, 544.1.1

Maximum demand - calculation of

Question

How do I calculate the maximum demand of a domestic electrical installation?

Answer

Before carrying out an assessment of the maximum demand of an electrical installation, the designer should consider all the factors that may have an influence on the effective and safe operation of the installation. Information relating to the characteristics of the available supply will also be required.

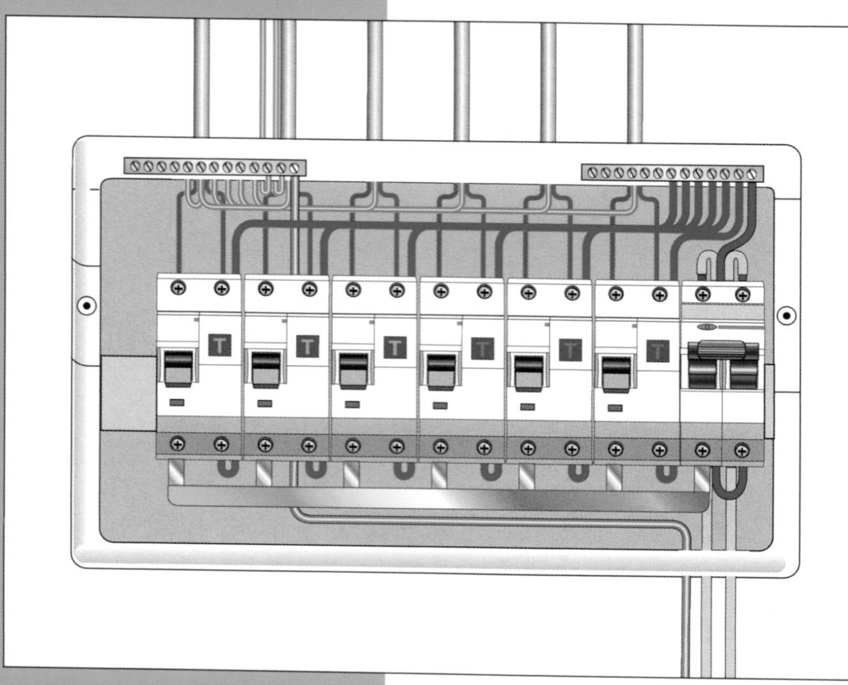

Regulation 311.1 of *BS 7671* requires that the maximum demand of an installation, expressed in amperes, is assessed. The purpose of the assessment is to establish whether or not the supply to the installation will be of sufficient current-carrying capacity for the purpose for which the installation is intended. For assessing maximum demand, sufficient information is needed about the connected load, how the installation is likely to be used and any diversity factors that may be applied.

By allowing for diversity, the designer recognizes that the maximum demand of the installation is less than the connected load. This is because at any one time only a certain number of items of current-using equipment are likely to be in use. Failure to allow for diversity would normally lead to assessing the available supply as inadequate for the load. For example, there is no restriction within *BS 7671* on the number of 13 A socket-outlets that can be connected to a circuit. Without applying diversity factors, a circuit having fifteen 13 A socket-outlets would have a potential load of approximately 196 A, which would exceed the current-carrying capacity of any supply to a domestic installation (typically 60 A or 100 A). The economic design of an electrical installation will almost always mean that diversity factors have to be applied to relevant circuits.

A variety of methods exist for estimating the maximum demand of an installation. The adopted method will depend on the information available at the time the calculation is carried out. For most installations, the estimated maximum demand will be an approximation since there is no exact method for calculating maximum demand in all circumstances.

Where a diversity factor is not known, the designer may wish to adopt the method described in *Appendix H - IEE Guidance Note 1 – Selection and Erection* (GN1) *or Appendix 1 – IEE On-Site Guide* (OSG).

Standard applied
BS 7671

Regulations referred to
311.1

Part P - notifying

Question

What work needs notifying under the requirements of *Part P* of the *Building Regulations for England and Wales*?

Answer

Part P of the *Building Regulations for England and Wales* requires that certain electrical work in houses and flats and their surroundings in England and Wales is notified to a building control body before the work starts.

Pocket Guide 8, published by NICEIC, and available for download from **www.niceicgroup.com**, provides examples of notifiable and non-notifiable work. Information from the card is reproduced here.

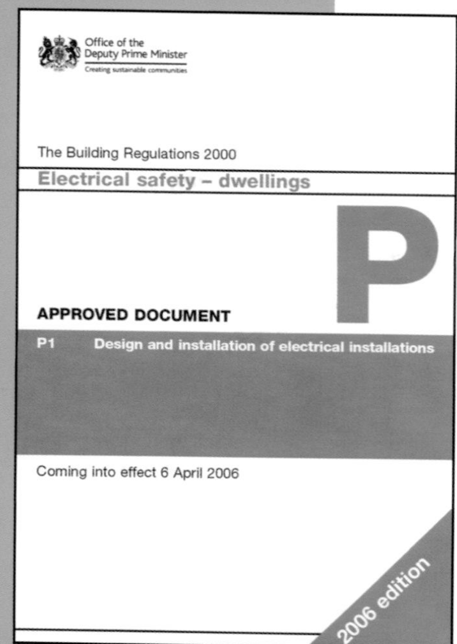
Office of the Deputy Prime Minister
Creating sustainable communities

The Building Regulations 2000
Electrical safety – dwellings

P

APPROVED DOCUMENT

P1 Design and installation of electrical installations

Coming into effect 6 April 2006

2006 edition

1. Examples of notifiable work

Anywhere in a dwelling or a surrounding:

- a complete new installation or rewire
- changing a consumer unit
- installing
  - a new final circuit, for example, for lighting, heating, socket-outlets, a shower or a cooker
  - **extra-low voltage** lighting (other than pre-assembled CE marked sets)
  - a solar photovoltaic power supply
  - electric ceiling or floor heating
  - an electricity generator
  - power or control wiring for a new central heating system.

Within a kitchen or special location:

- modifying a final circuit, for example, adding a lighting point, fused connection unit or socket-outlet

Within a special location:

- installing telephone or extra-low voltage wiring and equipment for the purposes of communications, information technology, signalling, control or similar purposes
- installing a prefabricated equipment set, for example, lighting, and associated flexible leads with integral plug and socket connections.

Outdoors:

- installing garden lighting or power, for example, a supply to a garden shed, detached garage, other outbuilding, electric gate or pond pump
- installing a socket-outlet
- installing a lighting point or other fixed current-using equipment, for example, air conditioning unit or a radon fan.

2. Examples of non-notifiable work

Anywhere in a dwelling or its surroundings:

- installing prefabricated **'modular'** wiring systems
- replacing a damaged cable for a single circuit, on a **like-for-like** basis
- replacing an accessory, such as a socket-outlet, control switch, ceiling rose or a fused connection unit
- providing **mechanical protection** to an existing fixed installation
- installing or upgrading main or supplementary equipotential bonding
- fitting or replacing an item of current-using equipment, such as a cooker, to an existing suitable circuit.

Within a garden shed, detached garage, or other outbuilding:

- modifying a final circuit, for example, adding a lighting point, fused connection unit or socket-outlet.

A company registered with a *Part P* self-certification scheme, such as the NICEIC Domestic Installer scheme, is not required to notify a building control body prior to carrying out 'notifiable work'. However, such a registered company would need to notify the self-certification scheme operator on completion of the notifiable work.

Notes for both notifiable work and non-notifiable work

Extra-low voltage	Defined in *BS 7671* as 'Not exceeding 50 V a.c. or 120 V ripple-free d.c., whether between conductors or to Earth'.
Kitchen	Defined in *The Building (Amendment) (No.3) Regulations 2004* as a 'room or part of a room which contains a sink and food preparation facilities'. A utility room, though it may contain a sink, does not fall within the definition of a kitchen if it does not contain food preparation facilities.
Special locations	Include locations containing a bath, shower, swimming pool, paddling pool or a hot air sauna.
Modular systems	The installation of prefabricated 'modular' systems, for example kitchen lighting systems and armoured garden cabling, linked by plug and socket connectors is not notifiable, provided that the products are CE-marked and that any final connection in a kitchen or special location is made to an existing suitable connection unit or point.
Outdoor equipment	Notification is not required for wiring to outdoor equipment, such as a lighting point, air conditioning unit or radon fan, where; (i) it is not a new circuit, and (ii) passes directly through an outside wall into the equipment, and (iii) is not an extension to a special location or kitchen circuit.
Like-for-like	Includes the condition that the replacement cable has the same current-carrying capacity and follows the same route.
Providing mechanical protection to an existing fixed installation	If the circuit protective measures and current-carrying capacity of conductors are unaffected by increased thermal insulation.

QUESTION 4

Part P - application of

Question

I am finding the requirements of *Part P* difficult to understand. What do they apply to?

Answer

Part P is a requirement under Schedule 1 of the *Building Regulations 2000 (England and Wales)* that applies to work carried out in houses and flats and their surroundings (such as gardens and outbuildings) in England and Wales.

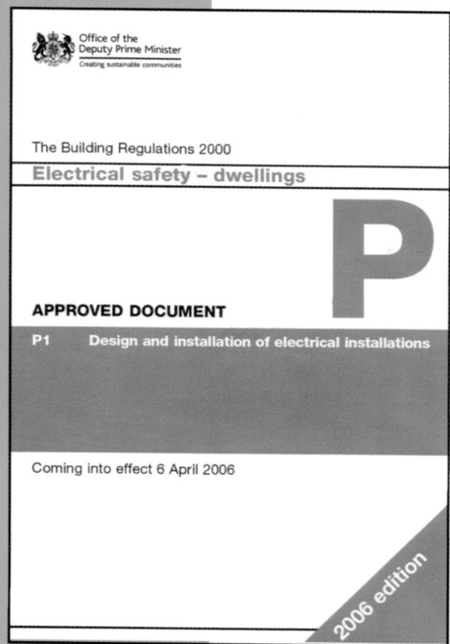
Office of the Deputy Prime Minister
Creating sustainable communities

The Building Regulations 2000

Electrical safety – dwellings

P

APPROVED DOCUMENT

P1 Design and installation of electrical installations

Coming into effect 6 April 2006

2006 edition

QUESTION 5

The document that many people consider to be *Part P* is actually *Approved Document P* (Electrical safety – dwellings) and this document provides guidance on how the requirements of Part P may be complied with.

Part P (P1) requires that, *'Reasonable provision shall be made in the design and installation of electrical installations in order to protect persons operating, maintaining or altering the installations from fire or injury'.*

The limits placed on the application of this requirement are that it only applies to electrical installations that are intended to operate at low or extra-low voltage and that are:

(a) in or attached to a dwelling, such as a house or flat,

(b) in the common parts of a building serving one or more dwellings, such as a stairway or communal corridor, but excluding power supplies to lifts,

(c) in a building that receives its electricity from a source located within or shared with a dwelling, such as a flat or maisonette, and

(d) in a garden or in or on land associated with a building where the electricity is from a source located within or shared with a dwelling.

Types of certificates and reports

Question

I have added a new circuit to an existing electrical installation. What type of certificate should be filled in?

Answer

Regulation 631.1 of *BS 7671* requires that after a new installation or changes to an existing installation have been verified (by inspection and testing), an Electrical Installation Certificate is provided. In addition to the requirement for such a certificate the regulation requires that a schedule of inspection and the results of testing be provided.

An Electrical Installation Certificate or a Domestic Electrical Installation Certificate, where applicable, must therefore be provided where any new circuits are added. Regulation 632.1 requires that the certificate and the schedule of inspection and results of any tests are given to the person ordering the work.

Where the contractor or other person responsible for the new work is adding circuits to an existing installation, Regulation 633.2 requires that any defects found in the existing installation shall, so far as is reasonably practicable, be recorded on the Electrical Installation Certificate.

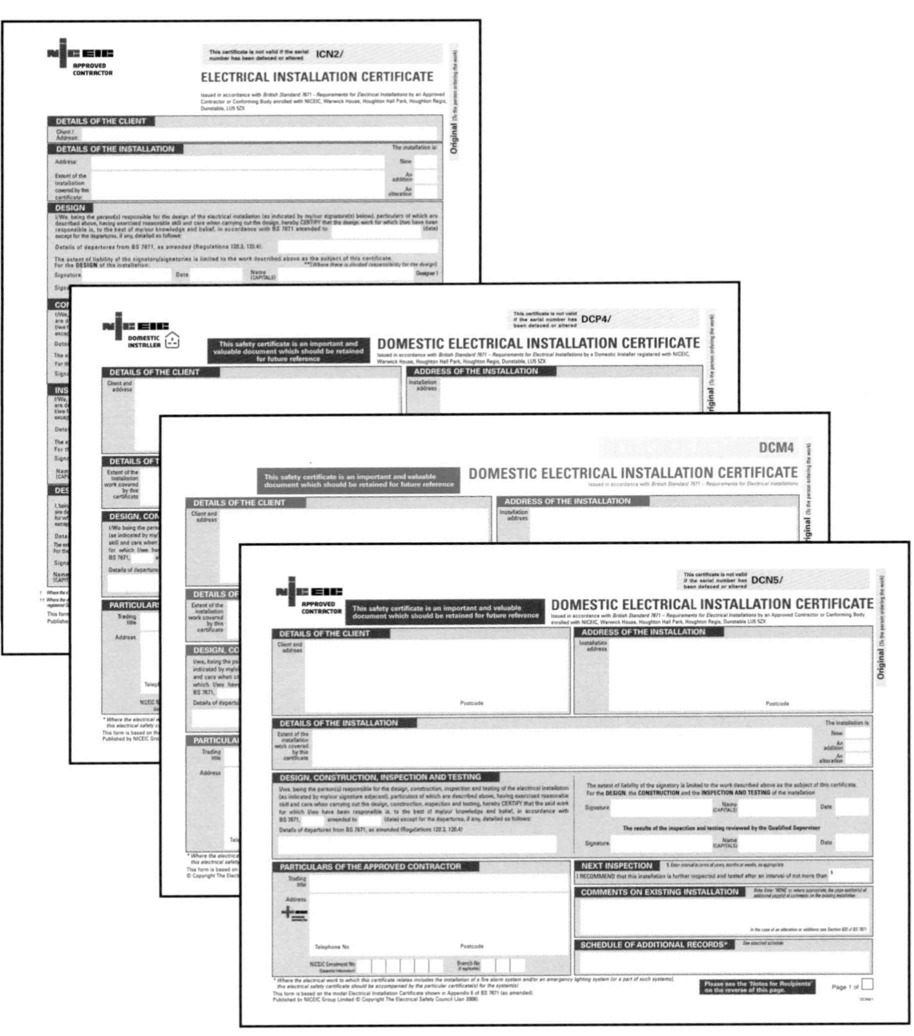

NICEIC APPROVED CONTRACTOR

This certificate is not valid if the serial number has been defaced or altered ICN2/

ELECTRICAL INSTALLATION CERTIFICATE

Issued in accordance with British Standard 7671 – Requirements for Electrical Installations by an Approved Contractor or Conforming Body enrolled with NICEIC, Warwick House, Houghton Hall Park, Houghton Regis, Dunstable, LU5 5ZX

DETAILS OF THE CLIENT

DETAILS OF THE INSTALLATION

DESIGN

NICEIC DOMESTIC INSTALLER

This safety certificate is an important and valuable document which should be retained for future reference

This certificate is not valid if the serial number has been defaced or altered DCP4/

DOMESTIC ELECTRICAL INSTALLATION CERTIFICATE

DCM4

DOMESTIC ELECTRICAL INSTALLATION CERTIFICATE

NICEIC APPROVED CONTRACTOR

This safety certificate is an important and valuable document which should be retained for future reference

This certificate is not valid if the serial number has been defaced or altered DCN5/

DOMESTIC ELECTRICAL INSTALLATION CERTIFICATE

Issued in accordance with British Standard 7671 – Requirements for Electrical Installations by an Approved Contractor or Conforming Body enrolled with NICEIC, Warwick House, Houghton Hall Park, Houghton Regis, Dunstable LU5 5ZX

Original (To the person ordering the work)

DETAILS OF THE CLIENT

Client and address

Postcode

ADDRESS OF THE INSTALLATION

Installation address

Postcode

DETAILS OF THE INSTALLATION

Extent of the installation work covered by this certificate

The installation is: New / An addition / An alteration

DESIGN, CONSTRUCTION, INSPECTION AND TESTING

I/we, being the person(s) responsible for the design, construction, inspection and testing of the electrical installation (as indicated by my/our signature adjacent), particulars of which are described above, having exercised reasonable skill and care when carrying out the design, construction, inspection and testing, hereby CERTIFY that the said work for which I/we have been responsible is, to the best of my/our knowledge and belief, in accordance with BS 7671, ______ amended to ______ (date) except for the departures, if any, detailed as follows:

Details of departures from BS 7671, as amended (Regulations 120.3, 120.4)

The extent of liability of the signatory is limited to the work described above as the subject of this certificate. For the **DESIGN**, the **CONSTRUCTION** and the **INSPECTION AND TESTING** of the installation

Signature / Name (CAPITALS) / Date

The results of the inspection and testing reviewed by the Qualified Supervisor

Signature / Name (CAPITALS) / Date

PARTICULARS OF THE APPROVED CONTRACTOR

Trading title

Address

Telephone No / Postcode

NICEIC Enrolment No / Branch No (if applicable)

NEXT INSPECTION

I RECOMMEND that this installation is further inspected and tested after an interval of not more than

COMMENTS ON EXISTING INSTALLATION

SCHEDULE OF ADDITIONAL RECORDS*

See attached schedule

* Where the electrical work to which this certificate relates includes the installation of a fire alarm system and/or an emergency lighting system (or a part of such systems), this electrical safety certificate should be accompanied by the particular certificate(s) for the system(s)

This form is based on the model Electrical Installation Certificate shown in Appendix 6 of BS 7671 (as amended).

Published by NICEIC Group Limited © Copyright The Electrical Safety Council (Jan 2008)

Please see the 'Notes for Recipients' on the reverse of this page.

Page 1 of

Standard applied

BS 7671

Regulations referred to

631.1, 632.1, 632.3, 633.2.

Record keeping

Question

Why is it necessary to have so much form filling when electrical installation work or periodic inspection and testing of an installation has been carried out?

Answer

BS 7671 requires that:

- on completion of an installation or an addition or alteration to an installation, appropriate inspection and testing shall be carried out to verify that the requirements of the standard have been met (Regulation 134.2.1 refers). Additionally, Regulations 631.1, 631.3 and 633.2 require that relevant documentation shall be completed
- periodic inspection and testing of an electrical installation must be carried out to determine whether the installation is in a satisfactory condition for continued service (Regulation 621.1 refers). Additionally, Regulation 631.2 requires that relevant documentation shall be completed
- a legible diagram, chart or table or equivalent form of information must be provided indicating a variety of information about an installation. For simple installations this may be provided on a schedule (Regulation 514.9.1 refers).

Additionally, where the installation is in an agricultural or horticultural premise, Regulation 705.514.9.3 requires that documentation must be provided to the user of the installation, which consists of:

- A plan indicating the location of all electrical equipment, and
- The routing of all concealed cables, and
- A single-line distribution diagram, and
- An equipotential bonding diagram indicating locations of bonding connections.

An Electrical Installation Certificate or, where appropriate, a Domestic Electrical Installation Certificate or a Minor Electrical Installation Works Certificate is an important declaration that the installation work has been designed, constructed and inspected and tested in accordance with the requirements of *BS 7671*. Similarly, a Periodic Inspection Report or, where appropriate a Domestic Periodic Inspection Report, is a declaration that the inspection and testing has been carried out in accordance with the requirements of *BS 7671*. All of these forms contain, or are accompanied by, a record of the particulars of the installation, the work carried out and of the results of the inspection and testing.

It is also a requirement of regulation 4(2) of the *Electricity at Work Regulations 1989* (EWR) that:

> *"As may be necessary to prevent danger, all systems shall be maintained so as to prevent, so far as is reasonably practicable such danger."*

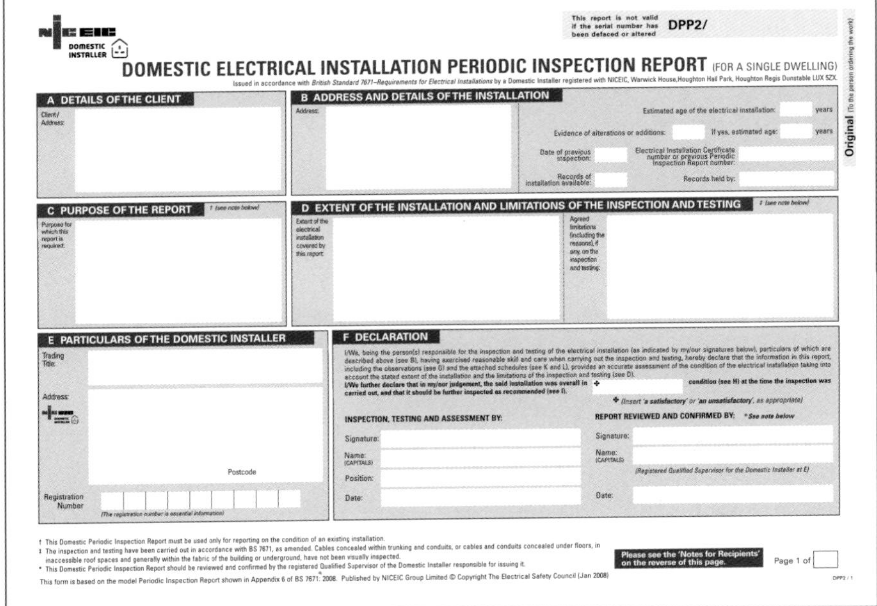

NICEIC DOMESTIC INSTALLER

This report is not valid if the serial number has been defaced or altered DPP2/

Original (To the person ordering the work)

DOMESTIC ELECTRICAL INSTALLATION PERIODIC INSPECTION REPORT (FOR A SINGLE DWELLING)

Issued in accordance with *British Standard 7671–Requirements for Electrical Installations* by a Domestic Installer registered with NICEIC, Warwick House,Houghton Hall Park, Houghton Regis Dunstable LUX 5ZX.

A DETAILS OF THE CLIENT

Client / Address:

B ADDRESS AND DETAILS OF THE INSTALLATION

Address:

Estimated age of the electrical installation: years

Evidence of alterations or additions: If yes, estimated age: years

Date of previous inspection: Electrical Installation Certificate number or previous Periodic Inspection Report number:

Records of installation available: Records held by:

C PURPOSE OF THE REPORT † (see note below)

Purpose for which this report is required:

D EXTENT OF THE INSTALLATION AND LIMITATIONS OF THE INSPECTION AND TESTING ‡ (see note below)

Extent of the electrical installation covered by this report:

Agreed limitations (including the reasons), if any, on the inspection and testing:

E PARTICULARS OF THE DOMESTIC INSTALLER

Trading Title:

Address:

Postcode

Registration Number

(The registration number is essential information)

F DECLARATION

I/We, being the person(s) responsible for the inspection and testing of the electrical installation (as indicated by my/our signatures below), particulars of which are described above (see B), having exercised reasonable skill and care when carrying out the inspection and testing, hereby declare that the information in this report, including the observations (see G) and the attached schedules (see K and L), provides an accurate assessment of the condition of the electrical installation taking into account the stated extent of the installation and the limitations of the inspection and testing (see D).

I/We further declare that in my/our judgement, the said installation was overall in ✤ condition (see H) at the time the inspection was carried out, and that it should be further inspected as recommended (see I).

✤ *(Insert 'a satisfactory' or 'an unsatisfactory', as appropriate)*

INSPECTION, TESTING AND ASSESSMENT BY:

Signature:

Name: (CAPITALS)

Position:

Date:

REPORT REVIEWED AND CONFIRMED BY: **See note below*

Signature:

Name: (CAPITALS)

(Registered Qualified Supervisor for the Domestic Installer at E)

Date:

† This Domestic Periodic Inspection Report must be used only for reporting on the condition of an existing installation.

‡ The inspection and testing have been carried out in accordance with BS 7671, as amended. Cables concealed within trunking and conduits, or cables and conduits concealed under floors, in inaccessible roof spaces and generally within the fabric of the building or underground, have not been visually inspected.

* This Domestic Periodic Inspection Report should be reviewed and confirmed by the registered Qualified Supervisor of the Domestic Installer responsible for issuing it.

Please see the 'Notes for Recipients' on the reverse of this page.

Page 1 of

This form is based on the model Periodic Inspection Report shown in Appendix 6 of BS 7671: 2008. Published by NICEIC Group Limited © Copyright The Electrical Safety Council (Jan 2008)

DPP2 / 1

In general, to demonstrate that the necessary inspection and testing has been carried out, and that relevant maintenance activities have been undertaken, to comply with the requirements of the EWR, records should be kept of the inspection and testing performed on an electrical installation. The *Memorandum of guidance on the Electricity at Work Regulations* states that records of maintenance, including test results, should preferably by kept throughout the life of an electrical system. This enables the condition of the electrical equipment and the effectiveness of maintenance policies to be monitored.

The requirements for maintenance as detailed by the EWR may not apply to dwellings in the same way as for normal work situations. For example, the EWR does not impose any duties on the householder to keep records of the maintenance of the electrical installation in a dwelling. However, electrical safety certification and Periodic Inspection Reports (PIRs) are a good way to demonstrate to prospective purchasers of a house that the installation was properly installed and has been appropriately maintained.

In summary, correctly compiled certificates and reports:

- are a record of your involvement and responsibility
- demonstrate that you have carried out the necessary inspection and testing
- can be significant in providing you with, if necessary, a defence under Regulation 29 of the *Electricity at Work Regulations*.

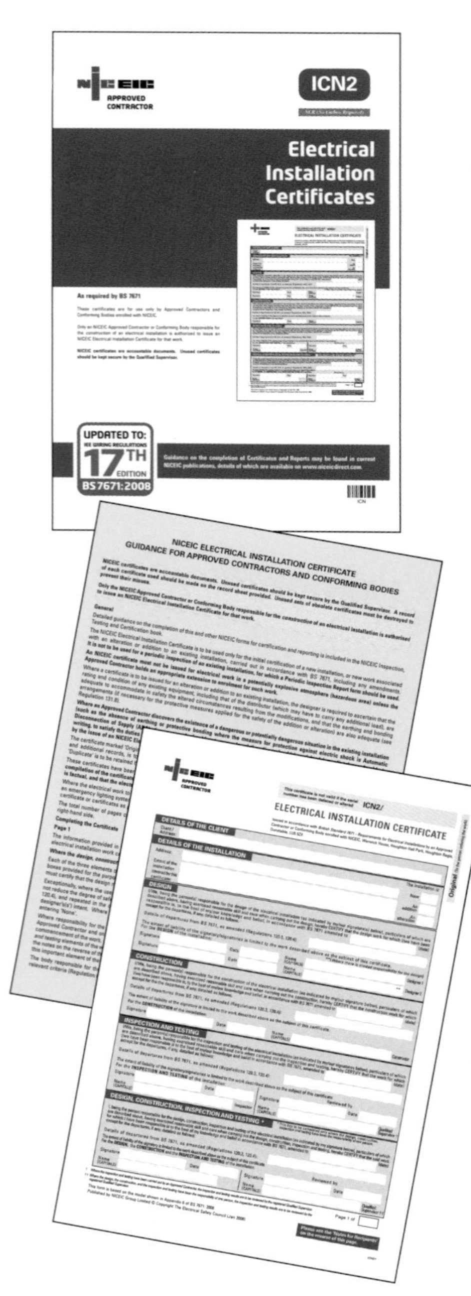

QUESTION 7

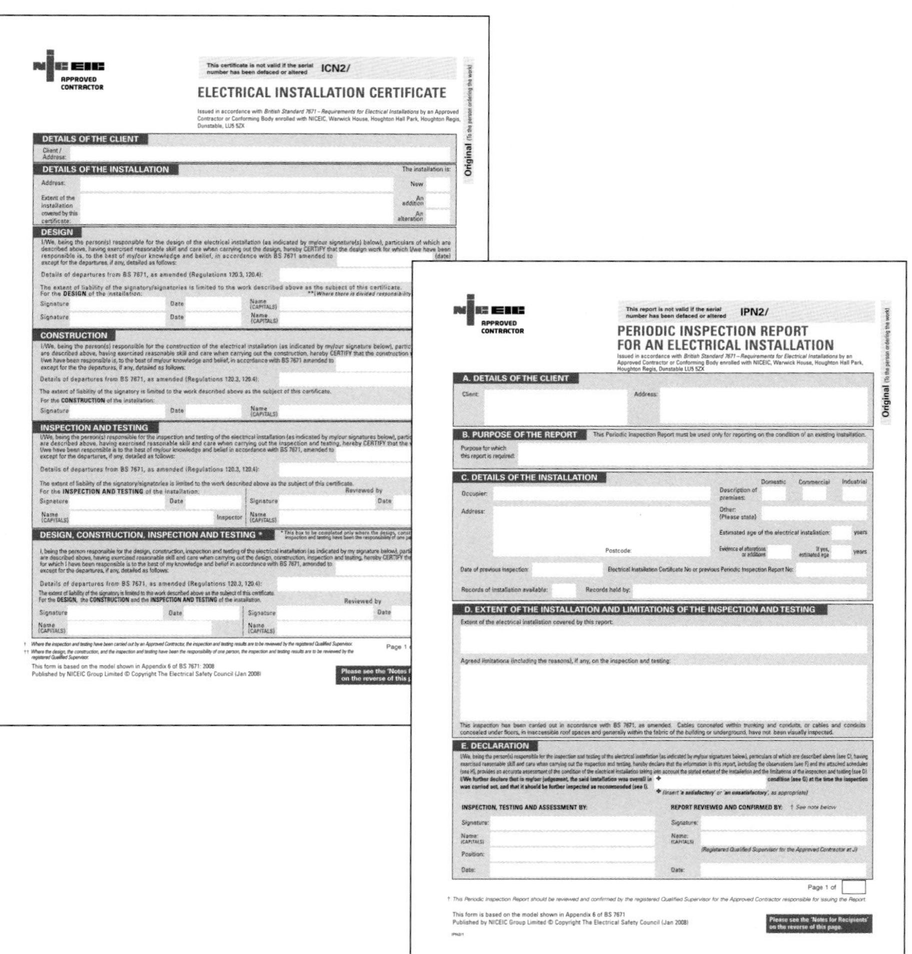

NICEIC APPROVED CONTRACTOR

This certificate is not valid if the serial number has been defaced or altered ICN2/

ELECTRICAL INSTALLATION CERTIFICATE

Issued in accordance with *British Standard 7671 – Requirements for Electrical Installations* by an Approved Contractor or Conforming Body enrolled with NICEIC, Warwick House, Houghton Hall Park, Houghton Regis, Dunstable, LU5 5ZX

Original (To the person ordering the work)

DETAILS OF THE CLIENT

Client / Address:

DETAILS OF THE INSTALLATION

The installation is:

Address: | New

Extent of the installation covered by this certificate: | An addition | An alteration

DESIGN

I/We, being the person(s) responsible for the design of the electrical installation (as indicated by my/our signature(s) below), particulars of which are described above, having exercised reasonable skill and care when carrying out the design, hereby CERTIFY that the design work for which I/we have been responsible is, to the best of my/our knowledge and belief, in accordance with BS 7671 amended to (date) except for the departures, if any, detailed as follows:

Details of departures from BS 7671, as amended (Regulations 120.3, 120.4):

The extent of liability of the signatory/signatories is limited to the work described above as the subject of this certificate.
For the **DESIGN** of the installation: **(Where there is divided responsibility

Signature | Date | Name (CAPITALS)

Signature | Date | Name (CAPITALS)

CONSTRUCTION

I/We, being the person(s) responsible for the construction of the electrical installation (as indicated by my/our signature below), partic are described above, having exercised reasonable skill and care when carrying out the construction, hereby CERTIFY that the construction I/we have been responsible is, to the best of my/our knowledge and belief, in accordance with BS 7671 amended to except for the the departures, if any, detailed as follows:

Details of departures from BS 7671, as amended (Regulations 120.3, 120.4):

The extent of liability of the signatory is limited to the work described above as the subject of this certificate.
For the **CONSTRUCTION** of the installation:

Signature | Date | Name (CAPITALS)

INSPECTION AND TESTING

I/We, being the person(s) responsible for the inspection and testing of the electrical installation (as indicated by my/our signatures below), partic are described above, having exercised reasonable skill and care when carrying out the inspection and testing, hereby CERTIFY that the I/we have been responsible is to the best of my/our knowledge and belief in accordance with BS 7671, amended to except for the departures, if any, detailed as follows:

Details of departures from BS 7671, as amended (Regulations 120.3, 120.4):

The extent of liability of the signatory/signatories is limited to the work described above as the subject of this certificate.
For the **INSPECTION AND TESTING** of the installation: | Reviewed by

Signature | Date | Signature | Date

Name (CAPITALS) | Inspector | Name (CAPITALS)

DESIGN, CONSTRUCTION, INSPECTION AND TESTING *

* This box to be completed only where the design, cons inspection and testing have been the responsibility of one pe

I, being the person responsible for the design, construction, inspection and testing of the electrical installation (as indicated by my signature below), parti are described above, having exercised reasonable skill and care when carrying out the design, construction, inspection and testing, hereby CERTIFY the for which I have been responsible is to the best of my knowledge and belief in accordance with BS 7671, amended to except for the departures, if any, detailed as follows:

Details of departures from BS 7671, as amended (Regulations 120.3, 120.4):

The extent of liability of the signatory is limited to the work described above as the subject of this certificate.
For the **DESIGN**, the **CONSTRUCTION** and the **INSPECTION AND TESTING** of the installation. | Reviewed by

Signature | Date | Signature | Date

Name (CAPITALS) | Name (CAPITALS)

† *Where the inspection and testing have been carried out by an Approved Contractor, the inspection and testing results are to be reviewed by the registered Qualified Supervisor.*

†† *Where the design, the construction, and the inspection and testing have been the responsibility of one person, the inspection and testing results are to be reviewed by the registered Qualified Supervisor.*

Page 1

This form is based on the model shown in Appendix 6 of BS 7671: 2008
Published by NICEIC Group Limited © Copyright The Electrical Safety Council (Jan 2008)

Please see the 'Notes f on the reverse of this p

NICEIC APPROVED CONTRACTOR

This report is not valid if the serial number has been defaced or altered IPN2/

PERIODIC INSPECTION REPORT FOR AN ELECTRICAL INSTALLATION

Issued in accordance with *British Standard 7671 – Requirements for Electrical Installations* by an Approved Contractor or Conforming Body enrolled with NICEIC, Warwick House, Houghton Hall Park, Houghton Regis, Dunstable LU5 5ZX

Original (To the person ordering the work)

A. DETAILS OF THE CLIENT

Client: | Address:

B. PURPOSE OF THE REPORT This Periodic Inspection Report must be used only for reporting on the condition of an existing installation.

Purpose for which this report is required:

C. DETAILS OF THE INSTALLATION

Occupier: | Description of premises: Domestic | Commercial | Industrial

Address: | Other: (Please state)

Estimated age of the electrical installation: years

Postcode: | Evidence of alterations or additions | If yes, estimated age | years

Date of previous inspection: | Electrical Installation Certificate No or previous Periodic Inspection Report No:

Records of installation available: | Records held by:

D. EXTENT OF THE INSTALLATION AND LIMITATIONS OF THE INSPECTION AND TESTING

Extent of the electrical installation covered by this report:

Agreed limitations (including the reasons), if any, on the inspection and testing:

This inspection has been carried out in accordance with BS 7671, as amended. Cables concealed within trunking and conduits, or cables and conduits concealed under floors, in inaccessible roof spaces and generally within the fabric of the building or underground, have not been visually inspected.

E. DECLARATION

I/We, being the person(s) responsible for the inspection and testing of the electrical installation (as indicated by my/our signatures below), particulars of which are described above (see C), having exercised reasonable skill and care when carrying out the inspection and testing, hereby declare that the information in this report, including the observations (see F) and the attached schedules (see H), provides an accurate assessment of the condition of the electrical installation taking into account the stated extent of the installation and the limitations of the inspection and testing (see D). **I/We further declare that in my/our judgement, the said installation was overall in ✤ condition (see G) at the time the inspection was carried out, and that it should be further inspected as recommended (see I).**

✤ *(insert '**a satisfactory**' or '**an unsatisfactory**', as appropriate)*

INSPECTION, TESTING AND ASSESSMENT BY: | **REPORT REVIEWED AND CONFIRMED BY:** † *See note below*

Signature: | Signature:

Name: (CAPITALS) | Name: (CAPITALS)

Position: | *(Registered Qualified Supervisor for the Approved Contractor at J)*

Date: | Date:

Page 1 of

† *This Periodic Inspection Report should be reviewed and confirmed by the registered Qualified Supervisor for the Approved Contractor responsible for issuing the Report.*

This form is based on the model shown in Appendix 6 of BS 7671
Published by NICEIC Group Limited © Copyright The Electrical Safety Council (Jan 2008)

Please see the 'Notes for Recipients' on the reverse of this page.

IPN2/1

Standards applied

BS 7671 • Electricity at Work Regulations 1989
Memorandum of guidance on the Electricity at Work Regulations

Regulations referred to

134.2.1, 514.9.1, 621.1, 631.1, 631.2, 631.3, 633.3, 705.514.9.3

Insulation resistance tests - when current-using equipment is connected

Question

How do I carry out an insulation resistance test on a fixed installation when current-using equipment is connected?

Answer

Effective insulation provides basic protection against contact with live parts, and prevents short-circuits and earth faults. An insulation resistance test of an installation is intended to give an indication of the condition of the insulation of the installation's conductors.

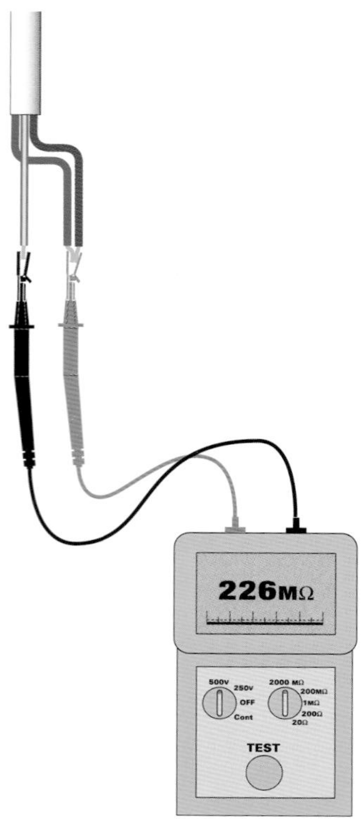

It is always preferable to carry out an insulation resistance test prior to current-using equipment being connected. Indeed, for new installations, the insulation resistance test is one of the tests that can reasonably be carried out during erection, as well as on completion of the installation (Regulation 610.1 refers).

However, there are situations where it may be necessary to carry out insulation resistance tests whilst current-using equipment is connected to the fixed installation. This might be the case, for example, where periodic inspection and testing is taking place, or where it is not practicable to disconnect electronic equipment or other items of current-using equipment.

Regulation 612.3.3 states that, when testing circuits including electronic devices, only a measurement to protective earth shall be made with the live conductors connected together. The note attached to the regulation also states that precautions may be necessary to avoid damage to electronic devices.

Where an insulation resistance test is performed under such conditions, it must be recognized that not all of the fixed wiring will be tested.

The NICEIC publication, *Inspection, Testing and Certification*, provides further guidance on carrying out an insulation resistance test.

Standard applied
BS 7671

Regulations referred to
610.1, 612.3.3.

Insulation resistance tests - position for testing

Question

At what positions should the insulation resistance be measured when testing a new electrical installation or an alteration or addition to an existing installation?

Answer

The are two purposes for which insulation resistance measurements are necessary:

- to check that the overall insulation resistance for the whole installation, or all new or altered/extended circuits, is sufficient to meet the requirements of *BS 7671*, and
- for the compilation of schedules of test results.

For the whole installation, the overall insulation resistance is considered satisfactory by Regulation 612.3.2 if the main switchboard, and each distribution circuit tested separately with all its final circuits connected but with current-using equipment disconnected, has an insulation resistance not less than the appropriate value given in Table 61 of *BS 7671*. The application of this requirement may differ depending on the size of the installation.

For a domestic installation, the overall insulation resistance requirement of Regulation 612.3.2 can usually be checked by testing at the consumer unit with all final circuits and distribution circuits (if any) connected.

QUESTION 9

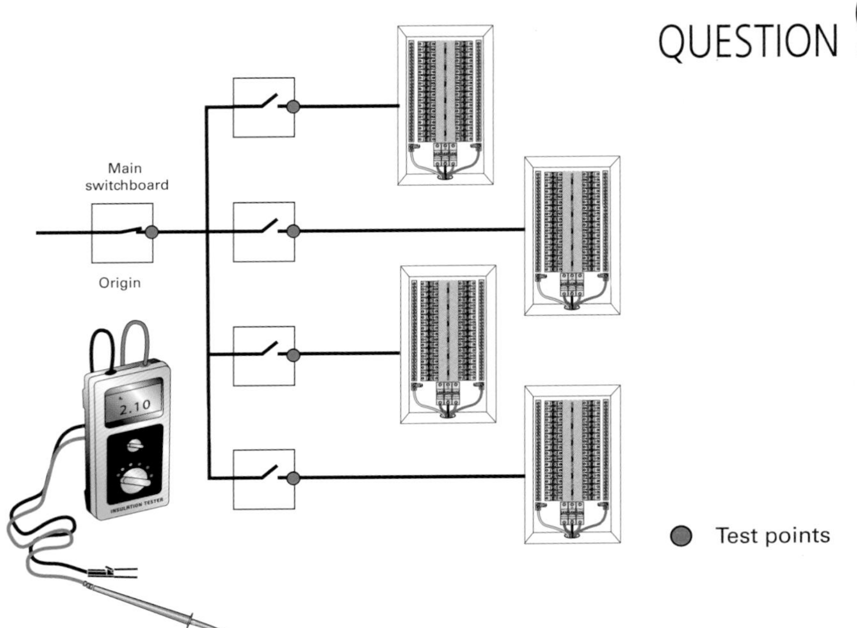

For a larger installation, because of the combination of a large number of circuits and long cable runs, it may be found that the insulation resistance measured at the main switchboard with all final circuits and distribution circuits connected is less than the appropriate value given in Table 61 of *BS 7671* (such as 1 MΩ for circuits of nominal voltage up to 500 V). In such a case, the insulation requirement of Regulation 612.3.2 should be checked by taking separate measurements at the main switchboard and at the origin of each distribution circuit (with final circuits connected), as indicated in the regulation.

To compile schedules of test results, the insulation resistance of each new circuit, or each altered/extended circuit, should be measured individually from the origin of the circuit. This is because the readings should be recorded on a schedule of test results based on the model given in Appendix 6 of *BS 7671*, which necessitates the readings for each circuit being recorded individually. Current-using equipment should be disconnected during the tests.

Standard applied
BS 7671

Regulations referred to
612.3.2

Time/current characteristics

Question

What are time/current characteristics and how are they used?

Answer

What are they?

The time/current characteristics in Appendix 3 of *BS 7671* are curves on graphs that provide details on the time that protective devices will take to operate when a particular magnitude of current flows. Information is given for the following protective devices:

- Fuses to *BS 1361*
- Semi-enclosed fuses to *BS 3036*
- Fuses to *BS EN 60269-2* and *BS 88-6*
- Type B circuit-breakers to *BS EN 60898* and RCBOs to *BS EN 61009*
- Type C circuit-breakers to *BS EN 60898* and RCBOs to *BS EN 61009*
- Type D circuit-breakers to *BS EN 60898* and RCBOs to *BS EN 61009*

In all cases the time/current characteristics in Appendix 3 of *BS 7671* are based on the slowest operating times that comply with the relevant standard. Additionally, information from the time/current characteristics has been used to derive the limiting values of earth fault loop impedance listed in the tables in Section 411 of *BS 7671*.

How do I use them?

The simplest way to make sense of the time/current characteristics for a particular type of protective device in Appendix 3 of *BS 7671* is to read off the values of current for the quoted disconnection times in the table in the top right-hand corner of the applicable set of time/current characteristics.

The time/current characteristics themselves are plotted on log-log graph paper. This type of graph paper enables large ranges to be included on the same page. It is divided into a series of 'cycles' – that is, repeated bands, each containing a series of unevenly spaced lines constantly repeated.

Considering the horizontal axis, the first line represents 1 A, with each subsequent vertical line (each one getting closer to the next) representing a further 1 A increase until a value of 10 A is reached. The cycle is then repeated with a 10 A increase per line until 100 A is reached. A further cycle is then repeated with a 100 A increase per line etc.

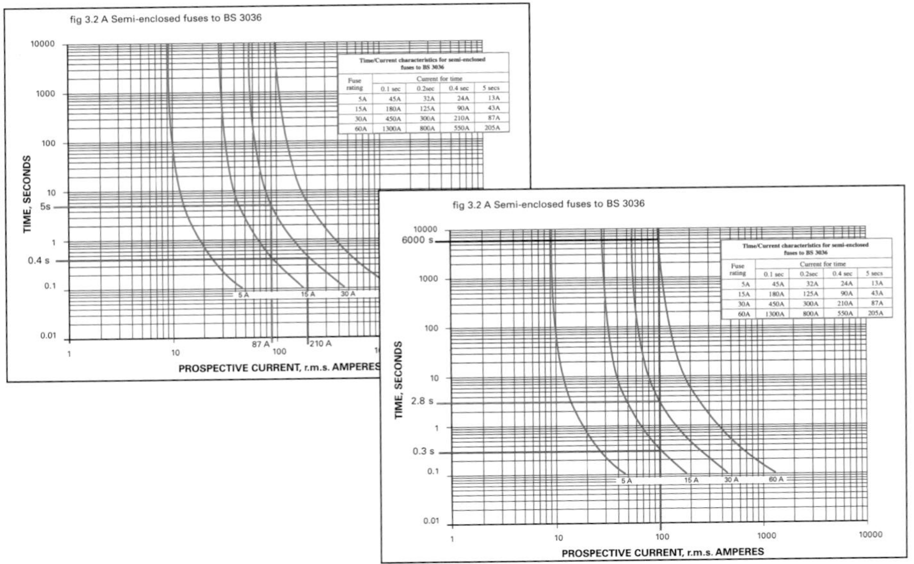

Time/Current characteristics for semi-enclosed fuses to BS 3036

Fuse rating	Current for time			
	0.1 sec	0.2sec	0.4 sec	5 secs
5A	45A	32A	24A	13A
15A	180A	125A	90A	43A
30A	450A	300A	210A	87A
60A	1300A	800A	550A	205A

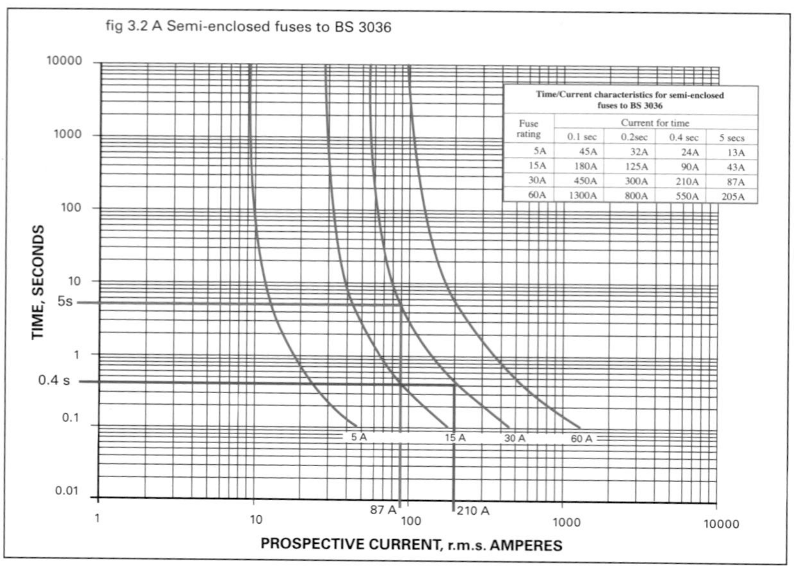

Required current for disconnection time of 0.4 s and 5 s

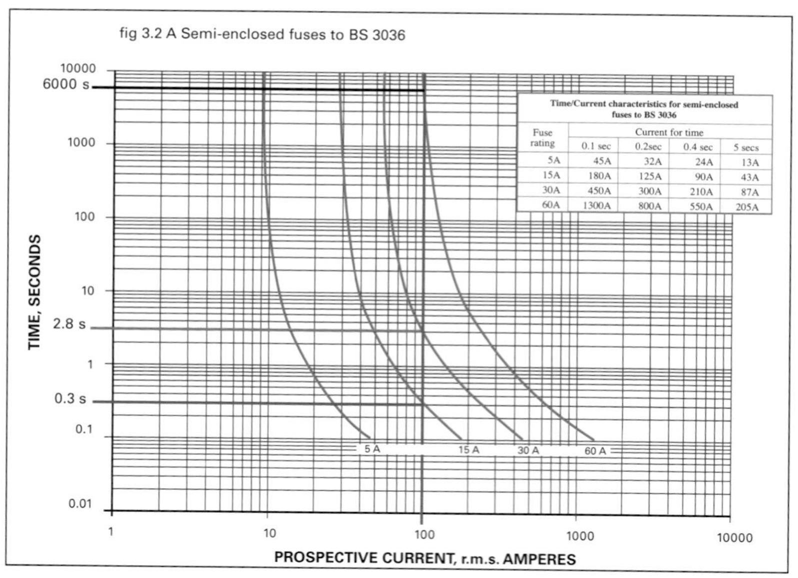

Disconnection times for a range of fuses for a fault current of 100 A

A similar process occurs with the vertical axis starting at 0.01 s.

Each individual line, say between 1 A and 2 A, is also subdivided into a series of unevenly spaced lines (not shown on the graph), so that a value of 1.5 A would not fall half way between the 1 A and 2 A values, but rather be set a little closer to the 2 A line.

To understand how to read the graphs, consider as an example a 30 A semi-enclosed fuse to *BS 3036*. For a 0.4 s disconnection time, a line is drawn horizontally until it crosses the 30 A curve. Reading down from where it crosses to the prospective current axis, it will be seen that a current of 210 A will cause a 30 A *BS 3036* fuse to operate in 0.4 s.

For a 5 s disconnection time, a horizontal line is drawn to the point where it crosses the characteristic curve of the device. For a 30 A *BS 3036* fuse, for example, a current of 87 A will cause the fuse to operate within 5 s.

Alternatively, if the prospective current is known, then the disconnection time can be determined. Consider a fault current of 100 A for each of the fuses on the diagram. Reading up from the 100 A position on the prospective current (horizontal) axis:

- 100 A will cause a 5 A fuse to operate faster than 0.1 s (it never crosses the characteristic curve)
- 100 A will cause a 15 A fuse to operate in 0.3 s
- 100 A will cause a 30 A fuse to operate in 2.8 s
- 100 A will cause a 60 A fuse to operate in approximately 6 000 s

Standard applied
BS 7671

Regulations referred to
Appendix 3

Earth fault loop impedance - when not listed in BS 7671

Question

If the maximum permitted value of earth fault loop impedance for a circuit is not given in Tables 41.2, 41.3 or 41.4 of *BS 7671*, how can it be determined?

Answer

For certain types of overcurrent protective device, such fuses rated at more than 200 A to *BS EN 60269* and *BS 88*, maximum permitted values of earth fault loop impedance are not given in the tables of maximum earth fault loop impedance in *BS 7671*.

Where this is the case, use can be made of the formula given in Appendix 3 of *BS 7671*:

$$Z_s = \frac{U_o}{I_a}$$

Where:

U_o is the nominal a.c. rms line voltage to earth

I_a is the current causing operation of the protective device within the specified time. This time will commonly be either 0.4 s or 5 s for circuits where the nominal voltage to earth is 230 V. The current may be determined from the time/current characteristics published by the manufacturer of the device, or by consulting the manufacturer for the value.

QUESTION 11

Example

What are the maximum earth loop impedance values for a 63 A HBC fuse to *BS EN 88-2.2 and BS 88-6* for disconnection times of 0.4 s?

Using data drawn from the time/current characteristics of Appendix 3 of *BS 7671*:

- a 0.4 s disconnection time for a 63 A HBC fuse requires a fault current (I_a) of 500 A

Assuming U_o =230 V

For 0.4 s

$$Z_s = \frac{230}{500} = 0.46\ \Omega$$

This process can be repeated for all fuse values that are not listed in *BS 7671*. For the fuse ratings not listed by Tables 41.2, the maximum earth fault loop values are:

For 0.4 s disconnection time:

General purpose (gG) fuses to *BS EN 88-2.2* and *BS 88-6*

Rating (A)	40	50	63	80	100	125	160	200
Z_s (ohms)	0.82	0.60	0.46	0.31	0.23	0.18	0.14	0.10

Fuses to BS 1361

Rating (A)	60	80	100					
Z_s (ohms)	0.38	0.29	0.20					

Fuses to BS 3036

Rating (A)	60	100						
Z_s (ohms)	0.42	0.20						

Standard applied

BS 7671

Regulations referred to

Table 41.2, Appendix 3.

Earth fault loop impedance - calculation of

Question

How should the earth loop impedance of a circuit in an installation be calculated?

Answer

Before a circuit is installed, the designer of the electrical installation should establish that the earth fault loop impedance will not exceed the appropriate maximum permitted value given in *BS 7671*. This is so that, under earth fault conditions, sufficient current will flow to cause the protective device to operate within the appropriate maximum permitted disconnection time.

The total earth fault loop impedance is generally considered in two parts: the external earth fault loop impedance (Z_e) and the internal resistance (R_1+R_2).

R_1+R_2 is the sum of the resistances of the line conductor and the circuit protective conductor between the origin of the installation and the electrically most remote point or accessory of the circuit.

The external earth loop impedance (Z_e) consists of:

- for TN systems, the metallic return path or, for TT and IT systems, the earth return path
- the path through the earthed neutral point of the transformer
- the transformer winding
- the line conductor of the distributor up to the origin of the installation.

The internal resistance consists of the resistance of:

- the line conductor from the origin of the installation to the electrically most remote point or accessory of the circuit *(R_1)* and
- the earthing conductor of the installation and the circuit protective conductor from the origin of the installation to the electrically most remote point or accessory of the circuit *(R_2)*.

$$Z_s = Z_e + (R_1 + R_2)$$

The values of resistance for the line conductor *(R_1)* and the earthing conductor and circuit protective conductor *(R_2)* may be determined from data provided in guidance material such as Table E1 of *IEE Guidance Note 1* or Table 9A of the *IEE On-Site Guide*[1]. Where resistance data is listed at a temperature lower than the normal operating temperature of the cable, a correction factor should be applied.

To determine the value of *(Z_e)*, the designer may use either measured data or data supplied by the distributor. Regulation 28 of the *Electricity Safety, Quality and Continuity Regulations 2002* (ESQCR) requires, amongst other things, that the value of the external impedance *(Z_e)* is declared by the distributor upon request.

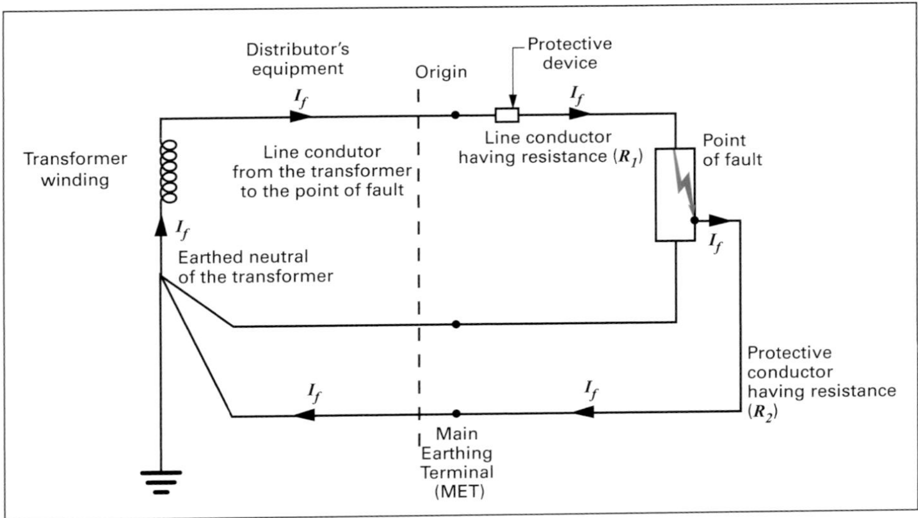

Diagram of earth fault loop for a TN-S system

[1] Published by The IEE.

Example

A fixed electric water heater in an indoor location is supplied through a 1.5/1.0 mm^2 pvc-insulated and sheathed twin and earth cable. The length of run is 21 m and the circuit is protected by a 15 A fuse to *BS 3036*. The external earth loop impedance as declared by the distributor is 0.8 Ω and the nominal voltage of the supply is 230 V. The earthing conductor is very short and its resistance may therefore be neglected.

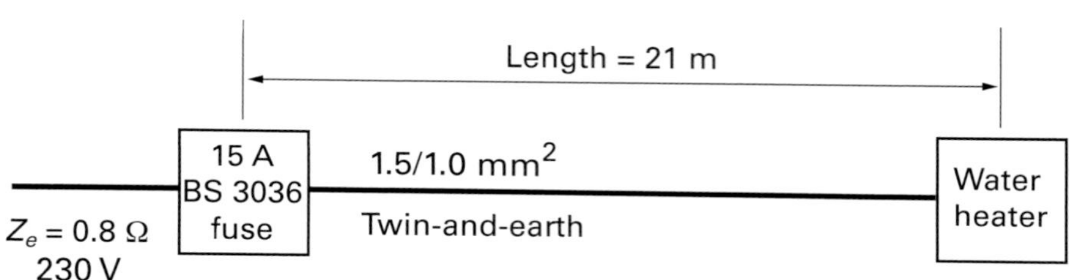

[2] No temperature correction factor need be applied to the external impedance.

Answer

From Table E1 of IEE Guidance Note 1 (or Table 9A IEE On-Site Guide):

$$(R_1+R_2)/m = 30.20\ m\,\Omega$$

Correction factor to convert resistance at 20 °C to the resistance at the normal operating temperature of 70 °C from Table E2 of IEE *Guidance Note 1* (or Table 9C IEE *On-Site Guide*):

$$F = 1.2$$

Total internal impedance:

$$(R_1+R_2) = \frac{m\Omega/m \times I \times F}{1000} = \frac{30.20 \times 21 \times 1.2}{1000} = 0.761\ \Omega$$

Total impedance:

$$Z_s = Z_e + (R_1+R_2) = 0.8 + 0.761 = 1.561\ \Omega$$

The maximum permitted disconnection time for the water heater, being rated at more than 32 A is 0.4 s (Regulation 411.3.2.2 refers).

From Table 41.2 of *BS 7671*, for a 0.4 s disconnection time, the maximum permitted earth fault loop impedance for a 15 A *BS 3036* fuse is 2.55 Ω. Therefore, for this example, the fuse will operate quickly enough to comply with Regulation 411.3.2.2.

Standards applied

BS 7671 • Regulation 28 ESQCR

Regulations referred to

411.3.2.2, Table 41.1, Table 41.2, Appendix 3.

Earth fault loop impedance testing - operation of protective devices

Question

Certain protective devices, such as residual current devices (RCDs), trip when an earth loop impedance test is carried out. Why is this and what should I do where this occurs?

Answer

During a test, a typical earth fault loop impedance test instrument causes a current of about 20 A to 25 A a.c. to flow from the line conductor to the protective conductor of the circuit. This test current is liable to cause unwanted tripping of any RCD or 6 A Type B circuit-breaker to *BS EN 60898* protecting the circuit, due to their particular time/current characteristics.

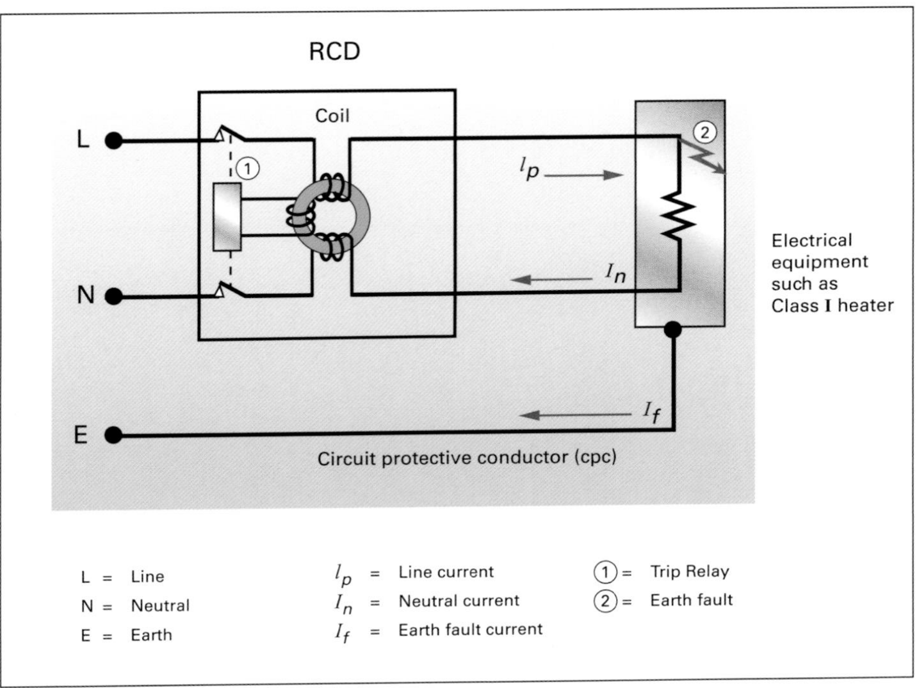

Operating principle of an RCD

1. Residual current device

An RCD operates when there is an imbalance between the line and neutral conductor currents in the circuit which exceeds the rated residual operating current ($I_{\Delta n}$) of the device. The imbalance is generally created when there is either a line to earth or a neutral to earth fault. Therefore, if any test instrument,that creates a sufficient imbalance between line and neutral conductor currents will cause the RCD to operate. Earth loop impedance test instruments can create such an imbalance, causing unwanted operation of the RCD when the test is performed.

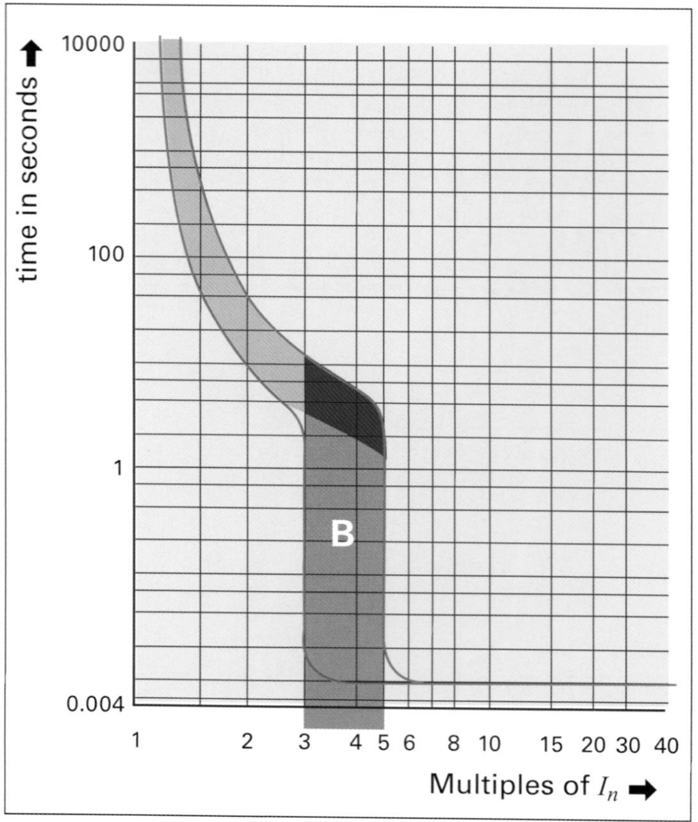

Time current characteristic for a 6 A Type B circuit-breaker

2. Circuit-breaker to BS EN 60898

A 6 A Type B circuit-breaker to *BS EN 60898* is required to operate within 0.1 s when a current five times its nominal current rating flows. The device may also operate within 0.1 s at values of current between three and five times the nominal rating of the device.

As the earth fault loop impedance test instrument can cause a current of up to 25 A to flow, this may cause unwanted operation of the circuit-breaker.

3. What to do

Where it is likely that unwanted tripping of either an RCD or a 6 A Type B circuit-breaker will occur during testing, use may be made of an earth fault loop impedance test instrument that 'tricks' the RCD or circuit-breaker into not tripping. This might be achieved by, for example, reducing the current during the test or by speeding up the test process.

Where such a test instrument is not used, or where the instrument still causes unwanted operation of the RCD or circuit-breaker, a combination of measured values may be used (explained below) for circuits rated at less than about 100 A. Under no circumstances should the verifier bypass any means of protection whilst the circuit is being tested. Such practice is dangerous.
Regulation 612.9 permits the earth fault loop impedance of a circuit to be either measured or determined by an alternative method.

Where the earth fault loop impedance value is to be measured by using a combination of values:

- the external earth fault loop impedance (Z_e)[1] should be measured using an earth fault loop test instrument, and the result recorded
- the resistance of the line conductor and protective conductor (R_1+R_2) should be measured at the furthest point in the circuit, using a low-resistance ohmmeter, and the result recorded.

The total earth fault loop impedance (Z_S) is the sum of the external earth fault loop impedance and the internal resistance values,
i.e. $Z_S = Z_e + (R_1+R_2)$.

It should be noted that the (R_1+R_2) test should be carried out only after having securely isolated the supply. Guidance on testing can be found in the book, *Inspection, Testing and Certification*, published by NICEIC.

[1] For a local distribution board rather than the origin of the installation Z_e becomes Z_{db}.

Standards applied
BS 7671• BS EN 60898 • IEE Guidance Note 3

Regulations referred to
612.9

Verification of steel conduit

Question

Where an existing steel conduit system is used as the circuit protective conductor, how can I verify its suitability for continued use for this purpose when carrying out periodic inspection and testing on the installation?

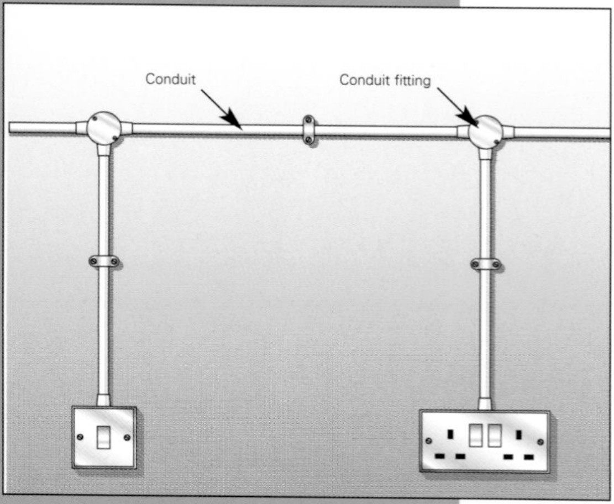

Conduit

Conduit fitting

Answer

The principal requirements of *BS 7671* relating to the use of steel conduit as a circuit protective conductor (cpc) are given in Regulations 543.2.5, and 543.3.6. A rigid steel conduit system will generally meet these requirements, for use as the cpc for the circuits it contains, provided that:

- the conduit and associated fittings comply with a British Standard. (The original csa of rigid steel conduit made to a British Standard can be expected to be sufficient to meet the relevant requirement of *BS 7671*, which is given in indent (ii) of Regulation 543.2.4, referred to in Regulation 543.2.5),
- the conduit system was properly installed and is in good condition (Regulation 621.2 requires it to be verified that the conduit is not damaged or deteriorated so as to impair safety, and that there are no installation defects and departures from the requirements of this standard that may give rise to danger),

- the joints in the conduit are mechanically and electrically continuous (Regulation 543.3.6 refers),
- the earthing terminal of each accessory is connected by a separate protective conductor to an earthing terminal in the associated box or other enclosure (Regulation 543.2.7 refers).

The conduit system should be inspected along its length, as far as practicable, to check the above points.

Particular attention should be paid to checking that there is no significant corrosion or other deterioration that could impair the electrical continuity of the conduit or reduce its csa such that it may be unsuitable to carry fault current, and that the joints are not loose.

Where the system is buried in the fabric of the building, cover plates should be removed to inspect the condition of couplers and bushes. In addition, information on the building construction may need to be acquired to establish if there have been any problems such as corrosion of structural steel reinforcement of the building, to assist in assessing the likely condition of the conduit system.

Testing should be carried out to verify that the conduit system provides good electrical continuity throughout its length and that the earth fault loop impedance of all circuits using conduit as the protective conductor is sufficiently low to meet the requirements of *BS 7671* for fault protection.

General guidance carrying out inspection and testing is given in the NICEIC book *Inspection, Testing and Certification* and in *IEE Guidance Note 3 Inspection & Testing*.

Standard applied
BS 7671

Regulations referred to
543.2.4, 543.2.5, 543.2.7, 543.3.6, 621.2.

Selection and erection

Questions 15-31

FROM THE HELPLINE ...

Rewireable fuses

Question

Does *BS 7671* require existing rewireable (semi-enclosed) fuses complying with *BS 3036* to be replaced with circuit-breakers or cartridge fuses?

Answer

No, *BS 7671* does not preclude the use of rewireable fuses complying with *BS 3036* (although, where a fuse is to be used, Regulation 533.1.1.4 expresses a preference for a cartridge fuse). Therefore, rewireable fuses to *BS 3036* may still be used both for new and existing installations.

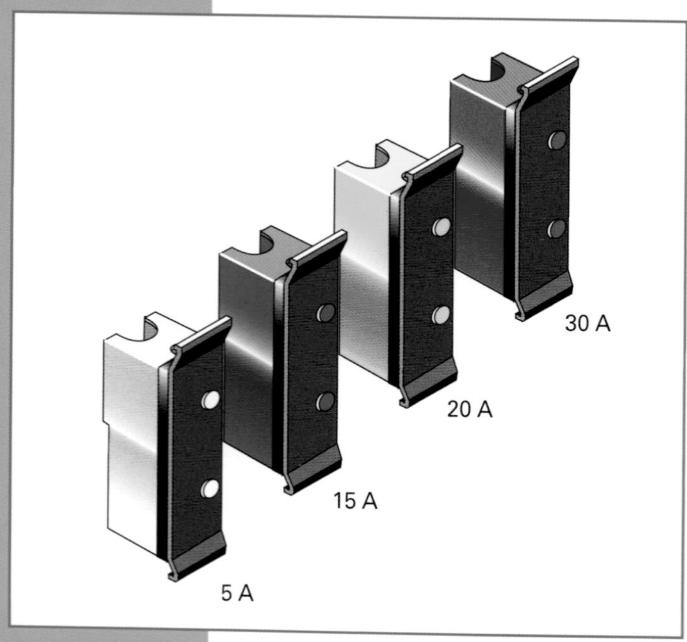

A number of factors need to be considered before installing new rewirable fuses:

- For reasons of protection against overload, Regulation 433.1.3 requires that the rated current of the fuse shall not exceed 0.725 times the current-carrying capacity of the lowest rated conductor in the circuit protected. The effect, therefore, of choosing such a fuse is that the cross-sectional area (csa) of the cable may need to be greater than if another type of protective device had been chosen, such as a *BS 1361* fuse or a *BS EN 60898* circuit-breaker.
- Regulation 533.1.1.2 requires that fuses having fuse links (fuse wire or cartridge) likely to be replaced by a person other than a skilled or instructed person shall be of a type that complies with the safety requirements of *BS 88 and* shall preferably be of a type that cannot be replaced inadvertently by one having a higher nominal current. These requirements are met if the fuse carrier will not fit into the fuse base of a lower rated fuse. For example, a 30 A fuse carrier must not fit into either a 15 A fuse base or a 5 A fuse base.
- To meet the requirement of Regulation 434.5.1, a rewireable fuse, like any other fault current protective device, must be chosen so that its rated short-circuit breaking capacity is not less than the maximum prospective fault current at the point where the fuse is installed. The only exception is where back-up protection is provided by another device, meeting specified requirements. Complying with the requirement of Regulation 434.5.1 may seem to be difficult with *BS 3036* fuses, as they have a relatively low short-circuit breaking capacity rating of between 1 kA – 4 kA, depending on category of duty. Fortunately, however, *BS 3036* fuses incorporated in a consumer unit are considered adequate for 16 kA prospective fault current provided that:
  - the consumer unit complies with Part 3 of *BS EN 60439: 1991 (Annex ZA of Corrigendum June 2006)*, and
  - the consumer unit is fed by a single-phase supply, the service cut-out having an HBC fuse to *BS 1361: 1971* Type II, rated at not more than 100 A.

Standards applied
BS 7671 • BS 3036 • BS 1361: 1971 Specification for cartridge fuses for a.c. circuits in domestic and similar premises • BS EN 60439: 1991 Low-voltage switchgear and control gear assemblies

Regulations referred to
433.1.3, 434.5.1, 533.1.1.2, 533.1.1.3.

Unswitched socket-outlets

Question

If socket-outlets to *BS 1363* do not have a switch do they need replacing?

Answer

No, unswitched socket-outlets do not need replacing and are permitted in an electrical installation.

Regulation 553.1.4 of *BS 7671* requires that socket-outlets used for household and similar use shall be of the shuttered type and, for an a.c. installation, shall preferably be of a type complying with *BS 1363*. Additionally, in Table 53.2 of *BS 7671*, a plug and socket-outlet may be used for isolation, switching off for mechanical maintenance and functional switching.

It should be noted, however, that Regulation 537.4.2.8 precludes a plug and socket-outlet from being selected as a device for emergency switching.

QUESTION 16

Standards applied
BS 7671 • BS 1363

Regulations referred to
Table 53.2, 537.4.2.8, 553.1.4.

Switches in bathrooms

Question

Is it permitted for a wall-mounted switch to be installed in a bathroom?

Answer

A wall-mounted switch may be installed in a bathroom. Historically, installers have made use of a pull-cord switch to control lighting in a bathroom. However, whilst Regulation 701.512.4 of *BS 7671* does not permit wall-mounted switches to be installed in zones 0, 1 or 2, it does not preclude a wall-mounted switch being installed outside of these zones. Regulation 512.2.1 does, however, require that due account be taken of external influences.

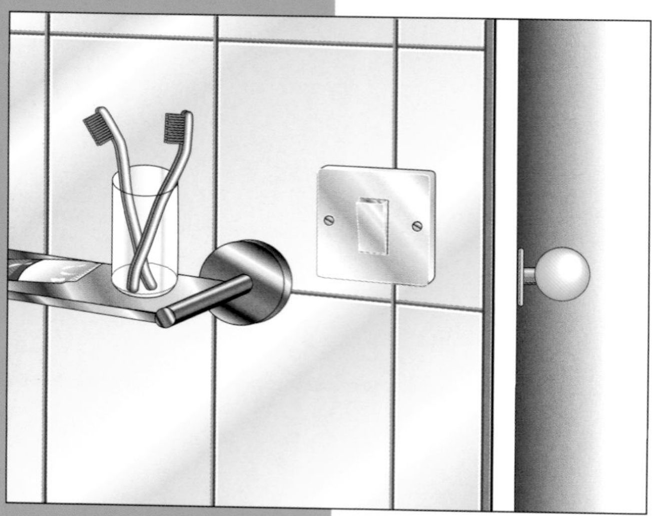

In particular, the electrical installation designer will need to be satisfied that a wall-mounted switch has the appropriate degree of protection from water ingress for installation in a bathroom. Where water jets are likely to be used, such as might occur in a communal shower area, Regulation 701.512.2 requires that electrical equipment has an International Protection (IP) rating of IPX5. In a bathroom where water jets are not likely to be used, such as in a dwelling, the designer will have to choose a wall-mounted switch having an IP rating relevant for the level of risk of water ingress. Alternatively, the designer may specify that a pull-cord switch complying with *BS 3676* with an IP rating suitable for its location is installed. The pull-cord switch body must be installed outside of zones 1 and 2; however, the insulated cord may enter either zone.

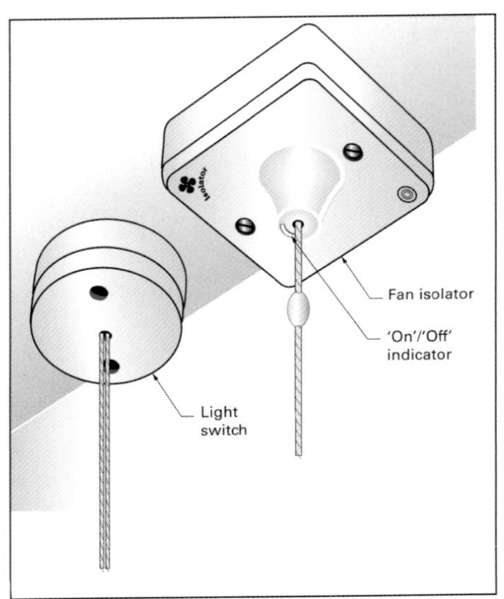

Standard applied
BS 7671 • BS 3676 • BS EN 60669-1

Regulations referred to
512.2.1, 701.512.2, 701.512.4.

Sockets-outlets near sinks

Question

Is it permitted for a socket-outlet to be installed near to a kitchen sink?

Answer

BS 7671 does **not** specify a minimum distance between a sink and a socket-outlet. However, Regulation 512.2.1 does require due account to be taken of external influences.

For domestic premises, to avoid the effects of splashing, as a 'rule of thumb' *BS 1363* socket-outlets ideally should be installed 1000 mm away from the sink. In many instances this is impractical, and where this is the case 300 mm is a minimum acceptable distance.

For commercial premises the same principle applies. However, the designer may consider it appropriate, due to the increased risk of splashing, to require *BS EN 60309* socket-outlets with degrees of protection of IPX4 or IPX5, as appropriate.

QUESTION 18

Standard applied
BS 7671

Regulations referred to
512.2.1.

Socket-outlets installed on or in wooden panels

Question

I want to install a socket-outlet in a wooden panel. Do I need to use an accessory box?

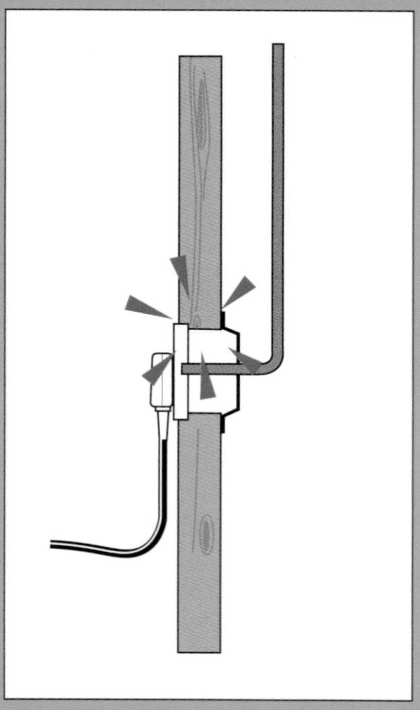

Answer

Regulation 526.7 requires that where a connection is made in an enclosure, it shall provide adequate mechanical protection and protection against relevant external influences (such as water). Where the termination or joint is in a live conductor (line or neutral) it must be contained within one (or combination) of the types of enclosure listed items in Regulation 526.5. The list includes:

i) a suitable accessory complying with the appropriate product standard

ii) an equipment enclosure complying with the appropriate product standard

iii) an enclosure partially formed or completed with building material non-combustible when tested to *BS 476-4*.

Additionally, Regulations 526.9 requires that the cores of cables from which sheath has been removed shall be enclosed.

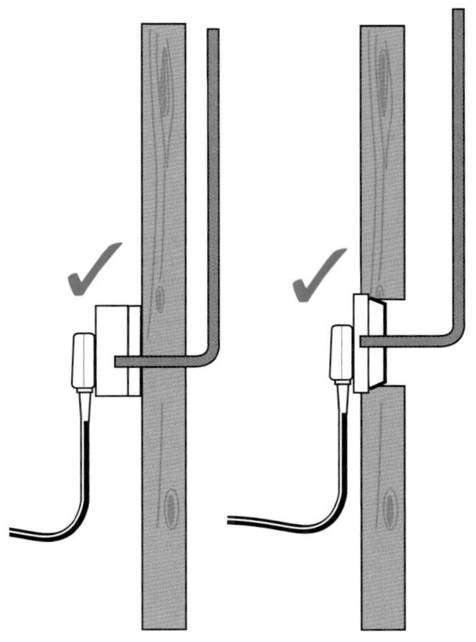

Assuming that a wooden panel failed to comply with the requirements of (iii) of Regulation 526.5, for non-combustibility, the connections for the socket-outlet, and the cable cores from which the sheath has been removed, must be contained within a proprietary accessory box or enclosure to the appropriate product standard. In this example, either a surface mounted or recessed box may be used to provide the necessary enclosed connections for compliance with Regulation 526.9.

The installer should also note that a wiring system must be selected and erected to avoid, during installation, use or maintenance, damage to the sheath or insulation of cables and their terminations (Regulation 522.8.1 refers). Enclosures should, therefore, be of adequate depth to ensure that this requirement is met.

Standards applied
BS 7671 • BS 476-4

Regulations referred to
522.8.1, 526.5, 526.7, 526.9.

Grommets for metal back boxes

Question

Does a metal back box require a grommet where an insulated and sheathed cable enters it?

Answer

There is a general requirement in Regulation 522.8.1 of *BS 7671* that 'a wiring system shall be selected and erected to avoid during installation, use or maintenance, damage to the sheath or insulation of cables and their terminations'.

However, failure to provide a grommet where a cable such as thermoplastic (pvc) insulated and sheathed twin-and-earth flat cable enters a metal back box is not, in its own right, a deficiency.

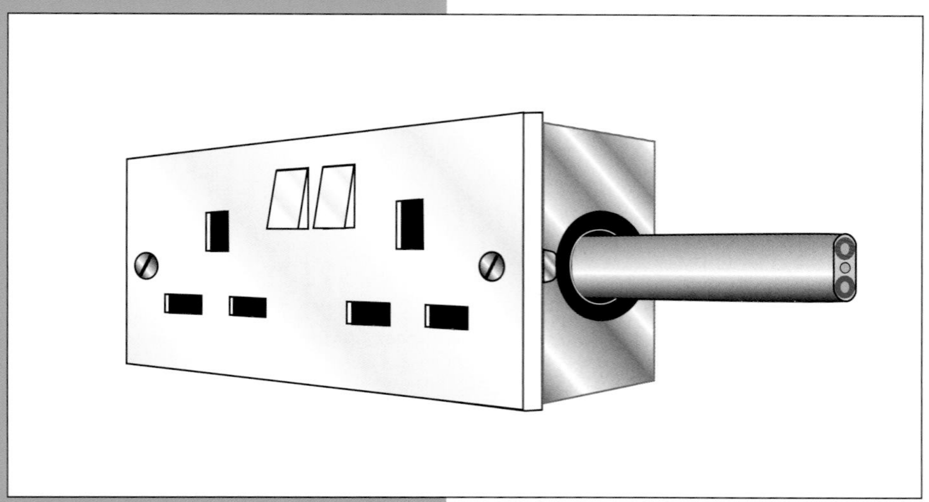

To comply with the requirements of Regulation 522.8.1, cable sheaths must be protected from any sharp edges along the whole of their length as well as at the entry point into the accessory. There are different ways of achieving this at the entry to enclosures, including deburring the entry hole, or providing suitable physical protection for the cable, or providing an appropriate grommet or both.

It should also be noted that Regulation 526.9 requires that cores of sheathed cables from which the sheath has been removed must be enclosed as required by Regulation 526.5. To comply with this requirement, the cable sheath must enter the accessory. Care must therefore be taken, when removing the sheath of a cable to expose the cores, that an excessive amount of sheath is not removed.

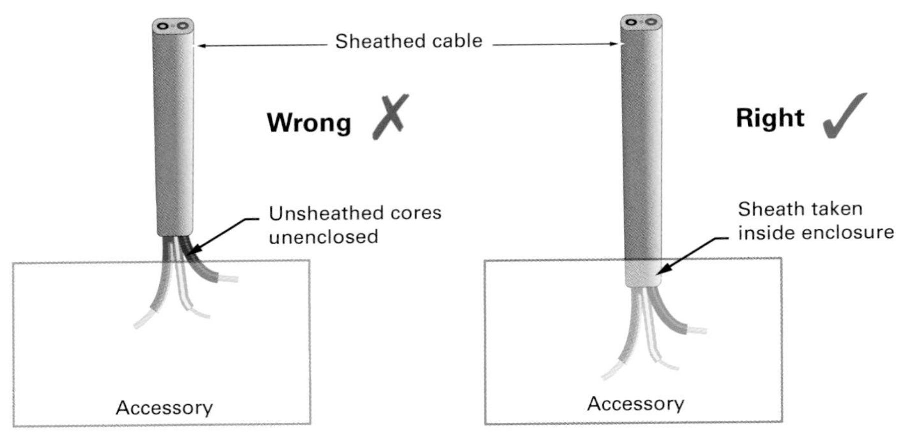

Standard applied
BS 7671

Regulations referred to
522.8.1, 526.5, 526.9.

Cables installed within cavity walls

Question

Is it permitted to install insulated and sheathed cables within a cavity wall?

Answer

There is no specific regulation that forbids an installer installing a cable within a cavity wall. However, *BS 7671*, the *Building Regulations 2000 for England and Wales (2004 Edition)* and Mandatory Standard 3.10 of the *Scottish Building Regulations* highlight a number of reasons why this practice is undesirable:

- the cable may be damaged during installation – Regulation 522.8.1 refers

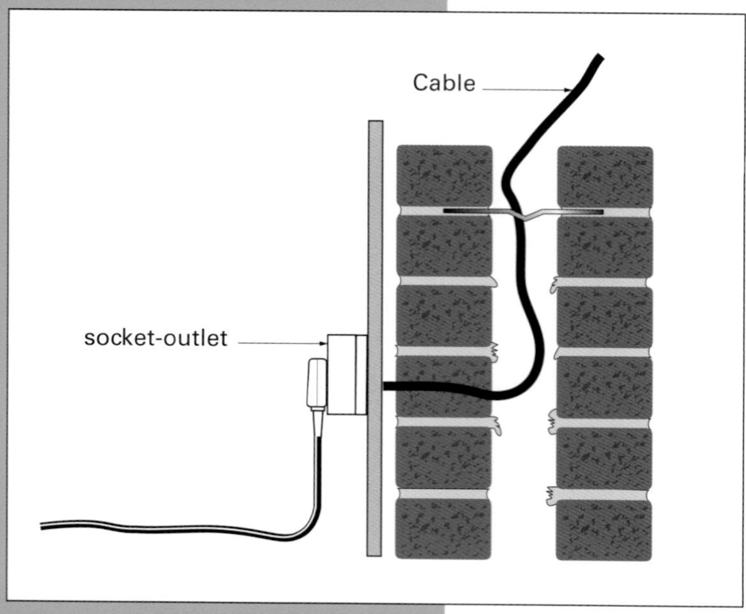

- the cable lacks support and where the cable passes through an opening, damage may occur to the sheath due to the cable's own weight – Regulation 522.8.4 refers
- thermoplastic (pvc) insulation in contact with polystyrene may cause the plasticizer within the insulation to migrate leading to reduced flexibility and a 'softening' of the cable sheath – Regulation 522.5.3 refers
- cables installed within thermal insulation will have their current-carrying capacity significantly reduced, which may require cable sizes to be increased – Regulation 523.7 refers
- the cable may be in contact with the outer and inner wall and hence provide a route for water (generally condensate) to drain into accessories - *Approved Document C* for England and Wales, Section 5: Walls, paragraph 5.13b
- a route for precipitation might be provided where a hole exist from the outer wall - Mandatory Standard 3.10 of the *Scottish Building Regulations* refers.

In summary, the installation of cables within cavity walls should be avoided. However, where it is necessary for cables to be installed in or through a cavity wall, the cables and their installation should be selected and erected to take account of the items listed above.

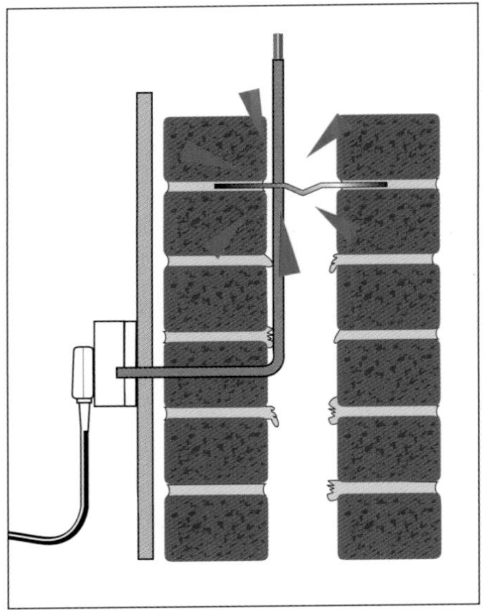

Standards applied

BS 7671 • Approved Document C, Site preparation and resistance to contaminants and moisture, of the Building Regulations for England and Wales 2000 (2004 Edition)
Scottish Building Regulations

Regulations referred to

522.5.3, 522.8.1, 522.8.4, 523.7.

Cables installed under a floor or above a ceiling - holes

Question

Where an insulated and sheathed cable is to be installed through a hole in a timber joist under a floor or above a ceiling, at what depth in the joist should the hole be drilled?

Answer

Regulation 522.6.5 of *BS 7671* requires that a cable installed under a floor or above a ceiling is run in such a position that it is not liable to be damaged by contact with the floor or the ceiling or their fixings. The regulation also states that a cable passing through a timber joist within a floor or ceiling construction or through a ceiling support shall:

i) be at least 50 mm measured from the top or bottom of the joist or batten, or

ii) incorporate an earthed metallic covering which complies with the requirements of these Regulations for a protective conductor of the circuit concerned, the cable complying with *BS 5467*, *BS 6346*, *BS 6724*, *BS 7846*, *BS EN 60702-1* or *BS 8436*, or

iii) be enclosed in earthed conduit complying with *BS EN 61386* and satisfying the requirements of these Regulations for a protective conductor, or

iv) be enclosed in earthed trunking or ducting complying with *BS EN 50085* and satisfying the requirements of these Regulations for a protective conductor, or

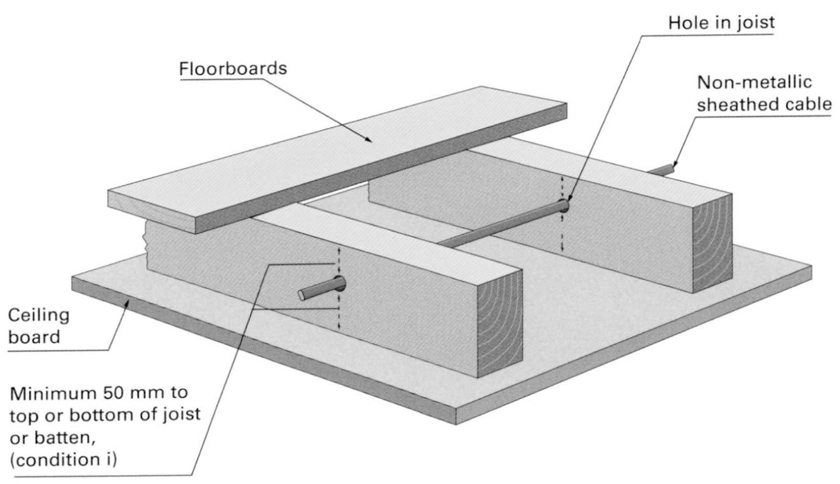

v) be mechanically protected against damage sufficient to prevent penetration of the cable by nails, screws and the like.

Where the joist has a depth less than 100 mm any hole must inevitably be less than 50 mm from either the top or bottom of the joist. In this instance, one solution would be for a notch to be cut and the requirements of parts (ii) to (v) of Regulation 522.6.5 (listed above) must be complied with, along with the requirements of *BS 5268-2: 2002 (Structural use of timber. Code of practice for permissible stress design, materials and workmanship).*

Where the depth of the joist does permit holes to be drilled, in addition to the requirements of Regulation 522.6.5, *BS 5268-2* details the position and size of holes such that their effect on the strength of the building structure need not be calculated.

BS 5268-2 recommends that the effect of holes need not be calculated in simply supported floor and roof-joists not more than 250 mm deep where holes drilled at the neutral axis with diameter not exceeding 0.25 of the depth of a joist and not less than three diameters (centre to centre) apart are located between 0.25 and 0.4 of the span from the support.

BS 8103-3: 1996 (Structural design of low-rise buildings. Code of practice for timber floors and roofs for housing) provides diagrams showing the application of *BS 5268-2* regarding guidance on the maximum depth of holes, their size and distance from one another, and their position in relation to the supporting wall. The diagrams are reproduced below for ease of reference.

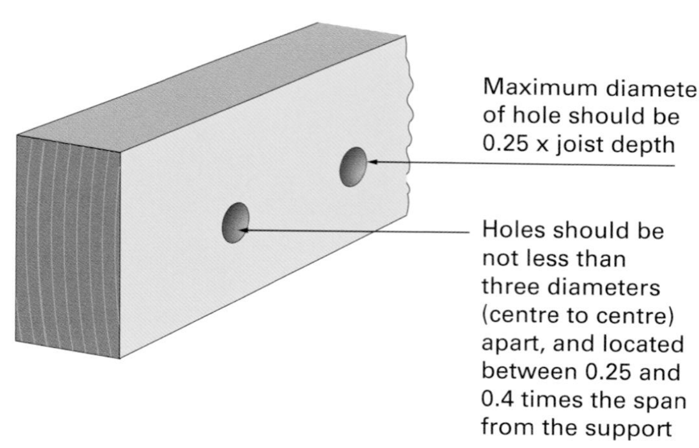
Maximum diameter of hole should be 0.25 x joist depth
Holes should be not less than three diameters (centre to centre) apart, and located between 0.25 and 0.4 times the span from the support

QUESTION 22

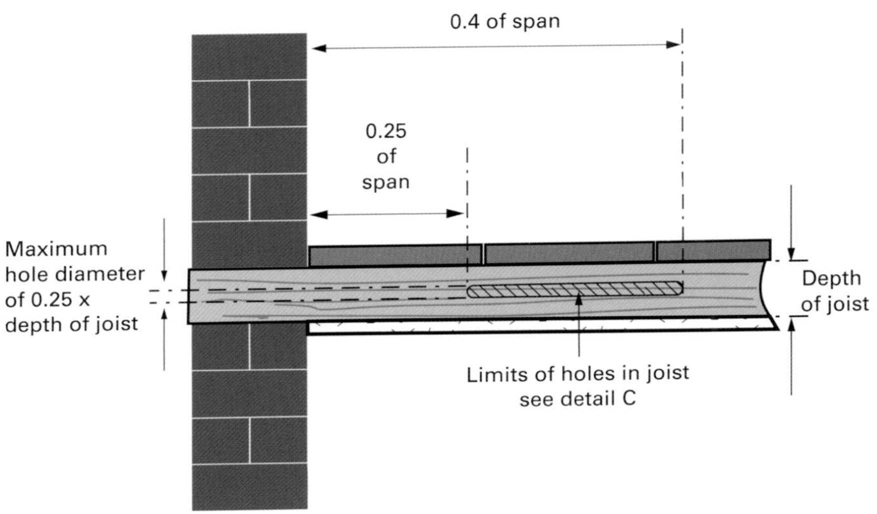

NOT TO SCALE

Standards applied

BS 7671 • BS 5268-2: 2002 clause 2.10.9 (part) • BS 8103-3: 1996

Regulations referred to

522.6.5

Cables installed under a floor or above a ceiling - notches

Question

When installing insulated and sheathed cables under a floor or above a ceiling, is it permissible to use a notch in a timber joist?

Answer

An installer is permitted to run insulated and sheathed cables through a notch in a joist, provided certain precautions are taken.

Regulation 522.6.5 of *BS 7671* requires that a cable installed under a floor or above a ceiling is run in such a position that it is not liable to be damaged by contact with the floor or the ceiling or their fixings. The regulation also states that a cable passing through a timber joist within a floor or ceiling construction or through a ceiling support shall:

i) be at least 50 mm measured from the top or bottom of the joist or batten, or

ii) incorporate an earthed armour or metallic covering which complies with the requirements of these Regulations for a protective conductor of the circuit concerned, the cable complying with *BS 5467*, *BS 6346*, *BS 6724*, *BS 7846*, *BS EN 60702-1* or *BS 8436*, or

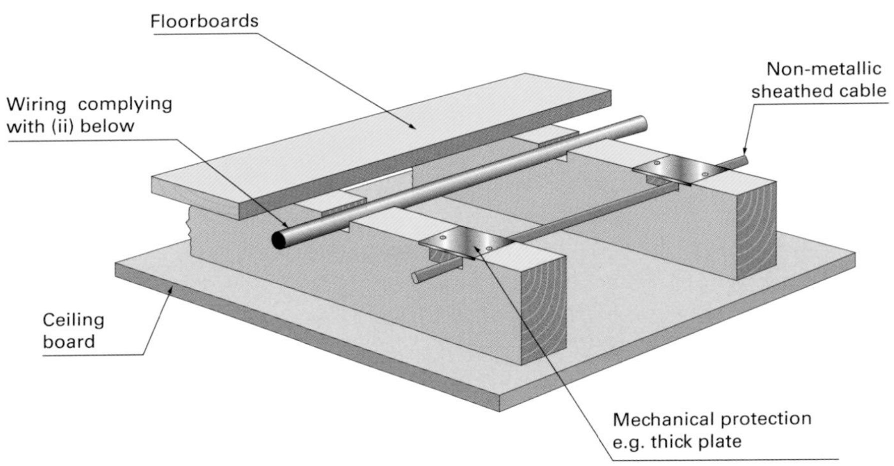

iii) be enclosed in earthed conduit complying with *BS EN 61386* and satisfying the requirements of these Regulations for a protective conductor, or

iv) be enclosed in earthed trunking or ducting complying with *BS EN 50085* and satisfying the requirements of these Regulations for a protective conductor, or

v) be mechanically protected against damage sufficient to prevent penetration of the cable by nails, screws and the like.

Where the cable is not protected by a securely supported and earthed length of metal conduit, and a metal protective plate is used, the plate should be at least 3 mm thick. Where the installer is concerned that shot fixings may be used, additional thought should be given to changing the cable type to one that incorporates an earthed armour or earthed metal sheath or, alternatively, installing the cable at a depth complying with the requirements of indent (i) of Regulation 522.6.5 (i.e. by passing it through a hole through the joist).

In addition to the requirements of *BS 7671*, *BS 5268-2: 2002 (Structural use of timber. Code of practice for permissible stress design, materials and workmanship)* details the maximum permitted depths of notches such that their effect on the strength of the building structure need not be calculated. *BS 5268-2: 2002* indicates that the effect of notches need not be calculated in simply supported floor and roof-joists not more than 250 mm deep where the notch does not exceed 0.125 of the depth of a joist and is located between 0.07 and 0.25 of the span from the support.

BS 8103-3: 1996 (Structural design of low-rise buildings. Code of practice for timber floors and roofs for housing) provides diagrams showing the application of *BS 5268-2: 2002* regarding guidance on the maximum depth of notches, their size and distance from one another, and their position in relation to the supporting wall. The diagrams are reproduced below for ease of reference.

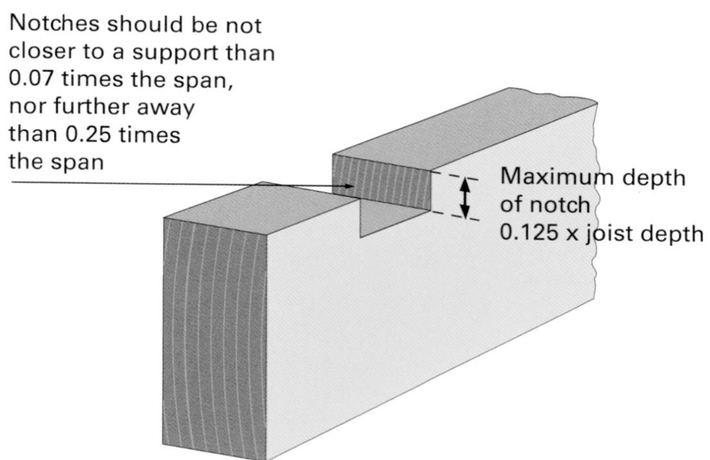
Notches should be not closer to a support than 0.07 times the span, nor further away than 0.25 times the span
Maximum depth of notch 0.125 x joist depth

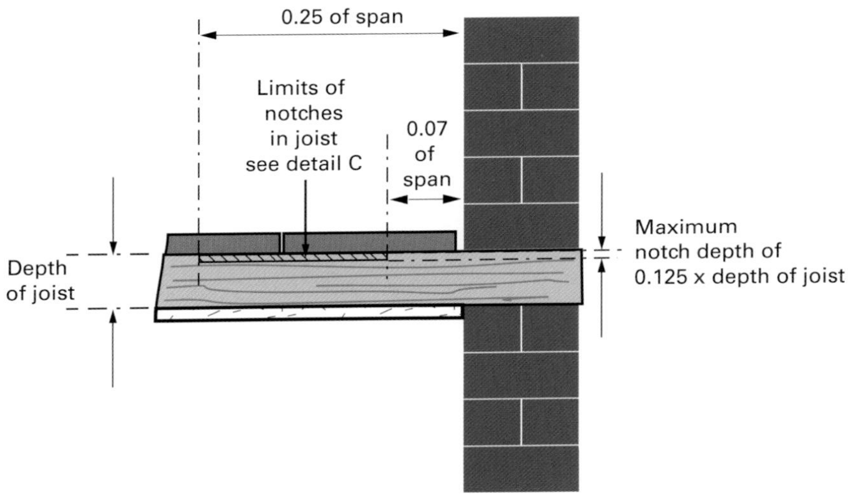

NOT TO SCALE

Standards applied

BS 7671 • BS 5268-2: 2002 clause 2.10.9 (part) • BS 8103-3: 1996

Regulations referred to

522.6.5

Dedicated circuit for an immersion heater

Question

Must an immersion heater be supplied through its own dedicated circuit?

Answer

BS 7671 does not require an immersion heater to be supplied through a dedicated circuit. However, Topic S225-17 of the *Electrical Safety Council Technical Manual* suggests that a water heater fitted to storage vessels having a capacity in excess of 15 litres should be supplied through its own circuit and connected through a 13 A fused-connection unit with cord-outlet complying with *BS 1363-4* or a double-pole switch with cord-outlet complying with *BS EN 60669-1* or *BS EN 60669-2-4*.

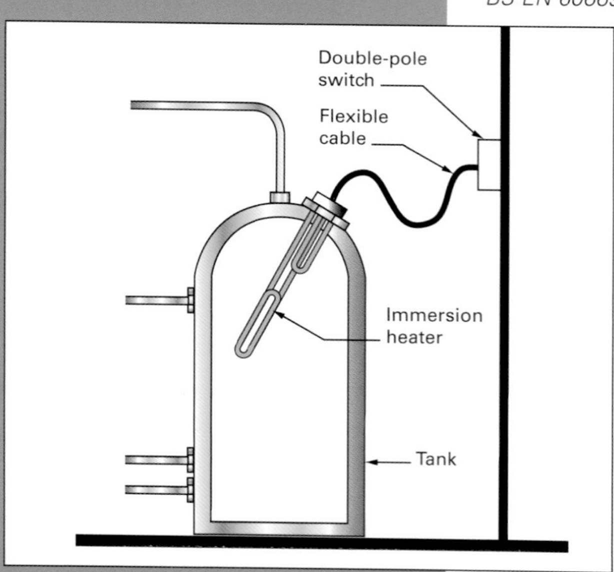

The reasons for having a separate circuit are twofold:

1. Possibility of overload

Although an immersion heater element is not liable to overload there is a risk of an overload on a circuit supplying both the water heater and other items of current-using equipment, such as would be the case with a ring final circuit.

Water storage tanks into which 2.7 kW immersion heater elements are installed hold between 80 and 210 litres of water. With such a heater element, operating from a supply of nominal voltage 230 V, a current of 12 A flows. Such a volume of water takes a significant period of time to heat up, during which there is a potential for overload should any other load be added to the final circuit.

2. Compliance with Regulation Group 314.1

Regulation 314.1 requires that an electrical installation is divided into circuits, amongst other things to, 'avoid danger and minimize inconvenience in the event of a fault.' Should the immersion heater be supplied from the same circuit as, for example, socket-outlets (such as may form part of a ring or radial final circuit), the automatic disconnection of the circuit would lead to a loss of supply to both the socket-outlets and the immersion heater, possible causing inconvenience.

Standard applied
BS 7671

Regulations referred to
314.1.

Fan control

Question

Is it permitted to supply a fan fitted in a location containing a bath or shower or in a kitchen from a lighting circuit?

Answer

It is quite acceptable for a fan in a bathroom, shower room or kitchen to be supplied from a local lighting circuit. Indeed, *Approved Document F, Ventilation* of the *Building Regulations for England and Wales* requires a ventilation fan for an internal, windowless room to be controlled by the light switch for that room and to have a 15 minute overrun[1]. Additionally, Table 1.1a of *Approved Document F* specifies the minimum extract levels for rooms.

To achieve appropriate rates of ventilation a electric fan is rarely rated above 0.5 A at a voltage of 230 V, and will commonly be rated at less than 0.25 A at 230 V. However, as with any item of current-using equipment, an appropriate assessment of load should be made. Additionally, a fan supplied from a local lighting circuit must meet the requirements for isolation and for switching off for mechanical maintenance.

[1]Table 1.5 Controls for ventilation devices refers.

1. Isolation

Whilst *BS 7671* no longer requires that every motor circuit be provided with a means of isolation, it does require that every fixed electric motor is provided with an efficient means of switching off, which is readily accessible and easily operated, and so placed as to prevent danger (Regulation 132.15.2 refers). Additionally, clause 5.3 of *BS EN 60204-1: 2006 Safety of machinery - Electrical equipment of machines - Part 1: General requirements* requires that a supply disconnecting device is provided. In the case of an extract fan for a bathroom, shower room or kitchen, this provides the means of isolation necessary for the safety of persons carrying out work such as inspecting, testing or replacing an extractor fan, where such work involves working on or near live parts.

Regulation 537.2.2.6 requires the device used for isolation to be clearly identified to show the electrical equipment which it isolates. Where the device is remote from the equipment to be isolated, Regulation 537.2.1.5 requires it to be capable of being secured in the open position.

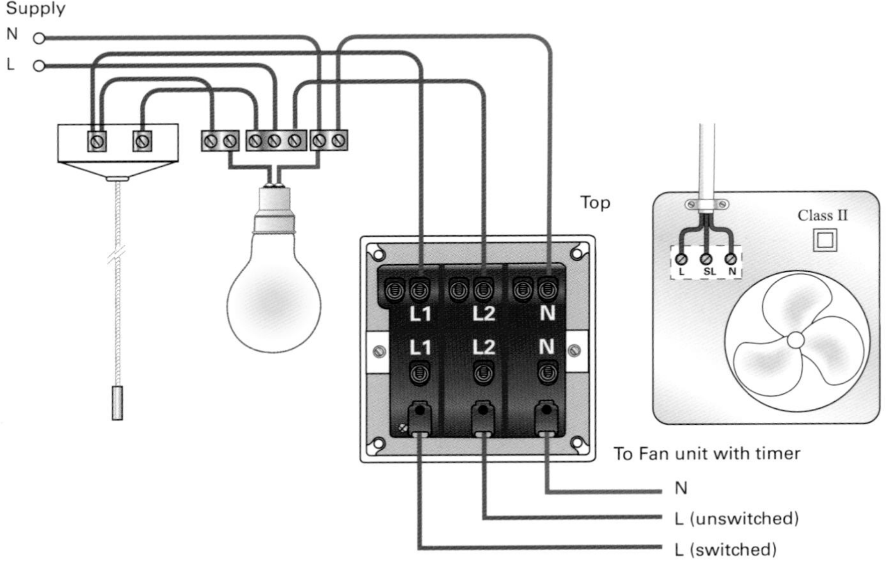

Rear view of Fan Isolator

Note: The circuit protective conductor is omitted from the diagram for clarity

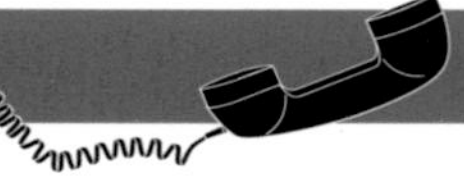

2. Switching off for mechanical maintenance

In addition to the requirements for isolation, Regulation 537.3.1 requires that where electrically powered equipment falls within the scope of *BS EN 60204*, such as a motor for a fan, the requirements for switching off for mechanical maintenance of that Standard apply. In particular, clause 5.6 requires that where a device used for switching off for prevention of unexpected start-up or a device used for disconnecting electrical equipment is located outside an enclosed electrical operating area, it shall be equipped with a means of securing in the OFF position. Where a plug and socket-outlet combination is so positioned that it can be kept under the immediate supervision of the person carrying out the work, means of securing in the disconnected state need not be provided. The device, irrespective of its type, must also be identified by durable marking where necessary (Regulation 537.3.2.4 refers).

A single device may be used both for isolation and for switching off for mechanical maintenance provided the requirements both of *BS 7671* and *BS EN 60204* are met.

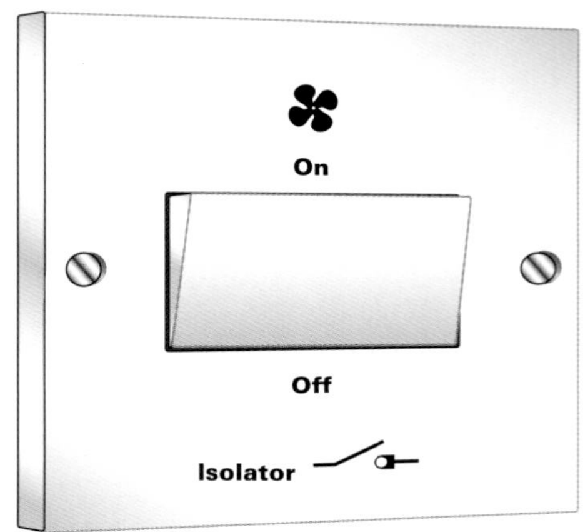

3. Zone

The designer should be aware that a bathroom or shower room is a special location covered by Section 701 of *BS 7671*. Regulation 701.55 permits an item of fixed current-using equipment, such as a fan, to be installed within zone 1 if it is suitable for that zone. However, the supply circuit must be protected by a residual current device having a rated residual operating current ($I_{\Delta n}$) not exceeding 30 mA and an operating time not exceeding 40 ms at a residual current of 5 $I_{\Delta n}$. Regulation 701.411.3.3 refers.

Standards applied

BS 7671 • Approved Document F Ventilation of the Building Regulations for England and Wales 2000 • BS EN 60204-1: 2006 Safety of machinery - Electrical equipment of machines - Part 1: General requirements

Regulations referred to

132.15.2, 537.2.1.5, 537.2.2.6, 537.3.1, 537.3.2.4, 701.411.3.3, 701.55, Section 701.

Fire hoods for downlighters

Question

Do I need to install a fire hood behind a downlighter?

Answer

There is no specific requirement in *BS 7671* to fit a fire hood to any downlighter.

However, a hole in a fire-resisting ceiling, whether for the purpose of accommodating a recessed luminaire, or indeed for any other reason, would need to be assessed to ascertain the impact it is likely to have on the performance of the ceiling.

There is no definitive answer to this issue, as the circumstances will vary on a case by case basis. The problems caused by installing a recessed luminaire into a timber floor/ceiling structure can be resolved in a number of ways, including the installation of a fireproof box behind the lamp or mounting an intumescent hood over the luminaire. However, such a solution should not be adopted unless the luminaire manufacturer has confirmed that the installation of the box or hood will not lead to overheating of the luminaire. Alternatively, a luminaire of a type which maintains the integrity of the ceiling in terms of structural performance, fire and sound insulation may be installed.

In cases of doubt the Local Authority Building Control office should be consulted so that the specific circumstances can be taken into account.

In any event, Regulation 421.2 requires that the heat generated by electrical equipment shall not cause danger of harmful effects to adjacent materials. Additionally, Regulation 421.1 requires that fixed electrical equipment is selected and erected such that its temperature in normal operation will not cause a fire. There have been instances where luminaires have generated sufficient heat to cause materials laid on top of them to catch fire; the installer must be satisfied that there is no risk of the heat generated by the luminaire causing a fire.

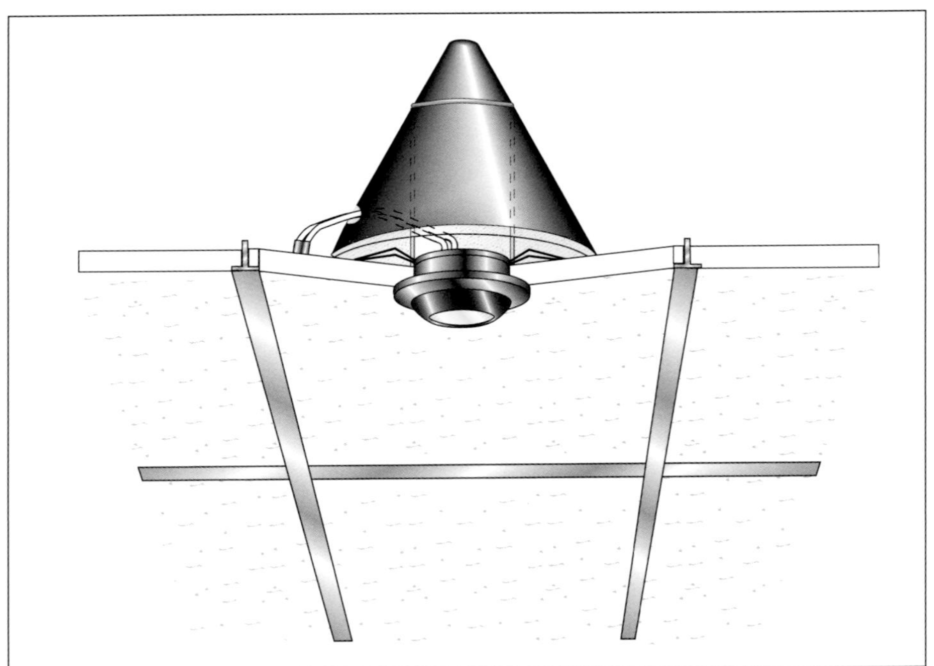

Standards applied

BS 7671 • Approved Document B, Fire safety, of the Building Regulations for England and Wales 2000 • Scottish Building Regulations

Regulations referred to

421.1, 421.2

Outside lighting fixed to a building

Question

I am planning to install an outside light on the external wall of a building. Are there any particular requirements of *BS 7671* that I need to take into account?

Answer

For equipment on the external wall of a building, such as an outside luminaire and the associated circuit wiring, certain requirements of *BS 7671* additional to those applying to an indoor installation should be taken into account. These requirements relate to (amongst other things):

- the particular external influences in the outdoor location
- the disconnection time of the circuit supplying the luminaire, and
- the requirements for isolation and switching off for mechanical maintenance.

1. External influences

Regulation 512.2.1 requires that

> *'Equipment shall be of a design appropriate to the situation in which it is to be used or its mode of installation shall take account of the conditions likely to be encountered'.*

Amongst the external influences liable to affect luminaire and circuit wiring are:

- direct sunlight (solar radiation and ultra-violet radiation) – Regulation 522.11.1 refers
- presence of moisture (water or high humidity) – Regulation Group 522.3 refers
- impact – Regulation Group 522.6 refers
- presence of flora and fauna – Regulation 522.9.1 refers

The designer will need to ensure that the luminaire, the circuit wiring and any other equipment installed externally, such as a switch or photo-electric control unit, are suitably selected and erected to withstand the external influences to which they are likely to be exposed.

Where the cables are liable to damage by impact they will need either to have additional mechanical protection, or be placed in an area of reduced risk. This might include, amongst other things:

- where there is the presence of flora, such as trees or bushes, then cables should be installed in such a way that the growth of the plant-life has no long-term detrimental effect

- where there is the presence of fauna, such as rats or mice, then cables should be installed with additional mechanical protection or away from the runs of the animals
- where cables are installed on the surface and are exposed to direct sunlight, the designer will need to protect the cable from the effects of prolonged exposure to direct sunlight. If this is not practicable, then cables with a sheath that the cable manufacturer states is resistant to ultra-violet radiation should be used.

2. Disconnection times

Regulation 411.3.2.2 of *BS 7671* requires for final circuits not exceeding 32 A that the disconnection time of the circuit must comply with Table 41.1 of *BS 7671* (0.4 s for a 230 V TN system or 0.2 s for a 230 V TT system).

3. Isolation and switching off for mechanical maintenance

The means of isolation for a lighting circuit will usually be the circuit-breaker or fuse protecting the circuit from overcurrent. Regulation 537.2.2.2 requires, amongst other things, that the position of the contacts or other means of isolation is either externally visible or clearly and reliably indicated. When maintenance is to be carried out, because of the position of the outside luminaire, it is possible that the means of isolation is not readily identifiable. It is, therefore, necessary for the schedule of results, or other form of notice complying with Regulation 514.9.1 to indicate the position of the outside luminaire.

Where it is necessary to switch off for mechanical maintenance, for example where a hot lamp requires replacing, a suitable device should be inserted, where practicable in the main supply circuit Regulation 537.3.2.1 refers. A suitable device might be a fused-connection unit, circuit-breaker or other form of switch. However, Regulation 537.3.2.2 does require that the chosen device is manually operated and the open position of the contacts of the device are visible or clearly and reliably indicated.

In addition, Regulation 537.3.2.3 requires that the device used for switching off for mechanical maintenance is designed and/or installed so as to prevent inadvertent or unintentional switching on. This may be achieved by the switch being labelled or by means of its position.. This may be achieved by the switch being labelled or by means of its position.

QUESTION 27

Standard applied
BS 7671

Regulations referred to
411.3.2.2, 512.2.1, 514.9.1, 522.3, 522.6, 522.9.1, 522.11.1, 537.2.2.2, 537.3.2.1, 537.3.2.2, 537.3.2.3.

Lighting circuit without a cpc

Question

I am thinking of extending and altering an existing lighting circuit wired in pvc-insulated and sheathed twin cable without a circuit protective conductor, by adding lighting points and switches and changing the existing lighting switches from the all-insulated type to the type having metal plates.

Is it permissible to do this or must the existing circuit be rewired?

Answer

The 13th Edition, and earlier, of the *IEE Wiring Regulations* did not require a circuit protective conductor (cpc) to be run to and terminated at every point and accessory of a lighting circuit, as is the current requirement.

There is no legal requirement, and no regulation in *BS 7671*, requiring an existing lighting circuit to be rewired or otherwise upgraded to current standards.

Furthermore, it is permissible to extend or alter an existing lighting circuit having no cpc. However, the new work must be carried out in accordance with the current edition of *BS 7671*, and the safety of the existing installation must not be impaired.

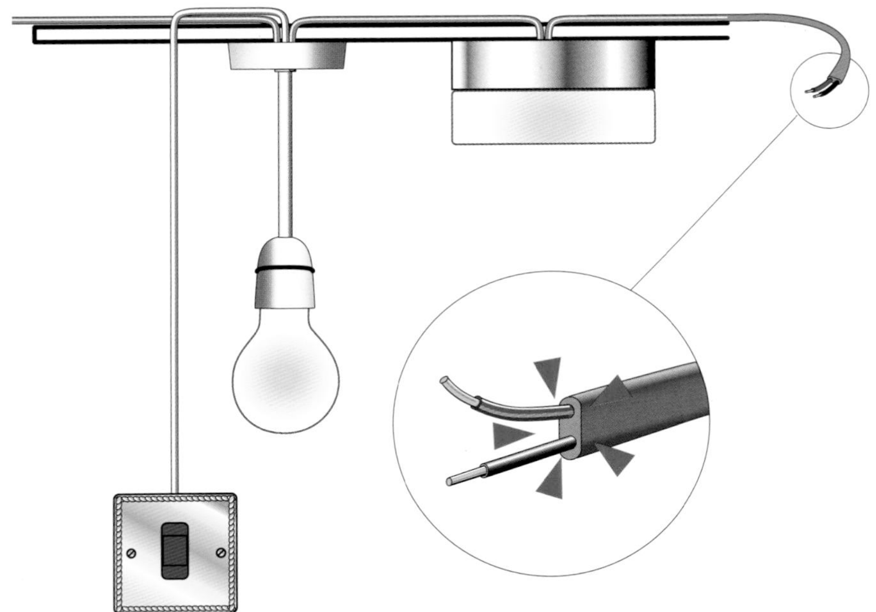

The following are some of the main requirements of *BS 7671* that must be taken into account where an existing lighting circuit without cpc is to be extended or altered:

1. No alteration or addition may be made to an existing installation unless it has been ascertained that that the rating and the condition of any existing equipment, including that of the distributor, will be adequate for the altered circumstances. Furthermore, the earthing and bonding arrangements, if necessary for the protective measure applied for the safety of the addition or alteration, shall be adequate (Regulation 131.8 refers). Amongst other things, the adequacy of the cross-sectional-area (csa) of the existing circuit conductors and the type and rating of the protective device must be established.

If, as is likely, protection against electric shock is provided by Automatic Disconnection of Supply, a cpc must be run to and terminated at each new point in wiring and at each new accessory (Regulation 411.3.1.1 refers).

2. A cpc must also be run to and terminated at any existing point or accessory that is changed from the all-insulated type to the type having metallic parts required to be earthed.
3. Furthermore, it is advisable that a cpc should be connected to any existing Class I equipment connected to the

circuit if this equipment is not already satisfactorily earthed. Advice on dealing with existing Class I equipment that may not be earthed is given in a best practice guide entitled *Replacing a Consumer Unit in Domestic Premises Where Lighting Circuits Have No Protective Conductor*, published by the Electrical Safety Council. This may be downloaded from NICEIC Group Ltd at **www.niceicgroup.com**

4. Like a cpc used for any other purpose, a cpc installed to an existing point or accessory may consist of a separate green-yellow covered copper conductor. However, where a cpc is not an integral part of a cable (such as a twin and earth cable) and is not contained in an enclosure formed by a wiring system (such as trunking), it must have a cross-sectional area not less than:
   - 2.5 mm² if protection against mechanical damage is provided, or
   - 4 mm² if protection against mechanical damage is not provided (Regulations 543.1.1 and 543.3.1 refer).

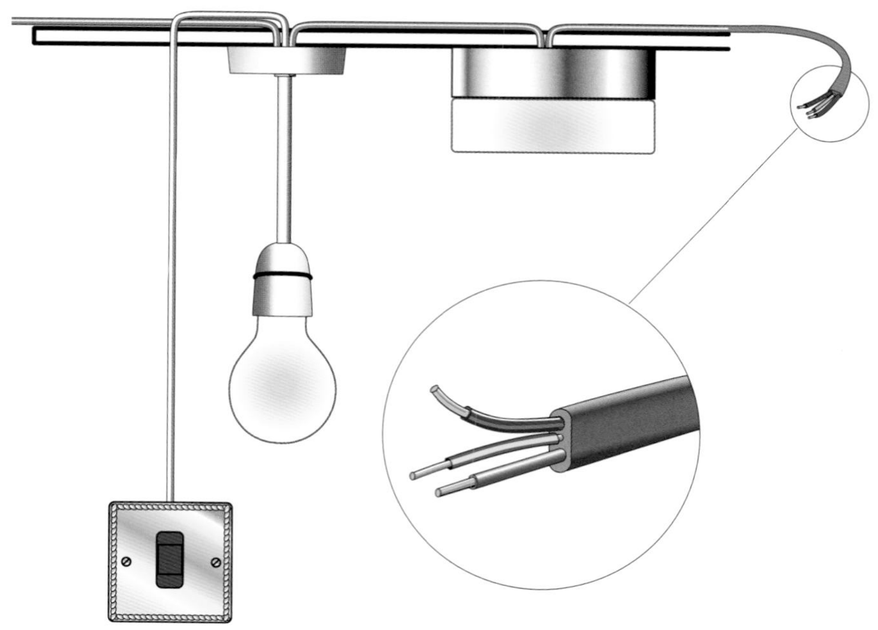

5. Where a cpc consists of a separate green-yellow covered copper conductor, it must still be incorporated in the same wiring system as the live conductors or in their immediate proximity (Regulation 543.6.1 refers). This would require the cpc to be run along the same cable route(s) as the existing cables. The requirement does not apply where a residual current device is used for protection against electric shock.

In practice, rather than making changes to an existing lighting circuit having no cpc, the designer or contractor may persuade the customer that it would be safer and more practicable to rewire the circuit.

Standard applied
BS 7671

Regulations referred to
131.8, 411.3.1.1, 543.1.1, 543.3.1, 543.6.1.

Instantaneous electric showers installed in a bathroom or shower room

Question

Does the supply circuit to an electric shower installed in zone 1 of a bathroom or shower room have to be protected by a residual current device (RCD)?

Answer

BS 7671 does require that the supply circuit to an electric shower in zone 1 of a location containing a bath or shower is provided with additional protection by means of a residual current device (RCD). The RCD must have a rated residual operating current not exceeding 30 mA, meeting the requirements given in Regulation 415.1.1 of *BS 7671*. (Regulation 701.411.3.3 refers).

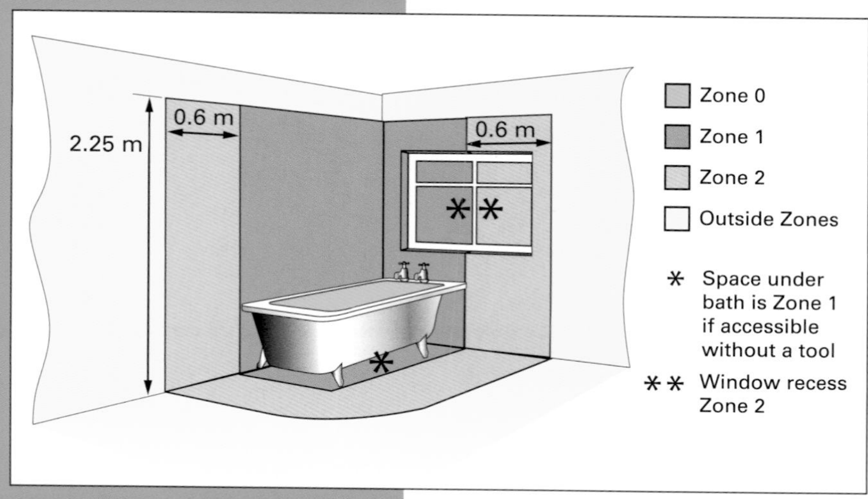

QUESTION 29

Standard applied
BS 7671

Regulations referred to
415.1.1, 701.411.3.3, 701.55.

Length of meter tails

Question

Why do meter tails longer than 3 m require additional switchgear?

Answer

Meter tails are a particular type of distribution circuit. Like all conductors they are required to be protected against overcurrent and to be provided with a means of isolation.

Traditionally, meter tails have not required any protection against overcurrent, or any provision for isolation, in addition to that provided by the electricity distributor. Regulations 433.3.1, 434.2.1 and 434.3 refer.

Although most electricity distributors will permit their cut-out fuse to be the means of overcurrent protection and isolation for the meter tails, they will only do so if the tails do not exceed a certain maximum permitted length.

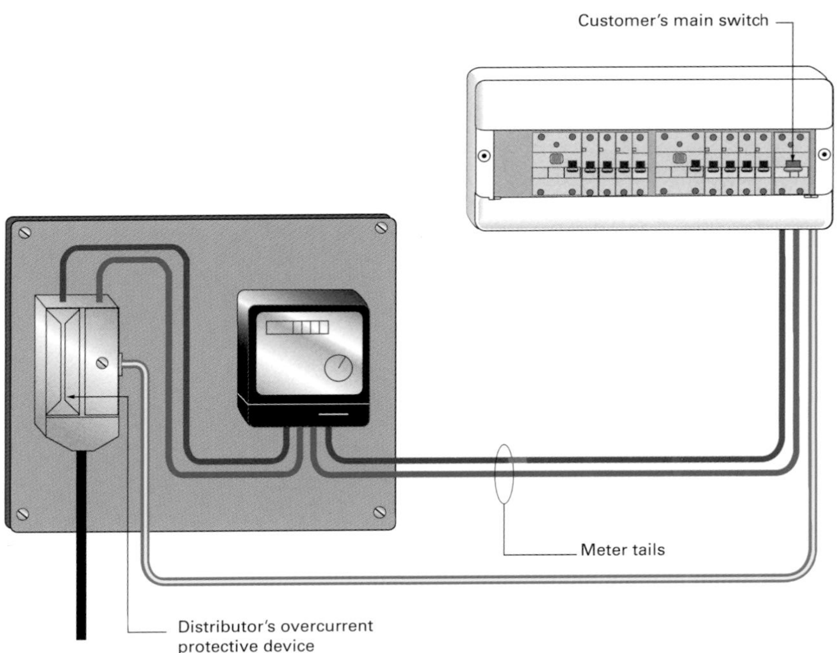
Customer's main switch
Meter tails
Distributor's overcurrent
protective device

The maximum permitted length of meter tails is determined by the distributor. Different distributors may have different requirements. Normally, the distributor will decide on the position of the cut-out and meter and will state the maximum permitted length for meter tails, such as 2 or 3 metres.

In the event that the distributor's requirements cannot be met, the electrical installation designer will be obliged to design a suitable distribution circuit (sub-main) to connect the consumer unit (or distribution board) to the origin of the installation. This will normally be accomplished by providing, close to the origin, a device such as a switch-fuse to permit the requirements for isolation, overcurrent protection and discrimination to be met for the distribution circuit.

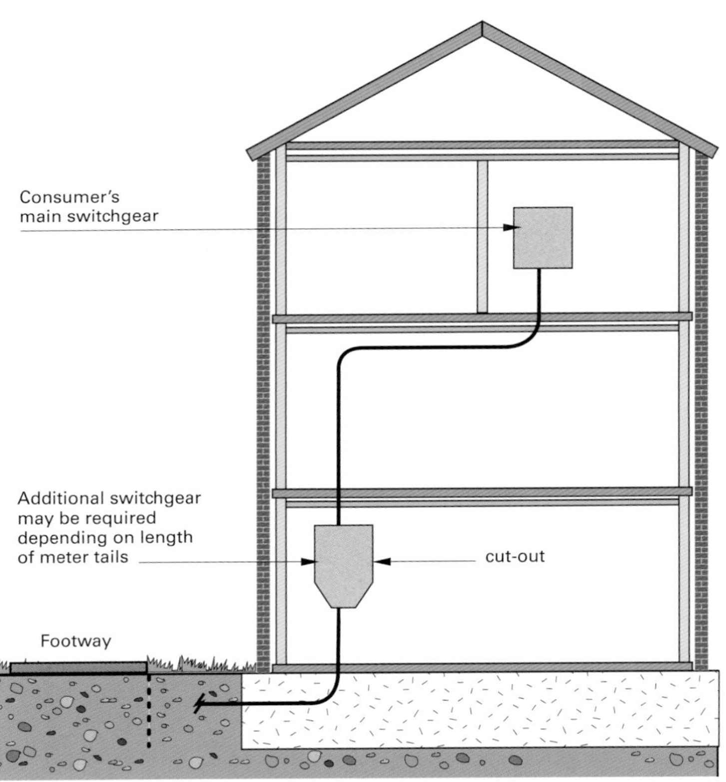

Note: Metering equipment omitted for clarity

Standard applied
BS 7671

Regulations referred to
433.3.1, 434.2.1, 434.3.

Fixing heights of accessories

Question

When adding new accessories to an existing electrical installation in a dwelling that does not comply with the requirements of *Part M* of the *Building Regulations for England and Wales,* must I comply with the fixing heights recommended by *Approved Document M* of the *Building Regulations for England and Wales*?

Answer

There is no requirement for new accessories to be installed at heights that comply with *Part M* of the *Building Regulations* for *England and Wales,* in an existing electrical installation in a dwelling that does not comply with *Part M.*

Approved Document M applies to new dwellings and non-domestic buildings, or where an existing non-domestic building is extended or undergoes a material alteration, or where there is a material change of use.

Clause 0.4 of *Approved Document M* states that a material alteration of a dwelling is work (electrical or otherwise) that would result in the dwelling not complying with the requirements of *Part M* where previously it did. However, the same clause also states that, if a dwelling previously did not comply with Part M, then, it should not be more unsatisfactory in relation to *Part M* after the material alteration.

Therefore, for an existing electrical installation which does not comply with the current requirements of *Part M*, new accessories may be positioned at the same heights as existing accessories.

Where a complete re-wire is being carried out an opportunity for compliance with *Approved Document M* is presented, and the designer may want to suggest to the client that the new electrical installation is installed in compliance with the Approved Document. However, there is no specific requirement for rewires and alterations to comply with *Part M* mounting heights.

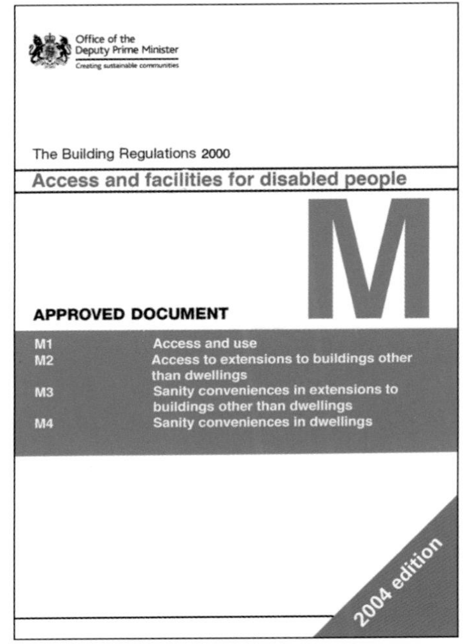

Standard applied

Approved Document M of the Building Regulations for England and Wales

Regulations referred to

Clause 0.4

Earthing and bonding
Questions 32 - 44

FROM THE HELPLINE ...

Earthing and bonding - what is the difference?

Question

What is the difference between earthing and bonding?

Answer

It is easy to confuse earthing and bonding because of the visual similarities between them. For example, green-and-yellow colour identification of the protective conductors is used for both, and both are associated with fault protection. However, earthing and bonding are quite distinct from each other in their purposes, their general arrangements, and in many of the requirements of *BS 7671* that they have to satisfy.

Both earthing and bonding must be provided in an installation, each meeting the respective safety requirements of *BS 7671*.

Generally, conductors provided for earthing are required to be designed to carry earth fault current, whereas conductors provided for bonding are not. Additionally, earthing is intended to limit the **duration** of touch voltages, while bonding is intended to limit the **magnitude** of touch voltages.

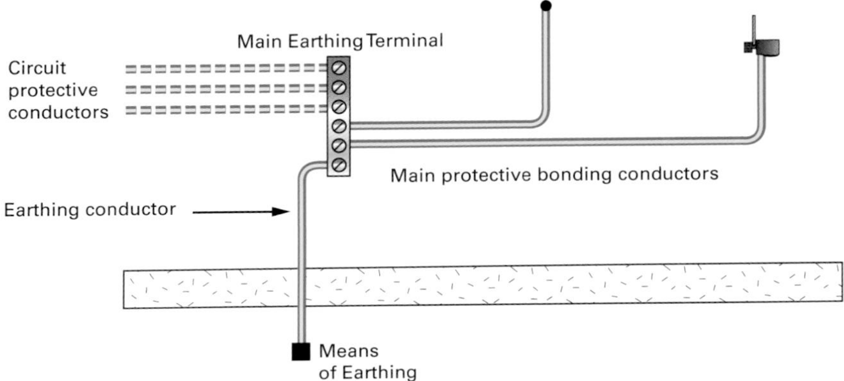

1. Touch voltage

The danger of electric shock due to an earth fault arises from the following voltages (sometimes called touch voltages) which may occur under such conditions in an installation:

a) voltages between exposed-conductive-parts[1] and other exposed-conductive-parts

b) voltages between extraneous-conductive-parts[2] and other extraneous-conductive-parts

c) voltages between exposed-conductive-parts and extraneous-conductive-parts

d) voltages between exposed-conductive-parts and Earth, or extraneous-conductive-parts and Earth.

---

[1] Exposed-conductive-part is a conductive part of equipment which can be touched and which is not a live part but which may become live under fault conditions.

[2] Extraneous-conductive-part is a conductive part liable to introduce a potential, generally earth potential, and not forming part of the electrical installation.

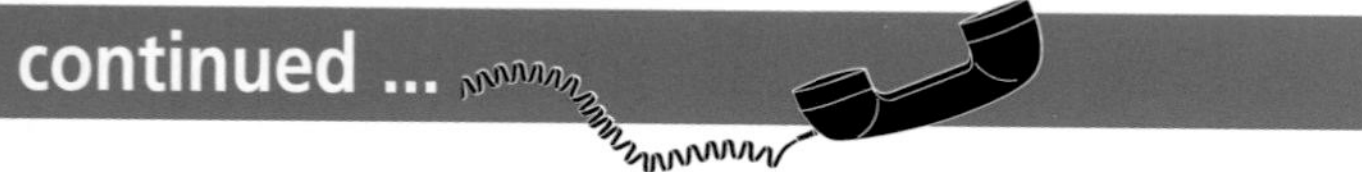

2. Earthing

The purpose of earthing, where used for protective purposes within an installation, is to limit the duration of the voltages in (a), (b), (c) and (d) above. This is achieved by the operation of the relevant protective device (such as a fuse or circuit-breaker) under earth fault conditions. This removes the voltages by causing the automatic disconnection of the supply to the faulty circuit within the time specified in *BS 7671*. Without an adequate earthing arrangement, the protective device could not operate as required under earth fault conditions.

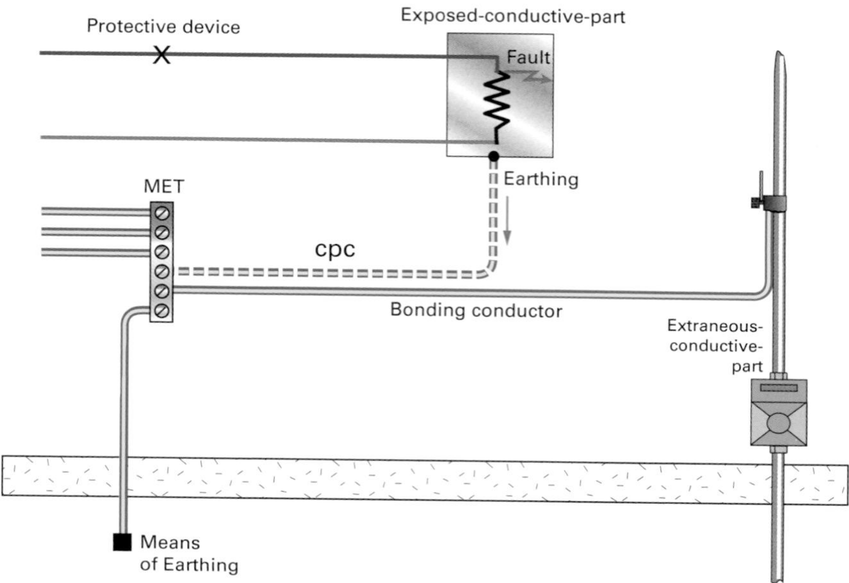

Labelled protective conductors under an earth-fault condition

3. Bonding

The purpose of bonding is to limit the magnitude of the voltages in (a), (b) and (c). This is achieved by electrically connecting together those conductive parts. The main safety benefit of adequate bonding is that the magnitude of voltages occurring between simultaneously accessible exposed-conductive-parts and extraneous-conductive-parts under earth fault conditions is insufficient to cause danger during the time taken for the relevant protective device to disconnect the supply to the faulty circuit.

A by-product of 'protective equipotential' (main and supplementary) bonding is that, under earth fault conditions, it may reduce the duration (not just magnitude) of the touch voltages in the installation. The reduction in touch voltage duration is related to the additional conductive paths that the bonding provides, which are in parallel with the earthing arrangement of the installation. The parallel paths allow a greater magnitude of earth fault current to flow, which may reduce the time taken for the relevant protective device to automatically disconnect the supply to the faulty circuit, and consequently reduces the touch voltage duration. Even so, bonding must not be relied upon to satisfy the disconnection time requirements of *BS 7671*, which is the function of earthing.

Standard applied
BS 7671

Regulations for further reading
Part 2, 411.1, 411.3, 543.1, 543.2, Part 7.

Main and supplementary bonding - what is the difference?

Question

What is the difference between main equipotential bonding and supplementary equipotential bonding?

Answer

The two principal types of equipotential bonding recognized by *BS 7671* are 'main' and 'supplementary'.

- Main equipotential bonding is part of the protective measure Automatic Disconnection of Supply, which is used in virtually every electrical installation in the United Kingdom.
- Supplementary equipotential bonding is a complementary measure for fault protection required in certain special installations or locations of increased shock risk, such as some of those in Part 7 of *BS 7671*.

Main bonding conductors only connect extraneous-conductive-parts, such as metallic gas and water service pipes at their points of entry into the premises, to the Main Earthing Terminal (MET) of the electrical installation (Regulation 411.3.1.2 refers).

Supplementary bonding conductors do not connect to the MET. Where relevant, supplementary bonding conductors connect between

- exposed-conductive-parts, for example, between simultaneously accessible metallic trunking and items of Class I equipment

- exposed-conductive-parts and extraneous-conductive-parts
- extraneous-conductive-parts, for example, between a metal water pipe and a rolled steel joist (RSJ).

A supplementary bonding conductor is also required to connect to the terminal of certain protective conductors in some of the locations of increased shock risk covered in Part 7 of *BS 7671*, such as locations containing a swimming pool or other basin (Regulation 702.411.3.3 refers).

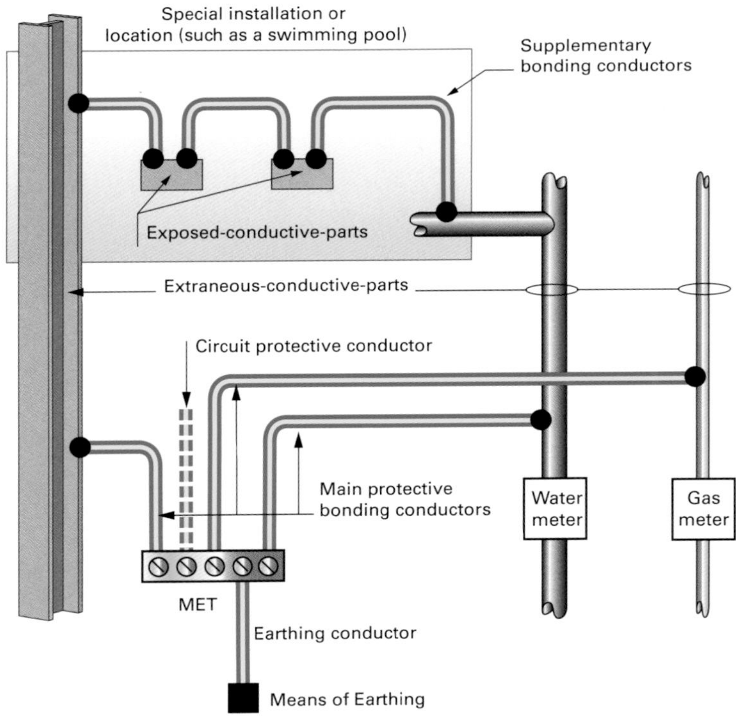

Standard applied
BS 7671

Regulations referred to
Part 2, 411.3.1.2, Part 7, 702.411.3.3.

Extraneous-conductive-parts - metal staircase

Question

In a brick built industrial unit there is an internal staircase leading to an upper level. The staircase has an exposed structural metal frame bolted to the concrete ground floor slab of the building. Is there a requirement to carry out main equipotential bonding to the frame of the staircase?

Answer

Any exposed metallic structural parts of a building must be main equipotentially bonded if they are extraneous-conductive-parts. Regulation 411.3.1.2 refers.

QUESTION 34

If the fixings securing the metal frame of the staircase to the ground floor slab do not extend through the damp-proof membrane, it is probable that the metal frame is isolated metalwork, and therefore not an extraneous-conductive-part. In such a case, main equipotential bonding of the metal frame would not be required.

However, if the fixings do extend through the membrane and into the foundations or the ground, the metal frame of the staircase should be considered to be an extraneous-conductive-part because it is liable to introduce earth potential. This situation would require the metal frame to be main equipotentially bonded in accordance with Regulation 411.3.1.2.

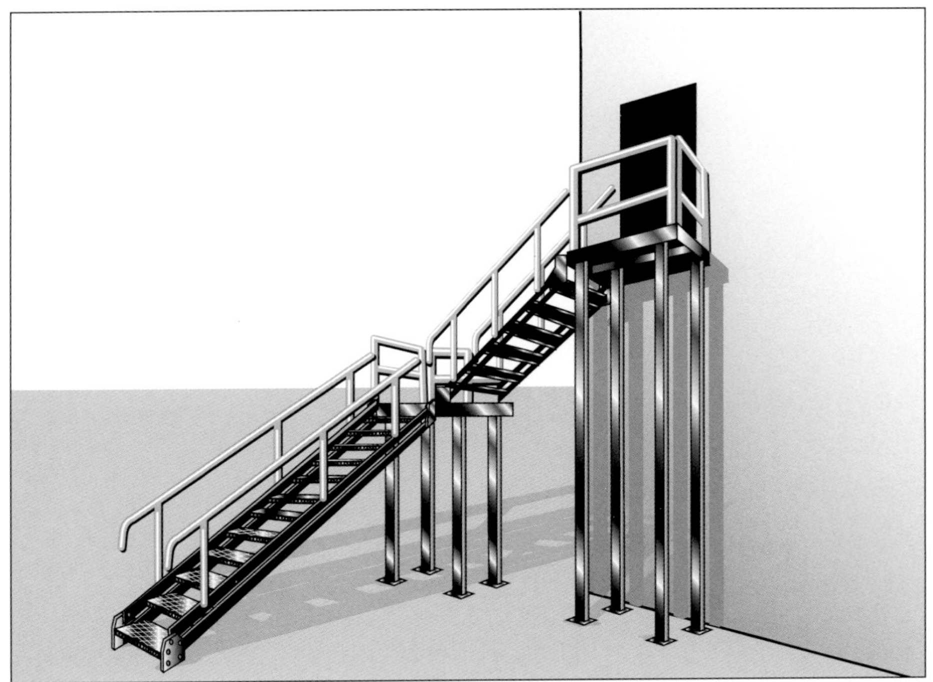

Standard applied
BS 7671

Regulations referred to
411.3.1.2

Extraneous-conductive-parts - plastic pipework

Question

A mains water service enters a building and connects to the supply side of a stopcock close to the point of entry. From the discharge side of the stopcock, plastic installation pipework within the building runs for a distance and then changes to copper pipework for the rest water installation. Is there a requirement to carry out main or supplementary bonding to the copper pipework?

Answer

If there is more than about a metre length of plastic pipework between the discharge side of the stopcock and the start of the copper pipework installation (assuming a pipe diameter of up to about 22 mm), there is normally no requirement to main bond the copper installation pipework, as it is then unlikely to be an extraneous-conductive-part.

Nevertheless, it is still good advice to main bond the copper pipework, the bonding conductor being connected to the hard metal pipework as near as practicable to where the pipework changes from plastic to copper and before any branch pipework.
The copper pipework should always be main bonded, in accordance with Regulation 411.3.1.2, if it makes electrical contact with the general mass of Earth, such as may occur if part of the run is buried beneath the ground floor. In these circumstances the bonding conductor should connect to the hard metal pipework as near a practicable to where it emerges from the floor.

Supplementary equipotential bonding should be provided to the copper pipework in certain of the locations of increased shock risk covered in Part 7 of *BS 7671*, such as agricultural and horticultural premises and swimming pools.

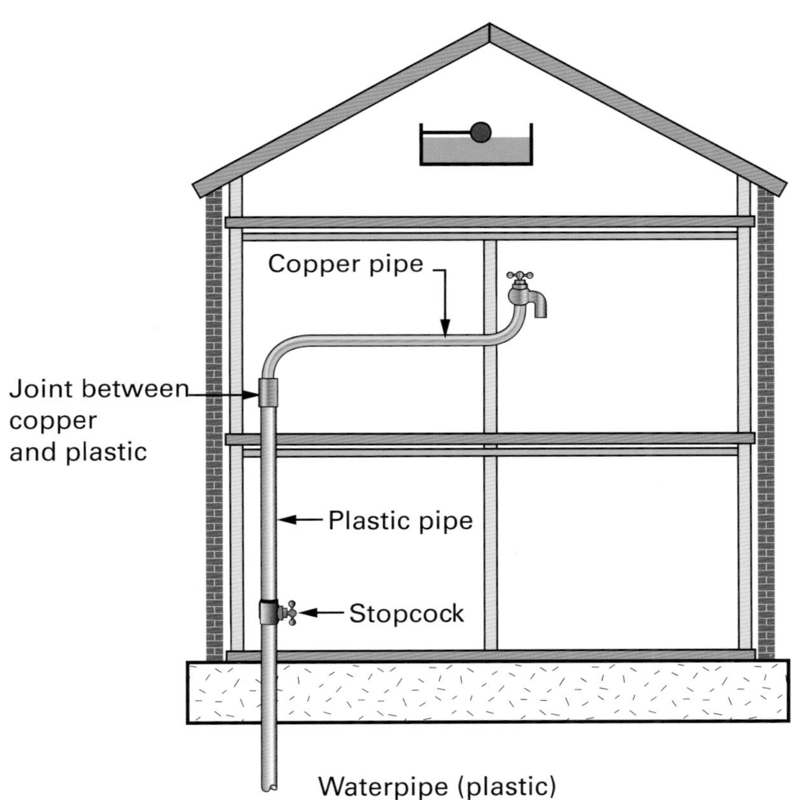

Standard applied
BS 7671

Regulations referred to
411.3.1.2, Part 7.

Earthing or bonding to metal cable tray or cable basket

Question

A number of multicore cables are grouped together on a length of metal cable tray or metal cable basket. Is it necessary to earth or bond the tray or basket?

Answer

Generally, as the cable cores are insulated and sheathed, it is not required either to earth or to bond the cable tray or basket, unless there are exceptional circumstances, which would need to be taken into account by the electrical installation designer.

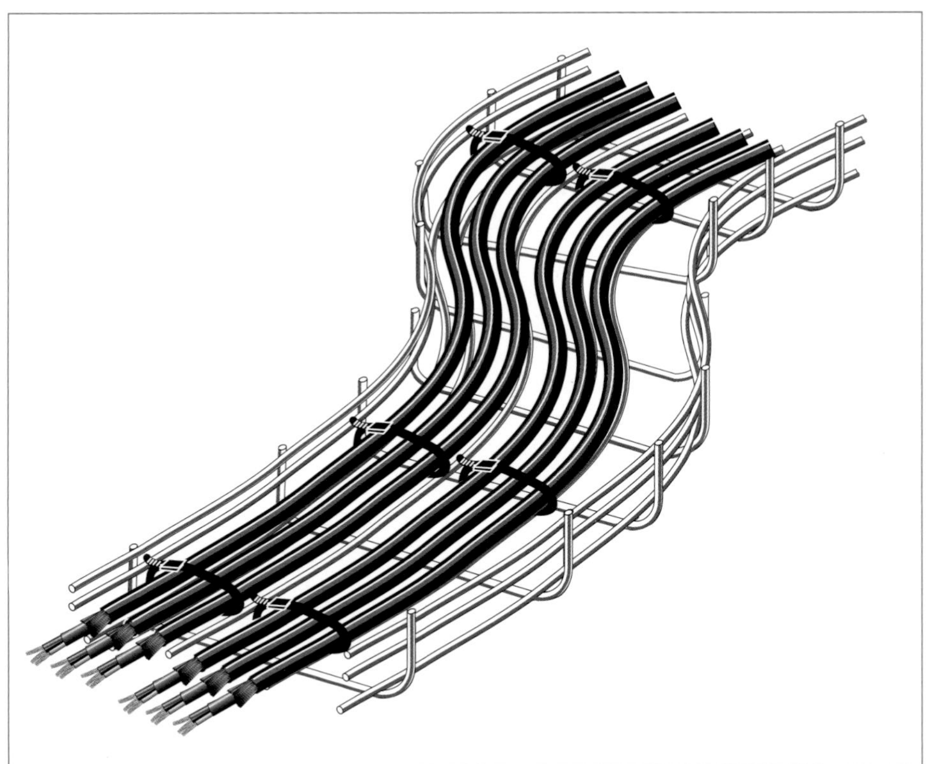

Exceptional circumstances may include:

i) if the installation designer has selected the cable tray or basket for use as a protective conductor, which is permitted under part indent (vi) of Regulation 543.2.2, subject to all the relevant requirements of *BS 7671* being met

ii) if the cable tray or basket meets the definition of an extraneous-conductive-part, main bonding is required.

In practice, it is unlikely that the cable tray or cable basket will be an extraneous-conductive-part or an exposed-conductive-part, or be selected as a protective conductor. Consequently, cable tray or cable basket generally need not be earthed or bonded.

1. Earthing

Cables mounted on a metallic cable tray or metallic cable basket will normally be of either of Class I construction (such as mineral-insulated copper-sheathed cable or steel wire armoured cable), or the equivalent of Class II equivalent construction (such as thermoplastic insulated and sheathed cable).

Exposed-conductive-parts of cables (for example a metal sheath or armour) are required to be connected to the main earthing terminal of the installation by a circuit protective conductor designed to conduct fault current. The cable tray or basket onto which Class I equipment is mounted is not, in consequence, an exposed-conductive-part and hence need not be earthed.

Where a cable complying with the appropriate standard has a non-metallic sheath or a non-metallic enclosure, it is deemed to provide satisfactory mechanical protection of the basic insulation (Regulation 412.2.4.1 refers). Hence the metal cable tray or basket need not be earthed.

Although the conductive parts of a metal cable or basket need not be deliberately earthed, some of these conductive parts may be earthed fortuitously by virtue of contact with exposed-conductive-parts.

2. Bonding

Unless a metal cable tray or metal cable basket system will introduce a potential that does not normally exist in the location in which the system is installed, it will not meet the definition of an extraneous-conductive-part. In normal circumstances, therefore, there is no need to arrange for the conductive parts of such a support system to be connected to either a main bonding conductor or to any supplementary bonding conductor.

Where either a cable tray or basket tray is installed in such a way as to introduce a potential from outside the location, such as may occur when running cable tray or basket between two buildings, then the tray or basket is likely to be an extraneous-conductive-part, and a main protective bonding conductor will be required to be connected between the Main Earthing Terminal (MET) and with the tray or basket (as applicable) near to its point of entry to each building.

QUESTION 36

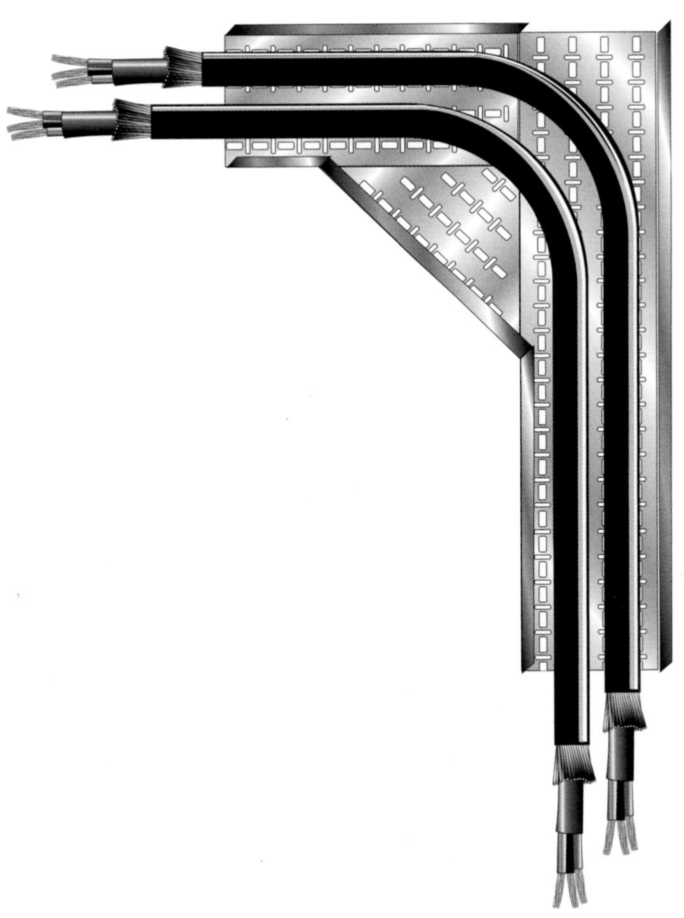

Standard applied
BS 7671

Regulations referred to
412.2.4.1, 543.2.2.

Metal sink - bonding

Question

Is it necessary to bond a metallic kitchen sink?

Answer

Supplementary equipotential bonding to a metallic kitchen sink is generally not required.

Although supplementary bonding is required in certain locations of increased shock risk, such as those defined in Part 7 of *BS 7671* (swimming pools and agricultural or horticultural premises etc), a kitchen is not defined in *BS 7671* as a location requiring additional fault protection; hence supplementary bonding is not required.

Furthermore, a metallic sink will almost certainly not, in its own right, be an extraneous-conductive-part[1] (as defined in Part 2: Definitions of *BS 7671*), and therefore the need for main equipotential bonding of the sink is unlikely to arise.

A note attached to Regulation 413-7 of the *15th Edition of the IEE Wiring Regulation* indicated that sinks might need to be bonded in areas where local supplementary bonding was provided. However, such a note was not included in the *16th Edition or the 17th Edition (BS 7671: 2008).*

---

[1] Extraneous-conductive-part is 'a conductive part liable to introduce a potential, generally earth potential, and not forming part of the electrical installation'.

QUESTION 37

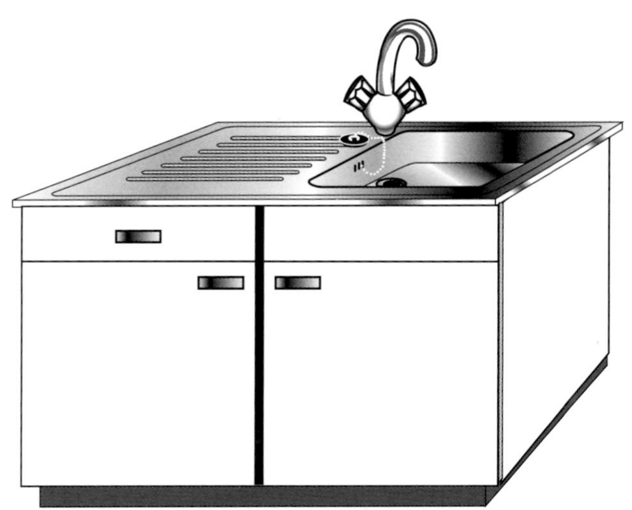

Standard applied
BS 7671 • 15th Edition IEE Wiring Regulations

Regulations referred to
Part 2, Part 7, 413-7 (15th Ed.).

Earthing of metal back boxes

Question

When installing a socket-outlet or a metallic wall-mounted switch, do I need to provide an earthing tail between the accessory and the accessory box?

Answer

The answer depends on the specific circumstances.

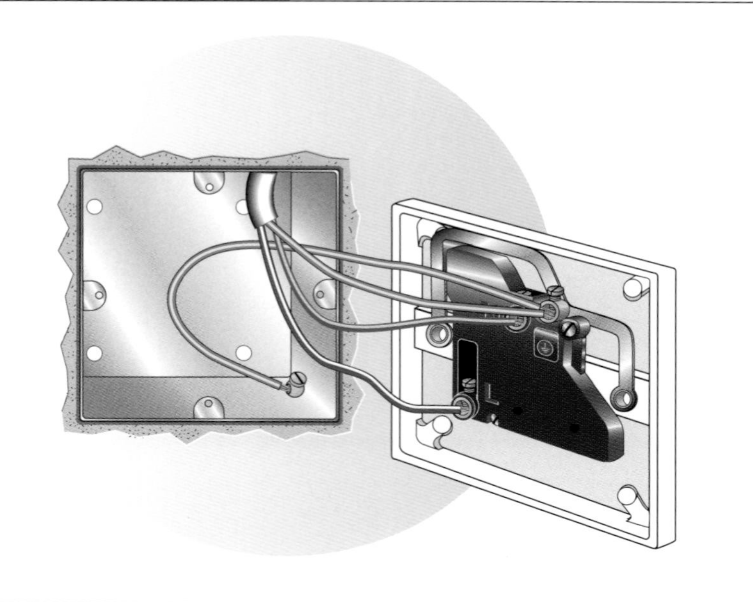

A metal back box for a surface-mounted accessory such as a socket-outlet is an exposed-conductive-part. Furthermore, a metal back box for a flush-mounted socket-outlet is deemed to be an exposed-conductive-part, (even though it may not be accessible to touch under normal conditions). Therefore, such back boxes, no less than every other exposed-conductive-part, are required to be earthed in accordance with Regulations 411.4.2 (TN systems) or 411.5.1 (TT systems).

Whether an earthing tail is required depends upon whether one or both of the lugs on the back box are adjustable (to permit the socket-outlet to be levelled) and upon the earthing strap and eyelet arrangement of the socket-outlet or other accessory. There are three conditions that may exist:

1) Where an accessory has an earthing strap and either one or two eyelets, and the metallic accessory box has two fixed (non-adjustable) lugs, there is no requirement to fit an earthing tail between the accessory and the accessory box (although the fitting of an earthing tail is still desirable).
2) Where a metallic accessory box has two adjustable lugs an earthing tail must be fitted between the accessory and the metallic accessory box. The reliability of the connection via the metal fixing screws may be compromised and, during the lifetime of the installation, effects such as corrosion may result in poor connection between the accessory and the metal accessory box.
3) Where an accessory box has one fixed and one adjustable lug, because some accessories have only one earthing strap and eyelet, it must be ensured that the earthing eyelet is located at the fixed lug position otherwise an earthing tail must be provided.

An earthing tail is an additional protective conductor consisting of a length of suitably-sized, green-yellow covered copper conductor connecting the earthing terminal of the socket-outlet (or other accessory) with the earthing terminal of the metal back box. In practice, a protective conductor from the accessory to the metal box will ensure that continuity will be maintained.

In addition to the general requirements stated above, Regulation 543.2.7 requires that where the protective conductor of the circuit is formed by conduit, trunking, ducting, or a metal sheath or armour of cable, then the earthing terminal of the accessory is connected by a separate protective conductor to an earthing terminal in the box or enclosure.

Standard applied

BS 7671

Regulations referred to

411.4.2, 411.5.1, 543.2.7.

Locations containing a bath or shower

Question

What needs to be connected together when carrying out supplementary bonding in a room containing a bath or shower?

Answer

Where the room containing a bath or shower is in a building with a protective equipotential bonding system in accordance with Regulation 411.3.1.2, which would commonly be the case, supplementary equipotential bonding may be omitted where all of the following conditions are met:

(i) all final circuits of the location comply with the requirements of disconnection according to Regulation 411.3.2.2. For a 230 V TN system this requires a maximum disconnection time of 0.4 s, and for a 230 V TT system this requires a 0.2 s disconnection time, and

(ii) all final circuits of the location have additional protection by means of an RCD having a rated residual operating current not greater than 30 mA and an operating time of not more than 40 ms at a residual current of 5 $I_{\Delta n}$, and

(iii) all extraneous-conductive-parts of the location are effectively connected to the protective equipotential bonding to 411.3.1.2.

In a location containing a bath or shower, the risk of electric shock is increased due to a reduction in body resistance or by contact with earth potential. Where the above three conditions are not met, supplementary bonding is required within a room containing a bath or shower to prevent the occurrence of voltages between exposed-conductive-parts and extraneous-conductive-parts of such magnitude as could cause risk of electric shock.

Regulation 701.415.2 requires that local supplementary equipotential bonding is established, connecting together the terminals of the protective conductor of each circuit supplying Class I and Class II equipment to the accessible extraneous-conductive-parts within a room containing a bath or shower.

Examples of parts that may be extraneous-conductive-parts, include:

- metallic pipes supplying services and metallic waste pipes (e.g. water, gas)
- metallic central heating pipes and air conditioning systems
- accessible metallic structural parts of the building; (metallic door architraves, window frames and similar parts are not considered to be extraneous-conductive-parts unless they are connected to metallic structural parts of the building).

However, exposed-conductive-parts of SELV circuits are excluded from the supplementary bonding requirements and must not be connected to such bonding. Regulation 414.4.4 refers.

The required supplementary bonding must be carried out either within the location containing the bath or shower or in close proximity (such as in an adjoining roof void or an airing cupboard opening into, or adjoining, the room) (Regulation 701.415.2 refers).

The type of conductor permitted to be used may include a supplementary conductor, a conductive part of a permanent and reliable nature, such as copper pipework, or a combination of both (Regulation 544.2.4 refers).

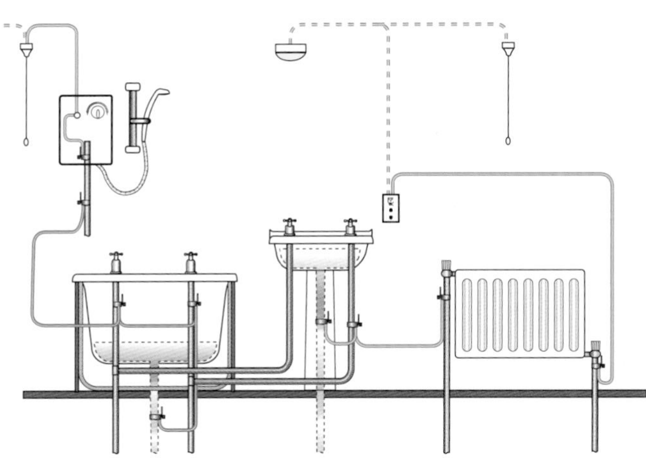

Standard applied
BS 7671

Regulations referred to
411.3.1.2, 411.3.2.2, 414.4.4, 415.1, 415.2, 544.2.4, 701.415.2.

Lightning protection systems

Question

What are the requirements for connecting a lightning protection system to an electrical installation's Main Earthing Terminal?

Answer

Where a structure has a lightning protection system, *BS 7671* requires the lightning protection system to be connected to the main earthing terminal (MET) of the electrical installation by main bonding conductor(s) complying with Section 544 (Regulation 411.3.1.2 refers).

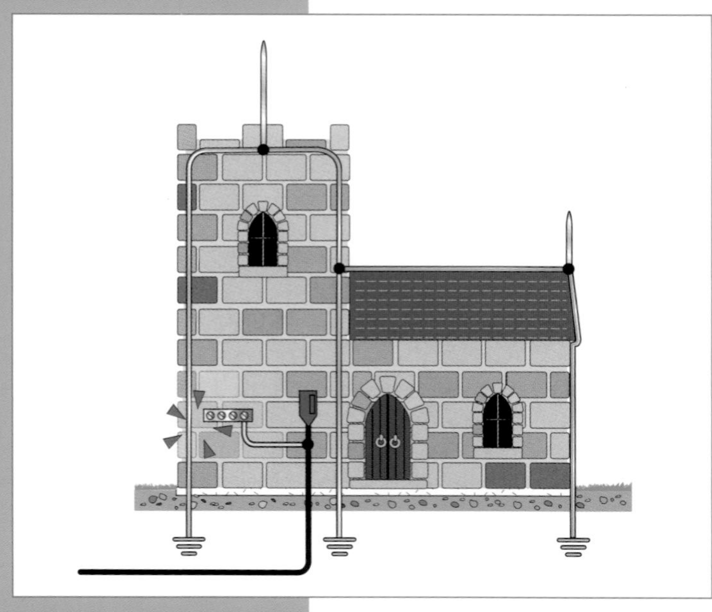

Whilst the electrical installation contractor may be required to install the bonding conductor, the choice of type and size of conductor is the responsibility of the lightning protection system designer, although the conductor must meet the relevant requirements of *BS 7671*. Additionally, it may be the case, that the final connection to the lightning protection system is the responsibility of the lightning protection specialist and **not** the contractor.

Due account must be taken of the recommendations of *BS EN 62305-3: 2006*[1] *Protection against lightning*. The lightning protection system itself is, however, excluded from the scope of *BS 7671* by Regulation 110.2.

It is advisable that the exact positions of bonding connections are determined by the lightning protection system designer, due to the complexity of the requirements of *BS EN 62305-3: 2006*. Normally, the connection should be from the down conductor of the lightning protection system closest to the MET of the electrical installation, by the most direct route available.

1 *BS EN 62305: 2006* supersedes *BS 6651: 1999 Code of practice for protection of structures against lightning* which is still current but will be withdrawn on 31st August 2008.

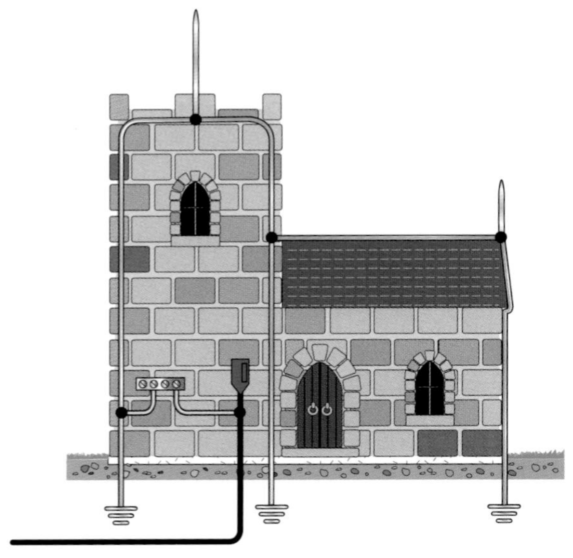

Bonding connections should not be made without consulting the designer of the lightning protection system, the system maintenance contractor or other competent person. Bonding connections to a lightning protection system are normally made outdoors, and may involve conductors of different shapes and dissimilar metals. Accordingly, special consideration should be given to the requirement of Regulation 526.1 for electrical connections to provide durable electrical continuity and adequate mechanical strength, and those of Regulation Group 522.5 regarding measures to avoid corrosion.

Generally, the means of connection should be discussed and agreed with the lightning protection system designer and installer. It is often best for the actual making of a connection to the system to be carried out by the lightning protection installer, although it is still the electrical contractor's responsibility to see that this is done satisfactorily.

Exceptionally, for reasons of safety, lightning protection system designers may advise that a main bonding connection should not be made to a lightning protection system. In such circumstances, the consequent departure from Regulation 411.3.1.2 must be recorded on the Electrical Installation Certificate and reference made to the last sentence of Regulation 120.3. The departure must be drawn to the customer's attention. For a connection not to be made between the lightning protection system and the electrical installation's equipotential bonding arrangement is permissible only where the electrical contractor has requested the main bonding connection be made, and has obtained the lightning protection system designer's written objection to the connection being made on grounds of safety.

QUESTION 40

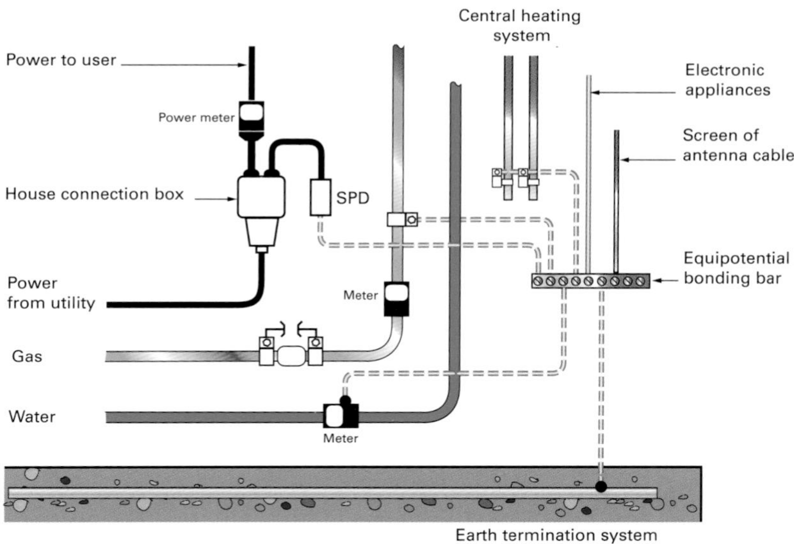

Based on Figure E.45 of *BS EN 62305* - Example of an equipotential bonding arrangement

Standards applied

BS EN 62305-3: 2006 • BS 7671

Regulations referred to

110.2, 120.3, 411.3.1.2, 522.5, 526.1, 544.

Supplies from a PME system - caravan pitches

Question

Are there any special earthing requirements that must be taken into account where a caravan park is supplied from a Protective Multiple Earthing (PME) supply?

Answer

Yes. The electricity distributor's PME earthing terminal earthing must not be used for earthing caravan pitch socket-outlets (Regulation 708.411.4 refers). Alternative earthing arrangements must be made for the pitch socket-outlets, as explained later.

This is because Regulation 9(4) of the *Electrical Safety, Quality and Continuity Regulations 2002* effectively prohibits the electricity distributor from offering the PME earthing facility for use as the means of earthing for the installation in a caravan or boat. The prohibition is intended to prevent the risk of metalwork in the caravan (or boat) becoming raised to line conductor potential in the event of the combined neutral and earth conductor of the supply became disconnected from Earth. Under such circumstances, a person entering or leaving the caravan would be at risk of electric shock.

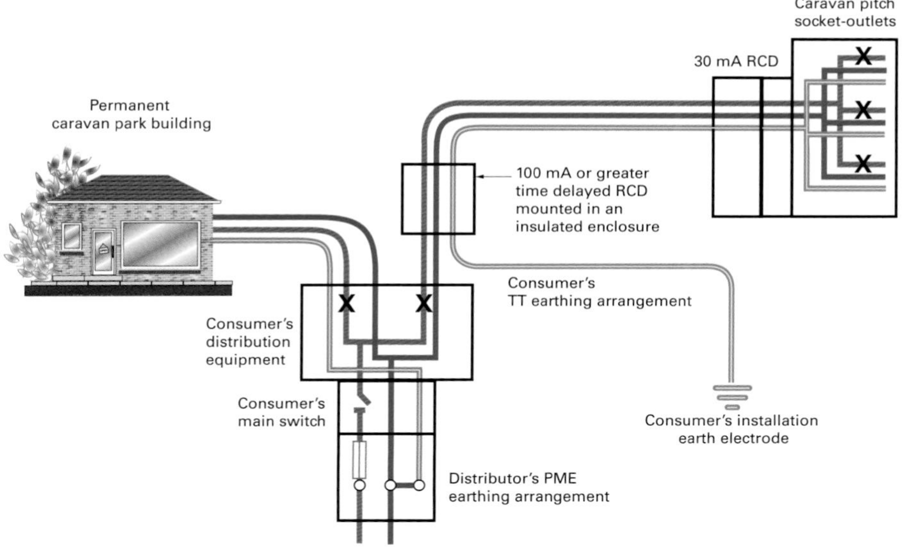

Fig 1

Regulation 708.553.1.14 of *BS 7671*, relating to the pitch socket-outlets on a caravan park, requires that the protective conductor of each socket-outlet circuit shall not be connected to the PME terminal.

Furthermore, the regulation requires that the protective conductor of the socket-outlet circuit shall be connected to an installation earth electrode and that the requirement of Regulation 411.5 for a TT system shall be met.

Whilst the note attached to Regulation 708.530.3 permits no more than four socket-outlets to be grouped in one supply/board, the socket-outlets at a pitch must be protected individually by a residual current device (RCD) complying with the requirements of Regulation 411.5 for TT systems. (Regulation 708.553.1.13 refers)

The separation of the caravan pitch TT earthing arrangement from the distributor's PME earthing terminal may be made at one of a number of places, the two main possibilities being:

- at the consumer's distribution position, where a time delay RCD would be used to provide discrimination with the RCDs protecting the pitch socket-outlets, as shown in Fig 1.
- at the pitch supply position, as shown in Fig 2.

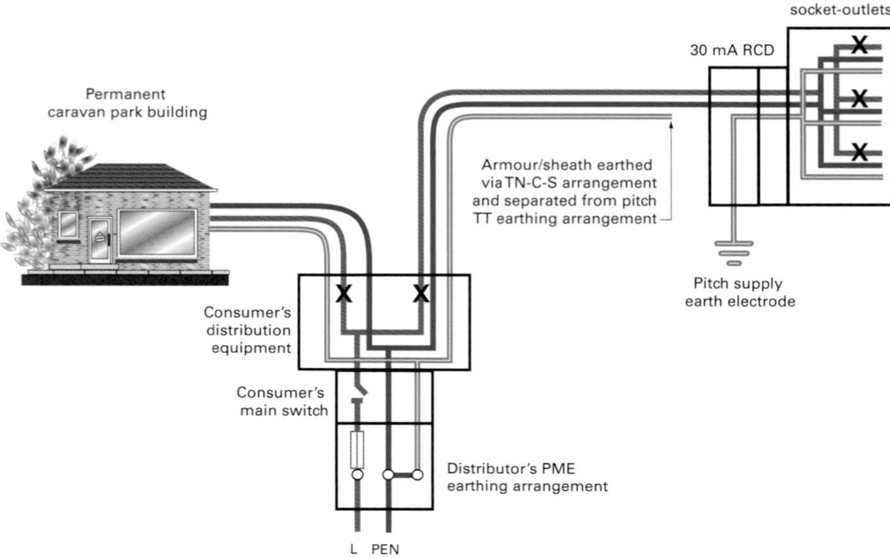

Fig 2.1

Note 2 to Table 41.5 of *BS 7671*, recommends that the installation earth electrode resistance does not exceed 200 Ω, and Regulation 411.5.3 requires that:

$$R_A I_{\Delta n} \leq 50\,\text{V}$$

Where

R_A = the sum of the resistances of the earth electrode and the protective conductor(s) connecting it to the exposed-conductive-parts

$I_{\Delta n}$ = rated residual operating current of the RCD

and the disconnection time shall be that required by Regulation 411.3.2.2 or 411.3.2.4, which, for a final circuit in a 230 V TT system shall not exceed 0.2 s, and for a distribution circuit or a circuit not covered by Regulation 411.3.2.2 shall not exceed 1 s.

QUESTION 41

Standards applied
BS 7671 • The Electricity, Safety, Quality and Continuity Regulations 2002

Regulations referred to
411.3.2.2, 411.3.2.4, 411.5, 411.5.3, 708.411.4, 708.530.3, 708.553.1.13, 708.553.1.14.

Cross-sectional area of an earthing conductor – TN system

Question

How should I size a single-core green-yellow pvc-covered copper cable for use as the earthing conductor for an installation forming part of a TN system?

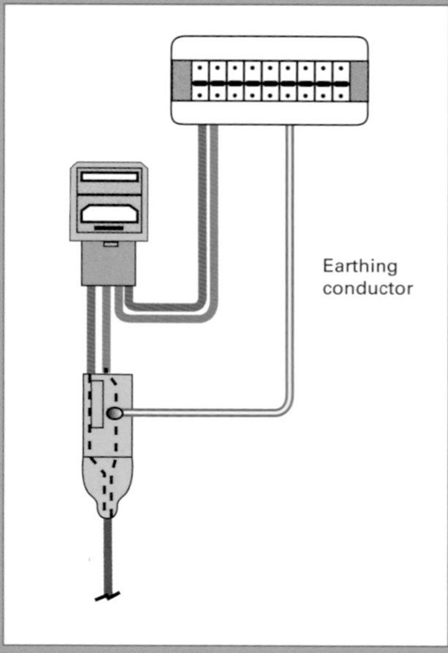

Answer

It is necessary to take the following into account to size an earthing conductor consisting of a single-core green-yellow covered copper cable:

- the form and material of the conductor
- the electricity distributor's requirements,
- whether or not the conductor will be buried in the ground,
- PME conditions, and
- the length of the earthing conductor, where the conductor is particularly long – as may be the case in a block of flats.

Where an electricity distributor's earthing facility is to be used as the means of earthing, the distributor may stipulate the type or types of conductor and the size of conductor which may be used for the earthing conductor of the installation. Most electricity distributors publish notes of guidance which include their requirements regarding (amongst other things) permitted types of earthing conductor.

1. Cross-sectional area (csa)

Subject to certain lower limits, referred to later, the csa of the earthing conductor must be either not less than that calculated in accordance with Regulation 543.1.3 (adiabatic equation) or not less than that selected in accordance with Regulation 543.1.4 (Table 54.7).

Generally, selection is the more commonly used method for determining the required csa. Selection makes use of Table 54.7 of *BS 7671* (reproduced below) together with knowledge of the csa and material of the associated line conductor.

Minimum cross-sectional area of the protective conductor in relation to the cross-sectional area of the associated line conductor

Cross-sectional area of line conductor S	Minimum cross-sectional area of the corresponding protective conductor	
	If the protective conductor is of the same material as the line conductor	If the protective conductor is not of the same material as the line conductor
(mm^2)	(mm^2)	(mm^2)
$S \leq 16$	S	$\frac{k_1}{k_2} \times S$
$16 < S \leq 35$	16	$\frac{k_1}{k_2} \times 16$
$S > 35$	$\frac{S}{2}$	$\frac{k_1}{k_2} \times \frac{S}{2}$

where: k_1 is the value of k for the line conductor, selected from Table 43.1 in Chapter 43 according to the materials of both conductor and insulation.

k_2 is the value of k for the protective conductor, selected from Tables 54.2 to 54.6, as applicable.

Whether determined by calculation or selection, the csa of an earthing conductor must not be less than certain lower limits. For a copper earthing conductor which is not an integral part of a cable (such as a core of a cable) and not contained in an enclosure (such as conduit) formed by a wiring system, the csa must be not less than 2.5 mm^2 where protection against mechanical damage is provided, and 4 mm^2 where such protection is not provided (Regulation 543.1.1 refers).

2. Where PME conditions apply

The earthing conductor of an installation that uses the earthing facility of a supply from a Protective Multiple Earthing (PME) network as its means of earthing also performs the function of a main protective bonding conductor. Accordingly, the csa of the conductor must be not less than that determined in accordance with Regulation 544.1.1 (refer to Table 54.8 of *BS 7671* reproduced below) for a main protective bonding conductor, or Section 543 for an earthing conductor, whichever is the greater.

Minimum cross-sectional area of the main protective bonding conductor in relation to the neutral of the supply

NOTE: Local distributor's network conditions may require a larger conductor.

Copper equivalent cross-sectional area of the supply neutral conductor (mm^2)	Minimum copper equivalent* cross-sectional area of the main protective bonding conductor (mm^2)
$\leq$ 35	10
$>$ 35 $\leq$ 50	16
$>$ 50 $\leq$ 95	25
$>$ 95 $\leq$ 150	35
$>$ 150	50

* The minimum copper equivalent cross-sectional area is given by a copper bonding conductor of the tabulated cross-sectional area or a bonding conductor of another metal affording equivalent conductance.

3. Csa for fault protection

Notwithstanding the considerations referred to above, the contribution that the impedance of the earthing conductor makes to the total earth fault loop impedance must also be considered. In some cases, the impedance of the circuit protective conductor may impose a constraint on the overall length of the circuit, in terms of affording fault protection.

Standard applied
BS 7671

Regulations referred to
543.1.1, 543.1.3, 544.1.1, Table 54.7, Table 54.8.

Installing earth electrodes - types for a TT system

Question

What may be used as the installation earth electrode in a TT system?

Answer

Many electrical installation installers and designers believe that the only type of installation earth electrode permitted for a TT system is a rod or pipe. This is not the case. Regulation 542.2.1 of *BS 7671* permits the following types of earth electrode:

- earth rods or pipes
- earth tapes or wires
- earth plates
- underground structural metalwork embedded in foundations
- welded metal reinforcement of concrete (except pre-stressed concrete) embedded in the earth
- lead sheaths and other metal coverings of cables, where not precluded by Regulation 542.2.5
- other suitable underground metalwork.

It should be noted that Regulation 542.2.4 specifically forbids the use of the metallic pipes of gases or flammable liquids or water utility supplies as earth electrodes, whilst not precluding them from being bonded within the electrical installation as required by Regulation 411.3.1.2. However, other metallic water supply pipework may be used as an earth electrode where precautions have been taken against its removal, and it has been considered for such a use.

Any earth electrode used must be capable of withstanding damage or corrosion (Regulation 542.2.3 refers). The rate of corrosion will depend on a range of factors, such as, the type of soil, the material the electrode is constructed of and the difference in electro-potential between different types of metal.

Particular problems may arise, however, where two dissimilar metals are in close proximity. Where steel is embedded in concrete and copper rods are installed they may be connected together with no increase in the rate of corrosion due to electrolytic action. However, where galvanized steel is not embedded in concrete it is strongly electronegative to both steel in concrete and copper and should not be bonded to either steel embedded in concrete or copper, otherwise electrolytic corrosion will occur, leading to a reduction in the mass of the steel. Any combination of dissimilar metals would require investigation prior to any interconnection. Further guidance can be found in Table 8 of *BS 7430 Code of practice for Earthing.*

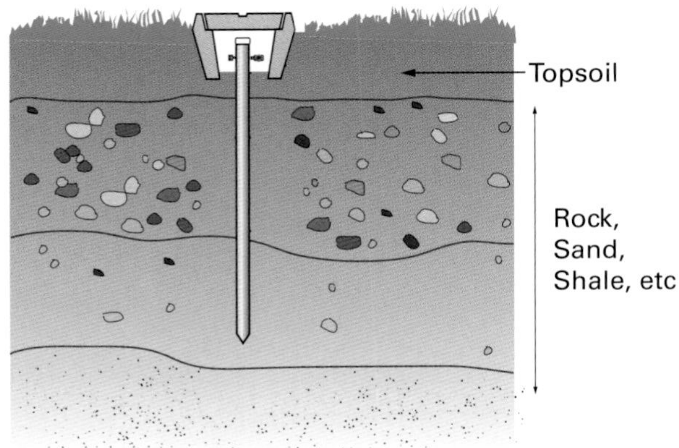

Standards applied

BS 7671 • BS 7430: 1998 Code of practice for earthing

Regulations referred to

411.3.1.2, 542.2.1, 542.2.3, 542.2.4, 542.2.5.

Installing earthing conductors – for a TT system

Question

In a TT system, what cross-sectional area of green-yellow pvc-covered copper earthing conductor should be used to connect between a Main Earthing Terminal of the installation and the installation earth electrode?

Answer

A designer determining the size of a green-yellow pvc copper earthing conductor for a TT system must combine the requirements of *BS 7671*, and in particular the requirements of Regulation 542.3.1 and Section 543.

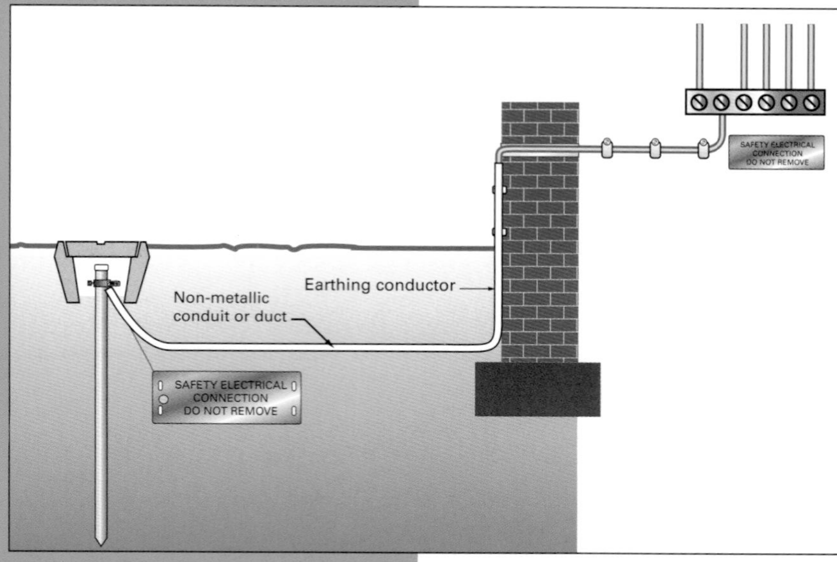

Size of earthing conductor

As with all protective conductors, Regulation 542.3.1 requires that an earthing conductor must have a cross-sectional area (csa) either complying with the requirements of Table 54.7 or calculated in accordance with Regulation 543.1.3. Additionally, where the earthing conductor is buried in the ground, the csa must comply with the requirements of Table 54.1 (reproduced below for ease of reference).

For a mechanically protected earthing conductor, the earthing conductor may be as small as 2.5 mm² (Regulation 543.1.1 refers).

However, it is generally the case that an earthing conductor is a green-yellow pvc-covered copper conductor and, where buried in the ground, unless the earthing conductor has a sheath surrounding the green-yellow covering, the smallest conductor csa must be 25 mm². Only where additional mechanical protection is provided, such as by a suitable non-metallic conduit or duct, may the size of the earthing conductor be smaller than 25 mm².

In practice, for a TT system, many installers will clip an earthing conductor to the surface of a building and then bury the conductor for the last part of the run into the earth electrode. If the earthing conductor has a csa smaller then 25 mm², to comply with Table 54.1, it will be necessary for mechanical protection to be provided where the cable is installed underground.

TABLE 54.1
Minimum cross-sectional area of a buried earthing conductor

	Protected against mechanical damage	Not protected against mechanical damage
Protected against corrosion by a sheath	2.5 mm² copper 10 mm² steel	16 mm² copper 16 mm² coated steel
Not protected against corrosion	25 mm² copper 50 mm² steel	

Standard applied
BS 7671

Regulations referred to
Table 54.1, Table 54.8, 542.3.1, 543.1.1, 543.1.3, Regulation Group 543.1.

Fire alarms and emergency lighting

Questions 45 - 50

FROM THE HELPLINE ...

Grades and Categories of fire detection and alarm systems in dwellings

Question

I am planning to install a fire alarm system in a dwelling. What are the meanings of the 'Grades' of system and 'Categories' of system?

Answer

1. Grades of system

BS 5839-6: 2004 Fire detection and fire alarm systems for buildings groups fire detection and fire alarm systems into six Grades, according to the equipment that they incorporate.

BRITISH STANDARD | BS 5839-6:2004

Fire detection and fire alarm systems for buildings —

Part 6: Code of practice for the design, installation and maintenance of fire detection and fire alarm systems in dwellings

NO COPYING WITHOUT BSI PERMISSION EXCEPT AS PERMITTED BY COPYRIGHT LAW

BSi British Standards

QUESTION **45**

The Grades relate to the engineering aspects of fire detection and fire alarm systems, and higher Grades of system tend to provide a greater level of control and monitoring of the system, or greater reliability and availability to perform correctly in the event of fire. General descriptions of Grades are:

Grade A	A fire detection and alarm system effectively designed and installed in accordance with the recommendations of *BS 5839-1: 2002* (as amended), except those in the clauses 16, 18, 20, 25.4e) and 27, which should be replaced by their corresponding clauses (13, 14, 18, 15.2c) and 21 respectively) in *BS 5839-6: 2004*.
Grade B	A fire detection and alarm system comprising fire detectors (other than smoke alarms and heat alarms), fire alarm sounders, and control and indicating equipment that either conforms to *BS EN 54-2* (and power supply to *BS EN 54-4*) or Annex C of this part of *BS 5839-6: 2004*
Grade C	A system of fire detectors and alarm sounders (which may be combined in the form of smoke alarms) connected to a common power supply, comprising the normal mains and a standby supply, with central control equipment.
Grade D	A system of one or more mains-powered smoke alarms, each with an integral standby supply. (The system may, in addition, incorporate one or more mains-powered heat alarms, each with an integral standby supply.)
Grade E	A system of one or more mains-powered alarms with no standby supply. (The system may, in addition, incorporate one or more mains-powered heat alarms, with or without standby supplies.)
Grade F	A system of one or more battery-powered smoke alarms. (The system may, in addition, incorporate one or more battery-powered heat alarms.)

2. Categories of system

System Categories relate to the level of protection afforded to the occupants of the dwelling. The Category of system appropriate for a dwelling will depend primarily on the fire risk.

General descriptions of Categories are:

Category LD	A fire detection and fire alarm system intended for the protection of life. This Category is further sub-divided into: • Category LD1 — a system installed throughout the dwelling, incorporating detectors in all circulation spaces that form part of the escape routes from the dwelling, and in all rooms and areas in which fire might start, other than toilets, bathrooms and shower rooms. • Category LD2 — a system incorporating detectors in all circulation spaces that form part of the escape routes from the dwelling, and in all rooms or areas that present a high fire risk to occupants. • Category LD3 — a system incorporating detectors in all circulation spaces that form part of the escape routes from the dwelling.
Category PD	A fire detection and fire alarm system intended for the protection of property. This Category is further sub-divided into: • Category PD1 — a system installed throughout the dwelling, incorporating detectors in all rooms and areas in which fire might start, other than toilets, bathrooms and shower rooms • Category PD2 — a system incorporating detectors only in defined rooms or areas of the dwelling in which the risk of fire to property is judged to warrant their provision.

QUESTION 45

Table 1 of *BS 5839-6: 2004* provides guidance on the minimum recommended Grade and Category of fire detection and fire alarm system for protection of life in typical dwellings.

Attention is also drawn to the requirements of the *Regulatory Reform (Fire Safety) Order 2005*, which applies to England and Wales, the *Fire and Rescue Services (Northern Ireland) Order 2006* and the *Fire (Scotland) Act 2005*.

Standards applied
BS 5839-6: 2004

Regulations referred to
BS 5839-1: 2002, BS EN 54-2, BS EN 54-4.

Wiring used in fire detection and alarm systems

Question

What type of wiring should be used for a fire alarm and detection system in a dwelling and what should be the sheath colour?

BRITISH STANDARD

BS 5839-6:2004

Fire detection and fire alarm systems for buildings —

Part 6: Code of practice for the design, installation and maintenance of fire detection and fire alarm systems in dwellings

NO COPYING WITHOUT BSI PERMISSION EXCEPT AS PERMITTED BY COPYRIGHT LAW

BSi British Standards

Answer

The type of cable used in a fire detection and fire alarm system will depend on the Grade of system that is to be installed.

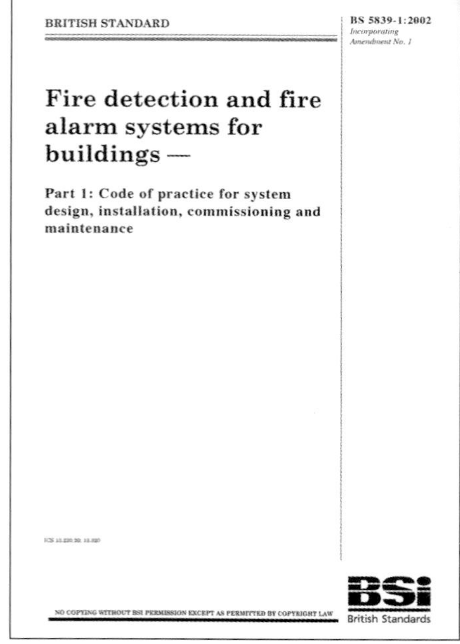

BRITISH STANDARD

BS 5839-1:2002
Incorporating Amendment No. 1

Fire detection and fire alarm systems for buildings —

Part 1: Code of practice for system design, installation, commissioning and maintenance

NO COPYING WITHOUT BSI PERMISSION EXCEPT AS PERMITTED BY COPYRIGHT LAW

BSi British Standards

Cables used for all parts of the critical signal paths (e.g. supplies to detectors), for the extra-low voltage supply from an external power supply unit (if any), and for the final circuit providing the low voltage mains supply to a Grade A systems should, as a minimum, comply with the recommendations of clause 26.2 of *BS 5839-1: 2002 (Fire detection and fire alarm systems for buildings)* for fire-resisting cables.

Amongst other things, for a Grade A system, the sheath of cables should be of a single common colour (preferably red) that is not used for cables of general electrical services in the building (clause 26.2(o) refers).

Cables used in Grade B systems should also, as a minimum, comply with the recommendations of *BS 5839-1: 2002* clause 26.2, except that the sheath need not be of a single common colour.

Cables for systems of Grades C, D, E and F need not be of the fire-resisting type, and no specific sheath colour is recommended by *BS 5839* for the purpose of identifying them as part of a fire detection and alarm system. As for any fire alarm system wiring, the electrical characteristics of the cables should be in accordance with relevant recommendations of *BS 7671*, and the wiring should not be susceptible to mechanical damage, such as may be due to impact, abrasion or rodent attack. Sufficient protection from mechanical damage may be achieved if the cables are installed in the building structure, under plaster within the prescribed zones or installed in conduit, trunking or ducting (clause 16.4 of *BS 5839-6* refers).

Standards applied
BS 5839-1: 2002 • BS 5839-6: 2004 • BS 5588-1: 1990

Regulations referred to
None listed

Segregation requirements for fire alarm cables in a dwelling

Question

What requirements for segregation (or separation) apply to the wiring of a fire detection and alarm system in a dwelling?

BRITISH STANDARD | BS 5839-6:2004

Fire detection and fire alarm systems for buildings —

Part 6: Code of practice for the design, installation and maintenance of fire detection and fire alarm systems in dwellings

ICS 13.220.20; 13.320

NO COPYING WITHOUT BSI PERMISSION EXCEPT AS PERMITTED BY COPYRIGHT LAW

BSi British Standards

Answer

To avoid electromagnetic interference with fire alarm signals from the wiring of other services or other voltages, any recommendations of the fire alarm system manufacturer with regard to segregation or separation of fire alarm wiring should be followed. (Clause 26.2(l) of *BS 5839-1: 2002* refers for Grade A and B systems, and clause 22.2 of *BS 5839-6: 2004* refers for Grade C systems.)

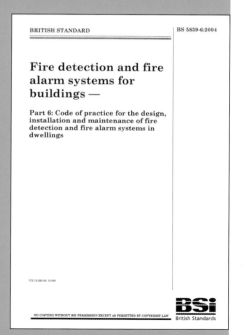

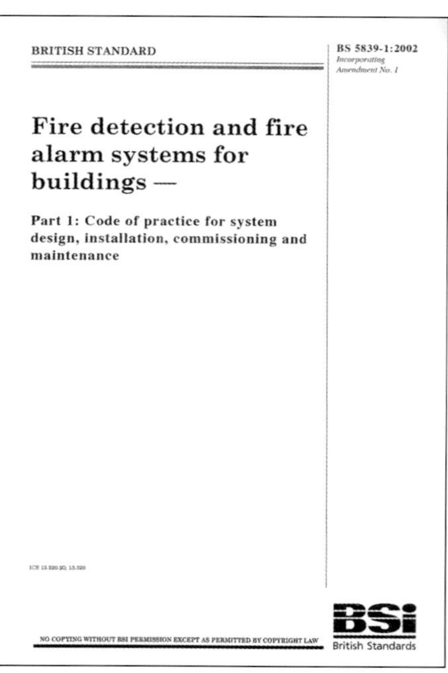

BRITISH STANDARD | BS 5839-1:2002 *Incorporating Amendment No. 1*

Fire detection and fire alarm systems for buildings —

Part 1: Code of practice for system design, installation, commissioning and maintenance

ICS 13.220.20; 13.320

NO COPYING WITHOUT BSI PERMISSION EXCEPT AS PERMITTED BY COPYRIGHT LAW

BSi British Standards

QUESTION 47

For a Grade A system, to avoid the risk of mechanical damage to the fire alarm cables, they should not be installed within the same conduit as the cables of other services. Where the fire alarm cables share common trunking, a compartment of the trunking, separated from other compartments by a strong, rigid and continuous partition, should be reserved solely for fire alarm cables (Clause 26.2(k) of *BS 5839-1*: 2002 refers.) Clause 28.1 of *BS 5839-1*: 2002 comments that the use of a continuous metal partition will also reduce the impact of electromagnetic interference (EMI).

For Grade A and B systems, the mains supply cable to any control, indicating or power supply equipment should not enter the equipment through the same entry as cables carrying extra-low voltage. Within the equipment, low voltage and extra-low voltage cables should, where this is practicable, be kept separate. (Clause 26.2(n) of *BS 5839-1: 2002* refers.)

Notwithstanding the recommendations just mentioned, the requirements of Regulation Group 528.1 of *BS 7671* must also be complied with. In particular, a band I circuit (e.g. extra-low voltage) must not be contained in the same wiring system as a band II circuit (e.g. 230 V) unless one of the methods in indents (i) to (vi) is adopted, such as every cable being insulated for the highest voltage present.

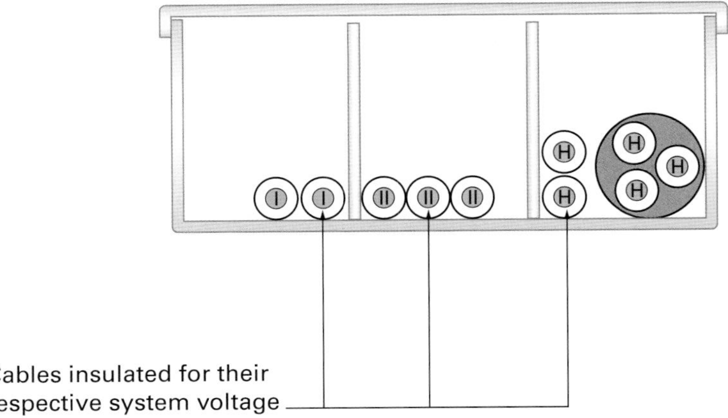

Standards applied
BS 5839-1: 2002 • BS 5839-6: 2004 • BS 7671

Regulations referred to
528.1

FROM THE HELPLINE ...

Tests on emergency lighting systems

Question

The model form of Emergency Lighting Periodic Inspection and Test Certificate in Annex D of *BS 5266-1: 2005* refers to daily, monthly and annual periodic tests. What should be covered during these tests?

Answer

The minimum servicing and testing that should be carried out where national regulations do not apply are given in clause 7 of *BS EN 50172: 2004 (Emergency escape lighting systems)* (dual numbered also as *BS 5266-8: 2004*).

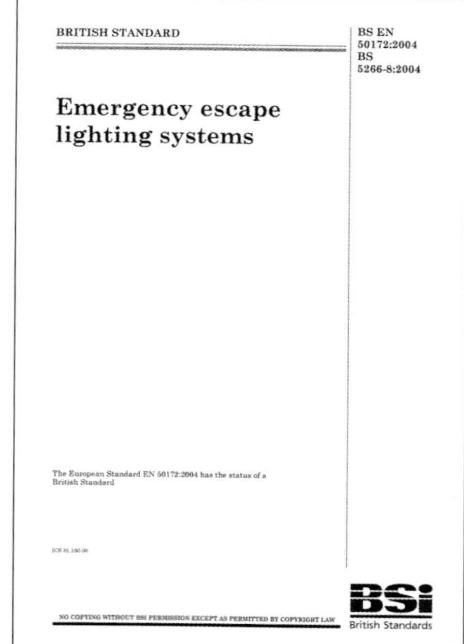
BRITISH STANDARD

BS EN 50172:2004
BS 5266-8:2004

Emergency escape lighting systems

The European Standard EN 50172:2004 has the status of a British Standard

NO COPYING WITHOUT BSI PERMISSION EXCEPT AS PERMITTED BY COPYRIGHT LAW

BSi British Standards

QUESTION 48

The specific daily, monthly and annual tests referred to are listed in the table.

Daily	**Monthly**	**Annually**
Indicators of central power supply shall be visually inspected for correct operation.	Switch on in emergency mode each luminaire and each internally illuminated exit sign from its battery by simulation of a failure of supply to the normal lighting for a period sufficient to ensure that each lamp is illuminated.	Each luminaire and internally illuminated sign shall be tested as for the monthly tests, but for its full duration in accordance with the manufacturer's information.
	All luminaires should be checked to ensure that they are present, clean and functioning properly.	The supply of the normal lighting shall be restored and any indicator lamp or device checked to ensure that it is showing the normal supply has been restored. The charging arrangements should be checked for proper functioning.
	At the end of the test period, the normal supply should be restored and any indicator lamp or device checked to see that the normal supply has been restored.	The date of the test and its results shall be recorded in the system logbook.
	For central battery systems, the correct operation of system monitors shall be checked.	For generating sets the requirements of *ISO 8528-12* shall be complied with.
	For generating sets the requirements of *ISO 8528-12* shall be complied with.	

It may be the case, however, that there is a need for a more onerous servicing or testing regime than listed above where the national standards are applied. For example, the need for additional servicing or testing requirements may be identified as the result of a 'risk assessment' carried out in accordance with the *Regulatory Reform (Fire Safety) Order 2005*, which applies to England and Wales.

Additional servicing and testing requirements may also arise from regulating authorities' requirements for licensing purposes.

It should also be noted that consultation with the client is necessary regarding the details of the contract and any relevant parts of the specification relating to documentation/certification, and the type of inspection to be undertaken. Where equipment is more specialized, it may be necessary to seek manufacturer's advice.

Emergency lighting systems are a safety service, and as such any tests should be carried out preceding a time of low risk. Carrying out the tests at such times will allow the battery supplying the emergency lighting system to recharge during the time of low risk. This is recognized by Clause 7 of the Standard, which specifies that:

> *'Because of the possibility of failure of the normal lighting supply occurring shortly after a period of testing of the emergency lighting system or during subsequent recharge period, all full duration tests shall wherever possible be undertaken preceding time of low risk to allow for battery recharge.'*

QUESTION **48**

Standards applied
BS 5266-1: 2005 • BS EN 50172: 2004 • BS 5266-8: 2004 • ISO 8528-12

Regulations referred to
None listed

Test facility for emergency lighting luminaires

Question

Is it a requirement of the emergency lighting standard or *BS 7671* to provide a test facility for an emergency lighting luminaire local to the luminaire's position?

Answer

Not necessarily. The recommendation of clause 9.3.3 of *BS 5266-1: 2005 (Emergency lighting – Part 1: Code of practice for the emergency lighting of premises)* is for each emergency lighting system to have a suitable means of simulating failure of the normal supply for test purposes.

However, *BS EN 60598-2-22: 1999 (Luminaires – Part 2-22: Particular requirements – Luminaires for emergency lighting)* does provide some detail on the nature of the test devices themselves. Specifically, clause 22.20.1 requires that,

> *'Self-contained emergency luminaires shall be provided with an integral test facility, or with the means of connection to a remote facility, for simulating failure of the normal supply. Manually operated test switches shall be self-resetting or key operated'.*

Additionally, clause 22.20.2 requires that,

> *'Any remote test device used in conjunction with emergency lighting luminaires shall not influence the normal operation of the luminaire, other than for testing'.*

In practice, where the layout of the emergency lighting system is simple, the testing facility may be located at the position of the distribution board associated with the emergency lighting. However, for more complex emergency lighting layouts, or where the building layout makes it difficult to undertake the testing of the lighting and observe the results reliably, it may be necessary to consider positioning test facilities in an accessible position locally to the corresponding emergency lighting.

It is also the case that some emergency lighting systems may have automatic testing facilities.

In addition to the requirements and recommendations of the other standards, Regulation 560.7.10 of *BS 7671* requires, amongst other things, that:

a copy of the drawings of the electrical safety installations shall be displayed at the origin of the installation showing the exact location of:

i) all electrical control equipment and distribution boards, with equipment designations

ii) safety equipment with final circuit designation and particulars and purpose of the equipment

iii) special switching and monitoring equipment for the safety power supply.

Standards applied

BS 5266-1: 2005 • BS 7671 • BS EN 60598-2-22: 1999

Regulations referred to

560.7.10

Lighting levels of an emergency lighting system

Question

When carrying out a periodic inspection and test on an emergency lighting system, how do I determine the lighting levels being achieved?

Answer

To comply with the requirements of *BS EN 1838: 1999* (dual numbered as *BS 5266-7: 1999*) Lighting applications – Emergency lighting, emergency escape route lighting should be checked either by measurement or by comparison with authenticated space data, such as:

- The Industry Committee for Emergency Lighting (ICEL) 1001: 1999 – The ICEL Scheme of Product and Authenticated Photometric Data Registration for Emergency Lighting Luminaires and Conversion Modules, or

- Calculations as detailed in the Chartered Institution of Building Services Engineers (CIBSE)/The Society of Light and Lighting (SLL) Guide L12: Emergency Lighting Design Guide, or
- An appropriate computer print-out of results, for example the printed results from recognized commercial emergency lighting design software.

(Annex C (informative) *BS 5266-1: 2005 Emergency lighting* refers).

Where authenticated data such as that mentioned above cannot be provided, Annex B (informative) of *BS 5266-1: 2005* permits a measurement of illuminance to be made. Annex A (normative) of *BS EN 1838: 1999* details the type of meter that should be used. The luminance and illuminance measurements must be made with a cosine photopic V(λ) – corrected meter. The meter must have an error tolerance not exceeding 10 %, with the error tolerance not exceeding 10 %, with the measurement taken up to 20 mm height above the floor.

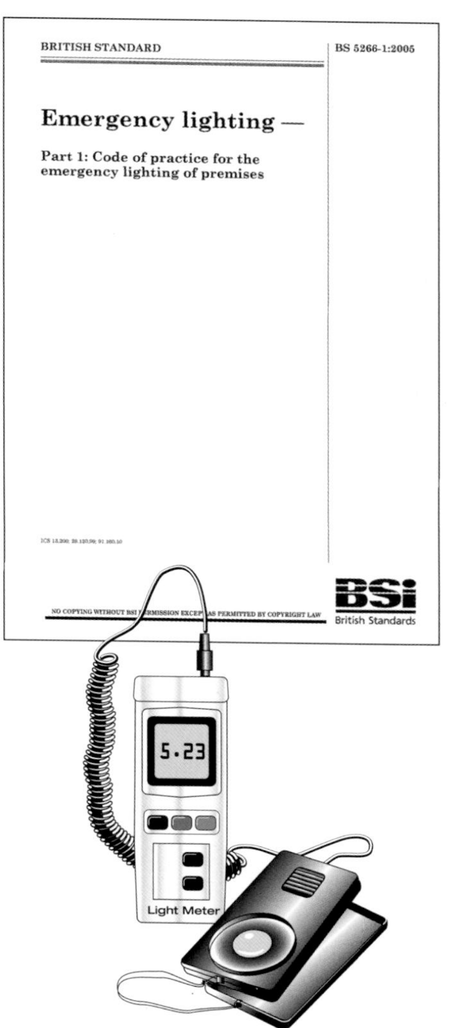

Standards applied

BS 5266-1: 2005 • BS EN 1838: 1999 (BS 5266-7) • ICEL 1001: 1999

Regulations referred to

None listed